PAGE
38

ON THE ROAD

YOUR COMPLETE DESTINATION GUIDE
In-depth reviews, recommendations
and insider tips

KU-431-014

**Orkney &
Shetland Islands**
p403

**Northern Highlands
& Islands**
p351

**Northeast
Scotland**
p223

**Inverness & the
Central Highlands**
p311

**Central
Scotland**
p180

**Southern Highlands
& Islands**
p259

Glasgow
p101

Edinburgh
p40

**Southern
Scotland**
p135

TOP EXPERIENCES MAP NEXT PAGE

PAGE
477

SURVIVAL GUIDE

YOUR AT-A-GLANCE REFERENCE
How to get around, get a room,
stay safe, say hello

FERRIES TO/FROM NORTH...

CROSSING	DURATION	FREQUE...
Belfast–Stranraer	3¼hr	2-4 daily
Belfast–Stranraer	1¾hr	4 daily
Larne–Cairnryan	1¾hr	8 daily
Larne–Cairnryan	1hr	2 daily (Mar-S...
Larne–Troon	1¾hr	2 daily (Mar-...

Train
...velling to Scotland by train
...lly faster and more
...ble than the bus, but...

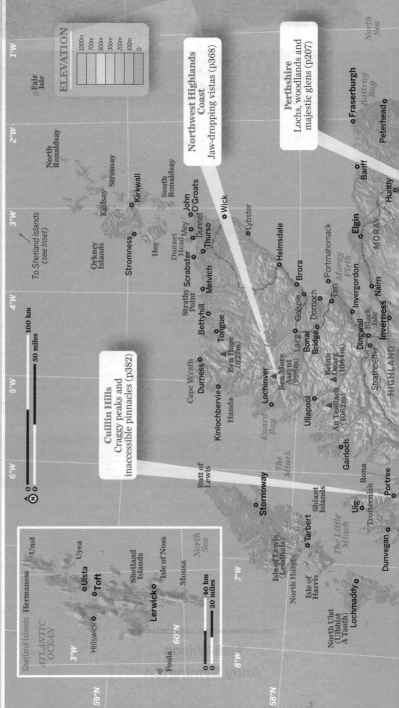

Scotland

Top Experiences

Cuillin Hills
Craggy peaks and inaccessible pinnacles (p382)

Northwest Highlands Coast
Jaw-dropping vistas (p368)

Perthshire
Lochs, woodlands and majestic glens (p207)

ELEVATION

1000m
700m
500m
300m
200m
100m
0

To Shetland Islands
(see inset)

Shetland Islands   Hermaness
Unst
Uyea
Ulsta
Toft
Hillswick
Foula
Lerwick
Mousa
Isle of Noss
Shetland Islands

ATLANTIC OCEAN

North Sea

3°W
60°N
59°N

0   40 km
0   20 miles

Butt of Lewis
Stornoway
Isle of Lewis (Leodhais)
North Harris
Isle of Harris
Tarbert
The Minch
Shiant Islands
North Uist (Uibhist A Tuath)
Lochmaddy
The Little Minch
Uig
Trotternish
Rona
Portree
Dunvegan

Cape Wrath
Durness
Kinlochbervie
Handa
Enard Bay
Lochinver
Ben More Assynt (998m)
Ullapool
An Teallach (1062m)
Gairloch
Ben Hope (927m)
Tongue
Bettyhill
Strathy Point
Melvich
Scrabster
Dunnet Head
Mey
Thurso
John O'Groats
Dunnet
Wick
Lybster
Helmsdale
Brora
Golspie
Dornoch
Portmahomack
Tain
Lairg
Bonar Bridge
Beinn Dearg (1084m)
Dingwall
Strathpeffer
Black Isle
Invergordon
Nairn
Inverness
HIGHLAND
Elgin
MORAY
Huntly
Banff
Fraserburgh
Peterhead
Rattray Bay

Fair Isle

North Sea

Orkney Islands
North Ronaldsay
Sanday
Stronsay
Eday
Kirkwall
South Ronaldsay
Stromness
Hoy

0   100 km
0   50 miles

N

8°W   7°W   6°W   5°W   4°W   3°W   2°W   1°W

Edinburgh
Famous for world-class festivals (p40)

Border Abbeys
Romantic, evocative, noble ruins (p138)

Climbing Ben Nevis
The highest Munro of them all (p341)

Glen Coe
Dramatic scenery meets deep history (p334)

Glasgow
Edgy and contemporary with great live music (p101)

55°N
56°N

Sunderland
Hartlepool
Newcastle-upon-Tyne
Durham
DURHAM
NORTHUMBERLAND
ENGLAND
CUMBRIA
Brampton
Carlisle
Berwick-upon-Tweed
Coldstream
Cockburnspath
St Abbs
Eyemouth
Coldingham
Duns
Kelso
Jedburgh
Hawick
Selkirk
Melrose
Galashiels
Newcastleton
Northumberland National Park
Lammermuir Hills
Moorfoot Hills
SCOTTISH BORDERS
EAST LOTHIAN
MID LOTHIAN
Dunbar
Haddington
Aberdour
Edinburgh
Peebles
Biggar
Moffat
Dumfries
Lanark
SOUTH LANARKSHIRE
Motherwell
Blantyre
Strathblane
Falkirk
FALKIRK
WEST LOTHIAN
Dunfermline
Kinross
Culross
Falkland
FIFE
Kirkcaldy
Firth of Forth
St Andrews
Broughty Ferry
Dundee
Perth
Crieff
Stirling
STIRLING
Dumbarton
Glasgow
Greenock
Dunoon
Helensburgh
INVERCLYDE
NORTH AYRSHIRE
EAST AYRSHIRE
Kilmarnock
Ayr
Ayr Bay
SOUTH AYRSHIRE
Girvan
Stranraer
Portpatrick
Mull of Galloway
DUMFRIES & GALLOWAY
Kirkcudbright
Castle Douglas
St John's Town of Dalry
Galloway Forest Park
Merrick (843m)
Machars Peninsula
Wigtown
Luce Bay
Burrow Head
Solway Firth
Brodick
Isle of Arran
Ardrossan
Firth of Clyde
Ailsa Craig
Isle of Bute
Inchmarnock
Kintyre
Campbeltown
Mull of Kintyre
Gigha
Isle of Islay
Sound of Jura
Isle of Jura
Isle of Colonsay
Oronsay
Laggan Bay
ATLANTIC OCEAN
North Channel
Larne
Belfast
NORTHERN IRELAND
ANTRIM
TYRONE
DERRY
Coleraine
Strabane
Buncrana
Letterkenny
DONEGAL
Gare Loch
Lochgilphead
Crinan
Kilmartine
Inveraray
ARGYLL & BUTE
Argyll Forest Park
Arrochar
Loch Lomond
Ben Lomond
Loch Lomond & the Trossachs National Park
Taynuilt
Connel
Oban
Lismore
Craignure
Salen
Mull
Tobermory
Coll
Tiree
Isle of Muck
Isle of Eigg
Isle of Rum
Canna
Barra (Barraigh)
Berneray (Bearnaraigh)
Sea of the Hebrides
Lochaline
Kinlochleven
Ben Nevis (1344m)
Glencoe
Fort William
Mallaig
Lochailort
Knoydart
Kingussie
Newtonmore
Morrone (859m)
Grampian Mountains
Braemar
Pitlochry
Kirriemuir
Blairgowrie
Forfar
Dunkeld
Aberfeldy
Glen Lyon
Ben Lawers (1214m)
PERTHSHIRE & KINROSS
ANGUS
Brechin
Edzell
Arbroath
Montrose
Stonehaven

Cuillin Hills

1 In a country famous for stunning scenery, the Cuillin Hills (p382) take top prize. This range of near-alpine craggy peaks has knife-edge ridges, jagged pinnacles, scree-filled gullies and acres of naked rock. Though a paradise for experienced mountaineers – the higher reaches of the Cuillin are off-limits to most walkers – there are easy trails through glens and corries where walkers can take in the views and share the landscape with red deer and golden eagles.

Edinburgh

2 Scotland's capital (p40) may be famous for its festivals, but there's much more to it than that. Edinburgh is a city of many moods: visit out of season to see the Old Town silhouetted against a blue spring sky, and a yellow haze of daffodils; or on a chill December morning with the fog snagging the spires of the Royal Mile, rain on the cobblestones and a warm glow beckoning from the window of a pub.

Charlotte Square, Edinburgh

Wildlife

3 Sparsely populated, and with large areas of wilderness, Scotland is an important sanctuary for animals of every kind. Amazing birdwatching is on offer everywhere, but the seabird cities of the Shetland Islands (p435) are the highlight. Capercaillie, corncrakes, ospreys, sea eagles and red kites are other avian drawcards, while red deer roam the uplands, pine martens and wildcats stalk the forests, and dolphins, whales, otters and orcas splash about in the northern waters.

Border Abbeys

4 The great Border abbeys were prosperous places with a turbulent history: their riches made them easy pickings for raiding parties from England. The Reformation meant that only their skeletons remain for us to see, but what romantic, evocative, noble ruins they are – at their best with their warm stone colours lit up by the evening sun. They sit in boutique, genteel Scottish town perfect for a quiet stay, and are all linked by a walking or cycling route. Jedburgh Abbey (p147)

KARL BLACKWELL

Boat Trips

5 No trip to Scotland is complete without taking to the high seas for a cruise along the coast. There's no better way to get a feeling for the history of the western seaboard and the northern isles, where until the second half of the 20th century sea travel was the easiest way to get around. There are countless boat trips on offer, from whale-watching or seabird-spotting cruises to island visits (Staffa, the Treshnish Isles and St Kilda are the most rewarding). And don't miss the chance to visit the Corryvreckan Whirlpool (p280).

GARETH MCCORMACK

Walking

6 The best way to really get inside Scotland's landscapes is to walk them. Despite the wind and midges and drizzle, walking (p26) here is a pleasure, with numerous short- and long-distance trails, hills and mountains begging to be tramped. Mild winters make it a year-round option, and the real bonus is the vibrant walking community here: you'll forge friendships on hillsides and, flushed and muddy, over a dram in a country pub or cosy Highland bothy at the end of the trail.

Ben Nevis, Lochaber Geopark

Glasgow

7 Scotland's biggest city (p101) lacks Edinburgh's classical beauty, but more than makes up for it with a barrelful of things to do and a warmth and energy that leave every visitor impressed. Edgy and contemporary, it's a great spot to browse art galleries and – despite the deep-fried-Mars-bar reputation – Scotlands's best place to eat. Add in what's perhaps Britain's best pub culture, and one of the world's best live-music scenes, and the only thing to do is live it. Ashton Lane, Glasgow

Castles

8 Desolate stone fortresses looming in the mist, majestic castles towering over historic towns, o luxurious palaces built on expansive grounds by lairds more concerned with pampering than with defence: Scotland has a full range of castles that reflect its turbulent history and tense relatio with its southern neighbour. Most castles have a story (or 10) to tell of plots, intrigues, imprisonments and treachery – as well as a ghost rumoured to stalk their halls. Eilean Donan Castle (p377)

SEAN CAFFREY

Golf

9 Scotland invented the game of golf and is still revered as its spiritual home by hackers and champions alike. Links courses are the classic experience here – bumpy coastal affairs where the rough is heather and machair and the main enemy is the wind, which can make a disaster of a promising round in an instant. St Andrews (p197), the historic Fife university town, is golf's headquarters, and an alluring destination for anyone who loves the sport. The Old Course, St Andrews

STEPHEN MEESE / ALAMY

Perthshire – Big Tree Country

10 Blue-grey lochs shimmer, reflecting the changing moods of the weather; swathes of noble woodland clothe the hills; majestic glens scythe their way into remote wildernesses; and salmon leap upriver to the place of their birth. In Perthshire (p207), the heart of the country, picturesque towns bloom with flowers, distilleries emit tempting malty odours and sheep graze in impossibly green meadows. There's a feeling of the bounty of nature that no other place in Scotland can replicate. Loch Tay

Northwest Highlands Coast

11 The Highlands abound in breathtaking views, but the far northwest is truly awe-inspiring. The coast road between Durness and Kyle of Lochalsh (p368) offers jaw-dropping scenes at every turn: the rugged mountains of Assynt, the desolate beauty of Torridon and the remote cliffs of Cape Wrath. These and the nooks of warm Highland hospitality found in classic rural pubs make this an unforgettable corner of the country. Stac Pollaidh and Inverpolly Nature Reserve seen from Suilven

Ancient Sites

12 Visiting ancient sites, it can be difficult to feel a connection with the people who built them, but Scotland's superb prehistoric remains have an immediate impact. Few better glimpses of Stone Age life exist than the Orkneys' Skara Brae (p413); the incredible cairns and chambered tombs found across the islands are equally impressive. Mysterious standing stones, muscular towers and richly symbolic Pictish stones make the distant past a constant presence. Skara Brae

JON ARNOLD IMAGES LTD / ALAMY

Whisky

13 Scotland's national drink (p459) – from the Gaelic *uisge bagh*, meaning 'water of life' – has been distilled here for more than 500 years. More than 100 distilleries are still in operation producing hundreds of varieties of single malt; learning to distinguish the smoky, peaty whiskies of Islay from, say, the flowery, sherried malts of Speyside has become a hugely popular pastime. Many distilleries offer guided tours, rounded off with a tasting session, and ticking off the local varieties is a great way to explore the whisky-making regions. Copper stills, Glenfiddich Whisky Distillery

Sea Kayaking

14 The convoluted coastline and countless islands of Scotland's western seaboard are widely recognised as some of the finest sea-kayaking (p378) areas in the world. Paddling your own allows you to explore remote islands, inlets, creeks and beaches that are inaccessible on foot, and also provides an opportunity to get close to wildlife such as seals, otters, dolphins and seabirds. Dozens of outfits offer guided kayaking tours for beginners, from a half-day to a week, either camping on wild beaches or staying in comfortable B&Bs. Isle of Lewis

Island Hopping

15 Much of western and northern Scotland's unique character comes from the more than 700 islands off Scotland's coast, of which almost 100 are inhabited. A network of ferry services links these islands to the mainland and each other; an Island Rover ticket (p489) – which offers unlimited ferry travel for 15 days – provides the best way to explore. It's possible to hop all the way from Arran or Bute to the Outer Hebrides, touching the mainland only at Kintyre and Oban. Oban Harbour

Climbing Ben Nevis

16 The allure of Britain's highest peak (p341) is strong – around 100,000 people a year set off up the summit trail, though not all make it to the top. Nevertheless, the highest Munro of them all is within the reach of anyone who's reasonably fit. Treat Ben Nevis with respect and your reward (weather permitting) will be a truly magnificent view and a great sense of achievement. Real walking enthusiasts can warm up by hiking the 95-mile West Highland Way (p261) first. View across the Mamores from Ben Nevis

Glen Coe

17 Scotland's most famous glen (p334) combines those two essential qualities of Highlands landscape: dramatic scenery and deep history. The peacefulness and beauty of this valley today belie the fact that it was the scene of a ruthless 17th-century massacre, when the local MacDonalds were murdered by soldiers of the Campbell clan. Some of the glen's finest walks – to the Lost Valley, for example – follow the routes used by the clanspeople trying to flee their attackers, and where many perished in the snow.

welcome to Scotland

Like a fine single malt, Scotland is a connoisseur's delight – an intoxicating blend of stunning scenery and sophisticated cities, of salt-tanged sea air and dark peaty waters, of outdoor adventure and deep history.

Outdoor Adventure

Scotland harbours some of the largest areas of wilderness left in Western Europe, a wildlife haven where you can see golden eagles soar above the lochs and mountains of the northern Highlands, spot otters tumbling in the kelp along the shores of the Outer Hebrides, and watch minke whales breach through shoals of mackerel off the coast of Mull. It's also an adventure playground where you can tramp the tundra plateaus of the Cairngorms, balance along tightrope ridges strung between the rocky peaks of the Cuillin, sea kayak among the seal-haunted isles of the Outer Hebrides, and take a speed-boat ride into the surging white water of the Corryvreckan whirlpool. And it's a place that changes with the seasons, offering something new each time you visit. Spring means a lilac haze of bluebells in the woods around Loch Lomond, while in summer the Hebridean beaches flaunt their golden sands and turquoise waters like Caribbean imposters. October brings a riot of autumn colour to the Perthshire forests, and in winter a fresh layer of crisp snow lends grandeur to the mountains of Glen Coe.

Deep History

Scotland is a land with a rich, multilayered history, a place where every corner of the landscape is steeped in the past – a deserted croft on an island shore, a moor that was once a battlefield, a beach where Vikings hauled their boats ashore, a cave that once sheltered Bonnie Prince Charlie. Hundreds of castles, from the plain but forbidding tower houses of Hermitage and Smailholm to the elaborate machicolated fortresses of Caerlaverock and Craigmillar testify to the country's often turbulent past. Battles that played a pivotal part in the building of a nation are remembered and brought to life at sites such as Bannockburn and Culloden. And museums and galleries such as Glasgow's Kelvingrove, Dundee's Discovery Point and Aberdeen's Maritime Museum recall the influence of Scottish engineers, artists, explorers, writers and inventors in shaping the modern world.

A Taste of Scotland

But it's not just connoisseurs of history and adrenalin who flock to Scotland's misty shores. An increasing number of visitors have discovered that its restaurants have shaken off their old reputation for deep-fried food and unsmiling service and can now compete with the best in Europe. A new-found respect for top-quality local produce means that you can feast on fresh seafood mere hours after it was caught, beef and venison that was raised just a few miles away from your table, and vegetables that were grown in your hotel's own organic garden. And top it all off with a dram of single malt whisky – rich, evocative and complex, the true taste of Scotland.

need to know

Currency
» Pounds Sterling (£)

Language
» English
» Gaelic and Lallans

When to Go

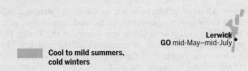

Cool to mild summers, cold winters

Lerwick
GO mid-May–mid-July

Stornoway
● GO May

Inverness
● GO May-Sep

Fort William
● GO May or Sep

Edinburgh
● GO Aug

High Season
(Jul & Aug, late Dec in Edinburgh)

» Accommodation prices 10%–20% higher (book in advance if possible)

» Warmest time of year, but often wet too

» Midges at their worst in Highlands and islands

Shoulder Season
(May, Jun & Sep)

» Wildflowers and rhododendrons bloom in May and June

» Statistically, best chance of dry weather, minus midges

» June evenings have daylight till 11pm

Low Season
(Oct–Apr)

» Rural attractions and accommodation often closed

» Snow on hills November to March

» In December it gets dark at 4pm

» Can be very cold and wet November to March

Your Daily Budget

Less than
£30

» Dorm beds: £10–£20

» Wild camping is free

» Cheap supermarkets for self-caterers

» Lots of free museums and galleries

Midrange
£30– £100

» Double room in mid-range B&B: £50–£90

» B&Bs often better value than midrange hotels

» Bar lunch: £10; dinner in midrange restaurant: £25

» Car hire: £30 a day

» Petrol costs: around 12p per mile

Top end over
£100

» Double room in high-end hotel: £120–£250

» Dinner at high-end restaurant: £40–£60

» Flights to islands: £60–£120 each

Money

» ATMs widely available. Credit cards widely accepted.

Visas

» Generally not needed for stays of up to six months. Not a member of the Schengen Zone.

Mobile Phones

» Uses the GSM 900/1800 network. Local SIM cards can be used in European and Australian phones.

Driving

» Drive on the left; steering wheel on right side of car.

Websites

» **Lonely Planet** (www. lonelyplanet.com/ Scotland) Destination information, forums, hotel bookings, shop.

» **VisitScotland** (www.visitscotland. com) Official tourism site; booking services.

» **Internet Guide to Scotland** (www. scotland-info.co.uk) Best online tourist guide to Scotland.

» **Traveline** (www. travelinescotland. com) Public transport timetables.

» **Scotland's People** (www. scotlandspeople. gov.uk) Explore your Scottish ancestry.

Exchange Rates

Australia	A$1	£0.62
Canada	C$1	£0.62
Euro zone	E1	£0.85
Japan	Y100	£0.75
New Zealand	NZ$1	£0.48
USA	US$1	£0.62

For current exchange rates see www.xe.com.

Important Numbers

Country code	+44
International access code	00
Ambulance	112 or 999
Fire	112 or 999
Police	112 or 999

Arriving in Scotland

» **Edinburgh Airport**
Buses – to Edinburgh city centre every 10 to 15 minutes from 4.30am to midnight
Night buses – every 30 minutes from 12.30am to 4am
Taxis – £15–£20; about 20 minutes to the city centre

» **Glasgow Airport**
Buses – to Glasgow city centre every 10 to 15 minutes from 6am to 11pm
Night buses – hourly 11pm to 4am, half-hourly 4am to 6pm
Taxis – £20–£25; about 30 minutes to city centre

Midges

If you've never been to the Scottish Highlands and islands before, be prepared for an encounter with the dreaded midge. These tiny, 2mm-long blood-sucking flies appear in huge swarms in summer, and can completely ruin a holiday if you're not prepared to deal with them.

They proliferate from late May to mid-September, but especially mid-June to mid-August – which unfortunately coincides with the main tourist season – and are most common in the western and northern Highlands. Midges are at their worst during the twilight hours, and on still, overcast days – strong winds and bright sunshine tend to discourage them.

The only way to combat them is to cover up, particularly in the evening. Wear long-sleeved, light-coloured clothing (midges are attracted to dark colours) and, most importantly, use a reliable insect repellent. See also p31.

if you like...

Castles

The clash and conflict of Scotland's colourful history has left a legacy of military strongholds scattered across the country, from the border castles raised against English incursions, to the island fortresses that controlled the seaways for the Lords of the Isles.

Edinburgh Castle The biggest, the most popular, the Scottish capital's reason for being (p46)

Stirling Castle Perched on a volcanic crag at the top of the town, this historic royal fortress and palace has the lot (p181 & p98)

Craigievar Castle The epitome of the Scottish Baronial style, all towers and turrets (p251)

Culzean Castle Enormous, palatial 18th-century mansion in a romantic coastal setting (p164)

Eilean Donan Perfect lochside location conveniently located just by the main road to Skye makes this the Highlands' most photographed fortress (p377)

Hermitage Castle Bleak and desolate borderland fortress speaking of turbulent times with England (p149)

Wild Beaches

Nothing clears a whisky hangover like a walk along a wind-whipped shoreline, and Scotland is blessed with a profusion of wild beaches. The west coast in particular has many fine strands of blinding white sands and turquoise waters that could pass for Caribbean beaches if it wasn't for the weather.

Kiloran Bay A perfect curve of deep golden sand – the perfect vantage point for stunning sunsets (p282)

Sandwood Bay A sea stack, a ghost story and 2 miles of windblown sand – who could ask for more? (p368)

Bosta A beautiful and remote cove filled with white sand beside an Iron Age house (p394)

Durness A series of pristine sandy coves and duney headlands surround this northwestern village (p366)

Scousburgh Sands Shetland's finest beach is a top spot for birdwatching as well as a bracing walk (p432)

Orkney's Northern Islands Most of these islands, especially Sanday, Westray and North Ronaldsay, have spectacular stretches of white sand with seabirds galore and seals lazing on the rocks (p418)

Good Food

Scotland's chefs have an enviable range of quality meat, game, seafood and vegetables at their disposal. The country has shaken off its once dismal culinary reputation as the land of deep-fried Mars Bars, and now boasts countless regional specialities, farmers markets, artisan cheese makers, smokeries and microbreweries.

Martin Wishart Michelin-starred perfection in Edinburgh's regenerated docklands (p78)

Contrast Brasserie French culinary art meets quality Highland produce in Inverness (p317)

Café Fish Perched on Tobermory waterfront, and serving fresh seafood and shellfish straight off the boat (p293)

Monachyle Mhor Utterly romantic location deep in the Trossachs and utterly wonderful food with sound sustainable principles (p193)

Peat Inn One of Scotland's most acclaimed restaurants sits in a hamlet amid the peaceful Fife countryside (p202)

The Albannach Fabulous gourmet retreat in the northwest; a real haven for relaxation (p369)

>> Bands play every night of the week at the legendary King Tut's Wah Wah Hut (p128), one of Glasgow's premier spots for seeing live music.

NEIL SETCHFIELD

Outdoor Adventures

Scotland is one of Europe's finest outdoor adventure playgrounds. The rugged mountain terrain and convoluted coastline of the Highlands and islands offer unlimited opportunities for hiking, mountain biking, surfing and snowboarding.

Fort William The self-styled Outdoor Capital of the UK, centre for hiking, climbing, mountain biking, winter sports... (p337)

Shetland One of Scotland's top coastlines for sea kayaking, with an abundance of bird and sea life to observe from close quarters (p431 & p435)

7 Stanes Mountain-biking trails for all abilities in the forests of southern Scotland (p175)

Cairngorms Winter skiing and summer walking amid the epic beauty of this high, subarctic plateau (p327)

Thurso Right up the top of Scotland, this is an unlikely surfing mecca, but once you've got the wetsuit on the waves are pretty good (p362)

Scapa Flow The scuttling of the German High Seas Fleet at the end of WWI has made this one of Europe's top diving sites (p416)

Live Music & Festivals

Scotland's festival calendar has seen an explosion of events in the last decade, with music festivals especially springing up in the most unlikely corners. The ones that have stood the test of time are full of character, with superb settings and a smaller, more convivial scale than monster gigs like Glastonbury and Reading.

RockNess Regularly praised as the most beautiful festival in the world, held in June with scenic Loch Ness as a backdrop (p338)

Arran Folk Festival June sees the fiddles pulled out all over this scenic island (p162)

T in the Park The country's biggest rock festival kicks off in mid-July near the town of Kinross (p209)

King Tut's Wah Wah Hut Live music nightly at this legendary Glasgow venue. Perhaps the best thing about it is that it's one of many great places in the city (p128)

Orkney Folk Festival Stromness vibrates to the wail of the fiddle and the stamping of feet in this good-natured, late-partying island festival (p415)

Rural Museums

Every bit as interesting and worthy of study as the 'big picture' history involving Mary Queen of Scots and Bonnie Prince Charlie – especially if you're investigating your Scottish ancestry – the history of rural communities is preserved in a wide range of fascinating museums, often in original farm buildings and historic houses.

Arnol Blackhouse Preserved in peat smoke since its last inhabitant left in the 1960s, a genuine slice of 'living history' (p393)

Highland Folk Museum Fascinating outdoor museum populated with real historic buildings reassembled here on site (p333)

Scottish Crannog Centre Head back to the Bronze Age in this excellent archaeological reconstruction of a fortified loch house (p215)

Tain Through Time Really entertaining local museum with a comprehensive display on Scottish history and Tain's silversmithing tradition (p355)

Stromness Museum Delightful small-town museum has details and artefacts about the Orkney fishing industry, the World Wars, and local marine wildlife (p415)

>> Winter hiking in the Nevis Range, near Fort William (p337) – the perfect base for exploring the mountains and glens of the western Highlands.

Pubs

No visit to Scotland is complete without a night in a traditional Scottish hostelry, supping real ales, sipping whisky and tapping your toes to traditional music. The choice of pubs is huge, but inn our opinion the old ones are the best.

Drovers Inn A classic Highland hostelry with kilted staff, candlelight and a stuffed bear (p263)

Sandy Bell's A stalwart of the Edinburgh folk scene, with real ale and live trad music (p82)

Glenelg Inn The beer garden here *is* actually a garden. What's more, it's got sensational views across the water to Skye (p377)

Horse Shoe This place – all real ales and polished brass – is Glasgow's best traditional pub (p124)

Stein Inn A lochside pub in Skye with fine ales, fresh seafood and a view to die for (p387)

Captain Flint's Don't plan on a quiet pint in this boisterous harbourside Shetland pub; a great place for a chat with locals (p429)

Shopping

Scotland offers countless opportunities for shoppers to indulge in retail therapy, from designer frocks and shoes in city malls, to local art, handmade pottery and traditional textiles in Highland and island workshops.

Glasgow The centre of Glasgow is a shopper's paradise, with everything from designer boutiques to second-hand records (p129)

Barras Glasgow's legendary flea market is a boisterous and intriguing place to browse for a taste of the city (p129)

Edinburgh Competes with Glasgow as the country's shopping epicentre, with its Harvey Nicks, malls, cashmere, tartan and quirky little gift shops (p84)

Wigtown An amazing array of second-hand and specialist bookshops cluster around the square in this small, out-of-the-way village (p176)

Isle of Skye It seems as if every second cottage on Skye is home to a workshop or an artist's studio, making the island a great place to find quality handmade arts and crafts (p385)

Classic Walks

Scotland's wild, dramatic scenery and varied landscape has made hiking a hugely popular pastime. There's something for all levels of fitness and enthusiasm, but the really keen hiker will want to tick off some (or all) of the classic walks.

West Highland Way The granddaddy of Scottish long-distance walks, the one everyone wants to do (p29)

Glen Affric to Shiel Bridge A classic two-day cross-country hike, with a night in a remote hostel (p321)

Southern Upland Way Crosses Southern Scotland's hills from coast to coast; longer and harder than the WHW (p138)

Ben Lawers One of central Scotland's classic hillwalks, with super views over Loch Tay (p216)

Fife Coastal Path Seascapes and clifftops galore on this picturesque route right around the 'Kingdom' (p195)

Cape Wrath Trail Head for the northwest corner from Fort William through some of Scotland's remotest scenery (p368)

If you like... unusual jewellery, take a look at the innovative, colourful items created by Heathergems (p218)

Hidden Gems

For those who enjoy exploring off the beaten track, Scotland is littered with hidden corners, remote road-ends and quiet cul-de-sacs where you can feel as if you are discovering the place for the first time.

Fossil Grove This strange fossilized forest is a relaxing place to escape Glasgow's bustle and ponder the immensity of geological time (p112)

Falls of Clyde Normally associated with shipbuilding, the River Clyde reveals the bucolic side of its character further upstream (p151)

Benmore Botanic Gardens Tucked away in a fold of the hills in the heart of the Cowal peninsula, this Victorian garden is a riot of colour in spring and early summer (p267)

Scotland's Secret Bunker It's back to the Cold War in this chilling but fascinating nuclear hideout hidden beneath a field in the middle of rural Fife (p206)

Cape Wrath A curious boat-minibus combo grinds you through a missile range to this spectacular headland at Britain's northwest tip (p368)

Islands

Scotland has more than 700 islands scattered around its shore. While the vast majority of visitors stick to the larger, better-known ones such as Arran, Skye, Mull and Lewis, it's often the smaller, lesser-known islands that provide the real highlights.

Iona Beautiful, peaceful (once the day-trippers have left) and of huge historic and cultural importance, Iona is the jewel of the Hebrides (p296)

Eigg The most intriguing of the Small Isles, with its miniature mountain, massacre cave and singing sands (p349)

Jura Wild and untamed, with more deer than people, and a dangerous whirlpool at its northern end (p279)

Isle of May Just a mile long, this spot off the Fife coast erupts to the clamour of tens of thousands of puffins in spring and summer (p205)

Westray & Papa Westray There's something magical about these adjacent islands at the north end of the Orkney archipelago. Great accommodation and eating options, plenty of coastal scenery, birdwatching and historic sights (p422 & p423)

Natural Wonders

Scotland's stunning landscapes harbour many awe-inspiring natural features, including spectacular sea stacks and rock formations, thundering waterfalls, impressive gorges and swirling tidal whirlpools.

Old Man of Hoy While most of the Orkneys is fairly flat, Hoy is rugged and rocky; its spectacular west coast includes Britain's tallest sea stack (p417)

Corryvreckan Whirlpool One of the world's three most powerful tidal whirlpools, squeezed between Jura and Scarba (p280)

Falls of Measach A trembling suspension bridge provides a scary viewpoint for one of Scotland's most impressive waterfalls (p372)

Fossil Grove This strange fossilized forest makes a relaxing place to visit to escape from Glasgow's bustle (p112)

Fingal's Cave Accessible only by boat, this columnar sea cave inspired Mendelssohn's *Hebrides Overture* (p298)

month by month

Top Events

1. **Edinburgh Festival and Fringe**, August
2. **T in the Park**, July
3. **Glasgow West End Festival**, June
4. **Celtic Connections**, January
5. **Braemar Gathering**, September

January

The nation shakes off its Hogmanay hangover and gets back to work, but only until Burns Night comes along. It's still cold and dark, but the skiing can be good.

Burns Night
Suppers all over the country (and the world for that matter) are held on 25 January to celebrate the anniversary of national poet Robert Burns, with much eating of haggis, drinking of whisky and reciting of poetry.

Celtic Connections
Glasgow hosts the world's largest winter music festival, a celebration of Celtic music, dance and culture, with participants arriving from all over the globe. Held mid- to late January. See www.celticconnections.com.

Up Helly Aa
Half of Shetland dresses up with horned helmets and battleaxes in this spectacular re-enactment of a Viking fire festival, with a torchlit procession leading the burning of a full-size Viking longship. Held in Lerwick on the last Tuesday in January. See www.uphellyaa.org.

February

The coldest month of the year is usually the best for hill walking, ice-climbing and skiing. The days are getting longer now, and snowdrops begin to bloom.

Six Nations Rugby Tournament
Scotland, England, Wales, Ireland, France and Italy battle it out in this prestigious tournament, held February to March; home games played at Murrayfield, Edinburgh. See www.rbs6nations.com.

Fort William Mountain Festival
The UK's Outdoor Capital celebrates the peak of the winter season with ski and snowboard learning workshops, talks by famous climbers, kids events and a festival of mountaineering films. See www.mountainfilmfestival.co.uk.

April

The bluebell woods on the shores of Loch Lomond come into flower, ospreys arrive at their Loch Garten nest. Weather improving, though heavy showers are still common.

Rugby Sevens
A series of week-end, seven-a-side rugby tournaments held in various towns throughout the Borders region in April and May, kicking off with Melrose in early April. Fast and furious rugby (sevens was invented here), crowded pubs and great craic. See www.melrose7s.com.

May

Wildflowers on the Hebridean machair, hawthorn hedges in bloom and cherry blossom in city parks – Scottish weather is often at its best in May.

Burns an' a' That
Ayrshire towns are the venues for performances of poetry and music, children's

events, art exhibitions and more in celebrations of the Scottish bard. See www.burnsfestival.com.

Spirit of Speyside

Based in the Moray town of Dufftown, this festival of whisky, food and music involves five days of distillery tours, knocking back the 'water of life', cooking, art and outdoor activities; held late April to early May in Moray and Speyside. See www.spiritof speyside.com.

June

Argyllshire is ablaze with pink rhododendron blooms as the long summer evenings stretch on till 11pm. Border towns are strung with bunting to mark gala days and Common Ridings.

Common Ridings

Following the age-old tradition that commemorates the ancient conflict with England, horsemen and -women ride the old boundaries of common lands, along with parades, marching bands and street parties. Held in various Border towns; Jedburgh (www.jethartcallantsfestival.com) is one of the biggest and best.

Glasgow Festivals

June is Glasgow's version of the Edinburgh festival, when the city hosts three major events – West End Festival (www.westend festival.co.uk), Glasgow's biggest music and arts

event; Glasgow International Jazz Festival (www.jazzfest.co.uk); and Glasgow Mela (www2. seeglasgow.com/glasgow mela), a celebration of the city's Asian community.

July

School holidays begin, as does the busiest time of year for resort towns. High season for Shetland birdwatchers.

T in the Park

Held annually since 1994, and headlined by world-class acts such as The Who, REM, Eminem and Kasabian, this major music festival is Scotland's answer to Glastonbury; held over a mid-July weekend at Balado, by Kinross. See www.tinthepark.com.

August

Festival time in Edinburgh and the city is crammed with visitors. On the west coast, this is the peak month for sighting Minke whales and basking sharks.

Edinburgh Festivals

You name it, Edinburgh has a festival event that covers it – books, art, theatre, music, comedy, dance, and the Military Tattoo (www.edintattoo.co.uk). The overlapping International Festival and Fringe keep the city jumping from the first week in August to the first week in September. See www.edinburgh festivals.co.uk.

September

School holidays are over, midges are dying off, wild brambles are ripe for picking in the hedgerows, and the weather is often dry and mild – an excellent time of year for outdoor pursuits.

Braemar Gathering

The biggest and most famous Highland Games in the Scottish calendar, traditionally attended by members of the Royal Family. Highland dancing, bagpipe-playing and caber-tossing; held early September in Braemar, Royal Deeside. See www.braemargathering.org.

December

Darkness falls mid-afternoon as the shortest day approaches. The often cold and wet weather is relieved by Christmas and New Year festivities.

Hogmanay

Christmas celebrations in Edinburgh (www.edinburghschristmas.com) culminate in a huge street party on Hogmanay (31 December). The fishing town of Stonehaven echoes an ancient, pre-Christian tradition with its procession of fireball-swinging locals who parade to the harbour and fling their blazing orbs into the sea (www.stonehavenfireballs.co.uk).

itineraries

Whether you've got six days or 60, these itineraries provide a starting point for the trip of a lifetime. Want more inspiration? Head online to lonelyplanet. com/thorntree to chat with other travellers.

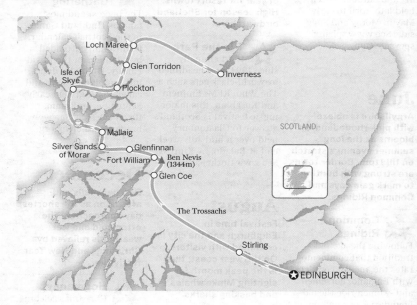

Two Weeks
A Highland Fling

❯ No trip to Scotland would be complete without a visit to **Edinburgh**. After two days of the capital's delights, head northwest to **Stirling** for Scotland's other great castle, then to the **Trossachs** for your first taste of Highland scenery (overnight in Callander).

As you continue north, the mountain scenery becomes more impressive, culminating in the grandeur of **Glen Coe**. Keen hill walkers will pause for a day at **Fort William** to climb **Ben Nevis** (plus another day to recover!) before taking the Road to the Isles past glorious **Glenfinnan** and the **Silver Sands of Morar**, to **Mallaig**. Overnight here and dine at one of its seafood restaurants.

Take the ferry to the **Isle of Skye**, and spend a day or two exploring Scotland's most famous island before crossing the Skye Bridge back to the mainland, then head north via the pretty village of **Plockton** to the magnificent mountain scenery of **Glen Torridon**. Spend a day or two hiking here, then follow the A832 alongside lovely **Loch Maree** and continue north into the big-sky wilderness of western Sutherland, before making your way back south with an overnight in **Inverness**.

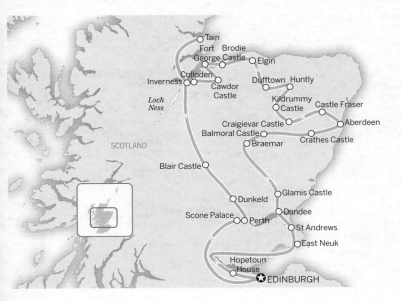

Two Weeks
Heart of Scotland

From **Edinburgh** head west to Queensferry to visit the elegant Adam-designed mansion of **Hopetoun House**, then go north across the Forth Road Bridge to Fife and turn east along the coastal road through the delightful fishing villages of the **East Neuk** (pause for a seafood lunch at Anstruther or St Monans) to the home of golf, **St Andrews**. Stay a night or two – heck, play a round of golf – before continuing north across the Tay Bridge to **Dundee** and **Glamis Castle**, with its royal associations. From here the A93 leads through the Grampian Mountains to reach **Braemar**, a good place to spend the night.

A feast of castles lies ahead as you make your way east along Royal Deeside – take your time, and visit (at the very least) the royal residence of **Balmoral Castle** and the fairy-tale **Crathes Castle** on your way to the granite city of **Aberdeen**. Plan to overnight here and try to get a table at Cafe 52 or the Silver Darling restaurant.

Now strike west again along the A944, making small detours to visit **Castle Fraser, Craigievar Castle** and **Kildrummy Castle** before turning north to **Huntly**, where you can combine a ruined castle with a night in the nearby Huntly Castle Hotel. Then it's west again to **Dufftown** in the heart of Speyside. Base yourself here for at least a day – there are two excellent restaurants to try, plus the nearby Mash Tun whisky bar – while you explore the many whisky distilleries nearby.

Strike northwest to **Elgin** to visit its magnificent ruined cathedral, then west on the A96 visiting **Brodie Castle, Fort George, Cawdor Castle** and **Culloden** on the way to Inverness (you'll probably need a stopover in Nairn). **Inverness** itself is worth a night or two – there are some excellent hotels and restaurants, and the opportunity for a side trip to **Loch Ness** (Drumnadrochit for monster spotters, Dores Inn for foodies).

Whisky fans can make another side trip north to the Glenmorangie Distillery at **Tain** before returning south to Edinburgh on the A9 and M9, stopping to visit **Blair Castle**, **Dunkeld** and **Scone Palace** (overnight at **Perth** if necessary).

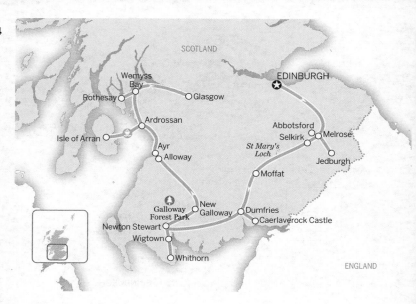

10 Days
Border Raid

> From **Edinburgh** the majority of tourists head north...which is a very good reason to head south, into the scenic Borders. Your first objective should be a visit to Sir Walter Scott's former home at **Abbotsford**, followed by a traipse around the beautiful Border abbeys of **Melrose** and Dryburgh; Melrose is a charming place to stay the night, with a choice of good hotels and eating places.

Next morning pay a visit to **Jedburgh** and yet another fine abbey, then return west to **Selkirk** and along the A708 to **Moffat**, passing through glorious scenery around St Mary's Loch. Continue to **Dumfries** (and stop for the night), where you can visit the first of several sights related to Scotland's national poet Robert Burns, and make a short side-trip to see spectacular **Caerlaverock Castle**.

Push on southwest around the Galloway coast to **Newton Stewart**, and detour south to visit the bookshops of **Wigtown** and the holy site of **Whithorn**. From Newton Stewart (a good overnight stop) drive up Glen Trool so that you can enjoy a hike amid the hills of Galloway Forest Park, before heading back east along the A712 to **New Galloway**, and then north on the A713 towards Ayr and Burns country.

At **Alloway** allow at least a day to visit the birthplace of Robert Burns (and other Burns-related sites), and perhaps a second day to enjoy the attractions of Culzean Castle – nearby **Ayr** has plenty of accommodation options (book a table at Fouter's bistro for a memorable meal).

From Ayr head north to Ardrossan and take the ferry from here across to the lovely **Isle of Arran** for a spot of hill walking, fishing or relaxing at one of the island's many pubs. Plan to spend two nights on the island – Brodick makes the best base.

Back on the mainland, head the short distance north to **Wemyss Bay** and take another ferry to **Rothesay** on the Isle of Bute, where you can spend one last night before making a visit to stunning Mount Stuart, one of Scotland's most impressive stately homes. Return to the mainland again and head east to **Glasgow**.

Two Weeks
Island Hopscotch

❯ This route is usually done by car, but the Oban–Barra–Stornoway–Ullapool–Inverness loop makes a brilliant cycle tour (around 270 miles, including the 60 miles from Ullapool ferry terminal to Inverness train station, making both start and finish accessible by rail). CalMac's Island Hopscotch ticket No 8 includes all the ferries needed for the Outer Hebrides part of this route.

From **Oban** it's a five-hour ferry crossing to **Barra**; you'll arrive in the evening so plan to spend the night there (book ahead). In the morning, after a visit to romantic Kisimul Castle and a tour around the island, take the ferry to **South Uist**. Walk along the wild beaches of the west coast, sample the local seafood and, if you've brought your fishing rod, look forward to a bit of sport on the island's many trout lochs. There are good places to stay at Polochar, Lochboisdale and Lochmaddy (two nights should be enough).

Keep your binoculars handy as you follow the road north through **Benbecula** and **North Uist**, as this is prime birdwatching country. If you're camping or hostelling, a night at **Berneray** is a must before taking the ferry to **Harris**. Pray for sun, as the road along Harris' west coast has some of the most spectacular beaches in Scotland. The main road continues north from **Tarbert** (good hotels) through the rugged Harris hills to **Lewis.**

Don't go directly to Stornoway, but take a turn west to the **Callanish Standing Stones**, **Dun Carloway** broch and **Arnol Blackhouse museum** – the highlights of the Western Isles – and if you have time (two days is ideal) detour west to the beautiful beaches around **Miavaig** and Traigh Uige; there's plenty of wild and semiwild camping, and an unusual overnight option in the Gallan Head Hotel.

Spend your final night in the Hebrides in **Stornoway** (eat at Digby Chick), then take the ferry to **Ullapool**, where you have the choice of heading direct to **Inverness**, or continuing north around the mainland coast through the jaw-dropping wilderness of **Inverpolly Nature Reserve**, **Cape Wrath** and **Durness** to **Thurso**, where the ferry to the **Orkney Islands** awaits.

Outdoor Activities

Best Time to Go

May, June and September are best months for hiking and biking – best chance of dry weather and less chance of midges

Best Outdoor Experiences

Hike the West Highland Way
Climb Ben Nevis
Cycle-tour the Outer Hebrides
Mountain-bike a black trail at Laggan Wolftrax
Sea-kayak in Shetland

Essential Hill Walking Gear

Good waterproofs
Spare warm clothing
Map and compass
Mobile phone (but don't rely on it)
First-aid kit
Head torch
Whistle (for emergencies)
Spare food and drink

Safety Checklist

Check the weather forecast first
Let someone know your plans
Set pace and objective to suit slowest member of party
Don't be afraid to turn back if it's too difficult

Scotland is a brilliant place for outdoor recreation and has something to offer everyone, from those who enjoy a short stroll to full-on adrenaline junkies. Although hiking, biking, fishing and golf are the most popular activities, there is an astonishing variety of things to do.

Most activities are well organised and have clubs and associations that can give visitors invaluable information and, sometimes, substantial discounts. **VisitScotland** (www.visitscotland.com) has brochures and dedicated websites covering the most popular activities.

Walking

Scotland's wild, dramatic scenery and varied landscape has made walking a hugely popular pastime for locals and tourists alike. There really is something for everyone, from after-breakfast strolls to the popular sport of Munro bagging (see boxed text, p30).

The best time of year for hill walking is usually May to September, although snow can fall on the highest summits even in midsummer. Winter walking on the higher hills of Scotland is for experienced mountaineers only, requiring the use of ice axe and crampons.

There is a tradition of relatively free access to open country in Scotland, especially on mountains and moorlands. You should, however, avoid areas where you might disrupt or disturb wildlife, lambing (generally mid-April to the end of May),

THE RIGHT TO ROAM

Access to the countryside has been a thorny issue in Scotland for many years. In Victorian times, belligerent landowners attempted to prevent walkers from using well-established trails. Moves to counter this led to successful legislation for the walkers and the formation of what later became the Scottish Rights of Way & Access Society.

In January 2003 the Scottish parliament formalised access to the countryside and passed the Land Reform (Scotland) Bill, creating statutory rights of access to land in Scotland for the first time (popularly known as 'the right to roam'). Basically, the Scottish Outdoor Access Code states that everyone has the right to be on most land and inland waters, providing they act responsibly.

As far as wild camping goes, this means that you can pitch a tent almost anywhere that doesn't cause inconvenience to others or damage to property, as long as you stay no longer than two or three nights in any one spot, take all litter away with you, and keep well away from houses and roads.

Scottish Outdoor Access Code (www.outdooraccess-scotland.com)
Scottish Rights of Way & Access Society (www.scotways.com)

---

grouse shooting (from 12 August to the third week in October) or deer stalking (1 July to 15 February, but the peak period is August to October). You can get up-to-date information on deer stalking in various areas through the **Hillphone** (www.hillphones. info) service.

Rights of way exist but local authorities aren't required to list and map them so they're not shown on Ordnance Survey (OS) maps of Scotland, as they are in England and Wales. However, the Scottish Rights of Way & Access Society (see boxed text, p27) keeps records of these routes, provides and maintains signposting, and publicises them in its guidebook, *Scottish Hill Tracks*.

What to Pack

Highland hikers should be properly equipped and cautious, as the weather can become vicious at any time of year. After rain, peaty soil can become boggy so always wear stout shoes or boots and carry extra food and drink – many unsuspecting walkers have had to survive an unplanned night in the open. Don't depend on mobile phones (although carrying one with you is a good idea, and can be a life-saver if you can get a signal). If necessary, leave a note with your route and expected time of return in the windscreen of your car.

Further Information

Every tourist office has leaflets (free or for a nominal charge) of suggested walks that take in local points of interest. Lonely Planet's *Walking in Scotland* is a comprehensive resource, covering short walks and long-distance paths; its *Walking in Britain* guide covers Scottish walks, too. For general advice, VisitScotland produces a **Walking Scotland** (http://walking. visitscotland.com) website that describes numerous routes in various parts of the country, and also offers safety tips and other useful information.

Other useful sources:

Mountaineering Council of Scotland (www.mcofs.org.uk)

Ordnance Survey (www.ordnancesurvey.co.uk)

Ramblers' Association Scotland (www.ramblers.org.uk/scotland)

Scottish Mountaineering Club (www.smc.org.uk)

Cycling

Cycling is an excellent way to explore Scotland. There are hundreds of miles of forest trails and quiet minor roads, and dedicated cycle routes along canal towpaths and disused railway tracks. Depending on your energy and enthusiasm, you can take a leisurely trip through idyllic farm country, stopping at the numerous pubs along the way, or head off-road for some serious, mud-spattered trail-riding. Cyclists in search of the wild and remote will enjoy northwestern Scotland and the Outer Hebrides, which offer peaceful pedalling through breathtaking landscapes.

WALK	DISTANCE	FEATURES	DURATION	DIFFICULTY	PAGE
Fife Coastal Path	78 miles	Firth of Forth, undulating country	5-6 days	easy	p195
Great Glen Way	73 miles	Loch Ness, canal paths, forest tracks	4 days	easy	p328
Pilgrims Way	25 miles	Machars peninsula, standing stones, burial mounds	2-3 days	easy	boxed text, p138
St Cuthbert's Way	62 miles	follows life of famous saint	6-7 days	medium	boxed text, p138
Southern Up-land Way	212 miles	remote hills & moorlands	9-14 days	medium-hard	boxed text, p138
Speyside Way	66 miles	follows river, whisky distilleries	3-4 days	easy-medium	boxed text, p32
West Highland Way	95 miles	spectacular scenery, mountains & lochs	6-8 days	medium	boxed text, p29

The beautiful forests, lochs, glens and hills in the central and southern areas of Scotland are more easily accessible and, like the gentle, undulating countryside in the beautiful Borders region, make for excellent cycling country.

Mountain Biking

Hardcore mountain bikers will also find plenty of challenges, from long off-road routes such as the **Great Glen Mountain Bike Trail** (p328), to forest trail centres such as the **7stanes** (see boxed text, p175), to world-class downhill courses such as those at **Laggan Wolftrax** (p333) and **Nevis Range** (p342).

Further Information

VisitScotland publishes a useful free booklet, *Cycle Scotland,* and has a dedicated website (cycling.visitscotland.com). Many regional tourist offices have information on local cycling routes and places to hire bikes. They also stock cycling guides and books.

For up-to-date, detailed information on Scotland's cycle-route network contact **Sustrans** (www.sustrans.org.uk). The **Cyclists' Touring Club** (www.ctc.org.uk) is a membership organisation offering comprehensive information about cycling in Britain.

Golf

Scotland is the home of golf. The game has been played in Scotland for centuries and there are more courses per head of population here than in any other country. Most clubs are open to visitors – details can be found on the web at www.scotlands-golf-courses.com.

St Andrews is the headquarters of the game's governing body, the Royal and Ancient Golf Club, and the location of the world's most famous golf course, the Old Course (see boxed text, p201). There are several major championship courses around the country including those at Royal Troon (p164) and Turnberry (p166).

VisitScotland publishes the *Official Guide to Golf in Scotland,* a free annual brochure listing course details, costs and clubs with information on where to stay. Some regions offer a **Golf Pass** (http://golf.visitscotland.com/golf-passes), costing between £40 and £120 for five days (Monday to Friday), which allows play on a range of courses.

Fishing

Fishing – coarse, sea and game – is enormously popular in Scotland, the lochs and rivers of which are filled with salmon, trout (sea, brown and rainbow), pike, Arctic char and many other species. Fly-fishing in particular is a joy in Scotland's many lochs and rivers – it's a tricky but rewarding form of angling, closer to an art form than a sport.

Fishing rights to most waters are privately owned and you must obtain a permit to fish in them – these are often readily available at the local fishing-tackle shop or hotel. Permits cost from around £15 per day but some salmon rivers – notably the Tweed, the Tay and the Spey – can be much more expensive.

There are numerous places throughout Scotland with stocked ponds where you can hire equipment and have a couple of lessons; they are a particularly good option for the kids. Examples include the Galloway Angling Centre (p175) and Rothiemurchus Trout Fishery (p329)

For wild brown trout the close season is early October to mid-March. The close season for salmon and sea trout varies between districts; it's generally from early November to early February.

The VisitScotland booklet *Fish in Scotland* (www.fishscotland.co.uk) is a good introduction and is available from tourist offices. Other organisations that can provide information include the following:

Scottish Anglers National Association (www.sana.org.uk)

Scottish Federation of Sea Anglers (www.fishsea.co.uk)

Skiing & Snowboarding

There are five ski centres in Scotland, offering downhill skiing and snowboarding:

Cairngorm Mountain (www.cairngormmountain.com) 1097m; has almost 30 runs spread over an extensive area; see p329.

Glencoe (www.glencoemountain.com) 1108m; has only five tows and two chairlifts; see p335.

WEST HIGHLAND WAY

This classic hike – the country's most popular long-distance path – stretches for 95 miles through some of Scotland's most spectacular scenery, from Milngavie (mull-*guy*), on the northwestern fringes of Glasgow, to Fort William.

The route begins in the Lowlands but the greater part of the trail is among the mountains, lochs and fast-flowing rivers of the western Highlands. After following the eastern shore of Loch Lomond and passing Crianlarich and Tyndrum, the route crosses the vast wilderness of Rannoch Moor and reaches Fort William via Glen Nevis, in the shadow of Britain's highest peak, Ben Nevis.

The path is easy to follow, making use of old drovers' roads (along which Highland cattle were once driven to Lowland markets), an old military road (built by troops to help subdue the Highlands in the 18th century) and disused railway lines.

Best done from south to north, the walk takes about six or seven days (the fastest time, set during the West Highland Way Race in 2006, is 15 hours 45 minutes!). Many people round it off with an ascent of Ben Nevis (p341). You need to be properly equipped with good boots, waterproofs, maps, a compass, and food and drink for the northern part of the walk. Midge repellent is also essential.

The West Highland Way Official Guide by Bob Aitken and Roger Smith is the most comprehensive guidebook. The Harveys map *West Highland Way* shows the entire route in a single waterproof map sheet.

Accommodation shouldn't be too difficult to find, though between Bridge of Orchy and Kinlochleven it's limited. At peak times (May, July and August), book accommodation in advance. There are some youth hostels and bunkhouses on or near the path, and it's possible to camp in some parts. A list of accommodation is available for free from tourist offices.

For more information check out the website www.west-highland-way.co.uk.

Glenshee (www.ski-glenshee.co.uk) 920m; situated on the A93 road between Perth and Braemar; offers the largest network of lifts and the widest range of runs in all of Scotland; see p222.

Lecht (www.lecht.co.uk) 793m; the smallest and most remote centre, on the A939 between Ballater and Grantown-on-Spey; see p251.

Nevis Range (www.nevisrange.co.uk) 1221m; near Fort William; offers the highest ski runs, the grandest setting and some of the best off-piste potential in Scotland; see p342.

The high season is from January to April but it's sometimes possible to ski from as early as November to as late as May. It's easy to turn up at the slopes, hire some kit, buy a day pass and off you go.

VisitScotland's *Ski Scotland* brochure is useful and includes a list of accommodation options. General information, and weather and snow reports, can be obtained from:

Ski Scotland (www.ski-scotland.com)

Snowsport Scotland (www.snowsportscot land.org)

WinterHighland (www.winterhighland.info)

Water Sports
Canoeing

Scotland, with its islands, sea lochs and indented coastline, is ideal for sea kayaking, while its inland lochs and Highland rivers are great for both Canadian and white-water canoeing.

For information contact the **Scottish Canoe Association** (www.canoescotland.org). It publishes coastal navigation sheets as well as organising tours, including introductory ones for beginners.

Diving

It may lack coral reefs and warm, limpid waters but Scotland offers some of the most spectacular and challenging scuba diving in Europe, if not the world. The seabed around St Abbs (p139) is Scotland's first voluntary marine nature reserve.

There are also hundreds of fascinating shipwrecks, the most famous of which are the seven remaining hulks of the WWI German High Seas Fleet, scuttled in 1919, which lie on the bed of Scapa Flow in the Orkney Islands (see boxed text, p416).

THE ANCIENT ART OF MUNRO BAGGING

At the end of the 19th century an eager hillwalker, Sir Hugh Munro, published a list of 545 Scottish mountains measuring over 3000ft (914m) – a height at which he believed they gained a special significance. Of these summits he classified 277 as mountains in their own right (new surveys have since revised this to a total of 283), the rest being satellites of lesser consequence (known as 'tops'). Sir Hugh couldn't have realised that his name would one day be used to describe any Scottish mountain over the magical 3000ft mark. Many keen hillwalkers now set themselves the target of reaching the summit of (or bagging) all 283 Munros.

The peculiar practice of Munro bagging started soon after the list was published – by 1901 the Reverend AE Robertson had become the first person to bag the lot. Between 1901 and 1981, only 250 people managed to climb all the Munros, but the huge increase in the popularity of hill walking from the 1980s onward saw the number of officially declared 'Munroists' soar to 4500 (see www. smc.org.uk/Munros) by 2010. Many people have completed the round more than once; the record for single-minded Munro bagging is held by Edinburgh's Steven Fallon (see boxed text, p375), who completed his 14th round in 2010.

To the uninitiated it may seem odd that Munro baggers see a day (or longer) spent plodding around in mist, cloud and driving rain to the point of exhaustion as time well spent. However, for those who can add one or more ticks to their list, the vagaries of the weather are part of the enjoyment, at least in retrospect. Munro bagging is, of course, more than merely ticking names on a list – it takes you to some of the wildest, most beautiful parts of Scotland.

Once you've bagged all the Munros you can move onto the Corbetts – hills over 2500ft (700m), with a drop of at least 500ft (150m) on all sides – and the Donalds, lowland hills over 2000ft (610m). And for connoisseurs of the diminutive, there are the McPhies: 'eminences in excess of 300ft (90m)' on the Isle of Colonsay.

BEATING THE MIDGES

Forget Nessie; the Highlands have a real monster in their midst – a voracious bloodsucking female, fully 2mm long and known as *Culicoides impunctatus*, or the Highland midge (the male midge is an innocent vegetarian). The bane of campers and as much a symbol of Scotland as the kilt or the thistle, they can drive sane folk to distraction as they descend in swarms of biting misery. Though mostly vegetarian too, the female midge needs a dose of blood in order to lay her eggs. And, like it or not, if you're in the Highlands in summer, you just volunteered as a donor.

The midge season lasts from late May to early September, with June to August being the worst months. Climate change has seen warmer, damper springs and summers, which seems to suit the midges just fine – in recent years they have increased both in numbers and in range. They are at their worst in the morning and evening, especially in calm, overcast weather; strong winds and strong sunshine help keep them away.

You can get an idea of how bad they are going to be in your area by checking the **midge forecast** (www.midgeforecast.co.uk).

Be Prepared

Cover up by wearing long trousers and long-sleeved shirts, and (if they're really bad) a head net (available in most outdoor shops for £3 to £5) worn over a brimmed hat. And use a repellent.

Many kinds of repellents have been formulated over the decades, some based on natural ingredients such as citronella and bog myrtle, but until recently there was only one that worked reliably – DEET, which is a nasty, industrial chemical that smells bad, stings your eyes and seems to be capable of melting plastic. Today a new repellent called Saltidin claims to be both effective and pleasant to use (marketed under the brand name Smidge).

However, there is another substance that has shot to prominence since 2005, despite not being marketed as an insect repellent. Avon's Skin So Soft moisturiser spray is so effective that it is regularly used as a midge repellent by professionals, including the Royal Marines, forestry workers and water engineers, as well as thousands of outdoor enthusiasts. You can find it in most outdoor stores in the west of Scotland. Not only does it keep the midges away, but it leaves your skin feeling 'velvety soft'...

For more information on the country's diving options contact the **Scottish Sub Aqua Club** (www.scotsac.com).

Sailing

The west coast of Scotland, with its myriad islands, superb scenery and challenging winds and tides, is widely acknowledged to be one of the finest yachting areas in the world.

Experienced skippers with suitable qualifications can charter a yacht from one of dozens of agencies; prices for bareboat charter start at around £1800 a week in high season for a six-berth yacht; hiring a skipper to sail the boat for you will cost £135 a day or £850 a week. Sailing dinghies can be rented from many places for around £60 a day.

Beginners can take a Royal Yachting Association training course in yachting or dinghy sailing at many sailing schools around the coast; for details of charter agencies, sailing schools and water-sports centres, get hold of VisitScotland's *Sail Scotland* brochure, or check out the website sail.visitscotland.com.

Surfing

Even with a wetsuit on you definitely have to be hardy to enjoy surfing in Scottish waters. That said, the country does have some of the best surfing breaks in Europe.

The tidal range is large, which means there is often a completely different set of breaks at low and high tides. It's the north and west coasts, particularly around Thurso (p362) and in the Outer Hebrides, which

THE SPEYSIDE WAY

This long-distance footpath follows the course of the River Spey, one of Scotland's most famous salmon-fishing rivers. It starts at Buckie and first follows the coast to Spey Bay, east of Elgin, then runs inland along the river to Aviemore in the Cairngorms (with branches to Tomintoul and Dufftown). At only 66 miles, the main walk can be done in three or four days, although including the branch trails to Dufftown and Tomintoul will push the total walking distance to 102 miles (allow seven days).

This route has also been dubbed the 'Whisky Trail' as it passes near a number of distilleries, including Glenlivet and Glenfiddich, which are open to the public. If you stop at them all, the walk may take considerably longer than the usual three or four days!

The Speyside Way, a guidebook by Jacquetta Megarry and Jim Strachan, describes the route in detail. Or check out the route at www.speysideway.org.

have outstanding, world-class surf. Indeed, Lewis has the best and most consistent surf in Britain, with around 120 recorded breaks and waves up to 5m. For more information contact **Hebridean Surf** (www.hebrideansurf.co.uk).

Birdwatching

Scotland is the best place in the British Isles (and in some cases, the only place) to spot bird species such as the golden eagle, white-tailed sea eagle, osprey, corncrake, capercaillie, crested tit, Scottish crossbill and ptarmigan, and the country's coast and islands are some of Europe's most important seabird nesting grounds.

There are more than 80 ornithologically important nature reserves managed by **Scottish Natural Heritage** (www.snh.gov.uk), the **Royal Society for the Protection of Birds** (www.rspb.org.uk) and the **Scottish Wildlife Trust** (www.swt.org.uk).

Further information can be obtained from the **Scottish Ornithologists Club** (www.the-soc.org.uk).

regions at a glance

Edinburgh

Culture ✓✓✓
History ✓✓✓
Food ✓✓✓

Culture
Dubbed the Athens of the North, the Scottish capital is a city of high culture and lofty ideals, art and literature, philosophy and science. It is here that each summer the world's biggest arts festival rises, phoenix-like, from the ashes of its rave reviews and box-office records to evoke yet another string of superlatives. Outside festival time, there's plenty to enjoy in the city's many theatres and world-class art galleries and museums.

p40

History
Perched on a brooding black crag overlooking the city centre, Edinburgh Castle has played a pivotal role in Scottish history. The growth of the city from its medieval Old Town to the Georgian elegance of the New Town and the parallel development of Scottish nationhood is well documented in its excellent museums and historic buildings. And on the edge of the city lies medieval Rosslyn Chapel, Scotland's most beautiful and enigmatic church.

Food
The last decade has seen a restaurant boom in Edinburgh, with more restaurants per person than in London. Eating out is commonplace, not just for special occasions, and the eateries range from stylish but inexpensive bistros and cafes to gourmet restaurants with Michelin stars. Scottish cuisine has been given a makeover too, with inventive chefs using top-quality local produce and adding contemporary twists to traditional favourites.

Glasgow

Museums ✓✓✓
Music ✓✓✓
Design ✓✓

Museums & Art Galleries
Glasgow's mercantile, industrial and academic history has left the city with a wonderful legacy of museums and art galleries, dominated by the grand Victorian cathedral of culture, Kelvingrove, boasting a bewildering variety of exhibits.

Live Music
Scotland's liveliest nightlife is found in the din and roar of Glasgow's drinking dens, from traditional Victorian pubs to its famed style bars. It's also the star of Scotland's live music scene, with many venues and bands, from top international acts to local start-ups.

Design
From Charles Rennie Mackintosh's iconic buildings and interiors and the centre's grand Victorian architecture, to the fashion boutiques of the Italian Centre and design exhibitions at the Lighthouse, Glasgow stakes its claim as Scotland's most stylish city.

p101

Southern Scotland

Historic Abbeys ✓✓✓
Stately Homes ✓✓
Activities ✓✓

Historic Abbeys

Rolling countryside and ruined abbeys dot Scotland's southern border. The Gothic ruins of Melrose, Jedburgh, Dryburgh and Sweetheart and the martial towers of Hermitage Castle, Caerlaverock Castle and Smailholm are eloquent testimony to a turbulent past.

Stately Homes

This region is rich in Adam-designed mansions such as Culzean Castle, Paxton House, Floors Castle and Mellerstain House, but the almost perfectly preserved Chippendale time-capsule Dumfries House takes top place.

Outdoor Activities

The rounded, heather-clad hills of the Southern Uplands can't compete with the Highlands for scenery, but the granite hills of Galloway and Arran are prime hill walking country, and the 7stanes trail centres offer some of the UK's best and most challenging mountain biking.

p135

Central Scotland

Golf ✓✓✓
Scenery ✓✓
Castles ✓✓

Golf

Scotland is the home of golf, and the Old Course at St Andrews – the oldest in the world – is on every golfer's wish list. The game has been played here for more than 600 years; the Royal & Ancient Golf Club, the game's governing body, was founded in 1754.

Scenery

From the picturesque Fife coastline, dotted with quaint fishing villages, and the wood-fringed lochs and hills of the Trossachs, to the big-tree country of Perthshire and the epic mountain scenery of Glen Lyon and Glenshee, central Scotland displays the full range of classic Scottish landscapes.

Castles

Some say that Stirling has the finest castle in the country, but the region has plenty of others worth visiting, including Scone Palace, Blair Castle, Kellie Castle, Doune Castle and St Andrews Castle.

p180

Northeast Scotland

Whisky ✓✓✓
Castles ✓✓✓
Royalty ✓✓

Whisky

Don't leave Scotland without visiting a whisky distillery; the Speyside region, around Dufftown in Moray, is the epicentre of the industry. More than 50 distilleries open their doors during the twice-yearly Spirit of Speyside festival; many open year-round.

Castles

Aberdeenshire and Moray have the greatest concentration of Scottish Baronial castles in the country, from the turreted splendour of Craigievar and Fyvie to the restrained elegance of Crathie and Balmoral.

Royalty

The valley of the River Dee (often called Royal Deeside) has been associated with the royal family since Queen Victoria acquired her holiday home, Balmoral Castle. Besides royal links with Balmoral and Ballater, there's Glamis Castle, family home of the late Queen Mother and birthplace of Princess Margaret.

p223

Southern Highlands & Islands

Wildlife ✓✓✓
Islands ✓✓✓
Food ✓✓✓

Wildlife
This region is home to some of Scotland's most spectacular wildlife, from magnificent white-tailed sea eagles at Mull, to majestic minke whales and basking sharks cruising the west coast. It's also where the beaver – extinct here for centuries – has been reintroduced into the wild.

Islands
Island-hopping is one of the best ways to explore the western seaboard, and the cluster of islands here – Islay with its whisky distilleries, wild and mountainous Jura, scenic Mull and the little jewel of Iona, and the gorgeous beaches of Colonsay, Coll and Tiree – provide a brilliant introduction.

Seafood
Whether you dine at a top restaurant in Oban or Tobermory, or eat with your fingers on the harbourside, the rich harvest of the sea is one of the region's biggest drawcards.

p259

Inverness & the Central Highlands

Activities ✓✓✓
Scenery ✓✓✓
Legends ✓✓

Activities
The Cairngorm towns of Aviemore and Fort William offer outdoor adventure galore. Be it climbing Ben Nevis, walking the West Highland Way, biking the trails around Loch Morlich or skiing the slopes of Cairngorm, there's something for everyone.

Scenery
Photographers are spoiled with classic views here, from the rugged beauty of Glen Coe and snow-patched Cairngorms summits to the Caledonian pine forests around Loch Affric and the golden beaches and island views of Arisaig and Morar.

Legends
Scotland's most iconic legend, the Loch Ness monster, lurks in the heart of this region. You might not spot Nessie, but the magnificent scenery of the Great Glen makes a visit worthwhile, as does Culloden battlefield, the undoing of another Scottish legend, Bonnie Prince Charlie.

p311

Northern Highlands & Islands

Scenery ✓✓✓
Activities ✓✓✓
History ✓✓

Scenery
From the peaks of Assynt and Torridon, to the jagged rock pinnacles of the Cuillin Hills, to the dazzling beaches of the Outer Hebrides, the big skies and lonely landscapes of the northern Highlands and islands are the very essence of Scotland, a wilderness of sea and mountains that remains one of Europe's most unspoilt regions.

Activities
The northwest's vast spaces are one huge adventure playground for hikers, bikers, climbers and kayakers, providing the chance to see some of the UK's most spectacular wildlife.

History
The abandoned rural communities of the north teach much about the Clearances, especially Arnol Blackhouse and Skye Museum of Island Life. The region is also rich in prehistoric remains, including the famous standing stones of Callanish.

p351

Orkney & Shetland Islands

History ✓✓✓
Birdwatching ✓✓✓
Music ✓

History

These treeless, cliff-bound islands have a fascinating Viking heritage and unique prehistoric villages, tombs and stone circles. Pre-dating the pyramids of Egypt, Skara Brae is northern Europe's best-preserved prehistoric village; Maes Howe is one of Britain's finest Neolithic tombs.

Birdwatching

Shetland is a birdwatcher's paradise, its cliffs teeming in summer with gannets, fulmars, kittiwakes, razorbills and puffins, and Europe's largest colony of Arctic terns. Several nature reserves include Hermaness on Unst, Scotland's northernmost inhabited island.

Music

The pubs of Kirkwall, Stromness and Lerwick are fertile ground for exploring the traditional music scene, with impromptu sessions of fiddle, bodhrán and guitar music. Both Orkney and Shetland host annual festivals of folk music.

p403

Look out for these icons:

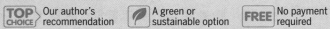

| TOP CHOICE | Our author's recommendation | | A green or sustainable option | FREE | No payment required |

See the Index for a full list of destinations covered in this book.

On the Road

Edinburgh

POP 430,000 / AREA 116 SQ KM

Best Places to Stay

» Witchery by the Castle (p69)

» Hotel Missoni (p69)

» Six Mary's Place (p71)

» Southside Guest House (p72)

» Prestonfield House Hotel (p72)

Best Places to Eat

» Outsider (p74)

» Ondine (p74)

» Oloroso (p76)

» Café Marlayne (p76)

» Fishers Bistro (p77)

Why Go?

Edinburgh is a city that begs to be explored. From the vaults and wynds (narrow lanes) that riddle the Old Town to the urban villages of Stockbridge and Cramond, it's filled with quirky, come-hither nooks that tempt you to walk just a little bit further. And every corner turned reveals sudden views and unexpected vistas – green sunlit hills, a glimpse of rust-red crags, a blue flash of distant sea.

But there's more to Edinburgh than sightseeing – there are top shops, world-class restaurants and a bacchanalia of bars to enjoy. This is a city of pub crawls and impromptu music sessions, mad-for-it clubbing and all-night parties, overindulgence, late nights and wandering home through cobbled streets at dawn.

All these superlatives come together in August at festival time, when it seems as if half the world descends on Edinburgh for one enormous party. If you can possibly manage it, join them.

When to Go
Edinburgh

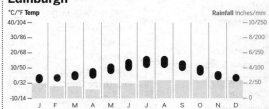

May Good weather (usually), flowers and cherry blossom everywhere, and (gasp!) no crowds.

August Festival time! Crowded and mad but unmissable.

December Christmas decorations, cosy pubs with open fires, ice skating in Princes Street Gardens.

Edinburgh Highlights

1 Taking in the views from the battlements of **Edinburgh Castle** (p46)

2 Feasting on steak and oysters at the **Tower Restaurant** (p74) as the sun sets over the city

3 Nosing around the Queen's private quarters on the former **Royal**

Yacht Britannia (p61) at Leith

4 Listening to live folk music at **Sandy Bell's** (p82)

5 Trying to decipher the Da Vinci Code at mysterious **Rosslyn Chapel** (p89)

6 Exploring Edinburgh's subterranean history in the haunted vaults of **South**

Bridge and **Real Mary King's Close** (p55)

7 Climbing to the summit of the city's miniature mountain, **Arthur's Seat** (p53)

EDINBURGH IN...

Two Days

A two-day trip to Edinburgh should start at **Edinburgh Castle**, followed by a stroll down the **Royal Mile** to the **Scottish parliament building** and the **Palace of Holyroodhouse**. You can work up an appetite by climbing **Arthur's Seat**, then satisfy your hunger with dinner at **Oloroso** while you watch the sun set over the **Firth of Forth**. On day two spend the morning in the **Museum of Scotland** then catch the bus to **Leith** for a visit to the **Royal Yacht Britannia**. In the evening have dinner at one of Leith's many excellent restaurants, or scare yourself silly on a guided **ghost tour**.

Four Days

Two more days will give you time for a morning stroll around the **Royal Botanic Garden**, followed by a trip to the enigmatic and beautiful **Rosslyn Chapel**. Relax with a visit to the seaside village of **Cramond** – bring along binoculars (for birdwatching and yacht-spotting) and a book (to read in the sun). Dinner at the **Cafe Royal Oyster Bar** could be before or after your sunset walk to the summit of **Calton Hill**. On day four head out to the pretty harbour village of **Queensferry**, nestled beneath the **Forth Bridges**, and take a cruise to **Inchcolm Island**.

History

Edinburgh owes its existence to the Castle Rock, the glacier-worn stump of a long-extinct volcano that provided a near-perfect defensive position guarding the coastal route from northeast England into central Scotland.

Back in the 7th century the Castle Rock was called Dun Eiden (meaning 'Fort on the Hill Slope'). When it was captured by invaders from the kingdom of Northumbria in northeast England in 638, they took the existing Gaelic name 'Eiden' and tacked it onto their own Old English word for fort, 'burh', to create the name Edinburgh.

Originally a purely defensive site, Edinburgh began to expand in the 12th century when King David I held court at the castle and founded the abbey at Holyrood. The royal court came to prefer Edinburgh to Dunfermline and, as parliament followed the king, Edinburgh became Scotland's capital. The city's first effective town wall was constructed around 1450, enclosing the Old Town as far east as Netherbow and south to the Grassmarket. This overcrowded area – by then the most populous town in Scotland – became a medieval Manhattan, forcing its densely packed inhabitants to build upwards instead of outwards, creating tenements five and six storeys high.

The capital played an important role in the Reformation (1560–1690), led by the Calvinist firebrand John Knox. Mary, Queen of Scots held court in the Palace of Holyroodhouse for six brief years, but when her son James VI succeeded to the English throne in 1603 he moved his court to London. The Act of Union in 1707 further reduced Edinburgh's importance, but its cultural and intellectual life flourished.

In the second half of the 18th century a planned new town was created across the valley to the north of the Old Town. During the Scottish Enlightenment (roughly 1740–1830), Edinburgh became known as 'a hotbed of genius', inhabited by leading scientists and philosophers such as David Hume and Adam Smith.

In the 19th century the population quadrupled to 400,000, not much less than today's, and the Old Town's tenements were taken over by refugees from the Irish famines. A new ring of crescents and circuses was built to the north of New Town, and grey Victorian terraces spread south of the Old Town.

In the 1920s the city's borders expanded again to encompass Leith in the north, Cramond in the west and the Pentland Hills in the south. Following WWII the city's cultural life blossomed, stimulated by the Edinburgh International Festival and its fellow traveller the Fringe, both held for the first time in 1947 and now recognised as world-class arts festivals.

Edinburgh entered a new era following the 1997 referendum vote in favour of a devolved Scottish parliament, which first convened in July 1999. The parliament is housed in a controversial new building at the foot of the Royal Mile, where the 2007 elections saw the Scottish National Party – whose long-term aim is independence for Scotland – take power for the first time.

⊙ Sights

Edinburgh's main attractions are concentrated in the city centre – on and around the Old Town's Royal Mile between the castle and Holyrood, and in New Town. A major exception is the Royal Yacht *Britannia,* which is in the redeveloped docklands district of Leith, 2 miles northeast of the centre.

If you tire of sightseeing, good areas for aimless wandering include the posh suburbs of Stockbridge and Morningside, the pretty riverside village of Cramond, and the winding footpaths of Calton Hill and Arthur's Seat.

OLD TOWN
Edinburgh's Old Town stretches along a ridge to the east of the castle, and tumbles down Victoria St to the broad expanse of the Grassmarket. It's a jagged and jumbled maze of masonry riddled with closes (alleys) and wynds (narrow lanes), stairs and vaults, and cleft along its spine by the cobbled ravine of the Royal Mile.

Until the founding of New Town in the 18th century, old Edinburgh was an overcrowded and insanitary hive of humanity squeezed between the boggy ground of the Nor' Loch (North Loch, now drained and occupied by Princes Street Gardens) to the north and the city walls to the south and east. The only way for the town to expand was upwards, and the five- and six-storey tenements that were raised along the Royal Mile in the 16th and 17th centuries were the skyscrapers of their day, remarked upon with wonder by visiting writers such as Daniel Defoe. All classes of society, from beggars to magistrates, lived cheek by jowl in these urban ants' nests, the wealthy occupying the middle floors – high enough to be above the noise and stink of the streets, but not so high that climbing the stairs would be too tiring – while the poor squeezed into attics, basements, cellars and vaults amid the rats, rubbish and raw sewage.

The renovated Old Town tenements still support a thriving city-centre community, and today the street level is crammed with cafes, restaurants, bars, backpacker hostels and tacky souvenir shops. Few visitors wander beyond the main drag of the Royal Mile, but it's worth taking time to explore the countless closes that lead off the street into quiet courtyards, often with unexpected views of city, sea and hills.

THE ROYAL MILE
This mile-long street earned its regal nickname in the 16th century when it was used by the king to travel between the castle and the Palace of Holyroodhouse. There are five sections (the Castle Esplanade, Castlehill, Lawnmarket, High St and Canongate), the names of which reflect their historical origins.

Castlehill: the short slope connecting the castle esplanade to the Lawnmarket.

Lawnmarket: a corruption of 'Landmarket', a market selling goods from the land outside the city. Takes its name from the large cloth market that flourished here until the 18th century. This was the poshest part of the Old Town, where many of its most distinguished citizens made their homes.

High St: stretches from George IV Bridge down to the Netherbow at St Mary's St; is the heart and soul of the Old Town, home to the city's main church, the Law Courts, the city council and – until 1707 – the Scottish parliament.

Canongate: the stretch of the Royal Mile from Netherbow to Holyrood takes its name from the Augustinian canons (monks) of Holyrood Abbey. From the 16th

CITY MAPS

For coverage of the whole city in detail, the best maps are Nicolson's *Edinburgh Citymap* and the Ordnance Survey's (OS) *Edinburgh Street Atlas*. You can buy these at the Edinburgh & Scotland Information Centre, bookshops and newsagents. Note that long streets may be known by different names along their length. For example, the southern end of Leith Walk is variously called Union Pl and Antigua St on one side, Elm Row and Greenside Pl on the other.

The OS's 1:50,000 Landranger map *Edinburgh, Penicuik & North Berwick* (Sheet No 66) covers the city and the surrounding region to the south and east at a scale of 1.25 inches to 1 mile; it's useful for walking in the Pentland Hills and exploring Edinburgh's fringes and East Lothian.

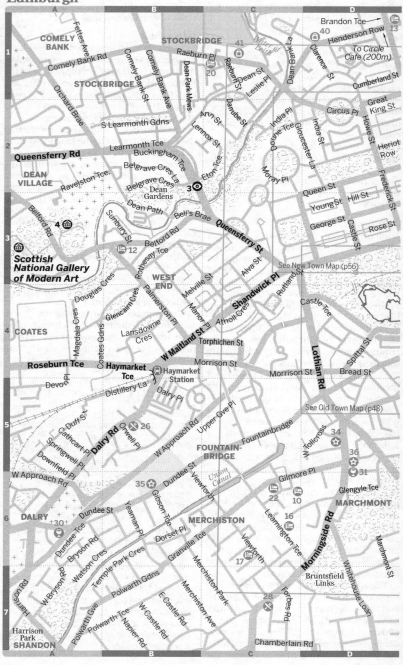

A map of Edinburgh showing the following areas and features:

COMELY BANK

STOCKBRIDGE

Brandon Tce
40
Henderson Row
13
To Circle
Cafe (200m)

Comely Bank Rd
Comely Bank Ave
Comely Bank St
Comely Bank Rd

Fettes Ave
Orchard Brae

Raeburn Pl
41
River of Leith
20
Dean Bank La
Clarence St
Cumberland St
Circus Pl
Great King St
Howe St
Heriot Row

Dean St
Leslie Pl
Raeburn St
Dean Bank La

Dean Park Mews
S Learmonth Gdns
Arn St
Danube St
Lennox St
India Pl
Doune Tce
India St
Gloucester La

Queensferry Rd
Learmonth Tce
Buckingham Tce
Belgrave Cres La
Eton Tce
Moray Pl
Queen St
Young St
Hill St
Frederick St

DEAN VILLAGE
Ravelston Tce
Belgrave Cres
Dean Gardens
3
Bell's Brae
Queensferry St
George St
Castle St
Rose St

4
Belford Rd
Sunbury St
Belford Rd
Rothesay Tce
WEST END
Dean Path
12
See New Town Map (p56)

Scottish National Gallery of Modern Art
3
Douglas Cres
Glencairn Cres
Melville St
Alva St
Shandwick Pl
Rutland St
Castle Tce

COATES
Magdala Cres
Coates Gdns
Palmerston Pl
Manor Pl
Atholl Cres
Lansdowne Cres
Torphichen St
Lothian Rd
Spittal St

Roseburn Tce
Haymarket Tce
Haymarket Station
W Maitland St
Morrison St
Morrison St
Bread St

Devon
Distillery La
Dalry Pl
See Old Town Map (p48)

Duff St
Cathcart Pl
Dalry Rd
Orwell Pl
26
Upper Gve Pl
W Approach Rd
Fountainbridge
34
Tollcross
36

Springwell Pl
Downfield Pl
W Approach Rd
FOUNTAIN-BRIDGE
31

35
Dundee St
Viewforth
Union Canal
Gilmore Pl
22
10
16
Glengyle Tce
MARCHMONT
Morningside Rd

DALRY
30
Dundee Tce
Bryson Rd
Dundee St
Yeaman Pl
Gibson Tce
MERCHISTON
Leamington Tce
17

W Bryson Rd
Watson Cres
Temple Park Cres
Dorset Pl
Granville Tce
Viewforth
Bruntsfield Links
Whitehouse Loan
Marchmont Rd

Harrison Rd
W Bryson Rd
Polwarth Gve
Polwarth Tce
Napier Rd
W Castle Rd
E Castle Rd
Merchiston Park
Merchiston Ave
28
Forbes Rd

Harrison Park
SHANDON
Chamberlain Rd

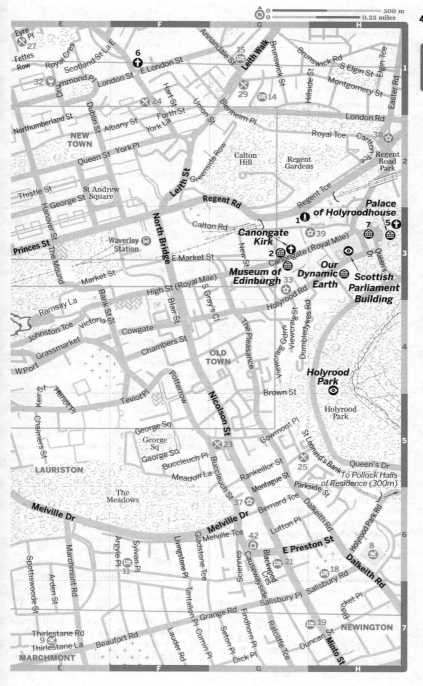

century it was home to aristocrats attracted to the Palace of Holyroodhouse. Originally governed by the monks, Canongate was an independent burgh separate from Edinburgh until 1856.

Edinburgh Castle CASTLE
(Map p48; www.edinburghcastle.gov.uk; Castlehill; adult/child incl audio guide £14/7.50; ⊙9.30am-6pm Apr-Sep, to 5pm Oct-Mar, last admission 45min before closing, closed 25 & 26 Dec) The brooding, black crags of Castle Rock rising above the western end of Princes St are the very reason for Edinburgh's existence. This rocky hill was the most easily defended hilltop on the invasion route between England and central Scotland, a route followed by countless armies from the Roman legions of the 1st and 2nd centuries AD to the Jacobite troops of Bonnie Prince Charlie in 1745.

Edinburgh Castle has played a pivotal role in Scottish history, both as a royal residence – King Malcolm Canmore (r 1058–93) and Queen Margaret first made their home here in the 11th century – and as a military stronghold. The castle last saw military action in 1745; from then until the 1920s it served as the British army's main base in Scotland. Today it is one of Scotland's most atmospheric, most popular – and most expensive – tourist attractions.

The **Entrance Gateway**, flanked by statues of Robert the Bruce and William Wallace, opens to a cobbled lane that leads up beneath the 16th-century **Portcullis Gate** to the cannons ranged along the Argyle and Mills Mount batteries. The battlements here have **great views** over New Town to the Firth of Forth.

At the far end of Mills Mount Battery is the famous **One O'Clock Gun**, where crowds gather to watch a gleaming WWII 25-pounder fire an ear-splitting time signal at exactly 1pm (every day except Sundays, Christmas Day and Good Friday).

South of Mills Mount, the road curls up leftwards through **Foog's Gate** to the highest part of Castle Rock, crowned by the tiny, Romanesque **St Margaret's Chapel**, the oldest surviving building in Edinburgh. It was probably built by David I or Alexander I in memory of their mother, Queen Margaret, sometime around 1130 (she was canonised in 1250). Beside the chapel stands **Mons Meg**, a giant 15th-century siege gun built at Mons (in what is now Belgium) in 1449.

The main group of buildings on the summit of Castle Rock are ranged around Crown Sq, dominated by the shrine of the **Scottish National War Memorial**. Opposite is the **Great Hall**, built for James IV (r 1488–1513) as a ceremonial hall and used as a meeting place for the Scottish parliament until 1639. Its most remarkable feature is the original, 16th-century hammer-beam roof.

The **Castle Vaults** beneath the Great Hall (entered from Crown Sq via the Prisons of War exhibit) were used variously as storerooms, bakeries and a prison. The vaults have been renovated to resemble 18th- and early-19th-century **prisons**, where graffiti carved by French and American prisoners can be seen on the ancient wooden doors.

On the eastern side of the square is the **Royal Palace**, built during the 15th and 16th centuries, where a series of historical tableaux leads to the highlight of the castle – a strongroom housing the **Honours of Scotland** (the Scottish crown jewels), the oldest surviving crown jewels in Europe. Locked away in a chest following the Act of Union in 1707, the crown (made in 1540 from the gold of Robert the Bruce's 14th-century coronet), sword and sceptre lay forgotten until they were unearthed at the instigation of the novelist Sir Walter Scott in 1818. Also on display here is the **Stone of Destiny** (p51).

Among the neighbouring **Royal Apartments** is the bedchamber where Mary, Queen of Scots gave birth to her son James VI, who was to unite the crowns of Scotland and England in 1603.

National War Museum of Scotland
(www.nms.ac.uk; admission incl in Edinburgh Castle ticket; ⏰9.45am-5.45pm Apr-Oct, to 4.45pm

DON'T MISS

CASTLE HIT LIST

If you're pushed for time, here's a hit list of the top things to see at Edinburgh Castle:

» Views from Argyle Battery
» One O'Clock Gun
» Great Hall
» Honours of Scotland
» Prisons of War

Nov-Mar) At the western end of the castle, to the left of the castle restaurant, a road leads down to the National War Museum of Scotland, which brings Scotland's military history vividly to life. The exhibits have been personalised by telling the stories of the original owners of the objects on display, making it easier to empathise with the experiences of war than any dry display of dusty weaponry ever could.

Highland Tolbooth Kirk   CHURCH
(Map p48; Castlehill; admission free; ⏰9.30am-7pm) Edinburgh's tallest spire (71.7m) is at the foot of Castlehill and is a prominent feature of the Old Town's skyline. The interior has been refurbished and it now houses the **Hub** (www.thehub-edinburgh.com), the ticket office and information centre for the Edinburgh Festival. There's also a good cafe here.

Scotch Whisky Experience
WHISKY EXHIBITION
(Map p48; www.scotchwhiskyexperience.co.uk; 354 Castlehill; adult/child incl tour & tasting £11.50/5.95; ⏰10am-6.30pm Jun-Aug, to 6pm Sep-May; 🚇) A former school houses this multimedia centre explaining the making of whisky from barley to bottle in a series of exhibits, demonstrations and tours that combine sight, sound and smell, including the world's largest collection of malt whiskies; look out for Peat the distillery cat! There's also a restaurant that serves traditional Scottish dishes with, where possible, a dash of whisky thrown in. It's a short distance downhill from the Castle Esplanade.

Camera Obscura   CAMERA OBSCURA
(Map p48; www.camera-obscura.co.uk; Castlehill; adult/child £9.25/6.25; ⏰9.30am-7.30pm Jul & Aug, 9.30am-6pm Apr-Jun, Sep & Oct, 10am-5pm Nov-Mar) Edinburgh's 'camera obscura' is a

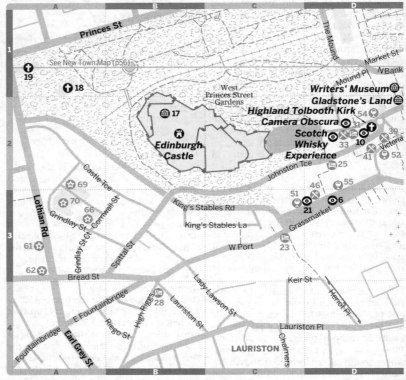

curious 19th-century device – in constant use since 1853 – that uses lenses and mirrors to throw a live image of the city onto a large horizontal screen. The accompanying commentary is entertaining and the whole experience has a quirky charm, complemented by an intriguing exhibition dedicated to illusions of all kinds. Stairs lead up through various displays to the **Outlook Tower**, which offers great views over the city.

Gladstone's Land HISTORIC HOUSE
(Map p48; NTS; www.nts.org.uk; 477 Lawnmarket; adult/child £5.50/4.50; ⊙10am-6.30pm Jul & Aug, to 5pm Apr-Jun, Sep & Oct) One of Edinburgh's most prominent 17th-century merchants was Thomas Gledstanes, who in 1617 purchased the tenement later known as Gladstone's Land. It contains fine painted ceilings, walls and beams, and some splendid furniture from the 17th and 18th centu-

ries. The volunteer guides provide a wealth of anecdotes and a detailed history.

FREE Writers' Museum LITERATURE MUSEUM
(Map p48; Lady Stair's Close, Lawnmarket; ⊙10am-5pm Mon-Sat year-round, 2-5pm Sun Aug) Tucked down a close just east of Gladstone's Land you'll find Lady Stair's House (1622), home to this museum which contains manuscripts and memorabilia belonging to three of Scotland's most famous writers: Robert Burns, Sir Walter Scott and Robert Louis Stevenson.

St Giles Cathedral CHURCH
(Map p48; www.stgilescathedral.org.uk; High St; £3 donation suggested; ⊙9am-7pm Mon-Fri, 9am-5pm Sat, 1-5pm Sun May-Sep, 9am-5pm Mon-Sat, 1-5pm Sun Oct-Apr) Dominating High St is the great grey bulk of St Giles Cathedral. Properly called the High Kirk of Edinburgh (it was only a true cathedral – the seat of a bishop – from 1633 to 1638 and from 1661 to

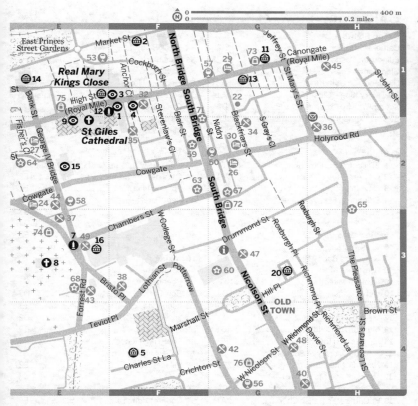

1689), St Giles Cathedral was named after the patron saint of cripples and beggars. A Norman-style church was built here in 1126 but was destroyed by English invaders in 1385; the only substantial remains are the central piers that support the tower.

The present church dates largely from the 15th century – the beautiful **crown spire** was completed in 1495 – but much of it was restored in the 19th century. The interior lacks grandeur but is rich in history: St Giles was at the heart of the Scottish Reformation, and John Knox served as minister here from 1559 to 1572. One of the most interesting corners of the kirk is the **Thistle Chapel**, built in 1911 for the Knights of the Most Ancient & Most Noble Order of the Thistle. The elaborately carved Gothic-style stalls have canopies topped with the helms and arms of the 16 knights – look out for the bagpipe-playing angel amid the vaulting.

By the side of the street, outside the western door of St Giles, is a cobblestone **Heart of Midlothian** set into the paving. This marks the site of the Tolbooth. Built in the 15th century and demolished in the early 19th century, the Tolbooth served variously as a meeting place for parliament, the town council and the General Assembly of the Reformed Kirk, before becoming law courts and, finally, a notorious prison and place of execution. Passers-by traditionally spit on the heart for luck (don't stand downwind!).

At the other end of St Giles is the **Mercat Cross**, a 19th-century copy of the 1365 original, where merchants and traders met to transact business and royal proclamations were read.

Real Mary King's Close   HISTORIC BUILDING
(Map p48; ☎0845 070 6255; www.realmarykings
close.com; 2 Warriston's Close, Writers Ct, High
St; adult/child £11/6; ⊙10am-9pm Apr-Oct, to
11pm Aug, 10am-5pm Sun-Thu, 10am-9pm Fri &

Old Town

Sat Nov-Mar) Across from St Giles is the City Chambers, originally built by John Adam (brother of Robert) between 1753 and 1761 to serve as the Royal Exchange – a covered meeting place for city merchants. However, the merchants preferred their old stamping ground in the street and the building became the city council offices in 1811.

Part of the Royal Exchange was built over the sealed-off remains of Mary King's Close, and the lower levels of this medieval Old Town alley have survived almost unchanged in the foundations of the City Chambers for 250 years. Now open to the public as the Real Mary King's Close, this spooky, subterranean labyrinth gives a fascinating insight into the daily life of 16th- and 17th-century Edinburgh. Costumed characters give tours through a 16th-century town house and the plague-stricken home of a 17th-century gravedigger. Advance booking recommended.

3D Loch Ness Experience   EXHIBITION
(Map p48; www.3dlochness.com; 1 Parliament Sq; adult/child £5.95/3.95; ◉9.30am-10pm Jul & Aug, 9.30am-8pm Apr-Jun, Sep & Oct, 10am-5pm Nov-Mar) The centrepiece of this exhibition dedicated to Scotland's most famous mythical beastie is a 3D documentary film (in five languages) exploring the various theories, eyewitness accounts and hoaxes surrounding the Loch Ness Monster (for more on Nessie, see the boxed text, p325). Plus, of course, a gift shop crammed with cheekily priced cuddly toys in the form of Nessie...

FREE **Museum of Childhood**   MUSEUM
(Map p48; 42 High St; ◉10am-5pm Mon-Sat, 2-5pm Sun) Halfway down the Royal Mile is 'the noisiest museum in the world'. Often filled with the chatter of excited children, it covers serious issues related to childhood – health, education, upbringing and so on – but also has an enormous collection of toys, dolls, games and books, recordings of school lessons from the 1930s, and film of kids playing street games in 1950s Edinburgh.

John Knox House   HISTORIC HOUSE
(Map p48; www.scottishstorytellingcentre.co.uk; 43-45 High St; adult/child £4/1; ◉10am-6pm Mon-Sat year-round, noon-6pm Sun Jul & Aug) The Royal Mile narrows at the foot of High St beside the jutting facade of John Knox House. This is the oldest surviving tenement in Edinburgh, dating from around 1490; John Knox, an influential church reformer and leader of the Protestant Ref

THE STONE OF DESTINY

On St Andrew's Day 1996 a block of sandstone – 26.5 inches by 16.5 inches by 11 inches in size, with rusted iron hoops at either end – was installed with much pomp and ceremony in Edinburgh Castle. For the previous 700 years it had lain in London, beneath the Coronation Chair in Westminster Abbey. Almost all English, and later British, monarchs from Edward II in 1307 to Elizabeth II in 1953 have parked their backsides firmly over this stone during their coronation ceremony.

The legendary Stone of Destiny – said to have originated in the Holy Land, and on which Scottish kings placed their feet during their coronation (not their bums; the English got that bit wrong) – was stolen from Scone Abbey near Perth by King Edward I of England in 1296. It was taken to London and there it remained for seven centuries – except for a brief removal to Gloucester during WWII air raids, and a three-month sojourn in Scotland after it was stolen by Scottish Nationalist students at Christmas in 1950 – an enduring symbol of Scotland's subjugation by England.

The Stone of Destiny returned to the political limelight in 1996, when the then Scottish Secretary and Conservative Party MP, Michael Forsyth, arranged for the return of the sandstone block to Scotland. A blatant attempt to boost the flagging popularity of the Conservative Party in Scotland prior to a general election, Forsyth's publicity stunt failed miserably. The Scots said thanks very much for the stone and then, in May 1997, voted every Conservative MP in Scotland into oblivion.

Many people, however, believe that Edward I was fobbed off with a shoddy imitation in 1296 and that the true Stone of Destiny remains safely hidden somewhere in Scotland. This is not impossible – some descriptions of the original state that it was made of black marble and decorated with elaborate carvings. Interested parties should read *Scotland's Stone of Destiny* by Nick Aitchinson, which details the history and cultural significance of Scotland's most famous lump of rock.

ormation in Scotland, is thought to have lived here from 1561 to 1572. The labyrinthine interior has some beautiful painted-timber ceilings and an interesting display on Knox's life and work.

FREE **People's Story** MUSEUM
(Map p44; 163 Canongate; ☺10am-5pm Mon-Sat year-round, 2-5pm Sun Aug) One of the surviving symbols of Canongate's former independence is the **Canongate Tolbooth**. Built in 1591, it served successively as a collection point for tolls (taxes), a council house, a courtroom and a jail. With picturesque turrets and a projecting clock, it's an interesting example of 16th-century architecture. It now houses a fascinating museum called the **People's Story**, which covers the life, work and pastimes of ordinary Edinburgh folk from the 18th century to today.

FREE **Museum of Edinburgh** MUSEUM
(Map p44; 142 Canongate; ☺10am-5pm Mon-Sat year-round, 2-5pm Sun Aug) Across the street from the People's Story is Huntly House. Built in 1570, it now houses a museum covering Edinburgh from its prehistory to the present. Exhibits of national importance include an original copy of the National Covenant of 1638, but the big crowd-pleaser is the dog collar and feeding bowl that once belonged to **Greyfriars Bobby**, the city's most famous canine citizen.

Canongate Kirk CHURCH
Downhill from Huntly House is the attractive curved gable of the Canongate Kirk (Map p44), built in 1688. The kirkyard contains the graves of several famous people, including the economist **Adam Smith** (1723–90), author of *The Wealth of Nations;* Mrs Agnes MacLehose (the 'Clarinda' of

---

HAVE YOUR SAY

Found a fantastic restaurant that you're longing to share with the world? Disagree with our recommendations? Or just want to talk about your most recent trip?

Whatever your reason, head to lonelyplanet.com, where you can post a review, ask or answer a question on the Thorntree forum, comment on a blog, or share your photos and tips on Groups. Or you can simply spend time chatting with like-minded travellers. So go on, have your say.

Robert Burns' love poems); and the 18th-century poet **Robert Fergusson** (1750–74). Fergusson was much admired by **Robert Burns**, who paid for the gravestone and penned the epitaph – take a look at the inscription on the back.

HOLYROOD

Palace of Holyroodhouse ROYAL PALACE
(Map p44; www.royalcollection.org.uk; Canongate; adult/child £10.25/6.20; ☺9.30am-6pm Apr-Oct, to 4.30pm Nov-Mar) This palace is the royal family's official residence in Scotland, but is most famous as the 16th-century home of the ill-fated **Mary, Queen of Scots**. The palace developed from a guesthouse attached to Holyrood Abbey, which was extended by King James IV in 1501. The oldest surviving part of the building, the northwestern tower, was built in 1529 as a royal apartment for James V and his wife, Mary of Guise. Mary, Queen of Scots spent six turbulent years here, during which time she debated with John Knox, married both her first and second husbands, and witnessed the murder of her secretary David Rizzio. The palace is closed to the public when the royal family is visiting and during state functions (usually in mid-May, and mid-June to early July; check the website for exact dates).

The guided tour leads you through a series of impressive royal apartments, ending in the **Great Gallery**. The 89 portraits of Scottish kings were commissioned by Charles II and supposedly record his unbroken lineage from Scota, the Egyptian pharaoh's daughter who discovered the infant Moses in a reed basket on the banks of the Nile.

But the highlight of the tour is **Mary, Queen of Scots' Bed Chamber**, home to the unfortunate Mary from 1561 to 1567, and connected by a secret stairway to her husband's bedchamber. It was here that her jealous first husband, Lord Darnley, restrained the pregnant queen while his henchmen murdered her secretary – and favourite – Rizzio. A plaque in the neighbouring room marks the spot where he bled to death.

Holyrood Abbey
(admission incl in palace ticket; ☺same as palace) The exit from the palace leads into the ruins of Holyrood Abbey. In summer you can join a **guided tour** of the ruins (included with your admission fee); the rest of the year you can explore them on your own. King David I founded the abbey here in the shadow of Salisbury Crags in 1128.

SCOTTISH PARLIAMENT BUILDING

The **Scottish parliament building** (Map p44; ☎0131-348 5200; www.scottish.parlia ment.uk; admission free; ☉9am-6.30pm Tue-Thu, 10am-5.30pm Mon & Fri in session, 10am-6pm Mon-Fri in recess Apr-Oct, 10am-4pm in recess Nov-Mar; ☎), built on the site of a former brewery close to the Palace of Holyroodhouse, was officially opened by HM the Queen in October 2005.

The public areas of the parliament building – the Main Hall, where there is an exhibition, a shop and cafe, and the **public gallery** in the Debating Chamber – are open to visitors (tickets needed for public gallery – see website for details). You can also take a free, one-hour **guided tour** (advance booking recommended) that includes a visit to the Debating Chamber, a committee room, the Garden Lobby and, when possible, the office of an MSP (Member of the Scottish Parliament). If you want to see the **parliament in session**, check the website to see when it will be sitting – business days are normally Tuesday to Thursday year-round.

Enric Miralles (1955–2000), the architect who conceived the Scottish parliament building, believed that a building could be a work of art. However, the weird concrete confection that has sprouted at the foot of Salisbury Crags has left the good people of Edinburgh staring and scratching their heads in confusion. What does it all mean? The strange forms of the exterior are all symbolic in some way, from the oddly shaped windows on the west wall (inspired by the silhouette of the *Reverend Robert Walker Skating on Duddingston Loch,* one of Scotland's most famous paintings), to the ground plan of the whole complex, which represents a 'flower of democracy rooted in Scottish soil' (best seen looking down from Salisbury Crags).

The **Main Hall**, inside the public entrance, has a low, triple-arched ceiling of polished concrete, like a cave, or cellar or castle vault. It is a dimly lit space, the starting point for a metaphorical journey from this relative darkness up to the **Debating Chamber** (sitting directly above the Main Hall), which is, in contrast, a palace of light – the light of democracy. This magnificent chamber is the centrepiece of the parliament, designed not to glorify but to humble the politicians who sit within it. The windows face Calton Hill, allowing MSPs to look up to its monuments (reminders of the Scottish Enlightenment), while the massive, pointed oak beams of the roof are suspended by steel threads above the MSPs' heads like so many Damoclean swords.

It was probably named after a fragment of the True Cross (rood is an old Scots word for cross), said to have been brought to Scotland by his mother, St Margaret. Most of the surviving ruins date from the 12th and 13th centuries, although a doorway in the far southeastern corner has survived from the original Norman church.

Queen's Gallery

(Map p44; adult/child £5.50/3, joint ticket incl admission to palace £14.30/8.30; ☉same as palace) The Queen's Gallery, beside the palace ticket office, is a showcase for a range of changing exhibitions of art from the Royal Collections.

Our Dynamic Earth   MULTIMEDIA EXHIBITION
(Map p44; www.dynamicearth.co.uk; Holyrood Rd; adult/child £10.50/7; ☉10am-6pm Jul & Aug, to 5.30pm Apr-Jun, Sep & Oct, to 5pm Wed-Sun Nov-Mar, last admission 90min before closing; ☎) The modernistic white marquee pitched beneath Salisbury Crags marks Our Dynamic Earth, billed as an interactive, multimedia journey of discovery through Earth's history from the big bang to the present day. Hugely popular with kids of all ages, it's a slick extravaganza of whiz-bang special effects and 3D movies cleverly designed to fire up young minds with curiosity about all things geological and environmental. Its true purpose, of course, is to disgorge you into a gift shop where you can buy model dinosaurs and souvenir T-shirts.

Holyrood Park   PARK
(Map p44) In Holyrood Park Edinburgh is blessed with a little bit of wilderness in the heart of the city. The former hunting ground of Scottish monarchs, the park covers 263 hectares of varied landscape, including crags, moorland and loch. The highest point is the 251m summit of **Arthur's Seat,**

the deeply eroded remnant of a long-extinct volcano. Holyrood Park can be circumnavigated by car or bike along Queen's Dr (it is closed to motorised traffic on Sunday), and you can hike from Holyrood to the summit in around 45 minutes.

NORTH OF THE ROYAL MILE

FREE **Fruitmarket Gallery**　　　GALLERY
(Map p56; www.fruitmarket.co.uk; 45 Market St; ☺11am-6pm Mon-Sat, noon-5pm Sun) One of Edinburgh's most innovative and popular galleries, the Fruitmarket showcases contemporary Scottish and international artists, and also has an excellent arts bookshop and cafe.

FREE **City Art Centre**　　　ART CENTRE
(Map p48; 2 Market St; fee for temporary exhibitions; ☺10am-5pm Mon-Sat, noon-5pm Sun) Across the street from the Fruitmarket Gallery is this art centre comprising six floors of exhibitions with a variety of themes, including an extensive collection of Scottish art.

SOUTH OF THE ROYAL MILE

FREE **National Museum of Scotland**
　　　　　　　　　　　　　　　MUSEUM
(Map p48; www.nms.ac.uk; Chambers St; fee for special exhibitions; ☺10am-5pm) Broad, elegant Chambers St is dominated by the long facade of the National Museum of Scotland. Its extensive collections are spread between two buildings, one modern, one Victorian.

The golden stone and striking modern architecture of the museum building, opened in 1998, is one of the city's most distinctive landmarks. The five floors of the museum trace the history of Scotland from geological beginnings to the 1990s, with many imaginative and stimulating exhibits – audio guides are available in several languages. Highlights include the **Monymusk Reliquary**, a tiny silver casket dating from AD 750, which is said to have been carried into battle with Robert the Bruce at Bannockburn in 1314, and some of the **Lewis chessmen**, a set of charming 12th-century chess pieces made from walrus ivory. Don't forget to take the lift to the **roof terrace** for a fantastic view of the castle.

The Museum of Scotland connects with the Victorian **Royal Museum** building, dating from 1861, the stolid, grey exterior of which gives way to a bright and airy, glassroofed hall. The museum houses an eclectic collection covering natural history, archaeology, scientific and industrial technology, and the decorative arts of ancient Egypt, Islam, China, Japan, Korea and the West.

(The Royal Museum was undergoing a major rebuild at the time of research; it is due to reopen in mid-2011.)

FREE **Greyfriars Kirk**　　　CHURCH
(Map p48; www.greyfriarskirk.com; Candlemaker Row; ☺10.30am-4.40pm Mon-Fri & 10.30am-2pm Sat, 1.30-3.30pm Thu only Nov-Mar) Candlemaker Row leads from the eastern end of the Grassmarket towards one of Edinburgh's most famous churches. **Greyfriars Kirk** was built on the site of a Franciscan friary and opened for worship on Christmas Day 1620. In 1638 the **National Covenant** was signed here, rejecting Charles I's attempts to impose episcopacy and a new English prayer book, and affirming the independence of the Scottish Church. Many who signed were later executed at the Grassmarket and, in 1679, 1200 Covenanters were held prisoner in terrible conditions in the southwestern corner of the kirkyard. There's a small exhibition inside the church.

Surrounding the church, hemmed in by high walls and overlooked by the brooding presence of the castle, **Greyfriars Kirkyard** is one of Edinburgh's most evocative cemeteries, a peaceful green oasis dotted with elaborate monuments. Many famous Edinburgh names are buried here, including the poet Allan Ramsay (1686–1758), architect William Adam (1689–1748) and William Smellie (1740–95), the editor of the first edition of the *Encyclopedia Britannica*.

In July and August you can join a **guided tour** (free; donation suggested) of the kirkyard; check the website for times and dates. If you want to experience the graveyard at its scariest – inside a burial vault, in the dark, at night – go on one of Black Hart Storytellers' guided tours.

Greyfriars Bobby Statue　　　MONUMENT
(Map p48) The memorials inside Greyfriars Kirkyard are interesting, but the one that draws the biggest crowds is outside, in front of the pub beside the kirkyard gate. It's the tiny statue of Greyfriars Bobby, a Skye terrier who, from 1858 to 1872, maintained a vigil over the grave of his master, an Edinburgh police officer. The story was immortalised (and romanticised) in a novel by Eleanor Atkinson in 1912, and in 1963 was made into a movie by – who else? – Walt Disney. Bobby's own grave, marked by a small, pink granite stone, is just inside the entrance to the kirkyard. You can see his original collar and bowl in the Museum of Edinburgh.

(Map p48) The site of a cattle market from the 15th century until the start of the 20th, the Grassmarket has always been a focal point of the Old Town. It was also the city's main **place of execution**, and over 100 martyred Covenanters are commemorated by a monument at the eastern end, where the gallows used to stand. The notorious murderers **Burke and Hare** operated from a now-vanished close off the western end. In 1827 they enticed at least 18 victims to their boarding house, suffocated them and sold the bodies to Edinburgh's medical schools. The law finally caught up with Burke and Hare – the latter turned King's evidence and testified against Burke, who was hanged outside St Giles in 1828. In an ironic twist, his corpse was donated to the anatomy school for public dissection, and a pocket book was made from his flayed skin (now on display in the Surgeons' Hall Museums).

Nowadays the broad, open square, edged by tall tenements and dominated by the looming castle, has many lively pubs and restaurants, including the **White Hart Inn**, which was once patronised by Robert Burns. **Cowgate** – the long, dark ravine leading eastwards from the Grassmarket – was once the road along which cattle were driven from the pastures around Arthur's Seat to the safety of the city walls. Today it is the heart of Edinburgh's nightlife, with around two dozen clubs and bars within five minutes' walk of each other.

NEW TOWN

Edinburgh's New Town lies north of the Old Town, on a ridge running parallel to the Royal Mile, separated from it by the valley

UNDERGROUND EDINBURGH

As Edinburgh expanded in the late 18th and early 19th centuries, many old tenements were demolished and new bridges were built to link the Old Town to the newly built areas to its north and south. South Bridge (built between 1785 and 1788) and George IV Bridge (built between 1829 and 1834) lead southwards from the Royal Mile over the deep valley of Cowgate, but so many buildings have been built closely around them that you can hardly tell they are bridges – George IV Bridge has a total of nine arches but only two are visible; South Bridge has no less than 18 hidden arches.

These **subterranean vaults** were originally used as storerooms, workshops and drinking dens. But as early-19th-century Edinburgh's population was swelled by an influx of penniless Highlanders cleared from their lands, and Irish refugees from the potato famine, the dark, dripping chambers were given over to slum accommodation and abandoned to poverty, filth and crime.

The vaults were eventually cleared in the late 19th century, then lay forgotten until 1994 when the **South Bridge vaults** were opened to guided tours (see Mercat Tours, p67). Certain chambers are said to be haunted and one particular vault was investigated by paranormal researchers in 2001.

Nevertheless, the most ghoulish aspect of Edinburgh's hidden history dates from much earlier – from the plague that struck the city in 1645. Legend has it that the disease-ridden inhabitants of **Mary King's Close** (a lane on the northern side of the Royal Mile on the site of the City Chambers – you can still see its blocked-off northern end from Cockburn St) were walled up in their houses and left to perish. When the lifeless bodies were eventually cleared from the houses, they were so stiff that workmen had to hack off limbs to get them through the small doorways and narrow, twisting stairs.

From that day on, the close was said to be haunted by the spirits of the plague victims. The few people who were prepared to live there reported seeing apparitions of severed heads and limbs, and the largely abandoned close fell into ruin. When the Royal Exchange (now the City Chambers) was constructed between 1753 and 1761, it was built over the lower levels of Mary King's Close, which were left intact and sealed off beneath the building.

Interest in the close revived in the 20th century when Edinburgh's city council began to allow occasional guided tours to enter. Visitors have reported many supernatural experiences – the most famous ghost is 'Sarah', a little girl whose sad tale has prompted people to leave gifts of dolls in a corner of one of the rooms. In 2003 the close was opened to the public as the Real Mary King's Close.

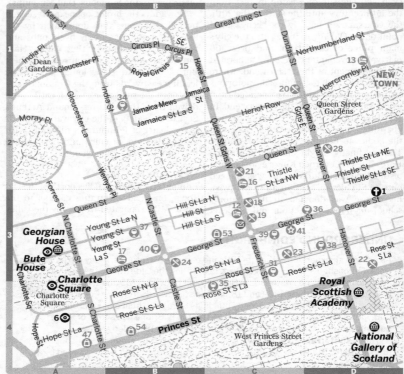

of Princes Street Gardens. Its regular grid of elegant Georgian terraces is a complete contrast to the chaotic tangle of tenements and wynds that characterise the Old Town.

Between the end of the 14th century and the start of the 18th, the population of Edinburgh – still confined within the walls of the Old Town – increased from 2000 to 50,000. The tottering tenements were unsafe and occasionally collapsed, fire was an ever-present danger, and the overcrowding and squalor became unbearable.

When the Act of Union in 1707 brought the prospect of long-term stability, the upper classes were keen to find healthier, more spacious living quarters, and in 1766 the lord provost of Edinburgh announced an architectural competition to design an extension to the city. It was won by an unknown 23-year-old, James Craig, a self-taught architect whose simple and elegant plan envisaged the main axis being George St, with

grand squares at either end, and with building restricted to one side only of Princes and Queen Sts so that the houses enjoyed views over the Firth of Forth to the north and to the castle and Old Town to the south.

During the 18th and 19th centuries New Town continued to sprout squares, circuses, parks and terraces, with some of its finest neoclassical architecture designed by Robert Adam. Today Edinburgh's New Town remains the world's most complete and unspoilt example of Georgian architecture and town planning. Along with the Old Town, it was declared a Unesco World Heritage Site in 1995.

PRINCES STREET

Princes St is one of the world's most spectacular shopping streets. Built up on the north side only, it catches the sun in summer and allows expansive views across Princes Street Gardens to the castle and the crowded skyline of the Old Town.

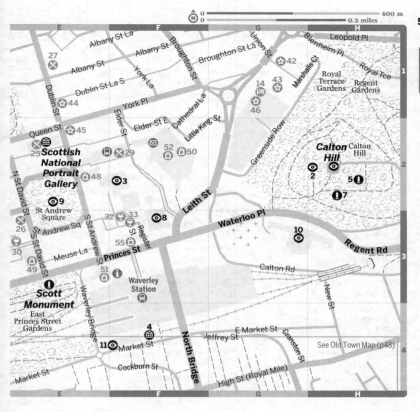

The western end of Princes St is dominated by the red-sandstone edifice of the Caledonian Hilton Hotel, and the tower of **St John's Church**, worth visiting for its fine Gothic Revival interior. It overlooks **St Cuthbert's Parish Church**, built in the 1890s on a site of great antiquity – there has been a church here since at least the 12th century, and perhaps since the 7th century. There is a circular **watchtower** in the graveyard – a reminder of the Burke and Hare days when graves had to be guarded against robbers.

At the eastern end is the prominent clock tower – traditionally three minutes fast so that you don't miss your train – of the **Balmoral Hotel** (originally the North British Hotel, built by the railway company of the same name in 1902) and the beautiful 1788 **Register House**, designed by Robert Adam, with a statue of the duke of Wellington on horseback in front. It houses the National Archives of Scotland and the ScotlandsPeople genealogical research centre.

Princes Street Gardens lie in a valley that was once occupied by the Nor' Loch, a boggy depression that was drained in the early 19th century. The gardens are split in the middle by **The Mound**, which was created by around two million cart-loads of earth excavated from the foundations of New Town being dumped here to provide a road link across the valley to the Old Town. It was completed in 1830.

Scott Monument　　MONUMENT
(Map p56; East Princes Street Gardens; admission £3; ◎10am-7pm Apr-Sep, 9am-4pm Mon-Sat, 10am-4pm Sun Oct-Mar) The eastern half of Princes Street Gardens is dominated by the massive Gothic spire of the Scott Monument, built by public subscription in memory of the novelist Sir Walter Scott after his death in 1832. The exterior is decorated with carvings of characters from his novels;

inside you can see an exhibition on Scott's life, and climb the 287 steps to the top for a superb view of the city.

FREE **National Gallery of Scotland**
ART GALLERY

(Map p56; www.nationalgalleries.org; The Mound; fee for special exhibitions; ◉10am-5pm, to 7pm Thu; ☎) Designed by William Playfair, this imposing classical building with its Ionic porticoes dates from the 1850s. Its octagonal rooms, lit by skylights, have been restored to their original Victorian decor of deep-green carpets and dark-red walls.

The gallery houses an important collection of **European art** from the Renaissance to post-Impressionism, with works by Verrocchio (Leonardo da Vinci's teacher), Tintoretto, Titian, Holbein, Rubens, Van Dyck, Vermeer, El Greco, Poussin, Rembrandt, Gainsborough, Turner, Constable, Monet, Pissarro, Gauguin and Cézanne; each year in January the gallery exhibits its collection of **Turner watercolours**, bequeathed by Henry Vaughan in 1900. Room X is graced by Antonio Canova's white marble sculpture **The Three Graces**; it is owned jointly with London's Victoria & Albert Museum.

The upstairs galleries house portraits by Sir Joshua Reynolds and Sir Henry Raeburn, and a clutch of **Impressionist** paintings including Monet's luminous *Haystacks,* Van Gogh's demonic *Olive Trees* and Gauguin's hallucinatory *Vision After the Sermon.* But the painting that really catches your eye is the gorgeous portrait of *Lady Agnew of Lochnaw* by John Singer Sargent.

The basement galleries dedicated to **Scottish art** include glowing portraits by Allan Ramsay and Sir Henry Raeburn, rural scenes by Sir David Wilkie and impressionistic landscapes by William MacTaggart. Look out for Raeburn's iconic *Reverend Robert Walker Skating on Duddingston Loch,* and Sir George Harvey's hugely entertaining *A Schule Skailin* (A School Emptying) – a stern dominie (teacher) looks on as the boys stampede for the classroom door, one reaching for a spinning top confiscated earlier. Kids will love the fantasy paintings of Sir Joseph Noel Paton in Room B5; the incredibly detailed canvases are crammed with hundreds of tiny fairies, goblins and elves.

FREE **Royal Scottish Academy** ART GALLERY
(Map p56; www.royalscottishacademy.org; The Mound; fee for special exhibitions; ⊙10am-5pm Mon-Sat, 2-5pm Sun; 🐾) The distinguished Greek Doric temple at the corner of The Mound and Princes St, its northern pediment crowned by a seated figure of Queen Victoria, is the home of the Royal Scottish Academy. Designed by William Playfair and built between 1823 and 1836, it was originally called the Royal Institution; the RSA took over the building in 1910. The galleries display a collection of paintings, sculptures and architectural drawings by academy members dating from 1831, and they also host temporary exhibitions throughout the year.

The RSA and the National Gallery of Scotland are linked via an underground mall – the **Weston Link** – which gives them twice the temporary exhibition space of the Prado in Madrid and three times that of the Royal Academy in London, as well as housing cloakrooms, a lecture theatre and a restaurant. The galleries have become famous in recent years for 'blockbuster' exhibitions such as 'The Age of Titian' and 'Impressionist Gardens'.

Until the 1990s George St – the major axis of New Town – was the centre of Edinburgh's financial industry and Scotland's equivalent of Wall St. Today the big financial firms have moved to premises in the Exchange office district west of Lothian Rd, and George St's former banks and offices house upmarket shops, pubs and restaurants.

At the western end of George St is **Charlotte Square**, the architectural jewel of New Town, designed by Robert Adam shortly before his death in 1791. The northern side of the square is Adam's masterpiece and one of the finest examples of Georgian architecture anywhere. **Bute House**, in the centre at No 6, is the official residence of Scotland's first minister.

FREE **National Trust for Scotland**
HISTORIC BUILDING
(Map p56; www.nts.org.uk; 28 Charlotte Sq; ⊙9.30am-5pm Mon-Sat) The headquarters of the National Trust is on the southern side of the square. As well as a shop, cafe and information desk, the building contains a restored 1820s **drawing room** (⊙11am-3pm Mon-Fri) with Regency furniture and a collection of 20th-century Scottish paintings.

Georgian House HISTORIC HOUSE
(Map p56; NTS; 7 Charlotte Sq; adult/child £5.50/4.50; ⊙10am-6pm Jul & Aug, 10am-5pm Apr-Jun, Sep & Oct, 11am-4pm Mar, 11am-3pm Nov) Next door to Bute House is the National Trust of Scotland's Georgian House, which has been beautifully restored and furnished to show how Edinburgh's wealthy elite lived at the end of the 18th century. The walls are decorated with paintings by Allan Ramsay, Sir Henry Raeburn and Sir Joshua Reynolds.

ST ANDREW SQUARE
Not as architecturally distinguished as its sister at the opposite end of George St, **St Andrew Square** is dominated by the fluted column of the **Melville Monument**, commemorating Henry Dundas, 1st Viscount Melville (1742–1811). Dundas was the most powerful Scottish politician of his time, often referred to when alive as 'Harry IX, the Uncrowned King of Scotland'. The impressive Palladian mansion of **Dundas House**, built between 1772 and 1774, on the eastern side of the square, was built for Sir Laurence Dundas (1712–81) – no relation to Viscount Melville. It has been the head office of the Royal Bank of Scotland since 1825 and

has a spectacular domed banking hall dating from 1857 (you can nip inside for a look).

A short distance along George St is the **Church of St Andrew & St George**, built in 1784 with an unusual oval nave. It was the scene of the Disruption of 1843, when 451 dissenting ministers left the Church of Scotland to form the Free Church.

FREE **Scottish National Portrait Gallery**   ART GALLERY
(Map p56; www.nationalgalleries.org; 1 Queen St; ⊙10am-5pm, to 7pm Thu) Just north of St Andrew Sq at the junction with Queen St is the Venetian Gothic palace of the Scottish National Portrait Gallery. Its galleries illustrate Scottish history through portraits and sculptures of famous Scottish personalities, from Robert Burns and Bonnie Prince Charlie to Sean Connery and Billy Connolly. Opening hours are extended during the Edinburgh Festival.

CALTON HILL

Calton Hill (100m; Map p56), rising dramatically above the eastern end of Princes St, is Edinburgh's acropolis, its summit scattered with grandiose memorials mostly dating from the first half of the 19th century. It is also one of the best viewpoints in Edinburgh, with a panorama that takes in the castle, Holyrood, Arthur's Seat, the Firth of Forth, New Town and the full length of Princes St.

On the southern side of the hill, on Regent Rd, is the modernist facade of **St Andrew's House** (Map p56), built between 1936 and 1939, which housed the civil servants of the Westminster government's Scottish Office until they were moved to the new Scottish Executive building in Leith in 1996.

Just beyond St Andrew's House and on the opposite side of the road is the imposing **Royal High School** building, dating from 1829 and modelled on the Temple of Theseus in Athens. Former pupils include Robert Adam, Alexander Graham Bell and Sir Walter Scott. It now stands empty. To its east, on the other side of Regent Rd, is the 1830 **Burns Monument** (Map p44), a Greek-style memorial to Robert Burns.

You can reach the summit of Calton Hill via the road beside the Royal High School or by the stairs at the eastern end of Waterloo Pl. The largest structure on the summit is the **National Monument** (Map p56), an over ambitious attempt to replicate the Parthenon and intended to honour Scotland's

dead in the Napoleonic Wars. Construction – paid for by public subscription – began in 1822, but funds ran dry when only 12 columns were complete.

Looking a bit like an upturned telescope – the similarity is intentional – and offering even better views, the **Nelson Monument** (Map p56; Calton Hill; admission £3; ⊙1-6pm Mon, 10am-6pm Tue-Sat Apr-Sep, 10am-3pm Mon-Sat Oct-Mar) was built to commemorate Admiral Lord Nelson's victory at Trafalgar in 1805.

The design of the **City Observatory** (Map p56), built in 1818, was based on the ancient Greek Temple of the Winds in Athens. Its original function was to provide a precise, astronomical time-keeping service for marine navigators, but smoke from Waverley train station forced the astronomers to move to Blackford Hill in the south of Edinburgh in 1895.

DEAN VILLAGE

If you follow Queensferry St northwards from the western end of Princes St, you come to **Dean Bridge** (Map p44), designed by Thomas Telford and built between 1829 and 1832. Down in the valley just west of the bridge is **Dean Village** (from 'dene', a Scots word for valley). It was founded as a milling community by the canons of Holyrood Abbey in the 12th century and by 1700 there were 11 watermills here operated by the Incorporation of Baxters (the bakers' trade guild). One of the old mill buildings has been converted into flats, and the village is now an attractive residential area.

FREE **Scottish National Gallery of Modern Art**   ART GALLERY
(Map p44; NGMA; www.nationalgalleries.org; 75 Belford Rd; fee for special exhibitions; ⊙10am-5pm) Set in an impressive neoclassical building surrounded by a landscaped sculpture park some 500m west of Dean Village is the Scottish National Gallery of Modern Art. The collection concentrates on **20th-century art**, with various European movements represented by the likes of Matisse, Picasso, Kirchner, Magritte, Miró, Mondrian and Giacometti. American and English artists are also represented, but most space is given to Scottish painters – from the Scottish colourists of the early 20th century to contemporary artists such as Peter Howson and Ken Currie. There's an excellent **cafe** downstairs, and the surrounding **park** features sculptures by Henry Moore, Rachel Whiteread and Barbara

Hepworth among others, as well as a 'landform artwork' by Charles Jencks.

A footpath and stairs at the rear of the gallery lead down to the **Water of Leith Walkway**, which you can follow along the river for 4 miles to Leith. This takes you past **6 Times**, a sculptural project by **Anthony Gormley** consisting of six human figures standing at various points along the river.

Dean Gallery

(Map p44; ☺10am-5pm) Directly across Belford Rd from the NGMA's main building, another neoclassical mansion houses its annexe, the Dean Gallery. The Dean holds the NGMA's collection of Dada and surrealist art, including works by Dali, Giacometti and Picasso, and a large collection of sculpture and graphic art created by the Edinburgh-born sculptor Sir Eduardo Paolozzi.

LEITH

Two miles northeast of the city centre, Leith has been Edinburgh's seaport since the 14th century and remained an independent burgh with its own town council until it was incorporated by the city in the 1920s. Like many of Britain's dockland areas, it fell into decay in the decades following WWII but has been undergoing a revival since the late 1980s. Old warehouses have been turned into luxury flats, and a lush crop of trendy bars and restaurants has sprouted along the waterfront. The area was given an additional boost in the late 1990s when the Scottish Executive (a government department) moved to a new building on Leith docks.

The city council has formulated a major redevelopment plan for the entire Edinburgh waterfront from Leith to Granton, the first phase of which is Ocean Terminal, a shopping and leisure complex that includes the former Royal Yacht *Britannia* and a berth for visiting cruise liners. Parts of Leith are still a bit rough but it's a distinctive corner of the city and well worth exploring.

Royal Yacht Britannia   HISTORIC SHIP

(Map p62; www.royalyachtbritannia.co.uk; Ocean Terminal, Leith; adult/child £10.50/6.75; ☺9.30am-6pm Jul-Sep, 10am-5.30pm Apr-Jun & Oct, 10am-5pm Nov-Mar, last admission 1½hr before closing; ☎) One of Scotland's biggest tourist attractions is the former Royal Yacht *Britannia*. She was the British royal family's floating home during their foreign travels from the time of her launch in 1953 until her decommissioning in 1997, and is now moored permanently in front of Ocean Terminal.

The tour, which you take at your own pace with an audio guide (available in 20 languages), gives an intriguing insight into the Queen's private tastes – *Britannia* was one of the few places where the royal family could enjoy true privacy. The entire ship is a monument to 1950s decor and technology, and the accommodation reveals Her Majesty's preference for simple, unfussy surroundings – the Queen's own bed is surprisingly tiny and plain.

There was nothing simple or unfussy, however, about the running of the ship. When the Queen travelled, along with her went 45 members of the royal household, five tons of luggage and a Rolls-Royce that was carefully squeezed into a specially built garage on the deck. The ship's company consisted of an admiral, 20 officers and 220 yachtsmen. The decks (of Burmese teak) were scrubbed daily, but all work near the royal accommodation was carried out in complete silence and had to be finished by 8am. A thermometer was kept in the Queen's bathroom to make sure that the water was the correct temperature, and when in harbour one yachtsman was charged with ensuring that the angle of the gangway never exceeded 12 degrees. And note the mahogany windbreak that was added to the balcony deck in front of the bridge. It was put there to stop wayward breezes from blowing up skirts and inadvertently revealing the royal undies.

Britannia was joined in 2010 by the 1930s racing yacht **Bloodhound**, which was owned by the Queen in the 1960s.

The Majestic Tour bus (see p66) runs from Waverley Bridge to *Britannia* during opening times. Alternatively, take Lothian Bus 11, 22, or 35 to Ocean Terminal.

GREATER EDINBURGH

Edinburgh Zoo   ZOO

(www.edinburghzoo.org.uk; 134 Corstorphine Rd; adult/child £15.50/11; ☺9am-6pm Apr-Sep, to 5pm Oct & Mar, to 4.30pm Nov-Feb) Opened in 1913, Edinburgh Zoo is one of the world's leading conservation zoos. Edinburgh's captive breeding program has saved many endangered species, including Siberian tigers, pygmy hippos and red pandas. The main attractions are the **penguin parade**

EDINBURGH

0   200 m
0   0.1 miles

(the zoo's penguins go for a walk every day at 2.15pm), the sea lion training session (daily at 11.15am), the rainbow lorikeet handling session (check the website for details) and the sun bears (newly arrived in 2010).

The zoo is 2.5 miles west of the city centre; take Lothian Bus 12, 26 or 31, First Bus 16, 18, 80 or 86, or the Airlink Bus 100 westbound from Princes St.

FREE **Royal Botanic Garden**   GARDEN
(Map p41; www.rbge.org.uk; 20a Inverleith Row; admission to glasshouses £4.50; ☺10am-7pm Apr-Sep, to 6pm Mar & Oct, to 4pm Nov-Feb) Just north of Stockbridge is the lovely Royal Botanic Garden. Twenty-eight beautifully landscaped hectares include splendid Victorian **palm houses**, colourful swathes of rhododendron and azalea, and a world-famous **rock garden**. The Terrace Cafe offers good views towards the city centre.

Take Lothian Bus 8, 17, 23 or 27 to the East Gate, or the Majestic Tour bus (see p66).

Cramond   HISTORIC DISTRICT
With its moored yachts, stately swans and whitewashed houses spilling down the hillside at the mouth of the River Almond, Cramond is the most picturesque corner of Edinburgh. It is also rich in history. The Romans built a fort here in the 2nd century AD (the village's name comes from Caer Amon, 'the fort on the River Almond'), but recent archaeological excavations have revealed evidence of a Bronze Age settlement dating from 8500 BC, the oldest known site in the whole of Scotland.

Cramond, which was originally a mill village, has a historic 17th-century church and a 15th-century tower house, as well as some rather unimpressive Roman remains, but most people come to enjoy the walks along the river to the ruined mills and to stroll along the seafront. On the riverside,

Leith

⊙ Top Sights
Royal Yacht Britannia A1

✕ Eating
1 Chop Chop C2
2 Daniel's Bistro B2
3 Diner 7 .... C3
4 Fishers Bistro C2
5 Martin Wishart C3

◎ Drinking
6 Port O'Leith D3
7 Teuchter's Landing C2

⊞ Shopping
8 Kinloch Anderson B2
9 Ocean Terminal A1

opposite the cottage on the far bank, is the Maltings (www.cramondassociation.org.uk; Cramond Village; admission free; ⊙2-5pm Sat & Sun Jun-Sep, daily during Edinburgh Festival), which hosts an interesting exhibition on Cramond's history.

Cramond is 5 miles northwest of the city centre; take bus 41 from central Princes St (westbound), Charlotte Sq (south side) or Queensferry St to Cramond Glebe Rd, then walk north for 400m.

Craigmillar Castle   CASTLE
(HS; Craigmillar Castle Rd; adult/child £4.20/2.50; ⊙9.30am-5.30pm Apr-Sep, to 4.30pm Oct, to 4.30pm Sat-Wed Nov-Mar) If you want to explore a Scottish fortress away from the crowds that throng Edinburgh Castle, try Craigmillar. Dating from the 15th century, the tower house rises above two sets of machicolated curtain walls. Mary, Queen of Scots took refuge here after the murder of Rizzio; it was here too that plans to murder her husband Darnley were laid. Look for the prison cell complete with built-in sanitation, something some 'modern' British prisons only finally managed in 1996.

The castle is 2.5 miles southeast of the city centre. Take bus 33 eastbound from Princes St to Old Dalkeith Rd and walk 500m up Craigmillar Castle Rd.

🏃 Activities

Walking
Edinburgh is lucky to have several good walking areas within the city boundary, including Arthur's Seat, Calton Hill, Blackford Hill, Hermitage of Braid, Corstorphine

Hill, and the coast and river at Cramond. The **Pentland Hills**, which rise to over 500m, stretch southwest from the city for 15 miles, offering excellent high- and low-level walking.

You can follow the Water of Leith Walkway from the city centre to Balerno (8 miles), and continue across the Pentlands to Silverburn (6.5 miles) or Carlops (8 miles), and return to Edinburgh by bus. Another good walk is along the Union Canal towpath, which begins in Fountainbridge and runs all the way to Falkirk (31 miles). You can return to Edinburgh by bus at Ratho (8.5 miles) or Broxburn (12 miles), and by bus or train from Linlithgow (21 miles).

Cycling
Edinburgh and its surroundings offer many excellent opportunities for cycling (see www.cyclingedinburgh.info and www.cycling-edinburgh.org.uk). The main off-road routes from the city centre out to the countryside follow the Union Canal towpath then the Water of Leith Walkway from Tollcross southwestwards to Balerno (7.5 miles) on the edge of the Pentland Hills, and the Innocent Railway Cycle Path from the southern side of Arthur's Seat eastwards to Musselburgh (5 miles) and on to Ormiston and Pencaitland.

There are several routes through the **Pentland Hills** that are suitable for mountain bikes. For details ask at any bike shop or check out the Pentland Hills Regional Park (www.edinburgh.gov.uk/phrp/biking) website. The Spokes *Edinburgh Cycle Map* (available from cycle shops for £6) shows all the city's cycle routes.

Edinburgh Cycle Hire & Scottish Cycle Safaris   BIKE HIRE
(Map p48; ☎0131-556 5560; www.cyclescotland.co.uk; 29 Blackfriars St; per day £10-15, per week £50-70; ⊙10am-6pm Mon-Sat) The friendly and helpful folk here rent out top-quality bikes; rates include helmet, lock and repair kit. You can hire tents and touring equipment too. The company also organises cycle tours in Edinburgh and all over Scotland – check the website for details.

Golf
There are no fewer than 19 golf courses in Edinburgh – the following are two of the best city courses.

Braid Hills Public Golf Course GOLF COURSE
(www.edinburghleisuregolf.co.uk; Braid Hills Approach; green fees weekday/weekend £20/24) A

scenic but challenging course to the south of the city centre.

Lothianburn Golf Course GOLF COURSE
(www.lothianburngc.co.uk; 106a Biggar Rd, Fairmilehead; green fees weekday/weekend £25/35) Enjoys a scenic setting at the foot of the Pentland Hills, south of the city.

Swimming

The Firth of Forth is a bit on the chilly side for enjoyable swimming, but there are several indoor facilities.

Royal Commonwealth Pool SWIMMING POOL
(Map p44; www.edinburghleisure.co.uk; 21 Dalkeith Rd) Edinburgh's main facility, with a 50m pool, diving pool, children's pool, flumes and fitness centre. Closed for refurbishment at time of research, reopening summer 2011.

Warrender Swim Centre SWIMMING POOL
(Map p44; www.edinburghleisure.co.uk; Thirlestane Rd; adult/child £3.90/2; ⊙6am-10pm Mon-Fri, 9am-6pm Sat, 9am-8pm Sun) Beautiful Victorian-era 23m pool, with gym and sauna.

Water Sports

The sheltered waters of the Firth of Forth host all kinds of water sports. **Port Edgar Marina & Sailing School** (www.edinburghleisure.co.uk; Shore Rd, Queensferry; ⊙9am-4.30pm) offers a wide range of courses in sailing, canoeing and power-boating.

Horse Riding

There are many scenic bridle paths suitable for horse riding in the countryside around Edinburgh, and a number of riding schools offer two- and three-hour treks as well as tuition, including **Tower Farm Riding Stables** (www.towerfarm.org; 85 Liberton Dr; per hr £26) in the south of the city.

Quirky Edinburgh

Edinburgh is full of unusual attractions and out-of-the-way corners that most visitors never see – even though they may be standing just a few metres away. Here are a few of the city's less mainstream attractions.

Mansfield Place Church CHURCH
(Map p44; www.mansfieldtraquair.org.uk; Mansfield Pl; ⊙1-4pm 2nd Sun of the month, 11am-1pm Sun-Thu during Edinburgh Festival Fringe) In complete contrast to the austerity of most of Edinburgh's religious buildings, this 19th-century, neo-Romanesque church at the foot of Broughton St contains a remarkable series of Renaissance-style frescos painted in the 1890s by Irish-born artist Phoebe Anna Traquair (1852–1936). Now undergoing restoration, the murals are on view to the public at certain times (check the website for any changes).

FREE **Museum on the Mound** MUSEUM
(Map p48; www.museumonthemound.com; The Mound; ⊙10am-5pm Tue-Fri, 1-5pm Sat & Sun) Housed in the Bank of Scotland's splendid Georgian HQ, this museum is a treasure trove of gold coins, bullion chests, safes, banknotes, forgeries, cartoons and lots of fascinating old documents and photographs charting the history of Scotland's oldest bank.

FREE **Edinburgh University Collection of Historic Musical Instruments** MUSEUM
(Map p48; www.music.ed.ac.uk/euchmi; Reid Concert Hall, Teviot Pl; ⊙3-5pm Wed, 10am-1pm Sat year-round, 2-5pm Mon-Fri during Edinburgh Festival) Musicians will enjoy this collection, which contains more than 1000 instruments ranging from a 400-year-old lute to a 1959 synthesiser.

Surgeons' Hall Museums MUSEUM
(Map p48; www.museum.rcsed.ac.uk, www.rcsed.ac.uk; Nicolson St; adult/child £5/3; ⊙noon-4pm Mon-Fri) The **History of Surgery Museum** is a fascinating look at surgery in Scotland from the 15th century – when barbers supplemented their income with blood-letting, amputations and other surgical procedures – to the present day. The highlight is the exhibit on Burke and Hare, which includes Burke's death mask and a pocket book bound in his skin. Covering dentistry, with its wince-inducing collections of extraction tools, is the adjacent **Dental Collection**. The **Pathology Museum** houses a gruesome but compelling 19th-century collection of diseased organs and massive tumours pickled in formaldehyde.

Gilmerton Cove HISTORIC BUILDING
(www.gilmertoncove.org.uk; 16 Drum St, Gilmerton; adult/child £5/4; ⊙tours 9.30am-6pm Mon-Sat, noon-4pm Sun) While ghost tours of Edinburgh's underground vaults and haunted graveyards have become a mainstream attraction, few tourists have yet explored Gilmerton Cove. Hidden in the southern suburbs, the mysterious cove is a series of manmade subterranean caverns hacked out of the rock, their origin and

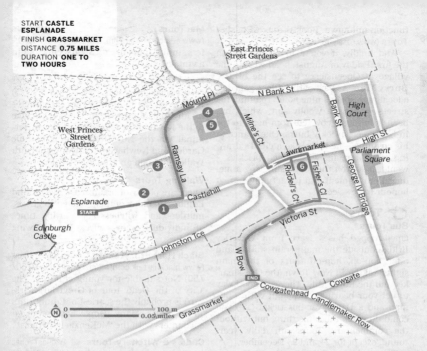

START **CASTLE ESPLANADE**
FINISH **GRASSMARKET**
DISTANCE **0.75 MILES**
DURATION **ONE TO TWO HOURS**

Walking Tour
Old Town Alleys

❭ This walk explores the alleys and closes around the upper part of the Royal Mile, and involves a bit of climbing up and down steep stairs.

From the Esplanade head down Castlehill. The 17th-century house on the right is known as ❶ **Cannonball House** because of the iron ball lodged in the wall (look between, and slightly below, the two largest windows). It was not fired in anger, but marks the gravitation height to which water would flow naturally from the city's first piped water supply.

The building across the street was originally the reservoir for the Old Town's water supply. On its west wall is the ❷ **Witches Well**, where a bronze fountain commemorates around 4000 people (mostly women) who were executed between 1479 and 1722 on suspicion of witchcraft.

Turn left down Ramsay Lane and take a look at ❸ **Ramsay Garden**, where late-19th-century apartments were built around the octagonal Ramsay Lodge, once home to

poet Allan Ramsay. The cobbled street continues around to ❹ **New College**, home to Edinburgh University's Faculty of Divinity. Nip into the courtyard to see the ❺ **statue of John Knox**.

Just past New College turn right and climb up the stairs into Milne's Court, a student residence. Exit into Lawnmarket, cross the street (bearing slightly left) and duck into ❻ **Riddell's Court** at No 322–328, a typical Old Town close. You'll find yourself in a small courtyard, but the house in front of you (built in 1590) was originally the edge of the street (the building you just walked under was added in 1726). The arch with the inscription *Vivendo discimus* (we live and learn) leads into the original 16th-century courtyard.

Go back into the street, turn right and right again down Fisher's Close, which leads to delightful Victoria Tce, poised above Victoria St. Go right, then down the stairs at the foot of Upper Bow and continue downhill to the Grassmarket where you can take your pick of cafes and bars.

function unknown. Book through **Rosslyn Tours** (www.rosslyntours.co.uk).

And finally, if you're in Edinburgh on the first Friday of August, head west to the village of Queensferry to see the bizarre **Burry Man**. As part of the village gala day, a local man spends nine hours roaming the streets wearing a woolly suit, which has been laboriously covered from head to toe in big, green, prickly burrs. One glance at his costume – he looks like a child's drawing of a Martian, with added prickles – would make you think he's suffering a medieval punishment, but it's actually a great honour to be selected.

☞ Tours

Bus Tours

Open-topped buses leave from Waverley Bridge outside the main train station and offer hop-on, hop-off tours of the main sights, taking in New Town, the Grassmarket and the Royal Mile. They're a good way to get your bearings, although with a bus map and a Day Saver bus ticket (£3) you could do much the same thing but without the commentary. Tours run daily, yearround, except for 24 and 25 December.

Tickets for the following three tours remain valid for 24 hours.

City Sightseeing   BUS TOURS
(www.edinburghtour.com; adult/child £12/5) Lothian Buses' bright-red open-top buses depart every 20 minutes from Waverley Bridge.

MacTours   BUS TOURS
(www.edinburghtour.com; adult/child £12/5) Offers similar tours to City Sightseeing, but in a vintage bus.

Majestic Tour   BUS TOURS
(www.edinburghtour.com; adult/child £12/5) Runs every 30 minutes (every 20 minutes in July and August) from Waverley Bridge to the Royal Yacht *Britannia* at Ocean Terminal via the New Town, Royal Botanic Garden and Newhaven, returning via Leith Walk, Holyrood and the Royal Mile.

Walking Tours

There are plenty of organised walks around Edinburgh, many of them related to ghosts, murders and witches. For starting times of individual walks, check the following websites:

Black Hart Storytellers   GHOST TOURS
(www.blackhart.uk.com; adult/concession £9.50/7.50) Not suitable for young children. The 'City of the Dead' tour of Greyfriars Kirkyard is probably the scariest of Edinburgh's 'ghost' tours. Many people have reported encounters with the 'McKenzie Poltergeist'.

Cadies & Witchery Tours   GHOST TOURS
(www.witcherytours.com; adult/child £7.50/5) The becloaked and pasty-faced Adam Lyal (deceased) leads a 'Murder & Mystery' tour of the Old Town's darker corners. These tours are famous for their 'jumper-ooters' – costumed actors who 'jump oot' when you least expect it.

LOCAL KNOWLEDGE

ADAM LYAL (DECEASED): GHOST

Adam Lyal (deceased) – aka Andrew Henderson – is the ghost of an Edinburgh highwayman who was hanged at the Tolbooth in 1811, and a tour leader with Cadies & Witchery Tours.

What are Edinburgh's spookiest places? The graveyards, though I would hesitate to recommend that anyone go to visit them at night! The spookiest by far is undoubtedly the Old Calton Burial Ground on Waterloo Rd, home to such departed notables as philosopher David Hume.

Where would a hard-working ghoul go to slake his thirst? We tend to do our carousing in some of the Old Town's marvellous little howffs (pubs), such as the Jolly Judge (p78) or the Last Drop (p78), and we can often be found in the Bow Bar (p78).

Can you recommend any good 'off-the-beaten-track' places? The wonderful thing about Edinburgh's Old Town is that so much of it is 'off the beaten track'! One of my favourite venues is Whistle Binkie's (p81). It's quite hard to spot, being located under the actual street with only a doorway on the pavement leading down, but it's well worth finding. Of course, there are other tours in Edinburgh, and the one I'd recommend to anyone is the Literary Pub Tour (p67). Booze, history and Scottish literature? It's a work of genius!

EDINBURGH FOR CHILDREN

Edinburgh has a multitude of attractions for children, and most things to see and do are child-friendly. Kids under five travel for free on Edinburgh buses, and five- to 15-year-olds pay a flat fare of 70p.

The Edinburgh & Scotland Information Centre has lots of info on children's events, and the handy guidebook *Edinburgh for Under Fives* can be found in most bookshops. The *List* magazine (www.list.co.uk) has a special kids section listing children's activities and events in and around Edinburgh. The week-long Imaginate Festival (www.imaginate.org.uk) of children's theatre, dance and puppetry takes place each year in late May/early June.

There are good, safe playgrounds in most Edinburgh parks, including Princes Street Gardens West, Inverleith Park (opposite the Royal Botanic Garden), George V Park (New Town), the Meadows and Bruntsfield Links.

Some more ideas for outdoor activities include exploring the Royal Botanic Garden, going to see the animals at Edinburgh Zoo, visiting the statue of Greyfriars Bobby and feeding the swans and playing on the beach at Cramond. During the Edinburgh and Fringe Festivals there is also plenty of street theatre for kids, especially on the High St and at the foot of The Mound, and in December there's an open-air ice rink and fairground rides in Princes Street Gardens.

If it's raining, you can visit the Discovery Centre, a hands-on activity zone on Level 3 of the Museum of Scotland, play on the flumes at the Royal Commonwealth Pool, try out the earthquake simulator at Our Dynamic Earth, or take a tour of the haunted Real Mary King's Close.

You should be aware that the majority of Scottish pubs, even those that serve bar meals, are forbidden by law to admit children under the age of 14; even in the family-friendly pubs (ie those in possession of a Children's Certificate), under-14s are only admitted between the hours of 11am and 8pm for a meal, and only when accompanied by an adult aged 18 or over. Sixteen- and 17-year-olds can buy and drink beer and wine with a meal in a restaurant.

Childminding Services

For information on government-approved childminding services, contact Edinburgh Childcare Information Service (☎0800 032 0323). The following are reliable Edinburgh agencies that charge from £7 an hour for babysitting:

Family Circle Care (☎0131-554 9500; www.familycircles.org; 22 Tower St, Leith)

Panda's Nanny Agency (☎0131-663 3967; www.pandasnannyagency.co.uk; 22 Durham Pl, Bonnyrigg)

Edinburgh Literary Pub Tour LITERARY TOURS (www.edinburghliterarypubtour.co.uk; adult/student £10/8) An enlightening two-hour trawl through Edinburgh's literary history – and its associated howffs (pubs) – in the entertaining company of Messrs Clart and McBrain. One of the city's best walking tours.

Mercat Tours HISTORY TOURS (www.mercattours.com; adult/child £9/5) Mercat offers a wide range of fascinating tours including history walks in the Old Town and Leith, 'Ghosts & Ghouls' tours and visits to haunted underground vaults.

Rebus Tours LITERARY TOURS (www.rebustours.com; adult/student £10/9) Tours of the 'hidden Edinburgh' frequented by novelist Ian Rankin's fictional detective John Rebus. Not recommended for children under 10.

Trainspotting Tours LITERARY TOURS (www.leithwalks.co.uk; per person £8) A tour of locations from Irvine Welsh's notorious 1993 novel *Trainspotting,* delivered with wit and enthusiasm. Not suitable for kids.

✯ Festivals & Events

Edinburgh hosts an amazing number of festivals throughout the year, notably the Edinburgh International Festival, the Edinburgh Festival Fringe and the Military Tattoo, which are all held around the same time in August. Hogmanay, Scottish New Year's celebrations, is also a peak party time.

EDINBURGH'S HOGMANAY

Traditionally, the New Year has always been a more important celebration for Scots than Christmas. In towns, cities and villages all over the country, people fill the streets at midnight on 31 December to wish each other a Guid New Year and, yes, to knock back a dram or six to keep the cold at bay.

In 1993 Edinburgh's city council had the excellent idea of spicing up Hogmanay by organising some events, laying on some live music in Princes St and issuing an open invitation to the rest of the world. Most of them turned up, or so it seemed, and had such a good time that they told all their pals and came back again the next year.

Now **Edinburgh's Hogmanay** (www.edinburghshogmanay.com) is the biggest winter festival in Europe. Events run from 29 December to 1 January, and include a torchlight procession, huge street party and a New Year's Day triathlon. To get into the main party area in the city centre after 8pm on 31 December you'll need a ticket – book well in advance.

April

Edinburgh International Science Festival SCIENCE & NATURE
(www.sciencefestival.co.uk) First held in 1987, it hosts a wide range of events, including talks, lectures, exhibitions, demonstrations, guided tours and interactive experiments designed to stimulate, inspire and challenge. From dinosaurs to ghosts to alien life forms, there's something to interest everyone. The festival runs over two weeks in April.

May

Imaginate Festival CHILDREN'S THEATRE
(www.imaginate.org.uk) This is Britain's biggest festival of performing arts for children, with events suitable for kids from three to 12. Groups from around the world perform classic tales like *Hansel and Gretel* as well as new material written specially for children. The festival takes place annually in the last week of May.

June

Scottish Real Ale Festival BEER
(www.scottishbeerfestival.org.uk; Assembly Rooms, 54 George St) A celebration of all things fermented and yeasty, Scotland's biggest beer-fest gives you the opportunity to sample a wide range of traditionally brewed beers from Scotland and around the world. Froth-topped bliss. The festival is held over a weekend in June.

Royal Highland Show AGRICULTURAL
(www.royalhighlandshow.org; Royal Highland Centre, Ingliston) Scotland's hugely popular national agricultural show is a four-day feast of all things rural, with everything from show-jumping and tractor-driving to sheep-shearing and falconry. Countless pens are filled with coiffed show-cattle and pedicured prize ewes. The show is held over a long weekend (Thursday to Sunday) in late June.

Edinburgh International Film Festival FILM
(www.edfilmfest.org.uk) One of the original Edinburgh Festival trinity, having first been staged in 1947 along with the International Festival and the Fringe, the two-week film festival is a major international event, serving as a showcase for new British and European films, and staging the European premieres of one or two Hollywood blockbusters.

July

Edinburgh International Jazz & Blues Festival JAZZ & BLUES
(www.edinburghjazzfestival.com) Held annually since 1978, the Jazz & Blues Festival pulls in top talent from all over the world. The festival runs for nine days, beginning on the last Friday in July (the week before the Fringe and Tattoo begin). The first weekend sees a Mardi Gras street parade on Saturday from the City Chambers, up the Royal Mile and down Victoria St into the Grassmarket, for an afternoon of free, open-air music. On the Sunday there's a series of free concerts at the Ross Bandstand in Princes Street Gardens.

August

See the boxed text, p70, for details of August's festivals.

December

For Edinburgh's Hogmanay, see the boxed text above.

Edinburgh's Christmas

(www.edinburghschristmas.com) The youngest of the Scottish capital's festivals, first held in 2000, the Christmas bash includes a big street parade, a fairground and Ferris wheel, and an open-air ice rink in Princes Street Gardens. The celebrations are held over the three weeks before Christmas Day.

🛏 Sleeping

A boom in hotel building has seen Edinburgh's tourist capacity swell significantly in the last decade, but you can guarantee that the city will still be packed to the gills during the festival period (August) and over Hogmanay (New Year). If you want a room during these periods, book as far in advance as possible – a year ahead if possible. In general, it's best to book ahead for accommodation at Easter and from mid-May to mid-September.

Hotels and hostels are found throughout the Old and New Towns; midrange B&Bs and guesthouses are concentrated outside the centre in the suburbs of Tollcross, Bruntsfield, Newington and Pilrig.

If you're driving, don't even think about staying in the city centre unless your hotel has its own private car park – parking in the centre is a nightmare. Instead, look for somewhere in a suburb like Newington, where there's a chance of finding free, on-street parking (even then, don't bet on getting a parking space outside the front door). Alternatively, stay outside the city and travel in by bus or train.

Edinburgh accommodation is slightly more expensive than in the rest of Scotland, so the price breakdown in these listings is different from that described on p478 – budget is less than £60, midrange £60 to £150, and top end is more than £150, based on the cost of a double room with bed and breakfast (B&B).

Accommodation Agencies

If you arrive in Edinburgh without a room, the Edinburgh & Scotland Information Centre (p86) booking service will try to find a room to suit you (and will charge a £5 fee if successful). If you have the time, pick up the tourist office's accommodation brochure and ring around yourself.

You can also try VisitScotland's Booking Hotline (☎0845 859 1006), which has a £3 surcharge; or search for accommodation on the Edinburgh & Lothians Tourist Board (www.edinburgh.org/accom) website.

OLD TOWN

Most of the interesting accommodation in the Old Town is either backpacker hostels or expensive hotels. For midrange options you'll have to resort to chain hotels – check the websites of Travelodge, Ibis etc.

TOP CHOICE Hotel Missoni
BOUTIQUE HOTEL £££

(Map p48; ☎0131-220 6666; www.hotelmissoni.com; 1 George IV Bridge; r £180; 🛜) The Italian fashion house has established a style icon in the heart of the medieval Old Town with this bold statement of a hotel – modernistic architecture, black-and-white decor with well-judged splashes of colour, impeccably mannered staff and – most importantly – very comfortable bedrooms and bathrooms with lots of nice little touches, from fresh milk in the minibar to plush bathrobes.

TOP CHOICE Witchery by the Castle
BOUTIQUE B&B £££

(Map p48; ☎0131-225 5613; www.thewitchery.com; Castlehill, Royal Mile; ste £295) Set in a 16th-century Old Town house in the shadow of Edinburgh Castle, the Witchery's seven lavish suites are extravagantly furnished with antiques, oak panelling, tapestries, open fires and roll-top baths, and supplied with flowers, chocolates and complimentary champagne. Overwhelmingly popular – you'll have to book several months in advance to be sure of getting a room.

Knight Residence
APARTMENTS £££

(Map p48; ☎0131-622 8120; www.theknightresidence.co.uk; 12 Lauriston St; d apt per night £169-199, 2-bedroom apt £249-289; 🛜) Works by contemporary artists adorn these modern one- and two-bedroom apartments (available by the night; the latter sleep up to four adults and one child), each with fully equipped kitchen and comfortable lounge with cable TV, video and stereo. It has a good central location in a quiet street only a few minutes' walk from the Grassmarket.

Smart City Hostel
HOSTEL £

(Map p48; ☎0870 892 3000; www.smartcityhostels.com; 50 Blackfriars St; dm £9-22, tw £80; @🛜) A big (620 beds), bright, modern hostel that feels more like a hotel, with a convivial cafe where you can buy breakfast, and mod cons such as keycard access and secure charging stations for mobile phones, MP3 players and laptops. Lockers in every room, bike parking and a central location just off the Royal Mile make this the city's new favourite place to stay.

FESTIVAL CITY

August in Edinburgh sees a frenzy of festivals, with half a dozen world-class events running at the same time.

Edinburgh Festival Fringe

When the first Edinburgh Festival was held in 1947, there were eight theatre companies who didn't make it onto the main program. Undeterred, they grouped together and held their own mini-festival, on the fringe, and an Edinburgh institution was born. Today the Edinburgh Festival Fringe (Map p48; ☎0131-226 0026; www.edfringe.com; Edinburgh Festival Fringe Office, 180 High St) is *the* biggest festival of the performing arts anywhere in the world.

Since 1990 the Fringe has been dominated by stand-up comedy, but the sheer variety of shows on offer is staggering – everything from chainsaw juggling to performance poetry to Tibetan yak-milk gargling. So how do you decide what to see? There are daily reviews in the *Scotsman* newspaper – one good *Scotsman* review and a show sells out in hours – but the best recommendation is word of mouth. If you have the time, go to at least one unknown show – it may be crap, but at least you'll have your obligatory 'worst show I ever saw' story.

The big names play at the mega-venues like the Assembly Rooms (www.assembly roomsedinburgh.co.uk; 54 George St) and the Pleasance (www.pleasance.co.uk/edin burgh; 60 Pleasance), and charge mega-prices (£12 a ticket and more, with one famous comic notoriously charging £37.50 in 2007), but there are plenty of good shows in the £5 to £8 range and, best of all, lots of free stuff. **Fringe Sunday** – usually the second Sunday – is a smorgasbord of free performances, staged in the Meadows park to the south of the city centre.

The Fringe takes place over 3½ weeks in August, the last two weeks overlapping with the first two of the Edinburgh International Festival.

Edinburgh International Festival

First held in 1947 to mark a return to peace after the ordeal of WWII, the Edinburgh International Festival (☎0131-473 2099; www.eif.co.uk) is festooned with superlatives – the oldest, the biggest, the most famous, the best in the world. The original was a modest affair, but today hundreds of the world's top musicians and performers congregate in Edinburgh for three weeks of diverse and inspirational music, opera, theatre and dance.

The festival takes place over the three weeks ending on the first Saturday in September; the program is usually available from April. Tickets for popular events – especially music and opera – sell out quickly, so it's best to book as far in advance as possible. You can buy tickets in person at the Hub (Map p48), or by phone or internet.

Edinburgh Military Tattoo

The month kicks off with the Edinburgh Military Tattoo (Map p56; ☎0131-225 1188; www.edintattoo.co.uk; Tattoo Office, 32 Market St), a spectacular display of military marching bands, massed pipes and drums, acrobats, cheerleaders and motorcycle display teams, all played out in front of the magnificent backdrop of the floodlit castle. Each show traditionally finishes with a lone piper, dramatically lit, playing a lament on the battlements. The Tattoo takes place over the first three weeks of August (from a Friday to a Saturday); there's one show at 9pm Monday to Friday and two (at 7.30pm and 10.30pm) on Saturday, but no performance on Sunday.

Edinburgh International Book Festival

Held in a little village of marquees in the middle of Charlotte Sq, the Edinburgh International Book Festival (☎0845 373 5888; www.edbookfest.co.uk) is a fun fortnight of talks, readings, debates, lectures, book signings and meet-the-author events, with a cafe and tented bookshop thrown in. The festival lasts for two weeks in August (usually the first two weeks of the Edinburgh International Festival).

Art Roch Hostel
HOSTEL £

(Map p48; 🕿0131-228 9981; www.artrochhostel. com; 2 West Port, Grassmarket; dm from £10; 🖳🛜) The new Art Roch Hostel tries to be all things to all people, and pretty much succeeds. There are mixed and female-only dorms, family rooms, an executive floor for business travellers, and a specially equipped room for wheelchair users. There's a very cool common room with loads of sofas, a hammock and pool table, 24-hour reception, and great location close to the castle.

Castle Rock Hostel
HOSTEL £

(Map p48; 🕿0131-225 9666; www.scotlands -top-hostels.com; 15 Johnston Tce; dm from £13.50, d £40-55; 🛜) With its bright, spacious, single-sex dorms, superb views and friendly staff, the 200-bed Castle Rock has lots to like. It has a great location – the only way to get closer to the castle would be to pitch a tent on the esplanade – a games room, reading lounge and big-screen video nights.

Budget Backpackers
HOSTEL £

(Map p48; 🕿0131-226 6351; www.budgetback packers.com; 39 Cowgate, The Grassmarket; dm from £12.50-16, tw £48; 🛜) This fun spot piles on the extras, with bike storage, pool tables, laundry and a colourful chill-out lounge. You'll pay a little more for four-bunk dorms, but larger dorms are great value. The only downside is that prices increase at weekends, but otherwise a brilliant spot to doss.

Edinburgh Metro
HOSTEL £

(SYHA; Map p48; 🕿0131-556 8718; 11/2 Robertson's Close, Cowgate; s £23-44; ☉Jul & Aug) Summer only, all single rooms in student accommodation.

Royal Mile Backpackers
HOSTEL £

Map p48; (🕿0131-557 6120; www.scotlands-top -hostels.com; 105 High St; dm from £13.50; 🛜) Small, cosy and quaint.

NEW TOWN & AROUND

TOP CHOICE Six Mary's Place
B&B ££

(Map p44; 🕿0131-3328965; www.sixmarys place.co.uk; 6 Mary's Pl, Raeburn Pl; s/d/f from £50/94/150; 🖳🛜) Six Mary's Place is situated in an attractive Georgian town house with a designer mix of period features, contemporary furniture and modern colours. The vegetarian-only breakfasts are served in an attractive conservatory that offers up a view of the garden, while the lounge, fitted out with big, comfy sofas, has free coffee and newspapers to linger over on a lazy morning.

One Royal Circus
B&B £££

(Map p56; 🕿0131-625 6669; www.oneroyalcircus. com; 1 Royal Circus; r £180-260; 🛜🚻) Live the New Town dream at this incredibly chic Georgian mansion where genuine antiques and parquet floors sit comfortably alongside slate bathrooms and Philippe Starck furniture. Bedrooms are kitted out with Egyptian cotton sheets, iPod docks and Arran Aromatics toiletries, and there are babyfoot and pool tables in the drawing room.

Gerald's Place
B&B ££

(Map p56; 🕿0131-558 7017; www.geraldsplace. com; 21b Abercromby Pl; d £119-149; 🖳🛜) Gerald is an unfailingly charming and helpful host, and his lovely Georgian garden flat (just two guest bedrooms) has a great location across from a peaceful park, an easy stroll from the city centre.

Tigerlily
BOUTIQUE HOTEL £££

(Map p56; 🕿0131-225 5005; www.tigerlilyedin burgh.co.uk; 125 George St; r from £195; 🛜) Georgian meets gorgeous at this glamorous, glittering boutique hotel (complete with its own nightclub) decked out in mirror mosaics, beaded curtains, swirling Timorous Beasties textiles and wall coverings, and atmospheric pink uplighting. Book the Georgian Suite (£375) for a truly special romantic getaway.

rick's
BOUTIQUE HOTEL ££

(Map p56; 🕿0131-622 7800; www.ricksedin burgh.co.uk; 55a Frederick St; r £115-175; 🛜) One of the first boutique hotels to appear in Edinburgh, rick's offers sharp styling and a laid-back atmosphere. The bedrooms boast walnut headboards and designer fabrics, with fluffy bathrobes, well-stocked minibars and Molton Brown toiletries.

Glasshouse
HOTEL £££

(Map p56; 🕿0131-525 8200; www.theetoncol lection.com; 2 Greenside Pl; r/ste from £285/450; 🅿🛜) A palace of cutting-edge design perched atop the Omni Centre at the foot of Calton Hill, and entered through the preserved facade of a 19th-century church, the Glasshouse sports luxury rooms with floor-to-ceiling windows, leather sofas, marble bathrooms and a rooftop garden.

Dene Guest House
B&B ££

(Map p44; 🕿0131-556 2700; www.deneguest house.com; 7 Eyre Pl; per person £25-50; 🚻) The Dene is a friendly and informal place, set in a charming Georgian town house, with a welcoming owner and spacious bedrooms. The inexpensive single rooms make it ideal for solo travellers; children under 10 staying in their parents' room pay half price.

Dukes of Windsor Street
BOUTIQUE B&B ££
(Map p44; ☎0131-556 6046; www.dukesofwind sor.com; 17 Windsor St; d £120-160; @☎) A relaxing eight-bedroom Georgian town house set on a quiet side street, only a few paces from Princes St, Dukes offers an appealing blend of modern sophistication and period atmosphere.

Belford Hostel
HOSTEL £
(Map p44; ☎0131-220 2200; www.hoppo.com; 6/8 Douglas Gardens; dm £13-20, d £45-65; @) An unusual hostel housed in a converted church. Although some people complain about noise – there are only thin partitions between dorms, and no ceilings – it's cheerful and well run with good facilities. This hostel is about 20 minutes' walk west of Waverley train station. If you're arriving by train from Glasgow or the north, get off at Haymarket station, which is much closer.

Balmoral Hotel
HOTEL £££
(☎0131-556 2414; www.thebalmoralhotel.com; 1 Princes St; s/d from £320/380; P☎❄) The sumptuous Balmoral – a prominent landmark at the eastern end of Princes St – offers some of the best accommodation in Edinburgh, including suites with 18th-century decor and some superb views over the city.

Frederick House Hotel
HOTEL ££
(Map p55; ☎0131-226 1999; www.townhouse hotels.co.uk; 42 Frederick St; s/d from £55/75; ☎) This well-positioned, good-value hotel has roomy double beds and large baths to soak away the day's walking aches. It's also one of few options in this price range that has a lift, which is ideal is you've got lots of baggage.

SOUTH EDINBURGH
There are lots of guesthouses in the South Edinburgh suburbs of Tollcross, Morningside, Marchmont and Newington, especially on and around Minto St and Mayfield Gardens (the continuation of North Bridge and Nicolson St) in Newington. This is the main traffic artery from the south and a main bus route into the city centre.

TOP CHOICE Southside Guest House
B&B ££
(Map p44; ☎0131-668 4422; www.southsideguesthouse.co.uk; 8 Newington Rd; s/d £70/90; ☎) Though set in a typical Victorian terrace, the Southside transcends the traditional guesthouse category and feels more like a modern boutique hotel. Its eight stylish rooms just ooze interior design, standing out from other Newington B&Bs through the clever use of bold colours and modern furniture.

TOP CHOICE Prestonfield House Hotel
BOUTIQUE HOTEL £££
(☎0131-668 3346; www.prestonfield.com; Priestfield Rd; r £275, ste £350-395; P☎) If the blonde wood, brown leather and brushed steel of modern boutique hotels leave you cold, then this is the place for you. A 17th-century mansion set in 20 acres of parkland (complete with peacocks and Highland cattle), Prestonfield House is draped in damask, packed with antiques and decorated in red, black and gold – look out for original tapestries, 17th-century embossed-leather panels, and £500-a-roll hand-painted wallpaper. The hotel's rooms are supplied with all mod cons, including internet access, Bose sound systems, DVD players and plasma-screen TVs. The hotel is southeast of the city centre, east of Dalkeith Rd.

45 Gilmour Rd
B&B ££
(☎0131-667 3536; www.edinburghbedbreakfast. com; 45 Gilmour Rd; s/d £60/110) A peaceful setting, large garden and friendly owners contribute to the appeal of this Victorian terraced house, which overlooks the local bowling green. The decor is a blend of 19th- and 20th-century influences, with bold Victorian reds, pine floors and period fireplace in the lounge, a rocking horse and art-nouveau lamp in the hallway, and a 1930s vibe in the three spacious bedrooms. Located 1 mile southeast of the city centre.

Aonach Mor Guest House
B&B ££
(Map p44; ☎0131-667 8694; www.aonachmor. com; 14 Kilmaurs Tce; r per person £30-70; @☎) This elegant Victorian terraced house is located on a quiet back street and has seven bedrooms, beautifully decorated, with many original period features. Our favourite is the four-poster bedroom with polished mahogany furniture and period fireplace. Located 1 mile southeast of the city centre.

Town House
B&B ££
(Map p44; ☎0131-229 1985; www.thetown house.com; 65 Gilmore Pl; per person £40-58; P☎) The five-room Town House is a plush little place, offering the sort of quality and comfort you might expect from a much larger and more expensive hotel. It's an elegant Victorian terraced house with big bay

windows, spacious bedrooms (all en suite) and a breakfast menu that includes salmon fishcakes and kippers alongside the more usual offerings.

Sherwood Guest House
B&B ££
(Map p44; ☑0131-667 1200; www.sherwood-edin burgh.com; 42 Minto St; s £30-60, d £40-75; P ⟨?⟩) One of the most attractive guesthouses on Minto St's B&B strip, the Sherwood is a re-furbished Georgian terraced house decked out with hanging baskets and shrubs. Inside are six en suite rooms that combine Regency-style striped wallpaper with modern fabrics and pine furniture.

Amaryllis Guest House
B&B ££
(Map p44; ☑0131-229 3293; www.amaryllisguest house.com; 21 Upper Gilmore Pl; per person £25-40; P) The Amaryllis is a cute little Georgian town house on a quiet back street. There are five bedrooms, including a spacious family room that can take two adults and up to four kids. Princes St is only 10 minutes' walk away.

Argyle Backpackers
HOSTEL £
(Map p44; ☑0131-667 9991; www.argyle-back packers.co.uk; 14 Argyle Pl; dm £14-20, d & tw £50-60; ⟨?⟩) The Argyle, spread across three adjacent terraced houses, is a quiet and relaxed hostel offering double and twin rooms as well as four- to eight-bed dorms (mixed sex). There is a comfortable TV lounge, an attractive little conservatory, and a pleasant walled garden at the back where you can sit outside in summer.

Pollock Halls of Residence
STUDENT ACCOMMODATION ££
(Map p44; ☑0131-651 2007; www.edinburghfirst. co.uk; 18 Holyrood Park Rd; s/d £48/80; P) This is a modern student complex belonging to the University of Edinburgh, with 1200 rooms (500 with en-suite bathroom). It's busy and often noisy, but close to the city centre and with Arthur's Seat as a backdrop. Available during Easter and summer vacations only (see website for dates).

Salisbury Hotel
HOTEL ££
(Map p44; ☑0131-667 1264; www.the-salisbury. co.uk; 45 Salisbury Rd; s/d/f £75/110/130; P ⟨?⟩) Boutique-style guesthouse in quiet, comfortable Georgian villa with large garden.

Menzies Guest House
B&B £
(Map p44; ☑0131-229 4629; www.menzies -guesthouse.co.uk; 33 Leamington Tce; s £50, d £45-65) Clean, friendly and well-run

place with seven high-ceilinged Victorian rooms spread over three floors. The cheaper rooms, with shared bathroom, are small but offer excellent value.

Robertson Guest House
B&B ££
(Map p44; ☑0131-229 2652; www.robertson -guesthouse.com; 5 Hartington Gardens; s/d £65/75; ⟨?⟩ ⟨♿⟩) Homely Victorian house in a quiet back street, with a range of healthy breakfasts including yogurt, fruit and vegetarian fry-up. Lower rates (from £35 a double) outside high season.

Kenvie Guest House
B&B ££
(Map p44; ☑0131-668 1964; www.kenvie.co.uk; 16 Kilmaurs Rd; r per person £27-40; ⟨?⟩) Situated in a quiet side street but close to a main bus route.

LEITH WALK & PILRIG ST
Northeast of the New Town, the area around Leith Walk and Pilrig St (Map p44) has lots of guesthouses, all within about a mile of the centre. To get there, take bus 11 from Princes St.

Millers 64
B&B ££
(☑0131-454 3666; www.millers64.com; 64 Pilrig St; s from £80, d £90-140; P ⟨?⟩) Luxury textiles, colourful cushions, stylish bathrooms and fresh flowers added to a warm Edinburgh welcome make this Victorian town house a highly desirable address. There are just two bedrooms (and a minimum three-night stay during festival periods) so book well in advance.

Ardmor House
B&B ££
(☑0131-554 4944; www.ardmorhouse.com; 74 Pilrig St; s £50-75, d £75-145; ⟨?⟩) The 'gay-owned, straight-friendly' Ardmor is a stylishly renovated Victorian house with five en-suite bedrooms, and all those little touches that make a place special – an open fire, thick towels, crisp white bed linen and free newspapers at breakfast.

Edinburgh Central Youth Hostel
HOSTEL £
(SYHA; Map p44; ☑0131-524 2090; www.edin burghcentral.org; 9 Haddington Pl, Leith Walk; dm £16-26, s/tw from £34/51; @ ⟨?⟩) This modern, purpose-built hostel, about a half-mile north of Waverley train station, is a big (300 beds), flashy, five-star establishment with its own cafe-bistro as well as self-catering kitchen, smart and comfortable eight-bed dorms and private rooms, and mod cons including keycard entry and plasma-screen TVs.

Balmoral Guest House   B&B **££**

(☑0131-554 1857; www.balmoralguesthouse.co.uk; 32 Pilrig St; r per person £30-50) Lots of word-of-mouth recommendations for this B&B set in an elegant, flower-bedecked, Victorian terraced house dating from 1856. The owners have a good eye for antiques (including, unusually, antique radios), and period furniture gives the bedrooms a pleasantly retro atmosphere.

OUTSIDE THE CENTRE

Globetrotter Inn   HOSTEL **£**

(☑0131-336 1030; www.globetrotterinns.com; 46 Marine Dr; dm £15-19, d & tw £46; @🛜) A large and comfortable hostel with luxury bunks, TV lounges, sauna and gym. Good value, but can occasionally be plagued by noisy stag-party groups. It's close to the waterfront about 4 miles northwest of the city centre, about 20 minutes by shuttle bus (£2.50 return, pick-up from Waterloo Place).

Mortonhall Caravan Park   CAMPSITE **£**

(☑0131-664 1533; www.meadowhead.co.uk; 38 Mortonhall Gate, Frogston Rd East; sites incl 1 car & 2 people £18-24, site & 1 person only £10.50; ☺Mar-Oct) Located in attractive parkland 5 miles southeast of the centre, Mortonhall has an on-site shop, bar and restaurant. Note – the one-person tent rate is not available during the Edinburgh International Festival. Take bus 11 from Princes St (westbound).

✖ Eating

In the last decade there has been a boom in the number of restaurants in Edinburgh – the city now has more restaurants per head of population than London. Eating out has become a commonplace event rather than something reserved for special occasions, and the choice of eateries ranges from stylish but inexpensive bistros and cafes to gourmet restaurants.

In addition, most pubs serve food, offering either bar meals or a more formal restaurant or both, but be aware that pubs without a Children's Certificate are not allowed to serve children under the age of 14.

If you want more listings than we can provide here, the excellent *Edinburgh & Glasgow Eating & Drinking Guide* (www.list.co.uk/food-and-drink), published annually by the *List* magazine, contains annual reviews of around 800 restaurants, cafes and bars.

OLD TOWN

TOP CHOICE **Outsider**   BISTRO **££**

(Map p48; ☑0131-226 3131; 15 George IV Bridge; mains £8-13; ☺noon-11pm) This Edinburgh stalwart is known for its rainforest interior (potted ferns in atmospheric dimness) and has a brilliant menu that jumps straight in with mains such as chorizo and chickpea casserole. The Sunday brunch features DJs and hangover-busting breakfasts. Very popular, so best to book ahead.

TOP CHOICE **Ondine**   SEAFOOD **£££**

(Map p48; ☑0131-226 1888; www.ondinerestaurant.co.uk; 2 George IV Bridge; mains £14-24; ☺noon-10pm) New on the scene in 2009 (part of the Hotel Missoni), Ondine has rapidly become one of Edinburgh's finest seafood restaurants, with a menu based on sustainably sourced fish. Take an octopus-inspired seat at the curved Crustacean Bar and tuck into lobster thermidor or a roast shellfish platter. The two-course lunch (noon to 2.30pm) and pretheatre (5pm to 6.30pm) menu costs £15.

Tower   SCOTTISH **£££**

(Map p48; ☑0131-225 3003; www.tower-restaurant.com; Museum of Scotland, Chambers St; mains £15-25; ☺noon-11pm) Chic and sleek, with a great view of the castle, Tower is set atop the Museum of Scotland building. A star-studded guest list of celebrities have enjoyed its menu of quality Scottish food, simply prepared – try half a dozen oysters followed by a fillet of Borders beef. A two-course pre-theatre menu (£15) is available from 5pm to 6.30pm.

Mums   CAFE **£**

(Map p48; www.monstermashcafe.co.uk; 4a Forrest Rd; mains £6-8; ☺8am-10pm Mon-Fri, 9am-10pm Sat, 10am-10pm Sun) After a change of name due to management fall-outs, the original founder of Monster Mash has re-opened it with a new name. This nostalgia-fuelled cafe continues to serve up classic British comfort food of the 1950s – bangers and mash, shepherd's pie, fish and chips. But there's a twist – the food is all top-quality nosh freshly prepared from local produce, including Crombie's gourmet sausages. And there's even a wine list!

Always Sunday   CAFE **£**

(Map p48; www.alwayssunday.co.uk; 170 High St, Royal Mile; mains £4-8; ☺8am-6pm Mon-Fri, 9am-6pm Sat & Sun) If the thought of a greasy fry-up is enough to put you off your breakfast, head instead for this bright and breezy

TOP FIVE EDINBURGH CAFES

Cafe culture is firmly ensconced in Edinburgh, and it is as easy to get your daily caffeine fix here as it is in New York or Paris. Most cafes offer some kind of food, from cakes and sandwiches to full-on meals.

» Forest (Map p48; www.theforest.org.uk; 2 Bristo Pl; mains £2-6; ☺noon-9pm; ☎) A chilled-out and comfortably scuffed-around-the-edges antidote to squeaky-clean style bars, this volunteer-run, not-for-profit art space and cafe serves up humongous helpings of hearty vegetarian and vegan fodder, ranging from burritos to falafel burgers.

» Circle Cafe (www.thecirclecafe.com; 1 Brandon Tce, Canonmills; mains £6-8; ☺8.30am-5pm Mon-Sat, 9am-4.30pm Sun) A great place for breakfast or a good-value lunch, Circle is a bustling neighbourhood cafe serving great coffee and cakes, and fresh, tasty lunch dishes ranging from chunky, home-baked quiches to smoked haddock and poached egg hollandaise.

» Elephant House (Map p48; www.elephanthouse.biz; 21 George IV Bridge; mains £6-8; ☺8am-11pm) Here you'll find counters at the front, tables and views of the castle at the back, and little effigies and images of elephants everywhere. Excellent coffee and tasty, homemade food – pizzas, quiches, pies, sandwiches and cakes – at reasonable prices make Elephant House deservedly popular with local students, shoppers and office workers.

» Glass & Thompson (Map p56; 2 Dundas St; mains £7-10; ☺8am-6pm Mon-Sat, 10.30am-4.30pm Sun) Grab a table in this spick-and-span New Town deli and sip a double espresso as you ogle the cheeses in the cold counter or watch the world go by through the floor-to-ceiling windows. Munchies include tasty platters such as dolmati and falafel, or parma ham and parmesan.

» Valvona & Crolla Caffè Bar (Map p44; www.valvonacrolla.co.uk; 19 Elm Row, Leith Walk; mains £9-13; ☺8.30am-5.30pm Mon-Thu, 8am-6pm Fri & Sat, 10.30am-3.30pm Sun; ☎) Try breakfast (served till 11.30am) with an Italian flavour – full *paesano* (meat) or *verdure* (veggie) fry-ups, or deliciously light and crisp *panettone* in *carrozza* (sweet brioche dipped in egg and fried) – or choose from almond croissants, muesli, yogurt and fruit, freshly squeezed orange juice and perfect Italian coffee. There's also a tasty lunch menu (noon to 3.30pm) of classic Italian dishes.

cafe that dishes up hearty but healthy grub such as fresh fruit smoothies, crisp salads, homemade soups and speciality sandwiches, washed down with fair-trade coffee or herbal tea.

Café Marlayne
FRENCH ££

(Map p48; www.cafemarlayne.com; 7 Old Fishmarket Close, High St; 2-course dinner £15; ☺lunch & dinner Tue-Sat) The second branch of the New Town French bistro (see p76) is a hidden gem, down a steep cobbled alley off the Royal Mile, with a changed-daily menu of market-fresh produce and a lovely little lunchtime sun-trap of an outdoor terrace.

Grain Store
FRENCH, SCOTTISH £££

(Map p48; ☎0131-225 7635; www.grainstore-restaurant.co.uk; 30 Victoria St; mains £14-28; ☺lunch & dinner) An atmospheric upstairs dining room on picturesque Victoria St, the Grain Store has a well-earned reputation for serving the finest Scottish produce, perfectly prepared – from seared scallops with peas and bacon, to tender wild hare cooked in a pastry parcel. Three-course lunch for £15 is good value. Booking recommended.

Mosque Kitchen
INDIAN £

(Map p48; 50 Potterrow; mains £2-5; ☺noon-7pm Sat-Thu, noon-1pm & 1.45-7pm Fri) Sophisticated it ain't – expect shared tables and disposable plates – but this is the place to go for cheap, authentic and delicious homemade curries, kebabs, pakora and naan bread washed down with lassi or mango juice. Caters to Edinburgh's Central Mosque, but welcomes all – local students have taken to it big time. No alcohol.

Maxie's Bistro
BISTRO ££

(Map p48; 5b Johnston Tce; mains £8-14; ☺11am-11pm) Maxie's candlelit bistro, with its cushion-lined nooks set amid stone walls and wooden beams is a pleasant enough setting for a cosy dinner, but at summer lunchtimes people queue for the outdoor tables on the terrace overlooking Victoria St. The food is dependable – Maxie's has been in the food business for more than 20 years – ranging from pastas, steaks and stir-fries to seafood platters and daily specials, and there's an excellent selection of wines.

Suruchi   INDIAN ££

(Map p48; www.suruchirestaurant.com; 14a Nicolson St; mains £7-11; ⊙noon-2.30pm & 5-11pm) A laid-back Indian eatery with handmade turquoise tiles, lazy ceiling fans and chilled-out jazz guitar, Suruchi offers a range of exotic dishes as well as the traditional tandoori standards, many with a Scottish twist. An amusing touch is provided by menu descriptions translated into broad Scots (*'a beezer o' a curry this...gey nippie oan the tongue'*).

Pancho Villa's   MEXICAN ££

(Map p48; ☎0131-557 4416; www.panchovillas. co.uk; 240 Canongate; mains £10-15; ⊙noon-10pm Mon-Sat, 5-10pm Sun) With a Mexican-born owner and lots of Latin American and Spanish staff, it's not surprising that this colourful and lively restaurant is one of the most authentic-feeling Mexican places in town. The dinner menu includes delicious steak fajitas and great vegetarian spinach enchiladas. It's often busy, so book ahead.

Amber   SCOTTISH ££

(Map p48; ☎0131-477 8477; www.amber-restau rant.co.uk; 354 Castlehill; mains £12-18; ⊙noon-3.45pm daily, 7-9pm Tue-Sat) You've got to love a place where the waiter greets you with the words, 'My name is Craig, and I'll be your whisky adviser for this evening'. Located in the Scotch Whisky Experience, this whisky-themed restaurant manages to avoid the tourist clichés and creates genuinely interesting and flavoursome dishes such as fillet of pork with black pudding and whisky and apple compote, or vegetarian haggis with a whisky cream sauce.

Engine Shed   VEGETARIAN £

(Map p44; www.theengineshed.org; 19 St Leonard's Lane; mains £3-6; ⊙10am-4pm Mon-Sat; ⊕) This fair-trade, organic vegetarian cafe is an ideal spot for a healthy lunch, or a cuppa and a bakery-fresh scone after climbing Arthur's Seat. It's been set up to help special-needs adults and as well as having their own bakery they also make their own tofu, which is used plentifully in their tasty curries.

NEW TOWN

TOP CHOICE Oloroso   SCOTTISH £££

(Map p56; ☎0131-226 7614; www.olo roso.co.uk; 33 Castle St; mains £16-25; ⊙restaurant noon-2.30pm & 7-10.30pm, bar 11am-1am) Oloroso is one of Edinburgh's most stylish restaurants, perched on a glass-encased New Town rooftop with views across a Mary Poppins' chimney-scape to the Firth of Forth and Fife hills. Swathed in sophisticated cream linen and charcoal upholstery enlivened with splashes of deep yellow, the dining room serves top-notch Scottish produce with Asian and Mediterranean touches. Two-course lunch £18.50.

TOP CHOICE Café Marlayne   FRENCH ££

(Map p56; ☎0131-226 2230; www.cafe marlayne.com; 76 Thistle St; mains £13-15; ⊙lunch & dinner) All weathered wood and candlelit tables, Café Marlayne is a cosy nook offering French farmhouse cooking – *brandade de morue* (salt cod) with green salad, slow roast rack of lamb, *boudin noir* (black pudding) with scallops and sautéed potato – at very reasonable prices. Booking recommended (there's a branch in the Old Town).

Valvona & Crolla VinCaffè   ITALIAN ££

(Map p56; ☎0131-557 0088; www.valvonacrolla. co.uk; 11 Multrees Walk, St Andrew Sq; mains £10-16; ⊙9.30am-late Mon-Sat, noon-5pm Sun; ⊛) Foodie colours dominate the decor at this delightful Italian bistro – bottle-green pillars and banquettes, chocolate-and-cream coloured walls, espresso-black tables – a perfect backdrop for VinCaffè's superb antipasto (£15 for two), washed down with a bottle of pink Pinot Grigio.

Mussel Inn   SEAFOOD ££

(Map p56; www.mussel-inn.com; 61-65 Rose St; mains £10-22; ⊙noon-3pm & 5.30-10pm Mon-Thu, noon-10pm Fri-Sun) Owned by west-coast shellfish farmers, the Mussel Inn provides a direct outlet for fresh Scottish seafood. The busy restaurant, decorated with bright beechwood indoors, spills out onto the pavement in summer. A kilogram pot of mussels with a choice of sauces – try leek, Dijon mustard and cream – costs £11.50.

Cafe Royal Oyster Bar   SEAFOOD £££

(Map p56; ☎0131-556 4124; www.caferoyal.org. uk; 17a West Register St; mains £17-24; ⊙noon-2pm & 7-10pm) Pass through the revolving doors on the corner of West Register St and you're transported back to Victorian times – a palace of glinting mahogany, polished brass, marble floors, stained glass, Doulton tiles, gilded cornices and starched table linen so thick that it creaks when you fold it. The menu is mostly classic seafood, from oysters on ice to *Coquilles St Jacques Parisienne* (scallops with mushrooms and white wine) and lobster thermidor, augmented by a handful of beef and game dishes.

Eteaket
CAFE £

(Map p56; www.eteaket.co.uk; 41 Frederick St; mains £4-6; ⊙8am-7pm Mon-Sat, 10am-7pm Sun) A 'tea boutique' serving more than 40 varieties of leaf tea, this cosy cafe also offers tempting breakfasts (bagels, toasted croissants, scrambled eggs), fresh sandwiches (ciabatta with hummus, feta cheese and sunblush tomatoes) and afternoon tea (scones with jam and clotted cream).

Stac Polly
SCOTTISH £££

(Map p56; ☎0131-556 2231; www.stacpolly.com; 29-33 Dublin St; mains £18-22; ⊙lunch Mon-Fri, dinner Mon-Sat) Named after a mountain in

northwestern Scotland, Stac Polly's kitchen adds sophisticated twists to fresh Highland produce. Dishes such as haggis in filo parcels with sweet plum and red wine sauce, and rump of lamb with chervil cake and puy lentils keep the punters coming back for more.

Blue Moon Cafe
CAFE £

(Map p44; www.bluemooncafe.co.uk; 1 Barony St; mains £7-8; ⊙10am-10pm) The Blue Moon is the focus of Broughton St's gay social life, always busy, always friendly, and serving up delicious nachos, salads, sandwiches and baked potatoes. It's famous for its homemade burgers (beef, chicken or falafel), which come with a range of toppings, and delicious daily specials.

LEITH

Fishers Bistro
TOP CHOICE
SEAFOOD ££

(Map p62; ☎0131-554 5666; www.fishers bistros.co.uk; 1 The Shore; mains £10-35; ⊙noon-10.30pm) This cosy little restaurant, tucked

---

TOP FIVE LUNCH SPOTS

Many restaurants in Edinburgh offer good-value lunches. Here are a few suggestions from various parts of the city.

» **Urban Angel** (Map p56; ☎0131-225 6215; www.urban-angel.co.uk; 121 Hanover St; mains £8-12; ⊙9am-10pm Mon-Sat, 10am-5pm Sun) A wholesome deli that puts the emphasis on fair-trade, organic and locally sourced produce, Urban Angel also has a delightfully informal cafe-bistro that serves all-day brunch (porridge with honey, French toast, eggs Benedict), tapas and a wide range of light, snacky meals.

» **First Coast** (Map p44; ☎0131-313 4404; www.first-coast.co.uk; 99-101 Dalry Rd; mains £9-15; ⊙noon-2pm & 5-10.30pm Mon-Sat) Our favourite neighbourhood bistro, First Coast has a striking main dining area with pale-grey wood panelling, stripped stone walls and Victorian cornices, and a short and simple menu offering hearty comfort food such as Thai marinated chicken salad, or glazed ham hough with mustard mash. At lunch, and from 5pm to 6.30pm, you can have an excellent two-course meal for £11.

» **Daniel's Bistro** (Map p62; ☎0131-553 5933; www.daniels-bistro.co.uk; 88 Commercial St; mains £8-15; ⊙10am-10pm) Daniel comes from Alsace, and his all-French kitchen staff combine top Scottish and French produce with Gallic know-how to create a wide range of delicious dishes. The Provencal fish soup is excellent, and main courses range from boeuf bourguignon to cassoulet. A seriously filling three-course lunch is £9.70.

» **La P'tite Folie** (Map p56; ☎0131-225 7983; 61 Frederick St; mains £16-18; ⊙noon-3pm & 6-11pm Mon-Sat, 6-11pm Sun) This is a delightful little restaurant with a Breton owner whose menu includes French classics – onion soup, *moules marinières* – alongside steaks, seafood and a range of *plats du jour*. The two-course lunch is a bargain at £9.

» **Petit Paris** (Map p48; ☎0131-226 2442; www.petitparis-restaurant.co.uk; 38-40 Grassmarket; mains £14-18; ⊙noon-3pm & 5.30-11pm, closed Mon Oct-Mar) Like the name says, this is a little piece of Paris, complete with checked tablecloths, friendly waiters and good-value grub – the *moules-frîtes* (mussels and chips) are excellent. There's a lunch deal offering the *plat du jour* and a coffee for £8; add a starter and it's £11.

beneath a 17th-century signal tower, is one of the city's best seafood places. The menu ranges widely in price, from cheaper dishes such as mackerel with beetroot, chilli and orange dressing, to more expensive delights such as North Berwick lobster served with garlic and herb butter.

Chop Chop CHINESE £
(Map p62; ☑0131-553 1818; 76 Commercial St; mains £7-10; ☺noon-2pm & 5.30-10pm Mon & Wed-Sat, noon-10pm Sun) Chop Chop is a Chinese restaurant with a difference, in that is serves dishes popular in China rather than Britain; as their slogan says, 'Can a billion people be wrong?'. No sweet and sour pork here, but a range of delicious dumplings filled with pork and coriander, beef and chilli, or lamb and leek, and unusual vegetarian dishes such as aubergine fried with garlic and Chinese spices.

Diner 7 CAFE ££
(Map p62; www.diner7.co.uk; 7 Commercial St; mains £8-12; ☺11.30am-11pm Thu-Sun, 4-11pm Mon-Wed) A neat local eatery with rust-coloured leather booths and banquettes, black and copper tables, and local art on the walls, this diner has a menu of succulent Aberdeen Angus steaks and home-made burgers, but also offers more unusual fare such as chicken and chorizo kebabs, or smoked haddock with black-pudding stovies.

Martin Wishart FRENCH £££
(Map p62; ☑0131-553 3557; www.martin-wishart.co.uk; 54 The Shore; 3-course lunch/dinner £28/60; ☺noon-2pm & 7-10pm Tue-Sat) In 2001 this restaurant became the first in Edinburgh to win a Michelin star. The eponymous chef has worked with Albert Roux, Marco Pierre White and Nick Nairn, and brings a modern French approach to the best Scottish produce, from roast scallop with Bellota ham and black cherry juice, to roast loin of lamb in a herb crust with asparagus tortellini.

Self-Catering
There are grocery stores and food shops all over the city, many of them open 9am to 10pm daily. Many petrol stations also have late-opening shops that sell groceries. There are several large supermarkets spread throughout the city including the following:
Sainsbury's (Map p56; 9-10 St Andrew Sq; ☺7am-10pm Mon-Sat, 9am-8pm Sun)

Tesco (Map p48; 94 Nicolson St; ☺6am-1am).

Marks & Spencer (Map p56; 54 Princes St; ☺9am-7pm Mon-Sat, 9am-8pm Thu, 11am-6pm Sun) Food hall sells high-quality ready-cooked meals.

Good delis for buying picnic goodies include the following:
Valvona & Crolla (Map p44; www.valvonacrolla.co.uk; 19 Elm Row, Leith Walk; ☺8am-6.30pm Mon-Sat, 11am-5pm Sun)
Peckham's (Map p44; www.peckhams.co.uk; 155-159 Bruntsfield Pl; ☺8am-midnight Mon-Sat, 9am-11pm Sun)

🍷 Drinking
Edinburgh has more than 700 bars, which are as varied as the population – everything from Victorian palaces to rough-and-ready drinking dens, and from bearded, real-ale howffs (pubs) to trendy cocktail bars.

OLD TOWN
The pubs in the Grassmarket have outdoor tables on sunny summer afternoons, but in the evenings are favoured by boozed-up lads on the pull, so steer clear if that's not your thing. The Cowgate – the Grassmarket's extension to the east – is Edinburgh's clubland.

Bow Bar PUB
(Map p48; 80 West Bow) One of the city's best traditional-style pubs (it's not as old as it looks) serving a range of excellent real ales and a vast selection of malt whiskies, the Bow Bar often has standing-room only on Friday and Saturday evenings.

Jolly Judge PUB
(Map p48; www.jollyjudge.co.uk; 7a James Crt; 🕿) A snug little howff tucked away down a close, the Judge exudes a cosy 17th-century atmosphere (low, timber-beamed painted ceilings) and has the added attraction of a cheering open fire in cold weather. No music or gaming machines, just the buzz of conversation.

Ecco Vino WINE BAR
(Map p48; www.eccovinoedinburgh.com; 19 Cockburn St) With outdoor tables on sunny afternoons, and cosy candlelit intimacy in the evenings, this comfortably cramped Tuscan-style wine bar offers a tempting range of Italian wines, though not all are available by the glass – best to share a bottle.

Villager BAR
(Map p48; www.villager-e.com; 49-50 George IV Bridge) A cross between a traditional pub and a pre-club bar, Villager has a comfort-

TOP FIVE VEGETARIAN RESTAURANTS

Many Edinburgh restaurants offer vegetarian options on the menu, some good, some bad, some indifferent. The places listed here are all 100% veggie and all fall into the 'good' category.

» **David Bann** (Map p48; ☎0131-556 5888; www.davidbann.com; 56-58 St Mary's St; mains £9-13; ☉noon-10pm Mon-Fri, 11am-10pm Sat & Sun) If you want to convince a carnivorous friend that cuisine à la veg can be as tasty and inventive as a meat-muncher's menu, take them to David Bann's stylish restaurant – dishes such as beetroot, apple and Dunsyre blue cheese pudding, and crepe of Thai-spiced broccoli and smoked tofu are guaranteed to win converts.

» **L'Artichaut** (Map p44; ☎0131-558 1608; www.lartichaut.co.uk; 14 Eyre Pl; 2-/3-course meal £15/20; ☉lunch & dinner Tue-Sat, 12.30-8pm Sun) Beautifully crafted Tim Stead tables and chairs reflect the care and craftsmanship that goes into the food at this new and inventive restaurant. Fresh, seasonal produce is used to create dishes such as rosemary and thyme pancake filled with aubergine and mozzarella, and spicy black bean stew with glazed chicory and spiced cauliflower.

» **Ann Purna** (Map p44; 45 St Patrick's Sq; mains £5-10; ☉noon-2pm & 5.30-11pm Mon-Fri, 5.30-11pm Sat & Sun) This little gem of an Indian restaurant serves exclusively vegetarian dishes from southern India, served with a smile by the family team who run the place. If you're new to this kind of food, opt for a *thali* – a self-contained platter that has about half a dozen different dishes, including a dessert. You can get a light lunch for £5.

» **Black Bo's** (Map p48; www.black-bos.com; 57-61 Blackfriars St; mains £10-13; ☉6-10pm) You can't accuse the chef at Black Bo's, a popular vegetarian and vegan eatery just off the Royal Mile, of being unadventurous. Check the daily specials, which are always interesting – beetroot and cashew balls stuffed with feta cheese, with chilli and garlic yogurt, for example.

» **Kalpna** (Map p48; www.kalpnarestaurant.com; 2-3 St Patrick Sq; mains £6-11; ☉noon-2pm & 5.30-10.30pm Mon-Sat year-round, plus 6-10.30pm Sun May-Sep) Another long-standing Edinburgh favourite, Kalpna is one of the best Indian restaurants in the country, vegetarian or otherwise. The cuisine is mostly Gujarati, with a smattering of dishes from other parts of India. The lunch buffet (£7) is superb value.

able, laid-back vibe. It can be standing-room only in the main bar in the evenings (the cocktails are excellent), but the side room, with its brown leather sofas and subtropical pot plants comes into its own for a lazy Sunday afternoon with the papers.

Royal Mile Tavern PUB
(Map p48; www.royalmiletavern.com; 127 High St) An elegant, traditional bar lined with polished wood, mirrors and brass, Royal Mile serves real ale (Deuchars IPA and Caledonian 80/-), good wines and decent pub grub – fish and chips, steak and Guinness pie, sausage and mash etc.

Last Drop PUB
(Map p48; 74 Grassmarket) The name commemorates the gallows that used to stand nearby, but the only swingers today are the pub's partying clientele, largely students and backpackers.

Beehive Inn PUB
(Map p48; 18-20 Grassmarket) The historic Beehive – a former coaching inn – is a big, buzzing party-pub, with a range of real ales, but the main attraction is sitting out the back in the Grassmarket's only beer garden, with views up to the castle.

Bannerman's PUB
(Map p48; www.myspace.com/bannermanslive; 212 Cowgate) A long-established favourite, Bannerman's straggles through a warren of old vaults. It pulls in crowds of students, locals and backpackers with live rock, punk and indie bands.

Pear Tree House PUB
(Map p48; 38 West Nicolson St) The Pear Tree is another student favourite, with comfy sofas and board games inside, plus the city's biggest and most popular beer garden in summer.

NEW TOWN

Rose St (between Princes St and George St) was once a famous pub crawl, where generations of students, sailors and rugby fans would try to visit every pub on the street (around 17 of them) and down a pint of beer in each one.

Oxford Bar PUB

(Map p56; www.oxfordbar.com; 8 Young St) The Oxford is that rarest of things these days, a real pub for real people, with no 'theme', no music, no frills and no pretensions. 'The Ox' has been immortalised by Ian Rankin, author of the Inspector Rebus novels, who is a regular here, as is his fictional detective.

Cumberland Bar PUB

(Map p44; www.cumberlandbar.co.uk; 1-3 Cumberland St) Immortalised as the stereotypical New Town pub in Alexander McCall-Smith's serialised novel *44 Scotland Street,* the Cumberland has an authentic, traditional wood-brass-and-mirrors look (despite being relatively new), and serves well-looked-after, cask-conditioned ales and a wide range of malt whiskies. There's also a pleasant little beer garden outside.

Guildford Arms PUB

(Map p56; www.guildfordarms.com; 1 West Register St) Located next door to the Cafe Royal Bar, the Guildford is another classic Victorian pub full of polished mahogany, brass and ornate cornices. The bar lunches are good – try to get a table in the unusual upstairs gallery, with a view over the sea of drinkers down below.

Kenilworth PUB

(Map p56; 152-154 Rose St) A gorgeous, Edwardian drinking palace, complete with original fittings – from the tile floors, mahogany circle bar and gantry, to the ornate

---

TOP FIVE TRADITIONAL PUBS

Edinburgh is blessed with a large number of traditional 19th- and early-20th-century pubs, which have preserved much of their original Victorian or Edwardian decoration and serve cask-conditioned real ales and a staggering range of malt whiskies.

» **Athletic Arms** (Diggers; Map p44; 1-3 Angle Park Tce) Named after the cemetery across the street – the grave-diggers used to nip in and slake their thirst after a hard day's interring – the Diggers dates from the 1890s. It's still staunchly traditional – the decor has barely changed in 100 years – and has recently revived its reputation as a real-ale drinker's mecca by serving locally brewed Diggers' 80-shilling ale. Packed to the gills with football and rugby fans on match days.

» **Abbotsford** (Map p56; www.theabbotsford.com; 3 Rose St) One of the few pubs in Rose St that has retained its Edwardian splendour, the Abbotsford has long been a hang-out for writers, actors, journalists and media people, and has many loyal regulars. Dating from 1902, and named after Sir Walter Scott's country house, the pub's centrepiece is a splendid mahogany island bar. Good selection of Scottish and English real ales.

» **Bennet's Bar** (Map p44; 8 Leven St) Situated beside the King's Theatre, Bennet's has managed to hang on to almost all of its beautiful Victorian fittings, from the leaded stained-glass windows and ornate mirrors to the wooden gantry and the brass water taps on the bar (for your whisky – there are over 100 malts to choose from).

» **Cafe Royal Circle Bar** (Map p56; www.caferoyal.org.uk; 17 West Register St) Perhaps the classic Edinburgh bar, the Cafe Royal's main claims to fame are its magnificent oval bar and the series of Doulton tile portraits of famous Victorian inventors. Check out the bottles on the gantry – staff line them up to look like there's a mirror there, and many a drink-befuddled customer has been seen squinting and wondering why he can't see his reflection.

» **Sheep Heid** (www.sheepheid.co.uk; 43-45 The Causeway, Duddingston) Possibly the oldest inn in Edinburgh (with a licence dating back to 1360) the Sheep Heid feels more like a country pub than an Edinburgh bar. Set in the semirural shadow of Arthur's Seat, it's famous for its 19th-century skittles alley and the lovely little beer garden.

mirrors and gas lamps – the Kenilworth was Edinburgh's original gay bar back in the 1970s. Today it attracts a mixed crowd of all ages, and serves a good range of real ales and malt whiskies.

Robertsons 37 Bar
PUB
(Map p56; 37 Rose St) No 37 is to malt whisky connoisseurs what the Diggers (now called the Athletic Arms) once was to real-ale fans. Its long gantry sports a choice of more than 100 single malts and the bar provides a quiet and elegant environment in which to sample them.

Kay's Bar
PUB
(Map p56; 39 Jamaica St) Housed in a former wine-merchant's office, tiny Kay's Bar is a cosy haven with a coal fire and a fine range of real ales. Good food is served in the back room at lunchtime, but you'll have to book a table – Kay's is a popular spot.

Amicus Apple
COCKTAIL BAR
(Map p56; www.amicusapple.com; 15 Frederick St) This laid-back cocktail lounge is the hippest hang-out in the New Town. The drinks menu ranges from retro classics such as Bloody Mary and mojito, to original and unusual concoctions such as the Cuillin Martini (Tanqueray No 10 gin, Talisker malt whisky and smoked rosemary).

Standing Order
BAR
(Map p56; www.jdwetherspoon.co.uk; 62-66 George St; ☏) One of several converted banks on George St, Standing Order is a cavernous beer hall with a fantastic vaulted ceiling and some cosy rooms off to the right – look for the one with the original 27-tonne safe. Despite its size, it can be standing-room only at weekends.

Tonic
COCKTAIL BAR
(Map p56; 34a North Castle St) As cool and classy as a perfectly mixed martini, from the chic decor to the Philippe Starck bar stools, Tonic prides itself on the authenticity of its cocktails, of which there are many – the menu goes on forever.

LEITH

Teuchter's Landing
PUB
(Map p62; 1 Dock Pl) A cosy warren of timber-lined nooks and crannies housed in a single-storey red-brick building (once a waiting room for ferries across the Firth of Forth), this real-ale and malt-whisky bar also has outdoor tables on a floating terrace in the dock.

Port O'Leith
PUB
(Map p62; 58 Constitution St) This is a good, old-fashioned, friendly local boozer, swathed with flags and cap bands left behind by visiting sailors – the harbour is just down the road. Pop in for a pint and you'll probably stay until closing time.

Starbank Inn
PUB
(www.starbankinn.co.uk; 64 Laverockbank Rd) The Starbank is an oasis of fine ales and good, homemade food on Edinburgh's windswept waterfront. In summer there's a sunny conservatory, and in winter a blazing fire to toast your toes in front of.

☆ Entertainment

Edinburgh has a number of fine theatres and concert halls, and there are independent art-house cinemas as well as mainstream movie theatres. Many pubs offer entertainment ranging from live Scottish folk music to pop, rock and jazz as well as karaoke and quiz nights, while a range of stylish modern bars purvey house, dance and hip-hop to the preclubbing crowd.

The comprehensive source for what's-on info is the *List* (www.list.co.uk), an excellent listings magazine covering both Edinburgh and Glasgow. It's available from most newsagents, and is published fortnightly on a Thursday.

Live Music

Check out the *List* and the *Gig Guide* (www.gigguide.co.uk), a free email newsletter and listings website, to see who's playing where.

JAZZ, BLUES & ROCK

Henry's Cellar
ROCK, INDIE
(Map p48; www.theraft.org.uk; 8a Morrison St) One of Edinburgh's most eclectic live-music venues, Henry's has something going on every night of the week, from rock and indie to 'Balkan-inspired folk', funk to hip-hop to hardcore, staging both local bands and acts from around the world. Open till 3am at weekends.

Whistle Binkie's
ROCK, BLUES
(Map p48; www.whistlebinkies.com; 4-6 South Bridge) This crowded cellar-bar just off the Royal Mile has live music every night till 3am, from rock and blues to folk and jazz. Open-mic night on Monday and breaking bands on Tuesday are showcases for new talent.

Jazz Bar   JAZZ

(Map p48; www.thejazzbar.co.uk; 1a Chambers St; ☎) This atmospheric cellar bar, with its polished parquet floors, bare stone walls, candlelit tables and stylish steel-framed chairs is owned and operated by jazz musicians. There's live music every night from 9pm to 3am, and on Saturday from 3pm.

Liquid Room   ROCK, INDIE

(Map p48; www.liquidroom.com; 9c Victoria St) The Liquid Room (see also Nightclubs) stages all kinds of gigs from local rock bands to tribute bands to the Average White Band. Check the program on the website.

TRADITIONAL

The capital is a great place to hear traditional Scottish (and Irish) folk music, with a mix of regular spots and impromptu sessions.

Sandy Bell's   FOLK

(Map p48; 25 Forrest Rd) This unassuming bar is a stalwart of the traditional-music scene (the founder's wife sang with The Corries). There's music almost every evening at 9pm, and from 3pm Saturday and Sunday.

Royal Oak   FOLK

(Map p48; www.royal-oak-folk.com; 1 Infirmary St) This popular folk pub is tiny, so get there early (9pm start weekdays, 2.30pm Saturday) if you want to be sure of a place. Sundays from 4pm to 7pm is open-session – bring your own instruments (or a good singing voice).

Pleasance Cabaret Bar   FOLK

(Map p48; www.edinburghfolkclub.co.uk; 60 The Pleasance) The Pleasance is home to the Edinburgh Folk Club, which runs a program of visiting bands and singers at 8pm on Wednesday nights.

Nightclubs

Edinburgh's club scene has some fine DJ talent and is well worth exploring; there are club-night listings in the *List*. Most of the venues are concentrated in and around the twin sumps of Cowgate and Calton Rd – so it's downhill all the way...

Bongo Club   MULTI-ARTS VENUE

(Map p44; www.thebongoclub.co.uk; Moray House, Paterson's Land, 37 Holyrood Rd) The weird and wonderful Bongo Club is home to Big N Bashy, a Saturday night club dedicated to reggae, grime, dubstep and jungle. Also worth checking out is the booming bass of roots and dub reggae night Messenger Sound System (boasting 'a sound system that could

knock you out'). The club is open as a cafe and exhibition space during the day.

Cabaret Voltaire   CLUB, LIVE MUSIC

(Map p48; www.thecabaretvoltaire.com; 36 Blair St) An atmospheric warren of stone-lined vaults houses Edinburgh's most 'alternative' club, which eschews huge dance floors and egotistical DJ worship in favour of a 'creative crucible' hosting an eclectic mix of DJs, live acts, comedy, theatre, visual arts and the spoken word. Well worth a look.

Liquid Room   CLUB, LIVE MUSIC

(Map p48; www.liquidroom.com; 9c Victoria St) Set in a subterranean vault deep beneath Victoria St, the Liquid Room is a superb club venue with a thundering sound system. There are regular club nights Wednesday to Saturday as well as live bands. The long-running and recently relaunched Evol (Friday from 10.30pm) is an Edinburgh institution catering to the indie-kid crowd, and is regularly voted as Scotland's top club night out.

Studio 24   CLUB

(Map p44; 24 Calton Rd) Studio 24 is the dark heart of Edinburgh's underground music scene, with a program that covers all bases, from house to nu metal via punk, ska, reggae, crossover, tribal, electro, techno and dance. Mission (Saturday from 11pm) is the city's classic hard-rock, metal and alt night.

Opal Lounge   CLUB

(Map p56; www.opallounge.co.uk; 51 George St) The Opal Lounge is jammed at weekends with affluent twenty-somethings who've spent £200 and two hours in front of a mirror to achieve that artlessly scruffy look. During the week, when the air-kissing crowds thin out, it's a good place to relax with an expensive but expertly mixed cocktail. Expect to queue on weekend evenings.

Lulu   CLUB

(Map p56; www.luluedinburgh.co.uk; 125 George St) Lush leather sofas, red satin cushions, fetishistic steel-mesh curtains and dim red lighting all help to create a decadent atmosphere in this drop-dead gorgeous club venue beneath the Tigerlily boutique hotel. Resident and guest DJs show a bit more originality than your average club.

Cinemas

Film buffs will find plenty to keep them happy in Edinburgh's art-house cinemas, while popcorn munchers can choose from a range of multiplexes.

Cameo
CINEMA

(Map p44; www.picturehouses.co.uk; 38 Home St) The three-screen, independently owned Cameo is a good, old-fashioned cinema showing an imaginative mix of mainstream and art-house movies. There is a good program of midnight movies and Sunday matinees, and the seats in Screen 1 are big enough to get lost in.

Filmhouse
CINEMA

(Map p48; www.filmhousecinema.com; 88 Lothian Rd; 🐾) The Filmhouse is the main venue for the annual Edinburgh International Film Festival and screens a full program of art-house, classic, foreign and second-run films, with lots of themes, retrospectives and 70mm screenings. It has wheelchair access to all three screens.

Cineworld Fountainpark
CINEMA

(Map p44; www.cineworld.co.uk; Fountainpark Complex, Dundee St) The Cineworld is a massive 12-screen multiplex complete with cafebar, movie-poster shop and frighteningly overpriced popcorn.

VUE Cinema
CINEMA

(Map p56; www.myvue.com; Omni Centre, Greenside Pl) Another 12-screen multiplex, with three 'VIP' screens where you can pay extra to watch from a luxurious leather reclining seat complete with side table for your drink and complimentary snacks.

Classical Music, Opera & Ballet

The following are the main venues for classical music.

Edinburgh Festival Theatre
BALLET, OPERA

(Map p48; www.eft.co.uk; 13-29 Nicolson St; ☺box office 10am-6pm Mon-Sat, to 8pm show nights, 4pm-showtime Sun) A beautifully restored art-deco theatre with a modern frontage, the Festival is the city's main venue for opera, dance and ballet, but also stages musicals, concerts, drama and children's shows.

Usher Hall
CLASSICAL MUSIC

(Map p48; www.usherhall.co.uk; Lothian Rd; ☺box office 10.30am-5.30pm, to 8pm show nights) The architecturally impressive Usher Hall hosts concerts by the Royal Scottish National Orchestra (RSNO) and performances of popular music.

St Giles Cathedral
CLASSICAL MUSIC

(Map p48; www.stgilescathedral.org.uk; High St) The big kirk on the Royal Mile plays host to a regular and varied program of classical music, including popular lunchtime and evening concerts and organ recitals. The cathedral choir sings at the 10am and 11.30am Sunday services.

Queen's Hall
CLASSICAL MUSIC

(Map p44; www.thequeenshall.net; Clerk St; ☺box office 10am-5.30pm Mon-Sat, or till 15min after show begins) The home of the Scottish Chamber Orchestra also stages jazz, blues, folk, rock and comedy.

Sport

Edinburgh is home to two rival **football** teams playing in the Scottish Premier League – **Heart of Midlothian** (aka Hearts) and **Hibernian** (aka Hibs). The domestic football season lasts from August to May, and most matches are played at 3pm on Saturday or 7.30pm on Tuesday or Wednesday.

Hearts has its home ground at **Tynecastle Stadium** (Map p44; www.heartsfc.co.uk; Gorgie Rd), southwest of the city centre in Gorgie. Hibernian's home ground is northeast of the city centre at **Easter Road Stadium** (Map p44; www.hibs.co.uk; 12 Albion Pl).

Each year, from January to March, Scotland's national **rugby** team takes part in the Six Nations Rugby Union Championship. The most important fixture is the clash against England for the Calcutta Cup. At club level the season runs from September to May. **Murrayfield Stadium** (www.scottishrugby.org; 112 Roseburn St), about 1.5 miles west of the city centre, is the venue for international matches.

Most other **sporting events**, including athletics and cycling, are held at **Meadowbank Sports Centre** (www.edinburghleisure.co.uk; 139 London Rd), Scotland's main sports arena.

Horse-racing enthusiasts should head 6 miles east to **Musselburgh Racecourse** (www.musselburgh-racecourse.co.uk; Linkfield Rd, Musselburgh), Scotland's oldest racecourse (founded 1816), where meetings are held throughout the year.

Theatre, Musicals & Comedy

Royal Lyceum Theatre
DRAMA, MUSICALS

(Map p48; www.lyceum.org.uk; 30b Grindlay St; ☺box office 10am-6pm Mon-Sat, to 8pm show nights) A grand Victorian theatre located beside the Usher Hall, the Lyceum stages drama, concerts, musicals and ballet.

Traverse Theatre
DRAMA, DANCE

(Map p48; www.traverse.co.uk; 10 Cambridge St; ☺box office 10am-6pm Mon-Sat, till 8pm on show nights) The Traverse is the main focus for new Scottish writing and stages an adventurous program of contemporary drama and dance. The box office is only open on Sunday (from 4pm) when there's a show on.

King's Theatre
DRAMA, MUSICALS

(Map p44; www.eft.co.uk; 2 Leven St, Bruntsfield; ☺box office open 1hr before show) King's is a traditional theatre with a program of musicals, drama, comedy and its famous Christmas pantomime.

Edinburgh Playhouse
MUSICALS

(Map p56; www.edinburgh-playhouse.co.uk; 18-22 Greenside Pl; ☺box office 10am-6pm Mon-Sat, to 8pm show nights) This restored theatre at the top of Leith Walk stages Broadway musicals, dance shows, opera and popular-music concerts.

Stand Comedy Club
COMEDY

(Map p56; www.thestand.co.uk; 5 York Pl) The Stand, founded in 1995, is Edinburgh's main comedy venue. It's an intimate cabaret bar with performances every night and a free Sunday lunchtime show.

🔒 Shopping

Princes St is Edinburgh's principal shopping street, lined with all the big high-street stores, with many smaller shops along pedestrianised Rose St, and more expensive designer boutiques on George St. There are also two big shopping centres in the New Town – **Princes Mall** (Map p56), at the eastern end of Princes St, and the nearby **St James Centre** (Map p56) at the top of Leith St, plus a designer shopping complex with a flagship Harvey Nichols store on the eastern side of St Andrew Sq. The huge **Ocean Terminal** (Map p62) in Leith is the biggest shopping centre in the city.

For more off-beat shopping – including fashion, music, crafts, gifts and jewellery – head for the cobbled lanes of Cockburn, Victoria and St Mary's Sts, all near the Royal Mile in the Old Town, William St in the western part of New Town, and the Stockbridge district, immediately north of the New Town.

Bookshops

Blackwell's Bookshop
BOOKSHOP

(Map p48; www.blackwell.co.uk; 53-62 South Bridge; ☺9am-8pm Mon & Wed-Fri, 9.30am-8pm Tue, 9am-6pm Sat, noon-6pm Sun) The city's principal bookstore; big selection of academic books.

Waterstone's
BOOKSHOP

(www.waterstones.com) East End (Map p56; 13 Princes St; ☺9am-8pm Mon-Fri, to 7.30pm Sat, 10am-7pm Sun); George St (Map p56; 83 George St; ☺9.30am-9pm Mon-Fri, to 8pm Sat, 11am-7pm Sun); West End (Map p56; 128 Princes St; ☺8.30am-8pm Mon-Sat, 10.30am-7pm Sun) The West End branch has an in-store cafe with great views.

Word Power
BOOKSHOP

(Map p48; www.word-power.co.uk; 43 West Nicolson St; ☺10am-6pm Mon-Fri, 10.30am-6pm Sat, noon-5pm Sun) Radical, independent bookshop with wide range of political, gay and feminist literature.

Cashmere & Wool

Woollen textiles and knitwear are one of Scotland's classic exports. Scottish cashmere – a fine, soft wool from young goats and lambs – provides the most luxurious and expensive knitwear and has been seen gracing the torsos of pop star Robbie Williams and England footballer David Beckham.

Kinross Cashmere
KNITWEAR

(Map p48; www.cashmerestore.com; 2 St Giles St) Wide range of traditional and modern knitwear.

Joyce Forsyth Designer Knitwear
KNITWEAR

(Map p48; www.joyceforsyth.co.uk; 42 Candlemaker Row; ☺closed Sun & Mon) Colourful designs that will drag your ideas about woollens firmly into the 21st century.

Edinburgh Woollen Mill
KNITWEAR

(Map p56; www.ewm.co.uk; 139 Princes St) An old stalwart of the tourist trade, with a good selection of traditional jerseys, cardigans, scarves, shawls and rugs.

Crafts & Gifts

Galerie Mirages
HANDICRAFTS

(Map p44; www.galeriemirages.co.uk; 46a Raeburn Pl) An Aladdin's Cave packed with jewellery, textiles and handicrafts from all over the world, best known for its silver, amber and gemstone jewellery in both ethnic and contemporary designs.

One World Shop
HANDICRAFTS

(Map p48; www.oneworldshop.co.uk; St John's Church, Princes St) Stocks a wide range of handmade crafts from developing countries, including paper goods, rugs, textiles, jewellery, ceramics, accessories, food and drink, all from accredited fair-trade suppliers. During the festival period (when the

Edinburgh has a small – but perfectly formed – gay and lesbian scene, centred on the area around Broughton St (known affectionately as the 'Pink Triangle') at the eastern end of New Town. Blue Moon Cafe (p77) at the foot of Broughton St is a friendly G&L caff offering good food and good company. It's also a good place to pick up on what's happening on the local scene.

Scotsgay (www.scotsgay.co.uk) is the local monthly magazine covering gay and lesbian issues, with listings of gay-friendly pubs and clubs. See also www.edinburgh gayscene.com for online listings.

Useful contacts:

Edinburgh LGBT Centre (www.lgbthealth.org.uk; 9 Howe St)

Lothian LGBT Helpline (☎0131-556 4049; ☺12.30-7pm Wed)

Pubs & Clubs

Edinburgh's most popular gay club night is the long-running **Taste** (www.taste-clubs. com).

» **CC Blooms** (Map p44; www.bebo.com/ccbloomsnightclub; 23 Greenside Pl, Leith Walk; ☺6pm-3am Mon-Sat, 7pm-3am Sun) The raddled old queen of the Edinburgh gay scene, CC's offers two floors of deafening dance and disco. It's a bit overpriced and overcrowded but worth a visit – go early, or sample the wild karaoke on Thursday and Sunday nights.

» **Regent** (Map p44; 2 Montrose Tce; ☺11am-1am Mon-Sat, 12.30pm-1am Sun) This is a pleasant gay local with a relaxed atmosphere (no loud music), serving coffee and croissants as well as excellent real ales, including Deuchars IPA and Caledonian 80/-. Meeting place for the Lesbian and Gay Real Ale Drinkers club (first Monday of month, 9pm).

» **Newtown Bar** (Map p56; www.newtownbar.co.uk; 26b Dublin St; ☺noon-1am Sun-Thu, to 2am Fri & Sat; ☎) Stylish modern bar serving good food and drink, and basement club with resident DJ that hosts regular men-only events.

---

shop stays open till 6pm) there's a crafts fair in the churchyard outside.

Meadows Pottery   STONEWARE
(Map p44; www.themeadowspottery.com; 11a Summerhall Pl) Sells colourful stoneware, all hand-thrown on the premises.

Adam Pottery   CERAMICS
(Map p44; www.adampottery.co.uk; 76 Henderson Row) Produces its own ceramics, mostly decorative, in a wide range of styles.

Department Stores

Jenners   DEPARTMENT STORE
(Map p56; www.houseoffraser.co.uk; 48 Princes St) Founded in 1838, Jenners is the grande dame of Scottish department stores. It stocks a wide range of quality goods, both classic and contemporary.

Harvey Nichols   DEPARTMENT STORE
(Map p56; www.harveynichols.com; 30-34 St Andrew Sq) The jewel in the crown of Edinburgh's shopping scene has four floors of designer labels and eye-popping price tags.

John Lewis   DEPARTMENT STORE
(Map p56; www.johnlewis.com; St James Centre) The place to go for good-value clothes and household goods.

Tartan & Highland Dress

There are dozens of shops along the Royal Mile and Princes St where you can buy kilts and tartan goods.

Kinloch Anderson   HIGHLAND DRESS
(Map p62; www.kinlochanderson.com; 4 Dock St, Leith) One of the best, this was founded in 1868 and is still family-run. Kinloch Anderson is a supplier of kilts and Highland dress to the royal family.

Geoffrey (Tailor) Inc   HIGHLAND DRESS
(Map p48; www.geoffreykilts.co.uk; 57-59 High St) Can fit you out in traditional Highland dress, or run up a kilt in your own clan tartan. Its offshoot, 21st Century Kilts, offers modern fashion kilts in a variety of fabrics.

ℹ Information

Emergency

In an emergency, dial ✆999 or ✆112 (free from public phones) and ask for police, ambulance, fire brigade or coastguard.

Edinburgh Rape Crisis Centre (✆08088 01 03 02; www.rapecrisisscotland.org.uk)

Lothian & Borders Police HQ (✆0131-311 3131; www.lbp.police.uk; Fettes Ave)

Lothian & Borders Police Information Centre (✆0131-226 6966; 188 High St; ☻10am-7.30pm Mar-Oct, to 6pm Nov-Feb) Report a crime or make lost-property inquiries here.

Internet Access

There are several internet-enabled telephone boxes (10p a minute, 50p minimum) scattered around the city centre, and countless wi-fi hot spots – search on www.jiwire.com. Internet cafes are spread around the city. Some convenient ones:

easyInternetcafe (www.easy-everything.com; 58 Rose St; ☻7.30am-10.30pm)

e-corner (www.e-cnr.co.uk; 54 Blackfriars St; per 20min £1; ☻7.30am-9pm Mon-Fri, 8am-9pm Sat & Sun)

G-Tec (www.grassmarket-technologies.com; 67 Grassmarket; per 20min £1; ☻10am-6pm Mon-Fri, to 5.30pm Sat)

Internet Resources

Edinburgh & Lothians Tourist Board (www.edinburgh.org) Official tourist-board site, with listings of accommodation, sights, activities and events.

Edinburgh Architecture (www.edinburgharchitecture.co.uk) Informative site dedicated to the city's modern architecture.

Events Edinburgh (www.eventsedinburgh.org.uk) The city council's official events guide.

Edinburgh Festival Guide (www.edinburghfestivals.co.uk) Everything you need to know about Edinburgh's many festivals.

List (www.list.co.uk) Listings of restaurants, pubs, clubs and nightlife.

Media

Edinburgh's home-grown daily newspapers include the *Scotsman* (www.scotsman.com), a quality daily covering Scottish, UK and international news, sport and current affairs, and the *Edinburgh Evening News* (www.edinburghnews.com), covering news and entertainment in the city and its environs; *Scotland on Sunday* is the weekend newspaper from the same publisher.

Medical Services

Boots (48 Shandwick Pl; ☻8am-9pm Mon-Fri, 8am-6pm Sat, 10.30am-4.30pm Sun) Chemist open longer hours than most.

Royal Hospital for Sick Children (✆0131-536 0000; www.nhslothian.scot.nhs.uk; 9 Sciennes Rd) Casualty department for children aged under 13 years; located in Marchmont.

Royal Infirmary of Edinburgh (✆0131-536 1000; www.nhslothian.scot.nhs.uk; 51 Little France Cres, Old Dalkeith Rd) Edinburgh's main general hospital; has 24-hour accident and emergency department.

Western General Hospital (✆0131-537 1330; www.nhslothian.scot.nhs.uk; Crewe Rd South; ☻9am-9pm) For non-life-threatening injuries and ailments, you can attend the Minor Injuries Unit without having to make an appointment.

For urgent medical advice you can call the **NHS 24 Helpline** (✆08454 24 24 24; www.nhs24.com). Chemists (pharmacists) can advise you on minor ailments. At least one local chemist remains open round the clock – its location will be displayed in the windows of other chemists.

For urgent dental treatment you can visit the walk-in **Chalmers Dental Centre** (3 Chalmers St; ☻9am-4.45pm Mon-Thu, to 4.15pm Fri). In the case of a dental emergency in the evenings or at weekends, call **Lothian Dental Advice Line** (✆0131-536 4800).

Post

Main post office (Map p56; St James Centre, Leith St; ☻8.30am-5.30pm Mon-Fri, to 6pm Sat) Hidden away inside shopping centre.

Tourist Information

Edinburgh & Scotland Information Centre (ESIC; Map p56; ✆0845 225 5121; www.edinburgh.org; Princes Mall, 3 Princes St; ☻9am-9pm Mon-Sat, 10am-8pm Sun Jul & Aug, 9am-7pm Mon-Sat, 10am-7pm Sun May, Jun & Sep, 9am-5pm Mon-Wed, 9am-6pm Thu-Sun Oct-Apr) Includes an accommodation booking service, currency exchange, gift and bookshop, internet access, and counters selling tickets for Edinburgh city tours and Scottish Citylink bus services.

Old Craighall tourist office (✆0131-653 6172; Old Craighall Junction, A1) In a service area on the main A1 road, about 5 miles east of the city centre.

Tourist & Airport Information Desk (✆0845 225 5121) At Edinburgh airport.

Travel Agencies

There are hundreds of travel agencies all over the city.

STA Travel (✆0871 702 9817; www.statravel.co.uk; 27 Forrest Rd; ☻10am-6pm Mon-Sat, 11am-5pm Sun) This one specialises in budget and student travel.

ⓘ Getting There & Away

Air

Edinburgh Airport (☎0131-333 1000; www.edinburghairport.com), 8 miles west of the city, has numerous flights to other parts of Scotland and the UK, Ireland and mainland Europe. See p487 for details of flights to Edinburgh from outside Scotland. **FlyBe/Loganair** (☎0871 700 2000; www.loganair.co.uk) operates daily flights to Inverness, Wick, Orkney, Shetland and Stornoway.

Bus

Edinburgh Bus Station (Map p56) is at the northeast corner of St Andrew Sq, with pedestrian entrances from the square and from Elder St. For timetable information, call **Traveline** (☎0871 200 22 33; www.travelinescotland.com).

Scottish Citylink (☎0871 266 3333; www.citylink.co.uk) buses connect Edinburgh with all of Scotland's cities and major towns. The following are sample one-way fares departing from Edinburgh.

DESTINATION	DETAILS		
Aberdeen	£26	3¼hr	3 daily
Dundee	£14	2hr	hourly
Fort William	£30	4-5hr	8 daily
Glasgow	£6	1¼hr	every 15min
Inverness	£26	4hr	hourly
Portree	£46	7hr	1 daily
Stirling	£7	1hr	hourly

It's also worth checking with **Megabus** (☎0900 160 0900; www.megabus.com) for cheap intercity bus fares (from as little as £3) from Edinburgh to Aberdeen, Dundee, Glasgow, Inverness and Perth.

See the Transport chapter, p488, for details of buses to Edinburgh from London and the rest of the UK.

Car & Motorcycle

Arriving in or leaving Edinburgh by car during the morning and evening rush hours (7.30am to 9.30am and 4.30pm to 6.30pm Monday to Friday) is an experience you can live without. Try to time your journey to avoid these periods.

Train

The main terminus in Edinburgh is Waverley train station (Map p56), located in the heart of the city. Trains arriving from, and departing for, the west also stop at Haymarket station (Map p44), which is more convenient for the West End.

You can buy tickets, make reservations and get travel information at the **Edinburgh Rail Travel Centre** (☺4.45am-12.30am Mon-Sat, 7am-12.30am Sun) in Waverley station. For fare and timetable information, phone the **National Rail Enquiry Service** (☎08457 48 49 50; www.nationalrail.co.uk) or use the Journey Planner on the website.

First ScotRail operates a regular shuttle service between Edinburgh and Glasgow (£11, 50 minutes, every 15 minutes), and frequent daily services to all Scottish cities including Aberdeen (£40, 2½ hours), Dundee (£20, 1¼ hours) and Inverness (£55, 3¼ hours).

See the Transport chapter, p488, for details of trains to Edinburgh from London.

ⓘ Getting Around

To/From the Airport

The Lothian Buses **Airlink** (www.flybybus.com) service 100 runs from Waverley Bridge, outside the train station, to the airport (£3/6 one way/return, 30 minutes, every 10 to 15 minutes) via the West End and Haymarket.

An airport taxi to the city centre costs around £16 and takes about 20 minutes. Both buses and taxis depart from outside the arrivals hall; go out through the main doors and turn left.

Bicycle

Thanks to the efforts of local cycling campaign group Spokes and a bike-friendly city council, Edinburgh is well equipped with bike lanes and dedicated cycle tracks. You can buy a map of the city's cycle routes from most bike shops.

Biketrax (www.biketrax.co.uk; 11 Lochrin Pl; ☺9.30am-6pm Mon-Fri, to 5.30pm Sat, noon-5pm Sun) rents out a wide range of cycles and equipment, including kids' bikes, tandems, recumbents, pannier bags and child seats. A mountain bike costs £16 for 24 hours, £12 for extra days, and £75 for one week. You'll need a £100 cash or credit-card deposit and photographic ID.

Car & Motorcycle

Though useful for day trips beyond the city, a car in central Edinburgh is more of a liability than a convenience. There is restricted access on Princes St, George St and Charlotte Sq, many streets are one way and finding a parking place in the city centre is like striking gold. Queen's Dr around Holyrood Park is closed to motorised traffic on Sunday.

CAR RENTAL

All the big, international car-rental agencies have offices in Edinburgh (see p490).

There are many smaller, local agencies that offer better rates. One of the best is **Arnold Clark**

([☎]0131-657 9120; www.arnoldclarkrental.co.uk; 20 Seafield Rd East) near Portobello, which charges from £26 a day, or £128 a week for a small car, including VAT and insurance.

PARKING

There's no parking on main roads into the city from 7.30am to 6.30pm Monday to Saturday. Also, parking in the city centre can be a nightmare. **On-street parking** is controlled by self-service ticket machines from 8.30am to 6.30pm Monday to Saturday, and costs £1 to £2 per hour, with a 30-minute to four-hour maximum. If you break the rules, you'll get a fine, often within minutes of your ticket expiring – Edinburgh's parking wardens are both numerous and notorious. The fine is £60, reduced to £30 if you pay up within 14 days. Cars parked illegally will be towed away. There are large, long-stay car parks at the St James Centre, Greenside Pl, New St, Castle Tce and Morrison St. Motorcycles can be parked free at designated areas in the city centre.

Public Transport

For the moment, Edinburgh's public transport system consists entirely of buses (a tram network is under construction, due to come into operation in 2012). The main operators are **Lothian Buses** (www.lothianbuses.co.uk) and **First** (www.firstedinburgh.co.uk); for timetable information contact **Traveline** ([☎]0871 200 22 33; www.travelinescotland.com).

Bus timetables, route maps and fare guides are posted at all main bus stops, and you can pick up a copy of the free *Lothian Buses Route Map* from **Lothian Buses Travelshops**:

Hanover St (27 Hanover St; [⊙]9am-6pm Mon-Fri, 10am-6pm Sat)

Shandwick Pl (7 Shandwick Pl; [⊙]9am-6pm Mon-Fri, 10am-6pm Sat)

Waverley Bridge (31 Waverley Bridge; [⊙]9am-6pm Mon-Fri, 10am-6pm Sat, 10am-5.15pm Sun)

Adult **fares** are £1.20 from the driver or £1.10 from automatic ticket machines at bus stops; children aged under five travel free and those aged five to 15 pay a flat fare of 70p. On Lothian Buses you must pay the driver the exact fare, but First buses will give change. Lothian Bus drivers also sell a Daysaver ticket (£3) that gives unlimited travel (on Lothian Buses only, excluding night buses) for a day. **Night-service buses** (www.nightbuses.com), which run hourly between midnight and 5am, charge a flat fare of £3.

You can also buy a **Ridacard** (from Travelshops; not available from bus drivers) that gives unlimited travel for one week for £15.

The **Lothian Buses lost property office** ([☎]0131-558 8858; lostproperty@lothianbuses.

co.uk; Main Depot, Annandale St; [⊙]10am-1.30pm Mon-Fri) is north of the city centre.

Taxi

Edinburgh's black taxis can be hailed in the street, ordered by phone (extra 80p charge), or picked up at one of the many central ranks. The minimum charge is £1.60 (£2.70 at night) for the first 450m, then 25p for every subsequent 210m or 45 seconds – a typical 2-mile trip across the city centre will cost around £6. Tipping is up to you – because of the high fares local people rarely tip on short journeys, but occasionally round up to the nearest 50p on longer ones. Some taxi companies:

Central Taxis ([☎]0131-229 2468)

City Cabs ([☎]0131-228 1211)

ComCab ([☎]0131-272 8000)

AROUND EDINBURGH

Edinburgh is small enough that, when you need a break from the city, the beautiful surrounding countryside isn't far away and is easily accessible by public transport, or even by bike. The old counties around Edinburgh are called Midlothian, West Lothian and East Lothian, often referred to collectively as 'the Lothians'.

Midlothian

QUEENSFERRY

Queensferry is at the narrowest part of the Firth of Forth, where ferries have sailed to Fife from the earliest times. The village takes its name from Queen Margaret (1046–93), who gave pilgrims free passage across the firth on their way to St Andrews. Ferries continued to operate until 1964 when the graceful **Forth Road Bridge** – now Europe's fifth longest – was opened.

Predating the road bridge by 74 years, the magnificent **Forth Bridge** – only outsiders ever call it the Forth Rail Bridge – is one of the finest engineering achievements of the 19th century. Completed in 1890 after seven years' work, its three huge cantilevers span 1447m and took 59,000 tonnes of steel, eight million rivets and the lives of 58 men to build.

In the pretty, terraced High St in Queensferry is the small **Queensferry Museum** (53 High St; admission free; [⊙]10am-1pm & 2.15-5pm Mon & Thu-Sat, noon-5pm Sun). It contains some interesting background information on the bridges, and a fascinating exhibit on the 'Burry Man', part of the village's summer gala festivities.

There are several good places to eat and drink along the High St, including the stylish **Orocco Pier** (www.oroccopier.co.uk; 17 High St; mains £13-20; ⊘9am-10pm), which has a modern dining area and outdoor terrace with a stunning view of the Forth Bridge.

The atmospheric **Hawes Inn** (www.vintageinn.co.uk; Newhalls Rd; mains £7-16; ⊘food served noon-10pm), famously mentioned in Robert Louis Stevenson's novel *Kidnapped,* serves excellent pub grub; it's opposite the Inchcolm ferry, right beside the railway bridge.

❶ Getting There & Away

Queensferry lies on the southern bank of the Firth of Forth, 8 miles west of Edinburgh city centre. To get there, take **First bus** 43 (£3, 30 minutes, three hourly) westbound from St Andrew Sq. It's a 10-minute walk from the bus stop to the Hawes Inn and the Inchcolm ferry.

Trains go from Edinburgh's Waverley and Haymarket stations to Dalmeny station (£3.60, 15 minutes, two to four hourly). From the station exit, the Hawes Inn is five minutes' walk along a footpath (across the road, behind the bus stop) that leads north beside the railway and then downhill under the bridge.

INCHCOLM

Known as the 'Iona of the East', the island of Inchcolm (meaning 'St Columba's Island') lies east of the Forth bridges, less than a mile off the coast of Fife. Only 800m long, it is home to the ruins of **Inchcolm Abbey** (HS; Inchcolm, Fife; adult/child £4.70/2.80; ⊘9.30am-5.30pm Apr-Sep, to 4.30pm Oct), one of Scotland's best-preserved medieval abbeys, founded by Augustinian priors in 1123.

The ferry boat **Maid of the Forth** (www.maidoftheforth.co.uk) sails to Inchcolm from Hawes Pier in Queensferry. There are one to four sailings most days from May to October. The return fare is £14.70/5.85 per adult/child, including admission to Inchcolm Abbey. It's a half-hour sail to Inchcolm and you get 1½ hours ashore. As well as the abbey, the trip gives you the chance to see the island's grey seals, puffins and other seabirds.

HOPETOUN HOUSE

One of Scotland's finest stately homes, **Hopetoun House** (www.hopetoun.co.uk; adult/child £8/4.25; ⊘10.30am-5pm Easter-Sep, last admission 4pm) has a superb location in lovely grounds beside the Firth of Forth. There are two parts – the older built to Sir William Bruce's plans between 1699 and 1702 and dominated by a splendid stairwell with (modern) trompe l'oeil paintings; and the newer designed between 1720 and 1750 by three members of the Adam family, William and sons Robert and John. The highlights are the red and yellow **Adam drawing rooms**, lined in silk damask, and the view from the roof terrace.

Britain's most elegant equine accommodation – where the marquis once housed his pampered racehorses – is now the stylish **Stables Tearoom** (mains £5-9; ⊘11am-4.30pm Easter-Sep), a delightful spot for lunch or afternoon tea.

Hopetoun House is 2 miles west of Queensferry along the coast road. Driving from Edinburgh, turn off the A90 onto the A904 just before the Forth Bridge and follow the signs.

ROSSLYN CHAPEL

The success of Dan Brown's novel *The Da Vinci Code* and the subsequent Hollywood film has seen a flood of visitors descend on Scotland's most beautiful and enigmatic church – **Rosslyn Chapel** (Collegiate Church of St Matthew; www.rosslynchapel.com; Roslin; adult/child £7.50/free; ⊘9.30am-6pm Mon-Sat, noon-4.45pm Sun Apr-Sep, 9.30am-5pm Mon-Sat, noon-4.45pm Sun Oct-Mar). The chapel was built in the mid-15th century for William St Clair, third earl of Orkney, and the ornately carved interior – at odds with the architectural fashion of its time – is a monument to the mason's art, rich in symbolic imagery. As well as flowers, vines, angels and biblical figures, the carved stones include many examples of the pagan 'Green Man'; other figures are associated with Freemasonry and the Knights Templar. Intriguingly, there are also carvings of plants from the Americas that predate Columbus' voyage of discovery. The symbolism of these images has led some researchers to conclude that Rosslyn is some kind of secret Templar repository, and it has been claimed that hidden vaults beneath the chapel could conceal anything from the Holy Grail or the head of John the Baptist to the body of Christ himself. The chapel is owned by the Episcopal Church of Scotland and services are still held here on Sunday mornings.

The chapel is on the eastern edge of the village of Roslin, 7 miles south of Edinburgh's centre. Lothian Bus 15 (not 15A) runs from the west end of Princes St in Edinburgh to Roslin (£1.20, 30 minutes, every 30 minutes).

A refreshing alternative to the mainstream tours is offered by **Celtic Trails** (www.celtictrails.co.uk) whose knowledgeable owner Jackie Queally leads guided tours of Rosslyn Chapel and other ancient and sacred sites covering subjects such as Celtic mythology, geomancy, sacred geometry and the Knights Templar. Half-/whole-day tours of the chapel and surrounding area are £33/60 per person, not including admission fees.

PENTLAND HILLS

Rising on the southern edge of Edinburgh, the **Pentland Hills** (www.edinburgh.gov.uk/phrp) stretch 16 miles southwest to near Carnwath in Lanarkshire. The hills rise to 579m at their highest point and offer excellent, not-too-strenuous walking with great views.

There are several access points along the A702 road on the southern side of the hills. MacEwan's bus 100 runs four times daily along the A702 from Princes St in Edinburgh to Biggar.

East Lothian

Beyond the former coalfields of Dalkeith and Musselburgh, the fertile farmland of East Lothian stretches eastwards along the coast to the seaside resort of North Berwick and the fishing harbour of Dunbar. In the middle lies the prosperous market town of Haddington.

HADDINGTON & AROUND
POP 8850

Haddington, straddling the River Tyne 18 miles east of Edinburgh, was made a royal burgh by David I in the 12th century. Most of the modern town, however, dates from the 17th to 19th centuries during the period of prosperity after the Agricultural Revolution. The prettiest part of town is the tree-lined Court St, with its wide pavement and grand 18th- and 19th-century buildings.

Church St leads from the eastern end of High St to **St Mary's Parish Church** (www.stmaryskirk.com; Sidegate; admission free; ⊙11am-4pm Mon-Sat, 2-4.30pm Sun Apr-Sep). Built in 1462, it's the largest parish church in Scotland and one of the finest pre-Reformation churches in the country.

A mile south of Haddington is **Lennoxlove House** (www.lennoxlove.com; Lennoxlove Estate; adult/child £5/3; ⊙guided tours 1.30-4pm Wed, Thu & Sun Apr-Oct), a hidden gem of a country house dating originally from around 1345, with major extensions and renovations from the 17th to the early 20th centuries. It contains fine furniture and paintings, and memorabilia relating to Mary, Queen of Scots. Chief among these are her death mask and a silver casket given to her by Francis II of France, her first husband. The house has been the seat of the duke of Hamilton since 1947.

First buses X6 and X8 run between Edinburgh and Haddington every 30 minutes. The nearest train station is at Drem, 3 miles to the north.

NORTH BERWICK
POP 6220

North Berwick is an attractive Victorian seaside resort with long sandy beaches, three golf courses and a small harbour. The **tourist office** (☏01620-892197; Quality St; ⊙9am-6pm Mon-Sat, 11am-4pm Sun Jun-Sep, 9am-6pm Mon-Sat Apr & May, 9am-5pm Mon-Sat Oct-Mar) is two blocks inland from the harbour.

⊙ Sights & Activities
Scottish Seabird Centre   WILDLIFE CENTRE
(www.seabird.org; The Harbour; adult/child £7.95/4.50; ⊙10am-6pm Apr-Sep, 10am-5pm Mon-Fri, 10am-5.30pm Sat & Sun Feb, Mar & Oct, 10am-4pm Mon-Fri, 10am-5.30pm Sat & Sun Nov-Jan) Top marks to the bright spark who came up with the idea for this centre, an ornithologist's paradise that uses remote-control video cameras sited on the Bass Rock and other islands to relay live images of nesting gannets and other seabirds – you can control the cameras yourself, and zoom in on scenes of cosy gannet domesticity. Off High St, a short steep path climbs up **North Berwick Law** (184m), a conical hill that dominates the town. When the weather's fine there are great views to spectacular **Bass Rock**, iced white in spring and summer with guano from thousands of nesting gannets. **Sea.fari** (www.seafari.co.uk) runs boat trips (adult/child £22/19, daily April to September) around Bass Rock and Craigleith Island, departing from North Berwick's harbour.

Dirleton Castle   CASTLE
(HS; Dirleton; adult/child £4.70/2.80; ⊙9.30am-5.30pm Apr-Sep, to 4.30pm Oct-Mar) Two miles

west of North Berwick is this impressive medieval fortress with massive round towers, a drawbridge and a horrific pit dungeon, surrounded rather incongruously by beautiful, manicured gardens.

Tantallon Castle   CASTLE

(HS; adult/child £4.70/2.80; ☺9.30am-5.30pm Apr-Sep, to 4.30pm Oct, 9.30am-4.30pm Sat-Wed Oct-Mar) Perched on a cliff 3 miles east of North Berwick is the spectacular ruin of Tantallon Castle. Built around 1350, it was the fortress residence of the Douglas earls of Angus (the 'Red Douglases'), defended on one side by a series of ditches and on the other by an almost sheer drop into the sea.

🛏 Sleeping & Eating

North Berwick has plenty of places to stay, though they can fill up quickly at weekends when golfers are in town. Recommended B&Bs include **Glebe House** (☎01620-892608; www.glebehouse-nb.co.uk; Law Rd; r per person £45-50; **P**), a beautiful Georgian country house with three spacious bedrooms, and homely **Beach Lodge** (☎01620-892257; www.beachlodge.co.uk; 5 Beach Rd; d £80-85), which offers sea views and vegetarian breakfasts.

The top eating places in the area are the **Grange** (www.grangenorthberwick.co.uk; 35 High St; 3-course lunch £11, mains £12-20; ☺lunch & dinner) in the centre of town, and the delightful **Deveau's Brasserie** (www.openarms hotel.com; Open Arms Hotel, Dirleton; mains £12-19; ☺lunch & dinner) in the village of Dirleton.

❶ Getting There & Away

North Berwick is 24 miles east of Edinburgh. First bus 124 runs between Edinburgh and North Berwick (1¼ hours, every 20 minutes). There are frequent trains between North Berwick and Edinburgh (£5, 35 minutes, hourly).

DUNBAR
POP 6350

Dunbar was an important Scottish fortress town in the Middle Ages, but little remains of its past save for the tottering ruins of **Dunbar Castle** overlooking the harbour. Today the town survives as a fishing port and seaside resort, famed in the USA as the birthplace of **John Muir** (1838–1914), pioneer conservationist and father of the US national park system.

The **tourist office** (☎01368-863353; 143 High St; ☺9am-5pm Mon-Sat, 11am-4pm Sun Jun-Sep, 9am-5pm Mon-Sat Apr, May & Oct) is near the town hall.

The town centre is home to **John Muir House** (www.jmbt.org.uk; 128 High St; admission free; ☺10am-5pm Mon-Sat, 1-5pm Sun Apr-Oct, 10am-5pm Wed-Sat, 1-5pm Sun Nov-Mar), the birthplace and childhood home of the great man himself. The nearby **Dunbar Town House Museum** (www.dunbarmuseum.org; High St; admission free; ☺12.30-4.30pm Apr-Oct, 2-4.30pm Sat & Sun Nov-Mar) provides an introduction to local history and archaeology (closed for refurbishment till summer 2011).

From the castle, a scenic 2-mile clifftop trail follows the coastline west to the sands of Belhaven Bay and **John Muir Country Park**.

First bus X6 (one hour, hourly) runs between Edinburgh and Dunbar. Trains from Edinburgh's Waverley train station serve Dunbar (£8, 20 minutes) every hour or so.

West Lothian

LINLITHGOW
POP 13,400

This ancient royal burgh is one of Scotland's oldest towns, though much of it 'only' dates from the 15th to 17th centuries. Its centre retains a certain charm, despite some ugly modern buildings and occasional traffic congestion, and the town makes an excellent day trip from Edinburgh.

The **tourist office** (☎01506-844600; ☺10am-5pm Apr-Oct) is in the Burgh Halls at the Cross.

◉ Sights & Activities

Linlithgow Palace   HISTORIC BUILDING

(HS; Church Peel; adult/child £5.20/3.10; ☺9.30am-5.30pm Apr-Sep, to 4.30pm Oct-Mar) The town's main attraction is this magnificent palace begun by James I in 1425. The building of the palace continued for over a century and it became a favourite royal residence – James V was born here in 1512, as was his daughter Mary (later Queen of Scots) in 1542, and Bonnie Prince Charlie visited briefly in 1745. The elaborately carved **King's Fountain**, the centrepiece of the palace courtyard, flowed with wine during Charlie's stay. The fountain, commissioned by James V in 1537, is the oldest in Britain, and was restored to full working order in 2005.

FREE **St Michael's Church**   CHURCH

(www.stmichaelsparish.org.uk; Church Peel; ☺10.30am-4pm Mon-Sat, 12.30-4.30pm Sun) Beside the palace is the Gothic St Michael's Church. Built between the 1420s and

1530s, it is topped by a controversial aluminium spire that was added in 1964. The church is said to be haunted by a ghost that foretold King James IV of his impending defeat at Flodden in 1513.

FREE **Annet House Museum** MUSEUM
(www.annethousemuseum.org.uk; 143 High St; ⊙11am-5pm Mon-Sat, 1-4pm Sun Apr-Oct) This small museum tells the story of the Stewart monarchy and the history of the town.

FREE **Linlithgow Canal Centre** CANAL CENTRE
(www.lucs.org.uk; Manse Rd Canal Basin; ⊙2-5pm Sat & Sun Easter-Sep, plus 2-5pm Mon-Fri Jul–mid-Aug) Just 150m south of the town centre lies the Union Canal and the pretty Linlithgow Canal Centre, where a little museum records the history of the canal. The centre runs three-hour canal boat trips (adult/child £8/4) west to the Avon Aqueduct departing at 2pm Saturday and Sunday, Easter to September, and occasionally to the Falkirk Wheel (see the boxed text, p189). Shorter 20-minute cruises (adult/child £3/1.50) leave every half-hour during the centre's opening times.

✖ Eating & Drinking

Four Marys PUB £
(www.thefourmarys.co.uk; 65-76 High St; mains £7-11; ⊙food served noon-3pm & 5-9pm Mon-Fri, noon-9pm Sat, 12.30-8.30pm Sun) The Four

Marys is an attractive traditional pub (opposite the palace entrance) that serves real ales and excellent pub grub, including haggis, neeps and tatties (haggis, mashed turnip and mashed potato).

Ship2Shore24 RESTAURANT £
(www.ship2shore24.co.uk; 57 High St; lunch mains £5-10; ⊙lunch & dinner Tue-Sat) A few doors along the street is this pleasant little seafood restaurant (two-/three-course dinner £26/30).

Champany Inn RESTAURANT £££
(☑01506-834532; www.champany.com; Champany; mains £16-26; ⊙12.30-2pm & 7-10pm Mon-Fri, 7-10pm Sat) This rustic inn is a trencherman's delight, famous for its excellent Aberdeen Angus steaks and Scottish lobsters (booking recommended). The neighbouring Chop & Ale House (mains £9-16) is a less expensive alternative to the main dining room, offering delicious homemade burgers and steaks. The inn is 2 miles northeast of Linlithgow on the A803/A904 road towards Bo'ness and Queensferry.

ℹ Getting There & Away

Linlithgow is 15 miles west of Edinburgh, and is served by frequent **trains** from the capital (£4, 20 minutes, four every hour); the train station is 250m east of the town centre.

You can also **cycle** from Edinburgh to Linlithgow along the Union Canal towpath (21 miles); allow 1½ to two hours.

Iconic Scotland

Royal Mile »
Rosslyn Chapel »
Stirling Castle »

busker plays bagpipes on the Edinburgh's Royal Mile (p43).

Royal Mile

A GRAND DAY OUT

Planning your own procession along the Royal Mile involves some tough decisions – it would be impossible to see everything in a single day, so it's wise to decide in advance what you don't want to miss and shape your visit around that. Remember to leave time for lunch, for exploring some of the Mile's countless side alleys and, during festival time, for enjoying the street theatre that is bound to be happening in High St.

The most pleasant way to reach the Castle Esplanade at the start of the Royal Mile is to hike up the zigzag path from the footbridge behind the Ross Bandstand in Princes Street Gardens (in springtime you'll be knee-deep in daffodils). Starting at Edinburgh Castle **1** means that the rest of your walk is downhill. For a superb view up and down the length of the Mile, climb the Camera Obscura's Outlook Tower **2** before visiting Gladstone's Land **3** and St Giles Cathedral **4**.

JONATHAN SMITH

Royal Visits to the Royal Mile

1561: Mary, Queen of Scots arrives from France and holds an audience with John Knox.
1745: Bonnie Prince Charlie fails to capture Edinburgh Castle, and instead sets up court in Holyroodhouse.
2004: Queen Elizabeth II officially opens the Scottish Parliament building.

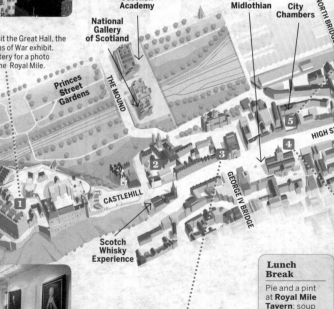

Edinburgh Castle
If you're pushed for time, visit the Great Hall, the Crown Jewels and the Prisons of War exhibit. Head for the Half-Moon Battery for a photo looking down the length of the Royal Mile.

Gladstone's Land
The 1st floor houses a faithful recreation of how a wealthy Edinburgh merchant lived in the 17th century. Check out the beautiful Painted Bedchamber, with its ornately decorated walls and wooden ceilings.

KARL BLACKWELL

Lunch Break

Pie and a pint at **Royal Mile Tavern**; soup and a sandwich at **Always Sunday**; bistro nosh at **Café Marlayne**.

If history's your thing, you'll want to add Real Mary King's Close **5**, John Knox House **6** and the Museum of Edinburgh **7** to your must-see list.

At the foot of the mile, choose between modern and ancient seats of power – the Scottish Parliament **8** or the Palace of Holyroodhouse **9**. Round off the day with an evening ascent of Arthur's Seat or, slightly less strenuously, Calton Hill. Both make great sunset viewpoints.

TAKING YOUR TIME

Minimum time needed for each attraction:

» **Edinburgh Castle:** two hours
» **Gladstone's Land:** 45 minutes
» **St Giles Cathedral:** 30 minutes
» **Real Mary King's Close:** one hour (tour)
» **Scottish Parliament:** one hour (tour)
» **Palace of Holyroodhouse:** one hour

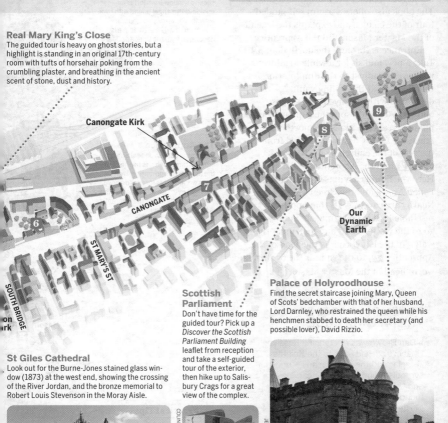

Real Mary King's Close
The guided tour is heavy on ghost stories, but a highlight is standing in an original 17th-century room with tufts of horsehair poking from the crumbling plaster, and breathing in the ancient scent of stone, dust and history.

Canongate Kirk

CANONGATE

ST MARY'S ST

SOUTH BRIDGE

Our Dynamic Earth

Scottish Parliament
Don't have time for the guided tour? Pick up a *Discover the Scottish Parliament Building* leaflet from reception and take a self-guided tour of the exterior, then hike up to Salisbury Crags for a great view of the complex.

Palace of Holyroodhouse
Find the secret staircase joining Mary, Queen of Scots' bedchamber with that of her husband, Lord Darnley, who restrained the queen while his henchmen stabbed to death her secretary (and possible lover), David Rizzio.

St Giles Cathedral
Look out for the Burne-Jones stained glass window (1873) at the west end, showing the crossing of the River Jordan, and the bronze memorial to Robert Louis Stevenson in the Moray Aisle.

COLIN PALMER PHOTOGRAPHY/ALAMY

JEAN-CHRISTOPHE GODET/ALAMY

Rosslyn Chapel

DECIPHERING ROSSLYN

Rosslyn Chapel is a small building, but the density of decoration inside can be overwhelming. It's well worth buying the official guidebook by the Earl of Rosslyn first; find a bench in the gardens and have a skim through before going into the chapel – the background information will make your visit all the more interesting. The book also offers a useful self-guided tour of the chapel, and explains the legend of the Master Mason and the Apprentice.

Entrance is through the north door **1**. Take a pew and sit for a while to allow your eyes to adjust to the dim interior; then look up at the ceiling vault, decorated with engraved roses, lilies and stars (can you spot the sun and the moon?). Walk left along the north aisle to reach the Lady Chapel, separated from the rest of the church by the Mason's Pillar **2** and the Apprentice Pillar **3**. Here you'll find carvings of Lucifer **4**, the Fallen Angel, and the Green Man **5**. Nearby are carvings **6** that appear to resemble Indian corn (maize). Finally, go to the western end and look up at the wall – in the left corner is the head of the Apprentice **7**; to the right is the (rather worn) head of the Master Mason **8**.

ROSSLYN CHAPEL & THE DA VINCI CODE

» Dan Brown was referencing Rosslyn Chapel's alleged links to the Knights Templar and the Freemasons – unusual symbols found among the carvings, and the fact that a descendant of its founder, William St Clair, was a Grand Master Mason – when he chose it as the setting for his novel's denouement. Rosslyn is indeed a coded work, written in stone, but its meaning depends on your point of view. See The Rosslyn Hoax? by Robert LD Cooper (www.rosslynhoax.com) for an alternative interpretation of the chapel's symbolism.

Explore Some More

After visiting the chapel, head downhill to see the spectacularly sited ruins of Roslin Castle, then take a walk along leafy Roslin Glen.

SANDRO VANNINI/CORBIS

Lucifer, the Fallen Angel
At head height, to the left of the second window from left is an upside-down angel bound with rope, a symbol often associated with Freemasonry. The arch above is decorated with the Dance of Death.

The Apprentice
High in the corner, beneath an empty statue niche, is the head of the murdered Apprentice, with a deep wound in his forehead above the right eye. The worn head on the side wall to the left of the Apprentice is that of his mother.

N
Doo

The Master Mason

8

Baptistery

Practical Tips

Buy your tickets in advance through the chapel's website (except in August, when no bookings are taken). No photography is allowed inside the chapel.

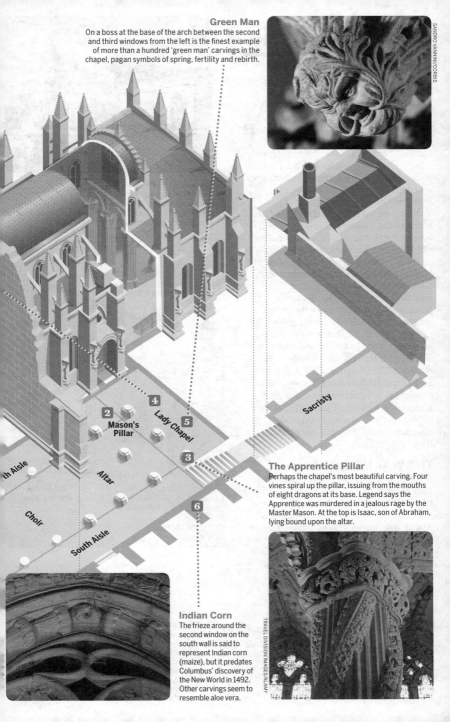

Green Man
On a boss at the base of the arch between the second and third windows from the left is the finest example of more than a hundred 'green man' carvings in the chapel, pagan symbols of spring, fertility and rebirth.

SANDRO VANNINI/CORBIS

2 **Mason's Pillar**

4

Lady Chapel **5**

3

Sacristy

th Aisle

Altar

Choir

South Aisle

6

The Apprentice Pillar
Perhaps the chapel's most beautiful carving. Four vines spiral up the pillar, issuing from the mouths of eight dragons at its base. Legend says the Apprentice was murdered in a jealous rage by the Master Mason. At the top is Isaac, son of Abraham, lying bound upon the altar.

Indian Corn
The frieze around the second window on the south wall is said to represent Indian corn (maize), but it predates Columbus' discovery of the New World in 1492. Other carvings seem to resemble aloe vera.

TRAVEL DIVISION IMAGES/ALAMY

Stirling Castle

PLANNING YOUR ATTACK

Stirling's a sizeable fortress, but not so huge that you'll have to decide what to leave out – there's time to see it all. Unless you've got a working knowledge of Scottish monarchs, head to the Castle Exhibition **1** first: it'll help you sort one James from another. That done, take on the sights at leisure. First, stop and look around you from the ramparts **2**; the views high over this flat valley, a key strategic point in Scotland's history, are magnificent.

Next, head down towards the back of the castle to the Tapestry Studio **3**, which is open for shorter hours; seeing these skilful weavers at work is a highlight.

Track back towards the citadel's heart, stopping for a quick tour through the Great Kitchens **4**; looking at all that fake food might make you seriously hungry, though. Then enter the main courtyard. Around you are the principal castle buildings. During summer there are events (such as Renaissance dancing) in the Great Hall **5** – get details at the entrance. The Museum of the Argyll & Sutherland Highlanders **6** is a treasure trove if you're interested in regimental history, but missable if you're not. Leave the best for last – crowds thin in the afternoon – and enter the sumptuous Royal Palace **7**.

THE WAY UP & DOWN

If you have time, take the atmospheric Back Walk, a peaceful, shady stroll around the Old Town's fortifications and up to the castle's imposing crag-top position. Afterwards, wander down through the Old Town to admire its facades.

DAVID ROBERTSON/ALAMY

Museum of the Argyll & Sutherland Highlanders
The history of one of Scotland's legendary regiments – now subsumed into the Royal Regiment of Scotland – is on display here, featuring memorabilia, weapons and uniforms.

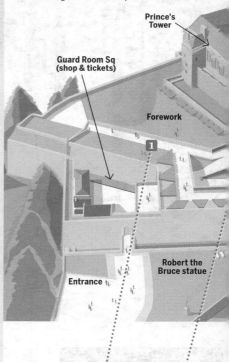

Prince's Tower

Guard Room Sq (shop & tickets)

Forework

1

Robert the Bruce statue

Entrance

TOP TIPS

» **Admission** Entrance is free for Historic Scotland members. If you'll be visiting several Scottish castles and ruins, a membership will save you plenty.

» **Vital Statistics** First constructed: before 1110; Number of sieges: at least 9; Last besieger: Bonnie Prince Charlie (unsuccessful); Money spent refurbishing the Royal Palace: £12 million.

Castle Exhibition
A great overview of the Stewart dynasty here will get your facts straight, and also offers the latest archaeological titbits from the ongoing excavations under the citadel. Analysis of skeletons has revealed surprising amounts of biographical data.

Royal Palace
The impressive new highlight of a visit to the castle is this recreation of the royal lodgings originally built by James V. The finely worked ceiling, ornate furniture and sumptuous unicorn tapestries dazzle.

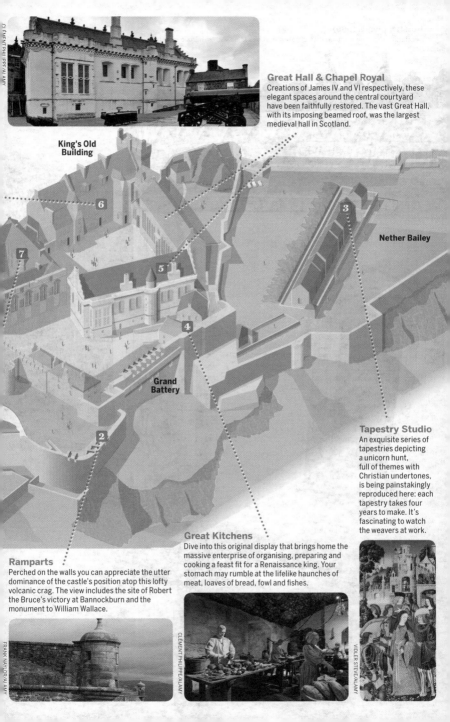

Great Hall & Chapel Royal
Creations of James IV and VI respectively, these elegant spaces around the central courtyard have been faithfully restored. The vast Great Hall, with its imposing beamed roof, was the largest medieval hall in Scotland.

King's Old Building

Nether Bailey

Grand Battery

Tapestry Studio
An exquisite series of tapestries depicting a unicorn hunt, full of themes with Christian undertones, is being painstakingly reproduced here: each tapestry takes four years to make. It's fascinating to watch the weavers at work.

Great Kitchens
Dive into this original display that brings home the massive enterprise of organising, preparing and cooking a feast fit for a Renaissance king. Your stomach may rumble at the lifelike haunches of meat, loaves of bread, fowl and fishes.

Ramparts
Perched on the walls you can appreciate the utter dominance of the castle's position atop this lofty volcanic crag. The view includes the site of Robert the Bruce's victory at Bannockburn and the monument to William Wallace.

Rosslyn Chapel (p89)
Scotland's most beautiful and enigmatic church is filled with symbolic carvings with both Christian and pagan themes.

Glasgow

POP 634,700

Includes »

Best Places to Stay

» Brunswick Hotel (p117)
» Malmaison (p117)
» Hotel du Vin (p119)
» Glasgow SYHA (p119)
» Blythswood Square (p117)

Best Places to Eat

» Café Gandolfi (p120)
» Left Bank (p123)
» Ubiquitous Chip (p123)
» Stravaigin (p123)
» Mother India (p123)

Why Go?

Regenerating and evolving at a dizzying pace, this city is edgy, modish and downright ballsy. Its Victorian architectural legacy is now swamped with stylish bars and top-notch restaurants, and a hedonistic club culture to bring out your nocturnal instincts. Glasgow's pounding live-music scene is one of the best in Britain, and accessible through countless venues dedicated to home-grown beats.

Yet nightlife is only the beginning. Top-drawer museums and galleries abound, and the city's proud industrial and artistic heritage is innovatively displayed. Charles Rennie Mackintosh's sublime works dot the town, while the River Clyde, traditionally associated with Glasgow's earthier side, is now a symbol of the city's renaissance.

Glaswegians are proud of their working-class background and leftist traditions. Glasgow combines urban mayhem and black humour and is so friendly, it's almost unnerving. Shrug off any restraint and immerse yourself in a down-to-earth metropolis that's all about fun.

When to Go

Glasgow

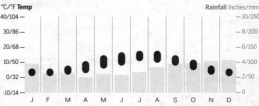

February The drizzle won't lift? Maroon yourself in one of Glasgow's fabulous pubs or clubs.

June The West End Festival, the Proms and the Jazz Festival make it music heaven.

August Glasgow's super-friendly at any time, but in sunshine there's no happier city in Britain.

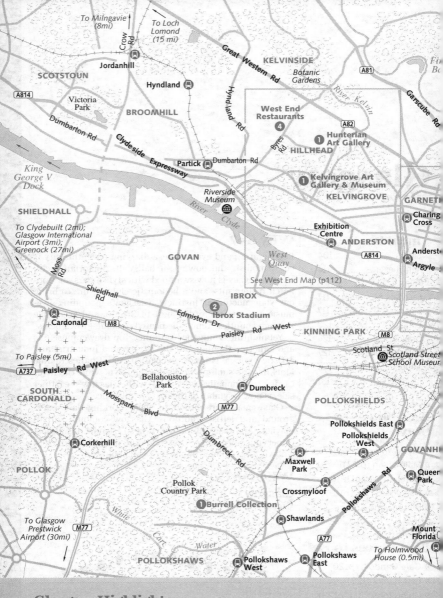

Glasgow Highlights

① Gazing at the Glasgow Boys' paintings in the **Burrell Collection** (p113), the **Kelvingrove Art Gallery & Museum** (p110) and the **Hunterian Art Gallery** (p111)

② Catching a match in one of Celtic or Rangers' massive cauldrons of **football** (p128)

③ Showing your latest dance moves among Glasgow's plethora of **nightclubs** (p127)

where the country's best DJs strut their stuff

④ Deciding just which one of the West End's excellent **restaurants** (p122) you are going to dine at next

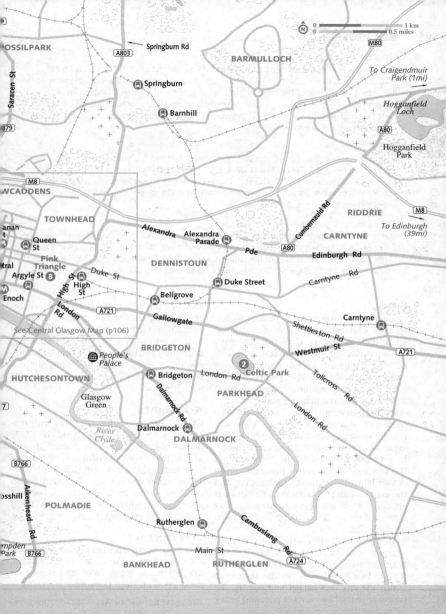

GLASGOW IN...

One Day
Glasgow deserves more time than this, but if you're squeezed, hit the East End for Glasgow Cathedral, St Mungo's Museum and a wander through the hillside necropolis. Later take on one of the city's top museums: either the Burrell Collection or the Kelvingrove. As evening falls, head to trendy Merchant City for a stroll and dinner – Café Gandolfi maybe, or the latest trendy newcomer. Make sure you head to Artá for a pre- or post-meal drink.

Two Days
Visit whichever museum you missed yesterday, and then it's Mackintosh time. Glasgow School of Art is his finest work: if you like his style, head to the West End for Mackintosh House. Hungry? Thirsty? Some of the city's best restaurants and bars are up this end of town, so you could make a night of it. Check out one of the numerous excellent music venues around the city.

Five Days
Better. Much better. Spend a day along the Clyde – the new Riverside Museum and the Science Centre. Plan your weekend around a night out at Arches or the legendary Sub Club, a day at the boutiques of the Italian Centre, earthier shopping at the Barras flea market and a football game. Don't miss trying at least one of the city's curry classics.

History
Glasgow grew around the cathedral founded by St Kertigan, later to become St Mungo, in the 6th century. Unfortunately, with the exception of the cathedral, virtually nothing of the medieval city remains. It was swept away by the energetic people of a new age – the age of capitalism, the Industrial Revolution and the British Empire.

In the 18th century much of the tobacco trade between Europe and the USA was routed through Glasgow and provided a great source of wealth. Even after the tobacco trade declined in the 19th century, the city continued to prosper as a centre of textile manufacturing, shipbuilding and the coal and steel industries. The outward appearance of prosperity, however, was tempered by the dire working conditions in the factories.

In the first half of the 20th century Glasgow was the centre of Britain's munitions industry, supplying arms and ships for the two world wars, in the second of which the city was carpet-bombed. In the post-war years, however, the port and heavy industries began to dwindle, and by the early 1970s, the city looked doomed. Unlike Edinburgh, working-class Glasgow had few alternatives when recession hit and the city became synonymous with unemployment, economic depression and urban violence, centred around high-rise housing schemes

such as the infamous Gorbals. More recently, urban development and a booming cultural sector have injected style and confidence into the city; though the standard of living remains low for Britain and life continues to be tough for many, the ongoing regeneration process gives grounds for optimism.

⊙ Sights

Glasgow's major sights are fairly evenly dispersed, with many found along the Clyde (focus of a long-term regeneration program), the leafy cathedral precinct in the East End and the museum-rich South Side. Many museums are free. The centre also contains a variety of attractions, particularly Mackintoshania. The trendy West End swarms with students during term time.

CITY CENTRE
The grid layout and pedestrian streets of the city centre make it easy to get around, and there are many cafes and pubs that make good pit stops between attractions.

Glasgow School of Art MACKINTOSH BUILDING
(Map p106; ☑0141-353 4526; www.gsa.ac.uk/tours; 167 Renfrew St; adult/child £8.75/7; ⊗9.30am-6.30pm Apr-Sep, 10am-5pm Oct-Mar) Mackintosh's greatest building, the Glasgow School of Art, still fulfils its original function, so just follow the steady stream of eclectically dressed students

up the hill to find it. It's hard not to be impressed by the thoroughness of the design; the architect's pencil seems to have shaped everything inside and outside the building. The interior design is strikingly austere, with simple colour combinations (often just black and cream) and those uncomfortable-looking high-backed chairs for which Mackintosh is famous. The library, designed as an addition in 1907, is a masterpiece. The visitor entrance is at the side of the building on Dalhousie St; here you'll find a shop with a small but useful interpretative display. Excellent hour-long guided tours (roughly hourly summer; 11am and 3pm winter) run by architecture students leave from here; this is the only way (apart from enrolling) you can visit the building's interior. They're worth booking by phone at busy times. Multilingual translations are available.

FREE **Gallery of Modern Art** GALLERY
(Map p106; www.glasgowmuseums.com; Royal Exchange Sq; ☺10am-5pm Mon-Wed & Sat, to 8pm Thu, 11am-5pm Fri & Sun; ☎) Scotland's most popular contemporary art gallery features modern works from artists worldwide in a graceful neoclassical building. The original interior is used to make a daring, inventive art display. Social issues are a focal point of the museum but it's not all heavy going: there's a big effort made to keep the kids entertained.

FREE **Willow Tearooms** MACKINTOSH BUILDING
(Map p106; www.willowtearooms.co.uk; 217 Sauchiehall St; ☺9am-5pm Mon-Sat, 11am-5pm Sun) Admirers of the great Mackintosh will love the Willow Tearooms, an authentic reconstruction of tearooms Mackintosh designed and furnished in the early 20th century for restaurateur Kate Cranston. Relive the original splendour of this unique tearoom and admire the architect's stroke in just about everything. He had a free rein and even the teaspoons were given his distinctive touch. Reconstruction took two years and the Willow opened as a tearoom again in 1980 (having been closed since 1926). The street name Sauchiehall means 'lane of willows', hence the choice of a stylised willow motif. See also p122.

Sharmanka Kinetic Gallery & Theatre
MECHANICAL THEATRE
(Map p106; ☎0141-552 7080; www.sharmanka. com; 103 Trongate; adult/child £8/free) Great fun for kids and fruit for reflection for adults: check out a show at this extraordinary mechanical theatre. Originally from St Petersburg, it brings inanimate objects to life; sculptured pieces of old scrap and tiny carved figures perform humorous and tragic stories of the human spirit to haunting music. It's joyful, ironic theatre: inspirational one moment and macabre the next, but always colourful, clever and thought-provoking. Full performances are at 7pm Thursday and Sunday, and there are shorter daily performances (£5 with two kids free) from Wednesday to Sunday (check by phone or online for times). The gallery is also open between performances.

FREE **Lighthouse** MACKINTOSH BUILDING
(Map p106; www.tlfe.org.uk; 11 Mitchell Lane; ☺10.30am-5pm Mon-Sat) Mackintosh's first building, designed in 1893, was a striking new headquarters for the *Glasgow Herald*. Tucked up a narrow lane off Buchanan St, it now serves as **Scotland's Centre for Architecture & Design**, with fairly technical temporary exhibitions, as well as the **Mackintosh Interpretation Centre**, a detailed if dryish overview of his life and work. On the top floor of the 'lighthouse', drink in great views over the rooftops and spires of the city centre.

FREE **City Chambers** TOWN HALL
(Map p106; George Sq) The grand City Chambers, the seat of local government, were built in the 1880s at the high point of the city's wealth. The interior is even more extravagant than the exterior, and the chambers have sometimes been used as a movie location to represent the Kremlin or the Vatican. Free guided tours are held at 10.30am and 2.30pm Monday to Friday.

Tenement House HISTORIC HOUSE
(NTS; Map p106; www.nts.org.uk; 145 Buccleuch St; adult/child £5.50/4.50; ☺1-5pm Mar-Oct) For a time-capsule experience, visit the small apartment in the Tenement House. It gives a vivid insight into middle-class city life in the late 19th century.

FREE **Royal Highland Fusiliers Museum** MUSEUM
(Map p106; www.rhf.org.uk; 518 Sauchiehall St; ☺9am-4pm Mon-Fri) Charts the history of this and previous regiments from 1678 to the present. The walls are dripping with exhibits, including uniforms, medals, pictures and other militaria. Wrought ironwork was designed by Mackintosh.

GLASGOW

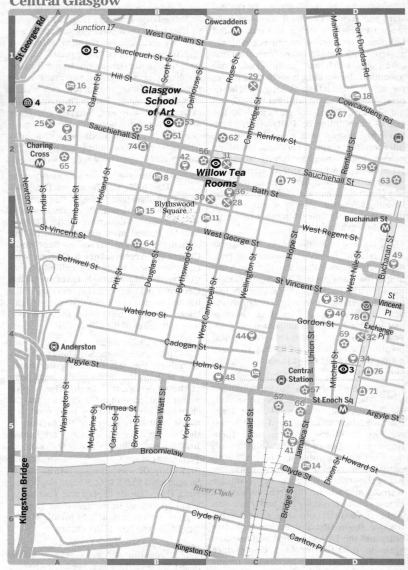

EAST END

The oldest part of the city, given a face-lift in the 1990s, is concentrated around Glasgow Cathedral, to the east of the modern centre. It takes 15 to 20 minutes to walk from George Sq, but numerous buses

pass nearby, including buses 11, 12, 36, 37, 38 and 42.

FREE **Glasgow Cathedral** CHURCH
(HS; Map p106; www.historic-scotland. gov.uk; Cathedral Sq; ☺9.30am-5.30pm Mon-Sat, 1-5pm Sun Apr-Sep, 9.30am-4.30pm Mon-Sat,

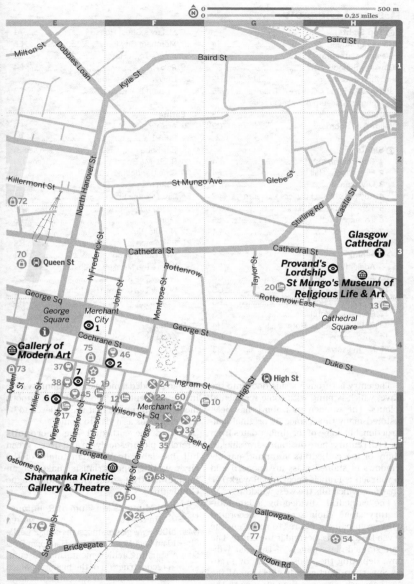

Glasgow Cathedral

Provand's Lordship

St Mungo's Museum of Religious Life & Art

Gallery of Modern Art

Sharmanka Kinetic Gallery & Theatre

1-4.30pm Sun Oct-Mar) An attraction that shouldn't be missed, Glasgow Cathedral has a rare timelessness. The dark, imposing interior conjures up medieval might and can send a shiver down the spine. It's a shining example of Gothic architecture, and the only mainland Scottish cathedral to have survived the Reformation. Most of the current building dates from the 15th century, and only the western towers were destroyed in the turmoil.

The entry is through a side door into the **nave**, which is hung with some regimental colours. The wooden roof above has been restored many times since its original construction, but some of the timber dates from the 14th century; note the impressive shields. Many of the cathedral's stunning, narrow windows of stained glass are modern and to your left is Francis Spear's 1958 work *The Creation*, which fills the west window.

The cathedral, divided by a late-15th-century stone choir screen, is decorated with seven pairs of figures to represent the Seven Deadly Sins. Beyond is the **choir**. The four stained-glass panels of the east window, depicting the Apostles (also by Francis Spear) are particularly effective. At the northeastern corner is the entrance to the 15th-century **upper chapter house**, where Glasgow University was founded. It's now used as a sacristy.

The most interesting part of the cathedral, the **lower church**, is reached by a stairway. Its forest of pillars creates a powerful atmosphere around St Mungo's tomb (St Mungo founded a monastic community here in the 5th century), the focus of a famous medieval pilgrimage that was believed to be as meritorious as a visit to Rome.

Behind the cathedral, the **necropolis** stretches picturesquely up and over a green hill. Its elaborate Victorian tombs of the city's wealthy industrialists make for an intriguing stroll, great views and a vague Gothic thrill.

TOP
CHOICE **St Mungo's Museum of Religious Life & Art**   MUSEUM
(Map p106; www.glasgowmuseums.com; 2 Castle St; ☉10am-5pm Mon-Thu & Sat, 11am-5pm Fri & Sun) A startling achievement, this museum, set in a reconstruction of the bishop's palace that once stood here in the cathedral forecourt, is an audacious attempt to capture the world's major religions in an artistic nutshell, while presenting the similarities and differences in how they approach common themes such as birth, marriage and death. The result is commendable. The attraction is twofold: firstly, impressive art that blurs

---

the lines between religion and culture; and secondly, the opportunity to delve into different faiths, an experience that can be as deep or shallow as you wish. There are three galleries, representing religion as art, religious life and, on the top floor, religion in Scotland. A Zen garden is outside.

FREE Provand's Lordship   HISTORIC HOUSE
(Map p106; www.glasgowmuseums.com; 3 Castle St; ⊙10am-5pm Mon-Thu & Sat, 11am-5pm Fri & Sun) Across the road from St Mungo's Museum is Provand's Lordship, the oldest house in Glasgow. A rare example of 15th-century domestic Scottish architecture, it was built in 1471 as a manse for the chaplain of St Nicholas Hospital. The ceilings and doorways are low, and the rooms are sparsely furnished with period artefacts, except for an upstairs room, which has been furnished to reflect the living space of an early-16th-century chaplain. The building's best feature is its authentic feel – if you ignore the tacky imitation-stone linoleum covering the ground floor.

FREE People's Palace   MUSEUM
(Map p102; www.glasgowmuseums.com; Glasgow Green; ⊙10am-5pm Mon-Thu & Sat, 11am-5pm Fri & Sun) Set in the city's oldest park, Glasgow Green, is the solid orange stone People's Palace. It is an impressive museum of social history, telling the story of the city from 1750 to the present. It has creative, inventive displays, which are great for families – the kids will love the re-creation of a WWII air raid. The palace was built in the late 19th century as a cultural centre for Glasgow's East End. The attached greenhouse, the Winter Gardens, has tropical plants and makes a nice spot for a coffee.

THE CLYDE
Once a thriving shipbuilding area, the Clyde sank into dereliction but is being rejuvenated. A major campaign to redevelop Glasgow Harbour, involving the conversion of former docklands into shops and public areas, is under way – to find out more about this project see www.glasgow harbour.com.

There are several good attractions along the Clyde, but the walk along its banks still isn't all it could be; it can feel bleak and impersonal, with oversized buildings dwarfing the humble pedestrian.

Riverside Museum FREE   MUSEUM
(Map p102; www.glasgowmuseums.com; ☺10am-5pm Mon-Thu & Sat, 11am-5pm Fri & Sun) The latest development along the Clyde is the building of this visually impressive new museum, designed by Iraqi architect Zaha Hadid, at Glasgow Harbour west of the centre. Due to open as this book hit the shelves, it was to house a varied collection, including three recreated Glasgow streets from various points in history, a display of maritime heritage and much of what was formerly in the Museum of Transport: a display of cars made in Scotland, plus assorted railway locos, trams, bikes (including the world's first pedal-powered bicycle from 1847) and model ships. The magnificent Tall Ship *Glenlee* (likely admission charge £5.95 with one child free per adult), a beautiful three-master launched in 1896, will also be berthed here. On board are displays about her history, restoration and shipboard life in the early 20th century.

Glasgow Science Centre   MUSEUM
(Map p112; ☏0141-420 5000; www.glasgowscience centre.org; 50 Pacific Quay; Science Mall adult/child £9.95/7.95, extras for IMAX, tower or planetarium £2.50; ☺10am-5pm) Scotland's flagship millennium project, the superb, ultramodern Glasgow Science Centre will keep the kids entertained for hours (that's middle-aged kids, too!). It brings science and technology alive through hundreds of interactive exhibits on four floors. Look out for the illusions (like rearranging your features through a 3-D head-scan) and the cloud chamber, showing tracks of natural radiation. It consists of an egg-shaped titanium-covered **IMAX** theatre (phone for current screenings) and an interactive **Science Mall** with floor-to-ceiling windows – a bounty of discovery for young, inquisitive minds. There's also a rotating **observation tower**, 127m high. And check out the planetarium, where the **Scottish Power Space Theatre** brings the night sky to life and a **Virtual Science Theatre** treats visitors to a 3-D molecular journey. To get here take Arriva bus 24 from Renfield St or First Glasgow bus 89 or 90 from Union St.

Clydebuilt   MUSEUM
(www.scottishmaritimemuseum.com; Kings Inch Rd, Braehead; adult/child £4.25/2.50; ☺10am-5.30pm Mon-Sat, 11am-5.30pm Sun) If immersing yourself in a city's heritage floats your boat, a visit to Clydebuilt will get you paddlin'. It's a superb collection of model ships, industrial displays and narrative, vividly painting the history of the Clyde, the fate of which has been inextricably linked with Glasgow and its people. It's a cleverly designed museum, with twists and turns that offer something new around every corner. Outside you can board *Kyles,* a typical 1872 vessel. Moored on the empty shores of the Clyde, with only the crying gulls above breaking the silence, it's a perfect place to contemplate the defunct shipyards that formed the cornerstone of Glasgow's industrial heritage.

Clydebuilt is a couple of miles west of Glasgow, not far from the airport. Several bus lines from Buchanan St bus station run to Braehead, including the X23 to Erskine.

WEST END

With its expectant buzz, trendy bars and cafes and nonchalant swagger, the West End is probably the most engaging area of Glasgow – it's great for people-watching, and is as close as Glasgow gets to bohemian. From the centre, buses 9, 16 and 23 run towards Kelvingrove, 8, 11, and 16 to the university, and 20, 44 and 66 to Byres Rd (among others).

Kelvingrove Art Gallery & Museum FREE
                MUSEUM, GALLERY
(Map p112; www.glasgowmuseums.com; Argyle St; ☺10am-5pm Mon-Thu & Sat, 11am-5pm Fri & Sun) In a magnificent stone building, this grand Victorian cathedral of culture has been revamped into a fascinating and unusual museum, with a bewildering variety of exhibits, but not so tightly packed as to overwhelm. Here you'll find fine art alongside stuffed animals, and Micronesian shark-tooth swords alongside a Spitfire plane, but it's not mix 'n' match: rooms are carefully and thoughtfully themed, and the collection is a manageable size. There's an excellent room of Scottish art, a room of fine French Impressionist works, and quality Renaissance paintings from Italy and Flanders. Salvador Dalí's superb *Christ of St John of the Cross* is also here. Best of all, everything – including every painting – has an easy-reading paragraph of

interpretation next to it: what a great idea. You can learn a lot about art and more here, and it's excellent for the children, with plenty for them to do and displays aimed at a variety of ages. Bus 17, among many others, runs here from Renfield St.

Hunterian Museum
FREE · MUSEUM

(Map p112; www.hunterian.gla.ac.uk; University Ave; ☉9.30am-5pm Mon-Sat) Housed in the glorious sandstone main building of the university, which is in itself reason enough to pay a visit, this quirky museum contains the collection of renowned one-time student of the university, William Hunter (1718–83). Hunter was primarily an anatomist and physician but, as one of those gloriously well-rounded Enlightenment figures, he interested himself in everything the world had to offer. Pickled organs in glass jars take their place alongside geological phenomena, potsherds gleaned from ancient brochs, dinosaur skeletons and a creepy case of deformed animals. The main halls of the exhibition, with their high vaulted roofs, are magnificent in themselves. A highlight is the 1674 'Map of the Whole World' in the World Culture section.

Hunterian Art Gallery
FREE · GALLERY

(Map p112; www.hunterian.gla.ac.uk; 82 Hillhead St; ☉9.30am-5pm Mon-Sat) Across the road from the Hunterian Museum, the bold tones of the Scottish Colourists (Samuel Peploe, Francis Cadell, JD Fergusson) are well represented in this gallery, which also forms part of Hunter's bequest to the university. There are also Sir William MacTaggart's impressionistic Scottish landscapes and a gem by Thomas Millie Dow. There's a special collection of James McNeill Whis-

tler's limpid prints, drawings and paintings. Upstairs, in a section devoted to late-19th-century Scottish art, you can see works by several of the Glasgow Boys.

Mackintosh House
TOP CHOICE · MACKINTOSH BUILDING

(Map p112; www.hunterian.gla.ac.uk; 82 Hillhead St; admission £3, after 2pm Wed free; ☉9.30am-5pm Mon-Sat) Attached to the Hunterian Art Gallery, this is a reconstruction of the first home that Charles Rennie Mackintosh bought with his wife, noted artist Mary Macdonald. It's fair to say that interior decoration was one of their strong points; the Mackintosh House is startling even today. The quiet elegance of the hall and dining room on the ground floor give way to a stunning drawing room. There's something otherworldly about the very mannered style of the beaten silver panels, the long-backed chairs and the surface decorations echoing Celtic manuscript illuminations. You wouldn't have wanted to be a guest that spilled a glass of red on this carpet.

Botanic Gardens
PARK

(Map p112; 730 Great Western Rd; ☉7am-dusk, glasshouse 10am-4.45pm) The best thing about walking into these beautiful gardens is the noise of Great Western Rd quickly receding into the background. Amazingly, the lush grounds don't seem that popular with locals (except on sunny weekends) and away from the entrance you may just about have the place to yourself. The wooded gardens follow the riverbank of the River Kelvin and there are plenty of tropical species to discover. Kibble Palace, an impressive Victorian iron and glass structure dating from 1873, is one of the largest glasshouses in Britain;

THE GLASGOW BOYS

The great rivalry between Glasgow and Edinburgh has also played out in the art world. In the late 19th century a group of Glaswegian painters challenged the domineering artistic establishment in the capital. Up to this point, paintings were largely confined to historical scenes and sentimental visions of the Highlands. These painters – including Sir James Guthrie, EA Hornel, George Henry and Joseph Crawhall – experimented with colour and themes of rural life, shocking Edinburgh's artistic society. Many of them went to study in Paris studios, and brought back a much-needed breath of European air into the Scottish art scene. Like Charles Rennie Mackintosh, the Glasgow Boys' work met with admiration and artistic recognition on the Continent.

The Glasgow Boys had an enormous influence on the Scottish art world, inspiring the next generation of Scottish painters – the Colourists. The Glasgow Boys' works can be seen in the main Glasgow galleries as well as Broughton House, Kirkcudbright (p172) and the National Gallery of Scotland in Edinburgh.

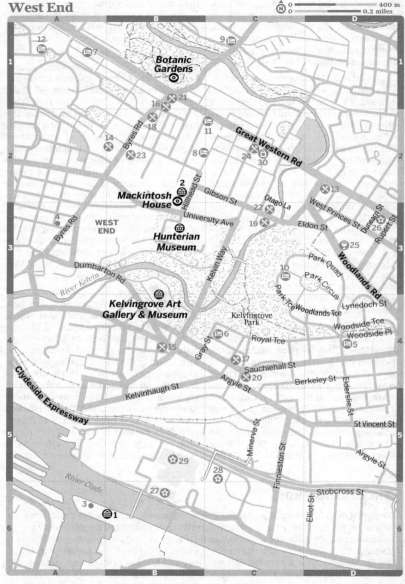

check out the herb garden, too, with its medicinal species. The gorgeous hilly grounds make the perfect place for a picnic lunch. There are also organised walks and concerts in summer – have a look at the noticeboard near the entrance to see what's on.

FREE **Fossil Grove** GEOLOGICAL SITE
(Victoria Park, Dumbarton Rd; ⊙10am-4pm Thu-Mon Apr-Sep) With sections of 350-million-year-old fossilised trees lying around just as they were found, Fossil Grove is an intriguing site.

To get here, take bus 44 from the city centre to Victoria Park.

SOUTH SIDE
The south side is a tangled web of busy roads with a few oases giving relief from the urban congestion. It does, however, contain some excellent attractions.

FREE **Burrell Collection** GALLERY
(Map p102; www.glasgowmuseums.com; Pollok Country Park; ⊙10am-5pm Mon-Thu & Sat, 11am-5pm Fri & Sun) One of Glasgow's top attractions is the Burrell Collection. Amassed by wealthy industrialist Sir William Burrell before being donated to the city, it is housed in an outstanding museum, 3 miles south of the city centre. This idiosyncratic collection of treasure includes everything from Chinese porcelain and medieval furniture to paintings by Renoir and Cézanne. It's not so big as to be overwhelming, and the stamp of the collector lends an intriguing coherence.

Visitors will find their own favourite part of this museum, but the exquisite tapestry galleries are outstanding. Intricate stories capturing life in Europe are woven into staggering wall-size pieces dating from the 13th century. The huge *Triumph of the Virgin* exemplifies the complexity in nature and theme of this medium, while posing the serious question: 'how long must this have taken?'.

Within the spectacular interior, carved-stone Romanesque doorways are incorporated into the structure so you actually walk through them. Floor-to-ceiling windows admit a flood of light, and enable the surrounding landscape outside to enhance the effect of the exhibits. It feels as if you're wandering in a huge tranquil greenhouse.

In springtime, it's worth making a full day of your trip here and spending some time wandering in the beautiful park, studded with flowers. Once part of the estates of Pollok House, which can be visited, the grounds have numerous enticing picnic spots; if you're not heading further north, here's the place to see shaggy Highland cattle, as well as heavy horses.

Many buses pass the park gates (including buses 45, 47, 48 and 57 from the city centre), and there's a twice-hourly bus service between the gallery and the gates (a pleasant 10-minute walk). Alternatively catch a train to Pollokshaws West from Central station (four per hour; you want the second station on the line for East Kilbride or Kilmarnock).

FREE **Scotland Street School Museum**
MACKINTOSH BUILDING
(Map p102; www.glasgowmuseums.com; 225 Scotland St; ☉10am-5pm Tue-Thu & Sat, 11am-5pm Fri & Sun) Mackintosh's Scotland Street School seems a bit forlorn these days, on a windswept industrial street with no babble of young voices filling its corridors. Nevertheless it's worth a visit for its supreme facade and interesting museum of education that occupies the interior. Reconstructions of classrooms from various points in the school's lifetime, combined with grumbling headmaster and cleaner will have older visitors recalling their own schooldays. It's right opposite Shields Rd subway station and there's an OK cafe here.

House for an Art Lover MACKINTOSH BUILDING
(☑0141-353 4770; www.houseforanartlover.co.uk; Bellahouston Park, Dumbreck Rd; adult/child £4.50/3; ☉10am-4pm Mon-Wed, 10am-1pm Thu-Sun) Although designed in 1901 as an entry in a competition run by a German magazine, the House for an Art Lover was not built until the 1990s. Mackintosh worked closely with his wife on the design and her influence is evident, especially in the rose motif. The overall effect of this brilliant architect's design is of space and light. Buses 3, 9, 54, 55 and 56 all run here from the city centre; always ring ahead before making the journey, as the house may be booked for events.

Holmwood House HISTORIC HOUSE
(NTS; www.nts.org.uk; 61-63 Netherlee Rd, Cathcart; adult/child £5.50/4.50; ☉noon-5pm Thu-Mon Apr-Oct) An interesting building designed by Alexander 'Greek' Thomson, Holmwood House dates from 1857. Despite constant ongoing renovations, it's well worth a visit. Look for sun symbols downstairs and stars upstairs in this attractive house with its adaptation of classical Greek architecture. Cathcart is 4 miles south of the centre; get a train via Queen's Park or a train to Neilston. Otherwise, take bus 44, 44A, 44D or 66 from the city centre. Follow

Rhannan Rd for about 800m to Holmwood House.

Scottish Football Museum MUSEUM
(The Hampden Experience; www.scottishfootball museum.org.uk; Hampden Park; adult/child £6/3; ☉10am-5pm Mon-Sat, 11am-5pm Sun) Football fans will just love the Scottish Football Museum, which features exhibits on the history of the game in Scotland and the influence of Scots on the world game. Football inspires an incredible passion in Scotland and the museum is crammed full of impressive memorabilia, including a cap and match ticket from the very first international football game (which took place in 1872 between Scotland and England, and ended with a score of 0-0). The museum's engrossing exhibits give insight into the players, the fans, the media and the way the game has changed over the last 140 years. You can also take a tour of the stadium (adult/child £6/3; combined ticket with museum £9/4.50), home ground of the national football side. The museum is at Hampden Park, off Aikenhead Rd. To get there, take a train to Mount Florida station or take bus 5, 31, 37 or 75 from Stockwell St.

NORTH SIDE
The north side doesn't have much of interest for visitors, apart from a unique church that also happens to be the headquarters of the Rennie Mackintosh Society.

Mackintosh Church MACKINTOSH BUILDING
(www.crmsociety.com; 870 Garscube Rd; adult/child £4/2; ☉10am-5pm Mon-Fri year-round, 2-5pm Sun Mar-Oct) Now the headquarters of the Charles Rennie Mackintosh Society, the church is the only one of Mackintosh's church designs to be built. It has excellent stained glass and relief carvings, and the wonderful simplicity and grace of the barrel-shaped design is particularly inspiring. Garscube Rd is the northern extension of Rose St in the city centre.

🏃 Activities
There are numerous green spaces within the city. **Pollok Country Park** (Map p102) surrounds the Burrell Collection and has several woodland trails. Nearer the centre of the city, the **Kelvin Walkway** follows the River Kelvin through Kelvingrove Park (Map p112), the Botanic Gardens and on to Dawsholm Park.

Great cities have great artists, designers and architects contributing to the cultural and historical roots of their urban environment while expressing its soul and individuality. Charles Rennie Mackintosh was all of these. His quirky, linear and geometric designs have had almost as much influence on the city as have Gaudí's on Barcelona. Many of the buildings Mackintosh designed in Glasgow are open to the public, and you'll see his tall, thin, art nouveau typeface repeatedly reproduced.

Born in 1868, Mackintosh studied at the Glasgow School of Art. In 1896, when he was aged only 27, he won a competition for his design of the School of Art's new building. The first section was opened in 1899 and is considered to be the earliest example of art nouveau in Britain, as well as Mackintosh's supreme architectural achievement. This building demonstrates his skill in combining function and style.

Although Mackintosh's genius was quickly recognised on the Continent, he did not receive the same encouragement in Scotland. His architectural career here lasted only until 1914, when he moved to England to concentrate on furniture design. He died in 1928, and it is only since the last decades of the 20th century that Mackintosh's genius has been widely recognised. For more about the man and his work, contact the **Charles Rennie Mackintosh Society** (☎0141-946 6600; www.crmsociety.com; Mackintosh Church, 870 Garscube Rd). Check its website for special events.

If you're planning to go CRM crazy, the Mackintosh Trail ticket, available at the tourist office or any Mackintosh building, gives you a day's admission to all his creations as well as unlimited bus and subway travel. It costs £16.

See Helensburgh (p264) for information on Hill House, another of Mackintosh's finest creations.

Walking & Cycling

The **Clyde Walkway** extends from Glasgow upriver to the Falls of Clyde near New Lanark (p151), some 40 miles away. The tourist office has a good leaflet pack detailing different sections of this walk. The 10-mile section through Glasgow has interesting parts, though modern buildings have replaced most of the old shipbuilding works.

The well-trodden, long-distance footpath called the **West Highland Way** begins in Milngavie, 8 miles north of Glasgow (you can walk to Milngavie from Glasgow along the River Kelvin), and runs for 95 spectacular miles to Fort William.

There are several long-distance pedestrian/cycle routes that begin in Glasgow and follow off-road routes for most of the way. Check www.sustrans.org.uk for more details.

The **Clyde–Loch Lomond route** traverses residential and industrial areas in a 20-mile ride from Bell's Bridge to Loch Lomond. This route continues to Inverness as part of the Lochs and Glens National Cycle Route.

The **Clyde to Forth cycle route** runs through Glasgow. One way takes you to Edinburgh via Bathgate, the other takes you via Paisley to Greenock and Gourock, the first section partly on roads. Another branch heads down to Irvine and Ardrossan, for the ferry to Arran. An extension via Ayr, Maybole and Glentrool leads to the Solway coast and Carlisle. See p131 for bike hire.

☞ Tours

City Sightseeing BUS TOUR
(☎0141-204 0444; www.citysightseeingglasgow. co.uk; adult/child £11/5) These double-decker tourist buses run a circuit along the main sightseeing routes, starting outside the tourist office on George Sq. You get on and off as you wish. A ticket, bought from the driver or in the tourist office, is valid for two consecutive days. All buses have wheelchair access and multilingual commentary.

Glasgow Taxis City Tour TAXI TOUR
(☎0141-429 7070; www.glasgowtaxis.co.uk) If you're confident you can understand the driver's accent, a taxi tour is a good way to get a feel of the city and its sights. The 80-minute tour takes you around all the centre's important landmarks, with commentary. The standard tour costs £35 for up to five people.

Loch Lomond Seaplanes SCENIC FLIGHTS
(Map p112; ☎0870 242 1457; www.lochlomondsea planes.com; Clyde River, Glasgow Science Centre)

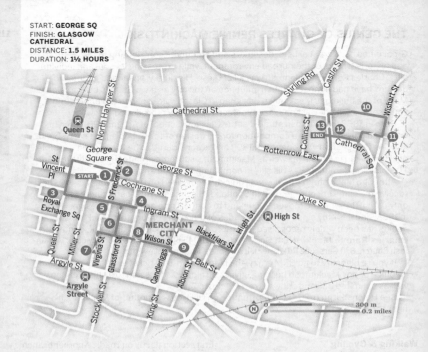

START: **GEORGE SQ**
FINISH: **GLASGOW CATHEDRAL**
DISTANCE: **1.5 MILES**
DURATION: **1½ HOURS**

Walking Tour
Glasgow

❯ This stroll takes you to Glasgow Cathedral through trendy Merchant City, once headquarters for Glasgow industrialists.

The tourist office on ❶ **George Square** is a good starting point. The square is surrounded by imposing Victorian architecture: the old post office, the Bank of Scotland and the grandiose ❷ **City Chambers**. Statues include Robert Burns, James Watt, and, atop a Doric column, Sir Walter Scott.

Walk one block south down Queen St to the ❸ **Gallery of Modern Art**. This striking colonnaded building was once the Royal Exchange and now hosts some of the country's best contemporary art displays.

The gallery faces Ingram St, which you should cross and then follow east four blocks to ❹ **Hutcheson's Hall**. Built in 1805, this elegant building is now maintained by the National Trust for Scotland (NTS). On your way, duck into the former Court House cells now housing the ❺ **Corinthian** pub/club for a glimpse of the extravagant interior. Retrace your steps one block and continue south down Glass-

ford St past ❻ **Trades Hall**, designed by Robert Adam in 1791 to house the trades guild. The exterior is best viewed from Garth St. Turn right into Wilson St and left along Virginia St, lined with the old warehouses of the Tobacco Lords; many of these have been converted into posh flats. The ❼ **Tobacco Exchange** became the Sugar Exchange in 1820.

Back on Wilson St, the ❽ **Sheriff Court** fills a whole block and was originally Glasgow's town hall. Continue east on Wilson St past Ingram Sq to ❾ **Merchant Square**, a covered courtyard that was once the city's fruit market but now bustles with cafes and bars.

Head up Albion St, then right into Blackfriars St. Emerging onto High St, turn left and follow it up to the ❿ **cathedral**. Behind the cathedral wind your way up through the ⓫ **Necropolis**, which offers great city views. On your way back check out the fabulous ⓬ **St Mungo's Museum of Religious Life & Art** and ⓭ **Provand's Lordship**.

This set-up uses the Clyde as its runway and will take you on scenic flights (£139) over Glasgow and Loch Lomond or even run you up to Oban.

Seaforce
BOAT TRIPS

(☑0141-221 1070; www.seaforce.co.uk; Riverside Museum) Departing from the new Riverside Museum, Seaforce offers speedy all-weather powerboat jaunts along the Clyde. There's a variety of trips, including a half-hour ride around central Glasgow (adult/child £10/6), an hour trip to the Erskine Bridge (£15/10) or four-hour rides to local wildlife hot spots (£50/35).

Waverley
BOAT TRIPS

(Map p112; www.waverleyexcursions.co.uk; Clyde River near Glasgow Science Centre) The world's last ocean-going paddle steamer (built in 1947), cruises the Firth of Clyde from April to September (tickets £15 to £40); the website details days of departure. It serves several towns and the islands of Bute, Great Cumbrae and Arran. It departs from Glasgow Science Centre (p110).

★ Festivals & Events

Not to be outdone by Edinburgh, Glasgow has some kicking festivals of its own.

Celtic Connections
MUSIC

(☑0141-353 8000; www.celticconnections.com) Two-week music festival held in January.

International Festival of Visual Art
VISUAL ART

(☑0141-276 8384; www.glasgowinternational.org) Held in late April in even years, this features a range of innovative installations, performances and exhibitions around town.

Glasgow Jazz Festival
JAZZ

(☑0141-552 3552; www.jazzfest.co.uk) Excellent festival held in June; George Sq is a good place for free jazz at this time.

RSNO Proms
CLASSICAL MUSIC

(☑0141-226 3868; www.rsno.org.uk) Classical music in June.

West End Festival
MUSIC, ARTS

(☑0141-341 0844; www.westendfestival.co.uk) This music and arts event is Glasgow's biggest festival, running for two weeks in June.

World Pipe Band Championships
PIPE BANDS

(☑0141-221 5414; www.rspba.org) Around 200 pipe bands; held in mid-August.

🛌 Sleeping

The city centre gets very rowdy at weekends, and accommodation options fill up fast, mostly with groups who will probably roll in boisterously some time after 3am. If you prefer an earlier appointment with your bed, you'll be better off in a smaller, quieter lodging or in the West End. Booking ahead is essential anywhere at weekends and in July and August.

CITY CENTRE

〔TOP CHOICE〕 Brunswick Hotel
HOTEL ££

(Map p106; ☑0141-552 0001; www.brunswickhotel.co.uk; 106 Brunswick St; compact d/standard d/d/king d £50/65/85/95; 🛜) Some places have dour owners threatening lockouts if you break curfew. Then there's the Brunswick, which every now and then converts the whole hotel into a party venue, with DJs in the lifts and art installations in the rooms. You couldn't ask for a more relaxed and friendly Merchant City base. The rooms are all stylish with a mixture of minimalism and rich, sexy colours. Compact and standard doubles will do if you're here for a night out, but king-size rooms are well worth the £10 upgrade. There's an excellent restaurant downstairs and occasional nightclub in the basement.

Malmaison
HOTEL £££

(Map p106; ☑0141-572 1000; www.malmaison.com; 278 West George St; standard r Fri-Sun £135, Mon-Thu £155; 🛜) Heavenly Malmaison is the ultimate in seductive urban accommodation. Cutting-edge but decadently stylish living at its best, this sassy sister of hospitality is super slinky and a cornerstone of faith in Glaswegian accommodation. Stylish rooms with their moody lighting have a dark, brooding tone, plush furnishings and a designer touch. It's best to book online, as it's cheaper, and various suite offers can be mighty tempting.

Blythswood Square
HOTEL £££

(Map p106; ☑0141-248 8888; www.blythswoodsquare.com; 11 Blythswood Sq; r £195-285; @🛜❄) Recently opened in a gorgeous Georgian terrace, this elegant five-star offers plenty of inner-city luxury, with grey and cerise tweeds providing casual soft-toned style throughout. Grades of rooms go from standard to penthouse with corresponding increases in comfort; it's hard to resist the traditional 'classic' ones with windows onto the delightful square, but at weekends

GLASGOW FOR CHILDREN

Although Glasgow is a bigger, busier city that Edinburgh, it's an easy city to travel around with children due to its extensive public transport system and friendly locals. The city boasts excellent family attractions, including the **Glasgow Science Centre** (p110) and **Sharmanka Kinetic Gallery & Theatre** (p105), which both vie for Glasgow's top child-friendly attraction. The new **Riverside Museum** (p110) and the **People's Palace** (p109) are also recommended.

For suggestions for short-term child-care agencies, get in touch with the council-run **Glasgow Childcare Information Service** (☑0141-287 5223; chis@education. glasgow.gov.uk; 100 Morrison St).

Most parks in Glasgow have playgrounds for children. In the centre of town, the major shopping complexes like Buchanan Galleries and St Enochs are handy stops, with baby-changing facilities and shops and activities designed to keep the kids occupied for an hour or two.

you'll have a quieter sleep in the new wing at the back. There's an excellent bar and superb restaurant, as well as a very handsome floorboarded and colonnaded salon space on the 1st floor that functions as an evening spot for cocktails. Other facilities include valet parking and, ready by the time you read this, a spa complex.

Artto HOTEL ££
(Map p106; ☑0141-248 2480; www.arttohotel. com; 37 Hope St; s/d £70/90; ☎) Right by the train station, this modish but affordable hotel has soft white, fawn, and burgundy tones in its compact but attractive rooms above a popular bar and eatery. Large windows make staying at the front appealing but, though the double glazing does a good job of subduing the street noise, light sleepers will be happier at the rear. Rates vary widely by the day; the above is a worst-case scenario.

Rab Ha's INN ££
(Map p106; ☑0141-572 0400; www.rabhas.com; 83 Hutcheson St; r £79-89; ☎) This Merchant City favourite is an atmospheric pub-restaurant with four stylish upstairs rooms. Each is a good size with a dark polished-wood theme and a spotless en suite. It's the personal touches, such as fresh flowers in the rooms and designer photographic prints on the walls, that make you feel special. Breakfast can be delivered to your room and you can come and go as you please, long after the bar downstairs has closed.

Pipers Tryst Hotel HOTEL ££
(Map p106; ☑0141-353 5551; www.thepipingcen tre.co.uk; 30-34 McPhater St; s/d £50/65; ☎) The name is no strategy to lure tartan tour-

ists; this intimate, cosy hotel is in a noble building actually run by the adjacent bagpiping centre. Cheery staff, great value and a prime city centre location make this a cut above other places. Of the eight well-appointed rooms, Nos 6 and 7 are our faves; you won't have far to migrate after a night of Celtic music and fine single malts in the snug bar-restaurant downstairs.

Euro Hostel HOSTEL £
(Map p106; ☑0141-222 2828; www.euro-hostels. co.uk; 318 Clyde St; dm £15-25, s £35-50, d £40-70; @☎) With hundreds of beds, this mammoth hostel is handily close to the station and centre. While it feels a bit institutional, it has excellent facilities, though the kitchen is very compact. Dorms range in size, and price varies on a daily basis, so book ahead for the best rates. Private rooms aren't great value. It's very popular with groups and has a rockin' bar on-site.

Adelaide's B&B ££
(Map p106; ☑0141-248 4970; www.adelaides. co.uk; 209 Bath St; s £35, s/d/f £50/60/82; @🖐) Quiet and cordial, this is ideal for folk who want location at a reasonable price. It's an unusual place – a simple, friendly guesthouse on prestigious Bath St set in a historic church conversion and still Baptist-run, though there's not a hint of preachiness in the air. Tariffs are room only – various breakfast options are available – and families are very welcome. Aim for the back to minimise weekend noise.

Babbity Bowster INN ££
(Map p106; ☑0141-552 5055; 16-18 Blackfriars St; s/d £45/60) Smack bang in the heart of the trendy Merchant City, this lively bar has

simple rooms with sleek furnishings and a minimalist design (No 3 is a good one). Staying here is an excellent Glaswegian experience – the building's design is attributed to Robert Adam. Unusually, room rates do not include breakfast – but that helps keep prices down.

McLay's Guest House
B&B £

(Map p106; ☎0141-332 4796; www.mclays.com; 260 Renfrew St; s/d £36/56, without bathroom £28/48; @☎) The string of cheapish guesthouses along the western end of Renfrew St are a mixed bag but offer a tempting location right by the Sauchiehall nightlife and a block or so from the College of Art. This is among the best of them; a solid choice with decent warm rooms and fair prices. It's sometimes a little cheaper via online booking agencies.

Merchant City Inn
HOTEL ££

(Map p106; ☎0141-552 2424; www.merchantcity inn.com; 52 Virginia St; s/d £50/80; ☎) Right in the heart of Merchant City alongside three of the city's key gay venues, this has snug rooms featuring pine fittings, wooden floors, and passable bathrooms. Rooms on the 2nd and 3rd floors have the better outlook.

EAST END

Cathedral House Hotel
HOTEL ££

(Map p106; ☎0141-552 3519; www.cathedralhou se.com; 28-32 Cathedral Sq; s/d £55/85; P☎) Who said you had to get out of town for those Scottish Baronial mansions, turrets and all? Right opposite the cathedral, this convivial spot has eight individual rooms above an attractive bar and restaurant. The corner rooms – No 7 is the best – offer sumptuous beds and great views of St Mungo's and the Necropolis. It's a great spot; the only catch is that the less mobile might struggle with the steep spiral stairs.

University of Strathclyde
Campus Village
UNIVERSITY ACCOMMODATION £

(Map p106; ☎0141-553 4148; www.rescat.strath. ac.uk; Rottenrow East; s £36, without bathroom £30; ☀mid-Jun–mid-Sep; ☎) The uni opens its halls of residence to tourists over summer. The Campus Village, opposite Glasgow Cathedral, offers B&B accommodation in single rooms (couples can relive the thrill of having to sneak into each others' room at midnight) at good prices. Cheaper, self-catering prices may also be available.

WEST END

Glasgow SYHA
HOSTEL £

(Map p112; ☎0141-332 3004; www.syha.org.uk; 8 Park Tce; dm/tw £23/62; @☎) Perched on a hill overlooking Kelvingrove Park in a charming town house, this place is simply fabulous and one of Scotland's best official hostels. Dorms are mostly four to six beds with padlock lockers and all have their own en suite - very posh. The common rooms are spacious, plush and good for lounging about. There's no curfew, a good kitchen, and breakfast is available. The prices above reflect maximums and are usually cheaper.

Hotel du Vin
HOTEL £££

(☎0141-339 2001; www.hotelduvin.com; 1 Devonshire Gardens; r from £150, ste from £410; P@☎) This is the favoured hotel for the rich and famous, and the patriarch of sophistication and comfort. A study in elegance, it's sumptuously decorated and occupies three classical terrace houses. There are 35 rooms, all individually furnished, and two fine restaurants are on-site with a wine selection exceeding 600 varieties.

Embassy Apartments
APARTMENTS ££

(Map p112; ☎0141-946 6698; www.mcquadeho tels.com; 8 Kelvin Dr; 2/4 person flat per night £77/95; ☎) If you're after a self-catering option, it's hard to go past this elegant place both for facilities and location. Situated in the leafy West End on a quiet, exclusive street right on the edge of the Botanical Gardens, it sleeps one to seven in studio-style apartments that have fully equipped kitchens and are sparkling clean. Particularly good option for couples and families with older kids. They are available by the day, but prices drop for three- and seven-day rentals. Prices vary extensively according to demand; the above are guides only.

Alamo Guest House
B&B ££

(Map p112; ☎0141-339 2395; www.alamoguestho use.com; 46 Gray St; d £84, s/d/tw without bathroom £42/64/68; ☎) The Alamo may not sound like a quiet, peaceful spot, but that's exactly what this great little place is. Opposite Kelvingrove Park, it feels miles from the hustle of the city, but the city centre and West End are within walking distance, and several of the best museums and restaurants in town are close by. The decor is an enchanting mixture of antique furnishings and modern design, and the breezy owners will make you very welcome. All rooms have DVD players and there's an extensive collection to borrow from.

Kirklee Hotel
HOTEL ££

(Map p112; ☑0141-334 5555; www.kirkleehotel.co.uk; 11 Kensington Gate; s/d £59/75; ☜) Want to spoil someone special? In a leafy neighbourhood, Kirklee is a quiet little gem that combines the luxury of a classy hotel with the warmth of staying in someone's home. The rooms are simply gorgeous, beautifully furnished and mostly looking onto lush gardens. For families there is an excellent downstairs room with enormous en suite. This could be Glasgow's most beautiful street.

Heritage Hotel
HOTEL ££

(Map p112; ☑0141-339 6955; www.theheritagehotel.net; 4 Alfred Tce, Great Western Rd; s/d £40/60; ☐☜) A stone's throw from all the action of the West End, this friendly hotel has a very open, airy and bright feel. Generally, the rooms on the 1st and 2nd floors are a bit more spacious (No 21 is best of the doubles) and have a better outlook. Rooms have been recently renovated, and you can smell the newness. This, the staff, and the fair prices, mark it out.

Bunkum Backpackers
HOSTEL £

(Map p112; ☑0141-581 4481; www.bunkumglasgow.co.uk; 26 Hillhead St; dm/tw £14/36; ☐☜) A tempting budget headquarters for assaults on the eateries and pubs of the West End, Bunkum Backpackers occupies a noble old Victorian terrace on a quiet street. The dorms are spacious – one exaggeratedly so – and the common room and kitchen are also large. There's no curfew but it's not a party hostel. Watch the street numbers; the place isn't well signposted.

Belhaven Hotel
HOTEL ££

(Map p112; ☑0141-339 3222; www.belhavenhotel.com; 15 Belhaven Tce; s £35, s/d/tw £52/72/75; ☜) Consistently friendly and blessed with some fantastically large rooms, Belhaven's rooms are lush little oases. A stylish art nouveau red pervades with subtle lighting, a hint of decadence and, in some rooms, almost floor-to-ceiling windows. Make sure you try a pint of the delicious Kingfisher lager in the in-house bar before you head out.

Acorn Hotel
HOTEL ££

(Map p112; ☑0141-332 6556; www.mcquadehotels.com; 140 Elderslie St; s/d £55/80; @☜) Enjoying a peaceful location by a park

yet just a block from Sauchiehall St, this smart little place has rooms that are compact but boast stylish colours and comfortable beds.

Craigendmuir Park
CAMPING £

(☑0141-779 4159; www.craigendmuir.co.uk; Campsie View, Stepps; sites for 1/2 £12.25/14.25; ☐) The nearest camping ground to town, Craigendmuir Park is about 800m from Stepps station. It has sites for caravans and tents and there are a few well-equipped chalets and holiday homes.

✖ Eating

Glasgow is the best place to eat in Scotland, with an excellent range of eateries. The West End is the culinary centre of the city, with Merchant City also boasting an incredible concentration of quality restaurants and cafes. Many Glasgow restaurants post offers on the internet (changing daily) at **5pm.co.uk** (www.5pm.co.uk). Note also that pubs and bars (see Drinking) are always a good lunchtime option.

CITY CENTRE

Café Gandolfi
CAFE, BISTRO ££

(Map p106; ☑0141-552 6813; 64 Albion St; mains £8-14; ☉9am-11.30pm Mon-Sat, noon-11.30pm Sun) In the fashionable Merchant City, this cafe was once part of the old cheese market. It's been pulling in the punters for years and packs an interesting clientele: die-hard Gandolfers, the upwardly mobile and tourists. It's an excellent, friendly bistro and upmarket coffee shop – very much the place to be seen. Book a Tim Stead–designed, medieval-looking table in advance for well-prepared Scottish and Continental food. There's an expansion, specialising in fish, next door.

Loon Fung
CHINESE ££

(Map p106; ☑0141-332 1240; www.loonfungglasgow.co.uk; 417 Sauchiehall St; mains £10-13; ☉noon-4am) It's rare to get such an authentically Chinese experience in Scotland and it's quite a surprise after a spot of late-night dining to emerge to Sauchiehall rather than Hong Kong. There are various set meal options but be adventurous and pick dishes off the pages of Chinese specials rather than the Westernised plates; there are some real gems here.

Brutti Ma Buoni
BISTRO ££

(Map p106; ☑0141-552 0001; www.brunswickhotel.co.uk; 106 Brunswick St; mains £8-13;

Glasgow has a vibrant gay scene, with the gay quarter found in and around the Merchant City (particularly Virginia, Wilson and Glassford Sts). The city's gay community has a reputation for being very friendly.

To tap into the scene, check out the *List*, the free *Scots Gay* (www.scotsgay.co.uk) magazine and the **GayScotland website** (www.gayscotland.com/glasgow/glasgow_index. htm). If you're in Glasgow in autumn check out **Glasgay** (☎0141-552 7575; www.glasgay. co.uk), a gay performing arts festival, held around October/November each year.

Many straight clubs and bars have gay and lesbian nights. The following are just a selection of gay and lesbian pubs and clubs in the city:

» **Bennet's** (Map p106; www.bennetsnightclub.co.uk; 90 Glassford St; ⊗11pm-3am Wed-Mon) Glasgow's longest-running gay club offers cheesy anthems that it probably hasn't changed since it opened in 1982 upstairs, and more contemporary dance sounds downstairs.

» **Delmonica's** (Map p106; 68 Virginia St; ⊗noon-midnight) Attached to the Polo Lounge, Delmonica's is a world away, with its predatory feeling of people on the pull. It's packed on weekday evenings. Friday night is glam night with chart tunes and Sunday is a karaoke free-for-all.

» **FHQ** (Map p106; 10 John St) In-fashion women-only location in the heart of the Pink Triangle.

» **Moda** (Map p106; cnr Virginia & Wilson Sts; ⊗5pm-midnight Mon, Tue & Thu, until 3am rest of the week) Blonde wood, fake tans and fluffy pink cocktails are the chief attributes of Moda, a place where beautiful folk strike a pose over daytime drinks, or recuperate before returning to the Polo Lounge next door or going downmarket at Delmonica's.

» **Polo Lounge** (Map p106; 84 Wilson St) Staff claim 'the city's best talent' is found here; a quick glance at the many glamour pusses – male and female – proves their claim. The downstairs club is packed on weekends; just the main bars open on other nights.

» **Revolver** (Map p106; www.revolverglasgow.com; 6a John St) Hip little Revolver, downstairs on cosmopolitan John St, sports a relaxed crowd and, crucially, a free jukebox. You'll be listening to indie rather than Abba here.

» **Waterloo Bar** (Map p106; 306 Argyle St) This is a traditional pub that's Scotland's oldest gay bar. It attracts punters of all ages. It's very friendly and, with a large group of regulars, a good place to meet people away from the scene.

⊗11am-10pm; ♿) If you like dining in a place that has a sense of fun, Brutti delivers – it's the antithesis of some of the pretentious places around the Merchant City. With dishes such as 'ugly but good' pizza and 'angry or peaceful' prawns, Brutti's menu draws a smile for its quirkiness and its prices. The Italian and Spanish influences give rise to tapas-like servings or full-blown meals, which are imaginative, fresh and frankly delicious.

Lily's Coffee Shop   CAFE £
(Map p106; 103 Ingram St; mains £4-6; ⊗9.30am-5pm Mon-Sat) Don't be put off by the slightly sterile feel: Lily's is a top lunch spot fusing a creative blend of East and West. It's a unique cross between a Chinese bistro and

chic cafe with made-to-order Chinese food (such as dumpling buns and mandarin-duck wraps) and standards like burgers and baked potatoes that are tarted up almost beyond recognition. The Chinese food is outstanding – fresh, lively and served with fruits and salad.

Dakhin   INDIAN ££
(Map p106; ☎0141-553 2585; www.dakhin.com; 89 Candleriggs; mains £6-16) This south Indian restaurant breathes some fresh air into the city's curry scene. Dishes are from all over the south, and include dosas – thin rice-based crêpes – and a yummy variety of fragrant coconut-based curries. If you're really hungry, try a thali: an assortment of Indian 'tapas'.

Bar Soba
ASIAN FUSION £

(Map p106; ☎0141-204 2404; www.barsoba.co.uk; 11 Mitchell Lane; mains £8-10) With seating around the edges of the room and candles flickering in windows there's a certain sense of intimacy in stylish and very friendly Bar Soba. You can eat in the plush downstairs restaurant, or in the bar. The food is Asian fusion and the laksas go down a treat – followed up of course with an irresistible chocolate brownie. Background beats are perfect for chilling and it can be a good spot to escape Friday evening crowds.

Where the Monkey Sleeps
CAFE £

(Map p106; www.monkeysleeps.com; 182 West Regent St; dishes £5-7; ☺7am-5pm Mon-Fri, 10am-5pm Sat) This funky little number in the middle of the business district is just what you need to get away from the ubiquitous coffee chains. Laid-back and a little hippy, the bagels and paninis, with names like maverick or renegade, are highlights, as are some very inventive dishes, such as the 'nuclear' beans, dripping with cayenne and Tabasco.

Mono
VEGAN £

(Map p106; www.myspace.com/monoglasgow; 12 Kings Ct, King St; mains £3-8) Combining vegetarian food with music, Mono is one of Glasgow's best vegan eateries. Monorail is in the same premises, which means you can browse through an indie record shop while waiting for your food to be prepared. The all-day bar-menu provides classics such as the breakfast fry-up while the main menu has a touch of flair demonstrating a Mediterranean influence. The lasagne is well worth ploughing through. Mono also makes a relaxing place for a coffee or a beer.

Willow Tearooms
CAFE £

(www.willowtearooms.co.uk; light meals £4-8; ☺9am-5pm Mon-Sat, 11am-5pm Sun) Buchanan St (Map p106; 97 Buchanan St); Sauchiehall St (Map p106; 217 Sauchiehall St) These re-creations of tearooms designed by Charles Rennie Mackintosh in 1904 – there are others cropping up around town – back up the design with excellent bagels, pastries or, more splendidly, champagne afternoon teas (£17). At busy times the queues for a table can be long.

Bar 91
BAR, BISTRO £

(Map p106; 91 Candleriggs; mains £7-10; ☺noon-9pm Mon-Thu, to 5pm Fri-Sun, bar until midnight daily) By day this happy, buzzy bar serves excellent meals, far better than average pub food. Salads, pasta and burgers are among the many tasty offerings, and in summer tables spill out onto the sidewalk – ideal for some people-watching of the bold and the beautiful variety.

West
BREWERY RESTAURANT £

(☎0141-550 0135; www.westbeer.com; Binnie Pl; mains £7-10) A cavernous room with an airy, industrial feel on the edge of Glasgow Green, this brewery churns out beers brewed in strict accordance with the Reinheitsgebot – traditional German purity law. Which basically means it's bloody good. Excellent German dishes accompany the amber fluid, such as bratwurst sausages, sauerkraut and schnitzels. Migrate to the beer garden overlooking the People's Palace in summer. To get there, head to the People's Palace and you'll see it opposite, next to the bizarrely ornate facade of the former carpet factory.

Arisaig
SCOTTISH ££

(Map p106; ☎0141-553 1010; www.arisaigrestaurant.co.uk; 1 Merchant Sq; mains £11-17) Relocated into the Merchant Sq building, a historical location converted into an echoing food court, Arisaig offers a good chance to try well-prepared Scottish cuisine at a fair price, with friendly service to boot. Candlelight and crisp linen makes for atmosphere, with both terrace and indoor seating.

Wee Curry Shop
INDIAN £

(Map p106; ☎0141-353 0777; www.theweecurryshopglasgow.com; 7 Buccleuch St; 2-course lunch £5.25, dinner mains £6-12; ☺lunch Mon-Sat, dinner daily) Great home-cooked curries. It's wise to book – it's a snug place with a big reputation, a limited menu and a sensational-value two-course lunch.

Red Onion
BISTRO ££

(Map p106; ☎0141-221 6000; www.red-onion.co.uk; 257 West Campbell St; mains £9-12; ⌨) An eclectic, French- and Asian-influenced menu drives the dining at the impressive Red Onion, run by a well-renowned chef.

Noodle Bar
DINER £

(Map p106; 482 Sauchiehall St; mains £6; ☺noon-4am) For large doses of late-night noodles with oodles of different combinations.

WEST END
There are numerous excellent restaurants in the West End. They cluster along Byres Rd and, just off it, on Ashton Lane and

Ruthven Lane. Gibson St and Great Western Rd also have plenty to offer.

Left Bank

BISTRO ££

(Map p112; ☏0141-339 5969; www.theleftbank. co.uk; 33 Gibson St; mains £8-14; ☺9am-10pm) Huge windows fronting the street greet patrons to this outstanding eatery specialising in gastronomic delights and lazy afternoons. There are lots of little spaces filled with couches and chunky tables reflecting a sense of intimacy. The large starter-menu can be treated like tapas, making it good for sharing plates. There are lots of delightful creations that use seasonal and local produce.

Ubiquitous Chip

SCOTTISH £££

(Map p112; ☏0141-334 5007; www.ubiquitous chip.co.uk; 12 Ashton Lane; 2-/3-course dinner £35/40) The original champion of Scottish produce, The Ubiquitous Chip has won lots of awards for its unparalleled Scottish cuisine, and for its lengthy wine list. Named to poke fun at Scotland's perceived lack of finer cuisine, it offers a French touch but resolutely Scottish ingredients, carefully selected and following sustainable principles. Above, **Upstairs at the Chip** (mains £12-20) provides cheaper, bistro-style food with a similarly advanced set of principles. There are also bar meals at the atmospheric upstairs pub, while the cute 'Wee Pub' down the side alley offers plenty of drinking pleasure.

Stravaigin

SCOTTISH ££

(Map p112; ☏0141-334 2665; www.stravaigin. com; 28 Gibson St; mains £10-19; ☺dinner Mon-Fri, lunch & dinner Sat & Sun) Stravaigin is a serious foodie's delight, with a menu constantly pushing the boundaries of originality and offering creative culinary excellence. The cool contemporary dining space in the basement has booth seating, and helpful, laid-back waiting-staff to assist in deciphering the audacious menu. Entry-level has a buzzing two-level bar that's open 11am to midnight daily; you can also eat here. There are always plenty of menu deals and special culinary nights.

Mother India

INDIAN ££

(Map p112; ☏0141-221 1663; www.motherindiagla sgow.co.uk; 28 Westminster Tce, Sauchiehall St; mains £9-14; ☺lunch Fri-Sun, dinner daily; ☝) Glasgow curry buffs are forever debating the merits of the city's numerous excellent south Asian restaurants, and Mother India features in every discussion. It may lack the trendiness of some of the up-and-comers

but it's been a stalwart for years and the quality and innovation on show is superb. It also makes a real effort for kids, with a separate menu.

Heart Buchanan

CAFE £

(Map p112; www.heartbuchanan.co.uk; 380 Byres Rd; light meals £4-7; ☺9am-6.30pm) The famous West End deli – give your nose a treat and drop in – has a small cafe space next door. Break any or all of the 10 commandments to bag a table, then enjoy some of Glasgow's best breakfasts, all with an exquisite quality of produce, a refreshing juice or milkshake, or regularly changing light-lunch options. If you failed in the table quest, the deli also does some of these meals to take away.

Stravaigin II

SCOTTISH ££

(Map p112; ☏0141-334 7165; www.stravaigin. com; 8 Ruthven Lane; mains £9-17) Top service makes all feel welcome at this relaxed eatery just off Byres Rd. The menu changes regularly but always features a few surprises from around the globe. Slow cooking features prominently in preparation of both meat and vegetables, so expect those flavours to burst out at you. But it's also got a legendary reputation for its burgers, fish 'n' chips, and haggis, so there's something here for any appetite.

Bothy

SCOTTISH ££

(Map p112; ☏0141-334 4040; ww.g1group.co.uk; 11 Ruthven Lane; mains £14-20) A bothy is not normally the most comfortable of abodes, but this West End player pays little heed to this tradition, boasting a combo of modern design and comfy retro furnishings. It also blows apart the myth that Scottish food is stodgy and uninteresting. The Bothy dishes out traditional, uniquely Scottish, homestyle fare with a modern twist. It's filling, but leave room for dessert. An £11 lunch will get you away cheaper.

Konaki

GREEK ££

(Map p112; ☏0141-342 4010; www.konakitaverna. co.uk; 920 Sauchiehall St; mains £9-13; ☺lunch Mon-Sat, dinner daily) Not far from the Kelvingrove museum, Konaki is a friendly and unpretentious Greek restaurant that makes a great morning or evening pitta stop. The starters are a particular highlight of the authentic menu – in fact, ordering a whole lot of them to share is the most enjoyable way to eat here. There are several Greek wines to accompany your meal; knock back a traditional thick coffee afterwards.

La Vallée Blanche
FRENCH £££

(Map p112; ☑0141-334 3333; www.lavalleebla nche.com; 360 Byres Rd; mains £17-21; ⊗Tue-Sun) Cosy and romantic, this upstairs venue is a haven from Byres Rd and sets up a most worthwhile 'Auld Alliance', combining the best of Scottish produce with a classical French flair in the kitchen. It's a prime venue for attempted seduction, or re-seduction, and neither the food nor the service will let you down.

Oran Mor Brasserie & Conservatory
SCOTTISH ££

(Map p112; ☑0141-357 6226; 731 Great Western Rd; mains £10-17) This temple to Scottish dining and drinking is a superb venue in an old church. Giving new meaning to the word 'conversion', the brasserie pumps out high-quality meals in a dark, Mackintosh-inspired space. There are also cheaper bistro-style meals, such as Cullen skink (soup made with smoked haddock, potato, onion and milk) or vegetarian haggis served with Arran mustard sauce, and more relaxed dining in the conservatory, adjoining the main bar (see p126).

Bay Tree Café
CAFE £

(Map p112; 403 Great Western Rd; mains £6-10; ⊗9am-10pm Mon-Sat, to 9pm Sun) The mostly vegetarian Bay Tree Café is excellent value. It has smiling staff, filling mains (mostly Middle Eastern and Greek), generous salads and a good range of hot drinks. The cafe is famous for its all-day Sunday brunch, including vegetarian burger, tattie scone, mushrooms, beans and tomato. It also serves a vegan breakfast.

Firebird
BISTRO ££

(Map p112; www.firebirdglasgow.com; 1321 Argyle St; mains £8-13) A combined bar and bistro with a cheery feel, Firebird has zany artwork on its bright walls and, more importantly, quality nosh whisked under the noses of its patrons. Local flavours and Mediterranean highlights (mainly Italian and Spanish) are evident and organic produce is used wherever possible. Taste sensations range from wood-fired pizzas to a Moroccan chicken and chickpea salad.

Wudon
JAPANESE £

(Map p112; www.wudon-noodlebar.co.uk; 535 Great Western Rd; dishes £5-8) Sushi, fried noodles, and ramen soups in a clean, contemporary setting.

🍷 Drinking

Some of Scotland's best nightlife is found in the din and sometimes roar of Glasgow's pubs and bars. There are as many different styles of bar as there are punters to guzzle in them; a month of solid drinking wouldn't get you past the halfway mark.

CITY CENTRE

Artà
BAR

TOP CHOICE (Map p106; www.arta.co.uk; 13-19 Walls St; ⊗until 3am) This extraordinary place is so baroque that when you hear a Mozart concerto over the sound system, it wouldn't surprise you to see the man himself at the other end of the bar. Set in a former cheese market, it really does have to be seen to be believed. As its door slides open, Artà's opulent, cavernous candle-lit interior is exposed. There's floor-to-ceiling velvet, with red curtains revealing a staircase to the tapas bar and restaurant above in a show of decadence that the Romans would have appreciated. Despite the luxury, it's got a relaxed, chilled vibe and a mixed crowd. The big cocktails are great.

Horse Shoe
PUB

(Map p106; www.horseshoebar.co.uk; 17 Drury St) This legendary city pub and popular meeting place dates from the late 19th century and is largely unchanged. It's a picturesque spot, with the longest continuous bar in the UK, but its main attraction is what's served over it – real ale and good food. Upstairs in the lounge is some of the best value pub food (dishes £3 to £6) in town.

Blackfriars
PUB

(Map p106; www.blackfriarsglasgow.com; 36 Bell St) Merchant City's most relaxed and atmospheric pub, Blackfriars' friendly staff and chilled-out house make it special. They take their cask ales seriously here, and there's a seating area with large windows that are great for people-watching.

Butterfly & Pig
PUB

(Map p106; www.thebutterflyandthepig.com; 153 Bath St) A breath of fresh air along trendy Bath St, the piggery is a little offbeat, a little zany and makes you feel comfortable as soon as you plunge into its basement depths. The decor is an eclectic bunch with a retro feel and this adds to its familiarity. You get the feeling that servicing this place regularly would be rewarded with your favourite pint being poured just as you enter the doorway. There's a sizeable menu of

CINDY-LOU RAMSAY, TV CAMERA OPERATOR & PHOTOGRAPHER

Top photography spot:

Pollok Park. The park itself is gorgeous and full of lots of good walks for walkers and cyclists to explore. It also takes you to the famous Burrell Collection, which may not look like much from the outside, but it's a really calming, beautiful building on the inside and jam-packed with exhibits from all over the world.

Something special people might miss?

The amazing architecture and statues, you have to look UP!

Glasgow in one word:

Charismatic.

Favourite spots for live music?

Barrowland and King Tut's Wah Wah Hut. Barrowland is an old, tired looking ballroom badly in need of a bit of a wee facelift, but you're guaranteed to get an unforgettable atmosphere; this is the reason that the biggest bands in the world continue to grace its stage. King Tut's is a much smaller venue for getting 'up close and personal' with some great bands.

And for clubbing?

I like jumping about the dance floor at the Classic Grand on Jamaica St. You have two different floors to choose from with classic rock anthems on the main floor to more indie or pop-punk downstairs. It's great for rock chicks like myself or people fed up with the trendy, expensive dance clubs and you don't have to worry about being knocked back at the door for not wearing the right kind of clothes.

Pub for a pint and read of the paper?

Blackfriars in the Merchant City.

Typical local words?

Blethering (chatting)! Glaswegians tend to do a lot of it, especially if you decide to ask them about their city!

pub grub, and more refined fare in the tearoom upstairs.

Babbity Bowster
PUB

(Map p106; 16-18 Blackfriars St) In a quiet corner of Merchant City, this handsome spot is perfect for a tranquil daytime drink, particularly in the adjoining beer garden. Service is attentive, and the smell of sausages may tempt you to lunch; there's also accommodation (see p118). This is one of the centre's most charming pubs, in one of its noblest buildings.

Arches
BAR

(Map p106; www.thearches.co.uk; 253 Argyle St) A one-stop culture/entertainment fix, Arches doubles as a theatre showing contemporary, avant-garde productions and there's also a club (p127). The hotel-like entrance belies the deep interior, which make you feel as though you've discovered Hades'

bohemian underworld. The crowd is mixed – hiking boots are as welcome as Versace.

Corinthian
BAR

(Map p106; www.thecorinthianclub.co.uk; 191 Ingram St) A breathtaking domed ceiling and majestic chandeliers make Corinthian an awesome venue. Originally a bank and later Glasgow's High Court, this regal building also houses a plush club, downstairs in old court cells, and a piano bar. Closed at time of research for renovation, it'll be open again by the time you read this.

Drum & Monkey
PUB

(Map p106; www.mbplc.com; 93-95 St Vincent St) Dark wood and marble columns frame this attractive drinking emporium, peppered with church pews and leather lounge chairs. Its cosy and relaxing vibe makes you want to curl up in an armchair with a pint for the afternoon. Its central location makes it popular with business folk after work.

Scotia
PUB

(Map p106; www.scotiabar.net; 112 Stockwell St) Drinks have been poured down throats at Scotia, arguably Glasgow's oldest pub, since 1792. And while the last good airing feels like it happened back in the mid-1850s, Scotia's cheery charm outweighs the grungy atmosphere.

Bar 10
BAR

(Map p106; 10 Mitchell Lane) A tiny city treasure that will cause the canny Glasgow drinker to give you a knowing glance if you mention its name. As laid-back as you could ask for in a hip city bar, the friendly, tuned-in staff complete the happy picture. It transforms from a quiet daytime bar to a happening weekend pub on Friday and Saturday nights. It also does decent, cheap paninis, salads, and the like during the day.

MacSorley's
BAR

(Map p106; www.macsorleys.com; 42 Jamaica St) There's nothing better than a good horseshoe-shaped bar in Glasgow, and here the elegantly moulded windows and ceiling add a touch of class to this happy place, which offers live music every night and some excellent, inventive pub food. DJs from the nearby Sub Club also play sets here.

Nice 'n' Sleazy
BAR, CLUB

(Map p106; www.nicensleazy.com; 421 Sauchiehall St) Students from the nearby School of Art make the buzz here reliably friendly on the rowdy Sauchiehall strip. If you're over 35 you'll feel like a professor not a punter, but retro decor, a big selection of tap and bottled beers, 3am closing, and nightly alternative live music downstairs followed by a club at weekends make this a winner.

Pivo Pivo
BAR

(Map p106; www.myspace.com/pivopivo; 15 Waterloo St) Cavernous downstairs beer hall with beers aplenty – 100 from 32 different countries to be exact. Add to that an impressive array of vodka and schnapps, and it may be a while before you see daylight.

Moskito
BAR

(Map p106; www.moskitoglasgow.com; 200 Bath St) A classic Bath St basement bar, Moskito is just the place to kick back, play pool and let the in-house DJs mellow you out with their deep beats and electronica.

Waxy O'Connors
PUB

(Map p106; www.waxyoconnors.co.uk; 46 West George St) This lager labyrinth could be an Escher sketch brought to life and is a cut above most Irish theme pubs.

WEST END

Uisge Beatha
PUB

(Map p112; www.uisgebeathabar.co.uk; 232 Woodlands Rd) If you enjoy a drink among dead things, you'll love Uisge Beatha (Gaelic for whisky, literally 'water of life'). This mishmash of church pews, stuffed animal heads and portraits of depressed nobility (the Maggie mannequin is our favourite) is patrolled by Andy Capp-like characters during the day and students at night. With 100 whiskies and four quirky rooms to choose from, this unique pub is one of Glasgow's best – an antidote to style bars.

Oran Mor
BAR

(www.oran-mor.co.uk; 731 Great Western Rd) Now some may be a little uncomfortable with the thought of drinking in a church. But we say: the Lord giveth. Praise be and let's give thanks – a converted church and an almighty one at that is now a bar, eating venue (see p124) and club venue. The bar feels like it's been here for years – all wood and thick, exposed stone giving it warmth and a celestial air. There's an excellent array of whiskies. The only thing missing is holy water on your way in.

Brel
BAR

(Map p112; www.brelbarrestaurant.com; 39 Ashton Lane) Perhaps the best on Ashton Lane, this bar can seem tightly packed, but there's a conservatory out the back so you can pretend you're sitting outside when it's raining, and when the sun does peek through there's a beer garden. They've got a huge range of Belgian beers, and they also do mussels and other Lowlands favourites.

Vodka Wodka
BAR

(Map p112; www.vodkawodka.co.uk; 31 Ashton Lane) Every vodka drinker's dream, Vodka Wodka has more varieties of the stealthy poison than you could possibly conquer in one sitting. Its brushed metal bar dishes out the liquid fire to students during the day and groups of mid-20s in the evening.

Jinty McGuinty's
PUB

(Map p112; www.jintys.com; 23 Ashton Lane) This is a popular Irish theme pub with unusual booth seating and a literary hall of fame.

☆ Entertainment

Glasgow is Scotland's entertainment city, from classical music, fine theatres and ballet, to cracking nightclubs pumping out state-of-the-art hip-hop, electro, or techno to cheesy chart tunes, and contemporary Scottish bands at the cutting edge of modern music.

To tap into your scene, check out *The List* (www.list.co.uk), an invaluable fortnightly events-guide available at newsagents and bookshops. The website www.nmbrs.net is good for clubs, while the *Herald* and the *Evening Times* newspapers list events happening around the city.

For theatre tickets book directly with the venue. For concerts, a useful booking centre is **Tickets Scotland** (✆0141-204 5151, 0870 220 1116; www.tickets-scotland.com; 239 Argyle St).

Nightclubs

Glasgow has one of Britain's biggest and best clubbing scenes, attracting devotees from afar. Glaswegians usually hit clubs after the pubs have closed, so many clubs offer discounted admission and cheaper drinks if you go before 10.30pm. Entry costs £5 to £10 (up to £25 for big events), although bars often hand out free passes. By law, clubs shut at 3am, so keep your ear to the ground to find out where the after parties are at.

Sub Club   NIGHTCLUB
(Map p106; www.subclub.co.uk; 22 Jamaica St) Saturdays at the Sub Club are one of Glasgow's legendary nights, offering serious clubbing with a sound system that aficionados usually rate the city's best. The claustrophobic, last-one-in vibe is not for those faint of heart.

Arches   NIGHTCLUB
(Map p106; www.thearches.co.uk; 253 Argyle St) R-e-s-p-e-c-t is the mantra with the Arches. The Godfather of Glaswegian clubs, it has a design based around hundreds of arches slammed together, and is a must for funk and hip-hop freaks. It is one of the city's biggest clubs pulling top DJs, and you'll also hear some of the UK's up-and-coming turntable spinners. It's off Jamaica St.

Classic Grand   NIGHTCLUB
(Map p106; www.classicgrand.com; 18 Jamaica St) Rock, industrial, electronic, and powerpop grace the stage and the turntables at this unpretentious central venue. It doesn't take

itself too seriously, drinks are cheap and the locals are welcoming.

Cathouse   NIGHTCLUB
(Map p106; www.cathouseglasgow.co.uk; 15 Union St; ◎Thu-Sun) Mostly rock, emo and metal at this long-standing indie, goth and alternative venue. There are two dance floors: upstairs is pretty intense with lots of metal and hard rock, downstairs is a little less scary if you're not keen on moshing.

ABC   NIGHTCLUB
(Map p106; www.o2abcglasgow.com; 300 Sauchiehall St) A beautiful creature of the clubbing world, ABC, also a music venue, has gorgeous bars, punters who scrub up pretty darn good and a varied music selection. It attracts heaps of students and is a good all-round venue. Indie lovers should check out Thursday nights.

Tunnel   NIGHTCLUB
(Map p106; www.tunnelglasgow.co.uk; 84 Mitchell St; ◎Wed-Sun) Tunnel is a good venue for young clubbers or those new to the scene, with plenty of cheap drink promos and a variety of beats. Wednesday (Home) is a big gay night (see p121), Friday is UN of Dance, while Saturday is devoted to RnB, funky tunes and disco – something for everyone.

Art School   NIGHTCLUB
(Map p106; 167 Renfrew St) An impressive occasional venue in the Glasgow School of Art (would CRM have approved?), this is where the style-cats of the student world hang out in force. It's a welcoming place and the dance nights are legendary. Cheap booze and a good selection of DJs rounds off the happy picture.

Live Music

Glasgow is the king of Scotland's live-music scene. Year after year, touring musicians, artists and travellers alike name Glasgow as one of their favourite cities in the world to enjoy live music. As much of Glasgow's character is encapsulated within the soul and humour of its inhabitants, the main reason for the city's musical success lies within its audience and the musical community it has bred and nurtured for years. On any given night you may find your breath taken by a wave of voices as the audience spontaneously harmonises with an artist on a chorus, a song or even, on special nights, an entire show.

There are so many venues it's impossible to keep track of them all. Pick up a copy of the *Gig Guide* (www.gigguide.co.uk), published monthly and available free in most pubs and venues for the latest on music gigs.

One of the city's premier live-music pub venues, the excellent **King Tut's Wah Wah Hut** (Map p106; www.kingtuts.co.uk; 272a St Vincent St) hosts bands every night of the week. Oasis were signed after playing here.

Two bars to see the best, and worst, of Glasgow's newest bands are **Brunswick Cellars** (Map p106; 239 Sauchiehall St) and **Classic Grand** (Map p106; 18 Jamaica St). Several of the bars mentioned under Drinking above are great for live music, including **MacSorley's** (p126) and **Nice 'n' Sleazy** (p126).

Other recommendations:

13th Note Café   CAFE
(Map p106; www.13thnote.co.uk; 50-60 King St) Also does decent vegetarian food.

ABC   CONCERT VENUE
(O2 ABC; Map p106; www.abcglasgow.com; 300 Sauchiehall St) Former cinema; medium- to large-size acts.

Barrowland   CONCERT VENUE
(Map p106; www.glasgow-barrowland.com; 244 Gallowgate) An exceptional old dancehall catering for some of the larger acts that visit the city.

Captain's Rest   PUB
(Map p112; www.captainsrest.co.uk; 185 Great Western Rd) Variety of indie bands.

Clyde Auditorium   AUDITORIUM
(Map p112; 0870 040 4000; www.secc.co.uk; Finnieston Quay) Also known as the Armadillo because of its bizarre shape, adjoins SECC, and caters for big national and international acts.

SECC   AUDITORIUM
(Map p112; 0870 040 4000; www.secc.co.uk; Finnieston Quay) Adjoins Clyde Auditorium and hosts major national and international acts. A new venue, Glasgow Arena, is being built alongside.

Cinemas

The two-screen **Glasgow Film Theatre** (Map p106; 0141-332 6535; www.gft.org.uk; 12 Rose St; adult/concession £6.50/5), off Sauchiehall St, screens art-house cinema and classics. **Cineworld** (Map p106; 0871 200 2000; www.cineworld.co.uk; 7 Renfrew St; adult/concession £7/5) shows mainstream films.

Theatres & Concert Halls

Theatre Royal   PERFORMANCE VENUE
(Map p106; 0141-332 3321; www.ambassadortickets.com; 282 Hope St) This is the home of Scottish Opera, and the Scottish Ballet often has performances here. Ask about standby tickets if you'll be in town for a few days.

City Halls   CONCERT HALL
(Map p106; www.glasgowconcerthalls.com; Candleriggs) In the heart of Merchant City, this has regular performances by the Scottish Chamber Orchestra and the Scottish Symphony Orchestra.

Glasgow Royal Concert Hall   CONCERT HALL
(Map p106; 0141-353 8080; www.grch.com; 2 Sauchiehall St) A feast of classical music is showcased at this concert hall, the modern home of the Royal Scottish National Orchestra.

King's Theatre   THEATRE
(Map p106; 0844 871 7648; www.kings-glasgow.co.uk; 297 Bath St) King's Theatre hosts mainly musicals; on rare occasions there are variety shows, pantomimes and comedies.

Citizens' Theatre   THEATRE
(0141-429 0022; www.citz.co.uk; 119 Gorbals St) This is one of the top theatres in Scotland and it's well worth trying to catch a performance here.

Tron Theatre   THEATRE
(Map p106; 0141-552 4267; www.tron.co.uk; 63 Trongate) Tron Theatre stages contemporary Scottish and international performances. There's also a good cafe.

Centre for Contemporary Arts   ARTS SPACE
(Map p106; www.cca-glasgow.com; 350 Sauchiehall St) This is a shmick venue making terrific use of space and light. It showcases the visual and performing arts, including movies, talks and galleries.

Tramway   ARTS SPACE
(www.tramway.org; 25 Albert Dr) Tramway theatre and exhibition space attracts cutting-edge theatrical groups, the visual and performing arts, and a varied range of artistic exhibitions. It's very near Pollokshields East train station.

Sport

Two football clubs dominate the sporting scene in Scotland, having vastly more resources than other clubs and a long history (and rivalry). This rivalry is also along partisan lines, with Rangers representing Protestant supporters, and Celtic, Catholic. It's worth going to a game; both play in magnificent arenas with great atmosphere. Games between the two (four a year) are fiercely contested, but tickets aren't sold to the general public; you'll need to know a season-ticket holder.

Celtic Football Club
FOOTBALL CLUB

(Map p102; ☎0871 226 1888; www.celticfc.co.uk; Celtic Park, Parkhead) There are daily stadium tours (adult/child £8.50/5.50). Get bus 61 or 62 from outside St Enoch centre.

Rangers Football Club
FOOTBALL CLUB

(Map p102; ☎0871 702 1972; www.rangers. co.uk; Ibrox Stadium, 150 Edmiston Dr) Tours of the stadium and trophy room run daily (£8/5.505 per adult/child). Get the subway to Ibrox station.

🛍 Shopping

Boasting the UK's largest retail phalanx outside London, Glasgow is a shopaholic's paradise. The 'Style Mile' around Buchanan St, Argyle St and Merchant City is a fashion hub, while the West End has quirkier, more bohemian shopping options.

Barras
FLEA MARKET

(Map p106; btwn Gallowgate & London Rd; ☺9am-4pm Sat & Sun) Glasgow's flea market, the Barras on Gallowgate, is the living, breathing heart of this city in many respects. It has almost a thousand stalls and people come here just for a wander as much as for their shopping, which gives the place a holiday air. The Barras is notorious for selling designer frauds, so be cautious. Watch your wallet, too.

Italian Centre
FASHION

(Map p106; John St) Fashion junkies can procure relief at Versace or Armani here.

Designer Exchange
FASHION

(Map p106; 3 Royal Exchange Ct) Designer Exchange stocks cheaper design samples and resale designer labels.

Buchanan Galleries
SHOPPING CENTRE

(Map p106; www.buchanangalleries.co.uk; Royal Exchange Sq) Huge number of contemporary clothing retailers.

Princes Square
FASHION

(Map p106; www.princessquare.co.uk; Buchanan St) Set in a magnificent 1841 renovated square. Beauty and fashion outlets including Vivienne Westwood.

WANT MORE?
129

For in-depth information, reviews and recommendations at your fingertips, head to the Apple App Store to purchase Lonely Planet's Glasgow City Guide iPhone app.

Alternatively, head to Lonely Planet (www.lonelyplanet.com/scotland/glasgow) for planning advice, author recommendations, traveller reviews and insider tips.

Argyll Arcade
JEWELLERY

(Map p106; www.argyll-arcade.com; Buchanan St) Splendid, jewellery-laden arcade.

Geoffrey (Tailor) Kiltmaker
KILTS

(Map p106; www.geoffreykilts.co.uk; 309 Sauchiehall St) The place to head to take some tartan home.

Tiso's
OUTDOOR

(Map p106; www.tiso.co.uk; 129 Buchanan St) Good for Munro baggers and other outdoor enthusiasts.

Adventure 1
OUTDOOR

(Map p106; www.adventure1.co.uk; 38 Dundas St) An excellent place to buy hiking boots.

Waterstone's
BOOKSHOP

(Map p106; www.waterstones.com; 153 Sauchiehall St) A major bookshop, also sells guidebooks and street maps of Glasgow.

Caledonia Books
BOOKSHOP

(Map p112; www.caledoniabooks.co.uk; 483 Great Western Rd) Characterful secondhand bookshop in the West End.

ℹ Information

The List (£2.20; www.list.co.uk), available from newsagents, is Glasgow and Edinburgh's invaluable fortnightly guide to films, theatre, cabaret, music, clubs – the works. The excellent *Eating & Drinking Guide* (£5.95), published by *The List* every April, covers Glasgow and Edinburgh.

Internet Access

Gallery of Modern Art (☎0141-229 1996; Royal Exchange Sq; ☺10am-5pm Mon-Wed & Sat, 10am-8pm Thu, 11am-5pm Fri & Sun) Basement library; free internet access. Bookings recommended.

ICafe (cnr Great Western Rd & Dunearn St; per hr £2; ☺10am-11pm) Sip a coffee and munch on a pastry while you check your emails on super-fast connections. Wi-fi too.

Mitchell Library (☏0141-287 2999; North St; ⊙9am-8pm Mon-Thu, to 5pm Fri & Sat) Free internet access; bookings recommended.

Yeeh@ (48 West George St; per hr £2; ⊙9.30am-7pm Mon-Fri, 10am-6pm Sat, 11am-6pm Sun)

Medical Services

To see a doctor, visit the outpatients department at any general hospital. Recommended hospitals:

Glasgow Dental Hospital (☏0141-211 9600; 378 Sauchiehall St)

Glasgow Royal Infirmary (☏0141-211 4000; 84 Castle St)

Western Infirmary (☏0141-211 2000; Dumbarton Rd)

Money

There are numerous ATMs around the centre. The post office and the tourist office have bureaux de change.

American Express (Amex; 66 Gordon St)

Post

There are post offices in some supermarkets; the larger ones are open Sunday as well.

Main post office (Map p106; 47 St Vincent St; ⊙Mon-Sat)

Tourist Information

Tourist office (Map p106; ☏0141-204 4400; www.seeglasgow.com; 11 George Sq; ⊙9am-5pm Mon-Sat) Excellent tourist office; makes local and national accommodation bookings (£4). Closes later and opens Sundays in summer.

Tourist office branch (☏0141-848 4440; Glasgow International Airport; ⊙7.30am-5pm)

⊙ Getting There & Away

Air

Ten miles west of the city, **Glasgow International Airport** (www.glasgowairport. com) handles domestic traffic and international flights. **Glasgow Prestwick Airport** (www. gpia.co.uk), 30 miles southwest of Glasgow, is used by **Ryanair** (www.ryanair.com) and some other budget airlines, with many connections to the rest of Britain and Europe.

Bus

All long-distance buses arrive at and depart from **Buchanan bus station** (Map p106; ☏0141-333 3708; www.spt.co.uk/bus/bbs; Killermont St), which has pricey lockers, ATMs, and a cafe with wi-fi.

Buses from London are very competitive. **Megabus** (www.megabus.com) should be your first port of call if you're looking for the cheapest

fare. It has one-way fares for around £11; check the website for your date of departure.

National Express (☏08717 81 81 81; www. nationalexpress.com) and **First** (☏0141-423 6600; www.firstgroup.com) also run to London (£25 to £35, eight hours). Most of these services are overnight. The 10.30pm National Express service stops at Heathrow. It's often cheaper to buy in advance online.

National Express also runs daily to several English cities. Check Megabus and the National Express website for heavily discounted fares on these routes: Birmingham (£50.90, seven to nine hours, four daily), Carlisle (£18.10, two hours, six daily), Manchester (£31.90, four to six hours, four daily), Newcastle (£30.90, four hours, daily) and York (£35.60, 7½ hours, daily).

Scottish Citylink (☏0870 550 5050; www.citylink.co.uk) has buses to most major towns in Scotland, including: Edinburgh (£6.30, 1¼ hours, every 15 minutes), Stirling (£6.60, 45 minutes, at least hourly), Inverness (£25.50, 3½ hours, eight daily), Aberdeen (£26.50, 2¾ to four hours, hourly), Oban (£16.40, three hours, four direct daily), Fort William (£20.50, three hours, seven daily), Portree on Skye (£38.20, 6¼ to seven hours, three daily) and Stranraer (£16.20, 2½ hours, three daily connecting with Belfast ferry).

Car & Motorcyle

There are numerous car-rental companies; the big names have offices at Glasgow and Prestwick airports. Companies include the following:

Arnold Clark (☏0141-423 9559; www.arnold clarkrental.com; 43 Allison St)

Avis (☏0141-544 6064; www.avis.co.uk; 70 Lancefield St)

Europcar (☏0141-249 4106; www.europcar. com; 76 Lancefield Quay)

Train

As a general rule, Glasgow Central station serves southern Scotland, England and Wales, and Queen St station serves the north and east. There are buses every 10 minutes between them. There are direct trains from London's King's Cross and Euston stations; they're much quicker (advance purchase single £60, full fare £144, 4½ hours, more than hourly) and more comfortable than the bus.

First ScotRail (☏08457 55 00 33; www. scotrail.co.uk) runs Scottish trains. Destinations include: Edinburgh (£11.50, 50 minutes, every 15 minutes), Oban (£19.30, three hours, three to four daily), Fort William (£23.40, 3¾ hours, four to five daily), Dundee (£22.60, 1½ hours, hourly), Aberdeen (£40.30, 2½ hours, hourly) and Inverness (£70.40, 3½ hours, 10 daily, four on Sunday).

ℹ Getting Around

To/From the Airport

There are buses every 10 or 15 minutes from Glasgow International Airport to Buchanan bus station (single/return £4.50/7). A taxi costs £20 to £25.

Bike

There are several places to hire a bike; the tourist office has a full list. Prices start at around £10/15/60 for a half-day/day/week. A couple of options:

Gear Bikes   BIKE HIRE
(☎0141-339 1179; www.gearbikes.com; 19 Gibson St) Decent hybrids.

West End Cycles   BIKE HIRE
(☎0141-357 1344; 16 Chancellor St) Good quality mountain bikes.

Car & Motorcycle

The most difficult thing about driving in Glasgow, as with most Scottish urban centres, is the confusing one-way system. For short-term parking (up to two hours) you've a decent chance of finding something on the street, paying at the meters. Otherwise, multistorey car parks are probably your best bet.

Public Transport

BUS City bus services, mostly run by **First Glasgow** (☎0141-423 6600; www.firstglasgow .com), are frequent. You can buy tickets when you board buses but on most you must have the exact change. Short journeys in town cost £1.25 or £1.70; a day ticket (£3.75) is good value and is valid until 1am, when a night network starts. The tourist office hands out the highly complicated SPT Bus Map, detailing all routes in and around the city.

TRAIN & UNDERGROUND There's an extensive suburban network of trains in and around Glasgow; tickets should be bought before travel if the station is staffed or from the conductor if it isn't. There's also an underground line that serves 15 stations in the centre, west and south of the city (single £1.20). The train network connects with the subway at Buchanan St station. The Discovery Ticket (£3.50) gives unlimited travel on the subway for a day, while the Roundabout ticket gives a day's unlimited train and subway travel for £5.25.

Taxi

There's no shortage of taxis and if you want to know anything about Glasgow, striking up a conversation with a cabbie is a good place to start.

You can pay by credit card with **Glasgow Taxis** (☎0141-429 7070; www.glasgowtaxis. co.uk) if you order by phone; most of its taxis are wheelchair accessible.

Good transport connections mean it's easy to plan day trips out of Glasgow. There are some excellent sights along the southern shore of the Clyde, where the ghosts of shipbuilding haunt places like Greenock, and Paisley's magnificent abbey tells a tale of nobler architectural times. Other appealing destinations within easy reach of Glasgow are covered in other chapters: New Lanark (p151), Helensburgh (p264) and Loch Lomond (p261) are examples of these.

Inverclyde

The ghostly remains of once-great shipyards still line the banks of the Clyde west of Glasgow.

The only places worth stopping along the coast west of the city are Greenock and Gourock, although there are a couple of items of interest in the otherwise unprepossessing town of **Port Glasgow**, including the fine 16th-century **Newark Castle** (HS; www.historic-scotland.org.uk; adult/child £3.70/2.20; ☺9.30am-5.30pm Apr-Sep), which is still largely intact and has a spectacular position on the shores of the Clyde.

GREENOCK & GOUROCK
POP 57,500

Fused together these days, the towns of Gourock and Greenock were always warming sights to a Glasgow mariner's heart as their ships rounded the point from the Firth of Clyde into the river proper and thence home. While Gourock's firthside views are spectacular, Greenock's historical buildings – despite the scrappy shopping complexes in its centre – and superior accommodation options invite a stop. In summer and on fine days, these become little resort towns for Glasgow families looking for a day out.

The **McLean Museum & Art Gallery** (www.inverclyde.gov.uk; 15 Kelly St, Greenock; admission free; ☺10am-5pm Mon-Sat) in the historic centre of Greenock is well worth checking out. It's quite an extensive collection, with displays charting the history of steam power and Clyde shipping. There's also a pictorial history of Greenock through the ages, while upstairs there are very good temporary exhibitions and small displays from China, Japan and Egypt. The natural history section highlights the sad

SHIPBUILDING ON THE CLYDE

One of the earliest permanent Lower Clyde shipyards was established in 1711 by John Scott at Greenock. Initial construction was for small-scale local trade but by the end of the 18th century large ocean-going vessels were being built. As the market expanded, shipyards also opened at Dumbarton and Port Glasgow.

The *Comet*, Europe's first steamship, was launched at Port Glasgow in 1812. By the 1830s and 1840s the Clyde had secured its position as the world leader in shipbuilding. Steel hulls came into use by the 1880s, allowing construction of larger ships with the latest and best engines.

In 1899 John Brown & Co, a Sheffield steelmaker, took over a Clydebank yard and by 1907 had become part of the world's largest shipbuilding conglomerate, producing ocean-going liners. Output from the Clyde shipyards steadily increased up to WWI and, with the advent of the war, there was huge demand for new shipping from both the Royal Navy and merchant navy.

During and after the war many small companies disappeared and shipbuilding giants, such as Lithgows Ltd, took their place. The depression years of the 1920s and 1930s saw many yards mothballed or closed. Another boom followed during WWII but these were to be the twilight years.

Many yards went into liquidation in the 1960s, and in 1972 Upper Clyde Shipbuilders was liquidated, causing complete chaos, a sit-in and a bad headache for Ted Heath's government.

Now the great shipyards of the Clyde are mostly derelict and empty. The remains of a once-mighty industry include just a handful of companies still operating along the Clyde.

reality of species extinction in the modern world.

Greenock was the birthplace of **James Watt**, the inventor whose work on the steam engine was one of the key developments of the Industrial Revolution. A statue of him marks his birthplace; behind this looms the spectacular Italian-style **Victoria Tower** on the municipal buildings, constructed in 1886.

🛏 Sleeping & Eating

Tontine Hotel   HOTEL **££**
(☏01475-723316; www.tontinehotel.co.uk; 6 Ardgowan Sq, Greenock; s/d £65/75; superior s/d £85/95; 🅿🛜) Spend the extra for the superior rooms at this noble hotel in the nicest part of Greenock. These spacious chambers are in the old part of the building, and have been recently refurbished, with good bathrooms. The standard rooms are good too, but just don't have the same appeal. Staff are most welcoming; book ahead in summer.

Spinnaker Hotel   HOTEL **££**
(☏01475-633107; www.spinnakerhotel.co.uk; 121 Albert Rd, Gourock; s/d £45/75) The Spinnaker is a pub looking out on Gourock's great view across the firth to Dunoon. Rooms (with either en suite or shared bathroom) have country-pine decor, are clean and spacious, and have large screen TVs. Downstairs the comfy bar is laid-back and has guest ales on tap. Pretty basic pub grub (mains £6 to £9) is also on offer.

James Watt College
UNIVERSITY ACCOMMODATION **£**
(☏01475-731360; enquiries@jameswatt.ac.uk; Custom House Way; s £25, without bathroom £17.50; 🅿) Fairly central and down on the waterfront, this residence hall has 164 single rooms, many with en suite. Families can arrange for a self-contained series of rooms, and there are well-equipped kitchens and cable broadband available for all.

Port & Harbour   BISTRO **££**
(Custom House Pl, Greenock; mains £9-16) On the waterfront in Greenock, this popular pub and restaurant offers a blend of Scottish and Indian cuisine.

ℹ Getting There & Away
Greenock is 27 miles west of Glasgow and Gourock 3 miles further west. The Glasgow-Greenock-Gourock leg of the Clyde to Forth pedestrian and cycle route (p115) follows an old train track for 10 miles. There are trains from Glasgow Central station (£5, 30 minutes, two to three per hour) and hourly buses stopping in both towns.

Gourock is an important ferry hub. **CalMac** (☎0800 066 5000; www.calmac.co.uk) ferries leave daily for Dunoon (passenger/car £3.65/8.80, 25 minutes, hourly) on Argyll's Cowal peninsula. Gourock's train station is next to the CalMac terminal.

There's a council-operated, passenger-only ferry service to Kilcreggan (£2.25, 12 minutes, 12 daily Monday to Saturday, three Sunday) and Helensburgh (£2.25, 40 minutes, three or four daily); buy tickets on board.

Western Ferries (☎01369-704452; www.western-ferries.co.uk) also has a service (passenger/car £3.80/10.50, 20 minutes, two to three hourly) to Dunoon from McInroy's Point, 2 miles from the train station; Scottish Citylink buses run to here.

WEMYSS BAY
POP 2500

Eight miles south of Gourock is Wemyss Bay (pronounced 'weemz'), where you can jump off a train and onto a ferry for Rothesay on the Isle of Bute (p268). There are trains from Glasgow (£5.65, one hour, hourly). **CalMac** (☎0800 066 5000; www.calmac.co.uk) ferries to Rothesay connect with most trains and cost £4.15/16.50 per passenger/car.

Blantyre
POP 17,300

Though technically part of Lanarkshire (p151), the birthplace of David Livingstone is an outlying suburb of Glasgow these days. It was founded as a cotton mill in the late 18th century and that zealous and pious doctor, missionary and explorer was raised in a one-room tenement and worked in the mill by day from the age of 10, going to the local school at night. Amazingly for a time in which most mill-workers were barely able to write their names, he managed to get himself into university, there to study medicine.

The **David Livingstone Centre** (NTS; www.nts.org.uk; adult/child £5.50/4.50; ◷10am-5pm Mon-Sat, 12.30-5pm Sun Apr-Dec) tells the story of his life from his early days in Blantyre to the 30 years he spent in Africa, where he named the Victoria Falls on one of his numerous journeys. It's a good display and brings to life the incredible hardships of his missionary existence, his battles against slavery, and his famous meeting with Stanley. There's a child-friendly African wildlife feature and the grassy park

---

WORTH A TRIP

PAISLEY

Once a proud weaving town, but these days effectively a southwestern suburb of Glasgow, Paisley's the place that gave its name to the funky patterned fabric. Though flanked by green countryside, it's not an engaging place, but it has an ace up its sleeve in the shape of its magnificent abbey. **Paisley Abbey** (www.paisleyabbey.org.uk; Abbey Close; admission free; ◷10am-3.30pm Mon-Sat) is well worth the short trip from Glasgow to see.

This majestic Gothic building was founded in 1163 by Walter Fitzalan, the first high steward of Scotland and ancestor of the Stuart dynasty. A monastery for Cluny monks, it was damaged by fire during the Wars of Independence in 1306 but rebuilt soon after. Most of the nave is 14th or 15th century. The building was mostly a ruin from the 16th century until the 19th-century restoration, not completed until 1928. Apart from the magnificent perspective down the nave, points of interest include royal tombs, some excellent 19th- and 20th-century stained glass, including three windows by Edward Burne-Jones, and the 10th-century Celtic **Barochan Cross**. A window commemorates the fact that William Wallace was educated by monks from this monastery.

If you've time, at the western end of the High St there's the **Paisley Museum** (www.renfrewshire.gov.uk; High St; admission free; ◷10am-5pm Tue-Sat, 2-5pm Sun), which features Paisley psychedelia! There are some marvellous exhibits, including contemporary displays of children in the modern world – it's worth at least a couple of hours. It also has collections of local and natural history, ceramics and 19th-century Scottish art.

Trains leave Glasgow's Central station for Paisley's Gilmour St station (10 minutes, eight per hour).

the museum is set in makes a perfect picnic spot.

It's a 30-minute walk along the river to **Bothwell Castle** (HS; www.historic-scotland. gov.uk; adult/child £3.70/2.20; ☺9.30am-5.30pm Apr-Sep, 9.30am-4.30pm Sat-Wed Oct-Mar), regarded as the finest 13th-century castle in Scotland. The stark, roofless, red-sandstone ruins are substantial and, largely due to their beautiful green setting, romantic.

Trains run from Glasgow Central station to Blantyre (20 minutes, three hourly). Head straight down the hill from the station to reach the museum.

The Campsies & Strathblane

The beautiful Campsies reach an altitude of nearly 600m and lie just 10 miles north of Glasgow. The plain of the River Forth lies to the north; Strathblane and Loch Lomond lie to the west.

One of several villages around the Campsies, attractive **Killearn** is known for its 31m-high obelisk, raised in honour of George Buchanan, James VI's tutor. Eight miles to the east, **Fintry** has carved itself a gorgeous spot deep in the Campsies on the banks of Endrick Water, which has an impressive 28m waterfall, the **Loup of Fintry**. In the west (on the West Highland Way) is **Drymen**, a pretty village with lots of character, which is popular due to its close proximity to Loch Lomond (p261).

🏃 Activities

One of the best walks in the area is the ascent of spectacular Dumgoyne hill (427m) from Glengoyne distillery, about 2 miles south of Killearn. Allow at least one hour for the ascent of Dumgoyne. It will take another hour to Earl's Seat, and 1½ hours to return from there to the distillery. From Drymen, the **Rob Roy Way** (www.robroyway. com) is a great week's walk through Central Scotland's most beautiful lochlands to Pitlochry.

🛏 Sleeping & Eating

Elmbank   B&B ££

(☎01360-661016; www.elmbank-drymen.co.uk; Stirling Rd, Drymen; d £70, without bathroom £58; P📶) Just off the square, this substantial property offers a variety of rooms and has a very friendly owner. The recommended rooms include the large double with en suite downstairs and the smallish double upstairs with king-size bed. The owner will happily do deals for singles and groups.

Culcreuch Castle   HOTEL ££

(☎01360-860555; www.culcreuch.com; Fintry; s/d from £83/116; P📶) Fancy a night in a 700-year-old castle? Culcreuch dates to 1296 and is a remarkably well-preserved historic building. The 14 rooms are individually styled with Victorian decor. Most rooms are sumptuous and look out onto the collage of greenery engulfing the surrounding estate. A little dowdy perhaps and popular with groups but this place, with its period furnishings, has real character.

Black Bull Hotel   HOTEL ££

(☎01360-550215; www.blackbullhotel.com; 2 The Square, Killearn; s/d £75/110; P📶) The heart of pretty Killearn is a refined pub serving posh bar meals (mains £10 to £14) and offering smart rooms that feel just a mite overpriced but are undoubtedly elegant, and tastefully decorated with black-and-white landscape photos. It's a relaxing base.

Clachan Inn   PUB £

(www.clachaninndrymen.co.uk The Square, Drymen; mains £7-10) One of several pubs in Scotland claiming the oldest inn title (opened 1734), this isn't as atmospheric as it could be – who thought the fruit machine was a good idea in an historic hostelry? Nevertheless, it serves a reliable menu of bar meals, augmented by a steak selection with various sauces in the evening. Order the local malt, Glengoyne, for dessert.

❶ Getting There & Away

First bus 10 runs from Glasgow to Killearn regularly. There are frequent daily services (except Sunday) between Balfron and Drymen on First bus 8.

Southern Scotland

Best Places to Stay

» Corsewall Lighthouse Hotel (p177)

» Churches Hotel (p140)

» Kildonan Hotel (p159)

» Cringletie House (p149)

» Lochranza SYHA (p159)

Best Places to Eat & Drink

» Cobbles Inn (p143)

» Sunflower Restaurant (p150)

» Fouter's (p163)

» Ship Inn (p155)

» Nightjar (p148)

Why Go?

Though folk in northern England are well aware of its charms, for many others southern Scotland is just something to drive through on the way to northern Scotland. Big mistake. But it does mean there's breathing room here in summer, and peaceful corners.

Southern Scotland's proximity to England brought raiding and strife; grim borderland fortifications saw skirmishing aplenty. There was loot to be had in the Borders, where large prosperous abbeys bossed agricultural communities. Regularly ransacked before their destruction in the Reformation, their ruins, linked by cycling and walking paths, are among Scotland's most atmospheric historic sites.

The hillier west enjoys extensive forest cover between bustling market towns. The hills cascade down to sandy stretches of coastline blessed with Scotland's sunniest weather. It's the land of Robert Burns, whose verse reflected his earthy attitudes and active social life. Offshore, Arran is an island jewel offering top cycling, walking and scenery.

When to Go

Ayr

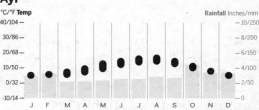

May If winter hasn't been too wet, lace the hiking boots and stride up Arran's hills.

June The perfect time to visit the region's numerous stately homes, with spectacular gardens in bloom.

Autumn Hit Galloway's forests to see red deer battling it out in the rutting season.

Southern Scotland Highlights

① Hiking or cycling between the noble ruins of the **Border Abbeys** (p138)

② Admiring 18th-century architectural genius at **Culzean Castle** (p164), perched on wild sea cliffs

③ Pondering the tough old life on the England–Scotland frontier at desolate **Hermitage Castle** (p149)

④ Exploring charming, dignified **Kirkcudbright**

(p172), and the creative flair of its inhabitants

⑤ Learning some Lallans words from the Scottish Bard's verses at the new **Robert Burns Birthplace Museum** (p163)

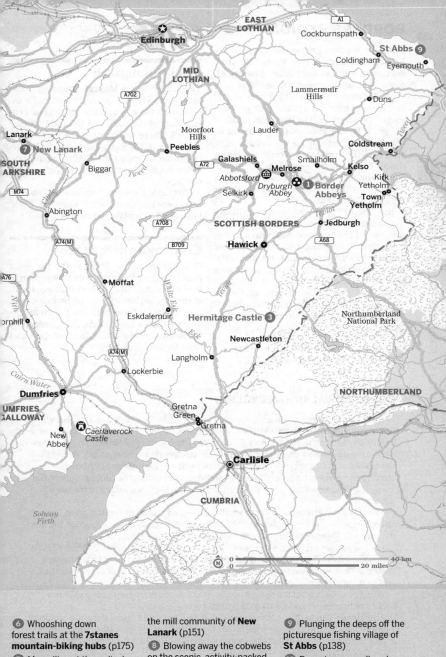

Edinburgh ✪

EAST
LOTHIAN

Cockburnspath ●
A1

St Abbs ❾
Coldingham ●
Eyemouth ●

MID
LOTHIAN

A702

Lammermuir
Hills
Duns ●

Moorfoot
Hills
Lauder ●

Coldstream ●

Lanark ●
❼ New Lanark

A72
Peebles ●

Galashiels ●
Melrose ●
Abbotsford 🏛
Dryburgh
Abbey
Selkirk ●

Smailholm ●
Kelso ●
Kirk
Yetholm ●
Town ●
Yetholm

❶ Border
Abbeys

SOUTH
~ARKSHIRE

Biggar ●

Tweed

SCOTTISH BORDERS

M74

Abington ●

Clyde

A708

Jedburgh ●
A68

Hawick ●

B709

A76

Moffat ●

White Esk

Teviot

A74(M)

Eskdalemuir ●

Hermitage Castle ❸

Northumberland
National Park

Esk

Nith

Newcastleton ●

A74(M)

Langholm ●

Lockerbie ●

NORTHUMBERLAND

Cairn Water

Dumfries ●

~UMFRIES
GALLOWAY

Gretna
Green ●
Gretna ●

New
Abbey ●
🏰 Caerlaverock
Castle

Carlisle ◎

CUMBRIA

Solway
Firth

Ⓝ 0   40 km
    0   20 miles

---

❻ Whooshing down
forest trails at the **7stanes
mountain-biking hubs** (p175)

❼ Marvelling at the radical
social reform instituted in

the mill community of **New
Lanark** (p151)

❽ Blowing away the cobwebs
on the scenic, activity-packed
Isle of Arran (p155)

❾ Plunging the deeps off the
picturesque fishing village of
St Abbs (p138)

❿ Browsing secondhand
books at **Wigtown** (p176)

BORDERS REGION

Domestic tourists grease the wheel of the Borders' economy – they flock here from north and south of the border, eager to explore links to the country's medieval past. It's a distinctive region – centuries of war and plunder have left a battle-scarred landscape, encapsulated by the remnants of the great Border abbeys. They were an irresistible magnet during the Border wars, and were destroyed and rebuilt numerous times. The monasteries met their scorched end in the 16th century and were never rebuilt. Today these massive stone shells are the region's finest attraction.

But there's more. Welcoming villages with ancient traditions pepper the countryside, one of the best cold-water diving sites in Europe is off the coast, and grandiose mansions await exploration. It's fine walking and cycling country too, the gentle hills lush with an artist's palette of shades of green. And don't miss Hermitage Castle; nothing encapsulates the region's turbulent history like this spooky stronghold.

ℹ Getting Around

There's a good network of local buses. **First** (☎01324-602200; www.firstgroup.com)

operates between most of the border towns and connects them with Edinburgh.

Cockburnspath

The 16th-century **Mercat Cross** in Cockburnspath village square, about a mile inland from the coast, is the official eastern-end start of the Southern Upland Way (see below). There are a couple of B&Bs here, but no pub; it's not a particularly inspiring place to spend the night, so jump on a bus to nearby Coldingham for accommodation.

Bus 253 running between Edinburgh and Berwick-upon-Tweed stops in Cockburnspath every two hours or so.

Coldingham & St Abbs

Coldingham and St Abbs are the two most popular places for tourists on this section of Scotland's east coast, a short distance north of the English border. This picturesque area is fantastic for those who love the great outdoors – there's loads to do, as evidenced by the anglers, scuba divers, birdwatchers and walkers who flock here.

BORDERS WALKING & CYCLING

The region's most famous walk is the challenging 212-mile **Southern Upland Way** (www.southernuplandway.gov.uk). If you want a sample, one of the best bits is the three- to four-day section from St John's Town of Dalry to Beattock. Another long-distance walk is the 62-mile **St Cuthbert's Way** (www.stcuthbertsway.fsnet.co.uk), inspired by the travels of St Cuthbert (a 7th-century saint who worked in Melrose Abbey), which crosses some superb scenery between Melrose and Lindisfarne (in England). In Galloway the **Pilgrims Way** follows a 25-mile trail from Glenluce Abbey to the Isle of Whithorn.

The **Borders Abbeys Way** (www.bordersabbeysway.com) links all the great Border abbeys in a 65-mile circuit. For shorter walks and especially circular loops in the hills, the towns of Melrose, Jedburgh and Kelso all make ideal bases.

For baggage transfer on these walks, contact **WalkingSupport** (☎01896-822079; www.walkingsupport.co.uk). In early September, look out for the **Scottish Borders Walking Festival** (www.borderswalking.com), with nine days of walks for all abilities and an instant social scene.

With the exception of the main A-roads, traffic is sparse, which, along with the beauty of the countryside, makes this ideal cycling country.

The **Tweed Cycle Way** is a waymarked route running 62 miles along the beautiful Tweed Valley, following minor roads from Biggar to Peebles (13 miles), Melrose (16 miles), Coldstream (19 miles) and Berwick-upon-Tweed (14 miles). Jedburgh tourist office (p148) has details.

For an island tour, the **Isle of Arran** offers excellent cycling opportunities. The 50-mile coast-road circuit is stunning and is worth splitting into two or three days.

☉ Sights & Activities

From the village of Coldingham, with its twisting streets, take the B6438 downhill to the small fishing village of St Abbs, a gorgeous, peaceful little community with a picture-perfect harbour nestled below the cliffs. St Abbs is a great place for walking – head for the car park at the harbour and have a stroll over the rocky sea walls to get a feel of this fabulous location.

The clear, clean waters around St Abbs form part of **St Abbs & Eyemouth Voluntary Marine Reserve** (www.marine-reserve. co.uk; Northfield, St Abbs), one of the best cold-water diving sites in Europe. The reserve is home to a variety of marine life, including grey seals and porpoises. Visibility is about 7m to 8m but has been recorded at 24m. Beds of brown kelp form a hypnotically undulating forest on the seabed.

Drop by the **St Abbs Dive Centre** (☎018907-71237; www.stabbs.org/postoffice. html) at the post office; these folk provide plenty of advice on diving in the area. They also sell and repair (no charge) equipment, and nothing seems to be too much trouble. Divers can charter boats from **Paul Crowe** (☎018907-71945, 07710-961050; www.divest abbs.info) or **Paul O'Callaghan** (☎018907-71525; www.stabbsdiving.com) among others.

Back in Coldingham try **Scoutscroft** (☎018907-71669; www.scoutscroft.co.uk; Scoutscroft Holiday Centre, St Abbs Rd) for pointers on the best places to dive in the area and what you'll likely see. You can also hire equipment here (full kit per day £60) and organise a boat dive. This professional set-up can kit you up with nitrox tanks, and do a full range of IANTD courses.

In Coldingham, a signposted turn-off to the east leads just under a mile down to away-from-it-all **Coldingham Bay**, which has a sandy beach and a clifftop walking trail to Eyemouth (3 miles). At St Vedas Hotel (p139) is **St Vedas Surf Shop** (www.stve das.co.uk) where you can hire surfboards and snorkelling gear. Surfing lessons are also available.

North of St Abbs, the 78-hectare **St Abb's Head National Nature Reserve** (NTS; www.nts.org.uk) is an ornithologist's wonderland, with large colonies of guillemots, kittiwakes, herring gulls, fulmars, razorbills and some puffins. You get to the reserve by following the 2-mile circular trail that begins beside the Northfield Farm car park (£2) on the road just west of St Abbs. The clifftop walks here are spectacular, especially on sunny days. There's a good little **nature exhibition** (☉10am-5pm Apr-Oct) in the Old Smiddy complex alongside.

🛏 Sleeping & Eating

Rock House　　　　　BUNKHOUSE, B&B **££**
(☎018907-71945; www.divestabbs.info; St Abbs; dm/s/d £18/30/60) Right by the harbour in St Abbs, this is run by a friendly dive skipper; you can almost roll out of bed onto the boat. There's a bunkhouse which is normally booked up by groups at the weekend, and a sweet room that can sleep up to three. There's also a self-catering cottage here.

St Vedas Hotel　　　　　　HOTEL **££**
(☎018907-71679; www.stvedas.co.uk; Coldingham Bay; s/tw without bathroom £35/60, d £70) Just opposite the path down to the beach, St Vedas is a cheery, British-beach-resort–style hotel. It has a touch of faded grandeur, and is very popular at weekends over summer. Rooms are plain but neat and tidy – No 1 is a good double with sea views and en suite. Meals are available at the **restaurant** (mains £6-9) and there's a cafe on the beach itself in summer.

ℹ Getting There & Away

Bus 253 between Edinburgh and Berwick-upon-Tweed (six daily Monday to Saturday, three Sunday) stops in Coldingham and St Abbs, as does bus 235, which runs at least hourly from Eyemouth.

Eyemouth

POP 3383

Eyemouth is a busy fishing port and popular domestic holiday destination. The harbour itself is very atmospheric – you may even spot seals frolicking in the water, and tourists frolicking around the boats, snapping pics of old fishing nets.

The community here suffered its greatest catastrophe in October 1881, when a storm destroyed the coastal fishing fleet, killing 189 fishermen, 129 of whom were locals.

☉ Sights

Eyemouth Museum　　　　　MUSEUM
(www.eyemouthmuseum.org.uk; Manse Rd; adult/child £2.50/free; ☉10am-4pm Mon-Fri, 11am-4pm Sat & Sun Apr-Oct) Captivating Eyemouth Museum has local-history displays, particularly relating to the town's fishing heritage.

Its centrepiece is the tapestry commemorating the 1881 fishing disaster.

Eyemouth Maritime Centre   MUSEUM
(www.worldofboats.org; Harbour Rd; adult/child/family £3.75/2.50/9; ◷10am-5pm) Situated right on Eyemouth's working fishing harbour, what was once the fish market has now been decked out to resemble an 18th-century man o'war. A changing yearly exhibition occupies most of the interior, drawing on the museum's large collection of well-loved wooden coastal craft. The museum guides are great for extra information.

Gunsgreen House   MUSEUM
(www.gunsgreenhouse.org; adult/child £5/3; ◷11am-5pm Thu-Mon Apr-Sep, weekends only Mar & Oct) Standing proud and four-square across the harbour, this elegant 18th-century John Adam mansion was built on the profits of smuggling: Eyemouth was an important landing point for the illegal cargoes of ships from northern Europe and the Baltic. The house has been beautifully restored to reflect this and other aspects of its varied past.

🛏 Sleeping & Eating

Churches Hotel   HOTEL **££**
TOP CHOICE
(☏01890-750401; www.churcheshotel.co.uk; Albert Rd; s £75, d £85-120; ◷Mar-Oct; 🅿🛜) This is a very stylish place set in an 18th-century building, with rooms exuding a cool demeanour and a classical look. Each room has a different theme but No 4, with its four-poster bed, and No 6, with huge windows overlooking the harbour, are our favourites. Little conveniences like bottled water and iPod docks are complemented by excellent personal service from the owners. The menu (mains £10 to £16) is blessed with the day's catch from the harbour – it's the best spot in town for fresh seafood.

Oblò   BISTRO **££**
(www.oblobar.com; 20 Harbour St; bar meals £6-10, dinner mains £12-15; ◷food 10am-9pm) For a meal pretty much anytime, find your way upstairs to this modern bar-bistro with its comfy seating and modish interior. It's urban, it's trendy, it's just down from the tourist office, and it's got a great deck to lap up the sunshine. Try the local seafood.

Bantry   B&B **££**
(Mackays; ☏018907-51900; www.mackaysofeyemouth.co.uk; 20 High St; s/d £40/60, without

bathroom £25/50) Plonked on top of the restaurant of the same name on the main drag, this place has redecorated and refurbished rooms with muted tones and a luxurious, modern feel, positioned right on the waterfront. Try to get No 3 if you're after a double, as it's the only one with sea views. Add £2.50 per person for continental breakfast, or a fiver for the works.

❶ Information

Tourist office (☏018907-50698; eyemouth@visitscotland.com; Manse Rd; ◷10am-4pm Mon-Sat, 11am-3pm Sun Apr-Oct) Very helpful; it's in Eyemouth Museum near the harbour.

❶ Getting There & Away

Eyemouth is 5 miles north of the Scotland-England border. Buses go to Berwick-upon-Tweed (15 minutes, frequent), which has a train station, and Edinburgh (£5.60, 1¾ hours, six daily Monday to Saturday, three Sunday).

South of Eyemouth

Further south, 3 miles west of the A1 along the B6461, **Paxton House** (www.paxtonhouse.com; adult/child £7.50/3.50; ◷11am-5pm Apr-Oct, grounds 10am-sunset Apr-Oct) is beside the River Tweed and surrounded by parkland and gardens. It was built in 1758 by Patrick Home for his intended wife, the daughter of Prussia's Frederick the Great. Unfortunately, she stood him up, but it was her loss; designed by the Adam family – brothers John, James and Robert – it's acknowledged as one of the finest 18th-century Palladian houses in Britain. It contains a large collection of Chippendale and Regency furniture, and its picture gallery houses paintings from the national galleries of Scotland. The nursery is a feature designed to provide insight into a child's 18th-century life. In the grounds are walking trails and a riverside museum on salmon fishing.

Duns & Around

POP 2594

Duns is a peaceful market town in the centre of Berwickshire, with some pleasant walks. You can get to **Duns Law** (218m) in Duns Castle Estate by following Castle St up from the square. The summit offers great views of the Merse and Lammermuir Hills. The Covenanter's Stone marks the spot where the Covenanting armies camped in 1639; a copy of the Covenant was later signed at Duns Castle.

Buses running between Galashiels and Berwick-upon-Tweed (six to nine daily) stop at Duns.

Lammermuir Hills

North of Duns, the low-lying Lammermuir Hills, with their extensive grouse moors, rolling farmland and wooded valleys, run east–west along the border with East Lothian. The hills are popular with walkers and there are numerous trails, including a section of the **Southern Upland Way** (see p138).

To the west, the Way can be accessed at Lauder, where it passes through the grounds of **Thirlestane Castle** (www.thirlestanecastle.co.uk; castle & grounds adult/child £10/6, grounds only £3/1.50; ☺10am-3pm Wed, Thu & Sun May-Sep, also Mon & Tue Jul-Aug). The narcissism of the aristocracy is evident here perhaps more than in most 'great homes'. Notice how many of the family portraits adorning the walls look similar? The extensive assemblage here is the result of the common practice of mass production used at the time. Many of the family have almost identical features, as the same bodies were used for their portraits with different clothes, faces and hands superimposed. Thirlestane is also home to some of the finest plasterwork ceilings in Europe.

Thirlestane is just outside town, off the A68, beside Leader Water. Munro's buses running between Kelso and Edinburgh pass by.

Coldstream

POP 1813

On a sweeping bend of the River Tweed, which forms the border with England, Coldstream is small and relatively hidden from the well-trodden Borders tourist beat. It can be a handy base when nearby Kelso is overflowing.

◉ Sights

FREE **Coldstream Museum** MUSEUM
(12 Market Sq; ☺10am-4pm Mon-Sat, 2-4pm Sun Apr-Sep, 1-4pm Mon-Sat Oct) The proud history of the Coldstream Guards is covered in this museum. Formed in 1650 in Berwick as part of Oliver Cromwell's New Model Army, the regiment took its present name from the town where it was stationed in 1659. It played a significant part in the restoration of the monarchy in 1660 and saw service at Waterloo, at Sebastopol during the Crimean War, in the Boer War, at the Somme and Ypres in WWI, and at Dunkirk and Tobruk in WWII. It remains the oldest regiment in continuous existence in the British army and is the only one directly descended from the New Model Army.

🛏 Sleeping & Eating

Eastbraes B&B B&B ££
(☏01890-883949; www.eastbraes.co.uk; 100C High St; s/d £45/70) Trundling down the main street in Coldstream, you simply don't expect the view you get out the back of this welcoming place; an idyllic vista over a grassy garden and a picturebook bend in the Tweed just beyond. A double and twin share a bathroom and there's one en suite double, which is simply enormous, and comes with a separate sitting area.

Calico House B&B ££
(☏07985-249207;www.bedandbreakfast-luxury.co.uk; 44 High St; d/ste £70/90) Set behind a shop that churns out high-quality interior designs, this is a superb B&B with sumptuous rooms blessed with great views and attention to detail. 'Cleanliness is next to godliness' could easily be the mantra here. Privacy from your hosts and value for money are two very strong points in this excellent accommodation option. The rate is £10 less if you stay more than one night.

Besom PUB £
(www.besom-inn.co.uk; 75 High St; mains £9-11; ☺lunch & dinner) Cosy, creeper-covered High Street pub with a beer garden and solid bar meals.

Garth House B&B ££
(☏01890-882477; 7 Market St; s/d £25/60) This old bastion is cheap and comfy with no frills attached. It's a basic, old-fashioned B&B – personable, good value and friendly – but nothing flash. If you want value for money – here it is.

❶ Getting There & Away

Coldstream is on the busy A697 linking Newcastle with Edinburgh. There are about six buses daily Monday to Saturday (three on Sunday) between Kelso (20 minutes) and Berwick-upon-Tweed (45 minutes) via Coldstream.

Kelso

POP 5116

Kelso, a prosperous market town with a broad, cobbled square flanked by Georgian buildings, has a French feel to it and a historic appeal. During the day it's a busy little place, but after 8pm you'll have the streets to yourself. The town has a lovely site at the junction of the Rivers Tweed and Teviot, and is one of the most enjoyable places in the Borders.

⊙ Sights

FREE **Kelso Abbey** ABBEY
(HS; www.historic-scotland.gov.uk; Bridge St; ⊙9.30am-6.30pm Apr-Sep, 9.30am-4.30pm Sat-Wed Oct-Mar) Once one of the richest abbeys in southern Scotland, Kelso Abbey was built by the Tironensians, an order founded at Tiron in Picardy and brought to the Borders around 1113 by David I. English raids in the 16th century reduced it to ruins, though what remains today is some of the finest surviving Romanesque architecture in Scotland.

Floors Castle CASTLE
(www.floorscastle.com; adult/child £7.50/3.50; ⊙11am-5pm May-Oct) Grandiose Floors Castle is Scotland's largest inhabited mansion and overlooks the Tweed about a mile

west of Kelso. Built by William Adam in the 1720s, the original Georgian simplicity was 'improved' in the 1840s with the addition of rather ridiculous battlements and turrets. Inside, view the vivid colours of the 17th-century Brussels tapestries in the drawing room and the intricate oak carvings in the ornate ballroom. Palatial windows reveal a ribbon of green countryside extending well beyond the estate.

Kelso Old Parish Church CHURCH
(The Butts; ⊙10am-4pm Mon-Fri May-Sep) Near the abbey, this rare, octagonal church built in 1773 is intriguing.

🏃 Activities

The **Pennine Way** (www.thepennineway.co.uk), which starts its long journey at Edale in the Peak district, ends at Kirk Yetholm Youth Hostel, about 7 miles southeast of Kelso on the B6352.

The **Borders Abbeys Way** (www.bordersabbeysway.com) links the great abbeys of Kelso, Jedburgh, Melrose and Dryburgh to create a 65-mile circuit. The Kelso–Jedburgh section (12 miles) is a fairly easy walk, largely following the River Teviot between the towns. The tourist office has a free leaflet with a map and description of the route.

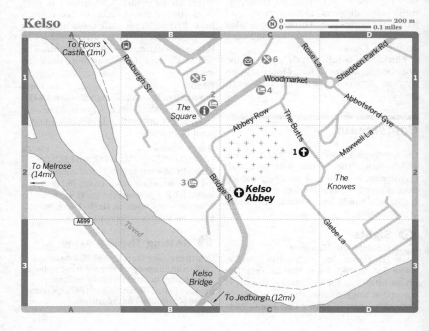

Kelso

Less-ambitious walkers should leave the Square by Roxburgh St and take the signposted alley to **Cobby Riverside Walk**, a pleasant ramble along the river to Floors Castle (although you have to rejoin Roxburgh St to gain admission to the castle).

🛌 Sleeping

TOP CHOICE **Old Priory**   B&B **££**
(📞01573-223030; www.theoldpriorykelso.com; 33 Woodmarket St; s/d £50/75; 🅿🛜) The doubles in this atmospheric place are fantastic and the family room has to be seen to be believed; rooms are both sumptuous and debonair with gorgeous dark polished wood pieces. The good news extends to the garden – perfect for a coffee in the morning – and a most comfortable sitting room. The huge windows are another feature, flooding the rooms with natural light.

Edenbank House   B&B **££**
(📞01573-226734; www.edenbank.co.uk; Sitchill Rd; s/d £35/70; 🅿) Half a mile down the road to Sitchill, this grand Victorian house (no sign) sits in spacious grounds where only the bleating of lambs in the green fields and birds in the garden break the silence. Opulent rooms, warm hospitality, and any-time-you-like breakfasts featuring homemade produce make for an utterly relaxing stay.

TOP CHOICE **Ednam House Hotel**   HOTEL **££**
(📞01573-224168; www.ednamhouse.com; Bridge St; s/d from £78/115; 🅿🛜📺) The genteel, Georgian Ednam House, touched with a quiet dignity, contains many of its original features and is the top place in town, with fine gardens overlooking the river and the excellent **Ednam House Restaurant**. It's very popular with fisher folk and during salmon season, from the end of August un-

til November, the hotel is very busy. Rooms with a river view cost more.

Central Guest House   B&B **£**
(📞01890-883664; www.thecentralguesthousekelso.co.uk; s/d £30/45) A bargain in sometimes pricey Kelso and just on the central square. The owners live off-site so call ahead first. The rooms are fine: spacious, with firm beds, new carpets and good bathrooms. Rates are room-only, but you get a fridge, toaster, and microwave so you can create your own breakfast.

🍴 Eating & Drinking

Cobbles Inn   PUB **££**
(📞01573-223548; www.thecobblesinn.co.uk; 7 Bowmont St; mains £10-16; ⏲lunch & dinner Tue-Sun) We've included the phone number for a reason: this pub off the main square is so popular you should book for a meal at weekends. Why does it pack out? Because it's cheery, very welcoming, warm, and serves excellent upmarket pub food in generous portions. There's a decent wine selection and proper coffee, but the wise leave room for dessert too. The bar always has an interesting guest ale or two as well. A cracking place.

Oscar's   BISTRO **££**
(📞01573-224008; www.oscars-kelso.com; 33 Horsemarket; mains £10-16; ⏲lunch Mon & Wed-Sat, dinner Wed-Mon) Posh comfort food and the work of local artists sit side by side in this likeable bar-restaurant-gallery in the centre of town. The menu changes, but when you see avocados, serrano ham, sea bass, sizzling lamb, hummus, and haggis on the same menu, it means one thing: you might have to come back again to try everything. A wide selection of wines accompanies the food, and you can browse the exhibition space downstairs while you wait for your plate.

ℹ Information

Kelso Hospital (📞01573-223441; Inch Rd)
Kelso Library (Bowmont St; ⏲Mon-Sat; @) Free internet access.

Tourist office (📞01573-223464; www.visit scottishborders.com; The Square; ⏲daily Apr-Nov, Mon-Sat Dec-Mar)

ℹ Getting There & Away

There are six buses daily (three on Sunday) to Berwick-upon-Tweed (one hour). Buses run to/from Jedburgh (25 minutes, up to 11 daily

---

Kelso

⊚ Top Sights

Monday to Saturday, five Sunday) and Hawick (one hour, seven daily Monday to Saturday, four Sunday). There are also frequent services to Edinburgh.

Around Kelso

SMAILHOLM TOWER

Perched on a rocky knoll above a small lake, the narrow, stone Smailholm Tower (HS; www.historic-scotland.gov.uk; Smailholm; adult/child £3.70/2.20; ☺9.30am-5.30pm Apr-Sep, 9.30am-4.30pm Sat & Sun Oct-Mar) provides one of the most evocative sights in the Borders and keeps the bloody uncertainties of its history alive. Although the displays inside are sparse, the panoramic view from the top is worth the climb.

The nearby farm, Sandyknowe, was owned by Sir Walter Scott's grandfather. As Scott himself recognised, his imagination was fired by the ballads and stories he heard as a child at Sandyknowe, and by the ruined tower a stone's throw away.

The tower is 6 miles west of Kelso, a mile south of Smailholm village on the B6397. You pass through the farmyard to get to the tower. Munro's bus 65 between Melrose and Kelso stops in Smailholm village.

MELLERSTAIN HOUSE

Finished in 1778, Mellerstain House (www.mellerstain.com; Gordon; adult/child £7/3.50; ☺12.30-5pm Sun & Wed May, Jun & Sep, plus Mon & Thu Jul & Aug, Sun only Oct) is considered to be Scotland's finest Robert Adam–designed mansion. It is famous for its classic elegance, ornate interiors and plaster ceilings; the library in particular is outstanding. Give the garish upstairs bedrooms a miss, but have a peek at the bizarre puppet-and-doll collection in the gallery.

It's about 10 miles northwest of Kelso, near Gordon. Munro's bus 65 between Melrose and Kelso passes about a mile from Mellerstain House.

TOWN YETHOLM & KIRK YETHOLM

The twin villages of Town Yetholm and Kirk Yetholm, separated by Bowmont Water, are close to the English border, about 6 miles southeast of Kelso. Hillwalking centres, they lie at the northern end of the Pennine Way (see p142) and on St Cuthbert's Way (see p138) between Melrose and Lindisfarne (Holy Island) in Northumberland.

As the last stop on the Pennine Way, Kirk Yetholm SYHA (☎0845 293 7373; www.syha.org.uk; Kirk Yetholm; dm £15.25; ☺Apr–mid-Sep) is often busy; book well in advance. Bus 81 from Kelso runs up to seven times a day Monday to Saturday (three times on Sunday).

Melrose

POP 1656

Tiny, charming Melrose is a polished village running on the well-greased wheels of tourism. This little enclave is a complete contrast to overbearing Galashiels, whose urban sprawl laps at its western edges. Sitting at the feet of the three heather-covered Eildon Hills, Melrose has a classic market square and one of the great abbey ruins.

◉ Sights

Melrose Abbey   ABBEY
(HS; www.historic-scotland.gov.uk; adult/child £5.20/3.10; ☺9.30am-5.30pm Apr-Sep, 9.30am-4.30pm Oct-Mar) Perhaps the most interesting of all the great Border abbeys, the red-sandstone Melrose Abbey was repeatedly destroyed by the English in the 14th century. The remaining broken shell is pure Gothic and the ruins are famous for their decorative stonework – see if you can glimpse the pig gargoyle playing the bagpipes on the roof. You can climb to the top for tremendous views.

The abbey was founded by David I in 1136 for Cistercian monks from Rievaulx in Yorkshire. It was rebuilt by Robert the Bruce, whose heart is buried here. The ruins date from the 14th and 15th centuries, and were repaired by Sir Walter Scott in the 19th century.

The adjoining museum (free for abbey ticket holders) has many fine examples of 12th- to 15th-century stonework and pottery found in the area. Note the impressive remains of the 'great drain' outside – a medieval sewerage system.

☯ Activities

There are many attractive walks in the Eildon Hills, accessible via a footpath off Dingleton Rd (the B6359) south of the town, or via the trail along the River Tweed. The tourist office has details of local walks.

The St Cuthbert's Way long-distance walking path starts in Melrose, while the coast-to-coast **Southern Upland Way** passes through town. You can do a day's walk along St Cuthbert's Way as far as Harestanes (16 miles), on the A68 near Jedburgh, and then return to Melrose on the hourly Jedburgh–Galashiels bus. The **Tweed Cycle Way** also passes through Melrose. See the boxed text, p138 for more details.

★ Festivals & Events

Melrose Rugby Sevens RUGBY
(www.melrose7s.com) In mid-April rugby followers fill the town to see the week-long competition.

Borders Book Festival BOOKS
(www.bordersbookfestival.org) Stretching over four days in late June.

🛏 Sleeping

Townhouse HOTEL ££
(☎01896-822645; www.thetownhousemelrose. co.uk; Market Sq; s/d £90/120; P 🛜) The classy Townhouse, exuding warmth and professionalism, has some of the best rooms in town – tastefully furnished with attention to detail. There are two superior rooms (£132) that are enormous in size with lavish furnishings; the one on the ground floor in particular has an excellent en suite, which includes a jacuzzi. It's well worth the price.

Old Bank House B&B ££
(☎01896-823712; www.oldbankhousemelrose. co.uk; 27 Buccleuch St; s/d £40/60) Right in the middle of town, this noble building offers B&B that stands out for its friendly welcome and helpful attitude. Spacious rooms and inviting beds make this a top Borders base.

Melrose SYHA HOSTEL £
(☎01896-822521; www.syha.org.uk; Priorwood; dm/tw £17/36; ⏰late Mar–late Oct; P @) A short walk from the abbey, this stately Georgian house is in a quiet location with a big grassy garden to relax in. The dorms vary substantially in number of beds and have no lockers, but it's all spotless and the common areas are good.

Braidwood B&B ££
(☎01896-822488; www.braidwoodmelrose.co. uk; Buccleuch St; s/d £45/60; 🛜) This popular town house near the abbey is an excellent place, with high-quality facilities and a warm welcome. The sparkling

rooms are finely decorated and the twin has great views. No singles are available in summer.

Burts Hotel HOTEL ££
(☎01896-822285; www.burtshotel.co.uk; Market Sq; s/d £70/130; P 🅿🛜) Set in an early-18th-century house, and with an enviable reputation, Burts retains much of its period charm and has been run by the same couple for over 30 years. It would suit older visitors or families. Room No 5 is the best. They do appealing food too.

🍴 Eating

Townhouse RESTAURANT ££
(☎01896-822645; www.thetownhousemelrose. co.uk; Market Sq; mains £11-13; ⏰lunch & dinner) The brasserie and restaurant here turn out just about the best gourmet cuisine in town – the sister hotel Burt's, opposite, comes a close second – and offers decent value. There's some rich, elaborate, beautifully presented fare here, but you can always opt for the range of creative lunchtime sandwiches for a lighter feed.

Marmion's Brasserie RESTAURANT ££
(☎01896-822245; www.marmionsbrasserie. co.uk; 5 Buccleuch St; mains £10-16; ⏰lunch & dinner Mon-Sat) This atmospheric, oak-panelled niche serves snacks all day, but the lunch and dinner menus include gastronomic delights, featuring things like local lamb, venison steaks, or pan-seared cod. For lunch the focaccias with creative fillings are a good choice.

Russell's CAFE £
(Market Sq; dishes £6-9; ⏰9.30am-5pm Tue-Sat, noon-5pm Sun) Solid wooden furniture and big windows looking out over the centre of Melrose make this stylish little tearoom/restaurant a popular option. There's a large range of snacks and more substantial lunch offerings, with daily specials.

Cellar CAFE £
(17 Market Sq; mains £4-8; ⏰10am-5pm) Drop into the Cellar for a caffeine hit. It's also good for a glass of wine on the town square, food platters and speciality cheeses.

ℹ Information

Melrose Library (18 Market Sq; ⏰Mon-Fri; @) Free internet access.

Tourist office (☎01896-822283; melrose@ visitscotland.com, Abbey St; ⏰10am-4.30pm

Mon-Sat, noon-4pm Sun Apr-Oct, 10am-4pm Fri & Sat Nov-Mar) By the abbey.

❶ Getting There & Away

First buses run to/from Edinburgh (£6, 2¼ hours, hourly) via Peebles. Change in Galashiels (20 minutes, frequent) for more frequent Edinburgh services and for other Borders destinations.

Around Melrose

DRYBURGH ABBEY

The most beautiful, complete Border abbey is **Dryburgh Abbey** (HS; www.historic-scotland.gov.uk; adult/child £4.70/2.80; ☺9.30am-5.30pm Apr-Sep, 9.30am-4.30pm Oct-Mar), partly because the neighbouring town of Dryburgh no longer exists (another victim of the wars) and partly because it has a lovely site in a sheltered valley by the River Tweed, accompanied only by a symphony of birdsong. The abbey conjures up images of 12th-century monastic life more successfully than its counterparts in nearby towns. Dating from about 1150, it belonged to the Premonstratensians, a religious order founded in France. The pink-hued stone ruins were chosen as the burial place for Sir Walter Scott.

The abbey is 5 miles southeast of Melrose on the B6404, which passes famous **Scott's View** overlooking the valley. You can hike there along the southern bank of the River Tweed, or take a bus to the nearby village of Newtown St Boswells.

ABBOTSFORD

Fans of Sir Walter Scott should visit his former residence, **Abbotsford** (www.scottsabbotsford.co.uk; adult/child £7/3.50; ☺9.30am-5pm Mon-Sat, 11am-4pm Sun late Mar–Oct, 9.30am-5pm Sun Jun-Sep). The inspiration he drew from the surrounding 'wild' countryside influenced many of his most famous works. A collection of Scott memorabilia is on display, including many personal possessions.

The mansion is about 2 miles west of Melrose between the River Tweed and the B6360. Frequent buses run between Galashiels and Melrose; alight at the Tweed bank roundabout and follow the signposts (it's a 15-minute walk). You can also walk from Melrose to Abbotsford in an hour along the southern bank of the Tweed.

Selkirk

POP 5742

While the noisy throb of machinery no doubt once filled the river valleys below Selkirk, a prosperous mill town in the early 19th century, today it sits placidly and prettily atop its steep ridge. Naughty millworkers on the wrong side of the law would have come face to face in court with Sir Walter Scott, who was sheriff here for three decades.

The helpful **tourist office** (☎01750-20054; selkirk@visitscotland.com; Halliwell's Close; ☺10am-5pm Mon-Sat, noon-3pm Sun Apr-Oct) is tucked away off Market Sq. Inside is **Halliwell's House Museum** (admission free), the oldest building (1712) in Selkirk. The museum charts local history with an engrossing exhibition, and the Robson Gallery has changing exhibitions.

Drop into **Sir Walter Scott's Courtroom** (Market Sq; admission free; ☺10am-4pm Mon-Fri, 11am-3pm Sat Apr-Sep, & 11am-3pm Sun May-Aug, noon-3pm Mon-Sat Oct), where there's an exhibition on the man's life and writings, plus a fascinating account of the courageous explorer Mungo Park (born near Selkirk) and his search for the River Niger.

🛏 Sleeping

Philipburn Country House Hotel HOTEL ££
(☎01750-20747; www.philipburnhousehotel.co.uk; r lodge/standard/luxury £90/125/175; ℗🛜) On the edge of town, this place makes a sound place to stay. New owners have pepped this former dower house up, and it features neat rooms and a snug bar and restaurant. The luxury rooms are great – some have a jacuzzi, while another is a split-level affair with a double balcony. There are room-only rates available in the separate **lodge** (single/double £60/70), which has self-catering facilities.

County Hotel HOTEL ££
(☎01750-721233; www.countyhotelselkirk.co.uk; Market Sq; s/d £45/89; ℗🛜) Located in the centre, this is a former coaching inn that has comfortable, recently refurbished rooms. It's popular with golfers and serves good upmarket bar meals (£9 to £12).

❶ Getting There & Away

First buses 95 and X95 run at least hourly between Hawick, Selkirk, Galashiels and Edinburgh (£6, two hours).

Sir Walter Scott (1771–1832) is one of Scotland's greatest literary figures. Born in Edinburgh, he moved to his uncle's farm at Sandyknowe in the Borders as a child. It was here, rambling around the countryside, that he gained a passion for historical ballads and Scottish heroes. After studying in Edinburgh he bought Abbotsford (p146), a country house in the Borders.

The Lay of the Last Minstrel (1805) was an early critical success. Further works earning him an international reputation included *The Lady of the Lake* (1810), set around Loch Katrine and the Trossachs. He later turned his hand to novels and virtually invented the historical genre. *Waverley* (1814), which dealt with the 1745 Jacobite rebellion, set the classical pattern of the historical novel. Other works included *Guy Mannering* (1815) and *Rob Roy* (1817). In *Guy Mannering* he wrote about Border farmer Dandie Dinmont and his pack of dogs, which became so popular that they became known as Dandie Dinmont Terriers, the only breed of dog named after a literary character.

Later in life Scott wrote obsessively to stave off bankruptcy. His works virtually single-handedly revived interest in Scottish history and legend in the early 19th century. Tourist offices stock a *Sir Walter Scott Trail* booklet, guiding you to many places associated with his life in the Borders.

Jedburgh

POP 4090

Attractive Jedburgh is a lush, compact oasis, where many old buildings and wynds (narrow alleys) have been intelligently restored, inviting exploration by foot. It's constantly busy with domestic tourists, but wander into some of the pretty side streets and you won't hear a pin drop.

◉ Sights

Jedburgh Abbey   ABBEY
(HS; www.historic-scotland.gov.uk; Abbey Rd; adult/child £5.20/3.10; ⊙9.30am-5.30pm Apr-Sep, 9.30am-4.30pm Oct-Mar) Dominating the town skyline, Jedburgh Abbey was the first great Border abbey to be passed into state care, and it shows – audio and visual presentations telling the abbey's story are scattered throughout the carefully preserved ruins (good for the kids or if it's raining). The red-sandstone ruins are roofless but relatively intact, and the ingenuity of the master mason can be seen in some of the rich (if somewhat faded) stone carvings in the nave (be careful of the staircase in the nave – it's slippery when wet). The abbey was founded in 1138 by David I as a priory for Augustinian canons.

FREE **Mary, Queen of Scots House**
                                          HISTORIC HOUSE
(Queen St; ⊙10am-4.30pm Mon-Sat, 11am-4.30pm Sun Mar-Nov) Mary stayed at this beautiful 16th-century tower house in 1566 after her famous ride to visit the injured earl of Bothwell, her future husband, at Hermitage Castle (p149). The interesting displays evoke the sad saga of Mary's life.

✦ Activities

The tourist office sells some handy walking booklets for short walks around the town, including sections of the **Southern Upland Way** (p138) or **Borders Abbeys Way** (p142).

✷ Festivals & Events

Jethart Callant's Festival   CULTURAL
(www.jethartcallantsfestival.com) For two weeks from late June marks the perilous time when people rode out on horseback checking for English incursions (see the boxed text, p148).

🛏 Sleeping

Maplebank   B&B £
(☎01835-862051; maplebank3@btinternet.com; 3 Smiths Wynd; s/d £25/40; ⊅) It's very pleasing to come across places like this, where it really feels like you're staying in someone's home. That someone in this case is like your favourite aunt: friendly and chaotic and generous. There's lots of clutter and it's very informal. The rooms are comfortable and large, and share a good bathroom. Breakfast (particularly if you like fruit, homemade yoghurts and a selection of everything) is better than you'll get at a posh guesthouse.

RIDING OF THE MARCHES

The Riding of the Marches, or Common Riding, takes place in early summer in the major Borders towns. Like many Scottish festivals it has ancient origins, dating back to the Middle Ages, when riders would be sent to the town boundary to check on the common lands. The colourful event normally involves extravagant convoys of horse riders following the town flag or standard as it's taken on a well-worn route. Festivities vary between towns but usually involve lots of singing, sport, pageants, concerts and a screaming good time! If you want to zero in on the largest of the Ridings, head to Jedburgh for the Jethart Callant's Festival (p147).

Willow Court   B&B ££
(☑01835-863702; www.willowcourtjedburgh. co.uk; The Friars; d £65-70; ℗🛜) With superb views over Jedburgh from the conservatory, where you are served a three-meals-in-one breakfast, Willow Court is a traditional B&B with homespun decor, smiling hosts and a large garden. Ask about the self-catering cottage just out of town.

Jedburgh Camping & Caravanning Club   CAMPING £
(☑01835-863393; www.campingandcaravanning club.co.uk/jedburgh; Elliot Park, A68; tent sites with/without car £15/7.50; ⊘Apr-Oct; ℗🛜) About a mile north of the town centre, opposite Jedburgh Woollen Mill, this site is set on the banks of Jed Water and is quiet and convenient, particularly if you're interested in fishing.

✖ Eating

Nightjar   RESTAURANT ££
(☑01835-862552; www.thenightjar.co.uk; 1 Abbey Close; mains £10-15; ⊘dinner Thu-Sat) Casual but classy, this is a highly commended restaurant dishing out a mix of creative meals, including seafood and Thai cuisine. The real highlight is if you're lucky enough to be here on the last Saturday of the month when a special Thai menu is revealed; locals rave about this night.

Carters Rest   PUB ££
(Abbey Pl; mains £9-12; ⊘lunch & dinner; 🛜) Right opposite the abbey, this offers up

market pub grub in an attractive lounge bar. The standard fare is fleshed out with an evening dinner menu featuring local lamb and other goodies. Portions are generous and served with a smile.

Sunrise   INDIAN £
(51 High St; mains £6-9; ⊘lunch & dinner) You'll pay slightly higher prices for the dishes at this curry house but it's well worth it. Featuring aromatic south Indian cooking, there's plenty on offer for vegetarians, including delicious homemade samosas stuffed with goodies, plus succulent, spicy tandoori chicken and generous side dishes.

❶ Information

There's a free wi-fi zone around the centre.
Library (Castlegate; ⊘Mon-Fri; @) Free internet access.

Tourist office (☑01835-863170; jedburgh@ visitscotland.com; Murray's Green; ⊘9.30am-5pm Mon-Sat, 10am-4pm Sun) Head tourist office for the Borders region. Extended hours in summer. Closed Sunday in winter.

❶ Getting There & Away

Jedburgh has good bus connections to Hawick (25 minutes, roughly hourly), Melrose (30 minutes, at least hourly Monday to Saturday) and Kelso (25 minutes, at least hourly Monday to Saturday, four Sunday). Munro's runs from Jedburgh to Edinburgh (£6, two hours, at least hourly Monday to Saturday, five Sunday).

Hawick

POP 14,573

Straddling the River Teviot, Hawick (pronounced 'hoik') is the largest town in the Borders and has long been a major production centre for knitwear.

In the centre of town, three buildings form what is labelled as 'The Heart of Hawick'. A former mill now holds the **tourist office** (☑01450-373993; hawick@visitscot land.com; Kirkstile; ⊘10am-5.30pm Mon-Thu, 10am-7.45pm Fri & Sat, noon-3.30pm Sun), and a cinema. Opposite, historic **Drumlanrig's Tower** is a solid stone mansion that was once a major seat of Douglas clan power in the Borders. It now holds the **Borders Textile Towerhouse** (www.heartofhawick. co.uk; Tower Knowe; admission free; ⊘10am-4pm Mon-Sat, also noon-3pm Sun Apr-Oct) that tells the story of the town's knitwear-producing history, while round the back of the tourist office, the **Heritage Hub** (www.scotborders.

gov.uk; Towerdykeside; ◎10am-4.45pm Mon, Fri & Sat, 10am-7.45pm Tue & Thu) is a state-of-the-art facility for anyone wishing to trace Scottish heritage, or other local archives.

Across the river, **Hawick Museum & Art Gallery** (☑01450-373457; Wilton Lodge Park; admission free; ◎10am-noon & 1-5pm Mon-Fri, 2-5pm Sat & Sun Apr-Sep, noon-3pm Mon-Fri, 1-3pm Sun Oct-Mar) has an interesting collection of mostly 19th-century manufacturing and domestic memorabilia.

There are several knitwear outlets in town, include **Hawick Cashmere of Scotland** (www.hawickcashmere.com; Arthur St); a full list is available from the tourist office.

You'll be met with a cheery welcome at the amiable **Bridgehouse B&B** (☑01450-370701; ginoscafebb@aol.com; Sandbed; s/d £30/58). Functional rooms, in former stables dating back to 1760, are brightly decorated and as neat as a pin, although en suites can be pokey. You can opt out of breakfast for a discount. There's a cafe and a bar overlooking the river, but if you feel like something more substantial, pop into **Sergio's** (www.sergiosofhawick.co.uk; pizza & pasta £6-9; ◎lunch & dinner) next door for pizza and pasta dishes or more elaborate, but overpriced, mains.

The half-hourly First buses 95 and X95 connect Hawick with Galashiels, Selkirk and Edinburgh (£6, two hours).

Hermitage Castle

The 'guardhouse of the bloodiest valley in Britain', **Hermitage Castle** (HS; www.historic-scotland.gov.uk; adult/child £3.70/2.20; ◎9.30am-5.30pm Apr-Sep) embodies the brutal history of the Scottish Borders. Desolate but proud with its massive squared stone walls, it looks more like a lair for orc raiding parties than a home for Scottish nobility, and is one of the bleakest and most stirring of Scottish ruins.

Strategically crucial, the castle was the scene of many a dark deed and dirty deal with the English invaders, all of which rebounded heavily on the perfidious Scottish lord in question. Here, in 1338, Sir William Douglas imprisoned his enemy Sir Alexander Ramsay and deliberately starved him to death. Ramsay survived for 17 days by eating grain that trickled into his pit (which can still be seen) from the granary above. In 1566, Mary Queen of Scots famously visited the wounded tenant of the castle, Lord Bothwell, here. Fortified, he recovered to (probably) murder her husband, marry her himself, then abandon her months later and flee into exile.

The castle is about 12 miles south of Hawick on the B6357.

Peebles

POP 8065

With a picturesque main street set on a ridge between the River Tweed and the Eddleston Water stream, Peebles is one of the most handsome of the Border towns. Though it lacks a major sight as a focus to things, the agreeable atmosphere and good walking options in the rolling, wooded hills hereabouts will entice you to linger for a couple of days.

◉ Sights & Activities

If it's sunny, the **riverside walk** along the River Tweed has plenty of grassed areas ideal for a picnic, and there's a children's playground (near the main road bridge). A mile west of the town centre, **Neidpath Castle** is a tower house perched on a bluff above the river; it's closed for the foreseeable future but worth a look from the riverbank.

Two miles east of town off the A72, in **Glentress forest**, is one of the **7stanes** (www.7stanes.gov.uk) mountain-biking hubs (see p175), as well as osprey viewing and marked walking trails. A **cafe** (☑01721-721736; www.thehubintheforest.co.uk) hires rigs and will put you on the right trail for your ability. These are some of Britain's best biking routes.

🛏 Sleeping & Eating

Cringletie House HOTEL £££
(☑01721-725750; www.cringletie.com; s/d from £210/230; 🅿@📶) Luxury without snobbery is this enchanting hotel's hallmark, and more power to them. To call it a house is being coy; it's an elegant baronial mansion, 2 miles north of Peebles on the A703 and set in lush, wooded grounds. Rooms are plush and feature genteel elegance and linen so soft you could wrap a newborn in it. There's an excellent **restaurant** (mains £23) and an excellent atmosphere.

Rowanbrae B&B ££
(☑01721-721630; www.aboutscotland.co.uk/peebles/rowanbrae.html; 103 Northgate; s/d £35/60; 📶) A marvellously hospitable couple run

LOCAL KNOWLEDGE

AMY HICKMAN: BIKE CLUB OFFICER

I work in Edinburgh for bikeclub.org.uk, an organisation which aims to encourage healthy lifestyles through cycling, and I'm a fanatical mountain biker myself. Scotland is a great place for mountain biking, and has developed an international reputation – the UCI World Cup competition is held annually in Fort William.

Best Mountain Biking Spots? I'm from the Borders originally, so I'm biased towards the 7stanes centres (see boxed text, p175) – Kirroughtree is the best, the trails there are great fun. I would also recommend Laggan Wolftrax (p333) for really challenging and technical terrain. These are both man-made centres; one of my favourite natural trails is the Gypsy Glen circuit at Cardrona, near the Glentress 7stanes centre (p149); the guys at Glentress can give you the route details.

Off the Beaten Track? My current favourite place for exploring is Fife – get hold of a map and go where looks interesting! Kelty Forest and Blairadam Forest (near the village of Kelty) are good places to start.

this great B&B in a quiet cul-de-sac not far from the main street; you'll soon feel like you're staying with friends. There are three upstairs bedrooms, two with en suite, and an excellent guest lounge for relaxation.

Sunflower Restaurant RESTAURANT **££**
(01721-722420; www.thesunflower.net; 4 Bridgegate; mains £10-15; lunch Mon-Sat, dinner Thu-Sat) The Sunflower, with its warm yellow dining room, is in a quiet spot off the main drag and has a reputation that brings lunchers from all over southern Scotland. It serves good salads for lunch and has an admirable menu in the evenings, with creative and elegant dishes that always include some standout vegetarian fare.

Tontine Hotel RESTAURANT WITH ROOMS **££**
(01721-720892; www.tontinehotel.com; High St; mains £7-14; lunch & dinner; P) Glorious is the only word to describe the Georgian dining room here, complete with musicians' gallery, fireplace, and windows the like of which we'll never see again. It'd be worth it even if they served catfood on mouldy bread, but luckily the meals – ranging from pub classics like steak-and-ale pie to more ambitious fare – are tasty and backed up by very welcoming service. Rooms (single/double £75/110) are decent too: there's a small supplement for river views.

Cross Keys Hotel HOTEL **££**
(01721-724222; www.crosskeyspeebles.co.uk; 24 Northgate; dm/s/d £22/35/60; P) The Cross Keys is a renovated 17th-century coaching inn, and the history shows in the curious rooms: glasses slide off the bedside tables

thanks to the time-warped floorboards. But that's character; the beds are comfortable, bathrooms good, and prices fair.

Rosetta Holiday Park CAMPING **£**
(01721-720770; www.rosettaholidaypark.co.uk; Rosetta Rd; tent site & 2 people £16; mid-Mar–Oct;) This camping ground, about 800m north of the town centre, has an exquisite green setting. There are plenty of amusements for the kids, such as a bowling green and a games room.

ℹ Information

Tourist office (01721-723159; bordersinfo@ visitscotland.com; High St; 9am-5pm Apr-Dec, 10am-4pm Mon-Sat Jan-Mar) To 6pm in summer.

ℹ Getting There & Away

The bus stop is beside the post office on Eastgate. First bus 62 runs half hourly to Edinburgh (1¼ hours), Galashiels (45 minutes) and Melrose (one hour).

Around Peebles

TRAQUAIR HOUSE

One of Scotland's great country houses, **Traquair House** (www.traquair.co.uk; Innerleithen; adult/child/family £7.50/4/21; 10.30am-5pm Jun-Aug, noon-5pm Apr-May & Sep, 11am-4pm Oct, 11am-3pm Sat & Sun Nov) has a powerful ethereal beauty, and an exploration here is like time travel. Odd, sloping floors and a musty odour bestow a genuine feel, and parts of the building are believed to have been constructed long before the first official record of its existence in 1107. The massive tower house was gradually expanded over the next 500 years but has remained virtually unchanged since 1642.

Since the 15th century, the house has belonged to various branches of the Stuart family, and the family's unwavering Catholicism and loyalty to the Stuart cause are largely why development ceased when it did. The family's estate, wealth and influence were gradually whittled down after the Reformation, and there was neither the opportunity nor, one suspects, the will to make any changes.

One of its most interesting places is the concealed room where priests secretly lived and performed Mass – up until 1829 when the Catholic Emancipation Act was finally passed. Other beautiful, time-worn rooms hold fascinating relics, including the cradle used by Mary for her son, James VI of Scotland (who also became James I of England), and many letters written by the Stuart pretenders to their supporters.

In addition to the house, there's a **garden maze**, an **art gallery**, a small **brewery** producing the tasty Bear Ale, and an active craft community. The **Traquair Fair** takes place here in early August.

Traquair is 1.5 miles south of Innerleithen, about 6 miles southeast of Peebles. Bus 62 from Edinburgh runs hourly to Innerleithen. Bus 62 runs from Edinburgh via Peebles to Innerleithen and on to Galashiels and Melrose.

SOUTH LANARKSHIRE

South Lanarkshire combines a highly urbanised area south of Glasgow with scenically gorgeous country around the Falls of Clyde and the World Heritage–listed area of New Lanark, by far the biggest drawcard of the region. If you're roaring up to Scotland on the M74, there are some fine places to break your journey.

See p133 for Blantyre, birthplace of David Livingstone.

Lanark & New Lanark

POP 8253

Below the market town of Lanark, in an attractive gorge by the River Clyde, is the World Heritage Site of New Lanark – an intriguing collection of restored mill buildings and warehouses.

Once the largest cotton-spinning complex in Britain, it was better known for the pioneering social experiments of Robert Owen, who managed the mill from 1800. New Lanark is really a memorial to this enlightened capitalist. He provided his workers with housing, a cooperative store (the inspiration for the modern cooperative movement), the world's first nursery school for children, a school with adult-education classes, a sick-pay fund for workers and a social centre he called the New Institute for the Formation of Character. You'll need at least half a day to explore this site, as there's plenty to see, and appealing walking along the riverside.

The best way to get the feel of New Lanark is to wander round the outside of this impressive place. What must once have been a thriving, noisy, grimy industrial village, pumping out enough cotton to wrap the planet, is now a peaceful oasis with only the swishing of trees and the rushing of the River Clyde to be heard.

⊙ Sights & Activities

New Lanark Visitor Centre   MUSEUM
(www.newlanark.org; adult/child/family £7/6/22; ⊙10am-5pm Apr-Sep, 11am-5pm Oct-Mar) You need to buy a ticket to enter the main attractions. These include a huge working spinning mule, producing woollen yarn, the **Historic Schoolhouse**, which contains an innovative, high-tech journey to New Lanark's past via a 3D hologram of the spirit of Annie McLeod, a 10-year-old mill girl who describes life here in 1820. The kids will love it as it's very realistic, although the 'do good for all mankind' theme is a little overbearing.

Also included in your admission is a **millworker's house**, Robert Owen's **home** and exhibitions on 'saving New Lanark'. There's also a 1920s-style **village store**.

Falls of Clyde Wildlife Centre

EXHIBITION, WALK
(www.swt.org.uk; adult/child £2/1; ⊙11am-5pm Mar-Dec, noon-4pm Jan & Feb) The wildlife centre is also by the river in New Lanark. This place has child-friendly displays focused on badgers, bats, peregrine falcons and other prominent species. In season, there's a live video feed of peregrines nesting nearby. Outside is a bee tree, where you can see honey being made.

From the centre, you can walk up to Corra Linn (30 minutes) and Bonnington Linn (one hour), two of the **Falls of Clyde** that inspired Turner and Wordsworth, through the beautiful nature reserve managed by the Scottish Wildlife Trust. You could return via the muddier path on the opposite bank, pass New Lanark, and cross the river a little further downstream to make a circular walk of it (three hours). The centre also organises various activities in summer, including badger-watching (adult/child £8/4).

Craignethan Castle   CASTLE
(HS; www.historic-scotland.gov.uk; Tillietudlem; adult/child £3.70/2.20; ⏱9.30am-5.30pm Apr-Sep, 9.30am-4.30pm Sat & Sun Oct-Mar) This castle has a very authentic feel – it hasn't been restored beyond recognition – and is in a stunning, tranquil spot, too. You'll feel miles from anywhere, so bring a picnic and make a day of it.

With a commanding position above the River Nethan, this extensive ruin includes a virtually intact tower house and a **caponier** (unique in the UK) – a small gun emplacement with holes in the wall so men with handguns could pick off attackers. The chilly chambers under the tower house are quite eerie.

Craignethan is 5 miles northwest of Lanark. If you don't have your own transport, take an hourly Lanark–Hamilton bus to Crossford, then follow the footpath along the northern bank of the River Nethan (20 minutes).

🛏 Sleeping & Eating

New Lanark makes a very relaxing, attractive place to stay.

New Lanark Mill Hotel   HOTEL ££
(☎01555-667200; www.newlanark.org; New Lanark; s/d £80/120; P@🖥♿) Cleverly converted from an 18th-century mill, this hotel is full of character and is a stone's throw from the major attractions. It has luxury rooms (only £25 extra for a spacious suite and added decadence) or self-catering accommodation in charming cottages (from £285/525 per week in winter/summer). The hotel also serves good meals (bar meals £6 to £9, two-course dinner £23).

New Lanark SYHA   HOSTEL £
(SYHA; ☎01555-666710; www.syha.org.uk; New Lanark; dm/tw £17/38; ⏱mid-Mar–mid-Oct; P@) This hostel has a great location in an old mill building by the River Clyde. It's been recently renovated and has a really good downstairs common area, and spruce en suite dormitories.

La Vigna   RESTAURANT ££
(☎01555-664320; www.lavigna.co.uk; 40 Wellgate, Lanark; 3-course lunch/dinner £13/24; ⏱lunch & dinner Mon-Sat, dinner Sun) This well established local favourite is a great spot, seemingly plucked from some bygone age with its quietly efficient service and, charmingly, a separate menu for ladies – without prices! The food is distinctly Italian, albeit using the sound Scottish venison, beef, and fish, and there are also vegetarian options. The set-price lunch is fine value at £13.

Crown Tavern   PUB £
(www.crown-tavern.com; 17 Hope St, Lanark; lunch mains £5-7, dinner mains £11-15; ⏱lunch & dinner) Off the main street, the Crowny is a local favourite. It's a highly regarded place that does good bar meals and even better food (pasta, seafood and vegetarian dishes) in the evenings in its restaurant. Try the local trout or the Highlander chicken.

ℹ Information

Tourist office (☎01555-661661; lanark@visitscotland.com; Ladyacre Rd, Lanark; ⏱10am-5pm) Close to the bus and train stations. Closed Sundays October to March.

ℹ Getting There & Around

Lanark is 25 miles southeast of Glasgow. Express buses from Glasgow, run by Irvine's Coaches, make the hourly run from Monday to Saturday (one hour).

Trains also run daily between Glasgow Central station and Lanark (£5.45, 55 minutes, every 30 minutes).

It's a pleasant walk to New Lanark, but there's also a half-hourly bus service from the train station (daily). If you need a taxi, call **Clydewide** (☎01555-663221).

Biggar
POP 2098

Biggar is a pleasant town in a rural setting dominated by Tinto Hill (712m). The town has a number of offbeat museums that give it a quirky appeal. It's also known for the nationalist, leftist poet Hugh MacDiarmid, who lived near here for nearly 30 years until his death in 1978.

◉ Sights

The **Biggar Museum Trust** (☎01899-221050; www.biggarmuseumtrust.co.uk) looks after most of the town's museums. It all relies on the goodwill of volunteers, so opening hours can be quite variable: it's worth ringing ahead if you've a special interest in one of them.

Gladstone Court   MUSEUM
(North Back Rd; adult/child £2/1; ⊙10.45am-4.30pm Apr-Oct) An intriguing indoor street museum with historic Victorian-era nook-and-cranny shops that you can pop into to steal a glimpse of the past. Don't miss the **old printing press** and the **Albion A2 Dogcart**, one of the oldest British cars still around.

Biggar Puppet Theatre   THEATRE
(www.purvespuppets.com; Broughton Rd; seats £7) Has miniature Victorian puppets and bizarre modern ones over 1m high that glow in the dark. Different shows are suitable for varying age groups, so inquire before you take along the kids. Check the website for performance times.

Tinto Hill   DAY HIKE
The hill dominates town. It is a straightforward ascent by the northern ridge from the car park, just off the A73 by Thankerton Crossroads. Look out for the **Stone Age fort** on your way up. Allow two hours for the return trip.

Moat Park Heritage Centre   MUSEUM
(Kirkstyle; adult/child £2/1; ⊙10.45am-4.30pm Apr-Oct) In a renovated church, covers the history of the area with geological and archaeological displays.

Greenhill Covenanter's House   MUSEUM
(Burnbrae; adult/child £1/50p; ⊙2-5pm Sat May-Sep) An intelligently reconstructed farmhouse with 17th-century furnishings and artefacts relating to the fascinating story of the local Covenanters, who valiantly defied their king to protect their religious beliefs.

Gasworks Museum   MUSEUM
(Gasworks Rd; adult/child £1/50p; ⊙11am-4pm Jun-Sep) The only reminder of the days when Scotland produced its gas by burning coal.

🛏 Sleeping & Eating

Cornhill House   HOTEL ££
(☎01899-220001; www.cornhillhousehotel.com; Coulter; s/d £75/90; [P]🛜) This is a well-

appointed place, complete with turrets, and is situated in a peaceful setting 2 miles southwest of Biggar. The rooms are good value, particularly those that have been refurbished, and a three-course breakfast is included. The restaurant is somewhat overpriced; you may want to eat elsewhere.

School Green Cottage   B&B ££
(☎01899-220388; isobel.burness@virgin.net; 1 Kirkstyle; s/d £35/60) Just off the sometimes noisy main road in the centre of town, this is an upright little place with courteous homespun hospitality. The neat double and twin here are well kitted out with New Zealand oak furnishings.

ℹ Information

Biggar Gallery (☎01899-221442; 139 High St; ⊙10am-5pm Mon-Sat, noon-5pm Sun) Doubles as a tourist information point. Good walking advice.

ℹ Getting There & Away

Biggar is 33 miles southeast of Glasgow. Bus 100 runs to/from Edinburgh (1¼ hours, hourly Monday to Saturday, three Sunday). Bus 191 runs hourly to/from Lanark (30 minutes), where you can change for Glasgow.

AYRSHIRE & ARRAN

Ayrshire is synonymous with golf and with Robert Burns – and there's plenty on offer here to satisfy both of these pursuits. Troon has six golf courses for starters, and there's enough Burns memorabilia in the region to satisfy his most fanatic admirers.

This region's main drawcard though is the irresistible Isle of Arran. With a gourmet culinary scene, atmospheric watering holes, and the most varied and scenic countryside of the southern Hebridean islands, this easily accessible island shouldn't be missed.

Back on the mainland, retro holiday towns by the seaside, such as Largs, give Ayrshire a unique flavour, while towns such as Irvine provide a link to the region's maritime heritage. There's also spectacular coastal scenery, best admired at Culzean Castle, one of the finest stately homes in the country.

The best way to appreciate the Ayrshire coastline is on foot: the **Ayrshire Coastal Path** (www.ayrshirecoastalpath.org) is 100 miles of spectacular waterside walking.

North Ayrshire

LARGS
POP 11,241

On a sunny day, there are few more beautiful places in southern Scotland than Largs, where green grass meets the sparkling water of the Firth of Clyde. It's a resort-style waterfront town that harks back to seaside days in times of gentler pleasures, and the minigolf, amusements, old-fashioned eateries and bouncy castle mean you should get into the spirit, buy an ice cream and go for a stroll to check out this slice of retro Scotland.

The main attraction in Largs is **Vikingar!** (www.kaleisure.com; Greenock Rd; adult/child £4.50/3.50; ⊙10.30am-4.30pm Apr-Sep, 10.30am-3.30pm Oct & Mar, 10.30am-3.30pm Sat & Sun Nov & Feb). This multimedia exhibition describes Viking influence in Scotland until its demise at the Battle of Largs in 1263. Tours with staff in Viking outfits run every hour. There's also a theatre, cinema, cafe, shop, swimming pool and leisure centre. It's on the waterfront road just north of the centre. You can't miss it, as it's the only place with a longship outside.

Largs hosts a **Viking festival** (www.largs vikingfestival.com) during the first week in September. The festival celebrates the Battle of Largs and the end of Viking political domination in Scotland.

🛏 Sleeping & Eating

Brisbane House Hotel   HOTEL **££**
(☎01475-687200; www.brisbanehousehotel.com; 14 Greenock Rd, Esplanade; s/d £80/85, d/ste with sea view £95/120; 🅿🛜🐾) We're not sure about the modern facade on this genteel old building, but the rooms are quite luxurious, and some – it's aimed at wedding parties – have jacuzzis and huge beds. It's on the waterfront road, so paying the extra for a sea view will reward in fine weather, as the sun sets over the island opposite. There's a decent bar and restaurant downstairs and a comfortable contemporary feel.

Nardini   CAFE, BISTRO **££**
(www.nardinis.co.uk; Esplanade; mains £11-18; ⊙9am-10pm; 🐾) Nothing typifies the old-time feel of Largs more than this giant art deco gelateria, well into its second century. The ice creams are decadently delicious, with rich flavours that'll have parents licking more than their fair share from the kids. There's also a cafe with outdoor seating, and a restaurant which does pizzas, pastas, and some surprisingly decent dishes like duck breast and delicious sardines on toast.

Haven House   B&B **£**
(☎01475-676389; m.l.mcqueen@btinternet.com; 18 Charles St; r per person £25) One of several good options on a street close to the water, this has comfortable rooms with good shared bathrooms. It's an easygoing place typical of the friendliness of this town. Room-only rates are a fiver less per person.

Glendarroch   B&B **££**
(☎01475-676305; www.glendarrochbedandbreak fast.co.uk; 24 Irvine Rd; s/d £34/56; 🅿) This B&B typifies Scottish hospitality – the rooms are well kept and the owner is friendly without being intrusive. If it's full, staff will probably ring around to try to find you something else.

❶ Information

Tourist office (☎01475-689962; www.ayrshire -arran.com; ⊙10.30am-3pm Mon-Sat Easter-Oct) At the train station, a block back from the waterfront on the main street.

❶ Getting There & Away

Largs is 32 miles west of Glasgow by road. There are very regular buses to Glasgow via Gourock and Greenock (45 minutes), and roughly one or two hourly to Ardrossan (30 minutes), Irvine (55 minutes) and Ayr (1¼ hours). There are trains to Largs from Glasgow Central station (£6.35, one hour, hourly).

ISLE OF GREAT CUMBRAE
POP 1200

Walking or cycling is the best way to explore this accessible, hilly island (it's only 4 miles long), ideal for a day-trip from Largs. **Millport** is the only town, strung out a long way around the bay overlooking neighbouring Little Cumbrae. With the frequent ferry service, the place buzzes with day-trippers and families (there's heaps of stuff for kids to do, such as crazy golf and a funfair). Walking around the bay admiring the views is one of the most pleasurable things to do in town, where you'll find a supermarket, bank (with ATM) and your choice of chippies.

The town boasts Britain's smallest cathedral, the lovely **Cathedral of the Isles** (☎01475-530353; College St; ⊙daylight hrs), which was completed in 1851. Inside it's quite ornate with a lattice woodwork ceiling and fragments of early Christian carved stones.

IRVINE

Boat lovers should check out the **Scottish Maritime Museum** (www.scottishmaritimemuseum.org; Gottries Rd, Harbourside; adult/child £3.50/2.50; ⏰10am-5pm Apr-Oct) in Irvine. In the massive **Linthouse Engine Shop** – an old hangar with a cast-iron framework – is an absorbing collection of boats and machinery. A ticket also gives admission to the **boat shop**, with its wonderful works of art and huge kids activity area. Free guided tours leave from the boat shop – guides will take you down to the pontoons where you can clamber over various ships and visitors can also see a shipyard worker's restored flat.

Further along the harbour road, make sure to drop into the wonderful **Ship Inn** (www.shipinnirvine.co.uk; 120 Harbour St; mains £7-8). It's the oldest pub in Irvine (1597), serves tasty bar meals (noon to 9pm) and has bucket loads of character.

Irvine is 26 miles from Glasgow. There are frequent buses from Ayr (30 minutes) and Largs (45 minutes). Trains run to/from Glasgow Central station (£5.75, 35 minutes, half-hourly); the other way they go to Ayr.

Just east of town is the interesting **Robertson Museum & Aquarium** (✆01475-530581; adult/child £2/1; ⏰9am-12.15pm & 2-4.15pm Mon-Fri Sep-Jun, 9am-4.30pm Mon-Fri, 10am-4pm Sat Jul & Aug). A short way along the coast from the aquarium is a remarkable rock feature, the **Lion**.

Little Cumbrae was bought in 2009 by a couple who plan to transform it into a yoga centre, overseen by controversial but massively popular guru Swami Ramdev.

The island's minor roads have well-marked **walking** and **cycling** routes. Take the Inner Circle route up to the island's highest point, **Glaid Stone**, where you get good views of Arran and Largs, and even as far as the Paps of Jura on a clear day. You can walk between the ferry and the town via here in about an hour. There are several bike-hire places in Millport.

If you're staying overnight on the island there are several choices. Try the unusual **College of the Holy Spirit** (✆01475-530353; www.island-retreats.org; College St; s/d £35/60, with en suite £50/70; 🛜), next to the cathedral; there's a refectory-style dining room and a library.

The **Dancing Midge** (www.thedancingmidgecafe.com; 24 Glasgow St; light meals £3-5; ⏰9am-5pm Thu-Mon; 🛜) is a cheerful cafe on the seafront providing healthy, tasty alternatives to the chippies in town, as well as an ideal spot to read the newspaper. Food is freshly prepared (sandwiches, salads and soups) and the coffee freshly brewed.

A very frequent 15-minute **CalMac** (www.calmac.co.uk) ferry ride links Largs with Great Cumbrae (passenger/car £4.70/20.35)

daily. Buses meet the ferries for the 3.5-mile journey to Millport (£1.80/2.80 single/return).

ARDROSSAN
POP 10,952

The main reason – OK the *only* reason – for coming here is to catch a CalMac ferry to Arran. Trains leave Glasgow Central station (£5.85, one hour, half-hourly) to connect with ferries (see p164).

Isle of Arran
POP 4800

Enchanting Arran is a jewel in Scotland's tourism crown. Strangely undiscovered by foreign tourists, the island is a visual feast, and boasts culinary delights, cosy pubs (including its own brewery) and stacks of accommodation. The variations in Scotland's dramatic landscape can all be experienced on this one small island, best explored by pulling on the hiking boots or jumping on a bicycle. Arran offers some challenging walks in the mountainous north, often compared to the Highlands, while the island's circular road is very popular with cyclists.

The ferry from Ardrossan docks at Brodick, the island's main town. To the south, Lamlash is actually the capital and, like nearby Whiting Bay, a popular seaside resort. From the pretty village of Lochranza in the north there's a ferry link to Claonaig on the Kintyre peninsula.

Camping isn't allowed without permission from the landowner, but there are several camping grounds. Good sleeping options are dotted all around the island, but especially in Brodick and the south. Accommodation is a good deal more expensive on Arran than on the mainland.

ℹ Information

There are banks with ATMs in Brodick. Websites include www.ayrshire-arran.com, www.visit-isle-of-arran.eu and www.visitarran.com.

Arran Library (☎01770-302835; Brodick Hall; ⏰10am-5pm Tue, 10am-7.30pm Thu & Fri, 10am-1pm Sat; @) Free internet access.

Hospital (☎01770-600777; Lamlash)

Tourist office (☎01770-303774; www.ayrshire-arran.com; ⏰9am-5pm Mon-Sat) Efficient; by Brodick pier. Also open Sundays in July and August.

ℹ Getting There & Away

CalMac runs a car ferry between Ardrossan and Brodick (passenger/car return £9.70/59, 55 minutes, four to eight daily), and from April to late October runs services between Claonaig and Lochranza (passenger/car return £8.75/39.10, 30 minutes, seven to nine daily).

ℹ Getting Around

BICYCLE Several places hire out bicycles in Brodick. Try these:

Arran Adventure Company (☎01770-302244; www.arranadventure.com; Shore Rd, Brodick; day/week £15/55)

Boathouse (☎01770-302868; Brodick Beach; day/week £12.50/45)

CAR Arran Transport (☎01770-700345; Brodick) at the service station near the ferry pier hires cars from £25/32 per half/full day.

PUBLIC TRANSPORT Four to seven buses daily go from Brodick pier to Lochranza (45 minutes), and many daily go from Brodick to Lamlash and Whiting Bay (30 minutes), then on to Kildonan and Blackwaterfoot. Pick up a timetable from the tourist office. An Arran Rural Rover ticket costs £4.75 and permits travel anywhere on the island for a day (buy it from the driver). For a **taxi**, call ☎01770-302274 in Brodick or ☎01770-600903 in Lamlash.

BRODICK & AROUND

Most visitors arrive in Brodick, the heartbeat of the island, and congregate along the coastal road to admire the town's long curving bay.

As you follow the coast along Brodick Bay, look out for **seals**, often seen on the rocks around **Merkland Point**. Two types live in these waters, the Atlantic grey seal and the common seal. The common seal has a face like a dog; the Atlantic grey seal has a Roman nose.

◉ Sights

Many of Brodick's attractions are just out of town, off the main road that runs north to Lochranza.

Brodick Castle & Park CASTLE
(NTS; www.nts.org.uk; adult/child castle & park £10.50/7.50, park only £5.50/4.50; ⏰castle 11am-4pm Sat-Wed Apr-Oct, open daily late Jun–early Sep, park 9.30am-sunset) The first impression of this estate 2.5 miles north of Brodick is that of an animal morgue as you enter via the hunting gallery, wallpapered with prized deer heads. On your way to the formal dining room (with its peculiar table furnishings), note the intricacy of the fireplace in the library. The castle has more of a lived-in feel than some NTS properties. Only a small portion is open to visitors. The extensive grounds, now a country park with various trails among the rhododendrons, justify the steep entry fee.

Arran Aromatics SOAP FACTORY
(☎01770-302595; www.arranaromatics.com; ⏰9.30am-5pm) In Duchess Court is this popular visitor centre where you can purchase any number of scented items and watch the production line at work. Free factory tours

run on Thursdays in summer at 6pm. The same people also run **Soapworks** (soapmaking from £7.50; ☺10am-4pm), a fun little place where kids (and adults!) can experiment by making their own soaps, combining colours and moulds to make weird and wonderful creations.

Isle of Arran Brewery

BREWERY

(✆01770-302353; www.arranbrewery.com; Cladach; ☺10am-5pm Mon-Sat, 12.30-5pm Sun Apr-Sep, 10am-3.30pm Mon & Wed-Sat) At the Cladach centre there's an excellent self-guided brewery tour for £2.50, which includes tastings in the shop. Arran beers are pure quality. Warning: Arran Dark is highly addictive. There's a good **outdoors shop** here too, if you're heading up Goatfell.

Marvin Elliott

GALLERY

Just beyond the Cladach centre, local artist Marvin Elliot creates impressive wooden sculptures in his workshop.

🏃 Activities

Drop into the tourist office for plenty of **walking** and **cycling** suggestions around the island. The 50-mile circuit on the coastal road is popular with cyclists and has few serious hills – more in the south than the north. There are plenty of walking booklets and maps available. There are many walking trails clearly signposted around the island. Several leave from Lochranza, including the spectacular walk to the island's northeast tip, **Cock of Arran**, and finishing in the village of Sannox (8 miles one-way).

The walk up and down **Goatfell** takes up to eight hours return, starting in Brodick and finishing in the grounds of Brodick Castle. If the weather's fine, there are superb views to Ben Lomond and the coast of Northern Ireland. It can, however, be very cold and windy up there; take the appropriate maps (available at the tourist office), waterproof gear and a compass.

Arran Adventure Company

OUTDOOR ACTIVITIES

(✆01770-302244; www.arranadventure.com; Shore Rd, Brodick; ☺Easter-Oct) Offers loads of activities, running a different one each day (such as gorge walking, sea kayaking, climbing, abseiling and mountain biking). All activities run for about three hours and cost around £48/38/28 for adults/solo teens/kids. Drop in to see what's available while you're around.

Auchrannie Resort

RESORT

(✆01770-302234; www.auchrannie.co.uk) Offers a bit of everything and can make a good destination if you're looking for something to do in Brodick. As well as tennis courts and gym, it has a pool and spa complex which nonguests can access for £4.60.

✦✦ Festivals & Events

There are local village festivals from June to September

Arran Folk Festival

FOLK MUSIC

(✆01770-302623; www.arranfolkfestival.org) A week-long festival in early June.

Arran Wildlife Festival

WILDLIFE

(www.arranwildlife.co.uk) This celebration of local fauna is held mid-May.

🛏 Sleeping

TOP CHOICE **Kilmichael Country House Hotel**

HOTEL £££

(✆01770-302219; www.kilmichael.com; Glen Cloy; s £95, d £160-199; P🐾) The island's best hotel, the Kilmichael is also the oldest building – it has a glass window dating from 1650. The hotel is a luxurious, tastefully decorated spot, a mile outside Brodick, with eight rooms and an excellent **restaurant** (3-course dinner £42). It's an ideal, utterly relaxing hideaway, and feels very classy without being overly formal.

🍴 Glenartney

B&B ££

(✆01770-302220; www.glenartney-arran.co.uk; Mayish Rd; s/d £56/78; ☺late Mar–Sep; P🐾) Uplifting bay views and genuine, helpful hosts make this a cracking option. Airy, stylish rooms make the most of the natural light available here at the top of the town. Cyclists will appreciate the bike wash and storage facilities, while hikers can benefit from the drying rooms and expert trail advice. The owners make big efforts to be sustainable too.

Fellview

B&B ££

(✆01770-302153; fellviewarran@yahoo.co.uk; 6 Strathwhillan Rd; r per person £30) This lovely house near the ferry is an excellent place to stay. The two rooms – which share a good bathroom – are full of thoughtful personal touches like bathrobes, and breakfast is in a pretty garden conservatory. The owner is warm, friendly and encapsulates Scottish hospitality; she doesn't charge a supplement for singles (because, in her words, 'it's not their fault'). To get here, head south out of Brodick and take the left-hand turn to Strathwhillan. Fellview is just up on the right.

Rosaburn Lodge
B&B ££

(☏01770-302383; www.rosaburnlodge.co.uk; d £70-80, ste £90-100; P) By the River Rosa, 800m from the centre of Brodick, this very friendly lodge gets heaps of natural light. There are three excellent rooms (and a chairlift to them). The Rosa suite overlooks the river via its bay window and is closer to an apartment than a bedroom. Note that there are no singles.

Belvedere Guest House
B&B ££

(☏01770-302397; www.vision-unlimited.co.uk; Alma Rd; s £35, d £60-80; P🖵) Imperiously overlooking the town, bay and surrounding mountains, Belvedere has well-presented rooms and very welcoming hosts, who also offer reiki, healing and de-stressing packages. They provide very good island information and good breakfasts with vegetarian choices.

Glen Rosa Farm
CAMPING £

(☏01770-302380; sites per person £4; P) In a lush glen by a river, 2 miles from Brodick, this large place has plenty of nooks and crannies to pitch a tent. It's remote camping with cold water and toilets only. To get there from Brodick head north, take String Rd, then turn right almost immediately on the road signed to Glen Rosa. After 400m, on the left is a white house where you book in; the campground is further down the road.

✗ Eating & Drinking

Creelers (☏01770-302810; www.creelers.co.uk; mains £11-21; ⊙lunch & dinner Tue-Sun Easter-Oct) Creelers is likely to close in the near future, but if it's still going when you read this, get on the phone and book a table. Situated 1.5 miles north of Brodick, it's Arran's top choice for fresh seafood. It's not licensed, so bring a bottle.

Eilean Mòr
CAFE £

(www.eileanmorarran.com; Shore Rd; mains £8-10; ⊙food 10am-9pm, bar 11am-midnight; 🖵) Upbeat and modern, this likeable little cafe-bar does tasty meals through the day, with pizzas and pastas featuring. But it's not afraid to give them a Scottish twist; try the haggis ravioli.

Arran on a Plate
RESTAURANT ££

(☏01770-303886; www.arranonaplate.com; Shore Rd; 2-course lunch/dinner £10/20; ⊙lunch & dinner) Unprepossessing from the outside, this new restaurant makes up for it inside, with solicitous service, a striking mural, and great sunset views over the bay. Dishes focus on fresh seafood and are attractively presented if a little short on quantity.

Ormidale Hotel
PUB £

(☏01770-302293; www.ormidalehotel.co.uk; Glen Cloy; mains £8-10; ⊙lunch & dinner; 🖵) This hotel has decent bar food. Dishes change regularly, but there are always some good vegetarian options, and daily specials. Quantities and value-for-money are high, and Arran beers are on tap.

Island Cheese Co
CHEESE PRODUCER £

(www.islandcheese.co.uk; Duchess Ct) Anyone with a fetish for cheese should stop by this place where you can stock up on the famed local cheeses. There are free samples.

Wineport
CAFE ££

(☏01770-302101; Cladach Centre; lunch mains £7-11, dinner mains £12-19; ⊙lunch daily, dinner Fri & Sat Apr-Oct) Next to the brewery, this cafe-bar has a fine sunny terrace and does a nice line in sophisticated bistro fare in the summer months.

CORRIE TO LOCHRANZA

The coast road continues north to the small, pretty village of Corrie, where there's a shop and hotel, and one of the tracks up Goatfell (the island's tallest peak) starts here. After Sannox, with a sandy beach and great views of the mountains, the road cuts inland. Heading to the very north, on the island's main road, visitors weave through lush glens flanked by Arran's towering mountain splendour.

Moderate walks here include the trail through Glen Sannox, which goes from the village of Sannox up the burn, a two-hour return trip.

The traditional stone Corrie Hotel (☏01770-810273; www.corriehotel.co.uk; r per person £34, without bathroom £28; P🖵) offers simple but comfortable rooms, several with great views, above a pub with a wonderful beer garden that scrapes the water's edge. Groups of four or more can reserve a bunkroom (£15 per head, bed only).

LOCHRANZA

The village of Lochranza is in a stunning location in a small bay at the north of the island. On a promontory stand the ruins of the 13th-century Lochranza Castle (HS; www.historic-scotland.gov.uk; admission free; ⊙24hr), said to be the inspiration for the castle in *The Black Island,* Hergé's Tintin adventure. It's basically a draughty shell inside, with interpretative signs to help you decipher the layout.

Also in Lochranza is the Isle of Arran Distillery ([☎]01770-830264; www.arranwhisky. com; tours adult/child £5/free; ⊙10am-6pm Mon-Sat, 11am-6pm Sun mid-Mar–Oct), which produces a light, aromatic single malt. The tour is a good one; it's a small distillery, and the whisky-making process is thoroughly explained. Opening hours are reduced in winter.

The Lochranza area bristles with red deer, who wander into the village unconcernedly to crop the grass on the golf course.

🛏 Sleeping & Eating

Lochranza SYHA   HOSTEL £
([☎]01770-830631; www.syha.org.uk; Lochranza; dm/f £17.50/72; ⊙mid-Feb–Oct; [P][@][�]) A recent refurbishment has made a really excellent hostel of what was always a charming place, with lovely views. The rooms are great, with chunky wooden furniture, keycards, and lockers. Rainwater toilets, a heat exchange system, and an excellent disabled room shows the thought that's gone into the redesign, while plush lounging areas, a kitchen you could run a restaurant out of, laundry, drying room, red deer in the garden, and welcoming management make this a top option.

Apple Lodge   B&B ££
([☎]01770-830229; Lochranza; s/d/ste £54/78/90; [P]) Once the village manse, this rewarding choice is most dignified and hospitable. Rooms are individually furnished, and very commodious. One has a four-poster bed, while another is a self-contained suite in the garden. The guest lounge is perfect for curling up with a good book, and courteous hosts mean you should book this one well ahead in summer.

Catacol Bay Hotel   PUB ££
([☎]01770-830231; www.catacol.co.uk; Catacol; r per person £30; [P][@][�][�]) Genially run, and with a memorable position overlooking the water, this no-frills pub 2 miles south of Lochranza offers comfortable-enough rooms with shared bathroom and views to lift the heaviest heart. No-frills bar food comes out in generous portions, there's a Sunday lunch buffet (£10.50), and the beer garden is worth a contemplative pint or two as you gaze off across the water into the west.

Lochranza Hotel   HOTEL ££
([☎]01770-830223; www.lochranza.co.uk; s/d £58/94; [P]) The focus of the village, being the only place you can get an evening meal, this bastion of Arran hospitality has comfortable rooms decked out in pink. The showers are pleasingly powerful, and the double and twin at the front (room Nos 1 and 10) have super views. Rooms are a bit overpriced, but they get cheaper if you stay more than one night.

WEST COAST

On the western side of the island, reached by String Rd across the centre (or the coast road), is the Machrie Moor Stone Circle, upright sandstone slabs erected around 6000 years ago. It's an eerie place, and these are the most impressive of the six stone circles on the island. There's another group at nearby Auchagallon, surrounding a Bronze Age burial cairn.

Blackwaterfoot is the largest village on the west coast; it has a shop and hotel. You can walk to King's Cave from here, via Drumadoon Farm – Arran is one of several islands that lay claim to a cave where Robert the Bruce had his famous arachnid encounter (p445). This walk could be combined with a visit to the Machrie stones.

SOUTH COAST

The landscape in the southern part of the island is much gentler; the road drops into little wooded valleys, and it's particularly lovely around Lagg. There's a 10-minute walk from Lagg Hotel to Torrylinn Cairn, a chambered tomb over 4000 years old where at least eight bodies were found. Kildonan has pleasant sandy beaches, a gorgeous water outlook, a hotel, a campground and an ivy-clad ruined castle.

In Whiting Bay you'll find small sandy beaches, a village shop, a post office and Arran Art Gallery (www.arranartgallery.com; Shore Rd), which has exquisite landscape portraits of Arran. From Whiting Bay there are easy one-hour walks through the forest to the Giant's Graves and Glenashdale Falls, and back – keep an eye out for golden eagles and other birds of prey.

🛏 Sleeping & Eating

[TOP CHOICE] **Kildonan Hotel**   HOTEL ££
([☎]01770-820207; www.kildonanhotel. com; Kildonan; s/d/ste £70/95/125; [P][�][�]) Luxurious rooms and a grounded attitude – dogs and kids are made very welcome – combine

to make this one of Arran's best options. Oh, and it's right by the water, with fabulous views and seals basking on the rocks. The standard rooms are beautifully furnished and spotless, but the suites – with private terrace or small balcony – are superb. Other amenities include great staff, a bar serving good bar meals, a restaurant doing succulent seafood, an ATM, book exchange, and laptops lent to guests if you didn't bring one. Applause.

Royal Arran Hotel B&B ££
(☎01770-700286; www.royalarran.co.uk; Whiting Bay; s £50, d £90-105; P 📶) This personalised, intimate spot has just four rooms. The double upstairs is our idea of accommodation heaven – four-poster bed, big heavy linen, a huge room and gorgeous water views. Room No 1 downstairs is a great size and has a private patio. The hosts couldn't be more welcoming (except to kids under 12, who aren't allowed).

Lagg Hotel HOTEL ££
(☎01770-870255; www.lagghotel.com; Lagg; s/d £45/80; P 📶) An 18th-century coach house, this inn has a beautiful location and is the perfect place for a romantic weekend away from the cares of modern life. Rooms have been recently refurbished; grab a superior one (£90) with garden views. There's also a cracking beer garden, a fine bar with log fire, and an elegant restaurant (dinner mains £11 to £16).

Viewbank House B&B ££
(☎01770-700326; www.viewbank-arran.co.uk; Whiting Bay; s £35, d £60-79; P 📶) Appropriately named, this friendly place does indeed have tremendous views from its vantage point high above Whiting Bay. Rooms, of which there are a variety with and without bathroom, are tastefully furnished and well kept. It's well signposted from the main road.

Sealshore Campsite CAMPING £
(☎01770-820320; www.campingarran.com; Kildonan; sites per person £6, per tent £1-3; P) Living up to its name, this small campsite is right by sea (and, happily, the Kildonan Hotel) with one of Arran's finest views from its grassy camping area. There's a good washroom area with heaps of showers, and the breeze keeps the midges away.

Coast BISTRO £
(☎01770-700308; Shore Rd, Whiting Bay; mains £9-10; ⏰lunch Wed-Mon, dinner Thu-Sat) This funky place decked out in suave red tones and with a sun-drenched conservatory on the water's edge serves grills, seafood and salads in the evening, with lighter offerings during the day.

Isle of Arran Brewery Guesthouse B&B ££
(☎01770-700662; guesthouse@arranbrewery.co.uk; Shore Rd, Whiting Bay; s/d from £55/80; P 📶) Newly refurbished, this bright, light place offers five rooms named after Arran beers. The best of them have sea views, and cost slightly more.

Kilmory Lodge Bunkhouse HOSTEL £
(☎01770-870345; www.kilmoryhall.com; Kilmory; dm £20; P) This new bunkhouse in Kilmory normally only opens for groups but you may be able to grab a spare bed. The Lagg Hotel is a minute's walk away.

LAMLASH

An upmarket town (even the streets feel wider here), Lamlash is in a dazzling setting, strung along the beachfront. The bay was used as a safe anchorage by the navy during WWI and WWII.

Just off the coast is **Holy Island**, owned by the Samye Ling Tibetan Centre and used as a retreat, but day visits are allowed. Depending on tides, the **ferry** (☎01770-600998) makes around seven trips a day (adult/child return £10/5, 15 minutes) from Lamlash and runs between May and September. The same folk also run fun mackerel-fishing expeditions (£20 per person).

No dogs, bikes, alcohol or fires are allowed on the island. There's a good walk to the top of the hill (314m), taking two or three hours return. It is possible to stay on the island in accommodation belonging to the grandiosely named **Holy Island Centre for World Peace & Health** (☎01770-601100; www.holyisle.org; dm/s/d £25/45/65). These prices include full (vegetarian) board. Although it's designed more for groups doing yoga and meditation courses at the centre, individuals are welcome.

Sleeping & Eating

Lilybank Guest House B&B ££
(☎01770-600230; www.lilybank-arran.co.uk; Shore Rd, Lamlash; s/d £50/70; P 📶) Built in the 17th century, Lilybank retains its heritage but has been refurbished for 21st-century needs. Rooms are clean and comfortable, with one adapted for disabled use. The front ones have great views over Holy

Island. Breakfast includes oak-smoked kippers and Arran goodies.

Drift Inn
PUB £

(Shore Rd, Lamlash; mains £8-9; ⊘lunch & dinner; 🚣) There are few better places to be on the island on a sunny day than the beer garden at this child-friendly hotel, ploughing your way through an excellent bar meal while gazing over to Holy Island. There are pub faves and genuine Angus beef burgers, with generous portions all round.

Glenisle Hotel
PUB ££

(www.glenislehotel.com; Shore Rd, Lamlash; mains £9-12; ⊘lunch & dinner; 🕾) Excellent pub food; serves Scottish classics such as Cullen skink (soup made with smoked haddock, potato, onion and milk). Good wine list.

Lamlash Bay Hotel
PUB ££

(www.lamlashbayhotel.co.uk; Shore Rd, Lamlash; mains £10-16, pizzas £7-8; ⊘lunch & dinner) Locals love a big meal out here; known for its toothsome pizza and filling Italian-style dishes.

East Ayrshire

In **Kilmarnock**, where Johnnie Walker whisky has been blended since 1820, is **Dean Castle** (www.deancastle.com; Dean Rd; admission free; ⊘11am-5pm daily Apr-Sep, 10am-4pm Wed-Sun Oct-Mar; 🚣), a 15-minute walk from the bus and train stations. The castle, restored in the first half of the 20th century, has a virtually windowless keep (dating from 1350) and an adjacent palace (1468), with a superb collection of medieval arms, armour, tapestries and musical instruments. The grounds, an 81-hectare park, are a good place for a stroll or a picnic, or you can eat at the visitor centre's tearoom, where snacks and light meals cost around £5. Free guided tours are available and there are regular activities for kids. From Ayr there are frequent buses throughout the day.

South Ayrshire

AYR
POP 46,431

Reliant on tourism, Ayr, whose long sandy beach has made it a popular family seaside resort since Victorian times, has struggled in the recent economic climate. Parts of the centre have a neglected air, though there

DUMFRIES HOUSE

A Palladian mansion designed in the 1750s by the Adam brothers, **Dumfries House** (☎01290-425959; www.dumfries-house.org.uk; adult/child £10/5; ⊘11am-4pm Thu-Mon Apr-Sep) is an architectural jewel: such is its preservation that Prince Charles personally intervened to ensure its protection. It contains an extraordinarily well-preserved collection of Chippendale furniture and numerous objets d'art. Visits are by guided tour; you should phone ahead to reserve a space and check tour times. The house is located 13 miles east of Ayr, near Cumnock.

are many fine Georgian and Victorian buildings, and it makes a convenient base for exploring this section of coast.

◉ Sights

Most things to see in Ayr are Robert Burns-related. The bard was baptised in the **Auld Kirk** (Old Church) off High St. The atmospheric cemetery here overlooks the river and is good for a stroll, offering an escape from the bustle of High St. Several of his poems are set here in Ayr; in 'Twa Brigs', Ayr's old and new bridges argue with one another. The **Auld Brig** (Old Bridge) was built in 1491 and spans the river just north of the church. In Burns' poem 'Tam o'Shanter', Tam spends a boozy evening in the pub that now bears his name – Tam o'Shanter – at 230 High St (see p163).

St John's Tower (Eglinton Tce) is the only remnant of a church where a parliament was held in 1315, the year after the celebrated victory at Bannockburn. John Knox's son-in-law was the minister here, and Mary, Queen of Scots, stayed overnight in 1563.

✗ Activities

With only a few steep hills, the area is well suited to cyclists. From Ayr, you could cycle to Alloway and spend a couple of hours seeing the Burns sights before continuing to Culzean via Maybole. You could either camp here, after seeing Culzean Castle, or cycle back along the coast road to Ayr, a return trip of about 22 miles. **AMG Cycles** (☎01292-287580; www.irvinecycles.co.uk; 55 Dalblair Rd; day/weekend/week £12.50/15/35) hires out bikes.

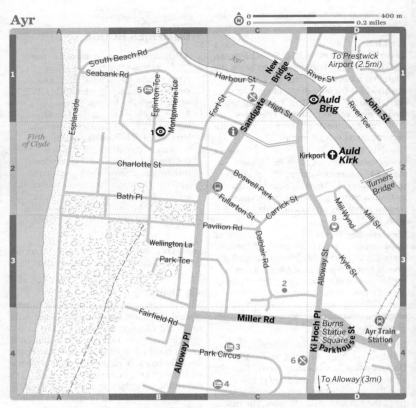

Ayr

The beachfront is good for a walk in sunny weather, especially at low tide when a huge sandy beach is revealed. The silhouettes of Arran's peaks over the bay form an impressive backdrop.

🎉 Festivals & Events

Burns an' a' That   CULTURAL
(www.burnsfestival.com) Held in Ayr in late May, this festival has a bit of everything, from wine-tasting to horseracing to concerts, some of it Burns-related.

🛏 Sleeping

Crescent   B&B ££
(☎01292-287329; www.26crescent.co.uk; 26 Bellevue Cres; s £50, d £70-80; ☏) When the blossoms are out, Bellevue Cres is Ayr's prettiest street, and this is an excellent place to stay on it. The rooms are impeccable – a tenner to upgrade to the spacious four-poster room is a sound investment – but it's the warm welcome given by the hosts that makes this

special. Numerous little extras, like Arran toiletries, bottled water in the rooms, and silver cutlery at breakfast, add appeal.

Eglinton Guest House
B&B ££

(☑01292-264623; www.eglinton-guesthouse -ayr.com; 23 Eglinton Tce; r per person £26; ☎) A short walk west of the bus station, this friendly family-run Georgian property is in a quiet cul-de-sac and has a range of traditional, tidy rooms. The location is brilliant – between the beach and the town, and it offers plenty of value, with comfortable beds and compact en suite bathrooms.

Belmont Guest House
B&B ££

(☑01292-265588; www.belmontguesthouse.co. uk; 15 Park Circus; s/d £35/56; ☎) There's a relaxing lounge and library for guests in this comfortable Victorian town house. It's a little deceptive inside, with the '70s decor punctuated by pictures of wildlife staring hungrily down at diners, but the rooms with Victorian furnishings are clean and mostly of a good size. Chocolates on your pillow give a romantic feel to the rooms. Note that over busy periods it doesn't accommodate singles.

Heads of Ayr Caravan Park
CAMPING £

(☑01292-442269; www.headsofayr.com; sites £17.50, chalets per week from £220; ☺Mar-Oct) This caravan park is in a lovely, quiet location close to the beach. From Ayr take the A719 south for about 5 miles.

✖ Eating & Drinking

Fouter's
RESTAURANT £££

(☑01292-261391; www.fouters.co.uk; 2a Academy St; mains £16-20; ☺dinner Tue-Sat) The best place to eat in town, Fouter's is a class act set in a former bank vault opposite the town hall. It's an ideal place to splash out on a top-class dinner without breaking the budget. It specialises in Ayrshire produce (such as new-season local lamb with pine nut, garlic and herb crust) and seafood prepared Mediterranean style. There's an early-dining menu (£15 for two courses) from 5pm to 7pm.

Beresford
BISTRO ££

(☑01292-280820; www.theberesfordayr.co.uk; 22 Beresford Tce; mains £10-16; ☺food 9am-9pm) Style and fun go hand in hand at this upbeat establishment serving afternoon martinis in teapots and luring churchgoing ladies with artisanal chocolates. The food is a creative fusion of influences based on solid local produce, with Ayrshire pork,

west coast oysters, and Scottish lamb often featuring. Some dishes hit real heights, and are solidly backed by a wide choice of wines, with 10 available by the glass. It stays open as a bar after the kitchen closes. Top service seals the deal.

Tam o'Shanter
PUB

(230 High St; mains £7) Opened in the mid-18th century and featured in the Burns poem whose name it now bears, this is an atmospheric old pub with traditional pub grub (served noon to 9pm).

❶ Information

Carnegie Library (12 Main St; ☺Mon-Sat; @) Offers fast, free internet access.

Tourist office (☑01292-290300; www. ayrshire-arran.com; 22 Sandgate; ☺9am-5pm Mon-Sat, 10am-5pm Sun Apr-Sep, 9am-5pm Mon-Sat Oct-Mar)

❶ Getting There & Around

Bus

Ayr is 33 miles from Glasgow and is Ayrshire's major transport hub. The main bus operator in the area is **Stagecoach Western** (☑01292-613500; www.stagecoachbus.com) which runs very frequent express services to Glasgow (one hour) and also serves Stranraer (£6.90, two hours, four to eight a day), other Ayrshire destinations, and Dumfries (£5.70, 2¼ hours, five to seven a day).

Train

There are at least two trains an hour that run to Ayr from Glasgow Central station (£6.70, 50 minutes), and some trains continue south from Ayr to Stranraer (£13, 1½ hours).

ALLOWAY

The pretty, lush town of Alloway (3 miles south of Ayr) should be on the itinerary of every Robert Burns fan – he was born here on 25 January 1759. Even if you haven't been seduced by Burns mania, it's still well worth a visit since the Burns-related exhibitions give a good impression of life in Ayrshire in the late 18th century.

◉ Sights

Robert Burns Birthplace Museum
MUSEUM

(NTS; www.nts.org.uk; adult/child £8/5; ☺10am-5pm Oct-Mar, 10am-5.30pm Apr-Sep) This brand new museum displays a solid collection of Burnsiana, including manuscripts and possessions of the poet like the pistols he packed in order to carry out his daily work – as a taxman. A Burns jukebox allows you to select readings of your favourite Burns verses, and there are other entertaining audio and visual performances.

The admission ticket (valid for three days) also covers the atmospheric **Burns Cottage**, by the main road from Ayr, and connected by a sculpture-lined walkway from the Birthplace Museum. Born in the little box bed in this cramped thatched dwelling, the poet spent the first seven years of his life here. It's an attractive display which gives you a context for reading plenty of his verse. Much-needed translation of some of the more obscure Scots farming terms he loved to use decorate the walls.

Alloway Auld Kirk   CHURCH
Near the Birthplace Museum are the ruins of the kirk, the setting for part of 'Tam o'Shanter'. Burns' father, William Burnes (his son dropped the 'e' from his name), is buried in the kirkyard; read the poem on the back of the gravestone.

Burns Monument & Gardens   GARDEN
The monument was built in 1823; the gardens afford a view of the 13th-century Brig o'Doon House.

🛏 Sleeping

Brig O'Doon House   HOTEL
(☎01292-442466; www.costley-hotels.co.uk; Alloway; s/d £85/120; P) On the main road right by the monument and bridge, a charming ivy-covered facade conceals the romantic, rather luxurious 190-year-old which will appeal greatly to Burns fans. The heavyish decor of plaid carpets is relieved by slate-floored bathrooms; rooms are spacious and very comfortable, and there are also a couple of cottages – Rose, more traditionally decorated, and Gables, more modern – across the bridge. Service is helpful, and there's a decent **restaurant** (3-course dinner £25), but the place is often booked up by wedding parties at weekends.

🛈 Getting There & Away

Stagecoach Western bus 57 operates hourly between Alloway and Ayr from 8.45am to 3.45pm Monday to Saturday (10 minutes). Otherwise, rent a bike and cycle here.

TROON
POP 14,766

Troon, a major sailing centre on the coast 7 miles north of Ayr, has excellent sandy beaches and six golf courses. The demanding championship course **Royal Troon** (☎01292-311555; www.royaltroon.co.uk; Craigend Rd) has offers on its website; the standard green fee is £165 (caddie hire is £40 extra).

Four miles northeast of Troon, **Dundonald Castle** (HS; www.historic-scotland. gov.uk; Dundonald; adult/child £3.50/1.50; ⊙10am-5pm Apr-Oct) commands impressive views and, in its main hall, has one of the finest barrel-vaulted ceilings preserved in Scotland. It was the first home of the Stuart kings, built by Robert II in 1371, and reckoned to be the third most important castle in Scotland in its time, after Edinburgh and Stirling. The visitor centre below the castle has good information on prior settlements, and scale models of the castle and its predecessors. Buses running between Troon and Kilmarnock stop in Dundonald village.

🛈 Getting There & Away

There are half-hourly trains to Ayr (10 minutes) and Glasgow (£6.15, 45 minutes).

P&O (☎0871 66 44 777; www.poirishsea.com) sails twice daily to Larne (£24 for passengers, £79 for a car and driver, two hours) in Northern Ireland.

CULZEAN CASTLE & COUNTRY PARK

The Scottish National Trust's flagship property, magnificent **Culzean** (NTS; ☎01655-884400; www.culzeanexperience.org; adult/child/family £13/9/32, park only adult/child £8.50/5.50; ⊙castle 10.30am-5pm Apr-Oct, park 9.30am-sunset year round) is one of the most impressive of Scotland's great stately homes. The entrance to Culzean (kull-*ane*) is a converted viaduct, and on approach the castle appears like a mirage, floating into view. Designed by Robert Adam, who was encouraged to exercise his romantic genius in its design, this 18th-century mansion is perched dramatically on the edge of the cliffs. Robert Adam was the most influential architect of his time, renowned for his meticulous attention to detail and the elegant classical embellishments with which he decorated his ceilings and fireplaces.

The beautiful oval staircase here is regarded as one of his finest achievements. On the 1st floor, the opulence of the circular saloon contrasts violently with the views of the wild sea below. Lord Cassillis' bedroom is said to be haunted by a lady in green, mourning for a lost baby. Even the

I see her in the dewy flowers,
I see her sweet and fair:
I hear her in the tunefu' birds,
I hear her charm the air:
There's not a bonnie flower that springs
By fountain, shaw, or green;
There's not a bonnie bird that sings,
But minds me o' my Jean.

Best remembered for penning the words of 'Auld Lang Syne', Robert Burns (1759–96) is Scotland's most famous poet and a popular hero whose birthday (25 January) is celebrated as Burns Night by Scots around the world.

Burns was born in 1759 in Alloway to a poor family, who scraped a living gardening and farming. At school he soon showed an aptitude for literature and a fondness for the folk song. He later began to write his own songs and satires. When the problems of his arduous farming life were compounded by the threat of prosecution from the father of Jean Armour, with whom he'd had an affair, he decided to emigrate to Jamaica. He gave up his share of the family farm and published his poems to raise money for the journey.

The poems were so well reviewed in Edinburgh that Burns decided to remain in Scotland and devote himself to writing. He went to Edinburgh in 1787 to publish a 2nd edition, but the financial rewards were not enough to live on and he had to take a job as a excise man in Dumfriesshire. Though he worked well, he wasn't a taxman by nature, and described his job as 'the execrable office of whip-person to the bloodhounds of justice'. He contributed many songs to collections published by Johnson and Thomson in Edinburgh, and a 3rd edition of his poems was published in 1793. To give an idea of the prodigious writings of the man, Robert Burns composed more than 28,000 lines of verse over 22 years. He died of rheumatic fever in Dumfries in 1796, aged 37.

Burns wrote in Lallans, the Scottish Lowland dialect of English that is not very accessible to the Sassenach (Englishman) or foreigner; perhaps this is part of his appeal. He was also very much a man of the people, satirising the upper classes and the church for their hypocrisy.

Many of the local landmarks mentioned in the verse-tale 'Tam o'Shanter' can still be visited. Farmer Tam, riding home after a hard night's drinking in a pub in Ayr, sees witches dancing in Alloway churchyard. He calls out to the one pretty witch, but is pursued by them all and has to reach the other side of the River Doon to be safe. He just manages to cross the Brig o'Doon, but his mare loses her tail to the witches.

The Burns connection in southern Scotland is milked for all it's worth and tourist offices have a *Burns Heritage Trail* leaflet leading you to every place that can claim some link with the bard. Burns fans should have a look at www.robertburns.org.

---

bathrooms are palatial, the dressing room beside the state bedroom being equipped with a Victorian state-of-the-art shower.

There are also two ice houses, a swan pond, a pagoda, a re-creation of a Victorian vinery, an orangery, a deer park and an aviary. Wildlife in the area includes otters.

If you really want to experience the magic of this place, it's possible to stay in the **castle** (s/d from £150/225, Eisenhower ste £250/375;) from April to October. There's also a **Camping & Caravanning Club**

(☎01655-760627; www.campingandcaravanning club.co.uk; tent sites members/non-members £9/16; ☎) at the entrance to the park, offering grassy pitches with great views.

❶ Getting There & Away

Culzean is 12 miles south of Ayr; Maybole is the nearest train station, but since it's 4 miles away it's best to come by bus from Ayr (30 minutes, 11 daily Monday to Saturday). Buses pass the park gates, from where it's a 20-minute walk through the grounds to the castle.

TURNBERRY
POP 200

Turnberry's **Ailsa golf course** (☏01655-334032; www.turnberry.co.uk) hosted the British Open in 2009 and is one of Scotland's most prestigious links courses, with spectacular views of Ailsa Craig (p166) offshore. You don't need a handicap certificate to play, just plenty of pounds – the standard green fee is £190. In summer though, take advantage of the after-3pm 'sunset' rate and you can go round for £90 a head.

Opposite the course, the super-luxurious **Turnberry Resort** (☏01655-331000; www.luxurycollection.com/turnberry; d from £279; P@⊛≋) offers everything you can think of, including an airstrip and helipad. As well as the luxurious rooms and excellent restaurant, 1906, there's a series of self-contained lodges.

KIRKOSWALD
POP 500

Just 2 miles east of Kirkoswald, by the A77, **Crossraguel Abbey** (HS; www.historic-scotland.gov.uk; adult/child £3.70/2.20; ⊙9.30am-5.30pm Apr-Sep) is a substantial ruin dating back to the 13th century that's good fun to explore. The renovated 16th-century gatehouse is the best part – you'll find decorative stonework and superb views from the top. Inside, if you have the place to yourself, you'll hear only the whistling wind – an apt reflection of the abbey's long-deceased monastic tradition. Don't miss the echo in the chilly sacristy.

Stagecoach Western runs Ayr-to-Girvan buses via Crossraguel Abbey and Kirkoswald (35 minutes, hourly Monday to Saturday, every two hours Sunday).

AILSA CRAIG

The curiously shaped island of Ailsa Craig can be seen from much of southern Ayrshire. While its unusual blue-tinted granite has been used by geologists to trace the movements of the great Ice Age ice sheet, birdwatchers know Ailsa Craig as the world's second-largest gannet colony – around 10,000 pairs breed annually on the island's sheer cliffs.

To see the island close up you can take a cruise from Girvan on the **MV Glorious** (☏01465-713219; www.ailsacraig.org.uk; 7 Harbour St, Girvan). It's possible to land if the sea is reasonably calm; a four-hour trip costs £20/15 per adult/child (£25 per person if you want three hours ashore).

Trains going to Girvan run approximately hourly (with only three trains on Sundays) from Ayr (30 minutes).

DUMFRIES & GALLOWAY

Some of the region's finest attractions lie in the gentle hills and lush valleys of Dumfries & Galloway. Ideal for families, there's plenty on offer for the kids and, happily, restaurants, B&Bs and guesthouses that are very used to children. Galloway Forest is a highlight, with its sublime views, mountain-biking and walking trails, red deer, kites and other wildlife, as are the dream-like ruins of Caerlaverock Castle.

Adding to the appeal of this enticing region is a string of southern Scotland's most idyllic towns, charming when the sun shines. And shine it does. Warmed by the Gulf Stream, this is the mildest region in Scotland, a phenomenon that has allowed the development of some famous gardens.

Dumfries
POP 31,146

Lovely, red-hued sandstone bridges crisscross pleasant Dumfries, which is bisected by the wide River Nith, with pleasant grassed areas along the river bank. Historically, Dumfries held a strategic position in the path of vengeful English armies. Consequently, although it has existed since Roman times, the oldest standing building dates from the 17th century. Plenty of famous names have passed through here: Robert Burns lived here and worked as a tax collector; JM Barrie, creator of Peter Pan, was schooled here; and the former racing driver David Coulthard hails from here.

◉ Sights

The red-sandstone bridges arching over the River Nith are the most attractive features of the town: **Devorgilla Bridge** (1431) is one of the oldest bridges in Scotland. You can download a multilingual MP3 audio tour of the town at www.dumgal.gov.uk/audiotour.

FREE **Burns House**   MUSEUM
(www.dumgal.gov.uk/museums; Burns St; ⊙10am-5pm Mon-Sat & 2-5pm Sun Apr-Sep, 10am-1pm & 2-5pm Tue-Sat Oct-Mar) This is a place of pilgrimage for Burns enthusiasts. It's here that the poet spent the last years of his life, and there are various items of his

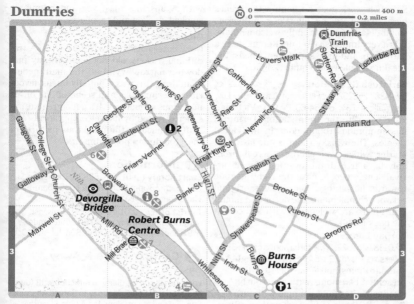

Dumfries

possessions in glass cases, as well as manuscripts and, entertainingly, letters: make sure you have a read.

FREE **Robert Burns Centre** MUSEUM
(www.dumgal.gov.uk/museums; Mill Rd; audiovisual presentation £2; ☺10am-5pm Mon-Sat & 2-5pm Sun Apr-Sep, 10am-1pm & 2-5pm Tue-Sat Oct-Mar) A worthwhile Burns exhibition in an old mill on the banks of the River Nith. It tells the story of the poet and Dumfries in the 1790s. The optional audiovisual presentations give more background on Dumfries, and explain the exhibition's contents.

You'll find Robert Burns' **mausoleum** in the graveyard at **St Michael's Kirk**; there's a grisly account of his reburial on the information panel. At the top of High St is a **statue** of the bard; take a close look at the sheepdog at his feet.

Ellisland Farm HISTORIC HOME
(www.ellislandfarm.co.uk; Auldgirth; adult/child £2.50/free; ☺10am-5pm Mon-Sat, 2-5pm Sun Apr-Sep, 10am-5pm Tue-Sat Oct-Mar) If you're not Burnsed out, you could head 6 miles northwest of town and visit the farm he leased. It still preserves some original features from when he and his family lived here, and there's a small exhibition. It's signposted off the A76 to Kilmarnock.

Dumfries

🛏 Sleeping

Merlin B&B ££
(☎01387-261002; 2 Kenmure Tce; r per person £30; ☏) Beautifully located on the riverbank across a pedestrian bridge from the centre, this is a top place to hole up in Dumfries.

So much work goes on behind the scenes here that it seems effortless: numerous small details and a friendly welcome make this a very impressive set-up. Rooms share a bathroom, and have super-comfy beds; the breakfast table is also quite a sight.

Ferintosh Guest House B&B ££
(☎01387-252262; www.ferintosh.net; 30 Lovers Walk; s £35, d £54-60; ☜) A Victorian villa, opposite the train station, Ferintosh has sumptuous rooms done in individual themes. The whisky room is our fave – no matter which you choose, there'll probably be a free dram awaiting you on arrival. These people have the right attitude towards hospitality. The owner's original artwork complements the decor and mountain bikers are welcomed with a shed out the back for bikes.

Torbay Lodge B&B ££
(☎01387-253922; www.torbaylodge.co.uk; 31 Lovers Walk; s/d £28/54; P☜) This high-standard guesthouse has beautifully presented bedrooms with generously sized en suites (and a single without); the good vibe is topped off with excellent breakfast.

✗ Eating & Drinking

Cavens Arms PUB £
(20 Buccleuch St; mains £7-12; ☺lunch & dinner Tue-Sun) Engaging staff, nine real ales on tap, and a warm contented buzz make this a legendary Dumfries pub. Generous portions of typical pub nosh backed up by a long list of more adventurous daily specials make it one of the town's most enjoyable places to eat too. If you were going to move to Dumfries, you'd make sure you were within a block or two of here.

Hullabaloo CAFE, RESTAURANT ££
(☎01387-259679; www.hullabaloorestaurant.co.uk; Mill Rd; lunch mains £5-9, dinner mains £10-15; ☺lunch daily, dinner Tue-Sat) At weekends locals flock to this contemporary restaurant at the Robert Burns Centre. For lunch there's wraps, melts and ciabattas, but come dinner time it's inventive angles on traditional creations – with imaginative fish dishes perhaps best on show.

One Bank St CAFE £
(1 Bank St; lunch £3-7; ☺10am-4pm Mon-Sat) This wee room upstairs around the corner from the tourist office (look for the sign on the street) does gourmet rolls and baked potatoes, but gets even more adventurous

with wraps like roast veg and humus or smoked chicken and raspberry.

Globe Inn PUB
(www.globeinndumfries.co.uk; 56 High St) A traditional, rickety old nook-and-cranny pub down a narrow wynd off the main pedestrian drag, this was reputedly Burns' favourite watering hole, and scene of one of his numerous seductions. It's got a great atmosphere created by its welcoming locals and staff as much as the numerous pictures of the 'ploughman poet' himself.

ℹ Information

Ewart library (☎01387-253820; Catherine St; ☺9.15am-7.30pm Mon-Wed & Fri, 9.15am-5pm Thu & Sat; @) Free internet access.

Tourist office (☎01387-245550; www.visit dumfriesandgalloway.co.uk; 64 Whitesands; ☺9.30am-5pm Mon-Sat, plus Sun Jul–mid-Oct)

ℹ Getting There & Away

Bus

Local buses run regularly to Kirkcudbright (one hour, roughly hourly Monday to Saturday, six on Sunday) and towns along the A75 to Stranraer (£7.40, 2¼ hours, eight daily Monday to Saturday, three on Sunday).

Bus 100/101 runs to/from Edinburgh (£7, 2¾ hours, four to seven daily), via Moffat and Biggar.

Train

There are trains between Carlisle and Dumfries (£8.60, 35 minutes, every hour or two Monday to Saturday), and direct trains between Dumfries and Glasgow (£12.90, 1¾ hours, eight daily Monday to Saturday); there's a reduced service on Sunday.

South of Dumfries

CAERLAVEROCK

The ruins of **Caerlaverock Castle** (HS; www.historic-scotland.gov.uk; adult/child £5.20/3.10; ☺9.30am-5.30pm Apr-Sep, 9.30am-4.30pm Oct-Mar), by Glencaple on a beautiful stretch of the Solway coast, are among the loveliest in Britain. Surrounded by a moat, lawns and stands of trees, the unusual pink-stoned triangular castle looks impregnable. In fact, it fell several times, most famously when it was attacked in 1300 by Edward I: the siege became the subject of an epic poem, 'The Siege of Caerlaverock'. The current castle dates from the late 13th century but, once defensive purposes were no longer a design necessity, it was refitted as a luxurious Scottish Renaissance mansion house in 1634. Ironically, the rampaging Covenanter militia sacked it a few years later. With nooks and crannies to explore, passageways and remnants of fireplaces, this castle is great for the whole family.

It's worth combining a visit to the castle with one to **Caerlaverock Wetland Centre** (www.wwt.org.uk; adult/child £6.70/3.30; ☺10am-5pm), a mile east. It protects 546 hectares of salt marsh and mud flats, the habitat for numerous birds, including barnacle geese. There's free, daily wildlife safaris with experienced rangers and a coffee shop that serves organic food.

From Dumfries, bus D6A runs several times a day (just twice on Sunday) to Caerlaverock Castle. By car take the B725 south.

RUTHWELL CROSS

A couple of miles beyond Caerlaverock, in the hamlet of Ruthwell, the **church** (☎0131-550 7612; ☺ring in advance to visit) holds one of Europe's most important early Christian monuments. The 6m-high 7th-century Ruthwell Cross is carved top to bottom in New Testament scenes and is inscribed with a poem called 'The Dream of the Rood'; written in a Saxon runic alphabet, it's considered one of the earliest examples of English-language literature.

Bus 79 running between Dumfries and Carlisle stops in Ruthwell.

NEW ABBEY

The small, picturesque village of New Abbey lies 7 miles south of Dumfries and contains the remains of the 13th-century Cistercian **Sweetheart Abbey** (HS; www.historic-scotland.gov.uk; adult/child £3/1.80; ☺9.30am-5.30pm Apr-Sep, to 4.30pm Oct, 9.30am-4.30pm Sat-Wed Nov-Mar). The shattered, red-sandstone remnants of the abbey are impressive and stand in stark contrast to the manicured lawns surrounding them. The abbey, the last of the major monasteries to be established in Scotland, was founded by Devorgilla of Galloway in 1273 in honour of her dead husband John Balliol (with whom she had founded Balliol College, Oxford). On his death, she had his heart embalmed and carried it with her until she died 22 years later. She and the heart were buried by the altar – hence the name.

On the edge of New Abbey, a historic house holds the **National Museum of Costume** (www.nms.ac.uk; adult/child £4/free; ☺10am-5pm Apr-Oct), which gives an over-view of what Scots have worn from Victorian times up to the postwar years. There are also picturesque gardens here.

Kids complaining about all the castles, historic sights and Robert Burns? Pack up the clan and get down to **Mabie Farm Park** (www.mabiefarmpark.co.uk; adult/child/family £5.50/5/20; ☺10am-5pm daily Apr-Oct, Sat & Sun Feb-Mar), between Dumfries and New Abbey off the A710. There are plenty of animals and activities for kids, including petting and feeding sessions, donkey rides, go-karting, slides, a soft play area, picnic areas...the list goes on – put a full day aside.

If you've got a range of ages, you could split up and take the older ones to the adjacent **Mabie Forest Park** (☎01387-270275; www.7stanes.gov.uk) which is one of the 7stanes mountain bike hubs (see p175. There are nearly 40 miles of trails for all levels; bike hire available.

Staying in New Abbey is a good alternative to Dumfries and the **Abbey Arms** (☎01387-850489; www.abbeyarmshotel.com; The Square; s/d £35/60) is a fine old inn with simple but clean and comfy rooms, and a good dose of homespun hospitality. The food is home cooked (mains £7 to £9) and a couple of dishes – Greek spanakopita and lamb rogan josh – deviate from the pub classics.

To get to New Abbey, take Bus 372 from Dumfries.

Annandale & Eskdale

These valleys, in Dumfries & Galloway's east, form part of two major routes that cut across Scotland's south. Away from the highways, the roads are quiet and there are some interesting places to visit, especially if you're looking to break a road trip.

GRETNA & GRETNA GREEN
POP 2705

Firmly on the coach tour circuit for its romantic associations (see the boxed text, p170), Gretna Green still hosts some 4000 weddings yearly. It's on the outskirts of the town of Gretna, just across the river from Cumbria in England, not far from Carlisle.

The touristy **Old Blacksmith's Shop** (www.gretnagreen.com; Gretna Green; adult/child £3.50/free; ☺9am-5pm Sep-Jun, to 7pm Jul-Aug) has an exhibition on Gretna Green's history, a sculpture park and a coach museum (there's even an anvil marriage room!).

TYING THE KNOT IN GRETNA GREEN

From the mid-18th century, eloping couples south of the border realised that under Scottish law people could (and still can) tie the knot at the age of 16 without parental consent (in England and Wales the legal age was 21; it's now 18). Gretna Green's location close to the border made it the most popular venue.

At one time anyone could perform a legal marriage ceremony, but in Gretna Green it was usually the local blacksmith, who became known as the 'Anvil Priest'. In 1940 the 'anvil weddings' were outlawed, but eloping couples still got married in the church or registry office.

Today many people take or even reaffirm their marriage vows in the village. If you want to get married over the famous anvil in the Old Blacksmith's Shop at Gretna Green, check out Gretna Green Weddings (www.gretnaweddings.com).

Smith's (☎01461-337007; www.smithsgretnagreen.co.uk; Gretna Green; s/d £115/135; P⊙⊛) is a large contemporary hotel with a reader-recommended **restaurant** (mains £12-19). Though the blocky exterior won't delight everybody, the interior is much more stylish. The rooms are decorated in a chic, restrained style with king-sized beds. Various grades are available; you'll get much cheaper rates booking online.

The very helpful **tourist office** (☎01461-337834; gretnatic@visitscotland.com; Gretna Gateway, Gretna; ⊙10am-6pm Apr-Sep, 10am-4.30pm Nov-Mar) is a good first stop for information on Scotland if you're driving across from England.

Bus 79 between Dumfries (1 hour) and Carlisle (35 minutes) stops in Gretna (hourly Monday to Saturday, every two hours Sunday). Trains also run from Gretna Green to Dumfries and Carlisle.

MOFFAT
POP 2135

Moffat lies in wild, hilly country near the upper reaches of Annandale. It's really enjoyed by the older brigade and is a popular tourist-coach spot. The former spa town is a centre for the local wool industry, symbolised by the bronze ram statue on High St.

At **Moffat Woollen Mill** (www.ewm-store.co.uk), near the tourist office, you can see a working weaving exhibition. This place is a retail bonanza – if that's your thing, you're going to love it here.

The flower-decked **Buchan Guest House** (☎01683-220378; www.buchanguesthouse.co.uk; Beechgrove; s/d £37/66; P⊛) is in a quiet street just a short walk north of the town centre. Room No 5 is a good choice, as it has a lovely outlook over nearby fields.

TOP CHOICE **Groom's Cottage** (☎01683-220049; Beattock Rd; d £60; P) is a beautifully presented, cosy self-contained nook with everything you could want for a comfortable stay. There are self-catering facilities (but breakfast is included). It has good privacy from the owner's residence, views over green fields and even an orthopaedic bed. It's a stylish job and very reasonably priced – weekly deals are available too. Look for 'The Lodge' sign coming in from the M74 – it's on your right before you hit the town centre. This option is ideally suited to couples.

The **tourist office** (☎01683-220620; Churchgate; ⊙10am-4pm Mon-Sat Apr-Oct) is also open Sunday in summer.

There are several daily buses to Edinburgh, Glasgow and Dumfries (buses 100 and 114). For Gretna, change at Lockerbie.

LANGHOLM
POP 2311

The waters of three rivers – the Esk, Ewes and Wauchope – meet at Langholm, a gracious old town at the centre of Scotland's tweed industry. Most people come for fishing and walking in the surrounding moors and woodlands; check out the **Langholm Walks website** (www.langholmwalks.co.uk) for details.

Border House (☎013873-80376; www.border-house.co.uk; High St; s/d £30/60; P) is an excellent central accommodation option with large rooms (the downstairs double in particular), a lovely hostess and big sink-in-and-smile beds. You may get fresh handmade chocolates if a batch has just been made!

Bus 112 has up to five daily connections with **Eskdalemuir** (no Sunday service). This goes on to Lockerbie, from where you can get buses to other destinations.

ESKDALEMUIR

Surrounded by wooded hills, Eskdalemuir is a remote settlement 13 miles northwest of Langholm. About 1.5 miles further north is the **Samye Ling Tibetan Centre** (☑013873-73232; www.samyeling.org; camping/dm/s/d incl full board £15/23/36/56; **P**), the first Tibetan Buddhist monastery built in the West (1968). The colourful prayer flags and the red and gold of the temple itself are a striking contrast to the stark grey and green landscape. You can visit the centre during the day (donation suggested, cafe on site), or stay overnight in simple accommodation which includes full vegetarian board. There are also meditation courses and weekend workshops available.

Bus 112 from Langholm/Lockerbie stops at the centre.

Castle Douglas & Around

POP 3671

Castle Douglas attracts a lot of day-trippers but hasn't been 'spruced up' for tourism. It's an open, attractive, well-cared-for town. There are some remarkably beautiful areas close to the centre, such as the small Carlingwark Loch. The town was laid out in the 18th century by Sir William Douglas, who had made a fortune in the Americas.

◉ Sights & Activities

Threave Castle   CASTLE
(HS; www.historic-scotland.gov.uk; adult/child incl ferry £4.20/2.50; ☉9.30am-5pm Apr-Sep) Two miles further west of Castle Douglas, Threave Castle is an impressive tower on a small island in the River Dee. Built in the late 14th century, it became a principal stronghold of the Black Douglases. It's now basically a shell, having been badly damaged by the Covenanters in the 1640s, but it's a romantic ruin nonetheless.

It's a 15-minute walk from the car park to the ferry landing, where you ring a bell for the custodian to take you across to the island in a small boat.

Loch Ken   LOCH, WATER SPORTS
Stretching for 9 miles northwest of Castle Douglas between the A713 and A762, Loch Ken is a popular outdoor recreational area. The range of water sports includes windsurfing, sailing, canoeing, power-boating and kayaking. Back on land, off-road buggies can also be hired. **Galloway Activity Centre** (☑01644-420626; www.lochken.co.uk;

☒), on the eastern bank north of Parton village, runs a wide range of activities, and also provides equipment and accommodation. Activities cost £16/26/38 for 1½/three/six hours. There are also walking trails and a rich variety of bird life. The Royal Society for the Protection of Birds (RSPB) has a **nature reserve** (www.rspb.org.uk) on the western bank, north of Glenlochar.

Sulwath Brewery   BREWERY
(www.sulwathbrewers.co.uk; 209 King St; adult/child £4/free; ☉10am-5pm Mon-Sat) You can see traditional brewing processes at Sulwath Brewery. Admission includes a half-pint of Galloway real ale (tea or coffee is also available). Recommended is the Criffel, an original pale ale, and Knockendoch, a dark brew with a delicious taste of roasted malt.

🛏 Sleeping & Eating

Douglas House   B&B ££
(☑01556-503262; www.douglas-house.com; 63 Queen St; s/d £38/78; ☎) A keen designer's eye is obviously present at this luxurious, attractively renovated place. Big beautiful bathrooms complement the light, stylish chambers, which include flatscreen digital TVs with inbuilt DVD player. The two upstairs doubles are the best, although the downstairs double is huge and has a king-size bed – you could sleep four in it...if you're into that kinda thing.

WORTH A TRIP

WANLOCKHEAD

'Lead mining': even the phrase has a sort of dulling effect on the brain, and you'd think it'd be a tough ask to make the subject interesting. But at the **Museum of Lead Mining** (www.leadminingmuseum.co.uk; adult/child £6.25/4.50; ☉11am-4.30pm Apr-Oct) at little Wanlockhead, off the motorway northwest of Moffat, they pull it off. It's apparently Scotland's highest village, and not necessarily a place you'd have chosen for quality of life back in the day. The tour of the place is fascinating, and family-friendly, taking in a real mine, miners' cottages, a unique library, and a display on lead-mining and other minerals. In summer, they also run gold-panning activities (£3).

Bus 224 heads to Wanlockhead from Dumfries.

Douglas Arms Hotel HOTEL ££

(☎01556-502231; www.douglasarmshotel.com; 206 King St; s/d dinner, bed & breakfast £55/80; 🛜) Smack bang in the middle of town, Douglas Arms was originally a coaching inn, but these days all the mod cons comfort the weary traveller. If you want to splash out, go for the honeymoon suite, which has a four-poster bed, jacuzzi and views over the main drag from a collage of windows. The lively bar serves scrumptious food (bar meals £8 to £12), although the atmosphere is a bit staid. The steak-and-ale pie made with Galloway beef is recommended.

Craig B&B ££

(☎01556-504840; www.thecraigcastledouglas.co.uk; 44 Abercromby Rd; s/d £33/60; P) This solid old property is a fine B&B with a conscientious owner, large rooms and fresh fruit served up for breakfast. It's old-fashioned hospitality – genuine and very comfortable. Would suit older visitors. It's on the edge of town on the road to New Galloway.

Lochside Caravan & Camping Site CAMPING £

(☎01556-502949; www.dumgal.gov.uk/caravanandcamping; Lochside Park; tent sites £15.50) Very central campsite attractively situated beside Carlingwark Loch; there's plenty of grass and fine trees providing shade.

Galloway Activity Centre HOSTEL, CAMPING £

(☎01644-420626; www.lochken.co.uk; Loch Ken; dm £15, tent sites £6 per person) Year-round dormitory accommodation and camping at this lakeside spot 10 miles north of Castle Douglas.

Deli 173 TAKEAWAY £

(173 King St; baguette or panini £2.80; ⏲8am-4pm Mon-Sat) For a truly awesome baguette drop into this fine-foods deli. We recommend 'the Godfather'.

Simply Delicious CAFE £

(134 King St; snacks £2-5; ⏲breakfast & lunch) Great cafe serving all-day brekky (£6.50), luxury melts and freshly ground coffee.

❶ Information

Library (☎502643; King St; ⏲10am-7.30pm Mon-Wed & Fri, 10am-5pm Thu & Sat; @) Free internet access.

Tourist office (☎01556-502611; King St; ⏲10am-5pm Mon-Sat Apr-Oct) In a small park on King St. Also open Sundays in July and August.

❶ Getting There & Away

Buses 501 and 502 pass through Castle Douglas roughly hourly en route to Dumfries (45 minutes) and Kirkcudbright (20 minutes). Bus 520 along the A713 connects Castle Douglas with New Galloway (30 minutes, six daily Monday to Saturday, one Sunday) and Ayr (£6.80, 2¼ hours, two or three daily Monday to Saturday, one Sunday).

Kirkcudbright

POP 3447

Kirkcudbright (kirk-*coo*-bree), with its dignified streets of 17th- and 18th-century merchants' houses and its appealing harbour, is the ideal base from which to explore the south coast. This delightful town has one of the most beautifully restored High Streets in Dumfries & Galloway. Look out for the nook-and-cranny wynds in the elbow of High St. With its architecture and setting, it's easy to see why Kirkcudbright has been an artists' colony since the late 19th century.

◉ Sights & Activities

Kirkcudbright is a charming town for a wander, dropping into galleries as you go; it won't be long before you stumble across its main sights. In June, the town's jazz festival (www.kircudbrightjazzfestival.co.uk) is four days of swing, trad, and dixie.

MacLellan's Castle CASTLE

(HS; www.historic-scotland.gov.uk; Castle St; adult/child £3.70/2.20; ⏲9.30am-5.30pm Apr-Sep) Near the harbour, this is a large, atmospheric ruin built in 1577 by Thomas MacLellan, then provost of Kirkcudbright, as his town residence. Inside look for the 'lairds' lug', a 16th-century hidey-hole designed for the laird to eavesdrop on his guests.

FREE Tolbooth Art Centre EXHIBITION SPACE

(High St; ⏲11am-4pm Mon-Sat, 2-5pm Sun) As well as catering for today's local artists, this centre has an exhibition on the history of the town's artistic development. The place is as interesting for the building itself as for the artistic works on display. It's one of the oldest and best-preserved tollbooths in Scotland and interpretative signboards reveal its past. Extended hours in summer.

Broughton House GALLERY

(NTS; www.nts.org.uk; 12 High St; adult/child £5.50/4.50; ⏲noon-5pm Apr-Oct) The 18th-century Broughton House displays paintings by EA Hornel (he lived and worked here), one of the Glasgow Boys group of painters (p111). Behind the house is a lovely Japanese-style garden (also open in February and March). The library with its wood panelling and stone carvings is probably the most impressive room.

Galloway Wildlife Conservation Park zoo (www.gallowaywildlife.co.uk; Lochfergus Plantation; adult/child £6/4; ⊙10am-dusk Feb-Nov) A mile from Kirkcudbright on the B727, this is an easy walk from town, and you'll see red pandas, wolves, monkeys, kangaroos, Scottish wildcats and many more creatures in a beautiful setting. An important role of the park is the conservation of rare and threatened species.

🛏 Sleeping & Eating

Kirkcudbright has a swathe of good B&Bs.

TOP CHOICE **Selkirk Arms Hotel** HOTEL ££
(☑01557-330402; www.selkirkarmshotel .co.uk; High St; s/d/superior d £82/116/136; P@🛜🍴) What a haven of good hospitality this is. Superior rooms are excellent – wood furnishings and views over the back garden give them a rustic appeal. Try No 20. The bistro (mains £10-18) serves top pub nosh – the fish and chips come wrapped in the hotel newsletter – and the restaurant, Artistas (2-course dinner £23), serves more refined but equally tasty fare. Staff are happy to be there, and you will be too.

Castle Restaurant RESTAURANT ££
(☑01557-330569; www.thecastlerestaurant.net; 5 Castle St; mains £12-14; ⊙lunch Thu-Sun, dinner Mon-Sat; 🍴) The Castle Restaurant is the best place to eat in town and uses organic produce where possible. It covers a few bases with chicken, beef and seafood dishes on offer as well as tempting morsels for vegetarians. Lunch mains are lighter and cheaper, and there's a good-value evening two-course offer for £16.

Gordon House Hotel HOTEL ££
(☑01557-330670; www.gordon-house-hotel.co. uk; 116 High St; s/d/f £40/70/80; 🛜) The small, laid-back hotel rooms are in good shape, but they vary a bit, so have a look at a few. No 2 is probably the best of the doubles. You can dine in the restaurant (mains £12 to £19), which serves posh nosh like pan-seared breast of guinea fowl with tarragon and grain mustard, or the lounge bar, and there's a beer garden for sunny afternoons.

Greengate B&B ££
(☑01557-331895; www.thegreengate.co.uk; 46 High St; s/d £50/70; 🛜) The artistically inclined should snap up the one double room in this lovely place, with both historic and current painterly connections.

Number One B&B ££
(☑01557-330540; www.number1bedandbreak fast.co.uk; 1 Castle Gdns; d £75; 🛜) Right by the castle, this tasteful spot offers high-end B&B with solicitous hosts who prepare great breakfasts and dinners and are happy to advise about walks in the area.

Anchorlee B&B ££
(☑01557-330197; www.anchorlee.co.uk; 95 St Mary St; s/d £55/75; P🛜) Top-floor rooms are a bit frilly but very spacious and neat as a pin. Very friendly.

Silvercraigs Caravan & Camping Site CAMPING £
(☑01557-330123; silvercraigs.caravan@dumgal. gov.uk; Silvercraigs Rd; sites for up to 2 £15.50; ⊙Mar-Oct; P) There are brilliant views from this campground; you feel like you're sleeping on top of the town. Great stargazing on clear nights. Good facilities, too, including a laundry.

ℹ Information

Check out www.kirkcudbright.co.uk and www. artiststown.org.uk for heaps of information on the town.

Tourist office (☑01557-330494; kirkcudbright tic@visitscotland.com; Harbour Sq; ⊙daily mid-Feb-Nov) Handy office with useful brochures detailing walks and road tours in the surrounding district.

ℹ Getting There & Away

Kirkcudbright is 28 miles southwest of Dumfries. Buses 501 and 505 run hourly to Dumfries (one hour) via Castle Douglas and Dalbeattie respectively. Change at Gatehouse of Fleet for Stranraer.

Gatehouse of Fleet
POP 892

Gatehouse of Fleet is an attractive little town stretched along a sloping main street, in the middle of which sits an unusual castellated clock tower. The town lies on the banks of the Water of Fleet, completely off the beaten track, and is surrounded by partly wooded hills.

In the centre of town, **Mill on the Fleet Visitor Centre** (www.millonthefleet.co.uk; High

St; admission free; ⊙10am-5pm Apr-Oct), in a converted 18th-century cotton mill, traces the history of the local industry. The town was originally planned as workers' accommodation. There's also tourist information and a cafe here.

One mile southwest on the A75, the well-preserved **Cardoness Castle** (HS; www.historic-scotland.gov.uk; adult/child £3.70/2.20; ⊙9.30am-5.30pm daily Apr-Sep, closed Thu & Fri Oct, to 4.30pm Sat & Sun Nov-Mar) was the home of the McCulloch clan. It's a classic 15th-century tower house with great views from the top.

Bobbin Guest House (☎01557-814229; bobbinguesthouse@sky.com; 36 High St; s/d £30/60; 🖳), situated right in the middle of town, is a home-from-home with a variety of spacious, well-appointed rooms with good en suite bathrooms.

The friendly, family-run **Bank of Fleet Hotel** (☎01557-814302; www.bankoffleet.co.uk; 47 High St; s/d £33/65; 🐾) has bright rooms with a blue decor that gives them a cool, contemporary feel. Live entertainment's on offer, plus good bar meals (mains £8 to £11) – try the grilled Galloway trout.

Buses X75 and 500 between Dumfries (one hour) and Stranraer (1¼ hours) stop here eight times daily (three on Sunday).

Around Gatehouse

Ideal for families, **Cream o' Galloway** (☎01557-815222; www.creamogalloway.co.uk; Rainton; visitor centre adult/child £2/4; incl all rides £10; ⊙10am-5pm mid-Mar–Oct, to 6pm Jul & Aug) has taken off big time. It offers a plethora of activities and events at the home of that delicious ice cream you'll see around the region. There are 4 miles of nature trails, an adventure playground for all ages, a 3-D maze, wildlife-watching, a farm to explore and plenty of ice cream to taste. Daily events include a farm tour and ice cream tasting, and there are regular special happenings. It's about 4 miles from Gatehouse off the A75 – signposted all the way. You can also hire bikes from here.

Galloway Forest Park

South and northwest of the small town of New Galloway is 300-sq-mile Galloway Forest Park, with numerous lochs and great whale-backed, heather- and pine-covered mountains. The highest point is **Merrick** (843m). The park is criss-crossed by some superb signposted walking trails, from gentle strolls to long-distance paths, including the **Southern Upland Way** (see the boxed text, p138). The park is very family focused; look out for the booklet of annual events, and the park newspaper, *The Galloway Ranger,* in tourist offices.

The park is also great for **stargazing**; it's been named a Dark Sky Park by the International Dark-Sky Association.

The 19-mile A712 (Queen's Way) between New Galloway and Newton Stewart slices through the southern section of the park.

On the shore of Clatteringshaws Loch, 6 miles west of New Galloway, is **Clatteringshaws Visitor Centre** (☎information 01671-402420; www.forestry.gov.uk/scotland; car-park fee £2; ⊙10.30am-4.30pm mid-Mar–Oct, to 5.30pm Jul & Aug), with an exhibition on the area's flora and fauna. Pick up a copy of the *Galloway Red Kite Trail* leaflet here, which details a circular route through impressive scenery that offers a good chance to spot one of these majestic reintroduced birds. From the visitor centre you can walk to a replica of a Romano-British homestead, and to Bruce's Stone, where Robert the Bruce is said to have rested after defeating the English at the Battle of Rapploch Moss (1307).

About a mile west of Clatteringshaws, **Raiders Rd** is a 10-mile drive through the forest with various picnic spots, child-friendly activities, and short walks marked along the way. It costs £2 per vehicle; drive slowly as there's plenty of wildlife about.

Further west is the **Galloway Red Deer Range** where you can observe Britain's largest land-based beast. During rutting season in autumn it's a bit like watching a bullfight as snorting, charging stags compete for the harem. During summer there are guided **ranger-led walks** (adult/child £3.50/2.50).

Walkers and cyclists head for **Glentrool** in the park's west, accessed by the forest road east from Bargrennan off the A714, north of Newton Stewart. Located just over a mile from Bargrennan is the **Glentrool Visitor Centre** (⊙10.30am-4.30pm mid-Mar–Oct, to 5.30pm Jul & Aug), which stocks information on activities, including mountain biking, in the area. There is a coffee shop with snacks and an opportunity to rest those weary legs. The road then winds and

MOUNTAIN-BIKING HEAVEN

A brilliant way to experience southern Scotland's forests is by pedal power. The **7stanes** (stones) are seven mountain-biking centres around the region with trails through some of the finest forest scenery you'll find in the country. **Glentrool** is one of these centres and the Blue Route here is 5.6 miles in length and a lovely ride climbing up to Green Torr Ridge overlooking Loch Trool. If you've more serious intentions, the Big Country Route is 36 miles of challenging ascents and descents that afford magnificent views of the Galloway Forest. It takes a full day and is not for wimps.

Another of the trailheads is at **Kirroughtree Visitor Centre**, 3 miles southeast of Newton Stewart. This offers plenty of singletrack at four different skill levels. You can hire bikes at both of these places (www.thebreakpad.com). For more information on routes see www.7stanes.gov.uk.

climbs up to Loch Trool, where there are magnificent views.

St John's Town of Dalry

St John's Town of Dalry is a charming village, hugging the hillside about 3 miles north of New Galloway on the A713. It's on the Water of Ken and gives access to the Southern Upland Way. It's a good base for Galloway Forest Park.

Lodgings ($\square$01644-430015; www.thelodgings.co.uk; St John's Town of Dalry; r per person £29.50) has just two very good rooms, one sleeping three and the other a family room sleeping four. Its advantage over other B&Bs here is privacy: the owners live offsite.

Vine-engulfed **Lochinvar Hotel** ($\square$01644-430107; www.lochinvarhotel.co.uk; St John's Town of Dalry; s/d £45/70, without bathroom £40/60; $\boxed{P}$), an old hunting lodge built in the 1750s with a stately interior, is a fine place to stay, or pop by for a pint. Front-facing rooms have the best views.

Bus 521 runs once or twice daily (except Sunday) to Dumfries (55 minutes). Bus 520/S2 connects New Galloway with Castle Douglas (30 minutes, three daily Monday to

Saturday, one Sunday); one to three services continue north to Ayr (1¼ to 1¾ hours).

175

Newton Stewart

POP 3600

On the banks of the sparkling River Cree, Newton Stewart is at the heart of some beautiful countryside, and is popular with hikers and anglers. On the eastern bank, across the bridge, is the older and smaller settlement of **Minnigaff**. With excellent accommodation and eating options, this makes a tempting base for exploring the Galloway Forest Park.

For advice on landing the big one, fishing gear and permits, drop into **Galloway Angling Centre** ($\square$01671-401333; 1 Queen St). Also see the very useful site at www.fishgalloway.co.uk.

🛏 Sleeping & Eating

Creebridge House Hotel   HOTEL **££**
($\square$01671-402121; www.creebridge.co.uk; Minnigaff; s/d/superior d £60/110/120; $\boxed{P}\boxed{\widehat{\ast}}\boxed{\#}$) This is a magnificent refurbished 18th-century mansion built for the Earl of Galloway. A maze inside, it has tastefully decorated rooms with modern furnishings and loads of character. Try to get a room overlooking the garden (No 7 is a good one). There's also good food here (mains £10 to £15).

Galloway Arms Hotel   HOTEL **££**
($\square$01671-402653; www.gallowayarmshotel.com; 54 Victoria St, Newton Stewart; s/d £39/75; $\boxed{P}\boxed{\widehat{\ast}}$) A traditional refurbished hotel offering excellent-value accommodation, with good-sized, well-furnished rooms and sparkling renovated en suites. Try No 11 if you're after a double. The hotel is walker- and cyclist-friendly, with bike storage and a drying room, while the bar and restaurant churn out excellent local fare: try the pork-and-apple burger.

Flowerbank Guest House   B&B **££**
($\square$01671-402629; www.flowerbankgh.com; Millcroft Rd, Minnigaff; s/d £30/60; $\boxed{P}$) This dignified 18th-century house is set in a magnificent landscaped garden on the banks of the River Cree. The two elegantly furnished rooms at the front of the house are slightly more expensive, but are spacious and have lovely garden views. Two-course dinners are £15.

Minnigaff Youth Hostel   HOSTEL **£**
(SYHA; $\square$01671-402211; www.syha.org.uk; Minnigaff; dm £15.25; $\odot$Apr-Sep; $\boxed{P}$) This converted

school is a well-equipped hostel with eight-bed dorms in a tranquil spot 800m north of the bridge on the eastern bank. Although it's popular with outdoor enthusiasts, you may just about have the place to yourself. Expect a lockout until 5pm.

Café Cree CAFE £
(www.cafecree.co.uk; 48 Victoria St, Newton Stewart; mains £6-10; ⊙lunch & dinner; ⌘) On the main street, this most hospitable place makes a real effort to source produce locally, and creates wraps, salads, and other dishes vibrant with flavour with it. To try the best of the region, go for a 'local hero platter', with smoked salmon, cheese and other goodies. They'll even spoil your canine companions.

ⓘ Information
Tourist office (⌕01671-402431; www.visit dumfriesandgalloway.com; Dashwood Sq; ⊙10am-4pm Mon-Sat Apr-Oct)

ⓘ Getting There & Away
Buses stop in Newton Stewart (Dashwood Sq) on their way to Stranraer (45 minutes) and Dumfries (1½ hours); both served several times daily. Frequent buses also run south to the Isle of Whithorn.

The Machars

South of Newton Stewart, the Galloway Hills give way to the softly rolling pastures of the triangular peninsula known as the Machars. The south has many early Christian sites and the loping 25-mile Pilgrims Way.

Bus 415 runs every hour or two between Newton Stewart and the Isle of Whithorn (one hour) via Wigtown (15 minutes).

WIGTOWN
POP 987

Wigtown is a huge success story. Economically run down for many years, the town's revival began in 1998 when it became Scotland's National Book Town. Today 24 bookshops offer the widest selection of books in Scotland and give book enthusiasts the opportunity to get lost here for days. A major **book festival** (www.wigtownbookfestival.com) is held here in late September.

The **Bookshop** (www.the-bookshop.com; 17 North Main St; ⊙9am-5pm Mon-Sat) claims to be Scotland's largest secondhand bookshop, and has a great collection of Scottish

and regional titles. **ReadingLasses Bookshop Café** (www.reading-lasses.com; 17 South Main St; ⊙10am-5pm Mon-Sat, also noon-5pm Sun May-Oct) sells caffeine to prolong your reading time and does a cracking smoked salmon salad sourced locally. It specialises in books on the social sciences and women's studies.

Folk in this town love their resident ospreys. It's a good conversation starter and if you'd like to learn a bit more about the majestic birds and see a live CCTV link to a nearby nest, drop by the **Wigtown County Buildings** (Market Sq; admission free; ⊙10am-5pm Mon, Thu & Sat, 10am-7.30pm Tue, Wed & Fri, 2-5pm Sun) for its osprey exhibition.

Browsing books can be thirsty work, so it's fortunate that **Bladnoch Distillery** (⌕01988-402605; www.bladnoch.co.uk; tours adult/child £3/free; ⊙9am-5pm Mon-Fri, also weekends Jul & Aug) is just a couple of miles away in the village of the same name. Ring for times of tours, which include a dram.

Four miles west of Wigtown, off the B733, the well-preserved recumbent **Torhouse Stone Circle** dates from the 2nd millennium BC.

Wow! That's what we said when we saw the rooms in **Hillcrest House** (⌕01988-402018; www.hillcrest-wigtown.co.uk; Station Rd; s £40, d £65-75; ⓟ⌾⌘). A noble stone building in a quiet part of town, the house features high ceilings and huge windows; spend the extra for one of the superior rooms, which have stupendous views overlooking rolling green hills and the sea beyond. This is all complemented by a ripper breakfast involving fresh local produce.

Pop into the bright dining room at **Café Rendezvous** (2 Agnew Cres; dishes £4-7; ⊙10am-4.30pm) for fresh, home-cooked paninis and filled crêpes. There's also decent coffee, gooey treats and outdoor seating.

WHITHORN
POP 867

Whithorn has a broad, attractive High St which is virtually closed at both ends (it was designed to enclose a medieval market). There are few facilities in town, but it's worth visiting because of its fascinating history.

In 397, while the Romans were still in Britain, St Ninian established the first Christian mission beyond Hadrian's Wall in Whithorn (pre-dating St Columba on Iona by 166 years). After his death, Whithorn Priory, the earliest recorded church in Scotland, was built to house his remains, and Whithorn became the focus of an important medieval pilgrimage.

Today the ruined priory is part of the excellent **Whithorn Trust Discovery Centre** (www.whithorn.com; 45 George St; adult/child £4.50/2.25; ☉10.30am-5pm Apr-Oct), which introduces you to the history of the place with a good audiovisual and very informative exhibition. There's ongoing archaeological investigation here, and you can see the site of earlier churches. There's also a museum with some fascinating early Christian stone sculptures, including the Latinus Stone (c 450), reputedly Scotland's oldest Christian artefact. Learn about the influences their carvers drew on, from around the British Isles and beyond.

ISLE OF WHITHORN
POP 400

The Isle of Whithorn, once an island but now linked to the mainland by a causeway, is a curious place with an attractive natural harbour and colourful houses. The roofless 13th-century **St Ninian's Chapel**, probably built for pilgrims who landed nearby, is on the windswept, evocative rocky headland. Around Burrow Head, to the southwest but accessed from a path off the A747 before you enter the Isle of Whithorn, is **St Ninian's Cave**, where the saint went to pray.

The 300-year-old **Dunbar House** (☎01988-500336; pompeylewis@aol.com; Tonderghie Rd; s/d £23/40) overlooking the harbour has two large, bright, perfect rooms that share a spotless bathroom. It's a bargain at this price, and cordially run. You can admire the view while tucking into your breakfast in the dining room.

The quayside **Steam Packet Inn** (☎01988-500334; www.steampacketinn.com; Harbour Row; r per person £35, without bathroom £30; ⊕) is a popular pub with real ales, scrumptious bar meals (mains £8 to £10), a snug bar and comfy lodgings. Try to get a room to the front of the building as they have lovely views over the little harbour (No 2 is a good one).

Stranraer
POP 10,851

The friendly but somewhat ramshackle ferry port of Stranraer is gradually seeing its boat services to Northern Ireland move up the road to Cairnryan. Though locals fear it'll turn their town into a ghostly shadow of what it was, it'll probably become a more pleasant place if the scheduled waterfront redevelopment takes place.

◎ Sights

FREE **St John's Castle** CASTLE
(George St; ☉10am-1pm & 2-5pm Mon-Sat Easter–mid-Sep) Worth a quick visit, St John's Castle was built in 1510 by the Adairs of Kihilt, a powerful local family. The old stone cells carry a distinctly musty smell. There are displays and a couple of videos that trace its history and, from the top of the castle, superb views of Loch Ryan and the ferries chugging out to Ireland.

FREE **Stranraer Museum** MUSEUM
(55 George St; ☉10am-5pm Mon-Fri, 10am-4pm Sat) This museum houses exhibits on local history and you can learn about Stranraer's polar explorers. The highlight is the carved stone pipe from Madagascar.

🛏 Sleeping & Eating

TOP CHOICE **Corsewall Lighthouse Hotel**
HOTEL £££
(☎01776-853220; www.lighthousehotel.co.uk; Kirkcolm; d incl 5-course dinner £150-250; ℗) It's just you and the cruel sea out here at this fabulously romantic 200-year-old lighthouse, right at the northwest tip of the peninsula, 13 miles northwest of Stranraer. On a sunny day, the water shimmers with light, and you can see Ireland, Kintyre, Arran, and Ailsa Craig. But when the wind and rain beat in, it's just great to be cosily holed up in the snug bar-restaurant or snuggling under the covers in your room. Rooms in the lighthouse building itself are attractive if necessarily compact; chalets are also available.

Balyett Farm Hostel & B&B B&B, HOSTEL £££
(☎01776-703395; www.balyettbb.co.uk; Cairnryan Rd; dm/s/d £20/45/65; ℗🐾) A mile north of town on the A77, Balyett provides tranquil accommodation in its tidy hostel section, which accommodates five people and has a kitchen/living area. The relaxed B&B at the nearby ivy-covered farmhouse could be the best deal in town. The rooms are light, bright and clean as a whistle. Room No 2 is our fave but all are beautifully furnished and come with lovely aspects over the surrounding country.

Ivy House B&B £££
(☎01776-704176; www.ivyplace.worldonline.co.uk; 3 Ivy Pl; s/d £30/56) This is a great guesthouse and does Scottish hospitality proud,

with excellent facilities, tidy en suite rooms and a smashing breakfast. Nothing is too much trouble for the hosts, who always have a smile for their guests. The room at the back overlooking the churchyard is particularly light and quiet.

North West Castle Hotel   HOTEL ££
(☎01776-704413; www.northwestcastle.co.uk; Port Rodie; s/d £85/130; [P][🏫][🛏]) Elegant and old fashioned, this is the most luxurious hotel in Stranraer and was formerly the home of Arctic explorer Sir John Ross. It's a little fussy, but even though an interior designer would tut-tut over the busy designs and clash of colours, the rooms are sumptuous indeed. Try to get a front-facing room for sea views. But here's the real puller: it was the first hotel in the world to have an indoor curling rink.

L'Aperitif   BISTRO ££
(☎01776-702991; London Rd; mains £11-14; ◷lunch & dinner Mon-Sat) Purgatory at dinnertime can look uncannily like Stranraer at times, so thank the powers that be for this cheerful local. It's definitely the town's best restaurant and is close to being its best pub too. Despite the name, dishes are more Italian than French, with great pastas alongside roasts, saltimbocca, and delicious appetisers featuring things like smoked salmon or greenlip mussels. Early dining (£13.50 for two courses) is lighter on the wallet.

Aird Donald Caravan Park   CAMPING £
(☎01776-702025; www.aird-donald.co.uk; London Rd; sites £12-13; [P]) The nearest tent-friendly campground is 1 mile east of the town centre. It has manicured lawns, plenty of trees and countless bunnies.

❶ Information
Library (North Strand St; ◷9.15am-7.30pm Mon-Wed & Fri, to 5pm Thu & Sat; [@]) Free internet access.

Tourist office (☎01776-702595; www.visitdumfriesandgalloway.com; stranraer@visitscotland.com; 28 Harbour St; ◷10am-4pm Mon-Sat) Efficient and friendly.

❶ Getting There & Away
Boat
Cairnryan is 6 miles north of Stranraer on the eastern side of Loch Ryan. Bus 358 runs frequently to Cairnryan (terminating at the post office). For a taxi to Cairnryan (around £8), contact **McLean's Taxis** (☎01776-703343; 21

North Strand St; ◷24hr), just up from the tourist office.

P&O (☎0871 66 44 777; www.poirishsea.com) Runs six to seven ferries a day from Cairnryan to Larne (Northern Ireland).

Stena Line (☎08447 70 70 70; www.stenaline.co.uk; passenger/car £27/100) Runs five to seven HSS and Superferries from Stranraer to Belfast. This service is set to move to Cairnryan in late 2011.

Bus
Scottish Citylink buses run to Glasgow (£16.20, 2½ hours, twice daily) and Edinburgh (£18.80, 3¾ hours, twice daily).

There are also several daily local buses to Kirkcudbright and the towns along the A75, such as Newton Stewart (45 minutes, at least hourly) and Dumfries (£7.40, 2¼ hours, nine daily Monday to Saturday, three on Sunday).

Train
First Scotrail runs to/from Glasgow (£19.30, 2¼ hours, two to seven trains daily); it may be necessary to change at Ayr.

Around Stranraer
Magnificent **Castle Kennedy Gardens** (www.castlekennedygardens.co.uk; Rephad; adult/child £4/1; ◷10am-5pm daily Apr-Sep, 10am-5pm Sat & Sun Feb-Mar & Oct), 3 miles east of Stranraer, are among the most famous in Scotland. They cover 30 hectares and are set on an isthmus between two lochs and two castles (Castle Kennedy, burnt in 1716, and Lochinch Castle, built in 1864). The landscaping was undertaken in 1730 by the Earl of Stair, who used unoccupied soldiers to do the work. Buses 430 (hourly) and 500 from Stranraer stop here.

Portpatrick
POP 585

Portpatrick is a charming port on the rugged west coast of the Rhinns of Galloway peninsula. Until the mid-19th century it was the main port for Northern Ireland but it's now a quiet holiday resort.

It is also a good base from which to explore the south of the peninsula, and it's the starting point for the **Southern Upland Way** (p138). You can follow part of the way to Stranraer (9 miles). It's a clifftop walk, followed by sections of farmland and heather moor. Start at the way's information shelter at the northern end of the harbour.

The walk is waymarked until 800m south of Stranraer, where you get the first good views of the village.

Harbour House Hotel (☎01776-810456; www.theharbourhousehotel.co.uk; 53 Main St; s/d £40/80) was formerly the customs house but is now a popular, solid old pub. Some of the tastefully furnished rooms have brilliant views over the harbour. The hotel is also a warm nook for a traditional bar meal (£8 to £10).

For a real dose of luxury, head 3 miles southeast to **Knockinaam Lodge** (☎01776-810471; www.knockinaamlodge.com; dinner, bed & breakfast for 2 £320-420; P🖘), a former hunting lodge on a little sandy bay. It's where Churchill plotted the endgame of WWII – you can stay in his suite – and it's a very romantic place to get away from it all. The excellent French-influenced cuisine (lunch/dinner £38/50) is backed up by a great range of wines and single malts.

See also the Corsewall Lighthouse Hotel (p177) for accommodation not too far away.

Buses 358 and 367 run to Stranraer (20 minutes, eight Monday to Saturday, three Sunday).

South of Portpatrick

From Portpatrick, the road south to the Mull of Galloway passes coastal scenery that includes rugged cliffs, tiny harbours and sandy beaches. Dairy cattle graze on the greenest grass you've ever seen, and the warm waters of the Gulf Stream give the peninsula the mildest climate in Scotland.

This mildness is demonstrated at **Logan Botanic Garden** (www.rbge.org.uk/logan; adult/child £5/1; ☺10am-4pm Sun Feb, 10am-5pm daily Mar & Oct, 10am-6pm daily Apr-Sep), a mile north of Port Logan, where an array of subtropical flora includes tree ferns and cabbage palms. The garden is an outpost of the Royal Botanic Garden in Edinburgh. Port Logan itself is a sleepy place with a decent pub and excellent sandy beach.

Further south, **Drummore** is a fishing village on the east coast. From here it's another 5 miles to the **Mull of Galloway**, Scotland's most southerly point. It's a spectacular spot, with windswept green grass and views of Scotland, England, 19 miles south to the Isle of Man and 26 miles west to Northern Ireland. The 26m-high **lighthouse** (adult/child £2/1; ☺10am-4pm Sat & Sun Easter-Oct, plus Mon Jul & Aug) here was built by Robert Stevenson, grandfather of the writer, in 1826. You can learn more about the Stevenson clan of lighthouse builders in the small **exhibition** (adult/child £2/1; ☺10am-4pm) at the lighthouse's base. The Mull of Galloway RSPB nature reserve, home to thousands of seabirds, has a **visitor centre** (www.rspb.org.uk; ☺10am-5pm) with plenty of information on local species, including where to see them. There's also a cafe here.

The former homes of the lightkeepers are now available to stay in; check out www.ntsholidays.com.

Central Scotland

Best Places to Stay

» Monachyle Mhor (p193)

» Milton Eonan (p216)

» Moor of Rannoch Hotel (p217)

» Roman Camp Hotel (p191)

» Spindrift (p205)

» Dalmunzie House (p222)

Best Places to Eat & Drink

» Peat Inn (p202)

» Moulin Hotel (p220)

» Breizh (p210)

» Seafood Restaurant (p203)

Why Go?

The country's historic roots are deeply embedded in Central Scotland. Significant ruins and castles from the region's history pepper the landscape; key battles around Stirling shaped Scotland's fortunes; and Perth, the former capital, is where kings were crowned on the Stone of Destiny.

Arriving from Glasgow and Edinburgh, visitors begin to get a sense of the country further north as the lowland belt gives way to Highland splendour. It is here that the majesty of Scotland's landscape unfolds in deep, dark, steely-blue lochs that reflect the silhouettes of soaring, sentinel-like craggy peaks on still days.

Whether in the big-tree country of Perthshire, the bare landscapes of Glenshee, or the green Fife coastline dotted with fishing villages, opportunities to enjoy the landscape abound: walking, cycling, and mountaineering are all easy possibilities. The region also has some of the country's best pubs and eateries, which greet weary visitors at day's end.

When to Go

Stirling

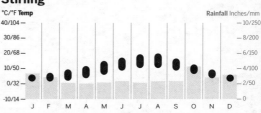

May If the weather's kind, it's a magical time for exploring before summer crowds arrive.

August Summer in Fife is a top time for coastal walks and crustacean feasts.

Winter Hit the slopes at Glenshee for the sight of Scottish crags blanketed with snow.

STIRLING REGION

Covering Scotland's wasplike waist, this region has always been a crucial strategic point dividing the Lowlands from the Highlands. For this reason, Scotland's two most important independence battles were fought here, within sight of Stirling's hilltop stronghold. Separated by 17 years, William Wallace's victory over the English at Stirling Bridge, followed by Robert Bruce's triumph at Bannockburn, established Scottish nationhood. The region remains a source of much national pride.

Stirling's Old Town perches on a spectacular crag, and the castle is among Britain's most fascinating. Within easy reach, the dreamy Trossachs, home to Rob Roy and inspiration to Walter Scott, offer great walking and cycling in the eastern half of Scotland's first national park (p261).

❶ Getting Around

Trains service Stirling but not the rest of the region, so you'll be relying on buses if you don't have your own transport. **First** (🕿01324-602200; www.firstgroup.com) is the main operator. The Central Scotland Rover rail ticket (£33), valid for three days out of seven, allows unlimited train travel between Edinburgh, Glasgow, Falkirk and Stirling.

Stirling

POP 32,673

With an utterly impregnable position atop a mighty wooded crag (the plug of an extinct volcano), Stirling's beautifully preserved Old Town is a treasure trove of noble buildings and cobbled streets winding up to the ramparts of its dominant castle, which offer views for miles around. Clearly visible is the brooding Wallace Monument, a strange Victorian Gothic creation honouring the legendary freedom fighter of *Braveheart* fame. Nearby is Bannockburn, scene of Robert the Bruce's major triumph over the English.

The castle makes a fascinating visit, but make sure you also spend time exploring the Old Town and the picturesque path that encircles it. Near the castle are a couple of snug pubs in which you can raise a dram to toast Scotland's hoary heroes. Below the Old Town, retail-minded modern Stirling doesn't offer the same appeal; stick to the high ground as much as possible and you'll love the place.

◉ Sights

Stirling Castle   CASTLE

181

(HS; www.historic-scotland.gov.uk; ⏰9.30am-6pm Apr-Sep, to 5pm Oct-Mar) Hold Stirling and you control Scotland. This maxim has ensured that a fortress of some kind has existed here since prehistoric times. Commanding superb views, you cannot help drawing parallels with Edinburgh castle – but many find Stirling's fortress more atmospheric; the location, architecture and historical significance combine to make it a grand and memorable sight. This means it draws plenty of visitors, so it's advisable to visit in the afternoon; many tourists come on day-trips from Edinburgh or Glasgow, so you may have the castle to yourself by about 4pm.

Admission costs for the castle will rise once the Royal Palace opens. The mooted price at time of research was £14 for adults, which would include an audioguide.

By the castle car park, the **Stirling tourist office** (admission free; ⏰9.30am-6pm Apr-Sep, to 5pm Oct-Mar) has an audiovisual presentation and exhibition about Stirling, including the history and architecture of the castle.

Great Hall, Gatehouse, Royal Palace & Chapel

The current castle dates from the late 14th to the 16th century, when it was a residence of the Stuart monarchs. The **Great Hall** and **Gatehouse** were built by James IV; observe the hammer-beam roof and huge fireplaces in the largest medieval hall in Scotland – the result of 35 years of restoration.

After a long restoration project, the **Royal Palace** is scheduled to reopen as this book hits the shelves. It'll be a sumptuous recreation of how this luxurious Renaissance palace would have looked when it was constructed by French masons under the orders of James V (in the early 16th century) to impress his (also French) bride and other crowned heads of Europe. Perhaps the most spectacular is the series of **tapestries** that have been painstakingly woven. Based on originals in New York's Metropolitan Museum, they depict the hunting of a unicorn – an event ripe with Christian metaphor – and are utterly beautiful. Until the last one is complete (probably in 2013) you can watch the weavers at work in the **Tapestry Studio**: it's fascinating to see.

James VI (r 1567–1625) remodelled the **Chapel Royal** and was the last King of Scots to live at Stirling.

Central Scotland Highlights

1 Opening your jaw in amazement at the epic splendour of **Glen Lyon** (p215)

2 Admiring the views from magnificent **Stirling Castle** (p181), overlooking ancient independence battlefields

3 Pacing through historic **St Andrews** (p197) to the famous Old Course

4 Strutting with peacocks at noble **Scone Palace** (p208), where Scottish kings were crowned

5 Crunching local seafood in the picturesque fishing villages of the **East Neuk of Fife** (p204)

6 Nursing a pint of Ale of Atholl by a roaring fire at the **Moulin Hotel** (p220)

7 Experiencing life at the end of the road amid the bleak landscapes of **Rannoch Moor** (p216)

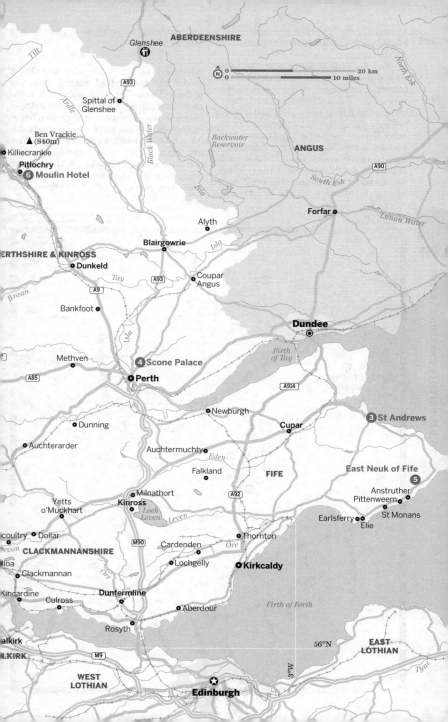

Museum of the Argyll & Sutherland
Highlanders, Great Kitchens & Castle
Exhibition

In the King's Old Building is the **Museum of the Argyll & Sutherland Highlanders** (donations encouraged), which traces the history of this famous regiment from 1794 to the present day. It has a great collection of ornately decorated dirks (daggers). In another part of the castle, the **Great Kitchens** are especially interesting, bringing to life the bustle and scale of the enterprise of cooking for the King. Near the entrance, the **Castle Exhibition** gives good background information on the Stuart kings and updates on current archaeological investigations

Argyll's Lodging

Admission to the castle also includes a guided tour of **Argyll's Lodging**, at the top of Castle Wynd near the bastion itself. Complete with turrets, this spectacular lodge is the most impressive 17th-century town house in Scotland. It's the former home of William Alexander, Earl of Stirling and noted literary figure. It has been tastefully restored and gives an insight into lavish, 17th-century aristocratic life. There are four or five guided tours daily (you can't enter by other means).

Stirling

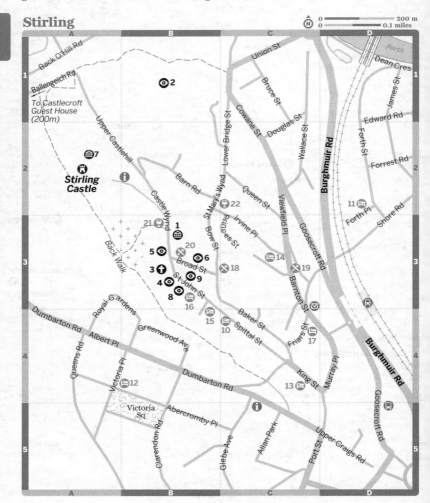

Old Town   HISTORIC DISTRICT

Below the castle, the steep Old Town has a remarkably different feel to modern Stirling, its cobblestone streets packed with 15th- to 17th-century architectural gems. Its growth began when Stirling became a royal burgh (about 1124), and in the 15th and 16th centuries rich merchants built their houses here.

Town Wall, Back Walk & Mar's Wark

Stirling has the best surviving **town wall** in Scotland. It was built around 1547 when Henry VIII of England began the 'Rough Wooing' – attacking the town in order to force Mary, Queen of Scots to marry his son so that the two kingdoms could be united. The wall can be explored on the **Back Walk**, which follows the line of the wall from Dumbarton Rd (near the tourist office) to the castle. You pass the town cemeteries

(check out the Star Pyramid, an outsized affirmation of Reformation values dating from 1863), then the path continues around the back of the castle to Gowan Hill where you can see the **Beheading Stone**, now encased in iron bars to prevent contemporary use.

Mar's Wark, on Castle Wynd at the head of the Old Town, is the ornate facade of what was once a Renaissance-style town house commissioned in 1569 by the wealthy Earl of Mar, regent of Scotland during James VI's minority.

Church of the Holy Rude & Cowane's Hospital

The **Church of the Holy Rude** (www.holyrude.org; St John St; admission free; ⊙11am-4pm May-Sep) has been the town's parish church for 600 years and James VI was crowned here in 1567. The nave and tower date from 1456, and the church has one of the few surviving medieval open-timber roofs. Stunning stained-glass windows and huge stone pillars create a powerful effect.

Behind the church is **Cowane's Hospital** (49 St John St; admission free; ⊙9am-5pm Apr-Sep, 10am-4pm Oct-Mar), built as an almshouse in 1637 by the merchant John Cowane. There's a family-tree database here, where you can search for your ancestors if they were born around this area.

Mercat Cross, Tolbooth & Old Town Jail

The **Mercat Cross**, in Broad St, is topped with a unicorn (known as 'The Puggie'), and was once surrounded by a bustling market. Nearby is the **Tolbooth**, built in 1705 as the town's administrative centre and renovated in 2001 to become the city's premier arts and music venue.

The **Old Town Jail** (www.oldtownjail.com; St John St; adult/child/family £6.50/4/17; ⊙10am-5pm Apr-Oct, 10.30am-4pm Nov-Mar) is a great one for kids, as actors take you through the complex, portraying a cast of characters that illustrate the hardships of Victorian prison life in innovative, entertaining style.

National Wallace Monument   MONUMENT (www.nationalwallacemonument.com; adult/child £7.50/4.50; ⊙10am-5pm Apr-Oct, to 6pm Jul & Aug, 10.30am-4pm Nov-Mar) Towering over Scotland's narrow waist, this nationalist memorial is so Victorian Gothic it deserves circling bats and ravens. It commemorates the bid for Scottish independence depicted in the film *Braveheart*. From the tourist office, walk or shuttle-bus up the hill to the building itself. Once there, break the climb up the narrow staircase inside to admire Wallace's 66 inches of broadsword and see the man himself re-created in a 3-D audiovisual display. More staid is the marble pantheon of lugubrious Scottish heroes, but the view from the top over the flat, green gorgeousness of the Forth Valley, including the site of Wallace's 1297 victory over the English at Stirling Bridge, justifies the steep entry fee.

Buses 62 and 63 run from Murray Pl in Stirling to the tourist office, otherwise it's a half-hour walk from central Stirling. There's a cafe here, too.

Bannockburn   BATTLEFIELD
Though Wallace's heroics were significant, it was Robert the Bruce's defeat of the English on 24 June 1314 at Bannockburn, just outside Stirling, that eventually established lasting Scottish nationhood. Exploiting the marshy ground, Bruce won a great tactical victory against a much larger and better-equipped force, and sent Edward II 'homeward, tae think again', as the song 'Flower of Scotland' commemorates.

At **Bannockburn Heritage Centre** (NTS; www.nts.org.uk; adult/child £5.50/4.50; ◷10am-5pm Mar-Oct, to 5.30pm Apr-Sep) the history pre- and post-battle is lucidly explained. The audiovisual could do with a remake, but there's lots to do for kids, and an intriguing recreation of Bruce's face which suggests that he may have suffered from leprosy in later life.

The battlefield itself (which never closes) is harder to appreciate; apart from a statue of the victor astride his horse and a misbegotten flag memorial, there's nothing to see. Bannockburn is 2 miles south of Stirling; you can reach it on bus 51 from Murray Pl in the centre.

🛌 Sleeping

Castlecroft Guest House   B&B ££
(☎01786-474933; www.castlecroft-uk.com; Ballengeich Rd; s/d £45/60; Ⓟ@◉❋) Nestling into the hillside under the back of the castle, this great hideaway feels like a rural retreat but is a short, spectacular walk from the heart of historic Stirling. The lounge boasts 180-degree views over green fields to the hills that gird the town, and the compact rooms are appealing and well maintained.

Willy Wallace Backpackers Hostel
     HOSTEL £
(☎01786-446773; www.willywallacehostel.com; 77 Murray Pl; dm/tw £17/36; @◉❋) This highly convenient central hostel is friendly, roomy and sociable. The colourful, spacious dormitories are clean and light, there's free tea and coffee, a good kitchen, and a laissez-faire atmosphere. Other amenities include a laundry service and free internet and wi-fi.

Sruighlea   B&B ££
(☎01786-471082; www.sruighlea.com; 27 King St; s/d £40/60; ❋) This place feels like a secret hideaway – there's no sign – but it's conveniently located smack-bang in the centre of town. You'll feel like a local staying here, and there are eating and drinking places practically on the doorstep. It's a B&B that welcomes guests with the kind of warmth that keeps them returning.

Stirling SYHA   HOSTEL £
(☎01786-473442; www.syha.org.uk; St John St; dm/tw £17.25/45; Ⓟ@◉❋) Right in the Old Town, this hostel has an unbeatable location and great facilities. Though its facade is that of a former church, the interior is modern and efficient. The dorms are compact but comfortable with lockers and en suite bathrooms; other highlights include a pool table, bike shed and, at busy times, cheap meals on offer. Lack of atmosphere can be the only problem.

Garfield Guesthouse   B&B ££
(☎01786-473730; www.garfieldgh.com; 12 Victoria Sq; small/large d £60/65) Though close to the centre of town, Victoria Sq is a quiet oasis, with noble Victorian buildings surrounding a verdant swathe of lawn. The Garfield's huge rooms, bay windows, ceiling roses and other period features make it a winner. There's a great family room, and some rooms have views to the castle towering above.

Forth Guest House   B&B ££
(☎01786-471020; www.forthguesthouse.co.uk; 23 Forth Pl; s/d £45/55; ❋) Just a couple of minutes' walk from town on the other side of the railway, this noble Georgian terrace offers attractive and stylish accommodation at a fair price. The rooms are very commodious, particularly the cute garret rooms with their coomed ceilings and good modern bathrooms. Credit cards not accepted.

Linden Guest House   B&B ££
(☎01786-448850; www.lindenguesthouse.co.uk; 22 Linden Ave; s/d £50/72; Ⓟ@) Handy if arriving by car from the south, this guesthouse's warm welcome and easy parking offer understandable appeal. The rooms,

William Wallace is one of Scotland's greatest heroes: a patriot whose exploits helped revive interest in Scottish history. Born in 1270, he was catapulted into fame and a place in history as a highly successful guerrilla commander who harassed the English invaders for many years.

In the wake of his victory over the English at Stirling Bridge in 1297, Wallace was knighted by Robert the Bruce and proclaimed Guardian of Scotland. However, it was only a short time before English military superiority and the fickle nature of the nobility's loyalties would turn against the defender of Scottish independence.

Disaster struck in July 1298 when King Edward's force defeated the Scots at the Battle of Falkirk. Wallace went into hiding and travelled throughout Europe to drum up support for the Scottish cause. Many of the Scottish nobility were prepared to side with Edward, and Wallace was betrayed after his return to Scotland in 1305, tried for treason at Westminster, and hanged, beheaded and disembowelled at Smithfield, London.

two of which are suitable for families, have fridges, and the gleaming bathrooms could feature in ads for cleaning products. Breakfast features fresh fruit and kippers, among other choices.

Stirling Highland Hotel HOTEL **£££**
(☏01786-272727; www.barcelo-hotels.co.uk; Spittal St; s/d £105/134; P@⊛☎) The smartest hotel in town, Stirling Highland Hotel is a sympathetic refurbishment of the old high school. This curious place still feels institutional in parts, but has great facilities that include pool, spa, gym, sauna and squash courts. It's very convenient for the castle and Old Town, and the rooms have been recently refitted, though they vary widely in size. Prices are flexible: those listed above are a guide.

Munro Guesthouse B&B **££**
(☏01786-472685; www.munroguesthouse.co.uk; 14 Princes St; s/d/f £42/65/85; ☎) Cosy and cheery, Munro Guesthouse is right in the centre of town, but locatd on a quiet side street. Things are done with a smile here, and the smallish rooms are most inviting, particularly the cute attic ones. The breakfast is also better than the norm, with fruit salad on hand. There's easy (pay) parking opposite.

Colessio Hotel HOTEL **£££**
(☏01786-448880; www.hotelcolessio.com; 33 Spittal St) This new luxury hotel and spa occupies an old hospital in the heart of the Old Town. It was still being built at time of research, but should be worth a look.

Cairns B&B **££**
(☏01786-479228; 12 Princes St; s/tw incl breakfast £30/54) Friendly, good-value,

central guesthouse that just has singles and twins. Rooms come with or without breakfast.

Neidpath B&B **££**
(☏01786-469017; www.neidpath-stirling.co.uk; 24 Linden Ave; d £58; P☎) Spotless rooms and a filling breakfast.

Witches Craig Caravan Park CAMPSITE **£**
(☏01786-474947; www.witchescraig.co.uk; Blairlogie; tent site for 1/2/2 plus car £9/11/17; ☺Apr-Oct; P) In a brilliant spot right at the foot of the Ochil Hills, which are just begging to be walked, Witches Craig is 3 miles east of Stirling by the A91.

✖ Eating & Drinking

Stirling isn't blessed with lots of excellent restaurants. Baker St is the main eating-and-drinking zone.

Portcullis PUB **£**
(☏01786-472290; www.theportcullishotel.com; Castle Wynd; bar meals £8-12; ☺lunch & dinner) Built in stone as solid as the castle that it stands below, this former school is just the spot for a pint and a pub lunch after your visit. With bar meals that would have had even William Wallace loosening his belt a couple of notches, a little beer garden, and a cosy buzz indoors, it's well worth a visit; there are also rooms here (single/double £67/87).

East India Company INDIAN **£**
(7 Viewfield Pl; mains £6-11; ☺dinner) This basement Indian restaurant is one of the best spots in Central Scotland for a curry. Sumptuously decorated to resemble a ship's stateroom, with portraits of tea barons on the wall to conjure images of the days of the clippers, it offers exquisite dishes from all

WANT MORE?

Head to **Lonely Planet** (www
.lonelyplanet.com/scotland/central-
scotland/stirling) for planning advice,
author recommendations, traveller
reviews and insider tips.

parts of India. There's a buffet dinner available Monday to Thursday (£8.95), but go à
la carte and savour the toothsome flavours.

Hermann's RESTAURANT £££
(☎01786-450632; www.hermanns.co.uk; 58
Broad St; 2-course lunch/3-course dinner £13/20,
mains £16-20; ⊙lunch & dinner) Solidly set on
a corner above the Mercat Cross and below
the castle, this elegant Scottish-Austrian
restaurant is a reliable and popular choice.
The solid, conservative decor is weirdly offset by magazine-style skiing photos, but the
food doesn't miss a beat and ranges from
Scottish favourites to gourmet schnitzel
and *spätzle* noodles. Vegetarian options are
good, and quality Austrian wines provide
an out-of-the-ordinary accompaniment.

Darnley Coffee House CAFE £
(www.darnley.connectfree.co.uk; 18 Bow St;
snacks £3.50-5; ⊙breakfast & lunch) Just down
the hill from the castle, beyond the end of
Broad St, Darnley Coffee House is a good
pit stop for home baking and speciality coffees during a walk around the Old Town.
The building is a historic 16th-century
house where Darnley, lover and later husband of Mary, Queen of Scots, once stayed
while visiting her.

Settle Inn PUB
(91 St Mary's Wynd) A warm welcome is guaranteed at Stirling's oldest pub (1733), a spot
redolent with atmosphere, what with its
log fire, vaulted back room, and low-slung
ceilings. Guest ales, atmospheric nooks for
settling in for the night, and a blend of local
characters make it a classic of its kind.

❶ Information

Library (Corn Exchange Rd; ⊙Mon-Sat; @)
Free internet access.

Stirling Royal Infirmary (☎01786-434000;
Livilands Rd) Hospital; south of the town
centre.

Stirling Visitor Centre (☎01786-450000;
⊙9.30am-6pm Apr-Sep, to 5pm Oct-Mar) Near
the castle entrance.

Tourist office (☎01786-475019; www.visitscott
ishheartlands.com; 41 Dumbarton Rd; ⊙10am-
5pm Mon-Sat year-round, plus Sun Jun–mid-
Sep; @)

❶ Getting There & Away

BUS The **bus station** (☎01786-446474) is on
Goosecroft Rd. **Citylink** (www.citylink.co.uk)
offers a number of services to/from Stirling:

Dundee £12.50, 1½ hours, hourly

Edinburgh £6.70, one hour, hourly

Glasgow £6.60, 45 minutes, hourly

Perth £7.70, 50 minutes, at least hourly

Some buses continue to Aberdeen, Inverness,
and Fort William; more frequently a change will
be required.

TRAIN First ScotRail (www.scotrail.co.uk)
has services to/from a number of destinations,
including these:

Aberdeen £38.60, 2¼ hours, regular services

Dundee £15.80, one hour, regular services

Edinburgh £6.90, 55 minutes, twice hourly
Monday to Saturday, hourly Sunday

Glasgow £7.10, 40 minutes, twice hourly Monday to Saturday, hourly Sunday

Perth £10.40, 35 minutes, regular services

Around Stirling

BRIDGE OF ALLAN
POP 5046

This upbeat former spa town, just 2.5 miles
north of Stirling, has an open street plan,
giving it a laid-back sense of space. It's a
good alternative to staying in Stirling.

At the **Bridge of Allan Brewery** (www.
bridgeofallan.co.uk; Queen's Lane; admission
free; ⊙daily Jul-Sep, Sat & Sun Oct-Jun), just off
Henderson St, you can learn about the mi-
crobrewing techniques behind traditional
Scottish ales. This is a great spot to taste local beers – it's very friendly and the quality
microbrews are recommended.

🛏 Sleeping & Eating

Adamo Hotel HOTEL £££
(☎01786-833268; www.adamohotels.com; 24
Henderson St; small s £60, s/d £100/140, 2-course
lunch/dinner £10.50/20; 🅿🛜) The gorgeous,
modern, plush rooms here have a dark and
fuzzy decor that makes you want to get naked and have a good roll around. All rooms
have car-wash showers, but only some come
with a bath. The rooms are different sizes,
so ask to see a selection. Ask about weekend
specials, too, and even if you're not staying,
drop in for lunch or dinner.

Anam Cara

B&B **££**

(☎01786-832030; caringclown@hotmail.com; 107 Henderson St; s/d £35/50; P) A simple B&B with a double and a twin room. The attraction here is your host – she's a laughter therapist! If everything is a bit grey outside and your time in Scotland is getting you down, this may be just the place for you.

Clive Ramsay Café

CAFE, DELI **£**

(www.cliveramsay.com; Henderson St; mains £8-10; ⊙breakfast & lunch) With a claim to 'sexy food', this little show-pony also has a wonderful deli next door selling fresh local produce. The cafe has a very trendy vibe and seems to be the centre of the town's universe. Scrumptious treats drawing from several world cuisines won't break your budget.

❶ Getting There & Away

You can walk to Bridge of Allan from Stirling in an hour. Frequent local buses from Stirling stop in Henderson St. Trains to Dunblane, Stirling, Glasgow and Edinburgh depart frequently from the station at the western end of Henderson St.

DUNBLANE

POP 7911

Dunblane, 5 miles northwest of Stirling, is a pretty town with a notable cathedral. It's difficult not to remember the horrific massacre that took place in the primary school in 1996, but happier headlines have come the town's way more recently with the rise of local tennis star Andy Murray.

Fabulous **Dunblane Cathedral** (HS; www. dunblanecathedral.org.uk; Cathedral Sq; admission free; ⊙9.30am-5.30pm Mon-Sat & 2-5.30pm Sun Apr-Sep, 9.30am-4.30pm Mon-Sat & 2-4.30pm Sun Oct-Mar) is well worth a detour. It's a superb, elegant sandstone building – a fine example of Gothic style. The lower parts of the walls date from Norman times, the rest making from the 13th to 15th centuries. A 10th-century carved Celtic stone is at the nave's head, and a standing stone commemorates the town's slain children.

The musty old **Leighton Library** (61 High St; admission free; ⊙11am-1pm Mon-Sat May-Sep), dating from 1684, is the oldest private library in Scotland. There are 4500 books in 90 languages.

You can walk to Bridge of Allan from Dunblane along Darn Rd in about an hour – it's an ancient path once used by monks. There are also frequent buses and trains from Stirling to Dunblane.

DOUNE

POP 1635

Doune is not far beyond Dunblane, on the road to Callander. Stop here to visit magnificent **Doune Castle** (HS; www.historic-scot land.gov.uk; adult/child £4.20/2.50; ⊙9.30am-5.30pm Apr-Sep, to 4.30pm Sat-Wed Oct-Mar), one of the best-preserved 14th-century castles in Scotland, having remained largely unchanged since it was built for the Duke of Albany. It was a favourite royal hunting lodge, but was also of great strategic importance because it controlled the route between the Lowlands and Highlands. Mary, Queen of Scots stayed here, as did Bonnie Prince

189

CENTRAL SCOTLAND AROUND STIRLING

WORTH A TRIP

THE FALKIRK WHEEL

Scotland's canals were once vital avenues for goods transportation, but the railway age left them to fall into dereliction. A millennium project restored two of Scotland's major canals, the Union and the Forth & Clyde. With a difference in level of 115ft, the two were once linked by an arduous series of 11 locks, but the construction of the unique **Falkirk Wheel** (www.thefalkirkwheel.co.uk; adult/child £7.95/4.95; ⊙10am-5.30pm daily Mar-Oct, 11am-4pm Wed-Sun Nov-Feb) changed all that. Its rotating arms literally scoop boats up and lift them to the higher waterway – it's an engineering marvel that makes a compelling visit.

Boat trips leave every half-hour (hourly in winter) from the nearby tourist office and travel into the wheel, which delivers you to the Union Canal high above. Boats then go through Roughcastle Tunnel before the return descent on the wheel. Anyone with an interest in engineering should not miss this boat ride – it's great for kids, too. The tourist office explains the workings of the mighty wheel – it only takes the power of about eight toasters for a full rotation! There's also a cafe here.

The Wheel is in Falkirk, a large town about 10 miles southeast of Stirling. Regular buses and trains link the two, and also connect Falkirk with Glasgow and Edinburgh.

Charlie, who used it to imprison government troops. There are great **views** from the castle walls, and the lofty **gatehouse** is very impressive, rising nearly 30m. Monty Python fans may recognise the castle from *Monty Python and the Holy Grail*.

Doune is 8 miles northwest of Stirling. **First** (www.firstgroup.com) buses run every hour or two (30 minutes), less frequently on Sunday.

DOLLAR
POP 2877

Charming Dollar is about 11 miles east of Stirling in the lower Ochil Hills. **Castle Campbell** (HS; www.historic-scotland.gov.uk; adult/child £4.70/2.80; ⊙9.30am-5.30pm Apr-Sep, to 4.30pm Sat-Wed Oct-Mar) is a 20-minute walk up **Dollar Glen**, into the wooded hills above the town. It's a spooky old stronghold of the Dukes of Argyll and stands between two ravines; you can clearly see why it was known as 'Castle Gloom'. There's been a fortress of some kind on this site from the 11th century, but the present structure dates from the 15th century. The castle was sacked by Cromwell in 1654, but the tower is well preserved. From the little car park near the castle there's a great ramble with sweeping views over Castle Campbell and the surrounding country.

Regular buses run to Dollar from Stirling.

The Trossachs

The Trossachs region has long been a favourite weekend getaway, offering outstanding natural beauty and excellent walking and cycling routes within easy reach of the southern population centres. With thickly forested hills, romantic lochs and an increasingly interesting selection of places to stay and eat, its popularity is sure to continue, protected by its national-park status (p261).

The Trossachs first gained popularity as a tourist destination in the early 19th century, when curious visitors came from all over Britain drawn by the romantic language of Walter Scott's poem *Lady of the Lake*, inspired by Loch Katrine, and *Rob Roy*, about the derring-do of the region's most famous son.

In summer the Trossachs can be overburdened with coach tours, but many of these are day-trippers – peaceful, long evenings gazing at the reflections in the nearest loch are still possible. It's worth timing your visit not to coincide with a weekend.

ABERFOYLE & AROUND
POP 576

Crawling with visitors on most weekends and dominated by a huge car park, little **Aberfoyle** is a fairly uninteresting place, easily overwhelmed by day-trippers. Instead of staying here, we recommend Callander or other Trossachs towns.

Half a mile north of Aberfoyle on the A821 is the **David Marshall Lodge tourist office** (www.forestry.gov.uk/qefp; admission free, car park £2; ⊙10am-4pm Nov-Mar, 10am-5pm Apr-Oct, to 6pm Jul & Aug) in the **Queen Elizabeth Forest Park**, which has info about the many walks and cycle routes in and around the park (many departing from the tourist office). The Royal Society for the Protection of Birds (RSPB) has a display here on local bird life, the highlight being a live video link to the resident osprey family. The centre is worth visiting solely for the views.

Three miles east is the **Lake of Menteith** (called lake not loch due to a mistranslation from Gaelic). A ferry takes visitors to the substantial ruins of **Inchmahome Priory** (HS; www.historic-scotland.gov.uk; adult/child incl ferry £4.70/2.80; ⊙9.30am-5.30pm Apr-Sep, last return ferry 4.30pm). Mary, Queen of Scots was kept safe here as a child during Henry VIII's 'Rough Wooing'. Henry attacked Stirling trying to force Mary to marry his son in order to unite the kingdoms (p446).

🏃 Activities

Several picturesque but busy waymarked **trails** start from the David Marshall Lodge tourist office centre in the forest park. These range from a light 20-minute stroll to a nearby waterfall to a hilly 4-mile circuit. Also here, **Go Ape!** (www.goape.co.uk; adult/child £30/20; ⊙daily Apr-Oct, Sat & Sun Mar & Nov) will bring out the monkey in you on its exhilarating adventure course of long ziplines, swings and rope bridges through the forest.

An excellent 20-mile circular **cycle route** links with the boat at Loch Katrine. From Aberfoyle, join the **Lochs & Glens Cycle Way** on the forest trail, or take the A821 over Duke's Pass. Following the southern shore of Loch Achray, you reach the pier on Loch Katrine. The ferry can take you to Stronachlachar (one way with bike £14) on the western shore, from where you can follow the beautiful B829 via Loch Ard back to Aberfoyle.

Sleeping & Eating

Lake of Menteith Hotel
HOTEL, RESTAURANT £££

(☎01877-385258; www.lake-hotel.com; Port of Menteith; d £130-190; P⊜) Soothingly situated on a lake (yes, it's the only non-loch in Scotland) 3 miles east of Aberfoyle, this makes a great romantic getaway. Rooms vary substantially in size, and are being upgraded, so it's worth shelling out a little extra for views and modernity. The restaurant serves sumptuous dinners (£40) with excellent service. Check the website for packages.

Mayfield Guest House
B&B ££

(☎01877-382962; www.mayfield-aberfoyle.co. uk; Main St; s/d £35/55; P) Nothing is too much trouble for the friendly hosts at this guesthouse. It has a double and two twin rooms, all very well kept, and a garage at the back for bikes. Pets welcome.

Forth Inn
PUB £

(☎01877-382372; www.forthinn.com; Main St; mains £6-9; ⊗breakfast, lunch & dinner; ⊞) In the middle of the village, the solid Forth Inn seems to be the lifeblood of the town, with locals and visitors alike queuing up for good, honest pub fare. The tasty bar meals are the best in town. It also provides accommodation and beer, with drinkers spilling outside into the sunny courtyard. Single/double rooms are available for £50/80, but they can be noisy at weekends.

ℹ Information
The **tourist office** (☎01877-382352; aberfoyle@ visitscotland.com; Main St; ⊗10am-5pm Apr-Oct, 10am-4pm Sat & Sun Nov-Mar; ⊚) details a history of the Trossachs and provides currency exchange and a soft play area.

ℹ Getting There & Away
First (www.firstgroup.com) has up to four daily buses from Stirling (40 minutes); you'll have to connect at Balfron on Sundays. See the Trossachs Transport boxed text for transport around the region.

CALLANDER
POP 2754

Callander has been pulling in the tourists for over 150 years, and has a laid-back ambience along its main thoroughfare. It's a far better place than Aberfoyle to spend time in, quickly lulling visitors into lazy pottering. There's also an excellent array of accommodation options here.

Sights & Activities

The **Hamilton Toy Collection** (www.theham iltontoycollection.co.uk; 111 Main St; adult/child £2/50p; ⊗10am-4.30pm Apr-Oct) is a powerhouse of 20th-century juvenile memorabilia, chock-full of dolls houses, puppets and toy soldiers. It's a guaranteed nostalgia trip.

The impressive **Bracklinn Falls** are reached by track and footpath from Bracklinn Rd (30 minutes each way from the car park). Also off Bracklinn Rd, a woodland trail leads up to **Callander Crags**, with great views over the surroundings; a return trip is about 4 miles from the car park.

The Trossachs is a lovely area to cycle around. On a cycle route and based at Trossachs Tryst hostel (see p192), the excellent **Wheels Cycling Centre** (☎01877-331100; www.wheelscyclingcentre.com) has a wide range of hire bikes starting from £10/15 per half-/full day.

Sleeping

TOP CHOICE **Roman Camp Hotel** HOTEL £££

(☎01877-330003; www.roman-camp-hot el.co.uk; s/d/superior d £95/145/185; P⊜) Callander's best hotel. It's centrally located but feels rural, set by the river in its own beautiful grounds with birdsong the only sound. Its endearing features include a lounge with blazing fire and a library with a tiny secret chapel. There are three grades of room; the standards are certainly luxurious, but the superior ones are even more appealing, with period furniture, armchairs and a fireplace. The upmarket restaurant is open to the public. Reassuringly, the name refers not to toga parties but to a ruin in the adjacent fields.

ℹ TROSSACHS TRANSPORT

In a bid to cut public transport costs, 'Demand Responsive Transport' (DRT) was being brought to the Trossachs when we researched this guide. Sounds complex, but basically it means you get a taxi to where you want to go, for the price of a bus (eg 10 miles for £3.30). Taxis run Monday to Saturday and need to be booked in advance; call or text ☎0844-567 5670 between 7am and 7pm Monday to Saturday, or book online at www. aberfoylecoaches.com.

Trossachs Tryst HOSTEL £

(☎01877-331200; www.scottish-hostel.co.uk; Invertrossachs Rd; dm/tw £17.50/45; P@?) Set up to be the perfect hostel for outdoorsy people, this cracking spot is in fresh-aired surroundings a mile from Callander. Facilities and accommodation are excellent, with dorms offering acres of space and their own bathrooms, and cycle hire with plenty of route advice. Help yourself to a continental breakfast in the morning, and enjoy the great feel that pervades this helpful place. To get there, take Bridge St off Main St, then turn right onto Invertrossachs Rd and continue for a mile.

Abbotsford Lodge B&B ££

(☎01877-330066; www.abbotsfordlodge.com; Stirling Rd; s/d £50/75; P@) This friendly Victorian house offers something different to the norm, with tartan and florals consigned to the bonfire, replaced by stylish comfortable contemporary design that enhances the building's original features. Ruffled fabrics and ceramic vases with flower arrangements characterise the renovated rooms. The top-floor ones share a bathroom (doubles £55), but the offbeat under-roof shapes are lovable. It's on the main road on the eastern side of town; look for the monkey puzzle tree.

Arden House B&B ££

(☎01877-330235; www.ardenhouse.org.uk; Bracklinn Rd; s/d £35/70; ⊗Apr-Oct; P?) A redoubt of peaceful good taste, this elegant home features faultlessly welcoming hospitality and a woodsy, hillside location close to the centre but far from the crowds. The commodious rooms have flatscreen TV and plenty of little extras, including a suite (£80) with great views. Homebaked banana bread and a rotating dish-of-the-day keep breakfast well ahead of the competition.

Callander Meadows B&B ££

(☎01877-330181; www.callandermeadows.co.uk; 24 Main St; s £45, d £70-80) Upstairs at this restaurant are three very appealing rooms, elegantly kitted-out with dark-varnished furnishings and striped wallpaper (one has a four-poster bed).

White Shutters B&B £

(☎01877-330442; 6 South Church St; s/d £22/39) A cute little house just off the main street, White Sutters offers pleasing rooms with shared bathroom and a friendly welcome. The mattresses aren't exactly new, but it's comfortable and offers great value for this part of the world.

Linley Guest House B&B ££

(☎01877-330087; www.linleyguesthouse.co.uk; 139 Main St; s/d incl breakfast £36/52) A spick-and-span B&B with bright rooms and helpful owners. The double en suite is worth the extra: it's beautifully appointed with a large window drawing in lots of natural light. Room-only rate available.

✖ Eating & Drinking

Mhor Fish BISTRO, TAKEAWAY ££

TOP CHOICE (☎01877-330213; www.mhor.net; 75 Main St; fish supper £5.50, mains £8-12; ⊗lunch & dinner Tue-Sun) Both chip shop and fish restaurant, but wholly different, this endearing black-and-white-tiled cafe displays the day's fresh catch. You can choose how you want it cooked, whether pan-seared and accompanied by one of many good wines, or fried and wrapped in paper with chips to take away. The fish and seafood comes from sustainable stock, and includes oysters and other goodies. If they run out of fresh fish, they shut, so opening hours can be a bit variable.

Callander Meadows RESTAURANT ££

(☎01877-330181; www.callandermeadows.co.uk; 24 Main St; lunch £7.95, mains £11-17; ⊗lunch & dinner Thu-Sun) Informal but smart, this well-loved restaurant in the centre of Callander occupies the two front rooms of a house on the main street. There's a contemporary flair for presentation and unusual flavour combinations, but a solidly British base underpins the cuisine, with things like mackerel, red cabbage, salmon and duck making regular and welcome appearances. It's also open on Mondays from April to September, and Wednesdays too in high summer.

Lade Inn PUB £

(www.theladeinn.com; Kilmahog; bar meals £8-11; ⊗lunch & dinner; ♿) Callander's best pub isn't in Callander – it's a mile north of town. It does decent, large and popular bar meals, doesn't mind kids, and pulls a good pint (the real ales here are brewed to a house recipe). Next door, the owners run a shop with a dazzling selection of Scottish beers. There's low-key live music here at weekends too, but it shuts early if it's quiet midweek.

ℹ Information

Loch Lomond & the Trossachs National Park tourist office (☎01389-722600; ww.lochlomond-trossachs.org; 52 Main St; ⊗9.30am-4.30pm Mon-Fri, 9.30am-12.30pm

Sat) This place is a useful centre for specific information on the park.

Rob Roy & Trossachs tourist office
(☎01877-330342; callander@visitscotland. com; Ancaster Sq; ☺10am-5pm daily Apr-Oct, 10am-4pm Mon-Sat Nov-Mar; ⊛) This centre has heaps of info on the area.

❶ Getting There & Away

First (www.firstgroup.com) operates buses from Stirling (45 minutes, hourly Monday to Saturday), while **Kingshouse** (www.kingshousetravel. co.uk) buses run from Killin (45 minutes, three to six daily Monday to Saturday). There are also **Citylink** (www.citylink.co.uk) buses from Edinburgh to Oban or Fort William via Callander (£15.10, 1¾ hours, daily).

Aberfoyle Coaches (www.aberfoylecoaches. com) runs between Callander and Aberfoyle (30 minutes, four times daily Monday to Saturday).

See the boxed text on p191 for other transport around the region.

LOCHS KATRINE & ACHRAY
This rugged area, 6 miles north of Aberfoyle and 10 miles west of Callander, is the heart of the Trossachs. From April to October two **boats** (☎01877-332000; www.lochkatrine.com; 1hr cruise adult/child £10/7) run cruises from Trossachs Pier at the eastern tip of Loch Katrine. At 10.30am there's a departure to Stronachlachar at the other end of the loch before returning (single/return adult £12/14, child £8/9). From Stronachlachar (also accessible by car via Aberfoyle), you can reach the eastern shore of Loch Lomond at isolated Inversnaid. A tarmac path links Trossachs Pier with Stronachlachar, so you can also take the boat out and walk/cycle back (12 miles). At Trossachs Pier, you can hire good bikes from **Katrinewheelz** (www.wheelscyclingcentre.com; hire per half-/full day from £10/15; ☺daily Apr-Oct). It even has electric buggies for the less mobile or inclined (£40 for two hours).

There are two good **walks** starting from nearby Loch Achray. The path to the rocky cone called **Ben A'an** (460m) begins at a car park near the old Trossachs Hotel. It's easy to follow, and the return trip is just under 4 miles (allow 2½ hours). A tougher walk is up rugged **Ben Venue** (727m) – there is a path all the way to the summit. Start walking from Loch Achray Hotel, follow the Achray Water westwards to Loch Katrine, then turn left and ascend the steep flanks of Ben Venue. There are great views of the Highlands and the Lowlands from the top. The return trip is about 5.5 miles – allow around four to five hours.

BALQUHIDDER & AROUND
Steeped in clan history, this mountainous and sparsely populated area is the wildest part of the Trossachs; get off the busy A84 for some tranquil lochscapes and great walking. North of Callander, you'll skirt past the shores of gorgeous Loch Lubnaig. Not as famous as some of its cousins, it's still well worth a stop for its sublime views of forested hills. In the small village of **Balquhidder** (ball-whidder), 9 miles north of Callander off the A84, there's a churchyard with **Rob Roy's grave**. It's an appropriately beautiful spot in a deep, winding glen in big-sky country. Rob Roy's wife and two of his sons are also interred here. In the church the 8th-century **St Angus' stone**, probably a marker to the original tomb of St Angus, an 8th-century monk who built the first church here.

TOP CHOICE **Monachyle Mhor** (☎01877-384622; www.mhor.net; dinner, bed & breakfast s/d from £166/220; ⓅⓈⓔⒶ), 4 miles on, is a luxury hideaway with a fantastically peaceful location overlooking two lochs. It's a great fusion of country Scotland and contemporary attitudes to design and food. The rooms and suites are superb and feature quirkily original decor. The restaurant offers set lunch (£20 for two courses) and dinner (£46) menus which are high in quality, sustainably sourced, and deliciously innovative. Enchantment lies in its successful combination of top-class hospitality with a relaxed rural atmosphere; dogs and kids happily romp on the lawns, and no-one looks askance if you come in flushed and muddy after a day's fishing or walking.

At the A84 junction, **Kings House Hotel** (☎01877-384646; www.kingshouse-scotland. co.uk; s/d £45/70; Ⓐ) is a classic inn built in 1779 for £40 at the request of passing drovers. Nowadays it offers B&B in more salubrious surroundings. The upstairs rooms are lovely, with fine views, and there's an ancient, narrow, sloping passageway that reminds visitors they're treading in the 200-year-old-plus footsteps of many a passing traveller. The cosy bar provides food and shelter from the elements.

The minor road at the A84 junction continues along pretty **Loch Voil** to Inverlochlarig, where you can climb **Stob Binnein** (1165m) by its southern ridge. Stob Binnein is one of the highest mountains in the area, and it has a most unusual shape, like a cone with its top chopped off.

ROB ROY

Nicknamed 'Red' ('ruadh' in Gaelic, anglicised to 'roy') for his ginger locks, Robert MacGregor (1671–1734) was the wild leader of the wildest of Scotland's clans. Although they had rights to the lands the clan occupied, these estates stood between powerful neighbours who had the MacGregors outlawed, hence their sobriquet 'Children of the Mist'. Incognito, Rob became a prosperous livestock trader, before a dodgy deal led to a warrant for his arrest.

A legendary swordsman, the fugitive from justice then became notorious for his daring raids into the Lowlands to carry off cattle and sheep. He was forever hiding from potential captors; he was twice imprisoned, but escaped dramatically on both occasions. He finally turned himself in, and received his liberty and a pardon from the King. He lies buried in the churchyard at Balquhidder (p193); his uncompromising epitaph reads 'MacGregor despite them'. His life has been glorified over the years due to Walter Scott's novel and the 1995 film. Many Scots see his life as a symbol of the struggle of the common folk against the inequitable ownership of vast tracts of the country by landed aristocrats.

Local buses between Callander and Killin stop at the Kings House Hotel, as do daily **Citylink** (www.citylink.co.uk) buses between Edinburgh and Oban/Fort William.

KILLIN
POP 666

A fine base for the Trossachs or Perthshire, this lovely village sits at the western end of Loch Tay (see also p215) and has a spread-out, relaxed sort of a feel, particularly around the scenic **Falls of Dochart** which tumble through the centre. On a sunny day people sprawl over the rocks by the bridge, pint or picnic in hand. Killin offers some fine walking around the town, and mighty mountains and glens close at hand.

The helpful, informative **tourist office** (☎01567-820254; killin@visitscotland.com) is in the **Breadalbane Folklore Centre** (www.breadalbanefolklorecentre.com; adult/child £2.95/1.95; ☉10am-4pm Wed-Mon Apr-Oct), in an old water mill overlooking the falls. There is an audiovisual presentation about St Fillan, a local saint whose religious teachings are said to have helped unite the ancient kingdoms of the Scots and the Picts in the 8th century. There are displays about local and clan history, including the Mac-Gregors and MacNabs. The **Clan MacNab burial ground** lies on an island in the river by the falls; ask at the tourist office for the gate key.

🏃 Activities

Five miles northeast of Killin, **Ben Lawers** (see the boxed text, p216) rises above Loch Tay. Other routes abound; one rewarding **circular walk** heads up into the Acharn forest south of town, emerging above the tree line to great views of Loch Tay and Ben Lawers. The tourist office has walking leaflets and maps covering the area.

Glen Lochay runs westwards from Killin into the hills of Mamlorn. You can take a **mountain bike** for about 11 miles up the glen to just beyond Batavaime. The scenery is impressive and the hills aren't too difficult to climb. It's possible, on a nice summer day, to climb over the top of **Ben Challum** (1025m) and descend to Crianlarich, but it's hard work. A potholed road also connects this glen with Glen Lyon (p215).

Killin is on the Lochs & Glens Cycle Way from Glasgow to Inverness. Hire bikes at **Killin Outdoor Centre** (☎01567-820652; www.killinoutdoor.co.uk; Main St; ☉daily). It also hires out canoes and kayaks.

🛏 Sleeping & Eating

There are numerous good guesthouses strung along the road through town, and a couple of supermarkets for trail supplies.

Falls of Dochart Inn   PUB ££
(☎01567-820270; www.falls-of-dochart-inn.co.uk; s/d from £60/80; 🅿🛜) In a prime position overlooking the falls, this is an excellent place to stay and eat. Handsome renovated rooms are comfortable, with slate bathrooms; it's worth the investment for one overlooking the falls themselves (double £95), but readers warn they can be chilly in winter. Downstairs is a very snug, atmospheric space with a roaring fire, personable service and really satisfying pub food, ranging from light meals to tasty, tender steaks and a couple of more advanced creations.

CENTRAL SCOTLAND STIRLING REGION

High Creagan CAMPSITE £
(☎01567-820449; Aberfeldy Rd; sites per person £6; ☺Mar-Oct) This place has a well-kept, sheltered campsite with plenty of grass set high on the slopes overlooking sparkling Loch Tay, just outside Killin. Kids under five aren't allowed in the tent area as there's a stream running through it.

Braveheart Backpackers HOSTEL £
(☎07796-886899; info@cyclescotland.co.uk; dm/s/d £17.50/20/40) Tucked away alongside the Killin Hotel (on the main road through town), these two adjoining cottages offer several types of room, all wood-clad with comfortable beds and bunks including sheets. The comfy kitchen and lounge area won't appeal to hygiene nuts, but make the place feel like a home rather than a hostel. There's a rather negotiable attitude to prices and bookings: in short, it's not for everyone, but we like it.

❶ Getting There & Away
Two daily **Citylink** (www.citylink.co.uk) buses between Edinburgh and Oban/Fort William stop here. There's also a **postbus** (www.royalmail. com) to Crianlarich and Tyndrum twice on weekdays and once on Saturday. **Kingshouse Travel** (www.kingshousetravel.co.uk) runs buses to Callander, where you can change to a Stirling service.

FIFE

Protruding like a serpent's head from Scotland's east coast, Fife (www.visitfife.com) is a tongue of land between the Firths of Forth and Tay. A royal history an atmosphere distinct from the rest of Scotland leads it to style itself as 'The Kingdom of Fife'.

Though overdeveloped southern Fife is commuter-belt territory, the eastern region's rolling green farmland and quaint fishing villages are prime turf for exploration and crab-crunching, and the fresh sea air feels like it's doing a power of good. Elsewhere in the county, little Falkland makes a great stop, and dignified Culross is a superbly preserved 17th-century burgh.

Fife's biggest attraction, St Andrews, has Scotland's most venerable university and a wealth of historic buildings. It's also, of course, the headquarters of golf and draws professionals and keen slashers alike to take on the Old Course – the classic links experience.

🏃 Activities
The **Fife Coastal Path** (www.fifecoastalpath. co.uk) runs more than 80 miles following the entire Fife coastline from the Forth Road Bridge to the Tay Bridge and beyond. It's well waymarked, picturesque and not too rigorous, though winds can buffet. It's easily accessed for shorter sections or day walks, and long stretches of it can be tackled on a mountain bike too.

❶ Getting Around
The main bus operator here is **Stagecoach Fife** (☎0871-2002233; www.stagecoachbus.com). For £6.80 you can buy a Fife Dayrider ticket, which gives unlimited travel around Fife on Stagecoach buses.

If you are driving from the Forth Road Bridge to St Andrews, a slower but much more scenic route than the M90/A91 is along the signposted **Fife Coastal Tourist Route**.

Culross
POP 500

An enchanting little town, Culross (*koo-ross*) is Scotland's best-preserved example of a 17th-century Scottish burgh: the National Trust for Scotland owns 20 of the town's buildings, including the palace. Small, red-tiled, whitewashed buildings line the cobbled streets, and the winding Back Causeway to the abbey is embellished with whimsical stone cottages.

As birthplace of St Mungo, Glasgow's patron saint, Culross was an important religious centre from the 6th century. The burgh developed, under laird George Bruce, by mining coal through extraordinary underwater tunnels. Vigorous trade resulted, enabling Bruce to build and complete the palace by 1611. When mining was ended by flooding of the tunnels, the town switched to making linen and shoes.

Culross Palace (NTS; www.nts.org.uk; adult/child £8/5; ☺noon-5pm Thu-Mon Apr-May & Sep, noon-5pm daily Jun-Aug, noon-4pm Thu-Mon Oct) is more a large house than a palace, and features extraordinary decorative painted woodwork, barrel-vaulted ceilings and an interior largely unchanged since the early 17th century. It's dark and spooky inside on an overcast day. The **Town House** (tourist office downstairs) and the **Study**, also completed in the early 17th century, are open to the public (via guided tour included in palace admission), but the other NTS properties can only be viewed from the outside.

Ruined **Culross Abbey** (HS; www.historic -scotland.gov.uk; admission free; ◷9.30am-7pm Mon-Sat & 2-7pm Sun Apr-Sep, 9.30am-4pm Mon-Sat & 2-4pm Sun Oct-Mar), founded by the Cistercians in 1217, is on the hill in a lovely peaceful spot with vistas of the firth. The choir of the abbey church is now the parish church.

Above a pottery workshop near the palace, **Biscuit Café** (www.culrosspottery.com; light meals £4-7; ◷breakfast & lunch) has a tranquil little garden and sells coffee, tempting organic cakes and scones, and tasty light meals.

Culross is 12 miles west of the Forth Road Bridge. **Stagecoach** (www.stagecoach bus.com) bus 78 runs to Culross from Dunfermline (25 minutes, hourly).

Dunfermline

POP 39,229

Historic, monastic Dunfermline is Fife's largest population centre, sprawling eastwards through once-distinct villages. Its noble history is centred on evocative **Dunfermline Abbey** (HS; www.historic-scotland. gov.uk; St Margaret St; adult/child £3.70/2.20; ◷9.30am-5.30pm daily Apr-Sep, 9.30am-4.30pm Mon-Wed & Sat, 9.30am-12.30pm Thu & 2-4.30pm Sun Oct-Mar), founded by David I in the 12th century as a Benedictine monastery. Dunfermline was already favoured by religious royals; Malcolm III married the exiled Saxon princess Margaret here in the 11th century, and both chose to be interred here. There were many more royal burials, none more notable than Robert the Bruce, whose remains were discovered here in 1818.

What's left of the abbey are the **ruins** of the impressive three-tiered refectory building, and the atmosphere-laden nave of the church, endowed with geometrically patterned columns and fine Romanesque and Gothic windows. It adjoins the 19th-century **church** (◷May-Sep) where Robert the Bruce now lies under the ornate pulpit.

Next to the refectory (and included in your abbey admission price) is **Dunfermline Palace**. Once the abbey guest house, it was converted for James VI, whose son, the ill-fated Charles I, was born here in 1600. Below stretches the bosky, strollable **Pittencrieff Park**.

The award-winning **Abbot House Heritage Centre** (www.abbothouse.co.uk; Maygate; adult/child £4/free; ◷10am-5pm Mar-Nov, 10am-4pm Dec-Feb), near the abbey, dates from the 15th century. History buffs could get lost for hours among the absorbing displays about the history of Scotland, the abbey and Dunfermline. Entry includes a guided tour.

Dunfermline is a culinary desert, but the good folk at **Fresh** (2 Kirkgate; light meals £4-7; ◷breakfast & lunch daily, dinner Sat & Sun; @), just up from the abbey, do decent sandwiches and coffee, as well as tasty daily specials based on deli produce. There's also wine, internet access, a gallery and book exchange.

There are frequent buses between Dunfermline and Edinburgh (40 minutes), Stirling (1¼ hours) and St Andrews (1¼ hours), and trains to/from Edinburgh (30 minutes).

Aberdour

POP 1690

It's worth stopping in this popular seaside town to ramble around impressive **Aberdour Castle** (HS; www.historic-scotland.gov. uk; adult/child £4.20/2.50; ◷9.30am-5.30pm daily Apr-Sep, 9.30am-4.30pm Sat-Wed Oct-Mar). Long a residence of the Douglases of Morton, the stately structure exhibits several architectural phases; it's worth purchasing the guidebook to better comprehend what you see. Most charming of all is the elaborate doocot (dovecote) at the bottom of the garden. Be sure to pop into the beautiful Romanesque church of **St Fillan's**, next door to the castle.

With real ales and good vegetarian choices on the menu, the family-run **Aberdour Hotel** (☎01383-860325; www.aberdourhotel. co.uk; 38 High St; s/d £60/85; Ⓟ☜) is not only a good place to stay, but also a tummy-warming meal stop (mains are £8 to £11), and there's an emphasis on hearty, home-cooked food.

There are regular trains to Edinburgh (40 minutes) and Dundee (one hour) from Aberdour, as well as buses to nearby Dunfermline (40 minutes).

Kirkcaldy

POP 46,912

Kirkcaldy (ker-caw-dee) sprawls along the edge of the sea for several miles and has a rather shabby promenade with spectacular pounding surf on windy days. It's worth stopping in town to visit the excellent museum. Kirkcaldy is famous as the birthplace of 18th-century Enlightenment philosopher and economist Adam Smith, the man who features on the English £20 note.

A short walk east from the train and bus stations, you'll find the **Kirkcaldy Museum & Art Gallery** (War Memorial Gardens; admission free; ⊘10.30am-5pm Mon-Sat, 2-5pm Sun), which combines historical accounts with contemporary exhibits. The kids will have a ball as there are plenty of hands-on attractions. There's also an impressive collection of **Scottish paintings** from the 18th to the 20th century, including work from the Scottish Colourists and the Glasgow Boys.

You're better off staying in Edinburgh, East Neuk or St Andrews than Kirkcaldy, but you'll be comfortable at **Ashgrove B&B** (☎01592-561354; www.ashgrovebnb.co.uk; 213 Nicol St; s/tw/f £40/60/80; ☐☎). The bustling, likeable Scot who runs this joint is as quirky as the rabbit-warren layout inside. Rooms are smallish but well set up, and exude a comforting homely warmth. Book in advance over summer.

The **tourist office** (☎01592-267775; www.visitfife.com; 339 High St; ⊘9.30am-5pm Mon-Sat Apr-Sep, 10am-4pm Mon-Sat Oct-Mar) is at the eastern end of the waterfront strip.

Frequent buses run to St Andrews (one hour), Anstruther (1¼ hours) and Edinburgh (one hour). Two to four trains an hour run to Edinburgh (£6.30, 45 minutes) and Dundee (£10.60, 40 minutes).

Falkland

POP 1183

Below the soft ridges of the Lomond Hills in the centre of Fife is the charming village of Falkland. Rising majestically out of the town centre and dominating the skyline is the outstanding 16th-century **Falkland Palace** (NTS; www.nts.org.uk; adult/child £10.20/7.10; ⊘11am-5pm Mon-Sat, 1-5pm Sun Mar-Oct), a country residence of the Stuart monarchs. Mary, Queen of Scots is said to have spent the happiest days of her life 'playing the country girl in the woods and parks' at Falkland. The palace was built between 1501 and 1541 to replace a castle dating from the 12th century; French and Scottish craftspeople were employed to create a masterpiece of Scottish Gothic architecture. The **King's bedchamber** and the **chapel**, with its beautiful painted ceiling, have both been restored. Don't miss the prodigious 17th-century Flemish hunting **tapestries** in the hall. One feature of the royal leisure centre

DEEP SEA WORLD

If the kids are tiring of historic buildings, a trip to **Deep Sea World** (www.deepseaworld.com; North Queensferry; adult/child/family £12/8.50/38.50; ⊘10am-5pm Mon-Fri, 10am-6pm Sat & Sun) might make them feel more kindly towards Fife. Situated at North Queensferry, just by the Forth bridges, it's a blockbuster aquarium with all those 'respect' species like sharks and piranhas, as well as seals and touch pools with rays and other sea creatures. You can even arrange guided dives with sharks. It's a little cheaper if you pre-purchase tickets online.

still exists: the oldest **royal tennis court** in Britain, built in 1539 for James V. It's in the grounds and still in use.

ⓉⓄⓅ Luigino's (Covenanter Hotel; ☎01337-857224; www.luiginos.co.uk; s/d/f £56/80/89; ☎), oppsite the church, is an old coaching inn that's a joyful marriage of wonderful traditional architecture and exuberant Italian gastronomy. Rooms have been made over with smart black slate and wallpaper, and the quality restaurant, **Luigino's** (mains £9-13, ⊘lunch and dinner), serves authentic and tasty *saltimbocca* (Italian veal-and-ham dish), pasta that you can watch being made fresh, and wood-fired pizza. The enthusiasm and cheeriness of the owners and staff is a high point.

Falkland is 11 miles north of Kirkcaldy. Bus 36 travels between Glenrothes and Auchtermuchty via Falkland. From either of those two places there are regular connections to St Andrews and other Fife destinations. Buses continue on to Perth (one hour) more or less hourly.

St Andrews

POP 14,209

For a small place, St Andrews made a big name for itself, firstly as religious centre, then as Scotland's oldest university town. But its status as the home of golf has propelled it to even greater fame, and today's pilgrims arrive with a set of clubs. But it's a lovely place to visit even if you've no interest in the game, with impressive medieval

St Andrews

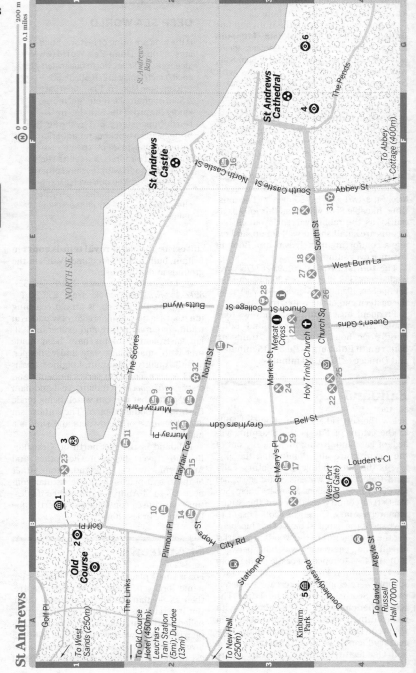

St Andrews Bay

NORTH SEA

St Andrews Castle

St Andrews Cathedral

The Pends

To Abbey Cottage (400m)

Abbey St

North Castle St

South Castle St

South St

West Burn La

Butts Wynd

The Scores

Murray Park

College St

Church St

Church Sq

Queen's Gdns

Market St

Mercat Cross

Holy Trinity Church

North St

Murray Park

Murray Pl

Greyfriars Gdn

Bell St

Playfair Tce

St Mary's Pl

West Port (Old Gate)

Louden's Cl

Pilmour Pl

Hope St

City Rd

Station Rd

Doubledykes Rd

Kinburn Park

Argyle St

To David Russell Hall (700m)

Old Course

Golf Pl

The Links

To West Sands (250m)

To Old Course Hotel (450m); Leuchars Train Station (5mi); Dundee (13mi)

To New Hall (250m)

0 · 200 m
0 · 0.1 miles

ruins, stately university buildings, idyllic white sands and excellent accommodation and eating options.

The Old Course, the world's most famous, has a striking seaside location at the western end of town. Although it's difficult to get a game (see the boxed text, p201), it's still a thrilling experience to stroll the hallowed turf. Between the students and golfers, St Andrews can feel like the least Scottish of places as, although technically a city, it's not very large.

History

St Andrews is said to have been founded by St Regulus, who arrived from Greece in the 4th century bringing the bones of St Andrew, Scotland's patron saint. The town soon grew into a major pilgrimage centre and St Andrews developed into the ecclesiastical capital of the country. The university was founded in 1410, the first in Scotland.

Golf has been played here for more than 600 years; the Royal & Ancient Golf Club, the game's governing body, was founded in 1754 and the imposing clubhouse was built a hundred years later. The British Open Championship takes place here every few years in July.

⊙ Sights

St Andrews Cathedral   CATHEDRAL RUINS
(HS; www.historic-scotland.gov.uk; The Pends; adult/child £4.20/2.50, incl castle £7.20/4.30; ⊙9.30am-5.30pm Apr-Sep, to 4.30pm Oct-Mar) The ruins of this cathedral are all that's left of one of Britain's most magnificent medieval buildings. You can appreciate the scale and majesty of the edifice from the small sections that remain standing. Although founded in 1160, it was not consecrated until 1318, but stood as the focus of this important pilgrimage centre until 1559 when it was pillaged during the Reformation.

St Andrew's supposed bones lie under the altar; until the cathedral was built, they had been enshrined in the nearby Church of St Regulus (Rule). All that remains of this church is **St Rule's Tower**, worth the climb for the view across St Andrews. The tourist office includes a **museum** with a collection of Celtic crosses and gravestones found on the site. The entrance fee only applies for the tower and museum; you can wander freely around the atmospheric ruins.

St Andrews Castle   CASTLE
(HS; www.historic-scotland.gov.uk; The Scores; adult/child £5.20/3.10, with cathedral £7.20/4.30;

St Andrews

⊘9.30am-5.30pm Apr-Sep, to 4.30pm Oct-Mar) Not far from the cathedral and with dramatic coastline views, the castle is mainly in ruins, but the site itself is evocative. It was founded around 1200 as the bishop's fortified home. After the execution of Protestant reformers in 1545, other reformers retaliated by murdering Cardinal Beaton and taking over the castle. They spent almost a year holed up, during which they and their attackers dug a complex of **siege tunnels**, said to be the best surviving example of castle-siege engineering in Europe; you can walk (or stoop) along their damp mossy lengths. A tourist office gives a good audiovisual introduction and has a small collection of Pictish stones.

The Scores   SIGNIFICANT AREA

From the castle, the Scores follows the coast west down to the first tee at the Old Course. Family-friendly **St Andrews Aquarium** (www.standrewsaquarium.co.uk; adult/child £6.50/4.60; ⊘10am-6pm Mar-Oct, 10am-4.30pm Nov-Feb, last entry 1hr before closing) has a seal pool, rays and sharks from Scottish waters and exotic tropical favourites. Once introduced to our finny friends, you can snack on them with chips in the cafe.

Nearby, the **British Golf Museum** (www.britishgolfmuseum.co.uk; Bruce Embankment; adult/child £6/3; ⊘9.30am-5pm Mon-Sat & 10am-5pm Sun Apr-Oct, 10am-4pm daily Nov-Mar) has an extraordinarily comprehensive overview of the history and development of the game and the role of St Andrews in it. Favourite fact: bad players were formerly known as 'foozlers'. Interactive panels allow you to relive former British Opens (watch Paul Azinger snapping his putter in frustration), and there's a large collection of memorabilia from Open winners both male and female.

Opposite the museum is the **Royal & Ancient Golf Club**, which stands proudly at the head of the **Old Course**, which you can stroll on once play is finished for the day, and all day on Sundays. Beside it stretches magnificent **West Sands** beach, made famous by the film *Chariots of Fire*.

FREE **St Andrews Museum**   MUSEUM
(www.fifedirect.org.uk/museums; Doubledykes Rd; ⊘10am-5pm Apr-Sep, 10.30am-4pm Oct-Mar) Near the bus station, St Andrews Museum has interesting displays that chart the history of the town from its founding by St Regulus to its growth as an ecclesiastical, academic and sporting centre. Local preservation work is a focal point.

🏃 Activities

Apart from the obvious one – **golf** (see the boxed text, p201) – the tourist office has a list of local **walks** and also sells OS maps. The **Fife Coastal Path** (www.fifecoastalpath.co.uk) stretches 78 miles from the Forth Road Bridge to beyond the Tay Bridge (Dundee), a wonderful long-distance walk. The section between St Andrews and East Neuk is fun either on foot or on a mountain bike. Parts of the track can be covered by the tide, so check tide times before you go. The tourist office has a detailed map.

All the East Neuk (p204) attractions are within easy **cycling** distance. You can also cycle north to the forest, beach and nature trail at **Tentsmuirs Sands** (10 miles).

👉 Tours

There is a **Witches Tour** (☏01334-655057; adult/child £7/5; ⊘7.30pm Thu & Fri) that recounts the history and folklore of St Andrews in an unusual fashion, with tales of ghosts and witches enlivened by theatrical stunts. It starts outside Greyfriars Hotel on North St.

🎊 Festivals & Events

Open Championship   GOLF
(www.opengolf.com) One of international golf's four 'majors', takes place in July. However, the tournament venue changes from year to year, and the Open only comes to St Andrews itself every five years – check the website for future venues.

St Andrews Highland Games
                        TRADTIONAL SPORTS
(www.albagames.co.uk) Held on the North Haugh on the last Sunday in July.

St Andrews Festival   ARTS, CULTURE
(www.standrewsfestival.co.uk) Five days of festivities leading up to St Andrews Day (30 November), the feast day of Scotland's patron saint. Celebrations include a festival of Scottish food and drink, and various arts events.

🛏 Sleeping

St Andrews accommodation is often heavily booked (especially in summer), so you're well advised to book in advance. Almost every house on Murray Park and Murray Pl is a guesthouse: this area couldn't be more convenient, but prices are on the high side.

TOP CHOICE **Abbey Cottage**   B&B ££
(☏01334-473727; www.abbeycottage.co.uk; Abbey Walk; s £40, d £59-64; ℗) You know

Golf has been played at St Andrews since the 15th century. By 1457 was so popular that James II placed a ban on it because it interfered with his troops' archery practice. Although it lies beside the exclusive, all-male (female bartenders, unsurprisingly, allowed) Royal & Ancient Golf Club, the Old Course is public.

You'll need to book in advance to play via **St Andrews Links Trust** (☎01334-466666; www.standrews.org.uk). You must reserve on or after the first Wednesday in September the year before you wish to play. No bookings are taken for Saturdays or the month of September.

Unless you've booked months in advance, getting a tee-off time is literally a lottery; enter the ballot at the **caddie office** (☎01334-466666) before 2pm on the day before you wish to play (there's no Sunday play). Be warned that applications by ballot are normally heavily oversubscribed, and green fees are £130 in summer. Singles are not accepted in the ballot and should start queuing as early as possible – 5.30am is good – in the hope of joining a group. You'll need a handicap certificate (24/36 for men/women). If your number doesn't come up, there are six other public courses in the area, including the prestigious, recently opened Castle Course (£120). Other summer green fees: New £65, Jubilee £65, Eden £40, Strathtyrum £25 and Balgove (nine-holer for beginners and kids) £12. There are various multiple-day tickets available. If you play on a windy day expect those scores to balloon: Nick Faldo famously stated, 'When it blows here, even the seagulls walk.'

Guided walks (£2.50) of the Old Course run at weekends in June and daily in July and August, and hit famous landmarks such as the Swilcan Bridge and the Road Hole bunker. They run from outside the shop roughly hourly from 11am to 4pm and last 50 minutes. On Sundays, a three-hour walk (£5) takes you around the whole course.

you've strayed from B&B mainstream when your charming host's hobby is photographing tigers in the wild – don't leave without browsing her albums. This engaging spot sits below the town, surrounded by stone walls which enclose a rambling garden; it feels like you are staying in the country. There are three excellent rooms, all different, with patchwork quilts, sheepskins, and antique furniture.

Hazelbank Hotel
HOTEL **£££**
(☎01334-472466; www.hazelbank.com; 28 The Scores; s/d £90/151; @☎) Offering a genuine welcome, the family-run Hazelbank is the most likeable of the hotels along the Scores. The front rooms have marvellous views along the beach and out to sea; those at the back are somewhat cheaper and more spacious. Prices drop significantly outside the height of summer. There are good portents if you are playing a round – Bobby Locke won the Open in 1957 while staying here.

Five Pilmour Place
B&B **££**
(☎01334-478665; www.5pilmourplace.com; 5 Pilmour Pl; s £75, d £105-130; @☎) Just around the corner from the Old Course, this luxurious and intimate spot offers stylish, compact rooms with an eclectic range of styles

as well as modern conveniences such as flatscreen TV and DVD player. The king-size beds are especially comfortable, and the lounge area is a stylish treat.

Meade B&B
B&B **££**
(☎01334-477350; annmeade10@hotmail.com; 5 Albany Pl; s with/without bathroom £55/30, d £60/40; ☎) It's always sweet relief to find a B&B unconcerned with VisitScotland's fussy regulations. This economical gem is run by a friendly family and their pets, including a portly marmalade cat and affectionate black lab. The two comfortable rooms are colour-coded and have readable novels, photo albums and films on DVD. The B&B might have moved to a new location by the time you read this, but the phone number will be the same.

Old Fishergate House
B&B **££**
(☎01334-470874; www.oldfishergatehouse.co.uk; North Castle St; s/d £75/100; ☎) This historic 17th-century town house, furnished with period pieces, is in a great location – the oldest part of town, close to the cathedral and castle. The two twin rooms are very spacious and even have their own sitting room and cushioned ledges on their window sills. On a scale of one to 10 for quaintness, we'd

rate it about a 9½. Cracking breakfasts feature fresh fish and pancakes.

St Andrews Tourist Hostel   HOSTEL £

(☎01334-479911; www.standrewshostel.com; St Marys Pl; dm £13-14; ☎) Laid-back and central, this hostel down the side of the Grill House restaurant is a little bit hard to spot. Occupying a stately old building, it has high corniced ceilings, especially in the huge lounge, and a laissez-faire approach. The dorms could use new mattresses, but are clean and bright. There's a supermarket close by.

⌁ University of St Andrews
UNIVERSITY ACCOMODATION £££
(www.discoverstandrews.com; ☼mid-Jun–mid-Sep; P@☎) When the university is out of session, three student residences open up as visitor accommodation. There's the hotel-style **New Hall** (☎01334-467000; North Haugh; s/d £56/83); self-catering rooms at **David Russell Hall** (☎01334-467100; Buchanan Gdns; apt for 3/7 days £290/560); and budget single rooms in the central **McIntosh Hall** (☎01334-467035; Abbotsford Cres; s/d £34/60). These prices are all good value for the standard of accommodation on offer.

Cameron House   B&B ££

(☎01334-472306; www.cameronhouse-sta.co.uk; 11 Murray Park; s/d £45/90; ☎) Beautifully decorated rooms and warm, cheerful hosts make this a real home-away-from-home on this guesthouse-filled street. The two single rooms share a bathroom. Prices drop £10 per person outside peak season.

Ogstons on North Street   HOTEL £££

(☎01334-473387; www.ogstonsonnorthst.com; 127 North St; s/d £100-120, d £120-160; ☎☝) If you want to eat, drink and sleep in the same stylish place then this classy inn could be for you. Smartened-up rooms feature elegant contemporary styling and coolly beautiful bathrooms, some with jacuzzi. There are also DVD players, iPod docks, crisp white linen and large windows that give the rooms an airy feel. The Oak Rooms (serving lunch and dinner) is the place for meals and a read of the paper. The bar is perfect for a snug tipple, and the Lizard Lounge in the basement is a late-night bar that cranks up with live gigs and regular DJs.

Old Course Hotel   HOTEL £££

(☎01334-474371; www.oldcoursehotel.co.uk; d with/without view £410/360, ste £680; P@☎☒) A byword for golfing luxury,

this hotel is right alongside the famous 17th and has huge rooms, excellent service and a raft of facilities. Fork out the extra £50 or so for a view over the Old Course.

Aslar House   B&B ££

(☎01334-473460; www.aslar.com; 120 North St; s/d £48/96; ☎) Mod-cons in the rooms at this upmarket pad include iPod docks, DVD players and silent fridges, but they don't detract from the house's historical features, including a whimsical turret room.

Cairnsmill Caravan Park   CAMPSITE £

(☎01334-473604; cairnsmill@aol.com; Largo Rd; sites for 2 people £15-16; ☼Apr-Oct; P☒) About a mile west of St Andrews on the A915, this camping ground has brilliant views over the town. There's not much space between sites, though – they pack 'em in.

Lorimer House   B&B ££

(☎01334-476599; www.lorimerhouse.com; 19 Murray Park; d £90-110; ☎) Smallish, sparklingly clean rooms with extra-comfy beds and a fab deluxe double on the top floor.

Burness House   B&B ££

(☎01334-474314; www.burnesshouse.com; 1 Murray Park; d per person £36-46; ☼Mar-Nov; ☎) Rich, Asian-inspired fabrics, golf pictures and shiny new bathrooms.

✗ Eating

St Andrews has a great range of eating options. Places compete heavily on price for the student custom, so there are good deals to be had everywhere. Two great options for self-catering or picnic fare are the fine fishmonger **Andrew Keracher** (www.keracher.co.uk; 73 South St), and **IJ Mellis** (www.mellischeese.co.uk; 149 South St), with a wealth of cheeses you can smell halfway down the street.

TOP CHOICE   Peat Inn   RESTAURANT £££

(☎01334-840206; www.thepeatinn.co.uk; 3-course lunch/dinner £16/32; ☼lunch & dinner Tue-Sat) The Peat Inn is one of the best restaurants in Scotland, housed in a rustic country inn about 6 miles west of St Andrews. Its award-winning French-influenced menu is culinary heaven. To get there, head west on the A915 then turn right on the B940.

Vine Leaf
RESTAURANT ££

(☎01334-477497; www.vineleafstandrews.co.uk; 131 South St; 2-course dinner £23.50; ⊙dinner Tue-Sat) Classy, comfortable, and well-established, the friendly Vine Leaf offers a changing menu of sumptuous Scottish seafood, game and vegetarian dishes. It's down a close off South St.

🌿 Seafood Restaurant
RESTAURANT £££

(☎01334-479475; www.theseafoodrestaurant.com; The Scores; lunch/dinner £22/45; ⊙lunch & dinner) The Seafood Restaurant occupies a stylish glass-walled room, built out over the sea, with plush navy carpet, crisp white linen, an open kitchen and panoramic views of St Andrews Bay. It offers top seafood and an excellent wine list, and has won a clutch of awards. Look out for its special winter deal – three-course lunch for £15, or dinner for £20.

Doll's House
RESTAURANT ££

(☎01334-477422; www.dolls-house.co.uk; 3 Church Sq; mains £10-15; ⊙lunch & dinner) With its high-backed chairs, bright colours and creaky wooden floor, the Doll's House blends a Victorian child's bedroom with modern stylings. The result is a surprising warmth and no pretensions. The menu makes the most of local fish and other Scottish produce, and the two-course lunch for £6.95 is unbeatable value. The early-evening two-course deal for £12.95 isn't bad either.

Zest
CAFE £

(www.zestjuicing.co.uk; 95 South St; juices £2-4; ⊙breakfast & lunch) Serving toasties, paninis and filled rolls along with a good coffee selection, this slick place is popular with students. French doors opening onto the street make it a great spot for people-watching on a breezy summer day. The juices and smoothies here are great, and priced very fairly.

Byre Theatre Bistro
BISTRO ££

(www.byretheatre.com; Abbey St; mains £9-15; ⊙breakfast, lunch & dinner Tue-Sat; 🛜👶) A happy, buzzy spot with comfy couches, works of art on the wall and a well-developed menu that encompasses some delicious fusion cooking. Lunchtime sandwiches come with interesting fillings, such as hummus and red pepper. Dinner gets more sophisticated, featuring dishes such as seared tuna steak on sultana-and-nutmeg couscous with smoked-tomato dressing.

Tailend
BISTRO £

(130 Market St; mains £6-10; ⊙breakfast, lunch & dinner) Delicious fresh fish sourced from Arbroath just up the coast put this new St Andrews arrival a class above most chippies. The array of exquisite smoked delicacies at the counter will have you planning a picnic or fighting for a table out the back.

B Jannetta
ICE CREAM £

(www.jannettas.co.uk; 31 South St; 2-dip cone £2.40; ⊙breakfast & lunch Mon-Sat) B Jannetta is a St Andrews institution, offering 52 varieties of ice-cream from the weird (Irn-Bru sorbet) to the decadent (strawberries-and-champagne). There's also a decent cafe next door.

🌿 Balaka
BANGLADESHI ££

(www.balaka.com; 3 Alexandra Pl; mains £10-12; ⊙lunch & dinner Mon-Sat, dinner Sun) Long-established Bangladeshi restaurant with both standard choices and more inspiring discoveries – all delicious and seasoned with herbs the owners grow themselves. The £6.95 lunch deal is a bargain.

Grill House
BISTRO £

(www.grillhouserestaurant.co.uk; St Mary's Pl; mains £6-15; ⊙lunch & dinner) This cheerful, sometimes boisterous restaurant offers something for every taste and bank balance, with a big selection ranging from Mexican, pizza and pasta to char-grilled salmon and quality steaks. The upbeat atmosphere and service are pluses, as is the £5 lunchtime deal.

Zizzi
BISTRO £

(www.zizzi.co.uk; 87 South St; pasta £7-10; ⊙lunch & dinner) Beloved of local students, this Italian eatery has atmosphere without the tack. Rather than Mona Lisas, moribund love songs and phallic pepper grinders, it's got contemporary decor, an open kitchen, a chatty buzz and fast service. The food won't wow but it will satisfy.

🍺 Drinking

Central Bar
PUB

(77 Market St) Rather staid compared to some of the wilder student-driven drinking options, this likeable pub keeps it real with traditional features, an island bar, lots of Scottish beers, decent service and filling (if uninspiring) pub grub.

West Port
PUB

(www.maclay.com; 170 South St; 🛜) Just by the gateway of the same name, this sleek, modernised pub has several levels, and a great beer garden out the back. Cheap cocktails rock the uni crowd, mixed drinks are above average, and there's some OK bar food.

Victoria PUB
(1 St Mary's Pl) Upstairs at the Victoria is popular with all types of students and serves good bar meals. There's a grungy cafe-bar here with plenty of natural light or a classier lounge bar where you can sink into a sofa. Check out the jazz on Sunday nights.

☆ Entertainment

There's always something on in the pubs around town during term-time.

Byre Theatre THEATRE
(☎01334-475000; www.byretheatre.com; Abbey St) This theatre company started life in a converted cow byre in the 1930s, and now occupies a flashy premises making clever use of light and space.

New Picture House CINEMA
(www.nphcinema.co.uk; North St) Two-screen cinema showing current films.

ℹ Information

J&G Innes (107 South St) Plenty of local-interest books, such as Fife's history of burning witches.

Library (Church Sq; ☺9.30am-5pm Mon, Fri & Sat, to 7pm Tue-Thu; @) Free internet access – drop-in only; no bookings.

St Andrews Memorial Hospital (☎01334-472327; Abbey Walk) Located south of Abbey St.

Tourist office (☎01334-472021; www.visit-st andrews.co.uk; 70 Market St; ☺9.15am-6.30pm Mon-Sat & 9.30am-5pm Sun Jul-Sep, 9.15am-5pm Mon-Sat mid-Oct–Jun, 11am-4pm Sun Apr-Jun; @) Helpful staff with good knowledge of St Andrews and Fife.

ℹ Getting There & Away

BUS All buses leave from the bus station on Station Rd. There are frequent services to the following:

Anstruther, 40 minutes, regularly

Crail, 30 minutes, regularly

Dundee, 30 minutes, half-hourly

Edinburgh via Kirkcaldy, £9.40, two hours, hourly

Glasgow, £9.40, 2 ½ hours, hourly

Stirling, £7.30, two hours, six to seven Monday to Saturday

TRAIN There is no train station in St Andrews itself, but you can take a train from Edinburgh (grab a seat on the right-hand side of the car-

riage for great firth views) to Leuchars, 5 miles to the northwest (£11.20, one hour, hourly). From here, buses leave regularly for St Andrews.

ℹ Getting Around

To order a cab, call **Golf City Taxis** (☎01334-477788). A taxi between Leuchars train station and the town centre costs around £10.

Spokes (☎01334-477835; www.spokes cycles.com; 37 South St; hire per half-/full day £8.50/13; ☺9am-5.30pm Mon-Sat) hires out mountain bikes.

East Neuk

This charming stretch of coast runs south from St Andrews to the point at Fife Ness, then west to Leven. Neuk is an old Scots word for corner, and it's certainly an appealing nook of the country to investigate, with picturesque fishing villages, some great restaurants and pretty coastal walks; the Fife Coastal Path's most scenic stretches are in this area. It's easily visited from St Andrews, but also makes a very pleasant place to stay.

CRAIL
POP 1695

Pretty and peaceful, little Crail has a much-photographed stone-sheltered harbour surrounded by wee cottages with red-tiled roofs. You can buy lobster and crab from a kiosk (☺lunch Sat & Sun) there. The benches in the nearby grassed area are perfectly placed for munching your alfresco crustaceans while admiring the view across to the Isle of May.

The village's history and involvement with the fishing industry is outlined in the **Crail Museum** (www.crailmuseum.org.uk; 62 Marketgate; admission free; ☺10am-1pm & 2-5pm Mon-Sat, 2-5pm Sun Jun-Sep, 2-5pm Sat & Sun Apr & May), which also offers tourist information.

Eighteenth-century **Selcraig House** (☎01333-450697; www.selcraighouse.co.uk; 47 Nethergate; s/d from £50/70; ☎) is a characterful, well-run place with a variety of rooms. Curiously shaped top-floor chambers will appeal to the quirky, while the fantastic four-poster room on the 1st floor (£80) will charm those with a taste for luxury and beautiful furnishings.

Hazelton Guest House (☎01333-450250; www.thehazelton.co.uk; 29 Marketgate North; d/superior d £70/80; ☺Mar-Oct; ☎) is a welcoming, walker-friendly guest house across the road from the museum, while **Caiplie House** (☏01333-450564; www.caipliehouse.co.uk; 53 High St N; s/d £39/64; ☺Apr-Nov; ☜) has large rooms with lots of lights, and big soft beds perfect for flopping at the end of the day. The top room here has views across to East Lothian. It also does reader-recommended evening meals.

Crail is 10 miles southeast of St Andrews. **Stagecoach** (www.stagecoachbus.com) bus 95 between Leven, Anstruther, Crail and St Andrews passes through Crail hourly every day (30 minutes to St Andrews).

ANSTRUTHER
POP 3442

Once among Scotland's busiest ports, cheery Anstruther has ridden the tribulations of the fishing industry better than some, and now has a very pleasant mixture of bobbing boats, historic streets, and visitors ambling around the harbour grazing on fish and chips or contemplating a trip to the Isle of May.

◉ Sights

The displays at the excellent **Scottish Fisheries Museum** (www.scotfishmuseum.org; adult/child £6/free; ☺10am-5.30pm Mon-Sat & 11am-5pm Sun Apr-Sep, 10am-4.30pm Mon-Sat & noon-4.30pm Sun Oct-Mar) include the **Zulu Gallery**, which houses the huge, partly restored hull of a traditional Zulu-class fishing boat, redolent with the scent of tar and timber. Afloat in the harbour outside the museum lies the *Reaper*, a fully restored Fifie-class fishing boat built in 1902.

The mile-long **Isle of May**, 6 miles southeast of Anstruther, is a stunning nature reserve. Between April and July the intimidating cliffs are packed with breeding kittiwakes, razorbills, guillemots, shags and around 40,000 puffins. Minke whales have also been spotted around the island in early summer. Inland are the remains of the 12th-century **St Adrian's Chapel**, dedicated to a monk who was murdered on the island by the Danes in 875.

The five-hour trip to the island on the **May Princess** (☏01333-310054; www.isleofmayferry.com; adult/child £19/9.50), including two to three hours ashore, sails almost daily from May to September. Make reservations and buy tickets at the harbour kiosk near the museum at least an hour before departure. Departure times vary depending on the tide – check upcoming times by

phone or via the website. There's also a faster boat, the 12-seater rigid-hull inflatable *Osprey*, which makes non-landing circuits of the island (adult/child £20/12.50) and longer visits (£25/15).

🍽 Sleeping & Eating

| TOP CHOICE | **Spindrift** | B&B ££ |

(☏01333-310573; www.thespindrift.co.uk; Pittenweem Rd; s/d £55/80; P☜) Arriving from the west, there's no need to go further than Anstruther's first house on the left, a redoubt of Scottish cheer and warm hospitality. The rooms are elegant, classy and extremely comfortable – some have views across to Edinburgh and one is like a ship's cabin, courtesy of the sea-captain who once owned the house. There are DVD players and teddies for company, an honesty-bar with characterful ales and malts and fine company from your hosts. Breakfast includes porridge once voted the best in the kingdom. Dinner (from £22) is also available.

Crichton House B&B ££
(☏01333-310219; www.crichtonhouse.com; High St W; d £70; P) You'll spot this B&B on the right as you approach the centre of town from the west. Sparklingly clean rooms with fresh fruit and slate-floored bathrooms are complemented by a cheery host and plenty of breakfast options. The door is a little bit further along the street than you think it'll be.

Sheiling B&B ££
(☏01333-310697; 32 Glenogil Gardens; r per person £25-30; P) Sheiling offers two genteel, elegantly furnished rooms with shared bathroom and a homespun vibe. It also has an excellent breakfast menu. Good for solo travellers.

Dreel Tavern PUB £
(16 High St W; mains £8-12; ☺lunch & dinner; 🚻) This charming old pub on the banks of the Dreel Burn has bucket-loads of character and serves reliably tasty bar meals, with excellent handwritten daily specials. Chow down in the outdoor beer garden in summer. There are also some top-quality cask ales here.

Wee Chippie TAKEAWAY £
(4 Shore St; fish supper £5; ☺lunch & dinner) The Anstruther Fish Bar is one of Britain's best chippies, but we – and plenty of locals – reckon this one is even better. The fish is of a very high quality, portions are larger and

there's less of a queue too. Eat your catch by the water.

Cellar Restaurant
RESTAURANT £££

(☏01333-310378; www.cellarrestaurant.co.uk; 24 East Green; 2/3-course set dinner £35/40; ☺lunch Fri & Sat, dinner Tue-Sat) Tucked away in an alley behind the museum, the Cellar is famous for its seafood and fine wines. Try the local crab, lobster or whatever delicacies they've brought in that day. Inside it's elegant and upmarket. Advance bookings are essential.

❶ Information

Tourist office (☏01333-311073; anstruther@visitscotland.com; Harbourhead; ☺10am-5pm Mon-Sat, 11am-4pm Sun Apr-Oct) The best tourist office in East Neuk.

❶ Getting There & Away

Stagecoach (www.stagecoachbus.com) bus 95 runs daily from Leven (more departures from St Monans) to Anstruther and on to St Andrews (40 minutes, hourly) via Crail.

AROUND ANSTRUTHER

A magnificent example of Lowland Scottish domestic architecture, **Kellie Castle** (NTS; www.nts.org.uk; adult/child/parking £8.50/5.50/3; ☺castle 1-5pm Thu-Mon Apr-Oct, garden 10am-5pm daily Apr-Oct, 10am-4pm Mon-Fri Nov-Mar) has creaky floors, crooked little doorways and some marvellous works of art, giving it an air of authenticity. It's set in a beautiful garden, and many rooms contain superb plasterwork, the Vine room being the most exquisite. The original part of the building dates from 1360; it was enlarged to its present dimensions around 1606.

The castle is 3 miles northwest of Pittenweem on the B9171. Bus 95 from St Andrews gets you closest – about 1.5 miles away. You can get straight to the castle by booking a **Go-Flexi** (☏01334-840340; www.go-flexi.org; £2) 'taxibus' from Anstruther.

Three miles north of Anstruther, off the B9131 to St Andrews, is **Scotland's Secret Bunker** (www.secretbunker.co.uk; adult/child/family £9.50/6.50/27; ☺10am-5pm Apr-Oct; @). This fascinating Cold War relic must be to one of Britain's underground command centres and a home for Scots leaders in the event of nuclear war. Hidden 30m underground and surrounded by nearly 5m of reinforced concrete are the austere operation rooms, communication centre and dormitories. It's very authentic and uses artefacts from the period, which make for an absorbing exploration. The Scottish Campaign for Nuclear Disarmament (CND) has an exhibit, bringing home the realities of Britain's current nuclear Trident policy. The bunker is a gripping experience and highly recommended.

To get to the bunker, book a **Go-Flexi** (☏01334-840340; www.go-flexi.org; £2) 'taxibus' from Anstruther, or it's a £15 standard taxi from St Andrews. Alternatively, jump off an X26 bus from Anstruther to St Andrews at the Drumrack crossroads and walk east for about 1.5 miles along the B940.

PITTENWEEM
POP 1747

Just a short stroll from Anstruther, Pittenweem is now the main fishing port on the East Neuk coast, and there are lively fish sales at the harbour from 8am. On a sunny day, buy an ice cream and stroll the short, breezy promenade, admiring the picturesque waterfront. The village name means 'place of the cave', referring to **St Fillan's Cave** (adult/child £1/free) in Cove Wynd, which was used as a chapel by a 7th-century missionary. The saint reputedly possessed miraculous powers – apparently, when he wrote his sermons in the dark cave, his arm would throw light on his work by emitting a luminous glow. The cave is protected by a locked gate, but a key is available from a nearby house (see the sign on the gate).

Drop into **Heron Bistro** (www.herongallery.co.uk; 15a High St; mains £5-8; ☺breakfast & lunch) for a snack or meal. Dressed crab and homemade smoked mackerel pâté feature on the menu, and you dine among local works of art that inject some real colour into this pretty harbour town – good for a browse, and everything is for sale.

Bus details for Pittenweem are as for Anstruther.

ST MONANS
POP 1450

This ancient fishing village is just over a mile west of Pittenweem and is named after another cave-dwelling saint who was probably killed by pirates. Apart from a picturesque historic windmill overlooking the sea, its main sight is the **parish church**, at the western end of the village. The church was built in 1362 on the orders of a grateful King David II, who was rescued by villagers from a shipwreck in the Firth of Forth.

A model of a full-rigged ship, dating from 1800, hangs above the altar. The church commands sweeping views of the firth, and the past echoes inside its cold, whitewashed walls.

St Monans Heritage Collection (5 West Shore; admission free; ☺11am-1pm & 2-4pm Tue, Thu, Sat & Sun May-Oct), on the harbour, is a wonderful small gallery devoted to the history of the St Monans' fishing industry through a collection of 20th-century black-and-white photos and several artefacts. Most of the photos were taken by a local photographer and the collection changes regularly.

There are a couple of B&Bs in St Monans, but more options in nearby Anstruther.

Harbour Howff Café (6 Station Rd; light meals £3-5; ☺breakfast & lunch Wed-Sun) is a community-run cafe promoting healthy eating and serving excellent sandwiches and fresh cakes.

TOP Seafood Restaurant (☑01333-730327; www.theseafoodrestaurant.com; 16 West End; 2-course lunch/dinner £22/40; ☺lunch & dinner Wed-Sun Apr-May, daily Jun-Aug) is a comfortable, but classy, fishy stalwart on the harbour. The menu changes – bouillabaisse, Dover sole, scallops – but just swim with the tide. The menu details the provenance of these sustainable morsels.

Stagecoach (www.stagecoachbus.com) bus 95 runs daily from St Monans to St Andrews (50 minutes, at least hourly), via Anstruther.

ELIE & EARLSFERRY
POP 1500

These two attractive villages mark the southwestern end of East Neuk. There are great sandy beaches and good walks along the coast, and there's nothing better than a lazy summer Sunday in Elie, watching the local team play cricket on the strand below.

Elie Watersports (☑01333-330962; www.eliewatersports.com; ☺daily), on the harbour at Elie, hires out windsurfers (per two hours £30), sailing dinghies (Lasers/Wayfarers per hour £18/22), canoes (per hour £10) and mountain bikes (per day £12), and provides instruction as well.

Ship Inn (www.ship-elie.com; Elie; mains £8-11; ☺lunch & dinner; ☒), down by Elie harbour, is a pleasant and popular place for a bar lunch. Seafood and Asian dishes feature on the menu and, on a sunny day, you can tuck-in at an outside table overlooking the wide sweep of the bay.

For sheer scenic variety, Perthshire is the pick of Scotland's regions and a place where everyone will find a special, personal spot – whether it's a bleak moor, snaking loch, postcard-perfect village or magnificent forest. Highlights are many: the enchanting valley of Glen Lyon strikes visitors dumb with its wild and remote beauty; stunning Loch Tay is nearby (the base for ascending Ben Lawers); and the River Tay runs east from here towards Dunkeld, whose cathedral is among the most beautifully situated in the country.

Things begin sedately in the southeast corner with Perth itself, a fine country town with a fabulous attraction in lavish Scone Palace, and get gradually wilder as you move northwards and westwards, moving through wooded slopes and river-blessed valleys and culminating in the bleak expanse of Rannoch Moor.

ⓘ Getting Around
The A9 cuts across the region through Perth and Pitlochry. It's the fast route into the Highlands and to Inverness, and very busy.

The council produces a useful public transport map available at tourist offices. **Stagecoach** (☑01382-227201; www.stagecoachbus.com) runs local services.

Trains run alongside the A9, destined for Inverness. Another line connects Perth with Stirling (in the south) and Dundee (in the east).

Kinross & Loch Leven
POP 4681

Kinross, just off the M90, sits on the banks of pretty Loch Leven. Stretch your legs or take a bike on the **Loch Leven Heritage Trail** (www.lochlevenheritagetrail.co.uk), which runs 8 miles around three-quarters of the loch, or head across to the island in its centre to visit evocative **Loch Leven Castle** (HS; www.historic-scotland.gov.uk; adult/child incl Kinross ferry £4.70/2.80; ☺9.30am-5.30pm Apr-Sep, last sailing 4pm), which served as a fortress and prison from the late 14th century. Its most famous captive was Mary, Queen of Scots, who was incarcerated here in 1567. Her famous charms bewitched Willie Douglas, who managed to get hold of the cell keys to release her, then rowed her across to the shore. The castle is now roofless but basically intact and makes an atmospheric visit. A bistro by the ferry dock, near the centre of Kinross, serves decent light meals.

Nearby, on the main street, **Roxburghe Guest House** (☎01577-862498; www.roxburgheguesthouse.co.uk; 126 High St, Kinross; r per person £25-35; Ⓟ📶) is a lovely guesthouse with cool, tastefully furnished rooms and a fabulous garden. Roxburghe feels like a home-away-from-home, and the owner is a professional masseuse and acupuncturist if you need any creases ironed out.

Citylink (www.citylink.co.uk) runs bus services between Perth (30 minutes, hourly) and Kinross. In the other direction buses go to Edinburgh (1½ hours, hourly).

Perth

POP 43,450

Sedately arranged along the banks of the Tay, this former capital of Scotland is a most liveable place with large tracts of enticing parkland surrounding an easily managed centre. On its outskirts lies Scone Palace, a country house of staggering luxury built alongside the mound that was the crowning place of Scotland's kings. It's really a must-see, but the town itself, ennobled by stately architecture, fine galleries and a few excellent restaurants, merits exploration, and is within easy striking distance of both Edinburgh and Glasgow.

Sights

Scone Palace PALACE

(www.scone-palace.co.uk; adult/child/family £9/6/26; ⏲9.30am-5pm Apr-Oct) 'So thanks to all at once and to each one, whom we invite to see us crowned at Scone.' This line from *Macbeth* indicates the importance of this place (pronounced 'skoon'), 2 miles north of Perth. The palace itself was built in 1580 on a site intrinsic to Scottish history. Here in 838, Kenneth MacAlpin became the first king of a united Scotland and brought the **Stone of Destiny** (see the boxed text, p51),

Perth

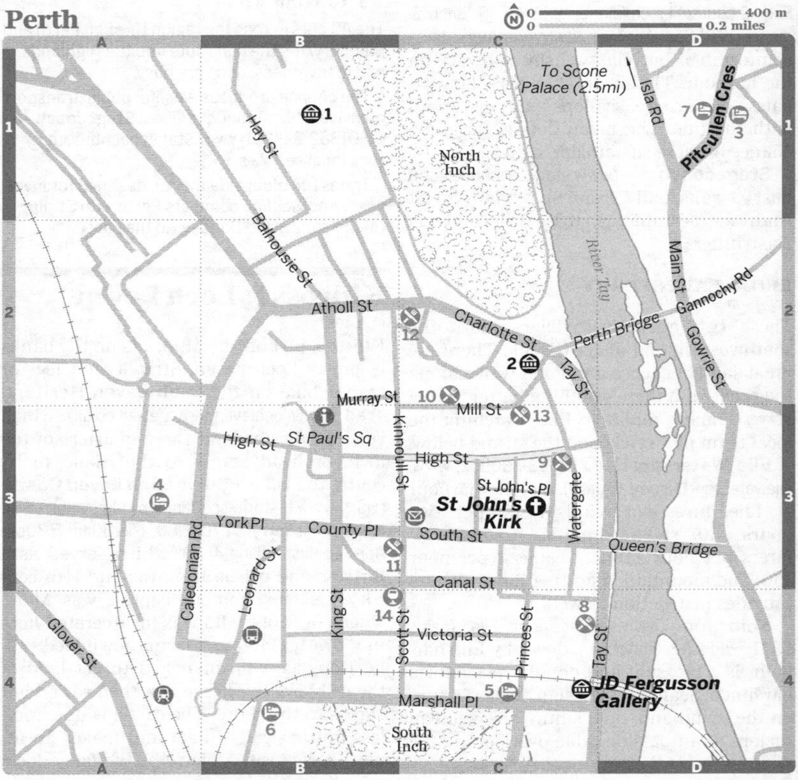

on which Scottish kings were ceremonially invested, to Moot Hill. In 1296 Edward I of England carted the talisman off to Westminster Abbey, where it remained for 700 years before being returned to Scotland.

These days, however, Scone doesn't really conjure up ye olden days of bearded warrior-kings swearing oaths in the mist since the palace, rebuilt in the early 19th century, is a Georgian mansion of extreme elegance and luxury.

The visit takes you through a succession of sumptuous **rooms** filled with fine French furniture and noble artworks. There's an astonishing collection of porcelain and fine portraits here, as well as a series of exquisite Vernis Martin papier-mâché. Scone has belonged for centuries to the Murray family, Earls of Mansfield, and many of the objects have fascinating history attached to them (friendly guides are on hand). Each room has comprehensive multilingual information; there are also panels relating histories of some of the Scottish kings crowned at Scone over the centuries.

Outside, peacocks – all named after a monarch – strut around the magnificent **grounds**, which incorporate woods, a butterfly garden, and a maze.

Perth

T TIME

Scotland's biggest music festival, **T in the Park** (www.tinthepark.com) rocks this nook of the country over the second weekend in July. A major event, with six stages and top-name acts, it takes place on the former Balado airfield near Kinross. It's a three-day affair, with camping available from the night before. The park is off the A91 just west of junction 7 of the M90.

Ancient kings were crowned atop **Moot Hill**, topped by a chapel, next to the palace. It's said that the hill was created by bootfuls of earth, brought by nobles attending the coronations as an acknowledgement of the king's rights over their lands, although it's more likely the site of an ancient motte-and-bailey castle.

From Perth's centre, cross the bridge, turn left, and keep bearing left until you reach the gates of the estate (15 to 20 minutes). From here, it's a half-mile to the palace. Various buses from town stop here roughly hourly; the tourist office has a printout. There's a good cafe at the palace, too.

FREE **St John's Kirk**   CHURCH
(www.st-johns-kirk.co.uk; St John St; ☺10am-4pm Mon-Sat, 10am-1pm Sun May-Sep) Daunting St John's Kirk, founded in 1126, is surrounded by cobbled streets and is still the centrepiece of the town. In 1559 John Knox preached a powerful sermon here that helped begin the Reformation, inciting a frenzied destruction of Scone abbey and other religious sites. Perth used to be known as St John's Town after this church; the football team here is still called St Johnstone.

FREE **JD Fergusson Gallery**   GALLERY
(www.pkc.gov.uk; cnr Marshall Pl & Tay St; ☺10am-5pm Mon-Sat) Beautifully set in the round waterworks building, this gallery exhibits much of the work of the Scottish Colourist JD Fergusson in a most impressive display. Fergusson spent time in Paris, and the influence of artists like Matisse on his work is evident; his voluptuous female portraits against a tropical-looking Riviera background are memorable, as is the story of his lifelong relationship with noted Scottish dancer Margaret Morris.

FREE **Perth Museum** MUSEUM
(www.pkc.gov.uk; cnr George & Charlotte Sts; ☉10am-5pm Mon-Sat) The city's main museum is worth wandering through for the elegant neoclassical interior alone. There's a varied shower of exhibits, ranging from portraits of dour lairds to interesting local social history. A geological room provides more entertainment for the young, while there are often excellent temporary exhibitions.

Black Watch Museum MUSEUM
(www.theblackwatch.co.uk; Hay St; adult/child £4/2; ☉9.30am-5pm Mon-Sat, also 10am-4pm Sun Apr-Oct) Housed in a mansion on the edge of North Inch, this museum honours what was once Scotland's foremost regiment. Formed in 1725 to combat rural banditry, the Black Watch fought in numerous campaigns, re-created here with paintings, memorabilia and anecdotes. Little attempt at perspective is evident: there's justifiable pride in the regiment's role in the gruelling trench warfare of WWI, where it suffered nearly 30,000 casualties, but no sheepishness about less glorious colonial engagements, such as against the 'Fuzzy Wuzzies' of Sudan. In 2006 the Black Watch was subsumed into the new Royal Regiment of Scotland

🛏 Sleeping

Someone should open a hostel in Perth.

Parklands HOTEL ££
(☎01738-622451; www.theparklandshotel.com; 2 St Leonard's Bank; s/d £89/129; P@🛜) Tucked away near the train station, this relaxing hotel sits amidst a lush hillside garden overlooking the parklands of South Inch. While the rooms – which vary in size and shape – conserve the character of this beautiful building, formerly the residence of the town's mayors, they also offer modern conveniences such as flatscreen TVs and CD/DVD players. The restaurant has a fine reputation and a terrace to lap up the Perthshire sun.

Comely Bank Cottage B&B ££
(☎01738-631118; www.comelybankcottage.co.uk; 19 Pitcullen Cres; s/d £48/55; P🛜) Pitcullen Cres is bristling with upmarket, flowery B&Bs. This is one of our favourites, a perfectly maintained family home offering large and commodious rooms with spacious bathrooms, and a solicitous owner who doesn't disappoint come breakfast time.

Pitcullen Guest House B&B ££
(☎01738-626506; www.pitcullen.co.uk; 17 Pitcullen Cres; d £68; P@🛜) Readers rave about this place, and rightly so. Good B&B depends on the host, and this one gets it spot-on, with helpful tips to guide your stay in Perth and numerous small, thoughtful extras that make this more than the sum of its parts.

Kinnaird Guest House B&B ££
(☎01738-628021; www.kinnaird-guesthouse.co.uk; 5 Marshall Pl; s/d £45/75; P🛜) The best of the handful of guesthouses enjoying a privileged position across the road from the lovely South Inch parkland, this elegant old house has noble original features and boasts appealing, bright rooms with big beds. The owners are engaging and extremely helpful; they are justifiably proud of what Perth has to offer. The back rooms do receive occasional train noise.

Heidl Guest House B&B ££
(☎01738-635031; www.heidl.co.uk; 43 York Pl; s/d £28/58; P🛜) Though it lacks a little character from outside, the Heidl is a very reliable place offering plenty of staunch hospitality allied with bright, light rooms, with cheery bedspreads in marine colours. Most rooms come with excellent en suite bathrooms; those that don't have good private exterior bathrooms. Writer John Buchan (of *Thirty-Nine Steps* fame) was born in the house opposite.

🍴 Eating & Drinking

Perth has an exceptionally good dining scene and a strong cafe and outside-dining culture.

TOP **Breizh** BISTRO ££
CHOICE (☎01738-444427; www.cafebreizh.co.uk; 28 High St; mains £7-14; ☉breakfast Mon-Sat, lunch & dinner daily) This warmly decorated bistro – the place could define the word – is a treat. Dishes are served with real panache, and the salads, featuring all sorts of delicious ingredients, are a feast of colour, texture and subtle flavours. The blackboard meat and fish specials offer great value and a real taste of northwest France: breakfasts, *galettes* (Breton buckwheat crêpes), tasty wines... If you like quality food served in an unpretentious way, you'll love it here.

63 Tay Street RESTAURANT ££
(☎01738-441451; www.63taystreet.com; 63 Tay St; mains £13-18; ☉lunch & dinner Tue-Sat) Classy

and warmly welcoming, this understated restaurant is Perth's best, featuring a lightly decorated dining area, excellent service and quality food. In a culinary Auld Alliance, French influence is applied to the best of Scottish produce to produce memorable game, seafood, beef and vegetarian plates.

Deans@Let's Eat
RESTAURANT ££

(☏01738-643377; www.letseatperth.co.uk; 77 Kinnoull St; mains £14-19; ⊗lunch & dinner Tue-Sat) Noted for its excellent service, this award-winning bistro is the best place in town for splashing out on a special meal. Outstanding cuisine comes in the form of creative dishes on a short menu listed by main ingredient: halibut, lamb and beef reliably feature, but the manner of their cooking will change. Enjoy an aperitif on the comfy couches before indulging your palate.

Kerachers
SEAFOOD ££

(☏01738-449777; www.kerachers-restaurant.co.uk; 168 South St; 2-course dinner £22.50; ⊗dinner Tue-Sat) This classic seafood restaurant keeps things simple, combining fresh seafood with ingredients that add hints of flavour to complement but not overpower the dishes – a recipe for success!

Glassrooms
CAFE £

(www.horsecross.co.uk; Mill St; light meals £5-8; ⊗breakfast & lunch Mon-Sat) Occupying part of the foyer of the ambitious, inspiring Perth Concert Hall, this open-plan cafe offers an eclectic range of daytime dishes. Expect several healthy and vegetarian choices as well as sandwiches and breakfasts.

Paco's
BISTRO ££

(www.pacos.co.uk; 3 Mill St; mains £7-13; ⊗lunch Sat, dinner daily; ⊕) Something of an institution, Paco's keeps Perthers coming back over and over, perhaps because it would take dozens of visits to even try half of the menu. There's something for everyone: steaks, seafood, pizza, pasta and Mexican, all served in generous portions. The fountain-tinkled terrace is the place for a sunny day.

Twa Tams
PUB

(www.myspace.com/thetwatams; 79 Scott St) Perth's best pub has a strange outdoor space with windows peering out onto the street, an ornate entrance gate and large, cosy interior. There are regular events, including live music every Friday and Saturday night; it has a sound reputation for attracting talented young bands.

❶ PERTH FESTIVAL OF THE ARTS

If you're in Perth in the last two weeks of May, you'll come across this low-profile but high-quality **arts festival** (www.perthfestival.co.uk). Various venues around town host a diverse range of cultural events; don't be surprised to see some big-name band of yesteryear or quality ballet troupe appearing at very reasonable prices.

❶ Information

AK Bell Library (York Pl; ⊗9.30am-5pm Mon, Wed & Fri, to 8pm Tue & Thu, to 4pm Sat; @) Free internet; lots of terminals.

Perth Royal Infirmary (☏01738-623311; Taymount Tce) Hospital; west of the town centre.

Tourist office (☏01738-450600; www.perthshire.co.uk; West Mill St; ⊗9.30am-5pm Mon-Sat & 10.30am-3.30pm Sun Apr-Oct, 10am-4pm Mon-Sat Nov-Mar) Efficiently run tourist office. Closes an hour later in summer.

❶ Getting There & Away

Bus

From the bus station, **Citylink** (www.citylink.co.uk) operates buses to/from these cities:

Dundee £6.70, 40 minutes, hourly

Edinburgh £10.30, 1½ hours, hourly

Glasgow £10.70, 1½ hours, hourly

Inverness £18.80, 2½ hours, at least five daily

Further buses run from the Broxden Park & Ride on Glasgow Rd; this is connected regularly with the bus station by shuttle bus. These include **Megabus** (www.megabus.com) discount services to Aberdeen, Edinburgh, Glasgow, Dundee, and Inverness.

Stagecoach (www.stagecoachbus.com) buses serve Perthshire destinations regularly, with reduced Sunday service.

Train

Trains run between Perth and various destinations, including the following:

Edinburgh £12.90, 1¼ hours, at least hourly Monday to Saturday

Glasgow £12.90, one hour, at least hourly Monday to Saturday, every two hours Sunday, from Queen St

Pitlochry £11, 30 minutes, two hourly, fewer on Sunday

Stirling £10.40, 30 minutes, one or two per hour

Strathearn

West of Perth, the wide strath (valley) of the River Earn was once a great forest where medieval kings hunted. The whole area is known as Strathearn, a very attractive region of undulating farmland, hills and lochs. The Highlands begin in the western section of Strathearn.

DUNNING
POP 900

If you think you've entered spooky country around here, you may just be right. On the way into Dunning, about a mile west of the town by the B8062, there's a strange cross on a pile of stones, etched with the words 'Maggie Wall burnt here 1657 as a witch.'

The village is dominated by the 12th-century Norman tower of St Serfs Church (HS; www.historic-scotland.gov.uk; admission by donation; ⊙9.30am-5.30pm Apr-Sep), but most of the building dates from 1810. The main reason to come is the magnificent 9th-century Dupplin Cross, the finest Pictish cross known. Originally located near Forteviot (3 miles from Dunning), it's now the regal centrepiece here. The fascinating symbolism and artistic influences will be explained in superb detail by the warden. It's rare to get such detailed insight at these

places, and you'll walk out of there feeling like you've learned something new.

Opposite is the wonderful Kirkstyle Inn (www.kirkstyle-dunning.co.uk; mains £7-11; ⊙lunch & dinner), an eccentric little nook-and-cranny pub with a warm glow and a local touch (and the food's not half bad either). It closes mid-afternoon during the week.

Dunning is about 8 miles southwest of Perth. Stagecoach (www.stagecoachbus.com) bus 17 runs from Perth (40 minutes, at least hourly Monday to Saturday).

CRIEFF
POP 6579

Scraping the edge of the Highlands, elegant Crieff is an old resort-style town, as popular with tourists today as it was in Victorian times. It sits in a valley amid some glorious Perthshire countryside.

⊙ Sights

In the basement at the tourist office is a small but interesting free exhibition of the town stocks, the Drummond Cross (1400–1600) and a formidable 9th-century Pictish cross slab.

At the noble old Glenturret Distillery 1 mile north of town, the highly rated Famous Grouse Experience (www.thefamous grouse.com; tours from £8.50; ⊙9am-6pm) has a better-than-average tour that details the making of malt whisky and the blending process to create Famous Grouse whisky. There's also a high-tech bonanza that includes a giant virtual jigsaw and 'flying with the grouse' audiovisual.

About 5 miles southeast of Crieff on the B8062, Innerpeffray Library (www.inner peffraylibrary.co.uk; Innerpeffray; adult/child incl tour £5/free; ⊙10am-12.45pm & 2-4.45pm Wed-Sat, 2-4pm Sun Mar-Oct, by appointment only Nov-Feb), is Scotland's first lending library (founded in 1680). There's a huge collection of rare, interesting and ancient books here, some of them 500 years old.

🛏 Sleeping & Eating

TOP CHOICE Comrie Croft   HOSTEL £
(☎01764-670140; www.comriecroft.com; camping per person £7-9, dm/s/d £16/22/38; P@🐾📶♿) A rustic, hospitable place to stay with great facilities, Comrie Croft has a bit of everything, with camping; a pleasant, airy hostel with plenty of bedspace; and Sami-style tepees with woodstove that sleep up to four (£52). Activities include mountain-biking (bike hire available), fishing, walking, lots of games for the kids and plenty of

---

GLENEAGLES

Deep in rural Perthshire near the town of Auchterarder, one of Scotland's most famous lodgings can be found: the Gleneagles Hotel (☎01764-662231; www.gleneagles.com; d from £410; P@🐾📶♿♿). Not your typical bed-and-breakfast, this is a no-holds-barred luxury spot with three championship golf courses, Andrew Fairlie at Gleneagles – often referred to as Scotland's best restaurant (open dinner Tuesday to Saturday) – and a variety of extravagantly elegant rooms and suites designed to cope with anything from a serious romantic splash-out to a royal family in exile. Despite the imposing building and kilted staff snapping to attention, it's welcoming to non-VIPs, and family-friendly to boot, with lots of activities available. There's Gleneagles train station to arrive sustainably; if not, limousine transfers are available. Check the website for deals.

places to just laze about. The Croft is 4 miles out of Crieff on the A85 towards Comrie.

Yann's
B&B, RESTAURANT ££

(☎01764-650111; www.yannsatglenearnhouse.com; d £80, mains £11-15; ☺dinner Wed-Sun, lunch Sat & Sun; ℗🖥) On the main road heading east out of town, this most welcoming establishment offers commodious rooms done out in light shades with understated style. The excellent restaurant here serves French comfort food classics like crêpes and coq au vin, with a contemporary flair.

Comely Bank Guest House
B&B ££

(☎01764-653409; www.comelybank.demon.co.uk; 32 Burrell St; s with/without bathroom £38/30, d £60; @🖥) A top Scottish guesthouse just down from the main street, Comely Bank is homelike and neat as a pin. The downstairs double is huge and could accommodate four at a pinch, while upstairs rooms are equally appealing and are still a good size. Laundry service is available and a genuine welcome guaranteed.

Crieff Hydro
HOTEL ££

(☎01764-655555; www.crieffhydro.com; Ferntower Rd; d £148; ℗@🖥🏊🏇) This enormous spa hotel is nearly 150 years old, but apart from its monumental exterior it looks very different from its mannered Victorian past. It's attractively functional and really does have everything for a family holiday, from a cinema and gym to restaurants, activities and pools. It's exceptionally child-friendly, with free daily childcare. Room rates vary substantially, so check the website: the above prices (for dinner, bed and breakfast) are a guide only. Its sister hotel, Murraypark (double £93), is just around the corner, and offers a quieter, cheaper stay in a smaller, more couple-focused establishment (and you can still access all the leisure facilities at the Hydro).

Gallery
RESTAURANT ££

(☎01764-653249; 13 Hill St; mains £10-14; ☺dinner Tue-Sat) The classy mains are backed up by satisfying warm salads and pastas at this cosy (too cosy if your neighbours are loud) restaurant just uphill from the main street. Helpful staff add to the satisfying dining experience, as does a short but thoughtfully chosen wine selection.

Delivino
CAFE £

(www.delivino.net; 6 King St; light meals £5-8; ☺breakfast & lunch daily, dinner Fri & Sat) Delivino is an elegant cafe just down from the square on the main street. It offers something for everyone, from Crieff ladies-who-lunch to a traveller looking for a light bite. An extensive selection of antipasti allows you to graze several flavours at a time, while delicious bruschettas and pizzas, accompanied by a glass of Italian red, make this central Crieff's best lunch option.

ℹ Information

Tourist office (☎01764-652578; crieff@visitscotland.com; ☺daily Apr-Oct, Mon-Sat Nov-Mar) Most helpful. In a clocktower on the main street.

ℹ Getting There & Away

Hourly **Stagecoach** (www.stagecoachbus.com) buses link Crieff with Perth (45 minutes), less frequently on Sunday. Other buses run to Comrie (20 minutes, roughly hourly Monday to Saturday, every two hours Sunday), St Fillans (35 minutes, five daily Monday to Saturday) and Stirling (50 minutes, four to eight daily).

UPPER STRATHEARN

The Highland villages of **Comrie** and **St Fillans** in upper Strathearn are surrounded by forests and craggy, bare hilltops where deer and mountain hares both live in abundance. St Fillans enjoys an excellent location at the eastern end of **Loch Earn**, which reflects the silhouettes of distant, towering peaks in its glittering waters.

The **Four Seasons Hotel** (☎01765-685333; www.thefourseasonshotel.co.uk; St Fillans; standard/superior d £110/130; ☺Mar-Dec; ℗🖥🏇) is a refined hotel with a touch of elegance, with two beautifully appointed sitting rooms and a small bar with loch views – great places to relax. There are boundless activities to choose from here, including water-skiing, quad-biking and pony trekking. There are also six secluded chalets nestled in the slopes behind the hotel and a good restaurant.

Comrie is 24 miles west of Perth, and St Fillans is about 5 miles further west. **Stagecoach** (www.stagecoachbus.com) operates daily buses from Perth, via Crieff, to Comrie and St Fillans (one hour).

West Perthshire

The jewel in central Scotland's crown, West Perthshire achieves a Scottish ideal with rugged, noble hills reflected in some of the nation's most beautiful lochs. Bring your hiking boots and camera and prepare to stay a few days.

Aberfeldy is the gateway to west Perthshire, and a good base: adventure sports, art and castles all feature on the menu here. It's a peaceful, pretty place on the banks of the Tay, but if it's moody lochs and glens that steal your heart, you may want to push a little further on into the region.

☉ Sights & Activities

The **Watermill** (www.aberfeldywatermill.com; Mill St; admission free; ☉10am-5pm Mon-Sat, 11am-5pm Sun) is an unusual attraction in the centre of town, incorporating a book-shop with a great Scottish collection, a gallery with contemporary works of art and a coffee shop. You could while away several hours in this old mill.

Dewar's World of Whisky (www.dewars worldofwhisky.com; tour £6.50; ☉10am-6pm Mon-Sat & noon-4pm Sun Apr-Oct, 10am-4pm Mon-Sat Nov-Mar) is on the eastern outskirts of Aberfeldy. The tour is a good one, fully 90 minutes long; after the usual overblown film, there's a very entertaining interactive blending session as well as the tour of the whisky-making process.

About 1½ miles west of town by the B846, **Castle Menzies** (www.menzies.org; Weem; adult/child £6/2.50 ☉10.30am-5pm Mon-Sat, 2-5pm Sun Apr–mid-Oct) is the impressive restored 16th-century seat of the chief of the clan Menzies (*ming*-iss). The Z-plan tower house is magnificently located against a backdrop of Scottish forest. And inside it doesn't disappoint: the place smells just like a castle should – musty and lived in. It reeks of authenticity despite extensive restoration work and is a highly recommended ramble. Check out the fireplace in the dungeon-like kitchens and the gaudy great hall upstairs, with windows unfurling a ribbon of lush, green countryside extending into wooded hills beyond the estate. You'll get in for free if you share a surname with the castle.

Just past here, **Highland Safaris** (☎01887-820071; www.highlandsafaris.net; ☉9am-5pm) offers an ideal way to spot some wildlife or simply enjoy Perthshire's magnificent countryside. Standard trips include the 2½-hour Mountain Safari (per adult/child £37.50/15), which includes a dram in the wilderness; and the Safari Trek (adult/child £60/30), which includes a walk in the mountains and a picnic. You can hire mountain bikes here (per day £15), and for

another £15 they'll drive you up the top of the hill and you make your own way down (a good option for walkers too). Wildlife you may spot include golden eagles, osprey and red deer. There's also gold-panning for kids.

In Aberfeldy, **Splash** (☎01887-829706; www.rafting.co.uk; Dunkeld Rd; ☉9am-9pm) offers family-friendly whitewater rafting on the River Tay (per adult/child £25/40) and more advanced adult trips on the Tummel and the Orchy. It also runs canyoning trips and hires mountain bikes (per half-/full day £10/20).

🛏 Sleeping

Guinach House　　　　　　　　B&B ££
(☎01887-820251; www.guinachhouse.co.uk; Urlar Rd; d £95-125; P 🛜) More like a boutique hotel, Guinach House has modish rooms and a casual, relaxed ambience. Rooms have privacy from the rest of the house and are individually styled – our favourite is the zebra room, although the red room, with freestanding bathtub, runs a close second. The whole place is set on a large estate, so there are plenty of rambling options just beyond the front doorstep.

Tigh'n Eilean Guest House　　　　B&B ££
(☎01887-820109; www.tighneilean.com; Taybridge Dr; s/d £52/66; P 🛜) Everything about this property screams comfort. It's a gorgeous place overlooking the Tay, with individually designed rooms all creating a unique sense of space. For couples our fave is the jacuzzi room – it's huge, and the same price as the others. The Tay riverbank here is delightful, with birdsong above and ducks paddling below.

Balnearn Guest House　　　　　B&B ££
(☎01887-820431; www.balnearnhouse.com; Crieff Rd; s/d/f £40/65/95; P 🛜) Balnearn is a sedate, refined and quite luxurious mansion near the centre of town. Most rooms have great natural light, and there's a particularly good family room downstairs. Doubles with private but exterior bathroom are cheaper (£58). The hosts are attentive and cordial.

ℹ Information

Tourist office (☎01887-820276; The Square; ☉Mon-Sat Nov-Mar, daily Apr-Oct) In an old church on the central square.

ℹ Getting There & Away

Stagecoach (www.stagecoachbus.com) runs buses from Aberfeldy to Pitlochry (45 minutes, hourly Monday to Saturday, fewer on Sunday),

Blairgowrie (1¼ hours, two daily Monday to Friday) and Perth (1¼ hours, 10 daily Monday to Saturday).

Local buses run a circular route from Aberfeldy through Kenmore, Fortingall and back to Aberfeldy up to five times daily Monday to Friday. There's also a service through to Killin (one hour, up to five times daily Monday to Saturday, Saturday only June to September), connecting with an Oban service.

KENMORE

Pretty Kenmore lies at Loch Tay's eastern end, 6 miles west of Aberfeldy, and is dominated by church, clock tower, and the striking archway of privately owned **Taymouth Castle**. Just outside town on the loch is the fascinating **Scottish Crannog Centre** (www.crannog.co.uk; tours adult/child £6.50/4.50; ⏲10am-5.30pm mid-Mar–Oct, 10am-4pm Sat & Sun Nov). A crannog, perched on stilts in the water, was a favoured form of defence-minded dwelling in Scotland from the 3rd millennium BC onwards. This one has been superbly reconstructed, and the guided tour includes an impressive demonstration of firemaking. It's an excellent attraction.

Kenmore is a good activity base, and **Loch Tay Boating Centre** (☎01887-830291; www.loch-tay.co.uk; ⏲daily) can have you speeding off on a mountain bike (per half-/full day £12/20) or out on the loch itself, in anything from a canoe to a cabin cruiser that'll sleep a whole family.

The heart of the village, **Kenmore Hotel** (☎01887-830205, www.kenmorehotel.com; s/d £85/140; P@Wi-Fi) has a bar with a roaring fire and some verses scribbled on the chimneypiece by Robert Burns in 1787, when the inn was already a couple of centuries old. There's also a riverbank beer garden and a wide variety of rooms, some across the road. They sport modern conveniences; the nicest have bay windows and river views. Prices plummet off-season and midweek.

Regular buses link Aberfeldy with Kenmore, some continuing to Killin via the turnoff to the trailhead for Ben Lawers.

LOCH TAY

Serpentine and picturesque, long Loch Tay reflects the powerful forests and mountains around it. The bulk of mighty **Ben Lawers** (1214m) looms above and is part of a National Nature Reserve that includes the nearby **Tarmachan Range**.

The main access point for the ascent of Ben Lawers (see the boxed text, p216) is the now-defunct tourist office, a mile off the A827 five miles east of Killin. There's also an easier nature trail leaving from here.

There's good accommodation in Kenmore and Killin (p194), as well as **Culdees Bunkhouse** (☎01887-830519; www.culdeesbunkhouse.co.uk; dm/tw/f £17/44/66; P@Wi-Fi), a wonderfully offbeat hostel with utterly majestic vistas: the whole of the loch stretches out before and below you. It's a quirky place you could get lost in, with compact, spotless dorms, lovable family rooms with the best views in Perthshire, and a range of cluttered, homelike lounging areas. It's a top spot to relax but also a fine base for hill walking or for mucking-in with the volunteers who help run the sustainable farm here. It's half a mile above the village of Fearnan, 4 miles west of Kenmore.

FORTINGALL

Fortingall is one of the prettiest villages in Scotland, with 19th-century thatched cottages in a very tranquil setting. The **church** has impressive wooden beams and a 7th-century **monk's bell**. In the churchyard, there's a 2000-year-old **yew**, probably the oldest tree in Europe. This tree was around when the Romans camped in the meadows by the River Lyon: popular if unlikely tradition says that Pontius Pilate was born here. Today the tree is a shell of its former self – at its zenith it had a girth of over 17m! But souvenir hunters have reduced it to two much smaller trunks.

Fortingall Hotel (☎01887-830367; www.fortingallhotel.com; s/d £110/160; PWi-Fi), nearby, is a peaceful, old-fashioned country hotel with polite service and furnished with quiet good taste. The bedrooms are spotless with huge beds, modern bathrooms, and little extras like bathrobes, whisky and DVD players. They look out over green meadows; in all a perfect spot for doing very little except enjoying the clean air and excellent dinners.

GLEN LYON

This remote and stunningly beautiful glen runs for some 34 unforgettable miles of rickety stone bridges, Caledonian pine forest and sheer heather-splashed peaks poking through swirling clouds. It becomes wilder and more uninhabited as it snakes its way west, and is proof that hidden treasures still

BAG A MUNRO: BEN LAWERS

The trip to the top of Ben Lawers and back can take up to five hours: pack wet-weather gear, water and food. From the now-closed tourist office, take the nature trail that heads northeast. After the boardwalk protecting a bog, cross a stile then fork left and ascend along the Edramucky burn (to the right). At the next rise, fork right and cross the burn. A few minutes later ignore the nature trail's right turn and continue ascending parallel to the burn's left bank for just over half a mile. Leave the protected zone by another stile and steeply ascend Beinn Ghlas's shoulder. Reaching a couple of large rocks, ignore a northbound footpath and continue zigzagging uphill. The rest of the ascent is a straightforward succession of three false summits. The last and steepest section alternates between erosion-sculpted rock and a meticulously crafted cobbled trail. Long views of majestic hillscapes, and even the North Sea and Atlantic, are your reward on a clear day.

exist in Scotland. The ancients believed it to be a gateway to Faerieland, and even the most sceptical of people will be entranced by the valley's magic.

From Fortingall, a narrow road winds up the glen – another road from Loch Tay crosses the hills and reaches the glen halfway in, at **Bridge of Balgie**. The glen continues up to a dam (past a memorial to explorer Robert Campbell); bearing left here you can actually continue over a wild and remote road (unmarked on maps) to isolated **Glen Lochay** and down to Killin. **Cycling** through Glen Lyon is a wonderful way to experience this special place.

There's little in the way of attractions in the valley – the majestic and lonely scenery is the reason to be here – but at **Glenlyon Gallery** (www.glenlyongallery.co.uk; Bridge of Balgie; admission free; ⊙10am-5pm Thu-Tue), next to the Bridge of Balgie post office (which does more-than-decent lunches), a selection of fine handmade pieces are for sale.

TOP Milton Eonan (☑01887-866318; www. miltoneonan.com; Bridge of Balgie; d £70; P ♠) is a must for those seeking utter tranquillity in a glorious natural setting. On an effervescent stream where a historic watermill once stood, it's a working croft that offers a romantic one-bedroom cottage (breakfast available for a little extra) at the bottom of the garden. It can sleep three at a pinch. The lively owners do packed lunches and evening meals (£18.50) using local and homegrown produce. After crossing the bridge at Bridge of Balgie, you'll see Milton Eonan signposted to the right.

Between Fortingall and Bridge of Balgie about 8½ miles up the glen, **Wester Camusvrachan** (☑01887-866320; www.glenlyon

bb.co.uk; s/tw/d £24/48/60; P ♠) offers cosy, good-value B&B; there's an en suite double room and a twin with bunks. Evening meals (BYO bottle) are £15 a head.

There is no public transport in the glen.

LOCHS TUMMEL & RANNOCH

The route along Lochs Tummel and Rannoch is worth doing any way you can – by foot, bicycle or car – just don't miss it! Hills of ancient birch and forests of spruce, pine and larch make up the **Tay Forest Park** – the king of Scotland's forests. It's the product of a brilliant bit of forward thinking: the replanting of Tay Forest 300 years ago. These wooded hills roll into the glittering waters of the lochs; a visit in autumn is recommended, when the birch trees are at their finest.

Queen's View Centre (www.forestry.gov. uk; Strathtummel; ⊙10am-6pm late-Mar–mid-Nov) is at the eastern end of Loch Tummel. Despite the signage, the shop here is a shop and not an exhibition, so if you pay the parking fee (£2) it's for the magnificent viewpoint over the water and towards **Schiehallion** (1083m).

Waterfalls, towering mountains and a shimmering loch greet visitors to the hidden treasure of **Kinloch Rannoch**. It's a great base for cycle trips around **Loch Rannoch** and local walks, including the hike up Schiehallion, a relatively easy climb rewarded by spectacular views unobstructed by other hills, from Braes of Foss. See www.jmt.org/east-schiehallion-estate.asp for more information.

Far beyond, the road ends at romantic, isolated **Rannoch train station**, which is on the Glasgow–Fort William line. Beyond is desolate, intriguing **Rannoch Moor**, a winding, vaguely threatening peat bog stretching as far as the A82 and Glen Coe. There's a tearoom on the platform, and a welcoming small hotel situated alongside the station.

🛏 Sleeping & Eating

TOP CHOICE **Moor of Rannoch Hotel** HOTEL **££**
(☎01882-633238; www.moorofrannoch. co.uk; Rannoch Station; s/d £56/96; ☺mid-Feb–Oct) At the end of the road by the Rannoch station, it's just about you and the moorland. This is one of Scotland's most isolated places, but luckily this friendly hotel is here to keep your spirits up if the solitude gets too much. Great food, cosy rooms and great walks right from the doorstep – a magical getaway.

Bunrannoch House B&B **££**
(☎01882-632407; www.bunrannoch.co.uk; Kinloch Rannoch; s/d £40/80, with dinner £65/130; P🔊) This historic former shooting lodge is a short way from town but feels utterly isolated and makes a great away-from-it-all destination. There's an ongoing renovation process and a friendly, 'can-do' attitude that's missing from other such country places. Walkers are most welcome, and there's a variety of rooms (including some great family ones upstairs). Excellent meals (vegan/vegetarian diets catered for) feature the likes of pike fished from Loch Rannoch or locally stalked venison. Dinner for non-guests is £30.

Gardens B&B B&B **££**
(☎01882-632434; www.thegardensdunalastair. co.uk; Kinloch Rannoch; s/d £40/70; P) Right off the beaten track between Kinloch Rannoch and Tummel Bridge, this place has just two rooms – a double and a twin. But what rooms they are: effectively suites, each with their own bathroom and sitting room. The conservatory space is great for soaking up the sun and contemplating the stunning view of Schiehallion. If you're looking for solitude and a touch of eccentricity, this is the place.

Loch Tummel Inn PUB **££**
(☎01882-634272; Strathtummel; bar meals £6-10, restaurant mains £10-14; ☺lunch & dinner) This old coaching inn is a snug spot for a decent feed from a menu featuring seafood. The bar is open all day for a leisurely pint in the beer garden overlooking Loch Tummel. The inn is about 3 miles from Queen's View.

❶ Getting There & Away

Broons Buses (☎01882-632331) operates a service between Kinloch Rannoch and Pitlochry (50 minutes, up to five a day Monday to Saturday) via Queen's View and Loch Tummel Inn. The Pitlochry–Rannoch Station **postbus** (www. royalmail.com) has a once-daily service (Monday to Saturday) via Kinloch Rannoch and both sides of the loch.

ScotRail (www.scotrail.co.uk) runs two to four trains daily from Rannoch station north to Fort William (£8.40, one hour) and Mallaig, and south to Glasgow (£19.30, 2¾ hours).

Perth to Blair Castle

There are a number of major sights strung along the busy but scenic A9, the main route north to the Cairngorms (p327) and Inverness (p314).

DUNKELD & BIRNAM
POP 1005
Ever been to a feel-good town? Well, Dunkeld and Birnam, with their enviable location nestled in the heart of Perthshire's big-tree country, await. The River Tay runs like a storybook river between the two. As well as Dunkeld's lovely cathedral, there's much walking to be done in this area of magnificent forested hills. These same walks inspired Beatrix Potter to create her children's tales.

◉ Sights & Activities
Situated between open grassland and the River Tay on one side and rolling hills on the other, **Dunkeld Cathedral** (HS; www. historic-scotland.gov.uk; High St; admission free; ☺9.30am-6.30pm Mon-Sat & 2-6.30pm Sun Apr-Sep, 9.30am-4pm Mon-Sat & 2-4pm Sun Oct-Mar) is one of the most beautifully sited cathedrals in Scotland. Don't miss it on a sunny day, as there are few lovelier places to be. Half the cathedral is still in use as a church; the rest is in ruins, and you can explore it all. It partly dates from the 14th century; the cathedral was damaged during the Reformation and burnt in the battle of Dunkeld (Jacobites vs Government) in 1689. The **Wolf of Badenoch** (p253) is buried – undeservedly – here in a fine medieval tomb behind the wooden screen in the church.

If you're looking to entertain the kids for a few hours, drop by **Going Pottie** (www. goingpottie.com; Cathedral St; activities from £5; ☺10am-5pm Mon-Sat, 11am-4pm Sun) where kids can get a paintbrush in their hand and create colourful ceramics – and mayhem.

Across the bridge is Birnam, made famous by *Macbeth*. There's not much left of Birnam Wood, but there is a small, leafy **Beatrix Potter Park** (the children's author, who wrote the evergreen story of *Peter Rabbit*, spent childhood holidays in the area). Next to the park, in the Birnam Arts Centre, is a small **exhibition** (Station Rd, Birnam; admission £1; ☑10am-4.30pm) on Potter and her characters.

Loch of the Lowes Wildlife Centre (www.swt.org.uk; adult/child £4/50p; ☑10am-5pm Apr-Sep), 2 miles east of Dunkeld off the A923, has wildlife displays mostly devoted to the majestic osprey. There's also an excellent birdwatching hide (with binoculars provided), where you can see the birds nesting during breeding season.

🛏 Sleeping & Eating

Birnam Hotel   HOTEL **££**
(☎01350-728030; www.birnamhotel.com; Perth Rd, Birnam; s/d/f £79/98/135; P 🐾) This grand-looking place with crow-stepped gables has tastefully fitted rooms opposite the Beatrix Potter park. Superior rooms (double £130) are substantially larger than the standards. Service is very welcoming, and there's a fairly formal restaurant as well as a livelier pub alongside serving creative bar meals.

TOP CHOICE Taybank   PUB **£**
(www.thetaybank.com; Tay Tce, Dunkeld; bar mains £5-8) Top choice for a sun-kissed pub lunch by the river is the Taybank, a regular meeting place and performance space for musicians of all creeds and a wonderfully open and welcoming bar. The menu includes a tasty selection of traditional and offbeat stews.

❶ Information

Dunkeld's **tourist office** (☎01350-727688; dunkeld@visitscotland.com; The Cross; ☑daily Apr-Oct, Fri-Sun Nov-Mar) has information on local trails and paths.

❶ Getting There & Away

Dunkeld is 15 miles north of Perth. **Citylink** (www.citylink.co.uk) buses between Glasgow/Edinburgh and Inverness stop at Birnam House Hotel. Birnam to Perth (£7.90) or Pitlochry (£7.60) takes 20 minutes.

Stagecoach (www.stagecoachbus.com) has a bus between Blairgowrie (30 minutes) and Aberfeldy (40 minutes), via Dunkeld, twice daily Monday to Friday only.

Trains run to Edinburgh (£12.90, 1½ hours, approximately hourly Monday to Saturday, four on Sunday), Glasgow (£12.90, 1½ hours, roughly hourly Monday to Saturday, four on Sunday) and Inverness (£21.50, two hours, eight daily Monday to Saturday, five on Sunday).

PITLOCHRY
POP 2564

Pitlochry, with its air already smelling of the Highlands, is a popular stop on the way north and a convenient base for exploring northern Central Scotland. On a quiet spring evening it's a pretty place with salmon jumping in the Tummel and good things brewing at the Moulin Hotel. In summer the main street can be a conga-line of tour groups, but get away from that and it'll still charm you.

◉ Sights

One of Pitlochry's attractions is its beautiful **riverside**; the River Tummel is dammed here, and you can watch salmon swimming (not jumping) up a **fish ladder** to the loch above.

Bell's Blair Athol Distillery   DISTILLERY
(☎01796-482003; www.discovering-distilleries. com; Atholl Rd; tour £5; ☑Mon-Fri winter, plus Sat Apr-Oct, plus Sun Jun-Oct) One of two distilleries around Pitlochry, this is at the southern end of town. Tours focus on whisky making and the blending of this well-known drop. The tour price is discountable off a bottle purchase.

FREE Edradour Distillery   DISTILLERY
(☎01796-472095; www.edradour.co.uk; ☑daily) This is proudly Scotland's smallest distillery and a great one to visit: you can see the whole process easily-explained in one room. It's 2.5 miles east of Pitlochry along the Moulin road, and a pleasant walk there.

Explorers Garden   GARDEN
(www.explorersgarden.com; adult/child £3/1; Foss Rd; ☑10am-5pm Apr-Oct) At the Pitlochry Festival Theatre, this excellent garden commemorates 300 years of plant collecting and those who hunted down 'new' species. The whole collection is based on plants brought back to Scotland by Scottish explorers.

Heathergems   CRAFTS
(www.heathergems.com; 22 Atholl Rd; ☑9am-5.30pm May-Sep, 9am-5pm Mon-Sat Oct-Apr) Just behind the tourist office is Heathergems, the factory outlet of a most unusual and beautiful form of Scottish jewellery. The jewellery is made from natural heather stems, which are dyed and pressed to create colourful, original pieces. You can actually view the jewellery being made through

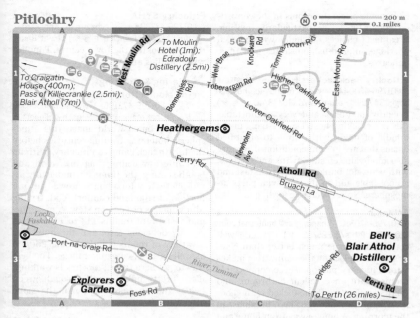

windows into the workshop. Definitely worth a browse.

✨ Festivals and Events

Pitlochry Festival Theatre　　THEATRE
(☏01796-484626; www.pitlochry.org.uk; Foss Rd; tickets £14-25) This well-known theatre stages a different mainstream play for six nights out of seven during its season from May to mid-October.

Étape　　CYCLE RACE
(www.etapecaledonia.co.uk) Étape, an 81-mile charity cycling event, brings competitors of all standards onto the beautiful highland roads around Pitlochry in mid-May. It's become a big deal; you'll have to prebook accommodation.

Enchanted Forest　　LIGHT SHOW
(www.enchantedforest.org.uk; adults £11-14, children £6) This spectacular sound-and-light show in a forest near Pitlochry is a major family hit in the last week of October and first week of November.

🛏 Sleeping

Craigatin House　　B&B **££**
(☏01796-472478; www.craigatinhouse.co.uk; 165 Atholl Rd; d standard/deluxe £78/88; P🐾🕾) Several times more tasteful than the average Pitlochry lodging, this noble house and

garden is set back from the main road at the western end of town. Chic contemporary fabrics covering expansive beds offer a standard of comfort above and beyond the reasonable price; the rooms in the converted stable block are particularly inviting. Breakfast choices include whisky-laced porridge, smoked-fish omelettes, and apple pancakes.

Pitlochry Backpackers Hotel   HOSTEL £
(☎01796-470044; www.scotlands-top-hostels.com; 134 Atholl Rd; dm/tw/d £15/38/40; P@) Friendly, laid-back and very comfortable, this is a cracking hostel smack-bang in the middle of town, with three- to eight-bed dorms that are in mint condition. There are also good-value en suite twins and doubles, with beds, not bunks. Cheap breakfast and a pool table add to the convivial party atmosphere. No extra charge for linen.

Ashleigh   B&B £
(☎01796-470316; nancy.gray@btinternet.com; 120 Atholl Rd; s/d £25/50; P) Genuine welcomes don't come much better than Nancy's, and her place on the main street makes a top Pitlochry pitstop. Three comfortable rooms share an excellent bathroom, and there's an open kitchen stocked with goodies where you make your own breakfast in the morning. A home-away-from-home and standout budget choice.

Knockendarroch House   HOTEL ££
(☎01796-473473; www.knockendarroch.co.uk; Higher Oakfield; dinner, bed & breakfast s/d £120/170; P) Top of the town and boasting the best views, this genteel, well-run hotel has a range of luxurious rooms with huge windows that take advantage of the Highland light. The standard rooms actually have better views than the larger, slightly pricier superior ones. A couple of rooms have great little balconies, perfect for a sundowner. Meals are highly commended here too.

Strathgarry   HOTEL ££
(☎01796-472469; www.strathgarryhotel.co.uk; 113 Atholl Rd; s/d £40/60, deluxe s/d £60/80;) With a top main-street location, Strathgarry is a hotel-bar-cafe-restaurant that's all done pretty well. En suite rooms are very snug and have some luxurious touches – we lost a researcher who sunk into one of the beds and was never seen again.

Tir Aluinn   B&B ££
(☎01796-473811; www.tiraluinn.co.uk; 10 Higher Oakfield Rd; s/d £32/64; P) Tucked away above the main street, this is a little gem of a place with bright rooms with easy-on-the-eye furniture, and an excellent personal welcome.

Pitlochry SYHA   HOSTEL £
(☎01796-472308; www.syha.org.uk; Knockard Rd; dm £17.25; ⊙Feb-Oct; P@) Great location overlooking the town centre. Popular with families and walkers.

🍴 Eating & Drinking

TOP CHOICE Moulin Hotel   PUB, HOTEL ££
(☎01796-472196; www.moulinhotel.co.uk; Moulin; bar mains £7-11; ⊙lunch & dinner) A mile away but a world apart, this atmospheric hotel was trading centuries before the tartan tack came to Pitlochry. With its romantic low ceilings, ageing wood and booth seating, the inn is a wonderfully atmospheric spot for a house-brewed ale or a portion of Highland comfort food: try the filling haggis or venison stew. A more formal restaurant (mains £13 to £16) serves equally delicious fare, and the hotel has a variety of rooms (single/double £60/75) as well as a self-catering annexe. The best way to get here from Pitlochry is walking: it's a pretty uphill stroll through green fields, and an easy roll down the slope afterwards.

Port-na-Craig Inn   RESTAURANT, PUB ££
(☎01796-472777; www.portnacraig.com; Port Na Craig; mains £13-17; ⊙lunch & dinner) Right on the river, this top little spot sits in what was once a separate hamlet. Delicious main meals are prepared with confidence and panache – scrumptious scallops or lamb steak bursting with flavour might appeal, but simpler sandwiches, kids' meals and light lunches also tempt. Or you could just sit out by the river with a pint and watch the anglers whisking away

McKay's Hotel   PUB £
(www.mckayshotel.co.uk; 138 Atholl Rd; mains £9; ⊙lunch & dinner) While the Moulin and the Port-na-Craig are perfect for a quiet beer in the Highland air, this is the place to go to meet locals and have a big night out. Live music at weekends, weekly karaoke and DJs make this Pitlochry's most popular. The action moves from the spacious front bar (which serves food) to the boisterous dancefloor out the back.

❶ Information
Computer Services Centre (☎473711; 67 Atholl Rd; per hr £3; ⊙9.30am-5.30pm Mon-Fri, to 12.30pm Sat; @) Internet access.

Tourist office (☎01796-472215; pitlochry@visitscotland.com; 22 Atholl Rd; ⊙8.30am-7pm Mon-Sat & 9.30am-5.30pm Sun Easter-Oct,

10am-4pm Mon-Sat Nov-Mar; @) Good information on local walks.

❶ Getting There & Away

Citylink (www.citylink.co.uk) buses run roughly hourly to Inverness (£15.10, two hours), Perth (£9.40, 40 minutes), Edinburgh (£14.40, two hours) and Glasgow (£14.40, 2¼ hours). **Megabus** (www.megabus.com) discount services also run these routes.

Stagecoach (www.stagecoachbus.com) runs to Aberfeldy (30 minutes, hourly Monday to Saturday, three Sunday), Dunkeld (25 minutes, up to 10 daily Monday to Saturday) and Perth (one hour, up to 10 daily Monday to Saturday).

Pitlochry is on the main railway from Perth (£11, 30 minutes, nine daily Monday to Saturday, five on Sunday) to Inverness.

❶ Getting Around

Escape Route (✆01796-473859; www.escape-route.biz; 3 Atholl Rd; bike hire per half-/full day from £10/18; ☉daily) rents out bikes; it's worth booking ahead at weekends. For a taxi, call **Broons** (✆01882-632331); a taxi to Blair Castle will cost you £15.

PASS OF KILLIECRANKIE

Drop into the **Killiecrankie tourist office** (NTS; www.nts.org.uk; ✆01796-473233; Killiecrankie; admission free, parking £2; ☉10am-5.30pm Apr-Oct) in this beautiful, rugged gorge, 3.5 miles north of Pitlochry. It has great interactive displays on the Jacobite rebellion and local flora and fauna. There's plenty to touch, pull and open – great for kids. There are some stunning walks into the wooded gorge, too; keep an eye out for red squirrels.

Almost halfway between Pitlochry and Blair Atholl, **Killiecrankie House Hotel** (✆01796-473220; www.killiecrankiehotel.co.uk; Killiecrankie; d standard/superior £230/250; ₱⚥) is brilliant for treating that someone special. Rates listed here are for dinner, bed and breakfast; bed-and-breakfast rate also available.

Local buses run between Pitlochry and Blair Atholl via Killiecrankie (10 minutes, three to seven daily).

BLAIR CASTLE & BLAIR ATHOLL

One of the most popular tourist attractions in Scotland, magnificent **Blair Castle** (www.blair-castle.co.uk; Blair Atholl; adult/child/family £8.75/5.25/24; ☉9.30am-5.30pm Apr-Oct) and the 108 square miles it sits on, is the seat of the Duke of Atholl, head of the Murray clan. It's an impressive white building set beneath forested slopes above the River Garry.

The original tower was built in 1269, but the castle has undergone significant remodelling since. Thirty rooms are open to the public and they present a wonderful picture of upper-class Highland life from the 16th century on. The **dining room** is sumptuous – check out the 9-pint wine glasses – and the **ballroom** is a vaulted chamber that's a virtual stag cemetery.

The current duke visits the castle every May to review the Atholl Highlanders, Britain's only private army.

For a great cycle, walk or drive, take the stunning road to Glenfender from Blair Atholl village. It's about 3 miles on a long, winding uphill track to a farmhouse; the views of snowcapped peaks along the way are spectacular.

Gothic **Atholl Arms Hotel** (✆01796-481205; www.athollarms.co.uk; Blair Atholl; s/d from £65/80; ₱⚥), a pub near the train station, is convenient for the castle and sometimes does special deals. The fussy rooms are of a high standard; book ahead on weekends. The Bothy Bar here is the sibling pub of the Moulin Hotel in Pitlochry, snug with booth seating, low-slung roof, bucket-loads of character and an enormous fireplace. There's no better place to be when the rain is lashing outside.

Blair Atholl is 6 miles northwest of Pitlochry, and the castle a further mile beyond it. Local buses run a service between Pitlochry and Blair Atholl (25 minutes, three to seven daily). Four buses a day (Monday to Saturday) go directly to the castle. There's a train station in the village, but not all trains stop here.

For a continuation of this route north up the A9, see the Cairngorms (p327).

Blairgowrie & Glenshee

The route along the A93 through Glenshee is one of the most spectacular drives in the country. Meandering burns and soaring peaks splotched with blinding-white snow dwarf open-mouthed drivers – it's surprising that there aren't more accidents! It's fantastic **walking** country in summer, and there's **skiing** in winter. Blairgowrie and Braemar (see p248) are the main accommodation centres for the Glenshee resort, although there is a small settlement 5 miles south of the ski runs at Spittal of Glenshee with a couple of good sleeping options.

🏃 Activities

Glenshee Ski Resort SKIING
(☎01339-741320; www.ski-glenshee.co.uk; half-/full-day lift pass £20/25) This resort has 38 pistes and is one of Scotland's largest skiing areas. After a good fall of snow and when the sun burns through the clouds, you will be in a unique position to drink in the beauty of this country; the skiing isn't half bad either. The chairlift can whisk you up to 910m, near the top of the Cairnwell (933m). Whenever there's enough snow in winter it opens daily. Prices are cheaper for beginners.

🛏 Sleeping & Eating

TOP CHOICE **Dalmunzie House** HOTEL £££
(☎01250-885224; www.dalmunzie.com; Glenshee; s £105-145, d £170-230, dinner £45; 🅿@🛜) A noble estate with a dash of antipodean hospitality thrown into the mix, this classy retreat lives up to the best Highland stereotypes: roaring fires, leather armchairs, antlers and decanters of malt. There are four classes of room, offering much comfort (some with four-poster beds). There's a beautiful library, set up to help research into Scottish forebears, and a restaurant: dinners are opulent affairs with three courses broken by a cleansing sorbet. As well as wonderful walks hereabouts, the property offers golf, tennis, fishing and other activities; bikes can also be hired.

Spittal of Glenshee Hotel HOTEL, HOSTEL ££
(☎01250-885215; www.spittalofglenshee.co.uk; Spittal of Glenshee; dm/s/d £16/55/65; 🅿🛜) This hotel is a very 'Scottish experience' – it's a great old country lodge that has burnt down numerous times, but don't worry: the insurers have calculated that it is likely the next fire won't be until 2029. There's a good bar, and a bunkhouse too (without cooking facilities).

Rosebank House B&B ££
(☎01250-872912; colhotel@rosebank35.fsnet. co.uk; Balmoral Rd, Blairgowrie; s/d £28/56; 🕙Jan-Nov; 🅿) This fine Georgian property is a great deal. Good-sized rooms upstairs are well kept and have small but clean en suites, and there's a large front garden. The friendly owners take good care of guests, and no surcharge is levied on solo travellers. Try to get a room overlooking the garden.

ℹ Information

Tourist office (☎01250-872960; blairgowrie@ visitscotland.com; 26 Wellmeadow; 🕙daily Apr-Oct & Dec, Mon-Sat Nov & Jan-Mar) On the central square in Blairgowrie with plenty of walking and skiing information.

ℹ Getting There & Away

Stagecoach (www.stagecoachbus.com) operates from Perth to Blairgowrie (50 minutes, three to seven daily). Buses also run from Dundee to Blairgowrie (50 minutes, hourly, less frequent on Sunday).

The only service from Blairgowrie to the Glenshee area, about 30 miles away, is Stagecoach bus 71 which runs twice on Wednesday and four times on Saturday to Spittal of Glenshee.

Around Blairgowrie

About 5 miles east of Blairgowrie, Alyth is a charming little historic village with a small canal and some exquisite stone bridges. Ask at Blairgowrie's tourist office for the *Walk Old Alyth* leaflet. If you're looking to escape the rain, perusing the displays on local history at Alyth Museum (www.pkc.gov.uk; Commercial St; admission free; 🕙1-5pm Wed-Sun May-Sep) is a fine way to pass an hour or so.

Alyth Hotel (☎01828-632447; www.alyth hotel.com; 6 Commercial St, Alyth; s/d £50/75, mains £8-11; 🅿) is a classic town pub that has had an excellent refurbishment. The old-style rooms upstairs are better than the renovated ones though, with a lot more space and a user-friendly design. Either way, try and get a room overlooking the Square; Room 1 is a good choice. The downstairs bar and restaurant is infinitely cosy with low-slung roof, stone walls and all manner of clutter giving it a homely feel.

Off the A94 and 8 miles east of Blairgowrie, Meigle is worth the trip for those with a fascination for Pictish stones. The tiny Meigle Museum (HS; www.historic-scotland.gov. uk; adult/child £3.20/1.90; 🕙9.30am-5.30pm Apr-Sep) has 26 such carved stones from the 7th to the 10th century, all found in the local area. The pieces range from the Nordic to the exotic – they include a Viking headstone and, bizarrely, a carving of a camel.

Northeast Scotland

Best Places to Stay

» Glen Clova Hotel (p235)
» 24 Shorehead (p246)
» Auld Kirk (p248)
» City Wharf Apartments
(p241)

Best Places to Eat

» Tolbooth (p246)
» Café 52 (p242)
» Metro (p228)
» Gathering Place (p250)

Why Go?

Many visitors pass by this corner of the country in their headlong rush to the tourist honeypots of Loch Ness and Skye. But they're missing out on a part of Scotland that's as beautiful and diverse as the more obvious attractions of the western Highlands and islands.

Within its bounds you'll find two of Scotland's four largest cities – Dundee, the city of jute, jam and journalism, the cradle of some of Britain's favourite comic characters, and home to Captain Scott's Antarctic research ship, the *Discovery;* and Aberdeen, the granite city, an economic powerhouse fuelled by the riches of North Sea oil.

Angus is a region of rich farmland and scenic glens dotted with the mysterious stones left behind by the ancient Picts, while Aberdeenshire and Moray are home to the greatest concentration of Scottish Baronial castles in the country, and dozens of distilleries along the River Spey.

When to Go
Aberdeen

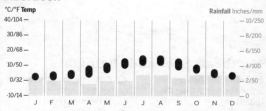

June/July Classic boats large and small fill Portsoy harbour for the Scottish Wooden Boat Festival.

September Braemar Gathering (Highland games); whisky and music festival in Dufftown.

December Spectacular fireball ceremony in Stonehaven on Hogmanay (New Year's Eve).

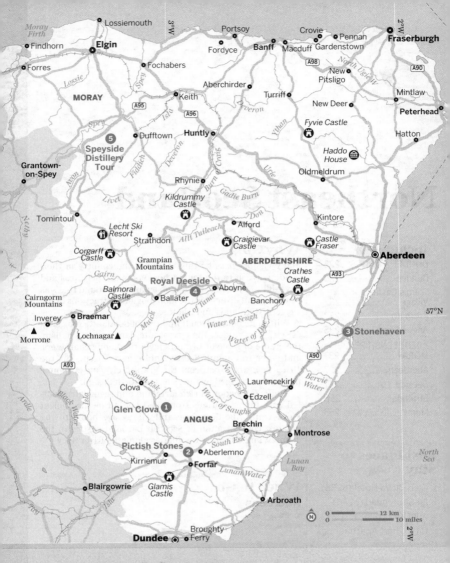

Northeast Scotland Highlights

1 Hiking through the hills around beautiful **Glen Clova** (p235)

2 Meditating on the meaning of the mysterious **Pictish stones** (p231) of Angus

3 Tucking into the freshest of Scottish seafood at the **Tolbooth Restaurant** (p246) in Stonehaven

4 Exploring the hills, forests, castles and pretty villages of **Royal Deeside** (p247)

5 Being initiated into the mysteries of malt whisky on a **Speyside distillery tour** (p255)

❶ Getting Around

You can pick up a **public transport map** from tourist offices and bus stations. For timetable information, call **Traveline** (☑0871 200 2233; www.travelinescotland.com).

BUS The Dundee to Aberdeen route is served by **Scottish Citylink** (www.citylink.co.uk) buses. **Stagecoach** (www.stagecoachbus.com) is the main regional bus operator, with services linking all the main towns and cities.

Stagecoach offers a **Highland Megarider** ticket (£24) that gives seven days unlimited bus travel in Inverness and as far as Strathpeffer, Beauly, Nairn, Elgin and Fochabers, and a **Bluebird Megarider** ticket (£70) that allows seven days unlimited travel on all its services in Aberdeenshire and Moray.

TRAIN The Dundee–Inverness railway line passes through Arbroath, Montrose, Stonehaven, Aberdeen, Huntly and Elgin.

DUNDEE & ANGUS

Angus is a region of fertile farmland stretching north from Dundee – Scotland's fourth-largest city – to the Highland border. It's an attractive area of broad straths (valleys) and low, green hills contrasting with the rich, red-brown soil of freshly ploughed fields. Romantic glens finger their way into the foothills of the Grampian Mountains, while the scenic coastline ranges from the red-sandstone cliffs of Arbroath to the long, sandy beaches around Montrose. This was the Pictish heartland of the 7th and 8th centuries, and many interesting Pictish symbol stones survive here.

Apart from the crowds visiting Discovery Point in newly confident Dundee and the coach parties shuffling through Glamis Castle, Angus is a bit of a tourism backwater and a good place to escape the hordes.

Dundee

POP 144,000

London's Trafalgar Sq has Nelson on his column, Edinburgh's Princes St has its monument to Sir Walter Scott and Belfast has a statue of Queen Victoria outside City Hall. Dundee's City Sq, on the other hand, is graced – rather endearingly – by the bronze figure of Desperate Dan. Familiar to generations of British school children, Dan is one of the best-loved cartoon characters from the children's comic the *Dandy,* published by Dundee firm DC Thomson since 1937.

Dundee enjoys perhaps the finest location of any Scottish city, spreading along the northern shore of the Firth of Tay, and can boast tourist attractions of national importance in Discovery Point and the Verdant Works museum. Add in the attractive seaside suburb of Broughty Ferry, some lively nightlife and the Dundonians themselves – among the friendliest, most welcoming and most entertaining people you'll meet – and Dundee is definitely worth a stopover.

History

During the 19th century Dundee grew from its trading port origins to become a major player in the shipbuilding, whaling, textile and railway engineering industries. Dundonian firms owned and operated most of the jute mills in India (jute is a natural fibre used in making ropes and sacking), and the city's textile industry employed as many as 43,000 people – little wonder Dundee earned the nickname 'Juteopolis'.

Dundee is often called the city of the 'Three Js' – jute, jam and journalism. According to legend, it was a Dundee woman, Janet Keillor, who invented marmalade in the late 18th century; her son founded the city's famous Keillor jam factory. Jute is no longer produced, and when the Keillor factory was taken over in 1988 production was transferred to England. Journalism still thrives, however, led by the family firm of DC Thomson. Best known for children's comics, such as the *Beano,* Thomson is now the city's largest employer.

In the late 19th and early 20th centuries Dundee was one of the richest cities in the country – there were more millionaires per head of population here than anywhere else in Britain – but the textile and engineering industries declined in the second half of the 20th century, leading to high unemployment and urban decay.

In the 1960s and '70s Dundee's cityscape was scarred with ugly blocks of flats, office buildings and shopping centres linked by unsightly concrete walkways – the view as you approach across the Tay Road Bridge does not look promising – and most visitors passed it by. Since the mid-1990s, however, Dundee has reinvented itself as a tourist destination, and a centre for banking, insurance and new industries, while its waterfront is currently undergoing a major redevelopment. It also has more university students – one in seven of the population – than any other town in Europe, except Heidelberg.

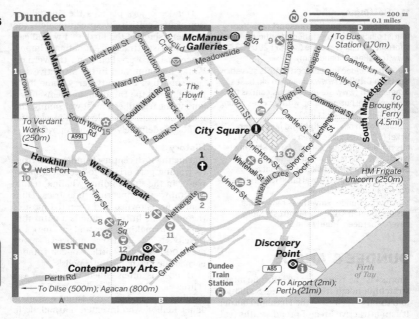

Sights

Discovery Point MUSEUM
(www.rrsdiscovery.com; Discovery Quay; adult/child £7.75/4.75; ⊙10am-6pm Mon-Sat, 11am-6pm Sun Apr-Oct, to 5pm Nov-Mar) The three masts of Captain Robert Falcon Scott's famous polar expedition vessel the **RRS Discovery** dominate the riverside to the south of the city centre. The ship was built in Dundee in 1900, with a wooden hull at least half a metre thick to survive the pack ice, and sailed for the Antarctic in 1901 where it spent two winters trapped in the ice. From 1931 on it was laid up in London where its condition steadily deteriorated, until it was rescued by the efforts of Peter Scott (son of Robert) and the Maritime Trust, and restored to its 1925 condition. In 1986 the ship was given a berth in its home port of Dundee, where it became a symbol of the city's regeneration.

Exhibitions and audiovisual displays in the main building provide a fascinating history of both the ship and Antarctic exploration, but *Discovery* itself – afloat in a protected dock – is the star attraction. You can visit the bridge, the galley and the mahogany-panelled officers' wardroom, and poke your nose into the cabins used by Scott and his crew.

A joint ticket that gives entry to both Discovery Point and the Verdant Works costs £11.50/7 per adult/child.

Verdant Works MUSEUM
(www.verdantworks.com; West Henderson's Wynd; adult/child £7/4; ⊙10am-6pm Mon-Sat, 11am-6pm Sun Apr-Oct, 10.30am-4.30pm Wed-Sat, 11am-4.30pm Sun Nov-Mar) One of the finest industrial museums in Europe, the Verdant Works explores the history of Dundee's jute industry. Housed in a restored jute mill, complete with original machinery still in working condition, the museum's interactive exhibits and computer displays follow the raw material from its origins in India through to the manufacture of a wide range of finished products, from sacking to rope to wagon covers for the pioneers of the American West. The mill is 250m west of the city centre.

FREE **McManus Galleries** MUSEUM
(www.mcmanus.co.uk; Albert Sq; ⊙10am-5pm Mon-Sat, 12.30-4.30pm Sun) Housed in a solid Victorian Gothic building designed by Gilbert Scott in 1867, the recently restored McManus Galleries is a city museum on a human scale – you can see everything there is to see, without feeling rushed or overwhelmed. The exhibits cover the history

Dundee

of the city from the Iron Age to the present day, including relics of the Tay Bridge Disaster and the Dundee whaling industry. Computer geeks will enjoy the Sinclair ZX81 and Spectrum (pioneering personal computers with a whole 16K of memory!) which were made in Dundee in the early 1980s.

HM Frigate Unicorn   MUSEUM
(www.frigateunicorn.org; Victoria Dock; adult/child £5/3; ⊙10am-5pm Apr-Oct, noon-4pm Wed-Fri, 10am-4pm Sat & Sun Nov-Mar) Unlike the polished and much-restored *Discovery,* Dundee's other floating tourist attraction retains the authentic atmosphere of a salty old sailing ship. Built in 1824, the 46-gun *Unicorn* is the oldest British-built ship still afloat – she was mothballed soon after launching and never saw action. By the mid-19th century sailing ships were outclassed by steam and the *Unicorn* served as a gunpowder store, then later as a training vessel.

When it was proposed to break up the ship for scrap in the 1960s, a preservation society was formed. Wandering around the four decks gives you an excellent impression of what it must have been like for the crew forced to live in such cramped conditions.

The *Unicorn* is berthed in Victoria Dock, just northeast of the Tay Road Bridge. The entry price includes a self-guided tour (also available in French and German).

FREE **Dundee Contemporary Arts**
                                      ART GALLERY
(www.dca.org.uk; Nethergate; ⊙10.30am-5.30pm Tue, Wed, Fri & Sat, 10.30am-8.30pm Thu, noon-5.30pm Sun) The focus for the city's emerging Cultural Quarter is Dundee Contemporary Arts, a centre for modern art, design and cinema. The galleries here exhibit work by contemporary UK and international artists, and there are **printmakers' studios** (print studio 11am-9pm Tue-Thu, 11am-6pm Fri & Sat) where you can watch artists at work, or even take part in craft demonstrations and workshops. There's also the Jute Cafe-Bar (see p229).

Dundee Law   PARK
It's worth making the climb up **Dundee Law** (174m) for great views of the city, the two Tay bridges and across to Fife. The **Tay Rail Bridge** – at just over 2 miles long, it was the world's longest when it was built – was completed in 1887 and replaced an earlier bridge whose stumps can be seen alongside. The original bridge collapsed during a storm in 1879, less than two years after it was built, taking a train and 75 lives along with it – the infamous Tay Bridge Disaster. The 1.5-mile **Tay Road Bridge** was opened in 1966. Dundee Law is a short walk northwest of the city centre, along Constitution Rd.

City Square   SIGNIFICANT AREA
The heart of Dundee is City Sq, flanked to the south by the 1930s facade of **Caird Hall**, which was gifted to the city by a textile magnate and is now home to the City Chambers. A more recent addition to the square, unveiled in 2001, is a bronze statue of **Desperate Dan**, the lantern-jawed hero of children's comic the *Dandy* (he's clutching a copy in his right hand), which has been published in Dundee since 1937.

Pedestrianised High St leads west into Nethergate, flanked to the north by **St Mary's Church**. Most of the church dates from the 19th century, but the **Old Steeple** was built around 1460.

✈️ Festivals & Events

If you're around in late July, look out for the **Dundee Blues Bonanza** (www.dundee bluesbonanza.co.uk), a two-day festival of free blues, boogie and roots music.

🛏️ Sleeping

Most of Dundee's city-centre hotels are business oriented, and offer lower rates on weekends. The main concentrations of B&Bs are along Broughty Ferry and Arbroath Rds east of the city centre, and on Perth Rd to the west. If you don't fancy a night in the city, consider staying at the nearby seaside town of Broughty Ferry.

Accommodation in Dundee is usually booked solid when the Open Golf tournament is staged at Carnoustie or St Andrews – check www.opengolf.com for future dates and venues.

Balgowan House   B&B ££
(📞01382-200262; www.balgowanhouse.co.uk; 510 Perth Rd; s/d £63/84; P🔊) Built in 1900 and perched in a prime location with stunning views over the Firth of Tay, Balgowan is a wealthy merchant's mansion converted into a luxurious guesthouse with two sumptuous en suite bedrooms. It's 2 miles west of the city centre, overlooking the university botanic gardens.

Apex City Quay Hotel   HOTEL ££
(📞01382-202404; www.apexhotels.co.uk; 1 West Victoria Dock Rd; r from £98; P🔊🏊) Though it looks plain from the outside, the Apex overlooks the city's redeveloping waterfront and sports the sort of stylish, spacious, sofa-equipped rooms that make you want to lounge around all evening munching chocolate in front of the TV. If you can drag yourself away from your room, there are spa treatments, saunas and Japanese hot tubs to enjoy. The hotel is just east of the city centre, close to the Frigate Unicorn.

Errolbank Guest House   B&B ££
(📞01382-462118; www.errolbank-guesthouse. com; 9 Dalgleish Rd; s/d £35/58; P) A mile east of the city centre, just north of the road to Broughty Ferry, Errolbank is a lovely Victorian family home with small but beautifully decorated en suite rooms set on a quiet street.

Dundee Backpackers   HOSTEL £
(📞01382-224646; www.hoppo.com; 71 High St; dm £13-15, s/tw from £25/40; @) New hostel in a beautifully converted historic building, with clean, modern kitchen, pool room, and an ideal location right in the city centre. Can get a bit noisy at night, but that's because it's close to pubs and nightlife.

Shaftesbury Hotel   HOTEL ££
(📞01382-669216; 1 Hyndford St; s/d from £55/85; 🔊) The family-run, 12-room Shaftesbury is a Victorian mansion built for a jute baron and has many authentic period features, including a fine marble fireplace in the dining room. It's 1.5 miles west of the city centre, just off Perth Rd.

Aabalree   B&B £
(📞01382-223867; www.aabalree.com; 20 Union St; s/d £24/40) This is a pretty basic B&B – there are no en suites – but the owners are welcoming (don't be put off by the dark entrance) and it couldn't be more central, close to both train and bus stations. This makes it popular, so book ahead.

Grampian Hotel   HOTEL ££
(📞01382-667785; www.grampianhotel.com; 295 Perth Rd; s/d from £55/70; P🔊) A small and welcoming hotel set in a restored Victorian town house with six spacious bedrooms (all en suite), just five minutes' walk from the West End.

Aauld Steeple Guest House   B&B £
(📞01382-200302; www.aauldsteepleguest house.co.uk; 94 Nethergate; s/d £27/44; 🔊) Just as central as Aabalree, but a bit more comfortable, the Aauld Steeple has spacious double and family rooms, some with views of St Mary's Church. Suffers a bit from street noise, though.

Riverview Caravan Park   CAMPSITE £
(📞01382-535471; www.riverview.co.uk; Marine Dr, Monifieth; tent or campervan sites £15; ⊘closed Feb) The nearest camping ground to Dundee is attractively sited near the beach, 5 miles east of the city centre.

🍴 Eating

TOP CHOICE **Metro**   BRASSERIE ££
(📞0845 365 0002; www.apexhotels.co. uk/eat; Apex City Quay Hotel, 1 West Victoria Dock Rd; mains £10-16) Sleek, slate-blue banquettes, white linen napkins, black-clad staff and a view of Victoria Dock lend an air of city sophistication to this stylish hotel brasserie, with a menu that ranges from steaks and burgers to Caribbean jerk chicken with coconut curry. There's a three-course dinner menu for £21.50. Located just east of the city centre, close to the Frigate Unicorn.

Playwright
BISTRO ££

(☑01382-223113; www.theplaywright.co.uk; 11 Tay Sq; mains £23-25; ☺10am-midnight) Next door to the theatre, and decorated with photos of Scottish actors, this innovative cafe-bar and bistro serves a 'grazing menu' of light meals (£5 to £8) from noon to 5pm, a lunch and pre-theatre menu (£17/20 for two/three courses) and a gourmet à la carte menu that concentrates on fine Scottish produce with dishes such as saddle of lamb with wild mushrooms and roast halibut with shellfish sauce.

Jute Cafe-Bar
BISTRO ££

(www.jutecafebar.co.uk; Dundee Contemporary Arts, 152 Nethergate; mains lunch £7-11, dinner £13-20; ☺10am-midnight Mon-Sat, noon-midnight Sun) The industrial-chic cafe-bar in the Dundee Contemporary Arts centre serves excellent deli sandwiches and steaks, as well as more adventurous Mediterranean-Asian fusion cuisine. Early-bird menu (5pm to 6.30pm daily) offers a two-course dinner for £12. Tables spill out into the sunny courtyard in summer.

Agacán
TURKISH ££

(☑01382-644227; 113 Perth Rd; mains £10-16; ☺dinner Tue-Sun) With a charismatic owner, quirky decor and wonderfully aromatic Turkish specialities (Iskender kebab is our favourite), it's no wonder that you have to book ahead at this little spot on a corner, a 20 minute walk up Perth Rd from the centre. If you can't get a table, you can settle for takeaway.

Dil'se
INDIAN ££

(www.dilse-restaurant.co.uk; 99 Perth Rd; mains £8-15; ☺noon-2.30pm & 4.30-11pm Sun-Thu, noon-2am Fri & Sat) Dundee loves a curry, and nobody does it better than this sleek modern Bangladeshi restaurant most of the way up Perth Rd. The bold, contemporary approach extends beyond the delicious old favourites to new dishes, such as Mas Bangla, which brings the subcontinent to Scots salmon.

Rep Theatre Cafe
CAFE-BAR ££

(www.dundeereptheatre.co.uk; Tay Sq; mains £9-15; ☺cafe 10am-late, restaurant noon-3pm & 5-10pm Mon-Sat) The city's arty types hang out in this Continental-style cafe-bar and restaurant in the foyer at the Dundee Rep Theatre. Great sandwiches and pizza, as well as tasty steaks, fishcakes and veggie dishes.

Fisher & Donaldson
TEAROOM £

(12 Whitehall St; ☺6.30am-5pm Mon-Sat) There's an excellent tearoom in the up-market bakery and patisserie.

Deep Sea
FISH & CHIPS £

(81 Nethergate; ☺9.30am-6.30pm Mon-Sat) Dundee's best fish and chips.

Tesco Metro
SELF-CATERING £

(Murraygate; ☺7am-midnight Mon-Fri, 7am-10pm Sat, 10am-7pm Sun)

🍷 Drinking

There are many lively pubs, especially in the West End and along West Port.

Nether Inn
PUB

(134 Nethergate) This large, stylish place, with comfy couches, pool table and drinks promos, is popular with students.

Social
BAR

(www.socialanimal.co.uk; 10 South Tay St) A lively style bar with a separate dining area.

Globe
BAR

(53-57 West Port; ☎) Serves good bar meals from noon to 7.30pm (6pm Sunday) and often has live music or sport on the big-screen TV.

☆ Entertainment

Dundee's nightlife may not be as hot as Glasgow's, but there are lots of places to go – pick up a free what's-on guide from the tourist office, or check out the What's On section of www.dundee.com. Tickets for most events are on sale at the Dundee Contemporary Arts centre.

Caird Hall
MUSIC, COMEDY

(www.cairdhall.co.uk; 6 City Sq; ☺box office 9am-4.30pm Mon-Fri, 9.30am-1.30pm Sat) The Caird Hall hosts regular concerts of classical music, as well as organ recitals, rock bands, dances, comedians, fetes and fairs. Check its website for details of coming events.

Dundee Rep Theatre
DRAMA

(www.dundeereptheatre.co.uk; Tay Sq; ☺box office 10am-6pm or start of performance) Dundee's main venue for the performing arts, the Rep is home to Scotland's only full-time repertory company and to the Scottish Dance Theatre.

Fat Sams
CLUB, LIVE MUSIC

(www.fatsams.co.uk; 31 South Ward Rd; ☺11pm-late) Fat Sams has been around for more than 20 years but is still one of the city's most popular clubs, with regular live gigs, DJs and student nights pulling in a young crowd (including lots of students from St Andrews University).

Reading Rooms CLUB, LIVE MUSIC
(www.myspace.com/thereadingrooms; 57 Blackscroft; admission £3-8; ☺8.30pm or 10.30pm-2.30am Wed-Sat) Dundee's hippest venue is an arty, bohemian hang-out in a run-down former library that hosts some of Scotland's best indie club nights. Live gigs have ranged from island singer-songwriter Colin MacIntyre (aka Mull Historical Society) to Ayrshire rock band Biffy Clyro.

ℹ Information

Ninewells Hospital (☎01382-660111; ☺casualty 24hr) At Menzieshill, west of the city centre.

Tourist office (☎01382-527527; www.angusanddundee.co.uk; Discovery Point; ☺10am-5pm Mon-Sat, noon-4pm Sun Jun-Sep, 10am-4pm Mon-Sat Oct-May)

ℹ Getting There & Away

AIR Two and a half miles west of the city centre, **Dundee Airport** (www.hial.co.uk/dundee-airport) has daily scheduled services to London City airport (CityJet), Birmingham and Belfast (FlyBe). Bus 8X runs between the airport and the city centre (five minutes, half-hourly Monday to Saturday). A taxi to the airport takes five minutes and costs £3.50.

BUS **National Express** (www.nationalexpress.com) operates one direct service a day from London to Dundee (£40, 11 hours).

Scottish Citylink (www.citylink.co.uk) has hourly buses from Dundee to Glasgow (£15, 2½ hours), Perth (£8, 35 minutes), Aberdeen (£15, 1½ hours) and Edinburgh (£14, two hours, change at Perth); book via www.megabus.com for fares as low as £5. Some Aberdeen buses travel via Arbroath, others via Forfar. There are also direct buses to Oban (£26, 3½ hours. two daily).

Stagecoach operates buses to Perth (one hour, hourly), Blairgowrie (one hour, hourly), Forfar (40 minutes, once or twice an hour), Kirriemuir (one hour, half-hourly), Brechin (1¼ hours, 10 daily, change at Forfar) and Arbroath (one hour, half-hourly). Bus 99 runs to St Andrews (one hour, every 15 minutes Monday to Saturday, hourly on Sunday).

TRAIN Trains run to Dundee from Edinburgh (£20, 1¼ hours) and Glasgow (£23, 1½ hours) at least once an hour Monday to Saturday, hourly on Sunday from Edinburgh, and every two hours on Sunday from Glasgow.

Trains from Dundee to Aberdeen (£24, 1¼ hours) travel via Arbroath and Stonehaven. There are around two trains an hour, fewer on Sunday.

ℹ Getting Around

The city centre is compact and is easy to get around on foot. For information on local public transport, contact **Travel Dundee** (www.traveldundee.co.uk; Forum Shopping Centre, 92 Commercial St; ☺9.15am-4.55pm Mon-Fri, 10am-3.55pm Sat).

BUS City bus fares cost 65p to £1.45 depending on distance; buy your ticket from the driver (exact fare only – no change given).

CAR Rental agencies:
Arnold Clark (☎01382-225382; East Dock St)
National Car Rental (☎01382-224037; 45-53 Gellatly St)
TAXI **Discovery Taxis** (☎01382-732111)

Broughty Ferry

Dundee's attractive seaside suburb, known locally as 'The Ferry', lies 4 miles east of the city centre. It has a castle, a long, sandy beach and a number of good places to eat and drink. It's also handy for the golf courses at nearby Carnoustie.

FREE **Broughty Castle Museum** MUSEUM
(Castle Green; ☺10am-4pm Mon-Sat, 12.30-4pm Sun, closed Mon Oct-Mar) A 16th-century tower house that looms imposingly over the harbour, guarding the entrance to the Firth of Tay. There's a fascinating exhibit on Dundee's whaling industry, and the view from the top offers the chance of spotting seals and dolphins offshore.

🛏 Sleeping

Hotel Broughty Ferry HOTEL ££
(☎01382-480027; www.hotelbroughtyferry.com; 16 W Queen St; s/d £68/88; ᴘ☏☲) It doesn't look like much from the outside, but this is the Ferry's swankiest place to stay, with 16 beautifully decorated bedrooms, a sauna and solarium and a small, heated pool. It's only a five-minute stroll from the waterfront.

Invermark House B&B ££
(☎01382-739430; www.invermark.co.uk; 23 Monifieth Rd; s/d from £30/50; ᴘ☏) Invermark is a grand Victorian villa set in its own grounds, built for a jute baron in the mid-19th century. There are five large en suite

The mysterious carved stones that dot the landscape of eastern Scotland are the legacy of the warrior tribes who inhabited these lands 2000 years ago. The Romans occupied the southern half of Britain from AD 43 to 410, but the region to the north of the firths of Forth and Clyde – known as Caledonia – was abandoned as being too dangerous, sealed off behind the ramparts of the Antonine Wall and Hadrian's Wall.

Caledonia was the homeland of the Picts, a collection of tribes named by the Romans for their habit of painting or tattooing their bodies. In the 9th century they were culturally absorbed by the Scots, leaving behind only a few archaeological remains, a scattering of Pictish place names beginning with 'Pit', and hundreds of mysterious carved stones decorated with intricate symbols, mainly in northeast Scotland. The capital of the ancient Southern Pictish kingdom is said to have been at Forteviot in Strathearn; Pictish symbol stones are to be found throughout this area and all the way up the eastern coast of Scotland into Sutherland and Caithness.

It is thought that the stones were set up to record Pictish lineages and alliances, but no-one is sure exactly how the system worked. They are decorated with unusual symbols, including z-rods (lightning bolt?), circles (the sun?), double discs (hand mirror?) and fantastical creatures, as well as figures of warriors on horseback, hunting scenes and (on the later stones) Christian symbols.

Local tourist offices provide a free leaflet titled the *Angus Pictish Trail*, which will guide you to the main Pictish sites in the area. The finest assemblage of stones in their natural outdoor setting is at Aberlemno (see the boxed text, p234), and there are excellent indoor collections at St Vigeans Museum (p232) and the Meigle Museum (p222). The Pictavia interpretive centre at Brechin (p237) provides a good introduction to the Picts and is worth a look before you visit the stones.

The Pictish Trail by Anthony Jackson lists 11 driving tours, while *The Symbol Stones of Scotland* by the same author provides more detail on the history and meaning of the Pictish stones.

bedrooms and an elegant lounge and dining room with a view of the gardens.

Ashley House B&B ££
(☎01382-776109; www.ashleyhousebroughtyferry.com; 15 Monifieth Rd; per person £30-35; P ☎) This spacious and comfortable guesthouse has long been one of Broughty Ferry's best. Its four cheerfully decorated bedrooms come equipped with hotel-grade beds and DVD player; one has a particularly grand bathroom.

Fisherman's Tavern B&B ££
(☎01382-775941; www.fishermanstavern.co.uk; 10-16 Fort St; s/d £39/64) A delightful 17th-century terraced cottage just a few paces from the seafront, the Fisherman's was converted into a pub in 1827. It now has 11 stylishly modern rooms, most with en suite, and an atmospheric pub (see p231).

✕ Eating & Drinking

Ship Inn PUB, RESTAURANT ££
(www.theshipinn-broughtyferry.co.uk; 121 Fisher St; mains £10-18; ⊙food noon-2pm & 5-10.30pm Mon-Fri, noon-10.30pm Sat & Sun) On the seafront around the corner from the Fisherman's is the snug, wood-panelled, 19th-century Ship Inn, which serves top-notch dishes ranging from gourmet haddock and chips to venison steaks; you can eat in the upstairs restaurant, or down in the bar (bar meals £7 to £9). It's always busy, so get there early to grab a seat.

Fisherman's Tavern PUB £
(10-16 Fort St; mains £6-12; ⊙food noon-2.30pm & 5-7.30pm) The Fisherman's – a maze of cosy nooks and open fireplaces in a 17th-century cottage – is a lively little pub where you can wash down smoked haddock fishcakes or steak and chips with a choice of Scottish real ales.

Visocchi's CAFE £
(40 Gray St; mains £7-10; ⊙9.30am-5pm Tue, 9.30am-8pm Wed, Thu & Sun, 9.30am-1pm Fri & Sat) Visocchi's – a 70-year-old institution – is a traditional, family-run Italian cafe that sells delicious homemade ice cream, good coffee and a range of burgers, pizzas and pasta dishes.

ℹ️ Getting There & Away

City bus 5 and Stagecoach bus 73 run from Dundee High St to Broughty Ferry (20 minutes) several times an hour from Monday to Saturday, and hourly on Sunday.

Glamis Castle & Village

Looking every inch the Scottish Baronial castle, with its roofline sprouting a forest of pointed turrets and battlements, Glamis Castle (www.glamis-castle.co.uk; adult/child £8.75/6; ⊙10am-6pm mid-Mar–Oct, 10.30am-4.30pm Nov & Dec, closed Jan–mid-Mar) claims to be the legendary setting for Shakespeare's *Macbeth*. A royal residence since 1372, it is the family home of the earls of Strathmore and Kinghorne – the Queen Mother (born Elizabeth Bowes-Lyon; 1900–2002) spent her childhood at Glamis (pronounced 'glams') and Princess Margaret (the Queen's sister; 1930–2002) was born here.

The five-storey, L-shaped castle was given to the Lyon family in 1372, but was significantly altered in the 17th century. Inside, the most impressive room is the **drawing room**, with its vaulted plasterwork ceiling. There's a display of armour and weaponry in the haunted crypt and frescoes in the chapel (also haunted). Duncan's Hall is named for the murdered King Duncan from *Macbeth* (though the scene actually takes place in Macbeth's castle in Inverness). As with Cawdor Castle, the claimed Shakespeare connection is fictitious – the real Macbeth had nothing to do with either castle, and died long before either was built.

You can also look around the royal apartments, including the Queen Mother's bedroom. The one-hour guided tours depart every 15 minutes (last tour at 4.30pm, or 3.30pm in winter).

The **Angus Folk Museum** (NTS; Kirkwynd, Glamis; adult/child £5.50/4.50; ⊙noon-5pm daily Jul & Aug, noon-5pm Sat & Sun only Easter-Jun, Sep & Oct), in a row of 18th-century cottages just off the flower-bedecked square in Glamis village, houses a fine collection of domestic and agricultural relics.

Glamis Castle is 12 miles north of Dundee. There are two to four buses a day from Dundee (35 minutes) to Glamis; some continue to Kirriemuir.

Arbroath

POP 22,800

Arbroath is an old-fashioned seaside resort and fishing harbour, home of the famous **Arbroath smokie** (a form of smoked haddock). The humble smokie achieved European Union 'Protected Geographical Indication' status in 2004 – the term 'Arbroath smokie' can be only be used legally to describe haddock smoked in the traditional manner within an 8km radius of Arbroath. No visit is complete without buying a pair of smokies from one of the many fish shops and eating them with your fingers while sitting beside the harbour. Yum.

◎ Sights

Arbroath Abbey   ABBEY

(HS; Abbey St; adult/child £4.70/2.80; ⊙9.30am-5.30pm Apr-Sep, 9.30am-4.30pm Oct-Mar) The magnificent, red-sandstone ruins of Arbroath Abbey, founded in 1178 by King William the Lion, dominate the town centre. It is thought that Bernard of Linton, the abbot here in the early 14th century, wrote the famous Declaration of Arbroath in 1320, asserting Scotland's right to independence from England (see the boxed text, p445). You can climb to the top of one of the towers for a grand view over the town.

St Vigeans Museum   MUSEUM

(HS; St Vigeans Lane; adult/child £3.70/2.20; ⊙10am-5pm Tue-Thu, Sat & Sun Apr-Oct, 11am-1pm Tue-Thu, Sat & Sun Nov-Mar) About a mile north of the town centre, this cottage museum houses a superb collection of Pictish and medieval sculptured stones. The museum's masterpiece is the **Drosten Stone**, beautifully carved with animal figures and hunting scenes on one side, and an interlaced Celtic cross on the other (look for the devil perched in the top left corner).

FREE **Arbroath Museum**   MUSEUM

(Ladyloan; ⊙10am-5pm Mon-Sat year-round, plus 2-5pm Sun Jul & Aug) This museum is housed in the elegant Signal Tower that was once used to communicate with the construction team working on the Bell Rock Lighthouse 12 miles offshore. It was undergoing refurbishment at the time of research, but will reopen in summer 2011 with new displays dedicated to Arbroath's maritime heritage and the Bell Rock lighthouse, which was built between 1807 and 1811 by the famous engineer Robert Stevenson (grandfather of writer Robert Louis Stevenson).

🏃 Activities

The coast northeast of Arbroath consists of dramatic red-sandstone cliffs riven by inlets, caves and natural arches. An excellent **clifftop walk** (leaflet from the tourist office) follows the coast for 3 miles to the quaint fishing village of **Auchmithie**, which claims to have invented the Arbroath smokie.

If you fancy catching your own fish, the **Marie Dawn** (☎01241-873957) and **Girl Katherine II** (☎01241-874510) offer three-hour sea-angling trips (usually from 2pm to 5pm) out of Arbroath harbour for £15 per person, including tackle and bait.

🛏 Sleeping

Harbour Nights Guest House B&B ££
(☎01241-434343; www.harbournights-scotland.com; 4 The Shore; s/d from £45/60) With a superb location overlooking the harbour, five stylishly decorated bedrooms and a gourmet breakfast menu, Harbour Nights is our favourite place to stay in Arbroath. Rooms 2 and 3, with harbour views, are a bit more expensive (doubles £70 to £80), but well worth asking for when booking.

Old Vicarage B&B ££
(☎01241-430475; www.theoldvicaragebandb.co.uk; 2 Seaton Rd; s/d from £55/80; P🐾) The three five-star bedrooms in this attractive Victorian villa have a pleasantly old-fashioned atmosphere, and the extensive breakfast menu includes Arbroath smokies. The house is on a quiet street close to the start of the clifftop walk to Auchmithie.

🍴 Eating

Gordon's Restaurant SCOTTISH £££
(☎01241-830364; www.gordonsrestaurant.co.uk; Main St, Inverkeillor; 3-course lunch £37, 4-course dinner £45; ☺noon-1.45pm Wed-Sun, 7-9pm Tue-Sun) Six miles north of Arbroath, in the tiny and unpromising-looking village of Inverkeillor, lies this hidden gem – an intimate and rustic eatery serving gourmet-quality Scottish cuisine. There are three comfortable bedrooms (single/double from £75/90) for those who don't want to drive back to a hotel after dinner.

But'n'Ben Restaurant SCOTTISH ££
(☎01241-877223; 1 Auchmithie; mains £8-15; ☺lunch & dinner Wed-Sat, lunch Sun, dinner Mon) Above the harbour in Auchmithie, this cosy, tartan-clad cottage restaurant serves the best of local seafood – the Arbroath smokie

pancakes are recommended – plus great homemade cakes and desserts. Best to book.

Smithie's CAFE £
(16 Keptie St; mains £3-6; ☺9.30am-4.30pm Mon-Fri, 9.30am-4pm Sat) Housed in a former butcher's shop, with hand-painted tiles and meat hooks on the ceiling, Smithie's is a great little neighbourhood deli and cafe serving Fairtrade coffee, pancakes, wraps and freshly made pasta – butternut squash and sage tortellini make a tasty change from macaroni cheese for a vegetarian lunch.

Sugar & Spice Tearoom CAFE £
(www.sugarandspiceshop.co.uk; 9-13 High St; mains £5-9; ☺10am-5pm Mon-Thu, 10am-9pm Fri & Sat, noon-7pm Sun, longer hours Jun-Sep; 👶) With its flounces, frills and black-and-white uniformed waitresses, this chintzy tearoom verges on the twee. However, the place is very child-friendly – there's an indoor play area and a Wendy (play) house out the back – and the tea and scones are sublime. You can even try an Arbroath smokie, grilled with lemon butter.

ℹ Information

Visitor centre & tourist office (☎01241-872609; Fishmarket Quay; ☺9.30am-5.30pm Mon-Sat, 10am-3pm Sun Jun-Aug, 9am-5pm Mon-Fri, 10am-5pm Sat Apr, May & Sep, 9am-5pm Mon-Fri, 10am-3pm Sat Oct-Mar) Beside the harbour.

Coldroom Computers (15 Westport; per 15 min 50p; ☺10am-5.30pm Mon-Fri, noon-4pm Sat; @) Internet access.

ℹ Getting There & Away

BUS Bus 140 runs from Arbroath to Auchmithie (15 minutes, six daily Monday to Friday, three daily on Saturday and Sunday).

THE FORFAR BRIDIE

Forfar, the county town of Angus, is the home of Scotland's answer to the Cornish pasty: the famous **Forfar bridie**. A shortcrust pastry turnover filled with cooked minced beef, onion and gravy, it was invented in Forfar in the early 19th century. If you fancy trying one, head for **James McLaren & Son** (8 The Cross, Forfar; ☺8am-4.30pm Mon-Wed, Fri & Sat, 8am-1pm Thu), a family bakery bang in the centre of Forfar, which has been selling tasty, home-baked bridies since 1893.

TRAIN Trains from Dundee to Arbroath (£4.50, 20 minutes, two per hour) continue to Aberdeen (£19, 55 minutes) via Montrose and Stonehaven.

Montrose

POP 11,800

Despite its seaside setting, broad main street of Victorian buildings and reputation as a golfing resort, Montrose exudes an austere and slightly down-at-heel atmosphere. It sits at the mouth of the River South Esk, where its industrial harbour serves the North Sea oil industry; and is backed by the broad, tidal mud flats of Montrose Basin, a rich feeding ground for thousands of resident and migrant birds.

At the southern edge of town, **Montrose Basin Visitor Centre** (www.montrose basin.org.uk; Rossie Braes; adult/child £4/3; ◷10.30am-5pm Mar-Oct, 10.30am-4pm Fri-Sun Nov-Feb) has indoor and outdoor hides, and viewing platforms with high-powered binoculars and remote-controlled TV cameras where you can zoom in on the local wildlife. In summer you can see curlews, oystercatchers and eider ducks – and perhaps an otter if you're lucky – and in autumn the basin is invaded by huge flocks of pink-footed and greylag geese. The birdwatching is best from two hours after high tide till two hours before the next high tide – check times at any tourist office.

THE ABERLEMNO STONES

Five miles northeast of Forfar, on the B9134, are the mysterious **Aberlemno stones**, some of Scotland's finest Pictish symbol stones. By the roadside there are three 7th- to 9th-century slabs with various symbols, including the z-rod and double disc, and in the churchyard at the bottom of the hill there's a magnificent 8th-century stone displaying a Celtic cross, interlace decoration, entwined beasts and, on the reverse, scenes of the Battle of Nechtansmere (where the Picts vanquished the Northumbrians in 685). The stones are covered up from November to March; otherwise there's free access at all times.

Prettier than Montrose's town beach, the 2-mile strand of **Lunan Bay** to the south is overlooked by the dramatic ruin of **Red Castle**.

Montrose lies on the Dundee to Aberdeen railway line.

Kirriemuir

POP 6000

Known as the Wee Red Town because of its close-packed, red-sandstone houses, Kirriemuir is famed as the birthplace of JM Barrie (1860–1937), writer and creator of the much-loved *Peter Pan*. A bronze statue of the 'boy who wouldn't grow up' graces the intersection of Bank and High Sts.

The tourist office is in the Gateway to the Glens Museum.

◉ Sights

JM Barrie's Birthplace (NTS; 9 Brechin Rd; adult/child £5.50/4.50; ◷11am-5pm Jul & Aug, noon-5pm Sat-Wed Apr-Jun, Sep & Oct) is the town's big attraction, a place of pilgrimage for Peter Pan fans from all over the world. The two-storey house where Barrie was born has been furnished in period style, and preserves Barrie's writing desk and the wash house at the back that served as his first 'theatre'. The ticket also gives admission to the **Camera Obscura** (adult/child Camera Obscura only £3/2; ◷noon-5pm Mon-Sat, 1-5pm Sun Jul-Sep, noon-5pm Sat & 1-5pm Sun Easter-Jun) on the hilltop northeast of the town centre, given to the town by Barrie himself.

The old Town House opposite the Peter Pan statue dates from 1604 and houses the **Gateway to the Glens Museum** (32 High St; admission free; ◷10am-5pm Mon-Sat Apr-Sep, closed Thu am Oct-Mar & Sun), a useful introduction to local history, geology and wildlife for those planning to explore the Angus Glens.

For generations of local school kids, the big treat when visiting Kirriemuir was a trip to the **Star Rock Shop** (27-29 Roods). Established in 1833, it still specialises in traditional Scottish 'sweeties' (candy), ranged in colourful jars along the walls – humbugs, tablet, cola cubes, pear drops, and the original Star Rock, still made to an 1833 recipe.

🛏 Sleeping & Eating

Airlie Arms Hotel HOTEL **££**
(☎01575-572847; www.theairliearms.co.uk; St Malcolm's Wynd; s/d £45/75; ℗) This attrac-

tive old coaching inn, just a few minutes' walk from the tourist office, has been recently revamped with modern, stylish en suite rooms and a candle-lit restaurant called the **Wynd** (mains £8-14; ⊙5-9pm Wed-Fri, noon-9pm Sat & Sun).

88 Degrees   CAFE, DELI **£**
(17 High St; mains £3-6; ⊙9am-5pm) A new cafe and deli that serves superb coffee (named for the ideal temperature of an espresso), delicious cakes and handmade chocolates. Breakfast till 10.30am and light lunches till 2.30pm.

❶ Getting There & Away
Stagecoach bus 20 runs from Dundee to Kirriemuir (£5.30, one hour, hourly Monday to Saturday, every two hours Sunday) via Glamis (20 minutes, two daily Monday to Saturday) and Forfar (25 minutes).

Angus Glens

The northern part of Angus is bounded by the Grampian Mountains, where five scenic glens – Isla, Prosen, Clova, Lethnot and Esk – cut into the hills along the southern edge of the Cairngorms National Park. All have attractive scenery, though each glen has its own distinct personality: Glen Clova and Glenesk are the most beautiful, while Glen Lethnot is the least frequented. You can get detailed information on walks in the Angus Glens from the tourist office in Kirriemuir and from the Glen Clova Hotel in Glen Clova.

Since the withdrawal of the postbus service, there is no public transport to the Angus glens other than a limited school-bus service along Glen Clova; ask at the tourist office in Kirriemuir or Dundee for details.

GLEN ISLA
At Bridge of Craigisla at the foot of the glen is a spectacular, 24m waterfall called **Reekie Linn**; the name Reekie (Scottish for 'smoky') comes from the billowing spray that rises from the falls.

A 5-mile walk beyond the road end at Auchavan leads into the wild and mountainous upper reaches of the glen, where the **Caenlochan National Nature Reserve** protects rare alpine flora on the high plateau.

GLEN PROSEN
Near the foot of Glen Prosen, 6 miles north of Kirriemuir, there's a good forest walk up

to the **Airlie monument** on Tulloch Hill (380m); start from the eastern road, about a mile beyond Dykehead.

From Glenprosen Lodge, at the head of the glen, a 9-mile walk along the **Kilbo Path** leads over a pass between Mayar (928m) and Driesh (947m), and descends to Glendoll Lodge at the head of Glen Clova (allow five hours).

Prosen Hostel (☎01575-540238; www.prosenhostel.co.uk; per person £18; ⊙year round; @) is an 18-bed bunkhouse with excellent facilities (including a red-squirrel viewing area in the lounge). It's 7 miles up the glen, just beyond Prosen village, but there's no public transport.

GLEN CLOVA
The longest and loveliest of the Angus Glens stretches north from Kirriemuir for 20 miles, broad and pastoral in its lower reaches but growing narrower and craggier as the steep, heather-clad Highland hills close in around its head.

The minor road beyond the Glen Clova Hotel ends at a Forestry Commission car park with toilets and a picnic area, which is the trailhead for a number of strenuous **walks** through the hills to the north.

Jock's Road is an ancient footpath that was used by cattle drovers, soldiers, smugglers and shepherds in the 18th and 19th centuries; 700 Jacobite soldiers passed this way during their retreat in 1746, en route to final defeat at Culloden. From the car park the path strikes west along Glen Doll, then north across a high plateau (900m) before descending steeply into Glen Callater and on to Braemar (15 miles; allow five to seven hours). The route is hard going and should not be attempted in winter; you'll need OS 1:50,000 maps, numbers 43 and 44.

An easier, but still strenuous, circular walk starts from the Glen Clova Hotel, making a circuit of the scenic corrie (glacial hollow) that encloses **Loch Brandy** (6 miles, four hours).

TOP ❯ Glen Clova Hotel (☎01575-
CHOICE 550350; www.clova.com; Glen Clova; s/d £60/90; ℗) is a lovely old drover's inn near the head of the glen and a great place to get away from it all. As well as 10 comfortable, country-style, en suite rooms (one with a four-poster bed), it has a bunkhouse out the back (£14 per person), a rustic, stone-floored climbers' bar with a roaring log fire, and a bay-windowed **restaurant** (mains £8-

13; ☺noon-8.15pm Sun-Thu, noon-8.45pm Fri & Sat) with views across the glen. The menu includes cock-a-leekie soup, venison in Drambuie sauce, and lamb and rosemary lasagne, and there are separate children's and vegetarian menus.

GLEN LETHNOT

This glen is noted for the Brown & White Caterthuns – two extraordinary Iron Age hill forts, defended by ramparts and ditches, perched on twin hilltops at its southern end. A minor road crosses the pass between the two summits, and it's an easy walk to either fort from the parking area in the pass; both are superb viewpoints. If you don't have a car, you can walk there from Brechin (6 miles) or from Edzell (5 miles).

GLENESK

The most easterly of the Angus Glens, Glenesk, runs for 15 miles from Edzell to lovely Loch Lee, surrounded by beetling cliffs and waterfalls. Ten miles up the glen from Edzell is Glenesk Folk Museum (The Retreat; adult/child £2/1; ☺noon-6pm daily Jun–mid-Oct, noon-6pm Sat & Sun only Easter-May; ☎), an old shooting lodge that houses a fascinating collection of antiques and artefacts documenting the local culture of the 17th, 18th and 19th centuries. It also has a tearoom, restaurant and gift shop, and has public internet access.

Five miles further on, the public road ends at Invermark Castle, an impressive ruined tower guarding the southern approach to the Mounth, a hill track to Deeside.

Edzell

POP 785

The picturesque village of Edzell, with its broad main street and grandiose monumental arch, dates from the early 19th century when Lord Panmure decided that the original medieval village, a mile to the west, spoiled the view from Edzell Castle. The old village was razed and the villagers moved to this pretty, planned settlement.

Lord Panmure's predecessors as owners of Edzell Castle (HS; adult/child £4.70/2.80; ☺9.30am-5.30pm Apr-Sep, to 4.30pm Oct, 9.30am-4.30pm Sat-Wed Nov-Mar) were the Lindsay earls of Crawford, who built this 16th-century L-plan tower house. Sir David Lindsay, a cultured and well-travelled man,

laid out the castle's beautiful **pleasance** in 1604 as a place of contemplation and learning. Unique in all of Scotland, this Renaissance walled garden is lined with niches for nesting birds, and sculptured plaques illustrating the cardinal virtues, the arts and the planetary deities.

Two miles north of Edzell, the B966 to Fettercairn crosses the River North Esk at Gannochy Bridge. From the lay-by just over the bridge, a blue-painted wooden door in the stone wall gives access to a delightful footpath that leads along the wooded river gorge for 1.5 miles to a scenic spot known as the Rocks of Solitude.

Alexandra Lodge (☎01365-648266; www.alexandralodge.co.uk; Inveriscandye Rd; s/d £45/70; ℗) is an attractive Edwardian villa with comfortable bedrooms and a lovely wood-panelled lounge, while the Panmure Arms Hotel (☎01365-648950; www.panmurearmshotel.co.uk; 52 High St; s/d from £55/80; ℗) is a pretty, mock-Tudor place serving excellent bar meals (£11 to £15) from noon till 2pm Monday to Friday and noon till 9pm Saturday and Sunday.

Bus 29 or 29A from Brechin to Laurencekirk stops at Edzell (15 minutes, seven a day Monday to Friday, five on Saturday).

Brechin

POP 7200

The name of the local football team, Brechin City, proclaims this diminutive town's main claim to fame – as the seat of Brechin Cathedral (now demoted to a parish church) it has the right to call itself a city, albeit the smallest one in Scotland. Adjacent to the cathedral is a 32m-high round tower built around 1000 as part of a Celtic monastery. It is of a type often seen in Ireland, but one of only three that survive in Scotland. Its elevated doorway, 2m above the ground, has carvings of animals, saints and a crucifix.

Housed nearby in the 18th-century former town hall, court room and prison, Brechin Town House Museum (St Ninian's Sq; admission free; ☺10am-5pm Mon-Sat Apr-Sep, 10am-5pm Mon, Tue & Thu-Sat, 10am-1pm Wed Nov-Mar) records the history of the round tower, cathedral and town.

The town's (OK, city's) picturesque Victorian train station dates from 1897 and is now the terminus of the restored Caledonian Railway (www.caledonianrailway.com; 2

Park Rd), which runs steam trains (adult/child £5/3 return) along a 3.5-mile stretch of track to Bridge of Dun. Trains run on Sunday from late May to mid-September, on Saturday in July and August, and at Easter and Christmas. From Bridge of Dun, it's a 15-minute signposted walk to the **House of Dun** (NTS; adult/child £8.50/5.50; ⊙11am-5pm Jul & Aug, noon-5pm Wed-Sun Apr-Jun, Sep & Oct), a beautiful Georgian country house built in 1730.

Adjoining Brechin Castle Centre (a gardening and horse-riding centre on the A90 just west of Brechin) is **Pictavia** (www.pictavia.org.uk; adult/child £3.25/2.25; ⊙9.30am-5.30pm Mon-Sat, 10.30am-5.30pm Sun Easter-mid Oct, 9am-5pm Mon-Sat, 10am-5pm Sun mid-Oct-Easter), an interpretive centre telling the story of the Picts, and explaining current theories about the mysterious carved symbol stones they left behind. It's worth making a trip here before going to see the Pictish stones at Aberlemno.

🛈 Getting There & Away

Scottish Citylink buses between Dundee and Aberdeen stop at Clerk St in Brechin. Stagecoach buses depart from South Esk St heading to Forfar (30 minutes, hourly), Aberlemno (15 minutes, six a day) and Edzell.

Bus 24 links Brechin and Stonehaven (55 minutes, three daily Sunday to Friday, five on Saturday).

ABERDEENSHIRE & MORAY

Since medieval times Aberdeenshire and its northwestern neighbour Moray have been the richest and most fertile regions of the Highlands. Aberdeenshire is famed for its Aberdeen Angus beef cattle, its many fine castles and the prosperous 'granite city' of Aberdeen. Moray's main attractions are the Speyside whisky distilleries that line the valley of the River Spey and its tributaries.

Aberdeen

POP 197,300

Aberdeen is the powerhouse of the northeast, fuelled by the North Sea petroleum industry. Oil money has made the city as expensive as London and Edinburgh, and there are hotels, restaurants and clubs with prices to match the depth of oil-wealthy pockets. Fortunately, most of the cultural attractions, such as the excellent Maritime Museum and the Aberdeen Art Gallery, are free.

Known throughout Scotland as the granite city, much of the town was built using silvery grey granite hewn from the now abandoned Rubislaw Quarry, at one time the biggest artificial hole in the ground in Europe. On a sunny day the granite lends an attractive glitter to the city, but when low, grey rain clouds scud in off the North Sea it can be hard to tell where the buildings stop and the sky begins.

Royal Deeside is easily accessible to the west, Dunnottar Castle to the south, sandy beaches to the north and whisky country to the northwest.

History

Aberdeen was a prosperous trading and fishing port centuries before oil became a valuable commodity. After the townspeople supported Robert the Bruce against the English at the Battle of Bannockburn in 1314, the king rewarded the town with land for which he had previously received rent. The rental income was used to establish the Common Good Fund, to be spent on town amenities, a fund that survives to this day: it helped to finance Marischal College, the Central Library, the art gallery and the hospital, and also pays for the colourful floral displays that have won the city numerous awards.

The name Aberdeen is a combination of two Pictish-Gaelic words, *aber* and *devana,* meaning 'the meeting of two waters'. The area was known to the Romans, and was raided by the Vikings when it was already an important port trading in wool, fish, hides and fur. By the 18th century paper- and rope-making, whaling and textile manufacture were the main industries, and in the 19th century it became a major herring-fishing centre.

Since the 1970s Aberdeen has been the main focus of the UK's offshore oil industry, home to oil company offices, engineering yards, a bustling harbour filled with supply ships, and the world's busiest civilian helilport. Unemployment rates, once among the highest in the country, are now among the lowest.

Aberdeen

400 m
0.2 miles

Streets & places

Commerce St
East North St
To Airport (6mi)
Justice St
Salvation Army Citadel
James St
Virginia St
Shore La
Castle Tce
Castle St
CASTLEGATE
Marischal St
Regent Quay
Regent Rd
Commercial Quay
Albert Basin
ABERDEEN HARBOUR
King St
Trinity Quay
Market St
Victoria Dock
Aberdeen Maritime Museum
Shiprow
Broad St
Marischal College & Museum
Provost Skene's House
Flourmill La
Netherkirkgate
Upperkirkgate
St Nicholas St
Back Wynd
Schoolhill
St Nicholas La
Correction Wynd
Union St
The Green
Exchange St
Stirling St
St
Market St
Rennie's Wynd
Guild St
Union Square Shopping Mall
Aberdeen Train Station
Union Bridge St
South College St
Bridge St
Crown Tce
St John's Pl
St Mary's Pl
Academy St
Windmill Brae
Denburn Rd
Aberdeen Art Gallery
Belmont St
Belmont St
Denburn Rd
Union Tce
Union Terrace Gardens
Blackfriars St
Harriet St
Blackfriars St
To Blue Lamp (150m)
Loch St
Spa St
Woolman Hill
Gilcomston Park St
Skene St
Skene Tce
Rosemount Viaduct
Diamond St
North Silver St
Crimon Pl
Golden Square
Union St
Crown St
Crown St
Dee St
Gordon St
Bon Accord St
Huntly St
Union Wynd
Union Row
To Butler's Islander Guest House (60m)
Langstane Pl
Summer St
Summer St
Chapel St
Rose St
Alford Pl
To Dee St
Glifordst St

Sights

City Centre

Union St is the city's main thoroughfare, lined with solid, Victorian granite buildings. The oldest area is **Castlegate**, at the eastern end, where the castle once stood. When it was captured from the English for Robert the Bruce, the password used by the townspeople was 'Bon Accord', which is now the city's motto.

In the centre of Castle St stands the 17th-century **Mercat Cross**, bearing a sculpted frieze of portraits of Stuart monarchs. The Baronial heap towering over the eastern end of Castle St is the **Salvation Army Citadel**, which was modelled on Balmoral Castle.

On the northern side of Union St, 300m west of Castlegate, is **St Nicholas Church**, the so-called 'Mither Kirk' (Mother Church) of Aberdeen. The granite spire dates from the 19th century, but there has been a church on this site since the 12th century; the early 15th-century **St Mary's Chapel** survives in the eastern part of the church.

FREE **Aberdeen Maritime Museum**

MUSEUM

(www.aagm.co.uk; Shiprow; ⊙10am-5pm Mon-Sat, noon-3pm Sun) Overlooking the nautical bustle of the harbour is the Maritime Museum. Centred on a three-storey replica of a North Sea oil production platform, its exhibits explain all you ever wanted to know about the petroleum industry. Other galleries, some situated in **Provost Ross's House**, the oldest building in the city and part of museum, cover the shipbuilding, whaling and fishing industries. Sleek and speedy Aberdeen clippers were a 19th-century shipyard speciality, used by British merchants for the importation of tea, wool and exotic goods (opium, for instance) to Britain, and, on the return journey, the transportation of emigrants to Australia.

FREE **Aberdeen Art Gallery** ART GALLERY

(www.aagm.co.uk; Schoolhill; ⊙10am-5pm Tue-Sat, 2-5pm Sun) Behind the grand facade of Aberdeen Art Gallery is a cool, marble-lined space exhibiting the work of contemporary Scottish and English painters, such as Gwen Hardie, Stephen Conroy, Trevor Sutton and Tim Ollivier. There are

Aberdeen

also several landscapes by Joan Eardley, who lived in a cottage on the cliffs near Stonehaven in the 1950s and '60s and painted tempestuous oils of the North Sea and poignant portraits of slum children. Among the Pre-Raphaelite works upstairs, look out for the paintings of Aberdeen artist William Dyce (1806–64), ranging from religious works to rural scenes.

Downstairs is a large, empty, circular white room, with fish-scaled balustrades evoking the briny origins of Aberdeen's wealth, commemorating the 165 people who lost their lives in the Piper Alpha oilrig disaster in 1988.

FREE Marischal College & Museum
MUSEUM

(www.abdn.ac.uk/marischal_museum; Marischal College, Broad St; ☺10am-5pm Mon-Fri, 2-5pm Sun) Across Broad St from Provost Skene's House is **Marischal College**, founded in 1593 by the 5th Earl Marischal, and merged with King's College (founded 1495) in 1860 to create the modern University of Aberdeen. The huge and impressive facade in Perpendicular Gothic style – unusual in having such elaborate masonry hewn from notoriously hard-to-work granite – dates from 1906 and is the world's second-largest granite structure (after L'Escorial near Madrid). At the time of research the building was being converted into Aberdeen City Council's new headquarters.

Founded in 1786, the **Marischal Museum** houses a fascinating collection of material donated by graduates and friends of the university over the centuries. In one room, the history of northeastern Scotland is depicted through its myths, customs, famous people, architecture and trade. The other gallery gives an anthropological overview of the world, incorporating objects from vastly different cultures, arranged thematically (Polynesian wooden masks alongside gas masks and so on). There are the usual Victorian curios, an Inuit kayak found in the local river estuary in the 18th century and Inuit objects collected by whalers. At the time of research, the museum was closed to the public during building work, but will reopen sometime in 2011.

FREE Provost Skene's House
HISTORIC BUILDING

(www.aagm.co.uk; Guestrow; ☺10am-5pm Mon-Sat) Surrounded by concrete and glass office blocks in what was once the worst slum in Aberdeen is Provost Skene's House, a late-medieval turreted town house occupied in the 17th century by the provost (the Scottish equivalent of a mayor) Sir George Skene. It was also occupied for six weeks by the Duke of Cumberland on his way to Culloden in 1746. The tempera-painted ceiling with its religious symbolism, dating from 1622, is unusual for having survived the depredations of the Reformation. It's a period gem featuring earnest-looking angels, soldiers and St Peter with crowing cockerels.

Gordon Highlanders Museum
MILITARY MUSEUM

(www.gordonhighlanders.com; St Lukes, Viewfield Rd; adult/child £5/2; ☺10.30am-4.30pm Tue-Sat, 12.30-4.30pm Sun Apr-Sep, 10am-4pm Tue-Sat Oct, Nov, Feb & Mar) The excellent Gordon Highlanders Museum records the history of one of the British Army's most famous fighting units, described by Winston Churchill as 'the finest regiment in the world'. Originally raised in the northeast of Scotland by the 4th Duke of Gordon in 1794, the regiment was amalgamated with the Seaforths and Camerons to form the Highlanders regiment in 1994. The museum is about a mile west of the western end of Union St – take bus 14 or 15 from Union St.

Aberdeen Harbour
Aberdeen has a busy, working harbour crowded with survey vessels and supply ships servicing the offshore oil installations, and car ferries bound for Orkney and Shetland. From dawn until about 8am the colourful **fish market** on Albert Basin operates as it has done for centuries.

Aberdeen Beach
Just 800m east of Castlegate is a spectacular 2-mile sweep of clean, **golden sand** stretching between the mouths of the Rivers Dee and Don. At one time Aberdeen Beach was a good, old-fashioned British seaside resort, but the availability of cheap package holidays has lured Scottish holidaymakers away from its somewhat chilly delights. On a warm summer's day, though, it's still an excellent beach. When the waves are right, a small group of dedicated **surfers** ride the breaks at the south end.

The Esplanade sports several traditional seaside attractions, including **Codona's Amusement Park** (www.codonas.com; Beach Blvd; all-day wristband £12; ☺11am-6pm Jul & Aug, check website rest of year, closed Nov-Easter), complete with stomach-churning waltzers, dodgems, a roller coaster, log flume and haunted house. The adjacent **Sunset Boulevard** (www.codonas.com; Beach Blvd; all-day wristband £12; ☺10am-midnight) is the indoor alternative, with tenpin bowling, dodgems, arcade games and pool tables.

Halfway between the beach and the city centre is **Satrosphere** (☎01224-640340; www.satrosphere.net; 179 Constitution St; adult/child £5.75/4.50; ☺10am-5pm), a hands-on, interactive science centre.

You can get away from the funfair atmosphere by walking north towards the more secluded part of the beach. There's a **bird-watching hide** on the south bank of the River Don, between the beach and King St, which leads back south towards Old Aberdeen.

Buses 14 and 15 (eastbound) from Union St go to the beach; or you can walk from Castlegate in 10 minutes.

Old Aberdeen

Just over a mile north of the city centre is the district called Old Aberdeen. The name is misleading – although Old Aberdeen is certainly old, the area around Castlegate is older still. This part of the city was originally called Aulton, from the Gaelic for 'village by the pool', and this was anglicised in the 17th century to Old Town.

It was here that Bishop Elphinstone established King's College, Aberdeen's first university, in 1495. The 16th-century **King's College Chapel** (College Bounds; admission free; ☺9am-4.30pm Mon-Fri) is easily recognised by its crown spire; the interior is largely unchanged since it was first built, with impressive stained-glass windows and choir stalls. The nearby **King's College Visitor Centre** (College Bounds; admission free; ☺10am-5pm Mon-Sat, 2-5pm Sun) houses a multimedia display on the university's history and a pleasant coffee shop.

Bus 20 from Littlejohn St (just north of Marischal College) runs to Old Aberdeen every 15 to 20 minutes.

FREE **St Machar's Cathedral**   CATHEDRAL
(www.stmachar.com; The Chanonry; ☺9am-5pm Mon-Sat Apr-Oct, to 4pm Nov-Mar) The 15th-century St Machar's Cathedral, with its massive twin towers, is a rare example of a fortified cathedral. According to legend, St Machar was ordered to establish a church where the river takes the shape of a bishop's crook, which it does just here. The cathedral is best known for its impressive **heraldic ceiling**, dating from 1520,

which has 48 shields of kings, nobles, archbishops and bishops. Sunday services are held at 11am and 6pm.

🛏 Sleeping

There are clusters of B&Bs on Bon Accord St and Springbank Tce (both 400m southwest of the train station) and along Great Western Rd (the A93, a 25-minute walk southwest of the city centre). They're usually more expensive than the Scottish average and, with so many oil industry workers staying the night before flying offshore, single rooms are at a premium. Prices tend to be lower on weekends.

TOP CHOICE **City Wharf Apartments**

SERVICED APARTMENTS ££
(☎0845 094 2424; www.citywharfapartments.co.uk; 19-20 Regent Quay; d from £95; ☎🖳) You can watch the bustle of Aberdeen's commercial harbour as you eat breakfast in one of these luxury serviced apartments, complete with stylish, fully equipped kitchen, champagne-stocked minibar and daily cleaning service. Available by the night or the week, with discounts for longer stays.

Globe Inn   B&B ££
(☎01224-624258; www.the-globe-inn.co.uk; 13-15 North Silver St; s/d £65/70) This popular pub (see p243) has seven appealing and comfortable guest bedrooms upstairs, done out in dark wood with burgundy bedspreads. There's live music in the pub on weekends so it's not a place for early-to-bed types, but the price vs location factor can't be beaten. No dining room, so breakfast is continental, served on a tray in your room.

Brentwood Hotel   HOTEL ££
(☎01224-595440; www.brentwood-hotel.co.uk; 101 Crown St; s £45-90, d £59-99; 🅿🖳) The friendly and flower-bedecked Brentwood, set in a granite town house, is one of the most attractive hotels in the city centre. It's comfortable and conveniently located, but often busy during the week – weekend rates (Friday to Sunday) are much cheaper.

Butler's Islander Guest House   B&B ££
(☎01224-212411; www.butlersguesthouse.com; 122 Crown St; s £40-65, d £60-80; @🖳) Just across the street from the Brentwood, and with a similar weekday/weekend price split, Butler's is a cosy place with a big breakfast menu that includes fresh fruit salad, kippers and kedgeree as alternatives to the traditional fry-up.

Aberdeen Douglas Hotel HOTEL **£££**
(☑01224-582255; www.aberdeendouglas.com; 43-45 Market St; r from £125; 🛜) You can't miss the grand Victorian facade of this historic landmark, which first opened its doors as a hotel in 1853. Now renovated, it offers classy modern rooms with polished woodwork and crisp white bedlinen, and is barely a minute's walk from the train station.

Simpson's Hotel BOUTIQUE HOTEL **££**
(☑01224-327777; www.simpsonshotel.co.uk; 59 Queen's Rd; s/d from £60/80; 🅿) Simpson's, a mile west of Union St, is a stylish boutique hotel decorated with a Mediterranean-Italian theme in shades of sand, terracotta and aqua. It's aimed at both business and private guests, and is totally wheelchair accessible. Cheaper rates on weekends.

Dunrovin Guest House B&B **££**
(☑01224-586081; www.dunrovinguesthouse.co. uk; 168 Bon Accord St; s/d from £45/70; 🅿🛜) Dunrovin is a typical granite Victorian house with eight bedrooms; the upstairs rooms are bright and airy. The friendly owners will provide a veggie breakfast if you wish. Located 400m south from the western end of Union St.

Royal Crown Guest House B&B **££**
(☑01224-586461; www.royalcrown.co.uk; 111 Crown St; s £35-70, d £60-80; 🅿🛜) The Royal Crown has eight small but nicely furnished bedrooms, and has a top location only five minutes' walk from the train station (though up a steep flight of stairs).

Aberdeen Youth Hostel HOSTEL **£**
(SYHA; ☑01224-646988; 8 Queen's Rd; dm £18-20; @🛜) This hostel, set in a granite Victorian villa, is a mile west of the train station. Walk west along Union St and take the right fork along Albyn Pl until you reach a roundabout; Queen's Rd continues on the western side of the roundabout.

Jurys Inn HOTEL **££**
(☑01224-381200; www.jurysinns.com; Union Sq, Guild St; s/d £88/96; 🛜) Stylish and comfortable new hotel right next to the train station.

Adelphi Guest House B&B **££**
(☑01224-583078; www.adelphiguesthouse.com; 8 Whinhill Rd; s/d from £40/50; 🛜) It's 400m south from western end of Union St.

Arden Guest House B&B **££**
(☑01224-580700; www.ardenguesthouse.co.uk; 61 Dee St; s/d from £50/60)

Kildonan Guest House B&B **££**
(☑01224-316115; www.kildonan-guesthouse. com; 410 Great Western Rd; s/d from £30/50; 🛜) 900m southwest of the city centre.

✖ Eating

TOP CHOICE **Café 52** BISTRO **££**
(☑01224-590094; www.cafe52.net; 52 The Green; mains £12-16; ⊗noon-9.30pm Mon-Sat, noon-6pm Sun; 🛜) This little haven of laid-back industrial chic – a high, narrow space lined with bare stonework, rough plaster and exposed ventilation ducts – serves some of the finest and most inventive cuisine in the northeast. Try starters such as wild game and garlic meatloaf with spiced swede chutney, or mains like roast-cumin-and-honey pork loin with baked black pudding.

Silver Darling SEAFOOD **£££**
(☑01224-576229; www.silverdarlingrestaurant. co.uk; Pocra Quay, North Pier; lunch mains £10-15, dinner mains £18-27; ⊗noon-1.45pm Mon-Fri & 7-9.30pm Mon-Sat) The Silver Darling (an old Scottish nickname for herring) is housed in a former Customs office, with picture windows overlooking the sea at the entrance to Aberdeen harbour. Here you can enjoy fresh Scottish seafood prepared by a top French chef while you watch the porpoises playing in the harbour mouth. The lunch menu offers good-value gourmet delights, such as pan-fried turbot with chorizo and herb croquette; bookings are recommended.

Moonfish Café FRENCH **££**
(☑01224-644166; www.moonfishcafe.co.uk; 9 Correction Wynd; 2-/3-course dinner £16/22; ⊗noon-11pm) The menu of this funky little eatery tucked away on a back street concentrates on good value French bistro fare (two-course lunch £10) such as classic French onion soup, *moules-frites* (mussels with fries) with saffron and Pernod cream sauce, and crisp sea bass fillet with chorizo, *boudin noir* (blood sausage) and salsa verde.

Foyer FUSION **££**
(☑01224-582277; www.foyerrestaurant. com; 82a Crown St; mains £10-19; ⊗11am-9.30pm Tue-Sat) A light, airy space filled with blond wood and bold colours, Foyer is an art gallery as well as a restaurant and is run by a charity that works against youth homelessness and unemployment. The seasonal menu is a fusion of Scottish, Mediterranean and Asian influences, with lots of good veg-

etarian (and gluten- or dairy-free) options. A light lunch menu is available from 11am to 4pm.

Musa Art Cafe
MODERN SCOTTISH ££

(☎01224-571771; www.musaaberdeen.com; 33 Exchange St; lunch mains £6-12, mains £16-19; ⊗noon-11pm) The bright paintings on the walls match the vibrant furnishings and smart gastronomic creations at this great cafe-restaurant, set in a former church that was later used to store bananas. As well as a menu that focuses on quality local produce cooked in a quirky way – think haggis-and-coriander spring rolls with apricot chutney – there are Brewdog beers from Fraserburgh, and interesting music, sometimes live.

Rendezvous@Nargile
TURKISH ££

(☎01224-323700; www.rendezvousatnargile.co.uk; cnr Forest Ave; mains £13-19; ⊗noon-10pm; ▪) A stylish West End venue specialising in Turkish cuisine. There are tasty spreads of mezes – *shakshuka* (a blend of roast peppers, tomatoes, aubergines and chilli), *dj-adjik* (yoghurt with garlic and cucumber) and *sigara boregi* (cheese pastries), for example – followed by delicious, melt-in-the-mouth kebabs and marinated meats, and vegetarian dishes such as *mantar guvec* (casserole of button mushrooms in creamy sauce with a cheese-and-couscous crust).

Beautiful Mountain
CAFE £

(www.thebeautifulmountain.com; 11-13 Belmont St; mains £6-9; ⊗8am-4.30pm Mon-Fri, 8am-5pm Sat, 5.30-11pm Thu-Sat) This cosy cafe is squeezed into a couple of tiny rooms (seating upstairs), but serves all-day breakfasts and tasty sandwiches (smoked salmon, Thai chicken, pastrami) on sourdough, bagels, ciabatta and lots of other breads, along with exquisite espresso and consummate cappuccino.

Sand Dollar Café
CAFE, BISTRO £

(www.sanddollarcafe.com; 2 Beach Esplanade; mains £4-7; ⊗9am-5pm) A cut above your usual seaside cafe – on sunny days you can sit at the wooden tables outside and share a bottle of chilled white wine, and there's a tempting menu that includes pancakes with maple syrup, homemade burgers and chocolate brownie with Orkney ice cream. An evening bistro menu (mains £11 to £20, served from 6pm Thursday to Saturday) offers steak and seafood dishes. The cafe is on the esplanade, 800m northeast of the city centre.

Ashvale Fish Restaurant
FISH & CHIPS £

(www.theashvale.co.uk; 42-48 Great Western Rd; takeaway £4-6, mains £8-10; ⊗11.45am-11pm; ▪) This is the flagship, 200-seat branch of the Ashvale, an award-winning fish-and-chip restaurant famed for its quality haddock. The Ashvale Whale – a 1lb fish fillet in batter (£10.65) – is a speciality; finish it off and you get a second one free (as if you'd want one by then!). There are branches in Elgin and Brechin.

Howie's
MODERN SCOTTISH ££

(☎639500; 50 Chapel St; 2-course lunch mains £6-8, dinner mains £10-13) A chic bistro dishing up great-value 'modern Scottish' cuisine accompanied by very reasonably priced house wine. Two-/three-course dinner £18/20.

Victoria Restaurant
CAFE £

(140 Union St; mains £6-9; ⊗9am-5pm Fri-Wed, 9am-6.30pm Thu) The Victoria, above the Jamieson & Carry jewellery shop, is a traditional, posh Scottish tearoom, with delicious fresh soups, salads and sandwiches. Breakfast served till 11.30am.

Poldino's
ITALIAN ££

(www.poldinos.co.uk; 7 Little Belmont St; mains £10-20; ⊗noon-2.30pm & 6-10.45pm Mon-Sat) Poldino's is a long-established Aberdeen eatery – an upmarket Italian family restaurant that never fails to impress with the quality of its food and service.

🍷 Drinking

Aberdeen is a great city for a pub crawl – it's more a question of knowing when to stop than where to start. There are lots of pre-club bars in and around Belmont St, with more traditional pubs scattered throughout the city centre.

Globe Inn
PUB

(www.the-globe-inn.co.uk; 13-15 North Silver St) This lovely Edwardian-style pub with wood panelling, marble-topped tables and walls decorated with old musical instruments is a great place for a quiet lunchtime or afternoon drink. It serves good coffee as well as real ales and malt whiskies, and has live music (rock, blues, soul) on Friday and Saturday evenings. And probably the poshest pub toilets in the country.

Prince of Wales
PUB

(7 St Nicholas Lane) Tucked down an alley off Union St, Aberdeen's best-known pub boasts the longest bar in the city, and a great range of real ales and good-value pub

grub. Quiet in the afternoons, but standing-room only in the evenings.

Old Blackfriars
PUB

(www.old-blackfriars.co.uk; 52 Castlegate) One of the most attractive traditional pubs in the city, with a lovely stone and timber interior, stained-glass windows and a relaxed atmosphere – a great place for an afternoon pint.

Blue Lamp
PUB

(121 Gallowgate) A long-standing feature of the Aberdeen pub scene, the Blue Lamp is a favourite student hang-out – a dark and slightly dingy drinking den with beer, good *craic* (lively conversation) and a jukebox selection that has barely changed since Elvis died. There are regular sessions of live jazz, folk and acoustic music. The pub is 150m north of the city centre, along Broad St.

Cameron's
PUB

(6 Little Belmont St; 🕾) Known as Ma Cameron's, this is Aberdeen's oldest pub (established in 1789). It has a pleasantly old-fashioned atmosphere, with lots of wood, brick and stone, and a range of excellent real ales and malt whiskies.

Lemon Tree Cafe
CAFE-BAR

(www.boxofficeaberdeen.com; 5 West North St; ☺noon-4pm Fri-Sun) The bohemian cafe-bar at the Lemon Tree theatre does excellent coffee, and stages live rock on Friday, folk on Saturday and jazz on Sunday.

☆ Entertainment

Cinemas

Belmont Cinema
CINEMA

(www.picturehouses.co.uk; 49 Belmont St) The Belmont is a great little art-house cinema, with a lively programme of cult classics, director's seasons, foreign films and mainstream movies.

Vue Cinema
CINEMA

(www.myvue.com; 10 Shiprow) A seven-screen multiplex, conveniently located just off Union St, that shows mainstream, first-run films.

Clubs & Live Music

Check out what's happening in the club and live-music scene at local record shops – try One Up Records (www.oneupmusic.co.uk; 17 Belmont St).

Snafu
CLUB, LIVE MUSIC

(www.clubsnafu.com; 1 Union St) Aberdeen's coolest club – though admittedly there isn't much competition – cosy Snafu offers a wide range of rotating club nights and guest DJs, as well as a Tuesday night comedy club and live music gigs.

Tunnels
CLUB, LIVE MUSIC

(www.thetunnels.co.uk; Carnegie's Brae) This cavernous, subterranean club – the entrance is in a road tunnel beneath Union St – is a great live music venue, with a packed programme of up-and-coming Scottish bands. It also hosts regular DJ nights – check the website for the latest program.

O'Neill's
PUB, LIVE MUSIC

(www.oneills.co.uk; 9 Back Wynd) Upstairs at O'Neill's you're guaranteed a wild night of pounding, hardcore Irish rock, indie and alternative tunes Friday to Sunday; downstairs is a (slightly) quieter bar packed with rugby types downing large quantities of Murphy's stout.

Theatre & Concerts

You can book tickets for most concerts and other events at the Box Office (www.boxofficeaberdeen.com; ☺9.30am-6pm Mon-Sat) next to the Music Hall (Union St), the main venue for classical music concerts.

Lemon Tree Theatre
DRAMA, MUSIC

(www.boxofficeaberdeen.com; 5 West North St) An interesting program of dance, music and drama, and often has live rock, jazz and folk bands playing. There are also children's shows, ranging from comedy to drama to puppetry.

His Majesty's Theatre
BALLET, OPERA

(www.boxofficeaberdeen.com; Rosemount Viaduct) The main theatre in Aberdeen hosts everything from ballet and opera to pantomimes and musicals.

Aberdeen Arts Centre
DRAMA

(www.aberdeenartscentre.org.uk; King St) Stages regular drama productions in its theatre and changing exhibitions in its gallery.

ⓘ Information

Aberdeen Royal Infirmary (✆01224-681818; Foresterhill; @) Medical services. About a mile northwest of the western end of Union St.

Books & Beans (www.booksandbeans.co.uk; 22 Belmont St; per 15min £1; ☺8am-6pm Mon-Sat) Internet access; also Fairtrade coffee and secondhand books.

Main post office (St Nicholas Shopping Centre, Upperkirkgate; ☺9am-5.30pm Mon-Sat)

Post Office (489 Union St)

Tourist office (☎01224-288828; www.
aberdeen-grampian.com; 23 Union St; ◷9am-
6.30pm Mon-Sat, 10am-4pm Sun Jul & Aug,
9.30am-5pm Mon-Sat Sep-Jun; @). Internet
access too.

ℹ Getting There & Away

AIR Aberdeen Airport (www.aberdeenairport.
com) is at Dyce, 6 miles northwest of the city
centre. There are regular flights to numerous
Scottish and UK destinations, including Orkney
and Shetland, and international flights to the
Netherlands, Norway, Denmark and France.

Stagecoach Jet bus 727 runs regularly from
Aberdeen bus station to the airport (single
£1.70, 35 minutes). A taxi from the airport to the
city centre takes 25 minutes and costs £15.

BOAT Car ferries from Aberdeen to Orkney and
Shetland are run by **Northlink Ferries** (www.
northlinkferries.co.uk). For more details, see
p405. The **ferry terminal** is a short walk east of
the train and bus stations.

BUS The **bus station** is next to Jurys Inn, close
to the train station. National Express runs direct
buses from London (£45, 12 hours) twice daily,
one of them overnight. Scottish Citylink runs
services to Dundee (£15, 1½ hours), Perth (£21,
two hours), Edinburgh (£26, 3¼ hours) and
Glasgow (£26, 4¼ hours).

Stagecoach bus 10 runs hourly to Inverness
(£11, 3¾ hours) via Huntly, Keith, Fochabers, Elgin (£10, two hours) and Nairn. Service 201 runs
every half-hour (hourly on Sunday) to Crathes
Castle gate (45 minutes), continuing once an
hour (less frequently on Sunday) to Ballater (1¾
hours) and every two hours to Crathie (for Balmoral Castle) and Braemar (£9, 2¼ hours).

Other local buses serve Stonehaven, Fraserburgh, Peterhead, Banff and Buckie.

TRAIN The **train station** is south of the city
centre, next to the massive Union Square shopping mall. There are several trains a day from
King's Cross in London to Aberdeen (£122, 7½
hours); some are direct, but most services involve a change of train at Edinburgh.

Other destinations served from Aberdeen by
rail include Edinburgh (£40, 2½ hours), Glasgow
(£40, 2¾ hours), Dundee (£24, 1¼ hours) and
Inverness (£25, 2¼ hours).

ℹ Getting Around

BUS The main city bus operator is **First Aberdeen** (www.firstaberdeen.com). Local fares cost
from 70p to £2; pay the driver as you board the
bus. A FirstDay ticket (adult/child £3.90/2.70)
allows unlimited travel from the time of purchase until midnight on all First Aberdeen buses.
Information, route maps and tickets are available from the **First Travel Centre** (47 Union St;
◷8.45am-5.30pm Mon-Sat).

The most useful services for visitors are buses
16A and 19 from Union St to Great Western Rd
(for B&Bs); bus 27 from the bus station to Aberdeen Youth Hostel and the airport; and bus 20
from Marischal College to Old Aberdeen.

CAR For rental cars try **Arnold Clark** (☎01224-
249159; www.arnoldclarkrental.com; Girdleness
Rd) or **Enterprise Car Hire** (☎01224-642642;
www.enterprise.co.uk; 80 Skene Sq).

TAXI The main city-centre taxi ranks are at the
train station and on Back Wynd, off Union St. To
order a taxi, phone **ComCab** (☎01224-353535)
or **Rainbow City Taxis** (☎01224-878787).

Around Aberdeen

STONEHAVEN
POP 9600

Originally a small fishing village, Stonehaven has been the county town of Kincardineshire since 1600 and is now a thriving
family-friendly seaside resort. There's a
tourist office (☎01569-762806; 66 Allardice
St; ◷10am-7pm Mon-Sat, 1-5.30pm Sun Jul & Aug,
10am-1pm & 2-5.30pm Mon-Sat Jun & Sep, 10am-
1pm & 2-5pm Mon-Sat Apr, May & Oct) near Market Sq in the town centre.

◉ Sights & Activities

From the lane beside the tourist office, a
boardwalk leads south along the shoreline
to the picturesque cliff-bound harbour,
where you'll find a couple of appealing
pubs and the town's oldest building, the
Tolbooth, built about 1600 by the Earl
Marischal. It now houses a small museum
(admission free; ◷10am-noon & 2-5pm Mon &
Thu-Sat, 2-5pm Wed & Sun) and a restaurant.

At the northern end of town is the Open-
Air Swimming Pool (www.stonehavenopen
airpool.co.uk; adult/child £4.70/2.80; ◷10am-
7.30pm Mon-Fri, 10am-6pm Sat & Sun Jul–mid-
Aug, 1-7.30pm Mon-Fri, 10am-6pm Sat & Sun Jun &
late Aug), an Olympic-size (50m), heated, sea-
water pool in art deco style, dating from
1934. The pool is also open for 'midnight
swims' from 10pm to midnight on Wednesday from the end of June to mid-August.

A pleasant, 15-minute walk along the
clifftops south of the harbour leads to the
spectacular ruins of Dunnottar Castle
(www.dunnottarcastle.co.uk; adult/child £5/1;
◷9am-6pm daily Easter-Oct, 10.30am-dusk Fri-
Mon Nov-Easter), spread out across a grassy
promontory rising 50m above the sea. As
dramatic a film set as any director could
wish for, it provided the backdrop for Fran-
co Zeffirelli's *Hamlet,* starring Mel Gibson.

The original fortress was built in the 9th century; the keep is the most substantial remnant, but the drawing room (restored in 1926) is more interesting.

The **Lady Gail 2** (☑01569-765064; adult/ child £10/5) offers boat trips from the harbour to the nearby sea cliffs of Fowlsheugh nature reserve, which from May to July are home to around 160,000 nesting seabirds, including kittiwakes, guillemots, razorbills and puffins.

✵ Festivals & Events

The town hosts several special events, including the famous **Fireball Ceremony** (www.stonehavenfireballs.co.uk) at Hogmanay (31 December), when people parade along the High St at midnight swinging blazing fireballs around their heads, and the three-day **Stonehaven Folk Festival** (www.stone havenfolkfestival.co.uk) in mid-July.

🛏 Sleeping & Eating

TOP CHOICE 24 Shorehead   B&B ££
(☑01569-767750; www.twentyfourshore head.co.uk; 24 Shorehead; s/d £55/70; @) Location makes all the difference, and the location of this former cooperage offering peaceful and very stylish B&B accommodation can't be beaten – last house at the end of the road, overlooking the harbour, with lovely sea views. Using the binoculars provided, you can even spot seals from your bedroom. No credit cards.

Beachgate House   B&B ££
(☑01569-763155; www.beachgate.co.uk; Beachgate Lane; s/d £55/70; P) This luxurious modern bungalow is right on the seafront, just a few paces from the tourist office; two of its five rooms have sea views, as does the lounge/dining room.

TOP CHOICE Tolbooth Restaurant
                                    SEAFOOD £££
(☑01569-762287; www.tolbooth-restaurant.co.uk; Old Pier; mains £16-24; ⊙closed Mon year round & Sun Oct-Apr) Set in a 17th-century building overlooking the harbour, and decorated with local art and crisp white linen, this is one of the best seafood restaurants in the region. Daily specials include dishes such as scallops with samphire risotto, artichokes and saffron foam. From Tuesday to Saturday you can get a two-/three-course lunch for £13/16. Reservations recommended.

Marine Hotel   PUB, SEAFOOD ££
(www.marinehotelstonehaven.co.uk; 9-10 The Shore; mains £8-13; ⊙food noon-2.30pm &

5.30-9pm Mon-Fri, noon-9pm Sat & Sun) A recent makeover with bare timber, slate and dove-grey paintwork has given this popular harbourside pub a boutique look; there are still half a dozen real ales on tap, including Deuchars IPA and Timothy Taylor, and a bar-meals menu that includes fresh seafood specials.

Carron Restaurant   SCOTTISH ££
(www.carron-restaurant.co.uk; 20 Cameron St; mains £12-20; ⊙Tue-Sat) This beautiful art deco restaurant is a remarkable survival from the 1930s, complete with bow-fronted terrace, iron fanlights, deco mirrors, player piano and original tiled toilets. The French- and Mediterranean-influenced menu makes the most of local produce, matching the elegance of the surroundings.

Boathouse Café   CAFE £
(Old Pier; mains £6-8; ⊙9.30am-4pm Mon-Fri, 9.30am-5pm Sat & Sun) Excellent coffee, cakes and light lunches; outdoor terrace with a view of the sea,

Ship Inn   PUB, SEAFOOD £
(www.shipinnstonehaven.com; 12 5 Shorehead; mains £9-17; ⊙lunch & dinner Mon-Fri, noon-9.45pm Sat & Sun) Real ales, pub grub and outdoor tables with a view of the harbour. More formal dining in the neighbouring Captain's Table restaurant.

ℹ Getting There & Away

Stonehaven is 15 miles south of Aberdeen and is served by the frequent **buses** travelling between Aberdeen (45 minutes, hourly) and Dundee (1½ hours). **Trains** to Dundee are faster (£12, 55 minutes, hourly) and offer a more scenic journey.

CASTLE FRASER

The impressive 16th- to 17th-century **Castle Fraser** (NTS; adult/child £8.50/5.50; ⊙11am-5pm Jul & Aug, noon-5pm Thu-Sun Apr-Jun, Sep & Oct) is the ancestral home of the Fraser family. The largely Victorian interior includes the great hall (with a hidden opening where the laird could eavesdrop on his guests), the library, various bedrooms and an ancient kitchen, plus a secret room for storing valuables; Fraser family relics on display include needlework hangings and a 19th-century artificial leg. The 'Woodland Secrets' area in the castle grounds is designed as an adventure playground for kids.

The castle is 16 miles west of Aberdeen and 3 miles south of Kemnay. Buses from Aberdeen to Alford stop at Kemnay.

HADDO HOUSE

Designed in Georgian style by William Adam in 1732, **Haddo House** (NTS; Tarves; adult/child £8.50/5.50; ☉11am-5pm Jul & Aug, 11am-5pm Fri-Mon Apr-Jun, Sep & Oct) is best described as a classic English stately home transplanted to Scotland. Home to the Gordon family, it has sumptuous Victorian interiors with wood-panelled walls, Persian rug–scattered floors and a wealth of period antiques. The beautiful grounds and terraced gardens are open all year (9am to dusk).

Haddo is 19 miles north of Aberdeen, near Ellon. Buses run hourly Monday to Saturday from Aberdeen to Tarves/Methlick, stopping at the end of the Haddo House driveway; it's a mile-long walk from bus stop to house.

FYVIE CASTLE

Though a magnificent example of Scottish Baronial architecture, **Fyvie Castle** (NTS; adult/child £10.50/7.50; ☉11am-5pm Jul & Aug, noon-5pm Sat-Tue Apr-Jun, Sep & Oct) is probably more famous for its ghosts, which include a phantom trumpeter and the mysterious Green Lady. The castle's art collection includes portraits by Thomas Gainsborough and Sir Henry Raeburn. The grounds are open all year (9am to dusk).

The castle is 25 miles north of Aberdeen on the A947 towards Turriff. A bus runs hourly every day from Aberdeen to Banff and Elgin via Fyvie village, a mile from the castle.

Deeside

The valley of the **River Dee** – often called **Royal Deeside** because of the royal family's long association with the area – stretches west from Aberdeen to Braemar, closely paralleled by the A93 road. From Deeside north to Strathdon is serious castle country – there are more examples of fanciful Scottish Baronial architecture here than anywhere else in Scotland.

The Dee, world-famous for its **salmon fishing**, has its source in the Cairngorm Mountains west of Braemar, the starting point for long walks into the hills. The **Fish-Dee website** (www.fishdee.co.uk) has all you need to know about fishing on the river.

CRATHES CASTLE

The atmospheric, 16th-century **Crathes Castle** (NTS; adult/child £10.50/7.50; ☉10.30am-5pm Jun-Aug, 10.30am-4.30pm Sat-Thu Apr, May, Sep & Oct, 10.30am-3.45pm Sat & Sun Nov-Mar; ♿) is famous for its Jacobean painted ceilings, magnificently carved canopied beds, and the 'Horn of Leys', presented to the Burnett family by Robert the Bruce in the 14th century. The beautiful formal **gardens** include 300-year-old yew hedges and colourful herbaceous borders.

The castle is on the A93, 16 miles west of Aberdeen, on the main Aberdeen to Ballater bus route.

BALLATER
POP 1450

The attractive little village of Ballater owes its 18th-century origins to the curative waters of nearby Pannanich Springs (now bottled commercially as Deeside Natural Mineral Water) and its prosperity to nearby Balmoral Castle.

The **tourist office** (☎01339-755306; Station Sq; ☉9am-6pm Jul & Aug, 10am-5pm Sep-Jun) is in the Old Royal Station. For internet access, go to **Cybernaut** (www.cybernaut.org.uk; 14 Bridge St; per 15min £1; ☉9am-5pm Mon-Fri, 10am-4pm Sat; @).

☉ Sights & Activities

When Queen Victoria travelled to Balmoral Castle she would alight from the royal train at Ballater's **Old Royal Station** (Station Sq; admission £2; ☉9am-6pm Jul & Aug, 10am-5pm Sep-Jun). The station has been beautifully restored and now houses the tourist office, a cafe and a museum with a replica of Victoria's royal coach. Note the crests on the shop fronts along the main street proclaiming 'By Royal Appointment' – the village is a major supplier of provisions to Balmoral.

Also on Station Sq is **Dee Valley Confectioners** (www.dee-valley.co.uk; Station Sq; admission free; ☉9am-noon & 2-4.30pm Mon-Thu Apr-Oct), where you can drool over the manufacture of traditional Scottish sweeties.

As you approach Ballater from the east the hills start to close in, and there are many pleasant **walks** in the surrounding area. The steep woodland walk up **Craigendarroch** (400m) takes just over one hour. **Morven** (871m) is a more serious prospect, taking about six hours, but offers good views from the top; ask at the tourist office for more info.

You can hire bikes from **CycleHighlands** (www.cyclehighlands.com; The Pavilion, Victoria Rd; per day £16; ☉9am-6pm), who also offers guided bike rides and advice on local trails, and **Cabin Fever** (Station Sq; per 2hr £8; ☉9am-6pm), who can also arrange pony trekking, quad-biking, clay-pigeon shooting or canoeing.

🛏 Sleeping & Eating

Accommodation here is fairly expensive and budget travellers usually continue to Braemar.

TOP CHOICE **Auld Kirk**   RESTAURANT WITH ROOMS **££**
(☑01339-755762; www.theauldkirk.com; Braemar Rd; s/d from £73/110; ☎) Here's something a little out of the ordinary – a six-bedroom 'restaurant with rooms' housed in a converted 19th-century church. The interior blends original features with sleek modern decor, and the stylish Scottish restaurant (two-/three-course dinner £29/35) serves local lamb, venison and seafood.

Green Inn   RESTAURANT WITH ROOMS **££**
(☑01339-755701; www.green-inn.com; s/d from £58/76; ℗) A lovely old house dotted with plush armchairs and sofas, this is another 'restaurant with rooms' – three comfortable en suite bedrooms, with the accent on fine dining. The menu includes French-influenced dishes such as roast quail with crayfish, truffle and wild mushrooms. A two-/three-course dinner costs £34/41 and meals are served from 7pm till 9pm Tuesday to Saturday.

Celicall   B&B **££**
(☑01339-755699; www.celicallguesthouse.co.uk; 3 Braemar Rd; d from £54; ℗) Celicall is a friendly, family-run B&B in a modern cottage right across the street from Station Sq, within easy walking distance of all attractions.

Old Station Cafe   CAFE **££**
(Station Sq; mains £9-15; ☉10am-5pm daily, 6.30-8.30pm Thu-Sat) The former waiting room at Queen Victoria's train station is now an attractive dining area with black-and-white floor tiles, basketwork chairs, and marble fireplace and table tops. Daily specials make good use of local produce, from salmon to venison, and good coffee and home-baked goods are available all day.

ℹ Getting There & Away

Bus 201 runs from Aberdeen to Ballater (£9, 1¾ hours, hourly Monday to Saturday, six on Sunday) via Crathes Castle, and continues to Braemar (30 minutes) every two hours.

BALMORAL CASTLE

Eight miles west of Ballater lies **Balmoral Castle** (www.balmoralcastle.com; adult/child £8.70/4.60; ☉10am-5pm Apr-Jul, last admission 4pm), the Queen's Highland holiday home, screened from the road by a thick curtain of trees. Built for Queen Victoria in 1855 as a private residence for the royal family, it kicked off the revival of the Scottish Baronial style of architecture that characterises so many of Scotland's 19th-century country houses.

The admission fee includes an interesting and well thought-out audioguide, but the tour is very much an outdoor one through garden and grounds; as for the castle itself, only the ballroom, which displays a collection of Landseer paintings and royal silver, is open to the public. Don't expect to see the Queen's private quarters! The main attraction is learning about Highland estate management, rather than royal revelations. Guided tours are available on Saturdays from October to December – check the website for details.

The massive pointy-topped mountain that looms to the south of Balmoral is **Lochnagar** (1155m), immortalised in verse by Lord Byron, who spent his childhood years in Aberdeenshire:

England, thy beauties are tame and domestic
To one who has roamed o'er the mountains afar.
O! for the crags that are wild and majestic:
The steep frowning glories of dark Lochnagar.

Balmoral is beside the A93 at Crathie and can be reached on the Aberdeen–Braemar bus.

BRAEMAR
POP 400

Braemar is a pretty little village with a grand location on a broad plain ringed by mountains where the Dee valley and Glen Clunie meet. In winter this is one of the coldest places in the country – temperatures as low as -29°C have been recorded – and during spells of severe cold hungry deer wander the streets looking for a bite to eat. Braemar is an excellent base for hill walking, and there's also skiing at nearby Glenshee.

The **tourist office** (☎01399-741600; The Mews, Mar Rd; ⏰9am-6pm Aug, 9am-5pm Jun, Jul, Sep & Oct, 10am-1.30pm & 2-5pm Mon-Sat, 2-5pm Sun Nov-May), opposite the Fife Arms Hotel, has lots of useful info on walks in the area. There's a bank with an ATM in the village centre, a couple of outdoor equipment shops and an **Alldays** (⏰7.30am-9pm Mon-Sat, 9am-6pm Sun) grocery store.

◉ Sights & Activities

The **Braemar Highland Heritage Centre** (Mar Rd; admission free; ⏰9am-6.30pm Jul & Aug, 10am-6pm Jun & Sep, 10am-5.30pm Mon-Sat, noon-5pm Sun Mar-May, shorter hr winter), beside the tourist office, tells the story of the area with displays and videos.

Just north of the village, turreted **Braemar Castle** (www.braemarcastle.co.uk; adult/child £5/3; ⏰11am-6pm Sat & Sun, also Wed Jul & Aug) dates from 1628 and served as a government garrison after the 1745 Jacobite rebellion. It was taken over by the local community in 2007, and now offers guided tours of the historic castle apartments.

An easy walk from Braemar is up **Creag Choinnich** (538m), a hill to the east of the village above the A93. The route is waymarked and takes about 1½ hours. For a longer walk (three hours) and superb views of the Cairngorms, head for the summit of **Morrone** (859m), southwest of Braemar. Ask at the tourist office for details of these and other walks.

🛏 Sleeping

TOP CHOICE **Rucksacks Bunkhouse** BUNKHOUSE £ (☎01339-741517; 15 Mar Rd; bothy £7, dm £12-15, tw £36; P@) An appealing cottage bunkhouse, with comfy dorm and cheaper beds in an alpine-style bothy (shared sleeping platform for 10 people; bring your own sleeping bag). Extras including a drying room (for wet-weather gear), laundry and even a sauna (£10 an hour). Nonguests are welcome to use the internet (£3 per hour, 10.30am to 4.30pm), laundry and even the showers (£2), and the friendly owner is a fount of knowledge about the local area.

Craiglea B&B ££ (☎01339-741641; www.craigleabraemar.com; Hillside Dr; r £70; P) Craiglea is a homely B&B set in a pretty stone cottage with three en suite bedrooms. Vegetarian breakfasts are available and the owners can give advice on local walks.

There are Highland games in many towns and villages throughout the summer, but the best known is the **Braemar Gathering** (www.braemargathering.org), which takes place on the first Saturday in September. It's a major occasion, organised every year since 1817 by the Braemar Royal Highland Society. Events include Highland dancing, pipers, tug-of-war, a hill race up Morrone, tossing the caber, hammer- and stone-throwing and the long jump. International athletes are among those who take part.

These kinds of events took place informally in the Highlands for many centuries as tests of skill and strength, but they were formalised around 1820 as part of the rise of Highland romanticism initiated by Sir Walter Scott and King George IV. Queen Victoria attended the Braemar Gathering in 1848, starting a tradition of royal patronage that continues to this day.

Clunie Lodge Guesthouse B&B ££ (☎01339-741330; www.clunielodge.com; Cluniebank Rd; r per person from £30; P) A spacious Victorian villa set in beautiful gardens, the Clunie is a great place to relax after a hard day's hiking, with its comfortable residents lounge, bedrooms with views of the hills and red squirrels scampering through the neighbouring woods. There's a drying room and secure storage for cycles.

Braemar Lodge Hotel HOTEL, BUNKHOUSE ££ (☎01339-741627; www.braemarlodge.co.uk; Glenshee Rd; dm from £12, s/d £75/120; P) This Victorian shooting lodge on the southern outskirts of the village has bags of character, not least in the wood-panelled Malt Room bar, which is as well stocked with mounted deer heads as it is with single malt whiskies. There's a good restaurant with views of the hills, plus a 12-berth hikers' bunkhouse in the hotel grounds.

Braemar Youth Hostel HOSTEL £ (SYHA; ☎01339-741659; 21 Glenshee Rd; dm £16-17; ⏰Jan-Oct; @) This hostel is housed in a grand former shooting lodge just south of the village centre on the A93 to Perth. It has a comfy lounge with pool table, and a barbecue in the garden.

St Margarets
B&B ££

(☎01339-741697; 13 School Rd; s/tw £32/54; 🛜) Grab this place if you can, but there's only one room – a twin with a serious sunflower theme. The genuine warmth of the welcome is heart-warming.

Invercauld Caravan Club Site
CAMPSITE £

(☎01339-741373; tent sites £10-15; ☺late Dec-Oct) Good camping here, or you can **camp wild** (no facilities) along the minor road on the east bank of the Clunie Water, 3 miles south of Braemar.

✗ Eating

TOP CHOICE **Gathering Place**
BISTRO ££

(☎01339-741234; www.the-gathering-place.co.uk; 9 Invercauld Rd; mains £15-18; ☺dinner Tue-Sun) This bright and breezy bistro is an unexpected corner of culinary excellence, with a welcoming dining room and sunny conservatory, tucked below the main road junction at the entrance to the village.

Taste
CAFE £

(www.taste-braemar.co.uk; Airlie House, Mar Rd; mains £3-5; ☺10am-5pm Thu-Mon; 🚼) Taste is a relaxed little cafe with armchairs in the window, serving soups, snacks, coffee and cakes.

Hungry Highlander
FISH & CHIPS £

(14 Invercauld Rd; mains £3-7; ☺10am-10pm Mon-Sat, 10.30am-10pm, 10am-10pm Sun) Serves a range of takeaway meals and hot drinks.

❶ Getting There & Away

Bus 201 runs from Aberdeen to Braemar (£9, 2¼ hours, eight daily Monday to Saturday, five on Sunday). The 50-mile drive from Perth to Braemar is beautiful, but there's no public transport on this route.

INVEREY

Five miles west of Braemar is the tiny settlement of Inverey. Numerous mountain walks start from here, including the adventurous walk through the **Lairig Ghru** pass to Aviemore (see the boxed text, p331).

The **Glen Luibeg** circuit (15 miles, six hours) is a good day-walk. Start from the woodland car park 250m beyond the **Linn of Dee**, a narrow gorge at the road bridge about 1.5 miles west of Inverey, and follow the footpath and track to Derry Lodge and Glen Luibeg – there are beautiful remnants of the ancient Caledonian pine forest here.

Continue westwards on a pleasant path over a pass into Glen Dee, then follow the River Dee back downstream to the linn. Take OS 1:50,000 map sheet number 43.

A good short walk (3 miles, 1½ hours) begins at the **Linn of Quoich** – a waterfall that thunders through a narrow slot in the rocks. Head uphill on a footpath on the east bank of the stream, past the impressive rock scenery of the **Punch Bowl** (a giant pothole), to a modern bridge that spans the narrow gorge, and return via an unsurfaced road on the far bank.

Strathdon

The valley of the River Don, home to many of Aberdeenshire's finest castles, stretches westward from Kintore, 13 miles northwest of Aberdeen, taking in the villages of Kemnay, Monymusk, Alford (*ah*-ford) and tiny Strathdon. The A944 parallels the lower valley; west of Alford, the A944, A97 and A939 follow the river's upper reaches.

Stagecoach bus 220 runs from Aberdeen to Alford (1½ hours, seven a day Monday to Saturday, four on Sunday); bus 219 continues from Alford to Strathdon village (50 minutes, two daily Tuesday and Thursday, one on Saturday) via Kildrummy.

ALFORD
POP 1925

Alford has a **tourist office** (☎01975-562052; Old Station Yard, Main St; ☺10am-5pm Mon-Sat, 12.45-5pm Sun Jun-Aug, 10am-1pm & 2-5pm Mon-Fri, 10am-noon & 1.45-5pm Sat, 12.45-5pm Sun Apr, May & Sep), banks with ATMs and a supermarket.

The **Grampian Transport Museum** (www.gtm.org.uk; adult/child £6/3; ☺10am-5pm Apr-Sep, 10am-4pm Oct) houses a fascinating collection of vintage motorbikes, cars, buses and trams, including a Triumph Bonneville in excellent nick, a couple of Model T Fords (including one used by Drambuie), a Ferrari F40 and an Aston Martin V8 Mk II. Unusual exhibits include a 19th-century horse-drawn sleigh from Russia, a 1942 Mack snowplough and the Craigievar Express, a steam-powered tricycle built in 1895 by a local postman.

Next to the museum is the terminus of the narrow-gauge **Alford Valley Steam Railway** (☎01975-562811; www.alfordvalleyrailway.org.uk; adult/child £2.50/1.50; ☺11.30am-4pm May-Sep, Sat & Sun only Apr), a heritage line that runs from here to Haughton Country Park.

CRAIGIEVAR CASTLE

The most spectacular of the Strathdon castles is Craigievar (NTS; adult/child £10/7; ☺noon-5.30pm Jul & Aug, noon-5.30pm Fri-Tue Easter-Jun & Sep), located 9 miles south of Alford. A superb example of the original Scottish Baronial style, it has managed to survive pretty much unchanged since its completion in the 17th century (although the exterior has recently been restored to its original pink colour after a £500,000 facelift). The lower half is a plain tower house, the upper half sprouts corbelled turrets, cupolas and battlements – an extravagant statement of its builder's wealth and status.

KILDRUMMY CASTLE

Nine miles west of Alford lie the extensive remains of the 13th-century Kildrummy Castle (HS; adult/child £3.70/2.20; ☺9.30am-5.30pm Apr-Sep), former seat of the Earl of Mar and once one of Scotland's most impressive fortresses. After the 1715 Jacobite rebellion the earl was exiled to France and his castle fell into ruin.

If you're in the mood for a night of luxury, head for Kildrummy Castle Hotel (☎01975-571288; www.kildrummycastlehotel.co.uk; s/d from£90/139; P🖱🏷) just along the road, a splendid Baronial hunting lodge complete with original oak panelling, log fires and four-poster beds.

CORGARFF CASTLE

In the wild upper reaches of Strathdon, near the A939 from Corgarff to Tomintoul, is the impressive fortress of Corgarff Castle (HS; adult/child £4.70/2.80; ☺9.30am-5.30pm daily Apr-Sep, 9.30am-4.30pm Sat & Sun Oct-Mar). The tower house dates from the 16th century, but the star-shaped defensive curtain wall was added in 1748 when the castle was converted to a military barracks in the wake of the Jacobite rebellion.

Jenny's Bothy (☎01975-651449; www.jennysbothy.co.uk; dm £10) is a welcoming year-round bunkhouse set in a remote croft; look out for the sign by the main road, then follow the old military road (drivable) for 0.75 miles. Phone ahead before arriving.

LECHT SKI RESORT

At the head of Strathdon the A939 – a magnificent rollercoaster of a road, much loved by motorcyclists – crosses the Lecht pass (637m), where there's a small skiing area with lots of short easy and intermediate runs. Lecht 2090 (www.lecht.co.uk) hires out skis, boots and poles for £17 a day; a one-day lift pass is £25. A two-day package, including ski hire, lift pass and instruction, costs £90.

The ski centre opens in summer, too, when you can rent mountain bikes (£20 for four hours) and quad bikes (£10 for a 12-minute session).

Northern Aberdeenshire

North of Aberdeen, the Grampian Mountains fall away to rolling agricultural plains pocked with small, craggy volcanic hills. This fertile lowland corner of northeastern Scotland is known as Buchan, a region of traditional farming culture immortalised by Lewis Grassic Gibbon in his trilogy, A Scots Quair, based on the life of a farming community in the 1920s. The old Scots dialect called the Doric lives on in everyday use here – if you think the Glaswegian accent is difficult to understand, just try listening in on a conversation in Peterhead or Fraserburgh.

The Buchan coast alternates between rugged cliffs and long, long stretches of sand, dotted with picturesque little fishing villages such as Pennan, where parts of the film Local Hero were shot.

FRASERBURGH
POP 12.500

Fraserburgh, affectionately known to locals as the Broch, is Europe's largest shellfish port. Like Peterhead, Fraserburgh's fortune has been founded on the fishing industry and has suffered from its general decline. The harbour is still fairly busy, though, and is an interesting place to wander around; there are good sandy **beaches** east of the town. There's a tourist office (☎01346-518315; Saltoun Sq; ☺10am-1pm & 2-5pm Mon-Sat Apr-Oct), a supermarket and banks with ATMs.

The excellent Scottish Lighthouse Museum (www.lighthousemuseum.org.uk; Kinnaird Head; adult/child £5/2; ☺10am-6pm Mon-Sat, 11am-6pm Sun Jul & Aug, 11am-5pm Mon-Sat, noon-5pm Sun Sep & Oct, to 4pm Nov-Mar) provides a fascinating insight into the network of lights that have safeguarded the Scottish coast for over 100 years, and the men and women who built and maintained them (plus a sobering fact – that *all* the world's lighthouses are to be decommissioned by 1 January 2080). A guided tour takes you to the top of the old Kinnaird Head lighthouse, built on top of a converted 16th-century castle; the engineering is so precise that the 4.5-ton light assembly can be rotated by pushing with a single finger. The anemometer here measured the strongest wind speed ever recorded in the UK, with a gust of 123 knots (142mph) on 13 February 1989.

Maggie's Hoosie (26 Shore St, Inverallochy; admission free; ☺2-4pm Mon-Thu Apr-Sep), 4 miles east of Fraserburgh, is a traditional fishwife's cottage with earthen floors and original furnishings, a timeless reminder of a bygone age.

Buses 267 and 268 run to Fraserburgh from Aberdeen (1½ hours, every 30 minutes Monday to Saturday, hourly on Sunday) via Ellon.

PENNAN

Pennan is a picturesque harbour village tucked beneath red-sandstone cliffs, 12 miles west of Fraserburgh. The white-washed houses are built gable-end to the sea, and the waves break just a few metres away on the other side of the village's only street. Most of the cottages are now holiday homes.

The village featured in the 1983 film *Local Hero,* and fans of the film still come to make a call from the red telephone box that played a prominent part in the plot. However, the box in the film was just a prop, and it was only later that film buffs and locals successfully campaigned for a real one to be installed.

The interior of the village hotel, the **Pennan Inn**, also appeared in the film, though one of the houses further along the seafront to the east doubled for the exterior of the fictional hotel. The beach scenes were filmed on the other side of the country, at Camasdarach Beach in Arisaig, see p345.

Bus 273 from Fraserburgh to Banff stops at the Pennan road end (25 minutes, two a day, Saturday only), 350m south of (and a steep climb uphill from) the village.

GARDENSTOWN & CROVIE

The fishing village of **Gardenstown**, or Gamrie (*game*-rey), founded by Alexander Garden in 1720, is built on a series of cramped terraces tumbling down the steep cliffs above the tiny harbour. Drivers should beware of severe gradients and hairpin bends in the village, parts of which can only be reached on foot. **Crovie** (*criv*-vee), 800m to the east, is even more claustrophobically picturesque.

HUNTLY
POP 4400

An impressive ruined castle and an attractive main square make this small town worth a stopover between Aberdeen and Elgin. The **tourist office** (☎01466-792255; The Square; ☺10am-5.30pm Mon-Sat, 10am-3pm Sun Jul & Aug, 10am-1pm & 2-5pm Mon-Sat Apr-Jun, Sep & Oct) is on the main square, next to a bank with an ATM.

Castle St (beside the Huntly Hotel) runs north from the town square to an arched gateway and tree-lined avenue that leads to 16th-century **Huntly Castle** (HS; adult/child £4.70/2.80; ☺9.30am-5.30pm Apr-Sep, 9.30am-4.30pm Oct, 9.30am-4.30pm Sat-Wed Nov-Mar), the former stronghold of the Gordons on the banks of the River Deveron. Over the main door is a superb carving that includes the royal arms and the figures of Christ and St Michael.

Just off the A96, 3 miles northwest of Huntly, is the **Peregrine Wild Watch Centre** (www.forestry.gov.uk/huntlyperegrines; Bin Forest; admission free; ☺9.30am-5.30pm Apr-Aug), a centre where you can observe rare peregrine falcons, both live from a hide and via a remote camera monitoring their nest site.

🛏 Sleeping

There are a couple of hotels on the main square and a handful of B&Bs in the surrounding streets; the hospitable **Hillview** (☎01466-794870; www.hillviewbb.com; Provost St; s/d £30/50; P🛜) and its tasty breakfast pancakes are recommended.

If you want to spoil yourself, continue along the drive beyond the castle to the **Castle Hotel** (☎01466-792696; www.castle hotel.uk.com; s/d from £70/100; P🛜), a splendid 18th-century mansion set amid acres of parkland. It's comfortably old fashioned, with a grand wooden staircase, convoluted corridors, the odd creaky floorboard and rattling sash window, but must be among the most affordable country house hotels in Scotland.

❶ Getting There & Away

Bus 10 from Aberdeen (1½ hours, hourly) to Inverness passes through Huntly. There are also

THE WOLF OF BADENOCH

Of all the hard-man figures of medieval Scotland, few inspired as much terror as Alexander Stewart, Earl of Buchan (1343–1405), illegitimate son of the king and better known as the Wolf of Badenoch. A cruel landowner with a number of castles in the Strathspey region, he was not a man to get on the wrong side of, as the Bishop of Moray found out in 1390. When the earl ditched his wife in favour of his mistress, the bishop excommunicated him. The monk who bore the message of excommunication was thrown head first into a well, and the infuriated Wolf, accompanied by a band of 'wild wicked Highland men', embarked on an orgy of destruction, burning first Forres, then Elgin, to the ground, destroying the cathedral and nearby Pluscarden Abbey in the process. Amazingly, Stewart still managed to end up being buried in Dunkeld Cathedral. Legend says his death occurred on a dark, stormy night. The devil came calling on a black horse and challenged him to a game of chess. The Wolf was checkmated, and the devil took his life (and soul) as his prize.

regular trains from Aberdeen to Huntly (one hour, every two hours), continuing to Inverness.

Moray

The old county of Moray (*murr*-ree), centred on the county town of Elgin, lies at the heart of an ancient Celtic earldom and is famed for its mild climate and rich farmland – the barley fields of the 19th century once provided the raw material for the Speyside whisky distilleries, one of the region's main attractions for present-day visitors.

ELGIN
POP 21,000

Elgin's been the provincial capital of Moray for over eight centuries and was an important town in medieval times. Dominated by a hilltop monument to the 5th Duke of Gordon, Elgin's main attraction is its impressive ruined cathedral, where the tombs of the duke's ancestors lie.

◉ Sights

Elgin Cathedral   CATHEDRAL
(HS; King St; adult/child £4.70/2.80, joint ticket with Spynie Palace £6.20/3.70; ⓧ9.30am-5.30pm Apr-Sep, 9.30am-4.30pm Oct, 9.30am-4.30pm Sat-Wed Oct-Mar) Many people think that the ruins of Elgin Cathedral, known as the 'lantern of the north', are the most beautiful and evocative in Scotland. Consecrated in 1224, the cathedral was burned down in 1390 by the infamous Wolf of Badenoch, the illegitimate son of Robert II, following his excommunication by the Bishop of Moray. The octagonal chapter house is the finest in the country.

Elgin Museum   MUSEUM
(www.elginmuseum.org.uk; 1 High St; adult/child £4/1.50; ⓧ10am-5pm Mon-Fri, 11am-4pm Sat Apr-Oct) Palaeontologists and Pict lovers will enjoy Elgin Museum, where the highlights are its collections of fossil fish and Pictish carved stones.

Gordon & MacPhail   DELICATESSEN
(www.gordonandmacphail.com; 58-60 South St; ⓧ9am-5pm Mon-Sat) Not a sight as such, but a sight for sore eyes perhaps – Gordon & MacPhail is the world's largest specialist malt whisky dealer. Over a century old and offering around 450 different varieties, its Elgin shop is a place of pilgrimage for whisky connoisseurs, as well as housing a mouth-watering delicatessen.

Spynie Palace   HISTORIC BUILDING
(HS; adult/child £3.70/2.20; ⓧ9.30am-5.30pm Apr-Sep, 9.30am-4.30pm Sat & Sun Oct-Mar) This palace 2 miles north of Elgin was the residence of the medieval bishops of Moray until 1686. The massive tower house commands lovely views over Spynie Loch.

🛏 Sleeping & Eating

Croft Guesthouse   B&B ££
(☎01343-546004; www.thecroftelgin.co.uk; 10 Institution Rd; s/d from £55/70; ℗) The Croft offers a taste of Victorian high society, set in a spacious mansion built for a local lawyer back in 1848. The house is filled with period features – check out the cast-iron and tile fireplaces – and the three large bedrooms are equipped with easy chairs and crisp bed linen.

Mansefield Hotel   HOTEL ££
(☎01343-540883; www.themansefield.com; Mayne Rd; s/d from £90/110; ℗) Centred on a

19th-century manse (minister's house), but with extensive modern additions, the Mansfield offers elegant accommodation both in sleek, modern rooms aimed at business travellers and in more traditional rooms with four-poster beds.

Southbank Guest House
B&B ££

(☎01343-547132; www.southbank-guesthouse.co.uk; 36 Academy St; s/d from £50/75; P) The family-run, 12-room Southbank is set in a large Georgian town house in a quiet street south of Elgin's centre, just five minutes' walk from the cathedral and other sights.

Mezzo
BISTRO ££

(cnr Hay & South Sts; mains £8-15; ⊘lunch & dinner Mon-Sat, dinner Sun) This lively bar and restaurant is part of the Mansefield Hotel complex, and serves tasty bistro fare, including pasta, pizza, burgers and various vegetarian dishes.

Xoriatiki
GREEK ££

(☎01343-546868; 89 High St; mains £7-12; ⊘lunch & dinner Tue-Sat) Likeable place which brings an authentic taste of Greece to Elgin at competitive prices. Access is via an alleyway off the main street.

Ashvale
FISH & CHIPS £

(11 Moss St; mains £6-12; ⊘10.45am-10pm) A branch of the famous Aberdeen fish-and-chip shop, sit in or takeaway.

ⓘ Information
Moray Business & Computer Centre (20 Commerce St; per 15min £1; ⊘9am-5pm Mon-Sat; @) Internet access.

Post office (Batchen St; ⊘8.30am-6pm Mon-Fri, 8.30am-4pm Sat)

Tourist office (☎01343-542666; 17 High St; ⊘9am-6pm Mon-Sat, 11am-4pm Sun Jun-Aug, 9am-5pm Mon-Sat, 11am-3pm Sun Apr, May, Sep & Oct, 10am-4pm Mon-Sat Nov-Mar)

ⓘ Getting There & Away
The bus station is a block north of the High St, and the train station is 900m south of the town centre.

BUS Elgin is a stop on the hourly Stagecoach bus 10 service between Inverness (£8, one hour) and Aberdeen (£10, two hours). Bus 305 goes from Elgin to Banff and Macduff (£8, one hour), continuing to Aberdeen via Fyvie. Bus 336 goes to Dufftown (£4, 30 minutes, hourly Monday to Saturday).

TRAIN There are frequent trains from Elgin to Aberdeen (£15, 1½ hours) and Inverness (£10, 45 minutes).

LOSSIEMOUTH
POP 9000

Lossie, as it's known locally, is the former port of Elgin, now better known as a seaside resort, yachting harbour and air force base; it's also the birthplace of James Ramsay MacDonald (1866–1937), who was the UK's first Labour prime minister (served 1923–24 and 1929–31; there's a plaque at 1 Gregory Pl, where he was born).

Lossiemouth's big selling point is the **East Beach**, a beautiful golden-sand beach that stretches for several miles to the southeast of the town, reached via a footbridge over the River Lossie. The old harbour, now a yachting marina, is a pleasant place to stroll.

Good places for coffee and cake or a light lunch include **Harbour Lights** (5 Pitgaveny Quay; snacks £2-5; ⊘9am-5pm), a tearoom beside the marina, and **La Caverna** (20 Clifton Rd; mains £9-13; ⊘noon-2pm & 5-9.30pm), a stone-vaulted Italian cafe and restaurant – the outdoor tables have a view of the beach.

DUFFTOWN
POP 1450

Rome may be built on seven hills, but Dufftown's built on seven stills, say the locals. Founded in 1817 by James Duff, 4th Earl of Fife, Dufftown is 17 miles south of Elgin and lies at the heart of the Speyside whisky-distilling region.

The **tourist office** (☎01340-820501; ⊘10am-1pm & 2-5.30pm Mon-Sat, 11am-3pm Sun Easter-Oct) is in the clock tower in the main square; the adjoining museum contains some interesting local items.

ⓞ Sights & Activities
With seven working distilleries nearby, Dufftown has been dubbed Scotland's malt whisky capital. Ask at the tourist office for a **Malt Whisky Trail** (www.maltwhiskytrail.com) booklet, a self-guided tour around the seven stills plus the Speyside Cooperage.

Keith and Dufftown Railway
HERITAGE RAILWAY

(www.keith-dufftown-railway.co.uk; Dufftown Station) A heritage railway line running for 11 miles from Dufftown to Keith. Trains hauled by 1950s diesel motor units run on Saturdays and Sundays from June to September, plus Fridays in July and August; a return ticket costs £9.50/4.50 for an adult/child. There are also two 1930s 'Brighton Belle' Pullman coaches on display, and a cafe housed in a 1957 British Railways cafeteria car.

Visiting a distillery can be memorable, but only hardcore malthounds will want to go to more than two or three. Some are great to visit; others are depressingly corporate. The following are some recommendations.

» **Aberlour** (www.aberlour.com; tours £10; ⊙10.30am & 2pm daily Easter-Oct, Mon-Fri by appointment Nov-Mar) Has an excellent, detailed tour with a proper tasting session. It's on the main street in Aberlour.

» **Glenfarclas** (www.glenfarclas.co.uk; admission £3.50; ⊙10am-4pm Mon-Fri Oct-Mar, 10am-5pm Mon-Fri Apr-Sep, plus 10am-4pm Sat Jul-Sep) Small, friendly and independent, Glenfarclas is 5 miles south of Aberlour on the Grantown road. The last tour leaves 90 minutes before closing. The in-depth Ambassador's Tour (Fridays only) is £15.

» **Glenfiddich** (www.glenfiddich.com; admission free; ⊙9.30am-4.30pm Mon-Fri year-round, 9.30am-4.30pm Sat & noon-4.30pm Sun Easter–mid-Oct) It's big and busy, but handiest for Dufftown and foreign languages are available. The standard tour starts with an overblown video, but it's fun, informative and free. An in-depth Connoisseur's Tour (£20) must be prebooked. Glenfiddich kept single malt alive during the dark years.

» **Macallan** (www.themacallan.com; standard tours £5; ⊙9.30am-4.30pm Mon-Sat Apr-Oct, ring for winter hours) Excellent sherry-casked malt. Several small-group tours are available (last tour at 3.30pm), including an expert one (£15); all should be prebooked. Lovely location 2 miles northwest of Craigellachie.

» **Speyside Cooperage** (www.speysidecooperage.co.uk; admission £3.30; ⊙9am-4pm Mon-Fri) Here you can see the fascinating art of barrel-making in action. It's a mile from Craigellachie on the Dufftown road.

» **Spirit of Speyside** (www.spiritofspeyside.com) This biannual whisky festival in Dufftown has a number of great events. It takes place in early May and late September; both accommodation and events should be booked well ahead.

NORTHEAST SCOTLAND MORAY

Whisky Museum MUSEUM
(www.dufftown.co.uk; The Hub, 12 Conval St; ⊙1-4pm Mon-Fri May-Sep) As well as housing a selection of distillery memorabilia (try saying that after a few drams), the Whisky Museum (recently moved to new premises in Conval St) holds 'nosing and tasting evenings' where you can learn what to look for in a fine single malt (£8 per person; 8pm Wednesday in July and August). You can then test your new-found skills at the nearby **Whisky Shop** (www.whiskyshopdufftown.co.uk; 1 Fife St), which stocks hundreds of single malts.

🛏 Sleeping & Eating

Davaar B&B B&B ££
(☎01340-820464; www.davaardufftown.co.uk; 17 Church St; s/d from £40/60) Just along the street opposite the tourist office, Davaar is a sturdy Victorian villa with three smallish but comfy rooms; the breakfast menu is superb, offering the option of Portsoy kippers instead of the traditional fry-up (which uses eggs from the owners' own chickens).

Fife Arms Hotel HOTEL ££
(☎01340-820220; www.fifearmsdufftown.co.uk; 2 The Square; s/d from £35/60; [P]) This welcoming hotel offers slightly cramped but comfortable accommodation in a modern block around the back; its bar is stocked with a wide range of single malts, and the restaurant (mains £9 to £16) dishes up sizzling steaks, homemade steak pies and locally farmed ostrich steaks.

🌿 **La Faisanderie** FRENCH, SCOTTISH £££
(☎01340-821273; The Square; mains £18-21; ⊙noon-1.30pm & 5.30-8.30pm) This is a great place to eat, run by a local chef who shoots much of his own game, guaranteeing freshness. The interior is decorated in French *auberge* style with a cheerful mural and pheasants hiding in every corner. The set menus (three-course lunch £18.50, four-course dinner £32) won't disappoint, but you can order à la carte as well.

🌿 **A Taste of Speyside** SCOTTISH ££
(☎01340-820860; 10 Balvenie St; mains £16-20; ⊙noon-9pm Tue-Sun Easter-Sep, noon-

2pm & 6-9pm Tue-Sun Oct-Easter) This up-market restaurant prepares traditional Scottish dishes using fresh local produce, including a challenging platter of smoked salmon, smoked venison, brandied chicken liver pâté, cured herring, a selection of Scottish cheeses and homemade bread (phew!). A two-course lunch costs £13.50.

ⓘ Getting There & Away

Buses link Dufftown to Elgin (50 minutes, hourly), Huntly, Aberdeen and Inverness.

On summer weekends, you can take a train from Aberdeen or Inverness to Keith, and then ride the Keith and Dufftown Railway (see p254) to Dufftown.

TOMINTOUL
POP 320

This high-altitude (345m) village was built by the Duke of Gordon in 1775 on the old military road that leads over the Lecht pass from Corgarff, a route now followed by the A939 (usually the first road in Scotland to be blocked by snow when winter closes in). The duke hoped that settling the dispersed population of his estates in a proper village would help to stamp out cattle stealing and illegal distilling.

Tomintoul (tom-in-*towel*) is a pretty, stone-built village with a grassy, tree-lined main square, where you'll find the tourist office (☎01807-580285; The Square; ☺9.30am-1pm & 2-5pm Mon-Sat Easter-Oct, plus 1-5pm Sun Aug); and, next door, the Tomintoul Museum (The Square; admission free; ☺9.30am-5pm Mon-Sat Apr-Oct, plus 1-5pm Sun Jul & Aug), which has displays on a range of local topics.

The surrounding Glenlivet Estate (now the property of the Crown) has lots of **walking and cycling** trails – the estate's information centre (www.crownestate.co.uk/glenlivet; Main St) distributes free maps of the area – and a spur of the **Speyside Way** long-distance footpath (see the boxed text, p32) runs between Tomintoul and Ballindalloch, 15 miles to the north.

⌂ Sleeping & Eating

Accommodation for walkers includes the Tomintoul Youth Hostel (SYHA; ☎01807-580364; Main St; dm £15; ☺May-Sep), housed in the old village school. The excellent Argyle Guest House (☎01807-580766; www.argyletomintoul.co.uk; 7 Main St; d/f £59/100) is a more comfortable alternative.

For something to eat, try the Clock-house Restaurant (The Square; mains £10-12;

☺lunch & dinner), which serves light lunches and bistro dinners made with fresh Highland lamb, venison and salmon.

ⓘ Getting There & Away

There is a very limited bus service to Tomintoul from Elgin, Dufftown and Aberlour. Check with the tourist office in Elgin for the latest timetable.

BANFF & MACDUFF
COMBINED POP 7750

The handsome Georgian town of Banff and the busy fishing port of Macduff lie on either side of Banff Bay, separated only by the mouth of the River Deveron. Banff Links – 800m of clean golden sand stretching to the west – and Macduff's impressive aquarium pull in the holiday crowds.

The tourist office (☎01261-812419; Collie Lodge, High St; ☺10am-5pm Mon-Sat, noon-5pm Sun Apr-Sep) is beside St Mary's car park in Banff.

◉ Sights

Duff House   ART GALLERY
(www.duffhouse.org.uk; adult/child £6.55/5.45; ☺11am-5pm Apr-Oct, 11am-4pm Thu-Sun Nov-Mar) Duff House is an impressive baroque mansion on the southern edge of Banff (upstream from the bridge, and across from the tourist office). Built between 1735 and 1740 as the seat of the Earls of Fife, it was designed by William Adam and bears similarities to that Adam masterpiece, Hopetoun House. Since being donated to the town in 1906 it has served as a hotel, a hospital and a POW camp, but is now an art gallery. One of Scotland's hidden gems, it houses a superb collection of Scottish and European art, including important works by Raeburn and Gainsborough.

Nearby Banff Museum (High St; admission free; ☺10am-12.30pm Mon-Sat Jun-Sep) has award-winning displays on local wildlife, geology and history, and Banff silver.

Macduff Marine Aquarium   AQUARIUM
(www.macduff-aquarium.org.uk; 11 High Shore; adult/child £5.65/2.80; ☺10am-5pm; ⓐ) The centrepiece of Macduff's aquarium is a 400,000L open-air tank, complete with kelp-coated reef and wave machine. Marine oddities on view include the brightly coloured cuckoo wrasse, the warty-skinned lumpsucker and the vicious-looking wolf fish.

⌂ Sleeping & Eating

Bryvard Guest House   B&B £££
(☎01261-818090; www.bryvardguesthouse.co.uk; Seafield St, Banff; s/d from £40/70; ☎) The

Bryvard is an imposing Edwardian town house close to the town centre, with four beautiful period-furnished bedrooms (two with en suite). Go for the 'McLeod' room, which has a four-poster bed and a sea view. The guesthouse's **Hidden Corner** restaurant (mains £15-18) serves dinner Thursday to Saturday.

County Hotel   HOTEL **££**
(☎01261-815353; www.thecountyhotel.com; 32 High St, Banff; s/d from £45/80; **P**) The County occupies an elegant Georgian mansion in the town centre, and is owned by a French chef – the hotel's **bistro** serves light meals (mains £6 to £10), while **Restaurant L'Auberge** offers the finest French cuisine (à la carte mains £29 to £35, three-course dinner £31).

Banff Links Caravan Park   CAMPSITE **£**
(☎01261-812228; Banff; tent/campervan from £8/14; ☼Apr-Oct) This camp site is beside the beach, 800m west of town.

ⓘ Getting There & Away

Bus 305 runs from Banff to Elgin (1½ hours, hourly) and Aberdeen (two hours), while bus 273 runs less frequently to Fraserburgh (one hour, twice on Saturday only).

PORTSOY
POP 1730

The pretty fishing village of Portsoy has an atmospheric **17th-century harbour** and a maze of narrow streets lined with picturesque cottages. An ornamental stone known as Portsoy marble – actually a beautifully patterned green-and-pale-pink serpentine – was quarried near Portsoy in the 17th and 18th centuries, and was reputedly used in the decoration of some rooms in the Palace of Versailles. Beside the harbour, the **Portsoy Marble Shop & Pottery** (Shorehead; ☼10am-5pm Apr-Oct) sells handmade stoneware and objects made from the local marble.

Each year on the last weekend in June or first weekend in July, Portsoy harbour is home to the **Scottish Traditional Boat Festival** (www.scottishtraditionalboatfestival.co.uk), a lively gathering of historic wooden sailing boats accompanied by sailing races, live folk music, crafts demonstrations, street theatre and a food festival.

The 12-room **Boyne Hotel** (☎01261-842242; www.boynehotel.co.uk; 2 North High St; s/d £40/72) is a cosy and atmospheric place to stay, while the **Shore Inn** (Church St) is a characterful real-ale pub overlooking the harbour.

Portsoy is 8 miles west of Banff; the hourly bus between Elgin and Banff stops here.

FORDYCE
POP 150

This impossibly picturesque village lies about 3 miles southwest of Portsoy. The main attractions are the 13th-century **St Tarquin's Church**, with its extraordinary canopied Gothic tombs, and the impressive 16th-century tower house of **Fordyce Castle**. The castle isn't open to the public, but its whitewashed west wing provides atmospheric **self-catering accommodation** (☎01261-843722; www.fordycecastle.co.uk; per week £395-595, 3 nights in low season £295) for up to four people.

The nearby **Joiner's Workshop & Visitor Centre** (admission free; ☼10am-8pm Thu-Mon Jul & Aug, 10am-6pm Fri-Mon Sep-Jun) has a collection of woodworking tools and machinery, and stages woodwork demonstrations by a master joiner.

FOCHABERS & AROUND
POP 1500

Fochabers sits beside the last bridge over the River Spey before it enters the sea. The town has a pleasant square, with a church and clock tower dated 1798, and a handful of interesting antique shops.

West of the bridge over the Spey is **Baxters Highland Village** (www.baxters.com; admission free; ☼10am-5pm), which charts the history of the Baxter family and their well-known brand of quality Scottish foodstuffs, founded in 1868. There's a factory tour with cookery demonstrations on weekdays.

Four miles north of Fochabers, at the mouth of the River Spey, is the tiny village of **Spey Bay**, the starting point for the Speyside Way long-distance footpath (p32).

SUENO'S STONE

The tidy town of Forres, 4 miles south of Findhorn, is famous for **Sueno's Stone**, a remarkable, 6.5m-high Pictish stone. It is the tallest and most elaborately carved Pictish stone in Scotland, dating from the 9th or 10th century, and is thought to depict a battle between the Picts and invading Scots or Vikings. It's protected from the elements by a huge plate-glass box, and is signposted from the main A96 Inverness-to-Elgin road at Forres.

CULBIN FOREST

On the western side of Findhorn Bay is **Culbin Forest** (www.culbin.org.uk), a vast swathe of Scots and Corsican pine that was planted in the 1940s to stabilise the shifting sand dunes that buried the Culbin Estate in the 17th century. The forest is a unique wildlife habitat, supporting plants, birds and animals (such as the pine marten) that are normally found only in ancient natural pine woods.

The forest is criss-crossed by a maze of walking and cycling trails which lead to a fantastic beach near the mouth of Findhorn Bay, a great birdwatching spot. Check the website for more info, or pick up a leaflet from local tourist offices.

It's also home to the **WDCS Wildlife Centre** (www.wdcs.org; Tugnet Ice House; admission free; ☺10.30am-5pm Apr-Sep) with an interesting display on the Moray Firth **dolphins**, which can occasionally be seen off the mouth of the river, and a pleasant cafe.

Fochabers is on the Aberdeen-to-Inverness bus route.

FINDHORN
POP 885

The attractive village of Findhorn lies at the mouth of the River Findhorn, just east of the Findhorn Bay nature reserve. It's a great place for **birdwatching**, **seal-spotting** and **coastal walks**.

Findhorn Heritage Centre (www.findhorn -heritage.co.uk; admission free; ☺2-5pm daily Jun-Aug, 2-5pm Sat & Sun May & Sep), housed in a former salmon-fisher's bothy at the northern end of the village, records the history of the settlement. The beach is just over the dunes north of the heritage centre – at low tide, you can see seals hauled out on the sandbanks off the mouth of the River Findhorn.

Hippies old and new should check out the **Findhorn Foundation** (www.findhorn. org; ☺visitor centre 10am-5pm Mon-Fri year-round, plus 1-4pm Sat Mar-Nov & 1-4pm Sun May-Sep), an international spiritual community founded in 1962. There's a small permanent population of around 150, but the community receives thousands of visitors each year. With no formal creed, the community is dedicated to cooperation with nature, 'dealing with work, relationships and our environment in new and more fulfilling ways', and fostering 'a deeper sense of the sacred in everyday life'. Projects include an eco-village, a biological sewage-treatment plant and a wind-powered generator. Guided tours (£5) start from the visitor centre at 2pm on Monday, Wednesday, Friday and Saturday from April to November, and on Sunday as well from April to September, or you can take a self-guided tour with guidebook (£3.50).

There are two good places to eat: the **Bakehouse** (mains £5-10; ☺10am-5pm), an organic bakery and cafe in the village centre, and the **Blue Angel Cafe** (www.blueangelcafe. co.uk; mains £3-9; ☺10am-5pm; ☎), an organic and vegetarian eatery in the Findhorn Foundation's eco-village.

Southern Highlands & Islands

Best Places to Stay

» Highland Cottage Hotel (p292)

» Achnadrish House (p294)

» George Hotel (p271)

Best Places to Eat

» Café Fish (p293)

» Waterfront Restaurant (p286)

» Colonsay Hotel (p282)

» Argyll Hotel (p297)

Why Go?

From the rasping spout of a minke whale as it breaks the surface, to the 'krek-krek-krek' of a corncrake, the coast and islands of southwest Scotland are filled with unusual wildlife experiences. You can spot otters tumbling in the kelp, watch sea eagles snatch fish from a lonely loch, and thrill to the sight of dolphins riding the bow-wave of your boat.

Here, sea travel is as important as road and rail – dozens of ferries allow you to island-hop your way from the Firth of Clyde to Oban and beyond, via the whisky distilleries of Islay, the wild mountains of Jura and the scenic delights of diminutive Colonsay.

The bustling town of Oban is the gateway to the isles – from the peaceful backwaters of Kerrera and Lismore to the dramatic coastal scenery of Mull and the wild, windswept beaches of Coll and Tiree.

When to Go

Oban

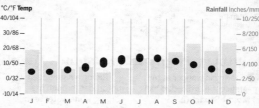

May Feis Ile (Islay Festival) celebrates traditional Scottish music and whisky.

June Roadsides and gardens become a blaze of colour with deep-pink rhododendron blooms.

August The best month of the year for whale watching off the west coast.

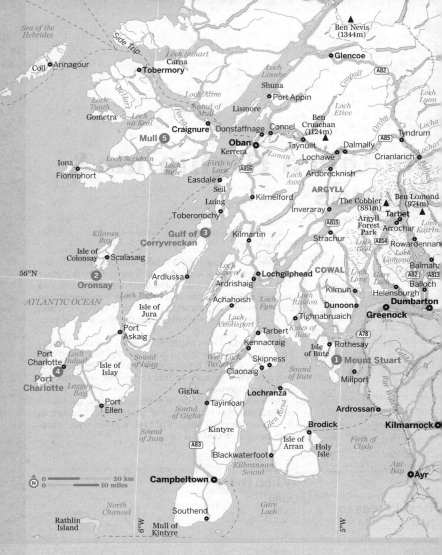

Southern Highlands & Islands Highlights

1 Staring in wonder at the magnificent marble-clad halls of **Mount Stuart** (p269)

2 Walking barefoot across the strand from Colonsay to **Oronsay** (p282) to visit the medieval priory

3 Riding a high-speed motorboat through the surging white water of the **Gulf of Corryvreckan** (boxed text, p280)

4 Sitting by a log fire in the **Port Charlotte Hotel** (p278), sampling some of Islay's finest single-malt whiskies

5 Whale watching in the waters off the west coast of **Mull** (boxed text, p295)

LOCH LOMOND & AROUND

The 'bonnie banks' and 'bonnie braes' of Loch Lomond have long been Glasgow's rural retreat – a scenic region of hills, lochs and healthy fresh air within easy reach of Scotland's largest city (Loch Lomond is within an hour's drive of 70% of Scotland's population). Since the 1930s Glaswegians have made a regular weekend exodus to the hills – by car, by bike and on foot – and today the loch's popularity shows no sign of decreasing.

The region's importance was recognised when it became the heart of Loch Lomond & the Trossachs National Park (www .lochlomond-trossachs.org) – Scotland's first national park, created in 2002.

Loch Lomond

Loch Lomond is the largest lake in mainland Britain and, after Loch Ness, perhaps the most famous of Scotland's lochs. Its proximity to Glasgow (20 miles away) means that the tourist honeypots of Balloch, Loch Lomond Shores and Luss get pretty crowded in summer. The main tourist focus is along the A82 on the loch's western shore, and at the southern end, around Balloch, which occasionally becomes a nightmare of jet skis and motorboats. The eastern shore, which is followed by the West Highland Way long-distance footpath, is a little quieter.

Loch Lomond straddles the Highland border and its character changes as you move north. The southern part is broad and island-studded, fringed by woods and Lowland meadows. However, north of Luss the loch narrows, occupying a deep trench gouged out by glaciers during the Ice Age, with 900m mountains crowding in on either side.

Activities

Walking

The big walk around here is the West Highland Way (www.west-highland-way.co.uk), which runs along the eastern shore of the loch. There are shorter lochside walks at Firkin Point on the western shore and at several other places around the loch. You can get further information on local walks from the national-park information centres at Loch Lomond Shores (p262) and Balmaha (p262).

Rowardennan is the starting point for an ascent of Ben Lomond (974m), a popular and relatively easy five- to six-hour round trip. The route starts at the car park just past the Rowardennan Hotel.

Boat Trips

The main centre for boat trips is Balloch, where Sweeney's Cruises (www.sweeney .uk.com; Balloch Rd) offers a range of trips including a one-hour cruise to Inchmurrin and back (adult/child £7/4, departs hourly), and a two-hour cruise (£12.50/6, departs 1pm and 3pm) around the islands. The quay is directly opposite Balloch train station, beside the tourist office. Sweeney's also runs hourly cruises from the Maid of the Loch jetty at Loch Lomond Shores.

Cruise Loch Lomond (www.cruiselochlo mondltd.com) is based in Tarbet and offers trips to Inversnaid and Rob Roy MacGregor's Cave. You can also be dropped off at Rowardennan and picked up at Inversnaid after a 9-mile hike along the West Highland Way.

The mail boat, run by Balmaha Boatyard (www.balmahaboatyard.co.uk; The Boatyard, Balmaha), cruises from Balmaha to the loch's four inhabited islands, departing at 11.30am and returning at 2pm with a one-hour stop on Inchmurrin (adult/child £9/4.50). Trips depart daily in July and August, and Monday, Thursday and Saturday in May, June and September.

Other Activities

The mostly traffic-free Clyde and Loch Lomond Cycle Way links Glasgow to Balloch (20 miles), where it links with the West Loch Lomond Cycle Path, which continues along the loch shore to Tarbet (10 miles).

You can rent rowing boats at Balmaha Boatyard for £10/30 per hour/day (or £20/50 for a boat with outboard motor). Lomond Adventure (☎01360-870218), also in Balmaha, rents out Canadian canoes (£30 per day) and sea kayaks (£25).

At Loch Lomond Shores (p262) you can hire canoes (£12/17 per half-/full hour) and bicycles (£12/17 per three hours/full day), take a guided canoe trip on the loch (£30 for two hours) or try power kiting (£30 for 2½ hours).

Information

Balloch tourist office (☎0870 720 0607; Balloch Rd; ◷9.30am-6pm Jun-Aug, 10am-6pm Apr & Sep)

Balmaha National Park Centre (☎01389-722100; Balmaha; ◷9.30am-4.15pm Apr-Sep)

National Park Gateway Centre (☎01389-751035; www.lochlomondshores.com; Loch Lomond Shores, Balloch; ◷10am-6pm Apr-Sep, to 5pm Oct-Mar; @🕾)

Tarbet tourist office (☎0870-720 0623; ◷10am-6pm Jul & Aug, to 5pm Easter-Jun, Sep & Oct) At the junction of the A82 and the A83.

❶ Getting There & Away

BUS First (www.firstgroup.com) Glasgow buses 204 and 215 run from Argyle St in central Glasgow to Balloch and Loch Lomond Shores (1½ hours, at least two per hour).

Scottish Citylink (www.citylink.co.uk) coaches from Glasgow to Oban and Fort William stop at Luss (£8, 55 minutes, six daily), Tarbet (£8, 65 minutes) and Ardlui (£14, 1¼ hours).

TRAIN There are frequent trains from Glasgow to Balloch (£4.15, 45 minutes, every 30 minutes) and a less-frequent service on the West Highland line from Glasgow to Arrochar & Tarbet station (£10, 1¼ hours, three or four daily), halfway between the two villages, and Ardlui (£13, 1½ hours), continuing to Oban and Fort William.

❶ Getting Around

Pick up the useful public transport booklet (free), which lists timetables for all bus, train and ferry services in Loch Lomond and the Trossachs National Park, available from any tourist office or park information centre.

BUS McColl's Coaches (www.mccolls.org.uk) bus 309 runs from Balloch to Balmaha (25 minutes, every two hours). An **SPT Daytripper ticket** (www.spt.co.uk/tickets) gives a family group unlimited travel for a day on most bus and train services in the Glasgow, Loch Lomond and Helensburgh area. Buy the ticket (£9.80 for one adult and one or two children, £17.50 for two adults and up to four children) from any train station or the main Glasgow bus station.

BOAT There are several passenger ferries on Loch Lomond, with fares ranging from £3 to £7 per person; bicycles are carried free. Except for the ferries out of Loch Lomond Shores, these are mostly small motorboats that operate on demand, rather than to a set timetable – telephone or visit for more information.

Ardlui to Ardleish (☎01307-704243; Ardlui Hotel; ◷9am-7pm May-Sep, to 6pm Apr & Oct) On demand.

Balmaha to Inchcailloch (☎01360-870214; Balmaha Boatyard, Balmaha; ◷9am-8pm daily) On demand.

Balmaha to Luss (www.cruiselochlomondltd.com; ◷Jul-Sep) Four daily.

Inveruglas to Inversnaid (☎01877-386223; Inversnaid Hotel) On demand; no fixed timetable.

Loch Lomond Shores to Balmaha (www.clydecruises.com; ◷late Jul-early Sep) Five daily.

Rowardennan to Luss (www.cruiselochlomondltd.com; ◷Jul-Sep) One daily. Departs Rowardennan at 9.30am; Luss at 4.15pm.

Tarbet to Inversnaid (www.cruiselochlomondltd.com; ◷Apr-Oct) Three daily.

Tarbet to Rowardennan (www.cruiselochlomondltd.com; ◷Apr-Oct) Twice daily. Departs Tarbet 10am and 4pm; Rowardennan at 10.45am and 4.45pm.

WESTERN SHORE

The town of **Balloch**, which straddles the River Leven where it flows from the southern end of Loch Lomond, is the loch's main population centre and transport hub. A Victorian resort once thronged by day-trippers transferring between the train station and the steamer quay, it is now a 'gateway centre' for Loch Lomond and the Trossachs National Park.

Loch Lomond Shores (www.lochlomondshores.com), a major tourism development a half-mile north of Balloch, sports a national-park information centre plus various visitor attractions, outdoor activities and boat trips. In keeping with the times, the heart of the development is a large shopping mall. It's also home to the **Loch Lomond Aquarium** (www.sealife.co.uk; adult/child £12/9; ◷10am-5pm), which has displays on the wildlife of Loch Lomond, an otter enclosure (housing short-clawed Asian otters, not Scottish ones), and a host of sea-life exhibits ranging from sharks to stingrays to sea turtles.

The vintage paddle steamer **Maid of the Loch** (www.maidoftheloch.com; admission free; ◷11am-4pm daily May-Oct, Sat & Sun only Nov-Apr), built in 1953, is moored here while awaiting full restoration – you can nip aboard for a look around.

Unless it's raining, give Loch Lomond Shores a miss and head for the little picture-postcard village of **Luss**. Stroll among the pretty cottages with roses around their doors (the cottages were built by the local laird in the 19th century for the workers on his estate), then pop into the **Clan Colquhoun tourist office** (adult/child £1/free; ◷10.30am-6pm Easter-Oct) for some background history before enjoying a cup of tea at the Coach House Coffee Shop.

Sleeping & Eating

TOP CHOICE **Drover's Inn** PUB £

(☎01301-704234; www.thedroversinn.co.uk; Inverarnan; bar meals £8-10, steaks £15-17; ⊙lunch & dinner; ℗) This is one howff (drinking den) you shouldn't miss – a low-ceilinged place with smoke-blackened stone, bare wooden floors spotted with candle wax, barmen in kilts, and walls festooned with moth-eaten stags' heads and stuffed birds. There's even a stuffed bear, and the desiccated husk of a basking shark. The bar serves hearty hill-walking fuel such as steak-and-Guinness pie with mustard mash, and hosts live folk music on Friday and Saturday nights. We recommend this inn more as a place to eat and drink than to stay – accommodation (single/double from £40/78) varies from eccentric, old-fashioned and rather run-down rooms in the old building (including a ghost in room 6), to more comfortable rooms (with en suite bathrooms) in the modern annexe across the road. Ask to see your room before taking it.

Loch Lomond Youth Hostel HOSTEL £

(SYHA; ☎01389-850226; www.syha.org.uk; Arden; dm £18; ⊙Mar-Oct; ℗@☎) Forget about roughing it, this is one of the most impressive hostels in the country – an imposing 19th-century country house set in beautiful grounds overlooking the loch. It's 2 miles north of Balloch and very popular, so book in advance in summer. And yes, it *is* haunted.

Ardlui Hotel HOTEL ££

(☎01301-704243; www.ardlui.co.uk; Ardlui; s/d £60/95; ℗) If the Drover's Inn is a little rough for your bedtime tastes, nip down the road to the plush Ardlui Hotel, a comfy country-house hotel with a great lochside location and a view of Ben Lomond from the breakfast room.

Coach House Coffee Shop CAFE £

(Luss; mains £5-11; ⊙10am-5pm) With its chunky pine furniture and deep, deep sofa in front of a rustic fireplace, the Coach House is one of the cosiest places to eat on Loch Lomond. The menu includes coffee and tea, home-baked cakes, scones, ciabattas and more substantial offerings such as haggis.

EASTERN SHORE

The road along the loch's eastern shore passes through the attractive village of **Balmaha**, where you can hire boats or take a cruise on the mail boat (see p261). There are several picnic areas along the lochside; the most attractive is at **Millarochy Bay** (1.5 miles north of Balmaha), which has a nice gravel beach and superb views across the loch to the Luss hills.

The road ends at **Rowardennan**, but the West Highland Way continues north along the shore of the loch. It's 7 miles to Inversnaid, which can be reached by road from the Trossachs, and 15 miles to Inverarnan on the main A82 road at the northern end of the loch.

Sleeping & Eating

Oak Tree Inn INN ££

(☎01360-870357; www.oak-tree-inn.co.uk; Balmaha; dm/s/d £30/60/75; ℗🍴) An attractive traditional inn built in slate and timber, the child-friendly Oak Tree offers luxurious guest bedrooms for pampered hikers, and two four-bed bunkrooms for hardier souls. The rustic **restaurant** dishes up hearty lunches and dinners (meals £8 to £15) such as steak-and-mushroom pie, and roast Arctic char with lime and chive butter, and cooks up an excellent bowl of Cullen skink (soup made with smoked haddock, potato, onion and milk).

Passfoot Cottage B&B ££

(☎01360-870324; www.passfoot.com; Balmaha; s/d from £55/64; ⊙Apr-Sep) Passfoot is a pretty little whitewashed cottage decked out with colourful flower baskets, with a lovely location overlooking Balmaha Bay. The bright bedrooms have a homely feel, and there's a large lounge with a wood-burning stove and loch view.

Rowardennan Hotel HOTEL ££

(☎01360-870273; www.rowardennanhotel.co.uk; Rowardennan; s/d £65/90, bar meals £7-11; ⊙lunch & dinner; ℗) Originally an 18th-century drovers' inn, the Rowardennan has two big bars (often crowded with rain-sodden hikers) and a good beer garden (often crowded with midges). It had just been taken over by new owners at the time of research, and much-needed refurbishment has made it a pleasant place to stay, with a choice of traditional but stylish hotel rooms and luxury self-catering lodges.

Rowardennan Youth Hostel HOSTEL £

(☎01360-870259; Rowardennan; dm £17; ⊙Mar-Oct) Housed in an attractive Victorian lodge, this hostel has a superb setting right on the loch shore, beside the West Highland Way.

Cashel Campsite CAMPSITE £
(☏01360-870234; www.forestholidays.co.uk;
Rowardennan; dm £6.50, tent sites per 2 people
incl car £15-17; ⊙Mar-Oct; ⊞) This is the most
attractive campsite in the area. It's 3 miles
north of Balmaha, by the loch.

CRIANLARICH & TYNDRUM
POP 350

Surrounded by spectacular hillscapes begging to be walked, and on the West Highland Way, these villages are well-visited
service junctions on the main A82 road,
just north of the Loch Lomond & the Trossachs National Park. Crianlarich has a train
station and more community atmosphere
than Tyndrum, but Tyndrum (*tyne*-drum),
5 miles up the road, has two stations, a bus
interchange, petrol station, late-opening
motorists' cafes and a flash **tourist office**
(☏01838-400246; ⊙10am-5pm Apr-Oct) – a
good spot for route information and maps
for walking and ascents of popular **An Cai-
steal** (995m), **Ben More** (1174m) and magnificent **Ben Lui** (1130m).

🛏 Sleeping & Eating

Crianlarich makes a more appealing base
than Tyndrum: vehicles slow down through
town and the views and food choice are
better.

Crianlarich SYHA HOSTEL £
(☏01838-300260; www.syha.org.uk; Station Rd,
Crianlarich; dm £18.75; ℗@🛜⊞) Well-run and
comfortable, with spacious kitchen, dining area and lounge, this is a real haven for
walkers or anyone passing through Crianlarich. Dorms vary in size – there are some
great en suite family rooms that should be
prebooked – but all are clean and roomy.

Strathfillan Wigwams CAMPING, CABINS £
(☏01838-400251; www.wigwamholidays.com/
strathfillan; camping per adult/child £6/3, wig-
wam d small/large £28/33, lodge d from £45;
℗@) This charismatic place, 3 miles from
Crianlarich and 2 miles from Tyndrum, is
off the A82 and has 16 heated 'wigwams' –
essentially wooden A-frame cabins with
fridge and foam mattresses that can sleep
four at a pinch. More upmarket are the self-
contained lodges with their own bathroom
and kitchen facilities. There's also camping
with access to all facilities.

🖋 Real Food Café CAFE £
(www.therealfoodcafe.com; Tyndrum; meals
£6-9; ⊙10am-10pm; ⊞) Don't be put off by the
decor of this former chain eatery – concentrate on the food. The menu looks familiar,
with fish and chips, soups, salads and sausages, but it makes an effort to source sustainably and locally, and the quality shines
through.

Crianlarich Hotel HOTEL, PUB ££
(☏01838-300272; www.crianlarich-hotel.co.uk;
Crianlarich; budget/standard d £90/105; ℗🛜)
On the junction where all roads meet, this
has large rooms with appealingly comfortable beds, compact bathrooms, and a feeling
that they spent more on the reception area
than the carpet. It's good value in the low
season. The bar meals (mains £8 to £13) are
pricey but served in a most elegant space,
with venison, lamb hotpot and salmon
available. The **restaurant** serves classier
dinners (two courses £28).

Tyndrum Lodge Hotel HOTEL, PUB ££
(☏01838-400219; www.glhotels.co.uk; Tyndrum;
s without bathroom £28, s/d £33/66; ℗🛜) The
heart of Tyndrum is this cheerily run pitstop that features decent-value rooms and
two convivial bars. Walkers should head for
rooms 1 to 12, which are towards the back
and a bit quieter, ensuring a decent night's
shut-eye. Shared bathrooms have baths not
showers; breakfast is a buffet affair, and bar
meals (£7 to £9) are supplemented by weekend all-you-can-eat curry nights.

ⓘ Getting There & Away

BUS Scottish Citylink (www.citylink.co.uk) runs
several buses daily to Edinburgh, Glasgow,
Oban and Skye from both villages. A **postbus**
(www.royalmail.com) links Crianlarich, Tyndrum
and Killin twice on each weekday and once on
Saturday.

TRAIN Trains run from Tyndrum and Crianlarich
to Fort William (£15, 1¾ hours, four daily Monday
to Saturday, two on Sunday), Oban (£8.90, one
hour, three or four daily) and Glasgow (£16.10,
two hours, three or four daily).

Helensburgh
POP 16,500

With the coming of the railway in the mid-
19th century, Helensburgh – named in the
18th century after the wife of Sir James
Colquhoun of Luss – became a popular
seaside retreat for wealthy Glaswegian
families. Their spacious Victorian villas now populate the neat grid of streets
that covers the hillside above the Firth
of Clyde, but none can compare with the
splendour of **Hill House** (NTS; www.nts.org.

uk; ✆01436-673900; Upper Colquhoun St; adult/child £8.50/5.50; ⏱1.30-5.30pm Apr-Oct). Built in 1902 for the Glasgow publisher Walter Blackie, it is perhaps architect **Charles Rennie Mackintosh**'s finest creation – its timeless elegance feels as chic today as it no doubt did when the Blackies moved in a century ago.

Helensburgh has a ferry connection with Gourock (p133) via Kilcreggan, and a frequent train service to Glasgow (£5, 50 minutes, two per hour).

Arrochar

POP 650

The village of Arrochar has a wonderful location, looking across the head of Loch Long to the jagged peaks of the **Cobbler** (881m). The mountain takes its name from the shape of its north peak (the one on the right, seen from Arrochar), which looks like a cobbler hunched over his bench. The village has several hotels and shops, a bank and a post office.

If you want to **climb the Cobbler**, start from the roadside car park at Succoth near the head of Loch Long. A steep uphill hike through the woods is followed by an easier section as you head into the valley below the triple peaks. Then it's steeply uphill again to the saddle between the north and central peaks. The central peak to the left (south) is the highest point, but it's awkward to get to – scramble through the hole and along the ledge to reach the airy summit. The north peak to the right is an easy walk. Allow five to six hours for the 5-mile round trip.

There's good camping at **Ardgartan Caravan & Campsite** (✆01301-702293; www.forestholidays.co.uk; Ardgartan; tent site plus car & 2 people £15-17; ⏱Apr-Oct) at the foot of Glen Croe. Bike hire also available.

The black-and-white, 19th-century **Village Inn** (✆01301-702279; www.villageinnarrochar.co.uk; Arrochar; s/d from £50/75; mains £8-18; ⏱lunch & dinner; 🅿🛜) is a lovely spot for lunch, or just a pint of real ale – the beer garden has a great view of the Cobbler. There are 14 en suite bedrooms; the ones at the top end of the price range have four-poster beds and a view over the loch.

Citylink (www.citylink.co.uk) buses from Glasgow to Inveraray and Campbeltown call at Arrochar and Ardgartan (£8, 1¼ hours, three daily). See p262 for trains to Arrochar & Tarbet station.

BOOTS, BOATS, BIKES & BUSES

A new service called **Loch Lomond 4Bs** (www.lochlomond4bs.co.uk) allows you to explore Loch Lomond's hiking and biking trails by using ferry services and buses with bike trailers to deliver you to the start and finish of your chosen route.

For example, if you don't have time for the full 95 miles of the West Highland Way, you can spend a day on one of its most scenic sections. Starting from Balloch train station, a bus takes you to Tarbet, then you travel by boat to Rowardennan and the start of the 7-mile hike along the eastern shore of Loch Lomond to Inversnaid, where the boat returns you to Tarbet and the bus back to Balloch (bus £5, ferry £14.50).

The service operates daily July to September, and on holiday weekends from Easter to June. See the website for full details of timetables and possible walking and cycling itineraries.

SOUTH ARGYLL

Cowal

The remote Cowal peninsula is cut off from the rest of the country by the lengthy fjords of Loch Long and Loch Fyne – it's an area more accessible by boat than by car. It comprises rugged hills and narrow lochs, with only a few small villages; the scenery around Loch Riddon is particularly enchanting. The only town on the mainland is the old-fashioned holiday resort of Dunoon.

From Arrochar, the A83 to Inveraray loops around the head of Loch Long and climbs up Glen Croe. The pass at the head of the glen is called the **Rest and Be Thankful** – when the original military road through the glen was repaired in the 18th century, a stone was erected at the top inscribed 'Rest, and be thankful. This road was made, in 1748, by the 24th Regt...Repaired by the 93rd Regt. 1786'. A copy of the stone can be seen at the far end of the parking area at the top of the pass.

There's a Forest Enterprise **tourist office** (✆01301-702432; Ardgartan; admission free;

⊙10am-5pm Apr-Oct) at the foot of the glen, with information on various walks on the Cowal peninsula.

As you descend Glen Kinglas on the far side of the Rest and be Thankful, the A815 forks to the left just before Cairndow; this is the main overland route into Cowal. From Glasgow, the most direct route is by ferry from Gourock to Dunoon (see p133 for details).

DUNOON & AROUND

Like Rothesay on the Isle of Bute, Dunoon (population 9100) is a Victorian seaside resort that owes its existence to the steamers that once carried thousands of Glaswegians

GAELIC & NORSE PLACE NAMES

Throughout the Highlands and islands of Scotland the indigenous Gaelic language has left a rich legacy of place names. They're often intermixed with Old Norse names left behind by the Viking invaders who occupied the western and northern islands between the 8th and 13th centuries. The spelling is now anglicised, but the meaning is still clear once you know what to look for. Here are a few of the more common Gaelic and Norse names and their meanings.

GAELIC PLACE NAMES

ach, auch – from *achadh* (field)
ard – from *ard* or *aird* (height, hill)
avon – from *abhainn* (river or stream)
bal – from *baile* (village or homestead)
ban – from *ban* (white, fair)
beg – from *beag* (small)
ben – from *beinn* (mountain)
buie – from *buidhe* (yellow)
dal – from *dail* (field or dale)
dow, dhu – from *dubh* (black)
drum – from *druim* (ridge or back)
dun – from *dun* or *duin* (fort or castle)
glen – from *gleann* (narrow valley)
gorm – from *gorm* (blue)
gower, gour – from *gabhar* (goat), eg Ardgour (height of the goats)
inch, insh – from *inis* (island, water-meadow or resting place for cattle)
inver – from *inbhir* (rivermouth or meeting of two rivers)
kil – from *cille* (church), eg Kilmartin (Church of St Martin)
kin, ken – from *ceann* (head), eg Kinlochleven (head of Loch Leven)
kyle, kyles – from *caol* or *caolas* (narrow sea channel)
more, vore – from *mor* or *mhor* (big), eg Ardmore (big height), Skerryvore (big reef)
strath – from *srath* (broad valley)
tarbert, tarbet – from *tairbeart* (portage), meaning a narrow neck of land between two bodies of water, across which a boat can be dragged
tay, ty – from *tigh* (house), eg Tyndrum (house on the ridge)
tober – from *tobar* (well), eg Tobermory (Mary's well)

NORSE PLACE NAMES

a, ay, ey – from *ey* (island)
bister, buster, bster – from *bolstaor* (dwelling place, homestead)
geo – from *gja* (chasm)
holm – from *holmr* (small island)
kirk – from *kirkja* (church)
pol, poll, bol – from *bol* (farm)
quoy – from *kvi* (sheep fold, cattle enclosure)
sker, skier, skerry – from *sker* (rocky reef)
ster, sett – from *setr* (house)
vig, vaig, wick – from *vik* (bay, creek)
voe, way – from *vagr* (bay, creek)

on pleasure trips 'doon the watter' (down the water) in the 19th and 20th centuries. As with Rothesay, Dunoon's fortunes declined in recent decades when cheap foreign holidays stole its market – however, while the Bute resort appears to be recovering, Dunoon is still a bit down in the dumps.

The **tourist office** (☎0845 225 5121; 7 Alexandra Pde; ☺9am-5.30pm Mon-Fri, 10am-5pm Sat & Sun Apr-Sep, shorter hr Oct-Mar; @) is on the waterfront 100m north of the pier.

◉ Sights & Activities

The town's main attraction is still, as it was in the 1950s, strolling along the **promenade**, licking an ice-cream cone and watching the yachts at play in the Firth of Clyde. On a small hill above the seafront is a **statue of Highland Mary** (1763–86), one of the great loves of Robert Burns' life. She was born near Dunoon, but died tragically young; her statue gazes longingly across the firth to Burns' home territory in Ayrshire.

Benmore Botanic Garden   GARDEN
(www.rbge.org.uk; Benmore; adult/child £5/1; ☺10am-6pm Apr-Sep, to 5pm Mar & Oct) This garden, 7 miles north of Dunoon, was originally planted in the 19th and early 20th centuries. It contains the country's finest collection of flowering trees and shrubs, including spectacular displays of **rhododendrons and azaleas**, and is entered along a spectacular avenue of giant **Californian redwoods** planted in 1863. A highlight is the recently restored **Victorian fernery**, nestled in an unlikely fold in the crags. The **cafe** here (which stays open all year) is a nice place for lunch or a coffee.

✵ Festivals & Events

Cowal Highland Gathering HIGHLAND CULTURE (www.cowalgathering.com) Held in Dunoon in mid-August. The spectacular finale traditionally features 3000 bagpipers playing en masse.

Cowalfest   ARTS, OUTDOORS
(www.cowalfest.org) A 10-day arts and walking festival featuring art exhibitions, film screenings, guided walks and bicycle rides throughout the Cowal peninsula.

⌂ Sleeping & Eating

Dhailling Lodge   B&B **££**
(☎01369-701253; www.dhaillinglodge.com; 155 Alexandra Pde; s/d £40/76; P@☎) You can experience some of Dunoon's former elegance

at this large Victorian villa overlooking the bay about 0.75 miles north of the CalMac ferry pier. The owners are the essence of Scottish hospitality, and can provide excellent evening meals (£20 per person) if you wish.

Chatters   RESTAURANT **££**
(☎01369-706402; 58 John St; mains lunch £5-9, dinner £15-22; ☺lunch & dinner Wed-Sat) Chatters is a pretty little cottage restaurant with tartan sofas in the sitting room and a few tables in the tiny garden. It serves a mix of lunchtime snacks and brasserie dishes, and is famous for its open sandwiches and tempting homemade puddings. Booking recommended.

❶ Getting There & Away

Dunoon is served by two competing ferry services from Gourock (p133) – the **CalMac** (www.calmac.co.uk) ferry is better if you are travelling on foot and want to arrive in the town centre.

TIGHNABRUAICH
POP 200

Sleepy little Tighnabruaich (tinna-*broo*-ach), a colony of seaside villas built by wealthy Glasgow families at the turn of the 20th century, is one of the most attractive villages on the Firth of Clyde. It was once a regular stop for Clyde steamers, and the old wooden pier is still occasionally visited by the paddle steamer *Waverley* (see p117).

The link with the sea continues in the **Tighnabruaich Sailing School** (www.tssargyll.co.uk; Carry Farm; ☺May-Sep), 2 miles south of Tighnabruaich. A five-day dinghy-sailing course costs £230, excluding accommodation.

The village is home to **An Lochan** (☎01700-811239; www.anlochan-argyll.co.uk; Tighnabruaich; mains £10-22; P), a luxurious boutique hotel (rooms £110 to £180) that's comfortable, but in our opinion, a tad over-priced. The food is exquisite, and uses fresh, locally sourced produce – summer-vegetable risotto with basil dressing, to seared scallops with black pudding, apple puree and curry oil.

If all you want to do is fill up with good, hearty homemade grub, go for the mussels and chips at the **Burnside Bistro** (mains £6-15; ☺breakfast, lunch & dinner) in the village centre, or a bar meal at the **Kames Hotel** (mains £8-15; ☺lunch & dinner), a mile to the south.

Isle of Bute

POP 7350

The island of Bute lies pinched between the thumb and forefinger of the Cowal peninsula, separated from the mainland by a narrow, scenic strait known as the Kyles of Bute. The Highland Boundary Fault cuts through the middle of the island so that, geologically speaking, the northern half is in the Highlands and the southern half is in the central Lowlands – a metal arch on Rothesay's Esplanade marks the fault line.

The Isle of Bute Discovery Centre (☏01700-505156; www.bestofbute.co.uk; Esplanade, Rothesay; ☺10am-6pm Mon-Fri, 9.30am-5pm Sat & Sun Jul & Aug, 10am-5pm daily Apr-Jun & Sep, shorter hr Oct-Mar; @) is in Rothesay's restored Winter Gardens.

The five-day Isle of Bute Jazz Festival (www.butejazz.com) is held over the first weekend of May.

ROTHESAY

From the mid-19th century until the 1960s, Rothesay – once dubbed the Margate of the Clyde – was one of the most popular holiday resorts in Scotland. Its Esplanade was bustling with day-trippers disembarking from the numerous steamers crowded around the pier, and its hotels were filled with elderly holidaymakers and convalescents taking advantage of the town's famously mild climate.

The fashion for foreign holidays that took off in the 1970s saw Rothesay's fortunes decline, and by the late 1990s it had become dilapidated and despondent. But in the last few years a nostalgia-fuelled resurgence of interest in Rothesay's holiday heyday has seen many of its Victorian buildings restored, the ferry terminal and harbour rebuilt and marinas constructed at Rothesay and Port Bannatyne. There's a new feeling of optimism in the air.

☉ Sights

Victorian Toilets
HISTORIC BUILDING

(Rothesay Pier; adult/child 20p/free) There aren't too many places where a public toilet would count as a tourist attraction, but Rothesay's Victorian toilets, dating from 1899, are a monument to lavatorial luxury – a disinfectant-scented temple of green marble, glistening white enamel, glass-sided cisterns and gleaming copper pipes. The attendant will escort ladies into the hallowed confines of the gents for a look around when the facilities are unoccupied.

Rothesay Castle
CASTLE

(HS; www.historic-scotland.gov.uk; King St; adult/child £4.20/2.50; ☺9.30am-5.30pm Apr-Sep, to 4.30pm Sat-Wed Oct-Mar) Just two blocks inland from the pier are the splendid ruins of 13th-century Rothesay Castle, with seagulls and jackdaws nesting in the walls. Once a favourite residence of the Stuart kings, it is unique in Scotland in having a circular plan, with four massive round towers. The landscaped moat, with its manicured turf, flower gardens and lazily cruising ducks, makes a picturesque setting.

Bute Museum
MUSEUM

(www.butemuseum.org; 7 Stuart St; adult/child £2/1; ☺10.30am-4.30pm Mon-Sat & 2.30-4.30pm Sun Apr-Sep, 2.30-4.30pm Tue-Sat Oct-Mar) The most interesting displays in Bute Museum are those recounting the history of the famous Clyde steamers. Other galleries cover natural history, archaeology and geology; the prize exhibit is a stunning jet necklace found in a Bronze Age burial on the island.

🛏 Sleeping

Boat House
B&B ££

(☏01700-502696; www.theboathouse-bute.co.uk; 15 Battery Pl; s/d from £45/65; 🛜) The Boat House brings a touch of class to Rothesay's guesthouse scene, with quality fabrics and furnishings and an eye for design that makes it feel a bit like a boutique hotel without the expensive price tag. Other features include sea views, a central location and a ground-floor room kitted out for wheelchair users.

Glendale Guest House
B&B ££

(☏01700-502329; www.glendale-guest-house.com; 20 Battery Pl; s/d/f from £35/60/90; 🅿🛜) Look out for the ornate, flower-bedecked facade on this beautiful Victorian villa, complete with pinnacled turret. All those windows mean superb sea views from the front-facing bedrooms, the elegant, 1st-floor lounge and the breakfast room, where you'll find homemade smoked haddock fishcakes on the menu as well as the traditional fry-up.

Moorings
B&B ££

(☏01700-502277; www.themoorings-bute.co.uk; 7 Mountstuart Rd; s/d from £37/55; 🅿) Another delightful Victorian lodge with good sea views, the family-friendly Moorings has an outdoor play area for kids and a high chair in the breakfast room. Vegetarian breakfasts are not a problem.

Roseland Caravan Park
CAMPSITE ££

(☑01700-504529; www.roselandcaravanpark
.co.uk; Roslin Rd, Canada Hill; tent site & 2 people
£8) The island's only official campsite is a
steep climb up the winding Serpentine Rd
from the ferry terminal. There's a small
but pleasant grassy area for tents amid the
static caravans.

✖ Eating

Waterfront Bistro
BISTRO ££

(www.thewaterfrontbistro.co.uk; 16 East Princes
St; mains £8-16; ☉dinner Thu-Mon) Cheerful
and informal, the wood-panelled Waterfront has a bistro menu that ranges from
haddock and chips to venison in red-wine
sauce to grilled langoustines with garlic butter. Bottled real ale from the Arran
Brewery complements the wine list.

Brechin's Brasserie
BRASSERIE ££

(01700-502922; 2 Bridgend St; mains £9-16;
☉lunch Tue-Sat, dinner Fri & Sat) A friendly
neighbourhood brasserie owned by jazz fan
Tim (check out the sheet music and posters
on the wall), Brechin's serves unpretentious
but delicious dishes such as homemade lasagne, local lamb chops with redcurrant
and red-wine sauce, and grilled salmon
with savoury herb butter.

Pier at Craigmore
BISTRO ££

(Mount Stuart Rd; mains £7-13; ☉lunch daily, dinner Sat) Housed in the former waiting room
of a Victorian pier on the eastern edge of
town, the Craigmore is a neat little bistro
with fantastic views. The lunch menu offers sandwiches, salads, homemade burgers
and quiche, while Saturday dinner is more
sophisticated with seafood, steak and roast
lamb. No credit cards.

Musicker
CAFE £

(11 High St; mains £3-5; ☉breakfast & lunch) This
cool little cafe, tricked out in pale minty
green, serves the best coffee on the island,
alongside a range of sandwiches with
imaginative fillings (haggis and cranberry,
anyone?). It also sells music CDs (folk, world
and country) and sports an old-fashioned
jukebox.

AROUND ROTHESAY

Mount Stuart
HISTORIC BUILDING

(www.mountstuart.com; adult/child £8/4; ☉11am-
5pm May-Sep) The Stuart Earls of Bute are
direct descendants of Robert the Bruce, and
have lived on the island for 700 years. When
a large part of the family seat was destroyed
by fire in 1877, the third Marquess of Bute,

John Patrick Crichton-Stuart (1847–1900) –
one of the greatest architecture patrons of
his day, and the builder of Cardiff Castle and
Castell Coch in Wales – commissioned Sir
Robert Rowand Anderson to create a new
one. The result – Mount Stuart – became
the finest neo-Gothic palace in Scotland,
and the first to have electric lighting, central
heating and a heated swimming pool.

The heart of the house is the stunning
Marble Hall, a three-storey extravaganza
of Italian marble that soars 25m to a dark-
blue vault spangled with constellations of
golden stars. Twelve stained-glass windows
represent the seasons and the signs of the
zodiac, with crystal stars casting rainbow-
hued highlights across the marble when the
sun is shining.

The design and decoration reflect the
third Marquess' fascination with astrology,
mythology and religion, a theme carried
over into the grand **Marble Staircase** beyond (where wall panels depict the six days
of the Creation), and the lavishly decorated
Horoscope Bedroom. Here the central
ceiling panel records the positions of the
stars and planets at the time of the Marquess' birth on 12 September 1847.

Yet another highlight is the **Marble
Chapel**, built entirely out of dazzling white
Carrara marble. It has a dome lit to spectacular effect by a ring of ruby-red stained-
glass windows – at noon on midsummer's
day a shaft of blood-red sunlight shines directly onto the altar. It was here that Stella
McCartney – daughter of ex-Beatle Sir Paul,
and friend of the present Marquess, former
racing driver Johnny Dumfries – was married in 2003.

Mount Stuart is 5 miles south of Rothesay. Bus 90 runs from the bus stop outside
the ferry terminal at Rothesay to Mount
Stuart (15 minutes, hourly May to September). You can buy a special Mount Stuart
day-trip ticket (adult/child £16/8) that includes return ferry and bus travel from Wemyss Bay ferry terminal to Mount Stuart, as
well as admission.

REST OF THE ISLAND
In the southern part of the island you'll
find the haunting 12th-century ruin of St
Blane's Chapel, set in a beautiful wooded
grove, and a sandy beach at Kilchattan Bay.

There are more good beaches on the west
coast. Scalpsie Bay is a 400m walk across
a field from the parking area, and has a
fantastic outlook to the peaks of Arran. You

THE MAIDS OF BUTE

One of the best walks on Bute is from the ferry pier at Rhubodach to the northern tip of the island (1.5 miles), where you can watch yachts negotiate the rocky narrows at the Burnt Islands. Just around the point are the Maids of Bute, two rocks painted to look like old women. The story goes that the distinctively shaped (but then unpainted) rocks were first noticed by the skipper of a pleasure steamer in the early 20th century, who always pointed them out to the passengers on his boat. Frustrated that the tourists could never see the resemblance, he sent a deckhand ashore with a couple of tins of paint to give them some clothes and recognisable faces. No one is quite sure who now maintains the maids, but every time the paint begins to peel, it's not long before a fresh coat brightens them up.

can often spot seals basking at low tide off Ardscalpsie Point, to the west.

Ettrick Bay is bigger, easier to reach, and has a tearoom (not the most attractive building on the island), but it's not as pretty as Scalpsie.

There are lots of easy walks on Bute, including the **West Island Way**, a waymarked, 30-mile walking route from Kilchattan Bay to Port Bannatyne; map and details are available from the Isle of Bute Discovery Centre (p268).

Cycling on Bute is excellent – the roads are well surfaced and fairly quiet. You can hire a bike from the **Bike Shed** (www.thebikeshed.org.uk; 23-25 East Princes St, Rothesay) for £10/15 per half-/full day.

Kingarth Trekking Centre (www.kingarthtrekkingcentre.co.uk; Kilchattan Bay) offers paddock rides for kids (£5; minimum age eight years), riding lessons (£20 per hour), and pony treks (£35 for two hours).

ⓘ Getting There & Away

BOAT CalMac (www.calmac.co.uk) ferries travel between Wemyss Bay and Rothesay (passenger/car £4.25/16.85, 35 minutes, hourly). Another CalMac ferry crosses the short stretch of water between Rhubodach in the north of the island and Colintraive (passenger/car £1.35/8.50, five minutes, every 15 to 20 minutes) in Cowal.

BUS West Coast Motors (www.westcoastmotors.co.uk) buses run four or five times a week from Rothesay to Tighnabruaich and Dunoon via the ferry at Colintraive. On Monday and Thursday a bus goes from Rothesay to Portavadie (via the Rhubodach–Colintraive ferry), where there's a ferry to Tarbert in Kintyre (passenger/car £3.60/16.25, 25 minutes, hourly).

Inveraray

POP 700

You can spot Inveraray long before you get here – its neat, whitewashed buildings stand out from a distance on the shores of Loch Fyne. It's a planned town, built by the Duke of Argyll in Georgian style when he revamped his nearby castle in the 18th century. The **tourist office** (☏0845 225 5121; Front St; ◷9am-6pm Jul & Aug, 10am-5pm Mon-Sat Apr-Jun, Sep & Oct, 10am-3pm Mon-Sat Nov-Mar; @) is on the seafront.

◉ Sights

Inveraray Castle   CASTLE
(www.inveraray-castle.com; adult/child £9/6.10; ◷10am-5.45pm Apr-Oct) Inveraray Castle has been the seat of the Dukes of Argyll – chiefs of Clan Campbell – since the 15th century. The 18th-century building, with its fairytale turrets and fake battlements, houses an impressive armoury hall, its walls patterned with a collection of more than 1000 pole arms, dirks, muskets and Lochaber axes. The castle is 500m north of town, entered from the A819 Dalmally road.

Inveraray Jail   MUSEUM
(www.inverarayjail.co.uk; Church Sq; adult/child £8.25/5.50; ◷9.30am-6pm Apr-Oct, 10am-5pm Nov-Mar) Inveraray Jail is an award-winning, interactive tourist attraction where you can sit in on a trial, try out a cell, and discover the harsh torture meted out to unfortunate prisoners. The attention to detail – including a life-sized model of an inmate squatting on a 19th-century toilet – more than makes up for the sometimes tedious commentary.

Inveraray Maritime Museum   MUSEUM
(www.inverarraypier.com; The Pier; adult/child £5/2.50; ◷10am-4pm) The *Arctic Penguin*, a three-masted schooner built in 1911 and one of the world's last surviving iron sailing ships, is permanently moored in Inveraray harbour and houses the Inveraray Maritime Museum. It has interesting photos and models of the old Clyde steamers and puffers, and a display about Para Handy, the fic-

tional sea captain created by local novelist Neil Munro (and celebrated in two successful TV series in the 1960s and 1990s). Kids will love exploring below the decks – there's a special play area in the bowels of the ship.

🛏 Sleeping & Eating

TOP CHOICE **George Hotel** HOTEL ££
(☎01499-302111; www.thegeorgehotel. co.uk; Main St E; s/d from £35/70; 🅿) The George Hotel boasts a magnificent choice of opulent rooms, complete with four-poster beds, period furniture, Victorian roll-top baths and private Jacuzzis (superior rooms cost £130 to £165 per double). The cosy wood-panelled bar, with its rough stone walls, flagstone floor and peat fires, is a delightful place for a bar meal (mains £7 to £10, open for lunch and dinner).

Claonairigh House B&B ££
(☎01499-302160; www.claonairighhouse.co.uk; Bridge of Douglas; s/d from £45/90; 🅿@🛜) This grand 18th-century house, built for the Duke of Argyll in 1745, is set in three hectares of grounds on the bank of a river (salmon-fishing available). There are three homely en suite rooms, one with a four-poster bed, and a resident menagerie of dogs, ducks, chickens and goats. It's 4 miles south of town on the A83.

Inveraray Youth Hostel HOSTEL £
(SYHA; ☎01499-302454; www.syha.org.uk; Dalmally Rd; dm £16; 🕑Apr-Oct; @) To get to this hostel, housed in a comfortable, modern bungalow, go through the arched entrance on the seafront – it's set back on the left of the road about 100m further on.

🍽 **Loch Fyne Oyster Bar** RESTAURANT ££
(www.lochfyne.com; Clachan, Cairndow; mains £10-22; 🕑breakfast, lunch & dinner) Six miles northeast of Inveraray in Cairndow, this rustic-themed restaurant serves excellent seafood, though the service can be a bit hit-and-miss. It's housed in a converted byre, and the menu includes locally farmed oysters, mussels and salmon. The neighbouring shop sells packaged seafood and other deli goods to take away, as well as bottled beer from the nearby Fyne Ales microbrewery.

ℹ Getting There & Away

Scottish Citylink (www.citylink.co.uk) buses run from Glasgow to Inveraray (£10, 1¾ hours, six daily Monday to Saturday, two Sunday). Three of these buses continue to Lochgilphead

and Campbeltown (£11, 2½ hours); the others continue to Oban (£9, 1¼ hours).

Crinan Canal

Completed in 1801, the picturesque Crinan Canal runs for 9 miles from Ardrishaig to Crinan allowing seagoing vessels – mostly yachts, these days – to take a short cut from the Firth of Clyde and Loch Fyne to the west coast of Scotland, avoiding the long and sometimes dangerous passage around the Mull of Kintyre. You can easily **walk** or **cycle** the full length of the canal towpath in an afternoon.

The canal basin at Crinan is the focus for the annual **Crinan Classic Boat Festival** (www.crinanclassic.com), held over the first weekend in July, when traditional wooden yachts, motor boats and dinghies gather for a few days of racing, drinking and music.

The basin is overlooked by the **Crinan Hotel** (☎01546-830261; www.crinanhotel.com; Crinan; s/d from £145/260 incl dinner; 🅿), which boasts one of the west coast's most spectacular sunset views and one of Scotland's top seafood restaurants. You're paying for that view, and for the olde-worlde atmosphere – don't expect five-star luxury. You can also eat in the hotel's **Crinan Bar** (mains £9-12; 🕑lunch & dinner) – the menu includes excellent local mussels with lemon, thyme and garlic.

The **coffee shop** (🕑10am-5:30pm) on the western side of the canal basin at Crinan has great home-baked cakes and scones.

If you want to walk along the canal and take the bus back, bus 425 from Lochgilphead to Tayvallich stops at Cairnbaan, Bellanoch and Crinan Cottages (20 minutes, three or four daily Monday to Saturday).

Kilmartin Glen

In the 6th century, Irish settlers arrived in this part of Argyll and founded the kingdom of Dalriada, which eventually united with the Picts in 843 to create the first Scottish kingdom. Their capital was the hill fort of Dunadd, on the plain to the south of Kilmartin Glen.

This magical glen is the focus of one of the biggest concentrations of prehistoric sites in Scotland. Burial cairns, standing stones, stone circles, hill forts and cup-and-ring-marked rocks litter the countryside. Within a 6-mile radius of Kilmartin village

RETURN OF THE BEAVER

Beavers have been extinct in Britain since the 16th century. But in 2009 they returned to Scotland, when a population of Norwegian beavers was released into the hill lochs of Knapdale in Argyllshire. In 2010 the beavers had their first offspring. The five-year **Scottish Beaver Trial** (www.scottishbeavers.org.uk) hopes to reveal whether the animals have a positive effect on habitat and biodiversity. If so, they could be introduced to other parts of the country.

Meanwhile, you can try and get a glimpse of them on the **Beaver Detective Trail**. It starts from the Loch Coille-Bharr forestry car park on the B8025 road to Tayvallich, about 1.5 miles south of the Crinan Canal.

there are 25 sites with standing stones and over 100 rock carvings.

◉ Sights

Your first stop should be **Kilmartin House Museum** (www.kilmartin.org; Kilmartin; adult/child £5/2; ☺10am-5.30pm Mar-Oct, 11am-4pm Nov-23 Dec), in Kilmartin village, a fascinating interpretive centre that provides a context for the ancient monuments you can go on to explore, alongside displays of artefacts recovered from various sites. The project was partly funded by midges – the curator exposed his body in Temple Wood on a warm summer's evening and was sponsored per midge bite!

The oldest monuments at Kilmartin date from 5000 years ago and comprise a linear cemetery of **burial cairns** that runs south from Kilmartin village for 1.5 miles. There are also ritual monuments (two stone circles) at **Temple Wood**, three-quarters of a mile southwest of Kilmartin. The museum bookshop sells maps and guides.

Kilmartin Churchyard contains some 10th-century Celtic crosses and lots of medieval grave slabs with carved effigies of knights. Some researchers have surmised that these were the tombs of Knights Templar who fled persecution in France in the 14th century.

The hill fort of **Dunadd**, 3.5 miles south of Kilmartin village, was the seat of power of the first kings of Dalriada, and may have

been where the Stone of Destiny (p51) was originally located. The faint rock carvings of a wild boar and two footprints with an Ogham inscription may have been used in some kind of inauguration ceremony. The prominent little hill rises straight out of the boggy plain of the **Moine Mhor Nature Reserve**. A slippery path leads to the summit where you can gaze out on much the same view that the kings of Dalriada enjoyed 1300 years ago.

🛏 Sleeping & Eating

Burndale B&B   B&B ££
(☎01546-510235; www.burndale.net; s/d from £35/54; P🐕) Set in a lovely Victorian manse (minister's house), this homely and hospitable B&B is just a short walk north from the Kilmartin House Museum. Expect a warm welcome and Loch Fyne kippers for breakfast. Credit cards not accepted.

Kilmartin Hotel   INN ££
(☎01546-510250; www.kilmartin-hotel.com; s/d £40/65; P) Though the rooms here are a bit on the small side, this attractively old-fashioned hotel is full of atmosphere. There's a restaurant here too, and a whisky bar with real ale on tap where you can enjoy live folk music at weekends.

TOP CHOICE | **Glebe Cairn Café**   CAFE £
(Kilmartin House Museum; mains £5-8; ☺breakfast & lunch, dinner Thu-Sat Jun-Aug) The cafe in the Kilmartin House Museum has a lovely conservatory with a view across fields to a prehistoric cairn. Dishes include homemade Cullen Skink, a Celtic cheese platter and hummus with sweet-and-sour beetroot relish. The drinks menu ranges from espresso to elderflower wine by way of Fraoch heather-scented ale.

❶ Getting There & Away

Bus 423 between Oban and Ardrishaig (four daily Monday to Friday, two on Saturday) stops at Kilmartin (£4.50, one hour 20 minutes).

You can walk or cycle along the Crinan Canal from Ardrishaig, then turn north at Bellanoch on the minor B8025 road to reach Kilmartin (12 miles one way).

Kintyre

The Kintyre peninsula – 40 miles long and 8 miles wide – is almost an island, with only a narrow isthmus at Tarbert connecting it to the wooded hills of Knapdale. During the Norse occupation of the Western Isles, the Scottish king decreed that the Vikings could claim as their own any island they could circumnavigate in a longship. So in 1098 the wily Magnus Barefoot stood at the helm while his men dragged their boat across this neck of land, thus validating his claim to Kintyre.

TARBERT
POP 1500

The attractive fishing village and yachting centre of Tarbert is the gateway to Kintyre, and well worth a stopover for lunch or dinner. There's a **tourist office** (☑01880-820429; Harbour St; ⊙9am-5pm Mon-Sat Apr-Oct) here.

◉ Sights & Activities

The picturesque harbour is overlooked by the crumbling, ivy-covered ruins of **Tarbert Castle**, built by Robert the Bruce in the 14th century. You can hike up to it via a signposted footpath beside the **Loch Fyne Gallery** (www.lochfynegallery.com; Harbour St; ⊙10am-5pm), which showcases the work of local artists.

Tarbert is the starting point for the 103-mile **Kintyre Way** (www.kintyreway.com), a walking route that runs the length of the peninsula to Southend at the southern tip. The first section, from Tarbert to Skipness (9 miles), makes a pleasant day-hike, climbing through forestry plantations to a high moorland plateau where you can soak up superb views to the Isle of Arran.

Highland Horse Riding (www.highlandhorseriding.com; An Tairbeart; per person per hr £25-30; ⊙Apr-Oct), on the western edge of the village, offers sightseeing and wildlife-spotting pony treks into the hills of Knapdale.

✵ Festivals & Events

Scottish Series Yacht Races   SAILING
(www.scottishseries.com) Held over five days around the last weekend in May. The harbour is crammed with hundreds of visiting yachts.

Tarbert Seafood Festival   FOOD & DRINK
(www.seafood-festival.co.uk) First weekend in July; food stalls, cooking demonstrations, music, family entertainment.

Tarbert Music Festival   MUSIC
(www.tarbertmusicfestival.com) On the third weekend in September: live folk, blues, beer, jazz, rock, *ceilidhs* (evening of traditional Scottish entertainment), more beer...

⌑ Sleeping & Eating

There are plenty of B&Bs and hotels here, but be sure to book ahead during festivals and major events.

Springside B&B   B&B ££
(☑01880-820413; www.scotland-info.co.uk/springside; Pier Rd; s/d £35/60; ℗) You can sit out the front of this attractive fisherman's cottage, which overlooks the entrance to the harbour, and watch the yachts and fishing boats come and go. There are four comfy rooms, three with en suite, and the house is just five minutes' walk from the village centre in one direction, and a short stroll from the Portavadie ferry in the other.

⌸ **Corner House Bistro**   SEAFOOD £££
TOP CHOICE (☑01880-820263; Harbour St; mains £14-26; ⊙lunch & dinner) It's worth making the trip to Tarbert just to eat at this relaxed and romantic restaurant, with its log fires, candlelight and award-winning French chef who knows exactly what to do with top-quality local seafood. The entrance is on the side street around the corner from the Corner House pub – look for the green awning. Best to book a table.

❶ Getting There & Away

BOAT CalMac (www.calmac.co.uk) operates a car ferry from Tarbert to Portavadie on the Cowal peninsula (passenger/car £3.60/16.25, 25 minutes, hourly).

Ferries to the islands of Islay and Colonsay depart from Kennacraig ferry terminal on West Loch Tarbert, 5 miles southwest of Tarbert.

BUS Tarbert is served by five **Scottish Citylink** (www.citylink.co.uk) coaches a day between Campbeltown and Glasgow (Glasgow to Tarbert £14, 3¼ hours; Tarbert to Campbeltown £7, 1¼ hours).

SKIPNESS
POP 100

The tiny village of Skipness is on the east coast of Kintyre, about 13 miles south of Tarbert, in a pleasant and quiet setting with great views of Arran. There's a post office and general store in the village.

Beyond the village rise the substantial remains of 13th-century **Skipness Castle** (admission free; ⊙24hr), a former possession of the Lords of the Isles. It's a striking building, composed of dark-green local stone trimmed with contrasting red-brown sandstone from Arran. The tower house was added in the 16th century and was occupied until the 19th century. From the top you can see the roofless, 13th-century **St Brendan's Chapel** down by the shore. The kirkyard contains some excellent carved grave slabs.

Skipness Seafood Cabin (sandwiches £3, mains £5-9; ⊙11am-6pm Sun-Fri late May-Sep), in the grounds of nearby Skipness House, serves tea, coffee and home baking, as well as local fish and shellfish dishes. In fine weather you can scoff the house special – crab sandwiches – at outdoor picnic tables with grand views of Arran.

Local bus 448 runs between Tarbert and Skipness (35 minutes, two daily Monday to Saturday).

At Claonaig, 2 miles southwest of Skipness, there's a daily car ferry to Lochranza on the Isle of Arran (passenger/car £5.20/23, 30 minutes, seven to nine daily).

ISLE OF GIGHA
POP 120

Gigha (*ghee*-ah; www.gigha.org.uk) is a low-lying island, 6 miles long by about a mile wide, that's famous for its sandy beaches and mild climate – subtropical plants thrive in the island's **Achamore Gardens** (www.gigha.org.uk/gardens; Achamore House; admission free, donation requested; ⊙9am-dusk).

Locally made **Gigha cheese** is sold in many parts of Argyll – there are several varieties produced on the island, including pasteurised goat's-milk cheese and oak-smoked cheddar.

The island's limited accommodation includes **Post Office House** (☎01583-505251; www.gighastores.co.uk; d £45; P), a Victorian house at the top of the hill above the ferry slip with two self-catering cottages (it houses the island post office and shop as well). There's also the **Gigha Hotel** (☎01583-505254; www.gigha.org.uk/accom; r per person £50), 100m south of the post office, which serves up bar meals, or if you're feeling peckish, four-course dinners. You can also eat at the **Boat House Café Bar** (☎01583-505123; www.boathouse-bar.com; mains £7-12; ⊙lunch & dinner) near the ferry slip.

There's a range of self-catering cottages available as well (see www.gigha.org.uk for details). Camping is allowed on a grassy area beside the Boat House near the ferry slip – there's no charge but space is limited, so call the Boat House in advance to check availability.

CalMac (www.calmac.co.uk) runs a ferry from Tayinloan in Kintyre to Gigha (passenger/car return £6.20/22.80, 20 minutes, hourly Monday to Saturday, six on Sunday). Bicycles travel free.

You can rent bikes from Post Office House for £12 per day.

CAMPBELTOWN
POP 6000

Campbeltown, with its ranks of gloomy, grey council houses, feels a bit like an Ayrshire mining town that's been placed incongruously on the shores of a beautiful Argyllshire harbour. It was once a thriving fishing port and whisky-making centre, but industrial decline and the closure of the former air-force base at nearby Machrihanish saw Campbeltown's fortunes decline.

The town feels a very long way from anywhere else, a feeling intensified by the continuing failure to reopen the ferry link from Campbeltown to Ballycastle in Northern Ireland (every year the message from the government is, 'Something will be done *next* year'). But renewal is in the air – the spruced-up seafront, with its flower beds, smart Victorian buildings and restored art-deco cinema, lends the town a distinctly optimistic air.

The **tourist office** (☎01586-552056; the Pier, Campbeltown; ⊙9am-5.30pm Mon-Sat) is beside the harbour.

⊙ Sights & Activities

There were once no fewer than 32 distilleries in the Campbeltown area, but most closed down in the 1920s. Today **Springbank Distillery** (www.springbankwhisky.com; tours £4; ⊙by arrangement 10am & 2pm Mon-Fri, 2pm only Oct-Apr) is one of only three that now operate in town. It is also one of the very few distilleries in Scotland that distils, matures and bottles all its whisky on the one site.

One of the most unusual sights in Argyll is in a **cave** on the southern side of the island of Davaar, at the mouth of Campbeltown Loch. On the wall of the cave is an eerie **painting of the Crucifixion** by local artist Archibald MacKinnon, dating from 1887. You can walk to the island at low tide across a shingle bar called the Dhorlinn (allow at least 1½ hours for the round trip), but make sure you're not caught by a rising tide – check tide times with the tourist office before you set off.

Mull of Kintyre Seatours (☎0870 720 0609; www.mull-of-kintyre.co.uk) operates two-hour, high-speed boat trips (adult/child from £30/20) out of Campbeltown harbour to look for wildlife: seals, porpoises, minke whales, golden eagles and peregrine falcons live in the turbulent tidal waters and on the spectacular sea cliffs of the Mull of Kintyre. Book in advance by phone or at the tourist office.

The **Mull of Kintyre Music Festival** (www.mokfest.com), held in Campbeltown in late August, is a popular event featuring traditional Scottish and Irish music.

ℹ Getting There & Away

AIR **Loganair/FlyBe** (www.loganair.co.uk) operates two flights daily, Monday to Friday, from Glasgow to Campbeltown (£50, 35 minutes).

BOAT From April to September, **Kintyre Express** (☐01294-270160; www.kintyre-express.com) operates a small, high-speed passenger ferry from Troon To Campbeltown (£50 one way, 1¼ hours, once daily Wednesday, Friday and Sunday). Tickets must be booked in advance.

BUS **Scottish Citylink** (www.citylink.co.uk) buses run from Campbeltown to Glasgow (£17, four hours, three daily) via Tarbert, Inveraray, Arrochar and Loch Lomond. It also runs to Oban (£15, four hours, three daily), changing buses at Inveraray.

MULL OF KINTYRE

A narrow winding road, about 18 miles long, leads south from Campbeltown to the **Mull of Kintyre**, passing some good **sandy beaches** near Southend. The name of this remote headland was immortalised in Paul McCartney's famous song – the former Beatle owns a farmhouse in the area. A **lighthouse** marks the spot closest to Northern Ireland, the coastline of which, only 12 miles away, is visible across the North Channel.

Isle of Islay

POP 3400

The most southerly island of the Inner Hebrides, Islay (*eye*-lah) is best known for its single-malt whiskies, which have a distinctive smoky flavour. There are eight working distilleries here, all of which welcome visitors and offer guided tours.

Islay's whisky industry contributes approximately £100 million a year to the government in excise duty and value-added tax (VAT); that's about £30,000 for every man, woman and child on the island. Little wonder that the islanders complain about the lack of government investment in the area.

With a list of over 250 recorded bird species, Islay also attracts birdwatchers. It's an important wintering ground for thousands of white-fronted and barnacle geese. As well as the whisky and wildfowl, there are miles of sandy beaches, pleasant walking trails, and good food and drink.

There's a campsite and bunkhouse at Kintra, near Port Ellen, and a campsite and youth hostel in Port Charlotte. If you want to camp elsewhere, ask permission first. Camping is prohibited on the Ardtalla and Dunlossit estates on the eastern side of Islay.

☞ Tours

Islay Birding   BIRDWATCHING
(www.islaybirding.co.uk) Birdwatching tours by bicycle (£30/60 per half-/full day). There are also 2½-hour wildlife walks (£30 per person) and family bushcraft courses (two adults plus children £60 per half-day) teaching outdoor-survival skills.

Islay Sea Safaris   CUSTOM TOURS
(www.islayseasafari.co.uk) Can arrange customised tours (£25 to £30 per person per hour) by sea from Port Ellen to visit some (or all) of Islay and Jura's distilleries in a single day. Also available are birdwatching trips, coastal explorations, and trips to Jura's remote west coast and the Corryvreckan Whirlpool.

Islay Stalking   WILDLIFE WATCHING
(www.thegearach.co.uk) Here's your chance to stalk deer and other wildlife in the company of a gamekeeper, and shoot them not with a gun but with a camera. Two-hour morning and evening photographic tours are £20/10 per adult/child.

✯ Festivals & Events

Fèis Ìle   SCOTTISH CULTURE
(Islay Festival; www.theislayfestival.co.uk) A week-long celebration of traditional Scottish music and whisky at the end of May. Events include *ceilidhs*, pipe-band performances, distillery tours, barbecues and whisky tastings.

Islay Jazz Festival   MUSIC
(www.islayjazzfestival.co.uk) This three-day festival takes place over the second weekend in September. A varied line-up of international talent plays at various venues across the island.

ℹ Information

Islay Service Point (Jamieson St, Bowmore; ⊙9am-12.30pm & 1.30-5pm Mon-Fri; @) Free internet access.

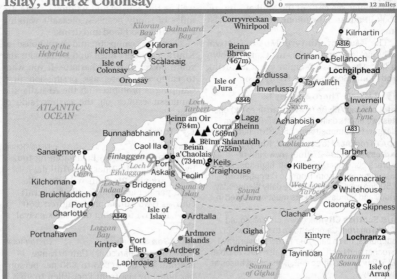

Islay tourist office (☎0870-720 0617; The Square, Bowmore; ⏰10am-5pm Mon-Sat, & 2-5pm Sun Apr-Aug, shorter hr Sep-Mar)

MacTaggart Community CyberCafé (www. islaycybercafe.co.uk; 30 Mansfield Pl, Port Ellen; ⏰9am-10pm Mon & Wed-Sat, to 5pm Tue & Sun; @⏰) Internet access.

MacTaggart Leisure Centre (School St, Bowmore; ⏰noon-9pm Mon-Fri, 10.30am-5.30pm Sat & Sun) Coin-operated laundrette.

ℹ Getting There & Away

There are two ferry terminals on the island, both served by ferries from Kennacraig in West Loch Tarbert – Port Askaig on the east coast, and Port Ellen in the south. Islay airport lies midway between Port Ellen and Bowmore.

AIR **Loganair/FlyBe** (www.loganair.co.uk) flies from Glasgow to Islay (£70 one way, 45 minutes, two or three flights daily Monday to Friday, one or two Saturday and Sunday).

Hebridean Air Services (☎0845 805 7465; www.hebrideanair.co.uk) operates flights (£65 one way, twice daily Tuesday and Thursday) from Connel Airfield (near Oban) to Colonsay (30 minutes) and Islay (40 minutes).

BOAT **CalMac** (www.calmac.co.uk) runs ferries from Kennacraig in West Loch Tarbert to Port Ellen (passenger/car £9.20/49, 2¼ hours, one to three daily) and Port Askaig (£9.20/49, two hours, one to three daily). On Wednesday only in

summer the ferry continues from Port Askaig to Colonsay (£4.85/24.70, 1¼ hours).

ℹ Getting Around

BICYCLE You can hire bikes from Bowmore Post Office (per day £10), and from the house opposite the Port Charlotte Hotel.

BUS A bus service links Ardbeg, Port Ellen, Bowmore, Port Charlotte, Portnahaven and Port Askaig (limited service on Sunday). Pick up a copy of the *Islay & Jura Public Transport Guide* from the tourist office.

CAR **D & N MacKenzie** (☎01496-302300; Port Ellen; from £30 a day) Hire cars.

TAXI Bowmore (☎01496-810449); Port Ellen (☎01496-302155).

PORT ELLEN & AROUND

Port Ellen is the main point of entry for Islay. It has a **Co-op Food** minimarket (⏰8am-8pm Mon-Sat, noon-7.30pm Sun), a pub and a bank (closed most afternoons and Wednesdays). There's an ATM in the Spar shop around the corner from the bank. While there's nothing to see in the town itself, the coast stretching northeast from Port Ellen is one of the loveliest parts of the island.

There are three whisky distilleries in close succession (check websites for tour times):

Laphroaig　　　　　　　DISTILLERY
(www.laphroaig.com; tours £3; ⊘9.30am-
5.30pm Mon-Fri, also 10am-4pm Sat & Sun
Mar-Dec)

Lagavulin　　　　　　　DISTILLERY
(www.discovering-distilleries.com; tours £6;
⊘9am-5pm Mon-Fri Apr-Oct, to 12.30pm Nov-Mar,
plus 9am-5pm Sat & 12.30-4pm Sun Jul & Aug)

Ardbeg　　　　　　　DISTILLERY
(www.ardbeg.com; tours £5; ⊘10am-5pm Jun-
Aug, 10am-4pm Mon-Fri Sep-May).

A pleasant **bike ride** leads past the distilleries to the atmospheric, age-haunted **Kildalton Chapel**, 8 miles northeast of Port
Ellen. In the kirkyard is the exceptional
late-8th-century **Kildalton Cross**, the only
remaining Celtic high cross in Scotland
(most surviving high crosses are in Ireland). There are carvings of biblical scenes
on one side and animals on the other.
There are also several extraordinary grave
slabs around the chapel, some carved with
swords and Celtic interlace patterns.

The kelp-fringed *skerries* (small rocky
islands or reefs) of the **Ardmore Islands**,
off the southeastern corner of Islay near
Kildalton, are a wildlife haven and home to
the second-largest colony of common seals
in Europe. For details of wildlife cruises see
the Tours section (p285).

🛏 Sleeping & Eating

TOP CHOICE **Kintra Farm**　　　CAMPSITE, B&B ££
(☎01496-302051; www.kintrafarm.co.uk;
Kintra; tent sites £4-10, plus per person £3, r per
person £30-38; ⊘Apr-Sep) At the southern
end of Laggan Bay, 3.5 miles northwest of
Port Ellen, Kintra offers three bedrooms
in a homely farmhouse B&B. There's also a
basic but beautiful campsite on buttercup-
sprinkled turf amid the dunes, with a sunset view across the beach.

Oystercatcher B&B　　　B&B ££
(☎01496-300409; www.islay-bedandbreakfast.
com; 63 Frederick Cres, Port Ellen; r per person
£32; @🕲) If you like your breakfasts fishy,
then this welcoming waterfront house is
the place for you – there's smoked haddock,
smoked salmon and kippers on the menu,
as well as the usual stuff. Bedrooms are
small but comfortable and nicely decorated.

TOP CHOICE **Old Kiln Café**　　　CAFE £
(Ardbeg; mains £4-10; ⊘breakfast & lunch
daily Jun-Aug, Mon-Fri only Sep-May) Housed in
the former malting kiln at Ardbeg Distill-

ery, this well-run cafe serves hearty homemade soups such as sweet-potato and chilli;
tasty light meals (try a panini sandwich
with haggis and apple chutney, or a platter of smoked Islay beef, venison and pastrami); and a range of home-baked desserts
including traditional clootie dumpling (a
rich steamed pudding filled with currants
and raisins) with ice cream.

BOWMORE

The attractive Georgian village of Bowmore was built in 1768 to replace the village
of Kilarrow, which just had to go – it was
spoiling the view from the laird's house.
Its centrepiece is the distinctive **Round
Church** at the top of Main St, built in circular form to ensure that the devil had no
corners to hide in.

Bowmore Distillery (www.bowmore.
co.uk; School St; tours adult/child £4/2; ⊘9am-
5pm Mon-Fri & 9am-noon Sat, also 9am-5pm Sat
Easter–mid-Sep & noon-4pm Sun Jul–mid-Sep)
is the only distillery on the island that still
malts its own barley. The tour (check website
for times), which begins with an overblown
10-minute marketing video, is redeemed by a
look at (and taste of) the germinating grain
laid out in golden billows on the floor of the
malting shed, and a free dram at the end.

Islay House Square, a collection of craft
shops and studios 3 miles northeast of Bowmore at Bridgend, is home to **Islay Ales**
(www.islayales.com; Bridgend; ⊘10.30am-5pm
Mon-Sat, plus noon-4pm Sun Jun-Aug), a microbrewery that produces a range of real ales,
all bottled by hand. After a complementary
tour of the premises, you can taste the ales
for free, and buy a bottle or two to drink
outdoors or back home (the brewery doesn't
have a bar licence). Our favourite is Saligo
Ale, a refreshing, summery pale ale.

🛏 Sleeping & Eating

Harbour Inn　　　RESTAURANT WITH ROOMS £££
(☎01496-810330; www.harbour-inn.com; The
Square; s/d from £95/130; @🕲) The plush
seven-room Harbour Inn, smartly decorated with a nautical theme, is the poshest
place in town. The **restaurant** (mains £16
to £24, open for lunch and dinner) has harbour views and serves fresh local oysters,
lobster and scallops, Islay lamb and Jura
venison.

Lambeth House　　　B&B ££
(☎01496-810597; lambethguesthouse@tiscali.
co.uk; Jamieson St; s/d £60/90; @🕭) A short

stroll from the harbour, the Lambeth is a simple, good-value guesthouse with comfy en suite bedrooms. Breakfasts are excellent, and it also offers a two-course evening meal for £12.

Lochside Hotel   HOTEL ££
(☎01496; 810244; www.lochsidehotel.co.uk; 19 Shore St; r per person from £50; �) The 10 en suite bedrooms at the Lochside are kitted-out with chunky pine furniture, including one room adapted for wheelchair users. The conservatory dining room provides sweeping views over Loch Indaal, plus the bar boasts a range of more than 250 single-malts, including many rare bottlings.

PORT CHARLOTTE
Eleven miles from Bowmore, on the opposite shore of Loch Indaal, is the attractive village of Port Charlotte. It has a general store (☺9am-12.30pm & 1.30-5.30pm Mon-Sat, 11.30am-1.30pm Sun) and post office.

Islay's long history is lovingly recorded in the Museum of Islay Life (www.islaymuseum.org; adult/child £3/1; ☺10am-5pm Mon-Sat, 2-5pm Sun Easter-Oct), housed in the former Free Church. Prize exhibits include an illicit still, 19th-century crofters' furniture, and a set of leather boots once worn by the horse that pulled the lawnmower at Islay House (so it wouldn't leave hoof prints on the lawn!). There are also touch-screen computers displaying archive photos of Islay in the 19th and early 20th centuries.

The Islay Natural History tourist office (www.islaynaturalhistory.org; adult/child £3/1.50; ☺10am-4pm Mon-Fri Apr-Oct, also Sat Jun-Aug), next to the youth hostel, has displays explaining the island's natural history, with advice on where to see wildlife and lots of interesting hands-on exhibits for kids.

The Bruichladdich Distillery (☎01496-850190; www.bruichladdich.com; tours £5; ☺9am-5pm Mon-Fri & 10am-4pm Sat), at the northern edge of the village, reopened in 2001 with all its original Victorian equipment restored to working condition. Independently owned and independently minded, Bruichladdich (brook-lah-day) produces an intriguing range of distinctive, very peaty whiskies. Call ahead to book a tour.

🛏 Sleeping & Eating
Port Charlotte Hotel   HOTEL £££
(☎01496-850360; www.portcharlottehotel.co.uk; Port Charlotte; s/d £95/160; P�) This lovely old Victorian hotel has stylish, in-

dividually decorated bedrooms with sea views, and a candlelit restaurant (mains £15 to £22, open for dinner) serving local seafood (seared scallops with braised leeks and truffle cream sauce), Islay beef, venison and duck. The bar (bar meals £7 to £10, open for lunch and dinner) is well stocked with Islay malts and real ales, and has a nook at the back with a view over the loch towards the Paps of Jura.

Debbie's Minimarket   CAFE £
(Bruichladdich; ☺9am-5.30pm Mon-Sat) The village shop and post office at Bruichladdich doubles as a deli that stocks good wine and posh picnic grub, and also serves the best coffee on Islay – sit at one of the outdoor tables and enjoy an espresso with a sea view.

Croft Kitchen   CAFE ££
(Port Charlotte; mains lunch £4-7, dinner £11-15; ☺lunch & dinner) This laid-back little bistro serves as a cafe during the day and transforms into a restaurant serving quality meals in the evening.

Port Mor Campsite   CAMPSITE £
(☎01496-850441; www.islandofislay.co.uk; Port Charlotte; tent sites per person £8; @�) The sports field to the south of the village doubles as a campsite – there are toilets, showers, laundry and a children's play area in the main building. Open all year.

Islay Youth Hostel   HOSTEL £
(SYHA; www.syha.org.uk; ☎01496-850385; Port Charlotte; dm £15; ☺Apr-Oct; @�) This modern and comfortable hostel is housed in a former distillery building with views over the loch.

PORTNAHAVEN
Six miles southwest of Port Charlotte the road ends at Portnahaven, another pretty village that was purpose-built as a fishing harbour in the 19th century. A mile north of the village is the pretty little shell-sand beach of Currie Sands, with a lovely view of Orsay island.

The next inlet to the north of the beach is occupied by the world's first commercially viable, wave-powered electricity generating station, built on cliffs that are open to the Atlantic swell. The 500kW plant – known as the Limpet (Land-installed, marine-powered energy transformer) – provides enough electricity to power 200 island homes.

LOCH GRUINART & AROUND

Seven miles north of Port Charlotte is **Loch Gruinart Nature Reserve**, where you can hear corncrakes in summer and see huge flocks of migrating ducks, geese and waders in spring and autumn; there's a hide with wheelchair access. The nearby **RSPB tourist office** (admission free; ☺10am-5pm Apr-Oct, to 4pm Nov-Mar) offers two- to three-hour guided walks around the reserve (£3 per person, 10am Thursday April to October).

Kilchoman Distillery (www.kilchomandis tillery.com; Rockfield Farm, Kilchoman; tours £4; ☺10am-5pm Mon-Fri, plus Sat Apr-Oct), 5 miles southwest of Loch Gruinart, is Islay's newest, going into production in 2005. The distillery grows its own barley on Islay, and the tourist office explores the history of farmhouse distilling on the island. Its first single-malt was released in 2010, and was so popular it sold out within days.

The **café** (mains £5-10; ☺lunch Mon-Fri Mar-Oct, plus Sat Apr-Sep, plus Sun Jul & Aug) at Kilchoman Distillery rustles up an excellent lunch – crusty brown rolls filled with hot-smoked salmon and dill mayo, and bowls of rich, smoky Cullen skink.

FINLAGGAN

Lush meadows swathed in buttercups and daisies slope down to reed-fringed Loch Finlaggan, the medieval capital of the Lords of the Isles. This bucolic setting, 3 miles southwest of Port Askaig, was once the most important settlement in the Hebrides, the central seat of power of the Lords of the Isles from the 12th to the 16th centuries. From the little island at the northern end of the loch the descendants of Somerled administered their island territories and entertained visiting chieftains in their great hall. Little remains now except the tumbled ruins of houses and a chapel, but the setting is beautiful and the history fascinating. A wooden walkway leads over the reeds and water lilies to the island, where information boards describe the remains.

Finlaggan tourist office (www.finlaggan. com; adult/child £3/1; ☺10.30am-4.30pm Mon-Sat & 1.30-4.30pm Sun Apr-Sep), in a nearby cottage (plus modern extension), explains the site's history and archaeology. The island itself is open at all times.

Buses from Port Askaig stop at the road's end, from where it's a 15-minute walk to the loch.

PORT ASKAIG & AROUND

Port Askaig is little more than a hotel, a shop (with ATM), a petrol pump and a ferry pier, set in a picturesque nook halfway along the Sound of Islay, the strait that separates the islands of Islay and Jura.

There are two distilleries within easy reach: **Caol Ila Distillery** (www.discovering -distilleries.com; tours £6; ☺9.15am-5pm Mon-Fri & 1.30-4.30pm Sat Apr-Oct, shorter hr in winter), pronounced 'cull *ee*-lah', a mile to the north, and **Bunnahabhain Distillery** (www.bunnaha bhain.com; tours £5; ☺9am-4.30pm Mon-Fri Mar-Oct, by appointment Nov-Feb), pronounced 'boo-na-*hah*-ven', 3 miles north of Port Askaig. Both enjoy wonderful locations with great views across to Jura.

The rooms at the **Port Askaig Hotel** (☏01496-840245; www.portaskaig.co.uk; s/d from £40/90; ℗), beside the ferry pier, seem pleasantly stuck in the 1970s, but the staff are warm and friendly, the breakfast is good and there's a great view of the Paps of Jura from the residents lounge. The beer garden is a popular spot to sit and watch the comings and goings at the quay.

Isle of Jura

POP 170

Jura lies off the coast of Argyll – long, dark and low like a vast Viking longship, its billowing sail the distinctive triple peaks of the Paps of Jura. A magnificently wild and lonely island, it's the perfect place to get away from it all – as George Orwell did in 1948. Orwell wrote his masterpiece *1984* while living at the remote farmhouse of Barnhill in the north of the island, describing it in a letter as 'a very un-get-at-able place'.

Jura takes its name from the Old Norse *dyr-a* (deer island) – an apt appellation, as the island supports a population of around 6000 red deer, outnumbering their human cohabitants by about 35 to one.

The community-run **Jura Service Point** (Craighouse; ☺10am-1pm Mon-Fri; @), 400m north of the Jura Hotel, provides tourist information and free internet access. **Jura Stores** (www.jurastores.co.uk; Craighouse; ☺9am-1pm & 2-5pm Mon-Fri, 9am-1pm & 2-4.30pm Sat) is the island's only shop. There's no bank or ATM, but you can get cash on a debit card at the Jura Hotel.

THE SCOTTISH MAELSTROM

It may look innocuous on the map, but the Gulf of Corryvreckan – the 1km-wide channel between the northern end of Jura and the island of Scarba – is home to one of the three most notorious tidal whirlpools in the world (the others are the Maelstrom in Norway's Lofoten Islands, and the Old Sow in Canada's New Brunswick).

The tide doesn't just rise and fall twice a day, it flows – dragged around the earth by the gravitational attraction of the moon. On the west coast of Scotland, the rising tide – known as the flood tide – flows northwards. As the flood moves up the Sound of Jura, to the east of the island, it is forced into a narrowing bottleneck jammed with islands and builds up to a greater height than the open sea to the west of Jura. As a result, millions of gallons of sea water pour westwards through the Gulf of Corryvreckan at speeds of up to 8 knots – an average sailing yacht is going fast at 6 knots.

The Corryvreckan Whirlpool forms where this mass of moving water hits an underwater pinnacle, which rises from the 200m-deep sea bed to within just 28m of the surface, and swirls over and around it. The turbulent waters create a magnificent spectacle, with white-capped breakers, standing waves, bulging boils and overfalls, and countless miniature maelstroms whirling around the main vortex.

Corryvreckan is at its most violent when a flooding spring tide, flowing west through the gulf, meets a westerly gale blowing in from the Atlantic. In these conditions, standing waves up to 5m high can form and dangerously rough seas extend more than 3 miles west of Corryvreckan, a phenomenon known as the Great Race.

You can see the whirlpool by making the long hike to the northern end of Jura (check tide times at Jura Hotel, and look under Activities, below, for walk details), or by taking a boat trip from Easdale (p289).

For more information, see www.whirlpool-scotland.co.uk.

◉ Sights

Apart from the superb wilderness walking and wildlife-watching, there's not a whole lot to do on the island except for visiting the Isle of Jura Distillery (www.isleofjura.com; admission free; ☺by appointment Mon-Fri) or wandering around the beautiful walled gardens of Jura House (www.jurahouseandgardens.co.uk; adult/child £2.50/free; ☺9am-5pm) at the southern end of the island. There's a lovely walk from the gardens down to a tiny white-sand beach where, if you're lucky, you might spot an otter. In summer a tea tent (☺11am-5pm Mon-Fri, to 4pm Sun Jun-Aug) sells hot drinks, home baking, crafts and plants.

There's also the Feolin Study Centre (www.theisleofjura.co.uk; admission free; ☺9am-5pm), just south of the ferry slip at Feolin, which has a small exhibition on Jura's history and provides information on all aspects of the island's history, culture and wildlife.

There are regular ceilidhs held throughout the year where visitors are made very welcome; check the notice board outside Jura Stores for announcements.

🏃 Activities

There are few proper footpaths on Jura, but any off-the-beaten-path exploration will involve rough-going through giant bracken, knee-deep bogs and thigh-high tussocks. Most of the island is occupied by deer-stalking estates, and access to the hills may be restricted during the stalking season (July to February); the Jura Hotel can provide details of areas to be avoided.

The only real trail is Evans' Walk, a stalkers' path that leads for 6 miles from the main road through a pass in the hills to a hunting lodge above the remote sandy beach at Glenbatrick Bay. The path leaves the road 4 miles north of Craighouse (just under a mile north of the bridge over the River Corran). The first 0.75 mile is hardgoing along an interwoven braid of faint, squelchy trails through lumpy bog; aim at or just left of the cairn on the near horizon. The path firms up and is easier to follow after you cross a stream. On the descent on the far side of the pass, look out for wild orchids and sundew, and keep an eye out for adders basking in the sun. Allow six hours for the 12-mile round trip.

Another good walk is to a viewpoint for the Corryvreckan Whirlpool (see boxed text, p280), the great tidal race between the northern end of Jura and the island of Scarba. From the northern end of the public road at Lealt you hike along a 4WD track past Barnhill to Kinuachdrachd Farm (6 miles). About 30m before the farm buildings a footpath forks left (there's an inconspicuous wooden signpost low down) and climbs up the hillside before traversing rough and boggy ground to a point 50m above the northern tip of the island. A rocky slab makes a natural grandstand for viewing the turbulent waters of the Gulf of Corryvreckan; if you have timed it right (check tide times at the Jura Hotel), you will see the whirlpool as a writhing mass of white water diagonally to your left and over by the Scarba shore. Allow five to six hours for the round trip (16 miles) from the road end.

Climbing the **Paps of Jura** is a truly tough hill-walk over ankle-breaking scree that requires good fitness and navigational skills (you'll need eight hours for the 11 long, hard and weary miles). A good place to start is by the bridge over the River Corran, 3 miles north of Craighouse. The first peak you reach is **Beinn a'Chaolais** (734m), the second is **Beinn an Oir** (784m) and the third is **Beinn Shiantaidh** (755m). Most people also climb **Corra Bheinn** (569m), before joining Evans' Walk to return to the road. If you succeed in bagging all four, you can reflect on the fact that the record for the annual Paps of Jura fell race is just three hours!

There are easier **short walks** (one or two hours) east along the coast from Jura House, and north along a 4WD track from Feolin. *Jura – A Guide for Walkers* by Gordon Wright (£2) is available from the tourist office in Bowmore, Islay (p276).

🛏 Sleeping & Eating

Places to stay on the island are very limited, so book ahead – don't rely on just turning up and hoping to find a bed. Most of Jura's accommodation is in self-catering cottages that are let by the week (see www.juradevelopment.co.uk).

You can camp for free in the field below the Jura Hotel (ask at the bar first, and pop a donation in the bottle); there are toilets and hot showers (£1 coin) in the block behind the hotel.

Sealladh Na Mara   B&B **££**
(☎01496-820349; www.isleofjura.net; Knockrome; per person from £25) A modern croft

house about 4 miles north of Craighouse, this place offers B&B in two cosy, IKEA-furnished bedrooms and a lovely guest lounge with a patio overlooking the sea. Evening meals can be provided, and there's also a self-catering two-bedroom chalet (from £200 a week).

Jura Hotel   HOTEL, PUB **££**
(☎01496-820243; www.jurahotel.co.uk; Craighouse; s/d from £50/84; ℗) The 18-room Jura is the most comfortable place to stay on the island; ask for a room at the front with a view of the bay. The hotel also serves decent bar meals (£7 to £12, open for lunch and dinner) and the bar itself is a very sociable place to spend the evening. Food is served from noon to 2pm and 6.30pm to 9pm.

🍴Antlers   BISTRO **££**
(☎01496-820123; www.theantlers.co.uk; Craighouse; mains £5-9, 2-/3-course dinner £25/29; ⏱10.30am-4.30pm daily, 6.30-9.30pm Tue-Sun; 🐾) This brand-new bistro makes the most of locally sourced produce, offering soup, sandwiches and burgers during the day, and an unexpectedly classy menu at dinner time, with dishes such as grilled goats cheese on black pudding with onion marmalade, glazed loin of pork with a cider reduction, and Cajun-style pan-fried venison.

ℹ Getting There & Away

A car ferry shuttles between Port Askaig on Islay and Feolin on Jura (passenger/car/bicycle £1.25/7.60/free, five minutes, hourly Monday to Saturday, every two hours Sunday). There is no direct car-ferry connection to the mainland.

From April to September **Jura Passenger Ferry** (☎07768-450000; www.jurapassengerferry.com) runs from Tayvallich on the mainland to Craighouse on Jura (£17.50, one hour, one or two daily except Wednesday). Booking recommended.

ℹ Getting Around

BICYCLE You can hire bikes from **Jura Bike Hire** (☎07092-180747; www.jurabikehire.com; Bramble Cottage, Keils; per day £12.50) a mile northeast of Craighouse.

BUS The island's only bus service runs between the ferry slip at Feolin and Craighouse (20 minutes), timed to coincide with ferry arrivals and departures. One or two of the runs continue north as far as Inverlussa.

TAXI **Mike Richardson** (☎07899-912116) operates a Landrover taxi service from the road's end at Lealt to Kinuachdrachd Farm for those wanting to shorten the hike to the Corryvreckan Whirlpool (minimum £20 per two people, plus £5 per extra person).

Isle of Colonsay

POP 100

Legend has it that when St Columba set out from Ireland in 563, his first landfall was Colonsay. But on climbing a hill he found he could still see the distant coast of his homeland, and pushed on further north to found his monastery in Iona, leaving behind only his name (Colonsay means 'Columba's Isle').

Colonsay is a connoisseur's island, a little jewel-box of varied delights, none exceptional but each exquisite – an ancient priory, a woodland garden, a golden beach – set amid a Highland landscape in miniature: rugged, rocky hills, cliffs and sandy strands, machair and birch woods, even a trout loch. Here, hill walkers bag **McPhies** – defined as 'eminences in excess of 300ft' (90m) – instead of Munros (see boxed text, p30). There are 22 in all; the supercompetitive will bag them all in one day.

The ferry pier is at Scalasaig, the main village, where you'll find a general store (☺9am-1pm & 2-5.30pm Mon & Wed-Fri, 9am-1pm Tue & Sat), post office, public telephone and free internet access at the Service Point (☺9.30am-12.30pm Mon-Fri;). There isn't a tourist office, bank or ATM on the island. General information is available at the CalMac waiting room beside the ferry pier, and at www.colonsay.org.uk.

The tiny Colonsay Bookshop (☎200232; Port Mor; ☺2-5pm Mon, Tue & Thu-Sat, 12.30-5pm Wed) at Kilchattan, on the west side of the island, has an excellent range of books on Hebridean history and culture.

☉ Sights & Activities

If the tides are right, don't miss the chance to walk across the half-mile of cockleshell-strewn sand that links Colonsay to the smaller island of Oronsay. Here you can explore the 14th-century ruins of Oronsay Priory, one of the best-preserved medieval priories in Scotland. There are two beautiful late-15th- century stone crosses in the kirkyard, but the highlight is the collection of superb 15th- and 16th-century carved grave slabs in the Prior's House; look for the ugly little devil trapped beneath the sword-tip of the knight on the right-hand side of the two horizontal slabs. The island is accessible on foot for about 1½ hours either side of low tide, and it's a 45-minute walk from the road-end on Colonsay to the priory. There are tide tables posted at the ferry terminal in Scalasaig.

The Woodland Garden (Colonsay House, Kiloran; admission free; ☺garden dawn-dusk, cafe breakfast & lunch Wed & Fri Easter-Sep) at Colonsay House, 1.5 miles north of Scalasaig, is tucked in an unexpected fold of the landscape and is famous for its outstanding collection of hybrid rhododendrons and unusual trees. The formal walled garden around the mansion has a terrace cafe.

There are good sandy beaches at several points around the coast, but Kiloran Bay in the northwest, a scimitar-shaped strand of dark golden sand, is outstanding. If there are too many people here for you, walk the 3 miles north to beautiful Balnahard Bay, accessible only on foot or by boat.

Back at Scalasaig, the Colonsay Brewery (www.colonsaybrewery.co.uk; ☺shop 10.30am-1pm & 2.30-5.30pm Wed, 4-7pm Fri & Sun, 10am-1pm Sat) offers you the chance to have a look at how it produces its hand-crafted ales – the Colonsay IPA is a grand pint.

Kevin & Christa Byrne (☎01951-200320; byrne@colonsay.org.uk) offer customised guided tours on foot (£25 per hour per tour for up to eight people), or by minibus (£50 per hour per tour for up to eight people). There's also a regular 'Hidden Colonsay' walking tour (adult/child £10/5) every Saturday in summer; booking essential.

🛏 Sleeping & Eating

Short-stay accommodation on Colonsay is limited and should be booked before coming to the island. Wild **camping** is allowed, as long as you abide by the provisions of the Scottish Outdoor Access Code (www.outdooraccess-scotland.com). See www.colonsay.org.uk for self-catering accommodation options.

TOP CHOICE **Colonsay Hotel** HOTEL ££ (☎01951-200316; www.colonsayestate.co.uk; Scalasaig; r £100-145; P🐾🛜) Completely refurbished in 2007, this wonderfully laid-back hotel is set in an atmospheric old inn dating from 1750, a short walk uphill from the ferry pier. The bar is a convivial melting pot of locals, guests, hikers, cyclists and visiting yachties, and the stylish **restaurant** (mains £11 to £18, open for lunch and dinner) offers down-to-earth cooking using local produce as much as possible, from Colonsay oysters and lobsters to herbs and salad leaves from Colonsay House gardens.

Backpackers Lodge
HOSTEL £

(☑01951-200312; www.colonsayestate.co.uk; Kiloran; dm £14-16, tw £36) Set in a former gamekeeper's house near Colonsay House, this lodge is about a 30-minute walk from the ferry terminal (you can arrange to be picked up at the pier). Advance bookings are essential. You can hire bikes here for £7 per day, and you can even use the tennis court at Colonsay House.

Island Lodges
SELF-CATERING ££

(☑01343-890752; www.colonsayislandlodges.co.uk; Scalasaig; chalets 2-night stay £150-250; ☎) These comfortable and modern self-catering holiday chalets, sleeping from two to five people, are just a 10-minute walk from the ferry pier at Scalasaig. You can check last-minute availability on the website.

Pantry
CAFE £

(Scalasaig; ⊙breakfast & lunch Mon-Sat, dinner Mon-Fri plus Sun Apr-Sep) This tearoom, close to the ferry pier, serves up light meals, snacks and ice creams. It also opens from October to March on the days that the ferry calls.

❶ Getting There & Around

AIR **Hebridean Air Services** (☑0845 805 7465; www.hebrideanair.co.uk) operates flights from Connel Airfield (near Oban) to Colonsay and Islay (£65 one way, twice daily Tuesday and Thursday).

BOAT From April to October, **CalMac** (www.calmac.co.uk) operates a car ferry from Oban to Colonsay (passenger/car £13/65, 2¼ hours, one daily except Saturday). From November to March the ferry runs on Monday, Wednesday and Friday only.

From April to October, on Wednesday only, the ferry from Kennacraig on the Kintyre peninsula to Islay's Port Askaig continues to Colonsay. A day-trip from Kennacraig or Port Askaig to Colonsay allows you six hours on the island; the day return fare from Port Askaig to Colonsay per passenger/car is £8.35/44.

BUS A 90-minute **minibus tour** (☑01951-200320; per person £10; ⊙11.30am Tue) of the island departs from the Colonsay Hotel; bookings essential. On Wednesdays, the minibus service is aimed at day-trippers, and makes two circuits of the island – you can be dropped off/picked-up at any point (per person £7.50). See www.colonsay.org.uk/walks.html for details.

Oban

POP 8120

Oban is a peaceful waterfront town on a delightful bay, with sweeping views to Kerrera and Mull. OK, that first bit about peaceful is true only in winter; in summer the town centre is a heaving mass of humanity, its streets jammed with traffic and crowded with holidaymakers, day-trippers and travellers headed for the islands. But the setting is still lovely.

There's not a huge amount to see in the town itself, but it's an appealingly busy place with some excellent restaurants and lively pubs, and it's the main gateway to the islands of Mull, Iona, Colonsay, Barra, Coll and Tiree.

◉ Sights

McCaig's Tower
HISTORIC BUILDING

(admission free; ⊙24hr) Crowning the hill above the town centre is the Victorian folly known as McCaig's Tower. Its construction was commissioned in 1890 by local worthy John Stuart McCaig, an art critic, philosophical essayist and banker, with the philanthropic intention of providing work for unemployed stonemasons. To reach it on foot, make the steep climb up **Jacob's Ladder** (a flight of stairs) from Argyll St and then follow the signs. The views over the bay are worth the effort.

Oban Distillery
DISTILLERY

(www.discovering-distilleries.com; Stafford St; tour £7; ⊙9.30am-5pm Mon-Sat Easter-Oct, plus noon-5pm Sun Jul-Sep, closed Sat & Sun Nov-Dec & Feb-Easter, closed Jan) This distillery has been producing Oban single-malt whisky since 1794. There are guided tours available (last tour begins one hour before closing time), but even without a tour, it's still worth a look at the small exhibition in the foyer.

FREE War & Peace Museum
MUSEUM

(www.obanmuseum.org.uk; Corran Esplanade; ⊙10am-6pm Mon-Sat & 10am-4pm Sun May-Sep, 10am-4pm daily Mar, Apr, Oct & Nov) Military buffs will enjoy the little War & Peace Museum, which chronicles Oban's role in WWII as a base for Catalina seaplanes and as a marshalling area for Atlantic convoys.

FREE Dunollie Castle
RUINS

(⊙24hr) A pleasant 1-mile stroll north along the coast road beyond Corran

SOUTHERN HIGHLANDS & ISLANDS OBAN & MULL

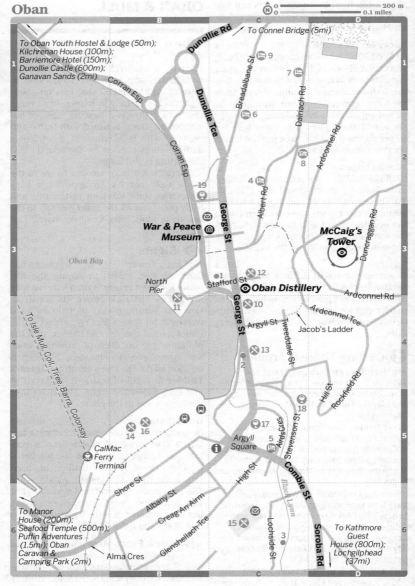

To Oban Youth Hostel & Lodge (50m);
Kilchrenan House (100m);
Barriemore Hotel (150m);
Dunollie Castle (600m);
Ganavan Sands (2mi)

To Connel Bridge (5mi)

Dunollie Rd

Dunollie Tce

Corran Esp

Corran Esp

Breadalbane St

Dalriach Rd

Ardconnel Rd

Albert Rd

George St

War & Peace Museum

Oban Bay

North Pier

McCaig's Tower

Duncraggan Rd

Stafford St

Oban Distillery

Ardconnel Rd

George St

Argyll St

Tweeddale St

Ardconnel Tce

Jacob's Ladder

To Isle Mull, Coll, Tiree, Barra, Colonsay

Hill St

Rockfield Rd

Stevenson St

Airds Cres

CalMac Ferry Terminal

Argyll Square

Shore St

High St

Combie St

Black Lynn

Albany St

Creag An Airm

Glenshellach Tce

Alma Cres

Lochside St

Soroba Rd

To Manor House (200m);
Seafood Temple (500m);
Puffin Adventures (1.5mi); Oban
Caravan &
Camping Park (2mi)

To Kathmore Guest House (800m);
Lochgilphead (37mi)

Esplanade leads to Dunollie Castle, built by the MacDougalls of Lorn in the 13th century and unsuccessfully besieged for a year during the 1715 Jacobite rebellion. It's always open but very much a ruin.

Pulpit Hill VIEWPOINT
An excellent viewpoint to the south of Oban Bay; the footpath to the summit starts to the right of Maridon House B&B on Dunuaran Rd.

Oban

◎ Top Sights

McCaig's Tower	D3
Oban Distillery	C3
War & Peace Museum	C3

Activities, Courses & Tours

1	Bowman's Tours	C3
2	Bowman's Tours	C4
3	Evo Bikes	C6

⊜ Sleeping

4	Heatherfield House	C2
5	Jeremy Inglis Hostel	C5
6	Oban Backpackers Lodge	C2
7	Old Manse Guest House	C1
8	Roseneath Guest House	C2
9	Sand Villa Guest House	C1

⊗ Eating

10	Cuan Mor	C4
11	Ee'usk	B4
12	Julie's Tearoom	C3
13	Kitchen Garden	C4
14	Shellfish Bar	B5
15	Tesco	C6
16	Waterfront Restaurant	B5

⊜ Drinking

17	Aulay's Bar	C5
18	Lorne Bar	C5
19	Oban Chocolate Company	B2

Ganavan Sands BEACH
Sandy, bucket-and-spade beach; 2.5 miles north of town along Corran Esplanade.

🏃 Activities

A tourist-office leaflet lists local bike rides, which include a 7-mile Gallanach circular tour, a 16-mile route to the Isle of Seil and routes to Connel, Glenlonan and Kilmore. You can hire mountain bikes from **Evo Bikes** (www.evobikes.co.uk; 29 Lochside St; ☺9am-5.30pm Mon-Sat), opposite Tesco supermarket, from £15 to £30 per day.

Based at North Connel, sea-kayaking coach **Rowland Woollven** (☑01631-710417; www.rwoollven.co.uk) offers instruction for beginners and guided tours (£100 for a full day for one person, £60 per person for two or three people) for more experienced paddlers in the waters around Oban.

If you fancy exploring the underwater world, **Puffin Adventures** (☑01631-566088; www.puffin.org.uk; Port Gallanach) offers a 1½-hour Try-a-Dive package (£87) for complete beginners.

Various operators offer **boat trips** to spot seals and other marine wildlife, departing from the North Pier slipway (adult/child £8/5.50); ask for details at the tourist office.

🖝 Tours

From April to October, **Bowman's Tours** (☑01631-563221/566809; www.bowmanstours .co.uk; 3 Stafford St & 1 Queens Park Pl) offers a Three Isles day-trip (adult/child £49/24.50, 10 hours, daily) from Oban that visits Mull, Iona and Staffa. Note that the crossing to Staffa is weather dependent.

Bowman's also runs a wildlife tour (adult/child £49/24.50) departing from Oban at 9.50am Sunday to Friday from May to July, and returning to Oban at 8pm. The trip takes in a ferry crossing to Craignure on Mull, travel by coach to Fionnphort, and a cruise around Staffa and the Treshnish Isles, plus two hours ashore on Lunga to visit a puffin colony.

🎊 Festivals & Events

West Highland Yachting Week SAILING
(www.whyw.co.uk) At the end of July/beginning of August, Oban becomes the focus of one of Scotland's biggest yachting events. Hundreds of yachts cram into the harbour and the town's bars are jammed with thirsty sailors.

Argyllshire Gathering HIGHLAND GAMES
(www.obangames.com; adult/child £8/4) Held over two days in late August, this is one of the most important events on the Scottish highland-games calendar and includes a prestigious pipe-band competition. The main games are held at Mossfield Park on the eastern edge of town.

🛏 Sleeping

Despite having lots of B&B accommodation, Oban's beds can still fill up quickly in July and August so try to book ahead. If you can't find a bed in Oban, consider staying at Connel, 4 miles to the north.

Barriemore Hotel B&B ££
(☑01631-566356; www.barriemore-hotel.co.uk; Corran Esplanade; s/d from £65/92; ℗) The Barriemore enjoys a grand location, overlooking the entrance to Oban Bay. There are 13 spacious rooms here (ask for one with a sea view), plus a guest lounge with

magazines and newspapers, and plump Loch Fyne kippers on the breakfast menu.

Heatherfield House
B&B ££

(☎01631-562681; www.heatherfieldhouse.co.uk; Albert Rd; s/d from £35/70; P@☎) The welcoming Heatherfield House occupies a converted 1870s rectory set in extensive grounds and has six spacious rooms. If possible, ask for room 1, complete with fireplace, sofa and a view over the garden to the harbour.

Kilchrenan House
B&B ££

(☎01631-562663; www.kilchrenanhouse.co.uk; Corran Esplanade; s/d £50/90; P) You'll get a warm welcome at the Kilchrenan, an elegant Victorian villa built for a textile magnate in 1883. Most of the rooms have views across Oban Bay, but rooms 5 and 9 are the best: room 5 has a huge freestanding bath tub, perfect for soaking weary bones.

Old Manse Guest House
B&B ££

(☎01631-564886; www.obanguesthouse.co.uk; Dalriach Rd; s/d from £62/74; P@☎) Set on a hillside above the town, the Old Manse commands great views over to Kerrera and Mull. The sunny, brightly decorated bedrooms have some nice touches (a couple of wine glasses and a corkscrew), and kids are made welcome with Balamory books, toys and DVDs.

Manor House
HOTEL £££

(☎01631-562087; www.manorhouseoban.com; Gallanach Rd; r £154-199; P) Built in 1780 for the Duke of Argyll as part of his Oban estates, the Manor House is now one of Oban's finest hotels. It has small but elegant rooms in Georgian style, a posh bar frequented by local and visiting yachties, and a fine restaurant serving Scottish and French cuisine. Children under 12 are not welcome.

Oban Backpackers Lodge
HOSTEL £

(☎01631-562107; www.obanbackpackers.com; Breadalbane St; dm £12.50-13.50; @☎) This is a friendly place with a good vibe and a large and attractive communal lounge with lots of sofas and armchairs. Breakfast is included in the price, there's free tea and coffee, a laundry service (£2.50) and powerful showers.

Oban Caravan & Camping Park
CAMPSITE £

(www.obancaravanpark.com; Gallanachmore Farm; tent & campervan sites £17; ☺Apr-Oct) This spacious campsite has a superb location overlooking the Sound of Kerrera, 2.5 miles south of Oban (bus twice a day). The quoted rate includes up to two people and a car; extra people are £2 each. A one-person tent with no car is £8. No prebooking – it's first-come, first-served.

Oban Youth Hostel & Lodge
HOSTEL £

(SYHA; ☎01631-562025; www.syha.org.uk; Corran Esplanade; dm £17, r per person £17-20; P@☎) Oban's SYHA hostel is set in a grand Victorian villa on the Esplanade, 0.75 miles north of the train station. The metal bunks are a bit creaky, but there are good showers and the lounge has great views across Oban Bay. The neighbouring lodge has three- and four-bedded rooms with en suite bathrooms.

Jeremy Inglis Hostel
HOSTEL £

(☎01631-565065; 21 Airds Cres; dm/s £15/22; ☎) This bargain place is more of an eccentric B&B than a hostel – most 'dorms' have only two or three beds, and are decorated with original artwork, books, flowers and cuddly toys. The kitchen is a little cramped, but the owner is friendly and knowledgeable (and makes delicious homemade jam). The price includes a continental breakfast.

Sand Villa Guest House
B&B ££

(☎01631-562803; www.holidayoban.co.uk; Breadalbane St; r per person £28-33; P☎) Ground floor room with wheelchair access. No credit cards.

Roseneath Guest House
B&B ££

(☎01631-562929; www.roseneathoban.com; Dalriach Rd; s/d from £40/60; P) Peaceful location with sea views.

Kathmore Guest House
B&B ££

(☎01631-562104; www.kathmore.co.uk; Soroba Rd; s £45-65, d £55-75; P) Good value, homely and welcoming.

✖ Eating

TOP CHOICE **Waterfront Restaurant**

SEAFOOD ££

(☎01631-563110; www.waterfrontoban.co.uk; Waterfront Centre, Railway Pier; mains £10-18; ☺lunch & dinner) Housed on the top floor of a converted seamen's mission, the Waterfront's stylish, unfussy decor – dusky pink and carmine with pine tables and local art on the walls – does little to distract from the superb seafood freshly landed at the quay just a few metres away. The menu ranges from crispy-battered haddock and chips to pan-fried scallops with lime, chilli and coriander pickle. There's an early evening menu (5.30pm to 6.45pm) offering two courses for £11.50, or soup followed by fish and chips for £9.75. Best to book for dinner.

TOP CHOICE | **Shellfish Bar** | SEAFOOD £
(Railway Pier; mains £2-7; ⊘breakfast & lunch) If you want to savour superb Scottish seafood without the expense of an up-market restaurant, head for Oban's famous seafood stall – it's the green shack on the quayside near the ferry terminal. Here you can buy fresh and cooked seafood to take away – excellent prawn sandwiches (£2.75), dressed crab (£4.75), and fresh oysters for only 65p each.

Seafood Temple | SEAFOOD £££
(☑01631-566000; Gallanach Rd; mains £15-25; ⊘dinner Thu-Sun) Locally sourced seafood is the god that's worshipped at this tiny temple – a former park pavilion with glorious views over the bay. Owned by a former fisherman who smokes his own salmon, what must be Oban's smallest restaurant serves up whole lobster cooked to order, scallops in garlic butter, plump langoustines, and the 'platter magnifique' (£60 for two persons), which offers a taste of everything. Booking essential.

Cuan Mor | BISTRO ££
(www.cuanmor.co.uk; 60 George St; mains £8-16; ⊘lunch & dinner) This always-busy bar and bistro sports a no-nonsense menu of old favourites – from haddock and chips to sausage and mash with onion gravy – spiced with a few more-sophisticated dishes such as scallops with black pudding, and a decent range of vegetarian dishes. And the sticky toffee pudding is not to be missed!

Ee'usk | SEAFOOD ££
(☑01631-565666; www.eeusk.com; North Pier; mains £12-20; ⊘lunch & dinner) Bright and modern Ee'usk (it's how you pronounce *iasg*, the Gaelic word for fish) occupies Oban's prime location on the North Pier. Floor-to-ceiling windows allow diners on two levels to enjoy views over the harbour to Kerrera and Mull, whilst sampling a seafood menu ranging from fragrant Thai fish cakes to langoustines with chilli and ginger. A little pricey, perhaps, but both food and location are first class.

Kitchen Garden | CAFE £
(www.kitchengardenoban.co.uk; 14 George St; mains £3-8; ⊘9am-5pm Mon-Sat, 10.30am-5pm Sun, 6-9pm Thu-Sat) Deli packed with

delicious picnic food. Also has a great little cafe above the shop – good coffee, scones, cakes, homemade soups and sandwiches.

Julie's Tearooms | CAFE £
(37 Stafford St; mains £4-10; ⊘breakfast & lunch Tue-Sat) Tea and scones, delicious Luca's ice-cream and homemade soup with crusty bread.

Tesco | SUPERMARKET
(Lochside St; ⊘8am-10pm Mon-Sat, 9am-6pm Sun) Self-caterers and campers can stock up here.

🍷 Drinking

Oban Chocolate Company | CAFE
(www.obanchocolate.co.uk; 34 Corran Esplanade; ⊘10am-5pm Mon-Sat, 12.30-4pm Sun Easter-Sep, shorter hr in winter, closed Jan) This shop that specialises in hand-crafted chocolates (you can watch them being made) also has a cafe serving excellent coffee and hot chocolate (try the chilli chocolate for a kick in the tastebuds), with big leather sofas in a window with a view of the bay.

Lorne Bar | PUB
(www.thelornebar.co.uk; Stevenson St; ☎) A traditional pub with a lovely old island bar, the Lorne serves Deuchars IPA and local Oban Brewery real ales, as well as above-average pub grub. Food is served from noon to 9pm, and there's a trad music session every Wednesday from 10pm.

Aulay's Bar | PUB
(8 Airds Cres) An authentic Scottish pub, Aulay's is cosy and low-ceilinged, its walls covered with old photographs of Oban ferries and other ships. It pulls in a mixed crowd of locals and visitors with its warm atmosphere and wide range of malt whiskies.

ℹ Information

Fancy That (112 George St; ⊘10am-5pm; @) Internet access.

Lorn & Islands District General Hospital (☑01631-567500; Glengallan Rd) Southern end of town.

Main post office (Lochside St; ⊘8am-6pm Mon-Sat, 10am-1pm Sun) Inside Tesco supermarket.

Tourist office (☑01631-563122; www.oban. org.uk; Argyll Sq; ⊘9am-7pm daily Jul & Aug, 9am-5.30pm Mon-Sat, 10am-5pm Sun May, Jun & Sep, 9am-5.30pm Mon-Sat Oct-Apr; @) Internet access available.

ⓘ Getting There & Away

The bus, train and ferry terminals are all grouped conveniently together next to the harbour on the southern edge of the bay.

BOAT **CalMac** (www.calmac.co.uk) ferries link Oban with the islands of Kerrera, Mull, Coll, Tiree, Lismore, Colonsay, Barra and Lochboisdale. See the relevant island entries for details of ferry services. Information and reservations for all CalMac ferry services are available at the ferry terminal on Oban's West Pier. Ferries to the Isle of Kerrera depart from a separate jetty, about 2 miles southwest of Oban town centre.

BUS **Scottish Citylink** (www.citylink.co.uk) buses run to Oban from Glasgow (£17, three hours, four daily) via Inveraray; and from Perth (£12, three hours, twice daily Friday to Monday) via Tyndrum and Killin.

West Coast Motors (www.westcoastmotors. co.uk) bus 423 runs from Oban to Lochgilphead (£5, 1¾ hours, four daily Monday to Friday, two on Saturday) via Kilmartin. Bus 918 goes to Fort William via Appin and Ballachulish (£9, 1½ hours, three daily Monday to Saturday).

TRAIN Oban is at the terminus of a scenic route that branches off the West Highland line at Crianlarich. There are up to three trains daily from Glasgow to Oban (£19, three hours).

The train isn't much use for travelling north from Oban – to reach Fort William requires a detour via Crianlarich (3¾ hours). Take the bus instead.

ⓘ Getting Around

BUS The main bus stop is outside the train station. **West Coast Motors** (www.westcoastmotors.co.uk) bus 417 runs from here to Ganavan Sands via Oban Youth Hostel (five minutes, two per hour Monday to Saturday). Bus 431 connects the train station with the Kerrera ferry and Oban Caravan & Camping Park (15 minutes, two or three daily Monday to Saturday from late May to September).

CAR **Hazelbank Motors** (☑01631-566476; www.obancarhire.co.uk; Lynn Rd; ◷8.30am-5.30pm Mon-Sat) hires out small cars per day/week from £40/225 including VAT, insurance and CDW (Collision Damage Waiver).

TAXI There's a taxi rank outside the train station. Otherwise, call **Oban Taxis** (☑01631-564666).

Around Oban

ISLE OF KERRERA
POP 40

Some of the best **walking** in the area is on Kerrera, which faces Oban across the bay. There's a 6-mile circuit of the island (allow three hours), which follows tracks or paths (use Ordnance Survey map 49) and offers the chance to spot wildlife such as Soay sheep, wild goats, otters, golden eagles, peregrine falcons, seals and porpoises. At Lower Gylen, at the southern end of the island, there's a **ruined castle**.

Kerrera Bunkhouse (☑01631-570223; www.kerrerabunkhouse.co.uk; Lower Gylen; dm £14) is a charming seven-bed bothy (hut or mountain shelter) in a converted 18th-century stable near Gylen Castle, a 2-mile walk south from the ferry (keep left at the fork just past the telephone box). Booking ahead is recommended. You can get snacks and light meals at the neighbouring Tea Garden (☑01631-570223; ◷lunch Wed-Sun Apr-Oct), which also has B&B (£20 per person).

There's a daily passenger ferry (www.kerrera-ferry.co.uk) to Kerrera from Gallanach, about 2 miles southwest of Oban town centre, along Gallanach Rd (adult/child return £5/2.50, bicycle free, 10 minutes). From Easter to October it runs half-hourly from 10.30am to 12.30pm and 2pm to 6pm daily, plus 8.45am Monday to Saturday. From November to Easter there are five or six crossings a day.

ISLE OF SEIL
POP 500

The small island of Seil, 10 miles southwest of Oban, is best known for its connection to the mainland – the so-called Bridge over the Atlantic, designed by Thomas Telford and opened in 1793. The graceful bridge has a single stone arch and spans the narrowest part of the tidal Clachan Sound.

On the west coast of the island is the pretty conservation village of Ellenbeich, with its whitewashed cottages. It was built to house workers at the local slate quarries, but the industry collapsed in 1881 when the sea broke into the main quarry pit – the flooded pit can still be seen. The Scottish Slate Islands Heritage Trust (www.slateislands.org.uk; Ellenbeich; admission free; ◷10.30am-1pm & 2-5pm Apr-Oct) displays fascinating old photographs illustrating life in the village in the 19th and early 20th centuries.

Coach tours flock to the Highland Arts Studio (www.highlandarts.co.uk; Ellenbeich; admission free; ◷9am-7pm Apr-Sep, to 5pm Oct-Mar), a crafts and gift shop and a shrine to the eccentric output of the late 'poet, artist and composer' C John Taylor. Please, try to keep a straight face.

Just offshore from Ellanbeich is the small island of Easdale, which has more old slate-workers' cottages and the interesting **Easdale Island Folk Museum** (www.easdale museum.org; Easdale; adult/child £2.25/50p; ☺11am-4.30pm Apr-Oct, to 5pm Jul & Aug). The museum has displays about the slate industry and life on the islands in the 18th and 19th centuries. Climb to the top of the island (a 38m peak!) for a great view of the surrounding area.

Anyone who fancies their hand at ducks and drakes should try to attend the **World Stone-Skimming Championships** (www. stoneskimming.com), held each year in Easdale on the last Sunday in September.

Boat Trips

From April to October **Sea.fari Adventures** (☎01852-300003; www.seafari.co.uk; Easdale Harbour) runs a series of exciting boat trips in high-speed rigid inflatable boats (RIBs) to the Corryvreckan Whirlpool (adult/child £35/27; call for the dates of 'Whirlpool Specials', when the tide is at its strongest), and the remote Garvellach Islands (£44/34). There are also three-hour whale-watching trips (£44/34), mostly in July and August, cruises to Iona and Staffa (£70/55), and a weekly day-trip to Colonsay (£44/34).

Sea Life Adventures (☎01631-571010; www.sealife-adventures.co.uk; Clachan Seil) offers similar trips, but is based on the eastern side of the island and has a bigger, more comfortable boat.

❶ Getting There & Around

West Coast Motors (www.westcoastmotors. co.uk) bus 418 runs four times a day, except Sunday, from Oban to Ellanbeich (45 minutes) and on to North Cuan (one hour) for the ferry to Luing.

Argyll & Bute Council (☎01631-562125) operates the daily passenger-only ferry service from Ellanbeich to Easdale island (£1.55 return, bicycles free, five minutes, every 30 minutes).

Isle of Mull

POP 2600

From the rugged ridges of Ben More and the black basalt crags of Burg to the blinding white sand, rose-pink granite and emerald waters that fringe the Ross, Mull can lay claim to some of the finest and most varied scenery in the Inner Hebrides. Add in two impressive castles, a narrow-gauge railway, the sacred island of Iona and easy access from Oban and you can see why it's

sometimes impossible to find a spare bed on the island.

Despite the number of visitors who flock to the island, it seems to be large enough to absorb them all; many stick to the well-worn routes from Craignure to Iona or Tobermory, returning to Oban in the evening. Besides, there are plenty of hidden corners where you can get away from the crowds.

The waters to the west of Mull provide some of the best whale-spotting opportunities in Scotland, with several operators offering whale-watching cruises (see the boxed texts, p295 and p294).

About two-thirds of Mull's population lives in and around Tobermory, the island's capital, in the north. Craignure, at the southeastern corner, has the main ferry terminal and is where most people arrive. Fionnphort is at the far-western end of the long Ross of Mull peninsula, and is where the ferry to Iona departs.

☞ Tours

See Bowman's Tours, p290 for details of day-trips from Oban to Mull, Staffa and Iona by ferry and bus.

Gordon Grant Marine   BOAT TOURS
(☎01681-700388; www.staffatours.com) Runs boat trips from Fionnphort to Staffa (adult/child £25/10, 2½ hours, daily April to October), and to Staffa and the Treshnish Isles (£45/20, five hours, Sunday to Friday May to July).

Mull Magic   WALKING TOURS
(☎01688-301213; www.mullmagic.com) Offers guided wildlife walking tours in the Mull countryside (£35 to £45 per person including packed lunch), as well as customised tours and four-day walking holidays.

✦✦ Festivals & Events

Mishnish Music Festival   MUSIC
(www.mishnish.co.uk) Last weekend of April; three days of foot-stomping traditional Scottish and Irish folk music at Tobermory's favourite pub.

Mendelssohn on Mull   MUSIC
(www.mullfest.org.uk) A week-long festival of classical music in early July.

Mull Highland Games   HIGHLAND GAMES
(www.mishnish.co.uk) Third Thursday in July; piping, highland dancing etc.

Mull & Iona Food Festival   FOOD & DRINK
(www.mict.co.uk) Five days of food- and drink-tastings in early September, with chef demonstrations, farm tours, produce

markets, restaurant visits and a host of other events.

Tour of Mull Rally
CAR RALLY

(www.2300club.org) Part of the Scottish Rally Championship, with around 150 cars involved. Public roads are closed for parts of the early-October weekend.

ℹ Information

MEDICAL Dunaros Hospital (☎01680-300392; Salen) Has a minor injuries unit; the nearest casualty department is in Oban.

MONEY Clydesdale Bank (Main St, Tobermory; ⊗9.15am-4.45pm Mon-Fri) The island's only bank and 24-hour ATM. You can get cash using a debit card from the post offices in Salen and Craignure, or get cash back with a purchase from Co-op food stores.

POST Post office (Main St, Tobermory; ⊗9am-1pm & 2-5.30pm Mon, Tue, Thu & Fri, 9am-1pm Wed & Sat) There are also post-office counters in Salen, Craignure and Fionnphort.

TOURIST INFORMATION Craignure tourist office (☎01680-812377; Craignure; ⊗8.30am-5pm Mon-Sat, 10.30am-5pm Sun)

Tobermory tourist office (☎01688-302182; The Pier, Tobermory; ⊗9am-6pm Mon-Sat & 10am-5pm Sun Jul & Aug, 9am-5pm Mon-Sat & 11am-5pm Sun May & Jun, shorter hrs rest of year)

ℹ Getting There & Away

There are frequent **CalMac** (www.calmac.co.uk) car ferries from Oban to Craignure (passenger/car £4.65/41.50, 40 minutes, every two hours). There's another car-ferry link from Lochaline to Fishnish, on the east coast of Mull (£2.80/12.55, 15 minutes, at least hourly).

A third CalMac car ferry links Tobermory to Kilchoan on the Ardnamurchan peninsula (£4.45/23, 35 minutes, seven daily Monday to Saturday). From June to August there are also five sailings on Sunday.

ℹ Getting Around

BICYCLE You can hire bikes for around £10 to £15 per day from the following places.

Brown's Hardware Shop (☎01688-302020; www.brownstobermory.co.uk; Main St, Tobermory)

On Yer Bike (☎01680-300501; Inverinate, Salen) Easter to October only. Also has an outlet by the ferry terminal at Craignure.

BUS Public transport on Mull is fairly limited.

Bowman's Tours (☎01680-812313; www.bowmanstours.co.uk) is the main operator, connecting the ferry ports and the island's main villages. Bus 495 goes from Craignure to Tobermory (£7 return, one hour, six daily Monday to Friday, four or five Saturday and Sunday), and bus 496 links Craignure to Fionnphort (£11 return, 1¼ hours, three or four daily Monday to Saturday, one Sunday). Bus 494 goes from Tobermory to Dervaig and Calgary (three daily Monday to Friday, two on Saturday).

CAR Almost all of Mull's road network consists of single-track roads. There are petrol stations at Craignure, Fionnphort, Salen and Tobermory.

TAXI Mull Taxi (☑07760 426351; www.mull taxi.co.uk) is based in Tobermory, and has a vehicle that is wheelchair accessible.

CRAIGNURE & AROUND

There's not much to see at Craignure other than the ferry terminal and the hotel, so turn left, walk 200m and hop onto the **Mull Railway** (www.mullrail.co.uk; Old Pier Station; adult/child return £5/3.50; ☺Apr-Oct), a miniature steam train that will take you 1.5 miles south to Torosay Castle.

Torosay Castle & Gardens (www.torosay. com; adult/child £7/4; ☺house 10.30am-5pm Apr-Oct, gardens 9am-sunset year-round) is a rambling Victorian mansion in the Scottish Baronial style, stuffed with antique furniture, family portraits and hunting trophies. You're left to wander at will: a sign advises, 'Take your time but not our spoons.'

Two miles beyond Torosay is **Duart Castle** (www.duartcastle.com; adult/child £5.30/2.65; ☺10.30am-5.30pm daily May–mid-Oct, 11am-4pm Sun-Thu Apr), a formidable fortress dominating the Sound of Mull. The seat of the Clan Maclean, this is one of the oldest inhabited castles in Scotland – the central keep was built in 1360. It was bought and restored in 1911 by Sir Fitzroy Maclean and has damp dungeons, vast halls and bathrooms equipped with ancient fittings. A bus to the castle meets the 9.50am, 11.55am and 2pm ferries from Oban to Craignure.

🛏 Sleeping

To **camp** within walking distance of the ferry, turn left and walk south for five minutes to **Shieling Holidays** (☑01680-812496; www.shielingholidays.co.uk; tent & 2 people £14, with car £16.50, dm £12.50; ☺late Mar-Oct), a well-equipped campsite with great views. Most of the permanent accommodation, including the hostel dorms and toilet block (dribbly showers), consists of 'cottage tents' made from heavy-duty tarpaulin, which gives the place a bit of a PVC-fetish feel.

Recommended B&Bs within 10 minutes' walk of the ferry include **Pennygate Lodge** (☑01680-812333; www.pennygatelodge.com; s/d from £50/70; 🅿🤙), next to the Shieling Holidays entrance, and **Dee-Emm B&B**

(☑01680-812440; www.dee-emm.co.uk; s/d from £50/60; 🅿), a half-mile south of Craignure on the road towards Fionnphort.

291

TOBERMORY
POP 750

Tobermory, the island's main town, is a picturesque little fishing port and yachting centre with brightly painted houses arranged around a sheltered harbour, with a grid-patterned 'upper town'. The village was the setting for the children's TV program *Balamory*, and while the series stopped filming in 2005 regular repeats mean that the town still swarms in summer with toddlers towing parents around looking for their favourite TV characters (frazzled parents can get a *Balamory* booklet from the tourist offices in Oban and Tobermory).

⊙ Sights & Activities

Places to go on a rainy day include **Mull Museum** (www.mullmuseum.org.uk; Main St; admission by donation; ☺10am-4pm Mon-Fri Easter-Oct), which records the history of the island. There are also interesting exhibits on crofting, and on the **Tobermory Galleon**, a ship from the Spanish Armada that sank in Tobermory Bay in 1588 and has been the object of treasure seekers ever since.

There's also **An Tobar Arts Centre** (www. antobar.co.uk; Argyll Tce; admission free; ☺10am-5pm Mon-Sat May-Sep, plus 1-4pm Sun Jul & Aug, 10am-4pm Tue-Sat Oct-Apr), an art gallery and exhibition space with a good vegetarian-friendly cafe; and the tiny **Tobermory Distillery** (www.tobermorymalt.com; tour £3; ☺10am-5pm Mon-Fri Easter-Oct), established in 1798.

The Hebridean Whale & Dolphin Trust's **Marine Discovery Centre** (www.whaledolph intrust.co.uk; 28 Main St; admission free; ☺10am-5pm Mon-Fri, 11am-4pm Sun Apr-Oct, 11am-5pm Mon-Fri Nov-Mar) has displays, videos and interactive exhibits on whale and dolphin biology and ecology, and is a great place for kids to learn about sea mammals. It also provides information about volunteering and reporting sightings of whales and dolphins.

Sea Life Surveys (☑01688-302916; www. sealifesurveys.com), based in the new harbour building beside the main car park, runs whale-watching boat trips out of Tobermory harbour; for more information see the boxed text, p295.

WALKING ON MULL

More information on the following walks can be obtained from the tourist offices in Oban, Craignure and Tobermory.

Ben More

The highest peak on the island, Ben More (966m) offers spectacular views of the surrounding islands when the weather is clear. A trail leads up the mountain from Loch na Keal, by the bridge on the B8035 over the Abhainn na h-Uamha (the river is 8 miles southwest of Salen – see Ordnance Survey (OS) 1:50,000 map sheet 49, grid reference 507368). Return the same way or continue down the narrow ridge to the eastern top, A'Chioch, then descend to the road via Gleann na Beinn Fhada. The glen can be rather wet and there's not much of a path. The round trip is 6.5 miles; allow five to six hours.

Carsaig Arches

One of the most adventurous walks on Mull is along the coast west of Carsaig Bay to the Carsaig Arches at Malcolm's Point. There's a good path below the cliffs most of the way from Carsaig, but it becomes a bit rough and exposed near the arches – the route climbs and then traverses a very steep slope above a vertical drop into the sea (not for the unfit or faint-hearted). You'll see spectacular rock formations on the way, culminating in the arches themselves. One, nicknamed the 'keyhole', is a freestanding rock stack; the other, the 'tunnel', is a huge natural arch. The western entrance is hung with curtains of columnar basalt – an impressive place. The round trip is 8 miles – allow three to four hours' walking time from Carsaig plus at least an hour at the arches.

Burg

At the tip of the remote Ardmeanach peninsula there is a remarkable 50-million-year-old fossil tree preserved in the basalt lava flows of the cliffs. A 4WD track leads from the car park at Tiroran to a house at Burg; the last 2.5 miles to the tree is on a very rough coastal path. About 500m before the tree, a metal ladder allows you to climb down to the foreshore, which is only accessible at low tide – check tide times at Tobermory tourist office before setting off. Allow six to seven hours for the strenuous 14-mile round trip.

🛏 Sleeping

Tobermory has dozens of B&Bs, but the place can still be booked solid in July and August, especially at weekends.

TOP CHOICE Highland Cottage Hotel
BOUTIQUE HOTEL ££££
(☑01688-302030; www.highlandcottage.co.uk; Breadalbane St; d £155-190; ☉mid-Mar–Oct; ℗☎) Antique furniture, four-poster beds, embroidered bedspreads and fresh flowers and candlelight lend this small hotel (only six rooms) an appealingly old-fashioned cottage atmosphere, but with all mod cons including cable TV, full-size baths and room service. There's also an excellent fine-dining restaurant here.

Sonas House
B&B ££
(☑01688-302304; www.sonashouse.co.uk; The Fairways, Erray Rd; s/d £80/125; ℗☎🏊) Here's a first – a B&B with a heated, indoor 10m swimming pool! Sonas is a large, modern house that offers luxury B&B in a beautiful setting with superb views over Tobermory Bay; ask for the 'Blue Poppy' bedroom, which has its own balcony.

Cuidhe Leathain
B&B ££
(☑01688-302504; www.cuidhe-leathain.co.uk; Salen Rd; r per person £35; ☎) A handsome 19th-century house in the upper town, Cuidhe Leathain (coo-lane), which means Maclean's Corner, exudes a cosily cluttered Victorian atmosphere. The breakfasts will set you up for the rest of the day, and the owners are a fount of knowledge about Mull and its wildlife.

2 Victoria St
B&B £
(☑01688-302263; 2 Victoria St; s/d £25/40; ☉Easter-Oct) Traditional, old-school B&B with simple, homely bedrooms (with shared bathroom) and a friendly and hospitable landlady.

Tobermory Campsite CAMPSITE £
(📞01688-302624; www.tobermorycamp
site.co.uk; Newdale, Dervaig Rd; tent sites per
adult/child £6/3; ⊘Mar-Oct; 🛉) A quiet,
family-friendly campsite a mile west of
town on the road to Dervaig.

Tobermory Youth Hostel HOSTEL £
(SYHA; 📞01688-302481; www.syha.org.uk; Main
St; dm £15; ⊘Mar-Oct; @) Great location in
a Victorian house right on the waterfront.
Bookings recommended.

✗ Eating & Drinking

Campers can stock up on provisions at the
Co-op supermarket (Main St; ⊘8am-8pm
Mon-Sat, 12.30-7pm Sun), and the **Tobermory
Bakery** (Main St; ⊘9am-5pm Mon-Sat), which
sells delicious, locally baked wholegrain
bread, cakes, biscuits and pastries, as well
as having a great deli counter.

TOP CHOICE **Café Fish** SEAFOOD ££
(📞01688-301253; www.thecafefish.com;
The Pier; mains £10-16; ⊘lunch & dinner) Seafood doesn't come much fresher than the
stuff served at this warm and welcoming
little restaurant overlooking Tobermory
harbour – as their motto says, 'The only
thing frozen here is the fisherman'! Langoustines and squat lobsters go straight
from boat to kitchen to join rich shellfish
bisque, fat scallops, seafood pie and catch-
of-the-day on the daily-changing menu.
Also has freshly baked bread, homemade
desserts and a range of Scottish cheeses on
offer.

Fish & Chip Van
(Main St; mains £4-7; ⊘12.30-9pm M
Dec) If it's a takeaway you're afte
tuck into some of Scotland's bes
fish and chips down on the water
where else will you find a chip
freshly cooked prawns and scallo

MacGochan's
(Ledaig; mains £9-15; ⊘lunch & dinn
pub beside the car park at the so
of the waterfront, MacGochan's
bar meals (haddock and chips
vegetable lasagne), and often I
barbecues on summer evening
more formal restaurant upstai
music in the bar on weekends.

Mishnish Hotel
(www.mishnish.co.uk; Main St; r
⊘lunch & dinner; 📶) 'The Mish'
hang-out for visiting yachties

place for a bar meal, or dinner at the more
formal restaurant upstairs. Wood-panelled
and flag-draped, this is a good old traditional pub where you can listen to live folk
music, toast your toes by the open fire, or
challenge the locals to a game of pool.

Tobermory Chocolate Factory CAFE £
(www.tobermorychocolate.co.uk; Main St; ⊘break-
fast & lunch) This tempting little shop not
only sells exquisite handmade chocolates,
but also has a cafe that serves excellent
espresso, cappuccino and hot chocolate.

☆ Entertainment

Mull Theatre THEATRE
(📞01688-302828; www.mulltheatre.com; Salen
Rd, Druimfin) One of Scotland's best-known
touring companies, putting on shows all
over Scotland. It is based at Druimfin,
about a mile south of Tobermory, which is
the venue for most of its Mull-based performances; check the website for details of the
latest shows.

NORTH MULL

The road from Tobermory west to Calgary
cuts inland, leaving most of the north coast
of Mull wild and inaccessible. Just outside
Tobermory a long, single-track road leads
north for 4 miles to majestic **Glengorm
Castle** (www.glengorm.com; Glengorm; admission free; ⊘10am-5pm Easter–mid-Oct) with
views across the sea to Ardnamurchan,
Rum and the Outer Hebrides. The castle
outbuildings house an art gallery featuring

Calgary: 2-p
P 🐾) This far
fantastic self-ca
ing from two to e
designed and fitted ou
ture and wood-burning s
(sleeps eight, £350 a week
includes a spectacular lounge/
with curved oak frames and lo
duced art work.

Bellachroy HOTEL, PUB
(📞01688-400314; www.bellachroyhotel.co.uk;
Dervaig; s/d from £65/90; P 🐾 🛉) The Bellachroy is an atmospheric 17th-century
droving inn with six plain but comfortable

THAR SHE BLOWS!

The North Atlantic Drift – a swirling tendril of the Gulf Stream – carries warm water into the cold, nutrient-rich seas off the Scottish coast, resulting in huge blooms of plankton. Small fish feed on the plankton, and bigger fish feed on the smaller fish... This huge seafood smorgasbord attracts large numbers of marine mammals, from harbour porpoises and dolphins to minke whales and even – though sightings are rare – humpback and sperm whales.

In contrast to Iceland and Norway, Scotland has cashed in on the abundance of minke whales off its coast by embracing whale-watching rather than whaling. There are now dozens of operators around the coast offering whale-watching boat trips lasting from a couple of hours to all day; some have whale-sighting success rates of 95% in summer.

While seals, porpoises and dolphins can be seen year-round, minke whales are migratory. The best time to see them is from June to August, with August being the peak month for sightings. The website of the **Hebridean Whale & Dolphin Trust** (www. whaledolphintrust.co.uk) has lots of information on the species you are likely to see, and how to identify them.

A booklet titled *Is It a Whale?* is available from tourist offices and bookshops, and provides tips on identifying the various species of marine mammal that you're likely to see.

Sleeping & Eating

Achnadrish House TOP CHOICE B&B ££
(☎01688-400388; www.achnadrish.co.uk; Dervaig Rd; d from £85; P@🖵) There aren't too many B&Bs where *pad Thai* noodles appear on the breakfast menu, but Achnadrish is one. The dish is a legacy of the owner's extensive Asian travels, as are many of the decorative touches in this wonderfully welcoming guest house. A three-course dinner (£30 per person) based on fresh local produce is also available, as is a dram of Tobermory single-malt (complementary) beside the open fireplace while Mike tells you all about the local wildlife (and his three friendly Labradors).

Calgary Farmhouse SELF-CATERING ££
(☎01688-400256; www.calgary.co.uk; person apt per 2 nights from £120; mhouse complex offers eight tering properties (sleep-ht people), beautifully with timber furni-oves. The Hayloft high season) lining room ally pro-

bedrooms. The bar is a focus for local social life and serves excellent meals (mains £9 to £15, plus kids' menu) based on fresh local produce: pork from a local Dervaig farm, lamb from Ulva, mutton from Iona, mussels from Inverlussa and Mull-landed seafood.

Glengorm Coffee Shop CAFE £
(www.glengorm.com; Glengorm Castle; mains £5-8; ⏱lunch) Set in a cottage courtyard in the grounds of Glengorm Castle, this cafe serves superb lunches (noon-4.30pm) – the menu changes daily, but includes sandwiches and salads (much of the salad veg is grown on the Glengorm estate), soups and specials such as curry-flavoured salmon fishcakes with mint and cucumber salad.

Calgary Farmhouse Tearoom CAFE £
(www.calgary.co.uk; Calgary; mains £5-8; ⏱lunch; P🖵) Just a few minutes' walk from the sandy beach at Calgary Bay, this tearoom serves soups, sandwiches, coffee and cake using fresh local produce as much as possible. There's also an art gallery and craft shop here. Open till 5.30pm in July and August.

Dervaig Hall Bunkhouse HOSTEL £
(☎01688-400491; www.dervaigbunkroomsmull. co.uk; Dervaig; dm/q £14/50; P) Basic but very comfortable bunkhouse accommodation in Dervaig's village hall, with self-ring kitchen and sitting room.

Calgary Bay CAMPSITE £

You can camp for free at the southern end of the beach at Calgary Bay – keep to the area south of the stream. There are no facilities other than the public toilets across the road; water comes from the stream.

CENTRAL MULL

The central part of the island, between the Craignure–Fionnphort road and the narrow isthmus between Salen and Gruline, contains the island's highest peak, Ben More (966m) and some of its wildest scenery (see the boxed text, p292).

The narrow B8035 road along the southern shore of Loch na Keal squeezes past some impressive cliffs before cutting south towards Loch Scridain. About a mile along the shore from Balmeanach, where the road climbs away from the coast, is **Mackinnon's Cave**, a deep and spooky fissure in the basalt cliffs that was once used as a refuge by Celtic monks. A big, flat rock inside, known as **Fingal's Table**, may have been their altar.

Balmeanach Park Caravan & Camping Site (☎01680-300342; per 2 people, tent & car £15; ☺Mar-Oct) is a peaceful camp-site a 10-minute walk from the Fishnish–Lochaline ferry, on the main road between Craignure and Tobermory (booking advised).

There's a very basic **campsite** (per person £3) at Killiechronan, half a mile north of Gruline (toilets and water are a five-minute walk away), and plenty of wild camping on the south shore of Loch na Keal below Ben More.

SOUTH MULL

The road from Craignure to Fionnphort climbs through some wild and desolate scenery before reaching the southwestern part of the island, which consists of a long peninsula called the **Ross of Mull**. The Ross has a spectacular south coast lined with black basalt cliffs that give way further west to white-sand beaches and pink granite crags. The cliffs are highest at Malcolm's Point, near the superb **Carsaig Arches** (see the boxed text, p295).

The little village of **Bunessan** has a hotel, tearoom, pub and some shops, and is home to the **Ross of Mull Historical Centre** (www.romhc.org.uk; admission £2; ☺10am-4pm Mon-Fri Apr-Oct), a cottage museum that

---

WATCHING WILDLIFE ON MULL

Mull's varied landscapes and habitats, from high mountains and wild moorland to wave-lashed sea cliffs, sandy beaches and seaweed-fringed skerries, offer the chance to spot some of Scotland's rarest and most dramatic wildlife, including eagles, otters, dolphins and whales.

Mull Wildlife Expeditions (☎01688-500121; www.torrbuan.com; Ulva Ferry) offers full-day Land Rover tours of the island with the chance of spotting red deer, golden eagles, peregrine falcons, white-tailed sea eagles, hen harriers, otters and perhaps dolphins and porpoises. The cost (adult/child £43/40) includes pick-up from your accommodation or from any of the ferry terminals, a picnic lunch and use of binoculars. The timing of this tour makes it possible as a day-trip from Oban, with pick-up and drop-off at the Craignure ferry.

Sea Life Surveys (☎01688-302916; www.sealifesurveys.com) runs whale-watching trips from Tobermory harbour to the waters north and west of Mull. An all-day whale-watch (£60 per person) gives up to seven hours at sea (not recommended for kids under 14), and has a 95% success rate for sightings. The four-hour family whale-watch is geared more towards children (£39/35 per adult/child).

Turus Mara (☎0800 085 8786; www.turusmara.com) runs boat trips from Ulva Ferry in central Mull to Staffa and the Treshnish Isles (adult/child £50/25, 6½ hours), with an hour ashore on Staffa and two hours on Lunga, where you can see seals, puffins, kittiwakes, razorbills and many other species of seabird.

Loch Frisa Sea Eagle Hide (☎01680-812556; www.forestry.gov.uk/mullseaeagles) runs escorted trips to a viewing hide on Loch Frisa where you can watch white-tailed sea eagles. Tours (£5/2 per adult/child) leave twice a day, Monday to Friday, from the Aros end of the Loch Frisa access trail (book in advance at the Craignure tourist office, p290).

houses displays on local history, geology, archaeology, genealogy and wildlife.

A minor road leads south from here to the beautiful white-sand bay of Uisken, with views of the Paps of Jura. You can camp beside the beach here (£1 per person; ask for permission at Uisken Croft), but there are no facilities.

At the western end of the Ross, 38 miles from Craignure, is Fionnphort (*finn*-a-fort) and the ferry to Iona. The coast here is a beautiful blend of pink granite rocks, white sandy beaches and vivid turquoise sea.

🛏 Sleeping & Eating

TOP CHOICE **Seaview** B&B ££
(☎01681-700235; www.iona-bed-br eakfast-mull.com; Fionnphort; s/d £55/75; P ☎) Barely a minute's walk from the Iona ferry, the Seaview has five beautifully decorated bedrooms and a breakfast conservatory with grand views across to Iona. The owner – a semiretired fisherman and his wife – offers tasty three-course dinners (£22 per person, September to April only), often based around local seafood. Bike hire available for guests only.

Staffa House B&B ££
(☎01681-700677; www.staffahouse.co.uk; Fionnphort; s/d from £48/66; P) This charming and hospitable B&B is packed with antiques and period features, and like the Seaview offers breakfast in a conservatory with a view of Iona. Solar panels top up the hot-water supply, and the hearty breakfasts, packed lunches (£5.50 to £7) and evening meals (£25 per person) make use of local and organic produce where possible.

Ninth Wave SEAFOOD ££
(☎01681-700757; www.ninthwaverestaurant .co.uk; Bruach Mhor; 4-course dinner £42; ☺dinner) A new venture based in a former croft a mile east of Fionnphort, this restaurant is owned and operated by a lobster fisherman and his Canadian wife. The daily menu makes use of locally landed shellfish and crustaceans, and vegetables and salad grown in the croft garden, served in a stylishly converted bothy. Advance booking essential.

Fidden Farm CAMPSITE £
(☎01681-700427; Fidden; tent sites per adult/ child £6/3; ☺Apr-Sep) A basic but beautifully situated campsite, with views over pink granite reefs to Iona and Erraid. It's 1.25 miles south of Fionnphort.

Isle of Iona
POP 130

There are few more uplifting sights on Scotland's west coast than the view of Iona from Mull on a sunny day – an emerald island set in a sparkling turquoise sea. From the moment you step off the ferry you begin to appreciate the hushed, spiritual atmosphere that pervades this sacred island. Not surprisingly, Iona attracts a lot of day-trippers, so if you want to experience the island's peace and quiet, the solution is to spend a night here. Once the crowds have gone for the day, you can wander in peace around the ancient graveyard where the early kings of Scotland are buried, attend an evening service at the abbey, or walk to the top of Dun I and gaze south towards Ireland, as St Columba must have done so many centuries ago.

History

St Columba sailed from Ireland and landed on Iona in 563 before setting out to spread Christianity throughout Scotland. He established a monastery on the island and it was here that the *Book of Kells* – the prize attraction of Dublin's Trinity College – is believed to have been transcribed. It was taken to Kells in Ireland when Viking raids drove the monks from Iona.

The monks returned and the monastery prospered until its destruction during the Reformation. The ruins were given to the Church of Scotland in 1899, and by 1910 a group of enthusiasts called the Iona Community (www.iona.org.uk) had reconstructed the abbey. It's still a flourishing spiritual community that holds regular courses and retreats.

◉ Sights & Activities

Head uphill from the ferry pier and turn right through the grounds of a ruined 13th-century nunnery with fine cloistered gardens, and exit at the far end. Across the road is the Iona Heritage Centre (adult/ child £2/free; ☺10.30am-4.30pm Mon-Fri Apr-Oct), which covers the history of Iona, crofting and lighthouses; the centre's **coffee shop** serves delicious home baking.

Turn right here and continue along the road to Reilig Oran, an ancient cemetery that holds the graves of 48 of Scotland's early kings, including Macbeth, and a tiny Romanesque chapel. Beyond rises the spiritual heart of the island – Iona Abbey (HS; www.iona.org.uk; adult/child £4.70/2.80; ☺9.30am-5.30pm Apr-Sep, to 4.30pm Oct-Mar).

The spectacular nave, dominated by Romanesque and early Gothic vaults and columns, contains the elaborate, white marble tombs of the 8th duke of Argyll and his wife. A door on the left leads to the beautiful Gothic cloister, where medieval grave slabs sit alongside modern religious sculptures. A replica of the intricately carved St John's Cross stands just outside the abbey – the massive 8th-century original is in the Infirmary Museum (around the far side of the abbey) along with many other fine examples of early Christian and medieval carved stones.

Continue past the abbey and look for a footpath on the left signposted Dun I (dunee). An easy walk of about 15 to 20 minutes leads to the highest point on Iona, with fantastic views in all directions.

Boat Trips

Alternative Boat Hire   BOAT TOURS
(☎01681-700537; www.boattripsiona.com) Offers cruises in a traditional wooden sailing boat for fishing, birdwatching, picnicking, or just drifting along admiring the scenery. One-/three-hour trips cost £9.50/18.50 per adult (child £5/8.50).

MV Iolaire   BOAT TOURS
(☎01681-700358; www.staffatrips.co.uk) Three-hour boat trips to Staffa (£25/10), departing Iona pier at 9.45am and 1.45pm, and from Fionnphort at 10am and 2pm, with one hour ashore on Staffa.

MV Volante   BOAT TOURS
(☎01681-700362; www.volanteiona.com) Four-hour sea-angling trips (£35 per person including tackle and bait), as well as 1½-hour round-the-island wildlife cruises (adult/child £15/8) and 3½-hour whale-watching trips (£35 per person).

🍴 Sleeping & Eating

TOP CHOICE **Argyll Hotel**   HOTEL ££
(☎01681-700334;   www.argyllhotel iona.co.uk; Baile Mor; s/d from £61/97; ⏲Mar-Oct) The terrace of cottages above the ferry slip houses this cute little hotel – it has 16 snug rooms (a sea view costs rather a bit more – £131 for a double) and a country-house restaurant (mains £8-15, ⏲lunch & dinner) with wooden fireplace and antique tables and chairs. The kitchen is supplied by a huge organic garden around the back, and the menu includes Cullen skink, home-grown salads, and venison-and-rabbit hotpot.

TOP CHOICE **Iona Hostel**   HOSTEL £
(☎01681-700781; www.ionahostel.co.uk; Lagandorain; dm £18.50; ⏲check-in 4-7pm) This hostel is set in an attractive, modern timber building on a working croft, with stunning views out to Staffa and the Treshnish Isles. Rooms are clean and functional, and the well-equipped lounge/kitchen area has an open fire. It's at the northern end of the island – to get here, continue along the road past the abbey for 1.5 miles (a 20- to 30-minute walk).

Tigh na Tobrach   B&B ££
(☎01861-700700; www.bandb-iona.co.uk; Baile Mor; per person £28; P) Comfortable B&B in modern house, with one family and one twin room. A short distance south of the ferry.

Cnocoran Campsite   CAMPSITE £
(☎01681-700112; cnocoran@yahoo.co.uk; Cnocoran; tent sites per person £5) Basic campsite about a mile west of the ferry. Open year-round.

ℹ️ Information

POST There's a tiny post office on the right as you head uphill from the ferry.

SHOPS Spar (⏲9am-5.15pm Mon-Sat, noon-4pm Sun) Grocery store above the ferry slip.

Finlay Ross Ltd (⏲9.30am-5pm Mon-Sat, 11.30am-4pm Sun) To the left of the ferry slip; sells gifts, books and maps, hires out bikes and provides a laundry service.

TOURIST INFORMATION Iona Community Council (www.isle-of-iona.com) There's a notice board at the top of the ferry slip that lists island accommodation and services.

ℹ️ Getting There & Away

The passenger ferry from Fionnphort to Iona (£4.30 return, five minutes, hourly) runs daily. There are also various day-trips available from Oban to Iona (see p290).

Isle of Coll

POP 100

Rugged and low-lying, Coll is Tiree's less fertile and less populous neighbour. The northern part of the island is a mix of bare rock, bog and lochans (small lochs), while the south is swathed in golden shell-sand beaches and machair dunes up to 30m high.

The island's main attraction is the peace and quiet – empty beaches, bird-haunted

SOUTHERN HIGHLANDS & ISLANDS OBAN & MULL

ISLE OF STAFFA

Felix Mendelssohn, who visited the uninhabited island of Staffa in 1829, was inspired to compose his *Hebrides Overture* after hearing waves echoing in the impressive and cathedral-like **Fingal's Cave**. The cave walls and surrounding cliffs are composed of vertical, hexagonal basalt columns that look like pillars (Staffa is Norse for 'Pillar Island'). You can land on the island and walk into the cave via a causeway. Nearby **Boat Cave** can be seen from the causeway, but you can't reach it on foot. Staffa also has a sizable puffin colony, north of the landing place.

Northwest of Staffa lies a chain of uninhabited islands called the **Treshnish Isles**. The two main islands are the curiously shaped **Dutchman's Cap** and **Lunga**. You can land on Lunga, walk to the top of the hill and visit the shag, puffin and guillemot colonies on the west coast at **Harp Rock**.

Unless you have your own boat, the only way to reach Staffa and the Treshnish Isles is on an organised boat trip – see p297, and the boxed text, p295, for details.

coastlines, and long walks along the shore. The biggest and most beautiful sandy beaches are at **Crossapol** in the south, and **Hogh Bay** and **Cliad** on the west coast.

In summer you may be lucky enough to hear the 'krek-krek-krek' of the corncrake at the **RSPB Nature Reserve** at Totronald in the southwest of the island; there's a **tourist office** (admission free; ⊙24hr) here. From Totronald a sandy 4WD track runs north past the dunes backing Hogh Bay to the road at Totamore, allowing walkers and cyclists to make a circuit back to Arinagour rather than returning the way they came.

There are two ruined castles about 6 miles southwest of Arinagour, both known as **Breachachadh Castle**, built by the Macleans in medieval times.

🛏 Sleeping & Eating

Most accommodation on Coll is self-catering, but a few places offer B&B, including **Taigh-na-Mara** (☎01879-230354; www.taighnamara.info; r per person £30-35) in Arinagour. You can camp for free on the hill above the Coll Hotel (no facilities); ask at the hotel first.

Coll Hotel   HOTEL **££**
(☎01879-230334; www.collhotel.com; Arinagour; s/d £55/100; Ⓟ) The island's only hotel is an atmospheric old place. It has quirkily shaped rooms with white-painted, wood-panelled walls, many of which have lovely views over the manicured hotel gardens and the harbour. The hotel also has a really good **restaurant** (mains £9-18; ⊙lunch & dinner) serving dishes ranging from crab chowder to lamb chops with herb-and-Parmesan crust.

Island Café   CAFE **£**
(Arinagour; mains £5-8; ⊙lunch Fri-Tue) This cheerful little cafe serves hearty, home-made meals such as sausage and mash with onion gravy, haddock and chips, and vegetarian cottage pie, accompanied by organic beer, wine and cider. Open till 7.30pm on Fridays and Saturdays.

Garden House Camping &
Caravan Site   CAMPSITE **£**
(☎01879-230374; Uig; per person £2, tent site £3-4; ⊙May-Sep) Basic campsite with toilets and cold water only, 4.5 miles southwest of Arinagour. Dogs are not allowed.

ℹ Information

Arinagour, a half-mile from the ferry pier, is the only village on Coll, and is home to the **Island Stores** (⊙10am-5.30pm Mon & Fri, 10am-1pm Tue & Thu, 9am-5.30pm Wed, 9.30am-5pm Sat) grocery shop, a post office (with ATM), some craft shops and a petrol pump. There is no reliable mobile-phone signal on the island; there are payphones at the pier and in the hotel. For more information see www.visitcoll.co.uk.

ℹ Getting There & Around

AIR Hebridean Air Services (☎0845 805 7465; www.hebrideanair.co.uk) operates flights from Connel Airfield (near Oban) to Coll (£65 one way, twice daily Monday and Wednesday).

BIKE Mountain bikes can be hired from the post office in Arinagour for £10 per day.

BOAT A **CalMac** (www.calmac.co.uk) car ferry runs from Oban to Coll (passenger/car £16.70/85.50 return, 2¾ hours, one daily) and continues to Tiree (one hour), except on Wednesday and Friday when the boat calls at

Tiree first. The one-way fare from Coll to Tiree is £2.60/12.75 per passenger/car.

On Thursdays only, you can take a ferry from Coll and Tiree to Barra in the Outer Hebrides (£7.10/35.25 one way, four hours).

Isle of Tiree

POP 765

Low-lying Tiree (tye-*ree*; from the Gaelic *tiriodh*, meaning 'land of corn') is a fertile sward of lush, green machair liberally sprinkled with yellow buttercups, much of it so flat that, from a distance, the houses seem to rise out of the sea. It's one of the sunniest places in Scotland, but also one of the windiest – cyclists soon find that although it's flat, heading west usually feels like going uphill. One major benefit – the constant breeze keeps away the midges.

The surf-lashed coastline here is scalloped with broad, sweeping beaches of white sand, hugely popular with windsurfers and kite-surfers. Most visitors, however, come for the birdwatching, beachcombing and lonely coastal walks.

◉ Sights

In the 19th century Tiree had a population of 4500, but poverty and overcrowding – plus food shortages following the potato famine of 1846 – led the landowner, the Duke of Argyll, to introduce a policy of assisted emigration. Between 1841 and 1881, more than 3600 people left the island, many of them emigrating to Canada, the USA, Australia and New Zealand.

An Iodhlann (www.aniodhlann.org.uk; Scarinish; admission free; ⊙9am-5pm Mon-Fri; 🕾) is a historical and genealogical library and archive, where many of the estimated 38,000 descendants of Tiree emigrants come to trace their ancestry. The centre stages a **summer exhibition** (adult/child £3/free; ⊙11am-5pm Tue-Fri Jul-Sep) on island life and history.

At **Sandaig**, in the far west of the island, is the **Island Life Museum** (admission free; ⊙2-4pm Mon-Fri Easter-Sep), a row of quaint thatched cottages each restored as a 19th-century crofter's home.

The picturesque harbour and hamlet of **Hynish**, near the southern tip of the island, was built in the 19th century to house workers and supplies for the construction of the Skerryvore Lighthouse, which stands 10 miles offshore. **Skerryvore Lighthouse Museum** (admission free; ⊙9am-5pm) occu-

pies the signal tower above the harbour, which was once used to communicate by semaphore with the lighthouse site.

For the best view on the island, walk up nearby **Ben Hynish** (141m), which is capped by a conspicuous radar station known locally as the Golf Ball.

🏃 Activities

Reliable wind and big waves have made Tiree one of Scotland's top windsurfing venues. The annual **Tiree Wave Classic** (www.tireewaveclassic.com) competition is held here in October.

Wild Diamond Watersports (☎01879-220399; www.wilddiamond.co.uk), based at Loch Bhasapoll in the northwest of the island, runs courses in windsurfing, kitesurfing, sand-yachting and stand-up paddleboarding, and rents out equipment. Six hours' equipment hire costs from £50, and a beginners course (six hours over two days) costs £100 including gear. Sand-yachting on Gott Bay beach at low tide is £25 per hour.

🛏 Sleeping & Eating

Scarinish Hotel HOTEL ££
(☎01879-220308; www.tireescarinishhotel.com; Scarinish; s/d £50/80; 🅿) There's hospitality on tap at the Scarinish, with enthusiastic owners who go out of their way to make you feel welcome. The refurbished rooms are crisp and clean, and the **restaurant** (mains £8-18, ⊙lunch & dinner) and traditional lean-to bar have a cosy atmosphere.

Ceabhar B&B ££
(☎01879-220684; www.ceabhar.com; Sandaig; r per person from £35; 🅿🕾) This snug little cottage B&B has a fantastic location at the western end of the island, looking out over the Atlantic towards the sunset. The owners are outdoor enthusiasts and can advise on kite-surfing, power-kiting and scuba diving. There's also a **restaurant** (mains £8-14, ⊙dinner Wed-Sat) in a sunny conservatory with sea views.

Kirkapol B&B ££
(☎01879-220729; www.kirkapoltiree.co.uk; Gott Bay; s/d £35/66; 🅿) Set in a converted 19th-century church overlooking the island's biggest beach, the Kirkapol has six homely rooms and a big lounge with a leather sofa. It's 2 miles north of the ferry terminal.

Millhouse Hostel HOSTEL £
(☎01879-220435; www.tireemillhouse.co.uk; Cornaigmore; dm/tw £15/35) Housed in a converted barn next to an old water mill,

this small but comfortable hostel is 5 miles west from the ferry pier.

Balinoe Croft Campsite CAMPSITE £ (☎01879-220399; www.wilddiamond.co.uk; Balinoe; tent sites per person £12; 🛜) A sheltered site with full facilities in the southwest of the island, near Balemartine, with great views of Mull.

❶ Information

There's a bank (without ATM), post office and Co-op supermarket (h8am-8pm Mon-Fri, 8am-6pm Sat, noon-6pm Sun) in Scarinish, the main village, a half-mile south of the ferry pier. You can get cash back with debit-card purchases at the Co-op.

Tourist information and internet access are available at the **Rural Centre** (☎01879-220677; Crossapol; ⊕11am-4pm Mon-Sat), and An Iodh-lann (see p299), but there is no accommodation booking service. For more information see www.isleoftiree.com.

❶ Getting There & Around

AIR Loganair/FlyBe (www.loganair.co.uk) flies from Glasgow to Tiree once daily (£56, 50 minutes) from Monday to Saturday.

Hebridean Air Services (☎0845 805 7465; www.hebrideanair.co.uk) operates flights from Connel Airfield (near Oban) to Tiree via Coll (one way from Oban/Coll £65/25, twice daily Monday and Wednesday).

BIKE You can rent bicycles from Millhouse Hostel (p299) and from **McLennan Motors** (☎01879-220555; Scarinish); the latter can also rent you a car.

BOAT Ferry connections and fares are the same as for Coll (see Getting There & Around, p298). Except on Wednesday and Friday the ferry goes to Coll first; journey time from Oban to Tiree is then four hours.

TAXI John Kennedy (☎01879-220419).

NORTH ARGYLL

Loch Awe

Loch Awe is one of Scotland's most beautiful lochs, with rolling forested hills around its southern end and spectacular mountains in the north. It lies between Oban and Inveraray and is the longest loch in Scotland – about 24 miles long – but is less than a mile wide for most of its length. See www.loch-awe.com for more information.

At its northern end, Loch Awe escapes to the sea through the narrow **Pass of Brander**, where Robert the Bruce defeated the Mac-

Dougalls in battle in 1309. In the pass, by the A85, you can visit **Cruachan power station** (www.visitcruachan.co.uk; Lochawe village; adult/child £6/2.50; ⊕9.30am-4.45pm Easter-Oct, tours every 30min). Electric buses take you more than half a mile inside Ben Cruachan, allowing you to see the pump-storage hydroelectric scheme which occupies a vast cavern hollowed out of the mountain.

Also at the northern end of Loch Awe are the scenic ruins of **Kilchurn Castle** (admission free; ⊕9am-5pm Apr-Sep), built in 1440, which enjoys one of Scotland's finest settings; you can climb to the top of the four-storey castle tower. It's a half-mile walk from the A85 road, just east of the bridge over the River Orchy.

Scottish **Citylink** (www.citylink.co.uk) buses from Glasgow to Oban go via Dalmally, Lochawe village and Cruachan power station. Trains from Glasgow to Oban stop at Dalmally and Lochawe village. See p288 for details.

Connel & Taynuilt

Hemmed in by dramatic mountain scenery, **Loch Etive** stretches for 17 miles from Connel to Kinlochetive (accessible by road from Glencoe). At Connel Bridge, 5 miles north of Oban, the loch is joined to the sea by a narrow channel partly blocked by an underwater rock ledge. When the tide flows in and out – as it does twice a day – millions of tons of water pour through this bottleneck, creating spectacular white-water rapids known as the **Falls of Lora**. You can park near the north end of the bridge and walk back into the middle to have a look.

Dunstaffnage Castle (HS; www.historic-scotland.gov.uk; Dunstaffnage; adult/child £3.70/2.20; ⊕9.30am-5.30pm Apr-Sep, to 4.30pm Oct, closed Thu & Fri Nov-Mar), 2 miles west of Connel, looks like a schoolkid's drawing of what a castle should look like – square and massive, with towers at the corners, and perched on top of a rocky outcrop. It was built around 1260 and was captured by Robert the Bruce during the Wars of Independence in 1309. The haunted ruins of the nearby 13th-century **chapel** contain lots of Campbell tombs decorated with skull-and-crossbone carvings.

One of the region's most unusual historical sights is **Bonawe Iron Furnace** (HS; www.historic-scotland.gov.uk; adult/child £4.20/2.50;

(Continued on page 309)

rquhart Castle (p325)
his ruined castle commands a brilliant location on the shores of Loch Ness – a popular place to keep watch for 'Nessie'.

JONATHAN SMITH

SEAN CAFFREY

GARETH MCCORMACK

1. Edinburgh Castle (p46)
This brooding, majestic castle stands guard above the medieval warren of Edinburgh's Old Town.

2. Rural B&Bs (p478)
The cosy hospitality of a traditional B&B, such as this one in Applecross, is a welcome treat after a long country walk.

3. Callanish Standing Stones (p394)

These mysterious pillars form one of Britain's most complete stone circles and one of the world's most atmospheric prehistoric sites.

4. Shetland Islands Birdwatching (p435)

The clifftop reserve at Hermaness is populated with gannets, fulmars, guillemots and puffins.

5. Neist Point Lighthouse (p386)

A remote corner of the Isle of Skye, with views of spectacular sea cliffs and the Outer Hebrides.

GRANT DIXON

1. Western Highlands

Accessible only by ferry or foot, the Knoydart peninsula (p347) is a remote wilderness.

2. Outer Hebrides

The windswept northern tip of Lewis is home to the 12th-century St Moluag's Church (p393).

3. Scone Palace (p208)

One of Scotland's most important royal seats, built on the original site of the Stone of Destiny.

4. Live Music in Glasgow (p127)

As befits Scotland's hippest city, Glasgow has the best live-music scene in the country.

NEIL SETCHFIELD

DAVID TIPLING

1. Caledonian Pine Forests
West Perthshire is 'big tree' country, where
you can ramble through ancient pine forests in
remote valleys such as Glen Lyon (p215).

2. Glen Affric (p321)
One of Scotland's most beautiful glens, a scenic
wonderland and national nature reserve.

3. Isle of Arran (p155)
The jewel in Scotland's tourism crown offers
dramatic landscapes in its mountainous north.

4. The Small Isles
The distinctive outline of the Isle of Rum (p348) offers a glorious sunset view from Scotland's western coast.

5. Balmoral Castle (p248)
This fairy-tale palace, built for Queen Victoria, has served as the royal family's holiday home since 1855.

FEARGUS COONEY

Edinburgh's Traditional Pubs (p80)
Bennet's Bar, with its original Victorian fittings and stained-glass windows, has over 100 malt whiskies to choose from.

⊙9.30am-5.30pm Apr-Sep), near Taynuilt. Dating from 1753, it was built by an iron-smelting company from the English Lake District because of the abundance of birchwood in the area. The wood was made into charcoal, which was needed for smelting the iron – to produce Bonawe's annual output of 700 tons of pig iron took 10,000 acres of woodland.

A fascinating self-guided tour leads you around the various parts of the site.

From the jetty opposite the entrance to Bonawe, **Loch Etive Cruises** (☏07721-732703, 01866-822430) runs boat trips to the head of Loch Etive and back between one and three times daily (except Saturday) from March to November. There are two-hour cruises (adult/child £10/8, departing 10am and noon) and three-hour cruises

---

LOCAL KNOWLEDGE

WHALE-WATCHING WISDOM: RUSSELL LEAPER

Russell Leaper works for the International Fund for Animal Welfare (IFAW), conducting scientific research to try and help reduce threats to whales around the world. He lives in Banavie, near Fort William.

How does Scotland's west coast compare in the league of world whale-watching spots? Rather like the weather, whale-watching in Scotland is less predictable than elsewhere. There is a good chance of seeing minke whales and harbour porpoises. Bottlenose and common dolphins are also seen regularly, and there is a small chance of seeing several other species of whales and dolphins. Basking sharks are also often seen on whale-watching trips. The whale-watching season tends to run from April to September because of the weather (they're easier to spot in calm conditions) but the whales may be around longer than this.

What was your most memorable whale sighting in Scottish waters? In 20 years of studying whales around the world, it's Scotland that has given me some of my most memorable encounters. On a small sailing boat on a glassy calm day in the Sound of Arisaig, myself and a group of children watched for nearly an hour as a minke whale played with the boat like a dolphin. The huge body with a small, curious eye would pass back and forth underneath us before surfacing to breathe out with a rasping blow that smelt of rotten vegetables. A special experience shared with my own children, but also with two girls from Belarus. Visiting Scotland for a month to escape a home still suffering from the effects of Chernobyl, they had never seen the sea before, let alone made eye contact with a whale.

Are whale and dolphin numbers in Scottish waters rising, falling, staying the same? We only have rather approximate estimates of numbers for a few species and almost no information on trends. The numbers of animals close to the coast varies from year to year but we don't really know how this relates to overall numbers. Unfortunately, Norway still kills several hundred minke whales a year from the same population that is watched around Scotland.

Does the whale-watching industry in Scotland have any negative impact on cetacean populations? There's certainly a risk that whale-watching can disturb whales but we don't have any evidence that this is a problem on the west coast of Scotland. The quantity of boat traffic, including whale-watching, is much lower than many other areas.

How can visitors ensure that their whale-watching activity has minimal impact? Scottish Natural Heritage has developed the **Scottish Marine Wildlife Watching Code** (www.marinecode.org). These are simple, common-sense measures to minimise disturbance. Feedback from customers is probably the most effective way of ensuring that operators stick to the code. You can contribute to minimising impact by knowing the code and telling the boat operator if they are not respecting it.

Are there any organisations that people can get involved with on a voluntary basis? IFAW is one of a number of groups campaigning on behalf of whales and dolphins at an international level. Locally, the Hebridean Whale & Dolphin Trust based in Tobermory (see p291) runs programs with volunteers and also collates sightings.

(£15/12, departing 2pm). You may spot eagles, otters, seals and deer, and at the head of the loch you can see the famous Etive slabs – dotted with rock climbers in dry weather. Bookings essential.

Buses between Oban and Fort William or Glasgow, and trains between Oban and Glasgow, all stop in Connel and Taynuilt. See p288 for details.

Appin & Around

The Appin region, once ruled over by the Stewarts of Appin from their stronghold at Castle Stalker, stretches north from the rocky shores of Loch Creran to the hills of Glencoe.

The **Scottish Sea Life Sanctuary** (www.sealsanctuary.co.uk; Barcaldine; adult/child £12.50/10; ⊙10am-5pm Mar-Oct), 8 miles north of Oban on the shores of Loch Creran, provides a haven for orphaned seal pups. As well as the seal pools there are tanks with herrings, rays and flatfish, touch pools for children, an otter sanctuary and displays on Scotland's marine environment.

North of Loch Creran, at Portnacroish, there's a wonderful view of **Castle Stalker** perched on a tiny offshore island – Monty Python buffs will recognise it as the castle that appears in the final scenes of the film *Monty Python and the Holy Grail*. **Port Appin**, a couple of miles off the main road, is a pleasant spot with a passenger ferry to the island of Lismore.

The delightfully quaint **Pierhouse Hotel** (☎01631-730302; www.pierhousehotel.co.uk; Port Appin; s £70-120, d £120-175; ℗⛾) sits on the waterfront above the ferry pier for Lismore, and has stylish modern rooms, a sauna and an excellent **restaurant** (mains £15-25, ⊙lunch & dinner) that enjoys a view across the water to Lismore, and specialises in local seafood and game.

You can hire bikes from **Port Appin Bike** (☎01631-730391), at the entrance to the village, for £8/12 per half-/full day.

Scottish Citylink (www.citylink.co.uk) buses between Oban and Fort William stop at the Sea Life Sanctuary and Appin village. See p288 for details.

Lismore

POP 170

The first thing you notice about the island of Lismore is how green it is (the Gaelic name

Lios Mor means 'Great Garden') – all lush grassland sprinkled with wildflowers, with grey blades of limestone breaking through the soil. And that's the secret – limestone is rare in the Highlands, but it weathers to a very fertile soil.

St Moluag's Centre (www.celm.org.uk; adult/child £3.50/free; ⊙11am-4pm May-Sep, noon-3pm Apr, Oct & Nov) houses a fascinating exhibition on Lismore's history and culture; alongside stands a reconstruction of a crofter's cottage. The **Lismore Café** (☎01631-760020; mains £3-6; ⊙lunch daily, dinner Fri & Sat Apr-Oct) here has an outdoor deck with a stunning view of the mainland mountains (booking necessary for dinner). The centre is in the middle of the island – if you're walking, you can take a short cut by starting along the coastal path north of the pier at Achnacroish (2 miles by road, just over 1 mile by the path).

The romantic ruins of 13th-century **Castle Coeffin** have a lovely setting on the west coast, a mile from Clachan (follow the waymarked path). **Tirefour Broch**, a defensive tower with double walls reaching 4m in height, is directly opposite on the east coast.

There is very little short-stay accommodation on Lismore. However, there are several self-catering options advertised on www.isleoflismore.com.

Lismore is long and narrow – 10 miles long and just over a mile wide – with a road running almost its full length. **Clachan**, a scattering of houses midway between Achnacroish and Point, is the nearest the island has to a village. **Lismore Stores** (⊙9am-5.30pm Mon, Tue, Thu & Fri, to 1pm Wed & Sat; ⓐ), between Achnacroish and Clachan, is a grocery store and post office, and has internet access.

ⓘ Getting There & Around

BIKE **Lismore Bike Hire** (☎01631-760213) will deliver your bike to the ferry slip; hire costs £6/10 per half-/full day.

BOAT A **CalMac** (www.calmac.co.uk) car ferry runs from Oban to Achnacroish, with two to five sailings Monday to Saturday (passenger/car £5.55/45.90 return, 50 minutes).

Argyll & Bute Council (www.argyll-bute.gov.uk) operates the passenger ferry from Port Appin to Point (£1.35, 10 minutes, hourly). Bicycles are carried for free.

TAXI Phone ☎01631-760220.

Inverness & the Central Highlands

Best Places to Stay

» Rocpool Reserve (p315)

» Lime Tree (p339)

» Lovat Arms Hotel (p327)

» Eagleview Guest House (p333)

» Trafford Bank (p315)

Best Places to Eat

» Lime Tree (p340)

» Contrast Brasserie (p317)

» Cross (p334)

» Lochleven Seafood Cafe (p337)

» Old Forge (p347)

Why Go?

From the high, subarctic plateau of the Cairngorms to the rugged, rocky peaks of Glen Coe and Ben Nevis, the central mountain ranges of the Scottish Highlands are testimony to the sculpting power of ice and weather. Here the landscape is at its grandest, with soaring hills of rock and heather bounded by wooded glens and rushing waterfalls.

Not surprisingly, this part of the country is an adventure playground for outdoor sports enthusiasts. Aviemore, Glen Coe and Fort William draw hill walkers and climbers in summer, skiers, snowboarders and ice climbers in winter. Inverness, the Highland capital, provides urban rest and relaxation, while nearby Loch Ness and its elusive monster add a hint of mystery.

From Fort William, base camp for climbing Ben Nevis, the Road to the Isles leads past the beaches of Arisaig and Morar to Mallaig, jumping-off point for the isles of Eigg, Rum, Muck and Canna.

When to Go
Inverness

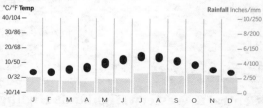

April–May The scenery is at its most spectacular, with snow lingering on the higher peaks.

June Fort William plays host to the UCI Mountain Bike World Cup, pulling in huge crowds of spectators.

September Ideal for hiking and hill walking: midges are dying off, but weather is still reasonably good.

Central & Western Highlands Highlights

① Hiking among the hills, lochs and forests of beautiful **Glen Affric** (p321)

② Wandering through the ancient Caledonian forest at **Rothiemurchus Estate** (p328)

③ Making it to the summit of **Ben Nevis** (p341) – and being able to see the view

④ Rattling your teeth loose on the championship downhill mountain-bike course at **Nevis Range** (p342)

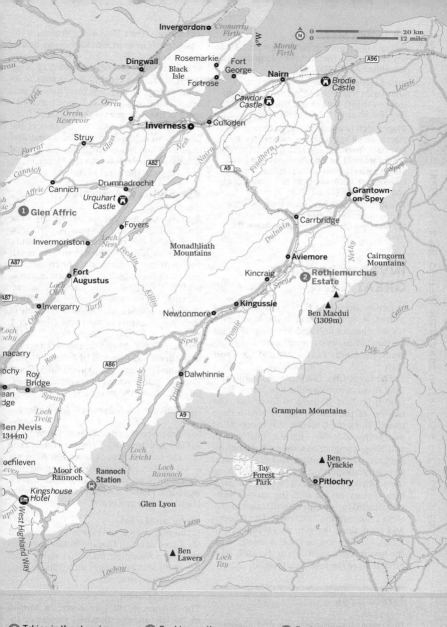

5 Taking in the stunning panorama from the summit of the **Sgurr of Eigg** (p349)

6 Soaking up the scenery (when you can see it!) in moody but magnificent **Glen Coe** (p334

7 Exploring the remote and rugged wilderness of the **Knoydart Peninsula** (p347)

ⓘ Getting Around

Pick up a free Highlands Public Transport Map at any tourist office. For timetable information, call **Traveline** (☎0871 200 2233).

BUS Scottish Citylink (www.citylink.co.uk) Runs buses from Perth to Inverness and from Glasgow to Fort William, and links Inverness to Fort William along the Great Glen.

Stagecoach (www.stagecoachbus.com) The main regional bus company, with offices in Aviemore, Inverness and Fort William. Dayrider tickets are valid for a day's unlimited travel on Stagecoach buses in various regions, including Inverness (£3.20), Aviemore and around (£6) and Fort William (£2.60).

TRAIN Two railway lines serve the region: the Perth–Aviemore–Inverness line in the east, and the Glasgow–Fort William–Mallaig line in the west.

INVERNESS & THE GREAT GLEN

Inverness, one of the fastest growing towns in Britain, is the capital of the Highlands. It's a transport hub and jumping-off point for the central, western and northern Highlands, the Moray Firth coast and the Great Glen.

The Great Glen is a geological fault running in an arrow-straight line across Scotland from Fort William to Inverness. The glaciers of the last ice age eroded a deep trough along the fault line that is now filled by a series of lochs – Linnhe, Lochy, Oich and Ness. The glen has always been an important communication route – General George Wade built a military road along the southern side of Loch Ness in the early 18th century, and in 1822 the various lochs were linked by the Caledonian Canal to create a cross-country waterway. The modern A82 road along the glen was completed in 1933 – a date that coincides neatly with the first modern sightings of the Loch Ness Monster (see the boxed text, p325).

Inverness

POP 55,000

Inverness, the primary city and shopping centre of the Highlands, has a great location astride the River Ness at the northern end of the Great Glen. In summer it overflows with visitors intent on monster hunting at nearby Loch Ness, but it's worth a visit in its own right for a stroll along the picturesque River Ness and a cruise on the Moray Firth in search of its famous bottlenose dolphins.

The city was probably founded by King David in the 12th century, but thanks to its often violent history few buildings of real age or historical significance have survived – much of the older part of the city dates from the period following the completion of the Caledonian Canal in 1822. The broad and shallow River Ness, which flows a short 6 miles from Loch Ness into the Moray Firth, runs through the heart of the city.

◉ Sights & Activities

Ness Islands   PARK

Save the indoor sights for a rainy day – the main attraction in Inverness is a leisurely stroll along the river to the Ness Islands. Planted with mature Scots pine, fir, beech and sycamore, and linked to the river banks and each other by elegant Victorian footbridges, the islands make an appealing picnic spot. They're a 20-minute walk south of the castle – head upstream on either side of the river (the start of the Great Glen Way), and return on the opposite bank. On the way you'll pass the red-sandstone towers of **St Andrew's Cathedral** (11 Ardross St), dating from 1869, and the modern Eden Court Theatre (p319), which hosts regular art exhibits, both on the west bank.

FREE Inverness Museum & Art Gallery
MUSEUM

(www.inverness.highland.museum; Castle Wynd; ☺10am-5pm Mon-Sat) Between the castle and the tourist office is Inverness Museum & Art Gallery, with wildlife dioramas, geological displays, period rooms with historic weapons, Pictish stones and contemporary Highland arts and crafts.

Victorian Market   MARKET

If the rain does come down, you could opt for a spot of retail therapy in the Victorian Market, a shopping mall that dates from the 1890s and has rather more charm than its modern equivalents.

Inverness Castle   CASTLE

The hill above the city centre is topped by the picturesque Baronial turrets of Inverness Castle, a pink-sandstone confection dating from 1847 that replaced a medieval castle blown up by the Jacobites in 1746; it serves today as the Sheriff's Court. It's not open to the public, but there are good views from the surrounding gardens.

⮕ Tours

Moray Firth Cruises   BOAT TOURS
(☏01463-717900; www.inverness-dolphin-cruises.co.uk; Shore St Quay, Shore St; ⊙10.30am-4.30pm Mar-Oct) Offers 1½-hour wildlife cruises (adult/child £14/10) to look for dolphins, seals and bird life. Sightings aren't guaranteed, but the commentaries are excellent, and on a fine day it's good just being out on the water. Follow the signs to Shore St Quay from the far end of Chapel St or catch the free shuttle bus that leaves from the tourist office 15 minutes before sailings (which depart every 1½ hours). In July and August there are also departures at 6pm.

Jacobite Cruises   BOAT TOURS
(☏01463-233999; www.jacobite.co.uk; Glenurquhart Rd) Cruise boats depart at 10.35am and 1.35pm from Tomnahurich Bridge for a 3½-hour trip along Loch Ness, including visits to Urquhart Castle and Loch Ness 2000 Monster Exhibition (adult/child £26/20 including admission fees). You can buy tickets at the tourist office and catch a free mini-bus to the boat. Other cruises, from one to 6½ hours, are available.

Happy Tours   WALKING TOURS
(www.happy-tours.biz; adult/child £10/free) Offers 1¼-hour guided walks exploring the town's history and legends. Tours begin outside the tourist office at 11am, 1pm and 3pm daily.

Inverness Taxis   TAXI TOURS
(☏01463-222900; www.inverness-taxis.co.uk) Wide range of day tours to Urquhart Castle, Loch Ness and Culloden, and even Skye. Fares per car (up to four people) range from £50 (two hours) to £200 (all day).

John O'Groats Ferries   BUS/FERRY TOURS
(☏01955-611353; www.jogferry.co.uk; ⊙departs 7.30am) From May to September, daily tours (lasting 13½ hours; adult/child £57/28.50) by bus and passenger ferry from Inverness bus station to Orkney.

🛏 Sleeping

Inverness has a good range of backpacker accommodation, and there are lots of guesthouses and B&Bs along Old Edinburgh Rd and Ardconnel St on the east side of the river, and on Kenneth St and Fairfield Rd on the west bank; all are within 10 minutes' walk of the city centre.

The city fills up quickly in July and August, so you should either prebook your accommodation or get an early start looking for somewhere to stay.

TOP CHOICE **Trafford Bank**   B&B ££
(☏01463-241414; www.traffordbankguesthouse.co.uk; 96 Fairfield Rd; s/d from £85/110; P🖥) Lots of word-of-mouth rave reviews for Trafford Bank, an elegant Victorian villa that was once home to a bishop, just a mitre-toss from the Caledonian Canal and only 10 minutes' walk west from the city centre. The luxurious rooms include fresh flowers and fruit, bathrobes and fluffy towels – ask for the Tartan Room, with its wrought-iron king-size bed and Victorian roll-top bath.

TOP CHOICE **Rocpool Reserve**   BOUTIQUE HOTEL £££
(☏01463-240089; www.rocpool.com; Culduthel Rd; s/d from £160/195; P🖥) Boutique chic meets the Highlands in this slick and sophisticated little hotel, where an elegant Georgian exterior conceals an oasis of contemporary cool. A gleaming white entrance hall lined with contemporary art leads to designer rooms in shades of chocolate, cream and coffee; expect lots of high-tech gadgetry in the more expensive rooms, ranging from iPod docks to balcony hot tubs with aquavision TV. A new restaurant by Albert Roux completes the package.

Ardconnel House   B&B ££
(☏01463-240455; www.ardconnel-inverness.co.uk; 21 Ardconnel St; per person from £35; 🖥) The six-room Ardconnel is another of our favourites – a terraced Victorian house with comfortable en-suite rooms, a dining room with crisp white table linen, and a breakfast menu that includes Vegemite for homesick Antipodeans. Kids under 10 not allowed.

Ach Aluinn   B&B ££
(☏01463-230127; www.achaluinn.com; 27 Fairfield Rd; per person £25-35; P) This large, detached Victorian house is bright and homely, and offers all you might want from a guesthouse – private bathroom, TV, reading lights, comfy beds with two pillows each, and an excellent breakfast. Five minutes' walk west from city centre.

Loch Ness Country House Hotel   HOTEL £££
(☏01463-230512; www.lochnesscountryhousehotel.co.uk; Dunain Park; d from £165; P🖥) This sumptuous country-house hotel offers traditional decor, featuring Victorian four-poster beds, Georgian-style furniture and Italian marble bathrooms, all set in beautiful

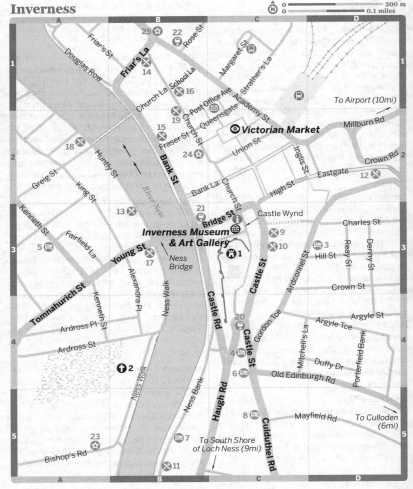

wooded grounds just five minutes' stroll from the Caledonian Canal and River Ness. The hotel is a mile southwest of Inverness on the A82 to Fort William.

Crown Hotel Guest House   B&B ££
(☏01463-231135; www.inverness-guesthouse. info; 19 Ardconnel St; s/d from £36/56; P⊞) Similar in layout to the ever-popular Ardconnel next door, but child-friendly, the Crown has kind and helpful owners. Two of the six bedrooms are family rooms (with a double, single, and folding bed in each), and there's a spacious lounge equipped with games consoles, DVDs and board games.

MacRae Guest House   B&B ££
(☏01463-243658; joycemacrae@hotmail.com; 24 Ness Bank; s/d from £45/64; P) This pretty, flower-bedecked Victorian house on the eastern bank of the river has smart, tastefully decorated bedrooms – one is wheelchair accessible – and vegetarian breakfasts are available. Minimum two-night bookings in July and August.

Bazpackers Backpackers Hotel   HOSTEL £
(☏01463-717663; 4 Culduthel Rd; dm/tw £14/38; @) This may be Inverness' smallest hostel (30 beds), but it's hugely popular – it's a friendly, quiet place with a convivial lounge

Inverness

◎ Top Sights
Inverness Museum & Art Gallery C3
Victorian Market C2

◎ Sights
1 Inverness Castle C3
2 St Andrew's Cathedral B4

◎ Sleeping
3 Ardconnel House D3
4 Bazpackers Backpackers
   Hotel C4
5 Bluebell House A3
   Crown Hotel Guest House .... (see 3)
   Glenmoriston Town House
   Hotel ....(see 11)
6 Inverness Student Hotel C4
7 MacRae House.....................................B5
8 Rocpool Reserve.................................C5

◎ Eating
9 Café 1 ....C3
10 Castle Restaurant...............................C3
11 Contrast Brasserie B5
12 Délices de Bretagne D2
13 Kitchen B3
14 Leakey's B1
15 Mustard Seed B2
16 Red Pepper B1
17 Rocpool B3
18 River House..A2
19 Sam's Indian Cuisine.........................B2

◎ Drinking
20 Castle Tavern.......................................C4
21 Johnny Foxes B3
22 Phoenix.. B1

◎ Entertainment
23 Eden Court Theatre............................A5
24 Hootananny B2
25 Ironworks B1

centred on a wood-burning stove, a small garden and great views. Though the dorms can be a bit cramped, the showers are great.

Inverness Student Hotel　HOSTEL £
(☏01463-236556; www.scotlands-top-hostels. com; 8 Culduthel Rd; dm from £14; @) Set in a rambling old house with comfy beds and views across the River Ness, this hostel has more of a party atmosphere than chilled out Bazpackers, and runs organised pub crawls in town. It's a 10-minute walk from the train station, just past the castle.

Inverness Millburn Youth Hostel　HOSTEL £
(SYHA; ☏01463-231771; Victoria Dr; dm £18.50; ☉Apr-Dec; P@⊕) Inverness' modern 166-bed hostel is 10 minutes' walk northeast of the city centre. With its comfy beds and flashy stainless-steel kitchen, some reckon it's the best hostel in the country. Booking is essential, especially at Easter, and in July and August.

Glenmoriston Town House Hotel
BOUTIQUE HOTEL £££
(☏01463-223777; www.glenmoristontownhouse. com; 20 Ness Bank; s/d from £105/150; P⊕) Luxurious boutique hotel on the banks of the River Ness. Can organise golfing and fishing for guests.

Mardon Guest House　B&B ££
(☏01463-231005; www.mardonguesthouse. co.uk; 37 Kenneth St; r per person £30-38; P⊕) Friendly B&B, with six cosy rooms (all en suite), just five minutes' walk west from the city centre.

Moyness House Hotel　B&B ££
(☏01463-233836; www.moyness.co.uk; 6 Bruce Gardens; r per person £40-50; P⊕) Elegant Victorian villa with a beautiful garden and peaceful setting, 10 minutes' walk southwest of the city centre.

Bluebell House　B&B ££
(☏01463-238201; www.bluebell-house.com; 31 Kenneth St; r per person £30-45; P⊕) Warm and welcoming hosts, top breakfasts, close to city centre.

Amulree　B&B ££
(☏01463-224822; amulree@btinternet.com; 40 Fairfield Rd; per person £30; P⊕) Comfortable, four-bedroom Victorian B&B less than 10 minutes' walk west of the city centre.

Bught Caravan Park & Campsite
CAMPSITE £
(☏01463-236920; www.invernesscaravanpark. com; Bught Lane; tent site per person £7, campervan £15; ☉Easter–mid-Oct) A mile southwest of the city centre near Tomnahurich Bridge, this camping ground is hugely popular with backpackers.

✖ Eating

TOP CHOICE **Contrast Brasserie**　BRASSERIE ££
(☏01463-227889; www.glenmoristonto wnhouse.com/contrast; 22 Ness Bank; mains £10-19; ☉noon-2.30pm & 5-10pm) Book early for what we think is the best restaurant in Inverness – a dining room that drips designer style, smiling professional staff,

a jug of water brought to your table without asking, and truly delicious food. Try mussels with Thai red curry, wild mushroom risotto, or pork belly with glazed walnuts and watercress; 10 out of 10. And at £10 for a two-course lunch, the value is incredible.

TOP CHOICE **Café 1** BISTRO ££
(☎01463-226200; www.cafe1.net; 75 Castle St; mains £10-20; ◷noon-2pm & 5.30-9.30pm Mon-Sat) Café 1 is a friendly and appealing little bistro with candlelit tables amid elegant blonde-wood and wrought-iron decor. There is an international menu based on quality Scottish produce, from succulent Aberdeen Angus steaks to crisp sea bass with chilli, lime and soy sauce. Lunch and early-bird menu (two courses for £9.50) is served noon to 6.45pm weekdays, and noon to 3pm Saturday.

Rocpool MEDITERRANEAN ££
(☎01463-717274; www.rocpoolrestaurant. com; 1 Ness Walk; mains £13-18; ◷noon-2.30pm & 5.45-10pm) Lots of polished wood, navy-blue leather and crisp white linen lend a nautical air to this relaxing bistro, which offers a Mediterranean-influenced menu that makes the most of quality Scottish produce, especially seafood. The two-course lunch (noon to 2.30pm Monday to Saturday) is £12.

Mustard Seed MODERN SCOTTISH ££
(☎01463-220220; www.mustardseedrest aurant.co.uk; 16 Fraser St; mains £12-16; ◷noon-10pm) This bright and bustling bistro brings a dash of big-city style to Inverness. The menu changes weekly, but focuses on Scottish and French cuisine with a modern twist. Grab a table on the upstairs balcony if you can – it's the best outdoor lunch spot in Inverness, with a great view across the river. And a two-course lunch for £6 – yes, that's right – is hard to beat.

Sam's Indian Cuisine INDIAN ££
(77-79 Church St; mains £8-13; ◷noon-2.30pm & 6-11pm) The stylish decor in Sam's is a cut above your average curry shop, and so is the food – lots of fresh and flavoursome spices and herbs make dishes such as jeera chicken (cooked with cumin seed) really zing. Wash it down with Indian Cobra beer.

River House MODERN SCOTTISH £££
(☎01463-222033; www.riverhouseinver ness.co.uk; 1 Greig St; mains £16-22; ◷noon-2pm & 5.30-9.30pm Tue-Sat, 6-9.30pm Sun)

The River House is an elegant restaurant of the polished-wood and crisp-white linen variety, serving the best of British venison, beef, lamb, duck and seafood.

Délices de Bretagne FRENCH £
(6 Stephen's Brae; mains £3-7; ◷9am-5pm Mon-Sat, 10am-5pm Sun) This cafe brings a little taste of France to the Highlands, with its art-nouveau decor and a menu of tasty *galettes* (savoury pancakes), crepes, Breton cider and excellent coffee.

Kitchen MODERN SCOTTISH ££
(☎01436-259119; www.kitchenrestaurant. co.uk; 15 Huntly St; mains £12-16; ◷noon-3pm & 5.30-10pm) This spectacular glass-fronted restaurant is under the same management as the Mustard Seed, and offers a similar menu with a view of the river.

Leakey's CAFE £
(Greyfriars Hall, Church St; mains £3-5; ◷10am-5.30pm Mon-Sat) Cafe in secondhand bookshop.

Castle Restaurant CAFE £
(41-43 Castle St; mains £4-8; ◷9am-8.30pm) Classic old-fashioned cafe.

Red Pepper CAFE £
(74 Church St; mains £3-4; ◷9am-5.30pm) Cool coffee and sandwich place.

Drinking

TOP CHOICE **Clachnaharry Inn** PUB
(www.clachnaharryinn.co.uk; 17-19 High St; Clachnaharry) Just over a mile northwest of the city centre, on the bank of the Caledonian Canal just off the A862, this is a delightful old coaching inn (with beer garden out back) serving an excellent range of real ales and good pub grub.

Castle Tavern PUB
(www.castletavern.net; 1-2 View Pl) Under the same management as the Clachnaharry Inn and with a tasty selection of real ales, this pub has a wee suntrap of a terrace out the front, a great place for a pint on a summer afternoon.

Phoenix PUB
(108 Academy St) This is the best of the traditional pubs in the city centre, with a mahogany horseshoe bar, a comfortable, family friendly lounge, and good food at both lunchtime and in the evening. Real ales on tap include the rich and fruity Orkney Dark Island.

Johnny Foxes

BAR

(www.johnnyfoxes.co.uk; 26 Bank St) Stuck beneath the ugliest building on the riverfront, Johnny Foxes is a big and boisterous Irish bar, with a wide range of food served all day and live music nightly. Part of the premises, The Den, is now a smart cocktail bar.

☆ Entertainment

Hootananny

LIVE MUSIC

(www.hootananny.com; 67 Church St) Hootananny is the city's best live-music venue, with traditional folk- and/or rock-music sessions nightly, including big-name bands from all over Scotland (and, indeed, the world). The bar is well stocked with a range of beers from the local Black Isle Brewery.

Eden Court Theatre

THEATRE

(www.eden-court.co.uk; Bishop's Rd) The Highlands' main cultural venue, with theatre, art-house cinema and conference centre, Eden Court stages a busy program of drama, dance, comedy, music, film and children's events, and has a good bar and restaurant. Pick up a program from the foyer or check the website.

Ironworks

LIVE MUSIC, COMEDY

(www.ironworksvenue.com; 122 Academy St) With live bands (rock, pop, tribute) and comedy shows two or three times a week, the Ironworks is the town's main venue for big-name acts.

Vue Cinema

CINEMA

(www.myvue.com; Inverness Retail & Business Park, Eastfield Way) This is a seven-screen multiplex cinema way out on the eastern edge of the city, just south of the A96 to Nairn.

ℹ️ Information

ClanLAN (22 Baron Taylor St; ⏰10am-8pm Mon-Fri, 11am-8pm Sat, noon-5pm Sun) Internet access £1 per 20 minutes.

New City Laundrette (17 Young St; ⏰8am-8pm Mon-Fri, to 6pm Sat, 10am-4pm Sun) Charges £3 per load, £1.40 to dry. Internet access £1 per 20 minutes.

Tourist office (☎01436-234353; www.visithighlands.com; Castle Wynd; ⏰9am-6pm Mon-Sat, 9.30am-5pm Sun Jul & Aug, 9am-5pm Mon-Sat, 10am-4pm Sun Jun, Sep & Oct, 9am-5pm Mon-Sat Apr & May) Bureau de change and accommodation booking service; also sells tickets for tours and cruises. Internet access £1 per 20 minutes. Opening hours limited November to March.

ℹ️ Getting There & Away
Air

Inverness airport (www.hial.co.uk/inverness-airport) At Dalcross, 10 miles east of the city on the A96 towards Aberdeen. There are scheduled flights to London, Bristol, Manchester, Belfast, Stornoway, Benbecula, Orkney, Shetland and several other British airports. For more information, see p489.

Stagecoach Jet (www.stagecoachbus.com) Buses run from the airport to Inverness bus station (£3, 20 minutes, every 30 minutes). A taxi costs around £15.

Bus

National Express (www.nationalexpress.com) operates a direct overnight bus from London to Inverness (£45, 13 hours, one daily), with more frequent services requiring a change at Glasgow.

Scottish Citylink (www.citylink.co.uk) has connections to Glasgow (£26, 3½ to 4½ hours, hourly), Edinburgh (£26, 3½ to 4½ hours, hourly), Fort William (£11, two hours, five daily), Ullapool (£9, 1½ hours, two daily except Sunday), Portree (£17, 3½ hours, five daily) on the Isle of Skye and Thurso (£18, 3½ hours, two daily).

If you book far enough in advance, **Megabus** (www.megabus.com) offers fares from as little as £5 for buses from Inverness to Glasgow and Edinburgh, and £15 to London.

Buses to Aberdeen (3¾ hours, hourly) and Aviemore (1¾ hours, three daily Monday to Friday) via Grantown-on-Spey are operated by Stagecoach; both Stagecoach and Citylink have buses to Fort William (two hours, hourly).

Train

There is one direct train daily from London to Inverness (£99, eight hours); others require a change at Edinburgh (nine hours, five daily). There are several direct trains a day from Glasgow (£55, 3½ hours), Edinburgh (£55, 3¼ hours) and Aberdeen (£25, 2¼ hours), and three daily Monday to Saturday (one or two on Sunday) to Thurso and Wick (£16, four hours).

The line from Inverness to Kyle of Lochalsh (£18, 2½ hours, four daily Monday to Saturday, two Sunday) provides one of Britain's great scenic train journeys.

ℹ️ Getting Around
Bicycle

Great Glen Cycle Hire (☎07752 102700; www.greatglencyclehire.com; 18 Harbour Rd) Hire mountain bikes for £20 a day. Will deliver bikes to local hotels and B&Bs.

Bus

City services and buses to places around Inverness, including Nairn, Forres, the Culloden battlefield, Beauly, Dingwall and Lairg, are operated by Stagecoach. An Inverness City Dayrider ticket costs £3.20 and gives unlimited travel for a day on buses throughout the city.

Car
Sharp's Vehicle Rental (☎01436-236694; www.sharpsreliablewrecks.co.uk; Inverness train station) Has rates starting at £30 per day.

Taxi
Highland Taxis (☎01436-222222)

Around Inverness

CULLODEN BATTLEFIELD
The Battle of Culloden in 1746, the last pitched battle ever fought on British soil, saw the defeat of Bonnie Prince Charlie and the end of the Jacobite dream when 1200 Highlanders were slaughtered by government forces in a 68-minute rout. The duke of Cumberland, son of the reigning king George II and leader of the Hanoverian army, earned the nickname 'Butcher' for his brutal treatment of the defeated Scottish forces. The battle sounded the death knell for the old clan system, and the horrors of the Clearances soon followed. The sombre moor where the conflict took place has scarcely changed in the ensuing 260 years.

The impressive new **visitor centre** (NTS; www.nts.org.uk/culloden; adult/child £10/7.50 ⊙9am-6pm Apr-Oct, 10am-4pm Nov-Mar) presents detailed information about the battle, including the lead-up and the aftermath, with perspectives from both sides. An innovative film puts you on the battlefield in the middle of the mayhem, and a wealth of other audio presentations must have kept Inverness' entire acting community in business for weeks. The admission fee includes an audioguide for a self-guided tour of the battlefield itself.

Culloden is 6 miles east of Inverness. Bus No 1 runs from Queensgate in Inverness to Culloden battlefield (30 minutes, hourly).

FORT GEORGE
The headland guarding the narrows in the Moray Firth opposite Fortrose is occupied by the magnificent and virtually unaltered 18th-century artillery fortification of **Fort George** (HS; adult/child £6.70/4; ⊙9.30am-5.30pm Apr-Sep, to 4.30pm Oct-Mar). One of the finest examples of its kind in Europe, it was established in 1748 as a base for George II's army of occupation in the Highlands – by the time of its completion in 1769 it had cost the equivalent of around £1 billion in today's money. The mile-plus walk around the ramparts offers fine views out to sea and back to the Great Glen. Given its size, you'll need at least two hours to do the place justice. The fort is off the A96 about 11 miles northeast of Inverness.

NAIRN
POP 11,000

Nairn is a popular golfing and seaside resort with a good sandy beach. The town has a **tourist office** (☎01667-452763; 62 King St; ⊙Apr-Oct), banks with ATMs and a post office.

The most interesting part of Nairn is the old fishing village of **Fishertown**, down by the harbour. **Nairn Museum** (www.nairn museum.co.uk; Viewfield House; adult/child £3/50p; ⊙10am-4.30pm Mon-Fri, to 1pm Sat Apr-Oct), a few minutes' walk from the tourist office, has displays on the history of Fishertown, as well as on local archaeology, geology and natural history.

You can spend many pleasant hours wandering along the **East Beach**, one of the finest in Scotland.

The big event in the town's calendar is the **Nairn Highland Games** (www.nairnhigh landgames.co.uk), held in mid-August. Also in August is the week-long **Nairn International Jazz Festival** (www.nairnjazz.com). Contact the tourist office for details of both events.

🛏 Sleeping & Eating
Glebe End   B&B **££**
(☎01667-451659; www.glebe-end.co.uk; 1 Glebe Rd; r per person £25-40; P🐾🛜) It's people as much as place that make a good B&B, and the owners here are all you could wish for – helpful and welcoming. The house is lovely too, a spacious Victorian villa with home-from-home bedrooms and a sunny conservatory where breakfast is served.

Sunny Brae Hotel   HOTEL **££**
(☎01667-452309; www.sunnybraehotel.com; Marine Rd; s £92, d from £99; P🛜) Beautifully decked out with fresh flowers and pot plants, the Sunny Brae enjoys an enviable location with great views across the Moray Firth. The hotel restaurant specialises in Scottish produce cooked with continental flair, with dishes such as rack of local lamb with ratatouille and garlic jus.

Boath House Hotel   HOTEL **£££**
(☎01667-454896; www.boath-house.com; Auldearn; s/d from £180/220; P) This beautifully restored Regency mansion, set in private

woodland gardens 2 miles east of Nairn on the A96, is one of Scotland's most luxurious country-house hotels, and includes a spa offering holistic treatments and a Michelin-starred **restaurant** (6-course dinner £65).

Classroom
BAR-BISTRO **££**

(☏01667-455999; www.theclassroombistro.com; 1 Cawdor St; mains £13-20; ☺10am-midnight Mon-Sat, noon-10.30pm Sun) Recently revamped in an appealing mixture of modern and traditional styles – lots of richly glowing wood with designer detailing – the Classroom doubles as cocktail bar and gastropub with a tempting menu that goes from Cullen skink (soup made with smoked haddock, potato, onion and milk) to slow-roast pork belly with black pudding and scallops.

ⓘ Getting There & Away
Buses run hourly (less frequently on Sunday) from Inverness to Aberdeen via Nairn. The town also lies on the Inverness–Aberdeen railway line; there are five to seven trains a day from Inverness (£6, 20 minutes).

CAWDOR
Cawdor Castle (www.cawdorcastle.com; adult/child £8.30/5.20; ☺10am-5.30pm May–mid-Oct) was the 14th-century home of the Thanes of Cawdor, one of the titles prophesied by the three witches for the eponymous character of Shakespeare's *Macbeth*. Macbeth couldn't have moved in, though, since the central tower dates from the 14th century (the wings were 17th-century additions) and he died in 1057. The castle is 5 miles southwest of Nairn.

Cawdor Tavern (www.cawdortavern.co.uk; bar meals £8-15; ☺lunch & dinner) in the nearby village is worth a visit, though it can be difficult deciding what to drink as it stocks over 100 varieties of whisky. There's also good pub food, with tempting daily specials.

BRODIE CASTLE
Set in 70 hectares of parkland, **Brodie Castle** (NTS; adult/child £8/5; ☺10.30am-5pm daily Jul & Aug, 10.30am-4.30pm Sun-Wed Apr-Jun, Sep & Oct) has several highlights, including a library with more than 6000 peeling, dusty volumes. There are wonderful clocks, a huge Victorian kitchen and a 17th-century dining room with wildly extravagant moulded plaster ceilings depicting mythological scenes. The Brodies have been living here since 1160, but the present structure dates mostly from 1567, with many additions over the years.

The castle is 8 miles east of Nairn. Stagecoach bus 10A or 11 from Inverness to Elgin stops at Brodie (35 minutes, hourly Monday to Saturday).

West Of Inverness

BEAULY
POP 1160

Mary, Queen of Scots is said to have given this village its name in 1564 when she exclaimed, in French: *'Quel beau lieu!'* (What a beautiful place!). Founded in 1230, the red-sandstone **Beauly Priory** is now an impressive ruin; a small information kiosk next door has information on the history of the priory.

The central **Priory Hotel** (☏01463-782309; www.priory-hotel.com; The Square; s/d £53/90; P☐☎) has bright, modern rooms and serves good bar meals. However, the best place for lunch is across the street at the **Corner on the Square** (www.corneronthesquare.co.uk; 1 High St; mains £5-7; ☺9am-5pm Mon-Sat), a superb little delicatessen and cafe that serves breakfast (till 11.30am), daily lunch specials (noon to 4.30pm) and excellent coffee.

Buses 28 and 28A from Inverness run to Beauly (45 minutes, hourly Monday to Saturday, five on Sunday), and the town lies on the Inverness–Thurso railway line.

STRATHGLASS & GLEN AFFRIC
The broad valley of Strathglass extends about 18 miles inland from Beauly, followed by the A831 road to **Cannich** (the only village in the area), where there's a grocery store and a post office.

Glen Affric (www.glenaffric.org), one of the most beautiful glens in Scotland, extends deep into the hills beyond Cannich. The upper reaches of the glen, now designated as **Glen Affric National Nature Reserve**, is a scenic wonderland of shimmering lochs, rugged mountains and native Scots pine, home to pine marten, wildcat, otter, red squirrel and golden eagle.

About 4 miles southwest of Cannich is **Dog Falls**, a scenic spot where the River Affric squeezes through a narrow, rocky gorge. A waymarked walking trail leads there easily from Dog Falls car park.

The road continues beyond Dog Falls to a parking area and picnic site at the eastern end of **Loch Affric** where there are several short walks along the river and the loch shore. The circuit of Loch Affric (10 miles, allow five hours) follows good paths right around the loch and takes you deep into the heart of some very wild scenery.

It's possible to walk all the way from Cannich to Glen Shiel on the west coast (35 miles) in two days, spending the night at the remote Glen Affric Youth Hostel (p322).

The minor road on the east side of the River Glass leads to the pretty little conservation village of Tomich, 3 miles southwest of Cannich, built in Victorian times as accommodation for estate workers. The road continues (unsurfaced for the last 2 miles) to a forestry car park, the starting point for a short (800m) walk to Plodda Falls. A restored Victorian viewing platform extends above the top of the falls like a diving board, giving a dizzying view straight down the cascade into a remote and thickly forested river gorge. Keep your eyes peeled for red squirrels and crossbills.

The Glen Affric Bar (Cannich; ⏰11am-11pm; 🐾) is a friendly hill-walkers' pub (walking guides are scattered around the place) serving cappuccino and bar meals as well as An Teallach real ale; it also has the only ATM for miles around.

🛏 Sleeping & Eating

Kerrow House   B&B ££
(📞01456-415243; www.kerrow-house.co.uk; Cannich; per person £35-40; 🅿) This wonderful Georgian hunting lodge has bags of old-fashioned character – it was once the home of Highland author Neil M Gunn – and has spacious grounds with 3.5 miles of private trout fishing. It's a mile south of Cannich on the minor road along the east side of the River Glass.

Tomich Hotel   HOTEL ££
(📞01456-415399; www.tomichhotel.co.uk; Tomich; s/d from £74/117; 🅿🐾🏊) About 3 miles southwest of Cannich on the southern side of the river, this Victorian hunting lodge has a blazing log fire, a Victorian restaurant, eight comfortable en-suite rooms and – a bit of a surprise out here in the wilds – a small, heated indoor swimming pool.

Glen Affric Youth Hostel   HOSTEL £
(SYHA; 📞bookings 0845 293 7373; Allt Beithe, Glen Affric; dm £18.50; ⏰Apr–mid-Sep) This remote and rustic hostel is set amid magnificent scenery at the halfway point of the cross-country walk from Cannich to Glen

Shiel, 8 miles from the nearest road. Facilities are basic and you'll need to take all supplies with you. Book in advance. There is no phone at the hostel.

Cannich Caravan Park   CAMPSITE £
(📞01456-415364; www.highlandcamping.co.uk; Cannich; tent sites per person £5.50, plus per car £1; 🐾) Good, sheltered site. Mountain bikes for hire at £15 a day.

Glen Affric Backpackers   HOSTEL £
(📞01456-415263; www.glenaffric.info/affric_backpackers; Charrein Lodge, Cannich; dm £10)

ℹ Getting There & Away

Stagecoach bus 17 runs from Inverness to Cannich (one hour, three a day Monday to Saturday) via Drumnadrochit; there are also three buses a day (except Sunday) from Cannich to Tomich (10 minutes).

Ross's Minibuses (www.ross-minibuses.co.uk) Operates a service from Inverness to the Glen Affric car park via Beauly and Cannich (two hours, once daily Monday, Wednesday and Friday only, July to mid-September). Check the website for the latest timetables.

Black Isle

The Black Isle – a peninsula rather than an island – is linked to Inverness by the Kessock Bridge.

ℹ Getting There & Away

Stagecoach buses 26 and 26A run from Inverness to Fortrose and Rosemarkie (30 to 40 minutes, twice hourly Monday to Saturday); half of them continue to Cromarty (one hour).

FORTROSE & ROSEMARKIE

At Fortrose Cathedral you'll find the vaulted crypt of a 13th-century chapter house and sacristy, and the ruinous 14th-century south aisle and chapel. Chanonry Point, 1.5 miles to the east, is a favourite dolphin-spotting vantage point – there are one-hour dolphin-watching cruises (www.dolphintripsavoch.co.uk; adult/child £12/8) departing from the harbour at Avoch (pronounced 'auch'), 3 miles southwest.

In Rosemarkie, the Groam House Museum (www.groamhouse.org.uk; admission by donation; ⏰10am-5pm Mon-Sat, 2-4.30pm Sun May-Oct, 2-4pm Sat & Sun Apr & Nov) has a superb collection of Pictish stones engraved with designs similar to those on Celtic Irish stones.

ERLEND & PAMELA TAIT: ARTISTS

Erlend and Pamela Tait are artists from Fortrose in the Black Isle. Erlend specialises in stained glass – he has worked on restoration projects in St Magnus Cathedral, Orkney, and the Great Hall at Stirling Castle, as well as creating original works for local schools. Pamela has recently exhibited in Scotland, USA and Germany. You can see their work at www.erlendtait.com and www.pamelatait.co.uk.

Highland artists whose work you admire?

Erlend Michael Forbes, Tim Maclean, Allan MacDonald, Gordon Robin Brown, Ronald Plowman, Shaun MacDonald...
Pamela There's also Jennifer Houliston, Gerald Laing, Fin MacRae, Alex Dunn and the late Alex Main.

Best secret spots?

Erlend The Black Isle is worth exploring – Learnie Red Rock for mountain biking, Groam House Museum (p322) for everything Pictish, Hugh Miller's Cottage (p323) for local geology and folklore. And the Clootie Well is a magical place where you hang a piece of your clothing to cure an ailment or bring you good luck.
Pamela Dogs Falls over at Glen Affric, and there's a lovely wee walk at Reelig Forest near Beauly which has some of the tallest trees in Britain. You must visit the Pirates Graveyard in Cromarty followed by the Cromarty bakery which sells the nicest bread ever, and great pies!

Good place for a drink?

We both love the Anderson (p323) in Fortrose – it has the best selection of whiskies and beers, great food too, and is just a lovely pub to be in.

From the northern end of Rosemarkie's High St, a short but pleasant signposted walk leads you through the gorges and waterfalls of the **Fairy Glen**.

Once you've worked up a thirst, retire to the bar at the **Anderson Hotel** (www.theanderson.co.uk; Union St, Fortrose) to sample its range of real ales (including Belgian beers and Somerset cider) and more than 200 single-malt whiskies.

CROMARTY
POP 720

The pretty village of Cromarty at the northeastern tip of the Black Isle has lots of 18th-century red-sandstone houses, and a lovely green park beside the sea for picnics and games. An excellent walk, known as the **100 Steps**, leads from the north end of the village to the headland viewpoint of South Sutor (4 miles round trip).

The 18th-century **Cromarty Courthouse** (www.cromarty-courthouse.org.uk; Church St; adult/child £2/free; ⊙11am-4pm Apr-Sep) details the town's history using contemporary references. Kids will love the talking mannequins.

Near the courthouse is **Hugh Miller's Cottage & Museum** (NTS; Church St; adult/child £5.50/4.50; ⊙1-5pm Sun-Wed May-Sep), the thatch-roofed birthplace of Hugh Miller (1802–56), a local stonemason and amateur geologist who later moved to Edinburgh and became a famous journalist and newspaper editor. The Georgian villa next door is home to a museum celebrating his life and achievements.

From Cromarty harbour, **Ecoventures** (☑01381-600323; www.ecoventures.co.uk) runs 2½-hour boat trips (adult/child £22/16) into the Moray Firth to see bottlenose dolphins and other wildlife.

Also at the harbour, **Sutor Creek** (☑01381-600855; www.sutorcreek.co.uk; 21 Bank St; mains £10-15; ⊙11am-9pm Wed-Sun) is an excellent little cafe-restaurant serving wood-fired pizzas and fresh local seafood – we can recommend the Cromarty langoustines with garlic and chilli butter.

For something lighter, there's good tea and scones at **Pantry** (1 Church St; ⊙10am-5pm Easter-Sep), or delicious filled rolls and savoury pies at the **Cromarty Bakery** (8 Bank St; ⊙9am-5pm Mon-Sat).

Loch Ness

Deep, dark and narrow, Loch Ness stretches for 23 miles between Inverness and Fort Augustus. Its bitterly cold waters have been extensively explored in search of Nessie, the elusive Loch Ness monster, but most visitors see her only in cardboard-cutout form at the monster exhibitions. The busy A82 road runs along the northwestern shore, while the more tranquil and picturesque B862 follows the southeastern shore. A complete circuit of the loch is about 70 miles – travel anticlockwise for the best views.

Activities

The 73-mile **Great Glen Way** (www.greatglen way.com) long-distance footpath stretches from Inverness to Fort William, where walkers can connect with the **West Highland Way**. It is described in detail in *The Great Glen Way*, a guide by Jacquetta Megarry and Sandra Bardwell.

The Great Glen Way footpath shares some sections with the 80-mile **Great Glen Mountain Bike Trail**, a waymarked mountain-bike route that follows canal towpaths and gravel tracks through forests, avoiding roads where possible.

The climb to the summit of **Meallfuar-vonie** (699m), on the northwestern shore of Loch Ness, makes an excellent short hill walk: the views along the Great Glen from the top are superb. It's a 6-mile round trip, so allow about three hours. Start from the car park at the end of the minor road leading south from Drumnadrochit to Bunloit.

Festivals & Events

RockNess Music Festival   MUSIC
(www.rockness.co.uk) A vast lochside field at the village of Dores hosts this annual festival, a three-day smorgasbord of the best in Scottish and international DJs and bands. Recent headliners include Fat Boy Slim, Leftfield and The Strokes.

DRUMNADROCHIT
POP 800

Seized by monster madness, its gift shops bulging with Nessie cuddly toys, Drumnadrochit is a hotbed of beastie fever, with two monster exhibitions battling it out for the tourist dollar.

Sights & Activities

Loch Ness Exhibition Centre

MONSTER EXHIBITION
(www.loch-ness-scotland.com; adult/child £6.50/4.50; ⊙9am-6.30pm Jul & Aug, to 6pm Jun & Sep, 9.30am-5pm Feb-May & Oct, 10am-3.30pm Nov-Jan) This is the better of the two Nessie-themed attractions, with a scientific approach that allows you to weigh the evidence for yourself, and featuring original footage of monster sightings plus exhibits of equipment used in the various underwater monster hunts.

Nessieland Castle Monster Centre

MONSTER EXHIBITION
(www.lochness-hotel.com; adult/child £5.50/4; ⊙9am-8pm Jul & Aug, 10am-5.30pm Apr-Jun, Sep & Oct, 10am-4pm Nov-Mar) This more homely option is more of a miniature theme park aimed squarely at the kids, but its main

---

WORTH A TRIP

DORES INN

While crowded tour coaches pour down the west side of Loch Ness to the hotspots of Drumnadrochit and Urquhart Castle, the narrow B862 road along the eastern shore is relatively peaceful. It leads to the village of Foyers, where you can enjoy a pleasant hike to the **Falls of Foyers**.

But it's worth making the trip just for the **Dores Inn** (☎01463-751203; www.thedores inn.co.uk; Dores; mains £8-20; ⊙lunch & dinner; 🐾), a beautifully restored country pub furnished with old church seating, local landscape paintings and fresh flowers. The menu specialises in quality Scottish produce, from haggis, neeps and tatties, and haddock and chips, to steaks, scallops and seafood platters.

The pub garden enjoys a stunning view along the length of Loch Ness, and even has a dedicated monster-spotting vantage point. The nearby campervan, emblazoned with Nessie-Serry Independent Research, has been home to dedicated Nessie hunter Steve Feltham (www.haveyouseenityet.co.uk) since 1991; he sells clay models of the monster, and is a fund of fascinating stories about the loch.

Highland folklore is filled with tales of strange creatures living in lochs and rivers, notably the kelpie (water horse) that lures unwary travellers to their doom. The use of the term 'monster', however, is a relatively recent phenomenon, the origins of which lie in an article published in the *Inverness Courier* on 2 May 1933, entitled 'Strange Spectacle on Loch Ness'.

The article recounted the sighting of a disturbance in the loch by Mrs Aldie Mackay and her husband: 'The creature disported itself, rolling and plunging for fully a minute, its body resembling that of a whale, and the water cascading and churning like a simmering cauldron.'

The story was taken up by the London press and sparked off a rash of sightings that year, including a notorious on-land encounter with London tourists Mr and Mrs Spicer on 22 July 1933, again reported in the *Inverness Courier*:

It was horrible, an abomination. About 50 yards ahead, we saw an undulating sort of neck, and quickly followed by a large, ponderous body. I estimated the length to be 25 to 30 feet, its colour was dark elephant grey. It crossed the road in a series of jerks, but because of the slope we could not see its limbs. Although I accelerated quickly towards it, it had disappeared into the loch by the time I reached the spot. There was no sign of it in the water. I am a temperate man, but I am willing to take any oath that we saw this Loch Ness beast. I am certain that this creature was of a prehistoric species.

The London newspapers couldn't resist. In December 1933 the *Daily Mail* sent Marmaduke Wetherall, a film director and big-game hunter, to Loch Ness to track down the beast. Within days he found 'reptilian' footprints in the shoreline mud (soon revealed to have been made with a stuffed hippopotamus foot, possibly an umbrella stand). Then in April 1934 came the famous 'long-necked monster' photograph taken by the seemingly reputable Harley St surgeon Colonel Kenneth Wilson. The press went mad and the rest, as they say, is history.

In 1994, however, Christian Spurling – Wetherall's stepson, by then 90 years old – revealed that the most famous photo of Nessie ever taken was in fact a hoax, perpetrated by his stepfather with Wilson's help. Today, of course, there are those who claim that Spurling's confession is itself a hoax. And, ironically, the researcher who exposed the surgeon's photo as a fake still believes wholeheartedly in the monster's existence.

Hoax or not, there's no denying that the bizarre mini-industry that has grown up around Loch Ness and its mysterious monster since that eventful summer 75 years ago is the strangest spectacle of all.

function is to sell you Loch Ness monster souvenirs.

Nessie Hunter CRUISE
(☎01456-450395; www.lochness-cruises. com; adult/child £10/8) One-hour monster-hunting cruises, complete with sonar and underwater cameras. Cruises depart from Drumnadrochit hourly from 9am to 6pm daily from Easter to December.

URQUHART CASTLE
Commanding a brilliant location with outstanding views (on a clear day), **Urquhart Castle** (HS; adult/child £7/4.20; ⊙9.30am-6pm Apr-Sep, to 5pm Oct, to 4.30pm Nov-Mar) is a popular Nessie-watching hot spot. A huge visitor centre (most of which is beneath ground level) includes a video theatre (with a dramatic 'unveiling' of the castle at the end of the film), displays of medieval items discovered in the castle, a huge gift shop and a restaurant. The site is often very crowded in summer.

The castle was repeatedly sacked and rebuilt (and sacked and rebuilt) over the centuries; in 1692 it was blown up to prevent the Jacobites from using it. The five-storey tower house at the northern point is the most impressive remaining fragment and offers wonderful views across the water.

🛏 Sleeping & Eating

Loch Ness Inn
INN ££

(☎01456-450991; www.staylochness.co.uk; Lewiston; s/d/f £69/99/140; P🐕) Conveniently located in the quiet hamlet of Lewiston, between Drumnadrochit and Urquhart Castle, the Loch Ness Inn ticks all the weary traveller's boxes with comfortable bedrooms (the family suite sleeps two adults and two children), a cosy bar pouring real ales from the Cairngorm and Isle of Skye breweries, and a rustic restaurant (mains £8-16) serving hearty, wholesome fare such as smoked haddock chowder, and venison sausages with mash and onion gravy.

Drumbuie Farm
B&B ££

(☎01456-450634; www.loch-ness-farm.co.uk; Drumnadrochit; per person from £30; ☺Mar-Oct; P) A B&B in a modern house on a working farm – the surrounding fields are full of sheep and highland cattle – with views over Urquhart Castle and Loch Ness. Walkers and cyclists are welcome.

Loch Ness Backpackers Lodge
HOSTEL £

(☎01456-450807; www.lochness-backpackers. com; Coiltie Farmhouse, East Lewiston; dm/d/f £12.50/30/45; P) This snug, friendly hostel housed in a cottage and barn has six-bed dorms, one double and a large barbecue area. It's about 0.75 miles from Drumnadrochit, along the A82 towards Fort William; turn left where you see the sign for Loch Ness Inn, just before the bridge.

Loch Ness Youth Hostel
HOSTEL £

(SYHA; ☎01320-351274; dm £18; ☺Apr-Sep; @) This hostel is housed in a big lodge overlooking Loch Ness, and many dorms have loch views. It's located on the A82 road, 13 miles southwest of Drumnadrochit, and 4 miles northeast of Invermoriston. Buses from Inverness to Fort William stop nearby.

Fiddler's Coffee Shop & Restaurant
CAFE/RESTAURANT ££

(www.fiddledrum.co.uk; Drumnadrochit; mains £8-16; ☺11am-11pm) The coffee shop does cappuccino and croissants, while the restaurant serves traditional Highland fare, such as venison casserole, and a wide range of bottled Scottish beers. There's also a whisky bar with huge range of single malts.

Borlum Farm
CAMPSITE £

(☎01456-450220; www.borlum.co.uk; Drumnadrochit; sites per person £5.50; ☺Mar-Oct) Campsite is beside main road 800m southeast of Drumnadrochit.

ℹ Getting There & Away

Scottish Citylink and Stagecoach buses from Inverness to Fort William run along the shores of Loch Ness (six to eight daily, five on Sunday); those headed for Skye turn off at Invermoriston. There are bus stops at Drumnadrochit (£6.20, 30 minutes), Urquhart Castle car park (£6.60, 35 minutes) and Loch Ness Youth Hostel (£10, 45 minutes).

Fort Augustus

POP 510

Fort Augustus, at the junction of four old military roads, was originally a government garrison and the headquarters of General George Wade's road-building operations in the early 18th century. Today it's a neat and picturesque little place, often overrun by tourists in summer.

◉ Sights & Activities

Caledonian Canal
CANAL

At Fort Augustus, boats using the Caledonian Canal are raised and lowered 13m by a 'ladder' of five consecutive locks. It's fun to watch, and the neatly landscaped canal banks are a great place to soak up the sun or compare accents with fellow tourists. The **Caledonian Canal Heritage Centre** (admission free; ☺10am-5pm Apr-Oct), beside the lowest lock, showcases the history of the canal.

Clansman Centre
MUSEUM

(www.scottish-swords.com; admission free; ☺10am-6pm Apr-Oct) An exhibition on 17th-century Highland life, with live demonstrations of how to put on a plaid (the forerunner of the kilt) and how the claymore (Highland sword) was made and used. There is also a workshop where you can purchase handcrafted reproduction swords, dirks and shields.

Royal Scot
CRUISE

(www.cruiselochness.com; ☺10am-4pm Mar-Oct, 2pm Sat & Sun only Nov & Dec) One-hour cruises (adult/child £11/6.50) on Loch Ness accompanied by the latest high-tech sonar equipment so you can keep an underwater eye open for Nessie.

Sleeping & Eating

TOP CHOICE Lovat Arms Hotel   HOTEL ££
(☎01456-459250;   www.thelovat.com;
Main Rd; d from £110; P 🛜 ♨) Recently given
a luxurious but eco-conscious boutique-
style makeover in shades of pink and grey,
this former huntin'-and-shootin' hotel is set
apart from the tourist crush around the canal. The bedrooms are spacious and stylishly furnished, while the lounge is equipped
with a log fire, comfy armchairs and grand
piano. The **restaurant** (mains £10-17), which
has a separate kids' menu, serves top quality cuisine, from posh fish and chips to roast
venison, seared sea bass, and wild mushroom risotto.

Morag's Lodge   HOSTEL £
(☎01320-366289; www.moragslodge.com; Bun-
noich Brae; dm/tw/f from £18/46/59; P @🛜)
This large and well-run hostel is based in a
big Victorian house with great views of Fort
Augustus' hilly surrounds, and has a convivial bar with open fire. It's hidden away in
the trees up the steep side road just north of
the tourist office car park.

Lorien House   B&B ££
(☎01320-366736; www.lorien-house.co.uk; Station Rd; s/d £45/70) Lorien is a cut above
your usual B&B – the bathrooms come
with bidets and the breakfasts with
smoked salmon, and there's a library of
walking, cycling and climbing guides in
the lounge.

Lock Inn   PUB ££
(Canal Side; mains £9-14) A superb little pub
right on the canal bank, the Lock Inn has a
vast range of malt whiskies and a tempting
menu of bar meals (served noon to 8pm)
that includes Orkney salmon, Highland
venison and daily seafood specials; the
house speciality is beer-battered haddock
and chips.

Cumberland's Campsite   CAMPSITE £
(☎01320-366257; www.cumberlands-campsite.
com; Glendoe Rd; sites per person £7-8; ☺Apr-
Sep) Southeast of the village on the B862
towards Whitebridge.

❶ Information

There's an ATM and bureau de change (in the
post office) beside the canal.

Tourist office (☎01320-366367; ☺9am-6pm
Mon-Sat, to 5pm Sun Easter-Oct) In the central
car park.

❶ Getting There & Away

Scottish Citylink and Stagecoach buses from
Inverness to Fort William stop at Fort Augustus
(£10, one hour, six to eight daily Monday to Saturday, five on Sunday).

THE CAIRNGORMS

The **Cairngorms National Park** (www.cairn
gorms.co.uk) encompasses the highest land-
mass in Britain – a broad mountain plateau,
riven only by the deep valleys of the Lairig
Ghru and Loch Avon, with an average altitude of over 1000m and including five of the
six highest summits in the UK. This wild
mountain landscape of granite and heather
has a sub-Arctic climate and supports rare
alpine tundra vegetation and high-altitude
bird species, such as snow bunting, ptarmigan and dotterel.

The harsh mountain environment gives
way lower down to scenic glens softened by
beautiful open forests of native Caledonian
pine, home to rare animals and birds such
as pine marten, wildcat, red squirrel, osprey, capercaillie and crossbill.

This is prime hill-walking territory, but
even couch potatoes can enjoy a taste of the
high life by taking the Cairngorm Mountain Railway up to the edge of the Cairngorm plateau.

Aviemore

POP 2400

Aviemore is the gateway to the Cairngorms,
the region's main centre for transport, accommodation, restaurants and shopping.
It's not the prettiest town in Scotland by
a long stretch – the main attractions are
in the surrounding area – but when bad
weather puts the hills off limits, Aviemore
fills up with hikers, cyclists and climbers
(plus skiers and snowboarders in winter)
cruising the outdoor-equipment shops or
recounting their latest adventures in the
cafes and bars. Add in tourists and locals
and the eclectic mix makes for a lively little
town.

Aviemore is on a loop off the A9 Perth–
Inverness road; almost everything of note
is to be found along the main drag, Grampian Rd. The train station and bus stop are
towards the southern end.

The Cairngorm skiing area and mountain railway lie 9 miles east of Aviemore

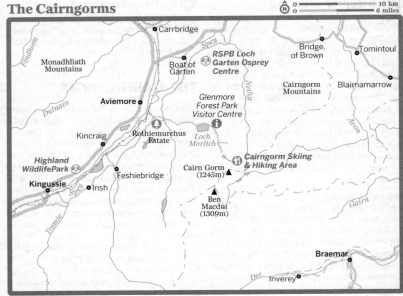

along the B970 (Ski Rd) and its continuation through Coylumbridge and Glenmore.

⊙ Sights

Strathspey Steam Railway   HERITAGE RAILWAY
(www.strathspeyrailway.co.uk; Station Sq) Aviemore's mainline train station is also home to the Strathspey Steam Railway, which runs steam trains on a section of restored line between Aviemore and Broomhill, 10 miles to the northeast, via Boat of Garten. There are four or five trains daily from June to September, and a more limited service in April, May, October and December; a return ticket from Aviemore to Broomhill is £10.50/5.25 per adult/child. An extension to Grantown-on-Spey is planned; in the meantime, you can continue from Broomhill to Grantown-on-Spey by bus.

Rothiemurchus Estate   WALKING, CYCLING
(www.rothiemurchus.net) The Rothiemurchus Estate, which extends from the River Spey at Aviemore to the Cairngorm summit plateau, is famous for having Scotland's largest remnant of **Caledonian forest**, the ancient forest of Scots pine that once covered most of the country. The forest is home to a large population of red squirrels, and is one of the last bastions of the Scottish wildcat.

The estate **visitor centre** (Inverdruie; admission free; ⊙9am-5.30pm), a mile southeast of Aviemore along the B970, sells an *Explorer Map* detailing more than 50 miles of footpaths and cycling trails, including the wheelchair-accessible 4-mile trail around **Loch an Eilein**, with its ruined castle and peaceful pine woods.

Craigellachie Nature Reserve

NATURE RESERVE
(www.snh.org.uk/nnr-scotland) A trail leads west from Aviemore Youth Hostel and passes under the A9 into the Craigellachie Nature Reserve, a great place for short hikes across steep hill sides covered in natural birch forest. Look out for birds and other wildlife, including the peregrine falcons that nest on the crags from April to July. If you're very lucky, you may even spot a capercaillie.

🏃 Activities

Aviemore Highland Resort   LEISURE COMPLEX
(www.aviemorehighlandresort.com) This complex of hotels, chalets and restaurants to the west of Grampian Rd includes a swimming pool, gym, spa, videogame arcade and a huge, shiny shopping mall. The **swimming pool** (adult/child £10/5; ⊙8am-

8pm) and other leisure facilities are open to nonresidents.

Bothy Bikes
MOUNTAIN BIKING

(www.bothybikes.co.uk; Inverdruie; ☺9am-5.30pm) Located just outside Aviemore on the way to Cairngorm, this place hires out mountain bikes for £15/20 per half-/full day. It can also advise on routes and trails; a good choice for beginners is the **Old Logging Way** which runs from the hire centre to Glenmore, where you can make a circuit of Loch Morlich before returning. For experienced bikers, the whole of the Cairngorms is your playground.

Cairngorm Mountain
WINTER SPORTS

(www.cairngormmountain.co.uk) Aspen or Val d'Isere it ain't, but with 19 runs and 23 miles of piste Cairngorm is Scotland's biggest ski area. When the snow is at its best and the sun is shining you can close your eyes and imagine you're in the Alps; sadly, low cloud, high winds and horizontal sleet are more common. The season usually runs from December until the snow melts, which may be as late as the end of April, but snowfall here is unpredictable – in some years the slopes can be open in November, but closed for lack of snow in February.

A ski pass for one day is £30/18 for adults/under 16s. Ski or snowboard hire is around £20/14.50 per adult/child a day; there are lots of hire outlets at Coire Cas, Glenmore and Aviemore.

During the season the tourist office displays snow conditions and avalanche warnings. You can check the latest snow conditions on the **Ski Hotline** (☏0900 165 4655) and at http://ski.visitscotland.com, or tune into Cairngorm Radio Ski FM on 96.6MHz.

Rothiemurchus Fishery
ANGLING

(www.rothiemurchus.net; Rothiemurchus Estate, Inverdruie) Cast for rainbow trout at this loch at the southern end of the village; buy permits (from £10 to £30 a day, plus £3.50 for tackle hire) at the Fish Farm Shop in Inverdruie. If you're a fly-fishing virgin, there's a beginner's package, including tackle hire, one hour's instruction and one hour's fishing, for £35. For experienced anglers, there's also salmon and sea-trout fishing on the River Spey – a day permit costs around £20; numbers are limited, so it's best to book in advance.

Cairngorm Sled-Dog Centre
DOG SLEDDING

(☏07767 270526; www.sled-dogs.co.uk; Ski Rd) If you prefer the smell of wet dog to the whiff of petrol, you can be taken on a two-to three-hour sled tour of local forest trails in the wake of a team of huskies (adult/child £60/40). The sleds have wheels, so snow's not necessary. There are also one-hour guided tours of the kennels (adult/child £8/4).

Alvie & Dalraddy Estate
QUAD BIKE

(☏01479-810330; www.alvie-estate.co.uk; Dalraddy Holiday Park; per person £39) Join a cross-country quad-bike trek at this estate, 3 miles south of Aviemore on the B9152 (call first).

🛏 Sleeping

Old Minister's House
B&B ££

(☏01479-812181; www.theoldministershouse.co.uk; Rothiemurchus; s/d £65/96; Ⓟ☎) This former manse dates from 1906 and has four rooms with a homely, country-farmhouse feel. It's in a lovely setting amid Scots pines on the banks of the River Druie, just 0.75 miles southeast of Aviemore.

Ardlogie Guest House
B&B £

(☏01479-810747; www.ardlogie.co.uk; Dalfaber Rd; s/d from £40/60; Ⓟ☎) Handy for the train station, the five-room Ardlogie has great views over the River Spey towards the Cairngorms. There's a boules pitch in the garden, and guests get free use of the local country club's pool, spa and sauna.

Aviemore Bunkhouse
HOSTEL £

(☏01479-811181; www.aviemore-bunkhouse.com; Dalfaber Rd; dm/tw/f £15/50/60; Ⓟ@☎) This independent hostel, next door to the Old Bridge Inn, provides accommodation in bright, modern six- or eight-bed dorms, each with private bathroom, and one twin/family room. There's a drying room, secure bike storage and wheelchair-accessible dorms. From the train station, cross the pedestrian bridge over the tracks, turn right and walk south on Dalfaber Rd.

Ravenscraig Guest House
B&B ££

(☏01479-810278; www.aviemoreonline.com; Grampian Rd; r per person £30-40; Ⓟ☎) Ravenscraig is a large, flower-bedecked Victorian villa with six spacious en-suite rooms, plus another six in a modern annexe at the back (one wheelchair accessible). It serves traditional and veggie breakfasts in an attractive conservatory dining room.

Cairngorm Hotel
HOTEL ££

(☏01479-810233; www.cairngorm.com; Grampian Rd; s/d £55/88; Ⓟ) Better known as the

Cairn, this long-established hotel is set in the fine old granite building with the pointy turret opposite the train station. It's a welcoming place with comfortable rooms and a determinedly Scottish atmosphere, all tartan carpets and stags' antlers. There's live music on weekends, so it can get a bit noisy – not for early-to-bedders.

Hilton Coylumbridge HOTEL ££
(☑01479-810661; www.coylumbridge.hilton.com; Coylumbridge; d from £98; P❄☎️⛲) This modern, low-rise Hilton, set amid the pine woods just outside Aviemore, is a wonderfully child-friendly hotel, with bedrooms for up to two adults and two children, indoor and outdoor play areas, a crèche and a baby-sitting service.

Kinapol Guest House B&B ££
(☑01479-810513; www.kinapol.co.uk; Dalfaber Rd; s/d from £30/40; P☎️) The Kinapol is a modern bungalow offering basic but comfortable B&B accommodation, across the tracks from the train station. All three rooms have shared bathrooms.

Aviemore Youth Hostel HOSTEL £
(SYHA; ☑01479-810345; 25 Grampian Rd; dm £17; P@☎️) Upmarket hostelling in a spacious, well-equipped building, five minutes' walk from the village centre. There are four- and six-bed rooms, and the doors stay open until 2am.

Rothiemurchus Camp & Caravan Park CAMPSITE £
(☑01479-812800; www.rothiemurchus.net; Coylumbridge; sites per person £7.50-8.50) The nearest camping ground is this year-round park set among Scots pines at Coylumbridge, 1.5 miles along the B970.

✖ Eating & Drinking

Old Bridge Inn PUB ££
(www.oldbridgeinn.co.uk; 23 Dalfaber Rd; mains £10-16; ☎️) The Old Bridge has a snug bar, complete with roaring log fire in winter, and a cheerful, chalet-style **restaurant** (food served noon to 3pm and 6pm to 9pm Sunday to Thursday, and to 10pm on Friday and Saturday) at the back serving quality Scottish cuisine.

Mountain Cafe CAFE £
(www.mountaincafe-aviemore.co.uk; 111 Grampian Rd; mains £4-9; ⊙8.30am-5pm Tue-Thu, to 5.30pm Fri-Mon; ⛲) Fresh, healthy breakfasts of muesli, porridge and fresh fruit (till 11.30am), hearty lunches of seafood chowder, salads or burgers, and homebaked breads, cakes and biscuits. Vegan, coeliac and nut-allergic diets catered for.

Ski-ing Doo BISTRO ££
(9 Grampian Rd; mains £7-11, steaks £14-16; ⊙noon-2.30pm & 5-11pm; ⛲) A long-standing Aviemore institution, the child-friendly Ski-ing Doo (it's a pun…oh, ask the waiter!) is a favourite with family skiers and hikers. An informal place offering a range of hearty, homemade burgers, chilli dishes and juicy steaks; the Doo Below cafe bar is open all day from noon.

Café Mambo CAFE-BAR £
(The Mall, Grampian Rd; mains £5-10; ⊙food noon-8.30pm Mon-Thu, noon-7.30pm Fri & Sat, 12.30-8.30pm Sun; ☎️) The Mambo is a popular chill-out cafe in the afternoon, serving burgers, steaks and Tex-Mex grub, and turns into a clubbing and live-band venue in the evenings.

Coffee Corner TEAROOM £
(85 Grampian Rd; snacks £3-5; ⊙9am-5pm) This cosy cafe is a good place to relax with newspapers and a steaming mug of coffee on a rainy day. It does good breakfasts, scones and ice-cream sundaes.

ℹ Information

There are ATMs outside the Tesco supermarket, and currency exchange at the post office and the tourist office, all located on Grampian Rd.

Old Bridge Inn (23 Dalfaber Rd; per 30min £1; ⊙11am-11pm Sun-Thu, to midnight Fri & Sat) Internet access.

Tourist office (☑01479-810363; www.visit aviemore.com; The Mall, Grampian Rd; ⊙9am-6pm Mon-Sat, 9.30am-5pm Sun Jul & Aug, 9am-5pm Mon-Sat, 10am-4pm Sun Easter-Jun, Sep & Oct) Hours are limited October to Easter.

ℹ Getting There & Away

BUS Buses stop on Grampian Rd opposite the train station; buy tickets at the tourist office. Services include:

Edinburgh (£23, 3¾ hours) Scottish Citylink

Glasgow (£23, 3¾ hours) Scottish Citylink-**Grantown-on-Spey** (35 minutes, five daily weekdays, two Saturday) Bus 33; runs via Carr bridge (15 minutes)

Grantown-on-Spey & Cairngorm car park (hourly, less frequent between Aviemore and Grantown-on-Spey on weekends) Bus 34.

Inverness (£9, 45 minutes) Scottish Citylink

Perth (£18, 2¼ hours) Scottish Citylink

TRAIN There are direct train services to Glasgow/Edinburgh (£40, three hours, three

MOUNTAIN WALKS IN THE CAIRNGORMS

The climb from the car park at the Coire Cas ski area to the summit of **Cairn Gorm** (1245m) takes about two hours (one way). From there, you can continue south across the high-level plateau to Ben Macdui (1309m), Britain's second-highest peak. This takes eight to 10 hours return from the car park and is a serious undertaking; for experienced and well-equipped walkers only.

The **Lairig Ghru trail**, which can take eight to 10 hours, is a demanding 24-mile walk from Aviemore through the Lairig Ghru pass (840m) to Braemar. An alternative to doing the full route is to make the six-hour return hike up to the summit of the pass and back to Aviemore. The path starts from Ski Rd, a mile east of Coylumbridge, and involves some very rough going.

Warning – the Cairngorm plateau is a sub-Arctic environment where navigation is difficult and weather conditions can be severe, even in midsummer. Hikers must have proper hill-walking equipment, and know how to use a map and compass. In winter it is a place for experienced mountaineers only.

daily) and Inverness (£10, 40 minutes, nine daily).

ⓘ Getting Around

BIKE Several places in Aviemore, Rothiemurchus Estate and Glenmore have mountain bikes for hire.

Bothy Bikes (www.bothybikes.co.uk; Ski Rd, Rothiemurchus) Charges £20 a day for a quality bike with front suspension and disc brakes.

BUS Bus 34 links Aviemore to Cairngorm car park (20 to 30 minutes, hourly, no Sunday service late October to late December) via Coylumbridge and Glenmore. A Strathspey Dayrider/Megarider ticket (£6/20) gives one/seven days unlimited bus travel from Aviemore as far as Cairngorm, Carrbridge and Kingussie (buy from the bus driver).

Around Aviemore

CAIRNGORM MOUNTAIN RAILWAY

Aviemore's most popular attraction is the **Cairngorm Mountain Railway** (☑01479-861261; www.cairngormmountain.co.uk; adult/child return £9.75/6.15; ◷10am-5pm May-Nov, 9am-4.30pm Dec-Apr), a funicular train that will whisk you to the edge of Cairngorm plateau (1085m) in just eight minutes. The bottom station is at the Coire Cas car park at the end of Ski Rd; at the top is an exhibition, a shop (of course) and a restaurant. Unfortunately, for environmental and safety reasons, you're not allowed out of the top station in summer, not even to walk down – you must return to the car park on the funicular. However, a trial project launched in 2010 offers 90-minute guided walks to the summit (adult/child £13/10) four times

a day from mid-July to October. Check the website for details.

LOCH MORLICH

Six miles east of Aviemore, Loch Morlich is surrounded by some 8 sq miles of pine and spruce forest that make up the **Glenmore Forest Park**. Its attractions include a sandy beach (at the east end).

◉ Sights & Activities

The park's visitor centre has a small exhibition on the Caledonian forest and sells the *Glen More Forest Park Map*, detailing local walks. The circuit of Loch Morlich (one hour) makes a pleasant outing; the trail is pram- and wheelchair-friendly.

Loch Morlich Watersports Centre
WATERSPORTS
(www.lochmorlich.com; Glenmore; ◷9am-5pm May-Oct) Popular outfit which rents out Canadian canoes (£18 an hour), kayaks (£8.50), windsurfers (£16.50), sailing dinghies (£20) and rowing boats (£18).

Cairngorm Reindeer Centre WILDLIFE PARK
(www.cairngormreindeer.co.uk; Glenmore; adult/child £9.50/5) The warden here will take you on a tour to see and feed Britain's only herd of reindeer, who are very tame and will even eat out of your hand. Walks take place at 11am, plus another at 2.30pm from May to September, and 3.30pm Monday to Friday in July and August.

Glenmore Lodge ADVENTURE SPORTS
(www.glenmorelodge.org.uk; Glenmore; Ⓟ) One of Britain's leading adventure sports training centres, offering courses in hill walking, rock climbing, ice climbing, canoeing,

mountain biking and mountaineering. The centre's comfortable **B&B accommodation** (per person £25-33) is available to all, even if you're not taking a course, as is the indoor-climbing wall, gym and sauna.

🛏 Sleeping

Cairngorm Lodge Youth Hostel HOSTEL £
(SYHA; ☎01479-861238; Glenmore; dm £17; ⊙closed Nov & Dec; @) Set in a former shooting lodge that enjoys a great location at the east end of Loch Morlich; prebooking is essential.

Glenmore Caravan & Camping Site
CAMPSITE £
(☎01479-861271; www.forestholidays.co.uk; Glenmore; tents & campervans £19-20; ⊙year round) Campers can set up base at this attractive lochside site with pitches amid the Scots pines; rates include up to four people per tent/campervan.

KINCRAIG & GLEN FESHIE

The **Highland Wildlife Park** (www.highland wildlifepark.org; Kincraig; adult/child £13.50/10; ⊙10am-5pm Apr-Oct, to 6pm Jul & Aug, to 4pm Nov-Mar) near Kincraig, 6 miles southwest of Aviemore, features a drive-through safari park and animal enclosures offering the chance to view rarely-seen native wildlife, such as wildcats, capercaillies, pine martens, white-tailed sea eagles and red squirrels, as well as species that once roamed the Scottish hills but have long since disappeared, including wolf, lynx, wild boar, beaver and European bison. Visitors without cars get driven around by staff (at no extra cost). Last entry is two hours before closing.

At Kincraig the Spey widens into Loch Insh, home of the **Loch Insh Watersports Centre** (www.lochinsh.com; Kincraig), which offers canoeing, windsurfing, sailing, bike hire and fishing, as well as B&B accommodation from £27 per person. The food here is good, especially after 6.30pm when the lochside cafe metamorphoses into a cosy restaurant.

Beautiful, tranquil **Glen Feshie** extends south from Kincraig, deep into the Cairngorms, with Scots pine woods in its upper reaches surrounded by big, heathery hills. The 4WD track to the head of the glen makes a great mountain-bike excursion (25-mile round trip).

CARRBRIDGE
POP 540

Carrbridge, 7 miles northeast of Aviemore, is a good alternative base for exploring the region. It takes its name from the graceful old bridge (spotlit at night), built in 1717, over the thundering rapids of the Dulnain.

The **Landmark Forest Heritage Park** (www.landmarkpark.co.uk; adult/child £11.55/9.25; ⊙10am-7pm mid-Jul–Aug, to 6pm Apr–mid-Jul, 5pm Sep-Mar), set in a forest of Scots pines, is a theme park with a difference; the theme is timber. The main attractions are the Ropeworx highwire adventure course, the Treetops Trail (a raised walkway through the forest canopy that allows you to view red squirrels, crossbills and crested tits), and the steam-powered sawmill.

Watching red squirrels from your bedroom window is just one of the things that makes **Pine Ridge B&B** (☎01479-841653; www.pineridgecarrbridge.com; Main St, Carrbridge; per person from £26; ℗) such an enticing place to stay; big, bright bedrooms and bounteous breakfasts seal the deal.

Bus 15 runs from Inverness to Carrbridge (45 minutes, four daily Monday to Friday, two on Saturday) and onwards to Grantown-on-Spey (20 minutes).

BOAT OF GARTEN

Boat of Garten is known as the Osprey Village because these rare and beautiful birds of prey nest nearby at the **RSPB Loch Garten Osprey Centre** (www.rspb.org.uk; Tulloch, Nethybridge; adult/child £3/50p; ⊙10am-6pm Apr-Aug). The ospreys migrate here each spring from Africa and nest in a tall pine tree – you can watch from a hide as the birds feed their young. The centre is signposted about 2 miles east of the village.

There is good-quality hostel accommodation at **Fraoch Lodge** (☎01479-831331; www.scotmountain.co.uk; Deshar Rd; per person £20; ℗). The **Boat Hotel** (☎01479-831258; www.boathotel.co.uk; s/d from £85/110; ℗ 🛜) offers luxurious accommodation and has a superb restaurant.

Boat of Garten is 6 miles northeast of Aviemore. The most interesting way to get here is on the Strathspey Steam Railway.

Grantown-on-Spey

POP 2170

Grantown (*gran-ton*) is an elegant Georgian town on the banks of the Spey, a favoured haunt of anglers and the tweed-cap-and-green-wellies brigade. Thronged with tourists in summer, it reverts to a quiet backwater in winter. Most hotels can kit you out for a day of fly-fishing or put you in touch with someone who can.

🛏 Sleeping & Eating

Brooklynn B&B ££
(☎01479-873113; www.woodier.com; Grant Rd; r per person £35-40; P🛜) This beautiful Victorian villa features original stained glass and wood panelling, and seven spacious, luxurious rooms (all doubles have en suites). The food – dinner is available as well as breakfast – is superb, too.

Craggan Mill SCOTTISH ££
(☎01479-872288; www.cragganmill.co.uk; Craggan Mill; mains £13-23; ⊘noon-2.30pm & dinner Wed-Mon) Housed in a restored 18th-century meal mill just south of town on the A95 towards Aviemore, the Craggan is strong on rustic atmosphere and friendly service. The menu doesn't disappoint either, with expertly prepared Scottish seafood, salmon, beef and venison, and desserts that include traditional clootie dumpling made to an old family recipe.

Glass House SCOTTISH £££
(☎01479-872980; www.theglasshouse-grantown .co.uk; Grant Rd; mains £18-22; ⊘noon-1.45pm Wed-Sat, 7-9pm Tue-Sat, 12.30-2pm Sun) Elegant but unpretentious restaurant famous for fresh, seasonal menus that focus on local produce.

Chaplin's Coffee House & Ice Cream Parlour ICE CREAM £
(High St; ⊘9.30am-5pm Mon-Sat, 10am-4.30pm Sun) Traditional family cafe selling delicious homemade ice cream.

ℹ Getting There & Away

For details of buses from Aviemore, see p330.

Kingussie & Newtonmore

The gracious old Speyside towns of Kingussie (kin-*yew*-see) and Newtonmore sit at the foot of the great heather-clad humps known as the Monadhliath Mountains. The towns are best known as the home of the excellent Highland Folk Museum.

◉ Sights & Activities

Highland Folk Museum FREE
OPEN-AIR MUSEUM
(www.highlandfolk.museum; Kingussie Rd, Newtonmore; ⊘10.30am-5.30pm Apr-Aug, 11am-4.30pm Sep & Oct) The open-air Highland Folk Museum comprises a collection of historical buildings and relics revealing many aspects of Highland culture and lifestyle. Laid out like a farming township, it has a community of traditional thatch-roofed cottages, a sawmill, a schoolhouse, a shepherd's bothy (hut) and a rural post office. Actors in period costume give demonstrations of woodcarving, spinning and peat-fire baking. You'll need two to three hours to make the most of a visit here.

Laggan Wolftrax FREE MOUNTAIN BIKING
(www.basecampmtb.com; Strathmashie Forest, Laggan; ⊘10am-6pm Mon, 9.30am-5pm Tue, Thu & Fri, 9.30am-6pm Sat & Sun) Ten miles southwest of Newtonmore, on the A86 road towards Spean Bridge, is one of Scotland's top mountain-biking centres, with purpose-built trails ranging from open-country riding to black-diamond downhills. Cycle hire is available on site, from £25 a day for a hardtail mountain bike to £40 for a full-suspension downhill rig.

Ruthven Barracks HISTORIC BUILDING
(admission free; ⊘24hr) The roofless Ruthven Barracks was one of four garrisons built by the British government after the first Jacobite rebellion of 1715 as part of a Hanoverian scheme to take control of the Highlands. Ironically, the barracks were last occupied by Jacobite troops awaiting the return of Bonnie Prince Charlie after the Battle of Culloden. Learning of his defeat and subsequent flight, they destroyed the barracks before taking to the glens. Perched dramatically on a river terrace and clearly visible from the main A9 road near Kingussie, the ruins are spectacularly floodlit at night.

🛏 Sleeping & Eating

Eagleview Guest House TOP CHOICE B&B ££
(☎01540-673675; www.eagleviewguest house.co.uk; Perth Rd, Newtonmore; r per person £25-35; P🛜♿) The family-friendly Eagleview is one of the nicest places to stay in the area, with beautifully decorated bedrooms, super-king-size beds, spacious bathrooms with power showers, and nice little touches like wall-mounted flatscreen TVs, cafetières with real coffee on your hospitality tray and real milk rather than that yucky UHT stuff.

Homewood Lodge B&B ££
(☎01540-661507; www.homewood-lodge -kingussie.co.uk; Newtonmore Rd, Kingussie; r per person £25-30; P) This elegant Victorian

lodge on the western outskirts of town offers double rooms with exquisite views of the Cairngorms – a nice way to wake up in the mornings! The owners are committed to recycling and energy efficiency, and have created a mini-nature reserve in the garden.

TOP CHOICE **Cross** RESTAURANT £££

(☎01540-661166; www.thecross.co.uk; Tweed Mill Brae, Ardbroilach Rd, Kingussie; 3-course dinner £50; ☺7-9pm Tue-Sat, closed Jan; P) Housed in a converted water mill beside the Allt Mor burn, the Cross is one of the finest restaurants in the Highlands. The intimate, low-raftered dining room has an open fire and a patio overlooking the stream, and serves a daily-changing menu of fresh Scottish produce accompanied by a superb wine list. If you want to stay the night, there are eight stylish **rooms** (double or twin £100 to £140) to choose from.

Blasta BISTRO ££

(☎01540-673231; www.blasta-restaurant.co.uk; Main St, Newtonmore; mains £13-18; ☺dinner Tue-Sat) An unpretentious interior of polished wood, plain white walls and black leather chairs puts the focus on the food at this popular local bistro (the name is Gaelic for 'tasty'). Local produce is showcased in dishes such as venison steak with sweet potato and ginger puree, and smoked salmon with egg mimosa and watercress dressing.

ⓘ Getting There & Away

BUS There are Scottish Citylink buses from Kingussie to Perth (£14, 1¾ hours, five daily), Aviemore (£7, 25 minutes, five to seven daily) and Inverness (£11, one hour, six to eight Monday to Saturday, three Sunday).

TRAIN From the train station at the southern end of town there are trains to Edinburgh (£32, 2½ hours, seven a day Monday to Saturday, two Sunday) and Inverness (£10, one hour, eight a day Monday to Saturday, four Sunday).

WEST HIGHLANDS

This area extends from the bleak blanket-bog of the Moor of Rannoch to the west coast beyond the valley Glen Coe and Fort William, and includes the southern reaches of the Great Glen. The scenery is grand throughout, with high and wild mountains dominating the glens. Great expanses of moor alternate with lochs and patches of commercial forest. Fort William, at the inner end of Loch Linnhe, is the only sizable town in the area.

Since 2007 the region has been promoted as **Lochaber Geopark** (www.lochabergeopark. org.uk), an area of outstanding geology and scenery.

Glen Coe

Scotland's most famous glen is also one of the grandest and, in bad weather, the grimmest. The approach to the glen from the east, watched over by the rocky pyramid of **Buachaille Etive Mor** – the Great Shepherd of Etive – leads over the Pass of Glencoe and into the narrow upper valley. The southern side is dominated by three massive, brooding spurs, known as the **Three Sisters**, while the northern side is enclosed by the continuous steep wall of the knife-edged Aonach Eagach ridge. The main road threads its lonely way through the middle of all this mountain grandeur, past deep gorges and crashing waterfalls, to the more pastoral lower reaches of the glen around Loch Achtriochtan and Glencoe village.

Glencoe was written into the history books in 1692 when the resident MacDonalds were murdered by Campbell soldiers in what became known as the Glencoe Massacre (see the boxed text, p335).

🏃 Activities

There are several short, pleasant walks around **Glencoe Lochan**, near the village. To get there, turn left off the minor road to the youth hostel, just beyond the bridge over the River Coe. There are three walks (40 minutes to an hour), all detailed on a signboard at the car park. The artificial lochan was created by Lord Strathcona in 1895 for his homesick Canadian wife Isabella and is surrounded by a North American–style forest.

A more strenuous hike, but well worth the effort on a fine day, is the climb to the **Lost Valley**, a magical mountain sanctuary still haunted by the ghosts of the murdered MacDonalds (only 2.5 miles round trip, but allow three hours). A rough path from the car park at Allt na Reigh (on the A82, 6 miles east of Glencoe village) bears left down to a footbridge over the river, then climbs up the wooded valley between Beinn Fhada and Gearr Aonach (the first and second of the Three Sisters). The route leads steeply up through a maze of giant, jum-

Glen Coe – Gleann Comhann in Gaelic – is sometimes (wrongly) said to mean 'the glen of weeping', a romantic mistranslation that gained popularity in the wake of the brutal murders that took place here in 1692.

Following the Glorious Revolution of 1688, in which the Catholic King James VII/II (VII of Scotland, II of England) was replaced on the British throne by the Protestant King William II/III, supporters of the exiled James – known as Jacobites, most of them Highlanders – rose up against William in a series of battles. In an attempt to quash Jacobite loyalties, King William offered the Highland clans an amnesty on the condition that all clan chiefs take an oath of loyalty to him before 1 January 1692.

Maclain, the elderly chief of the MacDonalds of Glencoe, had long been a thorn in the side of the authorities. Not only was he late in setting out to fulfil the king's demand, but he mistakenly went first to Fort William before travelling slowly through winter mud and rain to Inveraray, where he was three days late in taking the oath before the Sheriff of Argyll.

The secretary of state for Scotland, Sir John Dalrymple, decided to use the fact that Maclain had missed the deadline to punish the troublesome MacDonalds, and at the same time set an example to other Highland clans, some of whom had not bothered to take the oath.

A company of 120 soldiers, mainly from the Campbell territory of Argyll, were sent to the glen under cover of collecting taxes. It was a long-standing tradition for clans to provide hospitality to travellers and, since their commanding officer was related to Maclain by marriage, the troops were billeted in MacDonald homes.

After they'd been guests for 12 days, the government order came for the soldiers to 'fall upon the rebels the MacDonalds of Glencoe and put all to the sword under 70. You are to have a special care that the Old Fox and his sons do upon no account escape'. The soldiers turned on their hosts at 5am on 13 February, killing Maclain and 37 other men, women and children. Some of the soldiers alerted the MacDonalds to their intended fate, allowing them to escape; many fled into the snow-covered hills, where another 40 people died of exposure.

The ruthless brutality of the incident caused a public uproar, and after an inquiry several years later Dalrymple lost his job. There's a monument to Maclain in Glencoe village, and members of the MacDonald clan still gather here on 13 February each year to lay a wreath.

bled, moss-coated boulders before emerging – quite unexpectedly – into a broad, open valley with an 800m-long meadow as flat as a football pitch. Back in the days of clan warfare, the valley – invisible from below – was used for hiding stolen cattle; its Gaelic name, Coire Gabhail, means 'corrie of capture'.

The summits of Glen Coe's mountains are for experienced mountaineers only. Details of hill-walking routes can be found in the Scottish Mountaineering Club's guidebook *Central Highlands* by Peter Hodgkiss.

EAST OF THE GLEN

A few miles east of Glencoe proper, on the south side of the A82, is the car park and base station for the **Glencoe Mountain Resort** (www.glencoemountain.com), where commercial skiing in Scotland first began back in 1956. The Lodge Café-Bar has comfy sofas where you can soak up the view through the floor-to-ceiling windows.

The **chairlift** (adult/child £10/5; ⊙9.30am-4.30pm Thu-Mon May-Sep) continues to operate in summer – there's a grand view over the Moor of Rannoch from the top station – and provides access to a downhill mountain-biking track. In winter a lift pass costs £30 a day and equipment hire is £25 a day.

Two miles west of the ski centre, a minor road leads along peaceful and beautiful **Glen Etive**, which runs southwest for 12 miles to the head of Loch Etive. On a hot summer's day the River Etive contains many tempting pools for swimming in, and there are lots of good picnic sites.

The remote **King's House Hotel** (✆01855-851259; www.kingy.com; Glencoe; s/d £30/65; P) claims to be one of Scotland's oldest licensed inns, dating from the 17th century. It lies on the old military road from Stirling to Fort William (now followed by the West Highland Way; see boxed text, p29), and after the Battle of Culloden it was used as a Hanoverian garrison – hence the name. The hotel serves good pub grub (bar meals £8 to £12) and has long been a meeting place for climbers, skiers and hill walkers – the rustic **Climbers Bar** (⊙11am-11pm) is round the back. There's free **wild camping** across the wee bridge behind the hotel – no facilities, but you're allowed to use the toilets in the Climbers Bar.

GLENCOE VILLAGE
POP 360

The little village of Glencoe stands on the south shore of Loch Leven at the western end of the glen, 16 miles south of Fort William.

⊙ Sights & Activities

Glencoe Folk Museum MUSEUM
(Glencoe; adult/child £2/free; ⊙10am-5.30pm Mon-Sat Apr-Oct) The small, thatched museum houses a varied collection of military memorabilia, farm equipment, and tools of the woodworking, blacksmithing and slate-quarrying trades.

Glencoe Visitor Centre VISITOR CENTRE
(NTS; ☎01855-811307; www.glencoe-nts.org.uk; Inverigan; adult/child £5.50/4.50; ⊙9.30am-5.30pm Apr-Aug, 10am-5pm Sep & Oct, 10am-4pm Thu-Sun Nov-Mar) About 1.5 miles east of the village, towards the glen, is this modern facility with an ecotourism angle. The centre provides comprehensive information on the geological, environmental and cultural history of Glencoe via high-tech interactive and audiovisual displays, and tells the story of the Glencoe Massacre in all its gory detail.

Lochaber Watersports WATERSPORTS
(www.lochaberwatersports.co.uk; West Laroch; ⊙9.30am-5pm Apr-Oct) You can hire kayaks (£12 an hour), rowing boats (£15 an hour), sailing dinghies (£12 an hour), and even a 10m sailing yacht complete with skipper (£150 for three hours, up to five people) here.

⊨ Sleeping & Eating

TOP CHOICE **Clachaig Inn** HOTEL ££
(☎01855-811252; www.clachaig.com; Clachaig, Glencoe; s/d £70/88; ℗⊜) The Clachaig has long been a favourite haunt of hill walkers and climbers. As well as comfortable en-suite accommodation, there's a smart, wood-panelled lounge bar, with lots of sofas and armchairs, mountaineering photos and climbing magazines to leaf through. Climbers usually head for the lively Boots Bar on the other side of the hotel – it has log fires, serves real ale and good pub grub (mains £8 to £12), and has live Scottish, Irish and blues music every Saturday night.

Glencoe Independent Hostel HOSTEL £
(☎01855-811906; www.glencoehostel.co.uk; Glencoe; dm £12-15, bunkhouse £11-12; ℗) This handily located hostel, just 10 minutes' walk from the Clachaig Inn, is set in an old farmhouse with six- and eight-bed dorms, and a bunkhouse with another 16 bed spaces in communal, Alpine-style bunks. There's also a cute little wooden cabin that sleeps up to three (£48 to £54 per night).

Crafts & Things CAFE £
(www.craftsandthings.co.uk; Glencoe; mains £3-6; ⊙9.30am-5pm Mon-Fri, to 5.30pm Sat & Sun; ⊞) Just off the main road between Glencoe and Ballachulish, the coffee shop in this craft shop is a good spot for a lunch of homemade lentil soup with crusty rolls, ciabatta sandwiches, or just coffee and carrot cake. There are tables outdoors, and a box of toys to keep the little ones occupied.

Glencoe Youth Hostel HOSTEL £
(SYHA; ☎08155-811219; Glencoe; dm £18.50; ℗@⊜) Very popular with hikers, though the atmosphere is a little institutional. It's a 1.5-mile walk from the village along the minor road on the northern side of the river.

Invercoe Caravan & Camping Park
CAMPSITE £
(☎01855-811210; www.invercoe.co.uk; Glencoe; tent sites per person £8, campervan £20) Our favourite official campsite in Glencoe, this place has great views of the surrounding mountains and a covered area for campers to cook in.

ℹ Getting There & Away

Scottish Citylink buses run between Fort William and Glencoe (£7, 30 minutes, eight daily) and from Glencoe to Glasgow (£19, 2½ hours, eight daily). Buses stop at Glencoe village, Glencoe Visitor Centre, and Glencoe Mountain Resort.

Stagecoach bus 44 links Glencoe village with Fort William (35 minutes, hourly Monday to Saturday, three on Sunday) and Kinlochleven (25 minutes).

Kinlochleven

POP 900

Kinlochleven is hemmed in by high mountains at the head of the beautiful Loch Leven, about 7 miles east of Glencoe village. The aluminium smelter that led to the town's development in the early 20th century has long since closed, and the opening of the Ballachulish Bridge in the 1970s allowed the main road to bypass it completely. Hope was provided by the opening of the West Highland Way, which now brings a steady stream of hikers through the village.

The final section of the **West Highland Way** stretches for 14 miles from Kinlochleven to Fort William. The village is also the starting point for easier walks up the glen of the River Leven, through pleasant woods to the Grey Mare's Tail waterfall, and harder mountain hikes into the Mamores.

🏃 Activities

Ice Factor   CLIMBING
(www.ice-factor.co.uk; Leven Rd; ⊙9am-10pm Tue & Thu, to 7pm Mon, Wed & Fri) If you fancy trying your hand at ice-climbing, even in the middle of summer, head for the Ice Factor, the world's biggest indoor ice-climbing wall; a one-hour beginner's 'taster' session costs £30. There's also a rock-climbing wall, sauna and steam room, and a cafe and bar-bistro.

🛏 Sleeping & Eating

TOP/CHOICE Lochleven Seafood Cafe
                                           SEAFOOD ££
(☑01855-821048; www.lochlevenseafoodcafe. co.uk; Loch Leven; mains £8-18; ⊙noon-9pm Wed-Sun) This outstanding place serves superb shellfish freshly plucked live from tanks – oysters on the half shell, razor clams, scallops, lobster and crab – plus a daily fish special and some nonseafood dishes. For warm days, there's an outdoor terrace with a view across the loch to the Pap of Glencoe, a distinctive conical-shaped mountain.

Blackwater Hostel   HOSTEL £
(☑01855-831253; www.blackwaterhostel.co.uk; Lab Rd; dm/tw £14/32, tent sites per person £6) This 40-bed hostel has spotless dorms with en-suite bathrooms and TV, and a level, well-sheltered camping ground.

❶ Getting There & Away

Stagecoach bus 44 runs from Fort William to Kinlochleven (50 minutes, hourly Monday to Saturday, three on Sunday) via Ballachulish and Glencoe village.

Fort William

POP 9910

Basking on the shores of Loch Linnhe amid magnificent mountain scenery, Fort William has one of the most enviable settings in the whole of Scotland. If it wasn't for the busy dual carriageway crammed between the town centre and the loch, and one of the highest rainfall records in the country, it would be almost idyllic. Even so, the Fort has carved out a reputation as 'Outdoor Capital of the UK' (www.outdoorcapital. co.uk), and its easy access by rail and bus makes it a good place to base yourself for exploring the surrounding mountains and glens.

Magical **Glen Nevis** begins near the northern end of the town and wraps itself around the southern flanks of Ben Nevis (1344m) – Britain's highest mountain and a magnet for hikers and climbers. The glen is also popular with movie makers – parts of *Braveheart, Rob Roy* and the *Harry Potter* movies were filmed there.

History

There is little left of the original fort from which the town derives its name – it was pulled down in the 19th century to make way for the railway. The first castle here was constructed by General Monk in 1654 and called Inverlochy, but the meagre ruins by the loch are those of the fort built in the 1690s by General Mackay and named after King William II/III. In the 18th century it became part of a chain of garrisons (along with Fort Augustus and Fort George) that controlled the Great Glen in the wake of the Jacobite rebellions.

Originally a tiny fishing village called Gordonsburgh, the town took its present name with the opening of the railway in 1901, which, along with the building of the Caledonian Canal, helped it grow into a tourist centre. This has been consolidated in the last three decades by the huge increase in popularity of climbing, skiing, mountain biking and other outdoor sports.

⊙ Sights

Jacobite Steam Train   STEAM TRAIN
(☑01463-239026; www.steamtrain.info) From late May to early October, the Jacobite Steam Train makes the scenic two-hour run from Fort William to Mallaig, departing from Fort William train station at 10.20am Monday to Friday (plus weekends in July and August), returning from Mallaig at 2.10pm

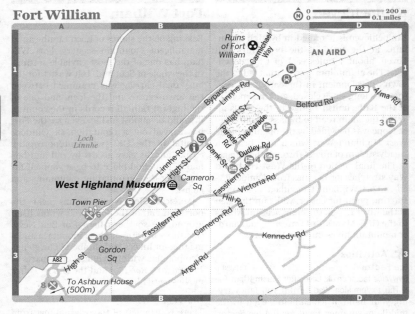

Fort William

⊙ Top Sights

West Highland Museum B2

⊜ Sleeping

1 Alexandra Hotel C2
2 Bank Street Lodge.................................C2
3 Fort William Backpackers...................D2
  Lime Tree .... (see 8)
4 No 6 Caberfeidh....................................C2
5 St Andrew's Guest House C2

⊗ Eating

6 Crannog Seafood Restaurant.............A3
7 Grog & Gruel B2
8 Lime Tree A3

⊙⊜ Drinking

9 Ben Nevis Bar B2
10 Fired Art Cafe.......................................A3

(adult/child £31/17.50 day return). There's a brief stop at Glenfinnan station, and you get 1½ hours in Mallaig. Classed as one of the great railway journeys of the world, the route crosses the historic **Glenfinnan Viaduct**, made famous in the *Harry Potter* films – the train's owners supplied the steam locomotive and rolling stock used in the film.

West Highland Museum   MUSEUM
(www.westhighlandmuseum.org.uk; Cameron Sq; adult/child £4/1; ⊙10am-5pm Mon-Sat Jun-Sep, plus 2-5pm Sun Jul & Aug, 10am-4pm Mon-Sat Oct-May) The small but fascinating West Highland Museum is packed with all manner of Highland memorabilia. Look out for the secret portrait of Bonnie Prince Charlie – after the Jacobite rebellions all things Highland were banned, including pictures of the exiled leader, and this tiny painting looks like nothing more than a smear of paint until viewed in a cylindrical mirror, which reflects a credible likeness of the prince.

Ben Nevis Distillery   DISTILLERY
(www.bennevisdistillery.com; Lochy Bridge; ⊙9am-5pm Mon-Fri year-round, plus 10am-4pm Sat Easter-Sep & noon-4pm Sun Jul & Aug) A tour of the distillery makes for a warming rainy-day alternative to exploring the hills; the guided tour costs £4/2 per adult/child.

✿ Events

UCI Mountain Bike World Cup

MOUNTAIN BIKING
(www.fortwilliamworldcup.co.uk) In June, Fort William pulls in crowds of more than 18,000 spectators for this World Cup downhill mountain-biking event. The gruelling

downhill course is at nearby Nevis Range ski area.

👉 Tours

Al's Tours TAXI TOURS
(☎01397-700700; www.alstours.com) Taxi tours with driver-guide around Lochaber and Glencoe cost £80/195 for a half-/full day.

Crannog Cruises BOAT TOURS
(☎01397-700714; www.crannog.net/cruises; Town Pier) Operates 1½-hour wildlife cruises (adult/child £10/5, four daily) on Loch Linnhe, visiting a seal colony and a salmon farm.

🛏 Sleeping

It's best to book well ahead in summer, especially for hostels. See also the Glen Nevis Sleeping & Eating section.

TOP CHOICE **Lime Tree** HOTEL ££
(☎01397-701806; www.limetreefortwilliam.co.uk; Achintore Rd; s/d from £70/100; P) Much more interesting than your average guesthouse, this former Victorian manse overlooking Loch Linnhe is an 'art gallery with rooms', decorated throughout with the artist-owner's atmospheric Highland landscapes. Foodies rave about the restaurant (see p340), and the gallery space – a triumph of sensitive design – stages everything from serious exhibitions (David Hockney in summer 2010) to folk concerts.

Grange B&B ££
(☎01397-705516; www.grangefortwilliam.com; Grange Rd; r per person £56-59; P) An exceptional 19th-century villa set in its own landscaped grounds, the Grange is crammed with antiques and fitted with log fires, chaise longues and Victorian roll-top baths. The Turret Room, with its window seat in the turret overlooking Loch Linnhe, is our favourite. It's 500m southwest of the town centre.

Crolinnhe B&B ££
(☎01397-702709; www.crolinnhe.co.uk; Grange Rd; r per person £56-64; P) If you can't get into the Grange try the neighbouring Crolinnhe, another grand 19th-century villa, with lochside location, beautiful gardens and sumptuous accommodation. A vegetarian breakfast is provided on request.

Calluna APARTMENT £
(☎01397-700451; www.fortwilliamholiday.co.uk; Heathercroft, Connochie Rd; dm/tw £15/34; P🖨)

Run by well-known mountain guide Alan Kimber and wife Sue, the Calluna offers self-catering apartments geared to groups of hikers and climbers, but also takes individual travellers prepared to share; there's a fully equipped kitchen and an excellent drying room for your soggy hiking gear.

St Andrew's Guest House B&B ££
(☎01397-703038; www.standrewsguesthouse.co.uk; Fassifern Rd; r per person £22-28; P🖨) Set in a lovely 19th-century building that was once a rectory and choir school, St Andrew's retains period features, such as carved masonry, wood panelling and stained-glass windows. It has six spacious bedrooms, some with stunning views.

Glenlochy Guest House B&B ££
(☎01397-702909; www.glenlochyguesthouse.co.uk; Nevisbridge; r per person £35-38; P) Convenient for Glen Nevis, Ben Nevis and the end of the West Highland Way, the Glenlochy is a sprawling modern place, with 12 en-suite rooms set in a huge garden beside the River Nevis; a pleasant place to sit on summer evenings.

Fort William Backpackers HOSTEL £
(☎01397-700711; www.scotlands-top-hostels.com; Alma Rd; dm/tw from £14/38; @) A 10-minute walk from the bus and train stations, this lively and welcoming hostel is set in a grand Victorian villa, perched on a hill side with great views over Loch Linnhe.

Bank Street Lodge HOSTEL £
(☎01397-700070; www.bankstreetlodge.co.uk; Bank St; dm/tw £14.50/48) Part of a modern hotel and restaurant complex, the Bank Street Lodge offers the most central budget beds in town, only 250m from the train station. It has kitchen facilities and a drying room.

No 6 Caberfeidh B&B ££
(☎01397-703756; www.6caberfeidh.com; 6 Caberfeidh, Fassifern Rd; r per person £22-35; 🖨) Friendly B&B; vegetarian breakfast on request.

Ashburn House B&B ££
(☎01397-706000; www.highland5star.co.uk; Achintore Rd; r per person £45-55; P🖨) Grand Victorian villa south of the centre; children under 12 not welcome.

Alexandra Hotel HOTEL ££
(☎01397-702241; www.strathmorehotels.com; The Parade; s/d from £69/109; P🖨) Large, traditional, family-oriented hotel bang in the middle of town.

✕ Eating & Drinking

TOP CHOICE **Lime Tree** MODERN SCOTTISH £££
(☎01397-701806; www.limetreefortwil
liam.co.uk; Achintore Rd; mains £19-25; ☺dinner
daily, noon-3pm Sun) Fort William is not over-
endowed with great places to eat, but the
restaurant at this small hotel and art gallery (see p339) has certainly put the UK's
Outdoor Capital on the gastronomic map.
The chef won a Michelin star in his previous restaurant, and turns out technically
accomplished dishes such as beer-braised
beef with shallot mousse, and slow-roast
pork belly with truffled honey. The two-
course Sunday lunch costs £13.

Crannog Seafood Restaurant SEAFOOD ££
☎01397-705589; www.crannog.net; Town Pier;
mains £14-20; ☺lunch & dinner) The Crannog
easily wins the prize for the best location in
town – it's perched on the Town Pier, giving
window-table diners an uninterrupted view
down Loch Linnhe. Informal and unfussy,
it specialises in fresh local seafood – there
are three or four daily fish specials plus the
main menu – though there are beef, poul-
try and vegetarian dishes too. Two-course
lunch £10.

Grog & Gruel PUB ££
(www.grogandgruel.co.uk; 66 High St; mains £9-
12; ☺bar meals noon-9pm) The Grog & Gruel
is a traditional-style, wood-panelled pub
with an excellent range of cask ales from
regional Scottish and English microbreweries. Upstairs is a lively Tex-Mex **restaurant**
(☺5-9pm), with a crowd-pleasing menu of
tasty enchiladas, burritos, fajitas, burgers,
steaks and pizza.

Fired Art Cafe CAFE £
(www.fired-art.co.uk; mains £3-4; ☺10am-5pm
Mon-Sat; 🛜🖶) Enjoy what is probably the
best coffee in town at this colourful cafe,
or go for a hot chocolate, milkshake or
smoothie; the kids can be kept busy painting their own coffee mugs in the pottery
studio at the back.

Ben Nevis Bar PUB
(105 High St) The Ben Nevis, the lounge bar
of which enjoys a good view over the loch,
exudes a relaxed, jovial atmosphere where
climbers and tourists can work off leftover
energy jigging to live music (Thursday and
Friday nights).

ⓘ Information

Belford Hospital (☎01397-702481; Belford
Rd) Opposite the train station.

Post office (☎0845 722 3344; 5 High St)
Tourist office (☎01397-703781; www.
visithighlands.com; 15 High St; ☺9am-6pm
Mon-Sat, 10am-5pm Sun Apr-Sep, limited hr
Oct-Mar) Internet access (£1 per 20 minutes).

ⓘ Getting There & Away

Bus
Scottish Citylink buses link Fort William with
Glasgow (£21, three hours, eight daily) and Edinburgh (£30, 4½ hours, one daily direct, seven
with a change at Glasgow) via Glencoe and Crianlarich, as well as Oban (£9, 1½ hours, three daily),
Inverness (£11, two hours, five daily) and Portree
(£28, three hours, four daily) on the Isle of Skye.

Shiel Buses service No. 500 runs to Mallaig
(1½ hours, three daily Monday to Friday only) via
Glenfinnan (30 minutes) and Arisaig (one hour).

Car
Fort William is 146 miles from Edinburgh, 104 miles
from Glasgow and 66 miles from Inverness. The
tourist office has listings of car-hire companies.

Easydrive Car Hire (☎01397-701616; www.
easydrivescotland.co.uk; Unit 36a, Ben Nevis
Industrial Estate, Ben Nevis Dr) Hires out small
cars from £32/185 a day/week, including tax
and unlimited mileage, but not Collision Damage Waiver (CDW).

Train
The spectacular West Highland line runs from
Glasgow to Mallaig via Fort William. There are
three trains daily (two on Sunday) from Glasgow
to Fort William (£24, 3¾ hours), and four daily
(three on Sunday) between Fort William and
Mallaig (£10, 1½ hours). Travelling from Edinburgh (£40, five hours), you have to change at
Glasgow's Queen St station.

There's no direct rail connection between
Oban and Fort William – you have to change at
Crianlarich, so it's faster to use the bus.

The overnight *Caledonian Sleeper* service
connects Fort William and London Euston (£103
sharing a twin-berth cabin, 13 hours).

ⓘ Getting Around

Bike
Off-Beat Bikes (☎01436-704008; www.off
beatbikes.co.uk; 117 High St; ☺9am-5.30pm;
half-/full-day mountain bike hire £12/17)

Bus
The Fort Dayrider ticket (£2.60) gives unlimited
travel for one day on Stagecoach bus services in
the Fort William area. Buy from the bus driver.

Taxi
There's a taxi rank on the corner of High St and
The Parade.

Around Fort William

GLEN NEVIS

You can walk the 3 miles from Fort William to scenic Glen Nevis in about an hour or so. The **Glen Nevis Visitor Centre** (☎01397-705922; www.bennevisweather.co.uk; ⊙9am-5pm Apr-Oct) is situated 1.5 miles up the glen, and provides information on walking as well as specific advice on climbing Ben Nevis.

From the car park at the far end of the road along Glen Nevis, there is an excellent 1.5-mile walk through the spectacular Nevis Gorge to **Steall Meadows**, a verdant valley dominated by a 100m-high bridal-veil waterfall. You can reach the foot of the falls by crossing the river on a wobbly, three-cable wire bridge – one cable for your feet and one for each hand – a real test of balance!

🛏 Sleeping & Eating

TOP CHOICE ⭐ **Ben Nevis Inn** HOSTEL **£**
(☎01397-701227; www.ben-nevis-inn.co.uk; Achintee; dm £14; P @) A good alternative to the youth hostel is this great barn of a pub (real ale and tasty bar meals available; mains £9 to £12), with a comfy 24-bed hostel downstairs. It's at the Achintee start of the path up Ben Nevis, and only a mile from the end of the West Highland Way. Food served noon to 9pm; closed Monday to Wednesday in winter.

Achintee Farm HOSTEL/B&B **£**
(☎01397-702240; www.achinteefarm.com; Achintee; dm/tw £15/34) This attractive farmhouse offers excellent B&B accommodation and also has a small bunkhouse attached. It's just 100m from the Ben Nevis Inn, and ideally positioned for climbing Ben Nevis.

CLIMBING BEN NEVIS

As the highest peak in the British Isles, Ben Nevis (1344m) attracts many would-be ascensionists who would not normally think of climbing a Scottish mountain – a staggering (often literally) 100,000 people reach the summit each year.

Although anyone who is reasonably fit should have no problem climbing Ben Nevis on a fine summer's day, an ascent should not be undertaken lightly. Every year people have to be rescued from the mountain. You will need proper walking boots (the path is rough and stony, and there may be soft, wet snowfields on the summit), warm clothing, waterproofs, a map and compass, and plenty of food and water. And don't forget to check the weather forecast (see www.bennevisweather.co.uk).

Here are a few facts to mull over before you go racing up the tourist track: the summit plateau is bounded by 700m-high cliffs and has a sub-Arctic climate; at the summit it can snow on any day of the year; the summit is wrapped in cloud nine days out of 10; in thick cloud, visibility at the summit can be 10m or less; and in such conditions the only safe way off the mountain requires careful use of a map and compass to avoid walking over those 700m cliffs.

The tourist track (the easiest route to the top) was originally called the Pony Track. It was built in the 19th century for the pack ponies that carried supplies to a meteorological observatory on the summit (now in ruins), which was manned continuously from 1883 to 1904.

There are three possible starting points for the tourist track ascent – Achintee Farm; the footbridge at Glen Nevis Youth Hostel; and, if you have a car, the car park at Glen Nevis Visitor Centre. The path climbs gradually to the shoulder at Lochan Meall an t-Suidhe (known as the Halfway Lochan), then zigzags steeply up beside the Red Burn to the summit plateau. The highest point is marked by a trig point on top of a huge cairn beside the ruins of the old observatory; the plateau is scattered with countless smaller cairns, stones arranged in the shape of people's names and, sadly, a fair bit of litter.

The total distance to the summit and back is 8 miles; allow at least four or five hours to reach the top, and another 2½ to three hours for the descent. Afterwards, as you celebrate in the pub with a pint, consider the fact that the record time for the annual Ben Nevis Hill Race is just under 1½ hours – up *and* down. Then have another pint.

Glen Nevis Youth Hostel HOSTEL £
(SYHA; ☎01397-702336; www.glennevishostel.
co.uk; Glen Nevis; dm £19; @🛜) Large, impersonal and reminiscent of a school camp,
this hostel is 3 miles from Fort William,
right beside one of the starting points for
the tourist track up Ben Nevis.

Glen Nevis Caravan & Camping Park
CAMPSITE £
(☎01397-702191; www.glen-nevis.co.uk; tent
£6.50, tent & car £11, campervan £11, per person
£3; ⊙mid-Mar–Oct) This big, well-equipped
site is a popular base camp for Ben Nevis
and the surrounding mountains.

ⓘ Getting There & Away

Bus 41 runs from Fort William bus station up
Glen Nevis to the youth hostel (10 minutes, five
daily Monday to Saturday, three on Sunday,
limited service October to April) and on to the
Lower Falls 3 miles beyond the hostel (20 minutes). Check at the tourist office for the latest
timetable, which is liable to alteration.

NEVIS RANGE

The **Nevis Range ski area** (☎01397-705825;
www.nevisrange.co.uk), 6 miles north of Fort
William, spreads across the northern
slopes of Aonach Mor (1221m). The gondola that gives access to the bottom of the
ski area at 655m operates year-round from
10am to 5pm; a return trip costs £10.50/6
for an adult/child (15 minutes each way).
At the top there's a restaurant and a couple
of walking routes through nearby **Lea-
nachan Forest**. During the ski season a
one-day lift pass costs £28/16.50 per adult/
child; a one-day package, including equipment hire, lift pass and two hours' instruction, costs £62.

A world championship **downhill
mountain-bike trail** (⊙11am-3pm mid-May–
mid-Sep) – for experienced riders only – runs
from the Snowgoose restaurant to the base
station; bikes are carried on a rack on the
gondola cabin. A single trip with your own
bike costs £12; full-suspension bike hire
costs from £40/70 per half-/full day depending on the bike. There are also 25 miles
of waymarked mountain-bike trails in the
nearby forest.

Bus 41 runs from Fort William bus station to Nevis Range (15 minutes, five daily
Monday to Saturday, three on Sunday, limited service October to April). Check at the
tourist office for the latest timetable, which
is liable to alteration.

CORPACH TO LOCH LOCHY

Corpach lies at the southern entrance to
the Caledonian Canal, 3 miles north of Fort
William; there's a classic picture-postcard
view of Ben Nevis from the mouth of the
canal. Nearby is the award-winning **Treasures of the Earth** (www.treasuresoftheearth.
co.uk; Corpach; adult/child £5/3; ⊙9.30am-7pm
Jul-Sep, 10am-5pm Mar-Jun & Oct, shorter hrs
Nov-Feb) exhibition, a rainy-day diversion
with a great collection of gemstones, minerals, fossils and other geological curiosities.

A mile east of Corpach, at Banavie, is
Neptune's Staircase, an impressive flight
of eight locks that allows boats to climb
20m to the main reach of the **Caledonian
Canal**. The B8004 road runs along the west
side of the canal to Gairlochy at the south
end of Loch Lochy, offering superb views of
Ben Nevis; the **canal towpath** on the east
side makes a great walk or bike ride (6.5
miles).

From Gairlochy the B8005 continues
along the west side of Loch Lochy to Achnacarry and the **Clan Cameron Museum**
(www.clan-cameron.org; adult/child £3.50/free;
⊙11am-5pm Jul & Aug, 1.30-5pm Easter-Jun &
Sep–mid-Oct), which records the history of
the clan and its involvement with the Jacobite rebellions, including items of clothing that once belonged to Bonnie Prince
Charlie.

From Achnacarry the **Great Glen Way**
and **Great Glen Mountain Bike Trail** continue along the roadless western shore of
Loch Lochy, and a dead-end minor road
leads west along lovely **Loch Arkaig**.

There are a couple of backpacker hostels in Corpach. At **Farr Cottage Lodge**
(☎01397-772315; www.farrcottage.com; dm/
tw £15/36; Ⓟ@) bike hire is also available,
while the folk at **Blacksmiths Backpackers Lodge** (☎01397-772467; www.highland
-mountain-guides.co.uk; dm £15; Ⓟ) can organise courses in climbing, kayaking and other
sports.

GLEN SPEAN & GLEN ROY

Near Spean Bridge, at the junction of the
B8004 and A82, 2.5 miles east of Gairlochy,
stands the **Commando Memorial**, which
commemorates the WWII special forces
soldiers who trained in this area.

Four miles further east, at Roy Bridge, a
minor road leads north up Glen Roy, which
is noted for its intriguing, so-called **parallel
roads**. These prominent horizontal terraces contouring around the hill side are ac-

tually ancient shorelines formed during the last ice age by the waters of an ice-dammed glacial lake. The best viewpoint is 3 miles up Glen Roy.

Ardgour & Ardnamurchan

The drive from Corran Ferry, 8 miles south of Fort William, to **Ardnamurchan Point** (www.ardnamurchan.com), the most westerly point on the British mainland, is one of the most beautiful in the western Highlands, especially in late spring and early summer when much of the narrow, twisting road is lined with the bright pink and purple blooms of rhododendrons. A car ferry (car £6.20, passenger free, 10 minutes, two an hour) crosses from the Fort William–Glencoe road to Ardgour at Corran Ferry.

The road clings to the northern shore of Loch Sunart, going through the pretty villages of **Strontian** – which gave its name to the element strontium, first discovered in ore from nearby lead mines in 1790 – and **Salen**.

The mostly single-track road from Salen to Ardnamurchan Point is only 25 miles long, but it'll take you 1½ hours each way. It's a dipping, twisting, low-speed roller coaster of a ride through sun-dappled native woodlands draped with lichen and fern. Just when you're getting used to the views of Morvern and Mull to the south, it makes a quick detour to the north for a panorama over the islands of Rum and Eigg.

⊙ Sights

Kilchoan
VILLAGE

The scattered crofting village of Kilchoan, the only village of any size west of Salen, is best known for the scenic ruins of 13th-century **Mingary Castle**. The village has a **tourist office** (☏01972-510222; Pier Rd; ☺Easter-Oct), a shop and a hotel, and there's a ferry to Tobermory on the Isle of Mull.

Ardnamurchan Natural History Centre
WILDLIFE CENTRE

(www.ardnamurchannaturalhistorycentre.co.uk; Glenmore; adult/child £4/2; ☺10.30am-5.30pm Mon-Sat, noon-5.30pm Sun Easter-Oct) Midway between Salen and Kilchoan is this fascinating centre, devised by local photographer Michael MacGregor, that tries to bring you face to face with the flora and fauna of the Ardnamurchan peninsula. The Living Building exhibit is designed to attract local wildlife, with a mammal den that is

occasionally occupied by hedgehogs or pine martens, an owl nest-box, a mouse nest and a pond. If the beasties are not in residence, you can watch recorded video footage of the animals. There's also live CCTV coverage of a golden eagle feeding site.

Ardnamurchan Lighthouse
HISTORIC LIGHTHOUSE

(www.nlb.org.uk; adult/child £3/1.70; ☺10am-5pm Apr-Oct) The final 6 miles of road from Kilchoan ends at the 36m-high, grey granite tower of Ardnamurchan Lighthouse, built in 1849 by the Stevensons to guard the westernmost point of the British mainland. There's a good tearoom, and the visitor centre will tell you more than you'll ever need to know about lighthouses, with lots of hands-on stuff for kids; the **guided tour** (£6) includes a trip to the top of the lighthouse. But the main attraction here is the expansive view over the ocean – this is a superb sunset viewpoint, provided you don't mind driving back in the dark.

🛏 Sleeping & Eating

Salen Hotel
INN ££

(☏01967-431661; www.salenhotel.co.uk; Salen; r £60; ℗) A traditional Highland inn with views over Loch Sunart, the Salen Hotel has three rooms above the pub (with sea views) and another three rooms (each with en suite) in a modern chalet out the back. The cosy lounge has a roaring fire and comfy sofa, and the bar meals, including seafood, venison and other game dishes, are very good.

Inn at Ardgour
INN ££

(☏01855-841225; www.ardgour.biz; Ardgour; d/f £90/120; ℗) This pretty, whitewashed coaching inn, draped in colourful flower baskets, makes a great place for a lunch break or overnight stop. The **restaurant** (mains £8 to £13) is set in the row of cottages once occupied by the Corran ferrymen, and serves traditional, homemade Scottish dishes.

Ardnamurchan Natural History Centre
CAFE £

(Glenmore; mains £4-8; ☺10.30am-5.30pm Mon-Sat, noon-5.30pm Sun Easter-Oct) The cafe at this wildlife centre serves delicious lunches, ranging from fresh salads and sandwiches to daily specials such as prawns and crayfish tails.

Resipole Caravan Park
CAMPSITE £

(☏01967-431235; www.resipole.co.uk; Resipole; tent sites £8, with car £13, per person £3)

Ardnamurchan Campsite CAMPSITE £
(☎01972-510766; www.ardnamurchanstudy centre.co.uk; Kilchoan; tent site & 1 person £7, extra person £6; ☺May-Sep; ℗) Just west of Kilchoan village.

ℹ Getting There & Away

Sheil Buses bus 502 runs from Fort William to Glenuig and Acharacle, continuing to Salen and Kilchoan on request (3¼ hours, one daily Monday to Saturday). For details of ferries between Kilchoan and Tobermory, see p290.

Salen to Lochailort

The A861 road from Salen to Lochailort passes through the low, wooded hills of Moidart. A minor road (signposted Dorlin) leads west from the A861 at Shiel Bridge to a picnic area looking across to the picturesque roofless ruin of 13th-century **Castle Tioram**. The castle sits on a tiny island in Loch Moidart, connected to the mainland by a narrow strand that is submerged at high tide (the castle's name, pronounced *chee*-ram, means 'dry'). It was the ancient seat of the Clanranald Macdonalds, but the Clanranald chief ordered it to be burned (to prevent it falling into the hands of Hanoverian troops) when he set off to fight for the Jacobite side in the 1715 rebellion. A proposal by the owner to restore the castle was turned down by Historic Scotland; it is now closed to the public due to its unsafe condition.

As the A861 curls around the north shore of Loch Moidart you will see a line of three huge beech trees (and two obvious stumps) between the road and the shore. Known as the **Seven Men of Moidart** (four have been blown down by gales and replaced with saplings), they were planted in the late 18th century to commemorate the seven local men who accompanied Bonnie Prince Charlie from France and acted as his bodyguards at the start of the 1745 rebellion.

Road to the Isles

The 46-mile A830 from Fort William to Mallaig is traditionally known as the Road to the Isles, as it leads to the jumping-off point for ferries to the Small Isles and Skye, itself a stepping stone to the Outer Hebrides. This is a region steeped in Jacobite history, having witnessed both the beginning and the end of Bonnie Prince Charlie's doomed attempt to regain the British throne.

The final section of this scenic route, between Arisaig and Mallaig, has recently been upgraded to a fast straight road. Unless you're in a hurry, instead opt for the old coastal road (signposted Alternative Coastal Route).

Between the A830 and the A87 far to the north lies Scotland's 'Empty Quarter', a rugged landscape of wild mountains and lonely sea lochs roughly 20 miles by 30 miles in size, mostly uninhabited and penetrated only by two minor roads (along Lochs Arkaig and Quoich). If you want to get away from it all, this is the place to go.

ℹ Getting Around

BUS Shiel Buses bus 500 runs to Mallaig (1½ hours, three daily Monday to Friday only) via Glenfinnan (30 minutes) and Arisaig (one hour).

TRAIN The Fort William–Mallaig railway line has four trains a day (three on Sunday), with stops at many points along the way, including Corpach, Glenfinnan, Lochailort, Arisaig and Morar.

GLENFINNAN
POP 100

Glenfinnan is hallowed ground for fans of Bonnie Prince Charlie; its monument to him is its central shrine.

◉ Sights & Activities

Glenfinnan Monument MONUMENT
This tall column, topped by a statue of a kilted Highlander, was erected in 1815 on the spot where the Young Pretender first raised his standard and rallied the clans on 19 August 1745, marking the start of the ill-fated campaign that would end in disaster 14 months later. The setting, at the north end of Loch Shiel, is hauntingly beautiful.

Glenfinnan Visitor Centre VISITOR CENTRE
(NTS; adult/child £3/2; ☺9.30am-5.30pm Jul & Aug, 10am-5pm Easter-Jun, Sep & Oct) The story of the '45, as the Jacobite rebellion of 1745 is known – when the prince's loyal clansmen marched and fought from Glenfinnan south to Derby, then back north to final defeat at Culloden – is recounted here.

Glenfinnan Station Museum MUSEUM
(www.glenfinnanstationmuseum.co.uk; adult/child £1/50p; ☺9am-5pm Jun–mid-Oct) A half-mile west of the visitor centre, this museum is a shrine of a different kind whose object of veneration is the great days of steam on the West Highland line. The famous 21-

arch **Glenfinnan Viaduct**, just east of the station, was built in 1901, and featured in the movie *Harry Potter & the Chamber of Secrets*. A pleasant walk of around 0.75 miles leads to a viewpoint for the viaduct and the loch.

Loch Shiel Cruises BOAT TRIP
(☏07801 537617; www.highlandcruises.co.uk; ☉Apr-Sep) Offers boat trips along Loch Shiel, departing from a jetty near Glenfinnan House Hotel. There are one- to 2½-hour cruises (£8 to £16 per person) daily except Saturday and Wednesday. On Wednesday the boat goes the full length of the loch to **Acharacle** (£15/22 one way/return), calling at Polloch and Dalilea, allowing for a range of walks and bike rides using the forestry track on the eastern shore.

🛏 Sleeping & Eating

Sleeping Car Bunkhouse BUNKHOUSE, CAFE **£**
(☏01397-722295; www.glenfinnanstationmuseum.co.uk; dm £14; ☉Jun–mid-Oct) Two converted railway carriages at Glenfinnan Station house the 10-berth bunkhouse and the atmospheric **Dining Car** (snacks £2-4; ☉9am-4.30pm Jun–mid-Oct), which serves scones with cream and jam and pots of tea, with superb views of the mountains above Loch Shiel.

Prince's House Hotel INN **££**
(☏01397-722246; www.glenfinnan.co.uk; s/d £69/100; P) A delightful old coaching inn from 1658, the Prince's House is a good place to pamper yourself – ask for the spacious, tartan-clad Stuart Room if you want to stay in the oldest part of the hotel. Note that only dinner, bed and breakfast rates (£160 to £190 a double) are available on weekends from Easter to October. There's no documentary evidence that Bonnie Prince Charlie actually stayed here in 1745, but then again it was the only sizable house in Glenfinnan at that time, so...

ARISAIG & MORAR

The 5 miles of coast between Arisaig and Morar is a fretwork of rocky islets, inlets and gorgeous silver-sand beaches backed by dunes and machair, with stunning sunset views across the sea to the silhouetted peaks of Eigg and Rum. The **Silver Sands of Morar**, as they are known, draw crowds of bucket-and-spade holidaymakers in July and August, when the many camping grounds scattered along the coast are filled to overflowing.

GLENUIG INN

Set on a peaceful bay on the Arisaig coast, halfway between Lochailort and Acharacle on the A830 road, the recently renovated **Glenuig Inn** (☏01687-470219; www.glenuig.com; Glenuig; B&B s/d/q £60/90/120, bunkhouse per person £25; P🐾) is a great place to get away from it all. As well as offering comfortable accommodation, good food (mains £9 to £19), and real ale on tap, it's a great base for exploring Arisaig, Morar and the Loch Shiel area.

Apart from the countless hiking and biking options, **Rockhopper Sea Kayaking** (www.rockhopperscotland.co.uk) can take you on a guided day tour (half/full £40/70) along the wild and beautiful coastline, starting and finishing at the inn.

👁 Sights

Camusdarach Beach BEACH
Fans of the movie *Local Hero* still make pilgrimages to Camusdarach Beach, just south of Morar, which starred in the film as Ben's beach. To find it, look for the car park 800m north of Camusdarach campsite; from here, a wooden footbridge and a 400m walk through the dunes lead to the beach. (The village that featured in the film is on the other side of the country, at Pennan.)

Land, Sea & Islands Visitor Centre VISITOR CENTRE
(www.arisaigcentre.co.uk; Arisaig; adult/child £2/free; ☉10am-4pm Mon-Fri, 1-4pm Sun) This centre in Arisaig village houses a small but fascinating exhibition on the part played by the local area as a base for training spies for the SOE (Special Operations Executive, forerunner of MI6) during WWII.

Loch nan Uamh HISTORIC SITE
The waters of Loch nan Uamh (loch nan *oo*-ah; 'the loch of the caves') lap at the southern shores of Arisaig; this was where Bonnie Prince Charlie first set foot on the Scottish mainland on 11 August 1745, on the shingle beach at the mouth of the Borrodale burn. Just 2 miles to the east of this bay, on a rocky point near a parking area, the **Prince's Cairn** marks the spot where he

finally departed Scottish soil, never to return, on 19 September 1746.

🛏 Sleeping & Eating

There are at least a half-dozen camping grounds between Arisaig and Morar; all are open in summer only, and are often full in July and August, so book ahead. Some are listed on www.road-to-the-isles.org.uk.

Garramore House　　B&B ££
(☑01687-450268; South Morar; r per person £25-35; 🅿🐾) Built as a hunting lodge in 1840, this house served as a Special Operations Executive HQ during WWII. Today it's a wonderfully atmospheric, child- and pet-friendly guesthouse set in lovely woodland gardens with great views to the Small Isles and Skye.

Old Library Lodge & Restaurant
RESTAURANT ££
(☑01687-450651; www.oldlibrary.co.uk; Arisaig; mains £10-15; ⏰food served noon-2.30pm & 6.30-9.30pm) The Old Library is a charming restaurant with **rooms** (B&B per person £45 to £55) set in converted 200-year-old stables overlooking the waterfront in Arisaig village. The lunch menu concentrates on soups and freshly made sandwiches, while dinner is a more sophisticated affair offering local seafood, game and lamb.

Camusdarach Campsite　　CAMPSITE £
(☑01687-450221; www.camusdarach.com; South Morar; tent sites £14; ⏰Mar-Oct) A small and beautiful site with good facilities, only three minutes' walk from the *Local Hero* beach.

MALLAIG
POP 800

If you're travelling between Fort William and Skye, you may find yourself overnighting in the bustling fishing and ferry port of Mallaig. Indeed, it makes a good base for a series of day-trips by ferry to the Small Isles and Knoydart.

👁 Sights & Activities

Mallaig Heritage Centre　HERITAGE CENTRE
(www.mallaigheritage.org.uk; Station Rd; adult/child £2/free; ⏰9.30am-4.30pm Mon-Sat, noon-4pm Sun) The village's rainy-day attractions are limited to this centre, which covers the archaeology and history of the region, including the heart-rending tale of the Highland Clearances in Knoydart.

MV Grimsay Isle　　TOURS
(☑07780 815158) Provides entertaining, customised sea-fishing trips and seal-watching tours (book at the tourist office).

🛏 Sleeping & Eating

Seaview Guest House　　B&B ££
(☑01687-462059; www.seaviewguesthousemallaig.com; Main St; r per person £28-35; ⏰Mar-Nov; 🅿) Just beyond the tourist office, this comfortable three-bedroom B&B has grand views over the harbour, not only from the upstairs bedrooms but also from the breakfast room. There's also a cute little cottage next door that offers self-catering accommodation (www.selfcateringmallaig.com; one double and one twin room) for £350 to £450 a week.

Springbank Guest House　　B&B £
(☑01687-462459; www.springbank-mallaig.co.uk; East Bay; r per person £25; 🅿📶) A little further around the bay than the Seaview, the Springbank is a traditional West Highland house with seven homely guest bedrooms, again with superb views across the harbour to the Cuillin of Skye.

Mallaig Backpacker's Lodge　　HOSTEL £
(☑01687-462764; www.mallaigbackpackers.co.uk; Harbour View; dm £14.50) Sheena's is a friendly, 12-bed hostel in a lovely old house overlooking the harbour. On a sunny day the hostel's Tea Garden **terrace cafe** (mains £5 to £10), with its flowers, greenery and cosmopolitan backpacker staff, feels more like the Med than Mallaig. The speciality of the house is a pint-glass full of Mallaig prawns with dipping sauce (£10). From late May to September the cafe opens in the evening with a bistro menu.

TOP CHOICE **Fish Market**　　SEAFOOD ££
(☑01687-462299; Station Rd; mains £9-20; ⏰lunch & dinner) At least half-a-dozen signs in Mallaig advertise 'seafood restaurant', but this bright, modern, bistro-style place next to the harbour is our favourite, serving simply prepared scallops with smoked salmon and savoy cabbage, grilled langoustines with garlic butter, and fresh Mallaig haddock fried in breadcrumbs, as well as the tastiest Cullen skink on the west coast. Upstairs is a **coffee shop** (mains £4-5; ⏰11am-5pm) that serves delicious hot roast-beef rolls with horseradish sauce, and scones with clotted cream and jam.

ℹ Information

There's a **tourist office** (☑01687-462170; ⏰10am-5.30pm Mon-Fri, 10.15am-3.45pm Sat, noon-3.30pm Sun), a post office, a bank with ATM and a **Co-op supermarket** (⊙8am-10pm Mon-Sat, 9am-9pm Sun).

ℹ Getting There & Away

BOAT

Ferries run from Mallaig to the Small Isles, the Isle of Skye and Knoydart; see the transport information for these areas for more details.

BUS

Shiel Buses bus 500 runs from Fort William to Mallaig (1½ hours, three daily Monday to Friday only) via Glenfinnan (30 minutes) and Arisaig (one hour).

TRAIN

The West Highland line runs between Fort William and Mallaig (£10, 1½ hours) four times a day (three on Sunday).

Knoydart Peninsula

POP 70

The Knoydart peninsula is the only sizable area in Britain that remains inaccessible to the motor car, cut off by miles of rough country and the embracing arms of Lochs Nevis and Hourn – Gaelic for the lochs of Heaven and Hell. No road penetrates this wilderness of rugged hills – **Inverie**, its sole village, can only be reached by ferry from Mallaig, or on foot from the remote road's end at Kinloch Hourn (a tough 16-mile hike).

The main reasons for visiting are to climb the remote 1020m peak of **Ladhar Bheinn** (*laar*-ven), which affords some of the west coast's finest views, or just to enjoy the feeling of being cut off from the rest of the world. There are no shops, no TV and no mobile-phone reception (although there *is* internet access); electricity is provided by a private hydroelectric scheme – truly 'off the grid' living! For more information and full accommodation listings, see www.knoydart.org.

🛏 Sleeping & Eating

Knoydart Lodge　　　　　　　　　B&B ££

(☎01687-460129; www.knoydartlodge.co.uk; Inverie; s/d £55/80; 🤙) This must be some of the most spacious and luxurious B&B accommodation on the whole west coast, let alone in Knoydart – on offer are large, stylish bedrooms in a fantastic, modern timber-built lodge reminiscent of an Alpine chalet. Gourmet evening meals are available on Wednesday and Saturday (£30 per person).

TOP
CHOICE **Old Forge**　　PUB, RESTAURANT ££

(☎01687-462267; www.theoldforge.co.uk; Inverie; mains £10-20; 🍴) The Old Forge is listed in the *Guinness Book of Records* as Britain's most remote pub. It's surprisingly sophisticated – as well as having real ale on tap, there's an Italian coffee machine for those wilderness lattes and cappuccinos, and the house special is a platter of langoustines with Marie Rose dipping sauce. In the evening you can sit by the fire, pint of beer in hand and join the impromptu *ceilidh* (an evening of traditional Scottish entertainment including music, song and dance) that seems to take place just about nightly.

Knoydart Foundation Bunkhouse

BUNKHOUSE £

(☎01687-462163; www.knoydart.org; Inverie; dm £14; @) A 15-minute walk east of the ferry pier.

Torrie Shieling　　　　　　BUNKHOUSE £

(☎01687-462669; torrie@knoydart.org; Inverie; dm £15) A 20-minute walk to the west.

Barisdale Bothy　　　　　　BUNKHOUSE £

(☎01764-684946; www.barisdale.com; Barisdale; dm £3, tent sites per person £1) Six miles west of Kinloch Hourn on the footpath to Inverie; has sleeping platforms without mattresses – you'll need your own sleeping bag and foam mat.

Long Beach　　　　　　　　　CAMPSITE £

(Long Beach; per tent £4) Basic but beautiful campsite, a 10-minute walk east of the ferry; water supply and composting toilet, but no showers.

ℹ Getting There & Away

Bruce Watt Cruises (☎01687-462320; www.knoydart-ferry.co.uk) Passenger ferry linking Mallaig to Inverie (£9/12 single/return, 45 minutes) twice daily Monday to Friday from mid-May to mid-September, and on Monday, Wednesday and Friday only the rest of the year (no weekend ferries). Taking the morning boat gives you four hours ashore in Knoydart before the afternoon return trip.

SMALL ISLES

The scattered jewels of the Small Isles – Rum, Eigg, Muck and Canna – lie strewn across the silvery-blue cloth of the Cuillin Sound to the south of the Isle of Skye. Their distinctive outlines enliven the glorious views from the beaches of Arisaig and Morar.

INVERNESS & THE CENTRAL HIGHLANDS KNOYDART PENINSULA

Rum is the biggest and boldest of the four, a miniature Skye of pointed peaks and dramatic sunset silhouettes. Eigg is the most pastoral and populous, dominated by the miniature sugarloaf mountain of the Sgurr. Muck is a botanist's delight with its wildflowers and unusual alpine plants, and Canna is a craggy bird sanctuary made of magnetic rocks.

If your time is limited and you can only visit one island, choose Eigg; it has the most to offer on a day-trip.

❶ Getting There & Away

The main ferry operator is **CalMac** (www. calmac.co.uk), which operates the passenger-only ferry from Mallaig to Eigg (£11 return, 1¼ hours, five a week), Muck (£17 return, 1½ hours, four a week), Rum (£16 return, 1¼ hours, five a week) and Canna (£20 return, two hours, two a week). You can also hop between the islands without returning to Mallaig, but the timetable is complicated and it requires a bit of planning – you would need at least five days to visit all four. Bicycles are carried for free.

From May to September **Arisaig Marine** (☎01687-450224; www.arisaig.co.uk) operates day cruises from Arisaig harbour to Eigg (£18 return, one hour, six a week), Rum (£24 return, 2½ hours, two or three a week) and Muck (£19 return, two hours, three a week). The trips include whale-watching, with up to an hour for close viewing. Sailing times allow four or five hours ashore on Eigg, two or three hours on Muck or Rum.

Isle of Rum

POP 30

The Isle of Rum – the biggest and most spectacular of the Small Isles – was once known as the Forbidden Island. Cleared of its crofters in the early 19th century to make way for sheep, from 1888 to 1957 it was the private sporting estate of the Bulloughs, a nouveau-riche Lancashire family who made their fortune in the textile industry. Curious outsiders who ventured too close to the island were liable to find themselves staring down the wrong end of a gamekeeper's shotgun.

The island was sold to the Nature Conservancy in 1957 and has since been a reserve noted for its deer, wild goats, ponies, golden and white-tailed sea eagles, and a 120,000-strong nesting colony of Manx shearwaters. Its dramatic, rocky mountains, known as the Rum Cuillin for their similarity to the peaks on neighbouring Skye, draw hill walkers and climbers.

◎ Sights & Activities

Kinloch Castle   CASTLE
(www.isleofrum.com; adult/child £6/3; ⊙guided tours Mon-Sat, to coincide with ferry times) When George Bullough – a dashing, Harrow-educated cavalry officer – inherited Rum along with half his father's fortune in 1891, he became one of the wealthiest bachelors in Britain. Bullough blew half his inheritance on building his dream bachelor pad – the ostentatious Kinloch Castle. The bachelor shipped in pink sandstone from Dumfriesshire and 250,000 tonnes of Ayrshire topsoil for the gardens, and paid his workers a shilling extra a day to wear tweed kilts – just so they'd look more picturesque. Hummingbirds were kept in the greenhouses and alligators in the garden, and guests were entertained with an orchestrion, the Edwardian equivalent of a Bose hi-fi system. Since the Bulloughs left, the castle has survived as a perfect time capsule of upper-class Edwardian eccentricity. The guided tour should not be missed.

Bullough Mausoleum   MAUSOLEUM
The only part of the island that still belongs to the Bullough family is this mausoleum in Glen Harris, a miniature Greek temple that wouldn't look out of place on the Acropolis; Lady Bullough was laid to rest here alongside her husband and father-in-law in 1967, having died at the age of 98.

Nature Trails   WALKING
There's some great coastal and mountain walking on the island, including a couple of easy, waymarked nature trails in the woods around Kinloch. **Glen Harris** is a 10-mile round trip from Kinloch, on a rough 4WD track – allow four to five hours' walking. The climb to the island's highest point, **Askival** (812m), is a strenuous hike and involves a bit of rock scrambling (allow six hours for the round trip from Kinloch).

🛏 Sleeping & Eating

Accommodation on Rum is strictly limited, and if you want to stay overnight on the island, you have to contact the **reserve office** (☎01687-462026) in advance. There are also two bothies (unlocked cottages for use of hikers) on the island.

Kinloch Castle Hostel   HOSTEL £
(☎01687-462037; www.isleofrum.com; Kinloch; dm £15, d £40-50; ⊙Mar-Oct; ☎) The castle has 45 hostel beds and four double bedrooms in its rear wing. There's a commu-

nal self-catering kitchen, and also a small restaurant offering a cooked breakfast and dinner to guests and nonguests alike.

Kinloch Campsite
CAMPSITE £

(www.isleofrum.com; tent sites per person £5) Situated near the castle, this basic campsite has toilets, a water supply and hot showers, but there's not much in the way of level ground! Book in advance with the reserve office. Wild camping in the rest of the island is allowed, but check with the reserve office first for advice on avoiding nesting areas and other wildlife that might suffer from disturbance.

ℹ️ Information

Kinloch, where the ferry lands, is the island's only settlement; it has a small **grocery shop** (⊙5-7.30pm), post office and public telephone, and a **visitor centre** (⊙8.30am-5pm) near the pier where you can get information and leaflets on walking and wildlife. There's a **tearoom** (⊙10am-4pm Apr-Sep) in the village hall, with internet access. The hall itself is open at all times for people to shelter from the rain (or the midges!). For more information see www.isleofrum.com.

Isle of Eigg
POP 70

The Isle of Eigg made history in 1997 when it became the first Highland estate to be bought out by its inhabitants. The island is now owned and managed by the **Isle of Eigg Heritage Trust** (www.isleofeigg.org), a partnership among the islanders, Highland Council and the Scottish Wildlife Trust.

🏃 Activities

The island takes its name from the Old Norse *egg* (edge), a reference to the Sgurr of Eigg (393m), an impressive minimountain that towers over Galmisdale. Ringed by vertical cliffs on three sides, it's composed of pitchstone lava with columnar jointing similar to that seen on the Isle of Staffa and at the Giant's Causeway in Northern Ireland.

Sgurr of Eigg
HIKING

The climb to the summit (4.5 miles round trip; allow three to four hours) begins on the stony road leading up from the pier, which continues uphill through the woods to a red-roofed cottage. Go through the gate to the right of the cottage and turn left; just 20m along the road a cairn on the right marks the start of a boggy footpath that leads over the eastern shoulder of the Sgurr, then tra-

verses beneath the northern cliffs until it makes its way up onto the summit ridge.

On a fine day the views from the top are magnificent – Rum and Skye to the north, Muck and Coll to the south, Ardnamurchan Lighthouse to the southeast and Ben Nevis shouldering above the eastern horizon. Take binoculars – on a calm summer's day there's a good chance of seeing minke whales feeding down below in the Sound of Muck.

Uamh Fraing
CAVE

A shorter walk (2 miles; allow 1½ hours round trip, and bring a torch) leads west from the pier to the spooky and claustrophobic Uamh Fraing (Massacre Cave). Start as for the Sgurr of Eigg, but 800m from the pier turn left through a gate and into a field. Follow the 4WD track and fork left before a white cottage to pass below it. A footpath continues across the fields to reach a small gate in a fence; go through it and descend a ridge towards the shore.

The cave entrance is tucked inconspicuously down to the left of the ridge. The entrance is tiny – almost a hands-and-knees job – but the cave opens out inside and runs a long way back. Go right to the back, turn off your torch, and imagine the cave packed shoulder to shoulder with terrified men, women and children. Then imagine the panic as your enemies start piling firewood into the entrance. Almost the entire population of Eigg – around 400 people – sought refuge in this cave when the MacLeods of Skye raided the island in 1577. In an act of inhuman cruelty, the raiders lit a fire in the narrow entrance and everyone inside died of asphyxiation. There are more than a few ghosts floating around in here.

Other Walks
HIKING

Other good walks are to the deserted crofts of **Grulin** on the southwest coast (5 miles, two hours round trip), and north to **Laig Beach** with its famous **singing sands** – the sand makes a squeaking noise when you walk on it (8 miles, three hours return). You can get more information on island walks from the craft shop in An Laimhrig.

🛏️ Sleeping & Eating

All accommodation should be booked in advance. For a full listing of self-catering accommodation, see www.iselofeigg.org.

Lageorna
B&B ££

(☎01687-482405; www.lageorna.com; Cleadale; dinner B&B per person £60; 🛜) This converted croft house and lodge in the island's north-west is Eigg's most luxurious accommodation. Rooms are fitted with beautiful, locally made 'driftwood-style' timber beds, and even have iPod docks (but no mobile-phone reception). Evening meals are part of the package, with the menu heavy on locally grown vegetables, seafood and venison.

Sandavore Bothy BOTHY £
(📞01687-482480; suehollands@talk21.com; Sandavore; per night £30) This tiny, one-room bothy, a 15-minute walk from the pier, has space for four people in one double bed and two bunk beds. It's a real Hebridean experience – accessible only on foot, no electricity (just gaslight and candles), cold running water only and an outside toilet.

Glebe Barn BUNKHOUSE £
(📞01687-482417; www.glebebarn.co.uk; Galmisdale; dm/tw £15/36) Excellent bunkhouse accommodation, with a smart, maple-floored lounge with central fireplace, modern kitchen, laundry, drying room, and bright, clean dorms and bedrooms.

Sue Holland's Croft CAMPSITE £
(📞01687-482480; suehollands@talk21.com; Cleadale; per tent £4) You can camp at this organic croft in the north of the island; basic facilities.

An Laimhrig CAFE £
(Galmisdale; ⏰10am-5pm May-Sep) There's a good cafe here at the ferry pier; winter opening times coincide with ferry arrivals and departures.

ℹ️ Information

The ferry landing is at Galmisdale in the south.
An Laimhrig (www.isleofeiggshop.co.uk; ⏰10am-5pm Mon-Wed & Fri, 11am-3pm Thu, 11am-5pm Sat, noon-1pm Sun May-Sep) The building above the pier houses a grocery store, post office, craft shop and tearoom; open shorter hours in winter. You can hire bikes here, too.

Isle of Muck

POP 30
The tiny island of **Muck** (www.isleofmuck.com), measuring just 2 miles by 1 mile, has exceptionally fertile soil, and the island is carpeted with wildflowers in spring and early summer. It takes its name from the Gaelic *muc* (pig), and pigs are still raised here.

Ferries call at the southern settlement of Port Mor. There's a **tearoom and craft shop** (⏰11am-4pm Jun-Aug, shorter hr May & Sep) above the pier, which also acts as an information centre.

It's an easy 15-minute walk along the island's only road from the pier to the sandy beach at **Gallanach** on the northern side of the island. A longer and rougher hike (1½ hours round trip) goes to the top of **Beinn Airein** (137m) for the best views. Puffins nest on the cliffs at the western end of Camas Mor, the bay to the south of the hill.

The cosy six-bed **Isle of Muck Bunkhouse** (📞01687-462042; dm £12), with its oil-fired Rayburn stove, is just above the pier, as is the welcoming eight-room **Port Mor House Hotel** (📞01687-462365; hotel@isleofmuck.com; r per person £50); rates include evening meals, which are also available to nonguests (£16, book in advance).

You can camp on the island for free – but ask at the craft shop first. For a full accommodation listing see www.isleofmuck.com.

Isle of Canna

POP 19
The roadless island of Canna is a moorland plateau of black basalt rock, just 5 miles long and 1.25 miles wide. **Compass Hill** (143m), at the northeastern corner, contains enough magnetite (an iron oxide mineral) to deflect the navigation compasses in passing yachts.

The ferry arrives at the hamlet of **A'Chill** at the eastern end of the island, where tourists have left extensive graffiti on the rock face south of the harbour. There's a tearoom and craft shop by the harbour, and a tiny post office in a hut. There is no mobile-phone reception.

You can walk to **An Coroghon**, just east of the ferry pier, a medieval stone tower perched atop a sea cliff, and continue to Compass Hill, or take a longer hike along the southern shore past a **Celtic cross** and the remains of the 7th-century **St Columba's Chapel**.

Accommodation is very limited. **Tighard** (📞01687-462474; www.peaceofcanna.co.uk; per person £35-50) is the only B&B (evening meals £25 to £30), and cafe-restaurant **Gille Brighde** (www.cannarestaurant.com; mains £7-17; ⏰11am-3pm & 6-9pm Tue-Fri, 10am-9pm Sat) the only eating place. Search www.ntsholidays.com for self-catering accommodation.

Canna Camping Holidays (📞01687-460166; www.cannafolk.co.uk) offers luxury camping in pre-pitched bell tents (£80 for two nights, up to five people).

Northern Highlands & Islands

Best Places to Stay

» Dornoch Castle Hotel (p357)

» Mackays (p367)

» Ceilidh Place (p371)

» Torridon (p374)

» Gearranan Blackhouse Village (p393)

» Toravaig House Hotel (p382)

Best Places to Eat

» Albannach (p369)

» Captain's Galley (p363)

» Three Chimneys (p387)

» Digby Chick (p392)

Why Go?

Scotland's vast and melancholy soul is here; an epic land whose stark beauty leaves an indelible imprint on the hearts of those who journey here. Mist and peat, heather and long sun-blessed summer evenings are the pay-off for so many days of horizontal drizzle.

Stone tells stories throughout. The monoliths of Lewis and the cairns of Caithness are testament left by prehistoric builders; walled castles and the broken stone of crofting communities shattered on the wheel of economic expedience tell of the Highlands' turbulent history.

Outdoors is where to be up here, whatever the weather; there's nothing like comparing windburn or mud-ruined boots over a dram by the fire of a Highland pub. The area lends itself to activity, from woodland strolls to Hebridean cycling circuits, sea kayaking to Munro-bagging, diving warship wrecks to puffin-spotting. Best are the locals, big-hearted and straight-talking: make it your business to get to know them.

When to Go
Portree

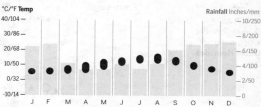

June The long, long evenings up here bathe heart-achingly sublime landscapes in a dreamlike light.

July The Hebridean Celtic Festival is a top time to experience the culture of the Outer Hebrides.

September Not as busy as summer, midges have gone and (if you're lucky) temperatures are still OK.

Northern Highlands & Islands Highlights

1 Gorging on fresh, succulent seafood in the delightful town of **Ullapool** (p370), with its picture-perfect harbour

2 Dipping your toes in the water at some of the world's most beautiful beaches on **Harris** (p395) and **Barra** (p400)

3 Shouldering the challenge of the **Cuillin Hills** (p382), the rugged silhouettes of which brood over the skyscape of Skye

4 Picking your jaw up off the floor as you marvel at the epic Highland scenery of the **far northwest** between Durness and Ullapool (p368)

5 Taking the trip out to the gloriously remote **Cape Wrath** (p368), Britain's northwestern shoulder

6 Relaxing in postcard-pretty **Plockton** (p376), where the Highlands meet the Caribbean

7 Launching yourself in a sea kayak to explore the otter-rich waters of the **Outer Hebrides** (p402)

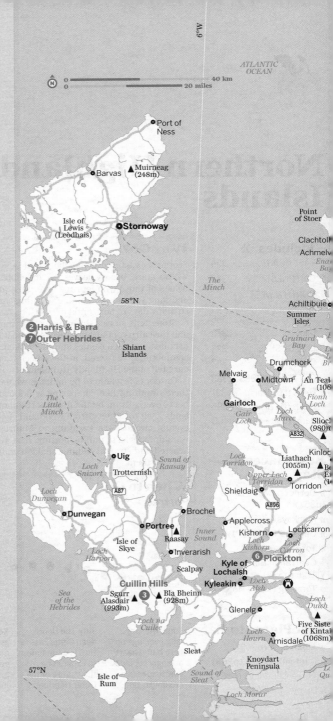

EAST COAST

In both landscape and character, the east coast is where the real barrenness of the Highlands begins to unfold. A gentle splendour and a sense of escapism mark the route along the twisting A9, as it heads north for the last of Scotland's far-flung, mainland population outposts. With only a few exceptions the tourism frenzy is left behind once the road traverses Cromarty Firth and snakes its way along wild and pristine coastline.

While the interior is dominated by the vast and mournful Sutherland mountain range, along the coast great heather-covered hills heave themselves out of the wild North Sea. Rolling farmland drops suddenly into the icy waters, and small, historic towns are moored precariously on the coast's edge.

Strathpeffer

POP 918

Strathpeffer is a delightful Highland town, its creaking old pavilions and grandiose hotels dripping with Victorian charm and a faded grandeur.

The village was a fashionable spa in Victorian and Edwardian times, when chic society folk congregated here to splash about in the sulphurous waters.

◉ Sights

The **Eagle Stone** (follow the signs from the main drag) is well worth a look when you're in town. It's a pre-7th-century Pictish stone connected to a figure from local history – the Brahan Seer, who predicted many future events. The **Strathpeffer & District Pipe Band** plays in the town square every Saturday from 8pm, May to September. There's also Highland dancing and a festive air.

Highland Museum of Childhood MUSEUM
(www.highlandmuseumofchildhood.org.uk; adult/child £2.50/1.50; ⊙10am-5pm Mon-Sat, 2-5pm Sun Apr-Oct) At the old Victorian train station is the Highland Museum of Childhood. It has a wide range of social-history displays about childhood in the Highlands, and also has activities for children, including a dressing-up box and a toy train. There's a good wee shop if you're after a present for a little somebody, and a peaceful cafe.

FREE **Pump Room** MUSEUM
(⊙10am-5pm Tue-Sat, Jun-Sep) The renovated Pump Room has some splendid displays showing the bizarre lengths Victorians went to in the quest for a healthy glow.

🛏 Sleeping & Eating

There are a couple of large hotels in town geared to coach tours of retirees, but no hostel.

Craigvar B&B ££
(☎01997-421622; www.craigvar.com; The Square; s/d £50/80; P🖛) Luxury living with a refined touch is what you'll find in this delightful Georgian town house. All the little extras that mark out a classy place are here, such as a welcome drink, bathrobes and fresh fruit. Couples should go for the 'Blue Room' with its sensational four-poster bed – you'll need to collapse back into it after the gourmet breakfast.

Coul House Hotel HOTEL £££
(☎01997-421487; www.coulhousehotel.com; Contin; s/d £85/155; P🖛) At Contin, not far south of Strathpeffer on the A835, Coul House is a very fine country mansion dating from 1821. Set in its own private wilderness, this charming country hotel with blazing log fire will entice you to linger. Luxury rooms include mountain views and four-poster beds. Its **restaurant** (mains £17-20) is open for dinner and serves eclectic modern fusion. Everything's delicious.

Maya CAFE £
(www.mayachocolates.co.uk; Main St; box of chocolates from £2.50; ⊙10am-5pm Tue-Sat) Ohhh, this place is dangerous. Bringing Belgian chocolates to the Highlands, Maya is the ultimate in sweet indulgence. It also serves up hot drinks, including hot chocolate... which goes perfectly with chocolate.

Red Poppy BISTRO ££
(☎01997-423332; www.redpoppyrestaurant.co.uk; mains £8-13; ⊙noon-8pm Tue-Sat, lunch Sun) In the restored historical Victorian spa pavilion is a much-needed dining option in town. There's a large selection of meals including game dishes such as wild boar steaks, and dining is in elegant surrounds. It's a little cheaper at lunchtime.

ℹ Information

The self-service **tourist office** (⊙10am-5pm Tue-Sat Jun-Sep) is in the Pump Room and has limited info. The bike shop on the square is good for information too.

❶ Getting There & Around

Stagecoach operates buses from Inverness to Strathpeffer (45 minutes, at least hourly Monday to Saturday, four on Sunday). The Inverness to Gairloch and Durness buses, plus some Inverness to Ullapool buses, also run via Strathpeffer.

Square Wheels Cycles (☑01997-421000; www.squarewheels.bizcom; The Square) Hires out mountain bikes for £10/15 per half-/full day. Price decreases with multiday hire. Staff can help with route information.

Tain

POP 3511

Scotland's oldest royal burgh, Tain is a proud sandstone town that rose to prominence as pilgrims descended to venerate the relics of St Duthac, who is commemorated by the 12th-century ruins of **St Duthac's Chapel**, and St Duthus Church. In the church grounds is entertaining **Tain Through Time** (www.tainmuseum.org.uk; Tower St; adult/child £3.50/2.50; ⊙10am-5pm Mon-Sat Apr-Oct), a heritage centre with a colourful and educational display on Duthac, King James IV and key moments in Scottish history. Another building focuses on the town's fine silversmithing tradition. Admission includes an audio-guided walk around town.

On Tain's northern outskirts, friendly **Glenmorangie Distillery** (www.glenmorangie .com; tours £2.50; ⊙9am-5pm Mon-Fri, plus 10am-4pm Sat & Sun Jun-Aug), with emphasis on the second syllable, produces a fine light malt, which is subjected to a number of different cask finishes for variation. The tour is less in-depth than some but finishes with a dram.

So much the heart of town that the main street has to detour around it, the **Royal Hotel** (☑01862-892013; www.royalhoteltain.co .uk; High St; s/d £50/85; ☎) is undergoing much-needed refurbishment that's leaving its good-sized rooms looking very spruce. For only a tenner more, you get a four-poster room in the old part of the hotel; these are great, with a choice of colour schemes, and well worth the upgrade. The restaurant is the best in town and bar meals are also decent.

Elegant B&B is available at **Golf View House** (☑01862-892856; www.golf-view.co.uk; 13 Knockbreck Rd; s £35-50, d £54-72; ℗☎), in an old manse in a secluded setting. Rooms are bright, and a couple have views of the sea. Breakfast is delicious, and hospitality excellent.

Scottish Citylink and Stagecoach buses from Inverness to Thurso pass through Tain several times daily (£8.50, 50 minutes to 1¼ hours, five daily).

There are up to three trains daily to Inverness (£11.20, one hour) and Thurso (£13.70, 2½ hours).

Portmahomack

POP 650

Portmahomack is a former fishing village in a flawless spot – right off the beaten track and gazing across the water at snowcapped peaks. The best place to enjoy the town is the grassy foreshore at the far end of Main St, near the little harbour.

The intriguing **Tarbat Discovery Centre** (www.tarbat-discovery.co.uk; Tarbatness Rd; adult/child £3.50/1; ⊙10am-5pm May-Sep, 2-5pm Apr & Oct) has some excellent carved Pictish stones. When 'crop circles' appeared in aerial photos a few years ago, the foundations of an Iron Age settlement were discovered around the village church; ongoing investigation revealed a Pictish monastery and evidence of production of illuminated manuscripts. The exhibition is excellent and includes the church's spooky crypt. Ask staff to pinpoint other Pictish sites in the region on a map for you.

There are good coastal walks at **Tarbat Ness**, 3 miles northeast of the village; the headland is marked by a tall, red-and-white-striped lighthouse.

Seafood aficionados shouldn't miss the bright and cheerful **Oystercatcher Restaurant** (☑01862-871560; www.the-oyster catcher.co.uk; Main St; lunch mains £8-14, dinner mains £15-20; ⊙lunch Wed-Sun, dinner Wed-Sat Apr-Oct). There's a bistro menu at lunchtime, where you can choose your serving size, and a classy brasserie evening menu with lots of lobster available among other delights. It also has three cosy **rooms** (s/d £43/98). The rate includes what has to be the most amazing breakfast in Scotland, with numerous gourmet options – you can book it even if you're not staying there overnight (£20).

Stagecoach Inverness runs from Tain to Portmahomack (25 minutes, four to five Monday to Friday).

Bonar Bridge & Around

The A9 crosses the Dornoch Firth, on a bridge and causeway, near Tain. An alternative route goes around the firth via the tiny settlements of **Ardgay**, where you'll find a train station, shop and hotel, and **Bonar Bridge**, where the A836 to Lairg branches west.

Mountain bikers will find two networks of **forest routes** (www.forestry.gov.uk/cycle northhighland) around here. From the car park below the Carbisdale youth hostel, there's a red and a blue trail (suitable for intermediate riders) with great views. At Balblair, a mile from Bonar Bridge off the Lairg road, 7 miles of black track will test anybody.

From Ardgay, a single-track road leads 10 miles up Strathcarron to **Croick**, the scene of notorious evictions during the 1845 Clearances. You can still see the evocative messages scratched by refugee crofters from Glencalvie on the eastern windows of Croick Church.

If a youth hostel could attract a five-star rating, opulent **Carbisdale Castle SYHA** (☎01549-421232; www.hostellingscotland.com; Culrain; dm/s/d £20/25/50; ☺mid-Mar–Oct; P@🛜🛝) would score six. Carbisdale Castle was built in 1914 for the dowager duchess of Sutherland – it is now Scotland's biggest and most luxurious hostel, its halls studded with statues and dripping with opulence. Kick back in the super-elegant library room or cook up a feast in the kitchen; catered

meals (£11.50 for a three-course dinner) are also available. It's 10 minutes' walk north of Culrain train station. Advance bookings are highly recommended. Mountain bikers coming off the trails can shower here for a small fee.

Trains running from Inverness to Thurso stop at Culrain (£13.50, 1½ hours, two to three daily), half a mile from Carbisdale Castle.

Lairg

POP 900

Lairg is an attractive village, although the tranquillity can be rudely interrupted by the sound of military jets heard whining and cracking overhead. At the southern end of Loch Shin, it's the gateway to the remote mountains and loch-speckled bogs of central Sutherland. The lonely A836 from Lairg to Tongue passes Ben Klibreck (961m) and Ben Loyal (764m).

In **Ferrycroft Visitor Centre** (☎01549-402160;www.highland.gov.uk/ferrycroft; ☺10am-4pm Apr-Oct; @), across the river from the town centre, you'll find displays on local history and a tourist information desk.

Four miles south of Lairg, the picturesque **Falls of Shin** is worth visiting, especially from June to September, when you can see salmon leaping up the cascades on their way upstream to spawn. There are marked forest trails here, as well as a large shop and cafe complex open daily – do

---

THE HIGHLANDS' JURASSIC PARK

In a pristine spot near Croick a revolutionary project is changing the concept of wildlife conservation in Scotland. **Alladale Wilderness Lodge & Reserve** (☎01863-755338; www.alladale.com; Ardgay), home to the country's most northerly tuft of ancient Scots pine forest, is releasing species once extinct in the area to roam on its vast estate. Wildlife on the reserve now includes elk, red deer, roe deer, wild boar, wild ponies and golden eagles. Longer-term plans include European bison and former predators, once abundant in Scotland, such as grey wolves, European brown bears and Eurasian lynx. There's plenty of local controversy over the project, with questions of public access and zoo licences being raised.

You can stay in the lodge, but it's for entire hire only, so you'd want a group of 10 or more. Smaller buildings accommodate up to four – rates start at around £600 per night, including full board. Call the lodge or see the website for details. Though broader public access, with activities like pony trekking and wildlife tours of the enclosed estate are planned, at time of research there was public access only on a few fixed dates throughout the summer; check the website for details.

Alladale is off the Croick road beyond Ardgay, where you can drop into **Alladale Country Stores** (☎01863-766323; Ardgay; ☺9am-5pm Mon-Sat, 10am-4pm Sun) for information.

they really shift all that chilled Harrods champagne?

Rooms are surprisingly modern and very good value at the solid **Lairg Highland Hotel** (☑01549-402243; www.highland-hotel.co.uk; Main St; s/d £39/78; [P][☎]). The decor is bright, en suites are sparkling and the inn caters for solo travellers. The **restaurant** is open for lunch and dinner (£10 to £14) and bar meals are also available (£7 to £9).

Trains from Inverness to Thurso stop at Lairg (£13.50, 1¾ hours) two or three times daily in each direction. There are no direct buses from Inverness; change at Tain.

Dornoch

POP 1206

It's difficult to believe that Scotland's last executed witch perished in a vat of boiling tar in Dornoch in 1722, because today this graceful village is all happy families. On the coast, 2 miles off the A9, this symphony in sandstone bewitches visitors with flowers, greenery and affable locals at every turn.

◎ Sights

Consecrated in the 13th century, **Dornoch Cathedral** (◷10am-7pm or later) is an elegant Gothic edifice with an interior softly illuminated through modern stained-glass windows. By the western door is the sarcophagus of Sir Richard de Moravia, who died fighting the Danes at the battle of Embo in the 1260s. Until he met his maker, the battle had been going rather well for him; he'd managed to slay the Danish commander with the unattached leg of a horse that was to hand.

Behind the Dornoch Castle Hotel, **Historylinks** (www.historylinks.org.uk; adult/child £2/free; ◷10am-4pm Mon-Fri Apr-Sep) is a child-friendly museum with displays on local history. It's open weekends from June to September, and Wednesdays and Thursdays over winter.

If you've struck Dornoch on a sunny day make sure you have a walk along its golden sand **beach**, which stretches for miles.

South of Dornoch, seals are often visible on the sand bars of **Dornoch Firth**.

🛏 Sleeping & Eating

TOP CHOICE **Dornoch Castle Hotel** HOTEL **££**
(☑01862-810216; www.dornochcastle hotel.com; Castle St; garden s/d £71/118, superi-

THE RIGHT SIDE OF THE TRACKS 357

Scotland has some unusual hostels and **Sleeperzzz.com** (☑01408-641343; www.sleeperzzz.com; Rogart Station; dm £14; ◷Mar–mid-Nov; [P]) in wee Pittentrail is one of them, set in three caringly converted railway carriages parked up in a siding by the station. It's on the A839, 10 miles east of Lairg but is also easily reached by train on the Inverness–Wick line (10% discount if you arrive this way) and has cute two-person dorms, kitchenettes and tiny lounges. The owners make an effort to run the hostel on sustainable lines, and there's a hearty local pub that does food, as well as beautifully lonely Highland scenery in the vicinity.

or/deluxe d £175/223; [P][☎][♿]) This 16th-century former bishop's palace makes a wonderful place to stay, particularly if you upgrade to one of the superior rooms, which have views, space, malt whisky and chocolates on the welcome tray, and, in some cases, four-poster beds; the deluxe rooms are unforgettable. Cheaper rooms (s/d £51/66) are also available in adjoining buildings. In the evening toast your toes in the cosy bar before dining in style at the first-rate **restaurant** (dinner mains £16-20) tucking into dishes featuring plenty of game and seasonal produce. The restaurant's open for lunch and dinner; bar meals are also available during the day.

2 Quail B&B **££**
(☑01862-811811; www.2quail.com; Castle St; s/d £110/130; [☎]) Intimate and upmarket, 2 Quail offers a warm welcome on the main street. The tasteful chambers are full of old-world comfort with sturdy metal bedframes, plenty of books and plump duvets; the downstairs guest lounge is an absolute delight.

Trevose Guest House B&B **££**
(☑01862-810269; jamackenzie@tiscali.co.uk; Cathedral Sq; s/d £35/60; ◷Mar-Sep; [☎]) First impressions deceive at Trevose Guest House, a lovely stone cottage right by the cathedral. It looks compact but actually boasts very spacious rooms with significant comfort and well-loved old wooden

furnishings. Character oozes from every pore of the place and a benevolent welcome is a given.

Rosslyn Villa ROOMS £
(☑01862-810237; Castle St; r per person £22) The best accommodation comes with simplicity and a smile. No breakfast.

Eagle Hotel PUB £
(www.eagledornoch.co.uk; Castle St; bar meals £8-10) Chow down at this top little boozer complete with eccentric ornamentation and simple bar food that comes in hefty portions and with a cheery smile.

ℹ Information

The **tourist office** (☑01862-255121; Castle St; ⏰9am-12.30pm, 1.30-5pm Mon-Fri, also Sat & Sun Jun-Aug) is in the Highland Council Building next to Dornoch Castle Hotel.

ℹ Getting There & Away

Scottish Citylink has four to five daily services to/from Inverness (£9, one hour) and Thurso (£14, 2¼ hours), which stop in the square at Dornoch.

Golspie

POP 1404

Golspie is an attractive town off the main drag and would be a congenial option for a day or two (particularly if you feel like pulling on the walking boots or exploring a castle).

One mile north of town is mighty **Dunrobin Castle** (www.dunrobincastle.co.uk; adult/child £8.50/5; ⏰10.30am-4.30pm Mon-Sat, noon-4.30pm Sun Apr, May & Sep–mid-Oct, 10.30am-5.30pm Jun-Aug), the largest house in the Highlands (187 rooms). Although it dates back to around 1275, most of what you see today was built in French style between 1845 and 1850. One of the homes of the earls and dukes of Sutherland, it's richly furnished and offers an intriguing insight into their opulent lifestyle. The house also displays innumerable gifts from farm tenants (probably grateful they weren't victims of the Clearances). The pitiless first Duke of Sutherland cleared 15,000 people from the north of Scotland while residing here.

Only 22 rooms are on display, with hunting trophies much to the fore. The **museum** offers an eclectic mix of archaeological finds, natural-history exhibits, more non-PC animal remains and an excellent collection of Pictish stones found in Sutherland. The formal gardens host impressive **falconry** displays two to three times a day.

Golspie is the starting point for some good walks. One trail leads north along the coast for 5 miles to Brora, passing the remains of the Iron Age broch (defensive tower) of **Carn Liath** about halfway along. The other trail climbs steeply above the village to the summit of **Ben Bhraggie** (394m), which is crowned by a massive monument to the duke of Sutherland that was erected in 1834 and is visible for miles around.

On the approach into town from Dornoch is **Blar Mhor** (☑01408-633609; www.blarmhor.co.uk; A9; s/d/f £30/50/70; 🅿), an excellent guesthouse with large, beautifully kept rooms (our fave is the double opposite the lounge) in a towering Victorian mansion. There are landscaped gardens and the lounge offers a chance to relax in the evening and socialise with other guests.

Buses between Inverness and Thurso stop in Golspie. There are also trains from Inverness (£15, two hours, two or three daily) to Golspie and to Dunrobin Castle.

Helmsdale

POP 900

Surrounded by hills with gorse that explodes mad yellow in springtime, this sheltered fishing town, like many other spots on this coast, was a major emigration point during the Clearances and also a booming herring port. It's surrounded by stunning, undulating coastline. The River Helmsdale is also one of the best salmon rivers in the Highlands.

In the centre of town, **Timespan** (www.timespan.org.uk; ⏰10am-5pm Mon-Sat, noon-5pm Sun Apr-Oct, 11am-4pm Sat & Sun, 2-5pm Tue Nov-Mar) has an impressive display covering local history (including the 1869 gold rush), and Barbara Cartland, late queen of romance novels, who was a Helmsdale regular. There are also local art exhibitions, a geology garden and a cafe.

🛏 Sleeping & Eating

Bridge Hotel HOTEL ££
(☑01431-821100; www.bridgehotel.net; Dunrobin St; s/d £65/105; 🅿) Ideally located, this early-19th-century lodging is the smartest place to stay and the best place to eat in town. Proud rather than furtive about its

Highland heritage, it displays a phalanx of antlers, even on the key fobs. But the rooms don't have the expected patina of age; they have wonderfully plush fabrics and a smart contemporary feel. The downstairs bar and restaurant hum with good cheer and relaxed hospitality; check out the replica of Britain's biggest landed salmon.

Helmsdale Hostel
HOSTEL £

(☎01431-821636; www.helmsdalehostel.co.uk; Stafford St; dm/tw/f £15/40/60; ☺Apr-Sep; ☜) This caringly run hostel is in very good nick and makes a cheerful, comfortable budget base for exploring Caithness. The dorm berths are mostly cosy single beds rather than bunks, and the en suite rooms are great for families. The lofty kitchen-lounge space has a wood stove and good kitchen.

La Mirage
BISTRO £

(www.lamirage.org; 7 Dunrobin St; mains £8-10; ☺noon-8.30pm) Created in homage to Barbara Cartland by the larger-than-life late owner, this minor legend is a medley of pink flamboyance, faded celebrity photos and show tunes. The meals aren't gourmet – think chicken Kiev – but the fish and chips (also available to take away: eat 'em down on the pretty harbour) are really tasty.

ℹ Getting There & Away

Buses from Inverness and Thurso stop in Helmsdale, as do trains (from Thurso £13.50, 1¼ hours, four daily).

CAITHNESS

Once you pass Helmsdale, you are entering Caithness, where cliffs topped with jagged gorse and grass hide tiny fishing harbours. This top corner of Scotland was Viking territory, historically more connected to Orkney and Shetland than to the rest of the mainland. It's a magical and mystical land with an ancient aura, peopled by wise folk with long memories who are fiercely proud of their corner of Scotland.

The region is bristling with ancient cairns and monuments, as well as Pictish and Viking remains. Most of the settlements you see today, however, are crofting villages set up when the Highland Clearances forced people to the coast. With the herring boom, these little fishing ports flourished and the region's chief town, Wick, became a harbour of international importance. In classic boom-and-bust way, the fish dried up and these places lapsed into painful decline: it's only in recent years that there's been some recovery. Inland, the lonely bogland is a real bird haven.

Caithness is the main gateway to Orkney, but make sure you spend some time getting to know this intriguing and isolated corner of the country.

Helmsdale to Lybster

About 7 miles north of Helmsdale is **Badbea**, which is a 15-minute walk east from the A9 (signposted). It's here that the ruins of crofts are perched on the clifftop. The **Berriedale Braes**, 2.5 miles beyond the Badbea parking area, is a difficult section of the A9, with steep gradients and hairpin bends.

Dunbeath has a spectacular setting in a deep glen – it makes a good stop on the way to the northern towns. There are a couple of shops and a **heritage centre** (www.dunbeath-heritage.org.uk; adult/child £2/free; ☺10am-5pm Sun-Fri Apr-Sep, 11am-3pm Mon-Fri Nov-Mar), which has a stone carved with runic graffiti, and a display on the work of Neil Gunn, whose wonderful novels evoke the Caithness of his boyhood.

Lybster is a purpose-built fishing village dating from 1810, with a stunning harbour area surrounded by grassy cliffs. In its heyday, it was Scotland's third busiest port: things have changed.

Down at the harbour is the **Waterlines Visitor Centre** (adult/child £2.50/50p; ☺11am-5pm May-Sep), with an exhibition on the fishing heritage of Lybster and a popular downstairs cafe. In summer it operates a smokehouse (giving visitors a whiff of the kippering process).

Stagecoach buses between Thurso and Inverness run via Lybster (one hour, up to four daily) and Dunbeath. There's also a coastal service from Wick to Helmsdale stopping at these places.

Around Lybster

At Ulbster, 5 miles north of Lybster on the A99, is **Whaligoe Steps**, a spectacular staircase cut into the cliff face. It provides access to a tiny natural harbour ringed by vertical cliffs and echoing with the cackle of nesting fulmars. The path begins at the end of the minor road beside the telephone box, opposite the road signposted 'Cairn of Get'. The **Cairn o'Get**, a prehistoric burial cairn, is a mile northwest of Ulbster. From the car park cross the stile and follow the black-and-white marker poles for approximately 1 mile. Wear decent shoes as the ground is boggy.

There are several interesting prehistoric sites near Lybster. Five miles to the northwest of Lybster, on the minor road to Achavanich, just south of Loch Stemster, are the unsigned 30 **Achavanich Standing Stones**. In a desolate setting, these crumbling monuments of the distant past still capture the imagination with their evocative location. It's all about colours: blue skies, a steely grey loch and the soft browns and greens of the land. The setting, and absence of modern tourism, makes this place special.

A mile east of Lybster on the A99, a turn-off leads 4 miles north to the **Grey Cairns of Camster**. Dating from between 4000 BC and 2500 BC, these burial chambers are hidden in long, low mounds rising from an evocatively desolate stretch of moor. The Long Cairn measures 60m by 21m. You can enter the main chamber, but must first crawl into the well-preserved Round Cairn, which has a corbelled ceiling. From the site you can then continue 7 miles north on this remote road to approach Wick on the A882.

Back on the A99, the **Hill o'Many Stanes**, 2 miles beyond the Camster turn-off, is a curious, fan-shaped arrangement of 22 rows of small stones that probably date from around 2000 BC. Staggeringly, there were 600 in the original pattern. On a sunny day, the views from this hill are stunning.

Wick

POP 7333

More gritty than pretty, Wick has been down on its luck since the collapse of the herring industry. It was once the world's largest fish port for the 'silver darlings' but when the market dropped off after WWII, job losses were huge and the town hasn't totally recovered. These days Wick is an important local service centre and transport terminus. It's well worth a look, particularly for its excellent museum, which puts everything in context.

👁 Sights & Activities

Wick Heritage Centre   MUSEUM

(www.wickheritage.org; 20 Bank Row; adult/child £3/50p; ⏱10am-5pm Mon-Sat Apr-Oct, last entry 3.45pm) Tracking the rise and fall of the herring industry, this great town museum displays everything from fishing equipment to complete herring fishing boats. It's a fantastic museum – without doubt one of the best in the country – and is absolutely huge inside, crammed with memorabilia and extensive displays describing Wick's heyday in the mid-19th century. The Johnston photographic collection is the museum's star exhibit. From 1863 to 1977, three generations of Johnstons photographed everything that happened around Wick, and the 70,000 photographs are an amazing portrait of the town's life. Prints of the early photos are for sale.

Castles   CASTLES

A path leads a mile south of town to the ruins of 12th-century **Old Wick Castle**, with the spectacular cliffs of the **Brough** and the **Brig**, as well as **Gote o'Trams**, a little further south. In good weather, it's a fine coastal walk to the castle, but take care on the final approach. Three miles northeast of Wick is the magnificently located clifftop ruin of **Castle Sinclair**.

Old Pulteney Distillery   DISTILLERY

(www.oldpulteney.com; Huddart St; ⏱10am-1pm & 2-4pm Mon-Fri) Old Pulteney is the most northerly distillery on mainland Scotland and runs excellent tours (£4) twice a day. Old Pulteney whisky has a light, earthy character with a hint of sea air and sherry.

Caithness Seacoast   BOAT TRIPS

(☏01955-609200; www.caithness-seacoast.co .uk) Wick's a boat town, and this outfit will take you out to sea to inspect the rugged coastline of the northeast. There are various options from a half-hour jaunt (adult/child £15/10) to a three-hour trip down to Lybster and back (adult/child £40/30).

🛏 Sleeping & Eating

Quayside   B&B ££

(☏01955-603229; www.quaysidewick.co.uk; 25 Harbour Quay; s/d/f without breakfast £30/50/75; P🕿) Quayside should be your first port of call for accommodation – they've been in the business for many years and know what they're doing. Right by the harbour in the nicest part of Wick, it's handy for everything worth seeing and eating in town. Spruce rooms – including a great family room with kitchenette – can be taken at B&B or bed-only rates and there are self-catering flats available too. The owners couldn't be more helpful. Book ahead. Good facilities for cyclists and motorcyclists.

Mackays Hotel   HOTEL **££**
(☑01955-602323; www.mackayshotel.co.uk; Union St; s/d £89/119; @�✿) The renovated Mackays is Wick's best hotel. Rooms vary in layout and size, so ask to see a few; prices drop if you're staying more than one night, and walk-up prices are usually quite a bit lower than the rack rates we list here. The 2.75m-long **Ebenezer Pl**, the shortest street in Britain, runs past one end of the hotel. The on-site **No 1 Bistro** (mains £10-13) is a fine-dining option for lunch or dinner. Service is friendly and the ingredients are sourced locally.

Bord de L'Eau   RESTAURANT **££**
(☑01955-604400; 2 Market St; mains £14-21; ☉lunch Tue-Sat, dinner Tue-Sun) This serene, upmarket French restaurant is the best place to eat in Wick. It overlooks the river and serves a changing menu of mostly meat French classics. The conservatory dining room overlooking the river is lovely on a sunny evening. It also opens for 'morning coffee' before lunch, when you can down tasty pastries with your cafe au lait.

ℹ Information

Tourist office (McAllans; 66 High St; ☉9am-5.30pm Mon-Sat) Good selection of information upstairs in McAllans Clothing Store.

Wick Carnegie Library (Sinclair Tce; ☉Mon-Sat) Free internet access.

ℹ Getting There & Away

Wick is a transport gateway to the surrounding area. **Flybe/Loganair** (☑0871 700 2000; www.flybe.com) flies between Edinburgh and Wick airport once daily except Saturday. **Eastern Airways** (☑01652-680600; www.easternairways.com) flies to Aberdeen (three Monday to Friday).

Stagecoach/Citylink operates buses to/from Inverness (£17.50, three hours, five daily) and Thurso (30 minutes, five daily) and also to John O'Groats (45 minutes, up to five daily).

Rapsons/Highland Country runs the connecting service to John O'Groats (40 minutes, four to seven Monday to Saturday) for the passenger ferry to Burwick, Orkney. It also runs by the Gills Bay ferry to St Margaret's Hope, Orkney.

Trains service Wick from Inverness (£16.10, four hours, four daily).

John O'Groats

POP 500

A car park surrounded by tourist shops, John O'Groats offers little to the visitor beyond a means to get across to Orkney; even the pub has been shut for a while now (there are a couple of cafes). Though it's not the northernmost point of the British mainland (that's Dunnet Head), it still serves as the end-point of the 874-mile trek from Land's End in Cornwall, a popular if arduous route for cyclists and walkers, many of whom raise money for charitable causes.

Another thing making the trip here worthwhile is jumping on board **North Coast Marine Adventures** (☑01955-611797; www.northcoast-marine-adventures.co.uk; adult/child £25/15), which runs scenic wildlife trips every couple of hours. Seals, whales, dolphins and seabirds can all be spotted. There's also a half-hour 'white water' thrill-seeking option (£20), which will get you soaked as you take on the turbulent waters of the Pentland Firth.

Two miles east, **Duncansby Head** provides a more solemn end-of-Britain moment with a small lighthouse and 60m cliffs sheltering nesting fulmars. A 15-minute walk from here through a sheep paddock yields spectacular views of the sea-surrounded monoliths known as **Duncansby Stacks**.

Six miles south of John O'Groats, in Auckengill on the Wick road, the **Caithness Broch Centre** (www.caithnessbrochcentre.co.uk; admission free; ☉noon-4pm Tue-Sat) has a small archaeological exhibition based on finds from these imposing ancient monuments. There is a broch, as well as Viking ruins, nearby.

There's a campsite and a few B&Bs in and around John O'Groats, as well as an SYHA hostel not far away, but it's not a great place to stay. For accommodation try Wick, Mey or Thurso – all nearby.

The **tourist office** (☑01955-611373; ☉10am-5pm Apr-Oct) is the best thing about the place, with its fine selection of local novels and books about Caithness and the Highland Clearances.

ℹ Getting There & Away

Stagecoach runs buses between John O'Groats and Wick (40 minutes, four to seven Monday to Saturday). There are also three to eight services Monday to Saturday to/from Thurso.

From May to September, a passenger ferry shuttles across to Burwick in Orkney (see p405).

Ninety-minute wildlife cruises to the island of Stroma or Duncansby Head cost £15 (late June to August).

Mey

POP 200

Mey is a very small village scattered along the A836. The **Castle of Mey** (www.castle ofmey.org.uk; adult/child £9.50/4; ⊙10.30am–4pm May–mid-Oct), a big crowd-puller for its Queen Mother connections, is about 6 miles from John O'Groats, off the A836 to Thurso. The exterior may seem grand but inside it feels domestic and everything is imbued with the character of the late Queen Mum: from a surprisingly casual lounge area with TV showing her favourite shows (*Dad's Army*, since you asked) to a photo of the king in 1943 that's lovingly inscribed 'Bertie'. All the in-jokes are explained by staff who worked for the lady. Outside in the castle grounds there's an unusual walled garden that's worth a stroll and there are lovely views over the Pentland Firth. The castle closes for a couple of weeks at the end of July.

The nearby **Castle Arms Hotel** (☑01847-851992; www.castlearms.co.uk; s/d £40/70; ℗), a former 19th-century coaching inn, has a friendly bar downstairs and simple but comfortable rooms upstairs. Or try **Hawthorns** (☑01847-851710; www.thehawthorns mey.co.uk; s/d £35/60; ℗☎), where rooms are huge and the owner's cheery smile is just as big.

Dunnet Head

Turn off 8 miles east of Thurso to reach the most northerly point on the British mainland, dramatic Dunnet Head, which banishes tacky pretenders with its majestic cliffs dropping into Pentland Firth. There are inspiring views of the Orkneys, flopping seals and nesting seabirds below, and a lighthouse built by Robert Louis Stevenson's granddad. On the road to the headland, you can stay at **Dunnet Head B&B** (☑01847-851774; www.dunnethead.iberacal. com; s/d from £27/44; ☎), with simple, comfortable rooms in the former post office.

Just west, Dunnet Bay offers you one of Scotland's finest beaches, backed by high dunes. There's **Seadrift** (Dunnet; ⊙2-5pm Sun-Wed & Fri May-Sep), a small wildlife display and base for the local rangers, who organise walks in summer, as well as a caravan-dominated **campsite** (☑01847-821319; www.caravanclub.co.uk; members pitch £13.80; ⊙Apr-Sep; ℗) backing the beach. At the southern end of Dunnet Bay lies the tiny harbour of **Castlehill**. Here a heritage trail explains the evolution of the local flagstone industry.

Thurso & Scrabster

POP 7737

Britain's most northerly mainland town, Thurso makes a handy overnight stop if you're heading west or across to Orkney. There's a pretty town beach, riverbank strolls and a good new museum. Thurso, which gets its name from the Norse for 'Thor's river', is also an unlikely surfing centre, with the choppy Pentland Firth raising some very respectable waves. Ferries cross from Scrabster, 2.5 miles west of Thurso, to Orkney.

Tiny Scrabster, little more than a collection of BP oil storage containers, revolves around its port, where there are a couple of good eating options.

◎ Sights

FREE **Caithness Horizons**   MUSEUM
(www.caithnesshorizons.co.uk; High St; ⊙10am-6pm Mon-Sat, 11am-4pm Sun) All shiny and new, this museum brings much of the lore, history and sentiment of Caithness to life through its excellent displays. A couple of fine Pictish cross-slabs greet the visitor downstairs; the main exhibition is a wide-ranging look at local history that includes plenty of audiovisuals – check out the wistful one on the now-abandoned island of Stroma for an emotional slice of social history. There's also a gallery space, an exhibition on the Dounreay reactor and a cafe.

⚑ Activities

Thurso is an unlikely **surfing** centre but the nearby coast has arguably the best and most regular surf on mainland Britain. There's an excellent right-hand reef break on the eastern side of town, directly in front of Lord Thurso's castle (closed to the public), and another shallow reef break 5 miles west at Brimms Ness. Pack a drysuit: this is no Hawaii.

Thurso's idyllic country **riverside walk** will make you feel miles away from town.

Access is near Waterside House and you can walk upstream, retracing your footsteps to come back (there was a bridge you could cross to come back on the other side, but it has been washed out). It's a beautiful walk, taking about 45 minutes at a stroll, and is a very popular local pursuit in decent weather. You can also walk all the way to Scrabster (40 minutes) along cliffs for brilliant views. Take care in windy weather.

🛌 Sleeping

Forss House Hotel   HOTEL ££££
(☎01847-861201; www.forsshousehotel.co.uk; Forss by Thurso; s/d £95/125, superior s/d/ste £110/160/230; Ⓟ🖧) Tucked into a thicket of trees 4 miles west of Thurso is elegant accommodation in an old Georgian mansion that has both character and style. Sumptuous upstairs rooms are much better than basement rooms as they have lovely views of the garden. There are also separate, beautifully appointed suites in the garden itself, which provide both privacy and a sense of tranquillity. Thoughtful extras like a selection of CDs and books in every room add appeal. It's right alongside a beautiful salmon river – the hotel can sort out permits and equipment – and if you've had a chilly day in the waders, some 300 malt whiskies await in the hotel bar.

Sandra's Hostel   HOSTEL £
(☎01847-894575; www.sandras-backpackers.ukf.net; 24 Princes St; dm/d/f £14/34/50; Ⓟ@🖧) A byword for backpacker excellence, Sandra's was awash with free facilities back when some hostels still had you scrubbing floors before checkout. Sporting an excellent kitchen, it offers free internet and wi-fi, a help-yourself continental breakfast, laundry and downstairs chip shop. Dorms, mostly four-berthers, are en suite and spotless.

Murray House   B&B ££
(☎01847-895759; www.murrayhousebb.com; 1 Campbell St; s/d £35/70; 🖧) A solid 19th-century town house on a central corner, Murray House gives a good first impression with a genuine welcome. It continues with new carpets, smart rooms with solid wooden furniture, an appealing lounge space and the option of an evening meal, all at very punter-friendly prices. No cards.

Pentland Hotel   HOTEL ££
(☎01847-893202; www.pentlandhotel.co.uk; Princes St; s/d £40/70; 🖧) The business-style

rooms in this place are great value. They're big enough to have a couch and a separate nook with a desk. It's a stylish place and surprisingly tranquil inside, given its central location. There are plenty of open areas for lounging around while you wait for the ferry to Orkney.

Waterside House   B&B £
(☎01847-894751; www.watersidehouse.org; 3 Janet St; s £25, d £35-50; Ⓟ) This straight-up guesthouse is easy to find (turn left just after the bridge coming into town), and has parking outside and comfortable beds in well-priced rooms. There's a range of them, from double en suites to cheaper attic rooms that share a spotless bathroom. Breakfast choices include egg-and-bacon rolls or takeaway if you've got an early ferry. No cards.

Thurso Hostel   HOSTEL £
(Ormlie Lodge; ☎01847-896888; ormlielodge@btconnect.com; Ormlie Rd; s/d £15/25; Ⓟ) This scruffy hostel is a students' hall of residence a few minutes' walk from the train station. It has a decent, if slightly ragged, range of budget accommodation. It's the place to go if you want a single room at a low price.

Orcadia Guest House   B&B £
(☎01847-894395; 27 Olrig St; s/d £22/44) This old and central budget favourite has been doing no-frills, value-packed B&B for decades, with simple and comfortable rooms that share bathrooms.

🍴 Eating

🥇 Captain's Galley   RESTAURANT £££
(☎01847-894999; www.captainsgalley.co.uk; Scrabster; 3-course dinner £46; ☺dinner Tue-Sat) Right by the ferry terminal in Scrabster, Captain's Galley is a classy but friendly place offering a short, seafood-based menu that features local and sustainably sourced produce prepared in relatively simple ways, letting the natural flavours shine through. Most rate it the best eatery in Caithness.

Holborn   BAR, RESTAURANT ££
(☎01847-892771; www.holbornhotel.co.uk; 16 Princes St; mains £13-18) A trendy, comfortable place decked out in light wood, the Holborn is quite a contrast to more traditional Thurso watering holes. Its bar, Bar 16, is a modern space with couches and comfy chairs. Bar meals here (£7 to £10) are uncomplicated but decent. The Red Pepper restaurant takes things to a higher level, with very tasty seafood – delicious

home-smoked salmon – the mainstay of a short but solid menu. Desserts are delicious too.

Ferry Inn PUB, RESTAURANT **££**
(www.ferryinnscrabster.co.uk; Scrabster; mains £11-19; ☺food breakfast, lunch & dinner) Near the ferry dock in Scrabster, this traditional stone pub has rather ugly extensions, but these house the busy restaurant. It specialises in steaks – pick your size – and local haddock; we reckon it's a tad overpriced but the evening view over the harbour is great. Cheaper bar meals (£8 to £11) are downstairs, along with a pool table.

Le Bistro BISTRO **££**
(☑01847-893737; 2 Traill St; lunch £5-8, dinner mains £10-15; ☺lunch & dinner Tue-Sat) Less sophisticated than when it was Thurso's main gourmet option, this eatery buzzes with chatter on weekend evenings as locals of all ages chow down on its simple meat and carb creations. What it does, it does well: the respectably sized steaks come on a sizzling platter and service has a smile.

ℹ Information

Dunbar Hospital (☑01847-893263; Ormlie Rd)
Laundrette (Riverside Pl; ☺9am-6pm Mon-Fri, 10am-5.30pm Sat)
Library (☑01847-893237; Davidson's Lane; ☺10am-6pm Mon & Wed, to 8pm Tue & Fri, to 1pm Thu & Sat) Free internet.
Tourist office (☑01847-893155; thurso@visitscotland.com; Riverside Rd; ☺Mon-Sat Apr-May & Sep-Oct, daily Jun-Aug)

ℹ Getting There & Around

From Inverness, Stagecoach/Citylink run via Wick to Thurso/Scrabster (£17.50, 3½ hours, five daily) and also head to John O'Groats (one hour, three to eight Monday to Saturday).

There are two or three daily train services from Inverness in summer (£16.10, 3¾ hours) but space for bicycles is limited so book ahead.

It's a 2-mile walk from Thurso train station to the ferry port at Scrabster or there are buses from Olrig St.

NORTH & WEST COAST

Quintessential Highland country such as this, marked by single-track roads, breathtaking emptiness and a wild, fragile beauty, is a rarity on the modern, crowded, highly urbanised island of Britain. You could get lost up here for weeks – and that still wouldn't be enough time.

Carving its way from Thurso to Glencoul, the north and northwest coastline is a feast of deep inlets, forgotten beaches and surging peninsulas. Within the rugged confines, the deep interior is home to vast, empty spaces, enormous lochs and some of Scotland's highest peaks.

The remarkable thing about the landscape is that it makes you feel special. Whether it's blazing sunshine or a murky greyness, the character of the land is totally unique and constantly changing – for that window of time in which you glimpse it, you capture an exclusive snapshot of this ancient area in your mind (or on your camera). Park the car and gaze. This northernmost slab of the Highlands is the stuff of coastal-drive dreams.

Thurso to Durness

It's 80 winding – and often spectacular – coastal miles from Thurso to Durness.

DOUNREAY & MELVICH

Ten miles west of Thurso is the **Dounreay nuclear power station**, which was the first in the world to supply mains electricity and is currently being decommissioned. The clean-up is planned to be finished by 2025; it's still a major employment source for the region. Just beyond Dounreay, **Reay** has a shop and an interesting little harbour dating from 1830. **Melvich** overlooks a fine beach and there are great views from **Strathy Point** (a 2-mile drive from the coast road, then a 15-minute walk).

BETTYHILL
POP 550
The panorama of a sweeping, sandy beach backed by velvety green hills with bulbous, rocky outcrops makes a sharp contrast to the sad history of this area. Bettyhill is a crofting community of resettled tenant farmers kicked off their land during the Clearances.

Bettyhill **tourist office** (☑01641-521244; ☺10.15am-5pm Mon-Sat, also dinner Fri & Sat Apr-Oct) has limited information on the area, but if you're after a bite to eat, **Elizabeth's Cafe** (mains £4-7) here serves good home-cooked food (such as local Bettyhill crab).

Adjacent **Strathnaver Museum** (www.strathnavermuseum.org.uk; adult/child £2/50p; ☺10am-5pm Mon-Sat Apr-Oct), in an old church,

FORSINARD & STRATHNAVER

Tough though it is to tear yourself away from the coast, we recommend plunging down the A897 just east of Melvich. After 14 miles you reach the railway at Forsinard. On the platform is the **Forsinard Flows Visitor Centre** (www.rspb.org.uk; admission free; ⊙9am-5.30pm Apr-Oct), a small nature exhibition. There's a 1-mile trail here introducing you to the Flows peatland; 4 miles north of here is a 4-mile trail crossing golden plover and dunlin nesting grounds.

Once past the centre, you soon start to cross epic, lonely, peaty moorscapes that stir the heart with their desolate beauty. Take a right turn at the village of Kinbrace onto the B871, which covers more jaw-dropping scenery before bringing you to the village of Syre. Turn right up here to follow the Strathnaver valley back to the coast near Bettyhill. Strathnaver is famous for having been the site of some of the worst of the Clearances, and the Strathnaver Trail is a series of numbered points of interest along the valley relating to this and several prehistoric sites.

tells the sad story of the Strathnaver Clearances through posters written by local kids. The museum contains memorabilia of Clan Mackay, various items of crofting equipment and one of the rowing boats that the folk of St Kilda used to throw over their cliffs like a message-in-a-bottle when they needed help. Outside the back door of the church is the Farr Stone, a fine carved Pictish cross-slab.

Just west of town, an enormous stretch of white sand flanks the River Naver as it meets the sea.

Bettyhill Hotel (☎01641-521352; www.betty hill.info; s/d from £25/50, mains £10; ⊙lunch & dinner) is a friendly place, with a range of rooms: some are distinctly more modern than others. There are rip-roaring views from some (such as No 2) over the sandy beach fringing Torrisdale Bay.

COLDBACKIE & TONGUE
POP 450

Coldbackie has outstanding views over sandy beaches, turquoise waters and offshore islands. If you haven't seen that magical Scottish light at work yet, there's a good chance you'll see it here – park the car for a few minutes and watch. Only 2 miles further on is Tongue, with the evocative 14th-century ruins of **Castle Varrich**, once a Mackay stronghold. To get to the castle, take the trail next to the Royal Bank of Scotland, near Ben Loyal Hotel – it's an easy stroll. Tongue has a shop, post office, bank and petrol station.

🛏 Sleeping & Eating

Cloisters   B&B £
(☎01847-601286; www.cloistertal.demon.co.uk; Talmine; s/d £32.50/55; P) Vying for the position of best-located B&B in Scotland, Cloisters has three en-suite twin rooms with brilliant views over the Kyle of Tongue and offshore islands. Breakfast is in the artistically converted church alongside. To get here from Tongue, cross the causeway and take the turn-off to Melness, almost immediately on your right; Cloisters is a couple of miles down this road.

Tongue SYHA   HOSTEL £
(☎01847-611789; www.syha.org.uk; dm/tw £16.25/39; ⊙Apr-Oct; P) In a wonderful spot right by the causeway across the Kyle of Tongue, a mile west of town, Tongue SYHA is the top budget option in the area, with clean, comfortably refitted dorms, some with views, a decent kitchen and cosy lounge. The helpful warden has plenty of local advice and turns her hand to delicious home baking.

Tongue Hotel   HOTEL, PUB ££
(☎01847-611206; www.tonguehotel.co.uk; s/d £65/100, superior £75/120; P🌐📶) Tongue Hotel is a welcoming spot that offers cosy, recently renovated rooms in a former hunting lodge. It has upmarket Highland restaurant fare (mains £16 to £18) in the evenings and great-value bar meals (£6, lunch and dinner) in the snug Brass Tap bar in the basement, a good spot to chat with locals or shelter from the weather.

Tigh-nan-Ubhal   B&B ££
(☎01847-611281; www.tigh-nan-ubhal.com; Main St; d £65; P📶) At the junction of the A836 and A838 and within stumbling distance of two pubs is this charming B&B. There are snug, loft-style rooms with plenty of natural light, but the basement double with spa

CROFTING & THE CLEARANCES

The wild and empty spaces up in these parts of the Highlands are among Europe's least populated zones, but this wasn't always so. Ruins of cottages in the most desolate areas are mute witnesses to one of the most heartless episodes of Scottish history: the Highland Clearances.

Up until the 19th century the most common form of farming settlement here was the *baile*, a group of a dozen or so families who farmed the land granted to them by the local chieftain in return for military service and a portion of the harvest. The arable land was divided into strips called *rigs*, which were allocated to different families by annual ballot so that each took turns at getting the poorer soils; this system was known as *runrig*. The families worked the land communally and their cattle shared the grazing land.

After Culloden, however, the king banned private armies and new laws made the clan chiefs actual owners of their traditional lands, often vast tracts of territory. With the prospect of unimagined riches allied to a depressing failure of imagination, the lairds decided that sheep were more profitable than agriculture and proceeded to evict tens of thousands of farmers from their lands. The Clearances forced these desperate folk to head for the cities in the hope of finding work or to emigrate to the Americas or southern hemisphere. Those who chose not to emigrate or move to the cities to find work were forced to eke a living from narrow plots of marginal agricultural land, often close to the coast. This was a form of smallholding that became known as crofting. The small patch of land barely provided a living and had to be supplemented by other work such as fishing and kelp-gathering. It was always precarious, as rights were granted on a year-by-year basis, so at any moment a crofter could lose not only the farm but also the house they'd built on it.

The economic depression of the late 19th century meant many couldn't pay their rent. This time, however, they resisted expulsion, instead forming the Highland Land Reform Association and their own political party. Their resistance led to several of their demands being acceded to by the government, including security of tenure, fair rents and eventually the supply of land for new crofts. Crofters now have the right to purchase their farmland and recent laws have abolished the feudal system, which created so much misery.

is the pick of the bunch – it's the biggest en suite we've seen in northern Scotland.

Craggan Hotel RESTAURANT ££
(☎01847-601278; www.thecraggan.co.uk; mains £8-16; ⊗breakfast, lunch & dinner) On the same road as Cloisters, 2 miles from the other side of the Kyle, Craggan Hotel doesn't look much from outside but go in and you'll find smart, formal service and a menu ranging from exquisite burgers (£6.50) to classy game and seafood dishes, presented beautifully. The wine list's not bad for a pub either.

TONGUE TO DURNESS

From Tongue it's 37 miles to Durness – you can take the causeway across the **Kyle of Tongue** or the beautiful old road that goes around the head of the kyle. A detour to **Melness** and **Port Vasgo** may be rewarded with the sight of seals on the beach.

Continuing west, the road crosses a desolate moor past **Moine House** (a ruin built as a shelter for travellers in 1830) to the northern end of **Loch Hope**. A 10-mile detour south along the loch leads to **Dun Dornaigil**, a well-preserved broch in the shadow of **Ben Hope** (927m). If you'd like to bag this Munro (see the boxed text, p30), it's a 4.5-mile, four-hour round trip along the route from the car park, which is 2 miles before the broch, near a large barn. It's a relatively easy walk but often cold at the exposed top.

Beyond Loch Hope, on the main road, **Heilam** has stunning views out over **Loch Eriboll**, Britain's deepest sea inlet and a shelter for ships during WWII.

Durness
POP 350

The scattered village of Durness (www.durness.org) is strung out along cliffs, which rise from a series of pristine beaches. It has one of the finest locations in Scotland. When the sun shines the effects of blinding white sand, the cry of seabirds and the lime-coloured seas combine in a magical way.

There are shops, ATM, petrol and plenty of accommodation options in Durness.

◉ Sights & Activities

Walking around the sensational sandy coastline is a highlight here, as is a visit to Cape Wrath. Durness' beautiful beaches, include Rispond to the east, Sargo Sands below town and Balnakeil to the west; the sea offers scuba-diving sites complete with wrecks, caves, seals and whales. At Balnakeil, less than a mile beyond Durness, a craft village occupies what was once an early-warning radar station. A walk along the beach to the north leads to Faraid Head, where you can see puffin colonies in early summer.

A mile east of the village centre is a path, near the SYHA hostel, down to Smoo Cave. The vast cave entrance stands at the end of an inlet, or geo, and a river cascades through its roof into a flooded cavern, then flows out to sea. There's evidence the cave was inhabited about 6000 years ago. From the vast main chamber, you can head through to a smaller flooded cavern where a waterfall sometimes cascades from the roof. From here you can take a boat trip (adult/child £3/2; ⊘Apr-Sep) across to explore a little further into the interior.

John Lennon spent some of his childhood days around Durness. There's a memorial to him near the cave.

🛏 Sleeping & Eating

Mackays HOTEL ££
(☎01971-511202; www.visitmackays.com; Durness; d/deluxe d £110/125; ⊘Apr-Nov; 🛜) You literally feel you're at the top corner of Scotland here; this is where the road turns 90 degrees. But no matter whether you're heading east or south, you'll go far before you find a better place to stay than this family-run haven of Highland hospitality. With big beds and soft fabrics, it's a romantic spot, but what impresses more than anything is the warm-hearted personal service. The restaurant (mains £11-17) presents local seafood and robust meat dishes.

Lazy Crofter Bunkhouse HOSTEL £
(☎01971-511202; www.durnesshostel.com; dm £15) Run out of Mackays, Lazy Crofter Bunkhouse is Durness' best budget accommodation. A bothy (mountain shelter) vibe

gives it a Highland feel and it offers inviting dorms with plenty of room and lockers, a sociable shared table for meals and board games, and a great wooden deck with sea views, perfect for midge-free evenings.

Loch Croispol Bookshop CAFE £
(www.scottish-books.net; Balnakeil Craft Village; light meals £4-8; ⊘10.30am-5pm) At this place you can feed your body and your mind. Set among books featuring all things Scottish are a few tables where you can enjoy an all-day breakfast, sandwiches and other scrumptious fare at lunch, such as fresh Achiltibuie salmon.

Glengolly B&B B&B £
(☎01971-511255; www.glengolly.com; r per person £28-33; ℗) This B&B has quaint, cottage-style rooms in a working croft. The helpful owners have excellent breakfasts and numerous dogs, both ceramic and real.

Sango Sands Oasis CAMPING £
(☎01971-511222; www.sangosands.com; Durness; sites per adult/child £5.75/3.50; ℗) You couldn't imagine a better location for a campsite: great grassy areas on the edge of cliffs descend to two lovely sand beaches. Facilities are good and very clean and there's a pub next door.

Smoo Cave Hotel PUB ££
(www.smoocavehotel.co.uk; mains £8-13) Signposted off the main road at the eastern end of town, this no-frills local offers the top corner's best bar food in hefty portions. Haddock or daily specials are an obvious and worthwhile choice; there's also a restaurant area with clifftop views.

🍫 Cocoa Mountain CAFE £
(www.cocoamountain.co.uk; Balnakeil Craft Village; box of 9 truffles £7; ⊘9am-6pm summer, 10am-5pm winter) Handmade chocolates include a chilli, lemongrass and coconut white-chocolate truffle and many more unique flavours. Tasty espresso and – of course – hot chocolate warm the cockles on those blowy horizontal-drizzle days.

❶ Information

Durness Community Building (1 Bard Tce; per 30min £1) Coin-op internet access, opposite Mackays.

Health centre (☎01971-511273)

Tourist office (☎01971-511368; durness@ visitscotland.com; ⊘10am-5pm Mon-Sat Apr-Oct, plus Sun Apr-Aug) Organises guided walks in summer. Closes for an hour for lunch.

Durness to Ullapool

Perhaps Scotland's most spectacular road trip, the 69 miles connecting Durness to Ullapool is a scenic feast, almost too much to take in. A wide heathered valley gives way to rockier country studded with small lochs; gorse-covered hills preface the magnificent rugged ridge of Assynt, punctuated by its glacier-scoured mountains, including ziggurat-like Quinag, the distinctive saddle of Suilven and much-climbed Stac Pollaidh. It's no wonder the area has been dubbed a geopark (www.northwest-highlands-geopark.co.uk).

Kinlochbervie was one of Scotland's premier fish-landing ports and there's a lovely beach at Oldshoremore, a crofting settlement about 2 miles northwest of Kinlochbervie. South of Cape Wrath, Sandwood Bay boasts one of Scotland's best and most isolated beaches, guarded at one end by the spectacular rock pinnacle Am Buachaille. Sandwood Bay is about 2 miles north of the end of a track from Blairmore (approach from Kinlochbervie), or you could walk south from the cape (allow eight hours) and on to Blairmore. Sandwood House is a creepy ruin reputedly haunted by the ghost of a 16th-century shipwrecked sailor from the Spanish Armada.

The outlook from the Kinlochbervie Hotel (☑01971-521275; www.kinlochberviehotel.com; s/d £55/95; 🅿🛜) combines the muscular fishing boats of the commercial harbour with dreamy bay vistas. Traditionally furnished, rooms 1 and 2 are the best, with simply magnificent water views. Meals are available (mains £9 to £10).

Two miles short of Kinlochbervie in Inshegra, Old School (☑01971-521383; www.oldschoolklb.co.uk; s/d £50/75; 🅿) is a most welcoming B&B with a variety of rooms, as well as cheaper ones in a bungalow alongside, and good-value evening meals (mains £10 to £12).

Scourie is a pretty crofting community. If you're looking to spoil yourself, Scourie Lodge (☑01971-502248; s/d £50/75; 🅿), in a gorgeous building overlooking the bay, has old-style comfort and hospitality in a lovely setting; the garden's palm trees are proof of the Gulf Stream's good works. Dinner is available (£25). Cards aren't taken.

Ferries (☑07775-625890; adult/child £10/5, ⏰9am-2pm Mon-Sat Apr-early Sep) go to the important Handa Island (www.swt.org.uk) seabird sanctuary from Tarbet, 6 miles north of Scourie; call for times.

KYLESKU & LOCH GLENCOUL

Cruises on Loch Glencoul pass by treacherous-looking mountains, seal colonies and the 213m-drop of Eas a'Chual Aulin, Britain's highest waterfall. In summer the MV Statesman (☑01971-502345; ⏰daily Apr-Sep) runs two-hour trips twice daily from Kylesku pier for £15/5 per adult/child to see waterfalls and baby seals.

WORTH A TRIP

CAPE WRATH

Though its name actually comes from the Norse word for 'turning point', there is something daunting and primal about Cape Wrath, the northwesternmost point of the British mainland. It is crowned by a lighthouse (built by Robert Stevenson in 1828) and stands close to the seabird colonies of Clo Mor, Britain's highest coastal cliffs. The absence of non-natural noise out here is marvellous. Getting to Cape Wrath involves a boat (☑01971-511287) ride – passengers and bikes only – across the Kyle of Durness (return £5.50, 10 minutes) connecting with an optional minibus (☑01971-511343) running 12 miles to the cape (return £10, 40 minutes). This is a friendly but eccentric, sometimes shambolic service, with limited capacity, so plan on waiting in high season, and ring before setting out to make sure the ferry is running. The ferry leaves from Keoldale pier, a couple of miles southwest of Durness, and runs two or more times daily from Easter to September. It's a spectacular ride or hike to Cape Wrath over bleak scenery occasionally used by the Ministry of Defence as a firing range. There's a cafe at the lighthouse serving soup and sandwiches.

An increasingly popular walking route is the Cape Wrath Trail (www.capewrathtrail.co.uk), which runs up here from Fort William (200 miles). It's unmarked, so you may want to do it guided – C-n-Do (www.cndoscotland.com) are one operator – or buy North to the Cape (www.cicerone.co.uk).

While you wait for the boat you can toast your toes by a log fire, enjoy a pint (decent ales on tap) and tuck into a superb all-day bar meal at the **Kylesku Hotel** (☎01971-502231; www.kyleskuhotel.co.uk; Kylesku; bar mains £9-13; ☺noon-9pm; ☎) overlooking the pier. Seafood is the speciality including local mussels and smoked haddock and salmon fish cakes. There's also a restaurant open for even tastier fishy delights at dinner time (mains £13 to £17). If you fancy bunkering down for the night, a variety of **rooms** (small s/d £55/80, s/d 65/97) are available – the separate, motel-style ones with views are the best.

ACHMELVICH & AROUND

Not far south of Kylesku, a 30-mile detour on the narrow B869 rewards with spectacular views and fine beaches. From the lighthouse at **Point of Stoer**, a one-hour cliff walk leads to the **Old Man of Stoer**, a spectacular sea stack. On this stretch is the **Clachtoll Beach Campsite** (☎01571-855377; www.clachtollbeachcampsite.co.uk; tent £8-10 plus per person £2; ☺Apr-Sep), a great coastal spot, and the **Achmelvich Beach SYHA** (☎01571-844480; www.syha.org.uk; Achmelvich; dm £15; ☺Apr-Sep) a whitewashed cottage set beside a great beach at the end of a side road. There's a summer chip shop nearby, otherwise bring your own supplies; it's a 4-mile walk from Lochinver. Ullapool–Lochinver buses take you to the hostel on request. The hostel closes between 10am and 5pm.

LOCHINVER & ASSYNT

The distinctive region of Assynt comprises a landscape of spectacular peaks rising from the moorland. Lochinver is the main settlement; a busy little fishing port that's a popular port of call for tourists, with its laid-back attitude, good facilities, striking scenery and range of accommodation.

Using local landscapes as inspiration, **Highland Stoneware** (www.highlandstoneware.com; Lochinver; ☺Mon-Fri, plus Sat Easter-Oct) ensures that you can relive the majesty of the northwest every time you look into the bottom of your teacup. Even better are the mosaics outside, especially the car.

NorWest Sea Kayaking (☎01571-844281; www.norwestseakayaking.com; 6 Inver Tce, Lochinver) are the folk to speak to if you fancy a paddle on the open water.

The Lochinver–Lairg road (A837) meets the Durness road (A894) at **Skiag Bridge**, by Loch Assynt, about 10 miles east of Lochinver. Half a mile south of here, by the loch, there's the ruin of the late-15th-century MacLeod stronghold, **Ardvreck Castle**. There are wonderful summer sunsets over the castle and the loch.

The stunningly shaped hills of Assynt are popular with walkers and include peaks such as Suilven (731m), Quinag (808m), Ben More Assynt (998m) and Canisp (846m). The tourist office has plenty of walking information: leaflets and more detailed booklets.

🛏 Sleeping & Eating

There are several B&Bs; for magnificent vistas head a mile around the bay to Baddidarrach, which looks back at Lochinver and the magnificent bulk of Suilven behind.

TOP CHOICE **Albannach** HOTEL/RESTAURANT £££
(☎01571-844407; www.thealbannach.co.uk; Baddidarroch; s/d/ste with dinner from £200/260/340; ☺Mar-Dec; ℗☎) The Albannach is sheer indulgence, on a grand scale. You'll discover roaring fireplaces, furniture found only in antique shops and a demure, sophisticated atmosphere. Roomy lodgings decorated with elegant flair, spacious grounds studded with fruit trees, inspiring panoramas and wonderful dinners using organic ingredients and well-selected local produce (£55 for nonguests) combine to make it a special spot.

Veyatie B&B ££
(☎01571-844424; www.veyatie-scotland.co.uk; 66 Baddidarrach; s/d £48/76; ☺Jan-Nov; ℗☎) Overseen by a personable Belgian shepherd (dog), this choice at the end of the road across the bay has perhaps the best views of all, as well as sweet rooms, a little conservatory and a grassy garden.

Inchnadamph Lodge HOSTEL, B&B £
(☎01571-822218; www.inch-lodge.co.uk; Inchnadamph; dm/d £17.25/51; ℗@☎) Situated by the Lochinver–Lairg road, this place is a friendly 50-bed lodge with lots of rustic accommodation. Most rooms are spacious and clean and there's a separate music/TV lounge for late partying. The facilities are excellent and it's very popular with groups.

Lochinver Larder & Riverside Bistro CAFE, RESTAURANT ££
(www.lochinverlarder.co.uk; 3 Main St; pies £5.95, mains £10-16; ☺10am-8.30pm) With an outstanding ensemble of inventive food made with local produce, Lochinver pies are a

particular standout here and are famous in this part of the world: try the smoked haddock, or wild boar and apricot – very tasty. The bistro also churns out delicious seafood dishes in the evening. A top place.

ℹ Information

There's a supermarket in town, as well as a post office, bank (with an ATM) and petrol station.

Tourist office (☏01571-844373; lochinver@ visitscotland.com; Main St; ⊙10am-5pm Mon-Sat Easter-Oct, also 10am-4pm Sun Jun-Aug) Has leaflets on hill walks in the area and a display on the story of Assynt, from flora and fauna to clans, conflict and controversy.

INVERPOLLY NATURE RESERVE

The Inverpolly Nature Reserve has numerous glacial lochs, as well as the three peaks of Cul Mor (849m), Stac Pollaidh (613m) and Cul Beag (769m). **Stac Pollaidh** provides one of the most exciting walks in the area, with some good scrambling on its narrow sandstone crest. It takes just three hours on a round trip from the car park at Loch Lurgainn.

ACHILTIBUIE
POP 300

With sheep nibbling the grassy roadside verges, the gorgeous Summer Isles moored just off the coast and the silhouettes of mountains skirting the bay, this village personifies idyllic Scottish beauty and is the perfect place for some serious relaxation.

Summer Isles Cruises (☏01854-622200; www.summer-isles-cruises.co.uk; ⊙Mon-Sat May-Sep) operates boat trips to the Summer Isles from Achiltibuie – you'll see some magnificent island scenery. Three-hour trips cost £22/11 per adult/child and include one hour ashore on **Tanera Mor**, where the post office issues its own stamps. Time and price details will change a little as a faster, newer boat was to be in place by the time this book hit the shelves.

Summer Isles Hotel (☏01854-622282; www.summerisleshotel.co.uk; Achiltibuie; s £115-175, d £145-210; ⊙Easter-Oct; **P**) is a very special place indeed, with wonderfully snug rooms – some are suites in separate cottages sleeping two to six – plus cracking views, a wee pub with convivial outdoor seating, bar meals and a restaurant with a stratospheric reputation for seafood (five-course table d'hôte £56). It's the perfect spot for a romantic getaway or some quality time off life's treadmill.

The rudimentary 20-bed **Achininver SYHA** (☏01854-622482; www.syha.org.uk; Achininver, Achiltibuie; dm £15; ⊙mid-May–Aug) is designed for walkers and outdoor enthusiasts – you have to walk half a mile off the main road to reach it. Its remote, serene location has to be one of the best in the country.

There are buses operating Monday to Saturday from Reiff, Badenscallie (half a mile from the hostel) and Achiltibuie to Ullapool (1½ hours, two daily Monday to Friday, one Saturday).

Ullapool
POP 1308

The pretty port of Ullapool is one of the most alluring Highlands spots, a wonderful destination in itself as well as a gateway for the Western Isles. Offering a row of whitewashed cottages arrayed along the harbour and special views of Loch Broom and its flanking hills, the town has a very distinctive appeal.

Ullapool served as an eviction and emigration point during the Clearances, with thousands of Scots watching the loch recede behind them as the diaspora cast them across the world.

◉ Sights & Activities

Ullapool is a great centre for hill walking. A good path up **Gleann na Sguaib** heads for the top of **Beinn Dearg** from Inverlael, at the inner end of Loch Broom. Ridgewalking on the **Fannichs** is relatively straightforward, with numerous different routes possible. The tourist office can supply you with all the information and maps you need. Good walking books sold at the tourist office include *Walks in Wester Ross* (£2.95), or you can pick up a copy of the freebie guide to local woodland walks.

In summer the ferry company CalMac runs day-trips to Lewis and Harris.

Ullapool Museum   MUSEUM
(www.ullapoolmuseum.co.uk; 7 West Argyle St; adult/child £3/50p; ⊙10am-5pm Mon-Sat Apr-Oct) In a converted Telford Parliamentary church, this museum relates the pre-, natural and social history of the town and Lochbroom area with a particular focus on the emigration to Nova Scotia and other places; there's a genealogy section if you want to trace your Scottish roots.

Rhue Studio
GALLERY

(www.rhueart.co.uk; Rhue; ⊙Mon-Sat Apr-Sep)
This studio, 2.5 miles northwest of Ullapool, displays and sells the excellent art of contemporary landscape painter James Hawkins. The vivid and reflective works take a moment to adjust to but they are wonderful interpretations. His work on the Outer Hebrides is breathtaking. Call for winter opening hours.

Seascape
BOAT TRIPS

(☏01854-633708; www.sea-scape.co.uk) These guys run you out to the Summer Isles in an orange rigid inflatable boat (RIB). Their two-hour trip costs £28.50 for adults, £20 for kids.

Summer Queen
BOAT TRIPS

(☏07713-257219; www.summerqueen.co.uk) The stately *Summer Queen* takes you out around Isle Martin (£17/8.50 per adult/child, two hours) or to the Summer Isles (£26/13, four hours), with a stop on Tanera Mor.

🛏 Sleeping

Note that during summer Ullapool is very busy and finding accommodation can be tricky – the answer: book ahead.

TOP CHOICE Ceilidh Place
HOTEL ££

(☏01854-612103; www.theceilidhplace. com; 14 West Argyle St; d £100-146; P🖥) Ceilidh Place is a celebration of Scottish culture and one of the more unusual and delightful places to stay in the Highlands. That's culture with a capital C: we're talking literature and traditional music, not tartan and Nessie dolls. Rooms go for character rather than modern bathrooms or conveniences, and come with a selection of books personally chosen by Scottish literati, eclectic artwork and nice little touches like hot-water bottles. Best of all is the sumptuous guest lounge, with sofas, chaises longues and an honesty bar.

West House
B&B ££

(☏01854-613126; www.accommodationullapool. net; West Argyle St; d £70; 🖥) Slap bang in the centre of Ullapool, this welcoming place, a solid white house that was once a manse, offers excellent rooms with a contemporary style and great bathrooms. Breakfast is continental style: rooms come with a fridge stocked with fresh fruit salad and juice so you can eat at your leisure in your own chamber. It also hires out bikes to explore the surrounding area.

Woodlands
B&B £

(☏01854-612701; www.ullapoolbandb.com; 1a Pulteney St; d £50; ⊙May-Sep; P🖥) With just two comfortable rooms sharing a bathroom, this place should be booked ahead; effervescent hosts mean it's a great bet. The breakfast is memorable; they make marmalade, jams and bread and smoke their own fish out the back.

Ullapool SYHA
HOSTEL £

(☏01854-612254; www.syha.org.uk; Shore St; dm/tw £17.25/38; ⊙Mar-Oct) You've got to hand it to the SYHA; they've chosen some very sweet locations for their hostels. This is as close to the water as it is to the town's best pub; about four seconds' walk. The front rooms have harbour views but the busy dining area and little lounge are also good spots for contemplating the water.

Point Cottage
B&B ££

(☏01854-612494; www.pointcottage.co.uk; 22 West Shore St; d £70; ⊙Mar-Oct; P) A haven of good taste, the courteous and welcoming Point Cottage has a great headland location – even the back rooms have water views. It's one of those shorefront cottages you've already admired if you arrived by ferry, and it'll feel comfy for both hedonists – smoked fish for breakfast – and walkers, with plenty of maps and advice.

Ceilidh Clubhouse
HOSTEL £

(☏01854-612103; West Lane; r per person £18-20; P) Opposite the Ceilidh Place, this place is run by them as no-frills accommodation for walkers, journeypeople and staff. A big building, it has hostel-style rooms with sturdy bunks and basin. Though showers and toilets are a little institutional, the big bonus is that rooms are private: if you're woken by snores, at least they'll be familiar ones.

Old Surgery
B&B ££

(☏01854-612520; www.oldsurgery.co.uk; 3 West Tce; d £62) It's worth paying the extra few pounds to bag rooms 1 or 2 (£70), which have big bay windows with super water vistas, tables to sit at and contemplate them from, extra berths for kids and a shared balcony.

Broomfield Holiday Park
CAMPING £

(☏01854-612664; www.broomfieldhp.com; West Lane; 1/2 person tent £8/12, plus for car £4; ⊙May-Oct) Great grassy headland location very close to centre. Midge-busting machines in action.

✗ Eating & Drinking

Ferry Boat Inn
PUB ££

(☎01854-612366; www.ferryboat-inn.com; Shore St; mains £9-12) Known as the FBI, this inn is to Ullapool what the castle is to Edinburgh. The pub's a little less traditional-looking these days with its bleached wood and nonstained carpet but it's still the place where locals and visitors mingle. The food offering is interesting; some of the dishes are a little bland, but a well-run dining room, quality ingredients and great presentation compensate.

Arch Inn
RESTAURANT, PUB ££

(☎01854-612454; www.thearchinn.co.uk; West Shore St; bar meals £7-9, mains £14-18; ☎) We're pretty impressed with this newly remodelled waterfront inn and there's plenty to like about it, from its cosy bar (with pool table) serving comfort food like bangers and mash to its classy upstairs restaurant, with glorious loch views and smart creations using Scottish produce with a regional French twist. The outdoor tables right over the lapping water are a top spot for a pint.

Ceilidh Place
RESTAURANT, BAR ££

(☎01854-612103; 14 West Argyle St; mains £11-16; ☺breakfast, lunch & dinner) The restaurant of Ceilidh Place serves up inventive dishes catering for most palates. It was a little disappointing last time we visited but the bar is still a great place, with a cosy atmosphere, outdoor seating, good wines by the glass and regular live music and events.

Frigate Café
CAFE £

(www.ullapoolcatering.co.uk; Shore St; mains £7-9; ☺noon-9pm) Frigate Café, on the waterfront, is a popular venue for coffee, teas and ice cream; it also sells a very tasty local smoked cheese. But you can also sit down and graze the Italian-influenced menu of salads, pizzas and pastas, or just drop by for a glass of wine or a beer.

Seaforth
PUB £

(www.theseaforth.com; cnr Quay & Shore Sts; bar meals £7-11; ☺food served noon-10pm; ⊕) Family-friendly and always packed, this big establishment in the heart of town does good-value bar meals and takeaway fish and chips downstairs and pricier but more peaceful bistro fare upstairs, with serene harbour views.

ℹ Information

Library (Mill St; ☺9am-5pm Mon, Wed & Fri, 9am-5pm & 6-8pm Tue & Thu, closed Mon & Wed during holidays) Free internet access.

Tourist office (☎01854-612486; ullapool@ visitscotland.com; Argyle St; ☺daily Jun-Sep, Mon-Sat Apr-May & Oct, Mon-Fri Nov-Mar)

Ullapool Bookshop (Quay St; ☺daily; @) Lots of books on Scottish topics and maps of the area. Internet access available at £1 per 15 minutes.

Ullapool Laundry (☎01854-613123; 7a Latheron Centre; ☺Mon-Sat) Service washes for muddied walkers.

ℹ Getting There & Around

Citylink has three daily buses, Monday to Saturday and one on Sunday, from Inverness to Ullapool (£12, 1½ hours), connecting with the Lewis ferry. See p390 for details of this service.

Ullapool to Kyle of Lochalsh

Although it's less than 50 miles as the crow flies from Ullapool to Kyle of Lochalsh, it's more like 150 miles along the circuitous coastal road – but don't let that put you off. It's a deliciously remote region and there are fine views of beaches and bays backed by mountains all the way along.

The A832 doubles back to the coast from the A835, 12 miles from Ullapool. Just after the junction, the **Falls of Measach** ('ugly' in Gaelic) spill 45m into the spectacularly deep and narrow Corrieshalloch Gorge. You can cross from side to side on a wobbly suspension bridge, built by Sir John Fowler of Braemore. The thundering falls and misty vapours rising from the gorge are very impressive.

If you're in a hurry to get to Skye, head inland on the A835 (towards Inverness) and catch up with the A832 further down, near Garve.

DUNDONNELL & AROUND
POP 200

Dundonnell appears half-drowned after a good soaking, with a combination of imposing ridges overlooking the lowlands of this tiny settlement. **An Teallach** (1062m) is a magnificent mountain – the highest summit can be reached by a path starting less than 500m southeast of the Dundonnell Hotel (six hours return). Traversing the ridge to Sail Liath is a more serious proposition, with lots of scrambling in precarious places and difficult route-finding. Carry Ordnance Survey (OS) map 19, food, water and waterproofs – it's amazing how quickly the weather can turn foul here.

Badrallach Bothy (☎01854-633281; www.badrallach.com; Badrallach; bothy per person £6, sites per 2 people £8, r per person £35, P), 7 miles from the A832, has a good range of accommodation, as well as boats, bikes and fishing gear for hire. It's the perfect place to get away from it all and acquaint yourself with the rural beauty of this country. There's an extra charge of £1.50 per car.

Dundonnell Hotel (☎01854-633204; www.dundonnellhotel.com; Dundonnell; s/d £65/110) provides good refuge from the elements and has elegant, traditionally furnished rooms; the loch- and mountain-facing premier rooms have great views. Tempting food and friendly staff round out the experience.

GAIRLOCH & AROUND

POP 1100

Gairloch is a group of villages (comprising Achtercairn, Strath and Charlestown) around the inner end of a loch of the same name. The surrounding area has beautiful sandy beaches, good trout-fishing and birdwatching. Hill walkers also use Gairloch as a base for the Torridon hills and An Teallach.

Gairloch Heritage Museum (www.gairlochheritagemuseum.org; Achtercairn; adult/child £4/1; ⏲10am-5pm Mon-Sat Apr-Oct) tells of life in the western Highlands and includes a typical crofting cottage. **Gairloch Trekking Centre** (☎01445-712652; www.gairlochtrekkingcentre.co.uk; ⏲Fri-Wed Mar-Oct) offers pony treks in the ample grounds of a local estate.

The **Gairloch Marine Wildlife Centre** (☎01445-712636; www.porpoise-gairloch.co.uk; Pier Rd, Charlestown; admission free; ⏲10am-4pm Easter-Oct) has audiovisual and interactive displays, lots of charts and photos, and knowledgeable staff. Cruises (per adult/child £20/10) run from the centre and sail up to three times daily (weather permitting); during the two-hour trips you may see basking sharks, porpoises and minke whales. The crew collect data on water temperature and conditions, and monitor cetacean populations, so your fare is subsidising an important research project.

Six miles north, subtropical **Inverewe Garden** (NTS; www.nts.org.uk; adult/concession £8.50/5.50; ⏲10am-4pm Apr-Oct, to 3pm Nov-Mar), utilises Gulf Stream warmth to grow Mediterranean and Japanese plants, among others. The cafe provides a good pit stop and has great cakes.

Sleeping & Eating

Old Inn INN ££
(☎01445-712006; www.theoldinn.net; Charlestown; s/d £57/99; P 📶) This rustic classic has a range of excellent snug rooms, some (such as room 4) with four-poster beds. Downstairs, the **bar** is an atmospheric nook-and-cranny affair, with the best pint of ale in town, and serves recommended bar meals (£7 to £14) of the delectable seafood variety. The inn is just opposite Gairloch Pier.

Rua Reidh Lighthouse Hostel HOSTEL £
(☎01445-771263; www.ruareidh.co.uk; dm/d £10.50/28; P @) By Melvaig and 13 miles from Gairloch (at the end of the road), this is an excellent hostel and will give you a taste of a lighthouse-keeper's life. Buses from Gairloch run as far as Melvaig, then it's a 3-mile walk along the road to the lighthouse. En suite twins and doubles (£35 to £42) and family rooms are also available.

Wayside Guest House B&B ££
(☎01445-712008; issmith@msn.com; Strath; s/d £35/60) If you're looking for a place to hole up for the night in town, Wayside has water views from two cosy rooms, which share a bathroom. Another double and family room have no view but are en suite. It's right next to Strath Stores.

Mountain Coffee Company CAFE £
(Strath; light meals £3-6) Not the sort of cafe you expect to come across in a Highlands town, offbeat and cosy Mountain Coffee Company is a shrine to all things mountaineering and has a lazy, chilled-out vibe. It sells excellent hearty food for walkers, best consumed in the attached conservatory, and a range of decadent coffees and hot chocolates stuffed with sugary things. The attached Hillbillies Bookshop is worth a browse.

Information

Tourist office (☎01445-712071; ⏲daily May-Sep) At the car park in Achtercairn where a road branches off to the main centre at Strath.

KINLOCHEWE & AROUND

Tiny Kinlochewe is a good base for outdoor activities. You'll find an outdoor-equipment shop, a petrol station with a tearoom and a shop/post office that runs a cafe in summer. Check out the **Beinn Eighe Visitor Centre** (⏲10am-5pm Easter-Oct), a mile north of Kinlochewe, with interactive displays (good for kids, too) on local geography, ecology, flora, fauna and walking routes.

Kinlochewe Hotel (☑01445-760253; www.kinlochewehotel.co.uk; Kinlochewe; dm/s £12.50/45, d £70-90; P🐾🐕) is a welcoming place that's very walker-friendly. As well as comfortable rooms with prices dependent on facilities, there are nice features like a handsome lounge well stocked with books, a great bar with several real ales on tap and a thoughtful menu of locally sourced food. There's also a bunkhouse with one no-frills 12-bed dorm, a decent kitchen and clean bathrooms.

East of Kinlochewe, the single-track A832 continues to Achnasheen, where there's a train station.

TORRIDON & AROUND

Southwest from Kinlochewe, the A896 follows Glen Torridon, overlooked by multiple peaks, including Beinn Eighe (1010m) and Liathach (1055m). The drive along Glen Torridon is one of the most breathtaking in Scotland. Mighty, brooding mountains, often partly obscured by clumps of passing clouds, seemingly drawn to their peaks like magnets, loom over the tiny, winding, single-track road.

The road reaches the sea at Torridon, where there is a Countryside Centre (NTS; donation £3; ⊙10am-5pm Sun-Fri Easter-Sep) offering information on flora, fauna and walks in the rugged area. There's an unstaffed Deer Museum (⊙daylight hr year-round) nearby, which contains a collection of photos and odds and ends put together by a previous ranger.

The camping ground (☑01381-621252; Torridon; sites free) here has good showers and you get a grassy patch to pitch your tent, along with stunning views and wide-open, exhilarating space.

The modern, squat Torridon SYHA (☑01445-791284; www.syha.org.uk; dm/tw £16.25/40; ⊙Mar-Oct; P@) is in a magnificent location surrounded by spectacular mountains. It's a very popular walking base so book ahead in summer.

Ferroch (☑01445-791451; www.ferroch.co.uk; Annat, Loch Torridon; s/d £68/84; P), just southwest of Torridon village, is a guesthouse with a spacious garden in a fabulous position. Once you've woken up to the views, you'll never want to leave. It does top evening meals, too.

To stay in the lap of luxury try the Torridon (☑01445-791242; www.thetorridon.com; s £180, d standard/superior/master £295/345/505; P@🐕), a lavish Victorian shooting lodge that has a romantic lochside position overlooking the peaks, with Liathach looming impossibly large opposite. Rooms are gradually being converted from a classic look to a more contemporary (but most tasteful) one, so specify which you'd prefer. The standard rooms are swish, but the enormous master rooms will make you feel gloriously decadent. The dinners are sumptuous affairs and are open to nonresidents (£45). Friendly staff can organise any number of activities on land or water. Part of the same set-up, the adjacent Torridon Inn (d £87) offers motel-style rooms and a welcoming bar serving meals.

The A896 continues westwards to lovely Shieldaig, which boasts an attractive main street of whitewashed houses right on the water. Tigh an Eilean Hotel (☑01520-755251; www.tighaneilean.co.uk; Shieldaig; bar meals £8-13, 3-course dinner £45) dishes out locally caught seafood so fresh that it may still be squirming on your plate.

APPLECROSS
POP 200

A long side trip abandons the A896 to follow the coast road to the delightfully remote seaside village of Applecross. Or you can continue a bit further down the A896 to one of the best drives in the country (best in terms of the remote and incredibly rugged and spectacular scenery, not the actual road, which winds and twists and balances on sheer precipices). The road climbs steeply to the Bealach na Ba pass (626m), then drops dramatically to the village. This drive is pure magic and a must if you're in the area.

The remote settlement of Applecross feels like an island retreat, partly because of its isolation, and partly because of the magnificent views of Raasay and the hills of Skye that set the pulse racing, particularly at sunset. On a clear day it's an unforgettable place, but the tranquil atmosphere isn't quite the same when the campsite and pub fill to the brim in school holidays.

You can pitch your tent at the Applecross Camp Site (☑01520-744268; www.applecross.uk.com; sites per person £7, hut for 2 £30; P), which offers green grassy plots, cute little wooden cabins and a good cafe.

The hub of the spread-out community here is the Applecross Inn (☑01520-744262; www.applecross.uk.com; Shore St; s/d

TALES FROM A CHAMPION MUNRO BAGGER: STEVEN FALLON

Steven Fallon, a hill walker, fell runner and qualified Mountain Leader who lives in Edinburgh, is the world's most prolific Munro bagger, having climbed all of Scotland's 283 Munros (peaks of 3000ft and higher) no fewer than 14 times. At the time of writing, he was almost halfway to his 15th round, and had nearly ticked off all of the 221 Corbetts (peaks from 2500ft to 2999ft) as well.

How long have you been bagging Munros, and what got you interested in the first place? For Christmas 1988 my parents gave me the Scottish Mountaineering Club guidebook *The Munros* – I hadn't realised there were so many fabulous peaks in Scotland! So off I went and ticked them off one by one. This took me to so many wonderful parts of Scotland that I would never have visited otherwise, and once I'd 'completed' (ie bagged all the Munros), I started on the Corbetts with the intention of repeating only my favourite Munros. But before I knew it I was well through my second round of Munros and, well, the rest is history.

Do you have a favourite, and/or least favourite Munro? As to my favourites, practically anything in the northwest Highlands could feature – they tend to be pointy with great views. I'd single out Slioch by Loch Maree; Beinn Alligin, Liathach and Beinn Eighe in Torridon; the Five Sisters of Kintail and all of the mountains in the Cuillin of Skye. However, my most-most-favourite has to be Ladhar Bheinn on the Knoydart Peninsula. It's pretty remote and to reach it requires a long walk-in along the southern shore of Loch Hourn. It's just so beautiful there. The mountain itself is complex with corries and ridges, and the summit has great views over Eigg to Skye and beyond. I'm pining just thinking about it!

My least favourite, without debate, has to be Ben Klibreck, the most northerly Munro after Ben Hope. It rises above a desolate area where the ground is wet, tussocky and tiring to move over. The last pull up to the summit builds you up to expect wonderful views, but the vista from the summit is really quite disappointing, looking over flat ground in most directions.

Which is the easiest Munro, and which is the hardest? With only 430m of ascent over 5km, the easiest Munros have to be the Cairnwell and Carn Aosda from the Glenshee ski resort. Good paths and ski-tows make for simple navigation over these two peaks, and if you time it right, you'll be back at the cafe in time for something to eat. Check out my website (www.stevenfallon.co.uk) for the 10 easiest Munro walks (click on Hill Lists and Maps/Munros/Easiest Munros).

The hardest peak depends entirely on your thinking. A'Mhaighdean in Wester Ross is the most remote, and most people have to backpack in over one or two or three days to tick this one off. Well worth it though! The most difficult technically has to be the aptly named Inaccessible Pinnacle in the Cuillin Hills on Skye. It's a clamber up a long fin of rock with sensational, tremble-inducing exposure, followed by an abseil down a short but vertical drop. Most Munro baggers will have to enlist the help of their rock-climbing friends or hire a guide.

For more information about bagging Munros, see the boxed text, p30.

£70/100; ☻food noon-9pm; ℗), which has a perfect shoreside location for a sunset pint, a wide variety of food (mains £7 to £13; mostly daily blackboard specials) and rooms with a view.

Back on the main road, the A896 runs south from Shieldaig to **Kishorn**, where there's a general store and post office – as well as spectacular views westwards to the steep, sandstone Applecross hills.

LOCHCARRON
POP 950

The appealing, whitewashed village of Lochcarron is a veritable metropolis with two supermarkets, a bank (with an ATM), post office and petrol station. A long shoreline footpath at the loch's edge provides the perfect opportunity for a stroll to walk off breakfast.

Old Manse (☎01520-722208; www.theold manselochcarron.com; Church St; s/d £35/60, tw with loch view £65; ℗) is a top-notch Scottish guesthouse, beautifully appointed and in a prime lochside position. Rooms are simply gorgeous and the twin overlooking the water is larger and well worth the extra fiver. Breakfast is great and this place would really suit couples: it's made for snuggling.

If you stay at the small, quiet **Rockvilla Hotel** (☎01520-722379; www.rockvilla-hotel. co.uk; Main St; r £70-79) choose rooms 1 or 2 – they are slightly cheaper and have private facilities and dreamy views. Open for lunch and dinner (mains £8 to £13), the hotel kitchen serves some wonderful fresh seafood and is renowned for its scallops.

PLOCKTON
POP 450

There's something distinctly tropical about idyllic little Plockton, a village that looks straight off a film set, with palm trees, whitewashed houses and a small bay dotted with islets and hemmed in by green-fuzzed mountains. It's a delightfully endearing place made famous as a location for the TV series *Hamish Macbeth*. It's on the tour-bus circuit these days but once evening comes, things settle into an easy tranquillity.

Calum's Seal Trips (☎01599-544306; www.calums-sealtrips.com; cruises adult/child £8/5) runs seal-watching cruises. There are swarms of the slippery fellas just outside the harbour and the trip comes with an excellent commentary. Trips leave daily at 10am, noon, 2pm and 4pm. You may even spot an otter.

Airily set in the one-time train station (it's now opposite), **Plockton Station Bunkhouse** (☎01599-544235; gillcoe@btinternet.com; dm £13; P⊕) has cosy four-bed dorms, a garden and kitchen-lounge with plenty of light and good perspectives over the frenetic comings and goings (OK, that last bit's a lie) of the platforms below. The owners also do good-value B&B (single/double £25/45) next door in the inaccurately named 'Nessun Dorma'.

Slap-bang by the sea, characterful **Shieling** (☎01599-544282; www.lochalsh.net/shieling; d £60; ⊙Easter-Oct) is surrounded by an expertly trimmed garden and has two carpeted rooms with views and big beds. Next door is an historic thatched blackhouse (a low-walled stone cottage with a turf roof and earthen floor).

The black-painted **Plockton Hotel** (☎01599-544274; www.plocktonhotel.co.uk; 41 Harbour St; s/d £85/120, cottage s/d £55/80, mains £8-13; ⊙lunch & dinner; ⊕) is one of those classic Highland spots that manages to make everyone happy, whether it's thirst, hunger or fatigue that brings you knocking. The assiduously tended rooms are a delight, with excellent facilities and thoughtful touches like bathrobes. Those without a water view are consoled with more space and a balcony with rock-garden perspectives. Just down the way, the cottage offers simpler comfort. The cosy bar (or wonderful beer garden on a sunny day) are memorable places for a pint, and food ranges from sound-value bar meals to seafood platters and local langoustines brought in on the afternoon boat.

Across the bay from town, **Duncraig Castle** (☎01599-544295; www.duncraigcastle. co.uk; d standard/superior £109/119; P) offers luxurious, offbeat hospitality as long as dead animals don't offend you. It needs a bit of work still – the curiously ugly school building alongside is thankfully destined for removal – but ongoing improvements are in progress. It's very close to Plockton but has its own train station.

Kyle of Lochalsh
POP 739

Before the controversial bridge, Kyle of Lochalsh was Skye's main ferry-port. Visitors now tend to buzz through town, but Kyle has an intriguing attraction if you're interested in marine life.

The tourist office is where to book for the **Seaprobe Atlantis** (☎0800 980 4846; www. seaprobeatlantis.com; ⊙Easter-Oct), a glass-hulled boat that takes a spin around the kyle to spot seabirds, seals and maybe an otter or two. The basic trip (£9.50/4.75 adult/child) includes an entertaining guided tour and plenty of beautiful jellyfish; longer trips also take in a WWII shipwreck.

There's a string of B&Bs just outside of town on the road to Plockton. The best place to eat is the **Waverley** (☎01599-534337; Main St; mains £12-20; ⊙dinner Fri-Wed). This superb restaurant is an intimate place with excellent service; try the taste of land and sea, combining Aberdeen Angus fillet steak with fresh local prawns.

The **tourist office** (☎01599-534276; ⊙daily Easter-Oct), beside the main seafront car park, stocks information on Skye. Next to it is one of Scotland's most lavishly decorated public toilets.

Citylink runs to Kyle a few times daily from Inverness (£18.60, 2¼ hours), and Glasgow (£34, 5¾ hours).

The train ride between Inverness and Kyle of Lochalsh (£18.20, 2½ hours, up to four daily) is one of Scotland's most scenic train routes.

Kyle to the Great Glen

It's 55 miles southeast via the A87 from Kyle to Invergarry, which lies between Fort William and Fort Augustus, on Loch Oich.

EILEAN DONAN CASTLE

Photogenically sited at the entrance to Loch Duich, near Dornie village, **Eilean Donan Castle** (www.eileandonancastle.com; Dornie; adult/child £5.50/4.50; ⊙9.30am-6pm mid-Mar–mid-Nov) is one of Scotland's most evocative castles, and must be represented in millions of photo albums. It's on an off-shore islet, magically linked to the mainland by an elegant, stone-arched bridge. It's very much a re-creation inside with an excellent introductory exhibition. Keep an eye out for the photos of castle scenes from the movie *Highlander*. There's also a sword used at the battle of Culloden in 1746. The castle was ruined in 1719 after Spanish Jacobite forces were defeated at the Battle of Glenshiel, and it was rebuilt between 1912 and 1932.

Citylink buses from Fort William and Inverness to Portree stop opposite the castle.

GLEN SHIEL & GLENELG

From Eilean Donan Castle, the A87 follows Loch Duich into spectacular Glen Shiel, with 1000m-high peaks soaring up on both sides of the road. At Shiel Bridge, home to a famous wild-goat colony, a narrow side road goes over the **Bealach Ratagain** (pass) to Glenelg, where there's a community-run ferry to Skye.

There are several good walks in the area, including the low-level route from Morvich to Glen Affric Youth Hostel, via spectacular **Gleann Lichd** (17 miles). A traverse of the **Five Sisters of Kintail** is a classic and none-too-easy expedition; start a mile east of the Glen Shiel battle site and finish at Shiel Bridge (eight to 10 hours). For more information on these walks, contact the tourist office at Kyle of Lochalsh.

From the Bealach Ratagain, there are great views of the Five Sisters. Continue past Glenelg in the direction of Arnisdale to the two fine ruined Iron Age **brochs** – Dun Telve and Dun Troddan. Dun Telve still stands to a height of 10m.

From palindromic Glenelg round to the road's end at **Arnisdale**, the scenery becomes even more spectacular, with great views across Loch Hourn to the remote Knoydart Peninsula. **Billy Mackenzie** (☑01599-522247; www.arnisdaleferry.com) can zip walkers and cyclists across to Knoydart.

Ratagan SYHA (☑01599-511243; www.syha.org.uk; dm £16; ⊙mid-Mar–Oct; P @) is a particularly good hostel. It has excellent facilities and a to-die-for spot by Loch Duich. If you want a break from Munro bagging, this is the place. There's at least one local bus a day from the Kyle of Lochalsh to the hostel (half an hour). Turn towards Glenelg from Shiel Bridge, then take the turning on the right to Ratagan.

Kintail Lodge Hotel (☑01599-511275; www.kintaillodgehotel.co.uk; Shiel Bridge; dm/s/d £13.50/85/120; P ☎) has two bunkhouses, with self-catering facilities, sleeping six people each. With 10 of the 12 fine rooms facing the loch, you'd be unlucky not to get a decent outlook from a room inside the hotel. The tasty bar meals (£9 to £16), including local venison and seafood, are available for lunch and dinner.

One of the Highlands' most picturesque places for a pint or a romantic away-from-it-all stay (doubles £120), the **Glenelg Inn** (☑01599-522273; www.glenelg-inn.com; Glenelg; mains £11-19; ⊙lunch & dinner; P) has tables in a lovely garden with cracking views of Skye. The elegant dining room serves up posh fare, with the local catch always featuring.

Citylink buses between Fort William, Inverness and Skye operate along the A87. A bus runs weekdays from Broadford on Skye to Arnisdale, via Kyle of Lochalsh, Ratagan hostel and Glenelg.

The **Skye ferry** (www.skyeferry.com) runs every 20 minutes between 10am and 6pm from Easter to mid-October. Passengers are free and cars cost £12/15 single/return; there's no need to book.

CLUANIE INN

Beyond the top of Glen Shiel, the A87 passes the remote, but welcoming, **Cluanie Inn** (☑01320-340238; www.cluanieinn.com; Glenmoriston; s £70 d standard/luxury £110/135, mains £8-14; ⊙lunch & dinner; P ☎), which has a great lived-in feel to it, providing shelter and good cheer from the elements. It's a classy lodge and very popular with outdoor enthusiasts. The luxury room comes with a four-poster bed and sauna. The compact adjacent clubhouse provides cheaper accommodation (per person £37.50). From the inn, you can walk along several mountain ridges, bagging Munros to your heart's content. There's a low-level route through to Glen Affric Youth Hostel, which takes three hours, but it gets very wet at certain times of year.

ISLE OF SKYE

POP 9900

The Isle of Skye (an t-Eilean Sgiathanach in Gaelic) takes its name from the old Norse *sky-a*, meaning 'cloud island', a Viking reference to the often mist-enshrouded Cuillin Hills. It's the biggest of Scotland's islands, a 50-mile-long smorgasbord of velvet moors, jagged mountains, sparkling lochs and towering sea cliffs. The stunning scenery is the main attraction, but when the mist closes in there are plenty of castles, crofting museums and cosy pubs and restaurants to retire to.

Along with Edinburgh and Loch Ness, Skye is one of Scotland's top three tourist destinations. However, the hordes tend to stick to Portree, Dunvegan and Trotternish, and it's almost always possible to find peace and quiet in the island's further-flung corners. Come prepared for changeable weather: when it's fine it's very fine indeed, but all too often it isn't.

🏃 Activities

WALKING

Skye offers some of the finest – and in places the roughest and most difficult – walking in Scotland. There are many detailed guidebooks available, including a series of four walking guides by Charles Rhodes, available from the Aros Centre and the tourist office in Portree. You'll need Ordnance Survey (OS) 1:50,000 maps 23 and 32. Don't attempt the longer walks in bad weather or in winter.

Easy, low-level routes include: through Strath Mor from Luib (on the Broadford–Sligachan road) and on to Torrin (on the Broadford–Elgol road, allow 1½ hours, 4 miles); from Sligachan to Kilmarie via Camasunary (four hours, 11 miles); and

from Elgol to Kilmarie via Camasunary (2½ hours, 6.5 miles). The walk from Kilmarie to Coruisk via Camasunary and the 'Bad Step' (allow five hours, 11 miles round trip) is superb but slightly harder (the Bad Step is a rocky slab poised above the sea that you have to scramble across; it's easy in fine, dry weather, but some walkers find it intimidating).

Skye Walking Holidays (☎01470-552213; www.skyewalks.co.uk; Duntulm Castle Hotel, Trotternish) Organises three-day guided walking holidays for £400 per person, including four nights of hotel accommodation.

CLIMBING

The Cuillin Hills is a veritable playground for rock climbers, and the two-day traverse of the Cuillin Ridge is the finest mountaineering expedition in the British Isles. There are several mountain guides in the area who can provide instruction and safely introduce inexperienced climbers to the harder routes.

Skye Guides (☎01471-822116; www.skyeguides.co.uk) A five-day basic rock-climbing course costs around £800 and a private mountain guide can be hired for around £190 a day (both rates apply for up to two clients).

SEA KAYAKING

The sheltered coves and sea lochs around the coast of Skye provide water lovers with magnificent sea-kayaking opportunities. The centres listed here can provide kayaking instruction, guiding and equipment hire for both beginners and experts. It costs around £35 for a half-day kayak hire with instruction.

Whitewave Outdoor Centre (☎01470-542414; www.white-wave.co.uk; 19 Linicro, Kilmuir; ⊗Mar-Oct)

Skyak Adventures (☎01471-820002; www.skyakadventures.com; 29 Lower Breakish, Breakish)

👉 Tours

There are several operators who offer guided tours of Skye, covering history, culture and wildlife. Rates are from £140 for a six-hour tour for up to six people.

Red Deer Travel (☎01478-612142) Historical and cultural tours by minibus.

Isle of Skye Tour Guide Co (☎01471-844440; www.isle-of-skye-tour-guide.co.uk) Geology, history and wildlife by car.

Information

Portree and Broadford are the main population centres on Skye.

INTERNET ACCESS

Columba 1400 Community Centre (Staffin, Trotternish; per hr £1; 10.30am-8pm Mon-Sat Apr-Oct;)

Portree tourist office (Bayfield Rd, Portree; per 20min £1; 9am-6pm Mon-Sat, 10am-4pm Sun Jun-Aug, 9am-5pm Mon-Fri, 10am-4pm Sat Apr, May & Sep, limited opening hr Oct-Mar)

Seamus Bar (Sligachan Hotel, Sligachan; per 15min £1; 11am-11pm;)

Skye & Outer Hebrides

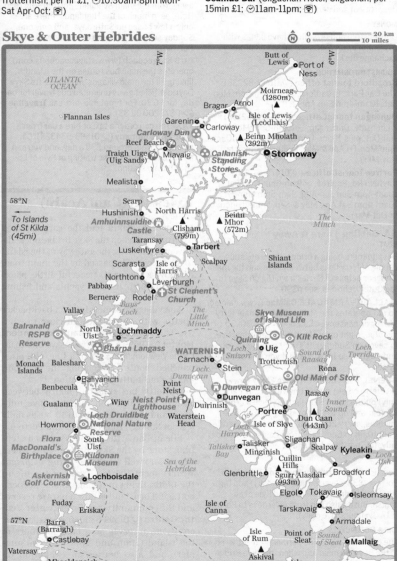

South Skye Computers (Old Corrie Industrial Estate, Broadford; per 15min £1.25; ⊘10am-5pm Mon-Fri, to 1pm Sat)

MEDICAL SERVICES

Portree Community Hospital (☏01478-613200; Fancyhill, Portree) There's a casualty department and dental surgery here.

MONEY

Only Portree and Broadford have banks with ATMs. Portree's tourist office has a currency exchange desk.

TOURIST INFORMATION

Broadford tourist office (☏01471-822361; The Car Park, Broadford; ⊘9.30am-5pm Mon-Sat, 10am-4pm Sun Apr-Oct)

Dunvegan tourist office (☏01470-521581; 2 Lochside, Dunvegan; ⊘10am-5pm Mon-Sat Jun-Oct, plus 10am-4pm Sun Jul & Aug, 10am-5pm Mon-Fri Apr & May, limited opening hr Nov-Mar)

Portree tourist office (☏01478-612137; Bayfield Rd, Portree; ⊘9am-6pm Mon-Sat & 10am-4pm Sun Jun-Aug, 9am-5pm Mon-Fri & 10am-4pm Sat Apr, May & Sep, limited opening hr Oct-Mar)

ⓘ Getting There & Away
BOAT

Despite there being a bridge, there are still a couple of ferry links between Skye and the mainland. For details of ferries from Uig on Skye to the Outer Hebrides, see p390.

MALLAIG–ARMADALE CalMac (www.calmac.co.uk) operates the Mallaig to Armadale ferry (driver or passenger £3.85, car £20.30, 30 minutes, eight daily Monday to Saturday, five to seven on Sunday). It's very popular in July and August, so book ahead if you're travelling by car.

GLENELG–KYLERHEA Skye Ferry (www.skyeferry.co.uk) runs a tiny vessel (six cars only) on the short Glenelg to Kylerhea crossing (car and up to four passengers £12, five minutes, every 20 minutes). The ferry operates from 10am to 6pm daily from Easter to October only, till 7pm June to August.

BUS

Scottish Citylink runs buses from Glasgow to Portree (£38, seven hours, four daily) and Uig via Crianlarich, Fort William and Kyle of Lochalsh. Buses also run from Inverness to Portree (£17, 3½ hours, five daily).

CAR & MOTORCYCLE

The Isle of Skye became permanently tethered to the Scottish mainland when the Skye Bridge opened in 1995. The controversial bridge tolls were abolished in 2004 and the crossing is now free.

There are petrol stations at Broadford (open 24 hours), Armadale, Portree, Dunvegan and Uig.

ⓘ Getting Around

Getting around the island by public transport can be a pain, especially if you want to explore away from the main Kyleakin–Portree–Uig road. Here, as in much of the Highlands, there are only a few buses on Saturdays, and only one Sunday service (between Kyle of Lochalsh and Portree).

BUS Stagecoach (www.stagecoachbus.com) operates the main bus routes on the island, linking all the main villages and towns. Its Skye Dayrider ticket gives unlimited bus travel for one day for £6.70. For timetable info, call **Traveline** (☏0871 200 22 33).

TAXI You can order a taxi or hire a car from **Kyle Taxi Company** (☏01599-534323). Car hire costs from around £38 a day, and you can arrange for the car to be waiting at Kyle of Lochalsh train station.

Kyleakin (Caol Acain)

POP 100

Poor wee Kyleakin had the carpet pulled from under it when the Skye Bridge opened – it went from being the gateway to the island to a backwater bypassed by the main road. It's now a pleasant, peaceful little place, with a harbour used by yachts and fishing boats.

The village is something of a backpacker ghetto, with four hostels in close proximity. The homely **Dun Caan Independent Hostel** (☏01599-534087; www.skyerover.co.uk; Castle View; dm from £15), in a fine, old, pine-panelled house overlooking the harbour, has the most attractive location.

A shuttle bus runs half-hourly between Kyle of Lochalsh and Kyleakin (five minutes), and there are eight to 10 buses daily (except Sunday) to Broadford and Portree.

Eilean Ban – the island used as a stepping stone by the Skye Bridge – was where Gavin Maxwell (author of *Ring of Bright Water*) spent the last years of his life in the 1960s, living in the lighthouse keeper's cottage. The island is now a nature reserve and the community-run **Brightwater Visitor Centre** (☏01599-530040; www.eileanban.org; Kyleakin) serves as a base for tours of the island (11am and 2pm daily in summer), and also houses an exhibition on Maxwell, the lighthouse and the island's wildlife. Opening times were uncertain at the time of research – best call ahead to check.

Broadford
(An T-Ath Leathann)

POP 1050

Broadford is a service centre for the scattered communities of southern Skye. The long, straggling village has a tourist office, a 24-hour petrol station, a large **Co-op supermarket** (⊙8am-10pm Mon-Sat, 9am-6pm Sun), a laundrette and a bank with an ATM.

There are lots of B&Bs in and around Broadford and the village is well placed for exploring southern Skye by car.

🛏 Sleeping & Eating

Broadford Hotel　　　　HOTEL **££**
(☑01471-822204; www.broadfordhotel.co.uk; Torrin Rd; s/d from £115/128; P⊛) The owners of the Bosville in Portree have converted the old Broadford Hotel into a glamourous and stylish retreat with luxury fabrics and designer colour schemes. There's a formal restaurant and the more democratic **Gabbro Bar** where you can enjoy a bar meal (mains £7 to £9, served noon to 9pm) of smoked haddock chowder or steak pie washed down with Isle of Skye Brewery ale.

Creelers　　　　SEAFOOD **££**
(☑01471-822281; www.skye-seafood-restaurant. co.uk; Lower Harrapool; mains £12-18; ⊙noon-9.30pm Mon-Sat) Broadford has several places to eat but one really stands out. Creelers is a small, bustling, no-frills restaurant that serves some of the best seafood on Skye; the house speciality is a rich, spicy seafood gumbo. Book ahead, and if you can't get a table then nip around to the back door, where you'll find Ma Doyle's Takeaway, for fish and chips (£5) to go.

Berabhaigh　　　　B&B **£**
(☑01471-822372; www.isleofskye.net/berab haigh; 3 Lime Park; r per person £34; ⊙Mar-Oct; P) Lovely old croft house with bay views. Just off the main road, near Creelers.

Luib House　　　　B&B **£**
(☑01471-820334; www.luibhouse.co.uk; Luib; r per person £30; P🐕) Large, comfortable and well-appointed house 6 miles north of Broadford.

Sleat

If you cross over the sea to Skye on the ferry from Mallaig you arrive in Armadale, at the southern end of the long, low-lying peninsula known as Sleat (pronounced 'slate'). The landscape of Sleat itself is not exceptional, but it provides a grandstand for ogling the magnificent scenery on either side – take the steep and twisting minor road that loops through **Tarskavaig** and **Tokavaig** for stunning views of the Isle of Rum, the Cuillin Hills and Bla Bheinn.

ARMADALE

POP 150

Armadale, where the ferry from Mallaig arrives, is little more than a store, a post office and a couple of houses. There are six or seven buses a day (Monday to Saturday) from Armadale to Broadford and Portree.

◉ Sights & Activities

Museum of the Isles　　MUSEUM, CASTLE
(www.clandonald.com; adult/child £6.95/4.95; ⊙9.30am-5.30pm Easter-Oct) Just along the road from the ferry is the part-ruined Armadale Castle, former seat of Lord Macdonald of Sleat. The neighbouring museum will tell you all you ever wanted to know about Clan Donald, as well as providing an easily digested history of the Lordship of the Isles. Prize exhibits include rare portraits of clan chiefs, and a wine glass that was once used by Bonnie Prince Charlie. The ticket also gives admission to the lovely castle gardens.

FREE **Aird Old Church Gallery**　ART GALLERY
(www.skyewatercolours.co.uk; ⊙10am-5pm Mon-Sat Easter-Sep) At the end of the narrow road that leads southwest from Armadale through Ardvasar village, this small gallery exhibits the powerful landscape paintings of Peter McDermott. The track beyond the gallery provides a good walk to the lighthouse and pretty little beach at **Point of Sleat** (5 miles round trip).

Sea.fari　　　　BOAT TRIPS
(☑01471-844787, 01471-833316; www.seafari. co.uk) Runs one- to three-hour boat trips (£27/37 per person) in high-speed RIBs. These trips have a high success rate for spotting minke whales in summer (an average of 180 sightings a year), with rarer sightings of bottlenose dolphins and basking sharks – even a humpback whale was spotted in August 2004, and two killer whales in 2007.

🛏 Sleeping & Eating

Flora MacDonald Hostel　　HOSTEL **£**
(☑01471-844272; www.skye-hostel.co.uk; The Glebe, Kilmore; dm/tw/q £14/36/65; P) Three

miles north of the ferry, on a farm full of Highland cattle and Eriskay ponies.

Pasta Shed CAFE £
(The Pier, Armadale; mains £6-12; ⊘9am-6pm) A cute little conservatory with some outdoor tables; serves good seafood dishes, pizzas, fish and chips, crab salads and coffees – you can sit in or take away.

ISLEORNSAY

This pretty harbour, 8 miles north of Armadale, is opposite Sandaig Bay on the mainland, where Gavin Maxwell lived and wrote his much-loved memoir *Ring of Bright Water*. **Gallery An Talla Dearg** (www.eilean-iarmain.co.uk/art-gallery; admission free; ⊘10am-6pm Mon-Fri, to 4pm Sat & Sun Apr-Oct) exhibits the works of artists who were inspired by Scottish landscapes and culture.

🛏 Sleeping & Eating

TOP CHOICE **Toravaig House Hotel** HOTEL £££
(☎01471-820200; www.skyehotel.co.uk; Sleat; r from £169; P🐾) This hotel, 3 miles south of Isleornsay, is one of those places where the owners know a thing or two about hospitality – as soon as you arrive you'll feel right at home – whether relaxing on the plump sofas by the log fire in the lounge or admiring the view across the Sound of Sleat from the lawn chairs in the garden. The spacious bedrooms – ask for room 1 (Eriskay), with its enormous sleigh bed – are luxuriously equipped, from the rich and heavy bed linen to the huge, high-pressure shower heads. The elegant **Iona restaurant** (four-course dinner £43) serves the best of local fish, game and lamb. After dinner you can retire to the lounge with a single malt and flick through the yachting magazines – you can even arrange a day-trip aboard the owners' 42ft sailing yacht.

Hotel Eilean Iarmain HOTEL £££
(☎01471-833332; www.eilean-iarmain.co.uk; s/d from £100/160; P) A charming old Victorian hotel with log fires, an excellent restaurant and 12 luxurious rooms, many with sea views. The hotel's cosy, wood-panelled **An Praban bar** serves delicious, gourmet-style bar meals (£7 to £10) – try the haddock in beer batter, venison burger or vegetarian lasagne.

Elgol (Ealaghol)

On a clear day, the journey along the road from Broadford to Elgol is one of the most scenic on Skye. It takes in two classic postcard panoramas – the view of Bla Bheinn across Loch Slapin (near Torrin), and the superb view of the entire Cuillin range from Elgol pier.

Bus 49 runs from Broadford to Elgol (40 minutes, three daily Monday to Friday, two Saturday).

🏃 Activities

Bella Jane BOAT TRIPS
(☎0800 731 3089; www.bellajane.co.uk; ⊘Easter–mid-Oct) *Bella Jane* offers a three-hour cruise (adult/child £20/8) from Elgol harbour to the remote **Loch na Cuilce**, an impressive inlet surrounded by soaring peaks and acres of bare rock slabs. On a calm day, you can clamber ashore here to make the short walk to **Loch Coruisk** in the heart of the Cuillin Hills. You get 1½ hours ashore and visit a seal colony en route.

Aquaxplore BOAT TRIPS
(☎0800 731 3089; www.aquaxplore.co.uk; ⊘Easter–mid-Oct) Runs 1½-hour high-speed boat trips from Elgol to an abandoned shark-hunting station on the island of Soay (adult/child £20/15), once owned by *Ring of Bright Water* author Gavin Maxwell. There are longer trips (£45/32, four hours) to Rum, Canna and Sanday to visit breeding colonies of puffins, with the chance of seeing minke whales on the way.

Misty Isle BOAT TRIPS
(☎01471-866288; www.mistyisleboattrips.co.uk; ⊘Apr-Oct) The prettier and more traditional wooden launch *Misty Isle* offers cruises to Coruisk with 1½ hours ashore for adult/child £18/7.50 (no Sunday service).

Cuillin Hills

The Cuillin Hills are Britain's most spectacular mountain range. Though small in stature (**Sgurr Alasdair**, the highest summit, is only 993m), the peaks are near-alpine in character, with knife-edge ridges, jagged pinnacles, scree-filled gullies and acres of naked rock. While they are a paradise for experienced mountaineers, the higher reaches of the Cuillin are off limits to the majority of walkers.

The good news is that there are also plenty of good low-level hikes within the ability of most walkers. One of the best (on a fine day) is the steep climb from Glenbrittle camping ground to **Coire Lagan** (6 miles round trip; allow at least three hours). The impressive upper corrie contains a lochan for bathing (for the hardy!), and the surrounding cliffs are a playground for rock climbers – bring along your binoculars.

There are two main bases for exploring the Cuillin – **Sligachan** to the north, and **Glenbrittle** to the south.

🛏 Sleeping & Eating

Sligachan Hotel　　　　　　HOTEL **££**
(☎01478-650204; www.sligachan.co.uk; Sligachan; per person from £59; P@🕾) The Slig, as it has been known to generations of climbers, is a near village in itself, encompassing a luxurious hotel, a microbrewery, self-catering cottages, a bunkhouse, a campsite, a big barn of a bar (see below) and an adventure playground.

Seamus's Bar　　　　　　　PUB **£**
(Sligachan Hotel, Sligachan; mains £8-10; ⊙food served 11am-11pm; @🕾🍴) This place dishes up decent bar meals, including haggis, neeps and tatties, steak and ale pie, and fish pie, and serves real ales from its own microbrewery plus a range of 200 malt whiskies in serried ranks above the bar. As well as the adventure playground outside, there are games, toys and a play area indoors.

Sligachan Bunkhouse　　　BUNKHOUSE **£**
(☎01478-650204; www.sligachan.co.uk; Sligachan Hotel, Sligachan; per person £15) Comfortable and modern bunkhouse opposite the hotel.

Sligachan Campsite　　　　CAMPSITE **£**
(Sligachan Hotel, Sligachan; sites per person £5; ⊙Apr-Oct) Across the road from the hotel is this basic campsite; be warned – this spot is a midge magnet. No bookings.

Glenbrittle Youth Hostel　　　HOSTEL **£**
(SYHA; ☎01478-640278; Glenbrittle; dm £15; ⊙Apr-Sep) Scandinavian-style timber hostel, quickly fills up with climbers on holiday weekends.

Glenbrittle Campsite　　　　CAMPSITE **£**
(☎01478-640404; Glenbrittle; sites per adult/child £5.50/3.50) Excellent site, close to mountains and sea; as at Sligachan, the midges here can be diabolical.

ℹ️ Getting There & Away

Sligachan, on the main Kyle–Portree road, is easily accessible by bus; Glenbrittle is harder to reach. Bus 53 runs five times a day Monday to Friday (once on Saturday) from Portree to Carbost via Sligachan (50 minutes); from there, you'll have to hitch or walk the remaining 8 miles to Glenbrittle (this can be slow, especially late in the day).

Minginish

Loch Harport, to the north of the Cuillin, divides the Minginish Peninsula from the rest of Skye. On its southern shore lies the village of Carbost, home to the smooth, sweet and smoky Talisker malt whisky, produced at **Talisker Distillery** (www.discovering -distilleries.com; Carbost; guided tour £5; ⊙9.30am-5pm Mon-Sat Easter-Oct, noon-5pm Sun Jul & Aug, 10–5pm Mon-Fri Nov-Easter). This is the only distillery on Skye; the guided tour includes a free dram. Magnificent **Talisker Bay**, 5 miles west of Carbost, has a sandy beach, sea stack and waterfall.

The **Old Inn** (☎01478-640205; www.carbost.f9.co.uk; Carbost; s/d £42/74; P) is an atmospheric wee pub, offering accommodation in bright B&B bedrooms and an appealing chalet-style bunkhouse (from £14 per person). The bar is a favourite with walkers and climbers from Glenbrittle – there's an outdoor patio at the back with great views over Loch Harport – and between noon and 10pm, it serves excellent pub grub (£8 to £12), from fresh oysters to haddock and chips.

Three miles northwest of Carbost is the **Skyewalker Independent Hostel** (☎01478-640250; www.skyewalkerhostel.com; Fiskavaig Rd, Portnalong; dm £13.50; @), housed in the old village school.

There are five buses a day on weekdays (one on Saturday) from Portree to Carbost via Sligachan.

Portree (Port Righ)

POP 1920

Portree is Skye's largest and liveliest town. It has a pretty harbour lined with brightly painted houses, and there are great views of the surrounding hills. Its name (from the Gaelic for King's Harbour) commemorates James V, who came here in 1540 to pacify the local clans.

◉ Sights & Activities

Aros Experience VISITOR CENTRE
(www.aros.co.uk; Viewfield Rd; ⊙9am-5.30pm; ⊞) On the southern edge of Portree, the Aros Experience is a combined visitor centre, book and gift shop, restaurant, theatre and cinema. The visitor centre (adult/child £3/2) offers a look at some fascinating, live CCTV images from local sea-eagle and heron nests, and a viewing of a (strangely commentary-free) wide-screen video of Skye's impressive scenery (it's worth waiting for the aerial shots of the Cuillin). The centre is a useful rainy-day retreat, with an indoor, soft play area for children.

MV Stardust BOAT TRIPS
(☑07798-743858; www.skyeboat-trips.co.uk; Portree Harbour) MV *Stardust* offers one- to two-hour boat excursions to the Sound of Raasay (£12 to £15 per person), with the chance to see seals, porpoises and – if you're lucky – white-tailed sea eagles. On Saturday there are longer cruises to the Isle of Rona (£25). You can also arrange to be dropped off for a hike on the Isle of Raasay and picked up again later.

✸✸ Festivals & Events

The annual **Isle of Skye Highland Games** (www.skye-highland-games.co.uk) are held in Portree in early August.

⊨ Sleeping

Portree is well supplied with B&Bs but many of them are in bland, modern bungalows that, though comfortable, often lack character. Accommodation fills up fast in July and August so be sure to book ahead.

TOP CHOICE **Ben Tianavaig B&B** B&B ££
(☑01478-612152; www.ben-tianavaig.co.uk; 5 Bosville Tce; r £65-75; ℗⊛) A warm welcome awaits the Aussie/Brit couple who run this appealing B&B bang in the centre of town. All four bedrooms have a view across the harbour to the hill that gives the house its name and breakfasts include free-range eggs and vegetables grown in the garden.

Bosville Hotel HOTEL ££
(☑01478-612846; www.bosvillehotel.co.uk; 9-11 Bosville Tce; s/d from £120/128; ⊛) The Bosville brings a little bit of metropolitan style to Portree with its designer fabrics and furniture, flatscreen TVs, fluffy bathrobes and bright, spacious bathrooms. It's worth splashing out a bit for the 'premier' rooms, with leather recliner chairs from which you can lap up the view over the town and harbour.

Peinmore House B&B ££
(☑01478-612574; www.peinmorehouse.co.uk; r per person £55; ℗) Located around 2 miles south of Portree, this former manse has recently been cleverly converted into a stylish and comfortable guesthouse with a spectacular oak-floored lounge, enormous bedrooms, excellent breakfasts and panoramic views.

Rosedale Hotel HOTEL ££
(☑01478-613131; www.rosedalehotelskye.co.uk; Beaumont Cres; s/d from £60/90; ⊙Mar-Nov) The Rosedale is a cosy, old-fashioned hotel – you'll be welcomed with a glass of whisky or sherry when you check in – delightfully situated down by the waterfront. Its three converted fishermen's cottages are linked by a maze of narrow stairs and corridors, and the excellent restaurant has a view of the harbour.

Woodlands B&B £
(☑01478-612980; www.woodlands-portree.co.uk; Viewfield Rd; r per person £32-34; ℗) A great location, with views across the bay, and unstinting hospitality make this modern B&B, a half-mile south of the town centre, a good choice.

Bayfield Backpackers HOSTEL £
(☑01478-612231; www.skyehostel.co.uk; Bayfield; dm from £13; @⊛) Clean, central and modern, this hostel provides the best backpacker accommodation in town. The owner really makes you feel welcome and is a fount of advice on what to do and where to go in Skye.

Bayview House B&B £
(☑01478-613340; www.bayviewhouse.co.uk; Bayfield; r per person from £23; ℗⊛) Bayview House is modern with spartan but sparklingly clean rooms and bathrooms with power showers. At this price and location, it's a bargain.

Torvaig Campsite CAMPSITE £
(☑01478-612209; www.portreecampsite.co.uk; Torvaig; sites per person £5; ⊙Apr-Oct) This is the closest camping ground to Portree; there's no shop on site so bring your own supplies. It's a mile north of town on the A87 to Uig.

✕ Eating & Drinking

TOP CHOICE Café Arriba CAFÉ £
(www.cafearriba.co.uk; Quay Brae; light meals £5-8, dinner mains £10-13; ☺7am-10pm May-Sep, 8am-5.30pm Oct-Apr) Arriba is a funky little cafe, brightly decked out in primary colours and offering the best choice of vegetarian grub on the island, ranging from a veggie breakfast fry-up to Indian-spiced bean cakes with mint yoghurt, as well as carnivorous treats such as slow-cooked haunch of venison with red wine and beetroot gravy. Also serves excellent coffee.

Bistro at the Bosville BISTRO ££
(☏01478-612846; www.bosvillehotel.co.uk; 7 Bosville Tce; mains £9-20; ☺noon-2.30pm & 5.30-10pm) This hotel bistro sports a relaxed atmosphere, an award-winning chef and a menu that makes the most of Skye-sourced produce – including lamb, game, seafood, cheese, organic vegetables and berries – and adds an original twist to traditional dishes.

Harbour View Seafood Restaurant
  SEAFOOD ££
(☏01478-612069; www.harbourviewskye.co.uk; 7 Bosville Tce; mains £10-19; ☺noon-2.30pm & 5.30-10pm) The Harbour View is Portree's most congenial place to eat. It has a homely dining room with a log fire in winter, books on the mantelpiece and bric-a-brac on the shelves. And on the table, superb Scottish seafood, such as fresh Skye oysters, seafood chowder, king scallops, langoustines and lobster.

Sea Breezes SEAFOOD ££
(☏01478-612016; 2 Marine Buildings, Quay St; mains £10-20; ☺noon-2.30pm & 5.30-10pm Tue-Sun, closed Nov, Jan & Feb) A good choice for seafood, Sea Breezes is an informal, no-frills restaurant specialising in local fish and shellfish fresh from the boat – try the impressive seafood platter, a small mountain of langoustines, crab, oysters and lobster. Book early, as it's often hard to get a table.

Isles Inn PUB
(Somerled Sq) Portree's pubs are nothing special but the Isles Inn is more atmospheric than most. The Jacobean bar, with its flagstone floor and open fires, pulls in a lively mix of young locals, backpackers and tourists.

Granary Bakery CAFÉ £
(Somerled Sq; light mains £5-8; ☺8am-5pm Mon-Sat) Most of Portree seems to congregate at the Granary's cosy coffee shop to snack on tasty sandwiches, filled rolls, pies, cakes and pastries.

Pier Hotel PUB
(Quay St) You can almost guarantee catching a weekend sing-song at this nautical-themed waterfront bar.

🛍 Shopping

Skye Batiks CRAFTS, GIFTS
(www.skyebatiks.com; The Green; ☺9am-6pm May, Jun & Sep, to 9pm Jul & Aug, to 5pm Mon-Sat Oct-Apr) Skye Batiks is a cut above your average gift shop, selling a range of interesting crafts such as carved wood, jewellery and batik fabrics with Celtic designs.

Over the Rainbow CRAFTS, GIFTS
(www.skyeknitwear.com; Quay Brae) Crammed with colourful knitwear, tweeds and country and casual clothing, as well as glassware, crafts and all kinds of interesting gifts.

Isle of Skye Soap Co COSMETICS
(www.skye-soap.co.uk; Somerled Sq; ☺9am-5.30pm Mon-Fri, to 5pm Sat) A sweet-smelling gift shop that specialises in handmade soaps and cosmetics made using natural ingredients and aromatherapy oils.

Carmina Gadelica MUSIC
(Bank St; ☺9am-5.30pm Mon-Sat, to 9pm Jul & Aug) Browse the shelves here for CDs of Gaelic music and books on local subjects.

ℹ Getting There & Around

BUS The main bus stop is in Somerled Sq. There are seven Scottish Citylink buses a day, including Sundays, from Kyle of Lochalsh to Portree (£13, one hour) and on to Uig.

Stagecoach services (Monday to Saturday only) run from Portree to Broadford (40 minutes, at least hourly) via Sligachan (15 minutes); to Armadale (1¼ hours, connecting with the ferries to Mallaig); to Carbost (40 minutes, four daily); to Uig (30 minutes, six daily) and to Dunvegan Castle (40 minutes, five daily Monday to Friday, three on Saturday). There are also five or six buses a day on a circular route around Trotternish (in both directions) taking in Flodigarry (20 minutes), Kilmuir (1¼ hours) and Uig (30 minutes). See p385 for details on buses from the mainland.

BIKE You can hire bikes at **Island Cycles** (☏01478-613121; The Green; ☺9am-5pm Mon-Sat) for £10/15 per half-/full day.

Dunvegan (Dun Bheagain)

Skye's most famous historic building, and one of its most popular tourist attractions, is **Dunvegan Castle** (www.dunvegancastle.com; Dunvegan; adult/child £8/4; ☺10am-5pm Easter-Oct, 11am-4pm Nov-Easter), seat of the chief of Clan MacLeod. It has played host to Samuel Johnson, Sir Walter Scott and, most famously, Flora MacDonald. The oldest parts are the 14th-century keep and dungeon but most of it dates from the 17th to 19th centuries.

In addition to the usual castle stuff – swords, silver and family portraits – there are some interesting artefacts, most famous being the **Fairy Flag**, a diaphanous silk banner that dates from some time between the 4th and 7th centuries. Bonnie Prince Charlie's waistcoat and a lock of his hair, donated by Flora MacDonald's granddaughter, share a room with **Rory Mor's Drinking Horn**, a beautiful 16th-century vessel of Celtic design that could hold half a gallon of claret. Upholding the family tradition in 1956, John Macleod – the 29th chief, who died in 2007 – downed the contents in one minute and 57 seconds 'without setting down or falling down'.

From the end of the minor road beyond Dunvegan Castle entrance, an easy walk of 1 mile leads to the **Coral Beaches** – a pair of blindingly white beaches composed of the bleached exoskeletons of coralline algae known as maerl.

On the way to Dunvegan from Portree you'll pass **Edinbane Pottery** (www.edinbane-pottery.co.uk; Edinbane; ☺9am-6pm, closed Sat & Sun Nov-Easter), one of the island's original craft workshops, established in 1971, where you can watch potters at work creating beautiful and colourful stoneware.

Duirinish & Waternish

The Duirinish Peninsula to the west of Dunvegan, and Waternish to the north, boasts some of Skye's most atmospheric hotels and restaurants, plus an eclectic range of artists' studios and crafts workshops. Portree tourist office provides a free booklet listing them all.

It's worth making the long drive beyond Dunvegan to the west side of the Duirinish Peninsula to see the spectacular sea cliffs of **Waterstein Head**, and to walk down to **Neist Point lighthouse** with its views to the Outer Hebrides.

At Stein on the Waternish Peninsula is **Dandelion Designs** (www.dandelion-designs.co.uk; Captain's House, Stein; ☺11am-5pm Easter-Oct), an interesting little gallery with a good range of colour and monochrome landscape photography, lino prints by Liz Myhill, and a range of handmade arts and crafts.

A few miles north of Stein you'll find **Shilasdair Yarns** (www.shilasdair-yarns.co.uk; Carnach; ☺10am-6pm Apr-Oct). The couple who run this place moved to Skye in 1971 and now raise sheep, hand-spin woollen yarn, and hand-dye a range of wools and silks using natural dyes. You can see the dyeing process in the workshop behind the studio, which sells finished knitwear as well as yarns.

FLORA MACDONALD

Flora MacDonald, who became famous for helping Bonnie Prince Charlie escape after his defeat at the Battle of Culloden, was born in 1722 at Milton in South Uist, where a memorial cairn marks the site of one of her early childhood homes.

In 1746 she helped Bonnie Prince Charlie make his way from Benbecula to Skye disguised as her Irish maidservant. With a price on the prince's head their little boat was fired on, but they managed to land safely and Flora escorted the prince to Portree where he gave her a gold locket containing his portrait before setting sail for Raasay.

Waylaid on the way home, the boatmen admitted everything. Flora was arrested and imprisoned in the Tower of London. She never saw or heard from the prince again.

In 1747 she returned to Skye, marrying Allan MacDonald and having nine children. Dr Samuel Johnson stayed with her in 1773 during his trip to the Western Isles, but later poverty forced her family to emigrate to North Carolina. There her husband was captured by rebels. Flora returned to Kingsburgh on Skye where she died in 1790. She was buried in Kilmuir churchyard, wrapped in the sheet on which both Bonnie Prince Charlie and Dr Johnson had slept.

📛 Sleeping & Eating

TOP CHOICE **Three Chimneys**

RESTAURANT WITH ROOMS £££

(☑01470-511258; www.threechimneys.co.uk; Colbost, Dunvegan; 3-course lunch/dinner £35/55; ⊙12.30-2pm Mon-Sat Mar-Oct, 6.30-9pm daily year-round; P) In Colbost, halfway between Dunvegan and Waterstein, Three Chimneys is a superb romantic retreat combining a gourmet restaurant in a candlelit crofter's cottage with sumptuous five-star rooms (double £285, dinner/B&B per couple £405) in the modern house next door. Book well in advance, and note that children are not welcome in the restaurant in the evenings.

Stein Inn INN ££

(☑01470-592362; www.steininn.co.uk; Stein, Waternish; bar meals £7-10; ⊙food served noon-4pm & 6-9.30pm Mon-Sat, 12.30-4pm & 6.30-9pm Sun Easter-Oct; P) This old country inn dates from 1790 and has a handful of bedrooms (per person £34 to £50) all with sea views, a lively little bar and a delightful beer garden – a real suntrap on warm summer afternoons – beside the loch. The bar serves real ales from the Isle of Skye Brewery and does an excellent crab sandwich for lunch.

Lochbay Seafood Restaurant SEAFOOD £££

(☑01470-592235; www.lochbay-seafood-restaurant.co.uk; Stein, Waternish; mains £13-22, lobster £28-40; ⊙lunch & dinner Tue-Fri) Just along the road from the Stein Inn is one of Skye's most romantic restaurants, a cosy farmhouse kitchen with terracotta tiles and a wood-burning stove, and a menu that includes most things that either swim in the sea or live in a shell. Best to book ahead.

Trotternish

The Trotternish Peninsula to the north of Portree has some of Skye's most beautiful – and bizarre – scenery.

EAST COAST

First up is the 50m-high, potbellied pinnacle of crumbling basalt known as the **Old Man of Storr**, prominent above the road 6 miles north of Portree. Walk up to its foot from the car park in the woods at the northern end of Loch Leathan (round trip 2 miles). This seemingly unclimbable pinnacle was first scaled in 1955 by English mountaineer Don Whillans, a feat that has been repeated only a handful of times since. North again, near Staffin (Stamhain), is spectacular **Kilt Rock**, a stupendous cliff of columnar basalt with vertical ribbing that's fancifully compared to the pleats of a kilt.

Staffin Bay is dominated by the dramatic basalt escarpment of the **Quiraing**: its impressive land-slipped cliffs and pinnacles constitute one of Skye's most remarkable landscapes. From a parking area at the highest point of the minor road between Staffin and Uig you can walk north to the Quiraing in half an hour. The adventurous (and energetic) can scramble up to the left of the slim pinnacle called the **Needle** to find a hidden, grass-topped plateau known as the **Table**.

📛 Sleeping & Eating

Flodigarry Country House Hotel HOTEL ££

(☑01470-552203; www.flodigarry.co.uk; Flodigarry; s/d from £90/120; P) Flora MacDonald lived in a farmhouse cottage at Flodigarry in northeast Trotternish from 1751 to 1759. The cottage and its pretty garden are now part of this delightful hotel – you can stay in the cottage itself (there are seven bedrooms), or in the more spacious rooms in the hotel itself. The bright, modern **bistro** (mains £10-25) has great views over the Inner Sound, and serves lunch and dinner featuring local produce such as langoustines, lobster, lamb and venison.

Dun Flodigarry Hostel HOSTEL £

(☑01470-552212; www.hostelflodigarry.co.uk; Flodigarry; dm/tw £13/30; @) If you find the local hotel too expensive, try this nearby hostel: it shares the same superb views, and you can still visit the hotel bar for afternoon tea. You can also camp nearby and use the hostel facilities (£6.50 per person).

WEST COAST

The peat-reek of crofting life in the 18th and 19th centuries is preserved in thatched cottages at **Skye Museum of Island Life** (www.skyemuseum.co.uk; Kilmuir; adult/child £2.50/50p; ⊙9.30am-5pm Mon-Sat Easter-Oct). Behind the museum is Kilmuir Cemetery, where a tall Celtic cross marks the **grave of Flora MacDonald**; the cross was erected in 1955 to replace the original, of which 'every fragment was removed by tourists'.

Whichever way you arrive at **Uig** (*oo-*ig), the picture-perfect bay, ringed by steep hills, rarely fails to impress. If you've time to kill while waiting for a ferry to the Outer Hebrides, visit the **Isle of Skye Brewery** (www.skyebrewery.co.uk; The Pier, Uig; ⊙9am-5pm Mon-Fri), which sells locally brewed cask ales and bottled beers.

Just south of Uig, a minor road (signposted 'Sheader and Balnaknock') leads in a mile or so to the **Fairy Glen**, a strange and enchanting natural landscape of miniature conical hills, rocky towers, ruined cottages and a tiny roadside lochan.

There's a cluster of B&Bs in Uig, as well as the **Uig Youth Hostel** (SYHA; ✆01470-542746; Uig; dm £15; ☉late Apr-Sep; ☎) and a lovely old coaching inn, the **Uig Hotel** (✆01470-542205; www.uighotel.com; Uig; s/d from £60/110; P).

Isle of Raasay

POP 160

Raasay is the rugged, 10-mile-long island that lies off Skye's east coast. There are several good walks here, including one to the flat-topped conical hill of **Dun Caan** (443m). Forest Enterprise publishes a free leaflet (available from the tourist offices in Portree or Kyle of Lochalsh) with suggested walks and forest trails.

The extraordinary ruin of **Brochel Castle**, perched on a pinnacle at the northern end of Raasay, was home to Calum Garbh MacLeod, an early-16th-century pirate. At the Battle of Culloden in 1746, Raasay supplied Bonnie Prince Charlie with around 100 fighting men and 26 pipers, but the people paid dearly for their Jacobite sympathies when victorious government forces arrived and proceeded to murder, rape and pillage their way across the island.

Set in a rustic cottage high on the hill overlooking Skye, **Raasay Youth Hostel** (SYHA; ✆01478-660240; Creachan Cottage; dm £16; ☉May-Sep) is a fair walk from the ferry pier (2.5 miles) but is a good base for exploring the island.

See www.raasay.com for a full listing of accommodation.

A CalMac ferry (passenger/car £3.10/11.90) runs from Sconser, on the road from Portree to Broadford, to the southern end of Raasay (15 minutes, hourly Monday to Saturday, twice daily Sunday). There are no petrol stations on the island.

OUTER HEBRIDES

POP 26,500

A professor of Spanish and a professor of Gaelic met at a conference and began discussing the relative merits of their respective languages. 'Tell me,' said the Spanish professor, 'do you have a Gaelic equivalent for the Spanish phrase *mañana, mañana*?' The Hebridean professor thought for a while, then replied, 'No, I do not think that we have in the Gaelic a word that conveys such a pressing sense of urgency'.

An old joke perhaps, but one that hints at the slower pace of life you can expect to find in the Gaelic-speaking communities of the Outer Hebrides, a place where the morning papers arrive in the afternoon and almost everything – in Lewis and Harris at least – closes down on Sundays.

The Outer Hebrides – also known as the Western Isles, or Na h-Eileanan an Iar in Gaelic – are a 130-mile-long string of islands lying off the northwest coast of Scotland. There are 119 islands in total, of which the five main inhabited islands are: Lewis and Harris (two parts of a single island, although often described as if they are separate islands), North Uist, Benbecula, South Uist and Barra. The middle three (often referred to simply as 'the Uists') are connected by road-bearing causeways.

The ferry crossing from Ullapool or Uig to the Western Isles marks an important cultural divide – more than a third of Scotland's registered crofts are in the Outer Hebrides, and no less than 60% of the population are Gaelic speakers. The rigours of life in the old island blackhouses are still within living memory.

Religion still plays a prominent part in public and private life, especially in the Protestant north where shops and pubs close their doors on Sundays and some accommodation providers prefer guests not to arrive or depart on the Sabbath. The Roman Catholic south is a little more relaxed about these things.

The name Hebrides is not Gaelic, and is probably a corruption of Ebudae, the Roman name for the islands. But the alternative derivation from the Norse *havbredey* – 'isles at the edge of the sea' – has a much more poetic ring, alluding to the broad vistas of sky and sea that characterise the islands' often bleak and treeless landscapes. But there is beauty here too, in the machair (grassy, wildflower-speckled dunes) and dazzling white-sand beaches, majesty in the rugged hills and sprawling lochs, and mystery in the islands' fascinating past. It's a past signalled by Neolithic standing stones, Viking place names, deserted crofts and folk memories of the Clearances.

Religion still plays a major role in island life, especially on predominantly Protestant Lewis and Harris where the Sabbath is still widely observed by members of the 'free churches'.

The Calvinist Free Church of Scotland (known as the 'Wee Frees'), and the even more fundamentalist Free Presbyterian Church of Scotland (the 'Wee Wee Frees'), which split from the established Church of Scotland in 1843 and 1893 respectively, are deeply conservative, permitting no ornaments, organ music or choirs. Their ministers deliver uncompromising sermons (usually in Gaelic) from central pulpits and precentors lead the congregation in unaccompanied but fervent psalm singing. Visitors are welcome to attend services, but due respect is essential.

The Protestants of the Outer Hebrides have succeeded in maintaining a distinctive fundamentalist approach to their religion, with Sunday being devoted largely to religious services, prayer and Bible reading. On Lewis and Harris, the last bastion of Sabbath observance in the UK, almost everything closes down on a Sunday. In fact, Stornoway must the only place in the UK to suffer a Sunday rush hour as people drive to church around 10.30am; it's then a ghost town for an hour and a half until the services are over. But a few cracks have begun to appear.

There was outrage when British Airways/Loganair introduced Sunday flights from Edinburgh and Inverness to Stornoway in 2002, with members of the Lord's Day Observance Society spluttering that this was the thin end of the wedge. They were probably right – in 2003 a Stornoway petrol station began to open on a Sunday, and now does a roaring trade in Sunday papers and takeaway booze. Then in 2006 the CalMac ferry from Berneray to Leverburgh in Harris started a Sunday service, despite strong opposition from the residents of Harris (ironically, they were unable to protest at the ferry's arrival, as that would have meant breaking the Sabbath).

If your time is limited, head straight for the west coast of Lewis with its prehistoric sites, preserved blackhouses and beautiful beaches. As with Skye, the islands are dotted with arts and crafts studios – the tourist offices can provide a list.

ℹ️ Information

INTERNET ACCESS

Community Library (Community School, Castlebay, Barra; ⊘9am-4.30pm Mon & Wed, 9am-4.30pm Tue & Thu, 6-8pm Fri, 10am-12.30pm Sat) Free access.

Stornoway Public Library (19 Cromwell St, Stornoway, Lewis; ⊘10am-5pm Mon-Wed & Sat, to 6pm Thu & Fri) Free access.

Taigh Chearsabhagh (Lochmaddy, North Uist; per 20min 50p; ⊘10am-5pm Mon-Sat Feb-Jun & Sep-Dec, 10am-5pm Mon-Thu & Sat, to 8pm Fri Jul & Aug)

INTERNET RESOURCES

CalMac (www.calmac.co.uk) Ferry timetables.

Visit Hebrides (www.visithebrides.com)

MEDICAL SERVICES

Both hospitals have casualty departments.

Uist & Barra Hospital (☏01870-603603; Balivanich, Benbecula)

Western Isles Hospital (☏01851-704704; MacAulay Rd, Stornoway, Lewis)

MONEY

There are banks with ATMs in Stornoway (Lewis), Tarbert (Harris), Lochmaddy (North Uist), Balivanich (Benbecula), Lochboisdale (South Uist) and Castlebay (Barra). Elsewhere, some hotels and shops offer cashback facilities.

TOURIST INFORMATION

Castlebay tourist office (☏01871-810336; Main St, Castlebay, Barra; ⊘9am-1pm & 2-5pm Mon-Sat, noon-4pm Sun Apr-Oct)

Lochboisdale tourist office (☏01878-700286; Pier Rd, Lochboisdale, South Uist; ⊘9am-1pm & 2-5pm Mon-Fri, 9.30am-5pm Sat, 9am-9.30pm Tue & Thu Apr-Oct)

Lochmaddy tourist office (☏01876-500321; Pier Rd, Lochmaddy, North Uist; ⊘9am-1pm & 2-5pm Mon-Fri, 9.30am-1pm & 2-5.30pm Sat, 8-9pm Mon, Wed & Fri Apr-Oct)

Stornoway tourist office (☏01851-703088; 26 Cromwell St, Stornoway, Lewis; ⊘9am-6pm & 8-9pm Mon, Tue & Thu, 9am-8pm Wed & Fri, 9am-5.30pm & 8-9pm Sat year-round)

Tarbert tourist office (☏01859-502011; Pier Rd, Tarbert, Harris; ⊘9am-5pm Mon-Sat, plus 8-9pm Tue, Thu & Sat Apr-Oct)

Getting There & Away

AIR There are airports at Stornoway (Lewis), and on Benbecula and Barra. There are flights to Stornoway from Edinburgh, Inverness, Glasgow and Aberdeen. There are also two flights a day (weekdays only) between Stornoway and Benbecula.

There are daily flights from Glasgow to Barra and Benbecula. At Barra, the planes land on the hard-sand beach at low tide, so the timetable depends on the tides.

Airlines serving the Western Isles:

FlyBe/Loganair (☑ 0871 700 2000; www.log anair.com)

Eastern Airways (☑ 0870 366 9100; www. easternairways.com)

Highland Airways (☑ 0845 450 2245; www.high landairways.co.uk)

BOAT **CalMac** (www.calmac.co.uk) runs car ferries from Ullapool to Stornoway (Lewis); from Uig (Isle of Skye) to Lochmaddy (North Uist) and Tarbert (Harris) and from Oban to Castlebay (Barra) and Lochboisdale (South Uist). One-way fares:

CROSSING	DURATION (HR)	CAR	DRIVER/ PASSENGER
Ullapool–Stornoway	2¾	£38	£7.55
Uig–Lochmaddy	1¾	£24	£5.15
Uig–Tarbert	1½	£24	£5.15
Oban–Castlebay	4¾	£51	£11.40
Oban–Lochboisdale	6¾	£51	£11.40

From Monday to Saturday there are two or three ferries a day to Stornoway, one or two a day to Tarbert and Lochmaddy, and one a day to Castlebay and Lochboisdale; on Sundays there are ferries (same frequency) to Castlebay, Lochboisdale and Lochmaddy, but none to Tarbert and Stornoway. You can also take the ferry from Lochboisdale to Castlebay (car/passenger £20/6.50, 1½ hours, one daily Monday, Tuesday and Thursday) and from Castlebay to Lochboisdale (one daily Wednesday, Friday and Sunday).

Advance booking for cars is essential in July and August; foot and bicycle passengers should have no problems. Bicycles are carried for free.

CalMac has 12 different Island Hopscotch tickets for set routes in the Outer Hebrides, offering a saving of around 10% (tickets are valid for one month). See the website for details.

Getting Around

Despite their separate names, Lewis and Harris are actually one island. Berneray, North Uist, Benbecula, South Uist and Eriskay are all linked by road bridges and causeways. There are car ferries between Leverburgh (Harris) and Berneray, Tarbert (Harris) and Lochmaddy (North Uist), Eriskay and Castlebay (Barra), and Lochboisdale (South Uist) and Castlebay (Barra).

The local council publishes two booklets of timetables (one covering Lewis and Harris, the other the Uists and Barra) that list all bus, ferry and air services in the Outer Hebrides. Timetables can also be found online at www.cne-siar. gov.uk/travel.

BICYCLE Many visiting cyclists plan to cycle the length of the archipelago, but if you're one of them, remember that the wind is often strong (you may hear stories of people pedalling downhill and freewheeling uphill), and the prevailing direction is from the southwest – so south to north is usually the easier direction. There are few serious hills, except for a stiff climb on the main road just north of Tarbert.

Bikes can be hired for around £10 a day or £45 a week in Stornoway (Lewis), Leverburgh (Harris), Howmore (South Uist) and Castlebay (Barra). **Rothan Cycles** (www.rothan.com) offers a delivery and pick-up service at various points between Eriskay and Stornoway.

BUS The bus network covers almost every village in the islands, with around four to six buses a day on all the main routes; however, there are no buses at all on Sundays. You can pick up timetables from the tourist offices, or call **Stornoway bus station** (☑ 01851-704327) for information.

CAR & MOTORCYCLE Away from the fast, two-lane road between Tarbert and Stornoway, most roads are single-track. The main hazard is posed by sheep wandering about or sleeping on the road. Petrol stations are far apart (almost all of those on Lewis and Harris are closed on Sunday), and fuel is about 10% more expensive than on the mainland.

There are petrol stations at Stornoway, Barvas, Borve, Uig, Breacleit (Great Bernera), Ness, Tarbert and Leverburgh on Lewis and Harris; Lochmaddy and Cladach on North Uist; Balivanich on Benbecula; Howmore, Lochboisdale and Daliburgh on South Uist; and Castlebay on Barra.

Cars can be hired from around £30 per day from the following:

Arnol Motors (☑ 018510-710548; www.arnol motors.com; Arnol, Lewis; ⊘closed Sun)

Lewis Car Rentals (☑ 01851-703760; www. lewis-car-rental.com; 14 Bayhead St, Stornoway; ⊘closed Sun)

Lewis (Leodhais)

POP 18,600

The northern part of Lewis is dominated by the desolate expanse of the Black Moor, a vast, undulating peat bog dimpled with glittering lochans, seen clearly from the Stornoway–Barvas road. But Lewis' finest scenery is on the west coast, from Barvas southwest to Mealista, where the rugged landscape of hill, loch and sandy strand is reminiscent of the northwestern Highlands. The Outer Hebrides' most evocative historic sites – Callanish Standing Stones, Dun Carloway, and Arnol Blackhouse Museum – are also to be found here.

The old blackhouses of this region may have been abandoned, but an increasing number are being restored as holiday homes. Most crofts still follow a traditional pattern dating back to medieval times, with narrow strips of land, designed to give all an equal share of good and bad soil, running from the foreshore (with its valuable seaweed, used as fertiliser), across the machair (the grassy sand dunes that provide the best arable land) to the poorer sheep-grazing land on hill or moor. Today few crofts are economically viable, so most islanders supplement their income with fishing, tweed-weaving and work on oil rigs and fish farms.

STORNOWAY (STEORNABHAGH)

POP 6000

Stornoway is the bustling 'capital' of the Outer Hebrides and the only real town in the whole archipelago. It's a surprisingly busy little place, with cars and people swamping the centre on weekdays. Though set on a beautiful natural harbour, the town isn't going to win any prizes for beauty or atmosphere, but it's a pleasant enough introduction to this remote corner of the country.

Stornoway is the Outer Hebrides' administrative and commercial centre, home to the Western Isles Council (Comhairle nan Eilean Siar) and the islands' Gaelic TV and radio stations. It's a bit of a ghost town on Sundays, especially from 11am to 12.30pm, when almost everyone is at church.

Sights

An Lanntair Art Centre
ARTS CENTRE

(www.lanntair.com; Kenneth St; ⊙10am-9pm Mon-Wed, to 10pm Thu, to midnight Fri & Sat; ☎) The modern, purpose-built An Lanntair

Art Centre, complete with art gallery, theatre, cinema and restaurant, is the centre of the town's cultural life; it hosts changing exhibitions of contemporary art and is a good source of information on cultural events.

FREE Museum nan Eilean
MUSEUM

(Francis St; ⊙10am-5.30pm Mon-Sat, shorter winter hr) This museum strings together a loose history of the Outer Hebrides from the earliest human settlements some 9000 years ago to the 20th century, exploring traditional island life and the changes inflicted by progress and technology.

Lewis Castle
CASTLE

The Baronial mansion across the harbour was built in the 1840s for the Matheson family, then owners of Lewis. It was gifted to the community by Lord Leverhulme in 1923 and was home to the local college for 40 years, but has lain empty since 1997 (the college now occupies modern buildings in the castle grounds); it is now slated for development as a museum and hotel. The beautiful grounds are open to the public and host the Hebridean Celtic Festival.

Lewis Loom Centre
WEAVING EXHIBITION

(3 Bayhead; adult/child £1/50p; ⊙9am-5.30pm Mon-Sat) The centre houses an exhibition on the history of Harris Tweed; the 40-minute guided tour (£2.50 extra) includes spinning and weaving demonstrations.

Festivals

Hebridean Celtic Festival
MUSIC

(www.hebceltfest.com) A four-day extravaganza of folk/rock/Celtic music held in the second half of July.

Sleeping

Braighe House
B&B ££

(☎01851-705287; www.braighehouse.co.uk; 20 Braighe Rd; r per person from £45; P) This spacious and comfortable guesthouse, 3 miles east of the town centre on the A866, has stylish, modern bedrooms and a great seafront location. Good bathrooms with powerful showers, hearty breakfasts and genuinely hospitable owners round off the perfect package.

Park Guest House
B&B ££

(☎01851-702485; www.theparkguesthouse.co.uk; 30 James St; s/d from £58/86; P) A charming Victorian villa with a conservatory and eight luxurious rooms (mostly en suite), the

SUNDAY EATS

Most restaurants in Stornoway are closed on Sundays. The few options for a sit-down meal include:

HS-1 Cafe-Bar (Royal Hotel, Cromwell St; mains £8-11; ⊙noon-4pm & 5-9pm)

Stornoway Balti House (24 South Beach; mains £8-13; ⊙noon-2.30pm & 6-11pm)

Park Guest House is comfortable and central and has the advantage of an excellent restaurant. Rooms overlooking the main road can be noisy on weekday mornings.

Royal Hotel HOTEL ££
(☎01851-702109; www.royalstornoway.co.uk; Cromwell St; s/d £79/109; P🐾) The 19th-century Royal is the most appealing of Stornoway's hotels – the rooms at the front retain period features such as wood panelling, and enjoy a view across the harbour to Lews Castle. Ask to see your room first, though, as some are a bit cramped.

Cabarfeidh Hotel HOTEL £££
(☎01851-702604; www.cabarfeidh-hotel.co.uk; Manor Park; s/d £125/165; P🐾) Owned by the same company as the Royal, the Cabarfeidh is bigger and more luxurious and is handy for the golf course, but lacks the Royal's old-fashioned character.

Thorlee B&B £
(☎01851-705466, 01851-706300; www.thorlee. com; 1-3 Cromwell St; d from £45; P) The family-oriented Thorlee has bright and cheerful rooms and a great central location with views over the harbour – an absolute bargain. If there's no answer at the guesthouse, ask at the Stag Bakery next door.

Laxdale Holiday Park CAMPSITE £
(☎01851-703234; www.laxdaleholidaypark.com; 6 Laxdale Lane; site £7-9 plus per person £3; ⊙Apr-Oct; 🐾) This camping ground, 1.5 miles north of town off the A857, has a sheltered woodland setting, though the tent area is mostly on a slope – get there early for a level pitch. There's also a bunkhouse (£15 per person) that stays open year-round.

Heb Hostel HOSTEL £
(☎01851-709889; www.hebhostel.co.uk; 25 Kenneth St; dm £15; @🐾) The Heb is a friendly, easygoing hostel close to the ferry, with comfy wooden bunks, a convivial living room with peat fire and a welcoming owner

who can provide all kinds of advice on what to do and where to go.

🍴 Eating

TOP CHOICE Digby Chick BISTRO £££
(☎01851-700026; 5 Bank St; mains £18-23; ⊙noon-10pm Mon-Sat) A modern restaurant that dishes up bistro cuisine such as haddock and chips, sesame-glazed pork belly or garlic-roasted mushroom with duck-egg salad at lunchtime, the Digby Chick metamorphoses into a candlelit gourmet restaurant in the evening, serving dishes such as grilled langoustines, seared scallops, roast lamb and steak. You can get a two-course lunch for £10 (11.30am to 2pm), and a three-course dinner for £20 (5.30pm to 6.30pm only).

Thai Café THAI £
(☎01851-701811; 27 Church St; mains £5-7; ⊙noon-2.30pm & 5.30-11pm Mon-Sat) Here's a surprise – authentic, inexpensive Thai food in the heart of Stornoway. This spick-and-span little restaurant has a genuine Thai chef, and serves some of the most delicious, best-value Asian food in the Hebrides. If you can't get a table, it does takeaway too.

An Lanntair Art Centre Café CAFE £
(Kenneth St; snacks £3-6, mains £10-16; ⊙10am-noon, noon-2.15pm & 5.30-9pm Mon-Sat) The stylish and family-friendly restaurant at the art centre serves a broad range of freshly prepared dishes, from tasty bacon rolls at breakfast, to burgers, baguettes or mince and tatties for lunch, to Thai curry, beef-and-Guinness pie or nut roast for dinner.

Park Guest House Restaurant
SCOTTISH £££
(☎01851-702485;www.theparkguesthouse.co.uk; 30 James St; mains £15-23; ⊙5-8.45pm Tue-Sat) The restaurant at the Park Guest House specialises in Scottish seafood, beef and game (plus one or two vegetarian dishes), simply prepared, allowing the flavour of the food to speak for itself. It offers a good-value, three-course dinner for £16.50 between 5pm and 6.30pm.

ℹ️ Information

Baltic Bookshop (8-10 Cromwell St; ⊙9am-5.30pm Mon-Sat) Good for local history books and maps.

Sandwick Rd Petrol Station (Sandwick Rd) The only shop in town that's open on a Sunday (from 10am to 4pm); the Sunday papers arrive around 2pm.

In the Outer Hebrides, where trees are few and far between and coal is absent, peat has been the main source of domestic fuel for many centuries. Although oil-fired central heating is now the norm, many houses have held on to their peat fires for nostalgia's sake.

Peat in its raw state is extremely wet and can take a couple of months to dry out. It is cut from roadside bogs, where the cuttings are at least a metre deep. Rectangular blocks of peat are cut using a long-handled tool called a *tairsgeir* (peat-iron); this is extremely hard work and can cause blisters even on hands that are used to manual labour.

The peat blocks are carefully assembled into a *cruach-mhonach* (peat stack), each balanced on top of the other in a grid pattern thus creating maximum air space. Once the peat has dried out it is stored in a shed.

Peat burns much more slowly than wood or coal and produces a not-unpleasant smell, but in the old blackhouses (which had no chimney) it permeated every corner of the dwelling, not to mention the inhabitants' clothes and hair, hence the expression 'peat-reek' – the ever-present smell of peat smoke that was long associated with island life.

❶ Getting There & Around

BUS The bus station is on the waterfront, next to the ferry terminal. Bus W10 runs from Stornoway to Tarbert (one hour, four or five daily Monday to Saturday) and Leverburgh (two hours).

The Westside Circular bus W2 runs a circular route from Stornoway through Callanish, Carloway, Garenin and Arnol; the timetable means you can visit one or two of the sites in a day.

BIKE You can hire bikes from **Alex Dan's Cycle Centre** (✆01851-704025; www.hebridean cycles.co.uk; 67 Kenneth St; ☺9am-6pm Mon-Sat).

BUTT OF LEWIS (RUBHA ROBHANAIS)

The Butt of Lewis (no snickering, please) – the extreme northern tip of the Hebrides – is windswept and rugged, with a very imposing lighthouse, pounding surf and large colonies of nesting fulmars on the high cliffs. There's a bleak sense of isolation here, with nothing but the grey Atlantic between you and Canada.

Just before the turn-off to the Butt at Eoropie (Eoropaidh), you'll find **St Moluag's Church** (Teampull Mholuidh), an austere, barn-like structure believed to date from the 12th century but still used by the Episcopal Church. The main settlement here is **Port of Ness** (Port Nis) with its attractive harbour. To the west of the village is the sandy beach of **Traigh**, which is popular with surfers and has a kids adventure playground nearby.

ARNOL

One of Scotland's most evocative historic buildings, the **Arnol Blackhouse** (HS; ✆01851-710395; adult/child £2.50/1.50; ☺9.30am-5.30pm Mon-Sat Apr-Sep, to 4.30pm Mon-Sat Oct-Mar, last admission 30min before closing) is not so much a museum as a perfectly preserved fragment of a lost world. Built in 1885, this traditional blackhouse – a combined byre, barn and home – was inhabited until 1964 and has not been changed since the last inhabitant moved out. The staff faithfully rekindle the central peat fire every morning so you can experience the distinctive peat-reek; there's no chimney, and the smoke finds its own way out through the turf roof, windows and door – spend too long inside and you might feel like you've been kippered! The museum is just off the A858, about 3 miles west of Barvas.

At nearby **Bragar**, a pair of whalebones form an arch by the road, with the rusting harpoon that killed the whale dangling from the centre.

GARENIN (NA GEARRANNAN)

The picturesque and fascinating **Gearrannan Blackhouse Village** is a cluster of nine restored thatch-roofed blackhouses perched above the exposed Atlantic coast. One of the cottages is home to the **Blackhouse Museum** (www.gearrannan.com; adult/child £2.20/1; ☺9.30am-5.30pm Mon-Sat Apr-Sep), a traditional 1955 blackhouse with displays on the village's history, while another houses the **Taigh an Chocair Cafe** (mains £3-6; ⏰9.30am-5.30pm Mon-Sat).

Garenin Crofters' Hostel (www.gatliff.org.uk; dm adult/child £10/6) occupies one of the village blackhouses, and is one of the most atmospheric hostels in Scotland (or anywhere else for that matter).

The other houses in the village are let out as self-catering **holiday cottages** (☎01851-643416; www.gearrannan.com; per 2 nights for 2 people £144-191) offering the chance to stay in a unique and luxurious modernised blackhouse with attached kitchen and lounge. There's a minimum five-night let from June to August.

CARLOWAY (CARLABAGH)

Dun Carloway (Dun Charlabhaigh) is a 2000-year-old, dry-stone broch, perched defiantly above a beautiful loch with views to the mountains of North Harris. The site is clearly signposted along a minor road off the A858, a mile southwest of Carloway village. One of the best-preserved brochs in Scotland, its double walls (with internal staircase) still stand to a height of 9m and testify to the engineering skills of its Iron Age architects.

The tiny, turf-roofed **Doune Broch Centre** (admission free; ⏰10am-5pm Mon-Sat Apr-Sep) nearby has interpretative displays and exhibitions about the history of the broch and the life of the people who lived there.

CALLANISH (CALANAIS)

The **Callanish Standing Stones**, 15 miles west of Stornoway on the A858 road, form one of the most complete stone circles in Britain and is one of the most atmospheric prehistoric sites anywhere. Its ageless mystery, impressive scale and undeniable beauty leave a lasting impression. Sited on a wild and secluded promontory overlooking Loch Roag, 13 large stones of beautifully banded gneiss are arranged, as if in worship, around a 4.5m-tall central monolith. Some 40 smaller stones radiate from the circle in the shape of a cross, with the remains of a chambered tomb at the centre. Dating from 3800 to 5000 years ago, the stones are roughly contemporary with the pyramids of Egypt.

The nearby **Calanais Visitor Centre** (www.callanishvisitorcentre.co.uk; admission free, exhibition £2; ⏰10am-9pm Mon-Sat Apr-Sep, to 4pm Wed-Sat Oct-Mar) is a tour de force of discreet design. Inside is a small **exhibition** that speculates on the origins and purpose

of the stones, and an excellent **cafe** (snacks £2-5).

If you plan to stay the night, you have a choice of **Eshcol Guest House** (☎01851-621357; www.eshcol.com; 21 Breascleit; r per person £43; P) and neighbouring **Loch Roag Guest House** (☎01851-621357; www.lochroag.com; 22a Breascleit; r per person £40-55; P), half a mile north of Callanish. Both are modern bungalows with the same friendly owner who is very knowledgeable about the local area.

GREAT BERNERA

This rocky island is connected to Lewis by a bridge built by the local council in 1953 – the islanders had originally planned to destroy a small hill with explosives and use the material to build their own causeway. On a sunny day, it's worth making the long detour to the island's northern tip for a picnic at the perfect little sandy beach of **Bosta** (Bostadh).

In 1996 archaeologists excavated an entire Iron Age village at the head of the beach. Afterwards, the village was reburied for protection, but a reconstruction of an **Iron Age house** (Bosta; adult/child £2/50p; ⏰noon-4pm Mon-Fri May-Sep) now sits nearby. Stand around the peat fire, above which strips of mutton are being smoked, while the custodian explains the domestic arrangements – truly fascinating, and well worth the trip.

There are five buses a day between Stornoway and the hamlet of Breacleit (one hour, Monday to Saturday) on Great Bernera; two or three a day will continue to Bosta on request. Alternatively, there's a signposted 5-mile **coastal walk** from Breacleit to Bosta.

MIAVAIG (MIABHAIG) & MEALISTA (MEALASTA)

The B8011 road (signposted Uig, on the A858 Stornoway–Callanish road) from Garrynahine to Timsgarry (Timsgearraidh) meanders through scenic wilderness to some of Scotland's most stunning beaches. At **Miavaig**, a loop road detours north through the Bhaltos Estate to the pretty, mile-long white strand of **Reef Beach**; there's a basic **camping ground** (per person £2) in the machair behind the beach.

From April to September, **Sea Trek** (☎01851-672469; www.seatrek.co.uk; Miavaig Pier) runs two-hour boat trips (adult/child £35/25; Monday to Saturday) to spot seals and nesting seabirds, and more adventurous, all-day trips (£90 per person; two per month, June and July only) in a high-speed RIB to the **Flannan Isles**, a remote group of tiny, uninhabited islands 25 miles northwest of Lewis. Puffins, seals and a ruined 7th-century chapel are the main attractions, but the isles are most famous for the mystery of the three lighthouse keepers who disappeared without trace in December 1900. There's also a 12-hour round trip to remote **St Kilda** (£180, once or twice weekly, May to September, weather permitting).

From Miavaig the road continues west through a rocky defile to Timsgarry and the vast, sandy expanse of **Traigh Uige** (Uig Sands) – the famous 12th-century Lewis chess pieces made of walrus ivory were discovered in the sand dunes here in 1831. Of the 78 pieces, 67 are in the British Museum in London, with 11 in Edinburgh's Museum of Scotland; you can buy replicas at various outlets on the island.

There's a very basic **campsite** (per person £2) on the south side of the bay (signposted 'Ardroil Beach'; toilet only, no showers). If you fancy dining or staying somewhere really unusual, head to the **Gallan Head Hotel** (✆01851-672474; www.gallanheadhotel. co.uk; Aird Uig; mains £11-17; ⏰lunch & dinner Mon-Sat), possibly the most remote fine-dining restaurant in Europe. It's housed in a converted, pine-clad military prefab that's perched above a wild, cliff-bound Atlantic cove 3 miles north of Timsgarry. The food is superb – local seafood, lamb and venison expertly prepared – and the setting unique. Booking is recommended. If you want to stay the night, there are five beautifully refurbished double rooms (from £35 per person).

The minor road that continues south from Timsgarry to **Mealista** passes a few smaller, but still spectacular, white-sand beaches; beware, though – the surf can make swimming treacherous.

Harris (Na Hearadh)

POP 2000

Harris, to the south of Lewis, is the scenic jewel in the necklace of islands that comprise the Outer Hebrides, a spectacular blend of rugged mountains, pristine beaches, flower-speckled machair and barren rocky landscapes. The isthmus at Tarbert splits Harris neatly in two: North Harris is dominated by mountains that rise forbiddingly above the peat moors to the south of Stornoway – Clisham (799m) is the highest point; South Harris is lower-lying, fringed by beautiful white-sand beaches on the west, and a convoluted rocky coastline to the east.

Harris is famous for Harris Tweed, a high-quality woollen cloth still hand-woven in islanders' homes. The industry employs around 400 weavers; staff at Tarbert tourist office can tell you about weavers and workshops that you can visit.

TARBERT (AN TAIRBEART)
POP 480

Tarbert is a harbour village with a spectacular location, tucked into the narrow neck of land that links North and South Harris. It has ferry connections to Uig on Skye.

Village facilities include a petrol station, bank, ATM and two general stores. The **Harris Tweed Shop** (www.isleofharristweed shop.co.uk; Main St; ⏰9.15am-5.30pm May-Sep) stocks a wide range of books on the Hebrides and sells gifts, crafts and the famous cloth itself.

🛏 Sleeping & Eating

Hotel Hebrides   HOTEL **££**
(✆01859-502364; www.hotel-hebrides.com; Pier Rd; per person £65-80; 🖥) The location and setting don't look promising – a drab new build squeezed between ferry pier and car park (you won't find any photos of the hotel exterior on the website) – but this new establishment brings a dash of urban design to Harris, with flashy fabrics and wall coverings, luxurious towels and toiletries, and a stylish restaurant and lounge bar.

Harris Hotel   HOTEL **££**
(✆01859-502154; www.harrishotel.com; s/d from £55/90; 🅿🖥) Run since 1903 by four generations of the Cameron family, Harris Hotel is a 19th-century sporting hotel, originally built for deer-stalkers visiting the North Harris Estates. It has spacious, comfy rooms and a good restaurant; look out for JM Barrie's initials scratched on the dining-room window (the author of *Peter Pan* visited in the 1920s). The hotel is on the way out of the village, on the road north towards Stornoway.

Rockview Bunkhouse   HOSTEL **£**
(✆01859-502081, 01859-502211; imacaskill@ tiscali.co.uk; Main St; dm £10) This hostel on the street above the harbour is a bit cell-like with its cramped dorms and air of neglect,

but it's close to the ferry. Not permanently staffed – if there's no answer, ask at the post office. The Rhenigidale hostel (see North Harris below) is a better bet for a longer stay.

Firstfruits CAFE £
(Pier Rd; mains £4-10; ⊘10am-4pm Mon-Sat Apr-Sep) This is a cosy little cottage tearoom near the tourist office – handy while you wait for a ferry.

NORTH HARRIS
Magnificent North Harris is the most mountainous region of the Outer Hebrides. There are few roads here, but many opportunities for climbing, walking and birdwatching.

The B887 leads west to Hushinish, where there's a lovely silver-sand beach, passing the impressive shooting lodge of Amhuinnsuidhe Castle, now an exclusive hotel. Just northwest of Hushinish is the uninhabited island of Scarp, the scene of bizarre attempts to send mail by rocket in 1934, a story that was recounted in the movie *The Rocket Post* (2001), which was shot in Harris.

Rhenigidale Crofters' Hostel (www.gatliff.org.uk; dm adult/child £10/6) can be reached on foot from Tarbert (6 miles, allow three hours). It's an excellent walk, but take all the necessary supplies for a mountain hike (map, compass, protective clothing etc). Take the road towards Kyles Scalpay for 2 miles and, at a bend in the road just beyond Laxdale Lochs, veer off to the left on a signposted track across the hills (marked on Ordnance Survey maps). The hostel is a small white cottage standing above the road on the eastern side of the glen; the warden lives in the house closest to the shore.

The remote hamlet of Rhenigidale can also be reached by road; bus W11 (request service) will take you there from Tarbert (30 minutes, two a day Monday to Saturday), but you'll have to book in advance (☏01859-502871).

SOUTH HARRIS
The west coast of South Harris has some of the most beautiful beaches in Scotland. The blinding white sands and turquoise waters of Luskentyre and Scarasta would be major holiday resorts if they were transported to somewhere with a warm climate; as it is, they're usually deserted.

The culture and landscape of the Hebrides are celebrated in the fascinating exhibition at Seallam! Visitor Centre (www.seallam.com; Northton; adult/child £2.50/2; ⊘10am-5pm Mon-Sat). *Seallam* is Gaelic for 'Let me show you'. The centre, which is in Northton, just south of Scarasta, also has a genealogical research centre for people who want to trace their Hebridean ancestry.

The east coast is a complete contrast to the west – a strange, rocky moonscape of naked gneiss pocked with tiny lochans, the bleakness lightened by the occasional splash of green around the few crofting communities. Film buffs will know that the psychedelic sequences depicting the surface of Jupiter in *2001: A Space Odyssey* were shot from an aircraft flying low over the east coast of Harris.

The narrow, twisting road that winds its way along this coast is known locally as the Golden Road, because of the vast amount of money it cost per mile. It was built in the 1930s to link all the tiny communities known as 'The Bays'. The MV Lady Catherine (☏01859-530310; www.scenic-cruises.co.uk), based at Flodabay harbour halfway down the east coast, offers three-hour wildlife cruises (adult/child £15/7) from May to September.

At the southernmost tip of this coastline stands the impressive 16th-century St Clement's Church (Rodel/Roghadal; admission free), which was abandoned in 1560 after the Reformation. Inside the echoing nave is the impressive tomb of Alexander MacLeod, the man responsible for the church's construction. Crude carvings show hunting scenes, a castle, a galleon and various saints, including St Clement clutching a skull.

The village of Leverburgh (An t-Ob; www.leverburgh.co.uk) is named after Lord Leverhulme (the creator of Sunlight soap, and the founder of Unilever), who bought Lewis and Harris in 1918. He had grand plans for the islands, and for Obbe, as Leverburgh was then known. It was to be a major fishing port with a population of 10,000, but the plans died with Lord Leverhulme in 1925 and the village reverted to a sleepy backwater. There is a post office with an ATM, a general store and a petrol station.

🛏 Sleeping & Eating
Carminish Guest House B&B ££
(☏01859-520400; www.carminish.com; 1a Strond, Leverburgh; s/d £50/68; ᴘ🤶) One of the few

B&Bs in Harris that is open all year, the welcoming Carminish is a modern house with three comfy guest bedrooms. There's a view of the ferry from the dining room, and lots of nice little touches such as handmade soaps, a tin of chocolate biscuits in the bedroom and the latest weather forecast posted on the breakfast table.

Sorrel Cottage
B&B £

(☎ 01859-520319; www.sorrelcottage.co.uk; 2 Glen, Leverburgh; r per person from £30) Sorrel Cottage is a pretty crofter's house, about 1.5 miles west of the ferry at Leverburgh. Evening meals can be provided (£16 a head), and vegetarians and vegans are happily catered for. Bike hire available.

Rodel Hotel
INN ££

(☎ 01859-520210; www.rodelhotel.co.uk; Rodel; s/d from £76/115; P) Don't be put off by the rather grey and grim exterior of this remote hotel – the interior has been refurbished to a high standard and offers four large, luxurious bedrooms; the one called Iona has the best view, across the little harbour. Open for dinner from 5.30pm to 9pm, the hotel restaurant (mains £14 to £18) serves delicious local seafood and game, with dishes such as local scallops with Stornoway black pudding and Hollandaise sauce.

Am Bothan
HOSTEL £

(☎ 01859-520251; www.ambothan.com; Leverburgh; dm £17.50; P 🤶) An attractive, chalet-style hostel, Am Bothan has small, neat dorms and a great porch where you can enjoy morning coffee with views over the creek. The hostel offers bike hire and can arrange wildlife-watching boat trips.

Skoon Art Café
CAFE £

(www.skoon.com; 4 Geocrab; mains £4-7; ⊙10am-4.30pm Tue-Sat Mar-Oct, noon-4pm Wed-Sat Nov-22 Dec, lunch served 11am-4pm) Set halfway along the Golden Road, this neat little art gallery doubles as an excellent cafe serving delicious homemade soups (broccoli and roast almond, and carrot and fennel are favourites), sandwiches, cakes and desserts (try the marmalade and ginger cake).

ℹ️ Getting There & Around

A CalMac car ferry zigzags through the reefs of the Sound of Harris from Leverburgh to Berneray (pedestrian/car £6.25/28.50, 1¼ hours, three or four daily Monday to Saturday). You can hire bicycles from Sorrel Cottage for £10 a day.

Berneray (Bearnaraigh)
POP 140

Berneray (www.isleofberneray.com) was linked to North Uist by a causeway in October 1998, but that hasn't altered the peace and beauty of the island. The beaches on its west coast are some of the most beautiful and unspoilt in Britain, and seals and otters can be seen in Bays Loch on the east coast.

The basic but atmospheric **Gatliff Hostel** (www.gatliff.org.uk; Baile; camping per person £5, dm adult/child £10/6), housed in a pair of restored blackhouses right by the sea, is the place to stay. You can camp outside, or on the grass above the gorgeous white-sand beach just to the north.

In summer snacks are available at the **Lobster Pot** (⊙9am-5.30pm Mon-Sat), the tearoom attached to Ardmarree Stores (a grocery shop near the causeway). The **Nurses Cottage** (⊙11am-3pm Mon-Fri Jun-Aug) provides tourist information.

Bus W19 runs from Berneray (Gatliff Hostel and Harris ferry) to Lochmaddy (30 minutes, six daily Monday to Saturday). For details of ferries to Leverburgh (Harris), see p390.

North Uist (Uibhist A Tuath)
POP 1550

North Uist, an island half-drowned by lochs, is famed for its fishing but also has some magnificent beaches on its north and west coasts. For birdwatchers this is an earthly paradise, with regular sightings of waders and wildfowl ranging from redshank to red-throated diver to red-necked phalarope. The landscape is less wild and mountainous than Harris but it has a sleepy, subtle appeal.

LOCHMADDY (LOCH NAM MADADH)

Little Lochmaddy is the first village you hit after arriving on the ferry from Skye. There's a **tourist office** (☎ 01876-500321; Pier Rd; ⊙9am-1pm & 2-5pm Mon-Fri, 9.30am-1pm & 2-5.30pm Sat, 8-9pm Mon, Wed & Fri Apr-Oct), a couple of stores, a bank with an ATM, a petrol station, a post office and a pub.

Taigh Chearsabhagh (admission free, museum £1; ⊙10am-5pm Mon-Sat Feb-Jun & Sep-Dec, 10am-5pm Mon-Thu & Sat, to 8pm Fri Jul & Aug; @) is a museum and arts centre that preserves and displays the history and culture of the Uists, and is also a thriving

INVASION OF THE KILLER HEDGEHOGS

In 1974 a couple of hedgehogs were introduced to South Uist by a local gardener in an attempt to control the slugs in his garden. Hedgehogs had never been native to the islands, and the incomers waddled innocently into a vacant ecological niche. They spread like wildfire, and by 2002 it was estimated that there were around 5000 of the spiny slug-munchers in the Uists. But what's more, they were posing a mortal threat to important colonies of rare ground-nesting birds – eggs are a favourite food of hedgehogs.

In 2002 Scottish Natural Heritage (SNH) announced that a cull was the only way to preserve the bird population and for the next few years each summer saw a battle between the SNH culling teams and animal rights organisations. While SNH combed the fields at night with flashlights, hog-spotters and lethal injections, the British Hedgehog Preservation Society and other campaign groups were offering £20 a head for live hedgehogs, which they transported to the mainland for release into the wild. The cull was ended in 2007 in favour of transporting live hedgehogs to the mainland.

If the Uist invaders had been rats rather than cute Mrs Tiggywinkles, the public reaction might have been different, as the inhabitants of Canna, in the Small Isles, will confirm. Rats were accidentally introduced to the tiny island (population 14) by a ship a century ago – by 2005 the rodent raiders numbered more than 10,000, forcing out native species including wood mice and birds – the island's population of burrow-nesting Manx shearwaters had ceased to nest there.

Canna's owner, the National Trust for Scotland, called in a crack team of rat-trappers from New Zealand, who trapped all the native wood mice and sent them for a nice holiday on the mainland, before wiping out the rats with poison bait. The plan seems to have worked. The woodmice were returned to their island home in 2006, and by summer 2007 the Manx shearwaters were nesting on Canna once more. Any public outcry? Not a squeak.

community centre, post office and meeting place. The centre's lively **cafe** (mains £3-6) dishes up lovely homemade soups, sandwiches and cakes.

🛏 Sleeping & Eating

Tigh Dearg Hotel HOTEL ££
(☎01876-500700; www.tighdearghotel.co.uk; Lochmaddy; s/d £99/139; 🅿🛜) It looks a little like a hostel from the outside but the 'Red House' (as the name means) is actually Lochmaddy's most luxurious accommodation, with nine designer bedrooms, a lounge with leather sofas around an open fire, a gym and even a sauna. There's a good restaurant too, with sea views from the terrace.

Old Courthouse B&B £
(☎01876-500358; oldcourthouse@tiscali. co.uk; Lochmaddy; r per person from £30; 🅿) This charming, Georgian-style villa has four guest rooms and is within walking distance of the ferry, on the road that leads to Uist Outdoor Centre. Excellent porridge for breakfast and kippers are on the menu too.

Lochmaddy Hotel HOTEL ££
(☎01876-500331; www.lochmaddyhotel.co.uk; s/d from £55/95; 🅿🛜) The Lochmaddy is a traditional anglers' hotel (you can buy fishing permits here) with comfy, recently refurbished rooms, many with harbour views. The lively hotel bar pulls in anglers, locals and tourists, and serves excellent pub grub (mains £9 to £13) including seafood, venison and king-size steaks.

Uist Outdoor Centre HOSTEL £
(☎01876-500480; www.uistoutdoorcentre. co.uk; Cearn Dusgaidh; dm £15; ⊙Mar–mid-Dec; 🅿@🛜) This shore-side activity centre has a smart bunkhouse with four-bed dorms and offers a range of activities including sea kayaking, rock climbing and diving.

❶ Getting There & Around

Buses from Lochmaddy to Berneray, Langass, Clachan na Luib, Benbecula and Lochboisdale run five or six times a day Monday to Saturday.

BHARPA LANGASS & POBULL FHINN

A waymarked circular path beside the Langass Lodge Hotel (just off the A867, 6 miles southwest of Lochmaddy) leads to the chambered Neolithic burial tomb of **Bharpa Langass** and the stone circle of **Pobull Fhinn** (Finn's People); both are reckoned to be around 5000 years old. There are lovely views over the loch, where you may be able to spot seals and otters.

The delightful **Langass Lodge Hotel** (☎01876-580285; www.langasslodge.co.uk; Locheport; s/d from £65/99; P🛇) is a former shooting lodge set in splendid isolation overlooking Loch Langais. Refurbished and extended, it now offers a dozen appealing rooms, many with sea views, and one of the Hebrides' best **restaurants** (2-/3-course dinner £28/34), noted for its fine seafood and game.

BALRANALD NATURE RESERVE

Birdwatchers flock to this Royal Society for the Protection of Birds (RSPB) nature reserve, 18 miles west of Lochmaddy, in the hope of spotting the rare red-necked phalarope or hearing the distinctive call of the corncrake. There's a **visitors centre** (☎01876-510372; ☺Apr-Sep) with a resident warden who offers 1½-hour guided walks (£5, depart visitor centre 10am on Tuesdays, May to August).

Benbecula (Beinn Na Faoghla)

POP 1200

Benbecula is a low-lying island whose flat, lochan-studded landscape is best appreciated from the summit of **Rueval** (124m), the island's highest point. There's a path around the south side of the hill (signposted from the main road; park beside the landfill site) that is said to be the route taken to the coast by Bonnie Prince Charlie and Flora MacDonald during the prince's escape in 1746.

The control centre for the British army's Hebrides Missile Range (located on the northwestern tip of South Uist) is the island's main source of employment, and **Balivanich** (Baile a'Mhanaich) – looking like a corner of a Glasgow housing estate planted incongruously on the machair – is the commercial centre serving the troops and their families. The village has a bank with an ATM, a post office, a large **Co-op supermarket** (☺8am-8pm Mon-Sat, 11am-6pm Sun) and a petrol station (open on Sundays).

South Uist (Uibhist A Deas)

POP 1900

South Uist is the second-largest island in the Outer Hebrides and saves its choicest corners for those who explore away from the main north–south road. The low-lying west coast is an almost unbroken stretch of white-sand beach and flower-flecked machair – a new waymarked hiking trail, the **Machair Way**, follows the coast – while the multitude of inland lochs provide excellent trout fishing. The east coast, riven by four large sea lochs, is hilly and remote, with spectacular **Beinn Mhor** (620m) the highest point.

Driving south from Benbecula you cross from the predominantly Protestant northern half of the Outer Hebrides into the mostly Roman Catholic south, a religious transition marked by the granite statue of **Our Lady of the Isles** on the slopes of Rueval (the hill with the military radomes on its summit), and the presence of many roadside shrines.

THE NORTH

The northern part of the island is mostly occupied by the watery expanses of Loch Bee and Loch Druidibeg. **Loch Druidibeg National Nature Reserve** is an important breeding ground for birds such as dunlin, redshank, ringed plover, greylag goose and corncrake; you can take a 5-mile self-guided walk through the reserve (pick up a leaflet from the Scottish Natural Heritage office on the main road beside the loch).

Two miles south of Loch Druidibeg is the attractive hamlet of **Howmore** (Tobha Mor), with several restored thatched black-houses. One houses the **Tobha Mor Crofters' Hostel** (www.gatliff.org.uk; dm adult/child £10/6).

You can hire bikes from **Rothan Cycles** (☎01870-620283; www.rothan.com; 9 Howmore; per day/week from £10/43) where the road to the hostel leaves the main road.

THE SOUTH

Six miles south of Howmore, **Kildonan Museum** (☎01878-710343; Kildonan; adult/child £1.50/free; ☺10am-5pm Mon-Fri, 2-5pm Sun Easter-Oct) explores the lives of local crofters through its collection of artefacts – an absorbing exhibition of black-and-white photography and first-hand accounts of harsh Hebridean conditions. There's also an excellent **tearoom** (mains £3-8; ☺11am-4pm Mon-Sat, 1-4pm Sun) and craft shop.

Amid Milton's ruined blackhouses, half a mile south of the museum, a cairn marks the site of **Flora MacDonald's birthplace**.

Askernish Golf Course (www.askernish golfclub.com), originally laid out by the legendary Tom Morris in 1891, was recently rediscovered among the dunes on South Uist. It has been restored and this classic, old-fashioned links course is once again open for play.

LOCHBOISDALE (LOCH BAGHASDAIL)

The ferry port of Lochboisdale is the island's largest settlement, with a tourist office, a bank with an ATM, a grocery store and a petrol station. There's a **Co-op supermarket** (⊙8am-8pm Mon-Sat, 12.30-6pm Sun) at Daliburgh, 3 miles west of the village.

🛏 Sleeping & Eating

TOP CHOICE **Polochar Inn** INN ££
(📞01878-700215; www.polocharinn.com; Polochar; s/d from £60/90; P) Run by local sisters Morag McKinnon and Margaret Campbell, this 18th-century inn has been transformed into a stylish, welcoming hotel with a stunning location looking out across the sea to Barra. The excellent restaurant and bar menu (mains £9 to £19) includes fish chowder, haddock and chips, local salmon and Uist lamb. Polochar is 7 miles southwest of Lochboisdale, on the way to Eriskay.

Lochboisdale Hotel HOTEL ££
(📞01878-700332; www.lochboisdale.com; s/d from £55/100; P) This old-fashioned huntin'-and-fishin' hotel has spacious, modernised rooms, many of which have stunning views across the Minch. The homely lounge bar has a roaring fire in winter, and hosts regular traditional music sessions; it also serves decent bar meals (£9 to £14).

Lochside Cottage B&B £
(📞01878-700472; www.lochside-cottage.co.uk; r per person from £25; P) Lochside Cottage is a friendly B&B, 1.5 miles west of the ferry, and has rooms with views and a sun lounge barely a fishing-rod's length from its own trout loch.

❶ Getting There & Around

For ferries from Lochboisdale to Oban, see p390.

Eriskay (Eiriosgaigh)

POP 170

In 1745 Bonnie Prince Charlie first set foot in Scotland on the west coast of Eriskay, on the sandy beach (immediately north of the ferry terminal) still known as **Prince's Strand** (Coilleag a'Phrionnsa).

More recently the SS *Politician* sank just off the island in 1941. The islanders salvaged much of its cargo of around 250,000 bottles of whisky and, after a binge of dramatic proportions, the police intervened and a number of the islanders landed in jail. The story was immortalised by Sir Compton Mackenzie in his comic novel *Whisky Galore,* later made into a famous film.

A CalMac car ferry links Eriskay with Ardmhor at the northern end of Barra (pedestrian/car £6.70/19.55, 40 minutes, four or five daily).

Barra (Barraigh)

POP 1150

With its beautiful beaches, wildflower-clad dunes, rugged little hills and strong sense of community, diminutive Barra – just 14 miles in circumference – is the Outer Hebrides in miniature. For a great view of the island, walk up to the top of **Heaval** (383m), a mile northeast of Castlebay.

Castlebay (Bagh a'Chaisteil), in the south, is the largest village. There's a tourist office, a bank with an ATM, a post office and two grocery stores.

◉ Sights & Activities

Kisimul Castle CASTLE
(HS; Castlebay; adult/child incl ferry £4.70/2.80; ⊙9.30am-5.30pm Apr-Sep) Castlebay takes its name from Kisimul Castle, first built by the MacNeil clan in the 11th century. It was sold in the 19th century and restored in the 20th by American architect Robert MacNeil, who became the 45th clan chief; he gifted the castle to Historic Scotland in 2000 for an annual rent of £1 and a bottle of whisky (Talisker single malt, if you're interested). A short boat trip (weather permitting) takes you out to the island castle, where you can explore the fortifications and soak up the view from the battlements.

Barra Heritage Centre HERITAGE CENTRE
(www.barraheritage.com; Castlebay; adult/child £2/1; ⊙10.30am-4.30pm Mon-Sat May-Aug, 10.30am-4.30pm Mon, Wed & Fri Mar, Apr & Sep) This heritage centre has Gaelic-themed displays about the island, local art exhibitions and a tearoom. It also manages a restored 19th-century thatched cottage, the **Black Shieling** (adult/child £2/75p; ⊙1-4pm Mon-Fri

May-Sep), 3 miles north of Castlebay on the west side of the island.

Traigh Mor
BEACH

In the north of the island, this vast expanse of firm golden sand (the name means 'Big Strand') serves as Barra's airport (a mile across at low tide, and big enough for three 'runways'), the only beach airport in the world that handles scheduled flights. Watching the little Twin Otter aircraft come and go is a popular spectator sport; in between flights, locals gather cockles, a local seafood speciality, from the sands.

🛏️ Sleeping & Eating

Accommodation on Barra is limited, so make a reservation before committing to a night on the island. Wild camping (on foot or by bike) is allowed almost anywhere; from 2010, campervans and car campers are restricted to official sites – check www.isleofbarra.com for details.

Castlebay Hotel
HOTEL ££

(☑01871-810223; www.castlebayhotel.com; Castlebay; s/d from £60/95; P) The recently refurbished Castlebay Hotel offers spacious bedrooms decorated with a subtle tartan motif – it's worth paying a bit extra for a sea view – and there's a comfy lounge and conservatory with grand views across the harbour to the islands south of Barra. The hotel bar is the hub of island social life, with regular sessions of traditional music, and the restaurant specialises in local seafood and game (rabbit is often on the menu).

THE EVEN FURTHER OUTER HEBRIDES

St Kilda (www.kilda.org.uk) is a collection of spectacular sea stacks and cliff-bound islands about 45 miles west of North Uist. The largest island, Hirta, measures only 2 miles by 1 mile, with huge cliffs along most of its coastline. Owned by National Trust for Scotland (NTS), the islands are a Unesco World Heritage Site and are the biggest seabird nesting site in the North Atlantic, home to more than a million birds.

History

Hirta was inhabited by a Gaelic-speaking population of around 200 until the 19th century, when the arrival of church missionaries and tourists began the gradual breakdown of St Kilda's traditional way of life. By the 1920s, disease and emigration had seen the islands' economy collapse, and the 35 remaining islanders were evacuated, at their own request, in 1930. The people had survived here by keeping sheep, fishing, growing a few basic crops such as barley and climbing the cliffs barefoot to catch sea birds and collect their eggs. Over the centuries, this resulted in a genetic peculiarity – St Kilda men had unusually long big toes.

Visiting St Kilda

The only way to spend any time in the islands is to join one of the two-week NTS work parties that visit St Kilda from mid-May to August. The NTS charges volunteers for doing archaeological and conservation work in and around the village ruins – you have to be physically fit and prepared to work for up to 36 hours per week. And you have to pay for the privilege – around £750 per person (including transport from Oban in a converted lifeboat and full board in dorm accommodation). To get an application form, send a stamped, self-addressed envelope to St Kilda Work Parties, NTS, Balnain House, 40 Huntly St, Inverness IV3 5HR. The closing date for applications is 31 January.

Boat tours to St Kilda are a major undertaking. For a full listing of tour operators, check out the website www.kilda.org.uk. Booking ahead is essential.

Sea Trek (☑01851-672469; www.seatrek.co.uk; Miavaig Pier, Lewis) Runs a 12-hour day-trip to St Kilda (£180 per person) once or twice weekly, May to September, weather permitting.

Kilda Cruises (☑01859-502060; www.kildacruises.co.uk; West Tarbert, Harris) Operates frequent day-trips to St Kilda (£180 per person) in summer, as well as customised cruises.

Dunard Hostel HOSTEL £

(☎01871-810443; www.dunardhostel.co.uk; Castlebay; dm/d from £15/38; P) Dunard is a friendly, family-run hostel just five minutes' walk from the ferry terminal. The owners can organise **sea-kayaking tours** for £30/55 a half-/full day.

Faire Mhaoldonaich B&B £

(☎01871-810511; www.fairemhaoldonaich.com; Nasg; r per person £28-33; ☺Mar-Oct; P) This B&B is a modern house with spacious, comfortable rooms and great views over Bagh Beag to the isle of Mhaoldonaich; it's a mile west of Castlebay on the road to Vatersay.

❶ Getting There & Around

See p390 for details of CalMac ferries from Castlebay to Oban and Lochboisdale (South Uist) and flights to the Scottish mainland; see p400 for the ferry from Ardmhor, at the northern end of Barra, to Eriskay.

Bus W32 makes a regular circuit of the island and also connects with flights at the airport.

You can hire bikes from **Island Adventures** (☎01871-810284; 29 St Brendan's Rd, Castlebay).

Pabbay (Pabaidh), Mingulay (Miughalaigh) & Berneray (Bearnaraigh)

These three uninhabited islands, gifted to the National Trust for Scotland (NTS) in 2000, are important breeding sites for seabird species such as fulmar, black guillemot, common and Arctic tern, great skua, puffin and storm petrel. There are boat trips to the islands from Castlebay, Barra, in settled weather for around £20 per person; ask at Barra tourist office for details. The puffin season lasts from June to early August.

Orkney & Shetland Islands

Best Places to Stay

» West Manse (p422)
» Woodwick House (p414)
» Links House (p414)
» Busta House Hotel (p434)
» Lighthouse cottages (p429)
» Almara B&B (p434)
» St Magnus Bay Hotel (p435)

Best Places to Eat:

» The Creel (p412)
» Hamnavoe Restaurant (p416)
» Monty's Bistro (p428)

Why Go?

Up here at Britain's top end it can feel more Scandinavian than Scottish, and no wonder. For the Vikings, the jaunt across the North Sea from Norway was as easy as a stroll down to the local mead hall and they soon controlled these windswept, treeless archipelagos, laying down longhouses alongside stony remains of ancient prehistoric settlements.

Though they are not as scenically splendid as Skye, say, an ancient magic hovers in the air above the Orkney and Shetland Islands, endowing them with an allure that lodges firmly in the soul. It's in the misty seas, where seals, whales and porpoises patrol lonely coastlines; it's in the air, where squadrons of seabirds wheel above huge nesting colonies; and it's on land, where standing stones catch late summer sunsets and strains of folk music disperse in the air before the wind gusts shut the pub door. Make the journey; open that door.

When to Go
Lerwick

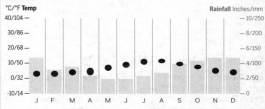

January The Shetlands' Up Helly Aa festival, for horned helmets and burning Viking ships on the beach.

June Orkney rocks to the St Magnus Festival: book accommodation ahead.

July Take advantage of the summer sunlight and Britain's longest daylight hours.

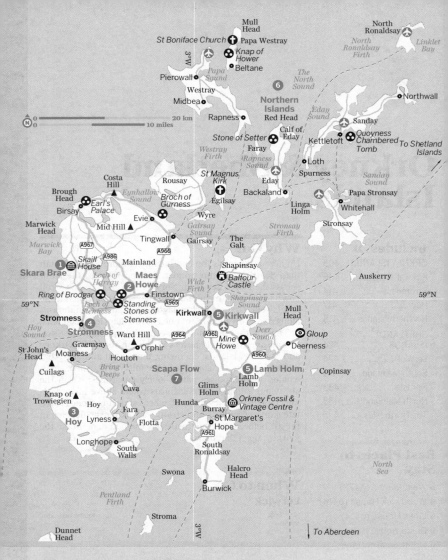

Orkney Islands Highlights

1 Shaking your head in astonishment at extraordinary **Skara Brae** (p413), a village of prehistoric perfection that pre-dates the pyramids

2 Plunging down the passageway into spooky **Maes Howe** (p412), an enormous Stone Age tomb livened up by some bawdy Viking graffiti

3 Exploring the scenic majesty of **Hoy** (p417) and – for serious rock climbers – scaling the Old Man there

4 Pacing the stone-flagged main street of **Stromness** (p414), as salty a fishing town as you'll ever find

5 Admiring the magnificent cathedral at **Kirkwall** (p406)

and the much humbler Italian Chapel at **Lamb Holm** (p410)

6 Island-hopping the magical **Northern Islands** (p418), where crystal azure waters lap against glittering white-sand beaches

7 Diving the sunken warships of **Scapa Flow** (p416)

ORKNEY ISLANDS

There's a magic to the Orkneys that you'll begin to feel as soon as the Scottish mainland slips away astern. Consisting of 70 flat, green-topped islands stripped bare of trees by the wind, it's a place of ancient standing stones and prehistoric villages, an archipelago of old-style hospitality and Viking heritage narrated in the *Orkneyinga Saga* and still strong today, a region whose ports tell of lives led with the blessings and rough moods of the sea, and a destination where seekers can find melancholy wrecks of warships and the salty clamour of remote seabird colonies.

Only a few short miles separate the archipelago from mainland Scotland, but Pentland Firth is one of Europe's most dangerous waterways, a graveyard of ships that adds an extra mystique to these islands shimmering in the sea mists.

The principal island, confusingly called Mainland, has the two major settlements – bustling market-town Kirkwall, and Stromness with its grey-flagged streets – and the standout ancient sites. Ferries and flights give access to the other 15 inhabited islands.

⌕ Tours

Orkney Island Holidays
ARCHAEOLOGICAL SITES, BIRDWATCHING
(☑01856-711373; www.orkneyislandholidays.com; Furrowend, Shapinsay) Based on Shapinsay, with guided tours of archaeological sites, birdwatching and wildlife trips and excursions to other islands. One-week, all-inclusive packages cost £1095.

Discover Orkney ARCHAEOLOGICAL SITES, WALKING
(☑01856-872865; www.discoverorkney.com; 44 Clay Loan, Kirkwall, Mainland) Offers guided tours and walks throughout the islands in the company of a qualified guide. Specific tours are tailored to your interests.

Orkney Archaeology Tours
ARCHAEOLOGICAL SITES
(☑01856-721217; www.orkneyarchaeologytours.co.uk) Runs private half- (£160 for up to four) and full-day (£240) tours with an archaeologist guide.

Wildabout Orkney WILDLIFE, HISTORICAL
(☑01856-877737; www.wildaboutorkney.com) Operates tours covering Orkney's history, ecology, folklore and wildlife. Day-trips operate year-round and cost £49, with pick-ups in Stromness and Kirkwall.

John O'Groats Ferries BOAT TRIPS
(☑01955-611353; www.jogferry.co.uk; John O'Groats) If you're in a hurry, these guys run a one-day tour of the main sites for £46, including the ferry from John O'Groats. You can do the whole thing as a long day-trip from Inverness.

Dawn Star Boat Trips BOAT TRIPS
(☑01856-876743; www.orkneyboattrips.co.uk; Berstane Rd, Kirkwall) Boat trips on Scapa Flow.

ⓘ Getting There & Away

AIR
Flybe/Loganair (☑0871 700 0535; www.flybe.com) flies daily from Kirkwall to Aberdeen, Edinburgh, Glasgow, Inverness and Sumburgh (Shetland). In summer it also serves Bergen (Norway).

BOAT
During summer, book ahead for car spaces. Fares vary according to season (low and peak fares are quoted here).

FROM SCRABSTER, SHETLANDS & ABERDEEN Northlink (☑0845 600 0449; www.northlinkferries.co.uk) operates ferries from Scrabster to Stromness (passenger £14 to £17, car £45 to £50, 1½ hours, three daily Monday to Friday, two on weekends). Northlink also sails from Aberdeen to Kirkwall (passenger £17 to £26, car £69 to £94, six hours, three or four weekly) and from Kirkwall to Lerwick (passenger one way £15 to £21, car one way £53 to £87, 7½ hours, three to four weekly) on the Shetland Islands.

FROM GILLS BAY Pentland Ferries (☑01856-831226; www.pentlandferries.co.uk) offers a shorter, cheaper car-ferry crossing. Boats leave from Gills Bay, about 3 miles west of John O'Groats, and head to St Margaret's Hope in Orkney (passenger/car £13/30, one hour). There are three to four crossings daily.

FROM JOHN O'GROATS From May to September, **John O'Groats Ferries** (☑01955-611353; www.jogferry.co.uk) operates a passenger-only service from John O'Groats (p361) to Burwick, on the southern tip of South Ronaldsay (one way/return £18/28). A bus to Kirkwall meets the ferry (all-included return from John O'Groats to Kirkwall is £30). There are four departures daily (two in May and September).

BUS
Citylink (☑0871 266-3333; www.citylink.co.uk) runs daily from Inverness to Scrabster (p364), connecting with the Stromness ferries.

John O'Groats Ferries (☑01955-611353; www.jogferry.co.uk) operates the summer-only Orkney bus service from Inverness to Kirkwall. Tickets (one way/return £34/46, five hours) include bus-ferry-bus travel from Inverness to Kirkwall. There are two buses daily from June to early September.

ⓘ Getting Around

The *Orkney Transport Guide,* a detailed schedule of all bus, ferry and air services around and to/from Orkney, is available free from tourist offices.

The largest island, Mainland, is joined by road-bearing causeways to Burray and South Ronaldsay. The other islands can be reached by air and ferry services.

AIR

Loganair (☑01856-872494; www.loganair.co.uk) operates interisland flights from Kirkwall to North Ronaldsay, Westray, Papa Westray, Stronsay, Sanday and Eday. See each island's entry in this chapter for details.

BICYCLE

Various locations on Mainland hire bikes, including **Cycle Orkney** (☑01856-875777; www.cycleorkney.com; Tankerness Lane, Kirkwall; per day £15; ☺Mon-Sat; 🖪) and **Orkney Cycle Hire** (☑01856-850255; www.orkneycyclehire.co.uk; 54 Dundas St, Stromness; per day £7.50-10).

BOAT

Orkney Ferries (☑01856-872044; www.orkneyferries.co.uk; Shore St, Kirkwall) operates car ferries from Mainland to the islands; see each island's entry in this chapter.

CAR

There are several car-hire companies on Mainland. Small-car rates begin at around £32/165 per day/week, although there are specials for as low as £28 per day.

Drive Orkney (☑01856-877551; www.driveorkney.com; Garrison Rd, Kirkwall)

Norman Brass Car Hire (☑01856-850850; www.stromnesscarhire.co.uk; North End Rd, Stromness) At the Blue Star Garage.

Orkney Campers (www.orkneycampers.com; Beesbreck, Orphir) Sturdy old VW campervans from £50 per day.

Orkney Car Hire (JD Peace Cars; ☑01856-872866; www.orkneycarhire.co.uk; Junction Rd, Kirkwall)

WR Tullock (☑01856-875500; www.orkneycarrental.co.uk; Castle St, Kirkwall)

PUBLIC TRANSPORT

Stagecoach (☑01856-878014; www.stagecoachbus.com) runs bus services on Mainland and South Ronaldsay. Most buses don't operate on Sunday. Dayrider (£7.25) and 7-Day Megarider (£16.25) tickets allow unlimited travel.

Kirkwall

POP 6206

Orkney's main town is the commercial centre of the islands and there's a comparatively busy feel to its main shopping street and ferry dock. It's set back from a wide bay and the atmospheric paved streets and twisting wynds (lanes) give Orkney's capital a distinctive character. Magnificent St Magnus Cathedral takes pride of place. Founded in the early 11th century, the original part of Kirkwall is one of the best examples of an ancient Norse town.

◉ Sights

St Magnus Cathedral   CATHEDRAL
(www.stmagnus.org; Broad St; ☺9am-6pm Mon-Sat, 1-6pm Sun Apr-Sep, 9am-1pm & 2-5pm Mon-Sat Oct-Mar) Founded in 1137 and built out of local red sandstone and yellow Eday stone, fabulous St Magnus Cathedral is Kirkwall's centrepiece. The powerful atmosphere of an ancient faith pervades the impressive interior. Lyrical and melodramatic epitaphs of the dead line the walls and emphasise the serious business of 17th- and 18th-century bereavement.

Earl Rognvald Brusason commissioned the cathedral in the name of his martyred uncle, Magnus Erlendsson, who was killed by Earl Hakon Paulsson on Egilsay in 1117. Work began in 1137, but the building is actually the result of 300 years of construction and alteration.

During summer, 40-minute tours of the cathedral's upper levels start at 11am and 2pm on Tuesday and Thursday and cost £5.50 per person.

Earl's Palace & Bishop's Palace   PALACES
(HS; www.historic-scotland.gov.uk; Watergate; adult/child £3.70/2.20; ☺9.30am-5.30pm Apr-Sep) Near the cathedral, these two ruined palaces are worth poking around. The better of the two, Earl's Palace, was once known as the finest example of French Renaissance architecture in Scotland. One room features an interesting history of its builder, Earl Patrick Stewart, who was executed in Edinburgh for treason. He started construction in about 1600, but he ran out of money and it was never completed.

The Bishop's Palace was built in the mid-12th century to provide comfortable lodgings for Bishop William the Old. There's a good view of the cathedral from the tower, and a plaque showing the different phases of the cathedral's construction.

FREE ### Orkney Museum
MUSEUM

(www.orkney.gov.uk; Broad St; ⊗10.30am-5pm Mon-Sat) Opposite the cathedral, this is a labyrinthine display in a former merchant's house. It has an overview of Orkney history and prehistory, including Pictish carvings and a display on the Ba'. Most engaging are the last rooms, covering 19th- and 20th-century social history; the earlier sections could do with a bit of a facelift but then again, it's free.

Highland Park Distillery
DISTILLERY

(☑01856-874619; www.highlandpark.co.uk; Holm Rd; tour £6; ⊗daily May-Aug, Mon-Fri Sep-Apr) Among Scotland's more respected whisky-makers, this distillery, where they malt their own barley, is great to visit. You can see this, and the peat kiln used to dry it, on the excellent, well-informed hour-long tour (hourly when open, and weekdays at 2pm in winter). The standard 12-year-old is a soft, balanced malt great for whisky novices and aficionados alike; the 18-year-old is among the world's finest drams. It, and other incarnations, can be tasted on more specialised tours (£15), which you can prearrange.

✺ Festivals & Events

St Magnus Festival (☑01856-871445; www. stmagnusfestival.com) takes place in June and is a colourful celebration of music and the arts.

⊙ Sleeping

Narvik
B&B ££

(☑01856-879049; carolevansnarvik@hotmail.co .uk; Weyland Tce; s/d £40/60; ℗) Dodge the B&B fascists who sweep you out of bed with a stiff-bristled broom for your seven-in-the-morning breakfast by staying at this charmingly peaceful spot. Accommodation is in a beautifully decorated separate flat, with a tiled floor, a wooden double bed, DVDs and a grassy garden. You've got your own kitchenette, which genial hosts stock with eggs, bacon, croissants and juices, so

your morning meal is wholly at your own pace. Head east down Berstane Rd, bear left onto East St, and Weyland Terrace is first on the left.

Orcades Hostel
HOSTEL £

(☑01856-873745; www.orcadeshostel.com; Muddisdale Rd; dm/d £17/50; ℗॰) Book ahead to get a bed in this cracking new hostel near the campsite on the western edge of town. It's a guesthouse conversion so there's a very smart kitchen and lounge area, and great-value doubles. Comfortable dorms with just four bunks make for sound sleeping, and young, enthusiastic owners give the place plenty of spark.

Mrs Muir
B&B ££

(☑01856-874805; www.twodundas.co.uk; 2 Dundas Cres; s/d £35/70; ℗) This former manse is a magnificent building that has four enormous rooms blessed with large windows and sizeable beds. There are plenty of period features, but the en suite bathrooms are not among them; they are sparklingly new, and one has a free-standing bathtub. Both the welcome and the breakfast will leave you more than satisfied.

Lynnfield Hotel
HOTEL ££

(☑01856-872505; www.lynnfieldhotel.co.uk; Holm Rd; s/d £80/110; ℗॰) Within whiffing distance of the Highland Park distillery, this recently refitted hotel is run with a professional, yet warmly personal, touch. With individual rooms featuring four-poster beds, a jacuzzi or antique writing desk, and a cosy dark-wood drawing room, it's an intimate place, which also boasts a good restaurant.

Crossford
B&B ££

(☑01856-876142; heatherandbobbo@yahoo.co. uk; Heatherly Loan; s/d £60/76; ℗) Situated just up the road from Highland Park Distillery, this excellent little B&B has just one double en suite room (with a lovely outlook), a small dining and sitting area and lots of privacy. It's very convenient to Kirkwall, but with a rural setting, you get the best of both worlds.

THE BA'

Every Christmas Day and New Year's Day, Kirkwall holds a staggering spectacle: a crazy ball game known as The Ba'. Two enormous teams, the Uppies and the Doonies, fight their way, no holds barred, through the streets, trying to get a leather ball to the other end of town. The ball is thrown from the Market Cross outside the cathedral to the waiting crowd; the Uppies have to get the ba' to the corner of Main St and Junction Rd, the Doonies must get it to the water. Violence, skulduggery and other stunts are common and the event, fuelled by plenty of strong drink, can last hours.

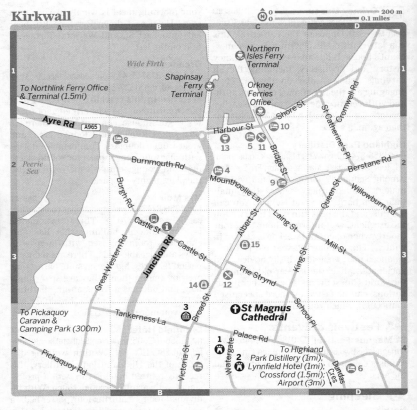

Pomona B&B
B&B **£**

(☏01856-872325; www.pomonacatering.co.uk; 9 Albert St; s/d £24/48) We rubbed our hands with glee when we found this old-fashioned B&B at the back of the cafe with the same name. With six en suite rooms it's not the roomiest lodging in Orkney, but it is a bargain and possibly the best located, just off the main drag in the heart of town.

Albert Hotel
HOTEL **££**

(☏01856-876000; www.alberthotel.co.uk; Mounthoolie Lane; s/d £110/128; ☎) Stylishly refurbished, this central but peaceful hotel is just about Kirkwall's finest address. Comfortable contemporary rooms in a variety of categories sport super-inviting beds and smart bathrooms. A great Orkney base, but you may end up spending more time in the excellent Bothy Bar downstairs.

Kirkwall Hotel
HOTEL **££**

(☏01856-872232; www.kirkwallhotel.com; Harbour St; s/d from £70/100; ☎) A grand old bastion of Orcadian hospitality, this hotel sits in a prime location gazing proudly over the harbour. Superior and superior-plus rooms are a little pricier, but are substantially grander and better value than the standards. They also face the front, with views of the harbour, from where you can watch the lifeboat drills.

Peedie Hostel
HOSTEL **£**

(☏01856-875477; kirkwallpeediehostel@talk21.com; Ayre Rd; dm £15) Nestling into a corner at the end of the Kirkwall waterfront, this cute hostel squeezes in all the necessary features for a comfortable stay in a small space. The dorms actually have plenty of room – it's only in the tiny kitchen that territorial squabbles might break out.

Kirkwall

Orkney Hotel   HOTEL ££
(☏01856-873477; www.orkneyhotel.co.uk; 40 Victoria St; s/d £85/109; P@☎) This historic hotel has been revitalised, with walls the colour of Shiraz and smartly refurbished rooms; some with disabled access are across the street. The best bed is a four-poster with cathedral views. Prices are usually £10 lower than the rack rates quoted here.

Kirkwall SYHA   HOSTEL £
(☏01856-872243; www.syha.org.uk; Old Scapa Rd; dm/s/tw £16/19/34; ⊙mid-Mar–Oct; P@) This functional hostel is a 15-minute walk from the centre, and set in a demountable former naval barracks. Never meant to last beyond the war, it now shows its age: long walks to the institutional showers, lockout till 5pm, a midnight curfew and no power points in the rooms. However, the big, sociable lounge and kitchen, and its large capacity are definite plus points.

Pickaquoy Caravan & Camping Park
CAMPING £
(☏01856-879900; www.pickaquoy.co.uk; Pickaquoy Rd; sites for 1 person for £6.50, 2-3 people £10.50; ⊙Apr-Sep; P) Plenty of grass and excellent modern facilities. Check in at the sports centre alongside.

Lerona   B&B ££
(☏01856-874538; Cromwell Cres; s/d £30/60, without bathroom £25/50; P) Guests come first, but the wee folk – a battalion of garden gnomes, and clans of dolls with lifelike stares – are close behind.

Shore   HOTEL ££
(☏01856-872200; www.theshore.co.uk; 6 Shore St; s/d £58/85; ☎) Smart contemporary rooms with a light Scandinavian touch above this lively harbourfront bar and restaurant. Those at the front are larger and (slightly) costlier. Breakfast extra.

✗ Eating & Drinking

Reel   CAFE £
(Albert St; sandwiches £3, ⊙9am-6pm) Part music shop and part cafe, Kirkwall's best coffee-stop sits alongside the cathedral, and bravely puts tables outside at the slightest threat of sunshine. It's a relaxed spot that's good for morning-after debriefing, as well as lunchtime panini and musically named sandwiches (along with their cheese one... Skara Brie). It's a centre for local folk musicians, with regular evening sessions.

Kirkwall Hotel   RESTAURANT ££
(☏01856-872232; www.kirkwallhotel.com; Harbour St; mains £9-15; ⊙lunch & dinner) This grand old Orcadian hotel on the waterfront is one of the capital's best places to dine. The elegant bar and eating area packs out; it's one of Kirkwall's favourite spots for an evening out with the clan. There's a fairly standard pub-food list that's complemented by a seasonal menu homing in on local seafood and meat – the lamb is delicious – that's well presented and very tasty. Starter portions are a bit lightweight.

Dil Se   SOUTH ASIAN £
(☏01856-875242; 7 Bridge St; mains £8-11; ⊙4-11pm) Upbeat and inventive, this main-street subcontinental choice tries to steer Orcadians away from the clichéd curry classics in favour of baltis – the spinach one is fabulous – and other creations. The late opening means you can enjoy those long summer evenings outdoors and not go hungry at the end of them.

Bothy Bar   PUB £
(www.alberthotel.co.uk; Mounthoolie Lane; mains £7-10; ⊙lunch & dinner) In the Albert Hotel,

the Bothy looks very smart these days with its modish floor and black-and-white photos of old-time Orcadian farming, but its low tables provide the customary cheer and sustaining food: think sausages, think haddock, think stews: good pub grub.

Shore
PUB ££

(www.theshore.co.uk; 6 Shore St; restaurant mains £8-15; ⊙food 8am-9pm) This popular harbourside eatery brings the gastropub concept to Kirkwall, offering bar meals combined with more adventurous fare in the restaurant section. It's a little hit-and-miss, but the local chefs are assured when it comes to the sea – monkfish is always a good bet.

Helgi's
PUB

(www.helgis.co.uk; 14 Harbour St) There's a traditional cosiness about this place, but the decor has moved beyond the time-honoured beer-soaked carpet to a comfortable contemporary slate floor and quotes from the *Orkneyinga Saga* plastering the walls. It's more find-a-table than jostle-at-the-bar and serves cheerful comfort food. Take your pint upstairs for quiet harbour contemplation.

Shopping

Kirkwall has some gorgeous jewellery and crafts along Albert St. Try **The Longship** (www.olagoriejewellery.com; 7 Broad St) for Orkney-made crafts and gifts, and exquisite designer jewellery. **Orcadian Bookshop** (www.orcadian.co.uk; 50 Albert St) has a great selection of local books and newspapers.

ⓘ Information

Balfour Hospital (☑01856-888000; New Scapa Rd)

Launderama (47 Albert St; ⊙Mon-Sat) Service washes for £9.

Orkney Library (☑01856-873166; 44 Junction Rd; ⊙Mon-Sat) Fast free internet access (one-hour maximum).

Support Training (cnr Junction Rd & West Tankerness Lane; per hr £4; ⊙Mon-Sat; ☎) Internet access.

Tourist office (☑01856-872856; www.visitorkney.com; 6 Broad St; ⊙9am-6pm summer, 9am-5pm Mon-Fri, 10am-4pm Sat winter) Has a good range of publications on Orkney.

ⓘ Getting There & Away

The **airport** (www.hial.co.uk) is 2.5 miles east of town. See p405 for flight information. For flights and ferries from Kirkwall to the islands, see the island sections.

Bus 1 runs direct from Kirkwall to Stromness (40 minutes, hourly, four to six Sunday); bus 2 runs to Orphir and Houton (20 minutes, four or five Monday to Saturday); bus 6 runs from Kirkwall to Evie (30 minutes, three to five daily Monday to Saturday) and the ferry at Tingwall to Rousay.

East Mainland To South Ronaldsay

When a German U-boat sneaked into Scapa Flow and sank the battleship *Royal Oak* right under the Royal Navy's nose in 1939, Churchill decided it was time to better protect this crucial naval harbour. Using concrete blocks and discarded ships, the sea channels between Lamb Holm, Glimps Holm, Burray, South Ronaldsay and Mainland were blocked; the **Churchill Barriers** still link the islands, and carry the main road from Kirkwall to Burwick. There are good sandy beaches by barriers 3 and 4.

ⓘ Getting There & Away

Bus 3 from Kirkwall runs to Deerness in East Mainland (30 minutes, three to five Monday to Saturday), with some buses calling at Tankerness. There are buses from Kirkwall to South Ronaldsay's St Margaret's Hope (30 minutes, almost hourly Monday to Saturday).

EAST MAINLAND

On a farm at Tankerness the mysterious Iron Age site of **Mine Howe** (adult/child £2.50/1.50; ⊙10am-4pm Jun-Aug, 11am-3pm Tue & Fri Sep & May) is an eerie underground chamber, the function of which is unknown; staff from the TV series *Time Team* carried out an archaeological dig here and concluded that it may have had some ritual significance, perhaps as an oracle or shrine.

Passing here, and continuing through Deerness, you reach the end of the road at Mull Head. A short walk brings you to the **Gloup**, a spectacular natural arch and narrow channel. Beyond here, a half-mile cliff walk brings you to the **Broch of Deerness**.

LAMB HOLM

On the tiny island of Lamb Holm, the **Italian Chapel** (admission free; ⊙9am-dusk) is all that remains of a POW camp that housed the Italian soldiers who worked on the Churchill Barriers. They built the chapel in their spare time, using two Nissen huts, scrap metal and their considerable artistic and decorative skills. One of the artists returned in 1960 to restore the paintwork. It's quite extraordinary inside and definitely worth seeing.

Alongside is the enthusiastic little shop of the **Orkney Wine Company** (www.orkney wine.co.uk; ☺Feb-Dec), which produces handmade wines made from berries, flowers and vegetables, all naturally fermented. Get stuck into some strawberry-rhubarb wine or carrot-and-malt-whisky liqueur – unusual flavours but surprisingly addictive.

BURRAY

Sleepy Burray village is on the southern side of this island. Nearby, **Orkney Fossil & Vintage Centre** (www.orkneyfossilcentre. co.uk; adult/child £3.50/2; ☺10am-5pm Apr-Sep) has a quirky collection of household and farming relics and 360-million-year-old Devonian fish fossils. There are also galleries devoted to the world wars.

Ankersted (☑01856-731217; www.anker sted.co.uk; r per person £24; P) is a great place to stay, with fine rooms, all with private bathroom. The upstairs lounge and balcony area overlook Watersound Bay and barrier 4, and are exclusively for guests' use. Stay a week and you get a free night.

Sands Hotel (☑01856-731298; www.the sandshotel.co.uk; Burray; s/d/ste £80/100/155; P☎) is a spiffy, refurbished 19th-century herring station, right on the pier. Very modern rooms have stylish furnishings, and all have great water views. Families and groups should consider a suite – these are two-level self-contained flats that sleep four and have a kitchen. The **restaurant** (mains £15, bar meals £8, ☺lunch and dinner), with its genteel, nautical feel, dishes out decent nosh, and tables in the sunlit conservatory migrate outside in sunny weather.

SOUTH RONALDSAY

The main village on South Ronaldsay is **St Margaret's Hope**, named after Margaret, the Maid of Norway, who died here in 1290 on the way from her homeland to marry the future Edward II of England. This is where the Gills Bay ferry docks.

⊙ Sights

Tomb of the Eagles ARCHAEOLOGICAL SITE (www.tomboftheeagles.co.uk; adult/child £6.50/3; ☺9.30am-5.30pm Apr-Oct, 10am-noon Mar, by arrangement Nov-Feb) At the island's southern tip, this is the result of a local farmer finding two significant archaeological sites on his land. The first is a Bronze Age stone building with a firepit, indoor well and plenty of seating; orthodox theory suggests it was a communal cooking site, but we reckon it's the original Orkney pub. Beyond here, in a spectacular clifftop position, the Neolithic tomb (wheel yourself in prone on a trolley) is an elaborate stone construction that held the remains of up to 340 people who died some five millennia ago. Before you head out to the sites, an excellent personal explanation is given to you at the visitor centre; you meet a few spooky skulls and can handle some of the artefacts found. It's about a mile's airy walk to the tomb from the centre.

Orkney Marine Life Aquarium AQUARIUM (B9044, Grimness; adult/child £6/4.25; ☺10am-6pm Easter-Oct) This aquarium showcases the fascinating and diverse collection of marine animals found in Scapa Flow and Orcadian coastal waters. Giant shellfish such as lobsters are a feature, and there's a rock pool that allows up-close and personal inspections of local creatures – great for everyone, especially kids. Injured seals that have been nursed back to health can be viewed in open-air pools, and there's also an old creel boat to clamber about on.

🛏 Sleeping & Eating

Bankburn House B&B ££ (☑08444 142310; www.bankburnhouse.co.uk; St Margaret's Hope; s/d £38/55, with en suite £48/65; P@☎) On the A961, just outside town, this place has four smashing upstairs rooms in a large rustic house. Two rooms have en suite, all are a brilliant size, and a lot of thought has been put into guests' comfort. There's also a huge stretch of lawn out the front, which overlooks the town and bay – perfect for sunbathing on those shimmering, summery Orkney days. There's a substantial discount if you stay more than one night.

Murray Arms Hotel PUB ££ (☑01856-831205; www.murrayarmshotel.com; St Margaret's Hope; hotel s/d £40/80; ☎) This friendly local has small but very cosy and well-kitted-out rooms above the village pub. Semiskylight windows mean you can see what the weather's doing without getting out of bed. The **bar** (mains £7-9) is popular with locals and a great spot to have a chinwag with some Orcadians.

St Margaret's Hope Backpackers

HOSTEL £

(☎01856-831225; www.orkneybackpackers.com; St Margaret's Hope; dm £13; P) The backpackers, next to the Murray Arms, and a short walk from the ferry, is a lovely stone cottage and has small, simple rooms with up to four berths – great for families. There's a great lounge, a kitchen, a laundry and good hot showers. It's an excellent set-up, particularly as the pub is right outside the front door and you can use the wi-fi in the adjacent cafe. Enquiries at the Trading Post shop next door.

Creel

RESTAURANT £££

(☎01856-831311; www.thecreel.co.uk; Front Rd, St Margaret's Hope; 2/3 courses £32/38; ⊗dinner Tue-Sun) On the waterfront in an unassuming house, on unpretentious wooden tables, some of Scotland's best seafood has been served up for well over 20 years. Upstairs and next door, the three **rooms** (singles/doubles £75/110) face the spectacular sunset over the water, and are most spacious and comfortable. It was up for sale at the time of research, so fingers crossed.

South Mainland

With its gently rolling landscape, South Mainland may not have the archaeological treasures of the north, but it does have its share of the island's history. There are a few things to see at **Orphir**, a scattered community with no shop, about 9 miles west of Kirkwall. The **Orkneyinga Saga Centre** (admission free; ⊗9am-5pm) has displays relating to the *Orkneyinga Saga* (see the boxed text, p413), and an interesting video depicting various of the saga's deeds.

Just behind the centre is **Earl's Bu** (admission free; ⊗24hr), the foundations of a 12th-century manor house belonging to the Norse earls of Orkney. There are also the remains of **St Nicholas' Church**, a unique circular building that was originally 9m in diameter. Built before 1136 and modelled on the rotunda of the Church of the Holy Sepulchre in Jerusalem, it was popular with pilgrims after the capture of the Holy Land during the First Crusade.

If it's sunny and you're thinking about a picnic, head to **Waulkmill Bay**, between Kirkwall and Orphir. The huge sandy beach is perfect for strolling and there is bench seating with impressive views.

🛏 Sleeping

Foinhaven

B&B ££

(☎01856-811249; www.foinhaven.co.uk; Germiston Rd, Orphir; s/d £40/60; P) For a farmstay, old-fashioned hospitality and one of the best breakfasts around, try the solitude at this place, 1.5 miles from Orphir, overlooking Waulkmill Bay. Rooms are traditional and bathrooms modern – a speck of dirt would feel lonely in here. The rate comes down if you stay more than one night.

Houton Bay Lodge

HOTEL ££

(☎01856-811320; www.houtonbaylodge.com; Houton; d/ste £75/95; P@ᖃ) Particularly good for families or business folk, this old seaplane base has been extensively refurbished, and the cool, stylish, contemporary rooms decked out with pine furniture are top notch (room 5 is a fave). Slick leather chairs, comfy beds and en suites complete the happy picture, as does a bar, a proper snooker table and other indoor games. The lodge is right behind the ferry terminal with departures for Flotta and Hoy.

❶ Getting There & Away

Bus 2 runs from Kirkwall to Houton (20 minutes, three to five daily Monday to Saturday) via Orphir. An extra bus, the Hoy Hopper, runs Wednesday to Friday in summer. For details of ferries from Houton to Hoy, see p418.

West & North Mainland

This part of the island is sprinkled with outstanding prehistoric monuments: the journey up to Orkney is worth it for these alone. The scattered village of Stenness, about 4 miles northeast of Stromness, consists of little more than some houses, a petrol station and a hotel. Around it, however, are three excellent attractions, easily accessible using the regular bus service between Stromness and Kirkwall (p410).

MAES HOWE

Egypt has the pyramids, Scotland has **Maes Howe** (HS; ☎01856-761606; www.historic-scotland.gov.uk; adult/child £5.20/3.10; ⊗tours hourly 10am-3pm Oct-Mar, also 4pm Apr-Sep). Constructed about 5000 years ago, it is an extraordinary place, a Stone Age tomb built from enormous sandstone blocks, some of which weighed many tons and were brought from several miles away. Creeping down the long stone passageway to the cen-

and was the site of a large settlement, inhabited throughout the Neolithic period (3500–1800 BC).

A short walk to the east are the excavated remains of **Barnhouse Neolithic Village**, thought to have been inhabited by the builders of Maes Howe. Don't skip this: it brings the area to life.

RING OF BRODGAR

Situated about a mile north of Stenness, along the road towards Skara Brae, is this wide circle of **standing stones** (www.historic -scotland.gov.uk; admission free; ⊙24hr), some over 5m tall. Last of the three Stenness monuments to be built (2500–2000 BC), it remains a most atmospheric location. Twenty-one of the original 60 stones still stand among the heather. These mysterious giants, their curious shapes mutilated by years of climatic onslaught, fire the imagination – what were they for? On a grey day with dark clouds thudding low across the sky, the stones look secretive and seem to be almost sneering at the jostling summer crowds. Free guided tours leave from the carpark at 1pm from June to August.

ORKNEY FOLKLORE & STORYTELLING VISITOR CENTRE

Between Brodgar and Skara Brae, this off-beat **centre** (☎01856-841207; www.orkney attractions.com) focuses on the islands' folkloric tradition. The best way to experience it is on one of their atmospheric storytelling evenings (Sunday, Tuesday and Friday at 8.30pm March to October, adult/child £10/6) where local legends are told around a peat fire. There's also a relaxing **B&B** (s/d £25/50; P), with traditional bannocks and oatmeal bread and locally cured bacon at breakfast, and meditation sessions.

SKARA BRAE & SKAILL HOUSE

A visit to extraordinary **Skara Brae** (HS; www.historic-scotland.gov.uk; Bay of Skaill; adult/child £6.70/4; ⊙9.30am-5.30pm Apr-Sep, to 4.30pm Oct-Mar), one of the world's most evocative prehistoric sites, offers the best opportunity in Scotland for a glimpse of Stone Age life. Idyllically situated by a sandy bay 8 miles north of Stromness, and predating Stonehenge and the pyramids of Giza, Skara Brae is northern Europe's best-preserved prehistoric village.

Even the stone furniture – beds, boxes and dressers – has survived the 5000 years since a community lived and breathed

---

ORKNEYINGA SAGA

Written around 1200, this saga is a rich tale of sorcery, political intrigue and cunning and unscrupulous acts among the Viking earls of Orkney. Part myth and part historical fact, it begins with the capture of the islands by the king of Norway and then recounts the next tumultuous centuries until they become part of Scotland. It's a wonderful piece of medieval literature. Head to the Orkneyinga Saga Centre for more background.

---

tral chamber, you feel the indescribable gulf of years that separate us from the architects of this mysterious place. Though nothing is known about who and what was interred here, the scope of the project suggests it was a structure of great significance.

By chance or design, for a few weeks around the winter solstice the setting sun shafts up the entrance passage and strikes the back wall of the tomb in spooky alignment. If you can't be there, check the webcams on www.maeshowe.co.uk.

In the 12th century, the tomb was broken into by Vikings searching for treasure. A couple of years later, another group sought shelter in the chamber from a blizzard that lasted three days. While they waited out the storm, they carved runic graffiti on the walls. As well as the some-things-never-change 'Olaf was 'ere' and 'Thorni bedded Helga', there are also more intricate carvings, including a particularly fine dragon and a knotted serpent.

Buy tickets in Tormiston Mill, on the other side of the road. Entry is by 45-minute guided tours that leave on the hour. Be sure to reserve your tour-slot ahead by phone. Due to the oversized groups, guides tend to only show a couple of the Viking inscriptions, but they'll happily show more if asked.

STANDING STONES OF STENNESS

Within sight of Maes Howe, four mighty **stones** (www.historic-scotland.gov.uk; admission free; ⊙24hr) remain of what was once a circle of 12. Recent research suggests they were perhaps erected as long ago as 3300 BC, and they impose by their sheer size; the tallest measures 5.7m in height. This narrow strip of land, the Ness of Brodgar, separates the Harray and Stenness lochs here. It was hidden until 1850, when waves whipped up by a severe storm eroded the sand and grass above the beach, exposing the houses underneath. There's an excellent interactive exhibit and short video, arming visitors with facts and theory, which will enhance the impact of the site. You then enter a reconstructed house, which gives the excavation that follows more meaning. The official guidebook, available from the visitors centre, includes a good self-guided tour.

The joint ticket will also get you into **Skaill House** (⊙Apr-Sep), an early-17th-century mansion built for the local bishop in 1620. It's a bit anticlimactic, catapulting straight from the Neolithic to the 1950s decor, but you can see a smart hidden compartment in the library as well as the bishop's original 17th-century four-poster bed.

Buses run to Skara Brae from Kirkwall and Stromness (Monday, Thursday and Saturday May to September only). It's possible to walk along the coast from Stromness to Skara Brae via Yesnaby Sea Stacks and the Broch of Borwick (9 miles).

BIRSAY

The small village of Birsay is 6 miles north of Skara Brae. The ruins of the **Earl's Palace** (admission free; ⊙24hr), built in the 16th century by the despotic Robert Stewart, earl of Orkney, dominate the village centre. Today it's a mass of half walls and crumbling columns that look like dilapidated chimney stacks. Nevertheless, the size of the palace is impressive, matching the reputed ego and tyranny of its former inhabitant.

At low tide (check tide times at the shop in Earl's Palace) you can walk out to the **Brough of Birsay** (HS; www.historic-scotland. gov.uk; adult/child £3.20/1.90; ⊙9.30am-5.30pm mid-Jun–Sep), about 0.75 miles northwest of the Earl's Palace. On the island, you'll find the extensive ruins of a Norse settlement and the 12th-century St Peter's Church.

Birsay makes a lovely, peaceful place to stay amid the Orkney countryside. **Birsay Hostel** (☑01856-873535; www.hostelsorkney. co.uk; small/medium tent £5/8, dm £13; ⊙May-Oct; P) is a former activity centre and school that now has dorms that vary substantially in spaciousness – go for one of the four-bedded ones. There's a big kitchen and grassy camping area. One of Orkney's most charming B&Bs is **Links House** (☑01856-721221; www.ewaf.co.uk; s/d £49/78; P), a most welcoming stone house near the sea. The beautiful rooms – one with

comforting sloping ceiling, one with a toilet that has wonderful vistas – are complemented by a great little gazebo space, where you can contemplate the scenery, or browse the books and maps kept here (along with a wee decanter of sherry). Breakfast is a treat – pancakes with blueberries and crème fraiche anyone?

EVIE

On an exposed headland at Aikerness, a 1.5-mile walk northeast from the straggling village of Evie, you'll find the **Broch of Gurness** (HS; www.historic-scotland.gov.uk; adult/child £4.70/2.80; ⊙9.30am-5.30pm Apr-Sep), a fine example of these drystone fortified towers that were both status symbol for powerful farmers and useful protection from raiders some 2200 years ago. The imposing entranceway and sturdy stone walls – originally 10m high – impress; inside you can see the hearth and where a mezzanine floor would have fitted. Around the broch are the remains of the settlement centred on it.

Eviedale Campsite (☑01856-751270; eviedale@orkney.com; Evie; sites £5-9; ⊙Apr-Sep; P🐾), at the northern end of the village, has a good grassed area for tent camping, with picnic tables. This would suit people looking to avoid the larger municipal sites. Next door is self-catering accommodation in excellent renovated farm cottages.

Down a turning about a mile west of the Tingwall ferry turnoff, **Woodwick House** (☑01856-751330; www.woodwickhouse.co.uk; s/d with shared bathroom £34/68, en suite s/d to £75/110; P🐾) is a mansion of understated elegance in a lovely setting. The sizeable, commodious rooms are in harmony with the relaxed rural atmosphere, as are the cosy lounges with a fire and books, and your courteous hosts do fine three-course dinners (£26; open to nonguests) and put on the odd cultural event. If you've been on Orkney for a while, you may not recognise those wooden things around the house. Trees.

Stromness

POP 1609

An elongated little port, Stromness lacks Kirkwall's size and punch but makes up for that with bucketloads of character. The rambling, winding streets flanking the town have changed little since the 18th century and the flagstone-paved main street curves along the waterfront, amid attractive stone cottages. Guesthouses, pubs and eateries interrupt traditional trade along the main street, where cars and pedestrians move at the same pace as each other.

◉ Sights

The main recreation in Stromness is simply strolling up and down the narrow, atmospheric main street.

Pier Arts Centre GALLERY
(www.pierartscentre.com; 30 Victoria St; ⊙10.30am-5pm Mon-Sat) Resplendently redesigned, this has really rejuvenated the Orkney modern-art scene with its sleek lines and upbeat attitude. It's worth a look as much for the architecture as its high-quality collection of 20th-century British art and changing exhibitions.

Stromness Museum MUSEUM
(www.orkneyheritage.com; 52 Alfred St; adult/child £3.50/1; ⊙10am-5pm Apr-Sep, 11am-3.30pm Mon-Sat Oct-Mar) A superb museum full of knick-knacks from maritime and natural-history exhibitions covering whaling, the Hudson's Bay Company and the sunken German fleet. You can happily nose around the place for a couple of hours. Across the street from the museum is the house where local poet and novelist George Mackay Brown (see p460) lived.

✯✯ Festivals & Events

The **Orkney Folk Festival** (www.orkneyfolk festival.com) is a four-day event based in Stromness in the third week of May, with a program of folk concerts, *ceilidhs* (evenings of traditional Scottish entertainment including music, song and dance) and casual pub sessions. The town packs out, and late-night buses from Kirkwall are laid on. Book ahead for event tickets and accommodation.

⌂ Sleeping

Orca Hotel HOTEL ££
(☎01856-850447; www.orcahotel.moonfruit.com; 76 Victoria St; s/d £40/54) Warm and homelike, this small hotel right in the heart of things is likeably out of the ordinary, and features cosy rooms with narrow, comfortable beds. Rates vary slightly depending on the room you choose; in winter you can use the hotel's kitchen.

Miller's House B&B ££
(☎01856-851969; www.millershouseorkney.com; 7 John St; s/d £50/70; ⊙Easter-Oct) Reached

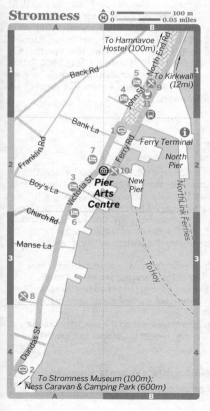

Stromness ⊙N 0 — 100 m / 0 — 0.05 miles

To Hamnavoe Hostel (100m)
To Kirkwall (12mi)
Back Rd
North End Rd
John St
Bank La
Ferry Rd
Franklin Rd
Ferry Terminal
North Pier
Boy's La
Victoria St
Pier Arts Centre
New Pier
Church Rd
NorthLink Ferries
Manse La
To Hoy
Dundas St
To Stromness Museum (100m);
Ness Caravan & Camping Park (600m)

from up a side alley, Miller's House is an historic Stromness residence – check out the wonderful 1716 stone doorway – but most of the rooms are actually in a different building (Harbourside Guest House) around the corner. Here you can smell the cleanliness, and there's plenty of light and an optimistic feel. Showers hit the spot, and you can use the laundry. Exceptional breakfasts include vegetarian options and daily baked bread.

Hamnavoe Hostel HOSTEL £
(☎01856-851202; www.hamnavoehostel.co.uk; 10a North End Rd; dm £16-18; ☎) This well-equipped hostel lacks a bit of character but makes up for that with excellent facilities, including a fine kitchen and a lounge room with great perspectives over the water. The dorms are very commodious, with duvets and reading lamps, and the showers are good.

Brown's Hostel HOSTEL £
(☎01856-850661; www.brownshostel.co.uk; 45 Victoria St; dm £14-15; @☎) On the main street, this handy, sociable place has cramped but cosy and homelike dorms (the upstairs ones are a pound more but have more space) as well as small private rooms. Life centres on its inviting common area, where you can browse the free internet or swap pasta recipes in the open kitchen. There are overflow rooms in a house up the street.

Stromness Hotel HOTEL ££
(☎01856-850298; www.stromnesshotel.com; Victoria St; s/d £55/98; ☎) Proudly surveying the main street and harbour, this lofty Victorian hotel is a reminder of the way things used to be, with its posh revolving door and imposing facade. The pink-hued rooms are spacious, but the yielding beds have seen better days and the claustrophobic lift means your suitcase'll have to find its own way.

Ness Caravan & Camping Park CAMPSITE £
(☎01856-873535; 1-person/2-person/family tents £5.80/9/11; ☺Apr-Sep; P) This breezy, fenced-in camping ground overlooks the bay at the southern end of town and is as neat as a pin.

✗ Eating & Drinking

Hamnavoe Restaurant RESTAURANT £££
(☎01856-850606; 35 Graham Pl; mains £13-19; ☺dinner Tue-Sun Apr-Oct) Tucked away off the main street, this long-standing Stromness classic specialises in excellent local seafood backed up by professional service. There's always something good off the boats, and the chef prides himself on his lobster. Booking is a must. From November to March, it's only open Saturday and Sunday for dinner, while in summer it also opens for lobster lunches on Saturday.

DIVING SCAPA FLOW'S WRECKS

One of the world's largest natural harbours, Scapa Flow has been in near-constant use by various fleets from the Vikings onwards. After WWI, 74 German ships were interned in Scapa; when the terms of the armistice were agreed on 6 May 1919, with the announcement of a severely reduced German navy, Admiral von Reuter, who was in charge of the fleet, decided to take matters into his own hands. On 21 June, a secret signal was passed from ship to ship and the British watched incredulously as every German ship began to sink. Fifty-two of them went to the bottom, with the rest left aground in shallow water.

Most of the ships were salvaged, but seven vessels remain to attract divers. There are three battleships – the *König*, the *Kronprinz Wilhelm* and the *Markgraf* – all of which weigh over 25,000 tonnes. The first two were subjected to blasting for scrap metal, but the *Markgraf* is undamaged and considered one of the best dives in the area.

As well as the German wrecks, numerous other ships rest on the sea bed in Scapa Flow. HMS *Royal Oak*, which was sunk by a German U-boat in October 1939, with the loss of 833 crew, is an official war grave.

Recommended diving contacts:

Diving Cellar (☎01856-850055; www.divescapaflow.co.uk; 4 Victoria St, Stromness)

Scapa Scuba (☎/fax 01856-851218; www.scapascuba.co.uk; Dundas St, Stromness)

Stromness Hotel
RESTAURANT, PUB **££**

(www.stromnesshotel.com; restaurant mains £8-15; ⊙lunch & dinner) This central hotel does excellent seafood dishes fused with tastes of the Orient, and there are vegetarian options. There's a lounge bar with harbour views, or the earthier, convivial Flattie Bar downstairs.

Julia's Café & Bistro
CAFE **£**

(20 Ferry Rd; mains £5-8; ⊙9am-5pm Sep-May, plus dinner Wed-Sun Jun-Aug; @🕾) This cafe with a conservatory, opposite the port, keeps all-comers happy, with massive fry-ups offset on the cardiac karma scale by wraps, salads and tempting vegetarian dishes such as nut roast or couscous. In summer it opens for dinner with elaborate fare (£10 to £13) on offer.

Ferry Inn
PUB **£**

(www.ferryinn.com; 10 John St; mains £7-11; ⊙breakfast, lunch & dinner) Every port has its pub, and in Stromness it's the Ferry. Convivial and central, it warms the cockles with folk music, local beers and characters, and pub food that's unsophisticated but generously proportioned and good value.

Stromness Cafe-Bar
CAFE **£**

(22 Victoria St; light meals £3-7; ⊙breakfast, lunch & dinner) This quirky little space, with attached shop, is good for a snack or something more substantial. Orkney beer is available and best enjoyed on the back terrace overlooking the water.

ℹ Information

Library (Alfred St; ⊙2-7pm Mon-Thu, 2-5pm Fri, 10am-5pm Sat) Free internet.

Tourist office (🕾01856-850716; ⊙10am-4pm Mon-Sat Apr-Oct) In the ferry terminal. Also open on Sunday in summer.

ℹ Getting There & Away

For information on ferries to Scrabster, Lerwick and Aberdeen, see p405.

Bus 1 runs regularly to Kirkwall (40 minutes) and on to St Margaret's Hope.

Hoy

Orkney's second-largest island, Hoy (meaning 'High Island'), got the lion's share of this archipelago's scenic beauty. Shallow turquoise bays lace the perimeter, while peat and moorland cover Orkney's highest

hills. The highest point is Ward Hill (479m), in the north of Hoy. Much of the northern part of the island is a Royal Society for the Protection of Birds (RSPB) reserve, with breeding guillemots, kittiwakes, fulmars, puffins and great skuas. Note that the ferry service from Mainland gets very busy over summer – book ahead.

◉ Sights

The northern part of the island boasts spectacular coastal scenery, including some of Britain's highest vertical cliffs – St John's Head on the northwest coast rises 346m. Hoy is probably best known for the **Old Man of Hoy**, a 137m-high rock stack that can be seen from the Scrabster–Stromness ferry. The northern part of Hoy has been maintained as a nature reserve by the RSPB since 1983.

Lyness, on the eastern side of Hoy, was an important naval base during both world wars, when the British Grand Fleet was based in Scapa Flow. With the dilapidated remains of buildings and an uninspiring outlook towards the oil terminal on Flotta island, this isn't a pretty place. However, the **Scapa Flow Visitor Centre** (admission by donation; ⊙9am-4.30pm Mon-Fri Mar-Oct, plus Sat & Sun May-Sep) is a fascinating naval museum and photographic display, located in an old pumphouse that once fed fuel to the ships. Take your time to browse the exhibits about WWI and WWII, and have a look at the folders that carry supplementary information; the letters home from a seaman lost when the *Royal Oak* was torpedoed are particularly moving.

At the southern end of the island, Long-hope's former lifeboat launching station holds a small **lifeboat museum**, centred round one of the old boats itself. Call the caretaker (🕾01856-701332) to have a look.

🏃 Activities

First scaled in 1966, the **Old Man of Hoy** is a rock-climber's delight. The easiest approach to the Old Man is from Rackwick Bay, a two- to three-hour walk by road from Moaness Pier (in Hoy village on the east coast, where the ferries dock) through the beautiful **Rackwick Glen**. You'll pass the 5000-year-old **Dwarfie Stane**, the only example of a rock-cut tomb in Scotland and, according to Sir Walter Scott, the favourite residence of Trolld, a dwarf from Norse legend. On your return you can take the path via the **Glens of Kinnaird** and **Berriedale**

Wood, Scotland's most northerly tuft of native forest.

The most popular walk climbs steeply westwards from Rackwick Bay, then curves northwards, descending gradually to the edge of the cliffs opposite the Old Man of Hoy. Allow seven hours for the return trip from Moaness Pier, or three hours from Rackwick, a village on the west coast – there's a hostel located at the point where the walk begins.

🛏 Sleeping & Eating

Uppersettir B&B **£**
(☎01856-791234; uppersettir@freeuk.com; Uppersettir; r per person £23; ℗) They're semi-retired and away quite often, so don't just turn up, but if you can snag a bed in this spectacularly situated hilltop farm 2.5 miles south of the Lyness ferry, count yourself fortunate. It's like staying at a friend's house: a comfortable room, a help-yourself attitude and hosts who couldn't be more welcoming. An out-of-the-ordinary B&B (plus pre-bedtime snack) experience. Two-night minimum – for your own good.

Hoy Centre HOSTEL **£**
(☎office hours only 01856-873535, ext 2415; www.hostelsorkney.co.uk; Moaness; dm/f £14/34; ℗) This is a pretty schmick place with an enviable location, around 15 minutes' walk from Moaness Pier, at the base of the rugged Cuilags. Rooms come with twin beds and a bunk bed, or there are family rooms, all with en suite.

Quoydale B&B **£**
(☎01856-791315; www.orkneyaccommodation. co.uk; s/d £25/42) There are several B&Bs on the island, including the welcoming Quoydale, nestled at the base of Ward Hill on a working farm 1 mile from the ferry terminal. It has spectacular views over Scapa Flow and offers tours and a taxi service.

Stromabank Hotel HOTEL, PUB **££**
(☎01856-701494; www.stromabank.co.uk; Longhope; s/d £42/64) Perched on the hill above Longhope, the small and atmospheric Stromabank has very acceptable refurbished en suite rooms, as well as an attractive bar (☉lunch Sun, dinner Fri-Wed), whose small menu offers tasty home-cooked meals (£6 to £10) using lots of local produce. Opens less in winter.

Rackwick Outdoor Centre HOSTEL **£**
(☎office hours only 01856-873535, ext 2415; www.hostelsorkney.co.uk; Rackwick; dm £11;

☉Apr-Sep; ℗) Newly refurbished, this cosy spot, 6 miles from the ferry at Moaness, is a snug (two four-bed dorms), clean place, popular with walkers. You can camp outside and use the facilities.

Wild Heather B&B **££**
(☎01856-791098; www.wildheatherbandb. co.uk; Lyness; s/d £32/50; ℗) Turn right from the ferry to reach this great place right on the bay. Plenty of thoughtful extras add value, and evening meals are available.

ℹ Getting There & Away

Orkney Ferries (☎01856-850624; www. orkneyferries.co.uk) runs passenger ferries between Stromness and Moaness Pier (£3.60, 30 minutes, two to five daily).

There's also a frequent **car ferry** (☎01856-811397) to Lyness (Hoy) from Houton on Mainland (passenger/car £3.60/11.50, 40 minutes, up to seven daily Monday to Friday, two or three Saturday and Sunday). The Sunday service only runs from May to September. Some services also drop in at the island of Flotta.

ℹ Getting Around

Transport on Hoy is very limited. Your best bet to explore is the **Hoy Hopper**, which runs Wednesday to Friday, mid-May to mid-September. It departs from Kirkwall, crosses to Hoy and then does circuits around the island, allowing you to hop on and off at will, before returning to Kirkwall in the evening. Total cost is £17/8.50 per adult/child.

There's no public transport to Rackwick Bay, so if you don't feel like walking call ☎01856-791315 or ☎01856-791263 for a minibus taxi service.

Northern Islands

The group of windswept islands north of Mainland provides a refuge for migrating birds and a nesting ground for seabirds; there are several RSPB reserves. Some of the islands are also rich in archaeological sites, but it's the beautiful scenery, with wonderful white-sand beaches and lime-green to azure seas, that is the main attraction.

The tourist offices in Kirkwall and Stromness have the useful *Islands of Orkney* brochure with maps and details of these islands. Note that the 'ay' at the end of each island name (from the Old Norse for 'island') is pronounced 'ee' (Shapinsay is pronounced '*shap*-in-see').

Getting There & Away

Orkney Ferries (☎01856-872044; www.orkneyferries.co.uk) and **Loganair** (☎01856-872494; www.loganair.co.uk) enable you to make day-trips to many of the islands from Kirkwall on most days of the week (Friday only to North Ronaldsay), but it's worth staying over.

There's also a new **fast ferry** (☎01857-616339; www.visiteday.com) service for passengers that zips between Stronsay, Sanday, Eday and Kirkwall on Tuesday and Thursday.

SHAPINSAY

Just 20 minutes by ferry from Kirkwall, Shapinsay is a low-lying, intensively cultivated island. **Balfour Castle** (www.balfourcastle.com), completed in 1848 in the turreted Scottish Baronial style, is Shapinsay's most impressive drawcard. Guided tours (2.15pm Sunday from May to September) must be booked in advance; the price (£20) includes the ferry, admission to the castle and afternoon tea. The castle can also be hired for group accommodation.

About 4 miles from the pier, at the far northeastern corner of the island, is the Iron Age **Burroughston Broch** (admission free; ☉24hr), one of the best-preserved brochs (defensive towers) in Orkney.

Orkney Ferries operates a ferry from Kirkwall (passenger/car £3.60/11.50, 25 minutes). Services are limited in winter.

ROUSAY

Just off the north coast of Mainland, hilly Rousay merits exploration for its fine assembly of prehistoric sites, great views and relaxing away-from-it-all ambience. Connected by regular ferry from Tingwall, it makes a great little day-trip, but you may well feel a pull to stay longer.

◉ Sights & Activities

Hire a bike at Trumland Farm (see p420) and take on the windy, hilly 14-mile circuit of the island.

FREE **Prehistoric Sites** ARCHAEOLOGICAL SITES (HS; www.historic-scotland.gov.uk; ☉24hr)
The major archaeological sites are clearly labelled from the 14-mile road that rings the island. Heading west (left) from the ferry, you soon come to **Taversoe Tuick**, an intriguing burial cairn constructed on two levels, with separate entrances – perhaps

---

LOCAL KNOWLEDGE

JOHN BAIN: INTERISLAND PILOT

Orkney's an archipelago; if the climate was different, it'd be similar to the Caribbean or Greece. There's a lot of unique aspects to it. Best time to visit? The summer, but it's the busiest. Not a lot of people like the climate in winter. We don't mind it, but for a visitor, a lot of places close down. Ferries are less frequent; you don't have the same chances to move around. But you do get some beautiful winter days.

Ferry or plane?

If you've got time, experience both. I'm biased but I would say that from the aircraft you see more, and you can fit more into your trip. We've just had a family in from Papa Westray (p423) to Kirkwall, and they're off to North Ronaldsay (p423) in the afternoon. You can see nearly all the main islands in a few days.

Most beautiful island?

Oh, no, no, no, I'd get hung, drawn, and quartered if I picked one! I live up on North Mainland and look out on the islet of Eynhallow [near Evie] every morning. The stories say that's where strange folk, the Finmen, lived. That's one of the great things about Orkney, the storytelling. Go to a storytelling night (p413), you'll be hooked.

On a rainy day?

Stay home! No, you can go round some of it, the craft shops in Kirkwall (p410). And the island's got some good pubs like Helgi's (p410) for a quiet drink.

Favourite out-of-the-way spot?

The Brough of Birsay (p414). Go up there for a picnic.

Local Words?

Peedie – it means small, or little. It's a very common word on the islands.

a joint tomb for different families; a semi-detached solution in posthumous housing. You can squeeze into the cairn to explore both levels, but there's not much space. Not far beyond here are two other significant cairns, **Blackhammer**, then **Knowe of Yarso**, the latter a fair walk up the hill but with majestic views.

Six miles from the ferry, the mighty **Midhowe Cairn** has been dubbed the 'Great Ship of Death'. Built around 3500 BC and enormous in size, it's divided into compartments, in which the remains of 25 people were found. Covered by a protective stone building, it's nevertheless a memorable sight. Next to it, **Midhowe Broch**, the sturdy stone lines of which echo the striations of the rocky shoreline, is a muscular Iron Age fortified compound with a mezzanine floor. The sites are by the water, a 10-minute walk downhill from the main road.

Trumland House GARDENS
(gardens £1.50; ⏰10am-5pm Mon-Fri May-Oct) Currently undergoing extensive restoration, this is probably the largest private house in Orkney. The grounds, with their thicket of native trees, are worth a stroll – you enter the walled garden through a medieval gate.

🛏 Sleeping & Eating

Trumland Farm Hostel HOSTEL £
(☎01856-821252; trumland@btopenworld.com; sites £5, dm £10, bedding £2; P) An easy stroll from the ferry, this organic farm has a wee hostel, with rather cramped six-bed dorms and a pretty little kitchen and common area. You can pitch tents outside and use the facilities; there's also a well-equipped self-catering cottage.

Taversoe Hotel HOTEL ££
(☎01856-821325; www.taversoehotel.co.uk; s/d £45/75; P) About 2 miles west from the pier, the island's only hotel is a low-key place with neat, simple doubles with water vistas that share a bathroom and a twin with en suite but no view. The best views, however, are from the dining room, which serves good-value meals. The friendly owners will pick you up from the ferry.

Pier Restaurant CAFE £
(meals £5-7; ⏰11am-11pm, closes 6.30pm Wed & Sun; @) Just above the ferry, this simple place does burgers and standard bar meals, and serves for a coffee or whisky while waiting for the boat, or a chat and a game of pool after a long day's walking. There's also internet access and a list of local residents who offer B&B.

ℹ Getting There & Around

A small **car ferry** (☎01856-751360; www.orkneyferries.co.uk) connects Tingwall on Mainland with Rousay (passenger/car £3.60/11.50, 30 minutes, up to six daily) and the nearby islands of Egilsay and Wyre.

Rousay Transport (☎01856-821234; www.visitrousay.co.uk) offers island tours, which include guided visits to the historic sites on Tuesday and Thursday (adult/child £16.50/3).

Bikes can be hired for £7 per day from Trumland Farm.

EGILSAY & WYRE

These two small islands lie east of Rousay. On Egilsay (population 37), a cenotaph marks the spot where Earl Magnus was murdered in 1117. After his martyrdom, pilgrims flocked to the island, and **St Magnus Church**, now roofless, was built. Today it provides a rare example of a round-towered Viking church. Much of Egilsay is an RSPB reserve; listen for the corncrakes at the southern end of the island.

Wyre (population 18) is even smaller. It was the domain of the Viking baron Kolbein Hruga ('Cubbie Roo'); the ruins of his castle, built around 1145, and the nearby 12th-century **St Mary's Chapel** can be visited free. Seal sightings at the beach on Wyre's western sliver are virtually guaranteed. These two islands are reached on the Rousay–Tingwall ferry (see p420).

STRONSAY

Shaped like a bent crucifix, Stronsay attracts walkers and cyclists for its lack of serious inclines, and beautiful landscapes over its four curving bays. You can spot wildlife, with chubby seals basking on the rocks, puffins and other seabirds.

◉ Sights & Activities

In the 19th century, Whitehall harbour became one of Scotland's major herring ports, but the fisheries collapsed in the 1930s. The old **Stronsay Fish Mart** (Whitehall; admission free; ⏰daily May-Sep) now houses a herring-industry interpretation centre. There's also a hostel and cafe here.

Just across the harbour is the small island of **Papa Stronsay**, where Earl Rognvald Brusason was murdered in 1046. The island is owned by a monastic order, the Transalpine Redemptorists; the monks will provide **boat trips** (☏01856-616389) to the island by prior arrangement. There are good coastal walks and, in the east, the **Vat O'Kirbister** is a fine example of a gloup (natural arch).

At the southern end of the island, you can visit the **seal-watch hide** on the beach. There's also a chance to see otters at nearby **Loch Lea-shun**.

🛏 Sleeping & Eating

Stronsay Hotel   HOTEL, PUB **££**
(☏01857-616213; www.stronsayhotelorkney.co .uk; Whitehall; s/d £38/76; 🛜) The island's watering hole has immaculate refurbished rooms. There's also recommended pub grub (meals from £7; open lunch and dinner) in the bar, with excellent seafood (including paella and lobster) in particular. There are good deals for multinight stays.

Stronsay Fish Mart   HOSTEL **£**
(☏01857-616386; Whitehall; dm £14) Part of the island's former herring station has been converted into a 10-bed hostel with shower and kitchen. It's clean and well run, and the neighbouring cafe serves takeaways, snacks and meals all day.

❶ Getting There & Away

Loganair (☏01856-872494; www.loganair. co.uk) flies from Kirkwall to Stronsay (£35 one way, 20 minutes, two daily Monday to Saturday). A **car ferry** (☏01856-872 044) links Kirkwall with Stronsay (passenger/car £7.05/16.75, 1½ hours, two to three daily) and Eday.

EDAY

Eday has a hilly centre, with cultivated fields situated around the coast. There is the impressive standing **Stone of Setter** and, close by, the chambered cairns of **Braeside**, **Huntersquoy** and **Vinquoy**. Huntersquoy is a two-storey cairn, like Taversoe Tuick (p419) on Rousay.

Eday Heritage and Visitor Centre (www. edayheritagecentre.org.uk; ⏱10am-6pm summer, Sun winter) has a range of local history exhibits, as well as an audiovisual about tidal energy initiatives. The early-17th-century **Carrick House** (☏01857-622260; adult/child £3/1; ⏱by appointment), with its floor bloodstained from a pirate skirmish, is worth a visit; tours of the house run in summer with advance notice.

It's worth getting hold of the *Eday Heritage Walk* leaflet from the Kirkwall tourist office, which details an interesting four-hour ramble from the Community Enterprises shop up to the cliffs of Red Head in the north of the island.

Eday Minibus Tour (☏01857-622206) offers 2¼-hour guided tours (adult/child £12/8) from the ferry pier on Monday, Wednesday and Friday from May to August. It also operates as a taxi service.

🛏 Sleeping & Eating

Eday Hostel   HOSTEL **£**
(☏07973-716278; www.syha.org.uk; dm £15; 🅿 ♿) Four miles north of the ferry pier, this recently renovated hostel is community-run and an excellent place to stay.

Blett B&B   B&B **££**
(☏01857-622248; Blett; B&B incl dinner per person £30, croft house per person £25) Mrs Popplewell has a charming cottage opposite the Calf of Eday islet with one double and one single room. There's also a couple of fully equipped, self-catering croft houses nearby sleeping three people each. Mrs Popplewell bakes fresh bread daily, and she serves snacks and meals at her craft shop.

Red House   CAFE **£**
(☏01857-622217; light meals £4-8; ⏱10am-5pm Tue-Fri Jun-Sep & by arrangement) Drop into this group of 19th-century croft buildings for home-cooked lunches, evening meals, local history and a chat.

❶ Getting There & Around

There are two flights from Kirkwall (one way £35, 30 minutes) to London airport – that's London, Eday – on Wednesday only. Ferries sail from Kirkwall, usually via Stronsay (passenger/car £7.05/16.75, two hours, two to three daily). There's also a link between Sanday and Eday (20 minutes).

SANDAY

Aptly named, blissfully quiet Sanday is ringed by Orkney's best beaches – with dazzling white sand of the sort you'd expect in the Caribbean. The island is almost entirely flat apart from a colossal sand dune and the cliffs at Spurness; the dunes are 12 miles long and growing, due to sand build-up.

There are several archaeological sites here, the most impressive being the **Quoyness chambered tomb** (admission free; ⏱24hr), similar to Maes Howe (see p412) and dating from the 3rd millennium BC. It has triple walls, a main chamber and six smaller cells. At the northeastern tip of Sanday, there's **Tafts Ness**, with around 500 prehistoric burial mounds.

Sleeping & Eating

Kettletoft Hotel
HOTEL, PUB ££

(☑01857-600217; www.kettletofthotel.co.uk; Kettletoft; s/d £35/70; P) The welcoming and family-friendly Kettletoft is a refurbished elderly statesman near the centre of the island. The pub here serves tasty bar meals for around £9, leaning towards the seaward side of things, with lobster even scuttling onto some dishes.

Ayre's Rock Hostel
HOSTEL, CAMPSITE £

(☑01857-600410; www.ayres-rock-sanday-ork ney.co.uk; 1-/2-person tents £5/7, dm/s £13.50/18; P) Cosy hostel sleeping eight in the outbuildings of a farm. There's a craft shop and chippie on site, breakfasts and dinners are available, and you can also pitch a tent.

Belsair
B&B, PUB ££

(☑01857-600206; www.belsairsanday.co.uk; Kettletoft; r per person £30) Overlooks the harbour; tidy en suite rooms that are good value. Bar meals and evening dinner feature Orcadian produce.

ℹ Getting There & Around

There are flights from Kirkwall to Sanday (one way £35, 20 minutes, twice daily Monday to Saturday) and ferries (passenger/car £7.05/16.75, 1½ hours), with a link to Eday.

WESTRAY

If you've only time to visit one of Orkney's northern islands, make delightful Westray the one. With an ecological bent, rolling farmland, handsome sandy beaches, coastal walks and appealing places to stay, it's a green emerald in the archipelago's jewel box.

The main settlement, Pierowall, is 7 miles from the Rapness ferry dock. Arrayed around a picturesque natural harbour, Pierowall was once a strategic Viking base.

⊙ Sights & Activities

In Pierowall, the **Westray Heritage Centre** (adult/child £2/50p; ⊙daily May-Sep) has interesting displays with finds from archaeological digs, the famous Neolithic 'Westray Wife' among them. A half-mile west of Pierowall stand the ruins of **Noltland Castle** (admission free), a tower house with a formidable array of shot holes from the defence of its deceitful owner Gilbert Balfour, who plotted to murder Cardinal Beaton and, after being exiled, the king of Sweden.

Westraak (☑01857-677777; www.westraak. co.uk) is a recommended operator that will take you on informative, engaging trips around the island, covering everything from Viking history to puffin mating habits.

The RSPB reserve at **Noup Head** coastal cliffs, in the northwest of the island, attracts vast numbers of breeding seabirds from April to July. There are big puffin posses here and at **Castle O'Burrian**, a mile north of Rapness.

Sleeping & Eating

West Manse
B&B, SELF-CATERING ££

(☑01857-677482; www.millwestray.com; Westside; r £30-35 per person; P⚡) Take the Westside road to its end to reach this imposing, noble house with arcing coastal vistas. Here no timetables reign; make your own breakfast when you feel like it. Your warmly welcoming hosts have introduced a raft of practical green solutions for heating, fuel and more. Kids will love this unconventional place; art exhibitions, cooking classes, venerably comfortable furniture and clean air are drawcards for parents.

The Barn
HOSTEL, CAMPSITE £

(☑01857-677214; www.thebarnwestray.co.uk; Chalmersquoy, Pierowall; sites £5 plus per person £1.50, dm £16; P) This excellent, intimate, modern 13-bed hostel is an Orcadian gem. It's heated throughout and has an inviting lounge, complete with DVD collection for when the weather turns foul. The price includes bed linen, shower and pristine kitchen facilities. Local advice comes free.

No 1 Broughton
B&B ££

(☑01857-677726; www.no1broughton.co.uk; Pierowall; s/d £35/60; P) This solid pinkish house sits right on Pierowall Bay and offers a very comfortable B&B with unusual extras such as original artworks on the walls and a sauna. There are three spacious rooms and a conservatory breakfast room where you can feel the sun but not that nasty wind.

Pierowall Hotel
PUB ££

(www.pierowallhotel.co.uk; Pierowall; mains £8-10; ⊙lunch & dinner) The heart of this island community, the local pub is famous throughout Orkney for its popular fish and chips – the fish is caught fresh by the hotel's boats and whatever has turned up in the day's catch is displayed on the blackboard. There are also some curries available, but the sea is the way to go here.

Bis Geos
SELF-CATERING ££

(☑01857-677420; www.bisgeos.co.uk; Bis Geos; per week from £292; P) Stunning views at this spectacular self-catering option between Pierowall and Noup Head.

ℹ️ **Getting There & Away**
There are flights from Kirkwall to Westray (one way £35, 20 minutes, one or two daily Monday to Saturday). A ferry links Kirkwall with Rapness (passenger/car £7.05/16.75, 1½ hours, daily).

PAPA WESTRAY

Known locally as Papay (*pa*-pee), this exquisitely peaceful, tiny island (4 miles long by a mile wide) attracts superlatives. It is home to Europe's oldest domestic building, the **Knap of Howar** (built about 5500 years ago), and to Europe's largest colony of arctic terns (about 6000 birds) at North Hill. Even the two-minute hop from Westray airfield is featured in *Guinness World Records* as the world's shortest scheduled air service. The island was also the cradle of Christianity in Orkney – **St Boniface's Church** was founded in the 8th century, though most of the recently restored structure is from the 12th century.

From May to September, **Jim Davidson** (📞01857-644259) runs boat trips to the **Holm of Papay**, a small island about a half-mile east of Papa Westray, for £5 per person. The main reason for a visit is to see the huge **chambered cairn**, with 16 beehive cells, and wall carvings. You enter through the roof – there's a torch so you can light the way as you crawl around in the gloomy interior.

Beltane Guest House & Hostel (📞01857-644224; www.papawestray.co.uk; dm/s/d £12/20/30; 🅿️), owned by the local community co-op, is the best place to stay on the island. It comprises a 20-bed hostel and a guesthouse with four simple and immaculate rooms with en suite. It's just over a mile north of the ferry.

B&B and tasty evening meals (dinner £17) are available at warm, welcoming **School Place** (📞01857-644268; sonofhewitj@aol.com; r per person £20). The conservatory is good for quiet reflection and the owners are *the* people to speak to about life in their beloved island community.

ℹ️ **Getting There & Away**
There are daily flights to Papa Westray (£17, 15 minutes) from Kirkwall, Monday to Saturday; there's an excellent £20 return offer.

There's also a passenger-only ferry from Pierowall to Papa Westray (£3.55, 25 minutes, three to six daily in summer); the crossing is free if you travel direct from the Rapness ferry. From October to April the boat sails by arrangement; phone 📞01857-677216.

NORTH RONALDSAY

Three miles long and almost completely flat, North Ronaldsay is a real outpost surrounded by rolling seas and big skies. The delicious peace and quiet and excellent birdwatching – fulmars, oystercatchers and terns are particularly numerous – lures visitors here; the island is home to cormorant and seal colonies and is an important stopover for migratory birds. There are enough old-style sheep here to seize power, but a 13-mile **drystone wall** right around the flat island keeps them off the grass; they make do with seaweed, which gives their meat a unique flavour.

At the north end of the island are two **lighthouses** – the old one was one of Scotland's earliest, while the new one is a Stevenson family special. Excellent **tours** (📞07703-112224; adult/child £4/2) of the latter and the adjacent **woollen mill** (adult/child £4/2, combined ticket £6/3) give you a real insight into the history and current lifestyle of the island. In the centre, the **New Kirk** (⊙24hr) holds an interesting exhibition of black-and-white photos that document various aspects of North Ronaldsay life.

Powered by wind and solar energy, **Observatory Guest House** (📞01857-633200; www.nrbo.co.uk; dm/s/d £14/33/66; 🅿️@📶) is a great spot next to the ferry pier, and offers first-rate accommodation and ornithological activities. There's a cafe-bar with lovely coastal views and convivial communal dinners (£12.50) in a sun-kissed (sometimes) conservatory: if you're lucky, local mutton might be on the menu. You can also camp here.

Garso Guest House (📞01857-633244; muir886@btinternet.com; B&B per person £35, cottage per person per night £30; 🅿️) is a comfortable B&B and self-catering cottage sleeping five, with an open fire and all your mod cons. It's at the northern end of the island, about 3 miles from the pier. It also offers a taxi and minibus service.

There are two or three daily flights to North Ronaldsay (£17, 20 minutes) from Kirkwall. There's a £20 return offer available that's great value. There's a weekly ferry from Kirkwall on Friday (passenger/car £7.05/16.75, 2½ hours).

SHETLAND ISLANDS

Adrift in the North Sea, and close enough to Norway geographically and historically to make nationality an ambiguous concept here, the Shetlands are Britain's northernmost outpost. There's a distinct Scandinavian lilt to the local accent, and walking down streets named King Haakon or St Olaf recalls the fact that the Shetlands were under Norse rule until 1469, when they were gifted to Scotland in lieu of the dowry of a Danish princess. The setting of this collection of mighty, wind-ravaged clumps of brown and green earth rising from the frigid waters of the North Sea is still uniquely Scottish, though, with deep, naked glens flanked by steep hills, twinkling, sky-blue lochs and, of course, sheep on the roads.

Despite the famous ponies and woollens, it's no agricultural backwater: the oil industry and military bases have ensured a certain prosperity, and a growing tourism industry takes advantage of its rich prehistoric heritage. Away from the semibustle of the capital, Lerwick, the isolation sweeps you off your feet – frequent thundering gales thrash across the raw landscape and mother nature whips up the wild Atlantic into white-cap frenzies that smash into imposing coastal cliffs.

One of the great attractions of the Shetlands is the birdlife (see boxed text, p435); it's worth packing binoculars even if you're not fanatical about it.

ⓘ Getting There & Around

AIR

The oil industry ensures that air connections are good. The main **airport** (www.hial.co.uk) is at Sumburgh, 25 miles south of Lerwick. **Flybe** (☑0871 700 0535; www.flybe.com) have daily services to Aberdeen, Kirkwall, Inverness, Edinburgh, and Glasgow; it also flies to Bergen (Norway) in summer. See individual islands for interisland flights.

BICYCLE

If it's fine, cycling on the islands' excellent roads can be an exhilarating way to experience the stark beauty of Shetland. It can, however, be very windy and there are few spots to shelter. Hire bikes from **Grantfield Garage** (☑01595-692709; www.grantfieldgarage.co.uk; North Rd, Lerwick; per day/week £7.50/40), among several other places, including Sumburgh Hotel, near the airport.

BOAT

Northlink Ferries (☑0845 600 0449; www.northlinkferries.co.uk) runs car ferries between Lerwick and Kirkwall in Orkney (see p405).

Northlink also runs overnight car ferries from Aberdeen to Lerwick (passenger £23 to £35, car £92 to £124, 12 to 14 hours, daily) leaving Aberdeen at 5pm or 7pm.

See individual islands for interisland ferries.

CAR & MOTORCYCLE

The wide roads seem more like motorways after Orkney's tiny, winding lanes. There are three car-hire outfits that process rentals with little fuss.

Bolts Car Hire (☑01595-693636; www.boltscarhire.co.uk; 26 North Rd, Lerwick) Small cars start from £39/177 per day/week. Office at airport.

Grantfield Garage (☑01595-692709; www.grantfieldgarage.co.uk; North Rd, Lerwick) The cheapest: from £23/118 per day/week.

Star Rent-a-Car (☑01595-692075; www.starrentacar.co.uk; 22 Commercial Rd, Lerwick) Opposite the bus station; from £36/164 per day/week. Office at airport.

Lerwick

POP 6830

Built on the herring trade, Lerwick is Shetland's only real town, home to about a third of the islands' population and dug into the hills of Bressay Sound on the island known as Mainland. It has a solid maritime feel, with aquiline oil-boats competing for harbour space with the dwindling fishing fleet. The water's clear blue tones makes wandering along atmospheric Commercial St a delightful stroll, and the town's excellent new museum provides all the cultural background you could desire.

◉ Sights

Shetland Museum | FREE | MUSEUM
(www.shetland-museum.org.uk; Hay's Dock; ◷10am-5pm Mon-Sat, noon-5pm Sun) This modern museum is an impressive recollection of 5000 years' worth of culture and people, and their interaction with this ancient landscape. Comprehensive but never dull, the display covers everything from the archipelago's geology to its fishing industry, via a great section on local mythology –find out about scary nyuggles, or use the patented machine for detecting trows. The Pictish carvings and replica jewellery are among the finest pieces; the museum also includes a working lighthouse mechanism, small

Shetland Islands Highlights

1 Discovering your inner Viking at Shetland's **Up Helly Aa** (p428) festival

2 Capering with puffins, spotting offshore orcas or dodging dive-bombing skuas in one of Shetland's fabulous **nature reserves** (p435)

3 Blowing away the cobwebs amid the raw, desolate and beautiful landscapes of **Unst** (p436) and **Yell** (p435)

4 Checking out Shetland's absorbing **museum** (p424), which details 5000 years' worth of history and landscapes

5 Watching the wild Shetland weather roll in to the spectacular cliffs of **Eshaness** (p434)

6 Exploring the islands' many layers of history at the ancient sights around **Sumburgh** (p432)

7 Taking advantage of the offbeat accommodation in a no-frills camping **böd** or a romantic **lighthouse cottage** (p429)

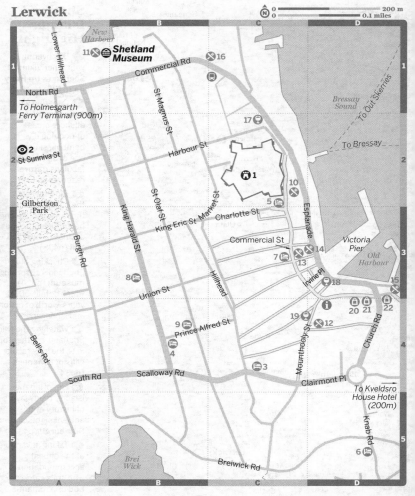

art gallery, and – what great smells – a boatbuilding workshop, where you can watch carpenters at work restoring and re-creating traditional Shetland fishing vessels.

FREE Clickimin Broch ARCHAEOLOGICAL SITE
(⊙24hr) This fortified site, just under a mile southwest of the town centre, was occupied from the 7th century BC to the 6th century AD. It's impressively large and its setting on a small loch gives it a feeling of being removed from the present day – unusual given the surrounding urban encroachment.

FREE Böd of Gremista HISTORIC BUILDING
(Gremista; ⊙10am-1pm & 2-5pm Tue-Sat May–mid-Sep) Across the harbour from the centre, this is well worth a visit. Once the headquarters of a fish-curing station, it was also the birthplace of Arthur Anderson, who went on to found P&O and who ploughed much of his wealth back into the local community. The friendly custodian is a delight.

FREE Fort Charlotte FORTIFICATION
(Charlotte St; ⊙9.30am-sunset) Above the town, there are excellent views from the battlements of Fort Charlotte, built in 1665 to protect the harbour from the Dutch navy.

Lerwick

Up-Helly-Aa Exhibition EXHIBITION
(www.uphellyaa.org; St Sunniva St; adult/child £3/1; 2-4pm & 7-9pm Tue, 7-9pm Fri, 2-4pm Sat mid-May–mid-Sep) This exhibition explains the truly bizarre, annual Viking fire festival (see the boxed text, p428).

✦ Festivals & Events
See also the boxed text, p428.
Folk Festival FOLK
(www.shetlandfolkfestival.com) Held during the last week of April.

Johnsmas Foy CULTURAL
(www.johnsmasfoy.com) Midsummer festival for four weeks in June.

Fiddle & Accordion Festival MUSIC
(www.shetlandaccordionandfiddle.com) Held in mid-October.

Fort Charlotte Guesthouse B&B ££
(01595-692140; www.fortcharlotte.co.uk; 1 Charlotte St; s £25-30, d £60;) Sheltering under the walls of the fortress, this great place offers very summery en suite rooms, including great singles. Views down the pedestrian street are on offer in some; sloping ceilings and oriental touches add charm to others. There's a bike shed and local salmon for breakfast. Very friendly; you'll need to book ahead.

Woosung B&B £
(01595-693687; sandraconroy43@btinternet.com; 43 St Olaf St; s/d £25/44) A budget gem in the heart of Lerwick B&B-land, this has a wise and welcoming host, and comfortable, clean, good-value rooms that share a bathroom. The solid stone house dates from the 19th century, built by a clipper captain who traded tea out of the port it's named after.

Isleburgh House Hostel HOSTEL £
(01595-745100; www.isleburgh.org.uk; King Harald St; dm/f £16.50/50; Apr-Sep; P@⌂♿) This typically grand Lerwick mansion houses an excellent hostel affiliated with the Scottish Youth Hostels Association (SYHA), with comfortable dorms, a shop, a laundry, a cafe and an industrial kitchen. Electronic keys offer excellent security and no curfew. It's wise to book ahead, and it's worth asking about winter availability as it sometimes opens for groups.

Kveldsro House Hotel HOTEL ££
(01595-692195; www.shetlandhotels.com; Greenfield Pl; s/d £98/120; P⌂) Shetland's most luxurious hotel overlooks the harbour. It's a dignified small hotel that will appeal to older visitors or couples looking for a treat. Rooms 415 and 417 are doubles with striking views over the harbour, or, if after a twin, try room 413, which has two walls of windows and Shetland views.

Clickimin Caravan & Camp Site CAMPSITE £
(01595-741000; www.srt.org.uk; Lochside; sites per small/large tent £8/11; P♿) By the loch on the western edge of town, Clickimin is a small and tidy park with good grassy sites. There's a laundry and shower block, and you've got a leisure centre with pool and more as part of the complex.

Carradale Guest House B&B ££
(01595-692251; carradale@btinternet.com; 36 King Harald St; s/d £35/60;) It's very amicable

ORKNEY & SHETLAND ISLANDS LERWICK

UP HELLY AA!!!

The long Viking history of the Shetlands has rubbed off in more ways than just street names and square-shouldered locals. Most villages have their own fire festival, a continuation of the old Viking midwinter celebrations of the rebirth of the sun. The most spectacular is in Lerwick.

Up Helly Aa (www.uphellyaa.org) takes place on the last Tuesday in January. Squads of 'guizers' dress in Viking costume and march through the streets with blazing torches, dragging a replica longship, which they then surround and burn, bellowing out Viking songs from behind bushy beards.

at Carradale and perpetually busy. The rooms, although a mix of old and new, are large and well furnished and provide a concoction of comforts for visitors. Couples should ask for the huge family room, which is traditionally decked out and has a private bathroom.

Grand Hotel HOTEL ££
(☏01595-692826; www.kgqhotels.co.uk; Commercial St; s/d £77/100; P🖳) Once the hub of town, this stately hotel isn't what it was when Victoria reigned, but ongoing modernisation is slowly bringing the rooms into the 21st century. Those on the top floors offer harbour views. Couples should go straight for room 330, which is an enormous room (refurbished with a four-poster bed) with dazzling harbour views.

Alderlodge Guest House B&B ££
(☏01595-695705; www.alder-lodge.co.uk; 6 Clairmont Pl; s/d £40/60; 🖳) This large stone building, a former bank, is a delightful place to stay. Imbued with a sense of space and light, common in these gracious old buildings, the rooms are large and, in this particular case, well furnished. The cordial hosts, who are flexible with checking-out and breakfast times, make the place special.

Eddlewood Guest House B&B ££
(☏01595-692772; catherinemarshall@live.co.uk; 8 Clairmont Pl; s/d £39/62) Run by a cheery soul, this sound selection has spacious, very well-kept rooms, some with limited sea views. The beds offer plenty of space to stretch out in, and these showers might just be Shetland's finest.

Glen Orchy House HOTEL ££
(☏01595-692031; www.guesthouselerwick.com; 20 Knab Rd, Breiwick Bay; s/d £60/85; P🖳) In a great spot close to the centre but also within a stone's throw of coastal walks, this huge place, once a convent, has spruce rooms and a large conservatory, complete with stunning coastal views. Friendly folk are complemented by good Thai food, among other choices.

✘ Eating

TOP CHOICE **Peerie Shop Cafe** CAFE £
(www.peerieshopcafe.com; Esplanade; snacks £2-5; ⊗9am-6pm Mon-Sat) If you've been craving proper espresso since leaving the mainland, head to this gem of a spot, with art exhibitions, wire-mounted halogens and industrial gantry chic. Newspapers, scrumptious cakes and sandwiches, hot chocolate that you deserve after that blasting wind outside, and, more rarely, outdoor seating, give everyone a reason to be here.

Monty's Bistro RESTAURANT ££
(☏01595-696555; 5 Mounthooly St; mains lunch £8-9, dinner £13-20; ⊗lunch Tue-Sat, dinner Mon-Sat) Though well tucked away behind the tourist office, this is far from a secret, and Shetlanders descend on its wee wooden tables with alacrity. The happy orange upstairs dining room is fragrant with aromas of Gressingham duck and local mussels from the short, quality menu, and the wine list has some welcome old friends.

Hay's Dock CAFE, RESTAURANT ££
(☏01595-741569; www.haysdock.co.uk; light lunches £3-6, dinner mains £13-18; ⊗lunch daily, dinner Thu-Sat) Upstairs in the Shetland Museum you'll find this place, with a glass front and optimistic balcony that look right over the water. Its clean lines and light wood recall Scandinavia, but the smart food relies on carefully selected local and Scottish produce on a short, quality menu.

Queen's Hotel RESTAURANT ££
(☏01595-692826; www.kqghotels.co.uk; mains £12-19; ⊗lunch & dinner) The dining room in this slightly run-down central hotel still wins marks for its big windows with sumptuous harbour views – ring ahead to book one of the ringside tables. While some of the roast-pork-with-delicate-fish combo platters are a bit strange, the seafood here is pretty good – the catch of the day is reliable, the Queen's stew is a feast of molluscs and crustaceans – and portions are generous.

Osla's Café

BISTRO £

(www.oslas.co.uk; 88 Commercial St; mains £7-13; ⊙lunch & dinner Mon-Sat, lunch Sun) Osla's is a sparky little joint that flips a mean pancake downstairs, but upstairs La Piazza is where you'll discover the joys of Italian cooking. Authentic, thin-crust pizzas are just like Papa used to make...well, almost.

Raba Indian Restaurant

SOUTH ASIAN £

(26 Commercial Rd; mains £5-8; ⊙lunch & dinner) Highly recommended curry house; Sunday buffet is a bargain at £9.50.

Fort Café

CAFE, TAKEAWAY £

(2 Commercial St; fish & chips £5-6; ⊙10am-8pm) Lerwick's salty air often creates fish-and-chip cravings. Eat in, or munch down on the pier if you don't mind the seagulls' envious stares.

Drinking & Entertainment

The Shetland Fiddlers Society plays at a number of locations and it's worth attending a session – inquire at the tourist office. Look out for Mareel, a new arts venue due to open on the waterfront near the museum in 2011.

Captain Flint's

PUB

(2 Commercial St; ⊙to 1am) This lively bar throbs with happy conversation and has a distinctly nautical, creaky-wooden feel. There's a cross-section of young 'uns, tourists, boat folk and older locals. There's live music some nights and a pool table upstairs. By some distance Lerwick's best pub.

Lounge

PUB

(4 Mounthooly St) A hospitable local bar patrolled by Andy Capp characters during the day, Lounge features a variety of live music performances several nights a week, including informal jam sessions.

Shopping

Best buys are the woollen jerseys, cardigans and sweaters for which Shetland is world-famous.

Spiders Web

KNITWEAR

(www.shetland-handknits.co.uk; 51 Commercial St) It's worth dropping in here as much for a chat as for the store's excellent array of hand-knitted garments, which are very high quality. The shop is opposite the Queen's Hotel.

Jamieson's Knitwear

KNITWEAR

(93 Commercial St) You'll find real Fair Isle sweaters with the distinctive OXOXO pattern here.

Shetland Times Bookshop

BOOKS

(www.shetland-times.co.uk; 71 Commercial St; ⊙Mon-Sat) Has every book you could possibly want to read about the Shetlands.

ℹ Information

Gilbert Bain Hospital (☎01595-743000; South Rd)

Shetland Library (Lower Hillhead; ⊙10am-7pm Mon, Wed & Fri, 10am-5pm Tue, Thu & Sat; @) Free internet.

Support Training (6a Mounthooly St; ⊙9am-5pm Mon-Fri) Free internet.

Tourist office (☎01595-693434; www.visit shetland.com; Market Cross; ⊙9am-5pm summer, 10am-4pm Mon-Sat winter) Helpful; good range of books and maps, and a comprehensive brochure selection.

ℹ Getting There & Around

For details of services to Lerwick, see p405. Ferries dock at Holmsgarth terminal, a 15-minute walk from the town centre. From Sumburgh airport, Leask's runs regular buses that meet flights.

If you need a taxi, call **Allied Taxis** (☎01595-690069; www.alliedtaxis.co.uk).

A LIGHT IN THE NORTH

Shetland offers intriguing options for getting off the beaten accommodation track. There's a great network of *böds* – simple rustic hostels with peat fires, which might mean bringing sleeping bag, coins for the meter, or even a campstove. We've listed some of these in the text, but there are more. Contact and book via **Shetland Amenity Trust** (☎01595-694688; www.camping-bods.com).

The same organisation runs three **lighthouse cottages** (☎01595-694688; www.lighthouse-holidays.com), all commanding dramatic views of rugged coastline: one near the airport at Sumburgh, one on the island of Bressay near Lerwick, and one in Mainland's northwest at Eshaness. Sleeping six to seven, the cottages cost from £190 to £230 for a three-night booking in high season.

Bressay & Noss

POP 350

Two islands lie across Bressay Sound east of Lerwick. The 34-sq-km island of Bressay (*bress*-ah) has some interesting walks, especially along the cliffs and up Ward Hill (226m), which has good views of the island.

The **Bressay Heritage Centre** (donation £2; ⊙10am-4pm Tue-Wed, Fri & Sat, 11am-5pm Sun May-Sep) is by the ferry dock and has an exhibition on Bressay life and history, as well as information about the mysterious Bronze Age mound that has been relocated alongside.

For serious **birdwatching**, visit Noss, a National Nature Reserve east of Bressay, to see huge seabird colonies on the island's 183m cliffs. Noss can only be visited from May to August, when Scottish Natural Heritage (SNH) operates a small visitor centre at Gungstie.

From Lerwick, **Seabirds & Seals** (☑07595-540224; www.seabirds-and-seals.com), among others, runs three-hour cruises (10am and 2pm) around Bressay and Noss for £40; you can book this by phone or at the Lerwick tourist office.

You can pause for an ale or excellent shellfish meal at **Maryfield Hotel** (☑01595-820207; mains £7-15; P), which offers secluded accommodation (singles/doubles £40/65) near the ferry. **Northern Lights Holistic Spa** (☑01595-820257; www.shetlandspa.com; Uphouse; d £100; P☎) offers colourful, relaxing en suite accommodation and various massage and spa treatments. Use of the sauna and steam room is included in the room rate, and it serves very smart meals.

ⓘ Getting There & Away

Daily ferries (passenger/car return £3.60/8.40, seven minutes, frequent) link Lerwick and Bressay. It's then 2.5 miles across the island (some people bring hired bikes from Lerwick) to take the inflatable dinghy to Noss (adult/child £3/1.50, 10am to 5pm Tuesday, Wednesday and Friday to Sunday late April to August), but check with the **SNH** (☑0800 107 7818) before leaving Lerwick, as the dinghy doesn't operate in bad weather.

Central & West Mainland

SCALLOWAY

POP 812

The former capital of Shetland, Scalloway (*scall*-o-wah), on the west coast 6 miles from Lerwick, is now a busy fishing village set around bare, rolling hills. The main landmark is **Scalloway Castle** (HS; www.historic-scotland.co.uk; admission free), with a well-preserved 15th-century keep. In theory, by the time you read this, the nearby Scalloway Museum – with displays on the town's glory days and the war years – should have moved to smart new premises next to the castle, which you would enter from it. However, at the time of research, the construction company had gone bust, leaving the project hanging. If the castle's not open, keys should be in the Scalloway Hotel.

During WWII the Norwegian resistance operated the 'Shetland Bus' from here. The trips carried agents, wireless operators and military supplies for the resistance movement, returning with refugees, recruits for the Free Norwegian Forces and, in December, Christmas trees for the treeless Shetlands! The **Shetland Bus Memorial** is a moving tribute on the waterfront, built of stones from both countries.

Close to the waterfront, the **Scalloway Hotel** (☑01595-880444; scalloway.hotel@btconnect.com; Main St; s/d £65/90; P) has modern, spotless rooms with small en suites. Some rooms have good views over the harbour and there's some really tasty, creative bar food here, as well as more upmarket fare in the restaurant.

Being in the North Atlantic Fisheries College, it's no surprise that the **Da Haaf Restaurant** (☑01595-880747; www.nafc.ac.uk; Port Arthur; mains £9-14; ⊙lunch Wed-Fri, dinner Thu-Fri) specialises in seafood – excellent local seafood at that. It's solid value, but ring ahead to check it's open.

Buses run from Lerwick (25 minutes, roughly hourly Monday to Saturday) to Scalloway.

WEISDALE

The gallery in the restored **Weisdale Mill** (Weisdale; admission free; ⊙10.30am-4.30pm Tue-Sat, noon-4.30pm Sun) has monthly, changing exhibitions, and everything – jewellery, crafts and paintings – is on sale. It's an excellent place to visit, and you're likely to meet some resident artists. There's also a cafe in a sunlit conservatory overlooking the burn (stream).

On the western shore of Weisdale Voe, south of the mill, are the ruins of the house where John Clunies Ross (1786–1853) was born. In 1827 he settled in the Indian Ocean's Cocos Islands, where he proclaimed himself king.

WESTERN SIDE

The western side of Mainland is notable for its varied scenery: bleak moors, sheer cliffs, rolling green hills and numerous cobalt-blue lochs and inlets. It's ideal for walking, cycling and fishing. The main settlement out here is Walls, which has basic services, B&Bs and a *böd* but doesn't really entice.

Out in the Atlantic 15 miles southwest of Walls, **Foula** (Bird Island) supports 42 people, 1500 sheep and 500,000 seabirds, including the rare Leach's petrel and Scotland's largest colony of great skuas. It's all amid dramatic cliff scenery, particularly the awesome, sheer Kame (372m). There isn't a shop on the island, but centrally located **Leraback B&B** (☑01595-753226; www.originart.com/leraback/leraback.html; Leraback; B&B incl dinner per person £35; P) offers accommodation and good food.

There are **ferries** (☑07881-823732; www.atlanticferries.co.uk) from Walls or Scalloway (passenger/car and driver one way £3.40/15.80, four hours, two to four weekly) and **flights** (☑01595-840246; www.directflight.co.uk) from Tingwall (return £53).

Northwest from Walls, the road crosses desolate moorland and then descends through green fields before arriving at the small crofting community of **Sandness**. Visible about a mile offshore is the island of **Papa Stour**, home to huge colonies of auks, terns and skuas. It's mostly made up of volcanic rock that has eroded to form sea caves, underground passages, arches and columns. Access to the island is by **ferry** (☑01957-722259) from West Burrafirth (passenger return £6.80, car and driver return £8.40, 40 minutes, daily except Tuesday and Thursday), east of Sandness, or Tuesday flights from Tingwall (return £37.50), with a day return possible. There's a **bunkhouse** (☑01595-873227; www.hurdibackhostel.co.uk; dm £20) on the island.

South Mainland

From Lerwick, the main road south winds 25 miles down the eastern side of this long, narrow, hilly tail of land to Sumburgh Head. The waters lapping against the cliffs are an inviting turquoise in many places. If it weren't for the raging Arctic gales, you may almost be tempted to have a dip.

DON'T MISS

SEA KAYAKING IN SHETLAND

Paddling is a top way to explore Shetland's tortuous coastline, and allows you to get up close to seals and bird life without the roar of the motor scaring them away. At Burra Island, 5 miles from Scalloway, **Sea Kayak Shetland** (☑07887-535659; www.seakayakshetland.co.uk) is a reliable, professional operator that caters for beginner and expert, and also offers simple accommodation.

SANDWICK & AROUND

Opposite the scattered village of Sandwick, where you pass the 60-degree latitude line, is the small isle of Mousa, an RSPB reserve protecting some 7000 breeding pairs of nocturnal storm petrels. Mousa is also home to rock-basking seals as well as impressive **Mousa Broch**, the best preserved of these northern fortifications. Rising to 13m, it's an imposing structure, typically double-walled, and with a spiral staircase to access a 2nd floor. It features in two Viking sagas as a hide-out for eloping couples; these days petrels favour it as a nesting spot.

From April to mid-September, **Tom Jamieson** (☑01950-431367; www.mousaboattrips.co.uk) runs daily boat trips (adult/child £13/6.50, 25 minutes) from Leebitton harbour in Sandwick, allowing two hours on Mousa. He also conducts night trips to view the petrels.

Back on Mainland, **Hoswick Visitor Centre** (Hoswick; admission free; ☉10am-5pm Mon-Sat, 11am-5pm Sun May-Sep; @) has a great collection of old wirelesses. There are displays on fishing, whaling, weaving and peat casting as well as internet access and a cafe.

Nearby, there's plenty of comfort at the **Orca Country Inn** (☑01950-431226; www.orcacountryinn.co.uk; Hoswick; s/d/f £43/65/73; P☎), which offers great views from its lounge area and its cosy chambers named after birds. They are decorated with great photos by one of the owners, who runs photography courses here.

In Sandwick, **Solbrekke** (☑01950-431410; Park Rd, Sandwick; s/d £25/50; P) is a welcoming spot that overlooks the isle of Mousa from its hilltop vantage point.

There are buses between Lerwick and Sandwick (25 minutes, three to seven daily).

BIGTON & AROUND
Buses from Lerwick stop twice daily (Monday to Saturday) in Bigton on the west coast, but it's another couple of miles to the **tombolo** (a narrow isthmus) that connects Mainland with St Ninian's Isle. This geologically important site is the largest shell-and-sand tombolo in Britain and is a Site of Special Scientific Interest (SSSI).

Walk across the tombolo to beautiful, emerald-capped **St Ninian's Isle**, where you'll find the ruins of a 12th-century church, beneath which are traces of an earlier Pictish church. During excavations in 1958, Pictish treasure, probably dating from AD 800 and consisting of 27 silver objects, was found beneath a broken sandstone slab. They're now kept in the Museum of Scotland in Edinburgh, though there are replicas in Lerwick's Shetland Museum.

BODDAM & SCOUSBURGH
From small Boddam a side road leads to the **Shetland Crofthouse Museum** (admission free; ◐10am-1pm & 2-5pm May-Sep). The years drop away when you enter, as you step back into a primitive existence. Built in 1870, it has been restored, thatched and furnished with 19th-century furniture and utensils. The Lerwick–Sumburgh bus stops right outside.

West of Boddam, Scousburgh sits placidly above Shetland's best beach, gloriously white **Scousburgh Sands**. Near Scousburgh is the **Spiggie Hotel** (☏01950-460409; www.thespiggiehotel.co.uk; s/d £55/100; P❡), with compact rooms and good seafood (lunch Wednesday to Sunday, dinner daily). The rooms and dining room boast great views down over the local loch, which offers fishing and birdwatching opportunities.

QUENDALE
South of Boddam, a minor road runs southwest to Quendale. Here you'll find the small but excellent, restored and fully operational 19th-century **Quendale Watermill** (www.quendalemill.co.uk; adult/child £2/50p; ◐10am-5pm mid-Apr–mid-Oct), the last of Shetland's watermills. There's a cafe here.

The village overlooks a long, sandy beach to the south in the Bay of Quendale. West of the bay there's dramatic cliff scenery and **diving** in the waters between Garth's Ness and Fitful Head and to the wreck of the oil tanker *Braer* off Garth's Ness.

From Lerwick there are two buses daily to Quendale, from Monday to Saturday.

SUMBURGH
With its clear waters, sea cliffs, and grassy headlands jutting out into sparkling blue waters, Sumburgh is one of the most scenic places to stay on the island. There's a seven-day tourist office at Sumburgh airport, with internet access.

◉ Sights

Jarlshof ARCHAEOLOGICAL SITE
(HS; www.historic-scotland.gov.uk; adult/child £4.70/2.80, 20% off with Old Scatness ticket; ◐9.30am-5.30pm Apr-Sep) Old and new collide at Mainland's southern tip, where Sumburgh airport is only a few metres from Jarlshof, a picturesque and instructive archaeological site covering various periods of occupation from 2500 BC to AD 1500. You can clearly see the complete change that happened when the Vikings arrived: their rectangular longhouses are in marked contrast to the brochs, roundhouses, and wheelhouses that preceded them. Atop the site is the Old House of Sumburgh, built in the 16th century and named 'Jarlshof' in a novel by Sir Walter Scott. There's an informative audio tour included with admission.

Old Scatness ARCHAEOLOGICAL SITE
(www.shetland-heritage.co.uk/amenitytrust; Dunrossness; adult/child £4/3, 20% discount with Jarlshof ticket; ◐10am-5pm Sun-Thu May-Oct) Brings Shetland's prehistoric past vividly and entertainingly to life; it's a must-see for archaeology buffs but fun for kids too. Clued-up guides in Iron Age clothes show you around the site, which is still being studied, and has provided important clues on the Viking takeover, and the dating of these northern Scottish sites in general. Discovered when building an airport access road, the site has revealed an impressive broch from around 300 BC, roundhouses and later wheelhouses. Best of all is the reconstruction of one of these, complete with smoky peat fire and working loom.

Sumburgh Head BIRDWATCHING
(www.rspb.org.uk) Near Jarlshof, and clearly visible from the site, the spectacular cliffs of Sumburgh Head, a mile from the main road, offer a good chance to get up close and personal with puffins, and also to see huge nesting colonies of fulmars, guillemots and razorbills. If you're lucky, you might spot dolphins or orcas; the car-park noticeboard

advises on recent sightings. The other important birdwatching area is the **Pool of Virkie**, the bay just east of the airport.

🛏 Sleeping & Eating

Another option is atmospheric Sumburgh Lighthouse cottage (see p429).

Betty Mouat's Böd   HOSTEL **£**
(Dunrossness; dm £8; P) Just behind Old Scatness, this is a simple and comfortable hostel with peat fire (£5 a bag), power and decent hot-water bathrooms. Book via the Trust (see boxed text, p429) or at Old Scatness.

Sumburgh Hotel   HOTEL **££**
(☎01950-460201;   www.sumburghhotel.com; Sumburgh; s/d £65/80; P@🛜) Next to Jarlshof is an upmarket, country-style hotel with a high standard of accommodation. There are fine views for birdwatchers, prehistorians and plane-spotters, comfortable pinkish rooms, and excellent restaurant and bar meals. Larger sea-view rooms cost more (singles/doubles £80/100).

🛈 Getting There & Away

To get to Sumburgh from Lerwick, take the airport bus (45 minutes, four to six daily).

Fair Isle

POP 70

It's a stomach-churning ferry ride to Fair Isle but it's worth it for the stunning cliff scenery, isolation and hordes of winged creatures. About halfway to Orkney, Fair Isle is one of Scotland's most remote inhabited islands. It's only 3 miles by 1.5 miles in size and is probably best known for its patterned knitwear, still produced in the island's co-operative, Fair Isle Crafts.

It's also a paradise for birdwatchers, who form the bulk of the island's visitors. Fair Isle is in the flight path of migrating birds, and thousands breed here. They're monitored by the **Bird Observatory**, which collects and analyses information year-round; visitors are welcome to participate.

Small **George Waterston Memorial Centre** (Taft; donations welcome; ⊙2-4pm Mon, 10.30am-noon Wed, 2-4pm Fri May-Sep) has photos and exhibits on the island's natural history, crofting, fishing, archaeology and knitwear.

The smart new **Fair Isle Lodge & Bird Observatory** (☎01595-760258; www.fairislebirdobs.co.uk; s/d with full board £55/100; ⊙May-Oct; P@🛜🛏) offers good en suite rooms.

Rates are full board, and there are free guided walks and other bird-related displays and activities.

🛈 Getting There & Away

From Tingwall, **DirectFlight** (☎01595-840246; www.directflight.co.uk) operates flights to Fair Isle (£60 return, 25 minutes, twice on Monday, Wednesday and Friday year-round and on Saturday May to September). A day-return ticket allows about seven hours on the island. **Ferries** (☎01595-760363) sail from Grutness (near Sumburgh) with the odd one from Lerwick to Fair Isle (person/car and driver one way £3.40/15.80, three hours, Tuesday and Saturday year-round and Thursday from May to early October). You can also book a boat charter with **Cycharters** (☎01595-696598; cycharters@ aol.com).

North Mainland

The north of Mainland is very photogenic – jumbles of cracked, peaty, brown hills blend with grassy pastureland and extend like bony fingers of land into numerous lochs and out into the wider, icy, grey waters of the North Sea. Different shades of light give it a variety of characters. Around Hillswick, there's stunning scenery and several good places to stay; this makes one of the best bases in the Shetlands.

VOE

Lower Voe is a pretty collection of buildings beside a tranquil bay on the southern shore of Olna Firth.

In previous incarnations, **Sail Loft** (☎01806-588327; www.camping-bods.co.uk; Lower Voe; dm £9), by the pier, was a fishing shed and knitwear factory, but it's now a camping *böd,* with coin-operated showers and fuel for sale (see boxed text, p429). Opposite, try the excellent seafood, including local salmon, in the appealing, wood-panelled **Pierhead Restaurant & Bar** (Lower Voe; mains £10-16; ⊙lunch & dinner). Eat at the upstairs restaurant or go for the cheaper bar meals downstairs.

There are buses from Lerwick to Voe (35 minutes, up to six daily Monday to Saturday).

WHALSAY & OUT SKERRIES

South of Voe, the B9071 branches east to Laxo, the ferry terminal for the island of **Whalsay**. This is one of the most prosperous islands, due to its large fishing fleet based at the modern harbour of **Symbister**.

Whalsay is popular for sea angling, and for trout fishing in its lochs. There are also scenic walks where colonies of seabirds breed and where you may catch sight of seals.

Grieve House (☎01595-694688; www.camping-bods.com; beds £8), the former home of poet Hugh MacDiarmid, is now a camping *böd*. There's no electricity or shower, but there is fuel for sale. Heading out of Symbister towards Isbister, it's on the left about half a mile from town. Not far beyond, the **Oot Ower** (☎01806-566658) offers self-catering bungalows and a weekend-only bar and Chinese restaurant. You can camp here too.

Regular **ferries** (☎01806-566259; www.shetland.gov.uk/ferries) link Laxo and Symbister (car/passenger return £3.60/8.40, 30 minutes, daily).

Northeast of Whalsay, another thriving fishing community occupies the tiny **Out Skerries**, made up of the three main islands of Housay, Bruray (these two connected by a road bridge) and Grunay, plus a number of islets. Their rugged cliffs teem with birdlife.

There are **ferries** (☎01806-515226) between Out Skerries and Lerwick on Tuesday and Thursday (passenger/car and driver return £5.60/8, 2½ hours), and Friday to Monday to Vidlin (only sails if booked; passenger/car and driver return £6.80/8.40, 1½ hours), 3 miles northeast of Laxo.

BRAE & AROUND

Accommodation is the reason to stop in the township of Brae; there are several guesthouses. However, you should book in advance, as they mainly cater to oil workers. There's fine **walking** on the peninsula west of Brae, and to the south on the red-granite island of **Muckle Roe**, which is connected to the peninsula by a bridge. Muckle Roe also offers good **diving** off its west and north coasts.

Just outside Brae and built in 1588, luxurious, genteel **Busta House Hotel** (☎01806-522506; www.bustahouse.com; s/d £90/110; Ⓟ⊛) is perhaps Shetland's most characterful hotel, with a long, sad history and inevitable rumours of a (friendly) ghost. Refurbished rooms are tastefully decked out, and retain a classy but homely charm. They're all individually designed and named after places in Shetland. Rooms with sea view and/or four-poster bed cost a little more. The **restaurant** (4-course dinner £35) is also excellent.

The Busta offers the best dining in the area, but there are a couple of pubs, a chippie and an Indian takeaway in Brae, so you won't be short of a cheaper bite. There's a supermarket at the road junction in the centre of town.

Buses from Lerwick to Eshaness and North Roe stop in Brae (35 minutes, up to seven daily Monday to Saturday).

ESHANESS & HILLSWICK

Eleven miles northwest of Brae the road ends at the red basalt cliffs of Eshaness, which form some of the most impressive, wild coastal scenery in Shetland. Howling Atlantic gales whip the ocean into a whitecap frenzy before it crashes into the base of the cliffs. When the wind subsides there is superb **walking** and panoramic views from the lighthouse (closed to the public) on the headland.

A mile east of Eshaness, a side road leads south to the **Tangwick Haa Museum** (admission free; ◷11am-5pm mid-Apr–Sep), housed in a restored 17th-century house. The wonderful collection of ancient B&W photos capture the sense of community here.

At **Hamnavoe**, which you reach from another side road heading north, about 3.5 miles east of Eshaness, is **Johnny Notions Camping Böd** (☎01595-694688; www.camping-bods.co.uk; beds £8; ◷Apr-Sep), offering four spacious berths in a cute wee stone cottage with a challengingly low door. It's very basic; there are no showers or electricity. This was the birthplace of Johnny 'Notions' Williamson, an 18th-century blacksmith who inoculated several thousand people against smallpox using a serum and method he had devised himself.

Decent campsites and tasty light meals served in a cafe with stunning views over St Magnus Bay, and its weird and wonderful rock formations, are on offer at **Braewick Café & Caravan Park** (☎01806-503345; www.eshaness.shetland.co.uk; Braewick; sites/wigwams £7/33; ◷10am-5pm Mar-Oct). It also offers 'wigwams' – wooden huts with fridge and kettle that sleep four, or six at a pinch.

Follow the puffin signpost a mile short of Hillswick to **Almara B&B** (☎01806-503261; www.almara.shetland.co.uk; Urafirth; s/d £30/60; Ⓟ⊛) and get the most wonderful welcome in the Shetlands. With sweeping views over the bay, this house has a great lounge, a few unusual features in the excellent rooms and bathrooms, and a good eye on the environ-

For birdwatchers, Shetland is paradise. As well as being a stopover for migrating Arctic species, there are vast seabird breeding colonies. Every bird seems to have its own name here: rain geese are red-throated divers, bonxies are great skuas, and alamooties are storm petrels.

Of the 24 sea-bird species that nest in the British Isles, 21 are found here; June is the height of the breeding season. The **Royal Society for the Protection of Birds** (RSPB; ☎01950-460800; www.rspb.org.uk) maintains several reserves on south Mainland and on the island of Fetlar. There are National Nature Reserves at **Hermaness** (where you can't fail to be entertained by the clownish antics of the almost tame puffins), **Keen of Hamar** and on the **Isle of Noss**. **Fair Isle** also supports large sea-bird populations.

But keep an eye on the sea itself: killer whales are regularly sighted, as are other cetaceans, as well as sea otters. A useful website for all species is www.nature-shetland.co.uk, which details latest sightings.

Take care when birdwatching as the cliff-edge sites can be dangerous.

---

ment. You'll feel completely at home and appreciated; this is B&B at its best.

In Hillswick itself, **St Magnus Bay Hotel** (☎01806-503372; www.stmagnusbayhotel.co.uk; s/d £65/95; P🐾) occupies a wonderful wooden mansion built in 1896 and transferred here from the Glasgow Exhibition. Enthusiastic new owners have injected some much-needed TLC and are renovating it beautifully. The rooms vary in size, shape, and views – grab one of the corner ones for a stunning double vista over the bay – but all are very appealing. There's a sauna for guests to use, and a lounge bar doing food: a great place to stay.

Down on the quay, **Da Böd** (www.shetlandwildlifesanctuary.com; Hillswick; suggested donation per dish £3-8; ⊙noon-6pm Thu-San May-Sep) serves vegetarian food in a hippy crofters' house, which is actually a 300-year-old former Hanseatic trading-post house and one of Shetland's oldest buildings. All proceeds go to the local wildlife sanctuary. Don't rely on it being open.

Buses from Lerwick run (evenings only) to Hillswick (1¼ hours) and Eshaness (1½ hours).

The North Isles

Yell, Unst and Fetlar make up the North Isles, all connected to each other by ferry.

YELL
POP 1100

Yell if you like but nobody will hear; the desolate peat moors here are typical Shetland scenery. The bleak landscape has an appeal though: Yell is all about colours – the browns and vivid, lush greens of the bogland, grey clouds thudding through the skies and the steely blue waters of the North Atlantic, which are never far away. The peat makes the ground look cracked and parched, although it's swimming most of the year. Though many folk fire on through to Unst, Yell offers several good hill walks, especially around the **Herra peninsula**, about halfway up the west coast.

Across Whale Firth from the peninsula is **Lumbister RSPB Reserve**, where red-throated divers (called rain geese in Shetland), merlins, skuas and other bird species breed. The area is home to a large otter population, too, best viewed around Whale Firth, where you may also spot common and grey seals.

South of Lumbister, on the hillside above the main road, stand the reputedly haunted ruins of **Windhouse**, dating from 1707. About a mile east of here is **Mid Yell**, the island's largest village. The road north to Gutcher passes **Basta Voe**, where many otters inhabit the shores. In the north, around **Cullivoe**, there's more good walking along the attractive coastline.

From the southern ferry terminal, the road leads 4 miles east to Burravoe. The **Old Haa Museum** (admission free; ⊙10am-4pm Tue-Thu & Sat, 2-5pm Sun Apr-Sep) has a medley of curious objects (pipes, a piano, a doll-in-cradle, tiny bibles, ships in bottles and a sperm-whale jaw) as well as an archive of local history and a tearoom.

🛏 Sleeping & Eating

After a couple of closures, sleeping options are limited, to say the least. But there are lots of excellent self-catering cottages dotted around the island: check www.visitshet land.com for options.

Windhouse Lodge HOSTEL £

(☎01957-702475; www.camping-bods.co.uk; Mid Yell; beds £9) Below the haunted ruins of Windhouse, and on the A968, you'll find this well-kept, clean, snug camping *böd* with a pot-belly stove to warm your toes. Book via phone or the website.

Wind Dog Café CAFE £

(www.winddogcafe.co.uk; Gutcher; snacks & light meals £3-5; ☺9am-5pm Mon-Fri, 10am-5pm Sat & Sun, dinner Jun-Aug; @) While you're waiting for the ferry to Unst, you can snack at this warm, eclectic little cafe. It serves up paninis, burgers and hot drinks. There's also a small library, ideal if the rain is pelting outside. It was up for sale at the time of research so may change.

ℹ Getting There & Away

Yell is connected with Mainland by **ferry** (☎01957-722259; www.shetland.gov.uk/ferries) between Toft and Ulsta (passenger/car and driver return £3.60/8.40, 20 minutes, frequent). Although you don't need to book, it's wise to do so in the summer months.

There are two buses Monday to Saturday from Lerwick to Yell and Unst, and a further one to Toft ferry pier (one hour). Connecting buses at Ulsta serve other parts of the island.

UNST

POP 1100

You're fast running out of Scotland once you cross to Unst, a rugged island of ponies and seabirds. It's prettier than Yell with bare, velvety-smooth hills and clusters of settlements that cling to their waterside locations, fiercely resisting the buffeting winds. It also feels less isolated and has more of a community.

Its stellar attraction is the marvellous headland of **Hermaness**, where a 4.5-mile round walk from the reserve entrance at the end of the road takes you to cliffs where gannets, fulmars and guillemots nest and numerous puffins frolic. The path is guarded by a small army of great skuas, known hereabouts as bonxies. They nest in the nearby heather, and dive-bomb at will if they feel threatened. They're damn solid birds too, but they don't usually make contact. From the cliffs, you can see Britain's most northerly point, the rocks of **Out Stack**, and **Muckle Flugga**, with its lighthouse built by Robert Louis Stevenson's uncle. Stevenson wrote *Treasure Island* while living on Unst. For more tips on wildlife-watching duck into the **Hermaness Visitor Centre** (admission free; ☺9am-5pm Apr–mid-Sep), near the reserve's entrance. You can book **boat trips** (☎01806-522447; www. muckleflugga.co.uk; ☺Tue, Thu, Sat Jun-Sep) to Muckle Flugga from here.

Unst has a wide variety of vegetation; some of the most unusual examples can be seen at the 30-hectare **Keen of Hamar National Nature Reserve**, located northeast of Baltasound.

Unst Heritage Centre (Haroldswick; adult/child £2/free, joint Unst Boat Haven ticket £3; ☺11am-5pm May-Sep) houses a modern museum with a history of the Shetland pony, and a nostalgic look at the past. There's a re-creation of a croft house complete with box bed and, for weather-obsessed Brits, a summary of the last 170 years of weather in the Shetlands.

Unst Boat Haven (Haroldswick; adult/child £2/free, joint Unst Heritage Centre ticket £3; ☺11am-5pm May-Sep) is housed in a large shed and is every boaty's delight, with rowing and sailing boats, photographs of more boats, and maritime artefacts.

Viking Unst (www.vikingshetland.com) is a project to promote the island's various Viking sites. The centrepiece, a reconstructed longhouse and replica longship, was being built on the main road just south of Haroldswick last time we passed by.

At the turn-off from the main road to Littlehamar, just north of Baltasound, don't miss what is certainly the most impressive **bus stop** (www.unstbusshelter.shetland. co.uk) in Britain. Enterprising locals, tired of waiting in discomfort, have installed an armchair, novels, flowers, a telly, an old Amstrad computer and a visitors' book to sign. It was all in orange when we visited, but the colour scheme changes yearly.

Also in Baltasound, but due to move to the Saxa Vord complex in Haroldswick, **Valhalla Brewery** (www.valhallabrewery.co.uk; ☺9am-5pm Mon-Fri) brews the most northerly beer in Britain, including its Island Bere, a throwback to original ale made with an indigenous barley variety.

🛏 Sleeping & Eating

Historic 18th-century **Belmont House** (www.belmontunst.org.uk), on the left as you leave the southern ferry terminal, was being restored at the time of research, and was due to offer en suite rooms. Self-caterers can stock up at shops in Uyeasound, Baltasound and Haroldswick.

TOP CHOICE **Gardiesfauld Hostel** HOSTEL **£**
(☎01957-755279; www.gardiesfauld.shetland.co.uk; Uyeasound; tent & 2 people £6, dm £12; ☺Apr-Sep; ℗) This 35-bed hostel is very clean, has most spacious dorms with lockers, family rooms, a garden, an elegant lounge and a wee conservatory dining area with great bay views. You can camp here too. Nonresidents are welcome to use common areas. The bus stops right outside. Bring 20p pieces for the shower.

Saxa Vord HOSTEL **£**
(☎01957-711711; www.saxavord.com; Haroldswick; s/d £18.50/37; ℗🖥) This former Royal Air Force base is something of a white elephant these days, but various plans are afoot. It's not the most atmospheric lodging place, but the barracks-style rooms offer great value for singles and couples, and there's something nice about watching the rain squalls through the window and skylight. The restaurant (open mid-May to September) dishes out reasonable local food, there's a bar – Britain's northernmost, by our reckoning – and a friendly, helpful atmosphere. Self-catering holiday houses here are good for families.

Prestegaard B&B **££**
(☎01957-755234; s/d £28/50; ℗) This solid old manse near the water in Uyeasound makes a great base. Rooms are spacious and very comfy, with water views and exterior, but private, bathroom. We particularly like the upstairs one. The breakfast room with Up Helly Aa shields and axes on the wall will bring out the Viking in you, and the kindly owner will make your stay a delightful one.

Baltasound Hotel HOTEL, PUB **££**
(☎01957-711334; www.baltasound-hotel.shetland.co.uk; Baltasound; s/d £49/78; ℗) The cottage-style rooms inside this solid place are better than the rooms in the nearby chalets, which

are a bit cramped. It's also a decent watering hole with a lovely country outlook, and does adequate bar meals in a dining room dappled by the evening sun.

❶ Getting There & Away

Unst is connected with Yell by a small car **ferry** (☎01957-722259; www.shetland.gov.uk/ferries) between Gutcher and Belmont (free, 10 minutes, frequent).

There are two buses Monday to Saturday from Lerwick to Yell and Unst.

FETLAR
POP 90
Fetlar is the smallest but most fertile of the North Isles. There's great **birdwatching** here, and the 705 hectares of grassy moorland around Vord Hill (159m) in the north form the **Fetlar RSPB Reserve**. Common and grey seals can also be seen on the shores. Much of the reserve is off limits in the summer breeding season but it's still the best time to see birds, including the red-necked phalarope.

Scenic **walking** is possible on much of the island, especially around the bay near Tresta, at Urie and Gruting in the north, and Funzie in the east.

There's no petrol on Fetlar, but there's a part-time shop in Houbie, the main village. The excellent **Fetlar Interpretive Centre** (www.fetlar.com; Houbie; adult/child £2/free; ☺1-5pm Mon-Fri, 2-5pm Sat & Sun May-Sep) has photos, audio recordings and videos on the island and its history.

The **Garths Campsite** (☎01957-733227; Gord; sites £5-9; ☺May-Sep), 2.5 miles from the ferry, overlooks the beach at Tresta and has great facilities. Run by the same people is friendly **Gord B&B** (☎01957-733227; nicboxall@btinternet.com; Gord; s/d/tw £35/50/70, dinner £15; ℗), with terrific sea views and two twin rooms and one double, all with en suite. There's also a camping *böd* (see boxed text, p429) on the island.

Four to seven daily free **ferries** (☎01957-722259; www.shetland.gov.uk/ferries) connect Fetlar with Gutcher on Yell and Belmont on Unst.

Understand
Scotland

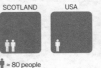

population per sq mile

SCOTLAND   USA   ENGLAND

👤 ≈ 80 people

Scotland Today

Scottish Politics

Although an integral part of Great Britain since 1707, Scotland has maintained a separate and distinct identity throughout the last 300 years. The return of a devolved Scottish parliament to Edinburgh in 1999 marked a growing confidence and pride in the nation's achievements.

The first decade of devolution has seen Scottish politics diverge significantly from the Westminster way, with Holyrood led by a minority Scottish National Party (SNP) administration since 2007. Distinctive policies that have been applied in Scotland but not in the rest of the UK include free long-term care for the elderly, the abolition of tuition fees for university students and higher pay for teachers. The SNP has committed itself to a referendum on whether Scotland should have full independence, but opinion polls show that most Scots are happy with the status quo.

The election of a Conservative/Lib Dem coalition government in Westminster in 2010 only served to heighten the political difference between Scotland and the rest of the UK – only one of Scotland's 59 constituencies returned a Conservative MP, while the Labour Party (which was defeated in Westminster) increased its share of the Scottish vote.

Transport

If you're unfortunate enough to find yourself driving into one of Scotland's cities during the weekday rush hour, you'll soon find that traffic congestion is one of the country's curses. Edinburgh has led the way in trying to discourage car use, with popular measures such as cycle routes, dedicated bus lanes and Park & Ride schemes, and unpopular ones such as increased parking charges and fines. Construction work is well under way on a scheme to reintroduce trams to the city by 2011 (try

» Highest point: Ben Nevis (1344m)

» Annual whisky export: 1 billion bottles

» Value of haggis sold for Burns Night: £1.2 million

» Number of times Scotland has won the football World Cup: 0

Top Books

Raw Spirit (Iain Banks) An enjoyable jaunt around Scotland in search of the perfect whisky.
Mountaineering in Scotland (WH Murray) Classic account of hiking in Scotland in the 1930s, when just getting to Glen Coe was an adventure in itself.

Adrift in Caledonia (Nick Thorpe) An insightful tale of hitchhiking around Scotland on a variety of vessels.
Stone Voices: The Search for Scotland (Neal Ascherson) A personal exploration of Scottish history and culture.

Classic DVDs

Tutti Frutti Iconic 1980s TV series about a fading rock band's last tour, with Robbie Coltrane and Emma Thompson.
The Maggie Classic 1950s Ealing comedy about the crew of a puffer on the west coast of Scotland.

belief systems
(% of population)

43
Church of
Scotland

28
Nonreligious

16
Roman
Catholic

6.8
Other
Christian

1.2
Other
0.8% Islamic
0.1% Buddhist
0.1% Sikh
0.1% Jewish
0.1% Hindu

if Scotland were 100 people

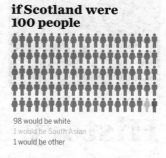

98 would be white
1 would be South Asian
1 would be other

---

asking an Edinburgh taxi driver what they think about the trams – if you have an hour or two to spare!).

In 2008 the Scottish Government introduced a scheme called the Road Equivalent Tariff (RET) on certain ferry crossings. This reduced the price of ferry transport to what it would cost to drive the same distance by road, in the hope of attracting more tourists and reducing business costs in the islands. The routes in the pilot scheme, which runs till 2012, are Ullapool to Stornoway; Uig (Skye) to Tarbert (Harris) and Lochmaddy (North Uist); Oban to Castlebay (Barra) and Lochboisdale (South Uist); and Oban to Coll and Tiree. Fares on these crossings have been cut by around 40%, and initial signs are that the scheme has been successful, with tourist numbers up by 25% to 40%.

Highlands & Islands

Crofting (smallholding in marginal areas) and land ownership are important issues in the Gaelic-speaking areas of northwest Scotland, especially since a headline-grabbing clause in the Land Reform (Scotland) Act (2003) allowed crofting communities to buy out the land that they live on with the aid of taxpayers' money, in the hope of reversing the gradual depopulation of the Highlands.

Several estates have followed Eigg, Gigha, Knoydart and North Harris into community ownership. In 2006 South Uist saw the biggest community buy-out yet. The latest case to make the headlines is the Pairc estate on Lewis, where a Warwickshire-based accountant, whose family has owned the estate since 1920, has leased the land to a power company that plans to erect a £200 million wind farm. The locals voted in favour of a community buy-out, but the landowner is challenging the legality of the Land Reform Act.

> Along with Wales and England, Scotland is part of Great Britain. Throw in Northern Ireland and you have the United Kingdom. It's OK to talk about Scotland's inhabitants as Scottish or British – but *never* English!

Vital Stats

» Population: 5.1 million
» Area: 78,722 sq km
» First Minister: Alex Salmond (SNP)
» GVA per capita: £20,066 (2008)
» Inflation: 2.9% (2010)
» Unemployment: 8.1% (2010)

Scottish Media

» *Caledonian Mercury* (www .caledonianmercury.com)
» *Herald* (www.heraldscotland .com)
» *Scotsman* (www.scotsman .com)
» *Press & Journal* (www. pressandjournal.co.uk)

Internet Radio

BBC Radio Scotland (www .bbc.co.uk/radioscotland) Find out what's hitting the headlines by listening to *Good Morning Scotland* from 6am weekdays.

History

For a geographically isolated place, Scotland has had a substantial share of incursions, immigrations and territorial struggles, and has been subjected to influences from Romans, the Norse lands, Ireland, France and, of course, England.

For from the decline of the Vikings onwards, Scottish history has been predictably and often violently bound to that of its southern neighbour. Battles and border raids were commonplace until shared kingship, then political union, drew the two together. Even then, Jacobite risings asserted a widely felt desire for freedom, finally partially realised with the devolution of the late 20th century.

Scotland's misty prehistory has left outstanding monuments, particularly in the northern islands, but the first outside reference to northern Britain's inhabitants comes with the Romans, whose struggles with the Picts caused the construction of two massive walls to keep them out.

If the Roman presence pushed formerly disparate tribes into union, the Vikings did the same. Their incursions led the Scots kingdom of Dalriada and the Pictish kingdom to unite, forming Scotland.

Once Viking power was broken, a familiar story of strong and weak monarchs, political intrigues and dynastic struggles played out over the centuries. The Wars of Independence freed Scotland from English interference and set up William Wallace and Robert the Bruce as heroes.

The Stewart line established Scotland as a major European player in Renaissance politics and art, but once James VI inherited the kingship of England royal attention was focused south of the border and, as fleets plied the seas to far-flung new colonies, Scotland was left behind. Political union in the early 18th century was born of pragmatism and widely resented. This, and the ousting of the Catholic King James in favour of his Dutch Protestant son-in-law led to widespread anger, and the Jacobite rebellions of the 18th century attempted to wrest power

Top Prehistoric Sights

» Jarlshof, Shetland

» Skara Brae, Orkney

» Maes Howe, Orkney

» Kilmartin Glen, Argyll

» Callanish, Lewis

» Tomb of the Eagles, Orkney

» Scottish Crannog Centre, Kenmore

TIMELINE

4000 BC	2200 BC	AD 43
Neolithic farmers move to Scotland from mainland Europe; sites from these ancient days dot Scotland, with the best concentrated in Orkney.	Beaker culture arrives in Scotland. The Bronze Age produces swords and shields. Construction of hill forts, crannogs and mystifying stone circles.	Claudius begins the Roman conquest of Britain, almost a century after Julius Caesar first invaded. By AD 80 a string of forts is built from the Clyde to the Forth.

back by putting James's son, then grandson, Bonnie Prince Charlie, on the throne.

Defeat at Culloden spelled the end of these dreams, and of the clan system. The Highlands had been ruled as a nation apart by clan leaders who now, stripped of power but possessed of vast lands, evicted their crofters in favour of estate-style sheep farming. This brutal period, the Clearances, left the Highlands an empty wilderness and forced hundreds of thousands to a precarious coastal life or emigration. Those that sought the cities were the fuel for the Industrial Revolution, building a spine of heavy industry across southern Scotland that lasted through to the late 20th century.

Early Days

Hunters and gatherers have left remains of shells and animal bones, providing fragments of evidence of the earliest human habitation in Scotland. These early people came in waves from northern Europe and Ireland as the glaciers retreated in the wake of the last Ice Age around 10,000 BC.

The Neolithic period was similarly launched by arrivals from mainland Europe. Scotland's Stone Age has left behind an astonishing diary of human development: Caithness, Orkney and Shetland have some of the world's best-preserved prehistoric villages, burial cairns and standing stones. Further south, crannogs (round structures built on stilts over a loch) were a favoured form of defensible dwelling through the Bronze Age.

The Iron Age saw the construction of a remarkable series of defence-minded structures of a different sort. Brochs (again a northeastern island development) were complex, muscular stone fortresses, some of which still stand well over 10m high.

Romans & Picts

The Roman invasion of Britain by Emperor Claudius began in AD 43, almost a century after Julius Caesar first invaded. However, the Roman onslaught ground to a halt in the north, not far beyond the present-day Scottish border. Between AD 78 and 84, the Roman Governor Agricola marched northwards and spent several years trying to subdue the wild tribes the Romans called the Picts (from the Latin *pictus,* meaning 'painted'). Little is known about these people, who inhabited northern and eastern Scotland. The Roman presence had probably helped to forge disparate Celtic tribes into a unified group; we can assume they were fierce fighters given the trouble the hardy Roman army had with them. The main material evidence of their culture is their fabulous carved symbol stones, found in many parts of eastern Scotland.

Some Top Pictish Stones

» St Vigeans Museum, Arbroath

» Aberlemno Stones, Angus

» Dupplin Cross, Dunning

» Groam House Museum, Rosemarkie

» Meigle Museum, Meigle

» Inverness Museum, Inverness

» Tarbat Discovery Centre, Portmahomack

» Elgin Museum, Elgin

AD 122

Romans have trouble with the people they call the Picts, and the 74-mile-long Hadrian's Wall is begun, designed to keep them in their place.

AD 142

Building of Antonine Wall marks northern limit of Roman Empire. It is patrolled for about 40 years, but after this the Romans decide northern Britain is too difficult to conquer.

DOUG MCKINLAY

» Walking the route of the Antonine Wall

ST COLUMBA

By the 2nd century Emperor Hadrian, tired of fighting the tribes in the north, decided to cut his losses and built the wall (AD 122–28) that bears his name across northern England between Carlisle and Newcastle. Two decades later Hadrian's successor, Antoninus Pius, invaded Scotland again and built a turf rampart, the Antonine Wall, between the Firth of Forth and the River Clyde. The Roman fort at Cramond marked its eastern end. In northern Britain, the Romans found they had met their match.

Christianity

Eventually the Romans left Britain and at this time there were at least two indigenous peoples in the northern region of the British Isles: the Picts in the north and east, and the Britons in the southwest. The Scots probably arrived around 500AD, crossing to Argyll from Northern Ireland and establishing a kingdom called Dalriada.

St Ninian was the earliest recorded teacher of Christianity in the region, establishing a mission in Whithorn in Scotland's southwest. He remains a mysterious figure shrouded in myth but there is little doubt that his influence was profound.

In the 6th century St Columba, Scotland's most famous missionary, resumed St Ninian's work. According to legend, Columba was a scholar and a soldier-priest who went into exile after involvement in a bloody battle. After fleeing Ireland in 563 he established a monastery on Iona, and also travelled to the northeast to take his message to the Picts. After his death he was credited with miraculous feats such as defeating what is today known as the Loch Ness monster. A visit to Iona today to see the reconstructed 13th-century abbey and the many fine stone carvings is a highlight of the Inner Hebrides. Down south, St Kertigan, later known as Mungo, founded what was to become Glasgow around this time.

The First Kings of Scotland

The Picts and Scots were drawn together by the threat of a Norse invasion and by the combination of political and spiritual power from their common Christianity. Kenneth MacAlpin, first king of a united Scotland, achieved power using a mixture of blood ties and diplomacy. Doubt has been cast recently as to whether he was of Pictish or Dalriadan origin; in any event, he set his capital in Pictland at Scone and brought to it the sacred Stone of Destiny, used in the coronation of Scottish kings.

Nearly two centuries later, Kenneth MacAlpin's great-great-great-grandson, Malcolm II (r 1005–18), defeated the Northumbrian Angles led by King Canute at the Battle of Carham (1018) near Roxburgh on the

St Columba was a man of fixed ideas. After arriving on Iona he promptly set about banishing women and cows as he believed 'where there is a cow there is a woman, and where there is a woman there is mischief'. His manner of living was austere – he slept on the bare floor with a stone for a pillow.

AD 397	5th century	Early 500s	6th century
The first Christian mission beyond Hadrian's Wall, in Whithorn, is initiated by St Ninian. The earliest recorded church in Scotland is built to house his remains.	Roman soldiers stationed in Britain are recalled to Rome as the Empire faces attack from barbarian tribes. The last Romans depart and Emperor Honorius tells Britons to fend for themselves.	A Celtic tribe, the Scots, cross the sea from northern Ireland and establish a kingdom in Argyll called Dalriada.	St Columba establishes a Christian mission on Iona. By the late 8th century the mission is responsible for the conversion of most of pagan Scotland.

River Tweed. This victory brought Edinburgh and Lothian under Scottish control and extended Scottish territory as far south as the Tweed.

With his Saxon queen, Margaret, Malcolm III Canmore (r 1058–93) – whose father Duncan was murdered by Macbeth (as described in Shakespeare's eponymous play) – founded a dynasty of able Scottish rulers. They introduced new Anglo-Norman systems of government and religious foundations.

Malcolm's son David I (r 1124–53) imported monks to found the great Border abbeys; their evocative remains are major attractions in Melrose, Jedburgh and Dryburgh. He increased his power by adopting the Norman feudal system, granting land to noble Norman families in return for military service.

But the Highland clans, inaccessible in their glens, remained a law unto themselves for another 600 years. The exploits of Rob Roy, especially his daring raids into the Lowlands and reputation as a champion of the poor, typified the romantic notion of these wild clans. A cultural and linguistic divide grew up between the Gaelic-speaking Highlanders and the Lowlanders who spoke the Scots tongue.

Robert the Bruce & William Wallace

When Alexander III fell to his death over a coastal cliff in Fife in 1286, there followed a dispute over the succession to the throne. There were no less than 13 claimants, but in the end it came down to a choice of two: Robert de Brus, lord of Annandale, and John Balliol, lord of Galloway. Edward I of England, as the greatest feudal lord in Britain, was asked to arbitrate. He chose Balliol, whom he thought he could manipulate more easily.

Seeking to tighten his feudal grip on Scotland, Edward – known as the 'Hammer of the Scots' – treated the Scots king as his vassal rather

THE DECLARATION OF ARBROATH

During the Wars of Independence, a group of Scottish nobles sent a letter to Pope John XXII requesting support for the cause of Scottish independence. Bearing the seals of eight earls and 31 barons, and written in Latin by the abbot of Arbroath in 1320, it is the earliest document that seeks to place limits on the power of a king.

Having railed against the tyranny of Edward I of England and having sung the praises of Robert the Bruce, the declaration famously states: 'For so long as a hundred of us remain alive, we will yield in no least way to English dominion. For we fight, not for glory nor for riches nor for honours, but only and alone for freedom, which no good man surrenders but with his life'.

685	**780**	**848**	**872**
The Pictish king Bridei defeats the Northumbrians at Nechtansmere in Angus, an against-the-odds victory that sets the foundations for Scotland as a separate entity.	From the 780s onwards, Norsemen in longboats from Scandinavia begin to pillage the Scottish coast and islands, eventually taking control of Orkney, Shetland and the Western Isles.	Kenneth MacAlpin unites the Scottish and Pictish thrones, thus uniting Scotland north of the Firth of Forth into a single kingdom.	The King of Norway creates an earldom in Orkney, and Shetland is also governed from here – these island groups become a vital Viking base for raids and colonisation down the west of Scotland.

than his equal. The humiliated Balliol finally turned against him and allied Scotland with France in 1295, thus beginning the enduring 'Auld Alliance' and ushering in the Wars of Independence.

Edward's response was bloody. In 1296 he invaded Scotland and Balliol was incarcerated in the Tower of London; in a final blow to Scots pride, Edward I removed the Stone of Destiny from Scone and took it back to London.

Enter arguably Scotland's most tragic hero, William Wallace. Bands of rebels were attacking the English occupiers and one such band, led by William Wallace, defeated the English army at the Battle of Stirling Bridge in 1297. After William Wallace was executed, Robert the Bruce, grandson of the lord of Annandale, saw his chance, defied Edward (whom he had previously aligned himself with), murdered his rival John Comyn and had himself crowned king of Scotland at Scone in 1306. Bruce mounted a campaign to drive the English out of Scotland but suffered repeated defeats. According to legend, while Bruce was on the run he was inspired to renew his efforts by a spider's persistence in spinning its web. And the inspiration was not in vain – he went on to secure an illustrious victory over the English at Bannockburn, enshrined in Scottish legend as one of the finest moments in the country's history.

Robert the Bruce Trail

» Melrose Abbey
» Dumfries
» Scone Palace
» Bannockburn, Stirling
» Arbroath Abbey
» Dunfermline Abbey

The Stewarts & the Renaissance

After the death of Robert the Bruce in 1329 – he's buried at Dunfermline, although his heart is buried in Melrose Abbey – the country was ravaged by civil disputes and continuing wars with England. Edinburgh was occupied several times by English armies and in 1385 the Kirk of St Giles was burned to the ground.

James IV (r 1488–1513) married the daughter of Henry VII of England, the first of the Tudor monarchs, thereby linking the two royal families through 'the Marriage of the Thistle and the Rose'. This didn't prevent the French from persuading James to go to war with his in-laws, and he was killed at the Battle of Flodden in 1513, along with 10,000 of his subjects.

Renaissance ideas flourished during James IV's reign. Scottish poetry thrived, created by *makars* (makers of verses) such as William Dunbar, the court poet of James IV, and Gavin Douglas. Much graceful Scottish architecture is from this period, and examples of Renaissance style can be seen in alterations to palaces at Holyrood, Stirling, Linlithgow and Falkland.

Mary, Queen of Scots & the Reformation

In 1542 King James V, childless, lay on his deathbed broken-hearted, it is said, after his defeat by the English at Solway Moss. On 8 December a

1018	1040	1263	1296
King Malcolm II defeats the Northumbrians at the Battle of Carham and gains the Lothian region for Scotland.	Macbeth takes the Scottish throne after defeating Duncan in battle. This, and the fact that he was later killed by Duncan's son Malcolm, are the only parallels to the Shakespeare version.	Norse power, which controlled the entire western seaboard, is finally broken at the Battle of Largs, which marks the retreat of Viking influence and eventually the handing back of the western isles to Scotland.	King Edward I marches on Scotland with an army of 30,000 men, razing ports, butchering citizens and capturing the castles of Berwick, Edinburgh, Roxburgh and Stirling.

In medieval times, when overland travel through the Scottish Highlands was slow, difficult and dangerous, the sea lochs, firths (estuaries), kyles (narrow sea channels) and sounds of the west coast were the motorways of their time. Cut off from the rest of Scotland, but united by these sea roads, the west coast and islands were a world – and a kingdom – unto themselves.

Descended from the legendary Somerled (a half-Gaelic, half-Norse warrior of the 12th century) the chiefs of Clan Donald claimed sovereignty over this watery kingdom. It was John Macdonald of Islay who first styled himself Dominus Insularum (Lord of the Isles) in 1353. He and his descendants ruled their vast territory from their headquarters at Finlaggan in Islay, backed up by fleets of swift *birlinns* and *nyvaigs* (Hebridean galleys), an intimate knowledge of the sea routes of the west and a network of coastal castles that included Skipness, Dunstaffnage, Duart, Stalker, Dunvegan and Kisimul.

Clan Donald held sway over the isles, often in defiance of the Scottish king, from 1350 to 1493. At its greatest extent, in the second half of the 15th century, the Lordship of the Isles included all the islands on the west coast of Scotland, the west-coast mainland from Kintyre to Ross-shire, and the Antrim coast of northern Ireland. But in challenging the Scottish king for territory, and siding with the English king against him, Clan Donald finally pushed its luck too far.

Following a failed rebellion in 1493, the Lordship was forfeited to King James IV of Scotland, and the title has remained in possession of the Scottish, and later British, royal family ever since. Lord of the Isles is one of the many titles held today by Prince Charles, heir to the British throne.

messenger brought word that his wife had given birth to a baby girl at the Palace of Linlithgow. Fearing the end of the Stewart dynasty, and recalling its origin through Robert the Bruce's daughter, James sighed, 'It cam' wi' a lass, and it will gang wi' a lass'. He died a few days later, leaving his week-old daughter, Mary, to inherit the throne as Queen of Scots.

She was sent to France at an early age and Scotland was ruled by regents, who rejected overtures from Henry VIII of England urging them to wed the infant queen to his son. Henry was furious, and sent his armies to take vengeance on the Scots. The 'Rough Wooing', as it was called, failed to persuade the Scots of the error of their ways. In 1558 Mary was married to the French dauphin and became queen of France as well as Scotland.

While Mary was in France, being raised as a Roman Catholic, the Reformation tore through Scotland. The preachings of John Knox, pupil of the Swiss reformer Calvin, found sympathetic ears. Knox,

» Stirling Castle

1298–1305

William Wallace is proclaimed Guardian of Scotland in March 1298. After Edward's force defeats the Scots at the Battle of Falkirk, Wallace resigns as guardian and goes into hiding, but is fatally betrayed after his return in 1305.

1314

Robert the Bruce wins a famous victory over the English at the Battle of Bannockburn – a victory which would turn the tide in favour of the Scots for the next 400 years.

concerned with the sway that political rulers wielded over the church, wrote *The First Blast of the Trumpet Against the Monstrous Regiment of Women*. It was an attack on three women rulers calling the shots in Scotland, England and France and linked his name to a hatred of women ever since.

Following the death of her sickly husband, the 18-year-old Mary returned to Scotland in 1561. She was formally welcomed to her capital city and held a famous audience at Holyrood Palace with John Knox. The great reformer harangued the young queen and she later agreed to protect the budding Protestant Church in Scotland while continuing to hear Mass in private.

She married Henry Stewart, Lord Darnley, in the Chapel Royal at Holyrood and gave birth to a son (later James VI) in Edinburgh Castle in 1565. Any domestic bliss was short-lived and, in a scarcely believable train of events, Darnley was involved in the murder of Mary's Italian secretary Rizzio (rumoured to be her lover), before he himself was murdered, probably by Mary's new lover and second-husband-to-be, the earl of Bothwell!

The Scots had had enough – Mary's enemies finally confronted her at Carberry Hill, just east of Edinburgh, and Mary was forced to abdicate in 1567 and thrown into prison at Castle Leven. She managed to escape, and confronted her enemies in battle at Langside but was forced to flee to England after her defeat. There, she was imprisoned for 19 years by Queen Elizabeth I before finally being executed in 1587.

Her son, the infant James VI (r 1567–1625) had meanwhile been crowned at Stirling, and a series of regents ruled in his place. In England, Elizabeth died childless, and the English, desperate for a male monarch, soon turned their attention north. James VI of Scotland became James I of England and moved his court to London. His plan to politically unite the two countries, however, failed. For the most part, the Stewarts (now spelled Stuart) ignored Scotland from then on. Indeed, when Charles I (r 1625–49) succeeded James, he couldn't be bothered to travel north to Edinburgh to be formally crowned as king of Scotland until 1633.

Covenanters & Civil War

Civil war strangled Scotland and England in the 17th century. Arrogant attempts by Charles I to impose episcopacy (the rule of bishops) and an English liturgy on the Presbyterian Scottish Church set off public riots in Edinburgh. The Presbyterians believed in a personal bond with God that had no need of mediation through priests, popes and kings. On 28 February 1638 hundreds gathered in Greyfriars Kirkyard to sign a Na-

Mary Queen of Scots by Antonia Fraser is the classic biography of Scotland's ill-starred queen, digging deep behind the myths to discover the real woman caught up in the labyrinthine politics of the period.

MARY QUEEN OF SCOTS

1320
The Declaration of Arbroath asserts Scotland's status as an independent kingdom in a submission to the pope. He agrees.

1328
Continuing raids on northern England force Edward II to sue for peace and the Treaty of Northampton gives Scotland its independence, with Robert I, the Bruce, as king.

1410
One of Europe's most venerable educational institutions, The University of St Andrews, is founded.

1468–69
Orkney and then Shetland are mortgaged to Scotland as part of a dowry from Danish King Christian I, whose daughter is to marry the future King James III of Scotland.

tional Covenant affirming their rights and beliefs. Scotland was divided between the Covenanters and those who supported the king.

In the 1640s civil war raged in England between the Royalists and Oliver Cromwell's Parliamentarians. Although there was an alliance between the Covenanters and the English parliament against Charles I, the Scots were appalled when the Parliamentarians executed the king in 1649. They offered his son the Scottish Crown provided he signed the Covenant and renounced his father, which he did. Charles II (r 1649–85) was crowned at Scone on 1 January 1651 but was soon forced into exile by Cromwell, who invaded Scotland and captured Edinburgh.

After Charles II's restoration in 1660, he reneged on the Covenant; episcopacy was reinstated and hardline Presbyterian ministers were deprived of their churches. Charles' brother and successor, the Catholic James VII/II (r 1685–89), made worshipping as a Covenanter a capital offence.

James had converted to Catholicism but as long as his Protestant daughter Mary was next in line a lid was kept on the simmering pot of religious conflict. When his second wife, however, gave birth to a son (a Catholic heir to the throne) in 1688, things erupted. Parliament called for James's Protestant son-in-law, William of Orange, to invade from the Netherlands, and James was forced into exile.

James' daughter, Mary, and her husband William (1689–1702) reigning jointly, restored the Presbyterian structure in the church and kicked out the bishops but the political and legal functions of the church were subject to parliamentary control. And so Scotland's turbulent Reformation came to an end.

A well-presented and easily absorbed introduction to Scottish history is at www.bbc.co.uk/history/scottish history. The accompanying images of historical sites help to bring it to life.

Union with England

The civil wars left the country and its economy ruined. Scotland couldn't compete in this new era of European colonialism and, to add to its woes, during the 1690s famine killed up to a third of the population in some areas. Anti-English feeling ran high: William was at war with France and was using Scottish soldiers and taxes – many Scots, sympathetic to the French, disapproved. This feeling was exacerbated by the failure of an investment venture in Panama (the so-called Darien Scheme, designed to establish a Scottish colony in the Americas), which resulted in widespread bankruptcy in Scotland.

The failure of the Darien Scheme made it clear to the wealthy Scottish merchants and stockholders that the only way they could gain access to the lucrative markets of developing colonies was through union with England. The English parliament favoured union through fear of Jacobite sympathies in Scotland being exploited by its enemies, the French.

GARETH McCORMACK

» Noup Head, Westray

1488–1513	1513	1560
The Scottish Renaissance produces an intellectual climate that encourages Protestantism, a reaction against the perceived wealth and corruption of the medieval Roman Catholic Church.	James IV invades northern England and is soundly defeated in Northumberland at the Battle of Flodden. It marks a watershed in war history, with artillery on the upswing and archery on the way out.	As a result of the Reformation, the Scottish parliament creates a Protestant Church independent of Rome and the monarchy. The Latin Mass is abolished and the pope's authority denied.

Bonnie Prince Charlie's flight after Culloden is legendary. He lived in hiding in the remote Highlands and islands for months before being rescued by a French frigate. His narrow escape from Uist to Skye, dressed as Flora MacDonald's maid, is the subject of the 'Skye Boat Song'.

BONNIE PRINCE CHARLIE

On receiving the Act of Union in Edinburgh, the chancellor of Scotland, Lord Seafield – leader of the parliament that the Act of Union abolished – is said to have murmured under his breath, 'Now there's an end to an auld sang'. Robert Burns later castigated the wealthy politicians who engineered the union in characteristically stronger language: 'We're bought and sold for English gold – such a parcel of rogues in a nation!'.

The Jacobites

The Jacobite rebellions of the 18th century sought to displace the Hanoverian monarchy (chosen by the English parliament in 1701 to succeed the house of Orange) and restore a Catholic Stuart king to the British throne.

James Edward Stuart, known as the Old Pretender, was the son of James VII/II. With French support he arrived in the Firth of Forth with a fleet of ships in 1708, causing panic in Edinburgh, but was seen off by English men-of-war.

The earl of Mar led another Jacobite rebellion in 1715 but proved an ineffectual leader better at propaganda than warfare. His campaign fizzled out soon after the inconclusive Battle of Sheriffmuir.

The Old Pretender's son, Charles Edward Stuart, better known as Bonnie Prince Charlie or the Young Pretender, landed in Scotland for the final uprising. He had little military experience, didn't speak Gaelic and had a shaky grasp of English. Nevertheless, supported by an army of Highlanders, he marched southwards and captured Edinburgh, except for the castle, in September 1745. He got as far south as Derby in England, but success was short-lived; a Hanoverian army led by the duke of Cumberland harried him all the way back to the Highlands, where Jacobite dreams were finally extinguished at the Battle of Culloden in 1746.

Although a heavily romanticised figure, Bonnie Prince Charlie was partly responsible for the annihilation of Highland culture, given the crackdown following his doomed attempt to recapture the crown. After returning to France he gained a reputation for drunkenness and mistreatment of mistresses. France had serious plans to invade Britain during the mid-18th century, but eventually ceased to regard the prince as a serious character.

The Highland Clearances

In the aftermath of the Jacobite rebellions, Highland dress, the bearing of arms and the bagpipes were outlawed. The Highlands were put under military control and private armies were banned.

The clansmen, no longer of any use as soldiers and uneconomical as tenants, were evicted from their homes and farms by the Highland

1567	1603	1692	1707
Mary, Queen of Scots is deposed and thrown in prison. Though her last stand is still to come, the days of wilful royal action in Scotland seem to be over.	James VI of Scotland inherits the English throne in the so-called Union of the Crowns, becoming James I of Great Britain.	The Massacre of Glencoe causes further rifts between those clans loyal to the crown and those loyal to the old ways.	Despite popular opposition, the Act of Union, which brings England and Scotland under one parliament, one sovereign and one flag, takes effect on 1 May.

chieftains to make way for the flocks – in Easter Ross the year 1792 was known for decades afterwards as the Year of the Sheep. A few stayed to work the sheep farms; many more were forced to seek work in the cities, or to eke a living from crofts (smallholdings) on poor coastal land. Men who had never seen the sea were forced to take to boats to try their luck at herring fishing, and many thousands emigrated – some willingly, some under duress – to the developing colonies of North America, Australia and New Zealand.

If you do much walking in the Highlands and islands, you are almost certain to come across a pile of stones among the bracken, all that remains of a house or cottage. Look around and you'll find another, and another, and soon you'll realise that this was once a crofting settlement. It's one of the saddest sights you'll see in Scotland – this emptiness, where once there was a thriving community. The Mull of Oa on the island of Islay, for example, once supported a population of 4000, but today there are barely 40 people living there.

The Scottish Enlightenment

During the period known as the Scottish Enlightenment (roughly 1740–1830) Edinburgh became known as 'a hotbed of genius'. The philosophers David Hume and Adam Smith and the sociologist Adam Ferguson emerged as influential thinkers, nourished on generations of theological debate. Medic William Cullen produced the first modern pharmacopoeia, chemist Joseph Black advanced the science of thermodynamics and geologist James Hutton challenged long-held beliefs about the age of the Earth.

After centuries of bloodshed and religious fanaticism, people applied themselves with the same energy and piety to the making of money and the enjoyment of leisure. There was a revival of interest in Scottish history and literature. The writings of Sir Walter Scott and the poetry of Robert Burns, a true man of the people, achieved lasting popularity.

The Industrial Revolution

The development of the steam engine ushered in the Industrial Revolution. The Carron Ironworks near Falkirk, established in 1759, became the largest ironworks and gun factory in Britain, and the growth of the textile industry saw the construction of huge weaving mills in Lanarkshire, Dundee, Angus and Aberdeenshire. The world's first steamboat, the *Charlotte Dundas,* sailed along the newly opened Forth and Clyde Canal in 1802, and the world's first seagoing steamship, the *Comet,* was launched on the Clyde in 1812.

Glasgow, deprived of its lucrative tobacco trade following the American War of Independence (1776–83), developed into an industrial

---

Jacobite, a term derived from the Latin for 'James', is used to describe the political movement committed to the return of the Stuart kings to the thrones of England and Scotland.

John Prebble's wonderfully written book *The Highland Clearances* tells the terrible story of how the Highlanders were driven out of their homes and forced into emigration.

1745–46	**1740s–1830s**	**Late 1700s**	**1888**
The culmination of the Jacobite rebellions: Bonnie Prince Charlie lands in Scotland, gathers an army and marches south. Though he gains English territory, he is eventually defeated at the Battle of Culloden.	Following the loss of the Scottish parliament in 1707, Edinburgh declines in political importance, but its cultural and intellectual life flourishes during a period known as the Scottish Enlightenment.	Scotland flourishes during the Industrial Revolution, becoming a world leader in the production of textiles, iron, steel and coal – and above all in shipbuilding and marine engineering.	The Scottish Labour Party, a trailblazer in the workers' movement, is founded by former miner James Keir Hardie.

powerhouse, the 'second city' of the British Empire (after London). Cotton mills, iron and steelworks, chemical works, shipbuilding yards and heavy-engineering works proliferated along the River Clyde in the 19th century, powered by the coal mines of Lanarkshire, Ayrshire, Fife and Midlothian.

The Clearances and the Industrial Revolution had shattered the traditional rural way of life and, though manufacturing cities and ports thrived in these decades of Empire, the wealth was generated for a se-

EXPLORING YOUR SCOTTISH ROOTS

Genealogy is a hugely popular pastime, and many visitors to Scotland take the opportunity to do some detective work on their Scottish ancestry.

One of the best guides is Tracing Your Scottish Ancestry by Kathleen B Cory, and there are many useful websites; **GenUKI** (www.genuki.org.uk) is a good starting point. **Ancestry** (www.ancestry.co.uk) is another.

At the excellent **Scotland's People Website** (www.scotlandspeople.gov.uk) you can search the indexes to Old Parish Registers and Statutory Registers as well as census returns, on a pay-per-view basis. **The International Genealogical Index** (www.familysearch.com), compiled by the Mormon Church, includes freely searchable records of Scottish baptisms and marriages.

The following places in Edinburgh can help out:

Scotland's People Centre (☎0131-314 4300; www.scotlandspeoplehub.gov.uk; 2 Princes St; ☺Mon-Fri) This collaboration between the General Register Office, the National Archives and the Court of the Lord Lyon brings together millions of useful records in one place. The main records used in Scottish genealogical research – the Statutory Registers of births, marriages and deaths (1855 to the present), the Old Parish Registers (1533–1854) and the 10-yearly census returns from 1841 to 1901 – are held here. The registration of births, marriages and deaths became compulsory in Scotland on 1 January 1855; before that date, the ministers of the Church of Scotland kept registers of baptisms and marriages. The oldest surviving parish registers date back to 1553, but these records are far from complete, and many births and marriages before 1855 went unrecorded. Daily search fee is £10 and there are tutorial sessions available.

National Archives of Scotland (☎0131-535 1334; www.nas.gov.uk; Register House, 2 Princes St, Edinburgh EH1 3YY; admission free; ☺Mon-Fri) You will need to ask for a reader's ticket (free) – bring some form of ID. Use of the Historical Search Room is free and is first come, first served.

Scottish Genealogy Society Library (☎0131-220 3677; www.scotsgenealogy.com; 15 Victoria Tce, Edinburgh EH1 2JL; ☺Mon-Thu & Sat) Maintains the world's largest library of Scottish gravestone inscriptions and a comprehensive records and family history collection. Entry is free for society members, £5 for nonmembers.

1890–1910	1914–1932	1919	1941–45
The 'Glasgow Boys' bring European influence and international recognition to Scottish art, breaking away from the Edinburgh mainstream.	Scottish industry slumps during WWI and collapses in its aftermath in the face of new Eastern production and the Great Depression. About 400,000 Scots emigrate between 1921 and 1931.	The Bloody Friday riot sees Glasgow strikers suppressed by the army, who feared a Bolshevik-style revolution.	Clydebank is blitzed by German bombers in 1941 with 1200 deaths; and by 1945 one out of four males in the workforce is employed in heavy industries to support the war effort.

lect few by an impoverished many. Deep poverty forced many into emigration and others to their graves. The depopulation was exacerbated by WWI, which took a heavy toll on Scottish youth. The ensuing years were bleak and marked by labour disputes.

War & Peace

Scotland largely escaped the trauma and devastation wrought by WWII on the industrial cities of England (although Clydebank was heavily bombed over a couple of days). Indeed, the war brought a measure of renewed prosperity to Scotland as the shipyards and engineering works geared up to supply the war effort. But the postwar period saw the collapse of shipbuilding and heavy industry, on which Scotland had become overreliant.

After the discovery of North Sea oil off the Scottish coast, excitement turned to bitterness for many Scots, who felt that revenues were being siphoned off to England. This issue, along with takeovers of Scots companies by English ones (which then closed the Scots operation, asset-stripped and transferred jobs to England), fuelled increasing nationalist sentiment in Scotland. The Scottish National Party (SNP) developed into a third force (later, a second as they eclipsed the Conservatives, and the first as they won power from the Labour Party) in Scottish politics.

Devolution

In 1979 a referendum was held on whether to set up a directly elected Scottish Assembly. Fifty-two per cent of those who voted said 'yes' to devolution, but Labour Prime Minister James Callaghan decided that everyone who didn't vote should be counted as a 'no'. By this devious reasoning, only 33% of the electorate had voted 'yes', so the Scottish Assembly was rejected.

From 1979 to 1997 Scotland was ruled by a Conservative government in London for which the majority of Scots hadn't voted. Separatist feelings, always present, grew stronger. Following the landslide victory of the Labour Party in May 1997, another referendum was held on the creation of a Scottish parliament. This time the result was overwhelmingly and unambiguously in favour.

Elections to the new parliament took place on 6 May 1999 and the Scottish parliament convened for the first time on 12 May in Edinburgh, with Labour's Donald Dewar, who died in office the very next year, becoming First Minister.

Most clan tartans are in fact a 19th-century invention (long after the demise of the clan system) partly inspired by the writings of Sir Walter Scott.

HISTORY

TARTANS

Between 1904 and 1931 around a million people emigrated from Scotland to begin a new life in North America and Australasia.

1970s	1999–2004
The discovery of oil and gas in the North Sea brings new prosperity to Aberdeen and the surrounding area, and also to the Shetland Islands.	Scottish parliament is convened for the first time on 12 May 1999. After scandals and huge expenses, a stunning new parliament building is opened in Edinburgh by Queen Elizabeth II in October of 2004.

WILL SALTER

» Interior, Scottish parliament building

The Scottish Larder

Traditional Scottish cookery is all about basic comfort food: solid, nourishing fare, often high in fat, that would keep you warm on a winter's day spent in the fields or out fishing, and sweet treats to come home to in the evening.

But a new culinary style known as Modern Scottish has emerged over the last two decades. It's a style that should be familiar to fans of Californian Cuisine and Mod Oz. Chefs take top-quality Scottish produce – from Highland venison, Aberdeen Angus beef and freshly landed seafood, to root vegetables, raspberries and Ayrshire cheeses – and prepare it simply, in a way that enhances the natural flavours, often adding a French, Italian or Asian twist.

Scotland's traditional drinks – whisky and beer – have also found a new lease of life in recent years, with single malts being marketed like fine wines, and a new breed of microbreweries springing up all over the country.

A Caledonian Feast by Annette Hope is a fascinating and readable history of Scottish cuisine, providing a wealth of historical and sociological background.

Breakfast, Lunch & Dinner

Haggis may be the national dish that Scotland is most famous for, but when it comes to what Scottish people actually cook and eat most often, the hands-down winner has to be mince and tatties (potatoes). Minced beef, browned in the pan and then stewed slowly with onion, carrot and gravy, is served with mashed potatoes (with a splash of milk and a knob of butter added during the mashing) – it's tasty, warming and you don't even have to chew.

The Full Scottish

Surprisingly few Scots eat porridge for breakfast – these days a cappuccino and a croissant is just as likely – and even fewer eat it in the traditional

EATING PRICE BANDS

In this guide, eating choices are flagged with price indicators, based on the cost of an average main course from the dinner menu:

» £ means a budget place where a main dish is less than £9.

» ££ means midrange; mains are £9 to £18

» £££ means top end; mains are more than £18

Note though that lunch mains are often cheaper than dinner mains, and many places offer an 'early bird' special with lower prices (usually available between 5pm and 7pm). See p480 for restaurant opening hours.

Scotland's national dish is often ridiculed by foreigners because of its ingredients, which admittedly don't sound promising – the finely chopped lungs, heart and liver of a sheep, mixed with oatmeal and onion and stuffed into a sheep's stomach bag. However, it actually tastes surprisingly good.

Haggis should be served with *champit tatties* and *bashed neeps* (mashed potatoes and turnips), with a generous dollop of butter and a good sprinkling of black pepper.

Although it's eaten year-round, haggis is central to the celebrations of 25 January, in honour of Scotland's national poet, Robert Burns. Scots worldwide unite on Burns Night to revel in their Scottishness. A piper announces the arrival of the haggis and Burns' poem *Address to a Haggis* is recited to this 'Great chieftan o' the puddin-race'. The bulging haggis is then lanced with a dirk (dagger) to reveal the steaming offal within, 'warm, reekin, rich'.

Vegetarians (and quite a few carnivores, no doubt) will be relieved to know that veggie haggis is available in some restaurants.

way; that is, with salt to taste, but no sugar. The breakfast offered in a B&B or hotel usually consists of fruit juice and cereal or muesli, followed by a choice of bacon, sausage, black pudding (a type of sausage made from dried blood), grilled tomato, mushrooms and a fried egg or two.

Fish for breakfast may sound strange, but was not unusual in crofting (smallholding) and fishing communities where seafood was a staple; many hotels still offer grilled kippers (smoked herrings) or smoked haddock (poached in milk and served with a poached egg) for breakfast – delicious with lots of buttered toast.

Broth, Skink & Bree

Scotch broth, made with mutton stock, barley, lentils and peas, is nutritious and tasty, while cock-a-leekie is a hearty soup made with chicken and leeks. Warming vegetable soups include leek and potato soup, and lentil soup (traditionally made using ham stock – vegetarians beware!).

Seafood soups include the delicious Cullen skink, made with smoked haddock, potato, onion and milk, and *partan bree* (crab soup).

Surf & Turf

Steak eaters will enjoy a thick fillet of world-famous Aberdeen Angus beef, and beef from Highland cattle is much sought after. Venison, from the red deer, is leaner and appears on many menus. Both may be served with a wine-based or creamy whisky sauce. Then there's haggis, Scotland's much-maligned national dish...

Scottish salmon is famous worldwide, but there's a big difference between the now-ubiquitous farmed salmon and the leaner, more expensive, wild fish. Also, there are concerns over the environmental impact of salmon farms on the marine environment.

Smoked salmon is traditionally dressed with a squeeze of lemon juice and eaten with fresh brown bread and butter. Trout, salmon's smaller cousin – whether wild, rod-caught brown trout or farmed rainbow trout – is delicious fried in oatmeal.

As an alternative to kippers you may be offered Arbroath smokies (lightly smoked fresh haddock), traditionally eaten cold. Herring fillets fried in oatmeal are good, if you don't mind picking out a few bones. Mackerel pâté and smoked or peppered mackerel (both served cold) are also popular.

Juicy langoustines (also known as Dublin Bay prawns), crabs, lobsters, oysters, mussels and scallops are also widely available.

Popular Scottish TV chef Nick Nairn's book *Wild Harvest* contains over 100 recipes based on the use of fresh, seasonal Scottish produce.

It is illegal to import haggis into the USA, as the US government has declared that sheep lungs are unfit for human consumption.

THE SCOTTISH LARDER BREAKFAST, LUNCH & DINNER

Clootie & Cranachan

Traditional Scottish puddings are irresistibly creamy, high-calorie concoctions. Cranachan is whipped cream flavoured with whisky, and mixed with toasted oatmeal and raspberries. Atholl brose is a mixture of cream, whisky and honey, flavoured with oatmeal. Clootie dumpling is a rich steamed pudding filled with currants and raisins.

Vegetarians & Vegans

Scotland has the same proportion of vegetarians as the rest of the UK – around 8% to 10% of the population – and vegetarianism has moved away from the hippie-student image of a few decades ago and is now firmly in the mainstream. Even the most remote Highland pub usually has at least one vegetarian dish on the menu, and there are many dedicated vegetarian restaurants in the cities. If you get stuck, there's almost always an Italian or Indian restaurant where you can get meat-free pizza, pasta or curry. Vegans, though, may find the options a bit limited outside of Edinburgh and Glasgow.

One thing to keep in mind is that lentil soup, a seemingly vegetarian staple of Scottish pub and restaurant menus, is traditionally made with ham stock.

Eating with Kids

Sadly, the majority of Scotland's eating places make no effort to welcome children, and many are actively hostile. There's no way of gauging restaurant attitudes other than by asking.

Top Seafood Restaurants

» Ondine, Edinburgh

» Café Fish, Tobermory

» Waterfront, Oban

» Silver Darling, Aberdeen

» Tolbooth, Stonehaven

» Lochleven Seafood Cafe, Kinlochleven

» Seafood Restaurant, St Monans

» Mhor Fish, Callander

SSSSSSMOKIN'!

Scotland is famous for its smoked salmon, but there are many other varieties of smoked fish – plus smoked meats and cheeses – to enjoy. Smoking food to preserve it is an ancient art that has recently undergone a revival, but this time it's more about flavour than preservation.

There are two parts to the process – first the cure, which involves covering the fish in a mixture of salt and molasses sugar, or soaking it in brine; and then the smoke, which can be either cold smoking (at less than 34°C), which results in a raw product, or hot smoking (at more than 60°C), which cooks it. Cold-smoked products include traditional smoked salmon, kippers and Finnan haddies. Hot-smoked products include *bradan rost* ('flaky' smoked salmon) and Arbroath smokies.

Arbroath smokies are haddock that have been gutted, beheaded and cleaned, then salted and dried overnight, tied together at the tail in pairs, and hot-smoked over oak or beech chippings for 45 to 90 minutes. Finnan haddies (named after the fishing village of Findon in Aberdeenshire) are also haddock, but these are split down the middle like kippers, and cold-smoked.

Kippers (smoked herring) were invented in Northumberland, in northern England, in the mid-19th century, but Scotland soon picked up the technique, and both Loch Fyne and Mallaig were famous for their kippers.

There are dozens of modern smokehouses scattered all over Scotland, many of which offer a mail-order service as well as an on-site shop; here are a few recommended ones:

Hebridean Smokehouse (www.hebrideansmokehouse.com; Cladach, North Uist, Outer Hebrides) Peat-smoked salmon and sea trout.

Inverawe Smokehouse & Fishery (www.smokedsalmon.co.uk; Inverawe, Dalmally, Argyllshire) Delicate smoked salmon, plump juicy kippers.

Marrbury Smokehouse (www.visitmarrbury.co.uk; Carsluith Castle, Creetown, Dumfries & Galloway) Supplier to Gleneagles Hotel and other top restaurants.

Salar Smokehouse (www.salar.co.uk; Lochcarnan, South Uist, Outer Hebrides) Famous for its flaky, hot-smoked salmon.

This situation is changing, albeit slowly, especially in the cities and more popular tourist towns where several restaurants and pubs now have family rooms and/or play areas. However, in many smaller towns and country areas kids will still get a frosty reception.

You should be aware that children under the age of 14 are not allowed into the majority of Scottish pubs, even those that serve bar meals; even in family-friendly pubs (those in possession of a Children's Certificate), under-14s are only allowed in between 11am and 8pm, and must be accompanied by an adult aged 18 or above.

Cookery Courses

There are two principal places that offer courses in Scottish cookery:
Kinloch Lodge Hotel (01471-833333; www.claire-macdonald.com; Kinloch Lodge, Isle of Skye IV43 8QY) Cookery demonstrations using fresh, seasonal Scottish produce given by Lady Claire Macdonald, author of *Scottish Highland Hospitality* and *Celebrations*.
Nairns Cook School (✆01877-389900; www.nairnscookschool.com; Port of Menteith, Stirling FK8 3JZ) Two-day courses in modern Scottish cooking at the school owned by Scotland's top TV chef Nick Nairn, author of *Wild Harvest* and *Island Harvest*.

What Are Ye Drinkin'?
A Pint...

Scottish breweries produce a wide range of beers. The market is dominated by multinational brewers such as Scottish & Newcastle, but smaller local breweries generally create tastier brews, some of them very strong. The aptly named Skull Splitter from Orkney is a good example, at 8.5% alcohol by volume.

Many Scottish beers use old-fashioned shilling categories to indicate strength (the number of shillings was originally the price per barrel; the stronger the beer, the higher the price). The usual range is from 60 to 80 shillings (written 80/-). You'll also see IPA, which stands for India Pale Ale, a strong, hoppy beer first brewed in the early 19th century for export to India (the extra alcohol meant that it kept better on the long sea voyage).

Draught beer is served in pints (usually costing from £2 to £3) or half-pints; alcoholic content generally ranges from 3% to 6%. What the English call bitter, Scots call heavy, or export – Caledonian 80/-, Maclays 80/- and Belhaven 80/- are all worth trying, but Deuchar's IPA from Edinburgh's Caledonian Brewery is our favourite.

BARR'S IRN BRU

Scotland's most famous soft drink is Barr's Irn Bru: a sweet fizzy drink, radioactive orange in colour, that smells like bubble gum and almost strips the enamel from your teeth. Many Scots swear by its restorative effects as a cure for a hangover.

Scottish Ales

The increasing popularity of real ales and a backlash against the bland conformity of globalised multinational brewing conglomerates has seen a huge rise in the number of specialist brewers and microbreweries springing up all over Scotland. They take pride in using only natural ingredients, and many try to revive ancient recipes, such as heather- and seaweed-flavoured ales.

These beers are sold in pubs, off-licences and delicatessens. Here are a few of our favourites to look out for:
Black Isle Brewery (www.blackislebrewery.com; Old Allangrance, Munlochy, Ross-shire) Range of organic beers.
Cairngorm Brewery (www.cairngormbrewery.com; Dalfaber Industrial Estate, Aviemore) Creator of multi-award-winning Trade Winds ale.

Colonsay Brewery (www.colonsaybrewery.co.uk; Scalasaig, Isle of Colonsay) Produces lager, 80/- and IPA.

Islay Ales (www.islayales.com; Islay House Sq, Bridgend, Isle of Islay) Refreshing and citrusy Saligo Ale.

Isle of Skye Brewery (www.skyebrewery.co.uk; The Pier, Uig) Distinctive Hebridean Gold ale, brewed with porridge oats.

Orkney Brewery (www.sinclairbreweries.co.uk; Quoyloo, Stromness, Orkney) Famous for its rich, chocolatey Dark Island ale, and the dangerously strong Skull Splitter.

Traquair House Brewery (www.traquair.co.uk; Traquair House, Innerleithen, Peeblesshire) Traquair House Ale, at 7.2% alcohol, is rich, dark and strong.

Williams Bros (www.fraoch.com; New Alloa Brewery, Alloa) Produces historic beers flavoured with heather flowers, seaweed, Scots pine and elderberries.

HOW TO BE A MALT WHISKY BUFF

'Love makes the world go round? Not at all! Whisky makes it go round twice as fast.'

Whisky Galore, Compton Mackenzie (1883–1972)

Whisky-tasting today is almost as popular as wine-tasting was in the yuppie heyday of the late 1980s. Being able to tell your Ardbeg from your Edradour is de rigueur among the whisky-nosing set, so here are some pointers to help you impress your friends.

What's the difference between malt and grain whiskies?

Malts are distilled from malted barley – that is, barley that has been soaked in water, then allowed to germinate for around 10 days until the starch has turned into sugar – while grain whiskies are distilled from other cereals, usually wheat, corn or unmalted barley.

So what is a single malt?

A single malt is a whisky that has been distilled from malted barley and is the product of a single distillery. A pure (vatted) malt is a mixture of single malts from several distilleries, and a blended whisky is a mixture of various grain whiskies (about 60%) and malt whiskies (about 40%) from many different distilleries.

Why are single malts more desirable than blends?

A single malt, like a fine wine, somehow captures the essence of the place where it was made and matured – a combination of the water, the barley, the peat smoke, the oak barrels in which it was aged, and (in the case of certain coastal distilleries) the sea air and salt spray. Each distillation varies from the one before, like different vintages from the same vineyard.

How should a single malt be drunk?

Either neat, or preferably with a little water added. To appreciate the aroma and flavour to the utmost, a measure of malt whisky should be cut (diluted) with one-third to two-thirds as much spring water (still, bottled spring water will do). Ice, tap water and (God forbid) mixers are for philistines. Would you add lemonade or ice to a glass of Chablis?

Where can I learn more?

If you're serious about spirits, the Scotch Malt Whisky Society (www.smws.com) has branches all round the world. Membership of the society costs from £100 for the first year (£52 a year thereafter) and includes use of members' rooms in Edinburgh and London.

...Or a Wee Dram?

Scotch whisky (always spelt without an 'e' – whiskey with an 'e' is Irish or American) is Scotland's best-known product and biggest export. The spirit has been distilled in Scotland at least since the 15th century.

As well as whiskies, there are whisky-based liqueurs such as Drambuie. If you must mix your whisky with anything other than water, try a whisky-mac (whisky with ginger wine). After a long walk in the rain there's nothing better to put a warm glow in your belly.

At a bar, older Scots may order a 'half' or 'nip' of whisky as a chaser to a pint or half-pint of beer (a 'hauf and a hauf'). Only tourists ask for 'Scotch' – what else would you be served in Scotland? The standard measure in pubs is either 25mL or 35mL.

The website www.scottishbrewing.com has a comprehensive list of Scottish breweries, both large and small.

Top 10 Single Malt Whiskies – Our Choice

After a great deal of diligent research (and not a few sore heads), Lonely Planet's *Scotland* authors have selected their 10 favourite single malts from across the country.

Ardbeg (Islay) The 10-year old from this noble Islay distillery is a byword for excellence. Peaty but well balanced. Hits the spot after a hill walk (p276).

Bowmore (Islay) Smoke, peat and salty sea air – a classic Islay malt. One of the few distilleries that still malts its own barley (p277).

Bruichladdich (Islay) A visitor-friendly distillery with a quirky, innovative approach – famous for very peaty special releases such as Moine Mhor (p278).

Glendronach (Speyside) Only sherry casks are used here, so the creamy, spicy result tastes like Grandma's Christmas trifle.

Highland Park (Island) Full and rounded, with heather, honey, malt and peat. Award-winning distillery tour (p407).

Isle of Arran (Island) One of the newest of Scotland's distilleries, offering a lightish, flavoursome malt with flowery, fruity notes (p159).

Macallan (Speyside) The king of Speyside malts, with sherry and bourbon finishes. Distillery set amid waving fields of Golden Promise barley (p255).

Springbank (Campbeltown) Complex flavours – sherry, citrus, pear-drops, peat – with a salty tang. Entire production process from malting to bottling takes place on site (p274).

Talisker (Island) Brooding, heavily peaty nose balanced by a satisfying sweetness from this lord of the isles. Great postdinner dram (p383).

The Balvenie (Speyside) Rich and honeyed, this Speysider is liquid gold for those with a sweet tooth.

THE SCOTTISH LARDER WHAT ARE YE DRINKIN'?

BREWERIES

Scottish Culture

Arts

Literature

Burns & Scott

Scotland's best-loved and most famous literary figure is, of course, Robert Burns (1759–96). His works have been translated into dozens of languages and are known and admired the world over.

In 1787 Burns was introduced to a 16-year-old boy at a social gathering in the house of an Edinburgh professor. The boy grew up to be Sir Walter Scott (1771–1832), Scotland's greatest and most prolific novelist. The son of an Edinburgh lawyer, Scott was born in Guthrie St (off Chambers St; the house no longer exists) and lived at various New Town addresses before moving to his country house at Abbotsford. Scott's early works were rhyming ballads, such as *The Lady of the Lake,* and his first historical novels – Scott effectively invented the genre – were published anonymously. He almost single-handedly revived interest in Scottish history and legend in the early 19th century, and was largely responsible for organising King George IV's visit to Scotland in 1822. Plagued by debt in later life, he wrote obsessively – to the detriment of his health – in order to make money, but will always be best remembered for classic tales such as *Waverley, The Antiquary, The Heart of Midlothian, Ivanhoe, Redgauntlet* and *Castle Dangerous.*

RLS & Sherlock Holmes

Along with Scott, Robert Louis Stevenson (1850–94) ranks as Scotland's best-known novelist. Born at 8 Howard Pl in Edinburgh into a family of famous lighthouse engineers, Stevenson studied law at Edinburgh University but was always intent on pursuing the life of a writer. An inveterate traveller, but dogged by ill health, he finally settled in Samoa in 1889, where he was revered by the natives as 'Tusitala' – the teller of tales. Stevenson is known and loved around the world for those tales: *Kidnapped, Catriona, Treasure Island, The Master of Ballantrae* and *The Strange Case of Dr Jekyll and Mr Hyde.* The Writers' Museum in Edinburgh celebrates the work of Burns, Scott and Stevenson.

Sir Arthur Conan Doyle (1859–1930), the creator of Sherlock Holmes, was born in Edinburgh and studied medicine at Edinburgh University. He based the character of Holmes on one of his lecturers, the surgeon Dr Joseph Bell, who had employed his forensic skills and powers of deduction on several murder cases in Edinburgh. There's a fascinating exhibit on Dr Bell in Edinburgh's Surgeons' Hall Museums.

McDiarmid to Muriel Spark

Scotland's finest modern poet was Hugh MacDiarmid (born Christopher Murray Grieve; 1892–1978). Originally from Dumfriesshire, he

---

Six Essential Scottish Novels

» *Waverley* (1814, Sir Walter Scott)

» *The Silver Darlings* (1941, Neil M Gunn)

» *A Scot's Quair* (1946, Lewis Grassic Gibbon)

» *The Prime of Miss Jean Brodie* (1962, Muriel Spark)

» *Greenvoe* (1972, George Mackay Brown)

» *Trainspotting* (1993, Irvine Welsh)

moved to Edinburgh in 1908, where he trained as a teacher and a journalist, but spent most of his life in Montrose, Shetland, Glasgow and Biggar. His masterpiece is 'A Drunk Man Looks at the Thistle', a 2685-line Joycean monologue.

Born in Edinburgh, Norman MacCaig (1910–96) is widely regarded as the greatest Scottish poet of his generation. A primary school teacher for almost 40 years, MacCaig wrote poetry that is witty, adventurous, moving and filled with sharp observation; poems such as 'November Night, Edinburgh' vividly capture the atmosphere of his home city.

The poet and storyteller George Mackay Brown (1921–96) was born in Stromness in the Orkney Islands, and lived there almost all his life. Although his poems and novels are rooted in Orkney, his work, like that of Burns, transcends local and national boundaries. His novel *Greenvoe* (1972) is a warm, witty and poetic evocation of everyday life in an Orkney community; his last novel, *Beside the Ocean of Time,* a wonderfully elegiac account of remote island life, was published in 1994.

Lewis Grassic Gibbon (born James Leslie Mitchell; 1901–35) is another Scots writer whose novels vividly capture a sense of place – in this case the rural northeast of Kincardineshire and Aberdeenshire. His most famous work is the trilogy of novels called *A Scot's Quair.*

Dame Muriel Spark (1918–2006) was born in Edinburgh and educated at James Gillespie's High School for Girls, an experience that provided material for perhaps her best-known novel, *The Prime of Miss Jean Brodie,* a shrewd portrait of 1930s Edinburgh. Dame Muriel was a prolific writer; her last novel, *The Finishing School,* published in 2004, was her 22nd.

The Contemporary Scene

The most widely known Scots writers today include the award-winning James Kelman (1946–), Iain Banks (1954–), Irvine Welsh (1961–) and Ian Rankin (1960–). The grim realities of modern Glasgow are vividly conjured up in Kelman's short story collection *Not Not While the Giro;* his controversial novel *How Late It Was, How Late* won the 1994 Booker Prize.

The novels of Irvine Welsh, who grew up in Edinburgh's working-class district of Muirhouse, describe a very different world from that inhabited by Miss Jean Brodie – the modern city's underworld of drugs, drink, despair and violence. Best known for his debut novel *Trainspot-*

AUTHOR PROFILE: IAIN BANKS

One of Scotland's most successful contemporary authors, Iain Banks (1954–) is also one of its most prolific. He has published 24 novels since 1984, 11 of them science fiction written under 'the world's most penetrable pseudonym', Iain M Banks.

Hailed as one of the most imaginative writers of his generation, Banks burst on to the Scottish literary scene with his dazzling debut novel *The Wasp Factory* (1984), a macabre but utterly compelling exploration of the inner world of Frank, a strange and deeply disturbed teenager. Though violent and unsettling, its dark humour and sharp dialogue keep the pages turning right to the bitter (and twisted) end.

Banks' 2009 novel, *Transition*, was seen as a merging of his science fiction and mainstream styles. Though enjoyable, it has a hard time living up to the impossibly high standard set by earlier books such as *Complicity* (1993), a gruesome and often hilarious thriller-satire on the greed and corruption of the Thatcher years, and the immensely likable *The Crow Road* (1992), a warm, witty and moving family saga based in the fictional Argyllshire town of Gallanach (a thinly disguised Oban transplanted to the shores of Loch Crinan). The latter provides one of Scottish fiction's most memorable opening sentences: 'It was the day my grandmother exploded'.

ting, Welsh's most accomplished work is probably *Marabou Stork Night-mares,* in which a soccer hooligan, paralysed and in a coma, reviews his violent and brutal life.

Ian Rankin's Edinburgh-based crime novels, featuring the hard-drinking, introspective Detective Inspector John Rebus, are sinister, engrossing mysteries that explore the darker side of Scotland's capital city. Rankin's novels are filled with sharp dialogue, telling detail and three-dimensional characters; he attracts a growing international following (his books have been translated into 22 languages). Rankin seems to improve with every book – the final Rebus novel, *Exit Music* (2007), is one of his best. In *The Complaints* (2009) he created a new and completely different character, Malcolm Fox, a cop who investigates other cops.

Music

Traditional Music

Scotland has always had a strong folk tradition. In the 1960s and 1970s Robin Hall and Jimmy MacGregor, the Corries and the hugely talented Ewan McColl worked the pubs and clubs up and down the country. The Boys of the Lough, headed by Shetland fiddler Aly Bain, was one of the first professional bands to promote the traditional Celtic music of Scotland and Ireland. It has been followed by the Battlefield Band, Runrig (who writes songs in Gaelic), Alba, Capercaillie and others.

The Scots folk songs that you will often hear sung in pubs and at *ceilidhs* (evenings of traditional Scottish entertainment, including music, song and dance) draw on Scotland's rich history. A huge number of them relate to the Jacobite rebellions in the 18th century and, in particular, to Bonnie Prince Charlie – 'Hey Johnnie Cope', the 'Skye Boat Song' and 'Will Ye No Come Back Again', for example – while others relate to the Covenanters and the Highland Clearances.

In recent years there has been a revival in traditional music, often adapted and updated for the modern age. Bands such as Runrig pioneered with their own brand of Celtic rock, while Shooglenifty blend Scottish folk music with anything from indie rock to electronica, producing a hybrid that has been called 'acid croft'.

But perhaps the finest modern renderings of traditional Scottish songs come from singer-songwriter Eddi Reader, who rose to fame with the band Fairground Attraction and their 1988 No 1 hit 'Perfect'. Since then her solo career has combined original songwriting with performances of traditional Scottish folk songs – her album *Eddi Reader Sings the Songs of Robert Burns* (2003, re-released with extra tracks in 2009) is widely regarded as one of the best interpretations of Burns' works.

Bagpipe music may not be to everyone's taste, but Scotland's most famous instrument has been reinvented by bands like the Red Hot Chilli Pipers, who use pipes, drums, guitars and keyboards to create rock versions of trad tunes that have been christened, tongue firmly in cheek, as 'Jock 'n' Roll'. They feature regularly at festivals throughout the country.

Rock & Pop

It would take an entire book to list all the Scottish artists and bands that have made it big in the world of rock and pop. From Glasgow-born King of Skiffle, Lonnie Donegan, in the 1950s, to the Glasgow-bred kings of guitar-pop Franz Ferdinand today, the roll call is long and impressive.

The 1960s saw Lulu shout her way into the charts, alongside Donovan and the Incredible String Band, while the '70s produced the Average White Band, Nazareth, the Sensational Alex Harvey Band, John Martyn and – God help us – the Bay City Rollers, a global phenomenon

The Living Tradition is a bimonthly magazine covering the folk and traditional music of Scotland and the British Isles, as well as Celtic music, with features and reviews of albums and live gigs. See also www.folkmusic.net.

The Traditional Music & Song Association (www.tmsa. org.uk) website has listings of music, dance and cultural festivals around Scotland.

whose allure remains a mystery to all except those who were teenage girls in the early 1970s.

The punk era produced the short-lived but superb Rezillos, plus the more durable Big Country, followed by a long roll call of other chart-toppers in the '80s – Simple Minds, the Waterboys, Primal Scream, Jesus and Mary Chain, Blue Nile, Lloyd Cole and the Commotions, Aztec Camera, the Associates, Deacon Blue, the Cocteau Twins, the Proclaimers, Wet Wet Wet, Texas, Hue and Cry, Runrig, the Bluebells – where do you stop?

The '90s saw the emergence of three bands that took the top three places in a vote for the best Scottish band of all time – melodic indie-pop songsters Belle and Sebastian, like-Oasis-only-better Brit-rock band Travis, and indie rockers Idlewild, who opened for the Rolling Stones in 2003 – as well as the Delgados, Trashcan Sinatras and Teenage Fanclub.

The bespectacled twin brothers Craig and Charlie Reid from Auchtermuchty in Fife, better known as the Proclaimers, produced a new album in 2009 *(Notes and Rhymes),* which is as passionate and invigorating as the songs that first made them famous back in the late '80s, 'Letter From America', and 'I'm Gonna Be (500 Miles)'.

Scottish artists who have made an impression in the last five years include award-winning Glasgow band Glasvegas, who played the Lollapalooza festival in Chicago in 2009; Ayrshire rockers Biffy Clyro; and the darlings of indie rock, the View, who should have released their third album by the time you read this.

The airwaves have been awash with female singer-songwriters in recent years, but few are as gutsy and versatile as Edinburgh-born, St Andrews–raised KT Tunstall. Although she's been writing and singing since the late 1990s, it was her 2005 debut album *Eye to the Telescope* that introduced her to a wider audience. And then there's Glasgow-born Amy Macdonald, who was only 20 years old when her first album *This is the Life* (2007) sold 3 million copies; her second, *A Curious Thing,* was released in 2010.

Painting
Monarch of the Glen

If asked to think of a Scottish painting, most people probably picture *Monarch of the Glen,* a romanticised portrait of a magnificent Highland red deer stag by Sir Edwin Landseer (1802–73). Landseer was not a Scot but a Londoner, though he did spend a lot of time in Scotland, leasing a cottage in Glen Feshie and visiting the young Queen Victoria at Balmoral to tutor her in drawing and etching.

Classical Portraitists

Perhaps the most famous Scottish painting is the portrait *Reverend Robert Walker Skating on Duddingston Loch* by Sir Henry Raeburn (1756–1823), in the National Gallery of Scotland. This image of a Presbyterian minister at play beneath Arthur's Seat, with all the poise of a ballerina and the hint of a smile on his lips, is a symbol of Enlightenment Edinburgh, the triumph of reason over wild nature.

Scottish portraiture reached its peak during the Scottish Enlightenment in the second half of the 18th century with the paintings of Raeburn and his contemporary Allan Ramsay (1713–84). You can see many fine examples of their work in the Scottish National Portrait Gallery. At the same time, Alexander Nasmyth (1758–1840) emerged as an important landscape painter whose work had an immense influence on the 19th century. One of the greatest artists of the 19th century was Sir David Wilkie (1785–1841), whose genre paintings depicted rustic scenes of rural Highland life.

Scottish Pop Playlist

» Franz Ferdinand: 'Take Me Out'

» KT Tunstall: 'Suddenly I See'

» The Proclaimers: 'Letter from America'

» The View: 'Same Jeans'

» Biffy Clyro: 'Bubbles'

» Amy Macdonald: 'This is the Life'

» Runrig: 'Loch Lomond'

» The Rezillos: 'Top of the Pops'

» Simple Minds: 'Don't You (Forget About Me)'

» Texas: 'Say What You Want'

The Scottish Colourists

In the early 20th century the Scottish painters most widely acclaimed outside of the country were the group known as the Scottish Colourists – SJ Peploe, Francis Cadell, Leslie Hunter and JD Fergusson – whose striking paintings drew on French post-Impressionist and Fauvist influences. Peploe and Cadell, active in the 1920s and 1930s, often spent the summer painting together on the Isle of Iona, and reproductions of their beautiful landscapes and seascapes appear on many a print and postcard. Aberdeen Art Gallery, Kirkcaldy Museum & Art Gallery and the JD Fergusson Gallery in Perth all have good examples of their work.

The Edinburgh School

In the 1930s a group of modernist landscape artists called themselves the Edinburgh School. Chief among them were William Gillies (1898–1978), Sir William MacTaggart (1903–81) and Anne Redpath (1895–1965). Following WWII, artists such as Alan Davie (1920–) and Sir Eduardo Paolozzi (1924–2005) gained international reputations in abstract expressionism and pop art. The Dean Gallery in Edinburgh has a large collection of Paolozzi's work.

Contemporary Artists

Among contemporary Scottish artists the most famous – or infamous – are Peter Howson and Jack Vettriano. Howson (1958–), best known for his grim portraits of Glasgow down-and-outs and muscular workers, hit the headlines when he went to Bosnia as an official war artist in 1993 and produced some disturbing and controversial works. *Croatian and Muslim,* an uncompromising rape scene, sparked a debate about what was acceptable in a public exhibition of art. More recently his nude portraits of pop icon Madonna garnered even more press. His work is much sought after and collected by celebrities such as David Bowie and Madonna herself. You can see examples of Howson's work at Aberdeen Art Gallery and Glasgow's Gallery of Modern Art.

Jack Vettriano (1954–) was formerly a mining engineer, but now ranks as one of Scotland's most commercially successful artists. An entirely self-taught painter, his work – realistic, voyeuristic, occasionally sinister and often carrying a powerful erotic charge – has been compared to that of the American painters Edward Hopper and Walter Sickert. You can see reproductions of his work in coffee-table books and posters, but not in any Scottish art gallery. The Scottish art establishment looks down its nose at him, despite – or perhaps because of – the enormous popularity of his work.

Top Five Scottish Films

» *The 39 Steps* (1935)

» *Whisky Galore!* (1949)

» *Local Hero* (1983)

» *Rob Roy* (1995)

» *Trainspotting* (1996)

Cinema

Perthshire-born John Grierson (1898–1972) is acknowledged around the world as the father of the documentary film. His legacy includes the classic *Drifters* (about the Scottish herring fishery) and *Seaward the Great Ships* (about Clyde shipbuilding). Filmmaker Bill Douglas (1934–91), the director of an award-winning trilogy of films documenting his childhood and early adult life, was born in the former mining village of Newcraighall just south of Edinburgh.

Glasgow-born writer-director Bill Forsyth (1946–) is best known for *Local Hero* (1983), a gentle comedy about an oil magnate seduced by the beauty of the Highlands, and *Gregory's Girl* (1980), about an awkward teenage schoolboy's romantic exploits. The directing credits of Gillies MacKinnon (1948–), another Glasgow native, include *Small Faces* (1996), *Regeneration* (1997) and *Hideous Kinky* (1998). Michael Caton-

Jones (1958–), director of *Memphis Belle* (1990) and *Rob Roy* (1995), was born in West Lothian and is a graduate of Edinburgh University.

In the 1990s the rise of the director-producer-writer team of Danny Boyle (English), Andrew Macdonald and John Hodge (both Scottish) – who wrote the scripts for *Shallow Grave* (1994), *Trainspotting* (1996) and *A Life Less Ordinary* (1997) – marked the beginnings of what might be described as a home-grown Scottish film industry. Writer and director David McKenzie hit the headlines in 2003 with *Young Adam*, which starred Ewan McGregor and Tilda Swinton, and won BAFTAs for best actor, best actress, best director and best film. McKenzie recently gave us *Hallam Foe* (2007) and *Perfect Sense* (2010).

Other Scottish directorial talent includes Kevin Macdonald, who made *Touching the Void* (2003), *The Last King of Scotland* (2006) and *State of Play* (2009), and Andrea Arnold, who directed *Red Road* (2006) and the BAFTA-winning *Fish Tank* (2009).

> For a guide to Scottish film locations check out www.scotlandthe movie.com.

Scottish Actors

Scotland's most famous actor is, of course, Sir Sean Connery (1930–), the original and best James Bond, and star of dozens of other hit films including *Highlander* (1986), *The Name of the Rose* (1986), *Indiana Jones and the Last Crusade* (1989), *The Hunt for Red October* (1990) and *The League of Extraordinary Gentlemen* (2003). Connery started life as 'Big Tam' Connery, sometime milkman and brickie, born in a tenement in Fountainbridge, Edinburgh.

Other Scottish actors who have achieved international recognition include Robert Carlyle, who starred in *Trainspotting* (1996), *The Full Monty* (1997) – the UK's most commercially successful film – *The World Is Not Enough* (1999) and *28 Weeks Later* (2007); Ewan McGregor, who appeared in *Trainspotting*, the most recent Star Wars films, *Angels and Demons* (2009) and *The Ghost* (2010); and Kelly Macdonald, yet another *Trainspotting* alumna who went on to appear in *Gosford Park* (2001), *No Country for Old Men* (2007) and *Boardwalk Empire* (2010).

> Despite dodgy Scottish accents from Liam Neeson and Jessica Lange, *Rob Roy* is a witty and moving cinematic version of Sir Walter Scott's tale of the outlaw MacGregor.

It's less widely known that Scotland produced some of the stars of silent film, including Eric Campbell (the big, bearded villain in Charlie Chaplin's films) and Jimmy Finlayson (the cross-eyed character in Laurel and Hardy films); in fact English-born Stan Laurel grew up and made his acting debut in Glasgow.

Architecture

There are interesting buildings all over Scotland, but Edinburgh has a particularly rich heritage of 18th- and early-19th-century architecture, and Glasgow is noted for its superb Victorian buildings.

Prehistoric

The northern islands of Scotland have some of the best surviving examples of prehistoric buildings in Europe. The best known are the stone villages of Skara Brae (from 3100 BC) in Orkney, and Jarlshof (from 1500 BC) in Shetland. The characteristic stone defensive towers known as brochs that can be seen in the north and west, including Glenelg (south of Kyle of Lochalsh), Dun Carloway (Lewis) and Mousa (Shetland), are thought to date from the Iron Age (2nd century BC to 1st century AD).

> **Top Prehistoric Sites**
> » Kilmartin Glen
> » Skara Brae
> » Broch of Gurness
> » Callanish
> » Maes Howe

Romanesque (12th Century)

The Romanesque style – with its characteristic round arches and chevron decoration – was introduced to Scotland via the monasteries that were founded during the reign of David I (1124–53). Good examples survive in Dunfermline Abbey, and St Magnus Cathedral in Kirkwall.

THE SCOTTISH LANGUAGE

Scottish Gaelic (Gàidhlig – pronounced 'gallic' in Scotland) is spoken by about 80,000 people in Scotland, mainly in the Highlands and islands, and by many native speakers and learners overseas. It is a member of the Celtic branch of the Indo-European family of languages, which has given us Gaelic, Irish, Manx, Welsh, Cornish and Breton.

Although Scottish Gaelic is the Celtic language most closely associated with Scotland, it was quite a latecomer to those shores. Other Celtic languages, namely Pictish and Brittonic, had existed prior to the arrival and settlement by Gaelic-speaking Celts (Gaels) from Ireland from the 4th to the 6th centuries AD. These Irish settlers, known to the Romans as Scotti, were eventually to give their name to the entire country. As their territorial influence extended so did their language, and from the 9th to the 11th centuries Gaelic was spoken throughout the country. For many centuries the language was the same as the language of Ireland; there is little evidence of much divergence before the 13th century. Even up to the 18th century the bards adhered to the strict literary standards of Old Irish.

Gaelic culture flourished in the Highlands until the 18th century and the Jacobite rebellions. After the Battle of Culloden in 1746 many Gaelic speakers were forced from their ancestral lands; this 'ethnic cleansing' by landlords and governments culminated in the Highland Clearances of the 19th century. Although still studied at academic level, the spoken language declined, being regarded as little more than a mere 'peasant' language of no modern significance.

It was only in the 1970s that Gaelic began to make a comeback with a new generation of young enthusiasts who were determined that it should not be allowed to die. After two centuries of decline, the language is now being encouraged through financial help from government agencies and the EU. Gaelic education is flourishing from playgroups to tertiary levels, flowing on into the fields of music, literature, cultural events and broadcasting, and people from all over Scotland, and indeed worldwide, are beginning to appreciate their Gaelic heritage.

Gothic (12th to 16th Centuries)

The more elaborate Gothic style – tall, pointed arches, ornate window tracery and ribbed vaulting – was adapted by the monastic orders. Examples of Early Gothic architecture can be seen in the ruins of the great Border abbeys of Jedburgh and Dryburgh, at Holyrood Abbey in Edinburgh and in Glasgow Cathedral. The more decorative Middle and Late Gothic styles appear in Melrose Abbey, the cathedrals of Dunkeld and Elgin, and the parish churches of Haddington and Stirling.

Best Gothic Abbeys

» Jedburgh
» Dryburgh
» Melrose
» Sweetheart
» Inchcolm
» Oronsay Priory

Post-Reformation (16th & 17th Centuries)

After the Reformation many abbeys and cathedrals were damaged or destroyed, as the new religion frowned on ceremony and ornament.

During this period the old style of castle, with its central keep and curtain wall such as at Dirleton Castle, was superseded by the tower house. Good examples include Castle Campbell, Loch Leven Castle and Neidpath Castle. The Renaissance style was introduced in the royal palaces of Linlithgow and Falkland.

Georgian (18th & Early 19th Centuries)

The leading Scottish architects of the 18th century were William Adam (1684–1748) and his son Robert Adam (1728–92), whose revival of classical Greek and Roman forms influenced architects throughout Europe. Among the many neoclassical buildings they designed are Hopetoun House, Culzean Castle and Edinburgh's Charlotte Sq, possibly the finest example of Georgian architecture anywhere.

The New Town of Edinburgh, and other planned towns such as Inveraray (Argyll) and Blair Atholl (Perthshire), are characterised by their elegant Georgian architecture.

Victorian (Mid- to Late-19th Century)

Alexander 'Greek' Thomson (1817–75) changed the face of 19th-century Glasgow with his neoclassical designs. Masterpieces such as the Egyptian Halls and Caledonia Rd Church in Glasgow combine Egyptian and Hindu motifs with Greek and Roman forms.

In Edinburgh, William Henry Playfair (1790–1857) continued Robert Adam's neoclassical tradition in the Greek temples of the National Monument on Calton Hill, the Royal Scottish Academy and the National Gallery of Scotland, before moving on to the neo-Gothic style in Edinburgh University's New College on The Mound.

The 19th-century boom in country-house building was led by architects William Burn (1789–1870) and David Bryce (1803–76). The resurgence of interest in Scottish history and identity, led by writers such as Sir Walter Scott, saw architects turn to the towers, pointed turrets and crow-stepped gables of the 16th century for inspiration. The Victorian revival of the Scottish Baronial style, which first made an appearance in 16th-century buildings such as Craigievar Castle, produced many fanciful abodes such as Balmoral Castle, Scone Palace and Abbotsford.

The 20th Century

Scotland's best known 20th-century architect and designer is Charles Rennie Mackintosh (1868–1928), one of the most influential exponents of the art-nouveau style. His finest building is the Glasgow School of Art (1896), which still looks modern more than a century after it was built. The art-deco style of the 1930s made little impact in Scotland; the few examples include St Andrews House in Edinburgh and the beautifully restored Luma Tower in Glasgow.

During the 1960s Scotland's larger towns and cities suffered badly under the onslaught of the motor car and the unsympathetic impact of large-scale, concrete building developments. However, modern architecture discovered a new confidence in the 1980s and 1990s, exemplified by the impressive gallery housing the Burrell Collection in Glasgow and the stunning modern buildings lining the banks of Glasgow's River Clyde.

Scotland's most controversial new structure is the Scottish parliament building in Edinburgh.

Sport
Football

Football (soccer) in Scotland is not so much a sport as a religion, with thousands turning out to worship their local teams on Wednesdays and weekends throughout the season (August to May). Sacred rites include standing in the freezing cold of a February day, drinking hot Bovril and eating a Scotch pie as you watch your team getting gubbed.

Scotland's top 10 clubs play in the Scottish Premier League (www .scotprem.com), but two teams – Glasgow Rangers and Glasgow Celtic – dominate the competition. On only 18 occasions since 1890 has a team other than Rangers or Celtic won the league; the last time was when Aberdeen won in 1985. Celtic was Premier League champion from 2006 to 2008, Rangers in 2009 and 2010.

Glasgow Celtic was the first British team to win the European Cup (1967) and, so far, the only Scottish club to have done so. The team that won back then was made up entirely of Scots players from the Glasgow area. In comparison, Rangers made history in 2000 by being the first to

Scotland's Castles by Chris Tabraham is an excellent companion for anyone touring Scottish castles – a readable, illustrated history detailing how and why they were built.

field a team composed entirely of non-Scottish players, and today half the players in the Premier League are of non-Scottish origin, a situation that angers many grassroots supporters and bodes ill for the future of the national team.

If supporting local teams is like a religion, supporting the Scottish national team is more like a penance. The beginning of each European Championship and World Cup is filled with hope, but usually ends in despair.

Despite their team's often poor results, Scotland fans – known as the Tartan Army – are famed for their friendliness and good behaviour abroad, to the extent that some English and French football fans have joined them. The non-Scottish contingent has been dubbed the 'Sporran Legion'.

Shinty (*camanachd* in Gaelic) is a fast and physical ball-and-stick sport similar to Ireland's hurling, with more than a little resemblance to clan warfare. It's an indigenous Scottish game played mainly in the Highlands, and the most prized trophy is the Camanachd Cup. For more information, see www.shinty.com.

Rugby Union

Traditionally, football was the sport of Scotland's urban working classes, while rugby union (www.scottishrugby.org) was the preserve of agricultural workers from the Borders and middle-class university graduates. Although this distinction is breaking down – rugby's popularity soared after the 1999 World Cup was staged in the UK, and the middle classes have invaded the football terraces – it persists to some extent.

Each year, starting in January, Scotland takes part in the Six Nations Rugby Union Championship. The most important fixture is the clash against England for the Calcutta Cup – it's always an emotive event; Scotland has won three times and drawn once in the last 10 years.

At club level, the season runs from September to May, and among the better teams are those from the Borders such as Hawick, Kelso and Melrose. At the end of the season, teams play a rugby sevens (seven-a-side) variation of the 15-player competition.

Curling, a winter sport which involves propelling a 19kg granite stone along the ice towards a target, was probably invented in Scotland in medieval times. For more information, see www. royalcaledonian curlingclub.org.

Golf

Scotland is the home of golf (www.scottishgolfunion.org). The game was probably invented here in the 12th century, and the world's oldest documentary evidence of a game being played (dating from 1456) was on Bruntsfield Links in Edinburgh.

Although St Andrews claims seniority in having the oldest golf course in the world, it was at Edinburgh's Leith Links in 1744 that the first official rules of the game were formulated by the Honourable Company of Edinburgh Golfers (now the famous Muirfield Golf Club). Rule number 9 gives some insight into the 18th-century game – 'If a ball be stop'd by any person, Horse, Dog or anything else, the Ball so stop'd must be played where it lyes'.

Today, there are more than 550 golf courses in Scotland – that's more per capita than in any other country. The sport is hugely popular and much more egalitarian than in other countries, with lots of affordable, council-owned courses. There are many world-famous championship courses too, from Muirfield in East Lothian and Turnberry and Troon in Ayrshire, to Carnoustie in Angus and St Andrews' Old Course in Fife.

In the realm of professional golf, Colin Montgomerie has been Scotland's top golfer for over a decade, consistently finishing in the top five in international tournaments. His best result was in the 2005 British Open Championship at St Andrews, where Montgomerie was runner-up to Tiger Woods, and he lost the 2006 US Open by a single shot – he's widely regarded as the best golfer never to have won a major tournament.

Caledonian Icons

Bagpipes

Highland soldiers were traditionally accompanied into battle by the skirl of the pipes, and the Scottish Highland bagpipe is unique in being the only musical instrument ever to be classed as a weapon. The playing of the pipes was banned – under pain of death – by the British government in 1747 as part of a scheme to suppress Highland culture in the wake of the Jacobite uprising of 1745 (p450). The pipes were revived when the Highland regiments were drafted into the British Army towards the end of the 18th century.

The bagpipe consists of a leather bag held under the arm, kept inflated by blowing through the blowstick; the piper forces air through the pipes by squeezing the bag with the forearm. Three of the pipes, known as drones, play a constant note (one bass, two tenor) in the background. The fourth pipe, the chanter, plays the melody.

Ceilidhs

The Gaelic word *ceilidh* (*kay*-lay) means 'visit'. A *ceilidh* was originally a social gathering in the house after the day's work was over, enlivened with storytelling, music and song. These days, a *ceilidh* means an evening of traditional Scottish entertainment including music, song and dance. To find one, check the village noticeboard, or just ask at the local pub; visitors are always welcome to join in.

Tartan

The oldest surviving piece of tartan – a patterned woollen textile now made into everything from kilts to key rings – dates back to the Roman period. Today tartan is popular the world over, and beyond – astronaut Al Bean took his MacBean tartan to the moon and back. Particular setts (tartan patterns) didn't come to be associated with particular clans until the 17th century, although today every clan, and indeed every Scottish football team, has one or more distinctive tartans.

The Kilt

The original Scottish Highland dress was not the kilt but the plaid – a long length of tartan cloth wrapped around the body and over the shoulder. The wearing of Highland dress was banned after the Jacobite rebellions but revived under royal patronage in the 19th century. George IV and his English courtiers donned kilts for their visit to Scotland in 1822. During the same century Sir Walter Scott, novelist, poet and dedicated patriot, did much to rekindle interest in Scottish ways. By then, however, many of the old setts had been forgotten, and as a result some tartans are actually Victorian creations. The modern kilt only appeared in the 18th century and was reputedly invented by Thomas Rawlinson, an Englishman!

The Falkirk Tartan is a piece of cream and brown cloth that was found with a hoard of Roman coins dating from around AD 320. It is now in the Museum of Scotland in Edinburgh.

TARTAN

You can search for your own clan tartan at www.tartansauthority.com.

Kilts don't have pockets, so kilted Scotsmen keep their beer money in a sporran, a pouch made of leather or animal skin that hangs in front of the kilt, suspended from a chain around the waist.

The Saltire & the Lion Rampant

Scottish football and rugby supporters can never seem to make up their minds which flag to wave, the Saltire or the Lion Rampant. The Saltire, or St Andrew's Cross – a diagonal white cross on a blue ground – is one of the oldest national emblems in the world, dating from at least the 12th century. Originally a religious symbol – St Andrew was crucified on a diagonal cross – it was adopted as Scotland's national flag in the late 14th century. According to legend, white clouds in the form of a saltire appeared in a blue sky during the battle of Nechtansmere between Scots and Saxons, urging the Scots to victory. It was incorporated in the Union Flag of the UK following the Act of Union in 1707.

The Lion Rampant – a red lion on a golden-yellow ground – is the Royal Banner of Scotland. It is thought to derive from the arms of King William I the Lion (r 1143–1214), and strictly speaking should only be used by a Scottish monarch. It is incorporated in the British Royal Standard, quartered with the three lions of England and the harp of Ireland.

For a modern designer take on the classic item of Scottish menswear, check out 21st Century Kilts (www.21st centurykilts.com).

Highland Games

Highland games are held in Scotland throughout the summer, and not just in the Highlands. You can find dates and details of Highland games held all over the country on the website VisitScotland (www.visitscot land.com) – follow the links What to See & Do/What's On/Highland Games.

The traditional sporting events are accompanied by piping and dancing competitions and attract locals and tourists alike. Some events are peculiarly Scottish, particularly those that involve trials of strength: tossing the caber (heaving a tree trunk into the air), throwing the hammer and putting the stone. Major Highland games are staged at Dunoon, Oban and Braemar.

More Scottish Inventions

» Antiseptic
» Breech-loading rifle
» Colour photography
» Kaleidoscope
» Lawnmower
» Logarithm
» Marmalade
» Refrigeration
» Ultrasound
» Vacuum flask

Famous Inventors

The Scots have made a contribution to modern civilisation that is out of all proportion to the size of their country. Although Scotland accounts for only 10% of Britain's population, it has produced more than 20% of leading British scientists, philosophers, engineers and inventors. Scots established the modern disciplines of economics, sociology, geology, electromagnetic theory, anaesthesiology and antibiotics, and pioneered the steam engine, the pneumatic tyre, the telephone and the TV.

Given the weather in Scotland perhaps it's not surprising that it was a Scot – the chemist Charles Macintosh (1766–1843) – who invented the waterproof material for the raincoat that still bears his name.

James Watt (1736–1819) didn't invent the steam engine (that was done by an Englishman, Thomas Newcomen), but it was Watt's modifications and improvements – notably the separate condenser – that led to its widespread usefulness in industry.

The chemical engineer James Young (1811–83), known as 'Paraffin' Young, developed the process of refining crude oil and established the world's first oil industry, based on extracting oil from the oil shales of West Lothian.

Not only did John Logie Baird (1888–1946) from Helensburgh invent TV, but it was his own company that produced (with the BBC) the world's first TV broadcast, the first broadcast with sound and the first outside broadcast. He also developed the concept of colour TV and took out a patent on fibre optics.

Alexander Graham Bell (1847–1922) was born in Edinburgh and emigrated to Canada and the USA, where he made a series of inventions, the most famous being the telephone in 1876.

The list of famous Scots goes on and on: James Gregory (1638–75), inventor of the reflecting telescope; John McAdam (1756–1836), who developed road-building and surfacing techniques; Thomas Telford (1757–1834), one of the greatest civil engineers of his time; Robert William Thomson (1822–73), who patented the pneumatic tyre in 1845; John Boyd Dunlop (1840–1921), who reinvented the pneumatic tyre in 1888; and Sir Robert Watson-Watt (1892–1973), a direct descendant of James Watt, who developed the radar system that helped Britain to victory in WWII.

There are an estimated 60 million people around the world who claim Scottish ancestry.

Wild Scotland

Visitors revel in the solitude and dramatic scenery encompassing so much of rural Scotland. Soaring peaks with veins of snow trickling down their summits, steely blue lochs, deep inlets, forgotten beaches and surging peninsulas are a taste of the astonishing natural diversity. The best wildlife in Britain – from the emblematic osprey to the red deer, its bellow reverberating among large strands of native forest – is found throughout the wild places of Scotland. Large chunks of land moored just offshore or miles out into the raging northern Atlantic Ocean, are havens for species hunted to extinction centuries ago in habitats further south. Cetaceans patrol the seas, and the remote archipelagos of the northeast are havens for seabird breeding colonies of extraordinary magnitude.

> Seventeen per cent of Scotland is forested, compared with England's 7%, Finland's 74% and a worldwide average of 30%.

The Land

Scotland's mainland can be neatly divided into thirds. The Southern Uplands, ranges of grassy rounded hills divided by wide valleys and bounded by fertile coastal plains, form the southern boundary to the Central Lowlands. The geological divide – the Southern Uplands Fault – runs in a line from Girvan (Ayrshire) to Dunbar (East Lothian).

The Central Lowlands lie in a broad band stretching from Glasgow and Ayr in the west to Edinburgh and Dundee in the east. This area is underlaid by sedimentary rocks, including the beds of coal and oil shale that fuelled Scotland's Industrial Revolution. Though it's only a fifth of the nation by land area, most of the country's industry, its two largest cities and 80% of the population are concentrated here.

Another great geological divide – the Highland Boundary Fault – runs from Helensburgh in the west to Stonehaven on the east coast, and marks the southern edge of the Scottish Highlands. These hills – most of their summits reach to around the 29500ft (900m) to 3280ft (1000m) mark – were deeply dissected by glaciers during the last Ice Age, creating a series of deep, U-shaped valleys: the long, narrow sea lochs that today are such a feature of Highland scenery. The Highlands form some 60% of the Scottish mainland, and are cut in two by the Great Glen, a rift valley running southwest to northeast.

> Scotland accounts for one third of the British mainland's surface area, but it has a massive 80% of Britain's coastline and only 10% of its population.

Despite their pristine beauty, the wild, empty landscapes of the western and northern Highlands are artificial wildernesses. Before the Highland Clearances (see p366) many of these empty corners of Scotland supported sizable rural populations.

Offshore, some 800 islands are concentrated in four main groups; the Shetlands, the Orkneys, the Outer Hebrides and the Inner Hebrides.

The Water

It rains a lot in Scotland – some parts of the western Highlands get over 4.5m of it a year – so it's not surprising there's plenty of water about. Around 3% of Scotland's land surface is fresh water; the numerous lochs, rivers and burns (streams) form the majority of this, but about a third is in the form of wetlands: the peat bogs and fens (mires) that form so much of the Highland and island landscape.

But it's the salt water that really shapes the country. Including the islands, there's over 10,000 miles of Scottish shoreline: tortuous, complex, coastline that doubles back on itself at the slightest opportunity. Scotland is defined as much by its water as by its land.

Wildlife

Scotland's wildlife is one of its big attractions, and the best way to see it is to get out there. Pull on the boots and sling on the binoculars, go quietly and see what you can spot. Many species that have disappeared from, or are rare in, the rest of Britain survive here.

Animals

While the Loch Ness monster still hogs headlines, Scotland's wild places harbour a wide variety of animals. Britain's largest land animal, the red deer, is present in numbers, as is the commoner roe deer. You'll see them if you spend any time in the Highlands: some are quite content to wander down the village street in the evening and crop at the lawns.

Otters are found in most parts of Scotland, around the coast and along salmon and trout rivers. The best places to spot them are in the northwest, especially in Skye and the Outer Hebrides. The piers at Kyle of Lochalsh and Portree are otter 'hot spots', as the otters have learned to scavenge from fishing boats.

Scotland is home to 75% of Britain's red-squirrel population; they've been pushed out in most of the rest of the country by the dominant greys, native to North America. The greys often carry a virus that's lethal to the reds, so measures are in place to try to prevent their further encroachment.

Other small mammals include the Orkney vole and various bats, as well as stoats and weasels. The blue mountain hare dwells in high mountain environments, and swaps a grey-brown summer coat for a pure white winter one.

Rarer beasts that were slaughtered to the point of extermination in the 19th century include pine martens, polecats and wildcats. Populations of these are small and remote, but are slowly recovering thanks to their protected status and greater awareness.

Some 90% of Britain's surface fresh water is found in Scotland, and Loch Lomond is Britain's biggest body of fresh water.

WINDING BACK THE CLOCK

Over the centuries many species have disappeared from Scotland, hunted into oblivion or left in the lurch after the destruction of their habitat or food supply. As a means of increasing biodiversity, there's a strong case for bringing some of them back. Though it has detractors, reintroduction of species has been implemented successfully in several instances. The red kite and the majestic white-tailed sea eagle, absent from Britain since the 19th century, are now soaring Scottish skies again. The former, distinguishable by their yellow beak and talons, are found along the west coast and in the Hebrides – visitors can see them (via TV cameras) at Aros Experience on Skye (p384). Galloway Forest Park (p174) is a good place to spot red kites.

The European beaver was released to the Scottish wilds in 2009 (see the boxed text, p272), a move opposed by some campaigners, who felt beavers might negatively impact the forests or water quality; the situation is being carefully monitored. The first beaver kits (young) were spotted in an Argyll forest in the summer of 2010.

But the mildly controversial beaver pales beside events at one Highland estate: the owner has already shipped in elk (moose), and wants to go for wolves next (see the boxed text, p356).

Of course, most animals you'll see will be in fields or getting in your way on single-track roads. Several indigenous sheep varieties are still around, smaller and stragglier than the purpose-bred supermodels we're used to. Other emblematic domestic animals include the Shetland pony and gentle Highland cow with its horns and shaggy reddish-brown coat and fringe.

The waters off Scotland's north and west coasts are rich in marine mammals. Dolphins and porpoises are fairly common, and in summer minke whales are regular visitors. Orcas, too, are regularly sighted around the Shetlands and Orkneys. Seals are widespread. Both the Atlantic grey (identified by its Roman nose) and the common seal (with a face like a dog) are easily seen along the coasts and, especially the islands.

Birds

Scotland has an immense variety of birds. For birdwatchers, the Shetland Islands (see p435) are paradise. Twenty-one of the British Isles' 24 seabird species are found here, breeding in huge colonies, and being entertained by the clownish antics of the puffin is a highlight for visitors.

Large numbers of grouse – a popular game bird – graze the heather on the moors. The ptarmigan (a type of grouse) is a native of the hills, seldom seen below 700m, with the unusual feature of having feathered feet. It is the only British bird that plays the Arctic trick of changing its plumage from mottled brown in summer to dazzling white in winter, the better to blend in with the snowfields. In heavily forested areas you may see a capercaillie, a black, turkeylike bird and the largest member of the grouse family. Millions of greylag geese winter on Lowland stubble fields.

News on endangered Scottish birds has generally been positive in the last couple of decades. The Royal Society for the Protection of Birds (RSPB, www.rspb.org.uk) is active here, and has overseen several success stories. As well as the reintroduction of species, the population of several precariously placed bird species has stabilised.

The majestic osprey (absent for most of the 20th century) nests in Scotland from mid-March through to September, after migrating from West Africa. There are around 200 breeding pairs and you can see nesting sites throughout the country, including at Loch Garten (p332) and Loch of the Lowes (p218). Other birds of prey too, such as the golden eagle, buzzards, peregrine falcon and hen harrier, are now protected and their populations are slowly recovering.

The habitat of the once common corncrake was almost completely wiped out by modern farming methods but farmers now mow in corncrake-friendly fashion and numbers have recuperated. Listen for their distinctive call – like a thumbnail drawn along the teeth of a comb – in the Uists (p399) and at Loch Gruinart Nature Reserve on Islay (p279).

> A beautifully written book about Scotland's wildlife, penned by a man who lived and breathed alongside the country's critters in a remote part of the Highlands, is *A Last Wild Place* by Mike Tomkies.

> One of the best-loved pieces of Scottish wildlife writing is *Ring of Bright Water* by Gavin Maxwell, in which the author describes life on the remote Glenelg peninsula with his two pet otters in the 1950s.

JOURNEY OF THE SALMON

One of Scotland's most thrilling sights is the salmon's leap up a fast-flowing cascade, resolutely returning to the very river of their birth several years before. The salmon's life begins in early spring, hatching in a stretch of fresh water in some Scottish glen. Called fry at this stage and only an inch long, they stay for a couple of years, growing through the 'parr' stage to become smolt, when they head out to sea.

Their destination could be anywhere in the North Atlantic, but they eventually, sometimes after several years, return home – scientists think they may use the Earth's magnetic field to navigate – to reproduce. Arriving all through the year, but most commonly in late spring, they regain strength after the arduous journey and spawn in late autumn. That job done, the salmon dies and the cycle begins anew.

As much as the untamed wildness of Scotland fills the spirit, another of the country's delights is a more managed beauty, in the shape of its numerous gardens, which emerge from harsh winter with a riotous explosion of colour in spring and summer. In the 19th century, every castle and stately home worth its salt had a planned garden in the grounds, and the warmer parts – the southwest, the Aberdeen and Moray area, and the Gulf Stream–warmed northwest coast – are absolutely studded with them.

From royal roses at Balmoral to unlikely subtropical species at Inverewe, there's a great deal more than anyone could reasonably expect at these latitudes. The National Trust for Scotland (www.nts.org.uk) manages many of the finest gardens; its website is a good first stop to plan a route through the blooms.

Plants & Trees

Although the thistle is Scotland's national flower, more characteristic are the Scottish bluebell (harebell), carpeting native woodlands in spring; and heather, the tiny pink and purple flowers of which emerge on the moors in August. Vivid pink rhododendrons are introduced but grow vigorously, and bright yellow gorse also flowers in May and June.

Only 1% of Scotland's ancient woodlands, which once covered much of the country, survive, and these are divided into small parcels across the land. Managed regeneration forests are slowly covering more of the landscape – especially in the Highlands. Some 5000 sq miles (1.3 million hectares) of tree cover (17% of the land area) now exists; not a huge figure, but an improvement on what it was. About a third of this is controlled by the government's Forestry Commission (www .forestry.gov.uk), which, as well as conducting managed logging, dedicates large areas of it to sustainable recreational use. The vast majority of this tree cover is coniferous, and there's a plan to increase it to 25% of land area by 2050.

Scottish Environment LINK (www. scotlink.org), the umbrella body for Scotland's voluntary environmental organisations, includes 36 bodies committed to environmental sustainability.

National Parks

Scotland has two national parks – Loch Lomond & the Trossachs National Park (www.lochlomond-trossachs.org) and the Cairngorms National Park (www.cairngorms.co.uk). But national parks are only part of the story. There's a huge range of protected areas with a bewildering array of 25 distinct classifications. Fifty-one National Nature Reserves span the country, and there are also marine areas under various levels of protection.

Environmental Issues

Scotland's abundance of wind and water means the government hasn't had to look far for sources of renewable energy. The grand plan is to generate half of the country's energy needs from renewable sources by 2020, and things look to be well on track. Scotland has been a European leader in the development of wind technology; wind farms now dot the hills and firths (estuaries), and the near-constant breeze in some areas means record-breaking output from some turbines. The latest proposal, the Clyde Wind Farm in Lanarkshire, will supply power to over a quarter of a million homes once completed.

Scottish Natural Heritage (www. snh.org.uk) is the government agency responsible for the conservation of Scotland's wildlife, habitats and landscapes. A key initiative is to reverse biodiversity loss.

The problem is, although everyone agrees that wind power is clean and economical, there's a powerful NIMBY (not in my back yard) element who don't want the windmills spoiling their view. And it's not just the whirring blades, of course. A remote Highland wind farm is all very well, but the power lines trailing all the way down to the south have a significant visual and environmental impact.

Sustainable Scotland (www.sustainable-scotland.net/climatechange) is a local government initiative to combat climate change and address sustainability in Scotland. Learn about community efforts to tackle a global problem.

SUSTAINABILITY

One of Scotland's major goals over the last decade or so has been to halt a worrying decline in biodiversity on land, in the air, and in the sea. You can see progress reports on the Scottish Natural Heritage website (www.snh.gov.uk) but a huge threat to existing species is, of course, climate change. A rise of a few degrees across the north would leave plenty of mountain plants and creatures with no place to go; it's already been speculated that the steady decline in Scotland's seabird population since the early '90s is partly caused by a temperature-induced decrease in certain plankton species.

But the main cause of the worrying level of some fish stocks is clear: we've eaten them all. In 2010, the Marine (Scotland) Act was passed. It's a compromise solution that tries to both protect vulnerable marine areas and stocks and sustain the flagging fishing industry. It may well be too little, too late.

Survival
Guide

Directory A–Z

Accommodation

Scotland provides a comprehensive choice of accommodation to suit all visitors. In this book accommodation choices are flagged with price indicators, based on the cheapest accommodation for two people in high season:

ACCOMMODATION PRICE INDICATORS

£	up to £50
££	from £50 to £130
£££	£130 and over

For budget travel, the options are campsites, hostels and cheap B&Bs. In highland areas you'll find bothies – simple walkers' hostels and shelters – and in the Shetlands there are *böds* (see boxed text, p429). Above this price level is a plethora of comfortable B&Bs and guesthouses (£25 to £40 per person per night). Midrange hotels are present in most places, while for high-end lodgings (£65-plus per person a night) there are some superb hotels, the most interesting being converted castles and mansions, or chic designer options in cities.

If you're travelling solo, expect to pay a supplement in hotels and B&Bs, meaning you'll often be forking over 75% of the price of a double for your single room.

Almost all B&Bs, guesthouses and hotels (and even some hostels) provide breakfast; if this is not the case, then it is mentioned in individual reviews throughout this book.

Prices increase over the peak tourist season (June to September) and are at their highest in July and August. Outside of these months, and particularly in winter, special deals are often available at guesthouses and hotels. Smaller establishments will often close from around November to March, particularly in more remote areas. If you're going to be in Edinburgh in the festival month of August or at Hogmanay (New Year), book as far in advance as you can – a year if possible – as the city will be packed.

Tourist offices have an accommodation booking service (£3 to £4, local and national), which can be handy over summer. However, note that they can only book the ever-decreasing number of places that are registered with **VisitScotland** (www.visitscotland.com/accommodation). There are many other fine accommodation options which, mostly for the hefty registration fee, choose not to register with the tourist board. Registered places tend to be a little pricier than nonregistered ones. Visit Scotland's star system is based on a rather stringent set of criteria, so don't set too much store by it.

B&Bs & Guesthouses

B&Bs are a Scottish institution. At the bottom end you get a bedroom in a private house, a shared bathroom and a fry-up (juice, coffee or tea, cereal and cooked breakfast – bacon, eggs, sausage, baked beans and toast). Midrange B&Bs have en suite bathrooms, TVs in each room and more variety (and healthier options) for breakfast. Almost all B&Bs provide hospitality trays (tea- and coffee-making facilities) in bedrooms. An excellent option are farm B&Bs, which offer traditional Scottish hospitality, huge breakfasts and a quiet rural setting – good for discharging urban grit. Pubs may also offer cheap (and sometimes noisy) B&B and can be good fun.

BOOK YOUR STAY ONLINE

For more accommodation reviews by Lonely Planet authors, check out hotels.lonelyplanet.com/Scotland. You'll find independent reviews, as well as recommendations on the best places to stay. Best of all, you can book online.

Guesthouses, often large converted private houses, are an extension of the B&B concept. They are normally larger and more upmarket than B&Bs, offering quality food and more luxurious accommodation.

Camping & Caravan Parks

Free 'wild' camping became a legal right under the Land Reform Bill. However, campers are obliged to camp on unenclosed land, in small numbers and away from buildings and roads (see the boxed text, p27).

Commercial camping grounds are geared to caravans and vary widely in quality. There are a lot of campsites covered in this book, but it was not possible to include every campsite in the much wider network. VisitScotland has a free map, available at tourist offices, showing caravan parks and campsites around Scotland.

Homestays & Hospitality Exchange

A convenient and increasingly popular holiday option is to join an international house-exchange organisation. You sign up for a year and place your home on a website giving details of what you're looking for, where and for how long. You organise the house swap yourself with people in other countries and arrange to swap homes, rent free, for an agreed period. Shop around, as registration costs vary between organisations. Check out Home Base Holidays (www.homebase-hols.com) and Home Link International (www.homelink.org.uk).

Organisations such as Hospitality Club (www.hospitalityclub.org) put people in contact for more informal free accommodation offers – a bit like blind-date couch-surfing. Even if you're not comfortable crashing in a stranger's house, these

PRACTICALITIES

» Leaf through Edinburgh's *Scotsman* newspaper or Glasgow's *Herald*, over 225 years old.

» Have a giggle at the popular Labour-influenced tabloid, the *Daily Record*, or try the *Sunday Post* for rose-tinted nostalgia.

» BBC Radio Scotland (AM 810kHz, FM 92.4-94.7MHz) provides a Scottish point of view.

» Watch BBC1 Scotland, BBC2 Scotland and ITV stations STV or Borders. Channel Four and Five are nationwide channels with unchanged content for Scotland.

» Use the metric system for weights and measures, with the exception of road distances (in miles) and beer (in pints). The pint is 570mL, more than the US version.

» In Scotland you can't smoke in any public place with a roof and at least half enclosed. That means pubs, bus shelters, restaurants and hotels – basically, anywhere you might want to.

sites are a great way to meet locals just to go out for a pint or two.

Hostels

Numerous hostels offer cheap accommodation and are great centres for meeting fellow travellers – in Scotland the standard of facilities is generally very good. The more upmarket hostels have en suite bathrooms in their dorms, and all manner of luxuries giving them the feel of hotels if it weren't for the bunk beds.

Hostels have facilities for self-catering, and many provide internet access and can usually arrange activities and tours.

From May to September and on public holidays, hostels – even the remote rural ones – can be booked out, sometimes by large groups, so phone in advance.

INDEPENDENT & STUDENT HOSTELS

There are a large number of independent hostels, most with prices around £10 to £16. Facilities vary considerably, but some of the best are listed in this book and

because they are aimed at young backpackers, they can often be great places to party. The free *Independent Backpackers Hostels Scotland* guide (www.hostel-scotland.co.uk), available from tourist offices, lists over 100 hostels in Scotland, mostly in the north.

SCOTTISH YOUTH HOSTEL ASSOCIATION

The SYHA (☏0845 293 7373; www.syha.org.uk) has a network of decent, reasonably priced hostels and produces a free booklet available from SYHA hostels and tourist offices. There are more than 60 to choose from around the country, ranging from basic walkers' digs to mansions and castles. You've got to be an HI member to stay, but nonmembers can pay a £2 supplement per night that goes towards the £10 membership fee. Prices vary according to the month, but average around £16 to £18 per adult in high season.

Most SYHA hostels close from mid-October to early March but can be rented out by groups.

Hotels

There are some wonderfully luxurious places, including rustic countryhouse hotels in fabulous settings, and castles complete with crenellated battlements, grand staircases and the obligatory rows of stag heads. Expect all the perks at these places, often including a gym, a sauna, a pool and first-class service. Even if you're on a budget, it's worth splashing out for a night at one of the classic Highland hotels, which function as community centres, including the local pub and restaurant.

In the cities, dullish chain options dominate the mid-range category, though there are some quirkier options to be had in Glasgow and Edinburgh.

Increasingly, hotels use an airline-style pricing system, so it's worth booking well ahead to take advantage of the cheapest rates. The website www.moneysavingexpert.com has a good guide to finding cheap hotel rooms.

Try these online discount sites:

www.hotels.com
www.lastminute.com
www.laterooms.com
www.priceline.co.uk

Self-Catering Accommodation

Self-catering accommodation is very popular in Scotland and staying in a house in a city or cottage in the country gives you an opportunity to get a feel for a region and its community. The minimum stay is usually one week in the summer peak season, three days or less at other times.

We've only listed limited self-catering options in this guide. The best place to start looking for this kind of accommodation is the website of **VisitScotland** (www.visitscotland.com), which lists numerous self-catering options all over Scotland.

These options also appear in the regional accommodation guides available from tourist offices.

Expect a week's rent for a two-bedroom cottage to cost from £160 in winter, and up to £280 July to September.

The following are other places to search:

CKD Galbraith (0131-556 4422; www.ckdgalbraith.co.uk) Offers a wide range of self-catering accommodation, from cottages to castles.

Cottage Guide (www.cottageguide.co.uk) Lots of Scottish cottages to browse online.

Ecosse Unique (01835-822277; www.uniquescotland.com) Offers furnished holiday homes all over the country.

Landmark Trust (01628-825925; www.landmarktrust.org.uk) A building preservation charity that restores historic buildings and lets them out as accommodation.

University Accommodation

Many Scottish universities offer their student accommodation to visitors during the holidays. Most rooms are comfy, functional single bedrooms, some with shared bathroom, but there are also twin and family units, self-contained flats and shared houses. Full-board, half-board, B&B and self-catering options are often available. Rooms are usually let out from late June to mid-September. Details are provided throughout regional chapters.

Activities

Scotland is a brilliant place for outdoor recreation and has something to offer everyone, from those who enjoy a short stroll to full-on adrenalin junkies. Although hiking, golf, fishing and cycling are the most popular activities, there is an astonishing variety of things to do.

Most activities are well organised and have clubs and associations that can give visitors invaluable information and, sometimes, substantial discounts. **Visit Scotland** (www.visitscotland.com) has information on most activities. Its website has useful pages on fishing, golf, skiing, cycling and adventure sports.

Detailed information can be found in the regional chapters throughout this guide. Some other useful sources:

Birdwatching The **Royal Society for the Protection of Birds** (www.rspb.org.uk) should be any birdwatcher's first port of call.

Cycling There are many excellent routes throughout the country. **Sustrans** (www.sustrans.org.uk) is the first place to go for more information.

Fishing Seasons and permits vary according to locality. Permits can usually be obtained at the local tackle shop.

Golf The Official Guide to Golf in Scotland is published by VisitScotland and can also be browsed on its website.

Walking Lonely Planet's Walking in Scotland is a comprehensive walkers' resource.

Business Hours

Shops open at least 9am to 5.30pm Monday to Friday and most open Saturday too; with late-night shopping usually until 8pm Thursday in the cities. A growing number also open Sunday, typically 11am to 5pm. In the Highlands and islands Sunday opening is restricted, and it's common for there to be little or no public transport.

In this guide, specific opening hours are only listed if they differ markedly from the following:

Banks 9.30am to 4pm Monday to Friday, plus some are

open 9.30am to 12.30pm Saturday.

Nightclubs 10pm to 4am Thursday to Saturday.

Post offices 9am to 5.30pm Monday to Friday, 9am to 12.30pm Saturday.

Pubs & Bars 11am to 11pm Monday to Thursday, 11am to 1am Friday and Saturday, 12.30pm to 11pm Sunday; lunch is served noon to 2.30pm, dinner 6pm to 9pm daily.

Shops 9am to 5.30pm (or 6pm in cities) Monday to Saturday, 11am to 5pm Sunday.

Restaurants Lunch noon to 2.30pm, dinner 6pm to 9pm or 10pm; in small towns and villages the chippy (fish-and-chip shop) is often the only place to buy cooked food after 8pm.

Children

Throughout this book we have listed child-friendly accommodation and recommended places and activities suitable for families. Reviews of accommodation and eating places that are especially child-friendly are indicated by the use of this icon: 🚸.

It's well worth asking in tourist offices for local family-focused publications. *List* magazine (available at newsagents and bookshops) has a section on children's activities and events in and around Glasgow and Edinburgh; also check local newspapers.

With the exception of many restaurants, children are well received around Scotland, and every area has some child-friendly attractions and B&Bs. Even dryish local museums usually make an effort with an activity sheet or child-focused information panels.

A lot of pubs are family-friendly and some have great beer gardens where kids can run around and exhaust themselves while you have a quiet pint. However, be aware that many Scottish pubs, even those that serve bar meals, are forbidden by law to admit children under 14; even in family-friendly pubs (ie those in possession of a Children's Certificate), under-14s are only admitted between 11am and 8pm, and only when accompanied by an adult.

Children under a certain age can often stay free with their parents in hotels, but be prepared for hotels and B&Bs (normally upmarket ones) that won't accept children; call ahead to get the low-down. More hotels and guesthouses these days provide child-friendly facilities, including cots. Many restaurants (especially the larger ones) have highchairs and decent children's menus available.

The larger car-hire companies can provide safety seats for children, but they're worth booking well ahead.

See Edinburgh for Children (p67) and Glasgow for Children (p118) for more on travel in those two cities with the kids. See also Lonely Planet's *Travel with Children*, by Brigitte Barta et al.

Customs Regulations

Travellers arriving in the UK from other EU countries don't have to pay tax or duty on goods for personal use, and can bring back as much EU duty-paid alcohol and tobacco as they like. However, if you bring in more than the following, you'll probably be asked some questions: 3200 cigarettes, 400 cigarillos, 200 cigars, 3kg of smoking tobacco, 10L of spirits, 20L of fortified wine (eg port or sherry), 90L of wine and 110L of beer. Those under 17 years cannot import any alcohol or tobacco. There are different allowances for tobacco products from the newer EU member countries, though (such as Estonia, Poland, Hungary, Latvia, Lithuania, Slovakia, the Czech Republic and Slovenia) – check the website of **HM Customs and Excise** (www.hmrc.gov.uk) for further details.

Travellers from outside the EU can bring in, duty-free:

» 200 cigarettes *or* 100 cigarillos *or* 50 cigars *or* 250g of tobacco

» 4L of still table wine

» 1L of spirits *or* 2L of fortified wine

» 60mL of perfume

» £300 worth of all other goods, including gifts and souvenirs.

Anything over this limit must be declared to customs officers on arrival.

For details of restrictions and quarantine regulations, see the customs website.

Discount Cards
Historic Sites

Membership of Historic Scotland (HS) and the National Trust for Scotland (NTS) is worth considering, especially if you're going to be in Scotland for a while. Both are nonprofit organisations dedicated to the preservation of the environment, and both care for hundreds of spectacular sites. Throughout this guide the abbreviations HS and NTS are used to indicate places that are under the care of these organisations. You can join up at any of their properties.

Historic Scotland (HS; ☎0131 668 8600; www.historic-scotland.gov.uk) A year's membership costs £40.50/76 per adult/family, and gives free entry to HS sites (half-price entry to sites in England and Wales). Also offers short-term Explorer membership – three days out of five for

£22, seven days out of 14 for £31.50.

National Trust for Scotland (NTS; ☎0131-243 9300; www.nts.org.uk) A year's membership of the NTS, costing £46/76 for an adult/family, offers free access to all NTS and National Trust properties (in the rest of the UK).

Hostel Cards

If travelling on a budget, membership of the **Scottish Youth Hostel Association/Hostelling International** (SYHA/HI; ☎0845 293 7373; www.syha.org.uk) is a must (annual membership over/under 16 years is £10/ free, life membership is £100).

Senior Cards

Discount cards for those over 60 years are available for train travel (see p492).

Student & Youth Cards

The most useful card is the International Student Identity Card (ISIC), which displays your photo. This can perform wonders, including producing discounts on entry to attractions and on many forms of transport.

There's a global industry in fake student cards, and many places now stipulate a maximum age for student discounts or substitute a 'youth discount' for 'student discount'. If under 26 but not a student, you can apply for the Euro/26 card, which goes by various names in different countries, or an International Youth Travel Card (IYTC) issued by the **International Student Travel Confederation** (ISTC; www.istc.org). These cards are available through student unions, hostelling organisations or youth travel agencies.

Electricity

230V/50Hz

Embassies & Consulates

Be aware that the Australian consulate in Edinburgh does not provide notarial services; travellers in need of these should contact the **Australian High Commission** (☎020-7379 4334) in London instead.

Food

In this guide eating choices are flagged with price indicators, based on the cost of an average main course from the dinner menu:

EATING PRICE INDICATORS

£	up to £9
££	from £9 to £18
£££	£18 and over

Note though that lunch mains are often cheaper than dinner mains, and many places offer an 'early bird' special with lower prices (usually available between 5pm and 7pm). See p480 for restaurant opening hours,

and the Scottish Larder chapter (p454) for information about tucking into Scottish cuisine.

Gay & Lesbian Travellers

Although many Scots are fairly tolerant of homosexuality, overt displays of affection aren't wise if conducted away from acknowledged 'gay' venues or districts – hostility may be encountered.

Edinburgh and Glasgow have small but flourishing gay scenes. The website www.gayscotland.com and the monthly magazine *Scotsgay* (www.scotsgay.com) keep gays, lesbians and bisexuals informed about gay-scene issues. See also the boxed texts in the Glasgow (p121) and Edinburgh (p85) chapters.

Health

» If you're an EU citizen, a European Health Insurance Card (EHIC) – available from health centres or, in the UK, post offices – covers you for most medical care. An EHIC will not cover you for non-emergencies, or emergency repatriation.

» Citizens from non-EU countries should find out if there is a reciprocal arrangement for free medical care between their country and the UK.

» If you do need health insurance, make sure you get a policy that covers you for the worst possible case, such as an accident requiring an emergency flight home.

» No jabs are required to travel to Scotland

» The most painful problems facing visitors to the Highlands and islands are midges (see boxed text, p31)

CONSULATES IN SCOTLAND

Most foreign diplomatic missions are in London, but many countries also have consulates in Edinburgh:

Australia	☎0131-538 0582	www.uk.embassy.gov.au	5 Mitchell St, Edinburgh
Canada	☎0131-473 6320	www.canadainternational.gc.ca	Festival Sq 50 Lothian Rd, Edinburgh
Denmark	☎0131-220 0300	www.amblondon.um.dk	48 Melville St, Edinburgh
France	☎0131-225 7954	www.ambafrance-uk.org	11 Randolph Cres, Edinburgh
Germany	☎0131-337 2323	www.edinburgh.diplo.de	16 Eglinton Cres, Edinburgh
Ireland	☎0131-226 7711	www.irishconsulatescotland.co.uk	16 Randolph Cres, Edinburgh
Japan	☎0131-225 4777	www.edinburgh.uk.emb-japan.go.jp	2 Melville Cres, Edinburgh
Netherlands	☎0131-524 9436	www.netherlands-embassy.org.uk	7 North St David St, Edinburgh
New Zealand	☎0131-222 8109	www.nzembassy.com/united-kingdom	5 Rutland Sq, Edinburgh
USA	☎0131-556 8315	www.usembassy.org.uk	3 Regent Tce, Edinburgh

Insurance

» This not only covers you for medical expenses, theft or loss, but also for cancellation of, or delays in, any of your travel arrangements.

» Lots of bank accounts give their holders automatic travel insurance – check if this is the case for you.

» Always read the small print carefully. Some policies specifically exclude 'dangerous activities', such as scuba diving, motorcycling, skiing, mountaineering and even trekking.

» There's a variety of policies and your travel agent can give recommendations. Make sure the policy includes health care and medication in the countries you may visit on your way to/from Scotland. See p482 for advice on health insurance.

» You may prefer a policy that pays doctors or hospitals directly rather than forcing you to pay on the spot and claim the money back later. If you have to claim

later, make sure you keep all documentation. Some policies ask you to call back (reverse charges) to a centre in your home country where an immediate assessment of your problem is made.

» Not all policies cover ambulances, helicopter rescue or emergency flights home. Most policies exclude cover for pre-existing illnesses.

Worldwide travel insurance is available at www.lonelyplanet.com/travel_services. You can buy, extend and claim online anytime – even if you're already on the road.

Internet Access

» If you're travelling with a laptop, you'll find a wide range of places offering a wi-fi connection. These range from cafes to B&Bs and public spaces.

» We've indicated accommodation and eating and drinking options that have wi-fi with the 🛜symbol in the text. Wi-fi is often free,

but some places (typically, upmarket hotels) charge.

» There are some increasingly good deals on pay-as-you-go mobile internet from mobile network providers.

» If you see the @symbol, then the place has an internet terminal.

» If you don't have a laptop, the best places to check email and surf the internet are public libraries – almost every town and village in the country has at least a couple of computer terminals devoted to the internet, and they are free to use, though there's often a time limit.

» Internet cafes also exist in the cities and larger towns and are generally good value, charging approximately £2 to £3 per hour.

» Many of the larger tourist offices across the country also have internet access.

Legal Matters

» The 1707 Act of Union preserved the Scottish legal

system as separate from the law in England and Wales.

» Police have the power to detain, for up to six hours, anyone suspected of having committed an offence punishable by imprisonment (including drugs offences). They can search you, take your photo and fingerprints, and question you. You are legally required to provide police with your correct name and address – not doing so, or giving false details, is an offence – but you are not obliged to answer any other questions. After six hours, the police must either formally charge you or let you go.

» If you are detained and/or arrested, you have the right to inform a solicitor and one other person, though you have no right to actually see the solicitor or to make a telephone call. If you don't know a solicitor, the police will inform the duty solicitor for you.

» The government can now detain foreigners suspected of terrorist activities, without charge, for a period of 28 days.

» If you need legal assistance, contact the **Scottish Legal Aid Board** (☑0131-226 7061; www.slab.org.uk; 44 Drumsheugh Gardens, Edinburgh).

» Possession of a small amount of cannabis is punishable by a fine, but possession of a larger amount of cannabis, or any amount of harder drugs, is much more serious, with a sentence of up to 14 years in prison. Police have the right to search anyone they suspect of possessing drugs.

» A maximum blood-alcohol level of 35mg/100mL when driving is allowable.

» Traffic offences (illegal parking, speeding etc) usually incur a fine, to be paid within 30 to 60 days. In Glasgow and Edinburgh the parking inspectors are numerous and without mercy – never leave your car around the city centres without a valid parking ticket as you risk a hefty fine.

» The legal minimum age in Scotland for drinking alcohol, smoking and voting is 18; for driving, it's 17.

» Travellers should note that they can be prosecuted under the law of their home country regarding age of consent, even when abroad.

Maps

If you're about to tackle Munros, you'll require maps with far greater detail than the maps in this guide, or the ones supplied by tourist offices. The Ordnance Survey (OS) caters to walkers, with a wide variety of maps at 1:50,000 and 1:25,000 scales. Alternatively, look out for the excellent walkers' maps published by Harveys; they're at scales of 1:40,000 and 1:25,000.

Money

The British currency is the pound sterling (£), with 100 pence (p) to a pound. 'Quid' is the slang term for pound.

Three Scottish banks issue their own banknotes, meaning there's quite a variety of different notes in circulation. They are legal tender in England too, but you'll sometimes run into problems changing them. They are also harder to exchange once you get outside the UK.

Euros are accepted in Scotland only at some major tourist attractions and a few upmarket hotels – it's always better to have sterling cash. For exchange rates see the inside front cover of this book. For information on costs, see p14.

ATMs

ATMs (called cashpoints in Scotland) are widespread and you'll usually find at least one in small towns and villages. You can use Visa, MasterCard, Amex, Cirrus, Plus and Maestro to withdraw cash from ATMs belonging to most banks and building societies in Scotland.

Cash withdrawals from some ATMs may be subject to a small charge, but most are free.

Credit Cards

Visa, MasterCard, Amex and Diners Club cards are widely recognised, although some places will charge for accepting them (generally for small transactions). Charge cards such as Amex and Diners Club may not be accepted in smaller establishments. Credit and credit/debit cards like Visa and MasterCard are more widely accepted, but smaller B&Bs may not take cards.

Moneychangers

Be careful using bureaux de change; they may offer good exchange rates but frequently levy outrageous commissions and fees. The best-value place to change money in the UK is at post offices, but only the ones in larger towns and cities offer this service. Larger tourist offices also have exchange facilities.

Tipping

» Tip 10% in sit-down restaurants, but not if there's already a service charge on the bill.

» In very classy places they may expect closer to 15%.

» Service is at your discretion: even if the charge is added to the bill, you don't have to pay it if you feel service has been poor.

» Don't tip in pubs: if the service has been exceptional over the course of an evening, you can say 'have one for yourself'.

» Tip taxi drivers in cities around 10%, or else just round up.

Public Holidays

Although bank holidays are general public holidays in the rest of the UK, in Scotland they only apply to banks and some other commercial offices.

Scottish towns normally have four days of public holiday, which they allocate themselves; dates vary from year to year and from town to town. Most places celebrate St Andrew's Day (30 November) as a public holiday.

General public holidays:

New Year 1 & 2 January
Good Friday March or April
Christmas Day 25 December
Boxing Day 26 December

Telephone

The famous red telephone boxes are a dying breed now, surviving mainly in conservation areas. You'll mainly see two types of phone booths in Scotland: one takes money (and doesn't give change), while the other uses prepaid phonecards and credit cards. Some phones accept both coins and cards. Payphone cards are widely available.

The cheapest way of calling internationally is to buy a discount call card; you'll see these in newsagents, along with tables of countries and the number of minutes you'll get for your money.

Mobile Phones

Codes for mobile phones usually begin with ☑07. The UK uses the GSM 900/1800 network, which covers the rest of Europe, Australia and New Zealand, but isn't compatible with the North American GSM 1900. Most modern mobiles, however, can function on both networks – check before you leave home.

International roaming charges can be prohibitively high, though, and you'll probably find it cheaper to get a UK number. This is easily done by buying a SIM card (around £10 including calling credit) and sticking it in your phone. Your phone may be locked to your home network, however, so you'll have to either get it unlocked, or buy a pay-as-you-go phone along with your SIM card (around £50).

Pay-as-you-go phones can be recharged by buying vouchers from shops.

Phone Codes & Useful Numbers

Dialling the UK Dial your country's international access code then ☑44 (the UK country code), then the area code (dropping the first 0) followed by the telephone number.

Dialling out of the UK The international access code is ☑00; dial this, then add the code of the country you wish to dial

Making a reverse charge (collect) international call Dial ☑155 for the operator. It's an expensive option, but not for the caller.

Area codes in Scotland Begin with ☑01xxx, eg Edinburgh ☑0131, Wick ☑01955.

Directory Assistance There are several numbers; ☑118500 is one.

Mobile phones Codes usually begin with ☑07.

Free calls Numbers starting with ☑0800 are free; calls to ☑0845 numbers are charged at local rates.

Time

Scotland is on GMT/UTC. The clocks go forward for 'summer time' one hour at the end of March, and go back at the end of October. The 24-hour clock is used for transport timetables, but plenty of folk still struggle to get the hang of it.

TIME DIFFERENCE BETWEEN SCOTLAND & MAJOR CITIES

Paris, Berlin, Rome	1hr ahead
New York	5hr behind
Sydney	9hr ahead Apr-Sep, 10hr Oct, 11hr Nov-Mar
Los Angeles	8hr behind
Mumbai	5½hr ahead, 4½hr Mar-Oct
Tokyo	9hr ahead, 8hr Mar-Oct

Tourist Information

The Scottish Tourist Board, known as **VisitScotland** (☑0845 225 5121; www.visitscotland.com, info@visitscotland.com; Ocean Point One, 94 Ocean Dr, Leith, Edinburgh EH6 6HJ), deals with inquiries made by post, email and telephone. You can request, online and by phone, for regional brochures be posted out to you.

Most larger towns have tourist offices that open 9am or 10am to 5pm Monday to Friday, and on weekends in summer. In small places, particularly in the Highlands, tourist offices only open from Easter to September. Details of tourist offices can be found throughout the guide.

Travellers with Disabilities

Travellers with disabilities will find Scotland a strange mix of user-friendliness and unfriendliness. Most new buildings are accessible to wheelchair users, so modern hotels and tourist attractions are fine. However, most B&Bs and guesthouses are in hard-to-adapt older buildings, which means that travellers with mobility problems may pay more for accommodation. Things are constantly improving, though.

It's a similar story with public transport. Newer buses have steps that lower for easier access, as do trains, but it's wise to check before setting out. Tourist attractions usually reserve parking spaces near the entrance for drivers with disabilities.

Many places such as ticket offices and banks are fitted with hearing loops to assist the hearing-impaired; look for a posted symbol of a large ear.

A few tourist attractions, such as Glasgow Cathedral, have Braille guides or scented gardens for the visually impaired.

VisitScotland produces the guide *Accessible Scotland* for wheelchair-bound travellers, and many tourist offices have leaflets with accessibility details for their area. Regional accommodation guides have a wheelchair-accessible criterion.

Many regions have organisations that hire wheelchairs; contact the local tourist office for details. Many nature trails have been adapted for wheelchair use.

For more information:

Disabled Persons Railcard (www.disabledpersons-railcard.co.uk) Discounted train travel (see p492).

Historic Scotland (HS; ☑0131-668 8600; www.historic-scotland.gov.uk) Has a free leaflet outlining access and facilities at HS properties, and also produces a large-print version of the HS promotional brochure.

Holiday Care Service (☑0845 124 9971; www.holidaycare.org.uk) Publishes regional information guides (£5) to Scotland and can offer general advice.

Royal Association for Disability & Rehabilitation (RADAR; ☑020-7250 3222; www.radar.org.uk; Information Dept, 12 City Forum, 250 City Rd, London EC1V 8AF) Excellent; publishes a guide (£10) on travel in the UK and has an accommodation website.

Visas

If you're a citizen of the EEA (European Economic Area) nations or Switzerland, you don't need a visa to enter or work in Britain – you can enter using your national identity card.

Visa regulations are always subject to change, so it's essential to check with your local British embassy, high commission or consulate before leaving home. Currently, if you're a citizen of Australia, Canada, New Zealand, Japan, Israel, the USA and several other countries, you can stay for up to six months (no visa required), but are not allowed to work.

Nationals of many countries, including South Africa, will need to obtain a visa: for more info, see www.ukvisas.gov.uk.

The Youth Mobility Scheme, for Australian, Canadian, Japanese, and New Zealand citizens aged 18 to 31, allows working visits of up to two years, but must be applied for in advance.

Commonwealth citizens with a UK-born parent may be eligible for a Certificate of Entitlement to the Right of Abode, which entitles them to live and work in the UK. Commonwealth citizens with a UK-born grandparent could qualify for a UK Ancestry Employment Certificate, allowing them to work full time for up to five years in the UK.

British immigration authorities have always been tough; dress neatly and carry proof that you have sufficient funds with which to support yourself. A credit card and/or an onward ticket will help.

Women Travellers

Women travelling alone are highly unlikely to have problems in Scotland, though there are still a few pubs where you'll turn heads if you walk in alone. Cosmopolitan city pubs and most rural pubs are fine – you'll get a pretty good idea as soon as you open the door.

The contraceptive pill is available only on prescription; however, the 'morning-after' pill (effective against conception for up to 72 hours after unprotected sexual intercourse) is available over the counter at chemists.

Work

» EU citizens don't need a permit to work in the UK, though citizens of some of those countries may need to register before starting work.

» See Visas (p486) for details of the Youth Mobility Scheme working holiday visa.

» Students and recent graduates are eligible to apply through BUNAC (www.bunac.org) for an internship allowing them to work for six months in the UK.

» Whatever your skills, it's worth registering with a number of temporary employment agencies – there are plenty in the cities.

» Low-paid seasonal work is often available in the tourist industry, usually in restaurants and pubs. Once the domain of Australian, South African and New Zealand travellers; the enlargement of the EU has seen many Eastern Europeans also travel to Scotland for these jobs. At Highland pubs, rates usually include bed and board, so it can be a good way to save money.

» Hostel notice boards sometimes advertise casual work. Without skills, it's difficult to find a job that pays enough to save money. Pick up a free copy of *TNT* (www.tntmagazine.com), found in larger cities – it lists jobs and employment agencies aimed at travellers.

Transport

GETTING THERE & AWAY

Flights, tours and rail tickets can be booked online at lonelyplanet.com/bookings.

Air

There are direct flights to Scottish airports from England, Wales, Ireland, the USA, Canada, Scandinavia and several countries in western and central Europe. From elsewhere, you'll probably have to fly into a European hub and catch a connecting flight to a Scottish airport – London, Amsterdam, Frankfurt and Paris have the best connections. If flying from North America, it's worth looking at Icelandair, which often has good deals to Glasgow via Reykjavik.

Airports & Airlines

Scotland has four main international airports: Aberdeen, Edinburgh, Glasgow and Glasgow Prestwick. A few short-haul international flights land at Inverness and Sumburgh, while London is the main UK gateway for long-haul flights.

Aberdeen (ABZ; www.aberdeenairport.com)

Edinburgh (EDI; www.edinburghairport.com)

Glasgow (GLA; www.glasgowairport.com)

Glasgow Prestwick (PIK; www.gpia.co.uk)

Inverness (INV; www.hial.co.uk/inverness-airport)

London Gatwick (LGW; www.gatwickairport.com)

London Heathrow (LHR; www.heathrowairport.com)

Sumburgh (LSI; www.hial.co.uk/sumburgh-airport).

There are many airlines serving Scottish airports. The main ones:

Aer Arann (RE; www.aerarann.com)

Aer Lingus (EI; www.aerlingus.com)

Air France (AF; www.airfrance.co.uk)

bmi (BD; www.flybmi.com)

bmibaby (WW; www.bmibaby.com)

British Airways (BA; www.ba.com)

Canadian Affair (www.canadianaffair.com)

Cimber Sterling (QI; www.cimber.com)

Cityjet (WX; www.cityjet.com)

Continental Airlines (CO; www.continental.com)

Eastern Airways (T3; www.easternairways.com)

easyJet (U2; www.easyjet.com)

Falcontravel (www.falcontravel.ch)

FlyBe (BE; www.flybe.com)

Germanwings (4U; www.germanwings.com)

Icelandair (FI; www.icelandair.com)

Jet2.com (LS; www.jet2.com)

CLIMATE CHANGE & TRAVEL

Every form of transport that relies on carbon-based fuel generates CO_2, the main cause of human-induced climate change. Modern travel is dependent on aeroplanes, which might use less fuel per kilometre per person than most cars but travel much greater distances. The altitude at which aircraft emit gases (including CO_2) and particles also contributes to their climate change impact. Many websites offer 'carbon calculators' that allow people to estimate the carbon emissions generated by their journey and, for those who wish to do so, to offset the impact of the greenhouse gases emitted with contributions to portfolios of climate-friendly initiatives throughout the world. Lonely Planet offsets the carbon footprint of all staff and author travel.

KLM Cityhopper (UK; www.
klmuk.com)

Lufthansa (LH; www.luft
hansa.co.uk)

Norwegian (DY; www.norwe
gian.com)

Ryanair (FR; www.ryanair.com)

Scandinavian Airlines (SK;
www.flysas.com)

Spanair (JKK; www.spanair.
com)

US Airways (US; www.usair
ways.com)

Wideroe (WF; www.wideroe.no)

Land
Bus

Buses are usually the cheapest way to get to Scotland
from other parts of the UK.
The main operators:

Megabus (www.megabus.
com) One-way fares from
London to Glasgow from as
little as £5.50 if you book
well in advance (up to eight
weeks).

National Express (www.
gobycoach.com) Regular
services from London and
other cities in England
and Wales to Glasgow and
Edinburgh.

Scottish Citylink (www.
citylink.co.uk) Daily service between Belfast and
Glasgow and Edinburgh via
Stranraer ferry.

Car & Motorcycle

Drivers of EU-registered vehicles will find bringing a car
or motorcycle into Scotland
fairly easy. The vehicle must
have registration papers
and a nationality plate, and
you must have insurance.
The International Insurance
Certificate (Green Card) isn't
compulsory, but it is excellent proof that you're covered. If driving from mainland Europe via the Channel
Tunnel or ferry ports, head
for London and follow the
M25 orbital road to the M1
motorway, then follow the
M1 and M6 north.

For rules of the road,
speed limits etc, see p490.

FERRIES TO/FROM NORTHERN IRELAND

CROSSING	DURATION	FREQUENCY	FARE (£)
Belfast–Stranraer	3¼hr	2-4 daily	25/89
Belfast–Stranraer	1¾hr	4 daily	25/99
Larne–Cairnryan	1¾hr	8 daily	24/69
Larne–Cairnryan	1hr	2 daily (Mar-Sep)	24/79
Larne–Troon	1¾hr	2 daily (Mar-Sep)	24/79

Train

Travelling to Scotland by train
is usually faster and more
comfortable than the bus, but
more expensive. Taking into
account check-ins and travel
time between city centre and
airport, the train is a competitive alternative, timewise, to
air travel on the London to
Edinburgh route.

East Coast (www.eastcoast.
co.uk) Trains between
London Kings Cross and
Edinburgh (four hours, every
half-hour).

Eurostar (www.eurostar.com)
You can travel from Paris or
Brussels to London in around
two hours on the Eurostar
service. From St Pancras it's
a quick and easy change to
Kings Cross or Euston for
trains to Edinburgh or Glasgow. Total journey time from
Paris to Edinburgh is about
eight hours.

First ScotRail (www.scotrail.
co.uk) Runs the Caledo-
nian Sleeper, an overnight
service connecting London
Euston with Edinburgh,
Glasgow, Stirling, Perth,
Dundee, Aberdeen, Fort William and Inverness.

National Rail Enquiry
Service (☑08457 484 950;
www.nationalrail.co.uk) Timetable and fares info for all
UK trains.

Virgin Trains (www.virgin
trains.co.uk) Trains between
London Euston and Glasgow
(4½ hours, hourly).

Sea
Continental Europe

Norfolk Line (www.norfolk
line.com) runs a car ferry
between Rosyth, 12 miles
northwest of Edinburgh,
and Zeebrugge in Belgium
(20 hours, three crossings
a week). Return passenger
fares in high season (July and
August) cost around €400
in a four-berth cabin. A car
adds €350 return to the fare.

Northern Ireland

Car-ferry links between
Northern Ireland and Scotland are operated by Stena
Line (www.stenaline.co.uk)
and P&O Irish Sea (www.
poirishsea.com). Stena Line
travels the Belfast–Stranraer route and P&O Irish
Sea the Larne–Troon and
Larne–Cairnryan routes.
There's a choice of standard
and high-speed ferries on
the Stranraer and Cairnryan
routes, high speed only on
the Troon route.

The prices in the above
table are advance purchase
one-way fares for a foot
passenger/car with driver,
in high season; fares vary
with time and day of departure, and are often less than
quoted here.

GETTING AROUND

Public transport in Scotland
is generally good, but it can
be costly compared with
other European countries.
Buses are usually the cheapest way to get around, but

FLYING IN STYLE

Loch Lomond Seaplanes (www.lochlomondseaplanes.com) operates Scotland's only seaplane passenger service, offering flights on demand from Glasgow to Oban (March to November, sea conditions permitting). Flights depart from the River Clyde next to Glasgow's Science Centre, and take only 25 minutes to reach Oban Bay; a return flight costs £169.

also the slowest. With a discount pass, trains can be competitive; they're also quicker and often take you through beautiful scenery.

Traveline (☑0871 200 2233; www.travelinescotland.com) provides timetable info for all public-transport services in Scotland, but can't provide fare information or book tickets.

Air

Most domestic air services are geared to business needs, or are lifelines for remote island communities. Flying is a pricey way to cover relatively short distances, and only worth considering if you're short of time and want to visit the Hebrides, Orkney or Shetland.

Airlines in Scotland

Eastern Airways (www.easternairways.com) Flies from Aberdeen to Stornoway and Wick.

Flybe/Loganair (www.loganair.co.uk) The main domestic airline in Scotland, with flights from Glasgow to Barra, Benbecula, Campbeltown, Islay, Kirkwall, Sumburgh, Stornoway and Tiree;

from Edinburgh to Inverness, Kirkwall, Sumburgh, Stornoway and Wick; from Aberdeen to Kirkwall and Sumburgh; and from Inverness to Kirkwall, Stornoway and Sumburgh. It also operates interisland flights in Orkney and Shetland, and from Barra to Benbecula.

Hebridean Air (www.hebrideanair.co.uk) Flies from Connel airfield near Oban to the islands of Coll, Tiree, Colonsay and Islay.

Bicycle

Scotland is a compact country, and travelling around by bicycle is a perfectly feasible proposition if you have the time. Indeed, for touring the islands a bicycle is both cheaper (in terms of ferry fares) and more suited to their small size and leisurely pace of life. For more information, see http://cycling.visitscotland.com and p27.

Boat

CalMac (www.calmac.co.uk) Serves the west coast and islands. Comprehensive timetable booklet available from tourist offices. **CalMac Island Hopscotch** offers more than two dozen tickets giving reduced fares for various combinations of crossings; these are listed on the website and in the CalMac timetables booklet.

CalMac Island Rover Ticket allowing unlimited travel on CalMac ferries, £48.50/70 for a foot passenger for eight/15 days, plus £232/348 for a car or £116/175 for a motorbike. Bicycles travel free with a foot passenger's ticket.

Northlink Ferries (www.northlinkferries.co.uk) Ferries from Aberdeen and Scrabster (near Thurso) to Orkney, from Orkney to Shetland and from Aberdeen to Shetland.

Bus

Scotland is served by an extensive bus network that covers most of the country. In remote rural areas, however, services are more geared to the needs of locals (getting to school or the shops in the nearest large town) and may not be conveniently timed for visitors.

First (www.firstgroup.com) Operates local bus routes in Aberdeen, Greater Glasgow, Edinburgh and southeast Scotland.

Royal Mail postbuses (www.postbus.royalmail.com) Minibuses, or sometimes four-seater cars, driven by postal workers delivering and collecting the mail – there are no official stops, and you can hail a postbus anywhere on its route. Although services have been cut severely in recent years, it's still the only public transport in some remote parts of Scotland.

Scottish Citylink (www.citylink.co.uk) National network of comfy, reliable buses serving all main towns. Away from main roads, you'll need to switch to local services.

Stagecoach (www.stagecoachbus.com) Operates local bus routes in many parts of Scotland.

Traveline (☑0871 200 2233; www.travelinescotland.com) Offers up-to-date timetable information.

Bus Passes

Scottish Citylink offers discounts to students, SYHA members and holders of the **NEC Smartcard** (www.youngscot.org), which gives discounts all over Scotland and Europe. Holders of a National Entitlement Card, available to seniors and disabled people who are UK citizens, gives free bus travel throughout the country.

The **Scottish Citylink Explorer Pass** offers unlimited travel on Scottish Citylink services within Scotland for any three days out of five (£35), any five days out of 10 (£59) or any eight days out of 16 (£79). Also gives discounts on various regional bus services, on Northlink and CalMac ferries, and in SYHA hostels. Can be bought in the UK by both UK and overseas citizens. It is not valid on National Express coaches.

Car & Motorcycle

Scotland's roads are generally good and far less busy than in England, so driving's more enjoyable. However, cars are nearly always inconvenient in city centres.

Motorways (designated 'M') are toll-free dual carriageways, limited mainly to central Scotland. Main roads ('A') are dual or single carriageways and are sometimes clogged with slow-moving trucks or caravans; the A9 from Perth to Inverness is notoriously busy.

Life on the road is more relaxed and interesting on the secondary roads (designated 'B') and minor roads (undesignated), although in the Highlands and islands there's the added hazard of suicidal sheep wandering

SINGLE TRACK ROADS

In many country areas, and especially in the Highlands and islands, you will find single track roads that are only wide enough for one vehicle. Passing places (usually marked with a white diamond sign, or a black and white striped pole) – are used to allow oncoming traffic to pass. Remember that passing places are also for overtaking – check your rear-view mirror often and pull over to let faster vehicles pass if necessary. Be aware that it's illegal to park in passing places.

onto the road (be particularly wary of lambs in spring).

At around £1.17p per litre (equivalent to more than US$8 per US gallon), petrol's expensive by American or Australian standards; diesel is about 3p per litre more expensive. Prices tend to rise as you get further from the main centres and are over 10% higher in the Outer Hebrides (around £1.27 a litre). In remote areas petrol stations are widely spaced and sometimes closed on Sunday.

Driving Licence

A non-EU licence is valid in Britain for up to 12 months from time of entry into the country. If bringing a car from Europe, make sure you're adequately insured.

Hire

Car hire is relatively costly here and it's often cheaper to arrange a fly/drive deal from home. The international hire companies charge from around £140 a week for a small car (Ford Fiesta, Peugeot 106); local companies, such as **Arnold Clark** (www. arnoldclarkrental.co.uk), start from £26 a day or £128 a week.

The main international hire companies:

Avis (www.avis.co.uk)
Budget (www.budget.co.uk)
Europcar (www.europcar. co.uk)
Hertz (www.hertz.co.uk)
Thrifty Car Rental (www. thrifty.co.uk)

Tourist offices have lists of local car-hire companies.

The minimum legal age for driving is 17 but to rent a car, drivers must usually be aged 23 to 65 – outside these limits special conditions or insurance requirements may apply.

If planning to visit the Outer Hebrides, Orkney or Shetland, it'll often prove cheaper to hire a car on the islands, rather than to pay to take a hire car across on the ferry.

Road Rules

The *Highway Code,* widely available in bookshops, details all UK road regulations. Vehicles drive on the left. Front seatbelts are compul-

ROAD DISTANCES (MILES)

	Aberdeen	Dundee	Edinburgh	Fort William	Glasgow	Inverness	Kyle of Lochalsh	Mallaig	Oban	Scrabster	Stranraer
Dundee	70										
Edinburgh	129	62									
Fort William	165	121	146								
Glasgow	145	84	42	104							
Inverness	105	131	155	66	166						
Kyle of Lochalsh	188	177	206	76	181	82					
Mallaig	189	161	180	44	150	106	34				
Oban	180	118	123	45	94	110	120	85			
Scrabster	218	250	279	185	286	119	214	238	230		
Stranraer	233	171	120	184	80	250	265	232	178	374	
Ullapool	150	189	215	90	225	135	88	166	161	125	158

sory; if the back seat has belts, they must be worn too. The speed limit is 30mph in built-up areas, 60mph on single carriageways and 70mph on dual carriageways. Give way to your right at roundabouts (traffic already on the roundabout has right of way). Motorcyclists must wear helmets.

It is a criminal offence to use a hand-held mobile phone or similar device while driving; this includes while you are stopped at traffic lights, or stuck in traffic, when you can expect to be moving again at any moment.

The maximum permitted blood-alcohol level when driving is 35mg/100mL; to stay under this level, drink no more than one pint of beer or one glass of wine.

Traffic offences (illegal parking, speeding etc) usually incur a fine for which you're allowed 30 to 60 days to pay. In Glasgow and Edinburgh the parking inspectors are numerous and without mercy – never leave your car around the city centres without a valid parking ticket, as you risk a hefty fine.

Hitching

Hitching is never entirely safe in any country and we don't recommend it. Travellers who hitch take a small but potentially serious risk. However, many people choose to hitch, and the advice that follows should help to make their journeys as fast and safe as possible.

Hitching is fairly easy in Scotland, except around big cities and built-up areas, where you'll need to use public transport. Although the northwest is more difficult because there's less traffic, waits of over two hours are unusual (except on Sunday in 'Sabbath' areas). On some islands, where public transport is infrequent, hitching is so much

a part of getting around that local drivers may stop and offer you lifts without you even asking.

It's against the law to hitch on motorways or their immediate slip roads; make a sign and use approach roads, nearby roundabouts or service stations.

Tours

There are lots of companies in Scotland offering all kinds of tours, including historical, activity-based and backpacker tours. It's a question of picking the tour that suits your requirements and budget. More companies are listed in destination chapters under Tours.

Classique Tours (www. classiquetours.co.uk) Bus tours of the western isles in vintage 1950s coaches, departing from Glasgow and staying in atmospheric country hotels.

Haggis Adventures (www. haggisadventures.com) Offers backpacker tours, with longer options taking in the Outer Hebrides or Orkney.

Heart of Scotland Tours (www.heartofscotlandtours. co.uk) Specialises in minicoach day tours of central Scotland and the Highlands, departing from Edinburgh.

Hebridean Princess (www. hebridean.co.uk) Luxury cruises around the west coast of Scotland, the Outer Hebrides and the Orkney and Shetland islands (HM the Queen chartered this ship for her summer holiday in 2010).

Macbackpackers (www. macbackpackers.com) Minibus tours for backpackers, using hostel accommodation, from Edinburgh to Loch Ness, Skye, Fort William, Glencoe, Oban and Stirling.

Mountain Innovations (www.scotmountain.co.uk) Guided activity holidays and courses in the Highlands;

walking, mountain biking and winter mountaineering.

Rabbie's Trail Burners (www.rabbies.com) One- to five-day tours of the Highlands in 16-seat minibuses with professional driver/ guide.

Scot-Trek (www.scot-trek. co.uk) Guided walks for all levels; ideal for solo travellers wanting to link up with others.

Train

Scotland's train network extends to all major cities and towns, but the railway map has a lot of large, blank areas in the Highlands and the Southern Uplands where you'll need to switch to bus or car. The West Highland line from Glasgow to Fort William and Mallaig, and the Inverness to Kyle of Lochalsh line offer two of the world's most scenic rail journeys.

National Rail Enquiry Service (☎08457 484 950; www.nationalrail.co.uk) For info on train timetables.

ScotRail (www.scotrail.co.uk) Operates most train services in Scotland; website has downloadable timetables.

Costs & Reservations

Train travel is more expensive than the bus, but usually more comfortable: a standard return from Edinburgh to Inverness is about £55 compared with £26 on the bus.

Reservations are recommended for intercity trips, especially on Fridays and public holidays; for shorter journeys, just buy a ticket at the station before you go. On certain routes, including the Glasgow–Edinburgh express, and in places where there's no ticket office at the station, you can buy tickets on the train.

Children under five travel free; those five to 15 usually pay half-fare. On weekends on some intercity routes you can upgrade a standard-class ticket to 1st class for £3 to £5 per single journey – ask the conductor on the train.

Bikes are carried free on all ScotRail trains but space is sometimes limited. Bike reservations are compulsory on certain train routes, including the Glasgow–Oban–Fort William–Mallaig line and the Inverness–Kyle of Lochalsh line; they are recommended on many others. You can make reservations for your bicycle from eight weeks to two hours in advance at main train stations, or when booking tickets by phone (☎0845 755 0033).

There are several types of ticket; in general, the further ahead you can book the cheaper your ticket will be:

Advance Purchase Book by 6pm on the day before travel; cheaper than Anytime.

Anytime Buy any time and travel any time, with no restrictions.

Off Peak There are time restrictions (you're not usually allowed to travel on a train that leaves before 9.15am); relatively cheap.

Discount Cards

Discount **railcards** (www. railcard.co.uk) are available for people aged 60 and over, for people aged 16 to 25 (or mature full-time students), and for those with a disability (☎0845 605 0525, text phone 0845 601 0132). The Senior Railcard (£26), Young Persons Railcard (£26) and Disabled Persons Railcard (£18) are each valid for one year and give one-third off most train fares in Scotland, England and Wales. Fill in an application at any major train station. You'll need proof of age (birth certificate, passport or driving licence) for the Young Persons and Seniors railcards (proof of enrolment for mature-age students) and proof of entitlement for the Disabled Persons Railcard.

Train Passes

ScotRail has a range of good-value passes for train travel. You can buy them at BritRail outlets in the USA, Canada and Europe, at the British Travel Centre in Regent St, London, at train stations throughout Britain, at certain UK travel agents and **ScotRail Telesales** (☎0845

755 0033) and online at www. scotrail.co.uk. Note that Travelpass and Rover tickets are not valid for travel on certain (eg commuter) services before 9.15am weekdays.

Central Scotland Rover Covers train travel between Glasgow, Edinburgh, North Berwick, Stirling and Fife; costs £33 for three days' travel out of seven.

Freedom of Scotland Travelpass Gives unlimited travel on all Scottish train services (some restrictions), all CalMac ferry services and on certain Scottish Citylink coach services (on routes not covered by rail). It's available for four days' travel out of eight (£114) or eight days out of 15 (£153).

Highland Rover Allows unlimited train travel from Glasgow to Oban, Fort William and Mallaig, and from Inverness to Kyle of Lochalsh, Aviemore, Aberdeen and Thurso; it also gives free travel on the Oban/Fort William to Inverness bus, on the Oban–Mull and Mallaig–Skye ferries, and on buses on Mull and Skye. It's valid for four days' travel out of eight (£74).

Glossary

For a glossary of Scottish place names, see the boxed text, p266.

bag – reach the top of (as in to 'bag a couple of peaks' or 'Munro bagging')

bailey – the space enclosed by castle walls

birlinn – Hebridean galley

blackhouse – low-walled stone cottage with thatch or turf roof and earth floors; shared by both humans and cattle and typical of the Outer Hebrides until the early 20th century

böd – once a simple trading booth used by fishing communities, today it refers to basic accommodation for walkers etc

bothy – hut or mountain shelter

brae – hill

broch – defensive tower

burgh – town

burn – stream

cairn – pile of stones to mark path or junction; also peak

camanachd – Gaelic for *shinty*

ceilidh (*kay*-lay) – evening of traditional Scottish entertainment including music, song and dance

Celtic high cross – a large, elaborately carved stone cross decorated with biblical scenes and Celtic interlace designs dating from the 8th to 10th centuries

chippy – fish-and-chip shop

Clearances – eviction of Highland farmers from their land by *lairds* wanting to use it for grazing sheep

Clootie dumpling – rich steamed pudding filled with currants and raisins

close – entrance to an alley

corrie – circular hollow on a hillside

craic – lively conversation

craig – exposed rock

crannog – an artificial island in a *loch* built for defensive purposes

crofting – smallholding in marginal agricultural areas following the Clearances

Cullen skink – soup made with smoked haddock, potato, onion and milk

dene – valley

dirk – dagger

dram – a measure of whisky

firth – estuary

gloup – natural arch

Hogmanay – Scottish celebration of New Year's Eve

howff – pub or shelter

HS – Historic Scotland

kyle – narrow sea channel

laird – estate owner

linn – waterfall

loch – lake

lochan – small *loch*

machair – grass- and wildflower-covered dunes

makar – maker of verses

Mercat Cross – a symbol of the trading rights of a market town or village, usually found in the centre of town and usually a focal point for the community

motte – early Norman fortification consisting of a raised, flattened mound with a keep on top; when attached to a *bailey* it is known as a motte-and-bailey

Munro – mountain of 3000ft (914m) or higher

Munro bagger – a hill walker who tries to climb all the *Munros* in Scotland

NNR – National Nature Reserve, managed by the *SNH*

NTS – National Trust for Scotland

nyvaig – Hebridean galley

OS – Ordnance Survey

Picts – early inhabitants of north and east Scotland (from Latin *pictus,* or 'painted', after their body-paint decorations)

provost – mayor

RIB – rigid inflatable boat

rood – an old Scots word for a cross

RSPB – Royal Society for the Protection of Birds

Sassenach – from Gaelic 'Sasannach': anyone who is not a Highlander (including Lowland Scots)

shinty – fast and physical ball-and-stick sport similar to Ireland's hurling

SMC – Scottish Mountaineering Club

SNH – Scottish Natural Heritage, a government organisation directly responsible for safeguarding and improving Scotland's natural heritage

sporran – purse worn around waist with the kilt

SSSI – Site of Special Scientific Interest

SYHA – Scottish Youth Hostel Association

wynd – lane

behind the scenes

SEND US YOUR FEEDBACK

We love to hear from travellers – your comments keep us on our toes and help make our books better. Our well-travelled team reads every word on what you loved or loathed about this book. Although we cannot reply individually to postal submissions, we always guarantee that your feedback goes straight to the appropriate authors, in time for the next edition. Each person who sends us information is thanked in the next edition – and the most useful submissions are rewarded with a free book.

Visit **lonelyplanet.com/contact** to submit your updates and suggestions or to ask for help. Our award-winning website also features inspirational travel stories, news and discussions.

Note: We may edit, reproduce and incorporate your comments in Lonely Planet products such as guidebooks, websites and digital products, so let us know if you don't want your comments reproduced or your name acknowledged. For a copy of our privacy policy visit lonelyplanet.com/privacy.

OUR READERS

Many thanks to the travellers who used the last edition and wrote to us with helpful hints, useful advice and interesting anecdotes:

Paul Adderley, Lisa Anderson, Sjoukje Appels, Alf B, Dolores Baldasare, Bettina Baur, Tim Bennetts, Ross Birnie, David Bremner, Gordon Bruce, Ruth Cameron, Mark Cameron, Stephanie Camillo, Henry Campbell, Del Chessell, Jenny Cheverst, Stefan Chivers, Lisa Colloby, Angela Costa, Gillian Cummins, James Davey, Andrew Douglas, Edward Dymock, Sinead Eaton, Erik Aalvik Evensen, Agata Falkowska-Gop, John Forsyth, Eli Franssens, Isabel Galan, Sally Gomery, Colum Goodchild, Giovanni Govoni, Anne Gracie, C Greig, Iris Kaeslin Grogg, Alan Halsall, Jo Hansen, Nick Hanson, Barbara Helm, Martina Hess, Martin Hoesli, Judy Holmes, Barbara Hood, Rebecca Jones, Robert Joy, Sue Justice, Andrew Kirk, Andrew P Kirk, Gordon Knight, Ravi Krishnan, Kaung Chiau Lew, Anne Little, Jean Livingstone, Lisa Lochrie, Maria Macdonald, Alasdair MacLeod, Jenny Mason, Golo Maurer, Aleks Mazurek, Trevor Mazzucchelli, Andrea McKenna, Mary McPherson, Kenny Meldrum, Sue Miles, Heather Monell, Diana Morgan, Brad Norris, Louise Nowell, Etain O'Carroll, Kathryn Peacocke, Jennifer Randolph-Quinney, Nicholas Rice, Cameron Ross, Sabrina Rossetti, Rosemary Samios, Richard Seaton, Amanda See, Sergei Shubin, Ian Smith, Ben Smits, David Squires, Andy Strangeway, Iana Strominger, Mukul Sukhwal, Scott Sutherland, Suzanne & John Sweek, Eveline Thoenes, Elizabeth Ulan, Betsie Van Coillie, Jordi van der Windt, René Vos, Hans-Werner Wabnitz, John Walker, David Wardrop-White, Sarah Weber, Karl Weis, Susan Weiss, Ben Wilcock, Henricus Willemsen, Benedict Wittet, Silvia Woodier, Hardy Zantke, Stanislav Zizka

AUTHOR THANKS

Neil Wilson

Many thanks to all the helpful and enthusiastic staff at tourist offices throughout the country, and to the many travellers I met on the road who chipped in with advice and recommendations. Thanks also to Carol Downie, and to Andrew Henderson, Steven Fallon, Russell Leaper, Amy Hickman, Erlend Tait and Pamela Tait. Finally, thanks to co-author Andy and to the ever-helpful and patient editors and cartographers at Lonely Planet.

Andy Symington

Special thanks to much-appreciated Edinburgh accommodation-option and on-the-road companion Jenny Neil, and ever-hospitable Juliette and David Paton, and to all my friends in Scotland. Particular thanks to Cindy-Lou Ramsay, John Bain, Len Bloom, Colin Bell and Amy Allanson, Andrew Burns, Riika Åkerlind, and Mark and Diane Hayward. Applause to helpful tourist-office staff, to co-author Neil, and to Cliff for a top organizing job. Gratitude too to my parents for first taking me to Scotland, and to Ruthy for solidarity and love despite the absences.

ACKNOWLEDGMENTS

Climate map data adapted from Peel MC, Finlayson BL & McMahon TA (2007) 'Updated World Map of the Köppen-Geiger Climate Classification', Hydrology and Earth System Sciences, 11, 163344.

Cover photograph: Ring of Brodgar, Orkney Islands/Bill Heinsohn, Getty. Many of the images in this guide are available for licensing from Lonely Planet Images: www.lonelyplanetimages.com.

THIS BOOK

This 6th edition of Scotland was researched and written by Neil Wilson (coordinating author) and Andy Symington. Neil also worked on the 5th edition along with Alan Murphy. The book was commissioned in Lonely Planet's London office and produced by the following people:

Commissioning Editors Clifton Wilkinson, Errol Hunt

Coordinating Editors Elisa Arduca, Ali Lemer

Coordinating Cartographer Csanad Csutoros

Coordinating Layout Designer Yvonne Bischofberger

Managing Editors Imogen Bannister, Bruce Evans, Liz Heynes

Managing Cartographers Herman So

Managing Layout Designers Indra Kilfoyle, Laura Jane

Assisting Editors Gina Tsarouhas, Carly Hall, Victoria Harrison, Angela Tinson, Charles Rawlings-Way, Helen Yeates

Assisting Cartographers Ildiko Bogdanovits, Amanda Sierp

Cover Research Naomi Parker

Internal Image Research Aude Vauconsant

Illustrator Javier Zarracina

Thanks to Mark Adams, Shahara Ahmed, David Connolly, Stefanie Di Trocchio, Janine Eberle, Joshua Geoghegan, Mark Germanchis, Michelle Glynn, Lauren Hunt, Paul Iacono, David Kemp, Nic Lehman, John Mazzocchi, Annelies Mertens, Wayne Murphy, Trent Paton, Adrian Persoglia, Piers Pickard, Averil Robertson, Lachlan Ross, Julie Sheridan, Laura Stansfeld, John Taufa, Sam Trafford, Juan Winata, Emily Wolman, Nick Wood

index

how to use this book

These symbols will help you find the listings you want:

◉ Sights	☆ Festivals & Events	☆ Entertainment
♣ Activities	🛏 Sleeping	🛍 Shopping
🎓 Courses	✕ Eating	ℹ Information/Transport
☞ Tours	🍷 Drinking	

Look out for these icons:

TOP CHOICE — Our author's recommendation

FREE — No payment required

🌿 — A green or sustainable option

Our authors have nominated these places as demonstrating a strong commitment to sustainability – for example by supporting local communities and producers, operating in an environmentally friendly way, or supporting conservation projects.

These symbols give you the vital information for each listing:

☑ Telephone Numbers	📶 Wi-Fi Access	🚍 Bus
⊙ Opening Hours	🏊 Swimming Pool	🚤 Ferry
P Parking	🥗 Vegetarian Selection	Ⓜ Metro
⊖ Nonsmoking	📖 English-Language Menu	Ⓢ Subway
❄ Air-Conditioning	👪 Family-Friendly	⊖ London Tube
@ Internet Access	🐾 Pet-Friendly	🚊 Tram
		🚆 Train

Reviews are organised by author preference.

Map Legend

Sights
- ● Beach
- ● Buddhist
- ● Castle
- ● Christian
- ● Hindu
- ● Islamic
- ● Jewish
- ● Monument
- ● Museum/Gallery
- ● Ruin
- ● Winery/Vineyard
- ● Zoo
- ● Other Sight

Activities, Courses & Tours
- ● Diving/Snorkelling
- ● Canoeing/Kayaking
- ● Skiing
- ● Surfing
- ● Swimming/Pool
- ● Walking
- ● Windsurfing
- • Other Activity/Course/Tour

Sleeping
- ● Sleeping
- ● Camping

Eating
- ● Eating

Drinking
- ● Drinking
- ● Cafe

Entertainment
- ● Entertainment

Shopping
- ● Shopping

Information
- ● Post Office
- ● Tourist Information

Transport
- ● Airport
- ● Border Crossing
- ● Bus
- ●+●+ Cable Car/Funicular
- ●● Cycling
- ●●●● Ferry
- Ⓜ Metro
- ●●● Monorail
- P Parking
- Ⓢ S-Bahn
- ● Taxi
- ●●●● Train/Railway
- ●●●● Tram
- ● Tube Station
- ⓤ U-Bahn
- • Other Transport

Routes
- Tollway
- Freeway
- Primary
- Secondary
- Tertiary
- Lane
- Unsealed Road
- Plaza/Mall
- Steps
- ⌇⌇ Tunnel
- Pedestrian Overpass
- Walking Tour
- Walking Tour Detour
- Path

Boundaries
- International
- State/Province
- Disputed
- Regional/Suburb
- Marine Park
- Cliff
- Wall

Population
- ● Capital (National)
- ◉ Capital (State/Province)
- ● City/Large Town
- ● Town/Village

Geographic
- ● Hut/Shelter
- ● Lighthouse
- ● Lookout
- ▲ Mountain/Volcano
- ● Oasis
- ● Park
-)(Pass
- ● Picnic Area
- ● Waterfall

Hydrography
- River/Creek
- Intermittent River
- Swamp/Mangrove
- Reef
- Canal
- Water
- Dry/Salt/Intermittent Lake
- Glacier

Areas
- Beach/Desert
- +++ Cemetery (Christian)
- ××× Cemetery (Other)
- Park/Forest
- Sportsground
- Sight (Building)
- Top Sight (Building)

OUR STORY

A beat-up old car, a few dollars in the pocket and a sense of adventure. In 1972 that's all Tony and Maureen Wheeler needed for the trip of a lifetime – across Europe and Asia overland to Australia. It took several months, and at the end – broke but inspired – they sat at their kitchen table writing and stapling together their first travel guide, *Across Asia on the Cheap*. Within a week they'd sold 1500 copies. Lonely Planet was born.

Today, Lonely Planet has offices in Melbourne, London and Oakland, with more than 600 staff and writers. We share Tony's belief that 'a great guidebook should do three things: inform, educate and amuse'.

OUR WRITERS

Neil Wilson

Coordinating Author, Edinburgh, Northeast Scotland, Southern Highlands & Islands, Central Highlands, Northern Highlands & Islands Neil was born in Scotland and save for a few years spent abroad has lived there most of his life. A lifelong enthusiasm for the great outdoors has inspired hiking, biking and sailing expeditions to every corner of the country. Memorable moments on his latest research trip included watching the sunset light up the hills of Applecross from a campsite high on Skye's Trotternish Ridge, and sighting two golden eagles thermalling over the wilds of central Mull. Stumbling across the magnificent menu at the Dores Inn near Inverness was an added bonus. Neil has been a full-time author since 1988 and has written more than 50 guidebooks for various publishers, including Lonely Planet's Encounter guide to his home town of Edinburgh.

Read more about Neil Wilson at:
lonelyplanet.com/members/neilwilson

Andy Symington

Glasgow, Southern Scotland, Central Scotland, Northern Highlands & Islands, Orkney & Shetland Islands Andy's Scottish forebears make their presence felt in a love of malt, a debatable ginger colour to his facial hair and a love of wild places. From childhood slogs up the M1 he graduated to making dubious road trips around the firths in a disintegrating Mini Metro and thence to peddling whisky in darkest Leith. Whilst living there, he travelled widely around the country in search of the perfect dram; now resident in Spain, he continues to visit very regularly.

Read more about Andy Symington at:
lonelyplanet.com/members/andy_symington

Published by Lonely Planet Publications Pty Ltd
ABN 36 005 607 983
6th edition – March 2011
ISBN 978 1 74179 324 6
© Lonely Planet 2011   Photographs © as indicated 2011
10 9 8 7 6 5 4 3 2
Printed in China